MW01140645

California Edition

GLENCOE LITERATURE

The Reader's Choice

Program Consultants

Beverly Ann Chin
Denny Wolfe
Jeffrey Copeland
Mary Ann Dudzinski
William Ray
Jacqueline Jones Royster
Jeffrey Wilhelm

Course 5

New York, New York Columbus, Ohio Chicago, Illinois Peoria, Illinois Woodland Hills, California

Acknowledgments

Grateful acknowledgment is given authors, publishers, photographers, museums, and agents for permission to reprint the following copyrighted material. Every effort has been made to determine copyright owners. In case of any omissions, the Publisher will be pleased to make suitable acknowledgments in future editions.

Acknowledgments continued on page R159.

The California English–Language Arts: Reading and Analyzing Test Questions pages in this book were written by The Princeton Review. Through its association with McGraw-Hill, The Princeton Review offers the best way to help students excel.

The Princeton Review is not affiliated with Princeton University or Educational Testing Service.

Glencoe/McGraw-Hill

A Division of The ***McGraw·Hill*** *Companies*

Printed in the United States of America

Send all inquiries to:
Glencoe/McGraw-Hill
8787 Orion Place
Columbus, OH 43240

ISBN 0-07-828145-8
(Student Edition)

ISBN 0-07-828150-4
(Teacher Wraparound Edition)

1 2 3 4 5 6 7 8 9 10 027/043 05 04 03 02 01

Senior Program Consultants

Beverly Ann Chin is Professor of English, Director of the English Teaching Program, Director of the Montana Writing Project, and former Director of Composition at the University of Montana in Missoula. In 1995–1996, Dr. Chin served as President of the National Council of Teachers of English. She currently serves as a Member of the Board of Directors of the National Board for Professional Teaching Standards. Dr. Chin is a nationally recognized leader in English language arts standards, curriculum, and assessment. Formerly a high school English teacher and adult education reading teacher, Dr. Chin has taught in English language arts education at several universities and has received awards for her teaching and service.

Denny Wolfe, a former high school English teacher and department chair, is Professor of English Education, Director of the Tidewater Virginia Writing Project, and Director of the Center for Urban Education at Old Dominion University in Norfolk, Virginia. For the National Council of Teachers of English, he has served as Chairperson of the Standing Committee on Teacher Preparation, President of the International Assembly, member of the Executive Committee of the Council on English Education, and editor of the SLATE Newsletter. Author of more than seventy-five articles and books on teaching English. Dr. Wolfe is a frequent consultant to schools and colleges on the teaching of English language arts.

Program Consultants

Jeffrey S. Copeland is Professor and Head of the Department of English Language and Literature at the University of Northern Iowa, where he teaches children's and young adult literature courses and a variety of courses in English education. A former public school teacher, he has published many articles in the professional journals in the language arts. The twelve books he has written or edited include *Speaking of Poets: Interviews with Poets Who Write for Children and Young Adults* and *Young Adult Literature: A Contemporary Reader.*

Mary Ann Dudzinski is a former high schoool English teacher and recipient of the Ross Perot Award for Teaching Excellence. She also has served as a member of the core faculty for the National Endowment for the Humanities Summer Institute for Teachers of Secondary School English and History at the University of North Texas. After fifteen years of classroom experience in grades 9–12, she currently is a language arts consultant.

William Ray has taught English in the Boston Public Schools; at Lowell University; University of Wroclaw, Poland; and, for the last fourteen years, at Lincoln-Sudbury Regional High School in Sudbury, Massachusetts. He specializes in world literature. He has worked on a variety of educational texts, as editor, consultant, and contributing writer.

Jacqueline Jones Royster is Professor of English and Associate Dean of the College of Humanities at The Ohio State University. She is also on the faculty of the Bread Loaf School of English at Middlebury College in Middlebury, Vermont. In addition to the teaching of writing, Dr. Royster's professional interests include the rhetorical history of African American women and the social and cultural implications of literate practices.

Jeffrey Wilhelm, a former English and reading teacher, is currently an assistant professor at the University of Maine where he teaches courses in middle and secondary level literacy. He is the author or co-author of several books on the teaching of reading and literacy, including *You Gotta BE the Book* and *Boys and Books.* He also works with local schools as part of the fledgling Adolescent Literacy Project and is the director of two annual summer institutes: the Maine Writing Project and Technology as a Learning Tool.

California Reading Advisory Board

Jane Fell Greene, Ed.D., is a literacy intervention expert with training and credentials in reading, linguistics, psycholinguistics, ESL, and clinical practice. A senior advisor for *The Reader's Choice*, Dr. Greene has 35 years of experience teaching English at the elementary, middle, adult education, and university levels. She and the National Council of *LANGUAGE!* Trainers provide professional development courses for literacy intervention specialists across the nation.

Cynthia Arceneaux, M.A.T., M.S., and Ed.D. in progress, is Coordinator of Reading/Language Arts for High Schools in the Los Angeles Unified School District. She has served as an assistant principal and cluster administrative specialist.

Jeri A. Balick, Ed.D., is a board member and immediate past president of the California Reading Association. She is the Director of Student and Family Advocacy for the San Bernardino County Superintendent of Schools.

Cheryl Caldera, M.A., is an ELL coach and trainer at Greenberg Elementary School in the Fresno Unified School District. She also is an adjunct faculty member in the Department of Literacy at California State University in Fresno.

Patty DiPaolo, a teacher and administrator, is coordinator of Professional Development in the Curriculum/Instruction Division of the Student and Teacher Excellence Project in San Bernardino.

Louisa C. Moats, Ed.D., a licensed psychologist, is a senior advisor for *The Reader's Choice* and is the author of several books, including *Speech to Print: Language Essentials for Teachers* and *Straight Talk About Reading*. She teaches at Simmons College in Boston and the Greenwood Institute in Vermont. Dr. Moats is currently the Project Director for the Early Interventions Program at the National Institute of Child, Health, and Human Development (NICHD).

Gay St. Cyr Hess, M.S., CCC-SLP, is an educator, speech/language pathologist, and learning disabilities specialist. She is a member of the National Council of *LANGUAGE!* Trainers.

Ronald M. Klemp is Coordinator of Reading/Language Arts for Middle Schools in the Los Angeles Unified School District. Dr. Klemp also has served as a lecturer in Education at California Lutheran University in Thousand Oaks.

Robert Pritchard is an incoming president of the California Reading Association and a professor of education at California State University in Fresno. He is co-editor of *Kids Come in All Languages: Reading Instruction for ESL Students.*

California Instructional Mentor Team

Jonica Bushman
Clovis USD
Clovis, California

Sharon Clause
Thurgood Marshall Middle School
San Diego, California

Renee Evon Crawford
O'Farrell Community School
San Diego, California

Sheila Felber
Halecrest Elementary School
Chula Vista, California

Essie Fischer
Wells Intermediate School
Riverside, California

Jan Gabay
The Preuss School-UCSD
La Jolla, California

Bobbi Ciriza Houtchens
Arroyo Valley High School
San Bernardino, California

George King
Turlock Junior High School
Turlock, California

Patrick Pierson
Gaspar de Portola Middle School
San Diego, California

Penny Rogers
Los Angeles USD A
Northridge, California

Jeannie Santos
Instructional Media Center
Fresno, California

Susie Shapiro
Los Angeles USD C
Van Nuys, California

Ginny Van Benthuysen
San Diego USD
San Diego, California

Harriette Ware
Los Angeles USD E
Los Angeles, California

Sheila Weiner
Gaspar de Portola Middle School
San Diego, California

Teacher Reviewers

Rahn Anderson
Arapahoe High School
Littleton Public Schools
Littleton, Colorado

Linda Antonowich
West Chester Area School District
West Chester, Pennsylvania

Mike Bancroft
Rock Bridge High School
Columbia, Missouri

Luella Barber
Hays High School
Hays, Kansas

Lori Beard
Cypress Creek High School
Houston, Texas

Hugh Beattie
Bergenfield Public School District
Bergenfield, New Jersey

Patricia Blatt
Centerville High School
Centerville, Ohio

Edward Blotzer III
Wilkinsburg High School
Pittsburgh, Pennsylvania

Ruby Bowker
Mt. View High School
Mt. View, Wyoming

Darolyn Brown
Osborn High School
Detroit, Michigan

Rob Bruno
Atholton High School
Columbia, Maryland

Mary Beth Crotty
Bridgetown Junior High
Cincinnati, Ohio

Susan Dawson
Sam Barlow High School
Portland, Oregon

Thomas A. Della Salla
Schenectady City School District
Schenectady, New York

Sandra Denton
East High School
Columbus, Ohio

Charles Eisele
St. John Vianney High School
St. Louis, Missouri

Mel Farberman
Benjamin Cardozo High School
Bayside, New York

Caroline Ferdinandsen
San Joaquin Memorial High School
Fresno, California

Tye Ferdinandsen
San Joaquin Memorial High School
Fresno, California

Randle Frink
East Rowan High School
Salisbury, North Carolina

Pamela Fuller
Capital High School
Charleston, West Virginia

Tara Gallagher
River Hill High School
Columbia, Maryland

June Gatewood
Rio Americano
Sacramento, California

Ellen Geisler
Mentor High School
Mentor, Ohio

Leslie Gershon
Annapolis Senior High
Mitchellville, Maryland

Kim Hartman
Franklin Heights High School
Columbus, Ohio

Charlotte Heidel
Gaylord High School
Gaylord, Michigan

Keith Henricksen
Sutton Public Schools
Sutton, Nebraska

Patricia Herigan
Central Dauphin High School
Harrisburg, Pennsylvania

Azalie Hightower
Paul Junior High School
Washington, D.C.

Bobbi Ciriza Houtchens
San Bernardino High School
San Bernardino, California

Cheri Jefferson
Atholton High School
Columbia, Maryland

Marsha Jones
Seymour High School
Seymour, Indiana

Cheryl Keast
Glendale High School
Glendale, California

Glenda Kissell
Littleton High School
Littleton, Colorado

Jan Klein
Cypress Lake High School
Fort Myers, Florida

Beth Koehler
Nathan Hale High School
West Allis, Wisconsin

Sister Mary Kay Lampert
Central Catholic High School
Portland, Oregon

Elaine Loughlin
Palo Duro High
Amarillo, Texas

Tom Mann
Franklin Heights High School
Columbus, Ohio

Carolyn Sue Mash
Westerville North High School
Westerville, Ohio

Eileen Mattingly
McDonough High School
Pomfret, Maryland

Wanda McConnell
Statesville High School
Statesville, North Carolina

Victoria McCormick
John Jay High School
San Antonio, Texas

Sandra Sue McPherson
McKeesport Area High School
McKeesport, Pennsylvania

Jill Miller
Odessa High School
Odessa, Texas

Karmen Miller
Cypress Falls High School
Houston, Texas

Catherine Morse
Shelby High School
Shelby, Ohio

Tom Omli
Rogers High School
Puyallup, Washington

John O'Toole
Solon High School
Solon, Ohio

Helen Pappas
Bridgewater-Raritan High School
Bridgewater, New Jersey

Jill Railsback
Seymour High School
Seymour, Indiana

Doug Reed
Franklin Heights High School
Columbus, Ohio

Mary Jane Reed
Solon High School
Solon, Ohio

Dorlea Rikard
Bradshaw High School
Florence, Alabama

Diane Ritzdorf
Arapahoe High School
Littleton, Colorado

Leonor Rodriguez
Breckenridge High School
San Antonio, Texas

Susanne Rubenstein
Wachusett Regional High School
Holden, Massachusetts

Steve Slagle
San Gabriel High School
San Gabriel, California

Tammy Smiley
Littleton High School
Littleton, Colorado

Carol Smith
Moses Lake School District
Moses Lake, Washington

Helen Spaith
Franklin Heights High School
Columbus, Ohio

Marsha Spampinato
High School of Enterprise,
Business, and Technology
Smithtown, New York

Nora Stephens
Huntsville High School
Huntsville, Alabama

David Stocking
Wachusett Regional High School
Holden, Massachusetts

Mark Tavernier
Norfolk Public Schools
Norfolk, Virginia

Martin Tierney
Bishop Dwenger High School
Fort Wayne, Indiana

Elysa Toler-Robinson
Detroit Public Schools
Detroit, Michigan

Megan Trow
Sprague High School
Salem, Oregon

Joseph Velten Jr.
Archbishop Wood High School
Warminster, Pennsylvania

Margaret Wildermann
McDonough High School
Pomfret, Maryland

Kathy Young
Walnut Ridge High School
Columbus, Ohio

Mary Young
Greenville High School
Greenville, Illinois

Letter to Students

Dear Student,

Welcome to ***Glencoe Literature: The Reader's Choice***. In this lively collection of classic and contemporary literature, you will find much to amuse, surprise, delight, engage, and inform you. A wide variety of selections—including poems, plays, short stories, essays, autobiographies, and news articles on a broad range of themes—offers you the chance to hear talented authors in all their diversity, as well as to experience and learn about the people, places, and ideas that moved them.

As you explore the literature selections in this book, you will also learn and review key reading and language arts skills. The questions and activities after each selection will help you to check your understanding of what you've read. They will also give you an opportunity to analyze important features of the literature. You will be asked to discuss and write about what you read and to explore how literature connects with your own experiences.

Your book is divided into six units, each focusing on a particular genre of writing. In addition, each unit is subdivided by theme. With every theme, you will complete an extended project and longer writing assignment along with many other individual, partner, and group activities. Keep your graded, completed assignments in a portfolio or as your teacher directs. Share your progress with your parents or guardians and also talk with them about the literature you are reading. Discuss your thoughts about the characters, themes, and other aspects of your reading.

The state of California has created a set of learning goals, or content standards, for you this year. We have included them on pages x–xv. Take some time to read over these standards with your parents or guardians. Then outline some steps that you can take to help you achieve these standards both inside and outside the classroom.

We hope that you enjoy the selections in ***Glencoe Literature: The Reader's Choice*** and that the lessons help you to succeed in mastering the content standards set for you.

Sincerely,

The Editors

Book Overview

Grade 10

CALIFORNIA

English-Language Arts Content Standards

READING

1.0 Word Analysis, Fluency, and Systematic Vocabulary Development

Students apply their knowledge of word origins to determine the meaning of new words encountered in reading materials and use those words accurately.

Vocabulary and Concept Development

1.1 Identify and use the literal and figurative meanings of words and understand word derivations.

1.2 Distinguish between the denotative and connotative meanings of words and interpret the connotative power of words.

1.3 Identify Greek, Roman, and Norse mythology and use the knowledge to understand the origin and meaning of new words (e.g., the word *narcissistic* drawn from the myth of Narcissus and Echo).

2.0 Reading Comprehension (Focus on Informational Materials)

Students read and understand grade-level-appropriate material. They analyze the organizational patterns, arguments, and positions advanced. The selections in *Recommended Literature, Grades Nine Through Twelve* (1990) illustrate the quality and complexity of the materials to be read by students. In addition, by grade twelve, students read two million words annually on their own, including a wide variety of classic and contemporary literature, magazines, newspapers, and online information. In grades nine and ten, students make substantial progress toward this goal.

Structural Features of Informational Materials

2.1 Analyze the structure and format of functional workplace documents, including the graphics and headers, and explain how authors use the features to achieve their purposes.

2.2 Prepare a bibliography of reference materials for a report using a variety of consumer, workplace, and public documents.

Comprehension and Analysis of Grade-Level-Appropriate Text

2.3 Generate relevant questions about readings on issues that can be researched.

2.4 Synthesize the content from several sources or works by a single author dealing with a single issue; paraphrase the ideas and connect them to other sources and related topics to demonstrate comprehension.

2.5 Extend ideas presented in primary or secondary sources through original analysis, evaluation, and elaboration.

2.6 Demonstrate use of sophisticated learning tools by following technical directions (e.g., those found with graphic calculators and specialized software programs and in access guides to World Wide Web sites on the Internet).

Expository Critique

2.7 Critique the logic of functional documents by examining the sequence of information and procedures in anticipation of possible reader misunderstandings.

2.8 Evaluate the credibility of an author's argument or defense of a claim by critiquing the relationship between generalizations and evidence, the comprehensiveness of evidence, and the way in which the author's intent affects the structure and tone of the text (e.g., in professional journals, editorials, political speeches, primary source material).

3.0 Literary Response and Analysis

Students read and respond to historically or culturally significant works of literature that reflect and enhance their studies of history and social science. They conduct in-depth analyses of recurrent patterns and themes. The selections in *Recommended Literature, Grades Nine Through Twelve* illustrate the quality and complexity of the materials to be read by students.

Structural Features of Literature

3.1 Articulate the relationship between the expressed purposes and the characteristics of different forms of dramatic literature (e.g., comedy, tragedy, drama, dramatic monologue).

3.2 Compare and contrast the presentation of a similar theme or topic across genres to explain how the selection of genre shapes the theme or topic.

Narrative Analysis of Grade-Level-Appropriate Text

3.3 Analyze interactions between main and subordinate characters in a literary text (e.g., internal and external conflicts, motivations, relationships, influences) and explain the way those interactions affect the plot.

3.4 Determine characters' traits by what the characters say about themselves in narration, dialogue, dramatic monologue, and soliloquy.

3.5 Compare works that express a universal theme and provide evidence to support the ideas expressed in each work.

3.6 Analyze and trace an author's development of time and sequence, including the use of complex literary devices (e.g., foreshadowing, flashbacks).

3.7 Recognize and understand the significance of various literary devices, including figurative language, imagery, allegory, and symbolism, and explain their appeal.

3.8 Interpret and evaluate the impact of ambiguities, subtleties, contradictions, ironies, and incongruities in a text.

3.9 Explain how voice, persona, and the choice of a narrator affect characterization and the tone, plot, and credibility of a text.

3.10 Identify and describe the function of dialogue, scene designs, soliloquies, asides, and character foils in dramatic literature.

Literary Criticism

3.11 Evaluate the aesthetic qualities of style, including the impact of diction and figurative language on tone, mood, and theme, using the terminology of literary criticism. (Aesthetic approach)

3.12 Analyze the way in which a work of literature is related to the themes and issues of its historical period. (Historical approach)

WRITING

1.0 Writing Strategies

Students write coherent and focused essays that convey a well-defined perspective and tightly reasoned argument. The writing demonstrates students' awareness of the audience and purpose. Students progress through the stages of the writing process as needed.

Organization and Focus

1.1 Establish a controlling impression or coherent thesis that conveys a clear and distinctive perspective on the subject and maintain a consistent tone and focus throughout the piece of writing.

1.2 Use precise language, action verbs, sensory details, appropriate modifiers, and the active rather than the passive voice.

Grade 10

Research and Technology

1.3 Use clear research questions and suitable research methods (e.g., library, electronic media, personal interview) to elicit and present evidence from primary and secondary sources.

1.4 Develop the main ideas within the body of the composition through supporting evidence (e.g., scenarios, commonly held beliefs, hypotheses, definitions).

1.5 Synthesize information from multiple sources and identify complexities and discrepancies in the information and the different perspectives found in each medium (e.g., almanacs, microfiche, news sources, in-depth field studies, speeches, journals, technical documents).

1.6 Integrate quotations and citations into a written text while maintaining the flow of ideas.

1.7 Use appropriate conventions for documentation in the text, notes, and bibliogrphies by adhering to those in style manuals (e.g., *Modern Language Association Handbook, The Chicago Manual of Style*).

1.8 Design and publish documents by using advanced publishing software and graphic programs.

Evaluation and Revision

1.9 Revise writing to improve the logic and coherence of the organization and controlling perspective, the precision of word choice, and the tone by taking into consideration the audience, purpose, and formality of the context.

2.0 Writing Applications (Genres and Their Characteristics)

Students combine the rhetorical strategies of narration, exposition, persuasion, and description to produce texts of at least 1,500 words each. Student writing demonstrates a command of standard American English and the research, organizational, and drafting strategies outlined in Writing Standard 1.0.

Using the writing strategies of grades nine and ten outlined in Writing Standard 1.0, students:

2.1 Write biographical or autobiographical narratives or short stories:

- a. Relate a sequence of events and communicate the significance of the events to the audience.
- b. Locate scenes and incidents in specific places.
- c. Describe with concrete sensory details the sights, sounds, and smells of a scene and the specific actions, movements, gestures, and feelings of the characters; use interior monologue to depict the characters' feelings.
- d. Pace the presentation of actions to accommodate changes in time and mood.
- e. Make effective use of descriptions of appearance, images, shifting perspectives, and sensory details.

2.2 Write responses to literature:

- a. Demonstrate a comprehensive grasp of the significant ideas of literary works.
- b. Support important ideas and viewpoints through accurate and detailed references to the text or to other works.
- c. Demonstrate awareness of the author's use of stylistic devices and an appreciation of the effects created.
- d. Identify and assess the impact of perceived ambiguities, nuances, and complexities within the text.

2.3 Write expository compositions, including analytical essays and research reports:

- a. Marshal evidence in support of a thesis and related claims, including information on all relevant perspectives.
- b. Convey information and ideas from primary and secondary sources accurately and coherently.
- c. Make distinctions between the relative value and significance of specific data, facts, and ideas.

d. Include visual aids by employing appropriate technology to organize and record information on charts, maps, and graphs.

e. Anticipate and address readers' potential misunderstandings, biases, and expectations.

f. Use technical terms and notations accurately.

2.4 Write persuasive compositions:

a. Structure ideas and arguments in a sustained and logical fashion.

b. Use specific rhetorical devices to support assertions (e.g., appeal to logic through reasoning; appeal to emotion or ethical belief; relate a personal anecdote, case study, or analogy).

c. Clarify and defend positions with precise and relevant evidence, including facts, expert opinions, quotations, and expressions of commonly accepted beliefs and logical reasoning.

d. Address readers' concerns, counterclaims, biases, and expectations.

2.5 Write business letters:

a. Provide clear and purposeful information and address the intended audience appropriately.

b. Use appropriate vocabulary, tone, and style to take into account the nature of the relationship with, and the knowledge and interests of, the recipients.

c. Highlight central ideas or images.

d. Follow a conventional style with page formats, fonts, and spacing that contribute to the documents' readability and impact.

2.6 Write technical documents (e.g., a manual on rules of behavior for conflict resolution, procedures for conducting a meeting, minutes of a meeting):

a. Report information and convey ideas logically and correctly.

b. Offer detailed and accurate specifications.

c. Include scenarios, definitions, and examples to aid comprehension (e.g., troubleshooting guide).

d. Anticipate readers' problems, mistakes, and misunderstandings.

WRITTEN AND ORAL ENGLISH LANGUAGE CONVENTIONS

The standards for written and oral English language conventions have been placed between those for writing and for listening and speaking because these conventions are essential to both sets of skills.

1.0 Written and Oral English Language Conventions

Students write and speak with a command of standard English conventions.

Grammar and Mechanics of Writing

1.1 Identify and correctly use clauses (e.g., main and subordinate), phrases (e.g., gerund, infinitive, and participial), and mechanics of punctuation (e.g., semicolons, colons, ellipses, hyphens).

1.2 Understand sentence construction (e.g., parallel structure, subordination, proper placement of modifiers) and proper English usage (e.g., consistency of verb tenses).

1.3 Demonstrate an understanding of proper English usage and control of grammar, paragraph and sentence structure, diction, and syntax.

Manuscript Form

1.4 Produce legible work that shows accurate spelling and correct use of the conventions of punctuation and capitalization.

1.5 Reflect appropriate manuscript requirements, including title page presentation, pagination, spacing and margins, and integration of source and support material (e.g., in-text citation, use of direct quotations, paraphrasing) with appropriate citations.

LISTENING AND SPEAKING

1.0 Listening and Speaking Strategies

Students formulate adroit judgments about oral communication. They deliver focused and coherent presentations of their own that convey clear and distinct perspectives and solid reasoning. They use gestures, tone, and vocabulary tailored to the audience and purpose.

Comprehension

1.1 Formulate judgments about the ideas under discussion and support those judgments with convincing evidence.

1.2 Compare and contrast the ways in which media genres (e.g., televised news, news magazines, documentaries, online information) cover the same event.

Organization and Delivery of Oral Communication

1.3 Choose logical patterns of organization (e.g., chronological, topical, cause and effect) to inform and to persuade, by soliciting agreement or action, or to unite audiences behind a common belief or cause.

1.4 Choose appropriate techniques for developing the introduction and conclusion (e.g., by using literary quotations, anecdotes, references to authoritative sources).

1.5 Recognize and use elements of classical speech forms (e.g., introduction, first and second transitions, body, conclusion) in formulating rational arguments and applying the art of persuasion and debate.

1.6 Present and advance a clear thesis statement and choose appropriate types of proofs (e.g., statistics, testimony, specific instances) that meet standard tests for evidence, including credibility, validity, and relevance.

1.7 Use props, visual aids, graphs, and electronic media to enhance the appeal and accuracy of presentations.

1.8 Produce concise notes for extemporaneous delivery.

1.9 Analyze the occasion and the interests of the audience and choose effective verbal and nonverbal techniques (e.g., voice, gestures, eye contact) for presentations.

Analysis and Evaluation of Oral and Media Communications

1.10 Analyze historically significant speeches (e.g., Abraham Lincoln's "Gettysburg Address," Martin Luther King, Jr.'s "I Have a Dream") to find the rhetorical devices and features that make them memorable.

1.11 Assess how language and delivery affect the mood and tone of the oral communication and make an impact on the audience.

1.12 Evaluate the clarity, quality, effectiveness, and general coherence of a speaker's important points, arguments, evidence, organization of ideas, delivery, diction, and syntax.

1.13 Analyze the types of arguments used by the speaker, including argument by causation, analogy, authority, emotion, and logic.

1.14 Identify the aesthetic effects of a media presentation and evaluate the techniques used to create them (e.g., compare Shakespeare's *Henry V* with Kenneth Branagh's 1990 film version).

2.0 Speaking Applications (Genres and Their Characteristics)

Students deliver polished formal and extemporaneous presentations that combine the traditional rhetorical strategies of narration, exposition, persuasion, and description. Student speaking demonstrates a command of standard American English and the organizational and delivery strategies outlined in Listening and Speaking Standard 1.0.

Using the speaking strategies of grades nine and ten outlined in Listening and Speaking Standard 1.0, students:

2.1 Deliver narrative presentations:

a. Narrate a sequence of events and communicate their significance to the audience.

b. Locate scenes and incidents in specific places.

c. Describe with concrete sensory details the sights, sounds, and smells of a scene and the specific actions, movements, gestures, and feelings of characters.

d. Pace the presentation of actions to accommodate time or mood changes.

2.2 Deliver expository presentations:

a. Marshal evidence in support of a thesis and related claims, including information on all relevant perspectives.

b. Convey information and ideas from primary and secondary sources accurately and coherently.

c. Make distinctions between the relative value and significance of specific data, facts, and ideas.

d. Include visual aids by employing appropriate technology to organize and display information on charts, maps, and graphs.

e. Anticipate and address the listener's potential misunderstandings, biases, and expectations.

f. Use technical terms and notations accurately.

2.3 Apply appropriate interviewing techniques:

a. Prepare and ask relevant questions.

b. Make notes of responses.

c. Use language that conveys maturity, sensitivity, and respect.

d. Respond correctly and effectively to questions.

e. Demonstrate knowledge of the subject or organization.

f. Compile and report responses.

g. Evaluate the effectiveness of the interview.

2.4 Deliver oral responses to literature:

a. Advance a judgment demonstrating a comprehensive grasp of the significant ideas of works or passages (i.e., make and support warranted assertions about the text).

b. Support important ideas and viewpoints through accurate and detailed references to the text or to other works.

c. Demonstrate awareness of the author's use of stylistic devices and an appreciation of the effects created.

d. Identify and assess the impact of perceived ambiguities, nuances, and complexities within the text.

2.5 Deliver persuasive arguments (including evaluation and analysis of problems and solutions and causes and effects):

a. Structure ideas and arguments in a coherent, logical fashion.

b. Use rhetorical devices to support assertions (e.g., by appeal to logic through reasoning; by appeal to emotion or ethical belief; by use of personal anecdote, case study, or analogy).

c. Clarify and defend positions with precise and relevant evidence, including facts, expert opinions, quotations, expressions of commonly accepted beliefs, and logical reasoning.

d. Anticipate and address the listener's concerns and counterarguments.

2.6 Deliver descriptive presentations:

a. Establish clearly the speaker's point of view on the subject of the presentation.

b. Establish clearly the speaker's relationship with that subject (e.g., dispassionate observation, personal involvement).

c. Use effective, factual descriptions of appearance, concrete images, shifting perspectives and vantage points, and sensory details.

Contents

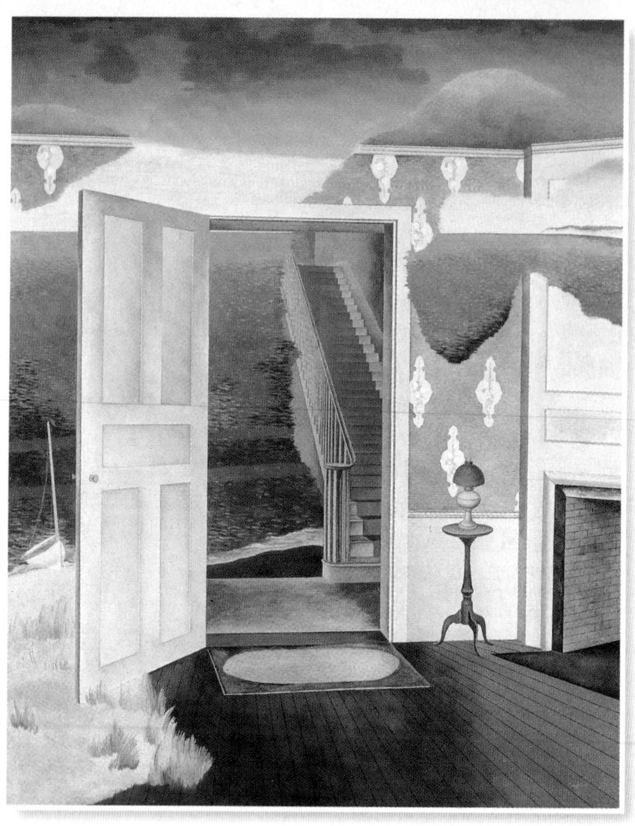

UNIT ONE

The Short Story

🌍 *indicates world literature*

Theme 4 Challenges and Consequences

UNIT ❧ TWO

Nonfiction

Sea and Tidal River, 1916 (detail).

UNIT THREE

Poetry

Theme 8 Issues of Identity .621

UNIT FOUR

Drama

UNIT ❦ SIX

Humor

Reference Section

MEDIA connection

COMPARING selections

Interdisciplinary Connection

Genre Focus

Literature FOCUS

Active Reading Strategies

Writing Workshop

Skills

Grammar Link

Listening, Speaking, and Viewing

Reading & Thinking Skills

Technology Skills

Vocabulary Skills

Writing Skills

Skill Minilessons

GRAMMAR AND LANGUAGE

READING AND THINKING

VOCABULARY

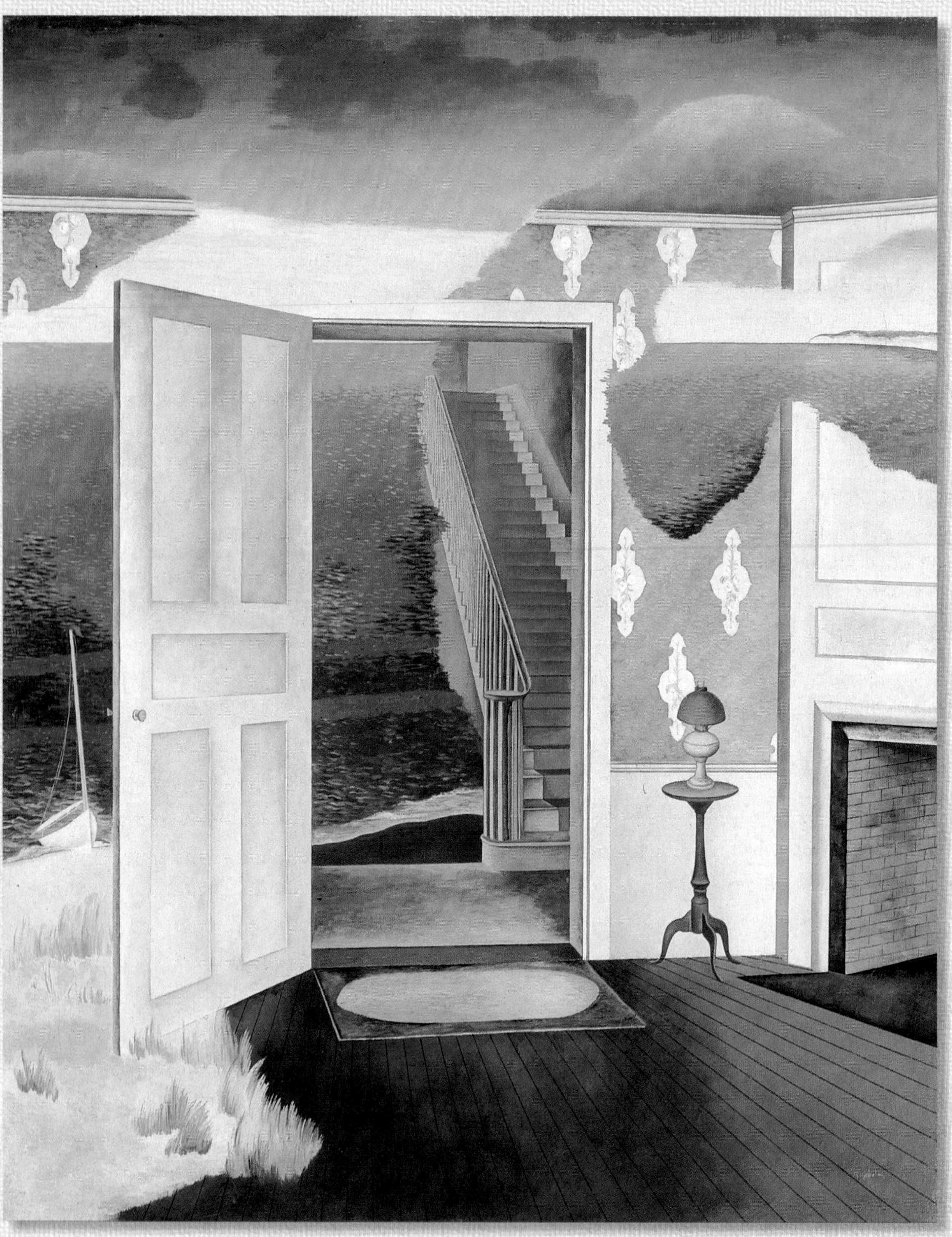

The Persistent Sea, No. 2. O. Louis Guglielmi (1906–1956). Oil on canvas, 29⅞ x 23¼ in. Private collection.

UNIT ✤ ONE

The Short Story

"[F]iction is like a spider's web, attached ever so lightly perhaps, but still attached to life at all four corners."

—Virginia Woolf

Genre Focus

Short Stories

When you talk about computers, you use terms that are specific to computers: megabytes, "log on," "boot up." Likewise, when people talk about literature, they use special terms—the language of literature analysis. You will find that learning to use that language can help you talk about how short stories are put together and what makes them effective.

What is a short story? It is a short piece of fiction that includes elements described in the charts on these pages. Look at how a story you probably know, the children's tale "Cinderella," can be analyzed in terms of these elements.

SHORT STORY ELEMENTS

MODEL: "Cinderella"

Setting

Setting is the time and place in which a story happens. The setting includes not only physical surroundings but also ideas, customs, values, and beliefs.

The story takes place a long time ago in a land ruled by a king and a queen.

Characters

Characters are the actors in a story's plot. They can be people, animals, or whatever the writer chooses.

- The **protagonist** is the main character.
- The **antagonist** is the person in conflict with the main character. Not all stories have antagonists.

The main characters are Cinderella, the stepsisters, their mother, the fairy godmother, the prince.
protagonist: Cinderella
antagonists: the stepsisters, their mother

Point of View

Point of view refers to the vantage point from which a story is told. The person telling the story is the narrator.

- **First-person point of view:** The narrator, a character in the story, uses "I" and "me" to tell the story.
- **Third-person point of view:** The narrator describes the characters and action from outside the story. A **third-person omniscient narrator** knows everything that goes on. A **third-person limited narrator** describes events as one character sees them.

"Cinderella" is told from the **third-person omniscient point of view:** the narrator knows what all the characters are doing and thinking.

Theme

Theme is the central message of a story that readers can apply to life. Common themes include insights into human nature and perceptions about life.

- **Stated themes** are directly presented in a story.
- **Implied themes** must be inferred. Readers need to consider all the elements of a story and ask what message about life they convey.

The theme of "Cinderella" is **implied.** The reader can infer the message that if you are in a bad situation, you should do the best that you can. In the end, things will work out for you.

Plot

Plot is the sequence of events in a story–a series of related incidents. Most plots deal with a **problem** and develop around a **conflict,** a struggle between opposing forces.

- An **external conflict** is a struggle between a character and an outside force, such as another character, nature, society, or fate.
- An **internal conflict** takes place within the mind of a character who struggles with opposing feelings or with indecision about how to act.

The events that make up the plot of "Cinderella" are shown in the diagram below.
problem: Cinderella wants to go to the ball, but her stepsisters prevent her from going.
conflict: The conflict is external—Cinderella versus the stepsisters and their mother.

Most plots develop in five stages.

- **Exposition** introduces the story's characters, setting, and conflict.
- **Rising action** develops the conflict with complications and twists.
- **Climax** is the emotional high point of the story.
- **Falling action** shows what happens to the characters after the climax.
- **Resolution** shows how the conflict is resolved or how the problem is solved.

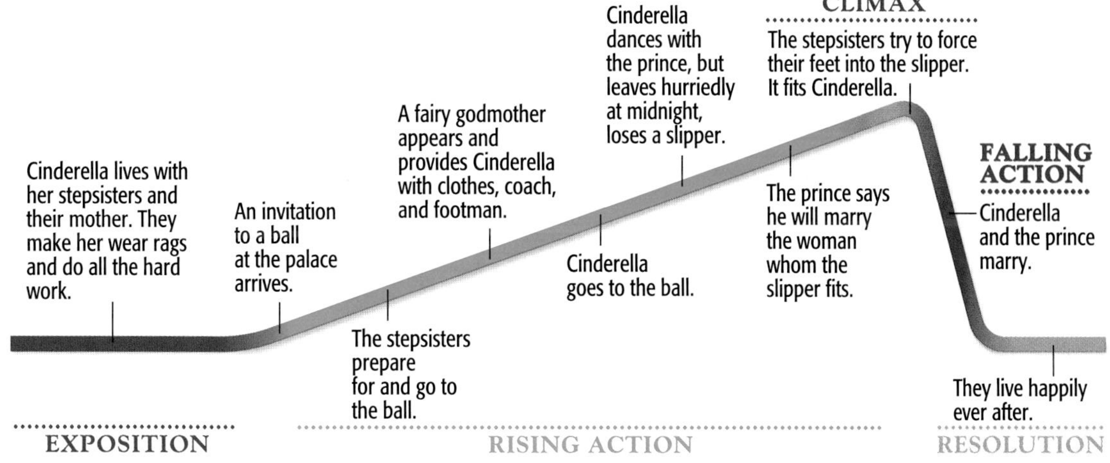
Cinderella lives with her stepsisters and their mother. They make her wear rags and do all the hard work.
An invitation to a ball at the palace arrives.
The stepsisters prepare for and go to the ball.
A fairy godmother appears and provides Cinderella with clothes, coach, and footman.
Cinderella goes to the ball.
Cinderella dances with the prince, but leaves hurriedly at midnight, loses a slipper.
The prince says he will marry the woman whom the slipper fits.
CLIMAX
The stepsisters try to force their feet into the slipper. It fits Cinderella.
FALLING ACTION
Cinderella and the prince marry.
They live happily ever after.
EXPOSITION
RISING ACTION
RESOLUTION

Active Reading Strategies

The Short Story

How can you get the most from your reading? Effective readers are active readers. As they read, they have conversations with themselves about the text; they get involved. Don't be a passive reader! Use the strategies below to help you read short stories actively and effectively.

- For more about related reading strategies, see **Reading Handbook,** pp. R78–R107.

PREDICT

Predicting helps you anticipate events and stay alert to the less obvious parts of a story. Make educated guesses about what will happen next by combining clues in the story with what you already know.

Say to yourself . . .

- From the title, I'd guess this story is about . . .
- This character will probably . . .
- The next thing that *has* to happen is . . .
- This story is different from my original prediction.

CONNECT

Draw parallels between the people, places, and events in the story and the people, events, and places in your own life.

Ask yourself . . .

- How would I act in the main character's situation?
- When have I felt the same way as this character?
- What parts of my life does this remind me of?
- What other stories does this remind me of?

QUESTION

Ask yourself questions to help you clarify the story as you go along.

Ask yourself . . .

- What's going on here?
- Why did he or she say that?
- What does this mean? Do I understand what I've just read?
- What might my teacher want me to notice about this story?

VISUALIZE In your mind, form pictures of what is happening in the story. Pay attention to the details the writer gives you, and make them a part of your reading experience.

Ask yourself . . .
- How does this scene/character/object look?
- Who is in this scene?
- Where are the characters in relation to one another and to their surroundings?

EVALUATE Form opinions and make judgments about the story while you are reading–not just after you've finished.

Ask yourself . . .
- Does this turn of events make sense?
- How would I judge this character's thoughts and actions?
- What is particularly effective about this writer's style?

REVIEW Pause from time to time to think about your reading. Summarize events in a story or rephrase difficult language to help you understand and remember what you've read.

Say to yourself . . .
- So far, . . .
- In other words, . . .

RESPOND Respond *while* you are reading. What are your immediate reactions?

Say to yourself . . .
- I like this, because . . .
- I'd like to ask the writer why . . .
- I think this character is . . .
- I wish I could see this place because . . .
- That was surprising!

Applying the Strategies

1. Read the next story, "Everyday Use," using the Active Reading Model in the margins.
2. Choose a story you have not read and practice using all of these strategies. Use stick-on notes to annotate the story as you read, or take notes on a separate piece of paper.

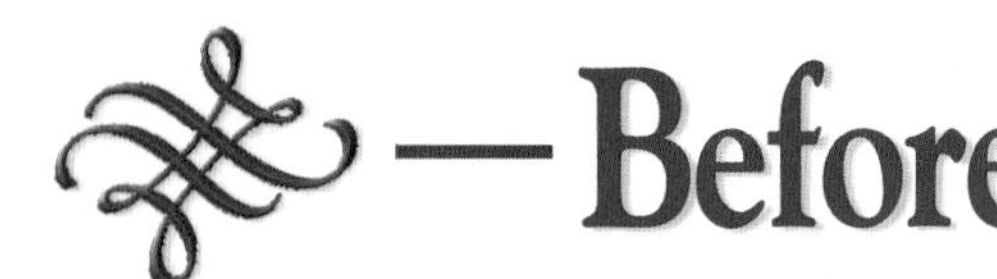

Before You Read

Everyday Use

Reading Focus

What objects have a special meaning for your family or for you?

Quickwrite List at least five objects that are prized by your family or by you. Briefly describe each one.

Setting a Purpose Read to discover how the value of a prized possession can be seen in different ways.

Building Background

The Time and Place

It is the 1970s somewhere in the South, deep in the country. The ancestors of the characters in "Everyday Use" probably were sharecroppers, like the author's parents. Sharecroppers rented land to farm, paid rent with a part of their crops, and sold the rest. In many cases, they worked brutally long hours and made just enough money to survive.

Did You Know?

Quilts developed as a way of making sure that nothing went to waste–even the scraps of fabric left over from making clothes. Women developed complicated patterns of arranging the scraps, and many quilts became works of art.

Vocabulary Preview

sidle (sīd′ əl) *v.* to move sideways, especially in a way that does not attract attention or cause disturbance; p. 8

furtive (fur′ tiv) *adj.* secret; shifty; sly; p. 11

oppress (ə pres′) *v.* to control or govern by the cruel and unjust use of force or authority; p. 12

doctrine (dok′ trin) *n.* a particular principle or position that is taught or supported, as of a religion; p. 13

priceless (prīs′ lis) *adj.* of greater value than can be measured; p. 16

Meet Alice Walker

If Alice Walker's brother had not accidentally shot her in the eye with a BB gun when she was eight, she might not have become a writer. The next year she had to go to a new school. The students made fun of her, and she became self-conscious and shy. Walker began spending her time alone, writing in her journal and reading. By the time she was fourteen and had eye surgery to improve her appearance, she was already hooked on writing and reading. Her most famous book is *The Color Purple*. It won a Pulitzer Prize and was made into a movie.

Alice Walker was born in 1944 in Georgia. She wrote this story in 1972.

Everyday Use

Alice Walker

I WILL WAIT FOR HER in the yard that Maggie and I made so clean and wavy yesterday afternoon. A yard like this is more comfortable than most people know. It is not just a yard. It is like an extended living room. When the hard clay is swept clean as a floor and the fine sand around the edges lined with tiny, irregular grooves, anyone can come and sit and look up into the elm tree and wait for the breezes that never come inside the house.

Maggie will be nervous until after her sister goes: she will stand hopelessly in corners, homely and ashamed of the burn scars down her arms and legs, eying her sister with a mixture of envy and awe. She thinks her sister has held life always in the palm of one hand, that "no" is a word the world never learned to say to her.

Active Reading Model

You've no doubt seen those TV shows where the child who has "made it" is confronted, as a surprise, by her own mother and father, tottering in weakly from backstage. (A pleasant surprise, of course: What would they do if parent and child came on the show only to curse out and insult each other?) On TV mother and child embrace and smile into each other's faces.

PREDICT

Based on the first paragraphs, what might this story be about?

Active Reading Model

Sometimes the mother and father weep, the child wraps them in her arms and leans across the table to tell how she would not have made it without their help. I have seen these programs.

Sometimes I dream a dream in which Dee and I are suddenly brought together on a TV program of this sort. Out of a dark and soft-seated limousine I am ushered into a bright room filled with many people. There I meet a smiling, gray, sporty man like Johnny Carson who shakes my hand and tells me what a fine girl I have. Then we are on the stage and Dee is embracing me with tears in her eyes. She pins on my dress a large orchid, even though she has told me once that she thinks orchids are tacky flowers.

Did You Know?
Johnny Carson hosted *The Tonight Show,* the popular late-night TV talk show, from 1962 to 1992.

In real life I am a large, big-boned woman with rough, man-working hands. In the winter I wear flannel nightgowns to bed and overalls during the day. I can kill and clean a hog as mercilessly as a man. My fat keeps me hot in zero weather. I can work outside all day, breaking ice to get water for washing; I can eat pork liver cooked over the open fire minutes after it comes steaming from the hog. One winter I knocked a bull calf straight in the brain between the eyes with a sledge hammer and had the meat hung up to chill before nightfall. But of course all this does not show on television. I am the way my daughter would want me to be: a hundred pounds lighter, my skin like an uncooked barley pancake. My hair glistens in the hot bright lights. Johnny Carson has much to do to keep up with my quick and witty tongue.

But that is a mistake. I know even before I wake up. Who ever knew a Johnson with a quick tongue? Who can even imagine me looking a strange white man in the eye? It seems to me I have talked to them always with one foot raised in flight, with my head turned in whichever way is farthest from them. Dee, though. She would always look anyone in the eye. Hesitation was no part of her nature.

QUESTION
Who is Dee?

"How do I look, Mama?" Maggie says, showing just enough of her thin body enveloped in pink skirt and red blouse for me to know she's there, almost hidden by the door.

"Come out into the yard," I say.

Have you ever seen a lame animal, perhaps a dog run over by some careless person rich enough to own a car, sidle up to someone who is ignorant enough to be kind to him? That is the way my Maggie walks. She has been like this, chin on chest, eyes on ground, feet in shuffle, ever since the fire that burned the other house to the ground.

VISUALIZE
How do you picture Maggie from these details?

Vocabulary
sidle (sīd′ əl) *v.* to move sideways, especially in a way that does not attract attention or cause disturbance

Girl in a Green Dress, 1930. William H. Johnson. Oil on canvas, 24¼ x 19½ in. National Museum of American Art, Washington, DC.

Viewing the painting: Which of the two sisters might be more like the girl in this portrait? Explain.

Active Reading Model

QUESTION
What happened to the sisters in the fire?

EVALUATE
How would you judge the narrator's feelings about Dee's behavior?

CONNECT
Can you think of anyone you know who is like Dee?

VISUALIZE
Stop and form a detailed mental image of the house.

Dee is lighter than Maggie, with nicer hair and a fuller figure. She's a woman now, though sometimes I forget. How long ago was it that the other house burned? Ten, twelve years? Sometimes I can still hear the flames and feel Maggie's arms sticking to me, her hair smoking and her dress falling off her in little black papery flakes. Her eyes seemed stretched open, blazed open by the flames reflected in them. And Dee. I see her standing off under the sweet gum tree she used to dig gum out of; a look of concentration on her face as she watched the last dingy gray board of the house fall in toward the red-hot brick chimney. Why don't you do a dance around the ashes? I'd wanted to ask her. She had hated the house that much.

I used to think she hated Maggie, too. But that was before we raised the money, the church and me, to send her to Augusta[1] to school. She used to read to us without pity; forcing words, lies, other folks' habits, whole lives upon us two, sitting trapped and ignorant underneath her voice. She washed us in a river of make-believe, burned us with a lot of knowledge we didn't necessarily need to know. Pressed us to her with the serious way she read, to shove us away at just the moment, like dimwits, we seemed about to understand.

Dee wanted nice things. A yellow organdy[2] dress to wear to her graduation from high school; black pumps to match a green suit she'd made from an old suit somebody gave me. She was determined to stare down any disaster in her efforts. Her eyelids would not flicker for minutes at a time. Often I fought off the temptation to shake her. At sixteen she had a style of her own: and knew what style was.

I never had an education myself. After second grade the school was closed down. Don't ask me why: in 1927 colored asked fewer questions than they do now. Sometimes Maggie reads to me. She stumbles along good-naturedly but can't see well. She knows she is not bright. Like good looks and money, quickness passed her by. She will marry John Thomas (who has mossy teeth in an earnest face) and then I'll be free to sit here and I guess just sing church songs to myself. Although I never was a good singer. Never could carry a tune. I was always better at a man's job. I used to love to milk till I was hooked in the side in '49. Cows are soothing and slow and don't bother you, unless you try to milk them the wrong way.

I have deliberately turned my back on the house. It is three rooms, just like the one that burned, except the roof is tin; they don't make shingle roofs any more. There are no real windows, just some holes cut in the sides, like the portholes in a ship, but not round and not square, with rawhide holding the shutters up on the outside. This house is in a pasture, too, like the other one. No doubt when Dee sees it she will want to tear it down. She wrote me once that no matter where we "choose" to live, she will manage to come see us. But

---

1. *Augusta* is a city in Georgia.
2. *Organdy* is a lightweight fabric, usually made of cotton.

Active Reading Model

she will never bring her friends. Maggie and I thought about this and Maggie asked me, "Mama, when did Dee ever *have* any friends?"

She had a few. Furtive boys in pink shirts hanging about on washday after school. Nervous girls who never laughed. Impressed with her they worshiped the well-turned phrase, the cute shape, the scalding humor that erupted like bubbles in lye. She read to them.

When she was courting Jimmy T she didn't have much time to pay to us, but turned all her faultfinding power on him. He *flew* to marry a cheap city girl from a family of ignorant flashy people. She hardly had time to recompose herself.

When she comes I will meet—but there they are!

Maggie attempts to make a dash for the house, in her shuffling way, but I stay her with my hand. "Come back here," I say. And she stops and tries to dig a well in the sand with her toe.

PREDICT
What do you think this family reunion will be like?

It is hard to see them clearly through the strong sun. But even the first glimpse of leg out of the car tells me it is Dee. Her feet were always neat-looking, as if God himself had shaped them with a certain style. From the other side of the car comes a short, stocky man. Hair is all over his head a foot long and hanging from his chin like a kinky mule tail. I hear Maggie suck in her breath. "Uhnnnh," is what it sounds like. Like when you see the wriggling end of a snake just in front of your foot on the road. "Uhnnnh."

Dee next. A dress down to the ground, in this hot weather. A dress so loud it hurts my eyes. There are yellows and oranges enough to throw back the light of the sun. I feel my whole face warming from the heat waves it throws out. Earrings gold, too, and hanging down to her shoulders. Bracelets dangling and making noises when she moves her arm up to shake the folds of the dress out of her armpits. The dress is loose and flows, and as she walks closer, I like it. I hear Maggie go "Uhnnnh" again. It is her sister's hair. It stands straight up like the wool on a sheep. It is black as night and around the edges are two long pigtails that rope about like small lizards disappearing behind her ears.

"Wa-su-zo-Tean-o!" she says, coming on in that gliding way the dress makes her move. The short stocky fellow with the hair to his navel is all grinning and follows up with "Asalamalakim,[3] my mother and sister!" He moves to hug Maggie but she falls back, right up against the back of my chair. I feel her trembling there and when I look up I see the perspiration falling off her chin.

"Don't get up," says Dee. Since I am stout it takes something of a push. You can see me trying to move a second or two before I make it. She turns,

3. *Wa-su-zo-Tean-o!* (wä so͞o′ zō tēn′ ō) and *Asalamalakim* (ä säl ä mä′ lä kēm) are greetings.

Vocabulary
furtive (fur′ tiv) *adj.* secret; shifty; sly

Active Reading Model

EVALUATE

Does it make sense for Dee to take pictures of a place she hates so much?

QUESTION

Why does the narrator keep calling him *Asalamalakim?*

REVIEW

Think about what you know about this family so far.

showing white heels through her sandals, and goes back to the car. Out she peeks next with a Polaroid. She stoops down quickly and lines up picture after picture of me sitting there in front of the house with Maggie cowering behind me. She never takes a shot without making sure the house is included. When a cow comes nibbling around the edge of the yard she snaps it and me and Maggie *and* the house. Then she puts the Polaroid in the back seat of the car, and comes up and kisses me on the forehead.

Meanwhile Asalamalakim is going through motions with Maggie's hand. Maggie's hand is as limp as a fish, and probably as cold, despite the sweat, and she keeps trying to pull it back. It looks like Asalamalakim wants to shake hands but wants to do it fancy. Or maybe he don't know how people shake hands. Anyhow, he soon gives up on Maggie.

"Well," I say. "Dee."

"No, Mama," she says. "Not 'Dee,' Wangero Leewanika Kemanjo!"[4]

"What happened to 'Dee'?" I wanted to know.

"She's dead," Wangero said. "I couldn't bear it any longer, being named after the people who oppress me."

"You know as well as me you was named after your aunt Dicie," I said. Dicie is my sister. She named Dee. We called her "Big Dee" after Dee was born.

"But who was *she* named after?" asked Wangero.

"I guess after Grandma Dee," I said.

"And who was she named after?" asked Wangero.

"Her mother," I said, and saw Wangero was getting tired. "That's about as far back as I can trace it," I said. Though, in fact, I probably could have carried it back beyond the Civil War through the branches.

"Well," said Asalamalakim, "there you are."

"Uhnnnh," I heard Maggie say.

"There I was not," I said, "before 'Dicie' cropped up in our family, so why should I try to trace it that far back?"

He just stood there grinning, looking down on me like somebody inspecting a Model A car. Every once in a while he and Wangero sent eye signals over my head.

"How do you pronounce this name?" I asked.

"You don't have to call me by it if you don't want to," said Wangero.

"Why shouldn't I?" I asked. "If that's what you want us to call you, we'll call you."

"I know it might sound awkward at first," said Wangero.

Did You Know?
The *Model A* was manufactured by the Ford Motor Company from 1927 to 1931.

4. ***Wangero Leewanika Kemanjo*** (wän gär′ ō lē wä′ nē kə ke män′ jō)

Vocabulary

oppress (ə pres′) *v.* to control or govern by the cruel and unjust use of force or authority

"I'll get used to it," I said. "Ream it out again."

Well, soon we got the name out of the way. Asalamalakim had a name twice as long and three times as hard. After I tripped over it two or three times he told me to just call him Hakim-a-barber.[5] I wanted to ask him was he a barber, but I didn't really think he was, so I didn't ask.

"You must belong to those beef cattle peoples down the road," I said. They said "Asalamalakim" when they met you, too, but they didn't shake hands. Always too busy: feeding the cattle, fixing the fences, putting up salt-lick shelters, throwing down hay. When the white folks poisoned some of the herd the men stayed up all night with rifles in their hands. I walked a mile and a half just to see the sight.

Hakim-a-barber said, "I accept some of their doctrines, but farming and raising cattle is not my style." (They didn't tell me, and I didn't ask, whether Wangero (Dee) had really gone and married him.)

We sat down to eat and right away he said he didn't eat collards and pork was unclean. Wangero, though, went on through the chitlins and corn bread, the greens and everything else. She talked a blue streak over the sweet potatoes. Everything delighted her. Even the fact that we still used the benches her daddy made for the table when we couldn't afford to buy chairs.

"Oh, Mama!" she cried. Then turned to Hakim-a-barber. "I never knew how lovely these benches are. You can feel the rump prints," she said, running her hands underneath her and along the bench. Then she gave a sigh and her hand closed over Grandma Dee's butter dish. "That's it!" she said. "I knew

Active Reading Model

QUESTION

Do you think this means that Mama knew all along that *Asalamalakim* was a greeting?

5. ***Hakim-a-barber*** (hä kēm′ ä bär′ bər)

Vocabulary

doctrine (dok′ trin) *n.* a particular principle or position that is taught or supported, as of a religion

Minnie, 1930. William H. Johnson. Oil on canvas, 17½ x 12¼ in. National Museum of American Art, Washington, DC.

Viewing the painting: What qualities might this woman share with the narrator of the story?

there was something I wanted to ask you if I could have." She jumped up from the table and went over in the corner where the churn stood, the milk in it clabber[6] by now. She looked at the churn and looked at it.

"This churn top is what I need," she said. "Didn't Uncle Buddy whittle it out of a tree you all used to have?"

"Yes," I said.

"Uh huh," she said happily. "And I want the dasher, too."

"Uncle Buddy whittle that, too?" asked the barber.

Dee (Wangero) looked up at me.

"Aunt Dee's first husband whittled the dash," said Maggie so low you almost couldn't hear her. "His name was Henry, but they called him Stash."

"Maggie's brain is like an elephant's," Wangero said, laughing. "I can use the churn top as a centerpiece for the alcove[7] table," she said, sliding a plate over the churn, "and I'll think of something artistic to do with the dasher."

When she finished wrapping the dasher the handle stuck out. I took it for a moment in my hands. You didn't even have to look close to see where hands pushing the dasher up and down to make butter had left a kind of sink in the wood. In fact, there were a lot of small sinks; you could see where thumbs and fingers had sunk into the wood. It was beautiful light yellow wood, from a tree that grew in the yard where Big Dee and Stash had lived.

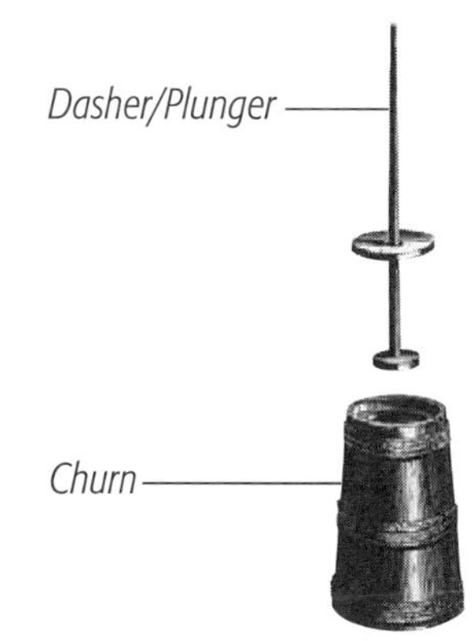

Did You Know?
A *dasher* is the plunger of a churn, a device used to stir cream to make butter.

After dinner Dee (Wangero) went to the trunk at the foot of my bed and started rifling through it. Maggie hung back in the kitchen over the dishpan. Out came Wangero with two quilts. They had been pieced by Grandma Dee and then Big Dee and me had hung them on the quilt frames on the front porch and quilted them. One was in the Lone Star pattern. The other was Walk Around the Mountain. In both of them were scraps of dresses Grandma Dee had worn fifty and more years ago. Bits and pieces of Grandpa Jarrell's Paisley shirts. And one teeny faded blue piece, about the size of a penny matchbox, that was from Great Grandpa Ezra's uniform that he wore in the Civil War.

PREDICT
Do you think Dee will end up with the quilts? Why?

"Mama," Wangero said sweet as a bird. "Can I have these old quilts?"

I heard something fall in the kitchen, and a minute later the kitchen door slammed.

"Why don't you take one or two of the others?" I asked. "These old things was just done by me and Big Dee from some tops your grandma pieced before she died."

"No," said Wangero. "I don't want those. They are stitched around the borders by machine."

6. *Clabber* is the thick, clotted part of sour milk.
7. An *alcove* (al′ kōv) is a small room or recessed opening off of a larger room.

Active Reading Model

"That'll make them last better," I said.

"That's not the point," said Wangero. "These are all pieces of dresses Grandma used to wear. She did all this stitching by hand. Imagine!" She held the quilts securely in her arms, stroking them.

"Some of the pieces, like those lavender ones, come from old clothes her mother handed down to her," I said, moving up to touch the quilts. Dee (Wangero) moved back just enough so that I couldn't reach the quilts. They already belonged to her.

"Imagine!" she breathed again, clutching them closely to her bosom.

"The truth is," I said, "I promised to give them quilts to Maggie, for when she marries John Thomas."

She gasped like a bee had stung her.

CONNECT

How does this statement relate to the story's title?

"Maggie can't appreciate these quilts!" she said. "She'd probably be backward enough to put them to everyday use."

"I reckon she would," I said. "God knows I been saving 'em for long enough with nobody using 'em. I hope she will!" I didn't want to bring up how I had offered Dee (Wangero) a quilt when she went away to college. Then she had told me they were old-fashioned, out of style.

QUESTION

Why does Dee want the quilts now, when she did not want to take one to college?

"But they're *priceless!*" she was saying now, furiously; for she has a temper. "Maggie would put them on the bed and in five years they'd be in rags. Less than that!"

"She can always make some more," I said. "Maggie knows how to quilt."

Dee (Wangero) looked at me with hatred. "You just will not understand. The point is these quilts, *these* quilts!"

"Well," I said, stumped. "What would *you* do with them?"

"Hang them," she said. As if that was the only thing you *could* do with quilts.

CONNECT

How would you feel if you were Maggie?

Maggie by now was standing in the door. I could almost hear the sound her feet made as they scraped over each other.

"She can have them, Mama," she said, like somebody used to never winning anything, or having anything reserved for her. "I can 'member Grandma Dee without the quilts."

I looked at her hard. She had filled her bottom lip with checkerberry snuff and it gave her face a kind of dopey, hangdog look. It was Grandma Dee and Big Dee who taught her how to quilt herself. She stood there with her scarred hands hidden in the folds of her skirt. She looked at her sister with something like fear but she wasn't mad at her. This was Maggie's portion. This was the way she knew God to work.

RESPOND

How do you feel about what Mama did?

When I looked at her like that something hit me in the top of my head and ran down to the soles of my feet. Just like when I'm in church and the spirit of God touches me and I get happy and shout. I did something I never

Vocabulary

priceless (prīs′ lis) *adj.* of greater value than can be measured

Quilts on the Line, 1994. Anna Belle Lee Washington. Oil on canvas, 20 x 30 in.

Viewing the painting: Compare and contrast the family and the setting of this painting with those in the story. What are the most striking differences? similarities?

had done before: hugged Maggie to me, then dragged her on into the room, snatched the quilts out of Miss Wangero's hands and dumped them into Maggie's lap. Maggie just sat there on my bed with her mouth open.

"Take one or two of the others," I said to Dee.

But she turned without a word and went out to Hakim-a-barber.

"You just don't understand," she said, as Maggie and I came out to the car.

"What don't I understand?" I wanted to know.

"Your heritage," she said. And then she turned to Maggie, kissed her, and said, "You ought to try to make something of yourself, too, Maggie. It's really a new day for us. But from the way you and Mama still live you'd never know it."

She put on some sunglasses that hid everything above the tip of her nose and her chin.

Maggie smiled; maybe at the sunglasses. But a real smile, not scared. After we watched the car dust settle I asked Maggie to bring me a dip of snuff. And then the two of us sat there just enjoying, until it was time to go in the house and go to bed.

RESPOND

"... the two of us sat there just enjoying ..." What do you think of this description of contentment?

Responding to Literature

Personal Response

The author has said that she thinks of Dee and Maggie and Mama as herself split into three parts. Which of the characters do you think is most like you? Explain in your journal.

Active Reading Response

Look back at the strategies described in the notes on pages 4 and 5. Which of these strategies do you use most often? Choose one and find three places in the story where you could apply it.

Analyzing Literature

Recall

1. Tell what Mama says about each daughter before Dee's arrival.
2. What reason does Dee give for changing her name? What is Mama's opinion of Dee's reason?
3. What is special about the two quilts that Dee wants?
4. How does Dee react when she learns what Mama plans to do with the quilts? What does Maggie say that Mama should do with them?
5. Why does Dee leave the house so abruptly?

Interpret

6. What can you infer about Mama's feelings toward Maggie and Dee, based on the information she gives before Dee arrives?
7. Do you think the reason Dee gives for changing her name is her only reason? Explain your answer.
8. How does the origin of the quilts affect Maggie's feelings about them? How does it affect Dee?
9. How does Dee feel about Maggie? Support your answer with details from the story.
10. Dee says at the end, "You just don't understand." In your opinion, does Mama understand? Explain.

Evaluate and Connect

11. Why, do you think, does the author begin the story with a description of the yard and a daydream about being on a television show?
12. How important a role does the **setting** play? How might the story be different if the characters lived in another time and another place?
13. Which sister do you like better, Maggie or Dee? Give reasons.
14. Do you feel that you understand your own heritage? Explain.
15. What advice would you like to give to Maggie? To Dee? To Mama?

Literary **ELEMENTS**

Point of View

In **first-person point of view,** the story is told by one of the characters, a narrator who uses "I" and "me" to relate the story. This point of view is limited because the reader "sees" the story only through that character's eyes. In "Everyday Use," for example, the author uses the first-person point of view to tell the story through Mama's eyes. The reader learns what Mama sees, thinks, feels, and experiences as she tells the story in her own voice.

1. The author might have told this story from the point of view of Dee or of Maggie. Why, do you think, did she choose to give Mama's version of what happened?
2. A reader must decide whether to trust the accuracy of the information a narrator presents. Do you trust Mama's version of events? Why or why not?
3. Retell or rewrite a scene from the point of view of Maggie, then of Dee.

- See **Literary Terms Handbook,** p. R9.

Literature and Writing

Writing About Literature

Comparing Characters In what ways are Dee and Maggie alike? In what ways are they different? Write several paragraphs in which you compare and contrast their personalities, values, attitudes toward life, and their development in the course of the story. Share your writing with one or two classmates. Are your views of the two sisters similar?

Creative Writing

Prized Possessions Look back at your response to the Reading Focus on page 6. Choose one of the listed prized objects that has special meaning for your family or for you. Describe the object carefully and explain what makes it so special. Also tell whether you would want it to be put to everyday use.

Extending Your Response

Literature Groups

Seeing Both Sides "Dee really deserved the quilts. She treasured them, not like Maggie. Besides, Dee knew how to take care of them. Maggie didn't even care about keeping them nice."

Do you agree with this statement? Did the right person get the quilts? First, make a list of reasons that Maggie should have gotten the quilts. Then do the same for Dee. Compare your reasons with those listed by other groups and decide which reasons are the most convincing.

Interdisciplinary Activity

Social Studies: Creating an Heirloom Create a piece of woodworking, needlework, or some other object that can be given "everyday use." If you have begun such a project, take this opportunity to complete it. After displaying the object, put it to "everyday use."

Learning for Life

Interview Talk to older relatives or friends about their childhoods or about the way things used to be when they were young. Use questions like these to get started:

- When you think of your childhood, what memories stand out most clearly?
- Where did you live when you were growing up? Where did you go to school? Where did you "hang out"?
- What special objects do you remember from your past? Why were they important to you?
- What was the best thing about the "good old days"? What was the worst thing?

Tape-record your interviews or take notes. Share the information you have gathered with the rest of the class.

Reading Further

You might enjoy these poems by Alice Walker:

"For My Sister Molly Who in the Fifties" and "Beyond What" from her collection *Revolutionary Petunias and Other Poems* present themes of family, transitions, and love.

Literary Criticism

"[Though Maggie] is not knowledgeable about the new 'blackness,'" observes Barbara T. Christian, "[she] truly understands heritage, because through her quilting she loves the people who have passed unto her a tradition of caring." Write a brief essay in which you compare Maggie's understanding of heritage with Dee's.

Save your work for your portfolio.

Skill Minilessons

GRAMMAR AND LANGUAGE • Possessive Pronouns

Possessive pronouns are pronouns that show ownership:

Dee acted as if the quilts were already *hers.*

Dee said, "You don't understand *your* heritage."

Other common possessive pronouns include *my, mine, his, its, our,* and *their.* Remember that apostrophes are not used with possessive pronouns. Thus, always write *its* (not *it's*) and *your* (not *you're*) to show possession.

For more about pronouns, see **Language Handbook,** p. R42.

PRACTICE On your paper, write the possessive pronoun that correctly completes each sentence.

1. Dee and Maggie both want a quilt with (its, it's) own special history.
2. Maggie and Dee have very different relationships with (they're, their) mother.
3. (Your, You're) grandmother and I made these quilts.
4. That blue one is (hers, her's).

READING AND THINKING • Chronological Order

Chronological order is the order, or sequence, in which events actually take place. In most short stories, the author relates the events of the story in chronological order. Sometimes, however, an author may describe events that occurred before or after the events of the story. In "Everyday Use," for example, as Mama sits in the yard waiting for Dee, she remembers an event from the past.

> "How long ago was it that the other house burned? Ten, twelve years? Sometimes I can still hear the flames . . ."

As you read a short story, think about the order in which the events actually occur.

PRACTICE On your paper, arrange these events in chronological order.

1. Dee told Mama that her new name was Wangero.
2. Dee told Maggie that she ought to try to make something of herself.
3. Maggie was badly burned in the fire.
4. Mama quit school after second grade, when her school closed down.
5. Mama snatched the quilts from Dee and gave them to Maggie.

For more about text structure, see **Reading Handbook,** pp. R86–R87.

VOCABULARY • Base Words

Sometimes prefixes or suffixes are added to whole words, called base words, which are often words you know. Although a final vowel may be dropped from a base word when a suffix is added, base words are usually easy to recognize. For example, now that you know the word *doctrine,* you can figure out that a doctrinaire approach would probably involve sticking to a principle or position. By knowing what *oppress* means, you can tell that an oppressive government would be one that controls by the cruel use of force.

PRACTICE Use the familiar base words contained in the words in the left column to match each word to its meaning, given in the right column.

1. inelegancies	a. friendly remarks
2. fatalities	b. to break up, as by spreading out
3. pleasantries	c. having to do with what is to come
4. decentralize	d. deaths
5. futuristic	e. crude behaviors

Transitions

Transitions are changes—passages from one place to another, saying good-bye to the old and welcoming the new, growing into adulthood. The characters you will meet in this theme all face changes in their lives. How do you approach transitions in your life? Do you ease into new stages, or do you resist change and want things to stay the same?

THEME PROJECTS

Performing

Critics' Choice You've probably seen a TV show in which two movie critics each give a thumbs-up or a thumbs-down review about a film. With a partner, create a similar show in which you review the stories in this theme.

1. Choose which elements of each story you will evaluate–for example, characters, plot, suspense, realism. Think about how well these elements work in the story.
2. Be prepared to defend your opinions if your partner challenges them. Use specific examples from the stories.
3. Consider having someone videotape your show so you can view it later.

Interdisciplinary Project

Art Choose three characters in this theme whose transitions are most interesting to you, and represent their changes visually.

1. Think about how each moment of transition would look. What objects could symbolize the characters' past life or their new condition? What colors best represent the before and after stages of their change?
2. Make a painting, collage, or diorama representing each of your characters' transitions.
3. Show your work to your classmates; see if they can tell which characters you've chosen.

The Family, Diana Ong (b. 1940). Private collection.

Before You Read

Chee's Daughter

Reading Focus

What would you do if someone took away something that was especially precious to you? Would you plot revenge, give up and feel very sad about the loss, or would you try to find a way to get the item back?

Chart It! Develop a flow chart like the one shown that details the steps you would take to get back something precious.

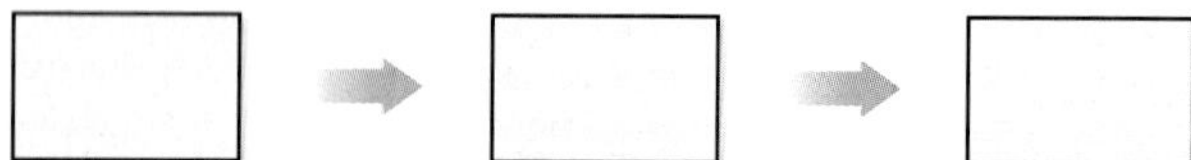

Setting a Purpose Read to learn how one Navajo man reacts to the loss of something precious.

Meet Juanita Platero and Siyowin Miller

Juanita Platero, a Navajo writer, began working in collaboration with California writer Siyowin Miller in 1929. Most of the stories the two wrote together explore the intersection of the traditional ways of the Navajo and the modern ways of twentieth-century America. The stories explore how these ways come into conflict, both in personal and family relationships, and how the conflicts are resolved. Platero and Miller also wrote a novel, *The Winds Erase Your Footprints*.

Building Background

The Time and Place

During the mid-1900s, a young Navajo (also spelled Navaho) father in the southwestern United States honors the ancient traditions and way of life despite the growth of modern civilization.

Did You Know?

Traditional Navajo culture is matrilineal—that is, a family traces its ancestry back through the mother's line, and children belong to the mother's clan. Typically, several generations of a family live close together. For example, a married daughter, her husband, and their children, and perhaps even her sisters and their families, would all live with or near her parents. The oldest woman in the family, usually the grandmother, enjoys a place at the center of family life.

Vocabulary Preview

gaudy (gô′ dē) *adj.* bright and showy to the point of being in bad taste; p. 26

indolence (ind′ əl əns) *n.* laziness; idleness; p. 27

acrid (ak′ rid) *adj.* irritating or upsetting; p. 30

banter (ban′ tər) *n.* good-natured, witty joking or teasing; p. 30

zealously (zel′ əs lē) *adv.* eagerly; enthusiastically; p. 31

flaunt (flônt) *v.* to display in a showy manner; p. 32

deference (def′ ər əns) *n.* courteous respect or regard for the judgment, opinions, or desires of another; p. 33

surmise (sər mīz′) *v.* to guess or conclude from little or no evidence; p. 33

Chee's Daughter

Juanita Platero
and Siyowin Miller

THE HAT TOLD THE STORY, the big, black, drooping Stetson. It was not at the proper angle, the proper rakish angle for so young a Navaho. There was no song, and that was not in keeping either.

There should have been at least a humming, a faint, all-to-himself "he he he heya," for it was a good horse he was riding, a slender-legged, high-stepping buckskin that would race the wind with light knee-urging. This was a day for singing, a warm winter day, when the touch of the sun upon the back belied the snow high on distant mountains.

Wind warmed by the sun touched his high-boned cheeks like flicker feathers, and still he rode on silently, deeper into Little Canyon, until the red rock walls rose straight upward from the stream bed and only a narrow piece of blue sky hung above. Abruptly the sky widened where the canyon walls were pushed back to make a wide place, as though in ancient times an angry stream had tried to go all ways at once.

This was home—this wide place in the canyon—levels of jagged rock and levels of rich red earth. This was home to Chee, the rider of the buckskin, as it had been to many generations before him.

He stopped his horse at the stream and sat looking across the narrow ribbon of water to the bare-branched peach trees. He was seeing them each springtime with their age-gnarled limbs transfigured beneath veils of blossom pink; he was seeing them in autumn laden with their yellow fruit, small and sweet. Then his eyes searched out the indistinct furrows of the fields beside the stream, where each year the corn and beans and squash drank thirstily of the overflow from summer rains. Chee was trying to outweigh today's bitter betrayal of hope by gathering to himself these reminders of the integrity of the land. Land did not cheat! His mind lingered deliberately on all the days spent here in the sun caring for the young plants, his songs to the earth and to the life springing from it—". . . In the middle of the wide field . . . Yellow Corn Boy . . . He has started both ways . . ." then the harvest and repayment in full measure. Here was the old feeling of wholeness and of oneness with the sun and earth and growing things.

Chee urged the buckskin toward the family compound where, secure in a recess of overhanging rock, was his mother's dome-shaped hogan, red rock and red adobe like the ground on which it nestled. Not far from the hogan was the half-circle of brush like a dark shadow against the canyon wall—corral for sheep and goats. Farther from the hogan, in full circle, stood the horse corral made of heavy cedar branches sternly interlocked. Chee's long thin lips curved into a smile as he passed his daughter's tiny hogan squatted like a round Pueblo oven beside the corral. He remembered the summer day when together they sat back on their heels and plastered wet adobe all about the circling wall of rock and the woven dome of piñon twigs. How his family laughed when the Little One herded the bewildered chickens into her tiny hogan as the first snow fell.

Did You Know?
Piñon (pin′ yōn), is any of several small pine trees found in Mexico and the southwestern United States.

Then the smile faded from Chee's lips and his eyes darkened as he tied his horse to a corral post and turned to the strangely empty compound. "Someone has told them," he thought, "and they are inside weeping." He passed his mother's deserted loom on the south side of the hogan and pulled the rude wooden door toward him, bowing his head, hunching his shoulders to get inside.

His mother sat sideways by the center fire, her feet drawn up under her full skirts. Her hands were busy kneading dough in the chipped white basin. With her head down, her voice was muffled when she said, "The meal will soon be ready, Son."

Chee passed his father sitting against the wall, hat over his eyes as though asleep. He passed his older sister, who sat turning mutton ribs on a crude wire grill over the coals, noticed tears dropping on her hands: "She cared more for my wife than I realized," he thought.

Then because something must be said sometime, he tossed the black Stetson upon a bulging sack of wool and said, "You have heard, then." He could not shut from his mind how confidently he had set the handsome new hat on his head that very morning, slanting the wide brim over one eye: he was going to see his wife, and today he would ask the doctors about bringing her home; last week she had looked so much better.

His sister nodded but did not speak. His mother sniffled and passed her velveteen sleeve beneath her nose. Chee sat down, leaning against the wall. "I suppose I was a fool for hoping all the time. I should have expected this. Few of our people get well from the coughing sickness.[1] But *she* seemed to be getting better."

His mother was crying aloud now and blowing her nose noisily on her skirt. His father sat up, speaking gently to her.

Chee shifted his position and started a cigarette. His mind turned back to the Little One. At least she was too small to understand what had happened, the Little One who had been born three years before in the sanitarium where his wife was being treated for the coughing sickness, the Little One he had brought home to his mother's hogan to be nursed by his sister, whose baby was a few months older. As she

1. *Coughing sickness* is a common name for tuberculosis, an infectious disease that affects the lungs and other body tissues and is characterized by a persistent cough.

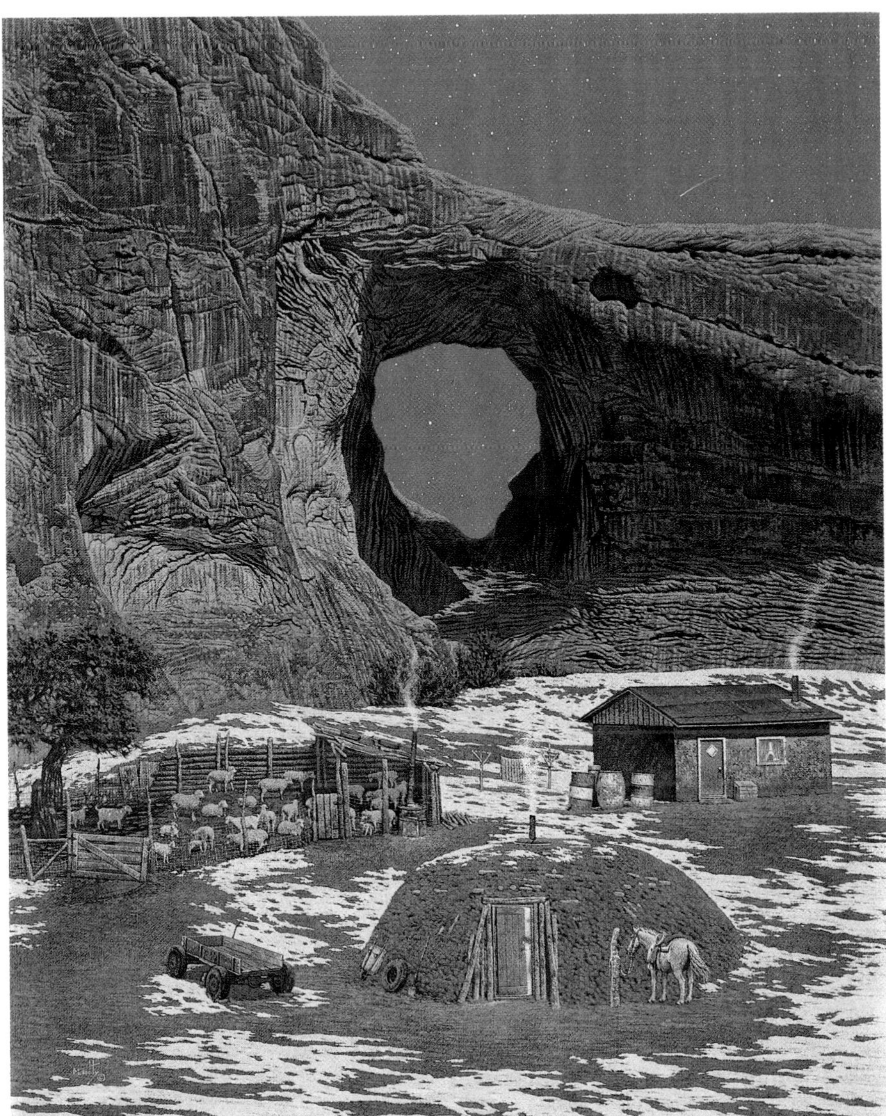

Moonlight. Marvin Toddy (b. 1954). Oil on canvas, 20 x 16 in. La Fonda Indian Shop and Gallery, Santa Fe.

Viewing the painting: How well does this painting help you visualize the place where Chee lives?

grew fat-cheeked and sturdy-legged, she followed him about like a shadow; somehow her baby mind had grasped that of all those at the hogan who cared for her and played with her, he—Chee—belonged most to her. She sat cross-legged at his elbow when he worked silver at the forge; she rode before him in the saddle when he drove the horses to water; often she lay wakeful on her sheep pelts until he stretched out for the night in the darkened hogan and she could snuggle warm against him.

Chee blew smoke slowly, and some of the sadness left his dark eyes as he said, "It is not as bad as it might be. It is not as though we are left with nothing."

Chee's sister arose, sobs catching in her throat, and rushed past him out the doorway. Chee sat upright, a terrible fear possessing him. For a moment his mouth could make no sound. Then: "The Little One! Mother, where is she?"

His mother turned her stricken face to him. "Your wife's people came after her this morning. They heard yesterday of their daughter's death through the trader at Red Sands."

Chee started to protest, but his mother shook her head slowly. "I didn't expect they would want the Little One either. But there is nothing you can do. She is a girl child and belongs to her mother's people; it is custom."

Frowning, Chee got to his feet, grinding his cigarette into the dirt floor. "Custom! When did my wife's parents begin thinking about custom? Why, the hogan where they live doesn't even face the east!" He started toward the door. "Perhaps I can overtake them. Perhaps they don't realize how much we want her here with us. I'll ask them to give my daughter back to me. Surely, they won't refuse."

His mother stopped him gently with her outstretched hand. "You couldn't overtake them now. They were in the trader's car. Eat and rest, and think more about this."

"Have you forgotten how things have always been between you and your wife's people?" his father said.

That night, Chee's thoughts were troubled—half-forgotten incidents became disturbingly vivid—but early the next morning he saddled the buckskin and set out for the settlement of Red Sands. Even though his father-in-law, Old Man Fat, might laugh, Chee knew that he must talk to him. There were some things to which Old Man Fat might listen.

Did You Know?
A *butte* (byūt) is an isolated, flat-topped land formation created by the erosion of all but a portion of a mesa or plateau. A *mesa* (mā′ sə) is a flat-topped hill or mountain with steep, rocky sides.

Chee rode the first part of the fifteen miles to Red Sands expectantly. The sight of sandstone buttes near Cottonwood Spring reddening in the morning sun brought a song almost to his lips. He twirled his reins in salute to the small boy herding sheep toward many-colored Butterfly Mountain, watched with pleasure the feathers of smoke rising against tree-darkened western mesas from the hogans sheltered there. But as he approached the familiar settlement sprawled in mushroom growth along the highway, he began to feel as though a scene from a bad dream was becoming real.

Several cars were parked around the trading store, which was built like two log hogans side by side, with red gas pumps in front and a sign across the tar-paper roofs: *Red Sands Trading Post—Groceries Gasoline Cold Drinks Sandwiches Indian Curios.* Back of the trading post an unpainted frame house and outbuildings squatted on the drab, treeless land. Chee and the Little One's mother had lived there when they stayed with his wife's people. That was according to custom—living with one's wife's people—but Chee had never been convinced that it was custom alone which prompted Old Man Fat and his wife to insist that their daughter bring her husband to live at the trading post.

Beside the post was a large hogan of logs, with brightly painted pseudo-Navaho[2] designs on the roof—a hogan with smoke-smudged windows and a garish blue door which faced north to the highway. Old Man Fat had offered Chee a hogan like this one. The trader would build it if he and his wife would live there and Chee would work at his forge, making silver jewelry where tourists could watch him. But Chee had asked instead for a piece of land for a cornfield and help in building a hogan far back from the highway and a corral for the sheep he had brought to this marriage.

A cold wind blowing down from the mountains began to whistle about Chee's ears. It flapped the gaudy Navaho rugs which were hung in one long bright line to attract tourists. It swayed the sign *Navaho Weaver at*

2. The prefix *pseudo-* (sōō′ dō) means "false or imitation."

Vocabulary
gaudy (gô′ dē) *adj.* bright and showy to the point of being in bad taste

Work beside the loom where Old Man Fat's wife sat hunched in her striped blanket, patting the colored thread of a design into place with a wooden comb. Tourists stood watching the weaver. More tourists stood in a knot before the hogan where the sign said: *See Inside a Real Navaho Home 25¢.*

Then the knot seemed to unravel as a few people returned to their cars; some had cameras; and there against the blue door Chee saw the Little One standing uncertainly. The wind was plucking at her new purple blouse and wide green skirt; it freed truant strands of soft dark hair from the meager queue into which it had been tied with white yarn.

Did You Know?
Here, *queue* (kyū) refers to a braid of hair at the back of the head.

"Isn't she cunning!" one of the women tourists was saying as she turned away.

Chee's lips tightened as he began to look around for Old Man Fat. Finally he saw him passing among the tourists collecting coins.

Then the Little One saw Chee. The uncertainty left her face, and she darted through the crowd as her father swung down from his horse. Chee lifted her in his arms, hugging her tight. While he listened to her breathless chatter, he watched Old Man Fat bearing down on them, scowling.

As his father-in-law walked heavily across the graveled lot, Chee was reminded of a statement his mother sometimes made: "When you see a fat Navaho, you see one who hasn't worked for what he has."

Old Man Fat was fattest in the middle. There was indolence in his walk even though he seemed to hurry, indolence in his cheeks so plump they made his eyes squint, eyes now smoldering with anger.

Some of the tourists were getting into their cars and driving away. The old man said belligerently to Chee, "Why do you come here? To spoil our business? To drive people away?"

"I came to talk with you," Chee answered, trying to keep his voice steady as he faced the old man.

"We have nothing to talk about," Old Man Fat blustered and did not offer to touch Chee's extended hand.

"It's about the Little One." Chee settled his daughter more comfortably against his hip as he weighed carefully all the words he had planned to say. "We are going to miss her very much. It wouldn't be so bad if we knew that *part* of each year she could be with us. That might help you too. You and your wife are no longer young people and you have no young ones here to depend upon." Chee chose his next words remembering the thriftlessness of his wife's parents, and their greed. "Perhaps we could share the care of this little one. Things are good with us. So much snow this year will make lots of grass for the sheep. We have good land for corn and melons."

Chee's words did not have the expected effect. Old Man Fat was enraged. "Farmers, all of you! Long-haired farmers! Do you think everyone must bend his back over the short-handled hoe in order to have food to eat?" His tone changed as he began to brag a little. "We not only have all the things from cans at the trader's, but when the Pueblos come past here on their way to town, we buy their salty jerked mutton, young corn for roasting, dried sweet peaches."

Vocabulary
indolence (ind′ əl əns) *n.* laziness; idleness

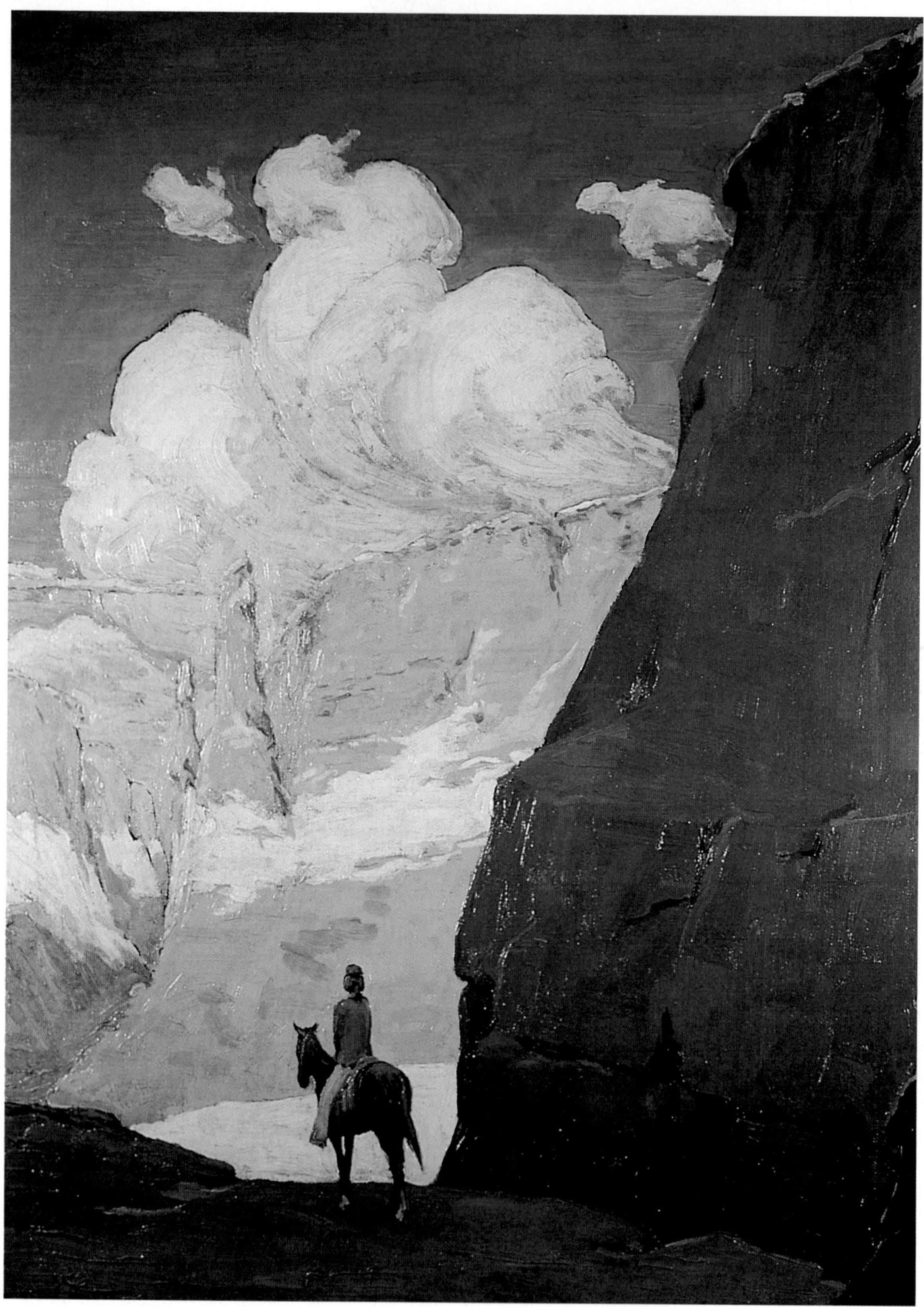

The Canyon, 1919. Frank Reed Whiteside. Oil on canvas, 20 x 16 in. David David Gallery, Philadelphia.

Viewing the painting: How does this scene reflect what Chee might have been feeling as he rode back to Little Canyon?

Chee's dark eyes surveyed the land along the highway as the old man continued to brag about being "progressive." *He* no longer was tied to the land. He and his wife made money easily and could *buy* all the things they wanted. Chee realized too late that he had stumbled into the old argument between himself and his wife's parents. They had never understood his feeling about the land—that a man took care of his land and it in turn took care of him. Old Man Fat and his wife scoffed at him, called him a Pueblo farmer, all during that summer when he planted and weeded and harvested. Yet they ate the green corn in their mutton stews, and the chili paste from the fresh ripe chilis,[3] and the tortillas from the cornmeal his wife ground. None of this working and sweating in the sun for Old Man Fat, who talked proudly of his easy way of living—collecting money from the trader who rented this strip of land beside the highway, collecting money from the tourists.

Yet Chee had once won that argument. His wife had shared his belief in the integrity of the earth, that jobs and people might fail one, but the earth never would. After that first year she had turned from her own people and gone with Chee to Little Canyon.

Old Man Fat was reaching for the Little One. "Don't be coming here with plans for my daughter's daughter," he warned. "If you try to make trouble, I'll take the case to the government man in town."

The impulse was strong in Chee to turn and ride off while he still had the Little One in his arms. But he knew his time of victory would be short. His own family would uphold the old custom of children, especially girl children, belonging to the mother's people. He would have to give his daughter up if the case were brought before the headman of Little Canyon, and certainly he would have no better chance before a strange white man in town.

He handed the bewildered Little One to her grandfather who stood watching every movement suspiciously. Chee asked, "If I brought you a few things for the Little One, would that be making trouble? Some velvet for a blouse, or some of the jerky she likes so well . . . this summer's melon?"

Old Man Fat backed away from him. "Well," he hesitated, as some of the anger disappeared from his face and beads of greed shone in his eyes. "Well," he repeated. Then as the Little One began to squirm in his arms and cry, he said, "No! No! Stay away from here, you and all your family."

The sense of his failure deepened as Chee rode back to Little Canyon. But it was not until he sat with his family that evening in the hogan, while the familiar bustle of meal preparing went on about him, that he began to doubt the wisdom of the things he'd always believed. He smelled the coffee boiling and the oily fragrance of chili powder dusted into the bubbling pot of stew; he watched his mother turning round crusty fried bread in the small black skillet. All around him was plenty—a half of mutton hanging near the door, bright strings of chili drying, corn hanging by the braided husks, cloth bags of dried peaches. Yet in his heart was nothing.

3. People string together *chilis,* or hot peppers, and preserve them by hanging them up to dry. The chilis are then used in cooking.

He heard the familiar sounds of the sheep outside the hogan, the splash of water as his father filled the long drinking trough from the water barrel. When his father came in, Chee could not bring himself to tell a second time of the day's happenings. He watched his wiry, soft-spoken father while his mother told the story, saw his father's queue of graying hair quiver as he nodded his head with sympathetic exclamations.

Chee's doubting, acrid thoughts kept forming: Was it wisdom his father had passed on to him, or was his inheritance only the stubbornness of a long-haired Navaho resisting change? Take care of the land and it will take care of you. True, the land had always given him food, but now food was not enough. Perhaps if he had gone to school, he would have learned a different kind of wisdom, something to help him now. A schoolboy might even be able to speak convincingly to this government man whom Old Man Fat threatened to call, instead of sitting here like a clod of earth itself—Pueblo farmer indeed. What had the land to give that would restore his daughter?

In the days that followed, Chee herded sheep. He got up in the half-light, drank the hot coffee his mother had ready, then started the flock moving. It was necessary to drive the sheep a long way from the hogan to find good winter forage. Sometimes Chee met friends or relatives who were on their way to town or to the road camp where they hoped to get work; then there was friendly banter and an exchange of news. But most of the days seemed endless; he could not walk far enough or fast enough from his memories of the Little One or from his bitter thoughts. Sometimes it seemed his daughter trudged beside him, so real he could almost hear her footsteps—the muffled pad-pad of little feet in deerhide. In the glare of a snowbank he would see her vivid face, brown eyes sparkling. Mingling with the tinkle of sheep bells he heard her laughter.

When, weary of following the small sharp hoof marks that crossed and recrossed in the snow, he sat down in the shelter of a rock, it was only to be reminded that in his thoughts he had forsaken his brotherhood with the earth and sun and growing things. If he remembered times when he had flung himself against the earth to rest, to lie there in the sun until he could no longer feel where he left off and the earth began, it was to remember also that now he sat like an alien against the same earth; the belonging together was gone. The earth was one thing and he was another.

It was during the days when he herded sheep that Chee decided he must leave Little Canyon. Perhaps he would take a job

Vocabulary

acrid (ak′ rid) *adj.* irritating or upsetting

banter (ban′ tər) *n.* good-natured, witty joking or teasing silversmithing for one of the traders in town. Perhaps, even though he spoke little English, he could get a job at the road camp with his cousins; he would ask them about it.

Springtime transformed the mesas. The peach trees in the canyon were shedding fragrance and pink blossoms on the gentled wind. The sheep no longer foraged for the yellow seeds of chamiso[4] but ranged near the hogan with the long-legged new lambs, eating tender young grass.

Chee was near the hogan on the day his cousins rode up with the message for which he waited. He had been watching with mixed emotions while his father and his sister's husband cleared the fields beside the stream.

"The boss at the camp says he needs an extra hand, but he wants to know if you'll be willing to go with the camp when they move it to the other side of the town?" The tall cousin shifted his weight in the saddle.

The other cousin took up the explanation. "The work near here will last only until the new cutoff beyond Red Sands is finished. After that, the work will be too far away for you to get back here often."

That was what Chee had wanted—to get away from Little Canyon—yet he found himself not so interested in the job beyond town as in this new cutoff which was almost finished. He pulled a blade of grass, split it thoughtfully down the center, as he asked questions of his cousins. Finally he said: "I need to think more about this. If I decide on this job, I'll ride over."

Before his cousins were out of sight down the canyon, Chee was walking toward the fields, a bold plan shaping in his mind. As the plan began to flourish, wild and hardy as young tumbleweed, Chee added his own voice softly to the song his father was singing: ". . . In the middle of the wide field . . . Yellow Corn Boy . . . I wish to put in."

Chee walked slowly around the field, the rich red earth yielding to his footsteps. His plan depended upon this land and upon the things he remembered most about his wife's people.

Through planting time Chee worked zealously and tirelessly. He spoke little of the large new field he was planting, because he felt so strongly that just now this was something between himself and the land. The first days he was ever stooping, piercing the ground with the pointed stick, placing the corn kernels there, walking around the field and through it, singing, ". . . His track leads into the ground . . . Yellow Corn Boy . . . his track leads into the ground." After that, each day Chee walked through his field watching for the tips of green to break through; first a few spikes in the center and then more and more, until the corn in all parts of the field was above ground. Surely, Chee thought, if he sang the proper songs, if he cared for this land faithfully, it would not forsake him now, even though through the lonely days of winter he had betrayed the goodness of the earth in his thoughts.

Through the summer Chee worked long days, the sun hot upon his back, pulling weeds from around young corn plants; he planted squash and pumpkin; he terraced a

Did You Know?
Tumbleweed is any of several kinds of bushy prairie plants that break off from their roots and get blown around by the wind.

4. *Chamiso* (chä mē′ sō), from the Spanish, is an evergreen shrub found in the western United States.

Vocabulary
zealously (zel′ əs lē) *adv.* eagerly; enthusiastically

small piece of land near his mother's hogan and planted carrots and onions and the moisture-loving chili. He was increasingly restless. Finally he told his family what he hoped the harvest from this land would bring him. Then the whole family waited with him, watching the corn: the slender graceful plants that waved green arms and bent to embrace each other as young winds wandered through the field, the maturing plants flaunting their pollen-laden tassels in the sun, the tall and sturdy parent corn with new-formed ears and a froth of purple, red, and yellow corn beards against the dusty emerald of broad leaves.

Summer was almost over when Chee slung the bulging packs across two pack ponies. His mother helped him tie the heavy rolled pack behind the saddle of the buckskin. Chee knotted the new yellow kerchief about his neck a little tighter, gave the broad black hat brim an extra tug, but these were only gestures of assurance and he knew it. The land had not failed him. That part was done. But this he was riding into? Who could tell?

When Chee arrived at Red Sands, it was as he had expected to find it—no cars on the highway. His cousins had told him that even the Pueblo farmers were using the new cutoff to town. The barren gravel around the Red Sands Trading Post was deserted. A sign banged against the dismantled gas pumps: *Closed until further notice.*

Old Man Fat came from the crude summer shelter built beside the log hogan from a few branches of scrub cedar and the sides of wooden crates. He seemed almost friendly when he saw Chee.

"Get down, my son," he said, eyeing the bulging packs. There was no bluster in his voice today, and his face sagged, looking somewhat saddened, perhaps because his cheeks were no longer quite full enough to push his eyes upward at the corners. "You are going on a journey?"

Chee shook his head. "Our fields gave us so much this year, I thought to sell or trade this to the trader. I didn't know he was no longer here."

Old Man Fat sighed, his voice dropping to an injured tone. "He says he and his wife are going to rest this winter; then after that he'll build a place up on the new highway."

Chee moved as though to be traveling on, then jerked his head toward the pack ponies. "Anything you need?"

"I'll ask my wife," Old Man Fat said as he led the way to the shelter. "Maybe she has a little money. Things have not been too good with us since the trader closed. Only a few tourists come this way." He shrugged his shoulders. "And with the trader gone—no credit."

Chee was not deceived by his father-in-law's unexpected confidences. He recognized them as a hopeful bid for sympathy and, if possible, something for nothing. Chee made no answer. He was thinking that so far he had been right about his wife's parents: their thriftlessness had left them with no resources to last until Old Man Fat found another easy way of making a living.

Old Man Fat's wife was in the shelter working at her loom. She turned rather wearily when her husband asked with noticeable

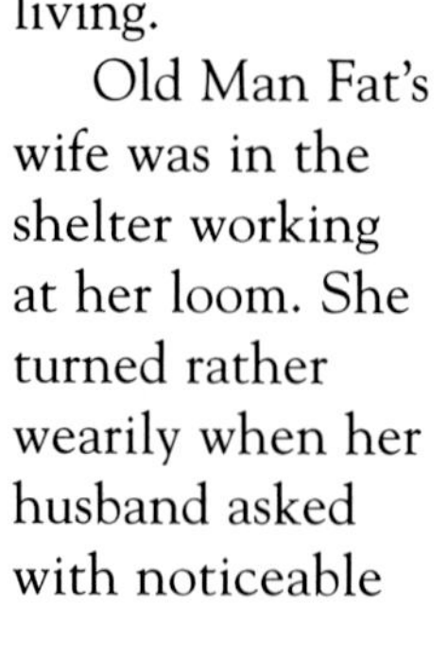

Vocabulary

flaunt (flônt) *v.* to display in a showy manner

it to the shelter where he untied the ropes. Pumpkins and hard-shelled squash tumbled out, and the ears of corn—pale yellow husks fitting firmly over plump ripe kernels, blue corn, red corn, yellow corn, many-colored corn, ears and ears of it—tumbled into every corner of the shelter.

"Yooooh," Old Man Fat's wife exclaimed as she took some of the ears in her hands. Then she glanced up at her son-in-law. "But we have no money for all this. We have sold almost everything we own—even the brass bed that stood in the hogan."

Old Man Fat's brass bed. Chee concealed his amusement as he started back for another pack. That must have been a hard parting. Then he stopped, for, coming from the cool darkness of the hogan was the Little One, rubbing her eyes as though she had been asleep. She stood for a moment in the doorway, and Chee saw that she was dirty, barefoot, her hair uncombed, her little blouse shorn of all its silver buttons. Then she ran toward Chee, her arms outstretched. Heedless of Old Man Fat and his wife, her father caught her in his arms, her hair falling in a dark cloud across his face, the sweetness of her laughter warm against his shoulder.

It was the haste within him to get this slow waiting game played through to the finish that made Chee speak unwisely. It

Friends in the Dark. Don Clark (b. 1955). Pastel, 30 x 20 in. Collection of the artist.

Viewing the painting: If this girl were Little One, would this picture be more typical of her life with Chee or with Old Man Fat? Explain.

deference if she would give him money to buy supplies. Chee surmised that the only income here was from his mother-in-law's weaving.

She peered around the corner of the shelter at the laden ponies, and then she looked at Chee. "What do you have there, my son?"

Chee smiled to himself as he turned to pull the pack from one of the ponies, dragged

Vocabulary

deference (def′ ər əns) *n.* courteous respect or regard for the judgment, opinions, or desires of another

surmise (sər mīz′) *v.* to guess or conclude from little or no evidence was the desire to swing her before him in the saddle and ride fast to Little Canyon that prompted his words. "The money doesn't matter. You still have something. . . ."

Chee knew immediately that he had overspoken. The old woman looked from him to the corn spread before her. Unfriendliness began to harden in his father-in-law's face. All the old arguments between himself and his wife's people came pushing and crowding in between them now.

Old Man Fat began kicking the ears of corn back onto the canvas as he eyed Chee angrily. "And you rode all the way over here thinking that for a little food we would give up our daughter's daughter?"

Chee did not wait for the old man to reach for the Little One. He walked dazedly to the shelter, rubbing his cheek against her soft dark hair, and put her gently into her grandmother's lap. Then he turned back to the horses. He had failed. By his own haste he had failed. He swung into the saddle, his hand touching the roll behind it. Should he ride on into town?

Then he dismounted, scarcely glancing at Old Man Fat, who stood uncertainly at the corner of the shelter, listening to his wife. "Give me a hand with this other pack of corn, Grandfather," Chee said, carefully keeping the small bit of hope from his voice.

Puzzled, but willing, Old Man Fat helped carry the other pack to the shelter, opening it to find more corn as well as carrots and round, pale yellow onions. Chee went back for the roll behind the buckskin's saddle and carried it to the entrance of the shelter, where he cut the ropes and gave the canvas a nudge with his toe. Tins of coffee rolled out, small plump cloth bags; jerked meat from several butcherings spilled from a flour sack; and bright red chilis splashed like flames against the dust.

"I will leave all this anyhow," Chee told them. "I would not want my daughter nor even you old people to go hungry."

Old Man Fat picked up a shiny tin of coffee, then put it down. With trembling hands he began to untie one of the cloth bags—dried sweet peaches.

The Little One had wriggled from her grandmother's lap, unheeded, and was on her knees, digging her hands into the jerked meat.

"There is almost enough food here to last all winter." Old Man Fat's wife sought the eyes of her husband.

Chee said, "I meant it to be enough. But that was when I thought you might send the Little One back with me." He looked down at his daughter noisily sucking jerky. Her mouth, both fists, were full of it. "I am sorry that you feel you cannot bear to part with her."

Old Man Fat's wife brushed a straggly wisp of gray hair from her forehead as she turned to look at the Little One. Old Man Fat was looking too. And it was not a thing to see. For in that moment the Little One ceased to be their daughter's daughter and became just another mouth to feed.

"And why not?" the old woman asked wearily.

Chee was settled in the saddle, the barefooted Little One before him. He urged the buckskin faster, and his daughter clutched his shirtfront. The purpling mesas flung back the echo: ". . . My corn embrace each other. In the middle of the wide field . . . Yellow Corn Boy embrace each other."

Responding to Literature

Personal Response

What was your response when Chee's plan to deal with Old Man Fat seemed to be falling apart?

Analyzing Literature

Recall

1. What is the way of life that Chee and his family live? How do Old Man Fat and his wife live?
2. Why does Little One go to live with Old Man Fat and his wife?
3. What does the building of the cutoff mean to Chee and his friends?
4. Why does Chee begin to doubt his way of life on the land?
5. What is finally decided by Chee and Old Man Fat about Little One?

Interpret

6. What do the differences in the two men's ways of life tell you about their attitudes toward their Navajo heritage?
7. Who do you think could provide Little One with the better life, Chee or Old Man Fat? Why?
8. In your opinion, was the new cutoff a positive or a negative addition to the area? Explain your opinion using details from the selection.
9. What might have happened if Chee had made a different decision about trusting the land?
10. How does Old Man Fat's attitude toward Chee change at the end of the story? What do you think accounts for this change?

Evaluate and Connect

11. **Irony** exists when a character's actions are the opposite of what people might expect. What is ironic about Old Man Fat and his wife taking Little One to live with them after her mother dies?
12. Look back at the flow chart you created for the Reading Focus on page 22. How does Chee's response to losing Little One compare to your predicted response if someone took something you valued?
13. Chee plans very carefully how he is going to get what he wants. In your opinion, was his planning worthwhile? Why or why not?
14. In your opinion, does Old Man Fat act true to character at the end of the story? Explain your answer.
15. **Theme Connections** Do you think traditional ways have value in a world of fast-paced changes? Support your response with examples from the selection and from your own experience.

Theme

The **theme** is the central message of a story that readers can apply to life. For example, the theme of many stories and movies is that goodness and courage will be rewarded. In some stories the theme is stated directly, but more often the theme is implied. To discover an implied theme, the reader might look at the experiences of the main characters and ask what message about life the story communicates.

1. Ideas about Navajo heritage are an important element in "Chee's Daughter." How do their attitudes toward their heritage affect the lives of Chee and Old Man Fat?
2. The writers could have chosen to state the theme of this selection directly. What might Chee have said that would summarize the story's message about heritage and tradition?
3. Explain how the theme of this story might apply to other life situations.

- See **Literary Terms Handbook**, p. R13.

Literature and Writing

Writing About Literature

The Importance of Place How important is the **setting** in this story? Write an analysis of the role the physical surroundings play in Chee's life and in his struggles with Old Man Fat. You might consider the natural landscape, the farmland and grazing lands, and the town where Old Man Fat lives and has his business. What attitudes and experiences do the authors associate with each part of the setting?

Creative Writing

Conversations with Chee Imagine that Chee and you are discussing a problem you have, and you have asked him for advice. For example, you might ask his advice on career planning or on what classes to sign up for next year. Or, you might wonder how to best get along with a classmate with whom you have very little in common. How would you describe your problem to Chee? How do you think he would respond? Record your conversation in writing.

Extending Your Response

Literature Groups

Life in Transition During the course of this story, Chee experiences several transitions, many of which involve permanent or temporary loss. In your group, identify as many of these transitions as you can. Then choose two or three and discuss how they affect Chee's life and the decisions he makes. Do you agree with the way he handles these transitions? Find examples from the selection to support your responses. Compare your ideas with those of other groups in the class.

Performing

Tell a Story In many Native American cultures, the storyteller is an important figure. Storytellers pass on through generations the stories important to the people. Imagine that you are a storyteller who feels that "Chee's Daughter" is an important story to preserve. Choose the most important elements of this story and turn them into an oral story. Share the story with a friend.

Interdisciplinary Activity

History: Navajo Heritage Find out more about traditional Navajo culture.

- Research the history of the people, as well as the customs, way of life, arts, and beliefs that contribute to Navajo heritage.
- Display your findings on a series of posters and share them with the class.

Reading Further

You might enjoy these works about Native American life:

Poetry: *The Book of Medicines,* by Linda Hogan, is a collection of poems that explore relationships between the author's Native American people, the land, and animals.

Short Story: Anna Lee Walters's story *"The Warriors,"* from her collection *The Sun Is Not Merciful,* explores the Native American tradition of oral storytelling and the lessons that an older relative passes down to younger generations.

Collection: In *The Way to Rainy Mountain,* N. Scott Momaday brings together Kiowa myths, legends, and historical anecdotes.

Save your work for your portfolio.

GRAMMAR AND LANGUAGE • Using Appositives

An appositive is a noun or pronoun placed next to another noun to identify or give more information about it. An appositive phrase is an appositive plus any words that modify it.

His father-in-law, Old Man Fat, might laugh. (*Old Man Fat* is an appositive identifying *father-in-law.*)

Chee was riding a good horse, a high-stepping buckskin. (The appositive phrase a *high-stepping buckskin* identifies the *horse.*)

Appositives are set off by commas unless they are essential to the meaning of the sentence.

PRACTICE On your paper write the appositive or appositive phrase in each of these sentences.

1. Chee rode toward his mother's home, a dome-shaped hogan.
2. Chee wanted to help his daughter, Little One.
3. He wanted to bring a gift, some velvet for a dress perhaps.
4. The family had only one source of income, his mother-in-law's weaving.

● For more about appositives, see **Language Handbook,** p. R27.

READING AND THINKING • Evaluating Generalizations

A generalization is a statement in which a collection of facts from specific situations is applied to more general circumstances. In "Chee's Daughter," Chee recalls the statement:

"Take care of the land and it will take care of you."

For Chee, this is a valid generalization because the land he has cared for has always provided him with food. If he had toiled in the fields and had gone hungry, then the generalization would have been invalid, or false.

PRACTICE Look back at the story to see the statement Chee's mother makes about "a fat Navaho." On a sheet of paper, explain the generalization she is making. Then write whether or not you think this is a valid generalization. Base your response on the facts in the story.

APPLY Use the facts in this story, or in another story you have read, to make another generalization. Share your generalization with a partner and discuss why you believe it is valid.

● For more on related reading skills, see **Reading Handbook,** pp. R78–R107.

VOCABULARY • Synonyms—Shades of Meaning

Synonyms are words that have the same or nearly the same meaning. For example, although *exhibit* and *flaunt* are synonyms, they do not mean exactly the same thing. To *exhibit* a talent is not obnoxious; to *flaunt* one is.

You will better understand what you read, and you will communicate more precisely when you write, if you pay attention to shades of meaning–those small but important differences that exist among many synonyms.

PRACTICE For each numbered word, choose the synonym that best matches the precise meaning.

	a.	b.	c.
1. acrid	a. bitter	b. tangy	c. penetrating
2. banter	a. heckling	b. talking	c. joking
3. deference	a. adoration	b. esteem	c. affection
4. zealously	a. spiritedly	b. insanely	c. carefully
5. indolence	a. laziness	b. inactivity	c. passivity

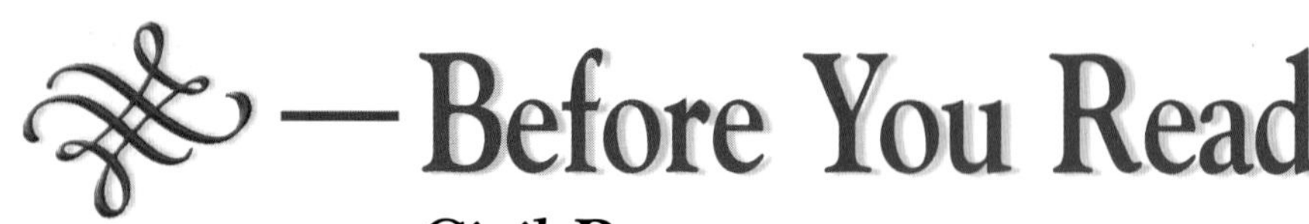

Civil Peace

Reading Focus

Imagine surviving a war or a natural disaster, such as a hurricane or flood. What would be absolutely essential to ensure your happy survival after such a catastrophic experience?

Map It! Complete a spider map like the one at the right with words that identify the people and things in your life that you consider essential to your happiness.

Happy survival

Setting a Purpose Read to learn the part that attitude plays in one man's happy survival.

Building Background

The Time and Place

This story takes place in Nigeria, probably in 1970, shortly after the end of the Nigerian civil war.

Did You Know?

Nigeria, located on the western coast of Africa, is the most densely populated country on the continent. Once a British colony, it became an independent nation in 1960. The Nigerian civil war began in 1967 when the Ibo—one of Nigeria's largest ethnic groups—tried to separate from Nigeria to form the independent Republic of Biafra. After enduring years of bloody battles, the Ibo were forced to surrender in 1970, ending the war. In connection with the war, Biafrans suffered a severe famine, in which nearly a million people died of starvation.

Vocabulary Preview

commandeer (kom′ ən dēr′) *v.* to seize for use by the military or government; p. 39

amenable (ə mē′ nə bəl) *adj.* responsive; able to be controlled; p. 40

retail (rē′ tāl) *v.* to sell directly to the consumer; p. 40

fortnight (fôrt′ nīt′) *n.* two weeks; p. 40

edifice (ed′ ə fis) *n.* a building, especially a large, important-looking one; p. 40

Meet Chinua Achebe

"It doesn't matter what language you write in, as long as what you write is good."

These words of Chinua Achebe (ə chā′ bā) refer to his use of English, rather than his native Ibo tongue, to write short stories and novels about Nigeria. In these works, he has tried to give English-speaking readers a deeper and more realistic view of African culture. Achebe's novel *Things Fall Apart* is recognized as a masterpiece of modern African literature.

Chinua Achebe was born in 1930 in Ogidi, Nigeria. This story was first published in 1971.

Civil Peace

Chinua Achebe

Jonathan Iwegbu counted himself extraordinarily lucky. "Happy survival!" meant so much more to him than just a current fashion of greeting old friends in the first hazy days of peace. It went deep to his heart. He had come out of the war with five inestimable blessings—his head, his wife Maria's head and the heads of three out of their four children. As a bonus he also had his old bicycle—a miracle too but naturally not to be compared to the safety of five human heads.

The bicycle had a little history of its own. One day at the height of the war it was commandeered "for urgent military action." Hard as its loss would have been to him he would still have let it go without a thought had he not had some doubts about the genuineness of the officer. It wasn't his disreputable rags, nor the toes peeping out of one blue and one brown canvas shoes, nor yet the two stars of his rank done obviously in a hurry in biro,[1] that troubled Jonathan; many good and heroic soldiers looked the same or

1. The stars signifying the officer's rank had been hand-drawn in ink. *Biro* (bi′ rō) is a British term for a ballpoint pen.

Vocabulary

commandeer (kom′ ən dēr′) *v.* to seize for use by the military or government

Did You Know?
A *raffia bag* is one woven from the fibers of the raffia palm tree.

worse. It was rather a certain lack of grip and firmness in his manner. So Jonathan, suspecting he might be amenable to influence, rummaged in his raffia bag and produced the two pounds with which he had been going to buy firewood which his wife, Maria, retailed to camp officials for extra stock-fish and corn meal, and got his bicycle back. That night he buried it in the little clearing in the bush where the dead of the camp, including his own youngest son, were buried. When he dug it up again a year later after the surrender all it needed was a little palm-oil greasing. "Nothing puzzles God," he said in wonder.

He put it to immediate use as a taxi and accumulated a small pile of Biafran money ferrying camp officials and their families across the four-mile stretch to the nearest tarred road. His standard charge per trip was six pounds and those who had the money were only glad to be rid of some of it in this way. At the end of a fortnight he had made a small fortune of one hundred and fifteen pounds.

Then he made the journey to Enugu[2] and found another miracle waiting for him. It was unbelievable. He rubbed his eyes and looked again and it was still standing there before him. But, needless to say, even that monumental blessing must be accounted also totally inferior to the five heads in the family. This newest miracle was his little house in Ogui Overside. Indeed nothing puzzles God! Only two houses away a huge concrete edifice some wealthy contractor had put up just before the war was a mountain of rubble. And here was Jonathan's little zinc house[3] of no regrets built with mud blocks quite intact! Of course the doors and windows were missing and five sheets off the roof. But what was that? And anyhow he had returned to Enugu early enough to pick up bits of old zinc and wood and soggy sheets of cardboard lying around the neighborhood before thousands more came out of their forest holes looking for the same things. He got a destitute carpenter with one old hammer, a blunt plane and a few bent and rusty nails in his tool bag to turn this assortment of wood, paper and metal into door and window shutters for five Nigerian shillings or fifty Biafran pounds. He paid the pounds, and moved in with his overjoyed family carrying five heads on their shoulders.

His children picked mangoes near the military cemetery and sold them to soldiers' wives for a few pennies—real pennies this time—and his wife started making breakfast akara balls[4] for neighbors in a hurry to start life again. With his family earnings he took his bicycle to the villages around and bought fresh palm wine which he mixed generously in his rooms with the water which had recently started running again in the public

2. *Enugu* (ā nōō′ gōō) is a city in southeastern Nigeria.

3. A *zinc house* is one with a zinc-coated metal roof.

4. *Akara balls* are ball-shaped bean cakes.

Vocabulary

amenable (ə mē′ nə bəl) *adj.* responsive; able to be controlled
retail (rē′ tāl) *v.* to sell directly to the consumer
fortnight (fôrt′ nīt′) *n.* two weeks
edifice (ed′ ə fis) *n.* a building, especially a large, important-looking one

tap down the road, and opened up a bar for soldiers and other lucky people with good money.

At first he went daily, then every other day and finally once a week, to the offices of the Coal Corporation where he used to be a miner, to find out what was what. The only thing he did find out in the end was that that little house of his was even a greater blessing than he had thought. Some of his fellow ex-miners who had nowhere to return at the end of the day's waiting just slept outside the doors of the offices and cooked what meal they could scrounge together in Bournvita tins. As the weeks lengthened and still nobody could say what was what Jonathan discontinued his weekly visits altogether and faced his palm wine bar.

But nothing puzzles God. Came the day of the windfall when after five days of endless scuffles in queues and counter queues in the sun outside the Treasury he had twenty pounds counted into his palms as ex gratia[5] award for the rebel money he had turned in. It was like Christmas for him and for many others like him when the payments began. They called it (since few could manage its proper official name) *egg rasher*.

Did You Know?
Here a *queue* (kyū) means a line of people.

As soon as the pound notes were placed in his palm Jonathan simply closed it tight over them and buried fist and money inside his trouser pocket. He had to be extra careful because he had seen a man a couple of days earlier collapse into near madness in an instant before that oceanic crowd because no sooner had he got his twenty pounds than some heartless ruffian picked it off him. Though it was not right that a man in such an extremity of agony should be blamed yet many in the queues that day were able to remark quietly on the victim's carelessness, especially after he pulled out the innards of his pocket and revealed a hole in it big enough to pass a thief's head. But of course he had insisted that the money had been in the other pocket, pulling it out too to show its comparative wholeness. So one had to be careful.

Jonathan soon transferred the money to his left hand and pocket so as to leave his right free for shaking hands should the need arise, though by fixing his gaze at such an elevation as to miss all approaching human faces he made sure that the need did not arise, until he got home.

He was normally a heavy sleeper but that night he heard all the neighborhood noises die down one after another. Even the night watchman who knocked the hour on some metal somewhere in the distance had fallen silent after knocking one o'clock. That must have been the last thought in Jonathan's mind before he was finally carried away himself. He couldn't have been gone for long, though, when he was violently awakened again.

"Who is knocking?" whispered his wife lying beside him on the floor.

"I don't know," he whispered back breathlessly.

The second time the knocking came it was so loud and imperious that the rickety old door could have fallen down.

"Who is knocking?" he asked then, his voice parched and trembling.

5. Something that is awarded *ex gratia* (eks gräsh′ ē ə) is given as a favor rather than as a legal right. The Latin word *gratia* means "kindness."

Children Dancing, c. 1948. Robert Gwathmey. Oil on canvas, 30 x 40 in. The Butler Institute of American Art, Youngstown, OH.

Viewing the painting: **How does the atmosphere these parents are creating for their children reflect the way Jonathan cares for his family?**

"Na tief-man and him people," came the cool reply. "Make you hopen de door." This was followed by the heaviest knocking of all.

Maria was the first to raise the alarm, then he followed and all their children.

"Police-o! Thieves-o! Neighbors-o! Police-o! We are lost! We are dead! Neighbors, are you asleep? Wake up! Police-o!"

This went on for a long time and then stopped suddenly. Perhaps they had scared the thief away. There was total silence. But only for a short while.

"You done finish?" asked the voice outside. "Make we help you small. Oya, everybody!"

"Police-o! Tief-man-o! Neighbors-o! we done loss-o! Police-o! . . ."

There were at least five other voices besides the leader's.

Jonathan and his family were now completely paralyzed by terror. Maria and the children sobbed inaudibly like lost souls. Jonathan groaned continuously.

The silence that followed the thieves' alarm vibrated horribly. Jonathan all but begged their leader to speak again and be done with it.

"My frien," said he at long last, "we don try our best for call dem but I tink say dem all done sleep-o . . . So wetin we go do now? Sometaim you wan call soja? Or you wan make we call dem for you? Soja better pass police. No be so?"

"Na so!" replied his men. Jonathan thought he heard even more voices now than before and groaned heavily. His legs were sagging under him and his throat felt like sandpaper.

"My frien, why you no de talk again. I de ask you say you wan make we call soja?"

"No."

"Awrighto. Now make we talk business. We no be bad tief. We no like for make trouble.

Trouble done finish. War done finish and all the katakata[6] wey de for inside. No Civil War again. This time na Civil Peace. No be so?"

"Na so!" answered the horrible chorus.

"What do you want from me? I am a poor man. Everything I had went with this war. Why do you come to me? You know people who have money. We . . ."

"Awright! We know say you no get plenty money. But we sef no get even anini.[7] So derefore make you open dis window and give us one hundred pound and we go commot. Orderwise we de come for inside now to show you guitar-boy like dis . . ."

A volley of automatic fire rang through the sky. Maria and the children began to weep aloud again.

"Ah, missisi de cry again. No need for dat. We done talk say we na good tief. We just take our small money and go nwayorly. No molest. Abi we de molest?"

"At all!" sang the chorus.

"My friends," began Jonathan hoarsely. "I hear what you say and I thank you. If I had one hundred pounds . . ."

"Lookia my frien, no be play we come play for your house. If we make mistake and step for inside you no go like am-o. So derefore . . ."

"To God who made me; if you come inside and find one hundred pounds, take it and shoot me and shoot my wife and children. I swear to God. The only money I have in this life is this twenty-pounds *egg rasher* they gave me today . . ."

6. The word *katakata* may be meant to imitate the sound of gunfire. The rest of the phrase is Nigerian dialect for "that went with it."
7. An *anini* (ä nē′ nē) is a small coin of Nigeria worth less than one cent.

"OK. Time de go. Make you open dis window and bring the twenty pound. We go manage am like dat."

There were now loud murmurs of dissent among the chorus: "Na lie de man de lie; e get plenty money . . . Make we go inside and search properly well . . . Wetin be twenty pound? . . ."

"Shurrup!" rang the leader's voice like a lone shot in the sky and silenced the murmuring at once. "Are you dere? Bring the money quick!"

"I am coming," said Jonathan fumbling in the darkness with the key of the small wooden box he kept by his side on the mat.

At the first sign of light as neighbors and others assembled to commiserate with him he was already strapping his five-gallon demijohn to his bicycle carrier and his wife, sweating in the open fire, was turning over akara balls in a wide clay bowl of boiling oil. In the corner his eldest son was rinsing out dregs of yesterday's palm wine from old beer bottles.

Did You Know?
A *demijohn* is a large earthenware or glass bottle, encased in wicker.

"I count it as nothing," he told his sympathizers, his eyes on the rope he was tying. "What is *egg rasher*? Did I depend on it last week? Or is it greater than other things that went with the war? I say, let *egg rasher* perish in the flames! Let it go where everything else has gone. Nothing puzzles God."

Responding to Literature

Personal Response

Do you share Jonathan Iwegbu's values? Look again at the "Happy Survival" map you made in the Reading Focus on page 38. Having read this story, what changes would you make to your map?

Analyzing Literature

Recall

1. What does Jonathan consider to be his greatest blessing?
2. Where are Jonathan and his family at the beginning of the story? Where is the rest of the story set?
3. What job did Jonathan have before the war? How do he and his family earn money after the war?
4. What are the official and unofficial names of the award Jonathan gets? Why does he receive the award?
5. Summarize what happens after Jonathan and his family are awakened by loud knocking at their door.

Interpret

6. What profound loss has Jonathan suffered? In your opinion, why does Jonathan dwell on his blessings and not on his losses?
7. How important is the story **setting?** Could this story have happened in another time or another place? Give reasons for your answer.
8. **Theme Connections** How does Jonathan seem to feel about the changes inflicted on him and his family by the war? Explain.
9. Do you think Jonathan would have collapsed "into near madness" if he had been robbed when he left the Treasury? Why or why not?
10. In your opinion, why is Jonathan able to deal with his latest loss so philosophically? Do you think his reaction is predictable? Explain.

Evaluate and Connect

11. Do you think Jonathan is a good role model for his children? Would he be a good role model for young people today? Explain.
12. In your opinion, should Jonathan have told the thieves about the *egg rasher?* What would you have done?
13. What do you think Jonathan means by "Nothing puzzles God"?
14. How does the author use **local color** (see page R7) to evoke the region he's writing about? Cite specific details from the story.
15. The author has said that "any good story . . . should have a message, . . . a purpose." In your opinion, what is the message of this story?

Literary ELEMENTS

Dialogue

Dialogue is conversation between characters in a literary work. Good dialogue sounds natural and flows smoothly. Used effectively, dialogue helps reveal a character's personality and can help readers understand the events of a story and predict what might happen next. Dialogue also can add drama and suspense to a story.

1. The only dialogue in this story is the conversation during the robbery. Why, do you think, did the author use dialogue in this scene? Why didn't the author just describe the robbery, as he did the other events in the story? Explain.
2. Why do you think the author has the thieves speak in a regional dialect, while Jonathan uses standard English?

- See **Literary Terms Handbook,** p. R3.

Literary Criticism

Critic G. D. Killam notes that although Jonathan "says that he can accept his losses in peacetime as he has accepted those in war, . . . there is really faint consolation for him and little to distinguish 'civil peace' from civil war." Respond to Killam's assessment in a brief essay examining the quality of Jonathan's life during this time of "peace."

Literature and Writing

Writing About Literature

Character Sketch Make a five-column chart with these headings: *Actions, Words, Thoughts, Appearance,* and *Reactions of others.* Go through the story, looking for details that reveal Jonathan's character and record each detail in the appropriate column. Then use the information in your chart as you write a character sketch of Jonathan. Compare your sketch with those of other students.

Creative Writing

Just the Facts Imagine that a police officer has come to Jonathan's house to interview him about the robbery. List questions that the police officer might ask. For each question, write the type of reply you would expect Jonathan to make.

Extending Your Response

Literature Groups

To See or Not to See A character in an Achebe novel entitled *Anthills of the Savannah* says: "It is the story that outlives the sound of war-drums and the exploits of brave fighters. . . . The story is our escort; without it, we are blind." Discuss how "Civil Peace" might help the reader "see" life in Nigeria after the civil war more clearly. Have one group member jot down the group's ideas about this topic. Share your ideas with the class.

Interdisciplinary Activity

Art: Nigerian Style The painting at the right is a celebration of the Nigerian tradition by an African American artist. Use library resources or the Internet to research Nigerian art. Then design your own cover for a collection of stories by Chinua Achebe, incorporating a piece of Nigerian art or a traditional Nigerian pattern.

Internet Connection

Web Insight Several universities have created Web sites dedicated to Chinua Achebe; some have links to sites related to the languages, customs, traditions, and people of Nigeria. Use these sites to explore a topic that you find particularly interesting. Be sure to narrow your topic to a manageable size. Report your findings to the class.

Save your work for your portfolio.

Reading Further

You might enjoy these other works by Chinua Achebe:

Novel: *Things Fall Apart,* set in an Ibo village in Nigeria, is a powerful and moving account of a "strong" man whose life is dominated by fear and anger.

Short Story Collection: *Girls at War and Other Stories* includes several stories that are rich in the folklore and traditions of Nigeria's Ibo culture.

Magic of Nigeria, 1971. Loïs Mailou Jones. Watercolor, 34 x 22 in. Collection of Dr. Tritobia Hayes Benjamin.

Skill Minilessons

GRAMMAR AND LANGUAGE • Using Descriptive Tag Lines

When the characters in "Civil Peace" speak, you know what they are feeling because Achebe has used descriptive tag lines to convey the tone of voice and emotional state of each speaker. For example, when Jonathan says "Nothing puzzles God," the tag line, "he said in wonder" conveys his awe and reverence of a higher power. Later, you know that Jonathan feels threatened and scared when he asks, "Who is knocking?" because "his voice is parched and trembling."

PRACTICE Review "Civil Peace," looking for tag lines with descriptive language. Pay particular attention to the tag lines used with the dialogue of the thieves. On your paper, write the tag lines and explain what they show about the emotions of the speaker or speakers.

APPLY Review a piece of your own writing that includes dialogue. Revise or add tag lines to convey the tone of voice and emotions of each speaker.

• For more about dialogue, see **Language Handbook,** p. R49.

READING AND THINKING • Analyzing Problems and Solutions

Often characters in stories come up against problems they need to solve. For example, at the beginning of "Civil Peace," Jonathan is confronted by an officer who wants his treasured old bicycle "for urgent military action." Jonathan would have given up the bike if he truly believed he had no other option. He accurately and cleverly suspects, however, that the officer will settle for a bribe. Jonathan keeps his bike and makes the officer happy at the same time.

PRACTICE Identify two other problems that Jonathan faces in "Civil Peace." On your paper, state each problem, describe how Jonathan solves it, and explain the thinking that leads to his solution.

APPLY Look at another story in this text that you have read. Explain how the main character in that story solves a problem.

• For more about comprehension strategies, see **Reading Handbook,** pp. R82–R94.

VOCABULARY • Etymology

English words come from many languages–Latin, Greek, French, Old English, Dutch, and others. Etymology is the study of the history of a word, from its origin to its current meaning. For example, *edifice* comes from the Latin word *aedificium* meaning "a building."

If you trace the history of *commandeer,* you will find the Afrikaans *kommandeer,* then the French *commander,* and eventually you will get to the Latin *com-* ("very much") and *mando* ("hand" plus "to give"). So, if you emphatically tell someone "Take care of this; it's in your hands now!" you've given a command. When you commandeer someone's property, you command them to turn it over to you.

Some word etymologies are easier to follow. *Fortnight,* for example, makes sense when you find out that it's an Old English word that means "fourteen nights."

PRACTICE Use a dictionary to look up the etymologies of *amenable* and *retail.* (A word's etymology is usually shown in brackets right after the abbreviation for the part of speech or at the end of the entry.) Then, for each word, briefly describe something that the etymology helps you to understand about the word.

Press Release

Have you read about or do you know anyone who has followed her heart and realized her dreams? Toshiko Akiyoshi has worked her way to the top of the American jazz scene, despite certain obstacles.

We, Too, Are One: Renowned Jazz Pianist Toshiko Akiyoshi Bridges the Gap

by Michael Henningsen

There was a time early in Toshiko Akiyoshi's career when she was convinced that she had no place in jazz. The musical culture from which Akiyoshi came was quite different from that which created the bulk of be-bop, swing, and big band jazz some 50 years ago. But it wasn't long before the gifted pianist realized that she could, indeed, contribute to jazz history while delicately infusing her music with her own rich Asian heritage. And since the mid-1970s, Toshiko Akiyoshi and her orchestra have done just that—and to much critical and audience acclaim.

Born in Manchuria, China, Akiyoshi was studying classical piano by the age of six. Upon her family's return to their native Japan, she considered a career in medicine before stumbling upon a "Pianist Wanted" sign posted outside one of the many dance halls that dotted the streets of the then still occupied country. She was hired on the spot. Her family insisted that she quit when school started. But, she says, "March came and went and no one noticed. I just kept on playing." She moved to Tokyo in the early 1950s and found herself quickly at the top of the city's burgeoning jazz scene, where she often played with touring American jazz artists. It was Oscar Petersen's rhythm section, in fact, who joined Akiyoshi on her first recording after Petersen hailed her the best female jazz pianist he'd ever heard.

Shortly thereafter, Akiyoshi moved to the United States to attend the Berklee College of Music and, in 1973, formed what would later become her 17-piece jazz orchestra. And in the 25 years that have followed, Akiyoshi has continued to define and redefine jazz with her unique melding of cultures and heritage. "I read a history book," she remembers, "that said the Israelis came through China to Japan, so I thought, we are all connected, hand in hand." And if music is indeed the international language, then Akiyoshi is truly fluent.

Analyzing Media

1. Explain how much of Akiyoshi's success you think is due to fate and how much is due to hard work.
2. Why do you think her family never pressed her to go into medicine as she had originally planned?

Before You Read

Two Kinds

Reading Focus

Just for a moment imagine yourself as an acclaimed musician or artist, a champion athlete, a brilliant scientist, or an award-winning actor.

Journal Write a description of yourself as a person who is at the top of his or her chosen field. Briefly tell what you have accomplished and what you enjoy most about your success.

Setting a Purpose Read to discover two different viewpoints on successful living.

Building Background

The Time and Place
The story takes place in Chinatown in San Francisco, probably during the early 1960s.

Did You Know?
Chinatown in downtown San Francisco is one of the largest Chinese communities outside of Asia. The neighborhood—with its fascinating mix of restaurants, shops, businesses, and religious and cultural institutions—is a crowded and bustling place. The area was settled by Chinese immigrants who arrived during the Gold Rush of 1849. Chinatown continues to grow, as immigrants arrive to begin a new life—just as the mother in "Two Kinds" had done in 1949.

Vocabulary Preview

prodigy (prod′ ə jē) *n.* an extraordinarily gifted or talented person, especially a child; p. 49
lament (lə ment′) *v.* to express sorrow or regret; p. 50
reproach (ri prōch′) *n.* blame; disgrace; discredit; p. 50
mesmerizing (mez′ mə rīz ing) *adj.* fascinating; p. 51
reverie (rev′ ər ē) *n.* fanciful thinking, daydream; p. 53
discordant (dis kôrd′ ənt) *adj.* not in agreement or harmony; p. 53
devastate (dev′ əs tāt) *v.* to destroy; overwhelm; p. 56
fiasco (fē as′ kō) *n.* a complete or humiliating failure; p. 56

Meet Amy Tan

Amy Tan enjoys performing music much more than the girl in this story does. She sings in a rock band as a way to relax and to raise money for worthy causes.

Tan's first published writing was an article titled, "What the Library Means to Me," written when she was eight years old. Since then she has become an award-winning author. Her first novel, *The Joy Luck Club*, was made into a feature film of the same name. The book, which includes the selection you are about to read, tells about four women from China and their Chinese American daughters.

Amy Tan was born in Oakland, California, in 1952. This story was published in 1989.

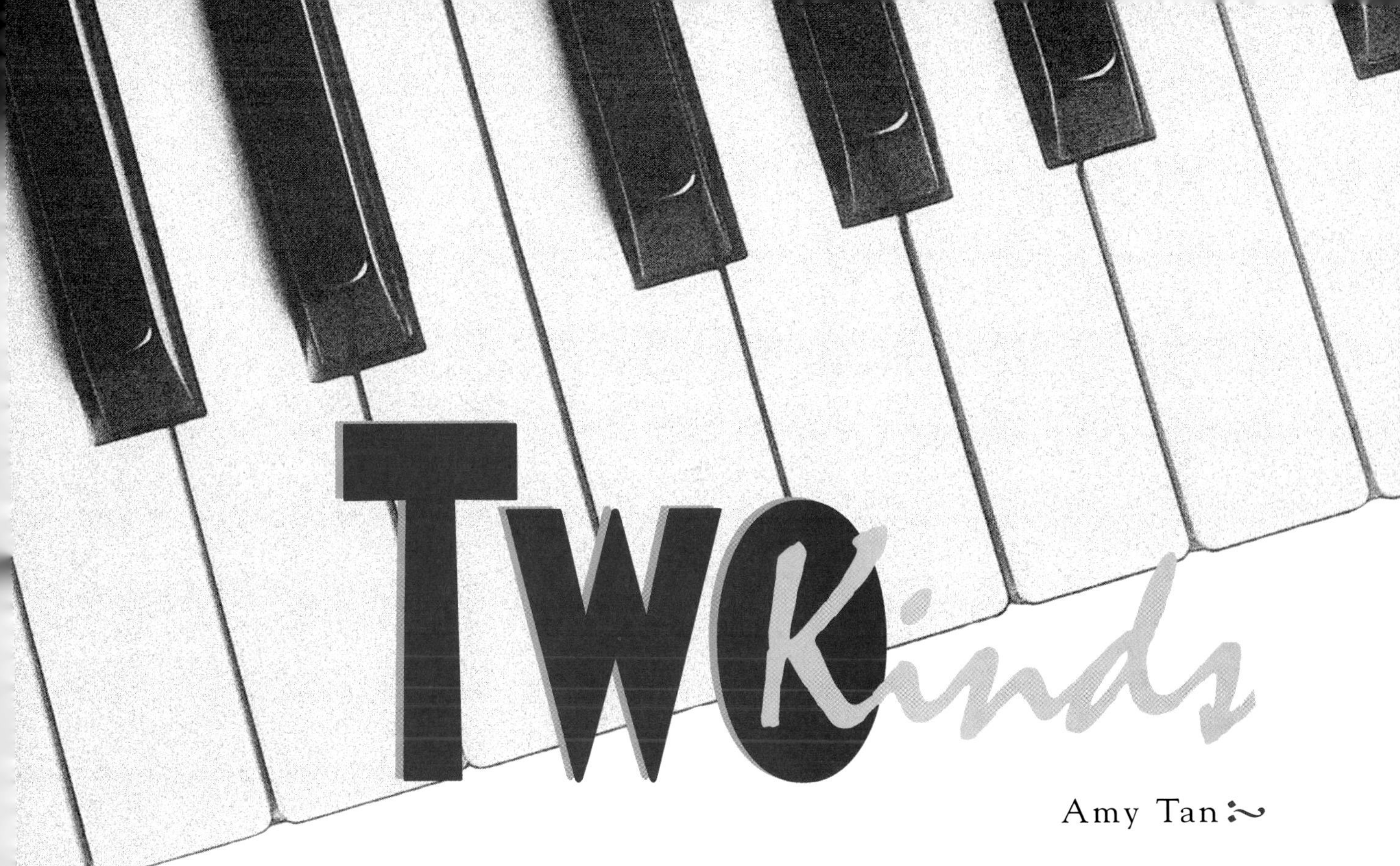

Two Kinds

Amy Tan

MY MOTHER BELIEVED YOU could be anything you wanted to be in America. You could open a restaurant. You could work for the government and get good retirement. You could buy a house with almost no money down. You could become rich. You could become instantly famous.

"Of course, you can be prodigy, too," my mother told me when I was nine. "You can be best anything. What does Auntie Lindo know? Her daughter, she is only best tricky."

America was where all my mother's hopes lay. She had come to San Francisco in 1949 after losing everything in China: her mother and father, her family home, her first husband, and two daughters, twin baby girls. But she never looked back with regret. Things could get better in so many ways.

We didn't immediately pick the right kind of prodigy. At first my mother thought I could be a Chinese Shirley Temple.[1] We'd watch Shirley's old movies on TV as though they were training films. My mother would poke my arm and say, "*Ni kan*. You watch." And I would see Shirley tapping her feet, or singing a sailor song, or pursing her lips into a very round O while saying "Oh, my goodness."

"*Ni kan*," my mother said, as Shirley's eyes flooded with tears. "You already know how. Don't need talent for crying!"

Soon after my mother got this idea about Shirley Temple, she took me to the beauty training school in the Mission District[2] and put me in the hands of a student who could barely hold the scissors without shaking. Instead of getting big fat curls, I emerged with an uneven mass of crinkly black fuzz. My

1. *Shirley Temple* was a popular child movie star of the 1930s.
2. The *Mission District* is a residential neighborhood in San Francisco.

Vocabulary
prodigy (prod′ ə jē) *n.* an extraordinarily gifted or talented person, especially a child

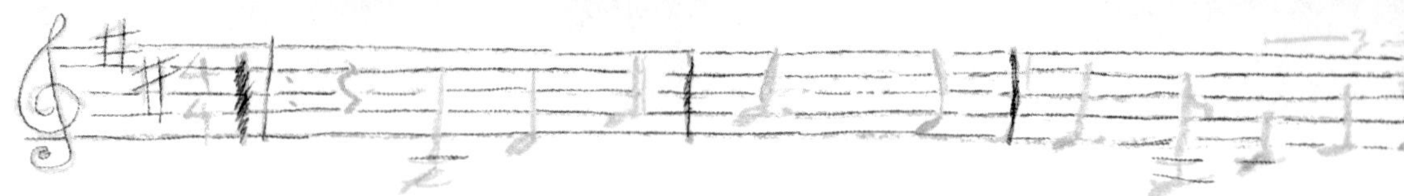

mother dragged me off to the bathroom and tried to wet down my hair.

"You look like Negro Chinese," she lamented, as if I had done this on purpose.

The instructor of the beauty training school had to lop off these soggy clumps to make my hair even again. "Peter Pan is very popular these days," the instructor assured my mother. I now had hair the length of a boy's, with curly bangs that hung at a slant two inches above my eyebrows. I liked the haircut, and it made me actually look forward to my future fame.

In fact, in the beginning I was just as excited as my mother, maybe even more so. I pictured this prodigy part of me as many different images, and I tried each one on for size. I was a dainty ballerina girl standing by the curtain, waiting to hear the music that would send me floating on my tiptoes. I was like the Christ child lifted out of the straw manger, crying with holy indignity. I was Cinderella stepping from her pumpkin carriage with sparkly cartoon music filling the air.

In all of my imaginings I was filled with a sense that I would soon become perfect. My mother and father would adore me. I would be beyond reproach. I would never feel the need to sulk, or to clamor for anything.

But sometimes the prodigy in me became impatient. "If you don't hurry up and get me out of here, I'm disappearing for good," it warned. "And then you'll always be nothing."

Every night after dinner my mother and I would sit at the Formica-topped[3] kitchen table. She would present new tests, taking her examples from stories of amazing children that she had read in *Ripley's Believe It or Not* or *Good Housekeeping*, *Reader's Digest*, or any of a dozen other magazines she kept in a pile in our bathroom. My mother got these magazines from people whose houses she cleaned. And since she cleaned many houses each week, we had a great assortment. She would look through them all, searching for stories about remarkable children.

The first night she brought out a story about a three-year-old boy who knew the capitals of all the states and even of most of the European countries. A teacher was quoted as saying that the little boy could also pronounce the names of the foreign cities correctly. "What's the capital of Finland?" my mother asked me, looking at the story.

All I knew was the capital of California, because Sacramento was the name of the street we lived on in Chinatown. "Nairobi!"[4] I guessed, saying the most foreign word I could think of. She checked to see if that might be one way to pronounce *Helsinki* before showing me the answer.

The tests got harder—multiplying numbers in my head, finding the queen of hearts in a deck of cards, trying to stand on my head without using my hands, predicting the daily temperatures in Los Angeles, New York, and London. One night I had to look at a page from the Bible for three minutes and then report everything I could remember. "Now Jehoshaphat[5] had riches and honor in abundance and . . . that's all I remember, Ma," I said.

3. *Formica* (fôr mī′ kə) is a plastic substance used to cover kitchen and bathroom surfaces because it is resistant to heat and water.

4. *Nairobi* (nī rō′ bē) is the capital of Kenya in east central Africa.

5. *Jehoshaphat* (ji hosh′ ə fat′) was a king of Judah in the ninth century B.C.

Vocabulary

lament (lə ment′) *v.* to express sorrow or regret

reproach (ri prōch′) *n.* blame; disgrace; discredit

And after seeing, once again, my mother's disappointed face, something inside me began to die. I hated the tests, the raised hopes and failed expectations. Before going to bed that night I looked in the mirror above the bathroom sink, and when I saw only my face staring back—and understood that it would always be this ordinary face—I began to cry. Such a sad, ugly girl! I made high-pitched noises like a crazed animal, trying to scratch out the face in the mirror.

And then I saw what seemed to be the prodigy side of me—a face I had never seen before. I looked at my reflection, blinking so that I could see more clearly. The girl staring back at me was angry, powerful. She and I were the same. I had new thoughts, willful thoughts—or, rather, thoughts filled with lots of won'ts. I won't let her change me, I promised myself. I won't be what I'm not.

So now when my mother presented her tests, I performed listlessly, my head propped on one arm. I pretended to be bored. And I was. I got so bored that I started counting the bellows of the foghorns out on the bay while my mother drilled me in other areas. The sound was comforting and reminded me of the cow jumping over the moon. And the next day I played a game with myself, seeing if my mother would give up on me before eight bellows. After a while I usually counted only one bellow, maybe two at most. At last she was beginning to give up hope.

Two or three months went by without any mention of my being a prodigy. And then one day my mother was watching the *Ed Sullivan Show*[6] on TV. The TV was old and the sound kept shorting out. Every time my mother got halfway up from the sofa to adjust the set, the sound would come back on and Sullivan would be talking. As soon as she sat down, Sullivan would go silent again. She got up—the TV broke into loud piano music. She sat down—silence. Up and down, back and forth, quiet and loud. It was like a stiff, embraceless dance between her and the TV set. Finally, she stood by the set with her hand on the sound dial.

She seemed entranced by the music, a frenzied little piano piece with a mesmerizing quality, which alternated between quick, playful passages and teasing, lilting[7] ones.

"*Ni kan*," my mother said, calling me over with hurried hand gestures. "Look here."

I could see why my mother was fascinated by the music. It was being pounded out by a little Chinese girl, about nine years old, with a Peter Pan haircut. The girl had the sauciness[8] of a Shirley Temple. She was proudly modest, like a proper Chinese child. And she also did a fancy sweep of a curtsy, so that the fluffy skirt of her white dress cascaded to the floor like the petals of a large carnation.

In spite of these warning signs, I wasn't worried. Our family had no piano and we couldn't afford to buy one, let alone reams of sheet music and piano lessons. So I could be generous in my comments when my mother bad-mouthed the little girl on TV.

"Play note right, but doesn't sound good!" my mother complained. "No singing sound." "What are you picking on her for?" I said carelessly. "She's pretty good. Maybe she's not the best, but she's trying hard."

6. The *Ed Sullivan Show* was a popular weekly variety show on TV in the 1950s and 1960s.

7. *Lilting* means "light and lively."

8. *Sauciness* means "boldness that is playful and lighthearted."

Vocabulary

mesmerizing (mez′ mə rīz ing) *adj.* fascinating

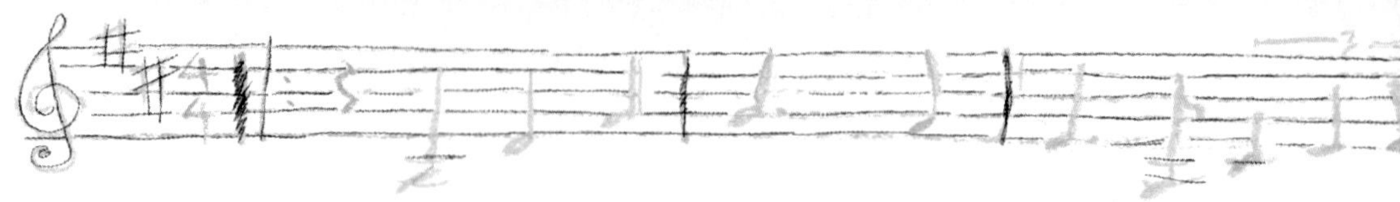

I knew almost immediately that I would be sorry I had said that.

"Just like you," she said. "Not the best. Because you not trying." She gave a little huff as she let go of the sound dial and sat down on the sofa.

Did You Know?
Edvard *Grieg* (grēg), 1843–1907, was a Norwegian composer.

The little Chinese girl sat down also, to play an encore of "Anitra's Tanz," by Grieg. I remember the song, because later on I had to learn how to play it.

Three days after watching the *Ed Sullivan Show* my mother told me what my schedule would be for piano lessons and piano practice. She had talked to Mr. Chong, who lived on the first floor of our apartment building. Mr. Chong was a retired piano teacher, and my mother had traded housecleaning services for weekly lessons and a piano for me to practice on every day, two hours a day, from four until six.

When my mother told me this, I felt as though I had been sent to hell. I whined, and then kicked my foot a little when I couldn't stand it anymore.

"Why don't you like me the way I am?" I cried, "I'm *not* a genius! I can't play the piano. And even if I could, I wouldn't go on TV if you paid me a million dollars!"

My mother slapped me. "Who ask you to be genius?" she shouted. "Only ask you be your best. For you sake. You think I want you to be genius! Hnnh! What for! Who ask you!"

"So ungrateful," I heard her mutter in Chinese. "If she had as much talent as she has temper, she'd be famous now."

Mr. Chong, whom I secretly nicknamed Old Chong, was very strange, always tapping his fingers to the silent music of an invisible orchestra. He looked ancient in my eyes. He had lost most of the hair on the top of his head, and he wore thick glasses and had eyes that always looked tired. But he must have been younger than I thought, since he lived with his mother and was not yet married.

I met Old Lady Chong once, and that was enough. She had a peculiar smell, like a baby that had done something in its pants, and her fingers felt like a dead person's, like an old peach I once found in the back of the refrigerator; its skin just slid off the flesh when I picked it up.

Did You Know?
Ludwig van *Beethoven* (bā′ tō vən), 1770–1827, was a German composer.

I soon found out why Old Chong had retired from teaching piano. He was deaf. "Like Beethoven!" he shouted to me. "We're both listening only in our head!" And he would start to conduct his frantic silent sonatas.[9]

Our lessons went like this. He would open the book and point to different things, explaining their purpose: "Key! Treble! Bass! No sharps or flats! So this is C major! Listen now and play after me!"

And then he would play the C scale a few times, a simple chord, and then, as if inspired by an old unreachable itch, he would gradually add more notes and running trills and a pounding bass until the music was really something quite grand.

---

9. *Sonatas* are instrumental compositions, commonly written for piano.

I would play after him, the simple scale, the simple chord, and then just play some nonsense that sounded like a cat running up and down on top of garbage cans. Old Chong would smile and applaud and say, "Very good! But now you must learn to keep time!"

So that's how I discovered that Old Chong's eyes were too slow to keep up with the wrong notes I was playing. He went through the motions in half time. To help me keep rhythm, he stood behind me and pushed down on my right shoulder for every beat. He balanced pennies on top of my wrists so that I would keep them still as I slowly played scales and arpeggios.[10] He had me curve my hand around an apple and keep that shape when playing chords. He marched stiffly to show me how to make each finger dance up and down, staccato,[11] like an obedient little soldier.

He taught me all these things, and that was how I also learned I could be lazy and get away with mistakes, lots of mistakes. If I hit the wrong notes because I hadn't practiced enough, I never corrected myself. I just kept playing in rhythm. And Old Chong kept conducting his own private reverie.

So maybe I never really gave myself a fair chance. I did pick up the basics pretty quickly, and I might have become a good pianist at that young age. But I was so determined not to try, not to be anybody different, that I learned to play only the most ear-splitting preludes, the most discordant hymns.

Over the next year I practiced like this, dutifully in my own way. And then one day I heard my mother and her friend Lindo Jong both talking in a loud, bragging tone of voice so that others could hear. It was after church, and I was leaning against a brick wall, wearing a dress with stiff white petticoats. Auntie Lindo's daughter, Waverly, who was my age, was standing farther down the wall, about five feet away. We had grown up together and shared all the closeness of two sisters, squabbling over crayons and dolls. In other words, for the most part, we hated each other. I thought she was snotty. Waverly Jong had gained a certain amount of fame as "Chinatown's Littlest Chinese Chess Champion."

"She bring home too many trophy," Auntie Lindo lamented that Sunday. "All day she play chess. All day I have no time do nothing but dust off her winnings." She threw a scolding look at Waverly, who pretended not to see her.

"You lucky you don't have this problem," Auntie Lindo said with a sigh to my mother.

And my mother squared her shoulders and bragged: "Our problem worser than yours. If we ask Jing-mei[12] wash dish, she hear nothing but music. It's like you can't stop this natural talent."

And right then I was determined to put a stop to her foolish pride.

A few weeks later Old Chong and my mother conspired to have me play in a talent show that was to be held in the church hall. By then my parents had saved up enough to

10. Arpeggios (är pej′ ē ōz) are chords in which the notes are played in succession instead of all at the same time.
11. To play music *staccato* (stə kä′ tō) is to produce sharp, distinct breaks between successive tones.

12. *Jing-mei* (jing′ mā)

Vocabulary
reverie (rev′ ər ē) *n.* fanciful thinking; daydream
discordant (dis kôrd′ ənt) *adj.* not in agreement or harmony

The Piano Lesson, 1994. Diana Ong. Watercolor. Private collection.

Viewing the painting: Compare how the girl in the painting approaches her piano practice with how Jing-mei approaches her practice.

Did You Know?
A *spinet* (spin′ it) is a small, upright piano.

buy me a secondhand piano, a black Wurlitzer spinet with a scarred bench. It was the showpiece of our living room.

For the talent show I was to play a piece called "Pleading Child," from Schumann's[13] *Scenes From Childhood.* It was a simple, moody piece that sounded more difficult than it was. I was supposed to memorize the whole thing. But I dawdled over it, playing a few bars and then cheating, looking up to see what notes followed. I never really listened to what I was playing. I daydreamed about being somewhere else, about being someone else.

The part I liked to practice best was the fancy curtsy: right foot out, touch the rose on the carpet with a pointed foot, sweep to the side, bend left leg, look up, and smile.

My parents invited all the couples from their social club to witness my debut. Auntie Lindo and Uncle Tin were there. Waverly and her two older brothers had also come. The first two rows were filled with children either younger or older than I was. The littlest ones got to go first. They recited simple nursery rhymes, squawked out tunes on miniature violins, and twirled hula hoops in pink ballet tutus, and when they bowed or curtsied, the audience would sigh in unison, "*Awww,*" and then clap enthusiastically.

When my turn came, I was very confident. I remember my childish excitement. It was as if I knew, without a doubt, that the prodigy side of me really did exist. I had no fear whatsoever, no nervousness. I remember thinking, This is it! This is it! I looked out over the audience, at my mother's blank face, my father's yawn, Auntie Lindo's stiff-lipped smile, Waverly's sulky expression. I had on a white dress, layered with sheets of lace, and a pink bow in my Peter Pan haircut. As I sat down, I envisioned people jumping to their feet and Ed Sullivan rushing up to introduce me to everyone on TV.

And I started to play. Everything was so beautiful. I was so caught up in how lovely I looked that I wasn't worried about how I would sound. So I was surprised when I hit the first wrong note. And then I hit another, and another. A chill started at the top of my head and began to trickle down. Yet I couldn't stop playing, as though my hands were bewitched. I kept thinking my fingers would adjust themselves back, like a train switching to the right track. I played this strange jumble through to the end, the sour notes staying with me all the way.

When I stood up, I discovered my legs were shaking. Maybe I had just been nervous, and the audience, like Old Chong, had seen me go through the right motions and had not heard anything wrong at all. I swept my right foot out, went down on my knee, looked up, and smiled. The room was quiet, except for Old Chong, who was beaming and shouting, "Bravo! Bravo! Well done!" But then I saw my mother's face, her stricken face. The audience clapped weakly, and as I walked back to my chair, with my whole face quivering as I tried not to cry, I heard a little boy whisper loudly to his mother, "That was awful," and the mother whispered back, "Well, she certainly tried."

And now I realized how many people were in the audience—the whole world, it seemed. I was aware of eyes burning into my back. I felt the shame of my mother and father as they sat stiffly through the rest of the show.

13. Robert *Schumann* (shōō′ män), 1810–1856, was a German composer.

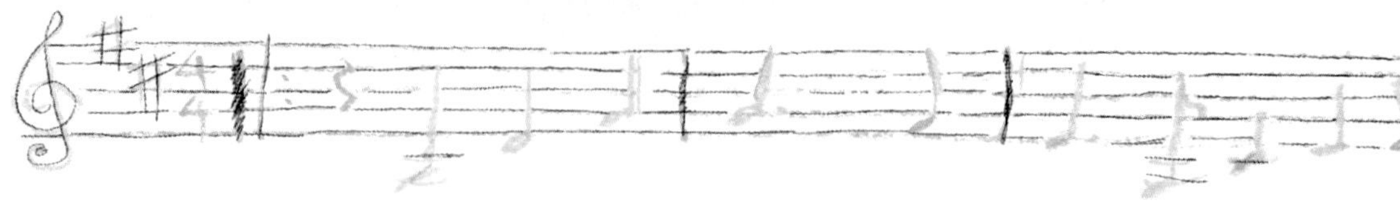

We could have escaped during intermission. Pride and some strange sense of honor must have anchored my parents to their chairs. And so we watched it all: The eighteen-year-old boy with a fake moustache who did a magic show and juggled flaming hoops while riding a unicycle. The breasted girl with white makeup who sang an aria[14] from *Madame Butterfly* and got an honorable mention. And the eleven-year-old boy who won first prize playing a tricky violin song that sounded like a busy bee.

Did You Know?
Madame Butterfly is a famous opera by Italian composer Giacomo Puccini.

After the show the Hsus, the Jongs, and the St. Clairs, from the Joy Luck Club, came up to my mother and father.

"Lots of talented kids," Auntie Lindo said vaguely, smiling broadly.

"That was somethin' else," my father said, and I wondered if he was referring to me in a humorous way, or whether he even remembered what I had done.

Waverly looked at me and shrugged her shoulders. "You aren't a genius like me," she said matter-of-factly. And if I hadn't felt so bad, I would have pulled her braids and punched her stomach.

But my mother's expression was what devastated me: a quiet, blank look that said she had lost everything. I felt the same way, and everybody seemed now to be coming up, like gawkers at the scene of an accident, to see what parts were actually missing.

When we got on the bus to go home, my father was humming the busy-bee tune and my mother was silent. I kept thinking she wanted to wait until we got home before shouting at me. But when my father unlocked the door to our apartment, my mother walked in and went straight to the back, into the bedroom. No accusations. No blame. And in a way, I felt disappointed. I had been waiting for her to start shouting, so that I could shout back and cry and blame her for all my misery.

I had assumed that my talent-show fiasco meant that I would never have to play the piano again. But two days later, after school, my mother came out of the kitchen and saw me watching TV.

"Four clock," she reminded me, as if it were any other day. I was stunned, as though she were asking me to go through the talent-show torture again. I planted myself more squarely in front of the TV.

"Turn off TV," she called from the kitchen five minutes later.

I didn't budge. And then I decided. I didn't have to do what my mother said anymore. I wasn't her slave. This wasn't China. I had listened to her before, and look what happened. She was the stupid one.

She came out from the kitchen and stood in the arched entryway of the living room. "Four clock," she said once again, louder.

"I'm not going to play anymore," I said nonchalantly. "Why should I? I'm not a genius."

She stood in front of the TV. I saw that her chest was heaving up and down in an angry way.

14. An *aria* (är′ ē ə) is an elaborate composition for solo voice.

Vocabulary

devastate (dev′ əs tāt) *v.* to destroy; overwhelm

fiasco (fē as′ kō) *n.* a complete or humiliating failure

"No!" I said, and I now felt stronger, as if my true self had finally emerged. So this was what had been inside me all along.

"No! I won't!" I screamed.

She snapped off the TV, yanked me by the arm and pulled me off the floor. She was frighteningly strong, half pulling, half carrying me toward the piano as I kicked the throw rugs under my feet. She lifted me up and onto the hard bench. I was sobbing by now, looking at her bitterly. Her chest was heaving even more and her mouth was open, smiling crazily as if she were pleased that I was crying.

"You want me to be someone that I'm not!" I sobbed. "I'll never be the kind of daughter you want me to be!"

"Only two kinds of daughters," she shouted in Chinese. "Those who are obedient and those who follow their own mind! Only one kind of daughter can live in this house. Obedient daughter!"

"Then I wish I weren't your daughter. I wish you weren't my mother," I shouted. As I said these things I got scared. It felt like worms and toads and slimy things crawling out of my chest, but it also felt good, that this awful side of me had surfaced, at last.

"Too late change this," my mother said shrilly.

And I could sense her anger rising to its breaking point. I wanted to see it spill over. And that's when I remembered the babies she had lost in China, the ones we never talked about. "Then I wish I'd never been born!" I shouted. "I wish I were dead! Like them."

It was as if I had said magic words. Alakazam!—her face went blank, her mouth closed, her arms went slack, and she backed out of the room, stunned, as if she were blowing away like a small brown leaf, thin, brittle, lifeless.

Portrait, c. 1950. Lawrence Chinn. Oil on canvas, 15 x 11 in. Collection of Frances Chinn.

Viewing the painting: Does the woman in this portrait fit your image of Jing-mei's mother? Why or why not?

It was not the only disappointment my mother felt in me. In the years that followed, I failed her many times, each time asserting my will, my right to fall short of expectations. I didn't get straight As. I didn't become class president. I didn't get into Stanford. I dropped out of college.

Unlike my mother, I did not believe I could be anything I wanted to be. I could only be me.

And for all those years we never talked about the disaster at the recital or my terrible declarations afterward at the piano bench. Neither of us talked about it again, as if it were a betrayal that was now unspeakable. So I never found a way to ask her why she had hoped for something so large that failure was inevitable.

And even worse, I never asked her about what frightened me the most: Why had she given up hope? For after our struggle at the piano, she never mentioned my playing again. The lessons stopped. The lid to the piano was closed, shutting out the dust, my misery, and her dreams.

So she surprised me. A few years ago she offered to give me the piano, for my thirtieth birthday. I had not played in all those years. I saw the offer as a sign of forgiveness, a tremendous burden removed.

"Are you sure?" I asked shyly. "I mean, won't you and Dad miss it?"

"No, this your piano," she said firmly. "Always your piano. You only one can play."

"Well, I probably can't play anymore," I said. "It's been years."

"You pick up fast," my mother said, as if she knew this was certain. "You have natural talent. You could be genius if you want to."

"No, I couldn't."

"You just not trying," my mother said. And she was neither angry nor sad. She said it as if announcing a fact that could never be disproved. "Take it," she said.

But I didn't, at first. It was enough that she had offered it to me. And after that, every time I saw it in my parents' living room, standing in front of the bay window, it made me feel proud, as if it were a shiny trophy that I had won back.

Last week I sent a tuner over to my parents' apartment and had the piano reconditioned, for purely sentimental reasons. My mother had died a few months before, and I had been getting things in order for my father, a little bit at a time. I put the jewelry in special silk pouches. The sweaters she had knitted in yellow, pink, bright orange—all the colors I hated—I put in mothproof boxes. I found some old Chinese silk dresses, the kind with little slits up the sides. I rubbed the old silk against my skin, and then wrapped them in tissue and decided to take them home with me.

After I had the piano tuned, I opened the lid and touched the keys. It sounded even richer than I remembered. Really, it was a very good piano. Inside the bench were the same exercise notes with handwritten scales, the same secondhand music books with their covers held together with yellow tape.

I opened up the Schumann book to the dark little piece I had played at the recital. It was on the left-hand page, "Pleading Child." It looked more difficult than I remembered. I played a few bars, surprised at how easily the notes came back to me.

And for the first time, or so it seemed, I noticed the piece on the right-hand side. It was called "Perfectly Contented." I tried to play this one as well. It had a lighter melody but with the same flowing rhythm and turned out to be quite easy. "Pleading Child" was shorter but slower; "Perfectly Contented" was longer but faster. And after I had played them both a few times, I realized they were two halves of the same song.

Responding to Literature

Personal Response

What was your opinion of Jing-mei's mother and the extremely ambitious goals she set for her daughter? Explain your answer.

Analyzing Literature

Recall

1. What two faces does Jing-mei see when she looks in the mirror after another failed prodigy training session?
2. What makes Jing-mei's mother decide that her daughter will study the piano? How does Jing-mei react to this news?
3. At her recital, how does Jing-mei feel when it is her turn to perform? How well does she perform?
4. Explain what provokes the nasty argument between Jing-mei and her mother.
5. What reasons does Jing-mei's mother give for offering Jing-mei the piano for her thirtieth birthday? How does Jing-mei interpret her mother's offer?

Interpret

6. Why, do you think, does Jing-mei decide to stop trying to become a prodigy?
7. In your opinion, why does Jing-mei have such a lazy attitude toward her piano studies?
8. Why, do you think, do Jing-mei and her parents feel so humiliated by her performance at the recital?
9. What is so brutal about the dreadful thing Jing-mei says to her mother at the end of their argument?
10. Do you think that Jing-mei's mother finally forgives her daughter for the dreadful thing she said? Explain.

Evaluate and Connect

11. In your opinion, why does Jing-mei's mother long for her to be famous?
12. Jing-mei and her mother seem to be fighting about the piano. In your opinion, what are they really fighting about?
13. Do you think that well-meaning parents–such as Jing-mei's mother–sometimes set unrealistic goals for their children? Explain.
14. To what does the title of this story refer? Do you think it's a good title for the story? Give a reason for your answer.
15. What do you think Jing-mei has learned by the end of the story?

Conflict

Most stories are based on a problem, or conflict, that gets resolved over the course of the story. **External conflicts** exist when a character struggles with an outside force, such as another person, society, fate, or a force of nature. An **internal conflict** exists in a character's mind, when he or she is torn between different feelings or goals. Many stories have more than one conflict. Typically, the conflicts are related in some way.

1. What is the main external conflict in "Two Kinds"?
2. Identify another external conflict in the story. How does this conflict get resolved?
3. Describe an internal conflict that Jing-mei or her mother might have. How does it relate to the main conflict you identified in question 1 above?

- See **Literary Terms Handbook,** p. R3.

Literature and Writing

Writing About Literature

Evaluate a Character's Actions Write a paragraph or two evaluating Jing-mei's actions. Do Jing-mei's actions seem appropriate for a girl her age and for her situation? What do you think of the way Jing-mei reacts to her mother? What does she think her mother wants? What does she want for herself? Support your opinions with details from the story.

Personal Writing

Side Effects of Success Look back at the journal entry you made in the Reading Focus on page 48, in which you described yourself at the top of your chosen field. Now imagine some of the possible drawbacks of such success—for example, the pressure to achieve, the fear of failure, the loss of privacy, the time demands of your career. Write another journal entry in which you describe what you like least about your success.

Extending Your Response

Literature Groups

Debating Issues Should parents ever require their children to take music lessons, as Jing-mei's mother did, or to play a sport or participate in any particular activity? First, look back at "Two Kinds" and list the reasons why the mother's requirements of Jing-mei were good and why they were bad. Use specific examples from the story as you develop your list. Then add to your list other reasons for and against mandatory after-school activities for children. Compare your lists with those made by other groups and debate whether it does more harm or more good to require a child to participate in an activity in which he or she has little or no interest.

Interdisciplinary Activity

History: Researching a Topic Jing-mei's mother represents one of about 2 million Chinese citizens who fled their homeland at the end of the 1940s and into the next decade. Do some research on this wave of Chinese migrations. What were the political and economic conditions in China at that time? Find out why so many Chinese left their homeland. Create a pamphlet with charts and pictures that details the results of your research.

Performing

Presentation Child prodigies—particularly in music—have been famous throughout history. Research a child prodigy and prepare a presentation about his or her work. For Mozart, for example, you might provide a brief biographical sketch and then play recordings of his music.

Leopold Mozart with Wolfgang and Nannerl, playing music, 1763 (detail). Louis Carrogis de Carmontelle. Watercolor, 33 x 20 cm. Musée Condé, Chantilly, France.

Reading Further

You might enjoy another work by Amy Tan:

Novel: *The Joy Luck Club* gives readers a moving look at the lives of four Chinese women in pre-1949 China and the lives of their American-born daughters.

Save your work for your portfolio.

Literary Criticism

"Schumann's music . . . serves as a metaphor used by Tan to highlight the relationship between mother and daughter," observes critic Gloria Shen. With a partner, discuss this metaphor. What does the music explain about Jing-mei's relationship with her mother?

Skill Minilessons

GRAMMAR AND LANGUAGE • Participles and Participial Phrases

Amy Tan uses **participles** (verb forms used as adjectives) and **participial phrases** to make her descriptions lively. For example:

I was a dainty ballerina girl standing by the curtains. (The participial phrase *standing by the curtains* describes *girl*.)

You can often improve your writing by using participles and participial phrases to combine short, choppy sentences. For example:

I dawdled over my piano piece. I daydreamed.
Daydreaming, I dawdled over my piano piece.

PRACTICE Combine each pair of sentences into one sentence that includes a participle or participial phrase.

1. Auntie wanted to scold Waverly. She gave Waverly a look.
2. Jing-mei returned to her seat. She fought back tears.
3. My mother called me over with hurried hand gestures. She said, "Look here."
4. My mother looked at the story. She asked, "What's the capital of Finland?"

• For more about participles, see **Language Handbook,** p. R41.

READING AND THINKING • Summarizing

To increase your reading comprehension and to follow the sequence of events in a story, stop periodically and summarize what you have read. A **summary** is a brief statement of the main idea of a passage. Notice the breaks in the text of "Two Kinds." These breaks, which indicate a change in time or topic, are good places to stop and summarize. The first section of the story might be summarized this way: *The narrator's mother, who lost everything in China, looked upon America as a land of opportunity.*

PRACTICE Review the remaining eight sections of the story. On your paper, write a one-sentence summary of each section.

APPLY Now summarize your summaries! Write a title for each section, such as "From China to America" for the first one.

• For more about summarizing, see **Reading Handbook,** p. R91.

VOCABULARY • Analogies

An analogy is a type of comparison that is based on the relationships between things or ideas. Some analogies are based on antonyms.

conceal : uncover :: persevere : quit

The opposite of *conceal* is *uncover;* the opposite of *persevere* is *quit*.

To finish an analogy, decide what relationship exists between the first two things or ideas. Then apply that relationship to another pair of words and see if it is the same.

• For more about analogies, see **Communications Skills Handbook,** p. R77.

PRACTICE Choose the word that best completes each analogy. Some of the analogies are based on antonyms.

1. lament : rejoice :: ignite :
   a. burn b. cool c. extinguish
2. harmonious : discordant :: mesmerizing :
   a. magical b. boring c. clashing
3. failure : fiasco :: meal :
   a. feast b. snack c. hunger
4. prodigy : talented :: giant :
   a. bold b. tall c. frightening
5. reproach : praise :: knowledge :
   a. learning b. criticism c. ignorance

Before You Read

Catch the Moon

Reading Focus

When was the last time you gave someone a special gift or did something really nice for another person?

List Ideas Think of your experience and other stories you know about people doing good deeds. List several possible reasons why someone might do something special for another person.

Setting a Purpose Read to discover how a teenager's gift-giving brings rewards to him in return.

Building Background

The Time and Place

It is toward the end of the 1900s in the *barrio* of a city in the northern United States. A *barrio* is an urban neighborhood in which most of the people are of Hispanic heritage. People in a *barrio* may have been born in the United States or come from Spanish-speaking countries, such as Mexico, Puerto Rico, the Dominican Republic, and Cuba.

Did You Know?

Hubcaps, or wheel covers, come in thousands of different styles. While they are mostly for show, hubcaps do keep dirt and moisture away from the wheel nuts and bearings in a car's wheel assembly. The flashiest hubcaps were made during the 1950s and 1960s. Some antique hubcaps have become collectors' items. People have even been known to "play" hubcaps as if they were cymbals.

Vocabulary Preview

harass (hə ras′, har′ əs) *v.* to bother or annoy repeatedly; p. 63

makeshift (māk′ shift′) *adj.* suitable as a temporary substitute for the proper or desired thing; p. 64

vintage (vin′ tij) *adj.* characterized by enduring appeal; classic; p. 64

decapitate (di kap′ ə tāt′) *v.* to cut off the head of; p. 66

relic (rel′ ik) *n.* an object that has survived decay, destruction, or the passage of time and is valued for its historic interest; p. 67

Meet Judith Ortiz Cofer

"Latina wherever I am," is the way Judith Ortiz Cofer sees herself. When she was a child, her family moved from Puerto Rico to Paterson, New Jersey. However, they made frequent visits back to Puerto Rico, so the writer has always felt close to her cultural roots. Vivid memories of her childhood in both countries, combined with a passion for reading literature, gave rise to Ortiz Cofer's dedication to her own writing, which includes poetry and fiction. Ortiz Cofer teaches creative writing at the University of Georgia, and has won many prizes for her own writing.

Ortiz Cofer was born in 1952 in Puerto Rico. This story was published in 1995.

Catch the Moon

Judith Ortiz Cofer

LUIS CINTRÓN SITS ON TOP OF A SIX-FOOT PILE OF HUBCAPS and watches his father walk away into the steel jungle of his car junkyard. Released into his old man's custody after six months in juvenile hall—for breaking and entering—and he didn't even take anything. He did it on a dare.

But the old lady with the million cats was a light sleeper, and good with her aluminum cane. He has a scar on his head to prove it.

Now Luis is wondering whether he should have stayed in and done his full time. Jorge Cintrón of Jorge Cintrón & Son, Auto Parts and Salvage, has decided that Luis should wash and polish every hubcap in the yard. The hill he is sitting on is only the latest couple of hundred wheel covers that have come in. Luis grunts and stands up on top of his silver mountain. He yells at no one, "Someday, son, all this will be yours," and sweeps his arms like the Pope blessing a crowd over the piles of car sandwiches and mounds of metal parts that cover this acre of land outside the city. He is the "Son" of Jorge Cintrón & Son, and so far his father has had more than one reason to wish it was plain Jorge Cintrón on the sign.

Luis has been getting in trouble since he started high school two years ago, mainly because of the "social group" he organized—a bunch of guys who were into harassing the local authorities. Their thing was taking something to the limit on a dare or, better still, doing something dangerous, like breaking into a house, not to steal, just to prove that they could do it. That was Luis's specialty, coming up with very complicated plans, like military strategies, and assigning the "jobs" to guys who wanted to join the Tiburones.[1]

Tiburón means "shark," and Luis had gotten the name from watching an old movie[2] about a Puerto Rican gang called the Sharks with his father. Luis thought it was one of the dumbest films he had ever seen. Everybody sang their lines, and the guys all pointed their toes and leaped in the air when they were supposed to be slaughtering each other. But he liked their name, the Sharks, so he made it Spanish and had it air-painted on his

1. *Tiburones* (tē′ boo rō′ nās)
2. *[old movie . . .]* The narrator is describing the feature film *West Side Story,* a 1961 musical based on Shakespeare's play *Romeo and Juliet* and set in the youth gang atmosphere of New York City in the late 1950s.

Vocabulary

harass (hə ras′, har′ əs) *v.* to bother or annoy repeatedly black T-shirt with a killer shark under it, jaws opened wide and dripping with blood. It didn't take long for other guys in the barrio to ask about it.

Man, had they had a good time. The girls were interested too. Luis outsmarted everybody by calling his organization a social club and registering it at Central High. That meant they were legal, even let out of last-period class on Fridays for their "club" meetings. It was just this year, after a couple of botched[3] jobs, that the teachers had started getting suspicious. The first one to go wrong was when he sent Kenny Matoa to *borrow* some "souvenirs" out of Anita Robles's locker. He got caught. It seems that Matoa had been reading Anita's diary and didn't hear her coming down the hall. Anita was supposed to be in the gym at that time but had copped out with the usual female excuse of cramps. You could hear her screams all the way to Market Street.

She told the principal all she knew about the Tiburones, and Luis had to talk fast to convince old Mr. Williams that the club did put on cultural activities such as the Save the Animals talent show. What Mr. Williams didn't know was that the animal that was being "saved" with the ticket sales was Luis's pet boa, which needed quite a few live mice to stay healthy and happy. They kept E.S. (which stood for "Endangered Species") in Luis's room, but she belonged to the club and it was the members' responsibility to raise the money to feed their mascot. So last year they had sponsored their first annual Save the Animals talent show, and it had been a great success. The Tiburones had come dressed as Latino Elvises and did a grand finale to "All Shook Up" that made the audience go wild. Mr. Williams had smiled while Luis talked, maybe remembering how the math teacher, Mrs. Laguna, had dragged him out in the aisle to rock-and-roll with her. Luis had gotten out of that one, but barely.

His father was a problem too. He objected to the T-shirt logo, calling it disgusting and vulgar. Mr. Cintrón prided himself on his own neat, elegant style of dressing after work, and on his manners and large vocabulary, which he picked up by taking correspondence courses in just about everything. Luis thought that it was just his way of staying busy since Luis's mother had died, almost three years ago, of cancer. He had never gotten over it.

All this was going through Luis's head as he slid down the hill of hubcaps. The tub full of soapy water, the can of polish, and the bag of rags had been neatly placed in front of a makeshift table made from two car seats and a piece of plywood. Luis heard a car drive up and someone honk their horn. His father emerged from inside a new red Mustang that had been totaled. He usually dismantled every small feature by hand before sending the vehicle into the *cementerio*,[4] as he called the lot. Luis watched as the most beautiful girl he had ever seen climbed out of a vintage white Volkswagen Bug. She stood in the sunlight in her white sundress waiting for

Did You Know?
Many people consider the *Volkswagen Beetle,* also nicknamed "VW" or "Bug," to be a classic car. Compact, durable, and affordable, the Bug was extremely popular in the 1960s and early 1970s.

3. *Botched* means "badly or clumsily done."

4. *Cementerio* (se men te′ rē ō) is Spanish for "cemetery."

Vocabulary

makeshift (māk′ shift′) *adj.* suitable as a temporary substitute for the proper or desired thing

vintage (vin′ tij) *adj.* characterized by enduring appeal; classic his father, while Luis stared. She was like a smooth wood carving. Her skin was mahogany, almost black, and her arms and legs were long and thin, but curved in places so that she did not look bony and hard—more like a ballerina. And her ebony hair was braided close to her head. Luis let his breath out, feeling a little dizzy. He had forgotten to breathe. Both the girl and his father heard him. Mr. Cintrón waved him over.

"Luis, the señorita here has lost a wheel cover. Her car is twenty-five years old, so it will not be an easy match. Come look on this side."

Luis tossed a wrench he'd been holding into a toolbox like he was annoyed, just to make a point about slave labor. Then he followed his father, who knelt on the gravel and began to point out every detail of the hubcap. Luis was hardly listening. He watched the girl take a piece of paper from her handbag.

"Señor Cintrón, I have drawn the hubcap for you, since I will have to leave soon. My home address and telephone number are here, and also my parents' office number." She handed the paper to Mr. Cintrón, who nodded.

"Sí, señorita, very good. This will help my son look for it. Perhaps there is one in that stack there." He pointed to the pile of caps that Luis was supposed to wash and polish. "Yes, I'm almost certain that there is a match there. Of course, I do not know if it's near the top or the bottom. You will give us a few days, yes?"

Luis just stared at his father like he was crazy. But he didn't say anything because the girl was smiling at him with a funny expression on her face. Maybe she thought he had X-ray eyes like Superman, or maybe she was mocking him.

"Please call me Naomi, Señor Cintrón. You know my mother. She is the director of the funeral home. . . ." Mr. Cintrón seemed surprised at first; he prided himself on having a great memory. Then his friendly expression changed to one of sadness as he recalled the

day of his wife's burial. Naomi did not finish her sentence. She reached over and placed her hand on Mr. Cintrón's arm for a moment. Then she said "Adiós" softly, and got in her shiny white car. She waved to them as she left, and her gold bracelets flashing in the sun nearly blinded Luis.

Mr. Cintrón shook his head. "How about that," he said as if to himself. "They are the Dominican owners of Ramirez Funeral Home." And, with a sigh, "She seems like such a nice young woman. Reminds me of your mother when she was her age."

Hearing the funeral parlor's name, Luis remembered too. The day his mother died, he had been in her room at the hospital while his father had gone for coffee. The alarm had gone off on her monitor and nurses had come running in, pushing him outside. After that, all he recalled was the anger that had made him punch a hole in his bedroom wall. And afterward he had refused to talk to anyone at the funeral. Strange, he did see a black girl there who didn't try like the others to talk to him, but actually ignored him as she escorted family members to the viewing room and brought flowers in. Could it be that the skinny girl in a frilly white dress had been Naomi? She didn't act like she had recognized him today, though. Or maybe she thought that he was a jerk.

Luis grabbed the drawing from his father. The old man looked like he wanted to walk down memory lane. But Luis was in no mood to listen to the old stories about his falling in love on a tropical island. The world they'd lived in before he was born wasn't his world. No beaches and palm trees here. Only junk as far as he could see. He climbed back up his hill and studied Naomi's sketch. It had obviously been done very carefully. It was signed "Naomi Ramirez" in the lower right-hand corner. He memorized the telephone number.

Luis washed hubcaps all day until his hands were red and raw, but he did not come across the small silver bowl that would fit the VW. After work he took a few practice Frisbee shots across the yard before showing his father what he had accomplished: rows and rows of shiny rings drying in the sun. His father nodded and showed him the bump on his temple where one of Luis's flying saucers had gotten him. "Practice makes perfect, you know. Next time you'll probably decapitate me." Luis heard him struggle with the word *decapitate*, which Mr. Cintrón pronounced in syllables. Showing off his big vocabulary again, Luis thought. He looked closely at the bump, though. He felt bad about it.

"They look good, hijo."[5] Mr. Cintrón made a sweeping gesture with his arms over the yard. "You know, all this will have to be classified. My dream is to have all the parts divided by year, make of car, and condition. Maybe now that you are here to help me, this will happen."

"Pop . . ." Luis put his hand on his father's shoulder. They were the same height and build, about five foot six and muscular. "The judge said six months of free labor for you, not life, okay?" Mr. Cintrón nodded, looking distracted. It was then that Luis suddenly noticed how gray his hair had turned—it used to be shiny black like his own—and that there were deep lines in his face. His father had turned into an old man and he hadn't even noticed.

"Son, you must follow the judge's instructions. Like she said, next time you get in

5. *Hijo* (ē′ hō) is Spanish for "son."

Vocabulary

decapitate (di kap′ ə tāt′) *v.* to cut off the head of

trouble, she's going to treat you like an adult, and I think you know what that means. Hard time, no breaks."

"Yeah, yeah. That's what I'm doing, right? Working my hands to the bone instead of enjoying my summer. But listen, she didn't put me under house arrest, right? I'm going out tonight."

"Home by ten. She did say something about a curfew, Luis." Mr. Cintrón had stopped smiling and was looking upset. It had always been hard for them to talk more than a minute or two before his father got offended at something Luis said, or at his sarcastic tone. He was always doing something wrong.

Luis threw the rag down on the table and went to sit in his father's ancient Buick, which was in mint condition. They drove home in silence.

After sitting down at the kitchen table with his father to eat a pizza they had picked up on the way home, Luis asked to borrow the car. He didn't get an answer then, just a look that meant "Don't bother me right now."

Before bringing up the subject again, Luis put some ice cubes in a Baggie and handed it to Mr. Cintrón, who had made the little bump on his head worse by rubbing it. It had GUILTY written on it, Luis thought.

"Gracias, hijo." His father placed the bag on the bump and made a face as the ice touched his skin.

They ate in silence for a few minutes more; then Luis decided to ask about the car again.

"I really need some fresh air, Pop. Can I borrow the car for a couple of hours?"

"You don't get enough fresh air at the yard? We're lucky that we don't have to sit in a smelly old factory all day. You know that?"

"Yeah, Pop. We're real lucky." Luis always felt irritated that his father was so grateful to own a junkyard, but he held his anger back and just waited to see if he'd get the keys without having to get in an argument.

"Where are you going?"

"For a ride. Not going anywhere. Just out for a while. Is that okay?"

His father didn't answer, just handed him a set of keys, as shiny as the day they were manufactured. His father polished everything that could be polished: doorknobs, coins, keys, spoons, knives, and forks, like he was King Midas counting his silver and gold. Luis thought his father must be really lonely to polish utensils only he used anymore. They had been picked out by his wife, though, so they were like relics. Nothing she had ever owned could be thrown away. Only now the dishes, forks, and spoons were not used to eat the yellow rice and red beans, the fried chicken, or the mouth-watering sweet plantains that his mother had cooked for them. They were just kept in the cabinets that his father had turned into a museum for her. Mr. Cintrón could cook as well as his wife, but he didn't have the heart to do it anymore. Luis thought that maybe if they ate together once in a while things might get better between them, but he always had something to do around dinnertime and ended up at a hamburger joint. Tonight was the first time in months they had sat down at the table together.

Did You Know?
A *plantain* (plant′ ən) is a tropical fruit similar to a banana, which must be cooked before eating.

Vocabulary

relic (rel′ ik) *n.* an object that has survived decay, destruction, or the passage of time and is valued for its historic interest

Luis took the keys. "Thanks," he said, walking out to take his shower. His father kept looking at him with those sad, patient eyes. "Okay. I'll be back by ten, and keep the ice on that egg," Luis said without looking back.

He had just meant to ride around his old barrio, see if any of the Tiburones were hanging out at El Building, where most of them lived. It wasn't far from the single-family home his father had bought when the business started paying off: a house that his mother lived in for three months before she took up residence at St. Joseph's Hospital. She never came home again. These days Luis wished he still lived in that tiny apartment where there was always something to do, somebody to talk to.

Instead Luis found himself parked in front of the last place his mother had gone to: Ramirez Funeral Home. In the front yard was a huge oak tree that Luis remembered having climbed during the funeral to get away from people. The tree looked different now, not like a skeleton, as it had then, but green with leaves. The branches reached to the second floor of the house, where the family lived.

For a while Luis sat in the car allowing the memories to flood back into his brain. He remembered his mother before the illness changed her. She had not been beautiful, as his father told everyone; she had been a sweet lady, not pretty but not ugly. To him, she had been the person who always told him that she was proud of him and loved him. She did that every night when she came to his bedroom door to say good-night. As a joke he would sometimes ask her, "Proud of what? I haven't done anything." And she'd always say, "I'm just proud that you are my son." She wasn't perfect or anything. She had bad days when nothing he did could make her smile, especially after she got sick. But he never heard her say anything negative about anyone. She always blamed *el destino*, fate, for what went wrong. He missed her. He missed her so much. Suddenly a flood of tears that had been building up for almost three years started pouring from his eyes. Luis sat in his father's car, with his head on the steering wheel, and cried, "Mami, I miss you."

When he finally looked up, he saw that he was being watched. Sitting at a large window with a pad and a pencil on her lap was Naomi. At first Luis felt angry and embarrassed, but she wasn't laughing at him. Then she told him with her dark eyes that it was okay to come closer. He walked to the window, and she held up the sketch pad on which she had drawn him, not crying like a baby, but sitting on top of a mountain of silver disks, holding one up over his head. He had to smile.

The plate-glass window was locked. It had a security bolt on it. An alarm system, he figured, so nobody would steal the princess. He asked her if he could come in. It was soundproof too. He mouthed the words slowly for her to read his lips. She wrote on the pad, "I can't let you in. My mother is not home tonight." So they looked at each other and talked through the window for a little while. Then Luis got an idea. He signed to her that he'd be back, and drove to the junkyard.

Luis climbed up on his mountain of hubcaps. For hours he sorted the wheel covers by make, size, and condition, stopping only to call his father and tell him where he was and what he was doing. The old man did not ask him for explanations, and Luis was grateful for that. By lamppost light, Luis worked and worked, beginning to understand a little why his father kept busy all the time. Doing something that had a beginning, a middle, and an end did something to your head. It was like the satisfaction Luis got out of planning "adventures" for his Tiburones, but there was

September 16, c. 1955. René Magritte. Oil on canvas, 14 x 10⅞ in. The Minneapolis Institute of Arts.

Viewing the painting: In what ways does this painting express the title and the mood of the story?

another element involved here that had nothing to do with showing off for others. This was a treasure hunt. And he knew what he was looking for.

Finally, when it seemed that it was a hopeless search, when it was almost midnight and Luis's hands were cut and bruised from his work, he found it. It was the perfect match for Naomi's drawing, the moon-shaped wheel cover for her car, Cinderella's shoe. Luis jumped off the small mound of disks left under him and shouted, "Yes!" He looked around and saw neat stacks of hubcaps that he would wash the next day. He would build a display wall for his father. People would be able to come into the yard and point to whatever they wanted.

Luis washed the VW hubcap and polished it until he could see himself in it. He used it as a mirror as he washed his face and combed his hair. Then he drove to the Ramirez Funeral Home. It was almost pitch-black, since it was a moonless night. As quietly as possible, Luis put some gravel in his pocket and climbed the oak tree to the second floor. He knew he was in front of Naomi's window—he could see her shadow through the curtains. She was at a table, apparently writing or drawing, maybe waiting for him. Luis hung the silver disk carefully on a branch near the window, then threw the gravel at the glass. Naomi ran to the window and drew the curtains aside while Luis held on to the thick branch and waited to give her the first good thing he had given anyone in a long time.

Responding to Literature

Personal Response

Were you surprised by Luis's actions at the end of the story? Why or why not?

Analyzing Literature

Recall

1. Why does Luis work at his father's car junkyard?
2. In what ways has Luis gotten into trouble?
3. Why does Naomi come to the junkyard? How does Luis react to seeing her?
4. Describe the relationship between Luis and his father.
5. What does Luis leave in the tree for Naomi?

Interpret

6. What do you think Luis's feelings are about his job at the junkyard? Cite details from the story to support your response.
7. How might the death of Luis's mother have affected his behavior? Explain.
8. How do Luis's feelings for Naomi help him deal with the loss of his mother?
9. Do you think there is a chance for Luis and his father to build a good relationship? Support your response with details from the story.
10. What do you think Luis discovers about himself as he searches for his gift to Naomi?

Evaluate and Connect

11. What do you think Luis's reasons were for giving the gift to Naomi? Think back to the Reading Focus on page 62 in which you listed reasons why a person might give a gift or do a good deed for someone. How do Luis's reasons compare with the reasons you listed?
12. Read Luis's description of his mother. In your opinion, what did Luis love most about her? Explain.
13. In addition to the gift he gives Naomi, Luis also will give something to his father. What will Luis give him?
14. In your opinion, what does Luis find so attractive about Naomi besides her good looks? Be specific and give examples to back up your opinion.
15. What does the title suggest about the **tone** of this story? Do you think it's a good title choice? Why or why not?

Literary ELEMENTS

Imagery

Writers make their work come alive by choosing words and phrases that appeal to readers' senses of sight, touch, taste, smell, and hearing. The use of these sensory details is called **imagery.**

1. What visual image is reflected in the title of the story? How does it show the tie between Luis and his father? Between Luis and Naomi?
2. What effect do the images of food on page 67 have on your reading of that part of the story?
3. How does the image of the oak tree outside Naomi's window help convey Luis's feelings at the times he saw the tree?

- See **Literary Terms Handbook,** p. R6.

Literary Criticism

Reviewer Nancy Vasilakis says of *An Island Like You: Stories of the Barrio,* "The narratives have universal resonance in the vitality, the brashness, the self-centered hopefulness, and the angst expressed by the teens as they tell of friendships formed, romances failed, and worries over work, family, and school." As a class, discuss how this observation applies to the story "To Catch a Moon."

Literature and Writing

Writing About Literature

Character Luis is the central character in this story. Analyze and describe him. Be sure to include the following in your analysis:

- a description of Luis's key personality traits
- a recap of what has happened to Luis and how he has responded to each event
- an explanation of how and why Luis changes

Creative Writing

On Love Write a poem that Luis might have written about his memories of his mother and his relationship with her; about his growing feelings for Naomi; or about his relationship with his father. Try including visual and other sensory images that help express his memories and his feelings about the person.

Extending Your Response

Literature Groups

Do the Tiburones Spell Trouble? Does the author suggest that Luis's association with the Tiburones is good or bad for him? Divide into two opposing groups to debate the question. Use evidence from the story as well as your own understanding of Luis and life to present your group's side. Then listen to the opposing group. When your debate is finished, vote on which side was more convincing, then share your results with the rest of the class.

Learning for Life

Car Talk Hubcaps aren't the only car part that Señor Cintrón sells at his salvage shop. He sells parts for all of the automotive systems that help a car run smoothly and safely. Find out about the various systems of a car. Then draw a diagram or build a simple model of one system and, using your diagram or model as a visual aid, explain to the class how that system works.

Interdisciplinary Activity

Art: Luis and His Logo Three works of art are described in this story: the Tiburones' logo, Naomi's drawing of the hubcap, and the drawing she made of Luis. Draw or paint one of these images as you imagine it. Share your work and any explanation of it with the class.

Reading Further

If you'd like to read more by Judith Ortiz Cofer, you might enjoy these stories:

Collection: *An Island Like You–Stories of the Barrio* is a set of twelve funny, poignant short stories about what it's like to be a Puerto Rican teenager growing up in the United States.

Save your work for your portfolio.

GRAMMAR AND LANGUAGE • Understanding Connotations

Connotations are the positive or negative feelings that most people associate with a word. These associations go beyond the **denotation,** or the literal dictionary definition of the word. Skilled writers choose their words with careful attention to connotations to evoke specific feelings or responses in readers. For example, when the narrator says that Luis "was released into his old man's custody," the term *old man* has a connotation of disrespect that is missing from the neutral word *father.*

PRACTICE On your paper, write an explanation of the differences in connotations between the two words in the following pairs.

1. unusual, peculiar
2. clever, tricky
3. youthful, immature
4. persistent, stubborn
5. adventurous, reckless

● For more about word choice, see **Reading Handbook,** p. R81.

READING AND THINKING • Recognizing Causes and Effects

A cause is the reason something happens; an effect is what happens as a result of the cause. For example, in "Catch the Moon," Luis is polishing hubcabs (effect) because a judge has sentenced him to work for his father for six months (cause).

PRACTICE On your paper, identify the cause of each of these events from the story.

1. Luis and his friends put on the Save the Animals talent show.
2. Luis's father takes several correspondence courses.
3. Naomi comes to the Auto Parts and Salvage yard.
4. Luis sits in his car outside the Ramirez Funeral Home and cries "like a baby."
5. Luis sorts through and organizes a mountain of wheel covers.

APPLY Return to the story. Find at least one effect for each of the events listed above. Write them on your paper.

● For more about text structure, see **Reading Handbook,** pp. R86–R87.

VOCABULARY • Compound Words

When two words are joined to form one, the result is a compound word. You can often figure out the meaning of an unfamiliar compound by thinking about the complete words that form it. For example, an outpouring of praise is a steadily flowing amount of praise. Some unfamiliar compounds are more difficult to figure out. *Makeshift* makes sense only if you know that *shift* can mean "a trick or scheme for use in an emergency."

● For more about compound words, see **Language Handbook,** p. R56.

PRACTICE Use your knowledge of the words that form the compounds in the left column to match each with its definition on the right.

1. underlying	a. achieved dishonestly
2. quitclaim	b. an uncredited author
3. soul-searching	c. basic and fundamental
4. ill-gotten	d. an honest look at one's true feelings
5. ghostwriter	e. the giving up of a right or the title to property

Grammar Link

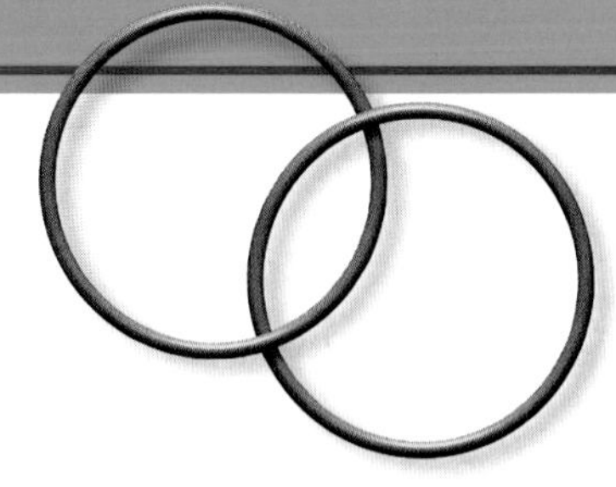

Avoiding Sentence Fragments

A fragment is an incomplete part of something. You might whistle a fragment of a song or sweep up the fragments of a china plate. A **sentence fragment** is a word or group of words that is only part of a sentence.

Problem 1 Some sentence fragments lack either a subject or a verb (or both).
Stands on a pile of hubcaps. [lacks a subject]
Hundreds of hubcaps in the pile. [lacks a verb]

Solution Add the missing subject and/or verb.
Luis stands on a pile of hubcaps.
Hundreds of hubcaps are rusting in the pile.

Problem 2 Some sentence fragments are really subordinate clauses that have been mistaken for a complete sentence. Although they have a subject and a verb, subordinate clauses do not express a complete thought and cannot stand alone as a sentence.
Because he broke into someone's house.

Solution A Join the subordinate clause to a main clause.
Luis was in juvenile hall because he broke into someone's house.

Solution B Remove the subordinating conjunction at the beginning of the clause.
He broke into someone's house.

People often use sentence fragments in conversation. The fragment "Got to run" lacks a subject. It could mean that the speaker has to go or that the listener should hurry, but it is unlikely to be misunderstood because the listener understands the context. In writing, however, a fragment that leaves out important information can be confusing.

For more about sentence fragments, see **Language Handbook,** pp. R14–R15.

ACTIVITIES

1. **Proofreading:** Use the strategies shown above to correct the sentence fragments in this paragraph.

   Naomi came to Mr. Cintrón's junkyard. Because she had lost a hubcap off her Volkswagon. She hoped they could find a replacement for it. Luis stared at her. The most beautiful girl in the world. Worked hard to find a match for her hubcap. Later that night, at Naomi's house. When she looked out the window and saw the gift Luis had brought her.

2. Revise a piece of your own writing using these strategies to eliminate sentence fragments.

MEDIA connection

Magazine Article

What lures people into the water and causes them to test their bodies against the challenges of the deep? For young diver Mehgan Heaney-Grier, it's the chance to set an underwater world record.

Where No One Has Gone Before?

by Paul Kvinta—*Outside* magazine, July 1997

The most peaceful part of Mehgan Heaney-Grier's life begins at 40 feet below sea level. This is the 19-year-old's "buoyancy point," the depth beyond which she can stop kicking her three-foot fins, straighten her long, slender frame, close her eyes, and fall headfirst like an anvil toward the bottom of the ocean. "Once I break 40 feet, I don't move a muscle," she explains. "I just put myself in God's hands, and he takes care of it."

. . . Heaney-Grier will take one deep breath and then attempt to propel herself past ten safety divers off Looe Key, Florida, snatch a tag at 210 feet, and swim back to the surface, delivering a new women's world record in the sport of free diving. Few observers doubt Heaney-Grier will break the current 204-foot mark held by Cuban Deborah Andollo—after all, some even think Heaney-Grier might be the finest free-diving prospect ever, male or female. . . .

In free diving, practitioners must master but two things: equalizing their air passages rapidly as pressure builds during descent, and slowing their metabolism to conserve what precious little oxygen they have. Thus any discussion of Heaney-Grier's prowess inevitably focuses on her ears and her gender. "Mehgan has a very special pair of ears," her coach explains. "She can equalize at any depth. And she is a woman, which is good, because women have a much lower metabolic rate than men. I'll make her into a diving machine."

Not that she wasn't headed that direction anyway. In 1995, when Heaney-Grier attempted her first free dive, she reached a phenomenal 87 feet. A year later, while setting her personal best and the American record of 155 feet, she surpassed her previous mark by a full 15 percent. Still, she remains a long way off from the men's record of 236 feet—and at least one observer doubts that she can ever get there. "I've heard she's very good, but I don't think she can make it," says Pipin Ferreras [champion Cuban free diver]. "Two hundred forty feet is very deep."

Analyzing Media

1. What do you think is the most important aspect of free diving for Mehgan Heaney-Grier?
2. What kinds of challenges do you set for yourself?

Before You Read

Through the Tunnel

Reading Focus

Think of times when you watched someone your age do something difficult or challenging. Perhaps you asked yourself, "Could I do that?"

Chart It! Make a chart like this one, and fill it in.

The Challenge	Did I try it?	What happened?
	yes no	
	yes no	

Setting a Purpose Read to see how one young boy faces a difficult challenge.

Building Background

The Time and Place

This story takes place at a seashore, perhaps on the Mediterranean coast of France. The time is most likely the 1940s or 1950s.

Did You Know?

Underwater diving with no equipment other than goggles is called breath-hold diving. This type of diving can be very dangerous due to the great force of water pressure: water is more than a thousand times as dense as air. Most breath-hold divers can remain submerged for less than one minute, although with training, some divers can stay underwater for two minutes.

Vocabulary Preview

conscientiously (kon′ shē en′ shəs lē) *adv.* thoughtfully and carefully; p. 76

contrition (kən trish′ ən) *n.* sorrow for one's sin or wrongdoing; repentance; p. 76

supplication (səp′ lə kā′ shən) *n.* an earnest and humble request; p. 78

beseeching (bi sēch′ ing) *adj.* begging; asking earnestly; p. 81

myriad (mir′ ē əd) *n.* great or countless numbers; p. 81

incredulous (in krej′ ə ləs) *adj.* unwilling or unable to believe; p. 83

convulsive (kən vul′ siv) *adj.* sudden and violent; p. 84

Meet Doris Lessing

"It's a good thing for kids to be alone: you get a sense of yourself and ideas of your own. . . ."

Solitude and independence have both been important to Lessing since she was very young. She grew up on an isolated farm with little supervision and spent much of her time roaming on her own.

Like the boy in this story, Lessing also has pushed herself to extremes in order to find out something about herself.

Doris Lessing was born in 1919 and lived in southern Africa until 1949, when she moved to England. This story was published in 1957.

Through the Tunnel

Doris Lessing

GOING TO THE SHORE ON THE FIRST MORNING OF THE VACATION, the young English boy stopped at a turning of the path and looked down at a wild and rocky bay, and then over to the crowded beach he knew so well from other years. His mother walked on in front of him, carrying a bright striped bag in one hand. Her other arm, swinging loose, was very white in the sun. The boy watched that white, naked arm, and turned his eyes, which had a frown behind them, toward the bay and back again to his mother. When she felt he was not with her, she swung around. "Oh, there you are, Jerry!" she said. She looked impatient, then smiled. "Why, darling, would you rather not come with me? Would you rather—" She frowned, conscientiously worrying over what amusements he might secretly be longing for, which she had been too busy or too careless to imagine. He was very familiar with that anxious, apologetic smile. Contrition sent him running after her. And yet, as he ran, he looked back over his shoulder at the wild bay; and all morning, as he played on the safe beach, he was thinking of it.

Next morning, when it was time for the routine of swimming and sunbathing, his mother said, "Are you tired of the usual beach, Jerry? Would you like to go somewhere else?"

"Oh, no!" he said quickly, smiling at her out of that unfailing impulse of contrition—a sort of chivalry.[1] Yet, walking down the path with her, he blurted out, "I'd like to go and have a look at those rocks down there."

She gave the idea her attention. It was a wild looking place, and there was no one there; but she said, "Of course, Jerry. When you've had enough, come to the big beach. Or just go straight back to the villa,[2] if you like." She walked away, that bare arm, now slightly reddened from yesterday's sun, swinging. And he almost ran after her again, feeling it unbearable that she should go by herself, but he did not.

1. Here, *chivalry* (shiv′ əl rē) means "an act of courtesy or politeness."
2. *Villa*, from the Italian, means "house," usually one in the country or at the seashore.

Vocabulary

conscientiously (kon′ shē en′ shəs lē) *adv.* thoughtfully and carefully
contrition (kən trish′ ən) *n.* sorrow for one's sin or wrongdoing; repentance

She was thinking, Of course he's old enough to be safe without me. Have I been keeping him too close? He mustn't feel he ought to be with me. I must be careful.

He was an only child, eleven years old. She was a widow. She was determined to be neither possessive nor lacking in devotion. She went worrying off to her beach.

As for Jerry, once he saw that his mother had gained her beach, he began the steep descent to the bay. From where he was, high up among red-brown rocks, it was a scoop of moving bluish green fringed with white. As he went lower, he saw that it spread among small promontories and inlets of rough, sharp rock, and the crisping, lapping surface showed stains of purple and darker blue. Finally, as he ran sliding and scraping down the last few yards, he saw an edge of white surf and the shallow, luminous movement of water over white sand, and, beyond that, a solid, heavy blue.

Did You Know?
Promontories are high points of land or rock overlooking the water.

Crowded Day at the Beach, 1922. Martha Walter. Oil on board, 16 x 20 in. David David Gallery, Philadelphia.

Viewing the painting: Why might Jerry not want to go to a beach like this one with his mother?

He ran straight into the water and began swimming. He was a good swimmer. He went out fast over the gleaming sand, over a middle region where rocks lay like discolored monsters under the surface, and then he was in the real sea—a warm sea where irregular cold currents from the deep water shocked his limbs.

When he was so far out that he could look back not only on the little bay but past the promontory that was between it and the big beach, he floated on the buoyant surface and looked for his mother. There she was, a speck of yellow under an umbrella that looked like a slice of orange peel. He swam back to shore, relieved at being sure she was there, but all at once very lonely.

On the edge of a small cape that marked the side of the bay away from the promontory was a loose scatter of rocks. Above them, some boys were stripping off their clothes. They came running, naked, down to the rocks. The English boy swam toward them, but kept his distance at a stone's throw. They were of that coast; all of them were burned smooth dark brown and speaking a language he did not understand. To be with them, of them, was a craving that filled his whole body. He swam a little closer; they turned and watched him with narrowed, alert dark eyes. Then one smiled and waved. It was enough. In a minute, he had swum in and was on the rocks beside them, smiling with a desperate, nervous supplication. They shouted cheerful greetings at him; and then, as he preserved his nervous, uncomprehending smile, they understood that he was a foreigner strayed from his own beach, and they proceeded to forget him. But he was happy. He was with them.

They began diving again and again from a high point into a well of blue sea between

Photograph by Douglass Faulkner.

Viewing the photograph: In what direction was the photographer shooting? How does this perspective reflect the feeling Jerry has about the diving boys?

rough, pointed rocks. After they had dived and come up, they swam around, hauled themselves up, and waited their turn to dive again. They were big boys—men, to Jerry. He dived, and they watched him; and when he swam around to take his place, they made way for him. He felt he was accepted, and he dived again, carefully, proud of himself.

Soon the biggest of the boys poised himself, shot down into the water, and did not come up. The others stood about, watching. Jerry, after waiting for the sleek brown head to appear, let out a yell of warning; they looked at him idly and turned their eyes back toward the water. After a long time, the boy came up on the other side of a big dark rock, letting the air out of his lungs in a sputtering gasp and a shout of triumph. Immediately the rest of them dived in. One moment, the morning seemed full of chattering boys; the next, the air and the surface of the water were empty. But through the heavy blue, dark shapes could be seen moving and groping.

Jerry dived, shot past the school of underwater swimmers, saw a black wall of rock looming at him, touched it, and bobbed up at once to the surface, where the wall was a low barrier he could see across. There was no one visible; under him, in the water, the dim shapes of the swimmers had disappeared. Then one, and then another of the boys came up on the far side of the barrier of rock, and he understood that they had swum through some gap or hole in it. He plunged down again. He could see nothing through the stinging salt water but the blank rock. When

Vocabulary

supplication (səp′ lə kā′ shən) *n.* an earnest and humble request

he came up the boys were all on the diving rock, preparing to attempt the feat again. And now, in a panic of failure, he yelled up, in English, "Look at me! Look!" and he began splashing and kicking in the water like a foolish dog.

They looked down gravely, frowning. He knew the frown. At moments of failure, when he clowned to claim his mother's attention, it was with just this grave, embarrassed inspection that she rewarded him. Through his hot shame, feeling the pleading grin on his face like a scar that he could never remove, he looked up at the group of big brown boys on the rock and shouted, *"Bonjour! Merci! Au revoir! Monsieur, monsieur!"*[3] while he hooked his fingers round his ears and waggled them.

Water surged into his mouth; he choked, sank, came up. The rock, lately weighted with boys, seemed to rear up out of the water as their weight was removed. They were flying down past him, now, into the water; the air was full of falling bodies. Then the rock was empty in the hot sunlight. He counted one, two, three. . . .

At fifty, he was terrified. They must all be drowning beneath him, in the watery caves of the rock! At a hundred, he stared around him at the empty hillside, wondering if he should yell for help. He counted faster, faster, to hurry them up, to bring them to the surface quickly, to drown them quickly —anything rather than the terror of counting on and on into the blue emptiness of the morning. And then, at a hundred and sixty, the water beyond the rock was full of boys blowing like brown whales. They swam back to the shore without a look at him.

He climbed back to the diving rock and sat down, feeling the hot roughness of it under his thighs. The boys were gathering up their bits of clothing and running off along

3. *["Bonjour! . . . monsieur!"]* These words are French for "Hello! Thanks! Good-bye! Sir, sir!"

the shore to another promontory. They were leaving to get away from him. He cried openly, fists in his eyes. There was no one to see him, and he cried himself out.

It seemed to him that a long time had passed, and he swam out to where he could see his mother. Yes, she was still there, a yellow spot under an orange umbrella. He swam back to the big rock, climbed up, and dived into the blue pool among the fanged and angry boulders. Down he went, until he touched the wall of rock again. But the salt was so painful in his eyes that he could not see.

He came to the surface, swam to shore, and went back to the villa to wait for his mother. Soon she walked slowly up the path, swinging her striped bag, the flushed, naked arm dangling beside her. "I want some swimming goggles," he panted, defiant and beseeching.

She gave him a patient, inquisitive look as she said casually, "Well, of course, darling."

But now, now, now! He must have them this minute, and no other time. He nagged and pestered until she went with him to a shop. As soon as she had bought the goggles, he grabbed them from her hand as if she were going to claim them for herself, and was off, running down the steep path to the bay.

Jerry swam out to the big barrier rock, adjusted the goggles, and dived. The impact of the water broke the rubber-enclosed vacuum, and the goggles came loose. He understood that he must swim down to the base of the rock from the surface of the water. He fixed the goggles tight and firm, filled his lungs, and floated, face down, on the water. Now, he could see. It was as if he had eyes of a different kind—fish eyes that showed everything clear and delicate and wavering in the bright water.

Under him, six or seven feet down, was a floor of perfectly clean, shining white sand, rippled firm and hard by the tides. Two grayish shapes steered there, like long, rounded pieces of wood or slate. They were fish. He saw them nose toward each other, poise motionless, make a dart forward, swerve off, and come around again. It was like a water dance. A few inches above them the water sparkled as if sequins were dropping through it. Fish again—myriads of minute fish, the length of his fingernail, were drifting through the water, and in a moment he could feel the innumerable tiny touches of them against his limbs. It was like swimming in flaked silver. The great rock the big boys had swum through rose sheer out of the white sand—black, tufted lightly with greenish weed. He could see no gap in it. He swam down to its base.

Again and again he rose, took a big chestful of air, and went down. Again and again he groped over the surface of the rock, feeling it, almost hugging it in the desperate need to find the entrance. And then, once, while he was clinging to the black wall, his knees came up, and he shot his feet out forward and they met no obstacle. He had found the hole.

He gained the surface, clambered about the stones that littered the barrier rock until he found a big one, and, with this in his arms, let himself down over the side of the rock. He dropped, with the weight, straight to the sandy floor.

Clinging tight to the anchor of stone, he lay on his side and looked in under the dark shelf at the place where his feet had gone. He could see the hole. It was an irregular, dark gap; but he could not see deep into it. He let go of his anchor, clung with his hands to the edges of the hole, and tried to push himself in.

Vocabulary

beseeching (bi sēch′ ing) *adj.* begging; asking earnestly

myriad (mir′ ē əd) *n.* great or countless numbers

He got his head in, found his shoulders jammed, moved them in sidewise, and was inside as far as his waist. He could see nothing ahead. Something soft and clammy touched his mouth; he saw a dark frond[4] moving against the grayish rock, and panic filled him. He thought of octopuses, of clinging weed. He pushed himself out backward and caught a glimpse, as he retreated, of a harmless tentacle[5] of seaweed drifting in the mouth of the tunnel. But it was enough. He reached the sunlight, swam to shore, and lay on the diving rock. He looked down into the blue well of water. He knew he must find his way through that cave, or hole, or tunnel, and out the other side.

First, he thought, he must learn to control his breathing. He let himself down into the water with another big stone in his arms, so that he could lie effortlessly on the bottom of the sea. He counted. One, two, three. He counted steadily. He could hear the movement of blood in his chest. Fifty-one, fifty-two. . . . His chest was hurting. He let go of

4. A *frond* is a large leaf with many divisions, or a leaflike part of a plant such as seaweed.
5. A *tentacle* is a long, flexible limb that could belong to a plant or to a creature such as an octopus.

(Rocky Sea Shore), 1916–1919. Edward Hopper. Oil on canvas panel, 9½ x 12 15/16 in. Collection of Whitney Museum of American Art, New York. Josephine N. Hopper Bequest. 70.166.

Viewing the painting: How does the scene portrayed here affect your understanding of the beach that Jerry goes to?

the rock and went up into the air. He saw that the sun was low. He rushed to the villa and found his mother at her supper. She said only, "Did you enjoy yourself?" and he said, "Yes."

All night the boy dreamed of the water-filled cave in the rock, and as soon as breakfast was over he went to the bay.

That night, his nose bled badly. For hours he had been underwater, learning to hold his breath, and now he felt weak and dizzy. His mother said, "I shouldn't overdo things, darling, if I were you."

That day and the next, Jerry exercised his lungs as if everything, the whole of his life, all that he would become, depended upon it. Again his nose bled at night, and his mother insisted on his coming with her the next day. It was a torment to him to waste a day of his careful self training, but he stayed with her on that other beach, which now seemed a place for small children, a place where his mother might lie safe in the sun. It was not his beach.

He did not ask for permission, on the following day, to go to his beach. He went, before his mother could consider the complicated rights and wrongs of the matter. A day's rest, he discovered, had improved his count by ten. The big boys had made the passage while he counted a hundred and sixty. He had been counting fast, in his fright. Probably now, if he tried, he could get through that long tunnel, but he was not going to try yet. A curious, most unchildlike persistence, a controlled impatience, made him wait. In the meantime, he lay underwater on the white sand, littered now by stones he had brought down from the upper air, and studied the entrance to the tunnel. He knew every jut and corner of it, as far as it was possible to see. It was as if he already felt its sharpness about his shoulders.

He sat by the clock in the villa, when his mother was not near, and checked his time. He was incredulous and then proud to find he could hold his breath without strain for two minutes. The words "two minutes," authorized by the clock, brought close the adventure that was so necessary to him.

In another four days, his mother said casually one morning, they must go home. On the day before they left, he would do it. He would do it if it killed him, he said defiantly to himself. But two days before they were to leave—a day of triumph when he increased his count by fifteen—his nose bled so badly that he turned dizzy and had to lie limply over the big rock like a bit of seaweed, watching the thick red blood flow on to the rock and trickle slowly down to the sea. He was frightened. Supposing he turned dizzy in the tunnel? Supposing he died there, trapped? Supposing—his head went around, in the hot sun, and he almost gave up. He thought he would return to the house and lie down, and next summer, perhaps, when he had another year's growth in him—*then* he would go through the hole.

But even after he had made the decision, or thought he had, he found himself sitting up on the rock and looking down into the water; and he knew that now, this moment, when his nose had only just stopped bleeding, when his head was still sore and throbbing—this was the moment when he would try. If he did not do it now, he never would. He was trembling with fear that he would not go; and he was trembling with horror at that long, long tunnel under the rock, under the sea. Even in the open sunlight, the barrier rock seemed very wide and very heavy; tons of rock pressed down on where he would go. If he died there, he would lie until

Vocabulary

incredulous (in krej′ ə ləs) *adj.* unwilling or unable to believe one day—perhaps not before next year—those big boys would swim into it and find it blocked.

He put on his goggles, fitted them tight, tested the vacuum. His hands were shaking. Then he chose the biggest stone he could carry and slipped over the edge of the rock until half of him was in the cool, enclosing water and half in the hot sun. He looked up once at the empty sky, filled his lungs once, twice, and then sank fast to the bottom with the stone. He let it go and began to count. He took the edges of the hole in his hands and drew himself into it, wriggling his shoulders in sidewise as he remembered he must, kicking himself along with his feet.

Soon he was clear inside. He was in a small rock-bound hole filled with yellowish-gray water. The water was pushing him up against the roof. The roof was sharp and pained his back. He pulled himself along with his hands—fast, fast—and used his legs as levers. His head knocked against something; a sharp pain dizzied him. Fifty, fifty-one, fifty-two. . . . He was without light, and the water seemed to press upon him with the weight of rock. Seventy-one, seventy-two. . . . There was no strain on his lungs. He felt like an inflated balloon, his lungs were so light and easy, but his head was pulsing.

He was being continually pressed against the sharp roof, which felt slimy as well as sharp. Again he thought of octopuses, and wondered if the tunnel might be filled with weed that could tangle him. He gave himself a panicky, convulsive kick forward, ducked his head, and swam. His feet and hands moved freely, as if in open water. The hole must have widened out. He thought he must be swimming fast, and he was frightened of banging his head if the tunnel narrowed.

A hundred, a hundred and one. . . . The water paled. Victory filled him. His lungs were beginning to hurt. A few more strokes and he would be out. He was counting wildly; he said a hundred and fifteen, and then, a long time later, a hundred and fifteen again. The water was a clear jewel-green all around him. Then he saw, above his head, a crack running up through the rock. Sunlight was falling through it, showing the clean, dark rock of the tunnel, a single mussel shell, and darkness ahead.

He was at the end of what he could do. He looked up at the crack as if it were filled with air and not water, as if he could put his mouth to it to draw in air. A hundred and fifteen, he heard himself say inside his head—but he had said that long ago. He must go on into the blackness ahead, or he would drown. His head was swelling, his lungs cracking. A hundred and fifteen, a hundred and fifteen pounded through his head, and he feebly clutched at rocks in the dark, pulling himself forward, leaving the brief space of sunlit water behind. He felt he was dying. He was no longer quite conscious. He struggled on in the darkness between lapses into unconsciousness. An immense, swelling pain filled his head, and then the darkness cracked with an explosion of green light. His hands, groping forward, met nothing; and his feet, kicking back, propelled him out into the open sea.

Did You Know?
A *mussel* is a kind of shellfish. Mussels are in the same scientific classification as clams, oysters, and scallops.

He drifted to the surface, his face turned up to the air. He was gasping like a fish. He felt he would sink now and drown; he could

Vocabulary
convulsive (kən vul′ siv) *adj.* sudden and violent

not swim the few feet back to the rock. Then he was clutching it and pulling himself up on to it. He lay face down, gasping. He could see nothing but a red-veined, clotted dark. His eyes must have burst, he thought; they were full of blood. He tore off his goggles and a gout[6] of blood went into the sea. His nose was bleeding, and the blood had filled the goggles.

He scooped up handfuls of water from the cool, salty sea, to splash on his face, and did not know whether it was blood or salt water he tasted. After a time, his heart quieted, his eyes cleared, and he sat up. He could see the local boys diving and playing half a mile away. He did not want them. He wanted nothing but to get back home and lie down.

In a short while, Jerry swam to shore and climbed slowly up the path to the villa. He flung himself on his bed and slept, waking at the sound of feet on the path outside. His mother was coming back. He rushed to the bathroom, thinking she must not see his face with bloodstains, or tearstains, on it. He came out of the bathroom and met her as she walked into the villa, smiling, her eyes lighting up.

"Have a nice morning?" she asked, laying her hand on his warm brown shoulder a moment.

"Oh, yes, thank you," he said.

"You look a bit pale." And then, sharp and anxious, "How did you bang your head?"

"Oh, just banged it," he told her.

She looked at him closely. He was strained; his eyes were glazed-looking. She was worried. And then she said to herself, Oh, don't fuss! Nothing can happen. He can swim like a fish.

They sat down to lunch together.

"Mummy," he said, "I can stay under water for two minutes—three minutes, at least." It came bursting out of him.

"Can you, darling?" she said. "Well, I shouldn't overdo it. I don't think you ought to swim any more today."

She was ready for a battle of wills, but he gave in at once. It was no longer of the least importance to go to the bay.

6. Here, *gout* refers to a mass of fluid that gushes or bursts forth.

Responding to Literature

Personal Response

If you had been in Jerry's place, do you think you would have tested yourself the way he did? If so, do you think you would have succeeded? Give reasons for your answers.

Analyzing Literature

Recall

1. How is Jerry's beach different from his mother's?
2. Describe the boys Jerry encounters, and trace the change in their attitude toward him.
3. Summarize what Jerry does when he goes to his beach the second time.
4. How is Jerry's preparation unlike the real test?
5. What happens after Jerry returns to the villa?

Interpret

6. In your opinion, why is Jerry first drawn to his beach?
7. Jerry begins clowning in the water while the boys are on the diving rock. In your opinion, why does Jerry do this?
8. Why, do you think, does Jerry decide that he must do what the other boys have done?
9. In your opinion, what is the most dramatic moment of Jerry's actual test? Explain your answer.
10. Why, do you think, doesn't Jerry feel a need to show his new ability to the other boys?

Evaluate and Connect

11. Was Jerry's decision to test himself a good one, or did he risk too much? Give reasons for your answer.
12. In your opinion, is Jerry a good son? Is his mother a good mother? Support your opinions with evidence from the story.
13. **Theme Connections** What do you think Jerry has learned about himself by the end of the story?
14. Stories sometimes contain a **symbol**—an object that stands for something else, often an idea or a concept. What do you think the tunnel in this story might symbolize?
15. Look back at the chart you made in the Reading Focus on page 75. How does Jerry's experience compare with the way you have handled difficulties or challenges in your own life?

Literary ELEMENTS

Plot

As the problem, or **conflict,** in a story is explored, the story often becomes more suspenseful. A story's **climax** is its turning point, the moment of greatest emotional intensity, interest, or suspense. Usually the climax is found at the point in a story where the conflict begins to be resolved. For instance, in a story about a race, the climax probably would occur as the main character or other characters approach the finish line.

1. What is the major conflict in this story? What other conflicts are present?
2. What is the climax of this story? Explain why you think this event is the story's turning point.
3. What conflict or conflicts are resolved by the end of the story? Explain your answer.

- See **Literary Terms Handbook,** p. R9.

Literature and Writing

Writing About Literature

Author's Choice of Details The author gives vivid descriptions of the physical effects that Jerry suffers during and after his breath-hold dives. Find at least five examples of such descriptions. Explain how each one helps the reader better understand the danger and the discomfort that Jerry faces as he struggles to meet the challenge he has set for himself.

Creative Writing

Dear Jerry Was Jerry brave or foolish? Write a letter to him expressing your opinion about his decision to try to swim through the tunnel. Support your opinion with reasons. Base your reasons on details from the story or on personal experience.

Extending Your Response

Literature Groups

Reading the Author's Mind Does the author believe it's a good idea to push oneself beyond one's limits? Debate this question in your group. Each group member should use evidence from the story to support his or her opinion. Tally your group's responses and share the results with the rest of the class.

Interdisciplinary Activity

Art: Illustrating a Scene Illustrate one of the underwater scenes that is described in a passage in this story. Reread the passage before you begin your illustration, so that you remember to include all of the details described in the scene.

Performing

You Can't Be Serious Imagine that you are Jerry's mother or another of his family members, and that he has told you he is planning to swim through the tunnel. What would you say to him? Work with a partner as you prepare a dialogue. One partner should take Jerry's role, and the other partner should take the family member's role. Perform your dialogue for the class.

Save your work for your portfolio.

VOCABULARY • Antonyms

Not all words have perfect antonyms. *Huge* has one *(tiny),* but no word means the opposite of *sigh* or *apple.* Then there are such words as *supplication.* What would be the opposite of an earnest and humble request? If you are asked to come up with an antonym for a word like this, think about the primary meaning of the word, in this case "a request." Thinking about *supplication* this way allows you to choose a word such as *requirement* or *order* as an antonym.

PRACTICE Use your knowledge of the words in the left column to match each one to its antonym in the right column. If a word is unfamiliar, use a dictionary to find out its meaning.

1. conscientiously	a. calm
2. convulsive	b. few
3. beseeching	c. gullible
4. myriads	d. carelessly
5. incredulous	e. demanding

Before You Read

The Vision Quest

Reading Focus

How important are goals? Can an experience be useful even if you fail to reach the goal you set?

List Ideas List some benefits a person might get from an experience even if the original goal is not reached.

Setting a Purpose Read to discover what one young Sioux learns from striving to reach a goal.

Building Background

The Time and Place

The events of "The Vision Quest" take place somewhere in or around South Dakota. The time is not specified, nor is it important, since the tale is timeless.

Did You Know?

Visions have always been an important part of Native American culture. Among some peoples, the quest for a vision is an initiation into adulthood, and the vision helps shape the young person's goals. However, individuals who face major life challenges or who feel the need for spiritual guidance might also seek a vision. Some vision quests involve fasting and solitude; others require physical suffering. The search for visions is still an important ritual in Native American culture.

Vocabulary Preview

brash (brash) *adj.* boldly disrespectful; p. 90

obliterate (ə blit′ ə rāt′) *v.* to destroy completely; p. 91

gaunt (gônt) *adj.* extremely thin and hollow-eyed, as from hunger or illness; looking like skin and bones; p. 91

humility (hū mil′ ə tē) *n.* the quality of being humble or modest; p. 91

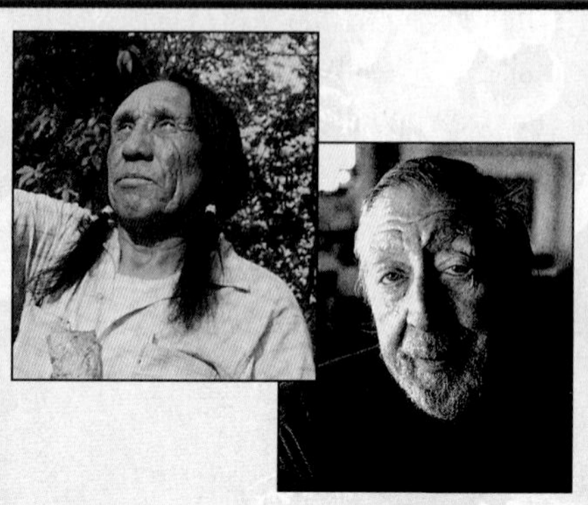

Meet Lame Deer and Richard Erdoes

Recalling his own vision quest, Lame Deer said,

"I thought of my forefathers who had crouched here before me . . . I felt their presence."

Lame Deer is a spiritual name that has been handed down from father to son in one Sioux family. The Lame Deer who told the story "Vision Quest" is also called John Fire.

Richard Erdoes was born in the early 1900s in what is now Austria. He came to New York in the 1940s. As an artist and writer on assignment in the United States, Erdoes met many Native Americans and became involved in their civil rights struggle.

John Fire Lame Deer was born in the late 1800s. He told this story to Richard Erdoes in 1967.

The Vision Quest

Told by Lame Deer
Recorded by Richard Erdoes

A YOUNG MAN WANTED TO GO ON A *HANBLECEYA*, or vision seeking, to try for a dream that would give him the power to be a great medicine man. Having a high opinion of himself, he felt sure that he had been created to become great among his people and that the only thing lacking was a vision.

The young man was daring and brave, eager to go up to the mountaintop. He had been brought up by good, honest people who were wise in the ancient ways and who prayed for him. All through the winter they were busy getting him ready, feeding him wasna,[1] corn, and plenty of good meat to make him strong. At every meal they set aside something for the spirits so that they would help him to get a great vision. His relatives thought he had the power even

1. *Wasna* is a high-energy food made of meat, fat, and berries pounded together.

Did You Know?
A *travois* (trə voi′) is a V-shaped sled made of hide or netting supported by two long poles that are harnessed to a horse or dog.

before he went up, but that was putting the cart before the horse, or rather the travois before the horse, as this is an Indian legend.

When at last he started on his quest, it was a beautiful morning in late spring. The grass was up, the leaves were out, nature was at its best. Two medicine men accompanied him. They put up a sweat lodge[2] to purify him in the hot, white breath of the sacred steam. They sanctified him with the incense of sweet grass, rubbing his body with sage, fanning it with an eagle's wing. They went to the hilltop with him to prepare the vision pit and make an offering of tobacco bundles. Then they told the young man to cry, to humble himself, to ask for holiness, to cry for power, for a sign from the Great Spirit, for a gift which would make him into a medicine man. After they had done all they could, they left him there.

He spent the first night in the hole the medicine men had dug for him, trembling and crying out loudly. Fear kept him awake, yet he was cocky, ready to wrestle with the spirits for the vision, the power he wanted. But no dreams came to ease his mind. Toward morning before the sun came up, he heard a voice in the swirling white mists of dawn. Speaking from no particular direction, as if it came from different places, it said: "See here, young man, there are other spots you could have picked; there are other hills around here. Why don't you go there to cry for a dream? You disturbed us all night, all us creatures and birds; you even kept the trees awake. We couldn't sleep. Why should you cry here? You're a brash young man, not yet ready or worthy to receive a vision."

But the young man clenched his teeth, determined to stick it out, resolved to force that vision to come. He spent another day in the pit, begging for enlightenment which would not come, and then another night of fear and cold and hunger.

When dawn arrived once more, he heard the voice again: "Stop disturbing us; go away!" The same thing happened the third morning. By this time he was faint with hunger, thirst, and anxiety. Even the air seemed to oppress him, to fight him. He was panting. His stomach felt shriveled up, shrunk tight against his backbone. But he was determined to endure one more night, the fourth and last. Surely the vision would come. But again he cried for it out of the dark and loneliness until he was hoarse, and still he had no dream.

Just before daybreak he heard the same voice again, very angry: "Why are you still here?" He knew then that he had suffered in vain; now he would have to go back to his people and confess that he had gained no knowledge and no power. The only thing he could tell them was that he got bawled out every morning. Sad and cross, he replied, "I can't help myself; this is my last day, and I'm crying my eyes out. I know you told me to go home, but who are you to give me orders? I don't know you. I'm going to stay until my uncles come to fetch me, whether you like it or not."

2. A *sweat lodge* is a hut made of branches bent and tied to form a framework, which is covered by hides or blankets. Inside, steam is produced by pouring or sprinkling water over red-hot rocks contained in a central pit.

Vocabulary
brash (brash) *adj.* boldly disrespectful

All at once there was a rumble from a larger mountain that stood behind the hill. It became a mighty roar, and the whole hill trembled. The wind started to blow. The young man looked up and saw a boulder poised on the mountain's summit. He saw lightning hit it, saw it sway. Slowly the boulder moved. Slowly at first, then faster and faster, it came tumbling down the mountainside, churning up earth, snapping huge trees as if they were little twigs. And the boulder was coming right down on him!

The young man cried out in terror. He was paralyzed with fear, unable to move. The boulder dwarfed everything in view; it towered over the vision pit. But just as it was an arm's length away and about to crush him, it stopped. Then, as the young man stared open-mouthed, his hair standing up, his eyes starting out of his head, the boulder *rolled up the mountain,* all the way to the top. He could hardly believe what he saw. He was still cowering motionless when he heard the roar and rumble again and saw that immense boulder coming down at him once more. This time he managed to jump out of his vision pit at the last moment. The boulder crushed it, obliterated it, grinding the young man's pipe and gourd rattle into dust.

Again the boulder rolled up the mountain, and again it came down. "I'm leaving, I'm leaving!" hollered the young man. Regaining his power of motion, he scrambled down the hill as fast as he could. This time the boulder actually leap-frogged over him, bouncing down the slope, crushing and pulverizing everything in its way. He ran unseeingly, stumbling, falling, getting up again. He did not even notice the boulder rolling up once more and coming down for the fourth time. On this last and most fearful descent, it flew through the air in a giant leap, landing right in front of him and embedding itself so deeply in the earth that only its top was visible. The ground shook itself like a wet dog coming out of a stream and flung the young man this way and that.

Gaunt, bruised, and shaken, he stumbled back to his village. To the medicine men he said: "I have received no vision and gained no knowledge. I have made the spirits angry. It was all for nothing."

"Well, you did find out one thing," said the older of the two, who was his uncle. "You went after your vision like a hunter after buffalo, or a warrior after scalps. You were fighting the spirits. You thought they owed you a vision. Suffering alone brings no vision nor does courage, nor does sheer will power. A vision comes as a gift born of humility, of wisdom, and of patience. If from your vision quest you have learned nothing but this, then you have already learned much. Think about it."

Vocabulary

obliterate (ə blit′ ə rāt′) *v.* to destroy completely

gaunt (gônt) *adj.* extremely thin and hollow-eyed, as from hunger or illness; "looking like skin and bones"

humility (hū mil′ ə tē) *n.* the quality of being humble or modest

Responding to Literature

Personal Response

What aspect of this story struck you most forcefully? Did anything surprise or impress you? Share your reactions with your classmates.

Analyzing Literature

Recall and Interpret

1. What kind of vision is the young man expecting? What does his expectation tell you about him?
2. What are some of the things the voice in the mountains says? How would you describe the vision quester's reaction to the voice?
3. How does the young man's vision quest end? Based on what he reports to the medicine men, what do you think his attitude is about his quest?
4. What response does the vision quester's uncle give him? In your opinion, is the response appropriate?

Evaluate and Connect

5. What is the central **conflict** in this story?
6. Do you think that the humor and modern language in the story added to or took away from its effectiveness for you? Use examples from the story to explain your answer.
7. Look over your response to the Reading Focus on page 88 and think of a time when you failed to reach a goal you had set for yourself. What did you learn from the experience?
8. **Theme Connections** In what way was this experience a transition for the young man? How was he different afterwards?

Literary ELEMENTS

Legend

A **legend** is a traditional narrative, such as a story or poem, that has been handed down from one generation to the next. It is presented as a type of history, even though it may not be factually accurate. Most legends help convey a culture's learning, knowledge, and values.

1. What Native American custom is central to this story?
2. Which parts of the story might be true and which parts could not be proven true?
3. What are some of the values that this story transmits?

- See **Literary Terms Handbook,** p. R7.

Extending Your Response

Literature Groups

Debate the Question Do you think the young man would ever undertake another vision quest? Form two groups, one that will support a *yes* answer, and one supporting *no*. Hold a debate, with each group giving details from the story to back up its position.

Creative Writing

Summary in Verse Write a song, poem, or limerick that summarizes the main points of "The Vision Quest." First, decide which elements of the story should be included. Then, include those elements in either a serious or humorous poem or song.

Save your work for your portfolio.

COMPARING *selections*

Through the Tunnel and The Vision Quest

COMPARE **GOALS**

Both Jerry and the vision quester set important goals for themselves.

1. How are their goals similar?
2. How are they different?
3. Think about what the two boys actually accomplish and how they feel about their accomplishments. How does the outcome of Jerry's experience compare with that of the vision quester's trial? Support your response with details from the stories.

COMPARE **CHALLENGES**

Who faced a greater challenge, Jerry or the vision quester?

- In a small group, take turns stating your opinion and supporting it with facts and reasons. Try to persuade other group members that your opinion is correct.
- Listen to fellow group members as they argue their side of this issue.
- As a group, decide which members presented the most persuasive arguments for their opinion and why those presentations were so convincing.
- Share your group's best arguments with the class. Try to decide, as a class, which character faced a greater challenge.

COMPARE **CUSTOMS**

The boys in both stories experienced a transition—a passage along the road from childhood to adulthood. Most societies have initiation rituals to mark that transition. Also, groups within societies often set tasks that must be accomplished before a person can be a full member of the group. Investigate the initiation customs of a society or a group, such as a club or service organization. You might interview members of the group or use the library or the Internet for your research. Then, based on your findings, write an analysis that compares the initiation customs of the group you studied with those of the culture in one of these stories.

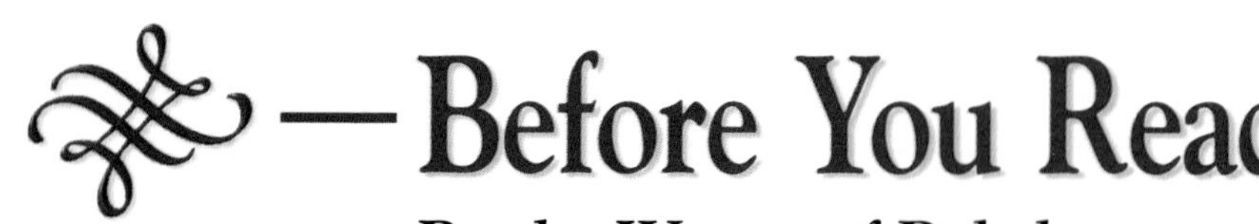

Before You Read

By the Waters of Babylon

Reading Focus

Have you ever accomplished—or wanted to accomplish—a task that is usually thought of as an adult responsibility?

Sharing Ideas List things that you have done, or would like to do, that are usually considered adult responsibilities. Share your list with a partner.

Setting a Purpose Read to discover the remarkable way in which one boy experiences the passage from adolescence to adulthood.

Building Background

The Time and Place

The events of this story unfold in a strange and forbidding landscape, at an unspecified time.

Did You Know?

The title "By the Waters of Babylon" alludes to Psalm 137, from the Bible, which begins:

"By the rivers of Babylon, there we sat down, yea, we wept, when we remembered Zion."

The psalm describes the Israelites' intense grief over the destruction of their sacred temple, their separation from their homeland Jerusalem (referred to here as Zion), and their enforced captivity at the hands of the Babylonians.

Vocabulary Preview

bade (bād) *v.* past tense of *bid,* to command, order, or ask; p. 96

anteroom (an′ tē ro͞om′) *n.* a small room serving as a waiting area or entrance to a larger, main room; p. 101

perplexed (pər plekst′) *adj.* troubled with doubt or uncertainty; puzzled; p. 103

Meet Stephen Vincent Benét

Stephen Vincent Benét (bə nā′) was fascinated and inspired by the American past. Historical themes and the American landscape dominate his work, which includes novels, poetry, plays, radio scripts, and short stories. Benét is most celebrated for his poetry, for which he was awarded two Pulitzer Prizes—the first, in 1929, for his epic poem *John Brown's Body*, and the second, in 1944, for another long poem entitled *Western Star*.

Stephen Vincent Benét was born in Bethlehem, Pennsylvania, in 1898; he died in New York City in 1943. This story was first published in 1937.

BY THE WATERS OF

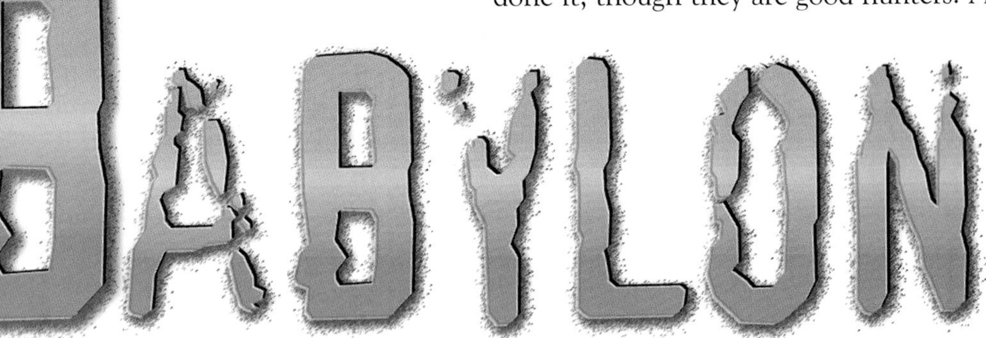

Stephen Vincent Benét

The north and the west and the south are good hunting ground, but it is forbidden to go east. It is forbidden to go to any of the Dead Places except to search for metal and then he who touches the metal must be a priest or the son of a priest. Afterwards, both the man and the metal must be purified. These are the rules and the laws; they are well made. It is forbidden to cross the great river and look upon the place that was the Place of the Gods—this is most strictly forbidden. We do not even say its name though we know its name. It is there that spirits live, and demons—it is there that there are the ashes of the Great Burning. These things are forbidden—they have been forbidden since the beginning of time.

My father is a priest; I am the son of a priest. I have been in the Dead Places near us, with my father—at first, I was afraid. When my father went into the house to search for the metal, I stood by the door and my heart felt small and weak. It was a dead man's house, a spirit house. It did not have the smell of man, though there were old bones in a corner. But it is not fitting that a priest's son should show fear. I looked at the bones in the shadow and kept my voice still.

Then my father came out with the metal—a good, strong piece. He looked at me with both eyes but I had not run away. He gave me the metal to hold—I took it and did not die. So he knew that I was truly his son and would be a priest in my time. That was when I was very young—nevertheless, my brothers would not have done it, though they are good hunters. After that, they gave me the good piece of meat and the warm corner by the fire. My father watched over me—he was glad that I should be a priest. But when I boasted or wept without a reason, he punished me more strictly than my brothers. That was right.

After a time, I myself was allowed to go into the dead houses and search for metal. So I learned the ways of those houses—and if I saw bones, I was no longer afraid. The bones are light and old—sometimes they will fall into dust if you touch them. But that is a great sin.

I was taught the chants and the spells—I was taught how to stop the running of blood from a wound and many secrets. A priest must know many secrets—that was what my father said. If the hunters think we do all things by chants and spells, they may believe so—it does not hurt them. I was taught how to read in the old books and how to make the old writings—that was hard and took a long time. My knowledge made me happy—it was like a fire in my heart. Most of all, I liked to hear of the Old Days and the stories of the gods. I asked myself many questions that I could not answer, but it was good to ask them. At night, I would lie awake and listen to the wind—it seemed to me that it was the voice of the gods as they flew through the air.

Did You Know?
A *grub* is the soft, wormlike larva of an insect, especially of a beetle.

We are not ignorant like the Forest People—our women spin wool on the wheel, our priests wear a white robe. We do not eat grubs from the tree, we have not forgotten the old writings, although they are hard to understand. Nevertheless, my knowledge and my lack of knowledge burned in me—I wished to know more. When I was a man at last, I came to my father and said, "It is time for me to go on my journey. Give me your leave."

He looked at me for a long time, stroking his beard, then he said at last, "Yes. It is time." That night, in the house of the priesthood, I asked for and received purification. My body hurt but my spirit was a cool stone. It was my father himself who questioned me about my dreams.

He bade me look into the smoke of the fire and see—I saw and told what I saw. It was what I have always seen—a river, and, beyond it, a great Dead Place and in it the gods walking. I have always thought about that. His eyes were stern when I told him—he was no longer my father but a priest. He said, "This is a strong dream."

"It is mine," I said, while the smoke waved and my head felt light. They were singing the Star song in the outer chamber and it was like the buzzing of bees in my head.

He asked me how the gods were dressed and I told him how they were dressed. We know how they were dressed from the book, but I saw them as if they were before me. When I had finished, he threw the sticks three times and studied them as they fell.

"This is a very strong dream," he said. "It may eat you up."

"I am not afraid," I said and looked at him with both eyes. My voice sounded thin in my ears but that was because of the smoke.

He touched me on the breast and the forehead. He gave me the bow and the three arrows.

"Take them," he said. "It is forbidden to travel east. It is forbidden to cross the river. It is forbidden to go to the Place of the Gods. All these things are forbidden."

Vocabulary
bade (bād) *v.* past tense of *bid*, to command, order, or ask

"All these things are forbidden," I said, but it was my voice that spoke and not my spirit. He looked at me again.

"My son," he said. "Once I had young dreams. If your dreams do not eat you up, you may be a great priest. If they eat you, you are still my son. Now go on your journey."

I went fasting, as is the law. My body hurt but not my heart. When the dawn came, I was out of sight of the village. I prayed and purified myself, waiting for a sign. The sign was an eagle. It flew east.

Sometimes signs are sent by bad spirits. I waited again on the flat rock, fasting, taking no food. I was very still—I could feel the sky above me and the earth beneath. I waited till the sun was beginning to sink. Then three deer passed in the valley, going east—they did not wind me or see me. There was a white fawn with them—a very great sign.

I followed them, at a distance, waiting for what would happen. My heart was troubled about going east, yet I knew that I must go. My head hummed with my fasting—I did not even see the panther spring upon the white fawn. But, before I knew it, the bow was in my hand. I shouted and the panther lifted his head from the fawn. It is not easy to kill a panther with one arrow but the arrow went through his eye and into his brain. He died as he tried to spring—he rolled over, tearing at the ground. Then I knew I was meant to go east—I knew that was my journey. When the night came, I made my fire and roasted meat.

Soleil Couchant. Eugene Boudin (1824–1898). Pastel on paper, 6⅛ x 8¼ in. Private collection.

Viewing the painting: How does this painting reflect the mood of John's dreams?

It is eight suns' journey to the east and a man passes by many Dead Places. The Forest People are afraid of them but I am not. Once I made my fire on the edge of a Dead Place at night and, next morning, in the dead house, I found a good knife, little rusted. That was small to what came afterward but it made my heart feel big. Always when I looked for game, it was in front of my arrow, and twice I passed hunting parties of the Forest People without their knowing. So I knew my magic was strong and my journey clean, in spite of the law.

Toward the setting of the eighth sun, I came to the banks of the great river. It was half-a-day's journey after I had left the god-road—we do not use the god-roads now for they are falling apart into great blocks of stone, and the forest is safer going. A long way off, I had seen the water through trees but the trees were thick. At last, I came out upon an open place at the top of a cliff. There was the great river below, like a giant in the sun. It is very long, very wide. It could eat all the streams we know and still be thirsty. Its name is Ou-dis-sun, the Sacred, the Long. No man of my tribe had seen it, not even my father, the priest. It was magic and I prayed.

Then I raised my eyes and looked south. It was there, the Place of the Gods.

How can I tell what it was like—you do not know. It was there, in the red light, and they were too big to be houses. It was there with the red light upon it, mighty and ruined. I knew that in another moment the gods would see me. I covered my eyes with my hands and crept back into the forest.

Surely, that was enough to do, and live. Surely it was enough to spend the night upon the cliff. The Forest People themselves do not come near. Yet, all through the night, I knew that I should have to cross the river and walk in the places of the gods, although the gods ate me up. My magic did not help me at all and yet there was a fire in my bowels, a fire in my mind. When the sun rose, I thought, "My journey has been clean. Now I will go home from my journey." But, even as I thought so, I knew I could not. If I went to the Place of the Gods, I would surely die, but, if I did not go, I could never be at peace with my spirit again. It is better to lose one's life than one's spirit, if one is a priest and the son of a priest.

Nevertheless, as I made the raft, the tears ran out of my eyes. The Forest People could have killed me without fight, if they had come upon me then, but they did not come. When the raft was made, I said the sayings for the dead and painted myself for death. My heart was cold as a frog and my knees like water, but the burning in my mind would not let me have peace. As I pushed the raft from the shore, I began my death song—I had the right. It was a fine song.

"I am John, son of John," I sang. "My people are the Hill People. They are the men.
I go into the Dead Places but I am not slain.
I take the metal from the Dead Places but I am not blasted.
I travel upon the god-roads and am not afraid. E-yah! I have killed the panther, I have killed the fawn!
E-yah! I have come to the great river. No man has come there before.
It is forbidden to go east, but I have gone, forbidden to go on the great river, but I am there.
Open your hearts, you spirits, and hear my song.
Now I go to the Place of the Gods, I shall not return.
My body is painted for death and my limbs weak, but my heart is big as I go to the Place of the Gods!"

All the same, when I came to the Place of the Gods, I was afraid, afraid. The current of the great river is very strong—it gripped my raft with its hands. That was magic, for the river itself is wide and calm. I could feel evil spirits about me, in the bright morning; I could feel their breath on my neck as I was swept down the stream. Never have I been so much alone—I tried to think of my knowledge, but it was a squirrel's heap of winter nuts. There was no strength in my knowledge any more and I felt small and naked as a new-hatched bird—alone upon the great river, the servant of the gods.

Yet, after a while, my eyes were opened and I saw. I saw both banks of the river—I saw that once there had been god-roads across it, though now they were broken and fallen like broken vines. Very great they were, and wonderful and broken—broken in the time of the Great Burning when the fire fell out of the sky. And always the current took me nearer to the Place of the Gods, and the huge ruins rose before my eyes.

I do not know the customs of rivers—we are the People of the Hills. I tried to guide my raft with the pole but it spun around. I thought the river meant to take me past the Place of the Gods and out into the Bitter Water of the legends. I grew angry then—my heart felt strong. I said aloud, "I am a priest and the son of a priest!" The gods heard me—they showed me how to paddle with the pole on one side of the raft. The current changed itself—I drew near to the Place of the Gods.

When I was very near, my raft struck and turned over. I can swim in our lakes—I swam to the shore. There was a great spike of rusted metal sticking out into the river—I hauled myself up upon it and sat there, panting. I had saved my bow and two arrows and the knife I found in the Dead Place but that was all. My raft went whirling downstream toward the Bitter Water. I looked after it, and thought if it had trod me under, at least I would be safely dead. Nevertheless, when I had dried my bowstring and restrung it, I walked forward to the Place of the Gods.

It felt like ground underfoot; it did not burn me. It is not true what some of the tales say, that the ground there burns forever, for I have been there. Here and there were the marks and stains of the Great Burning, on the ruins, that is true. But they were old marks and old stains. It is not true either, what some of our priests say, that it is an island covered with fogs and enchantments. It is not. It is a great Dead Place—greater than any Dead Place we know. Everywhere in it there are god-roads, though most are cracked and broken. Everywhere there are the ruins of the high towers of the gods.

How shall I tell what I saw? I went carefully, my strung bow in my hand, my skin ready for danger. There should have been the wailings of spirits and the shrieks of demons, but there were not. It was very silent and sunny where I had landed—the wind and the rain and the birds that drop seeds had done their work—the grass grew in the cracks of the broken stone. It is a fair island—no wonder the gods built there. If I had come there, a god, I also would have built.

How shall I tell what I saw? The towers are not all broken—here and there one still stands, like a great tree in a forest, and the birds nest high. But the towers themselves look blind, for the gods are gone. I saw a fish hawk, catching fish in the river. I saw a little dance of white butterflies over a great heap of broken stones and columns. I went there and looked about me—there was a carved stone with cut-letters, broken in half. I can read letters but I could not understand these. They said UBTREAS. There was also the shattered image of a man or a god. It had been made of white stone and he wore his hair tied back like a woman's. His name was ASHING, as I read on the cracked half of a stone. I thought it wise to pray to ASHING, though I do not know that god.

How shall I tell what I saw? There was no smell of man left, on stone or metal. Nor were there many trees in that wilderness of stone. There are many pigeons, nesting and dropping in the towers—the gods must have loved them, or, perhaps, they used them for sacrifices. There are wild cats that roam the god-roads, green-eyed, unafraid of man. At night they wail like demons but they are not demons. The wild dogs are more dangerous, for they hunt in a pack, but them I did not meet till later. Everywhere there are the carved stones, carved with magical numbers or words.

I went north—I did not try to hide myself. When a god or a demon saw me, then I would die, but meanwhile I was no longer afraid. My hunger for knowledge burned in me—there was so much that I could not understand. After a while, I knew that my belly was hungry. I could have hunted for my meat, but I did not hunt. It is known that the gods did not hunt as we do—they got their food from enchanted boxes and jars. Sometimes these are still found in the Dead Places—once, when I was a child and foolish, I opened such a jar and tasted it and found the food sweet. But my father found out and punished me for it strictly, for, often, that food is death. Now, though, I had long gone past what was forbidden, and I entered the likeliest towers, looking for the food of the gods.

I found it at last in the ruins of a great temple in the mid-city. A mighty temple it must have been, for the roof was painted like the sky at night with its stars—that much I could see, though the colors were faint and dim. It went down into great caves and tunnels—perhaps they kept their slaves there. But when I started to climb down, I heard the squeaking of rats, so I did not go—rats are unclean, and there must have been many tribes of them, from the squeaking. But near there, I found food, in the heart of a ruin, behind a door that still opened. I ate only the fruits from the jars—they had a very sweet taste. There was drink, too, in bottles of glass—the drink of the gods was strong and made my head swim. After I had eaten and drunk, I slept on the top of a stone, my bow at my side.

When I woke, the sun was low. Looking down from where I lay, I saw a dog sitting on his haunches. His tongue was hanging out of his mouth; he looked as if he were laughing. He was a big dog, with a gray-brown coat, as big as a wolf. I sprang up and shouted at him but he did not move—he just sat there as if he were laughing. I did not like that. When I reached for a stone to throw, he moved swiftly out of the way of the stone. He was not afraid of me; he looked at me as if I were meat. No doubt I could have killed him with an arrow, but I did not know if there were others. Moreover, night was falling.

I looked about me—not far away there was a great, broken god-road, leading north. The towers were high enough, but not so high, and while many of the dead-houses were wrecked, there were some that stood. I went toward this god-road, keeping to the heights of the ruins, while the dog followed. When I had reached the god-road, I saw that there were others behind him. If I had slept later, they would have come upon me asleep and torn out my throat. As it was, they were sure enough of me; they did not hurry. When I went into the dead-house, they kept watch at the entrance—doubtless they thought they

Abismo. David Alfaro Siqueiros (1896–1974). Piroxyline on Masonite, 23⅝ x 27½ in.

Viewing the painting: What elements in this painting remind you of the setting of the story?

would have a fine hunt. But a dog cannot open a door and I knew, from the books, that the gods did not like to live on the ground but on high.

I had just found a door I could open when the dogs decided to rush. Ha! They were surprised when I shut the door in their faces—it was a good door, of strong metal. I could hear their foolish baying beyond it but I did not stop to answer them. I was in darkness—I found stairs and climbed. There were many stairs, turning around till my head was dizzy. At the top was another door—I found the knob and opened it. I was in a long small chamber—on one side of it was a bronze door that could not be opened, for it had no handle. Perhaps there was a magic word to open it but I did not have the word. I turned to the door in the opposite side of the wall. The lock of it was broken and I opened it and went in.

Within, there was a place of great riches. The god who lived there must have been a powerful god. The first room was a small anteroom—I waited there for some time, telling the spirits of the place that I came in peace and not as a robber. When it seemed to me that they had had time to hear me, I went on. Ah, what riches! Few, even, of the windows had been broken—it was all as it had been. The great windows that looked over the city had not been broken at all though they were dusty and streaked with many years. There were coverings on the floors, the colors

Vocabulary

anteroom (an′ tē ro͞om′) *n.* a small room serving as a waiting area or entrance to a larger, main room not greatly faded, and the chairs were soft and deep. There were pictures upon the walls, very strange, very wonderful—I remember one of a bunch of flowers in a jar—if you came close to it, you could see nothing but bits of color, but if you stood away from it, the flowers might have been picked yesterday. It made my heart feel strange to look at this picture—and to look at the figure of a bird, in some hard clay, on a table and see it so like our birds. Everywhere there were books and writings, many in tongues that I could not read. The god who lived there must have been a wise god and full of knowledge. I felt I had right there, as I sought knowledge also.

Nevertheless, it was strange. There was a washing-place but no water—perhaps the gods washed in air. There was a cooking-place but no wood, and though there was a machine to cook food, there was no place to put fire in it. Nor were there candles or lamps—there were things that looked like lamps but they had neither oil nor wick. All these things were magic, but I touched them and lived—the magic had gone out of them. Let me tell one thing to show. In the washing-place, a thing said "Hot" but it was not hot to the touch—another thing said "Cold" but it was not cold. This must have been a strong magic but the magic was gone. I do not understand—they had ways—I wish that I knew.

It was close and dry and dusty in their house of the gods. I have said the magic was gone but that is not true—it had gone from the magic things but it had not gone from the place. I felt the spirits about me, weighing upon me. Nor had I ever slept in a Dead Place before—and yet, tonight, I must sleep there. When I thought of it, my tongue felt dry in my throat, in spite of my wish for knowledge. Almost I would have gone down again and faced the dogs, but I did not.

I had not gone through all the rooms when the darkness fell. When it fell, I went back to the big room looking over the city and made fire. There was a place to make fire and a box with wood in it, though I do not think they cooked there. I wrapped myself in a floor-covering and slept in front of the fire—I was very tired.

Now I tell what is very strong magic. I woke in the midst of the night. When I woke, the fire had gone out and I was cold. It seemed to me that all around me there were whisperings and voices. I closed my eyes to shut them out. Some will say that I slept again, but I do not think that I slept. I could feel the spirits drawing my spirit out of my body as a fish is drawn on a line.

Why should I lie about it? I am a priest and the son of a priest. If there are spirits, as they say, in the small Dead Places near us, what spirits must there not be in that great Place of the Gods? And would not they wish to speak? After such long years? I know that I felt myself drawn as a fish is drawn on a line. I had stepped out of my body—I could see my body asleep in front of the cold fire, but it was not I. I was drawn to look out upon the city of the gods.

It should have been dark, for it was night, but it was not dark. Everywhere there were lights—lines of light—circles and blurs of light—ten thousand torches would not have been the same. The sky itself was alight—you could barely see the stars for the glow in the sky. I thought to myself "This is strong magic" and trembled. There was a roaring in my ears like the rushing of rivers. Then my eyes grew used to the light and my ears to the sound. I knew that I was seeing the city as it had been when the gods were alive.

That was a sight indeed—yes, that was a sight: I could not have seen it in the body—my body would have died. Everywhere went the gods, on foot and in chariots—there were gods beyond number and counting and their chariots blocked the streets. They had turned night to day for their pleasure—they did not sleep with the sun. The noise of their coming and going was the noise of many waters. It was magic what they could do—it was magic what they did.

I looked out of another window—the great vines of their bridges were mended and the god-roads went east and west. Restless, restless, were the gods and always in motion! They burrowed tunnels under rivers—they flew in the air. With unbelievable tools they did giant works—no part of the earth was safe from them, for, if they wished for a thing, they summoned it from the other side of the world. And always, as they labored and rested, as they feasted and made love, there was a drum in their ears—the pulse of the giant city, beating and beating like a man's heart.

August, 1982. Avigdor Arikha. Oil on canvas, 31¾ x 39¼ in.

Viewing the painting: Compare the view in this picture with what John imagined he saw when he looked out the window.

Were they happy? What is happiness to the gods? They were great, they were mighty, they were wonderful and terrible. As I looked upon them and their magic, I felt like a child—but a little more, it seemed to me, and they would pull down the moon from the sky. I saw them with wisdom beyond wisdom and knowledge beyond knowledge. And yet not all they did was well done—even I could see that—and yet their wisdom could not but grow until all was peace.

Then I saw their fate come upon them and that was terrible past speech. It came upon them as they walked the streets of their city. I have been in the fights with the Forest People—I have seen men die. But this was not like that. When gods war with gods, they use weapons we do not know. It was fire falling out of the sky and a mist that poisoned. It was the time of the Great Burning and the Destruction. They ran about like ants in the streets of their city—poor gods, poor gods! Then the towers began to fall. A few escaped—yes, a few. The legends tell it. But, even after the city had become a Dead Place, for many years the poison was still in the ground. I saw it happen, I saw the last of them die. It was darkness over the broken city and I wept.

All this, I saw. I saw it as I have told it, though not in the body. When I woke in the morning, I was hungry, but I did not think first of my hunger for my heart was perplexed and confused. I knew the reason

Vocabulary

perplexed (pər plekst′) *adj.* troubled with doubt or uncertainty; puzzled for the Dead Places but I did not see why it had happened. It seemed to me it should not have happened, with all the magic they had. I went through the house looking for an answer. There was so much in the house I could not understand—and yet I am a priest and the son of a priest. It was like being on one side of the great river, at night, with no light to show the way.

Then I saw the dead god. He was sitting in his chair, by the window, in a room I had not entered before and, for the first moment, I thought that he was alive. Then I saw the skin on the back of his hand—it was like dry leather. The room was shut, hot and dry—no doubt that had kept him as he was. At first I was afraid to approach him—then the fear left me. He was sitting looking out over the city—he was dressed in the clothes of the gods. His age was neither young nor old—I could not tell his age. But there was wisdom in his face and great sadness. You could see that he would have not run away. He had sat at his window, watching his city die—then he himself had died. But it is better to lose one's life than one's spirit—and you could see from the face that his spirit had not been lost. I knew, that, if I touched him, he would fall into dust—and yet, there was something unconquered in the face.

That is all of my story, for then I knew he was a man—I knew then that they had been men, neither gods nor demons. It is a great knowledge, hard to tell and believe. They were men—they went a dark road, but they were men. I had no fear after that—I had no fear going home, though twice I fought off the dogs and once I was hunted for two days by the Forest People. When I saw my father again, I prayed and was purified. He touched my lips and my breast, he said, "You went away a boy. You come back a man and a priest." I said, "Father, they were men! I have been in the Place of the Gods and seen it! Now slay me, if it is the law—but still I know they were men."

He looked at me out of both eyes. He said, "The law is not always the same shape—you have done what you have done. I could not have done it in my time, but you come after me. Tell!"

I told and he listened. After that, I wished to tell all the people but he showed me otherwise. He said, "Truth is a hard deer to hunt. If you eat too much truth at once, you may die of the truth. It was not idly that our fathers forbade the Dead Places." He was right—it is better the truth should come little by little. I have learned that, being a priest. Perhaps, in the old days, they ate knowledge too fast.

Nevertheless, we make a beginning. It is not for the metal alone we go to the Dead Places now—there are the books and the writings. They are hard to learn. And the magic tools are broken —but we can look at them and wonder. At least, we make a beginning. And, when I am chief priest we shall go beyond the great river. We shall go to the Place of the Gods—the place newyork—not one man but a company. We shall look for the images of the gods and find the god ASHING and the others—the gods Lincoln and Biltmore[1] and Moses.[2] But they were men who built the city, not gods or demons. They were men. I remember the dead man's face. They were men who were here before us. We must build again.

1. The *Biltmore* is a famous hotel in New York City.
2. Robert *Moses* (1888–1981) was a New York state public official whose name appears on many bridges and other structures built during his administration.

Responding to Literature

Personal Response

Which line or passage in the story had the greatest impact on you? Why?

Analyzing Literature

Recall

1. Which event determines that John will one day be a priest? How does John's life change after this event?
2. In which direction does John decide to travel? Why?
3. Describe John's journey down the great river.
4. What does John find to be untrue about the Place of the Gods? What is his greatest discovery?
5. When John returns home, he wants to share his knowledge with all of the Hill People. What does his father tell him to do? Why?

Interpret

6. In your opinion, does John consider his priestly calling a privilege or a burden? Support your answer with evidence from the story.
7. What internal conflict must John overcome before choosing a direction for his journey? How does he know he has made the right choice?
8. What does John believe will happen to him when he reaches the Place of the Gods? In your opinion, what does John's decision to continue on his journey reveal about his character?
9. Name four objects or places that John sees in the Place of the Gods, and explain what you think they actually are.
10. **Theme Connections** How does John's journey change him? In your opinion, what long-term impact will his journey have on his people?

Evaluate and Connect

11. Do you believe that John is being disrespectful by ignoring his father's advice and the law? Explain your answer.
12. Compare the civilization of the Hill People with that of the people who once lived in the Place of the Gods.
13. In your opinion, is our society in danger of being destroyed in the same way as the Place of the Gods? Explain your answer.
14. John believes that "it is better to lose one's life than one's spirit." Do you agree? Why or why not?
15. How does knowing the source of the biblical **allusion** in the title of this story enrich your understanding of the story? (See page R1.)

Literary ELEMENTS

Moral

A **moral** is a practical lesson about right and wrong conduct. Do you recall Aesop's fable about the shepherd boy who, as a joke, kept shouting "Wolf!"? When a wolf really did come, no one answered the boy's cry. The moral is given at the end of the fable: *Even when liars tell the truth, they are seldom believed.* In most stories, however, the moral is not stated directly. The reader must infer the moral by thinking about the events of the story and by examining what the characters do, say, and think.

1. What do you think the moral of this story is? What details helped you determine the moral?
2. In your opinion, what does the story reveal about the author's convictions about right and wrong and about his views of the conflicts between good and evil in the world?

- See **Literary Terms Handbook,** p. R8.

Literature and Writing

Writing About Literature

Evaluate a Literary Technique Benét expects the reader to use clues to infer key aspects of the story. Evaluate the effectiveness of this technique. Does gradually revealing the truth about the Place of the Gods add suspense and interest to the story? Use details from the selection to support your ideas. Share your evaluation with others.

Personal Writing

Rites of Passage Compare the adult responsibilities John took on as part of his passage to adulthood with those that you and a partner discussed in the Reading Focus on page 94. Write a dialogue between you and John in which you share your thoughts and feelings about the passage from adolescence to adulthood.

Extending Your Response

Literature Groups

Full Disclosure? At the end of the story, John's father tells him: "Truth is a hard deer to hunt. If you eat too much truth at once, you may die of the truth." John then realizes that "the truth should come little by little." Do you agree with John and his father? Or do you think that John should immediately share all his knowledge with his people? Debate these issues in your group. Share your ideas with the class.

Interdisciplinary Activity

History: Lost Worlds Although this story is fantasy, history has shown that the knowledge and advancements of great civilizations—such as those of the ancient Maya, Egyptians, Greeks, and Romans—can be lost to subsequent generations. Investigate a lost civilization that was later rediscovered. Look for parallels between that civilization and the culture of the former dwellers of the Place of the Gods. Share your findings with the class.

Listening and Speaking

Rebuttal In 1877 British biologist Thomas Henry Huxley wrote: "If a little knowledge is dangerous, where is the man who has so much as to be out of danger?" Prepare a speech that John might give in response to this quote. Use the dialogue in the story to model John's speech patterns and manner of expressing himself. Then rehearse and perform the speech for the class.

Literary Criticism

Critic Joel Roache comments that many of Benét's stories "are enriched by the underlying assumption that the human being is a blend of negative and positive potential." Working with a partner, list the positive and negative aspects of human beings as displayed in "By the Waters of Babylon." Discuss the ending of the story in light of Roache's observation.

Save your work for your portfolio.

VOCABULARY • The Prefix *Ante-*

The prefix *ante-* means "before, in space or time"; therefore, a room that comes before a main room is called an *anteroom.* There are only three words in which *ante-* is joined to an English base word: *anteroom,* its synonym, *antechamber,* and *antedate.* All other words with the prefix *ante-* have Latin roots.

PRACTICE Read the definitions of the three words to the right. Then write a sentence for each word, using it correctly in a meaningful context.

antebellum: *adj.* before the war, usually used to describe the period before the American Civil War

antediluvian: *adj.* before the flood (the one in the biblical story about Noah's ark); usually used to refer to something extremely old or someone extremely old-fashioned

antecedent: *n.* a noun that is referred to by a pronoun (The noun usually comes before the pronoun.)

Reading & Thinking Skills

Visualizing

Imagine that your friend has just come back from visiting her relatives in another state. As she talks about that state's scenery–the overcast skies and the foothills covered with red-leaved maple trees–you can picture the scene even though you've never been there. That's because you're **visualizing** what your friend saw, or using her words to form a mental picture of what she's describing.

Good readers also visualize. Turning an author's verbal descriptions into mental images can help you enter into a story's world and better understand the action. In order to visualize, pay careful attention to the descriptive words the author uses. Read the passage slowly, then close your eyes and let the words form a picture.

If the passage describes movement, pay attention to the nouns and verbs the author uses to convey action and then turn the picture into a movie in your mind. For example, the narrator in "By the Waters of Babylon" says "I saw a little dance of white butterflies over a great heap of stone." This sentence provides information about the color of the butterflies, the size of the stone pile, and where the butterflies are in relation to the stones. Close your eyes and picture the butterflies dancing over the stones.

● For more reading strategies, see **Reading Handbook,** pp. R78–R107.

ACTIVITY

Before filmmakers start shooting a movie, they make a storyboard, or a series of sketches that show the scenes in order of sequence. Read the following paragraph from "By the Waters of Babylon." Then make a storyboard that shows what you visualize when you read this passage.

> **"I looked about me—not far away there was a great, broken god-road, leading north. The towers were high enough, but not so high, and while many of the dead-houses were wrecked, there were some that stood. I went toward this god-road, keeping to the heights of the ruins, while the dog followed. When I had reached the god-road, I saw that there were others behind him. If I had slept later, they would have come upon me asleep and torn out my throat. As it was, they were sure enough of me; they did not hurry. When I went into the dead-house, they kept watch at the entrance—doubtless they thought they would have a fine hunt. But a dog cannot open a door and I knew, from the books, that the gods did not like to live on the ground but on high."**

Before You Read

What I Have Been Doing Lately

Reading Focus

Have you ever dreamed that you were someplace that seemed familiar in certain ways, but was strange or even bizarre in other ways?

Freewrite Try to recall the most fantastic dream you've ever had. Jot down as many descriptive details as you can remember.

Setting a Purpose Read to experience the sights and sounds of a dream world.

Building Background

The Time and Place

"What I Have Been Doing Lately" is set in the recent past, probably on a tropical island in the Caribbean. The climate and landscape of this island, with its cloudless skies, monkeys, and flowering trees, seem similar to the island of Antigua, where the author grew up.

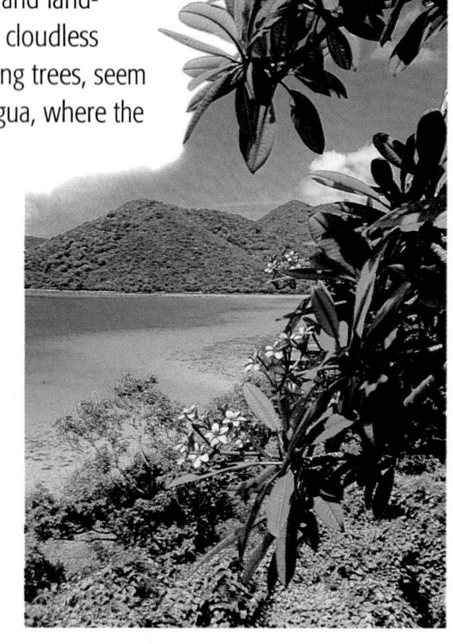

Did You Know?

Stream of consciousness is a literary technique that combines a series of thoughts and images into a flowing narrative. Feelings, impressions, and ideas—both rational and irrational—unfold in the same pattern and at the same speed that they occur in a character's mind.

Vocabulary Preview

verandah (və ran′də) *n.* a long porch, usually with a roof, that extends along one or more sides of a house; p. 110

interlaced (in′ tər lāst′) *adj.* connected by or as if by being woven together; interwoven; p. 111

psalm (sälm) *n.* a sacred poem, song, or hymn; p. 111

Meet Jamaica Kincaid

"I read *Jane Eyre* as a child, and I totally loved it and totally identified with it. I did not think about the race difference at all, and I think that's very natural."

Growing up in Antigua under the oppression of racism, Jamaica Kincaid found that books were a great equalizer. At sixteen, Kincaid moved to New York City, where her passion for books led her to a successful career in writing. Kincaid's writing focuses on the Caribbean and often deals with the relationship between mothers and daughters.

Jamaica Kincaid was born in 1949 in St. John's, Antigua. This story first appeared in The Paris Review.

Eight Huts in Haiti. D. Roosevelt (b. 1952.) Oil on canvas. Private collection.

What I Have Been Doing Lately

Jamaica Kincaid

What I Have Been Doing Lately

What I have been doing lately: I was lying in bed and the doorbell rang. I ran downstairs. Quick. I opened the door. There was no one there. I stepped outside. Either it was drizzling or there was a lot of dust in the air and the dust was damp. I stuck out my tongue and the drizzle or the damp dust tasted like government school ink. I looked north. I looked south. I decided to start walking north. While walking north, I noticed that I was barefoot. While walking north, I looked up and saw the planet Venus. I said, "It must be almost morning." I saw a monkey in a tree. The tree had no leaves. I said, "Ah, a monkey. Just look at that. A monkey." I walked for I don't know how long before I came up to a big body of water. I wanted to get across it but I couldn't swim. I wanted to get across it but it would take me years to build a boat. I wanted to get across it but it would take me I didn't know how long to build a bridge. Years passed and then one day, feeling like it, I got into my boat and rowed across. When I got to the other side, it was noon and my shadow was small and fell beneath me. I set out on a path that stretched out straight ahead. I passed a house, and a dog was sitting on the verandah but it looked the other way when it saw me coming. I passed a boy tossing a ball in the air but the boy looked the other way when he saw me coming. I walked and I walked but I couldn't tell if I walked a long time because my feet didn't feel as if they would drop off. I turned around to see what I had left behind me but nothing was familiar. Instead of the straight path, I saw hills. Instead of the boy with his ball, I saw tall flowering trees. I looked up and the sky was without clouds and seemed near, as if it were the ceiling in my house and, if I stood on a chair, I could touch it with the tips of my fingers. I turned around and looked ahead of me again. A deep hole had opened up before me. I looked in. The hole was deep and dark and I couldn't see the bottom. I thought, What's down there?, so on purpose I fell in. I fell and I fell, over and over, as if I were an old suitcase. On the sides of the deep hole I could see things written, but perhaps it was in a foreign language because I couldn't read them. Still I fell, for I don't know how long. As I fell I began to see that I didn't like the way falling made me feel. Falling made me feel sick and I missed all the people I had loved. I said, I don't want to fall anymore, and I reversed myself. I was standing again on the edge of the deep hole. I looked at the deep hole and I said, You can close up now, and it did. I walked some more without knowing distance. I only knew that I passed through days and nights, I only knew that I passed through rain and shine, light and darkness. I was never thirsty and I felt no pain. Looking at the horizon, I made a joke for myself: I said, "The earth has thin lips," and I laughed.

Looking at the horizon again, I saw a lone figure coming toward me, but I wasn't frightened because I was sure it was my mother. As I got closer to the figure, I could see that it wasn't my mother, but still I wasn't frightened because I could see that it was a woman.

When this woman got closer to me, she looked at me hard and then she threw up her hands. She must have seen me somewhere before because she said, "It's you. Just look at that. It's you. And just what have you been doing lately?"

I could have said, "I have been praying not to grow any taller."

I could have said, "I have been listening carefully to my mother's words, so as to make a good imitation of a dutiful daughter."

Vocabulary

verandah (və ran′ də) *n.* a long porch, usually with a roof, that extends along one or more sides of a house

I could have said, "A pack of dogs, tired from chasing each other all over town, slept in the moonlight."

Instead, I said, What I have been doing lately: I was lying in bed on my back, my hands drawn up, my fingers interlaced lightly at the nape of my neck.[1] Someone rang the doorbell. I went downstairs and opened the door but there was no one there. I stepped outside. Either it was drizzling or there was a lot of dust in the air and the dust was damp. I stuck out my tongue and the drizzle or the damp dust tasted like government school ink. I looked north and I looked south. I started walking north. While walking north, I wanted to move fast, so I removed the shoes from my feet. While walking north, I looked up and saw the planet Venus and I said, "If the sun went out, it would be eight minutes before I would know it." I saw a monkey sitting in a tree that had no leaves and I said, "A monkey. Just look at that. A monkey." I picked up a stone and I threw it at the monkey. The monkey, seeing the stone, quickly moved out of its way. Three times I threw a stone at the monkey and three times it moved away. The fourth time I threw the stone, the monkey caught it and threw it back at me. The stone struck me on my forehead over my right eye, making a deep gash. The gash healed immediately but now the skin on my forehead felt false to me. I walked for I don't know how long before I came to a big body of water. I wanted to get across, so when the boat came I paid my fare. When I got to the other side, I saw a lot of people sitting on the beach and they were having a picnic. They were the most beautiful people I had ever seen. Everything about them was black and shiny. Their skin was black and shiny. Their shoes were black and shiny. Their hair was black and shiny. The clothes they wore were black and shiny. I could hear them laughing and chatting and I said, I would like to be with these people, so I started to walk toward them, but when I got up close to them I saw that they weren't at a picnic and they weren't beautiful and they weren't chatting and laughing. All around me was black mud and the people all looked as if they had been made up out of the black mud. I looked up and saw that the sky seemed far away and nothing I could stand on would make me able to touch it with my fingertips. I thought, If only I could get out of this, so I started to walk. I must have walked for a long time because my feet hurt and felt as if they would drop off. I thought, If only just around the bend I would see my house and inside my house I would find my bed, freshly made at that, and in the kitchen I would find my mother or anyone else that I loved making me a custard. I thought, If only it was a Sunday and I was sitting in a church and I had just heard someone sing a psalm. I felt very sad so I sat down. I felt so sad that I rested my head on my own knees and smoothed my own head. I felt so sad I couldn't imagine feeling any other way again. I said, I don't like this. I don't want to do this anymore. And I went back to lying in bed, just before the doorbell rang.

1. The *nape of my neck* refers to the back of the neck.

Vocabulary

interlaced (in′ tər lāst′) *adj.* connected by or as if by being woven together; interwoven

psalm (sälm) *n.* a sacred poem, song, or hymn

Responding to Literature

Personal Response

How might you feel if you awoke from the dream described by the narrator?

Analyzing Literature

Recall

1. Who is the narrator of this story?
2. Where is the narrator at the beginning of the story? At the end?
3. The account the narrator gives is divided into two parts. What obstacles does the narrator face in the first part?
4. Describe the picnic scene in the second part of the story. What happens when the narrator gets close to the people?
5. Why does the narrator go back to lying in bed?

Interpret

6. What can you infer about the narrator's age and family relationships? Support your inferences with details from the story.
7. Do you think that the events in this story really happened? Give reasons for your answer.
8. Consider the obstacles faced by the narrator in the first part of the description. What might these obstacles **symbolize?** (See page R13.)
9. How does the change in the picnic scene affect the narrator? Explain your answer.
10. In your opinion, what might be causing the narrator's sadness and anxiety?

Evaluate and Connect

11. Some experts say that dreams are the result of subconscious hopes and fears. Do you think the narrator's hopes and fears are typical of people your age? Explain your answer.
12. How does the author's use of **repetition** affect your appreciation and understanding of the story?
13. **Theme Connections** What do you think the author is saying about transition and change?
14. Which images linger in your mind after reading the story?
15. Why, do you think, did the author choose to write this story in the first person, using the **stream-of-consciousness** technique? (See page R12.)

Literary ELEMENTS

Description

A **description** is a carefully detailed portrayal of a person, place, thing, or event. Writers often use **sensory details** in their descriptions to help readers understand what story characters see, hear, touch, taste, or smell. Notice the sensory details in the following description from this story: "I stuck out my tongue and the drizzle or the damp dust tasted like government school ink." These details help you "see" and "taste" what is being described.

1. Read the first paragraph of the story. Identify five sensory details that describe what the narrator experiences during her journey. Tell whether each detail appeals to the sense of sight, hearing, touch, taste, or smell.
2. After meeting the woman, the narrator retells the first part of the story. Write a brief comparison of the two descriptions. Which details in the two versions are alike? Which details are different?

- See **Literary Terms Handbook,** p. R3.

Literature and Writing

Writing About Literature

Analyze Events Choose one particular event from the first part of the story that is repeated in the second part. Write a two- or three-paragraph analysis comparing and contrasting the two versions. You might use a Venn diagram to organize your thoughts.

Personal Writing

You Must Be Dreaming Look back at the dream details you jotted down in the Reading Focus on page 108. Retell your dream in the first person, using the **stream-of-consciousness** technique employed in this story. Be sure to include sensory details.

Extending Your Response

Literature Groups

Responding to Imagery Some book reviewers find the imaginative images in Kincaid's stories difficult to understand and confusing; others like their poetic, musical quality and their ability to appeal to all kinds of people. Discuss with your group which reviews reflect your response to Kincaid's imagery.

Interdisciplinary Activity

Music: Compose a Calypso Song Listen to calypso—a type of folk music that originated in Trinidad and spread throughout the Caribbean region. With a partner, compose a calypso song using the story title "What I Have Been Doing Lately" as a refrain. Try to incorporate images from the story into your lyrics. Perform the song for the class.

Learning for Life

Dreaming Themes Researchers have identified several common dream themes. Often, dreams with these themes occur during times of stress or transition in people's lives. Investigate to learn what these common dream themes are, what researchers believe they mean, and when people are most likely to have such dreams. Try using an on-line periodical index, such as InfoTrack, to find magazine articles about recent dream research. Share your findings with the class.

Save your work for your portfolio.

VOCABULARY • Analogies

An analogy is a type of comparison that is based on the relationships between things or ideas. Some analogies are based on a relationship that could be called "class and member."

book : novel :: doctor : pediatrician

One type of *book* is a *novel;* one type of *doctor* is a *pediatrician.*

To finish an analogy, decide what relationship exists between the first two things or ideas. Then apply that relationship to another pair of words.

• For more about analogies, see **Communications Skills Handbook,** p. R77.

PRACTICE Choose the pair that best completes each analogy.

1. porch : verandah ::
   a. truck : car
   b. house : mansion
   c. painter : sculptor
   d. church : steeple
   e. playground : swing
2. poem : psalm ::
   a. island : peninsula
   b. ocean : lake
   c. mammal : reptile
   d. symphony : conductor
   e. institution : hospital

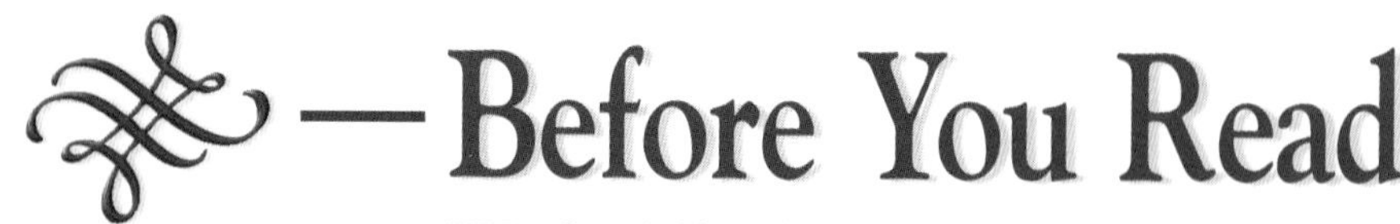

Before You Read

With All Flags Flying

Reading Focus

Do you know an elderly person who is no longer able to live on his or her own? Does that person live with family members, in a nursing home, or in another kind of situation?

Think/Pair/Share Think about the advantages and disadvantages of that elderly person's living arrangements. Jot down your reactions and then share them with a partner.

Setting a Purpose Read to learn about a choice one elderly man makes between self-reliance and loneliness.

Building Background

The Time and Place

This story takes place in and around Baltimore, Maryland, the area where Anne Tyler has lived and worked since 1976. Baltimore is a large industrial and port city on Chesapeake Bay, approximately forty miles northeast of Washington, D.C. The story probably takes place in the 1960s.

Did You Know?

Throughout history, ships' captains have used flags to communicate with each other at sea. During the era of great naval battles, a defeated captain could signal surrender by "striking his colors," or lowering the flag of his ship. If a captain meant never to surrender, he'd hoist all flags on board as a promise to fight on to victory or to go down "with all flags flying."

Vocabulary Preview

appurtenance (ə purt′ ən əns) *n.* an optional article or piece of equipment that adds to one's convenience or comfort; accessory; p. 117

wince (wins) *v.* to draw back slightly, as in pain; flinch; p. 119

subtle (sut′ əl) *adj.* not open or direct; not obvious; p. 121

doddering (dod′ ər ing) *adj.* trembling or shaking, as from age; p. 121

monosyllabic (mon′ ə si lab′ ik) *adj.* having only one syllable; p. 121

chronic (kron′ ik) *adj.* lasting a long time or returning repeatedly; p. 121

cavernous (kav′ ər nəs) *adj.* large and spacious, like a cavern; p. 122

Meet Anne Tyler

"I had never used a telephone and could strike a match on the soles of my bare feet."

Anne Tyler has used these words to describe herself at age eleven when her family moved to Raleigh, North Carolina. Tyler grew up in rural North Carolina, where, with her Quaker parents, she lived in utopian communes and followed the simple ideals of her family's religion. From this country life came many ideas that Tyler later developed in her writing. Her novels include *The Accidental Tourist* and the Pulitzer Prize–winning *Breathing Lessons*.

Anne Tyler was born in Minneapolis, Minnesota, in 1941. This story was published in 1971.

With All Flags Flying

Anne Tyler

Weakness was what got him in the end. He had been expecting something more definite—chest pains, a stroke, arthritis—but it was only weakness that put a finish to his living alone. A numbness in his head, an airy feeling when he walked. A wateriness in his bones that made it an effort to pick up his coffee cup in the morning. He waited some days for it to go away, but it never did. And meanwhile the dust piled up in corners; the refrigerator wheezed and creaked for want of defrosting. Weeds grew around his rosebushes.

He was awake and dressed at six o'clock on a Saturday morning, with the patchwork quilt pulled up neatly over the mattress. From the kitchen cabinet he took a hunk of bread and two Fig Newtons, which he dropped into a paper bag. He was wearing a brown suit that he had bought on sale in 1944, a white T-shirt and copper-toed work boots. These and his other set of underwear, which he put in the paper bag along with a razor, were all the clothes he took with him. Then he rolled down the top of the bag and stuck it under his arm, and stood in the middle of the kitchen staring around him for a moment.

Country Road in July, 1937. Charles Burchfield. Watercolor on paper, 26½ x 26½ in. Collection of Washington State University Museum of Art, Pullman, WA. Gift of Charles and Virginia Orton.

Viewing the painting: How does the mood of this painting reflect the emotions of the old man at this point in the story?

The house had only two rooms, but he owned it—the last scrap of the farm that he had sold off years ago. It stood in a hollow of dying trees beside a superhighway in Baltimore County. All it held was a few sticks of furniture, a change of clothes, a skillet and a set of dishes. Also odds and ends, which disturbed him. If his inventory were complete, he would have to include six clothespins, a salt and a pepper shaker, a broken-toothed comb, a cheap ballpoint pen—oh, on and on, past logical numbers. Why should he be so cluttered? He was eighty-two years old. He had grown from an infant owning nothing to a family man with a wife, five children, everyday and Sunday china and a thousand appurtenances, down at last to solitary old age and the bare essentials again, but not bare enough to suit him. Only what he needed surrounded him. Was it possible he needed so much?

Now he had the brown paper bag; that was all. It was the one satisfaction in a day he had been dreading for years.

He left the house without another glance, heading up the steep bank toward the superhighway. The bank was covered with small, crawling weeds planted especially by young men with scientific training in how to prevent soil erosion. Twice his knees buckled. He had to sit and rest, bracing himself against the slope of the bank. The scientific weeds, seen from close up, looked straggly and gnarled. He sifted dry earth through his fingers without thinking, concentrating only on steadying his breath and calming the twitching muscles in his legs.

Once on the superhighway, which was fairly level, he could walk for longer stretches of time. He kept his head down and his fingers clenched tight upon the paper bag, which was growing limp and damp now. Sweat rolled down the back of his neck, fell in drops from his temples. When he had been walking maybe half an hour he had to sit down again for a rest. A black motorcycle buzzed up from behind and stopped a few feet away from him. The driver was young and shabby, with hair so long that it drizzled out beneath the back of his helmet.

"Give you a lift, if you like," he said. "You going somewhere?"

"Just into Baltimore."

"Hop on."

He shifted the paper bag to the space beneath his arm, put on the white helmet he was handed and climbed on behind the driver. For safety he took a clutch of the boy's shirt, tightly at first and then more loosely when he saw there was no danger. Except for the helmet, he was perfectly comfortable. He felt his face cooling and stiffening in the wind, his body learning to lean gracefully with the tilt of the motorcycle as it swooped from lane to lane. It was a fine way to spend his last free day.

Half an hour later they were on the outskirts of Baltimore, stopped at the first traffic light. The boy turned his head and shouted, "Whereabouts did you plan on going?"

"I'm visiting my daughter, on Belvedere near Charles Street."

"I'll drop you off, then," the boy said. "I'm passing right by there."

The light changed, the motor roared. Now that they were in traffic, he felt more conspicuous, but not in a bad way. People in their automobiles seemed sealed in, overprotected; men in large trucks must envy the way the motorcycle

Vocabulary

appurtenance (ə purt′ ən əns) *n.* an optional article or piece of equipment that adds to one's convenience or comfort; accessory looped in and out, hornet-like, stripped to the bare essentials of a motor and two wheels. By tugs at the boy's shirt and single words shouted into the wind he directed him to his daughter's house, but he was sorry to have the ride over so quickly.

His daughter had married a salesman and lived in a plain, square stone house that the old man approved of. There were sneakers and a football in the front yard, signs of a large, happy family. A bicycle lay in the driveway. The motorcycle stopped just inches from it. "Here we are," the boy said.

"Well, I surely do thank you."

He climbed off, fearing for one second that his legs would give way beneath him and spoil everything that had gone before. But no, they held steady. He took off the helmet and handed it to the boy, who waved and roared off. It was a really magnificent roar, ear-dazzling. He turned toward the house, beaming in spite of himself, with his head feeling cool and light now that the helmet was gone. And there was his daughter on the front porch, laughing. "Daddy, what on *earth?*" she said. "Have you turned into a teeny-bopper?"[1] Whatever that was. She came rushing down the steps to hug him—a plump, happy-looking woman in an apron. She was getting on toward fifty now. Her hands were like her mother's, swollen and veined. Gray had started dusting her hair.

"You never *told* us," she said. "Did you ride all this way on a motorcycle? Oh, why didn't you find a telephone and call? I would have come. How long can you stay for?"

"Now . . ." he said, starting toward the house. He was thinking of the best way to put it. "I came to a decision. I won't be living alone any more. I want to go to an old folks' home. That's what I *want*," he said, stopping on the grass so she would be sure to get it clear. "I don't want to live with you—I want an old folks' home." Then he was afraid he had worded it too strongly. "It's nice *visiting* you, of course," he said.

"Why, Daddy, you know we always asked you to come and live with us."

"I know that, but I decided on an old folks' home."

"We couldn't do that. We won't even talk about it."

"Clara, my mind is made up."

Then in the doorway a new thought hit her, and she suddenly turned around. "Are you sick?" she said. "You always said you would live alone as long as health allowed."

"I'm not up to that any more," he said.

"What is it? Are you having some kind of pain?"

"I just decided, that's all," he said. "What I *will* rely on you for is the arrangements with the home. I know it's a trouble."

"We'll talk about that later," Clara said. And she firmed the corners of her mouth exactly the way her mother used to do when she hadn't won an argument but wasn't planning to lose it yet either.

In the kitchen he had a glass of milk, good and cold, and the hunk of bread and the two Fig Newtons from his paper bag. Clara wanted to make him a big breakfast, but there was no sense wasting what he had brought. He munched on the dry bread and washed it down with milk, meanwhile staring at the Fig Newtons, which lay on the smoothed-out bag. They were the worse for their ride—squashed and pathetic-looking, the edges worn down and crumbling. They seemed to have come from somewhere long ago and far away. "Here, now, we've got cookies I baked

1. *Teeny-bopper* is a slang word, commonly used in the 1960s and 1970s, that refers to a young teenager who follows the latest fad or craze, as in music or dress.

only yesterday," Clara said; but he said, "No, no," and ate the Fig Newtons, whose warmth on his tongue filled him with a vague, sad feeling deeper than homesickness. "In my house," he said, "I left things a little messy. I hate to ask it of you, but I didn't manage to straighten up any."

"Don't even think about it," Clara said. "I'll take out a suitcase tomorrow and clean everything up. I'll bring it all back."

"I don't want it. Take it to the colored people."

"Don't want any of it? But, Daddy—"

He didn't try explaining it to her. He finished his lunch in silence and then let her lead him upstairs to the guest room.

Clara had five boys and a girl, the oldest twenty. During the morning as they passed one by one through the house on their way to other places, they heard of his arrival and trooped up to see him. They were fine children, all of them, but it was the girl he enjoyed the most. Francie. She was only thirteen, too young yet to know how to hide what she felt. And what she felt was always about love, it seemed: whom she just loved, who she hoped loved her back. Who was just a darling. Had thirteen-year-olds been so aware of love in the old days? He didn't know and didn't care; all he had to do with Francie was sit smiling in an armchair and listen. There was a new boy in the neighborhood who walked his English sheepdog past her yard every morning, looking toward her house. Was it because of her, or did the dog just like to go that way? When he telephoned her brother Donnie, was he hoping for her to answer? And when she did answer, did he want her to talk a minute or to hand the receiver straight to Donnie? But what would she say to him, anyway? Oh, all her questions had to do with where she might find love, and everything she said made the old man wince and love her more. She left in the middle of a sentence, knocking against a doorknob as she flew from the room, an unlovable-looking tangle of blond hair and braces and scrapes and Band-Aids. After she was gone the room seemed too empty, as if she had accidentally torn part of it away in her flight.

Getting into an old folks' home was hard. Not only because of lack of good homes, high expenses, waiting lists; it was harder yet to talk his family into letting him go. His son-in-law argued with him every evening, his round, kind face anxious and questioning across the supper table. "Is it that you think you're not welcome here? You are, you know. You were one of the reasons we bought this big house." His grandchildren when they talked to him had a kind of urgency in their voices, as if they were trying to impress him with their acceptance of him. His other daughters called long distance from all across the country and begged him to come to them if he wouldn't stay with Clara. They had room, or they would make room; he had no idea what homes for the aged were like these days. To all of them he gave the same answer: "I've made my decision." He was proud of them for asking, though. All his children had turned out so well, every last one of them. They were good, strong women with happy families, and they had never given him a moment's worry. He was luckier than he had a right to be. He had felt lucky all his life, dangerously lucky, cursed by luck; it had seemed some disaster must be waiting to even things up. But the luck had held. When his wife died it was at a late age, sparing her the pain she would have had to face, and his life had continued in its steady, reasonable pattern with no more sorrow than any other

Vocabulary

wince (wins) *v.* to draw back slightly, as in pain; flinch man's. His final lot was to weaken, to crumble and to die—only a secret disaster, not the one he had been expecting.

He walked two blocks daily, fighting off the weakness. He shelled peas for Clara and mended little household articles, which gave him an excuse to sit. Nobody noticed how he arranged to climb the stairs only once a day, at bedtime. When he had empty time he chose a chair without rockers, one that would not be a symbol of age and weariness and lack of work. He rose every morning at six and stayed in his room a full hour, giving his legs enough warning to face the day ahead. Never once did he disgrace himself by falling down in front of people. He dropped nothing more important than a spoon or a fork.

Meanwhile the wheels were turning; his name was on a waiting list. Not that that meant anything, Clara said. "When it comes right down to driving you out there, I just won't let you go," she told him. "But I'm hoping you won't

Virgil Thompson, 1971. Alice Neel. Oil on canvas, 48 x 37 in. National Portrait Gallery, Washington, DC.

Viewing the painting: How would you describe the personality of this man? How is he similar to or different from the man in the story?

carry things that far. Daddy, won't you put a stop to this foolishness?"

He hardly listened. He had chosen long ago what kind of old age he would have; everyone does. Most, he thought, were weak, and chose to be loved at any cost. He had seen women turn soft and sad, anxious to please, and had watched with pity and impatience their losing battles. And he had once known a schoolteacher, no weakling at all, who said straight out that when she grew old she would finally eat all she wanted and grow fat without worry. He admired that—a simple plan, dependent upon no one. "I'll sit in an armchair," she had said, "with a lady's magazine in my lap and a box of homemade fudge on the lampstand. I'll get as fat as I like and nobody will give a hang." The schoolteacher was thin and pale, with a kind of stooped, sloping figure that was popular at the time. He had lost track of her long ago, but he liked to think that she had kept her word. He imagined her fifty years later, cozy and fat in a puffy chair, with one hand moving constantly between her mouth and the candy plate. If she had died young or changed her mind or put off her eating till another decade, he didn't want to hear about it.

He had chosen independence. Nothing else had even occurred to him. He had lived to himself, existed on less money than his family would ever guess, raised his own vegetables and refused all gifts but an occasional tin of coffee. And now he would sign himself into the old folks' home and enter on his own two feet, relying only on the impersonal care of nurses and cleaning women. He could have chosen to die alone of neglect, but for his daughters that would have been a burden too—a different kind of burden, much worse. He was sensible enough to see that.

Meanwhile, all he had to do was to look as busy as possible in a chair without rockers and hold fast against his family. Oh, they gave him no peace. Some of their attacks were obvious—the arguments with his son-in-law over the supper table—and some were subtle; you had to be on your guard every minute for those. Francie, for instance, asking him questions about what she called the "olden days." Inviting him to sink unnoticing into doddering reminiscence. "Did I see Granny ever? I don't remember her. Did she like me? What kind of person was she?" He stood his ground, gave monosyllabic answers. It was easier than he had expected. For him, middle age tempted up more memories. Nowadays events had telescoped. The separate agonies and worries—the long, hard births of each of his children, the youngest daughter's chronic childhood earaches, his wife's last illness—were smoothed now into a single, summing-up sentence: He was a widowed farmer with five daughters, all married, twenty grandchildren and three great-grandchildren. "Your grandmother was a fine woman," he told Francie; "just fine." Then he shut up.

Francie, not knowing that she had been spared, sulked and peeled a strip of sunburned skin from her nose.

Clara cried all the way to the home. She was the one who was driving; it made him nervous. One of her hands on the steering wheel held a balled-up tissue, which she had stopped using. She let

Vocabulary
subtle (sut′ əl) *adj.* not open or direct; not obvious
doddering (dod′ ər ing) *adj.* trembling or shaking, as from age
monosyllabic (mon′ ə si lab′ ik) *adj.* having only one syllable
chronic (kron′ ik) *adj.* lasting a long time or returning repeatedly

tears run unchecked down her face and drove jerkily with a great deal of brake-slamming and gear-gnashing.

"Clara, I wish you wouldn't take on so," he told her. "There's no need to be sad over *me*."

"I'm not sad so much as mad," Clara said. "I feel like this is something you're doing *to* me, just throwing away what I give. Oh, why do you have to be so stubborn? It's still not too late to change your mind."

The old man kept silent. On his right sat Francie, chewing a thumbnail and scowling out the window, her usual self except for the unexplainable presence of her other hand in his, tight as wire. Periodically she muttered a number; she was counting red convertibles, and had been for days. When she reached a hundred, the next boy she saw would be her true love.

He figured that was probably the reason she had come on this trip—a greater exposure to red convertibles.

Whatever happened to DeSotos? Didn't there used to be a car called a roadster?

They parked in the U-shaped driveway in front of the home, under the shade of a poplar tree. If he had had his way, he would have arrived by motorcycle, but he made the best of it—picked up his underwear sack from between his feet, climbed the front steps ramrod-straight. They were met by a smiling woman in blue who had to check his name on a file and ask more questions. He made sure to give all the answers himself, overriding Clara when necessary. Meanwhile Francie spun on one squeaky sneaker heel and examined the hall, a cavernous, polished square with old-fashioned parlors on either side of it. A few old people were on the plush[2] couches, and a nurse sat idle beside a lady in a wheel chair.

They went up a creaking elevator to the second floor and down a long, dark corridor deadened by carpeting. The lady in blue, still carrying a sheaf of files, knocked at number 213. Then she flung the door open on a narrow green room flooded with sunlight.

"Mr. Pond," she said, "this is Mr. Carpenter. I hope you'll get on well together."

Mr. Pond was one of those men who run to fat and baldness in old age. He sat in a rocking chair with a gilt-edged Bible on his knees.

"How-do," he said. "Mighty nice to meet you."

They shook hands cautiously, with the women ringing them like mothers asking their children to play nicely with each other. "Ordinarily I sleep in the bed by the window," said Mr. Pond, "but I don't hold it in much importance. You can take your pick."

"Anything will do," the old man said.

Clara was dry-eyed now. She looked frightened.

"You'd best be getting on back now," he told her. "Don't you worry about me. I'll let you know," he said, suddenly generous now that he had won, "if there is anything I need."

Clara nodded and kissed his cheek. Francie kept her face turned away, but she hugged him tightly, and then she looked up at him as she stepped back. Her eyebrows were tilted as if she were about to ask him one of

Did You Know?
The *DeSoto*, manufactured by Chrysler from 1928 to 1961, was so popular that it was called "America's family car." It was named after Spanish explorer Hernando de Soto.

2. *Plush* is a fabric (similar to velvet) that is used in furniture upholstery.

Vocabulary
cavernous (kav′ ər nəs) *adj.* large and spacious, like a cavern

her questions. Was it her the boy with the sheepdog came for? Did he care when she answered the telephone?

They left, shutting the door with a gentle click. The old man made a great business out of settling his underwear and razor in a bureau drawer, smoothing out the paper bag and folding it, placing it in the next drawer down.

"Didn't bring much," said Mr. Pond, one thumb marking his page in the Bible.

"I don't need much."

"Go on—take the bed by the window. You'll feel better after awhile."

"I *wanted* to come," the old man said.

"That there window is a front one. If you look out, you can see your folks leave."

He slid between the bed and the window and looked out. No reason not to. Clara and Francie were just climbing into the car, the sun lacquering the tops of their heads. Clara was blowing her nose with a dot of tissue.

"*Now* they cry," said Mr. Pond, although he had not risen to look out himself. "Later they'll buy themselves a milk shake to celebrate."

"I wanted to come. I made them bring me."

"And so they did. *I* didn't want to come. My son wanted to put me here—his wife was expecting. And so he did. It all works out the same in the end."

"Well, I could have stayed with one of my daughters," the old man said. "But I'm not like some I have known. Hanging around making burdens of themselves, hoping to be loved. Not me."

"If you don't care about being loved," said Mr. Pond, "how come it would bother you to be a burden?"

Then he opened the Bible again, at the place where his thumb had been all the time and went back to reading.

The old man sat on the edge of the bed, watching the tail of Clara's car flash as sharp and hard as a jewel around the bend of the road. Then, with nobody to watch that mattered, he let his shoulders slump and eased himself out of his suit coat, which he folded over the foot of the bed. He slid his suspenders down and let them dangle at his waist. He took off his copper-toed work boots and set them on the floor neatly side by side. And although it was only noon, he lay down full-length on top of the bedspread. Whiskery lines ran across the plaster of the ceiling high above him. There was a cracking sound in the mattress when he moved; it must be covered with something waterproof.

The tiredness in his head was as vague and restless as anger; the weakness in his knees made him feel as if he had just finished some exhausting exercise. He lay watching the plaster cracks settle themselves into pictures, listening to the silent, neuter voice in his mind form the words he had grown accustomed to hearing now: Let me not give in at the end. Let me continue gracefully till the moment of my defeat. Let Lollie Simpson be alive somewhere even as I lie on my bed; let her be eating homemade fudge in an overstuffed armchair and growing fatter and fatter and fatter.

Responding to Literature

Personal Response

What are your feelings about Mr. Carpenter? Do you admire him, pity him, or find him frustrating? Explain in your journal.

Analyzing Literature

Recall

1. What does Mr. Carpenter take with him when he leaves his house?
2. What choice has Mr. Carpenter made about how he will spend his old age? Summarize his reasons for making that choice.
3. What do the members of Mr. Carpenter's family want him to do?
4. What happens when Mr. Carpenter arrives at the old folks' home?
5. What does Mr. Carpenter do after Clara and Francie leave?

Interpret

6. Why, do you think, does the paper bag give Mr. Carpenter such satisfaction? Might the bag be a **symbol** for something else? Explain.
7. What does Mr. Carpenter's choice suggest about what he values above all else? Explain your answer.
8. Why, do you think, does Mr. Carpenter seem to reject the love his family offers him?
9. Does Mr. Pond seem to believe that Mr. Carpenter really wants to be at the old folks' home? Explain your answer.
10. What do you think Mr. Carpenter was thinking as he stretched out on the bed at the old folks' home? Do you think he is any less determined to maintain his dignity and independence? Explain.

Evaluate and Connect

11. In your opinion, why does Mr. Carpenter never discuss love with his family? Why, do you think, does hearing Francie talk about love give him so much pleasure?
12. What choice do you think you would have made in Mr. Carpenter's situation? How does that choice fit in with your response to the Reading Focus on page 114?
13. Mr. Carpenter seems to feel that only the weak depend on loved ones. Do you agree with him? Explain.
14. To what does the title of this story refer? What does it suggest about how Mr. Carpenter will face death?
15. Do you think this story presents a realistic view of the dilemmas faced by older people and their families? Explain.

Literary ELEMENTS

Characters

A short story may have one or many **characters** who take part in the story's action. The **main characters** are the most important to the story. Most stories also have **minor characters** who interact with the main characters, but who may not be especially important to the plot. Characters who reveal only one personality trait are called **flat characters.** Those who show varied traits, which may even seem contradictory, are called **round characters.**

1. Who are the main characters in "With All Flags Flying"? Who is the central character of the story?
2. In your opinion, is Mr. Pond a main character or a minor one? Support your response with examples from the story.
3. Do you think Mr. Carpenter is a round, fully developed character or a flat character showing only one or two traits? Give specific examples from the story to support your claim.

- See **Literary Terms Handbook,** p. R2.

Literature and Writing

Writing About Literature

The Author's Voice Write an analysis of the author's attitude toward Mr. Carpenter, his behavior, and his plans for his future. Does she agree with his decisions? Or is she trying to show that Mr. Carpenter is misguided in his plan? Use specific examples from the story to illustrate the author's feelings about the main character and the choices he makes for himself.

Creative Writing

Obituary Imagine that Mr. Carpenter has died after living at the old folks' home for several years. Write his obituary for the local newspaper. Feel free to make up details about his life, but make sure that they are consistent with what you know about Mr. Carpenter from the story. For models, refer to some of the obituaries in your local newspaper.

Extending Your Response

Literature Groups

Discussing Issues Mr. Carpenter tries to pare down his life before he goes to the old folks' home, to get rid of anything he doesn't need. He seems to think that love is not one of the essentials of life. What do you think? Is love essential to life, or can people get by without it? Can love be put away like an extra suit of clothes? Discuss the question in your group. Support your opinions with examples from the story and from your own experience. Finally, share the results of your discussion with the class.

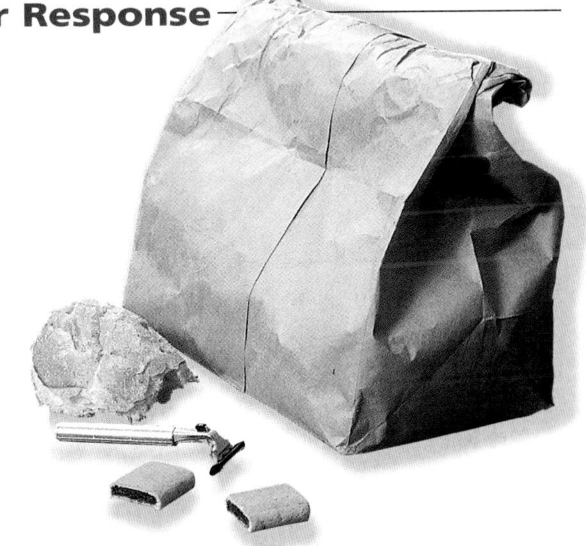

Learning for Life

Elder Care Working with a partner, find out what resources exist in your community for older people who can no longer live without assistance. These may include traditional "old folks' homes," also called nursing homes; "meals-on-wheels" programs; visiting nurse or housekeeping services; and retirement communities. Call or write to one of the resources to learn about the services offered. Share your findings with the class.

Performing

Dialogue With a partner, practice the dialogue between Mr. Pond and Mr. Carpenter. Add an answer that Mr. Carpenter might have given to Mr. Pond's final question: "If you don't care about being loved, how come it would bother you to be a burden?" Perform your dialogue for the class.

Reading Further

Anne Tyler has written a number of books. Here is one you might enjoy. A movie based on the novel is also available.

Novel: *The Accidental Tourist,* in which the main character hates to travel, but makes his living as the anonymous author of travel guidebooks.

Viewing: *The Accidental Tourist*

Literary Criticism

"[Tyler's] major theme," argues Mary Ellen Brooks, "is the obstinante endurance of the human spirit, reflected in every character's acceptance or rejection of his fate and in how that attitude affects his day to day life." Write an analysis of "With All Flags Flying," exploring how this theme is developed in the story.

Save your work for your portfolio.

GRAMMAR AND LANGUAGE • Quotation Marks in Dialogue

Dialogue is the conversation between characters in a literary work. Quotation marks are used to enclose the exact words spoken by a character. Each time the speaker changes, a new paragraph begins and a new set of quotation marks is used. Here's an example of dialogue from "With All Flags Flying."

"Give you a lift, if you like," he said. "You going somewhere?"

"Just into Baltimore."

"Hop on."

PRACTICE Copy several examples of dialogue from the story, omitting the quotation marks and the paragraph breaks. Exchange papers with a classmate. Rewrite each dialogue, adding quotation marks and paragraph breaks as needed. Check your work by comparing it with the dialogues in the story.

- For more about punctuating dialogue, see **Language Handbook,** p. R49.

READING AND THINKING • Identifying Assumptions

An assumption is something that is taken for granted without proof. In fiction, characters often base their actions on assumptions they make. For example, in "With All Flags Flying," Mr. Carpenter assumes that Clara will try to convince him to make his home with her. This assumption turns out to be correct. Mr. Carpenter also assumes that he would be a burden to Clara and her family. This assumption appears to be incorrect. Clara and her family try hard to convince Mr. Carpenter to live with them; it's unlikely that they would consider him a burden.

- For information on related comprehension skills, see **Reading Handbook,** pp. R78–R107.

PRACTICE Indicate whether you think each assumption below is correct or incorrect. Support your answers with information from the story or from your own experience.

1. Mr. Carpenter assumes that something definite, like a stroke or arthritis, will put an end to his living alone.
2. Mr. Carpenter assumes that his family will finally accept his decision to live in an old folks' home.
3. Mr. Carpenter assumes that older people who depend on their families are weak.
4. Clara assumes that her father is rejecting *her* when he refuses to live with her and her family.
5. Mr. Pond assumes that Mr. Carpenter is not as happy about being in the old folks' home as he pretends to be.

VOCABULARY • Prefixes Expressing Number

One of the vocabulary words for "With All Flags Flying" is *monosyllabic,* which means "having only one syllable." Like *uni-, mono-* is a prefix that means "one." If you speak in a monotone, you use only one tone. A monochromatic picture uses one color; a monologue is one person speaking.

Many prefixes and combining forms express number. *Bi-* (or *bin-*), *di-,* and *du-* mean "two"; *tri-* means three; *tetra-* and *quadri-* (or *quadru-*) mean four.

PRACTICE Use your knowledge of familiar words and prefixes to answer the following questions.

1. What word describes someone who can speak three languages? (Hint: Think about *bilingual.*)
2. What is a diarchy? (Hint: Think about *monarchy.*)
3. Name one animal that's a biped and one that's a quadruped. (Hint: Think about *pedal.*)
4. What is required to do a *bimanual* task? (Hint: Think about *manual labor.*)

Listening, Speaking, and Viewing

Debating

The story "With All Flags Flying" pits the wishes of an aging father against those of his daughter. The two characters could have held a debate to settle their differences. A debate is a contest between two people or teams who argue for or against an idea. In a debate, two sides take turns presenting their cases. Then, each side has a chance to refute the other's arguments. Finally, a panel of judges selects the winning side. The checklists below can help you plan and present a debate.

Gathering Information

- Choose a statement or question that has two clear sides.
- Take a position and back it up with facts, statistics, and examples.
- Make sure that each point you make includes accurate and relevant facts. Avoid information that can be interpreted in more than one way.
- Consider the knowledge and sympathies of the judges or your audience. Present your case in a way that will be understandable and convincing to them.
- Anticipate and address the arguments of your opponent.
- Write key ideas and facts on note cards that you can refer to when presenting the debate.

Presenting a Debate

- Speak clearly and loudly enough for everyone to hear. Put some enthusiasm in your voice.
- Stand straight, but be natural. Use hand gestures to emphasize important points. Vary your gaze to include every person in the room.

ACTIVITIES

1. Television news programs such as *Crossfire* and *NewsHour with Jim Lehrer* regularly invite guests to discuss their opposing views on current events. Watch one of these broadcasts and take notes on what the speakers say and how they say it. Then use the checklists above to evaluate which speaker was most convincing. Share your results with the class.
2. Brainstorm a list of debate topics with your class. Find a partner who will debate the opposite side of a topic you feel strongly about. Research the topic and prepare a short (five-minute) presentation of your case. With your partner, take turns giving your presentation. Then, as a class, discuss the ideas that each side should include when refuting the other's argument.

Before You Read

A Child, a Dog, the Night

Reading Focus

How would you define true friendship?

Sharing Ideas Write a definition of true friendship. Meet with a small group of classmates to compare and discuss your definitions.

Setting a Purpose Read to discover what a young boy learns about the power of friendship.

Building Background

The Time and Place
The time of this story is the not-too-distant past. The place is the rugged landscape of northern Chile–a country on the west coast of South America–in and around the town of Chuquicamata, site of the world's largest open-pit copper mines.

Did You Know?
The places mentioned in this story–Chuquicamata, Calama, and Antofagasta–are located in the northern desert region of Chile. The Atacama Desert, one of the driest places in the world, covers the northern half of this region. Chuquicamata, in the Atacama Desert, is known for its enormous copper mine, where one of the main characters in this story works. Exports of copper and other valuable minerals support Chile's economy.

Meet Amalia Rendic

In her native Chile, Amalia Rendic was a renowned author of literature for young people. She also was a teacher of Castilian Spanish, one of the more common forms of the language spoken in Spain. In addition, Rendic was a contributor to two Latin American newspapers, *El Mercurio*, of Santiago, Chile, and *La Nación*, published in Costa Rica.

Amalia Rendic was born in Chile in 1928; she died in 1988. This story appears in Landscapes of a New Land, *a collection of short stories by Latin American women.*

Vocabulary Preview

disperse (dis purs′) *v.* to go off in different directions; scatter; p. 129

intrigue (in trēg′) *v.* to excite the curiosity or interest of; fascinate; p. 130

monologue (mon′ ə lôg′) *n.* a long speech made by one person; p. 131

residue (rez′ ə do͞o′) *n.* what remains after part is removed; p. 131

contemplate (kon′ təm plāt′) *v.* to give intense attention to; consider carefully; p. 132

plaintive (plān′ tiv) *adj.* expressing sorrow; mournful; sad; p. 133

reciprocal (ri sip′ rə kəl) *adj.* given, felt, or shown in return; p. 133

A Child, a Dog, *the* Night

Amalia Rendic
Translated by Miriam Ben-Ur

THE SUN FADED SHORTLY IN GOLDEN RAYS. The faint light of the streetlamps could scarcely hold back the darkness and fog that invaded the entire mining camp. A large group of men handling the pile drivers, machinists, ore workers, and miners were going home. The return journey was slow and silent because of the breathing difficulty caused by the thin air. The Chuquicamata[1] mine is situated at over two thousand eight hundred meters above sea level.

As the group arrived at the Binkeroft neighborhood, it began to disperse toward different streets of the workers camp. Household lights could be seen through half-open windows and doors. The worker, Juan Labra,[2] a strong machinist and loyal friend, continued walking on one of the many narrow streets, still sighing because of the shrill whistles and sirens of the work areas. The wrinkles quickly vanished from his young face, which was already furrowed with deep wrinkles like veins of ore, and a burst of tenderness filled his eyes. He readily accepted his young family's loving welcome. Little Juan was waiting at the door of the house as he did every afternoon. He was a small nine-year-old boy, with lively, curious eyes, quite strong for his age and with feet that loved to walk. For him, the mine had no secrets. He knew every inch of the mine and all of its mysteries. He was a talkative child whose constant chatter could be interrupted only by smiles. With his face pressed against the

1. ***Chuquicamata*** (cho͞o kwē′ kə mä′ tə)
2. ***Juan Labra*** (wän lä′ brə)

Vocabulary
disperse (dis purs′) *v.* to go off in different directions; scatter

El Chico de la Gorra Verde (Juanito Laguna), c. 1954. Antonio Berni. Gouache, charcoal, and wax crayon on board, 28½ x 20½ in. Private collection.

Viewing the art: How would you describe the expression on this boy's face? Does he fit your image of Little Juan? Why or why not?

iron garden gate, he curiously watched a very tall North American who was walking behind his father.

"Dad, a gringo[3] is following you, he is coming to our house!" he whispered, frightened, to his father. The street was deserted.

Little Juan was intrigued by the presence of Black, the huge shepherd dog that followed Mr. Davies, his master. Black was one of the few beings that had managed to enter Davies' affections. A solitary companion in his lonely existence in a foreign land.

"Please come in, Mr. Davies. What can we do for you?" said the miner Juan Labra, respectfully taking off his metal hat and opening the small door of the gate. He could barely hide his astonishment at seeing one of the company's owners at his door.

"I'll be brief, Mr. Labra. I need a big favor from you. I soon must leave for Antofagasta[4] and want to leave in your custody for a few days my good friend, Black. You'll be kind. In Calama[5] you organized a society for the protection of animals. Everybody knows this," said Mr. Davies, looking at his dog.

"That's fine, Mr. Davies, thank you for your trust. He will be happy here. We will make sure the dog doesn't suffer. My son, Little Juan, will take care of him in my absence," promised Labra, adjusting his jacket and feeling strangely satisfied inside.

"I leave him in your hands and thank you very much. See you later, Mr. Labra. I'll return very soon, Black . . . Ah, I forgot! Here I'll leave his provisions of canned meat. It is his favorite food."

The master and his dog seemed sad. Black tugged at his master's pants, Davies

3. In Latin American countries, *gringo* refers to a foreigner, especially a non-Hispanic North American.

4. *Antofagasta* (än′ tō fə gäs′ tə)

5. *Calama* (kə lä′ mə)

Vocabulary

intrigue (in trēg′) *v.* to excite the curiosity or interest of; fascinate bent over to pet the dog's head, with its pointed snout, and left. The animal started to follow, but Little Juan's arms held him back like chains. Black barked falteringly, sniffing the air. His red, wet tongue was hanging out of his mouth. He panted anxiously. The boy closed the gate. Black stood erect, looking lonesome. His shining fur, his slenderness, his dignified bearing, were indications of his pedigree. He was an expensive dog and had won many dog shows because of his pedigree.

The dog's gaze was steady, and the boy's face was reflected in his eyes like tiny bright points.

The boy began talking to the dog as if it were a younger brother. For a long time they watched each other without even blinking. The dog's gaze was steady, and the boy's face was reflected in his eyes like tiny bright points. He shyly petted the back of the dog, who was sniffing the air and later responded with a reluctant movement of his tail.

Little Juan continued his strange monologue with Black. They started to become fond of each other. Across the dark, foggy hours of the night the dawn arrived. Then the day broke, as always, in the middle of the two huge mounds that formed the San Pedro and San Pablo volcanoes. Everything seemed to be a wet blue color.

Black awoke with the first sirens on the patio of the workers' house and watched the procession of miners; it was almost as if a great thing had awakened in his heart, too. He responded to these new impressions with barks that sounded like explosions. First thing in the morning, Little Juan, in a fantasy world, went out to see his new friend, and during the next few days they went everywhere together.

Challenging the wind, they ran along the winding ribbon that was the road to Calama. They tirelessly penetrated the immense vastness of the thin air.

They played together, diving into the gray residues of the copper mine pit, that shapeless, majestic mass of metallic land. They tried to collect the shining blue-green and yellow reflections that make bright colors in the sunlight.

They passed the hours this way until the nights came, the ties of the friendship that bound Little Juan and Black becoming stronger and stronger. A growing anxiety clouded the boy's short-lived happiness. He was dreading the day that their time together would end. It was certain that Mr. Davies would return.

"Papa, can't you ask the mister to give us Black? Why can't you buy him?"

"No, Little Juan, he will never be ours. He is very elegant, and worth his weight in gold. He is a rich man's dog. The gringos like to take walks with dogs like this one and present them in shows," answered the worker with a bitter smile.

"When I grow up I will buy him," responded little Juan decisively. "I don't want them to take him away! He's my friend!" he shouted at his father.

One day, as they returned from their walk on the banks of the Loa River, a nasty mountain wind began to blow. They were wet from

Vocabulary

monologue (mon′ ə lôg′) *n.* a long speech made by one person

residue (rez′ ə do͞o′) *n.* what remains after part is removed

Amanecer, c. 1917–1918. Dr. Atl. Oil on burlap, 15¾ x 24 in. Private collection.

Viewing the painting: What elements of this painting reflect Little Juan's mood when he returned Black to his owner?

the silky mist of Camanchaca.[6] When they came to the door, they stopped as if in fear and dread.

"Mr. Davies!" He had returned. The little boy tried to explain what the dog meant to him, but the words welled up in his heart and stayed in his parched throat. It was a sad moment.

"Good-bye, little friend, and good luck," he stammered, weeping and wringing his hands nervously.

Mr. Davies thanked him sincerely. Like a little gentleman, the child refused to accept any payment.

Black reluctantly started to walk behind his former owner, and eagerly examining the corners of the road, said good-bye to the workers' neighborhoods on the road toward the American camp. Now that Little Juan's first encounter with despair was over, he pondered the fact that he could never have an elegant dog. Black continued his walk. The harmony settled in both of them.

But the loneliness of night came, when souls contemplate themselves to the last fragment of life itself and then everything was useless. Little Juan's defenses collapsed and he began to cry. Something provoked a flow of communication between the boy and the animal across the space and at that very moment,

6. *Camanchaca* (kə′ män chä′ kə)

Vocabulary

contemplate (kon′ təm plāt′) *v.* to give intense attention to; consider carefully the dog began to howl in the American camp. Memories of Black were flashing through the boy's mind, and as if driven by a secret force, the dog barked furiously, asking the wind to transmit his message. It began as a plaintive concert, and then it became deafening.

Little Juan cried the whole night in a beseeching moan that became a strange concert that whipped through the still streets of the mining town.

Mr. Davies was bewildered by Black's behavior. What could a man do when faced with a crying dog? A new truth took possession of the gringo's mind. Black didn't belong to him anymore; he had lost his love.

Labra could not comfort his tearful and feverish little boy. For what could a man do when faced with a crying child? Labra wanted to see his son's quick, confident smile once again. He felt obliged to win back Little Juan's smile. Poverty had stung him many times, but he could not stand this. Something extraordinary would have to happen in the mining town on this uneasy night. As if the time had come for all men to be brothers, Labra threw his poncho on his shoulders, took the flashlight, and set off for the high neighborhood to see if a miracle could become reality. Yes, he must be courageous and daring. He, a simple laborer, always shy and silent, would ask for the elegant, beautiful, prize-winning Black from one of the company bosses. He inhaled the cold night air deeply and shuddered to think of his own boldness. He climbed up toward the American camp.

Suddenly, a pair of brown, phosphorescent[7] eyes were glowing in the light of the lantern. Labra was startled. The smell of a pipe and fine tobacco, and a familiar bark stopped him . . .

Mr. Davies had gone out to see him at that very moment and had been coming toward the workers' housing area!

Something touched the hearts of the two men. Words were not necessary.

"He doesn't belong to me anymore," stammered Mr. Davies, depositing Black's heavy metal leash in the worker's hands.

Labra took the animal in his trembling hands and a melancholy[8] happiness warmed his smile. There were no elaborate thanks, only a silent and reciprocal understanding. Black, tugging, forced him to continue following his tracks toward Little Juan's neighborhood.

In that miraculous moment, a new warmth tempered the night of Chuqui.

7. Here, *phosphorescent* (fos′ fə res′ ənt) means "glowing."
8. Here, *melancholy* (mel′ ən kol′ ē) means "thoughtful and serious."

Vocabulary

plaintive (plān′ tiv) *adj.* expressing sorrow; mournful; sad
reciprocal (ri sip′ rə kəl) *adj.* given, felt, or shown in return

Responding to Literature

Personal Response

How did the ending of the story make you feel? Describe your reactions in your journal.

Analyzing Literature

Recall

1. Who are the characters in this story? What is their relationship to one another?
2. Why does Mr. Davies choose Juan Labra to take care of Black?
3. Use details from the story to describe how the relationship between Little Juan and Black develops.
4. Describe how Little Juan and Black react to being separated after Mr. Davies returns. What does Labra decide to do?
5. How does the story end?

Interpret

6. Explain the characters' attitudes toward each other at the beginning of the story. How does the author convey these attitudes?
7. How does Labra feel about being asked to take care of Black? Cite evidence from the story to support your answer.
8. How do you think Labra feels when Little Juan asks him to buy Black from Mr. Davies? Explain your answer.
9. What is the **climax** of the story? Explain why you think this is the turning point in the story.
10. What is your interpretation of the last line of the story?

Evaluate and Connect

11. In your opinion, who is the **hero** of this story? Give reasons for your answer. (See Literary Terms Handbook, page R6.)
12. All of the characters in this story are male. In your opinion, might female characters, in the same situation, express their feelings differently? Explain.
13. Juan Labra and his family probably need the money Mr. Davies offers to Little Juan. Why do you think Little Juan will not accept the money? What would you have done?
14. **Theme Connections** How are the characters in this story transformed by the events that occur?
15. Do you think most dogs would become devoted to a new master as quickly and completely as Black did? Explain your answer.

Literary **ELEMENTS**

Narrator

The **narrator,** or storyteller, lets the reader know what is going on in a story. A fiction writer chooses the narrator's point of view from which to tell a story in the most appealing way. The author of "A Child, a Dog, the Night," for example, uses an **omniscient,** or "all knowing," narrator who stands outside the story and knows the thoughts and feelings of every character. As a result, the reader knows more than any one character does.

1. Why might Rendic have chosen to tell readers the thoughts and observations of all the main characters?
2. Choose one of the characters in the story: Juan Labra, Little Juan, Mr. Davies, or Black. In your opinion, would the story be as interesting if the point of view were limited to that one character's point of view? Explain.

- See **Literary Terms Handbook,** p. R8.

Literature and Writing

Writing About Literature

Literary Review Write a review of this story for the literary section of your school newspaper. Briefly describe the setting and the main characters. Then identify the central conflict of the story, but do not reveal how it is resolved. Tell what you think is the most important idea or issue explored in the story. You may want to discuss how effectively the author deals with that issue.

Personal Writing

Friends for Life Look back at the definition of true friendship that you wrote in the Reading Focus on page 128. After reading this story, is there anything you would change or add to your definition? Once you are satisfied with your definition, identify what you feel is the ultimate act of true friendship in this story. In a paragraph, tell what that act is and why you think it deserves that description.

Extending Your Response

Literature Groups

Look into the Future Imagine that on a trip to Chile, you encounter Little Juan, who is now thirty years old. After spending some time with him, you return home. Form a small group and share what you have learned about what has happened to "Little" Juan and his family. Compare your group's scenarios with those imagined by other groups.

Learning for Life

Letter of Inquiry Before this story began, Juan Labra had organized a society for the protection of animals. Write a letter to a local animal protection agency, requesting information about the history, goals, and accomplishments of the group. Share the information with the class.

Listening and Speaking

Create a Different Ending What might have happened if Labra had not met Mr. Davies on the road? What if he had continued on to the mine owner's home and confronted him there? Discuss what the two might have said to each other. Then take turns role-playing the dialogue between the two men. Present your dialogue to the class.

Save your work for your portfolio.

VOCABULARY • Analogies

An analogy is a type of comparison that is based on the relationships between things or ideas. Some analogies are based on a relationship that could be called "degree of intensity."

dislike : hate :: irritate : enrage

To intensely *dislike* is to *hate;* to intensely *irritate* is to *enrage.*

To finish an analogy, decide what relationship exists between the first two things or ideas. Then apply that relationship to another pair of words.

For more about analogies, see **Communications Skills Handbook,** p. R77.

PRACTICE Choose the pair that best completes each analogy.

1. think : contemplate ::
   a. look : inspect
   b. question : answer
   c. debate : discuss
   d. remember : recall
   e. surrender : escape
2. interest : intrigue ::
   a. awaken : doze
   b. perplex : mystify
   c. encourage : support
   d. criticize : correct
   e. instruct : demonstrate

Writing Workshop

Personal Writing:
Reflective Essay

First impressions are often wrong, and they're always incomplete—whether they're first impressions of people or of short stories. Upon reflection, you often discover more than you noticed at first. **In this workshop you will write a reflective essay that explores your impressions of a story you have read.** A reflective essay shows the progress of your thinking: from first impressions, through second thoughts, to a considered opinion.

- As you write your reflective essay, refer to the **Writing Handbook,** pp. R58–R71.

EVALUATION RUBRIC

By the time you complete this Writing Workshop, you will have

- begun by clearly identifying a story you have read and some aspects of it you will reflect upon
- elaborated on the ideas in the introduction to arrive at a considered opinion about the story
- used transitions to make clear the connections between your ideas
- supported your thoughts with appropriate passages from the text
- presented a reflective essay that is free of errors in grammar, usage, and mechanics

The Writing Process

PREWRITING

PREWRITING TIP

Use freewriting to begin reflecting on your responses to a work of literature. Let your ideas flow and jot them down as they come to you.

Explore ideas

Think about the short stories you've read so far in this unit. You'll base your essay on your reflections about a particular aspect of one of those stories. Begin exploring ideas for your reflective essay with questions such as the following:

- Which story made the strongest impression on you?
- What were your first impressions of this story?
- Upon further reflection, what other ideas occurred to you? What questions did the story raise in your mind?
- What experiences of your own came to mind as a result of reading the story?
- What new ideas about life's transitional moments did the story suggest to you?
- Which aspect of the story intrigued you the most or made the strongest impression on you?

Choose an audience

Do you want to write for people who have read the story or for people who have *not* read it? Remember to summarize the plot for those who aren't familiar with it.

Consider your purpose

The stories in this theme are about moving from one phase of life to another; your essay will move from first impressions to later ideas. You will take your reader through each step.

Make a plan

You'll be asking your audience to follow your thoughts over the course of your essay. In order to organize your reflections into a form that others can understand, jot down notes for the three parts of your essay.

STUDENT MODEL

Introduction	What is the story and what is it about? What aspect of the story will you reflect on?	"With All Flags Flying" is about an eighty-two-year-old man who is growing weaker but remains stubbornly independent. I'll reflect on his relationship with his family.
Body	Begin with your first impressions: What was your immediate response?	This old man is very stubborn and selfish.
	Then reconsider: What other responses are possible?	He may be afraid of dying and may want to be near his family.
	Arrive at a considered opinion: Upon reflection, what is your interpretation?	Maybe the old man loves his family and doesn't want to burden them.
Conclusion	Review the progress of your thinking: Where did you start? Where did you end up?	At first, I felt frustrated and angry towards the old man. He seemed selfish. After thinking about it more, though, my feelings changed. I saw that the old man loves his family and doesn't want to be a burden to them.

Complete Student Model on p. R108.

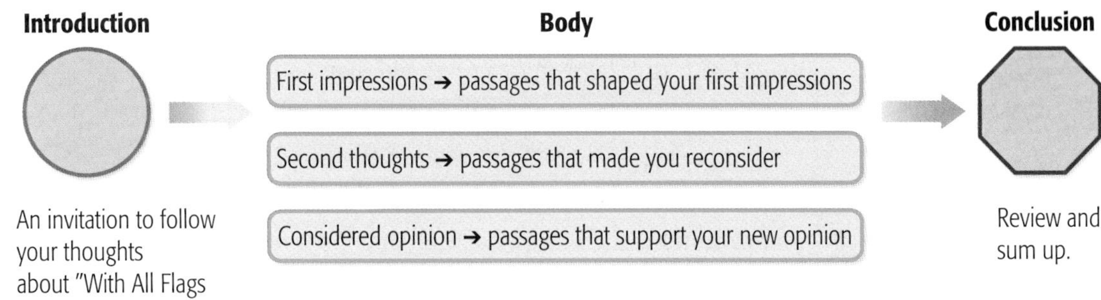

DRAFTING

TECHNOLOGY TIP

If you're working on a computer, save your notes under a new file name. Presto! You've started your draft. Now expand it.

Think on paper

Drafting a reflective essay should be like thinking on paper—or, if you're using a computer, thinking on the screen. Refer to the notes you made when you planned your essay. Then go ahead and "think."

Let one idea suggest another. This is a time to write too much rather than too little. Think, question, respond, react, meditate, and reflect. Put it all down without trying to measure one idea against another. If your ideas lead you in surprising directions, that's great! It means your thoughts are making new thoughts—you're reflecting.

Write your draft

Concentrate on getting your ideas down, not on phrasing everything perfectly. You can always change your draft later. As you write, refer to your plan to make sure you include each part of your introduction, body, and conclusion.

STUDENT MODEL

At first, I thought this old man was just a selfish and uncaring person. I kept thinking how much I would hate it if my grandfather was like him! He doesn't seem like he really loved his family, with the way he acted toward them. I read the story a couple of times, though, and finally my opinion changed. Maybe he just couldn't show his family his feelings very well.

But why couldn't he just show them that he loved them? I think it has something to do with him being afraid of being a burden to them. This old man seems like he really values independence more than anything. For instance, he goes all the way to his daughter's house by himself, without asking for her help. Also, in the story, it comes right out and says that he has decided to be independent on purpose, like that's a really important choice that he made about his life. So all of this makes me think that maybe he just doesn't know how to show his love, not that he doesn't love them.

Complete Student Model on p. R108.

REVISING

REVISING TIP

Take another look

After you finish your draft, you may be tempted to begin revising it right away. Resist the temptation! Instead, set your draft aside for a while. Then return to it with a fresh eye, and read it through without making any changes at all. Next, revise it, using the **Rubric for Revising** as a guide. You may want to repeat this process two or three times, constantly trying to convey your ideas more clearly to your audience.

REVISING TIP

Be sure to use transitions that help your audience follow your thinking.

Read your essay aloud

Read your work aloud to someone else to hear how it sounds. (Keep the written copy to yourself, since it hasn't been edited.) Ask your listener if he or she had any difficulty following the progress of your thinking. Go through the **Rubric for Revising** with him or her, but don't feel that you have to make every change your listener suggests. It's your essay, and it reports *your* reflections.

STUDENT MODEL

I think the old man is ~~trying~~ *fighting a battle* to retane his dignity in old age. We laern from the last lines of the story that he wants to "not give in" ~~so it really~~ *and to "continue gracefully until the moment of my defeat," which* shows his problem in terms of a "battle." ~~I'll bet that would make a great scene in a TV show.~~ The problem ~~was~~ *is* that the old man sees the need for love as a ~~type of thing~~ *weakness* that could ~~cost~~ *cause* him to loose this battle, this is a sad thing for ~~him and the others~~ *both the old man and his family* because they lost the most precious thing we have—time—too.

Complete Student Model on p. R108.

RUBRIC FOR REVISING

Your revised reflective essay should have

- ☑ an engaging introduction that tells what the story is about and where your reflections will lead
- ☑ a clear, logical progression from your initial impressions to your considered opinion
- ☑ appropriate passages from the text to support your impressions and thoughts
- ☑ vivid words and images that add interest to your writing
- ☑ a conclusion that briefly reviews and summarizes your ideas

Your revised essay should be free of

- ☑ information that does not relate to your main point
- ☑ wordy or awkward statements that make the meaning of your ideas unclear
- ☑ errors in grammar, usage, and mechanics

EDITING/PROOFREADING

PROOFREADING TIP

Use the **Proofreading Checklist** on the inside back cover of this book to help you mark errors that you find.

Are you satisfied with the content of your reflective essay? If so, then it's time to edit and proofread your essay carefully for errors in grammar, usage, mechanics, and spelling.

Grammar Hint

Do not shift, or change, verb tenses when you describe two or more events that occur at the same time.

INCORRECT: *In the story, the old man wants to remain independent, but his daughter and her family wished he would live with them.*

CORRECT: *In the story, the old man wants to remain independent, but his daughter and her family wish he would live with them.*

- For more about verb tenses, see **Language Handbook,** pp. R23–R24.

STUDENT MODEL

Complete Student Model

For a complete version of the model developed in this workshop, refer to **Writing Workshop Models**, p. R108.

Still, there was one thing that puzzles me: Mr. Pond and the old man's discussion. Mr. Pond will be the old mans roommate when he got to the old age home.

Complete Student Model on p. R108.

PUBLISHING/PRESENTING

PRESENTING TIP

Ask the members of your audience to read the story before you present your essay.

How you choose to present your essay depends on your audience. If you've written for family members, you might read your essay to them. To reach a wider audience, you could post your essay in an Internet forum devoted to the author of the story you reflected upon.

Reflecting

The great French writer Marcel Proust wrote that "great works of art do not begin by giving us all their best." In mediocre work, the obvious is all there is; in great work, the best is usually found only upon reflection. How does this idea relate to what you just wrote?

Read your essay one last time, reflecting upon its strengths and weaknesses. Plan to build on the strengths in your next piece of writing.

Save your work for your portfolio.

Theme 2 Making Choices

Thinking things over and deciding for oneself are freedoms that people value. Yet making choices can also be one of the most difficult aspects of life. Many of the characters you will meet in this theme are making choices that will forever define who they are. What are the major choices you can expect to face in your lifetime?

THEME PROJECTS

Journalism

Choose the Way Out Imagine that several characters from this theme are stranded in the African savanna. Their challenge is to get back to civilization and safety.

1. Working in a group, have each member pretend to be a character from a story in this theme. All the characters must act as a group to plan an escape from the savanna.
2. Stay in character as you argue for the choices you think will best help the group. Each character may choose one object from his or her story to help in the escape.
3. Afterward, write a press release for the newspaper stating how you made the decisions that brought you home safely.

Interdisciplinary Project

Geography From the sports you play to the food you eat, your surroundings influence everything in your life. The same is true for characters in fiction.

1. On a large sheet of paper, draw a world map. Identify the setting for each story in this theme and mark it on your map.
2. For each story, locate the place farthest away from its original setting and imagine that the story took place there.
3. On a note card, describe how the new setting might affect the story. Attach the note card to your map.

Before You Read

A White Heron

Reading Focus

Have you ever been tempted to reveal a secret? Can you recall why you did or did not reveal a particular secret?

Chart It! A secret may be told to you by another person, or you may discover a secret on your own. Think about secrets you have known. Then fill in a chart like this one.

The secret	Did you keep this secret?	Why or why not?

Setting a Purpose Read to discover how difficult the decision to keep or reveal a secret can be.

Building Background

The Time and Place

"A White Heron" is set in the early summer, probably in the late 1800s. The place is somewhere in rural New England, not far from the ocean.

Did You Know?

The heron in this story is most likely the *great egret*–a tall, white heron with a long, thin, yellow bill and black legs. In the late 1800s, some species of egrets were brought to the point of near extinction by hunters who killed the birds to obtain their showy feathers, used to decorate ladies' hats. Killing egrets is now illegal.

Vocabulary Preview

wary (wār′ ē) *adj.* cautious; on the alert; p. 144

discreetly (dis krēt′ lē) *adv.* in a manner showing good judgment; cautiously; p. 145

squalor (skwol′ ər) *n.* wretchedness; misery and filth; p. 146

wane (wān) *v.* to decrease gradually; p. 148

giddy (gid′ ē) *adj.* causing dizziness or lightheadedness; p. 151

vexed (vekst) *adj.* impatient or angry; annoyed; p. 151

perilous (per′ ə ləs) *adj.* dangerous; risky; p. 151

rebuke (ri būk′) *v.* to scold sharply; p. 152

Meet Sarah Orne Jewett

As a child, Sarah Orne Jewett loved to read. Fortunately for her—and for readers who have benefited from her exposure to fine literature—the Jewett home was filled with so many books that stacks of them had to be removed from chairs before guests could sit down. Jewett also spent time with her father, a country doctor, who took her along on visits to patients. On these outdoor rides, the author developed her keen perception of nature and her great love for the natural world.

Sarah Orne Jewett was born in South Berwick, Maine, in 1849, and died there in 1909. This story was published in 1886.

A White Heron

Sarah Orne Jewett

THE WOODS WERE ALREADY FILLED WITH SHADOWS one June evening, just before eight o'clock, though a bright sunset still glimmered faintly among the trunks of the trees. A little girl was driving home her cow, a plodding, dilatory,[1] provoking creature in her behavior, but a valued companion for all that.

1. *Dilatory* (dil′ ə tôr′ ē) means "causing delay; slow."

Taking a Walk, 1886. George Inness. Oil on canvas, 36 x 50 in. David David Gallery, Philadelphia.

They were going away from whatever light there was, and striking deep into the woods, but their feet were familiar with the path, and it was no matter whether their eyes could see it or not.

There was hardly a night the summer through when the old cow could be found waiting at the pasture bars; on the contrary, it was her greatest pleasure to hide herself away among the huckleberry bushes, and though she wore a loud bell she had made the discovery that if one stood perfectly still it would not ring. So Sylvia had to hunt for her until she found her, and call Co'! Co'! with never an answering Moo, until her childish patience was quite spent. If the creature had not given good milk and plenty of it, the case would have seemed very different to her owners. Besides, Sylvia had all the time there was, and very little use to make of it. Sometimes in pleasant weather it was a consolation to look upon the cow's pranks as an intelligent attempt to play hide and seek, and as the child had no playmates she lent herself to this amusement with a good deal of zest. Though this chase had been so long that the wary animal herself had given an unusual signal of her whereabouts, Sylvia had only laughed when she came upon Mistress Moolly at the swamp-side, and urged her affectionately homeward with a twig of birch leaves. The old cow was not inclined to wander farther; she even turned in the right direction for once as they left the pasture and stepped along the road at a good pace. She was quite ready to be milked now, and seldom stopped to browse. Sylvia wondered what her grandmother would say because they were so late. It was a great while since she had left home at half past five o'clock, but everybody knew the difficulty of making this errand a short one. Mrs. Tilley had chased the hornéd torment too many summer evenings herself to blame any one else for lingering, and was only thankful as she waited that she had Sylvia, nowadays, to give such valuable assistance. The good woman suspected that Sylvia loitered occasionally on her own account; there never was such a child for straying about out-of-doors since the world was made! Everybody said that it was a good change for a little maid who had tried to grow for eight years in a crowded manufacturing town, but, as for Sylvia herself, it seemed as if she never had been alive at all before she came to live at the farm. She thought often with wistful compassion of a wretched geranium that belonged to a town neighbor.

"'Afraid of folks,'" old Mrs. Tilley said to herself, with a smile, after she had made the unlikely choice of Sylvia from her daughter's houseful of children, and was returning to the farm. "'Afraid of folks,' they said! I guess she won't be troubled no great with 'em up to the old place!" When they reached the door of the lonely house and stopped to unlock it, and the cat came to purr loudly and rub against them, a deserted pussy, indeed, but fat with young robins, Sylvia whispered that this was a beautiful place to live in, and she never should wish to go home.

The companions followed the shady wood-road, the cow taking slow steps and the child very fast ones. The cow stopped long at the brook to drink, as if the pasture were not half a swamp, and Sylvia stood still and waited, letting her bare

Vocabulary
wary (wār′ ē) *adj.* cautious; on the alert

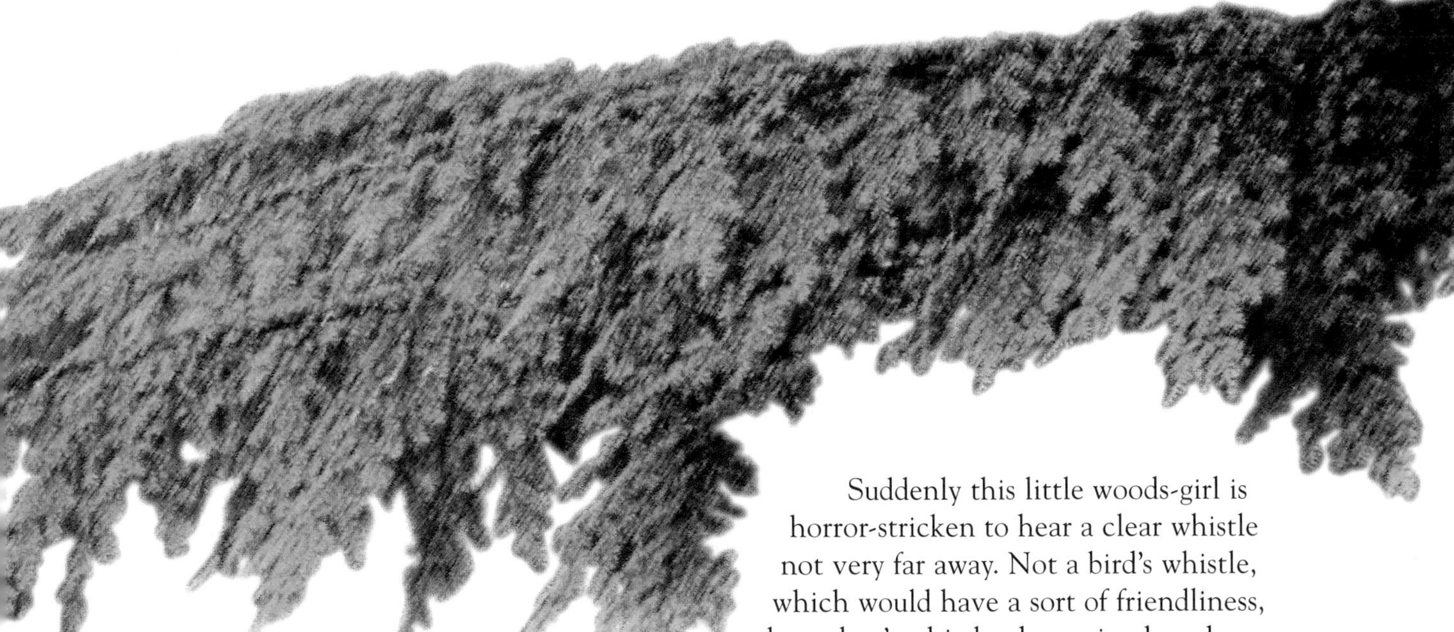

feet cool themselves in the shoal[2] water, while the great twilight moths struck softly against her. She waded on through the brook as the cow moved away, and listened to the thrushes with a heart that beat fast with pleasure. There was a stirring in the great boughs overhead. They were full of little birds and beasts that seemed to be wide awake, and going about their world, or else saying good night to each other in sleepy twitters. Sylvia herself felt sleepy as she walked along. However, it was not much farther to the house, and the air was soft and sweet. She was not often in the woods so late as this, and it made her feel as if she were a part of the gray shadows and the moving leaves. She was just thinking how long it seemed since she first came to the farm a year ago, and wondering if everything went on in the noisy town just the same as when she was there; the thought of the great red-faced boy who used to chase and frighten her made her hurry along the path to escape from the shadow of the trees.

2. *Shoal* means "shallow."

Suddenly this little woods-girl is horror-stricken to hear a clear whistle not very far away. Not a bird's whistle, which would have a sort of friendliness, but a boy's whistle, determined, and somewhat aggressive. Sylvia left the cow to whatever sad fate might await her, and stepped discreetly aside into the bushes, but she was just too late. The enemy had discovered her, and called out in a very cheerful and persuasive tone, "Halloa, little girl, how far is it to the road?" and trembling Sylvia answered almost inaudibly, "A good ways."

She did not dare to look boldly at the tall young man, who carried a gun over his shoulder, but she came out of her bush and again followed the cow, while he walked alongside.

"I have been hunting for some birds," the stranger said kindly, "and I have lost my way, and need a friend very much. Don't be afraid," he added gallantly. "Speak up and tell me what your name is, and whether you think I can spend the night at your house, and go out gunning early in the morning."

Sylvia was more alarmed than before. Would not her grandmother consider her much to blame? But who could have foreseen such an accident as this? It did not seem to be her fault, and she hung her head as if the stem of it were broken, but managed to answer "Sylvy," with much effort when her companion again asked her name.

Vocabulary

discreetly (dis krēt′ lē) *adv.* in a manner showing good judgment; cautiously

Mrs. Tilley was standing in the doorway when the trio came into view. The cow gave a loud moo by way of explanation.

"Yes, you'd better speak up for yourself, you old trial! Where'd she tucked herself this time, Sylvy?" But Sylvia kept an awed silence; she knew by instinct that her grandmother did not comprehend the gravity of the situation. She must be mistaking the stranger for one of the farmer lads of the region.

The young man stood his gun beside the door, and dropped a lumpy game bag beside it; then he bade[3] Mrs. Tilley good evening, and repeated his wayfarer's story, and asked if he could have a night's lodging.

"Put me anywhere you like," he said. "I must be off early in the morning, before day; but I am very hungry, indeed. You can give me some milk at any rate, that's plain."

"Dear sakes, yes," responded the hostess, whose long slumbering hospitality seemed to be easily awakened. "You might fare better if you went out to the main road a mile or so, but you're welcome to what we've got. I'll milk right off, and you make yourself at home. You can sleep on husks or feathers," she proffered[4] graciously. "I raised them all myself. There's good pasturing for geese just below here towards the ma'sh.[5] Now step round and set a plate for the gentleman, Sylvy!" And Sylvia promptly stepped. She was glad to have something to do, and she was hungry herself.

It was a surprise to find so clean and comfortable a little dwelling in this New England wilderness. The young man had known the horrors of its most primitive housekeeping, and the dreary squalor of that level of society which does not rebel at the companionship of hens. This was the best thrift of an old-fashioned farmstead, though on such a small scale that it seemed like a hermitage. He listened eagerly to the old woman's quaint talk, he watched Sylvia's pale face and shining gray eyes with ever growing enthusiasm, and insisted that this was the best supper he had eaten for a month, and afterward the new-made friends sat down in the doorway together while the moon came up.

It was a surprise to find so clean and comfortable a little dwelling in this New England wilderness.

Soon it would be berry-time, and Sylvia was a great help at picking. The cow was a good milker, though a plaguy[6] thing to keep track of, the hostess gossiped frankly, adding presently that she had buried four children, so Sylvia's mother, and a son (who might be dead) in California were all the children she had left. "Dan, my boy, was a great hand to go gunning," she explained sadly. "I never wanted for pa'tridges or gray squer'ls while he was to home. He's been a great wand'rer,

3. *Bade* is the past tense of *bid* and, here, means "said in greeting."
4. *Proffered* rhymes with, and means the same as, *offered.*
5. In the grandmother's New England dialect, *ma'sh* is *marsh,* a low-lying wetland.
6. Something that is *plaguy* (plā′ gē) is troublesome or annoying.

Vocabulary
squalor (skwol′ ər) *n.* wretchedness; misery and filth

I expect, and he's no hand to write letters. There, I don't blame him, I'd ha' seen the world myself if it had been so I could."

"Sylvy takes after him," the grandmother continued affectionately, after a minute's pause. "There ain't a foot o' ground she don't know her way over, and the wild creaturs counts her one o' themselves. Squer'ls she'll tame to come an' feed right out o' her hands, and all sorts o' birds. Last winter she got the jaybirds to bangeing[7] here, and I believe she'd 'a' scanted herself of her own meals to have plenty to throw out amongst 'em, if I hadn't kep' watch. Anything but crows, I tell her, I'm willin' to help support—though Dan he had a tamed one o' them that did seem to have reason same as folks. It was round here a good spell after he went away. Dan an' his father they didn't hitch,[8]—but he never held up his head ag'in after Dan had dared him an' gone off."

The guest did not notice this hint of family sorrows in his eager interest in something else.

"So Sylvy knows all about birds, does she?" he exclaimed, as he looked round at the little girl who sat, very demure but increasingly sleepy, in the moonlight. "I am making a collection of birds myself. I have been at it ever since I was a boy." (Mrs. Tilley smiled.) "There are two or three very rare ones I have been hunting for these five years. I mean to get them on my own ground if they can be found."

"Do you cage 'em up?" asked Mrs. Tilley doubtfully, in response to this enthusiastic announcement.

"Oh no, they're stuffed and preserved, dozens and dozens of them," said the ornithologist,[9] "and I have shot or snared every one myself. I caught a glimpse of a white heron a few miles from here on Saturday, and I have followed it in this direction. They have never been found in this district at all. The little white heron, it is," and he turned again to look at Sylvia with the hope of discovering that the rare bird was one of her acquaintances.

But Sylvia was watching a hop-toad in the narrow footpath.

"You would know the heron if you saw it," the stranger continued eagerly. "A queer tall white bird with soft feathers and long thin legs. And it would have a nest perhaps in the top of a high tree, made of sticks, something like a hawk's nest."

Sylvia's heart gave a wild beat; she knew that strange white bird, and had once stolen softly near where it stood in some bright green swamp grass, away over at the other side of the woods. There was an open place where the sunshine always seemed strangely yellow and hot, where tall, nodding rushes grew, and her grandmother had warned her that she might sink in the soft black mud underneath and never be heard of more. Not far beyond were the salt marshes just this side the sea itself, which Sylvia wondered and dreamed much about, but never had seen, whose great voice could sometimes be heard above the noise of the woods on stormy nights.

"I can't think of anything I should like so much as to find that heron's nest," the handsome stranger was saying. "I would give ten dollars to anybody who could show it to me," he added desperately, "and I mean to spend my whole vacation hunting for it if need be. Perhaps it was only migrating, or had been chased out of its own region by some bird of prey."

7. *Bangeing* (bān′ jing) is a New England expression meaning "gathering or lounging around in groups."

8. *Didn't hitch,* another New England expression, means "didn't get along."

9. An *ornithologist* is someone who studies, or is an expert on, birds.

Mrs. Tilley gave amazed attention to all this, but Sylvia still watched the toad, not divining,[10] as she might have done at some calmer time, that the creature wished to get to its hole under the doorstep and was much hindered by the unusual spectators at that hour of the evening. No amount of thought, that night, could decide how many wished-for treasures the ten dollars, so lightly spoken of, would buy.

The next day the young sportsman hovered about the woods, and Sylvia kept him company, having lost her first fear of the friendly lad, who proved to be most kind and sympathetic. He told her many things about the birds and what they knew and where they lived and what they did with themselves. And he gave her a jackknife, which she thought as great a treasure as if she were a desert islander. All day long he did not once make her troubled or afraid except when he brought down some unsuspecting singing creature from its bough. Sylvia would have liked him vastly better without his gun; she could not understand why he killed the very birds he seemed to like so much. But as the day waned, Sylvia still watched the young man with loving admiration. She had never seen anybody so charming and delightful; the woman's heart, asleep in the child, was vaguely thrilled by a dream of love. Some premonition of that great power stirred and swayed these young creatures who traversed[11] the solemn woodlands with soft-footed silent care. They stopped to listen to a bird's song; they pressed forward again eagerly, parting the branches—speaking to each other rarely and in whispers; the young man going first and Sylvia following, fascinated, a few steps behind, with her gray eyes dark with excitement.

She grieved because the longed-for white heron was elusive,[12] but she did not lead the guest, she only followed, and there was no such thing as speaking first. The sound of her own unquestioned voice would have terrified her—it was hard enough to answer yes or no when there was need of that. At last evening began to fall, and they drove the cow home together, and Sylvia smiled with pleasure when they came to the place where she heard the whistle and was afraid only the night before.

Half a mile from home, at the farther edge of the woods, where the land was highest, a great pine tree stood, the last of its generation. Whether it was left for a boundary mark, or for what reason, no one could say; the wood choppers who had felled its mates were dead and gone long ago, and a whole forest of sturdy trees, pines and oaks and maples, had grown again. But the stately head of this old pine towered above them all and made a landmark for sea and shore miles and miles away. Sylvia knew it well. She had always believed that whoever climbed to the top of it could see the ocean; and the little girl had often laid her hand on the great rough trunk and looked up wistfully at those dark boughs that the wind always stirred, no matter how hot and still the air might be below. Now she thought of the tree with a new excitement, for why, if one climbed it at break of day could not one see all the world, and easily discover from whence the white heron flew, and mark the place, and find the hidden nest?

10. Here, *divining* means "guessing."
11. To *traverse* is to pass across or through.
12. If a thing is *elusive* (i lo͞o′ siv), it is difficult to discover or catch.

Vocabulary
wane (wān) *v.* to decrease gradually

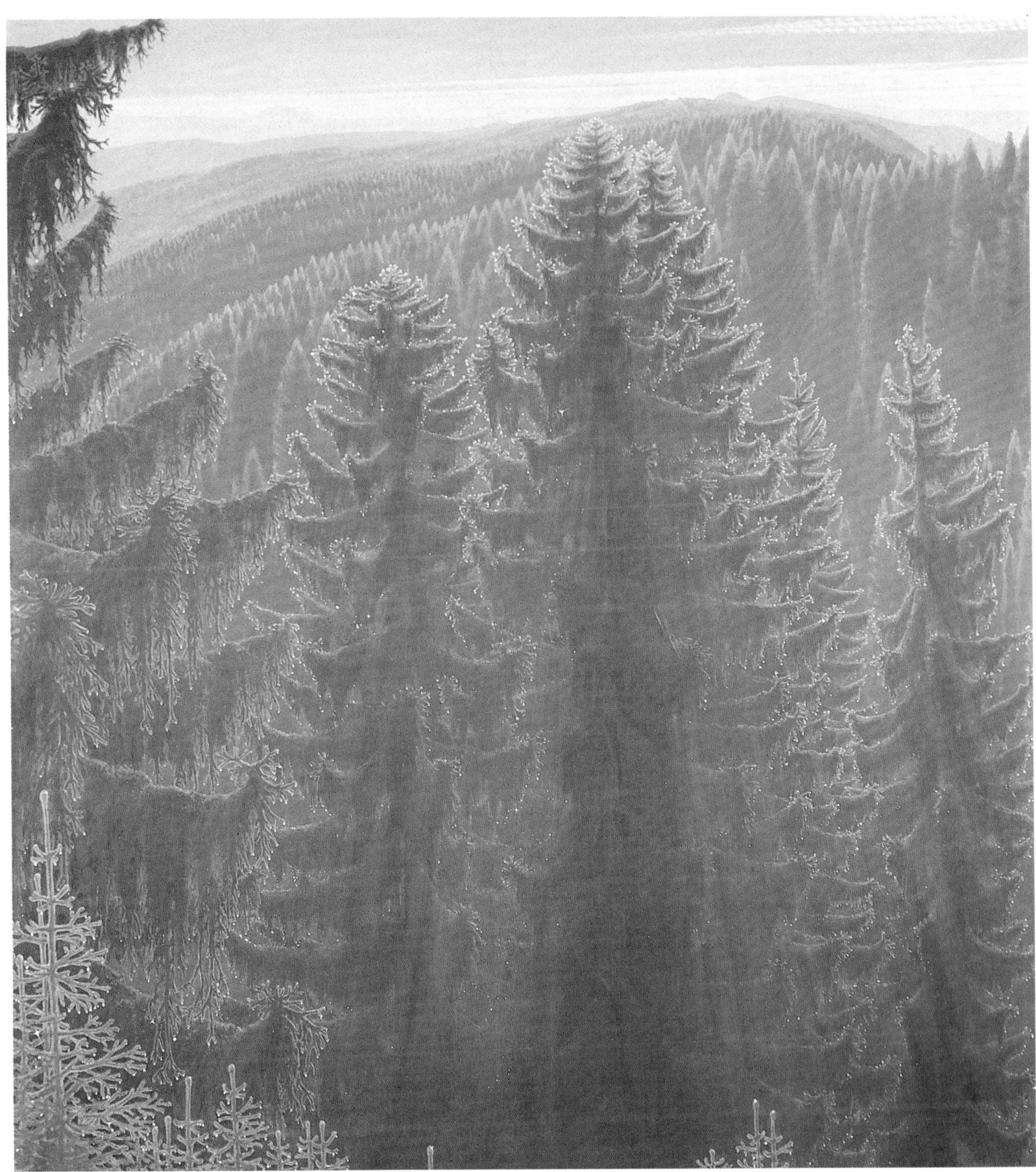

Forest in the Dew. Wolfgang Muller (b. 1877).

Viewing the painting: Imagine you are Sylvy, perched on the highest tree in the forest. What emotions do you feel as you look upon this vista?

What a spirit of adventure, what wild ambition! What fancied triumph and delight and glory for the later morning when she could make known the secret! It was almost too real and too great for the childish heart to bear.

All night the door of the little house stood open and the whippoorwills came and sang upon the very step. The young sportsman and his old hostess were sound asleep, but Sylvia's great design kept her broad awake and watching. She forgot to think of sleep. The short summer night seemed as long as the winter darkness, and at last when the whippoorwills ceased, and she was afraid the morning would after all come too soon, she stole out of the house and followed the pasture path through the woods, hastening toward the open ground beyond, listening with a sense of comfort and companionship to the drowsy twitter of a half-awakened bird, whose perch she had jarred in passing. Alas, if the great wave of human interest which flooded for the first time this dull little life should sweep away the satisfactions of an existence heart to heart with nature and the dumb life of the forest!

She crept out along the swaying oak limb at last, and took the daring step across into the old pine tree.

There was the huge tree asleep yet in the paling moonlight, and small and silly Sylvia began with utmost bravery to mount to the top of it, with tingling, eager blood coursing the channels of her whole frame, with her bare feet and fingers, that pinched and held like bird's claws to the monstrous ladder reaching up, up, almost to the sky itself. First she must mount the white oak tree that grew alongside, where she was almost lost among the dark branches and the green leaves heavy and wet with dew; a bird fluttered off its nest, and a red squirrel ran to and fro and scolded pettishly[13] at the harmless housebreaker. Sylvia felt her way easily. She had often climbed there, and knew that higher still one of the oak's upper branches chafed against the pine trunk, just where its lower boughs were set close together. There, when she made the dangerous pass from one tree to the other, the great enterprise would really begin.

She crept out along the swaying oak limb at last, and took the daring step across into the old pine tree. The way was harder than she thought; she must reach far and hold fast, the sharp dry twigs caught and held her and scratched her like angry talons, the pitch made her thin little fingers clumsy and stiff as she went round and round the tree's great stem, higher and higher upward. The sparrows and robins in the woods below were beginning to wake and twitter to the dawn, yet it seemed much lighter there aloft in the pine tree, and the child knew she must hurry if her project were to be of any use.

The tree seemed to lengthen itself out as she went up, and to reach farther and farther upward. It was like a great mainmast to the voyaging earth; it must truly have been amazed that morning through all its ponderous frame as it felt this determined spark of human spirit wending its way from higher branch to branch. Who knows how steadily the least twigs held themselves to advantage this light, weak creature on her way! The old pine

13. *Pettishly* means "crossly or irritably."

must have loved his new dependent. More than all the hawks, and bats, and moths, and even the sweet voiced thrushes, was the brave, beating heart of the solitary gray-eyed child. And the tree stood still and frowned away the winds that June morning while the dawn grew bright in the east.

Sylvia's face was like a pale star, if one had seen it from the ground, when the last thorny bough was past, and she stood trembling and tired but wholly triumphant, high in the treetop. Yes, there was the sea with the dawning sun making a golden dazzle over it, and toward that glorious east flew two hawks with slow-moving pinions.[14] How low they looked in the air from that height when one had only seen them before far up, and dark against the blue sky. Their gray feathers were as soft as moths; they seemed only a little way from the tree, and Sylvia felt as if she too could go flying away among the clouds. Westward, the woodlands and farms reached miles and miles into the distance; here and there were church steeples, and white villages; truly it was a vast and awesome world!

The birds sang louder and louder. At last the sun came up bewilderingly bright. Sylvia could see the white sails of ships out at sea, and the clouds that were purple and rose-colored and yellow at first began to fade away. Where was the white heron's nest in the sea of green branches, and was this wonderful sight and pageant of the world the only reward for having climbed to such a giddy height? Now look down again, Sylvia, where the green marsh is set among the shining birches and dark hemlocks; there where you saw the white heron once you will see him again; look, look! a white spot of him like a single floating feather comes up from the dead hemlock and grows larger, and rises, and comes close at last, and goes by the landmark pine with steady sweep of wing and outstretched slender neck and crested head. And wait! wait! do not move a foot or a finger, little girl, do not send an arrow of light and consciousness from your two eager eyes, for the heron has perched on a pine bough not far beyond yours, and cries back to his mate on the nest and plumes his feathers for the new day!

Did You Know?
When a heron *plumes its feathers,* it cleans and smooths them with its bill.

The child gives a long sigh a minute later when a company of shouting catbirds comes also to the tree, and vexed by their fluttering and lawlessness the solemn heron goes away. She knows his secret now, the wild, light, slender bird that floats and wavers, and goes back like an arrow presently to his home in the green world beneath. Then Sylvia, well satisfied, makes her perilous way down again, not daring to look far below the branch she stands on, ready to cry sometimes because her fingers ache and her lamed feet slip. Wondering over and over again what the stranger would say to her, and what he would think when she told him how to find his way straight to the heron's nest.

14. Here, the bird's *pinions* are its wings. The word may also be used to refer to a bird's feathers.

Vocabulary
giddy (gid′ ē) *adj.* causing dizziness or lightheadedness
vexed (vekst) *adj.* impatient or angry; annoyed
perilous (per′ ə ləs) *adj.* dangerous; risky

"Sylvy, Sylvy!" called the busy old grandmother again and again, but nobody answered, and the small husk bed was empty and Sylvia had disappeared.

The guest waked from a dream, and remembering his day's pleasure hurried to dress himself that might it sooner begin. He was sure from the way the shy little girl looked once or twice yesterday that she had at least seen the white heron, and now she must really be made to tell. Here she comes now, paler than ever, and her worn old frock is torn and tattered, and smeared with pine pitch. The grandmother and the sportsman stand in the door together and question her, and the splendid moment has come to speak of the dead hemlock tree by the green marsh.

But Sylvia does not speak after all, though the old grandmother fretfully rebukes her, and the young man's kind, appealing eyes are looking straight in her own. He can make them rich with money; he has promised it, and they are poor now. He is so well worth making happy, and he waits to hear the story she can tell.

No, she must keep silence! What is it that suddenly forbids her and makes her dumb? Has she been nine years growing and now, when the great world for the first time puts out a hand to her, must she thrust it aside for a bird's sake? The murmur of the pine's green branches is in her ears, she remembers how the white heron came flying through the golden air and how they watched the sea and the morning together, and Sylvia cannot speak; she cannot tell the heron's secret and give its life away.

Dear loyalty, that suffered a sharp pang as the guest went away disappointed later in the day, that could have served and followed him and loved him as a dog loves! Many a night Sylvia heard the echo of his whistle haunting the pasture path as she came home with the loitering cow. She forgot even her sorrow at the sharp report[15] of his gun and the sight of thrushes and sparrows dropping silent to the ground, their songs hushed and their pretty feathers stained and wet with blood. Were the birds better friends than their hunter might have been,—who can tell? Whatever treasures were lost to her, woodlands and summertime, remember! Bring your gifts and graces and tell your secrets to this lonely country child!

15. A gun's *report* is the explosive noise of its being fired.

Vocabulary
rebuke (ri būk′) *v.* to scold sharply

Responding to Literature

Personal Response

Were you surprised by the decision Sylvia makes at the end of the story? Why or why not?

Analyzing Literature

Recall

1. Summarize the information the author gives about Sylvia during the first part of the story, before she meets the young man.
2. What is Sylvia's initial reaction to the young man? How do her feelings toward him change as the story progresses?
3. What is the stranger looking for? What does he plan to do if he finds it?
4. Describe how Sylvia finds what the stranger is looking for.
5. At the end of the story, what does the stranger expect Sylvia to do? What course of action does Sylvia follow?

Interpret

6. What conclusions can you draw about Sylvia's **character,** from what you learn about her before she meets the young man?
7. Why do Sylvia's feelings toward the young man change?
8. What reasons does Sylvia have for wanting to help the stranger find what he is looking for? In your opinion, what reason matters the most to her?
9. What emotions do you think Sylvia experiences during her climb? How does she feel when she finally reaches the top?
10. **Theme Connections** What does the choice made by Sylvia reveal about her character and her values?

Evaluate and Connect

11. When Sylvia is high up in the pine tree, the narrator addresses her directly instead of speaking to the reader. How does this change in point of view affect your reading of the story?
12. What is your opinion of the young man? Would you have wanted to help him? Explain why or why not.
13. If you had been in Sylvia's situation, what choice do you think you would have made? Give reasons for your answer.
14. How does the author's use of **local color** (see page R7) affect your appreciation and enjoyment of the story? Give specific examples.
15. What environmental issues are raised in this story? Are these issues still relevant today? Explain your answer.

Literary ELEMENTS

Setting

Setting is the time and place in which the events of a story occur. "A White Heron" takes place in a rural area of New England, near the sea, probably in the late 1800s. The setting of a story often helps to create a particular atmosphere, or mood. For example, some reviewers have characterized the setting of this story as "benevolent and kind."

1. Do you agree that the setting of this story is "benevolent and kind"? Why or why not? What other words might you use to characterize the setting? Support your ideas with evidence from the story.
2. In your opinion, is the setting of this story essential to the plot? In other words, could this story occur in a different place? In a different time? Explain.

- See **Literary Terms Handbook,** p. R11.

Literature and Writing

Writing About Literature

Is It an Allegory? "A White Heron" can be read as an **allegory** in which the characters and events represent ideas and concepts that go beyond the literal meaning of the story. Write a paragraph about what you think the characters and events in this story might represent and why you think as you do. Compare your ideas with those of several classmates.

Creative Writing

Nature Journal As a nature lover, Sylvia may have kept a journal to record her observations of the natural world. Imagine that you are Sylvia. Write one or two entries in your nature journal using sensory details from the story. Describe not only what you perceive through your five senses but also the emotions that you experience.

Extending Your Response

Literature Groups

Debating a Character's Choice Do you think Sylvia made the right choice? Debate this issue with your group. Justify your opinion with evidence from the story or from your own experience. Feel free to ask fellow group members to do the same. Then tally the opinions of your group. Share the results with the class.

Interdisciplinary Activity

History Research the attitudes of Americans toward nature and the environment in the late 1800s and early 1900s. Find out what conservation laws were enacted during this era. Share what you learn with the class.

Internet Connection

Birds of a Feather Check out Web sites of the National Audubon Society or of a large university in your area to find out what birds are indigenous to your region. With a partner, make a poster with drawings or photographs of at least several of these birds. List information related to their nesting habits, diet, migratory patterns, and so on. Display the poster in the classroom.

Reading Further

If you would like to read more by Sarah Orne Jewett, you might enjoy these works:

Short Story Collection: *The King of Folly Island and Other People* contains stories that depict women as the guardians of community.

Novels: *The Country of the Pointed Firs* features a Maine village and its people.

A Country Doctor relates the conflicts of a woman physician.

Save your work for your portfolio.

Literary Criticism

"In 'A White Heron', . . ." writes one critic, "Jewett lodged a strong protest against the limitations women faced in society and literature. She reworked the conventional female bildungsroman [growing-up story], which typically ends in marriage or capitulation to a patriarchal and capitalist society." With a group of classmates, discuss the following questions: How does Sylvia move beyond traditional limitations? Does she have any regrets? Do you think Jewett's main purpose was to "lodge a strong protest"? Support your ideas with evidence from the selection.

GRAMMAR AND LANGUAGE • Using Semicolons

Good writers vary the length and structure of their sentences. One way to do this is to use a semicolon to join two shorter, related sentences to make a longer one. See how the author combined these two short sentences with a semicolon in "A White Heron."

The good woman suspected that Sylvia loitered occasionally on her own account; there never was such a child for straying about out-of-doors since the world was made!

She could have written this as two sentences.

The good woman suspected that Sylvia loitered occasionally on her own account.

There never was such a child for straying about out-of-doors since the world was made!

PRACTICE Review a piece of your own writing. Find passages where the flow of the writing could be improved by combining short sentences with related ideas. Then, using a semicolon to join those sentences, rewrite the passages.

- For more about semicolons, see **Language Handbook,** p. R47.

READING AND THINKING • Cause and Effect

Events in a story sometimes have a cause-and-effect relationship–that is, one event may be the **cause** of a second event, the **effect.** In "A White Heron," Sylvia's cow hides from her when it is time to go home (cause). As a result, Sylvia spends a lot of time hunting for the cow (effect). Sometimes an effect may be the cause of yet another event. Because Sylvia spends so much time looking for her cow (cause), she arrives home late (effect).

PRACTICE On your paper, write the effect of each cause or the cause of each effect listed.

1. **Cause:** The stranger sees a white heron near Mrs. Tilley's farm.
2. **Effect:** Sylvia leaves the house before daybreak.
3. **Cause:** Sylvia climbs to the top of the old pine tree.
4. **Effect:** The stranger goes away.

- For more about cause and effect, see **Reading Handbook,** pp. R78–R107.

VOCABULARY • Multiple-Meaning Words

Many words have more than one meaning. Some, such as *gravity,* have meanings so different from each other that they're unlikely to be confusing. Other words have several meanings that are extremely similar. For example, *rebuke* can be a verb or a noun; *vexed* can be a verb or an adjective, but in either case, the meanings are similar. Then there are words like *giddy,* for which you need to consider the context to determine the meaning.

In "A White Heron," *giddy* means "causing dizziness," but *giddy* can also mean "dizzy" or "lightheartedly silly." If the reference is to "a giddy height," you know *giddy* must mean "causing dizziness." A giddy smile, on the other hand, might mean that the smiler is dizzy, or that the smile itself is silly. You would need to keep reading and hope for enough context clues to make the meaning clear.

PRACTICE Each pair of phrases below uses the same word, once with a meaning that is probably familiar to you and once with a meaning that may not be familiar. For each pair, write two sentences using the underlined word, one with each meaning.

1. a. entertain a child   b. entertain a thought
2. a. offensive remark   b. on the offensive
3. a. a bad temper   b. temper the criticism

Before You Read

The Boar Hunt

Reading Focus

Have you ever had an experience that completely changed your attitude toward something? Perhaps you were injured while playing a dangerous sport, and you vowed never to play that sport again.

Journal Write about an experience that completely changed your attitude toward something. Explain how your outlook changed.

Setting a Purpose Read to learn what changes a hunter's attitude toward his sport.

Building Background

The Time and Place

"The Boar Hunt" takes place in the not-too-distant past, in a remote, unexplored jungle in Peru.

Did You Know?

Wild boars are wild hogs with razor-sharp tusks, pointy ears, straight tails, and a hard, thick hide covering their chests. They weigh an average of 200 pounds, although some may weigh as much as 500 pounds. Wild boars run much faster than domestic hogs and are naturally aggressive toward other creatures, including humans. The prospect of bagging a wild boar—despite the danger, or perhaps because of it—has challenged hunters since ancient times.

Vocabulary Preview

rejuvenate (ri jo͞o′ və nāt′) *v.* to make fresh or young again; p. 158
lethargy (leth′ ər jē) *n.* sluggish inactivity or drowsiness; p. 159
impotent (im′ pət ənt) *adj.* ineffective, powerless, or helpless; p. 160
horde (hôrd) *n.* a large group; multitude; p. 160
tenaciously (ti nā′ shəs lē) *adv.* stubbornly; persistently; p. 160
sporadic (spə rad′ ik) *adj.* irregular; occasional; p. 160
atonement (ə tōn′ mənt) *n.* something done to make up for a sin, injury, or loss; p. 163
implicit (im plis′ it) *adj.* suggested but not directly stated; p. 163
infamy (in′ fə mē) *n.* extreme wickedness or shameful evil; p. 163

Meet José Vasconcelos

In 1908, a year after he had graduated from law school, José Vasconcelos (hō sā′ väs cōn sā′ lōs) joined the revolutionary movement that led to the eventual resignation of Mexican dictator Porfirio Díaz. A prolific writer, philosopher, politician, educational reformer, and university president, Vasconcelos helped Mexicans discover a cultural identity that stressed the dignity and nobility of their Indian heritage. His belief in the superiority of Mexican culture helped to awaken a spirit of national pride.

José Vasconcelos was born in Oaxaca, Mexico, in 1882. He died in 1959.
A Mexican Ulysses *is an abridged translation of Vasconcelos's autobiography.*

The Boar Hunt

José Vasconcelos
Translated by Paul Waldorf

WE WERE FOUR COMPANIONS, and we went by the names of our respective nationalities: the Colombian, the Peruvian, the Mexican; the fourth, a native of Ecuador, was called Quito[1] for short. Unforeseen chance had joined us together a few years ago on a large sugar plantation on the Peruvian coast.

We worked at different occupations during the day and met during the evening in our off time. Not being Englishmen, we did not play cards. Instead, our constant discussions led to disputes. These didn't stop us from wanting to see each other the next night, however, to continue the interrupted debates and support them with new arguments. Nor did the rough sentences of the preceding wrangles indicate a lessening of our affection, of which we assured ourselves reciprocally with the clasping of hands and a look. On Sundays we used to go on hunting parties. We roamed the fertile glens, stalking, generally with poor results, the game of the warm region around the coast, or we entertained ourselves killing birds that flew in the sunlight during the siesta hour.

1. Perhaps he was called this because *Quito* (kē′ tō) is the capital of Ecuador.

We came to be tireless wanderers and excellent marksmen. Whenever we climbed a hill and gazed at the imposing range of mountains in the interior, its attractiveness stirred us and we wanted to climb it. What attracted us more was the trans-Andean[2] region: fertile plateaus extending on the other side of the range in the direction of the Atlantic toward the immense land of Brazil. It was as if primitive nature called us to her breast. The vigor of the fertile, untouched jungles promised to rejuvenate our minds, the same vigor which rejuvenates the strength and the thickness of the trees each year. At times we devised crazy plans. As with all things that are given a lot of thought, these schemes generally materialized. Ultimately nature and events are largely what our imaginations make them out to be. And so we went ahead planning and acting. At the end of the year, with arranged vacations, accumulated money, good rifles, abundant munitions, stone- and mudproof boots, four hammocks, and a half dozen faithful Indians, our caravan descended the Andean slopes, leading to the endless green ocean.

Did You Know?
The *Marañón* (mä′ rə nyōn′) *River* runs through northeast Peru and flows into the Amazon.

At last we came upon a village at the edge of the Marañón River. Here we changed our safari. The region we were going to penetrate had no roads. It was unexplored underbrush into which we could enter only by going down the river in a canoe. In time we came to the area where we proposed to carry out the purpose of our journey, the hunting of wild boars.

We had been informed that boars travel in herds of several thousands, occupying a region, eating grass and staying together, exploiting the grazing areas, organized just like an army. They are very easy to kill if one attacks them when they are scattered out satisfying their appetites—an army given over to the delights of victory. When they march about hungry, on the other hand, they are usually vicious. In our search we glided down river between imposing jungles with our provisions and the company of three faithful Indian oarsmen.

One morning we stopped at some huts near the river. Thanks to the information gathered there, we decided to disembark a little farther on in order to spend the night on land and continue the hunt for the boars in the thicket the following day.

Sheltered in a backwater, we came ashore, and after a short exploration found a clearing in which to make camp. We unloaded the provisions and the rifles, tied the boat securely, then with the help of the Indians set up our camp one half kilometer from the river bank. In marking the path to the landing, we were careful not to lose ourselves in the thicket. The Indians withdrew toward their huts, promising to return two days later. At dawn we would set out in search of the prey.

Though night had scarcely come and the heat was great, we gathered at the fire to see each other's faces, to look instinctively for protection. We talked a little, smoked, confessed to being tired, and decided to go to bed. Each hammock had been tied by one end to a single tree, firm though not very thick in the trunk. Stretching out from this

2. The prefix *trans-* means "across, through, or over." Here, *trans-Andean* refers to the Andes Mountains.

Vocabulary
rejuvenate (ri jo͞o′ və nāt′) *v.* to make fresh or young again

Selva, 1981. Luis Monje. Oil on canvas, 51⅛ x 67 in. Private collection.
Viewing the painting: What elements of this painting reflect the sense of foreboding in the story?

axis in different directions, the hammocks were supported by the other end on other trunks. Each of us carried his rifle, cartridges, and some provisions which couldn't remain exposed on the ground. The sight of the weapons made us consider the place where we were, surrounded by the unknown. A slight feeling of terror made us laugh, cough, and talk. But fatigue overcame us, that heavy fatigue which compels the soldier to scorn danger, to put down his rifle, and to fall asleep though the most persistent enemy pursues him. We scarcely noticed the supreme grandeur of that remote tropical night.

I don't know whether it was the light of the magnificent dawn or the strange noises which awakened me and made me sit up in my hammock and look carefully at my surroundings. I saw nothing but the awakening of that life which at night falls into the lethargy of the jungle. I called my sleeping companions and, alert and seated in our hanging beds, we

Vocabulary
lethargy (leth′ ər jē) *n.* sluggish inactivity or drowsiness

dressed ourselves. We were preparing to jump to the ground when we clearly heard a somewhat distant, sudden sound of rustling branches. Since it did not continue, however, we descended confidently, washed our faces with water from our canteens, and slowly prepared and enjoyed breakfast. By about 11:00 in the morning we were armed and bold and preparing to make our way through the jungle.

But then the sound again. Its persistence and proximity in the thicket made us change our minds. An instinct made us take refuge in our hammocks. We cautiously moved our cartridges and rifles into them again, and without consulting each other we agreed on the idea of putting our provisions safely away. We passed them up into the hammocks, and we ourselves finally climbed in. Stretched out face down, comfortably suspended with rifles in hand, we did not have to wait long. Black, agile boars quickly appeared from all directions. We welcomed them with shouts of joy and well-aimed shots. Some fell immediately, giving comical snorts, but many more came out of the jungle. We shot again, spending all the cartridges in the magazine.[3] Then we stopped to reload. Finding ourselves safe in the height of our hammocks, we continued after a pause.

We counted dozens of them. At a glance we made rapid calculations of the magnitude of the destruction, while the boars continued to come out of the jungle in uncountable numbers. Instead of going on their way or fleeing, they seemed confused. All of them emerged from the jungle where it was easy for us to shoot them. Occasionally we had to stop firing because the frequent shooting heated the barrels of our rifles. While they were cooling we smoked and were able to joke, celebrating our good fortune. The impotent anger of the boars amazed us. They raised their tusks in our direction, uselessly threatening us. We laughed at their snorts, quietly aimed at those who were near, and Bang! a dead boar. We carefully studied the angle of the shoulder blade so that the bullet would cross the heart. The slaughter lasted for hours.

At 4:00 P.M. we noticed an alarming shortage of our ammunition. We had been well supplied and had shot at will. Though the slaughter was gratifying, the boars must have numbered, as we had been informed previously, several thousands, because their hordes didn't diminish. On the contrary, they gathered directly beneath our hammocks in increasing groups. They slashed furiously at the trunk of the tree which held the four points of the hammocks. The marks of the tusks remained on the hard bark. Not without a certain fear we watched them gather compactly, tenaciously, in tight masses against the resisting trunk. We wondered what would happen to a man who fell within their reach. Our shots were now sporadic, well aimed, carefully husbanded.[4] They did not drive away the aggressive beasts, but only redoubled their fury. One of us ironically noted that from being the attackers we had gone on the defensive. We did not laugh very long at the joke. Now we hardly shot at all. We needed to save our cartridges.

3. A *magazine* is the supply chamber from which cartridges are fed into the firing chamber.

4. To *husband* something is to manage it in a careful, economic way.

Vocabulary

impotent (im′ pət ənt) *adj.* ineffective, powerless, or helpless
horde (hôrd) *n.* a large group; multitude
tenaciously (ti nā′ shəs lē) *adv.* stubbornly; persistently
sporadic (spə rad′ ik) *adj.* irregular; occasional

The afternoon waned and evening came upon us. After consulting each other, we decided to eat in our hammocks. We applauded ourselves for taking the food up—meat, bread, and bottles of water. Stretching ourselves on our hammocks, we passed things to each other, sharing what we needed. The boars deafened us with their angry snorts.

After eating, we began to feel calm. We lit cigars. Surely the boars would go. Their numbers were great, but they would finally leave peacefully. As we said so, however, we looked with greedy eyes at the few unused cartridges that remained. Our enemies, like enormous angry ants, stirred beneath us, encouraged by the ceasing of our fire. From time to time we carefully aimed and killed one or two of them, driving off the huge group of uselessly enraged boars at the base of the trunk which served as a prop for our hammocks.

Night enveloped us almost without our noticing the change from twilight. Anxiety also overtook us. When would the cursed boars leave? Already there were enough dead to serve as trophies to several dozen hunters. Our feat would be talked about; we had to show ourselves worthy of such fame. Since there was nothing else to do, it was necessary to sleep. Even if we had had enough bullets it would have been impossible to continue the fight in the darkness. It occurred to us to start a fire to drive the herd off with flames, but apart from the fact that we couldn't leave the place in which we were suspended, there were no dry branches in the lush forest. Finally, we slept.

We woke up a little after midnight. The darkness was profound, but the well-known noise made us aware that our enemies were still there. We imagined they must be the last ones which were leaving, however. If a good army needs several hours to break camp and march off, what can be expected of a vile army of boars but disorder and delay? The following morning we would fire upon the stragglers, but this painful thought bothered us: they were in large and apparently active numbers. What were they up to? Why didn't they leave? We thus spent long hours of worry. Dawn finally came, splendid in the sky but noisy in the jungle still enveloped inwardly in shadows. We eagerly waited for the sun to penetrate the foliage in order to survey the appearance of the field of battle of the day before.

What we finally saw made us gasp. It terrified us. The boars were painstakingly continuing the work which they had engaged in throughout the entire night. Guided by some extraordinary instinct, with their tusks they were digging out the ground underneath the tree from which our hammocks hung; they gnawed the roots and continued to undermine

them like large, industrious rats. Presently the tree was bound to fall and we with it, among the beasts. From that moment we neither thought nor talked. In desperation we used up our last shots, killing more ferocious beasts. Still the rest renewed their activity. They seemed to be endowed with intelligence. However much we concentrated our fire against them, they did not stop their attack against the tree.

Foresta Tropical 1 (Jungla), 1985. Armando Morales. Oil on canvas, 64 x 51 in. Private collection.

Viewing the painting: What emotions does the scene in this painting convey to you? How are they similar to the emotions depicted in the end of the story?

Soon our shots stopped. We emptied our pistols, and then silently listened to the tusks gnawing beneath the soft, wet, pleasant-smelling earth. From time to time the boars pressed against the tree, pushing it and making it creak, eager to smash it quickly. We looked on hypnotized by their devilish activity. It was impossible to flee because the black monsters covered every inch in sight. It seemed to us that, by a sudden inspiration, they were preparing to take revenge on us for the ruthless nature of man, the unpunished destroyer of animals since the beginning of time. Our imagination, distorted by fear, showed us our fate as an atonement for the unpardonable crimes implicit in the struggle of biological selection. Before my eyes passed the vision of sacred India, where the believer refuses to eat meat in order to prevent the methodical killing of beasts and in order to atone for man's evil, bloody, treacherous slaughter, such as ours, for mere vicious pleasure. I felt that the multitude of boars was raising its accusing voice against me. I now understood the infamy of the hunter, but what was repentance worth if I was going to die with my companions, hopelessly devoured by that horde of brutes with demonlike eyes?

Stirred by terror and without realizing what I was doing, I hung from the upper end of my hammock, I balanced myself in the air, I swung in a long leap, I grasped a branch of a tree facing the one on which the boars were digging. From there I leaped to other branches and to others, reviving in myself habits which the species had forgotten.

The next moment a terrifying sound and unforgettable cries told me of the fall of the tree and the end of my companions. I clung to a trunk, trembling and listening to the chattering of my jaws. Later, the desire to flee gave me back my strength. Leaning out over the foliage, I looked for a path, and I saw the boars in the distance, marching in compressed ranks and holding their insolent snouts in the air. I knew that they were now withdrawing, and I got down from the tree. Horror overwhelmed me as I approached the site of our encampment, but some idea of duty made me return there. Perhaps one of my friends had managed to save himself. I approached hesitantly. Each dead boar made me tremble with fear.

But what I saw next was so frightful that I could not fix it clearly in my mind: remains of clothing—and footwear. There was no doubt; the boars had devoured them. Then I ran toward the river, following the tracks we had made two days before. I fled with great haste, limbs stiff from panic.

Running with long strides, I came upon the boat. With a great effort, I managed to row to the huts. There I went to bed with a high fever which lasted many days.

I will participate in no more hunts. I will contribute, if I have to, to the extermination of harmful beasts. But I will not kill for pleasure. I will not amuse myself with the ignoble[5] pleasure of the hunt.

5. *Ignoble* means "without honor or worth" or, since *ig-* is a negative prefix, "not noble."

Vocabulary

atonement (ə tōn′ mənt) *n.* something done to make up for a sin, injury, or loss

implicit (im plis′ it) *adj.* suggested but not directly stated

infamy (in′ fə mē) *n.* extreme wickedness or shameful evil

Responding to Literature

Personal Response

What emotions did you experience as you read this story? Did any of your reactions surprise you? Explain in your journal.

Analyzing Literature

Recall

1. Who are the main characters in this story? What has brought them together?
2. What preparations do the men make for their journey? What is the purpose of their journey?
3. Describe the location and layout of the camp that the men and their helpers set up.
4. Summarize what happens during the men's first full day in the camp.
5. At what point in the story do the men realize their fate? How do the narrator's actions determine his particular fate?

Interpret

6. What conclusions can you draw about the main characters from the way they spend their free time? Use evidence from the story to support your answer.
7. Rate the preparations the men make for their journey–*Excellent, Good, Fair,* or *Poor*–in terms of usefulness. Explain your rating.
8. In camp the first evening, what do the men's actions and thoughts seem to indicate about their attitude toward their surroundings?
9. How do the roles played by the men and the boars change as the story progresses? What causes these changes?
10. The narrator says, "I now understood the infamy of the hunter." What do you think he means?

Evaluate and Connect

11. What techniques does the author use to build suspense? Give specific examples from the story.
12. Explain how the **mood** of the story changes as the plot develops. (See Literary Terms Handbook, page R8.)
13. Explain how the terms "self-preservation" and "survival of the fittest" might be applied to this story.
14. How do you feel about what happened to the men? Do you think justice was served? Why or why not?
15. In your opinion, what is the moral, or lesson, that this story teaches?

Literary ELEMENTS

Point of View

Point of view is the relationship of the narrator, or storyteller, to the story. In "The Boar Hunt," the author uses first-person point of view–that is, the story is told by one of the characters, referred to as "I." The reader sees everything through the eyes of this character, who is a participant in the hunt.

1. How does the narrator's eyewitness description of events affect your emotional reaction to the story?
2. Imagine that a different character in the story had been the narrator. Explain how the story might be different when told from that narrator's point of view. For example, in what ways might the descriptions of the characters and events change?

- See **Literary Terms Handbook,** p. R9.

Literature and Writing

Writing About Literature

Cause and Effect Write a paragraph in which you trace the narrator's change in attitude toward hunting. Identify specific events from the story that cause this change. In a second paragraph, compare the narrator's experience with the one you described in the Reading Focus on page 156.

Creative Writing

Eyewitness Account Television talk shows often invite survivors of terrible ordeals to tell their stories. The host usually prepares questions that will lead the guest to tell his or her story. With a partner, write a script for a talk show starring the survivor of "The Boar Hunt."

Extending Your Response

Literature Groups

Coping with Life An important aspect of Mexican philosophical thought is the idea that human beings are destined to lead tragic lives dominated by conflicts that can never be totally resolved. An individual must learn to cope with conflicts that arise from chance and circumstance, as well as conflicts created by personal desires. In your group, discuss how these ideas might be applied to the characters in "The Boar Hunt."

Internet Connection

Know the Law In the United States, the hunting of wild game has caused the extinction or near extinction of several species of wild animals and birds, including the bison, passenger pigeon, and whooping crane. As a result, laws have been enacted in many states to limit the hunting of wild animals. Use the Web to research hunting laws in your region. Share your findings with the class.

Interdisciplinary Activity

Art: Create a Mural José Vasconcelos was part of a cultural movement in Mexico that supported muralists. How do you think a muralist might depict "The Boar Hunt"? Draw a sketch of your ideas. Meet with a small group of classmates to compare and discuss your sketches. Then work together to create a mural, using a large piece of art paper, or pieces of poster board taped together. Display your mural in the classroom.

Save your work for your portfolio.

VOCABULARY • Analogies

An analogy is a type of comparison that is based on the relationships between things or ideas. Some analogies are based on synonyms.

sluggish : slow :: lucky : fortunate

Sluggish is a synonym for *slow; lucky* is a synonym for *fortunate.*

To finish an analogy, decide what relationship exists between the first two things or ideas. Then apply that relationship to the second pair of words.

For more about analogies, see **Communications Skills Handbook,** p. R77.

PRACTICE Choose the word that best completes each analogy.

1. horde : mob :: farming :
   a. farmer b. agriculture c. land
2. rejuvenate : renew :: annoy :
   a. irritate b. avoid c. torture
3. mischief : infamy :: drizzle :
   a. sprinkle b. moisture c. downpour
4. exact : precise :: implicit :
   a. stated b. understood c. picky

Before You Read

Delicious Death

Reading Focus

Have you ever tried to convince a parent or someone else in authority that you were mature enough to participate in a particular activity? Perhaps you wanted to attend a concert with a friend, camp in the wilderness, or get a job.

Discuss Identify the activity in which you wanted to participate and list the arguments you used. As a group, discuss which argument seems the most convincing. Then tell whether your arguments were successful—did you get permission to do what you wanted to do?

Setting a Purpose Read to discover how a mother responds to her son's hunting experience.

Building Background

The Time and Place

The speaker of this poem is recalling a time in the recent past when she and her son lived in a mountainous region of the country.

Did You Know?

A traditional belief common to Native American cultures is that all things on Earth—humans, animals, plants, even rocks—are endowed with a living spirit. Although humans are given the privilege of hunting and using animals for food, shelter, and clothing, they must hunt only what they need for survival, as game animals are considered kindred spirits and a revered gift. Thus, in traditional Native American cultures, hunting is not a sport engaged in for amusement or to prove one's skill but rather a necessary and often dangerous occupation.

Meet Alma Luz Villanueva

In response to a thank-you letter from one of her readers, Alma Luz Villanueva said that it forced her to "acknowledge the paradox, the mystery of writing: that when we touch the most personal, the most hidden within ourselves, we touch the universal."

Villanueva grew up in San Francisco's Mission District where she was raised by her grandmother, a Yaqui Indian from Mexico. Her work shows influences of her combined Native American and Mexican heritage. Villanueva's books of poetry include *Bloodroot* and *The Ultraviolet Sky*, for which she won the American Book Award in 1989.

Alma Luz Villanueva was born in 1944 in Santa Barbara, California.

Delicious Death

Alma Luz Villanueva

to my son, Marc

Memory: You were fifteen in the mountains,
your friends were going hunting,
you wanted to go.

Cold, autumn day-sky of steel
and rifles, the shade of bullets. We
fought. I didn't want to let you go.

And you stood up to me, "My friends are
going, their parents let them hunt, like
am I some kind of wimp or what, Mom . . ."

We walked into Thrifty's to buy the bullets,
you would use one of their rifles—I imagined
you being shot or shooting another eager boy/man.

"What you kill you eat, do you understand?"
I stared each word into your eyes. As you
walked away, I said to the Spirits, "Guard

this human who goes
in search of
lives."

✲ ✲ ✲ ✲ ✲

You brought home four small quail.
I took them saying, "Dinner." I stuffed
them with rice, apples, baked them in garlic,
onions, wine. "Tonight, Mom?" "Yes, tonight."
I plucked the softest tail feathers and as you
showered, I placed them in your pillow case:

"May the thunder and
the prey be
one.

May the hunter eat
and be eaten in
time.

May the boy always
be alive in the
man."

✲ ✲ ✲ ✲ ✲

We ate, mostly, in silence—
I felt you thinking, I just
killed this, what I'm chewing . . .

On the highest peaks the first
powder shines like the moon—
winter comes so quickly.

On your face soft, blonde hair (yes, this
son is a gringo) shines like manhood—
childhood leaves so quickly.

The wonder of the hunt is on my tongue,
I taste it—wild, tangy, reluctant—
this flesh feeds me well.

I light the candles and thank the quail
in a clear voice—I thank them for their
small bodies, their immense, winged souls.

"God, Mom, you're making me feel like a
killer." "Well, you are and so am I."
Swallowing, swallowing this delicious death.

New Mexico in Winter, 1922. Carlos Vierra. Oil on canvas, 28 x 38 in. Courtesy of the Gerald Peters Gallery, Sante Fe.

Viewing the painting: What sort of mood does the mixture of pastels and rich greys in this painting create? Does the mood of the painting fit the mood of the poem?

Responding to Literature

Personal Response

Do you think the mother should have allowed her son to go hunting? Why or why not?

Analyzing Literature

Recall and Interpret

1. What argument does the son use in trying to persuade his mother to let him go hunting? Compare his argument with those you listed in the Reading Focus on page 166. What do you think is the real reason for the mother's decision?
2. What does the mother say to her son right before he walks away? Why do you think she says this?
3. Describe the ritual that the mother performs using the quail feathers. What is your interpretation of her prayer or chant?
4. How does the boy react to what his mother says and does at dinner? Do you think that she wanted him to react this way? Explain.

Evaluate and Connect

5. **Theme Connections** How does the mother's decision seem to change the way she looks at her son? Explain your answer.
6. What two **images** does the speaker create in lines 37–42? In your opinion, what do these images seem to suggest? (See Literary Terms Handbook, page R6.)
7. How does the mother feel as she eats her dinner? How do you think the boy feels? Do you think you would have had the same feelings if you had been in their place? Explain.
8. This poem includes some dialogue between the mother and son. In your opinion, does this dialogue sound real? Why or why not?

Literary ELEMENTS

Colloquial Language

Colloquial language is a type of language used in everyday speech but not used in formal speech or formal writing. Colloquial language sometimes differs from formal language in grammar, vocabulary, or pronunciation. The expressions "That's cool" and "I'm out of here" are examples of colloquial language. Writers use colloquial language to create an informal, conversational tone. Colloquial expressions are not considered slang, although they may contain slang words.

1. What examples of colloquial language can you find in "Delicious Death"?
2. How does the use of colloquial language affect your appreciation of the poem? Explain.

- See **Literary Terms Handbook,** p. R2.

Extending Your Response

Creative Writing

Guess What Happened at Dinner? Imagine a conversation the son might have with one of his friends the day after the quail dinner. Write a dialogue in which the son describes the events of the previous evening, as well as his feelings about those events. Include the comments and questions of the son's friend.

Interdisciplinary Activity

Biology: On the Quail Trail About twenty species of quail live in North America. Gather information about one species. In a small group, create a poster-sized chart displaying the facts your group has gathered about different species of quail. Illustrate your chart.

Save your work for your portfolio.

COMPARING selections

The Boar Hunt and Delicious Death

COMPARE **PURPOSES**

Both Vasconcelos and Villanueva use literature to make a statement about choices and consequences.

- What is similar about the authors' messages?
- How are the messages different?
- In your opinion, which message is stronger? Why?

COMPARE **ATTITUDES**

How do your attitudes about hunting compare with the attitudes of the characters in the two selections?

- In a small group, list five to ten survey questions about hunting animals in the wild. For example: *Should hunters be allowed to kill wild animals for sport?*
- Discuss how you think the narrator of "The Boar Hunt" and the mother and son in "Delicious Death" would answer the survey questions. Record the answers you think these characters would give.
- Have group members write down their own answers to the survey questions. Compile your survey results and share them with the class, comparing your groups' attitudes with those of the characters in the two selections.

COMPARE **MEDIA USE**

Gather copies of a variety of articles, photographs, paintings, posters, and advertisements about hunting, as well as tapes of TV and radio programs about this topic, if possible. Label the items and display them in a central location. Then, give a brief oral presentation to the class telling which items you find most effective for conveying information about the topic. Include your reasons for your choices.

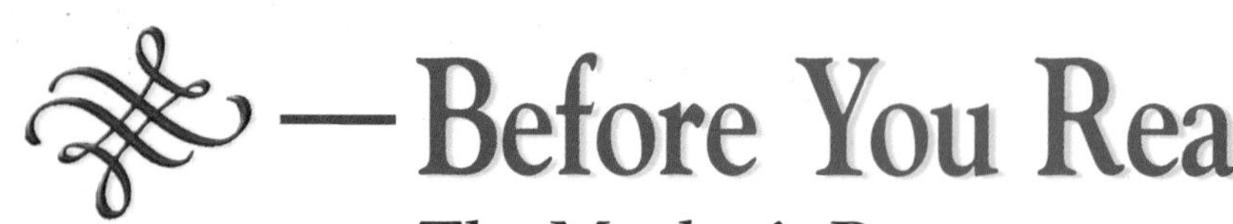

Before You Read

The Monkey's Paw

Reading Focus

What would you wish for if you could have three wishes granted? How might the granting of these wishes change your life and the lives of others around you? Would all the changes be positive?

Freewrite Make a list of wishes. Study the list and consider the possible consequences of each wish. Circle your top three wishes.

Setting a Purpose Read to learn how lives change when wishes are granted.

Building Background

The Time and Place

"The Monkey's Paw" takes place in Laburnam Villa, the cozy home of an elderly English couple and their grown son. It is probably sometime in the late 1800s.

Did You Know?

As this story opens, Mr. White and his son, Herbert, are playing chess, a board game for two players. Each player has sixteen pieces–a king, a queen, two rooks, two bishops, two knights, and eight pawns–to move strategically around the board. The game is won when one player attacks and then captures the opponent's king. A player usually announces the attack by saying "Check" and the final victory with the word "Checkmate."

Vocabulary Preview

amiably (ā′ mē ə blē) *adv.* in a friendly, good-natured way; p. 173
grimace (grim′ is) *n.* a twisting of the face; p. 175
presumptuous (pri zump′ cho͞o əs) *adj.* too forward; bold; p. 175
doggedly (dô′ gid lē) *adv.* stubbornly; firmly; p. 175
enthralled (en thrôld′) *adj.* fascinated; charmed; p. 176
credulity (kri do͞o′ li tē) *n.* a tendency to believe too readily; p. 176
prosaic (prō zā′ ik) *adj.* ordinary; commonplace; p. 177
avaricious (av′ ə rish′ əs) *adj.* greedy; p. 177
sinister (sin′ is tər) *adj.* threatening or suggesting evil; p. 178
oppressive (ə pres′ iv) *adj.* hard to bear; distressing; p. 181

Meet William Wymark Jacobs

William Wymark Jacobs, the son of an English wharf supervisor, was a bank employee and postal worker before he turned his writing hobby into a profession. Childhood memories of sailors and dock workers inspired the sea stories for which Jacobs became famous. He also wrote humorous stories and horror tales. "The Monkey's Paw"—the selection you are about to read—is the author's best-known story.

William Wymark Jacobs was born in London in 1863; he died in 1943. This story appeared in the collection The Lady of the Barge, *published in 1902.*

The Monkey's Paw

W. W. Jacobs

I

WITHOUT, THE NIGHT WAS COLD and wet, but in the small parlor of Laburnam Villa the blinds were drawn and the fire burned brightly. Father and son were at chess, the former, who possessed ideas about the game involving radical changes, putting his king into such sharp and unnecessary perils that it even provoked comment from the white-haired old lady knitting placidly[1] by the fire.

"Hark at the wind," said Mr. White, who, having seen a fatal mistake after it was too late, was amiably desirous of preventing his son from seeing it.

"I'm listening," said the latter, grimly surveying the board as he stretched out his hand. "Check."

"I should hardly think that he'd come tonight," said his father, with his hand poised over the board.

"Mate," replied the son.

"That's the worst of living so far out," bawled Mr. White, with sudden and unlooked-for violence; "of all the beastly, slushy, out-of-the-way places to live in, this is the worst. Pathway's a bog, and the road's a torrent. I don't know what people are thinking about. I suppose because only two houses on

1. *Placidly* (plas′ id lē) means calmly; peacefully.

Vocabulary

amiably (ā′ mē ə blē) *adv.* in a friendly, good-natured way the road are let, they think it doesn't matter."

"Never mind, dear," said his wife soothingly; "perhaps you'll win the next one."

Mr. White looked up sharply, just in time to intercept a knowing glance between mother and son. The words died away on his lips, and he hid a guilty grin in his thin gray beard.

"There he is," said Herbert White, as the gate banged too loudly and heavy footsteps came toward the door.

The old man rose with hospitable haste, and, opening the door, was heard condoling[2] with the new arrival. The new arrival also condoled with himself, so that Mrs. White said, "Tut, tut!" and coughed gently as her husband entered the room, followed by a tall burly man, beady of eye and rubicund of visage.[3]

"Sergeant Major Morris," he said, introducing him.

Frank John St. Jay, 1900. Thomas Eakins. Oil on canvas, 23⅞ x 19⅞ in. Fine Arts Museums of San Francisco. Gift of Mr. and Mrs. John D. Rockefeller, 3rd. 1979.7.7.

Viewing the painting: What does the posture of the man in the painting reveal about his character? How is this man similar to Sergeant Major Morris?

The sergeant major shook hands, and, taking the proffered seat by the fire, watched contentedly while his host got out whiskey and tumblers and stood a small copper kettle on the fire.

At the third glass his eyes got brighter, and he began to talk, the little family circle regarding with eager interest this visitor from distant parts, as he squared his broad shoulders in the chair and spoke of strange scenes and doughty[4] deeds, of wars and plagues and strange peoples.

"Twenty-one years of it," said Mr. White, nodding at his wife and son. "When he went away he was a slip of a youth in the warehouse. Now look at him."

"He don't look to have taken much harm," said Mrs. White politely.

"I'd like to go to India myself," said the old man, "just to look around a bit, you know."

"Better where you are," said the sergeant major, shaking his head. He put down the empty glass and, sighing softly, shook it again.

"I should like to see those old temples and fakirs[5] and jugglers," said the old man. "What was that you started telling me the other day about the monkey's paw or something, Morris?"

2. To *condole* is to express sympathy.
3. *Rubicund of visage* means reddish or rosy in the face.
4. A *doughty* (dou′ tē) deed is a brave or valiant one.
5. A *fakir* (fə kēr′) is a member of a Muslim or Hindu sect who takes a vow of poverty and lives by begging. Fakirs sometimes do extraordinary and dangerous tricks.

"Nothing," said the soldier hastily. "Leastways, nothing worth hearing."

"Monkey's paw?" said Mrs. White curiously.

"Well, it's just a bit of what you might call magic, perhaps," said the sergeant major offhandedly.

His three listeners leaned forward eagerly. The visitor absent-mindedly put his empty glass to his lips and then set it down again. His host filled it for him.

"To look at," said the sergeant major, fumbling in his pocket, "it's just an ordinary little paw, dried to a mummy."

He took something out of his pocket and proffered it. Mrs. White drew back with a grimace, but her son, taking it, examined it curiously.

"And what is there special about it?" inquired Mr. White as he took it from his son and, having examined it, placed it upon the table.

"It had a spell put on it by an old fakir," said the sergeant major, "a very holy man. He wanted to show that fate ruled people's lives, and that those who interfered with it did so to their sorrow. He put a spell on it so that three separate men could each have three wishes from it."

His manner was so impressive that his hearers were conscious that their light laughter jarred somewhat.

"Well, why don't you have three, sir?" said Herbert White cleverly.

The soldier regarded him in the way that middle age is wont[6] to regard presumptuous youth. "I have," he said quietly, and his blotchy face whitened.

"And did you really have the three wishes granted?" asked Mrs. White.

"I did," said the sergeant major, and his glass tapped against his strong teeth.

"And has anybody else wished?" inquired the old lady.

"The first man had his three wishes, yes," was the reply. "I don't know what the first two were, but the third was for death. That's how I got the paw."

His tones were so grave that a hush fell upon the group.

"If you've had your three wishes, it's no good to you now, then, Morris," said the old man at last. "What do you keep it for?"

The soldier shook his head. "Fancy, I suppose," he said slowly. "I did have some idea of selling it, but I don't think I will. It has caused enough mischief already. Besides, people won't buy. They think it's a fairy tale, some of them, and those who do think anything of it want to try it first and pay me afterward."

"If you could have another three wishes," said the old man, eyeing him keenly, "would you have them?"

"I don't know," said the other. "I don't know."

He took the paw, and dangling it between his front finger and thumb, suddenly threw it upon the fire. White, with a slight cry, stooped down and snatched it off.

"Better let it burn," said the soldier solemnly.

"If you don't want it, Morris," said the old man, "give it to me."

"I won't," said his friend doggedly. "I threw it on the fire. If you keep it, don't

6. *Wont* means accustomed; used. Different people (and dictionaries) are wont to pronounce it with a long *o*, a short *o*, or a short *u*.

Vocabulary

grimace (grim′ is) *n.* a twisting of the face
presumptuous (pri zump′ cho͞o əs) *adj.* too forward; excessively bold
doggedly (dô′ gid lē) *adv.* stubbornly; firmly

blame me for what happens. Pitch it on the fire again, like a sensible man."

The other shook his head and examined his new possession closely. "How do you do it?" he inquired.

"Hold it up in your right hand and wish aloud," said the sergeant major, "but I warn you of the consequences."

"Sounds like the *Arabian Nights*," said Mrs. White, as she rose and began to set the supper. "Don't you think you might wish for four pairs of hands for me?"

Her husband drew the talisman[7] from his pocket and then all three burst into laughter as the sergeant major, with a look of alarm on his face, caught him by the arm. "If you must wish," he said gruffly, "wish for something sensible."

Mr. White dropped it back into his pocket, and placing chairs, motioned his friend to the table. In the business of supper the talisman was partly forgotten, and afterward the three sat listening in an enthralled fashion to a second installment of the soldier's adventures in India.

"If the tale about the monkey paw is not more truthful than those he has been telling us," said Herbert, as the door closed behind their guest, just in time for him to catch the last train, "we shan't make much out of it."

"Did you give him anything for it, Father?" inquired Mrs. White, regarding her husband closely.

"A trifle," said he, coloring slightly. "He didn't want it, but I made him take it. And he pressed me again to throw it away."

"Likely," said Herbert, with pretended horror. "Why, we're going to be rich, and famous, and happy. Wish to be an emperor, Father, to begin with: then you can't be bossed around."

He darted round the table, pursued by the maligned[8] Mrs. White armed with an antimacassar.

Did You Know?
An *antimacassar* (an′ ti mə kas′ ər) is a small decorative covering put over the back and arms of a chair or sofa to prevent soiling.

Mr. White took the paw from his pocket and eyed it dubiously. "I don't know what to wish for, and that's a fact," he said slowly. "It seems to me I've got all I want."

"If you only cleared the house, you'd be quite happy, wouldn't you?" said Herbert, with his hand on his shoulder. "Well, wish for two hundred pounds, then; that'll just do it."

His father, smiling shamefacedly at his own credulity, held up the talisman, as his son, with a solemn face somewhat marred by a wink at his mother, sat down at the piano and struck a few impressive chords.

"I wish for two hundred pounds," said the old man distinctly.

A fine crash from the piano greeted the words, interrupted by a shuddering cry from the old man. His wife and son ran toward him.

"It moved," he cried, with a glance of disgust at the object as it lay on the floor. "As I wished it twisted in my hands like a snake."

"Well, I don't see the money," said his son, as he picked it up and placed it on the table, "and I bet I never shall."

"It must have been your fancy, Father," said his wife, regarding him anxiously.

7. A *talisman* is a charm believed to have magical powers.

8. If you are *maligned,* someone has spoken ill of you or told harmful untruths about you.

Vocabulary

enthralled (en thrôld′) *adj.* fascinated; charmed

credulity (kri do͞o′ li tē) *n.* a tendency to believe too readily

He shook his head. "Never mind, though; there's no harm done, but it gave me a shock all the same."

They sat down by the fire again while the two men finished their pipes. Outside, the wind was higher than ever, and the old man started nervously at the sound of a door banging upstairs. A silence unusual and depressing settled upon all three, which lasted until the old couple rose to retire for the night.

"I expect you'll find the cash tied up in a big bag in the middle of your bed," said Herbert, as he bade them good night, "and something horrible squatting up on top of the wardrobe watching you as you pocket your ill-gotten gains."

He sat alone in the darkness, gazing at the dying fire, and seeing faces in it. The last face was so horrible and so simian[9] that he gazed at it in amazement. It got so vivid that, with a little uneasy laugh, he felt on the table for a glass containing a little water to throw over it. His hand grasped the monkey's paw, and with a little shiver he wiped his hand on his coat and went up to bed.

His hand grasped the monkey's paw, and with a little shiver he wiped his hand on his coat and went up to bed.

II

In the brightness of the wintry sun next morning as it streamed over the breakfast table Herbert laughed at his fears. There was an air of prosaic wholesomeness about the room which it had lacked on the previous night, and the dirty, shriveled little paw was pitched on the sideboard with a carelessness which betokened[10] no great belief in its virtues.

"I suppose all old soldiers are the same," said Mrs. White. "The idea of our listening to such nonsense! How could wishes be granted in these days? And if they could, how could two hundred pounds hurt you, Father?"

"Might drop on his head from the sky," said the frivolous Herbert.

"Morris said the things happened so naturally," said his father, "that you might if you so wished attribute it to coincidence."

"Well, don't break into the money before I come back," said Herbert, as he rose from the table. "I'm afraid it'll turn you into a mean, avaricious man, and we shall have to disown you."

His mother laughed, and following him to the door, watched him down the road, and, returning to the breakfast table, was very happy at the expense of her husband's credulity. All of which did not prevent her from scurrying to the door at the postman's knock, nor prevent her from referring somewhat shortly to retired sergeant majors of bibulous[11] habits when she found that the post brought a tailor's bill.

"Herbert will have some more of his funny remarks, I expect, when he comes home," she said, as they sat at dinner.

9. To be *simian* is to resemble a monkey.

10. *Betokened* means "indicated."

11. A sergeant major or anyone else of *bibulous* (bib′ yə ləs) habits is fond of alcoholic beverages and drinks them regularly.

Vocabulary

prosaic (prō zā′ ik) *adj.* ordinary; commonplace
avaricious (av′ ə rish′ əs) *adj.* greedy

"I dare say," said Mr. White, pouring himself out some beer; "but for all that, the thing moved in my hand; that I'll swear to."

"You thought it did," said the old lady soothingly.

"I say it did," replied the other. "There was no thought about it. I had just—What's the matter?"

His wife made no reply. She was watching the mysterious movements of a man outside, who, peering in an undecided fashion at the house, appeared to be trying to make up his mind to enter. In mental connection with the two hundred pounds, she noticed that the stranger was well dressed and wore a silk hat of glossy newness. Three times he paused at the gate, and then walked on again. The fourth time he stood with his hand upon it, and then with sudden resolution flung it open and walked up the path. Mrs. White at the same moment placed her hands behind her, and hurriedly unfastening the strings of her apron, put that useful article of apparel beneath the cushion of her chair.

She brought the stranger, who seemed ill at ease, into the room. He gazed furtively at Mrs. White, and listened in a preoccupied fashion as the old lady apologized for the appearance of the room, and her husband's coat, a garment which he usually reserved for the garden. She then waited patiently for him to broach[12] his business, but he was at first strangely silent.

"I—was asked to call," he said at last, and stooped and picked a piece of cotton from his trousers. "I came from Maw and Meggins."

The old lady started. "Is anything the matter?" she asked breathlessly. "Has anything happened to Herbert? What is it? What is it?"

Her husband interposed. "There, there, Mother," he said hastily. "Sit down and don't jump to conclusions. You've not brought bad news, I'm sure, sir," and he eyed the other wistfully.

"I'm sorry—" began the visitor.

"Is he hurt?" demanded the mother wildly.

The visitor bowed in assent. "Badly hurt," he said quietly, "but he is not in any pain."

"Oh, thank God!" said the old woman, clasping her hands. "Thank God for that! Thank—"

She broke off suddenly as the sinister meaning of the assurance dawned upon her and she saw the awful confirmation of her fears in the other's averted face. She caught her breath, and turning to her husband, laid her trembling old hand upon his. There was a long silence.

"He was caught in the machinery," said the visitor at length, in a low voice.

"Caught in the machinery," repeated Mr. White, in a dazed fashion, "yes."

He sat staring blankly out at the window, and taking his wife's hand between his own, pressed it as he had been wont to do in their old courting days nearly forty years before.

"He was the only one left to us," he said, turning gently to the visitor. "It is hard."

The other coughed, and, rising, walked slowly to the window. "The firm wished me to convey their sincere sympathy with you in your great loss," he said, without looking around. "I beg that you will understand I am only their servant and merely obeying orders."

There was no reply; the old woman's face was white, her eyes staring, and her breath inaudible; on the husband's face was a look such as his friend the sergeant might have carried into his first action.

"I was to say that Maw and Meggins disclaim all responsibility," continued the other.

12. To *broach* a subject is to mention it for the first time.

Vocabulary

sinister (sin′ is tər) *adj.* threatening or suggesting evil

"They admit no liability at all, but in consideration of your son's services they wish to present you with a certain sum as compensation."

Mr. White dropped his wife's hand, and rising to his feet, gazed with a look of horror at his visitor. His dry lips shaped the words, "How much?"

"Two hundred pounds," was the answer.

Unconscious of his wife's shriek, the old man smiled faintly, put out his hands like a sightless man, and dropped, a senseless heap, to the floor.

The Old Version, 1881. Thomas Hovenden. Oil on canvas, 24 x 19 in. Fine Arts Museums of San Francisco. Gift of Mr. and Mrs. John D. Rockefeller, 3rd. 1993.35.17.

Viewing the painting: At what point in the story might Mr. and Mrs. White have resembled the couple in the painting? Explain.

III

In the huge new cemetery, some two miles distant, the old people buried their dead, and came back to a house steeped in shadow and silence. It was all over so quickly that at first they could hardly realize it, and remained in a state of expectation as though of something else to happen— something else which was to lighten this load, too heavy for old hearts to bear.

But the days passed, and expectations gave place to resignation—the hopeless resignation of the old, sometimes miscalled apathy. Sometimes they hardly exchanged a word, for now they had nothing to talk about, and their days were long to weariness.

It was about a week after that the old man, waking suddenly in the night, stretched out his hand and found himself alone. The room was in darkness, and the sound of subdued weeping came from the window. He raised himself in bed and listened.

"Come back," he said tenderly. "You will be cold."

"It is colder for my son," said the old woman, and wept afresh.

The sound of her sobs died away on his ears. The bed was warm, and his eyes heavy with sleep. He dozed fitfully, and then slept until a sudden wild cry from his wife awoke him with a start.

"*The paw!*" she cried wildly. "The monkey's paw!"

He started up in alarm. "Where? Where is it? What's the matter?"

She came stumbling across the room toward him. "I want it," she said quietly. "You've not destroyed it?"

"It's in the parlor, on the bracket," he replied, marveling. "Why?"

She cried and laughed together, and bending over, kissed his cheek.

"I only just thought of it," she said hysterically. "Why didn't I think of it before? Why didn't *you* think of it?"

"Think of what?" he questioned.

"The other two wishes," she replied rapidly. "We've only had one."

"Was not that enough?" he demanded fiercely.

"No," she cried triumphantly; "we'll have one more. Go down and get it quickly, and wish our boy alive again."

The man sat up in bed and flung the bedclothes from his quaking limbs. "You are mad!" he cried, aghast.

"Get it," she panted; "get it quickly, and wish— Oh, my boy, my boy!"

Her husband struck a match and lit the candle. "Get back to bed," he said unsteadily. "You don't know what you are saying."

"We had the first wish granted," said the old woman feverishly; "why not the second?"

"A coincidence," stammered the old man.

"Go and get it and wish," cried his wife, quivering with excitement.

The old man turned and regarded her, and his voice shook. "He has been dead ten days, and besides he—I would not tell you else, but—I could only recognize him by his clothing. If he was too terrible for you to see then, how now?"

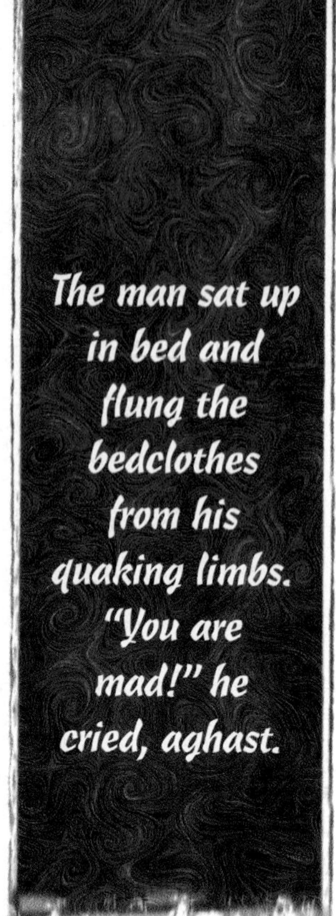
The man sat up in bed and flung the bedclothes from his quaking limbs. "You are mad!" he cried, aghast.

"Bring him back," cried the old woman, and dragged him toward the door. "Do you think I fear the child I have nursed?"

He went down in the darkness, and felt his way to the parlor, and then to the mantelpiece. The talisman was in its place, and a horrible fear that the unspoken wish might bring his mutilated son before him ere he could escape from the room seized upon him, and he caught his breath as he found that he had lost the direction of the door. His brow cold with sweat, he felt his way round the table, and groped along the wall until he found himself in the small passage with the unwholesome thing in his hand.

Even his wife's face seemed changed as he entered the room. It was white and expectant, and to his fears seemed to have an unnatural look upon it. He was afraid of her.

"*Wish!*" she cried, in a strong voice.

"It is foolish and wicked," he faltered.

"*Wish!*" repeated his wife.

He raised his hand. "I wish my son alive again."

The talisman fell to the floor, and he regarded it shudderingly. Then he sank trembling into a chair as the old woman, with burning eyes, walked to the window and raised the blind.

He sat until he was chilled with the cold, glancing occasionally at the figure of the old woman peering through the window. The candle end, which had burned below the rim of the china candlestick, was throwing pulsating shadows on the ceiling and walls, until, with a flicker larger than the rest, it expired. The old man, with an unspeakable sense of relief at the failure of the talisman, crept back to his bed, and a minute or two afterward the old woman came silently and apathetically beside him.

Neither spoke, but both lay silently listening to the ticking of the clock. A stair creaked, and a squeaky mouse scurried noisily through the wall. The darkness was oppressive, and after lying for some time screwing up his courage, he took the box of matches, and striking one, went downstairs for a candle.

At the foot of the stairs the match went out, and he paused to strike another, and at the same moment a knock, so quiet and stealthy as to be scarcely audible, sounded on the front door.

The matches fell from his hand and spilled in the passage. He stood motionless, his breath suspended until the knock was repeated. Then he turned and fled swiftly back to his room, and closed the door behind him. A third knock sounded through the house.

"*What's that?*" cried the old woman, starting up.

"A rat," said the old man, in shaking tones—"a rat. It passed me on the stairs."

His wife sat up in bed listening. A loud knock resounded through the house.

"It's Herbert!" she screamed. "It's Herbert!"

She ran to the door, but her husband was before her, and catching her by the arm, held her tightly.

"What are you going to do?" he whispered hoarsely.

"It's my boy; it's Herbert!" she cried, struggling mechanically. "I forgot it was two miles away. What are you holding me for? Let's go. I must open the door."

"Don't let it in," cried the old man, trembling.

"You're afraid of your own son," she cried, struggling. "Let me go. I'm coming, Herbert; I'm coming."

There was another knock, and another. The old woman with a sudden wrench broke free and ran from the room. Her husband followed to the landing, and called after her appealingly as she hurried downstairs. He heard the chain rattle back and the bottom bolt drawn slowly and stiffly from the socket. Then the old woman's voice, strained and panting.

"The bolt," she cried loudly. "Come down. I can't reach it."

But her husband was on his hands and knees groping wildly on the floor in search of the paw. If he could only find it before the thing outside got in. A perfect fusillade[13] of knocks reverberated through the house, and he heard the scraping of a chair as his wife put it down in the passage against the door. He heard the creaking of the bolt as it came slowly back, and at the same moment he found the monkey's paw, and frantically breathed his third and last wish.

The knocking ceased suddenly, although the echoes of it were still in the house. He heard the chair drawn back and the door opened. A cold wind rushed up the staircase, and a long loud wail of disappointment and misery from his wife gave him courage to run down to her side, and then to the gate beyond. The street lamp flickering opposite shone on a quiet and deserted road.

13. A *fusillade* (fyū′ sə läd′) is the firing of many guns in rapid succession or anything that resembles such a sound, as the knocks do here.

Vocabulary

oppressive (ə pres′ iv) *adj.* hard to bear; distressing

Responding to Literature

Personal Response

Consider Mr. White's actions at the end of the story. In his place, what would you have done? Give a reason for your answer.

Analyzing Literature

Recall

1. At what time of day does the story begin? Compare the weather outside with the atmosphere inside the parlor.
2. What is special about the monkey's paw that Sergeant Major Morris shows to the Whites? How do the Whites react to it?
3. What does Morris do with the paw after telling about its background? What does Mr. White immediately do?
4. What is Mr. White's first wish? What happens after he makes it? What is his second wish?
5. Summarize what happens after Mr. White makes the second wish.

Interpret

6. What is the **mood** at the beginning of the story? What details help to create this mood?
7. How does Morris feel about the paw? How do you know?
8. Do you think Morris regrets showing the monkey's paw to the Whites? Why or why not?
9. A situation is said to be **ironic** when what happens is the opposite of what is expected. What is ironic about Mr. White's first wish?
10. Why doesn't Mr. White want his wife to open the door? What do you think Mr. White's third wish is?

Evaluate and Connect

11. **Theme Connections** Do you think Mr. White's first wish was a sensible choice? Why or why not? Evaluate your wish list from the Reading Focus on page 172. Are your wishes sensible? Explain.
12. Before making his first wish, Mr. White says, "It seems to me I've got all I want." In your opinion, what point is the author making?
13. How does the author use **foreshadowing** to prepare the reader for the events to come (see page R5)? Give three examples.
14. Have you ever gotten something you wished for and then regretted that your wish was granted? Describe your experience.
15. In your opinion, what is the most unsettling aspect of this story? Explain your answer.

Literary ELEMENTS

Suspense

Suspense is a feeling of uncertainty, a sense that something disastrous is about to happen. Authors can build suspense through the characters' actions and words. For example, an ominous feeling is created when Morris throws the monkey's paw on the fire and Mr. White snatches it up. Suspense builds when Morris tells Mr. White, "If you keep [the paw], don't blame me for what happens." A description of the setting also can create suspense.

1. Look for examples of how the author creates suspense by telling what characters do or say. Find two examples of each.
2. In your opinion, what is the most suspenseful moment in the story? Explain your choice.

- See **Literary Terms Handbook,** p. R13.

Literature and Writing

Writing About Literature

Analyze Literary Techniques W. W. Jacobs was known for his ability to combine humor and a sense of adventure in his stories. Write a paragraph or two explaining how the author uses the elements of humor and adventure in "The Monkey's Paw." Describe how the use of these elements affects your appreciation and enjoyment of the story. Share and discuss your ideas in a small group.

Creative Writing

My Dear Friend Have you ever heard this old saying? "Be careful what you wish for, because you just might get your wish." Imagine that you are Mrs. White. Write a letter to a close friend, explaining the sad truth of this saying.

Extending Your Response

Literature Groups

Wasted Wishes? Mrs. White convinces her husband to make a horrifying second wish, which Mr. White then cancels out with the third wish. Do you think the Whites wasted their last two wishes? Why or why not? Is there something they could have wished for that might have eased the pain of their great loss? Or do you think the monkey's paw is such an evil thing that nothing but sorrow can come from it? Debate these questions in your group, supporting your ideas with evidence from the story. Share your opinions with the class.

Learning for Life

Horror Reviews Interview friends or family members about their favorite horror stories. Have them rate the "scariness level" of each story, using a rating scale you have created. For example: 1 = "Mildly scary–won't keep you up past your bedtime"; 5 = "Horrific–do not read at night or on a camping trip." Then make a pamphlet that includes the story titles, their ratings, and a brief review of each story. (Remember: Don't spoil the stories by giving away their endings!) Share the pamphlet with your classmates and then ask your school librarian to add it to the library's pamphlet file.

Performing

Drama "The Monkey's Paw" is often performed as a one-act play. If possible, obtain a script of the play version of this story or write a script of your own based on the text. Perform the play for other students, faculty, and family members.

Reading Further

If you would like to read other stories by William Wymark Jacobs, you might check out these books that contain stories about sailing and life at sea:

Many Cargoes
The Skipper's Wooing
Sea Urchins
Snug Harbour

You also might enjoy reading stories of suspense by other authors, such as Edgar Allan Poe and Nathaniel Hawthorne.

Save your work for your portfolio.

Literary Criticism

In "The Monkey's Paw," suggests Glenn S. Burne, "the consequences of acquiring the power to change destiny . . . are spelled out in nightmarish detail, with the implication that man does not have the knowledge or wisdom to control his own fate; he can only make things worse." As a class, find examples from the story to support Burne's interpretation. Do you agree with this explanation of the story? Why or why not?

Skill Minilessons

GRAMMAR AND LANGUAGE • Punctuating Dialogue

Read this dialogue between two characters from "The Monkey's Paw." Notice that the actual words spoken by the characters are enclosed in quotation marks and that the appropriate commas and end marks appear *inside* the closing quotation mark.

"I'd like to go to India myself," said the old man, "just to look around a bit, you know."

"Better where you are," said the sergeant major.

Did you notice that the tag lines, which identify the speakers, are set off by a comma or commas? Also, when a sentence within a quotation is interrupted by a tag line, the second part of the quoted sentence does not begin with a capital letter. When you write dialogue, remember to begin a new paragraph and use a new set of quotation marks each time the speaker changes.

PRACTICE Write a dialogue between Mr. White and Sergeant Major Morris in which the two men discuss Mr. White's three wishes. Be sure to punctuate your dialogue correctly.

● For more about punctuating dialogue, see **Language Handbook,** p. R47.

READING AND THINKING • Chronological Order

"The Monkey's Paw," like most short stories, is told in chronological, or actual time, order. The story is divided into three numbered parts, each of which corresponds to the two nights and one day on which the major events of the story take place.

● For more about related comprehension skills, see **Reading Handbook,** pp. R78–R107.

PRACTICE Copy the three headings listed below. Under each heading, list in chronological order the major events that occur in that part of "The Monkey's Paw."

I. A rainy night at Laburnam Villa
II. The next day
III. One night, ten days after Herbert's accident

VOCABULARY • Unlocking Meaning

When you learn a new word, your vocabulary rarely increases by only that one word. Many words share roots with other words. For example, knowing *credulity* gives you a good shot at understanding *incredulity, credible, incredulous, credibility, credence,* and *credo,* all of which have to do with beliefs or believability. The context in which each word appears will help you narrow down its possible meaning. (This isn't a foolproof system. If you put down a credenza, you're lowering a piece of furniture, not insulting a belief.)

PRACTICE Briefly state what you'd guess is the meaning of each underlined word.

1. Her calm and thoroughness made her a <u>credible</u> witness.
2. I wouldn't give too much <u>credence</u> to gossip if I were you.
3. All members of the group stood to recite its <u>credo</u>.
4. When I announced I'd received straight A's, Dad gave me an <u>incredulous</u> look.
5. The man's story was so bizarre that I found it <u>incredible</u>.

Writing Skills

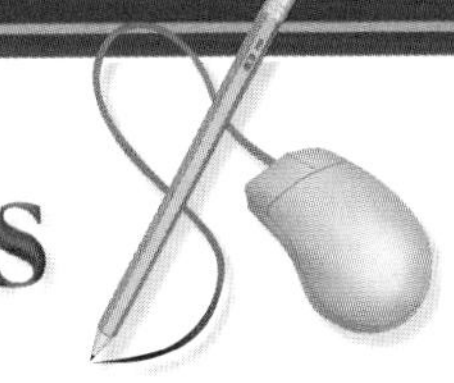

Creating Emphasis

To write persuasively, you must **emphasize,** or draw attention to, your most important ideas. Read the letter to the editor below to see how one writer makes a strong point about the factory mentioned in "The Monkey's Paw." Notice how the writer uses repetition and asks questions to create emphasis.

Dear Editor,

In your article about the work-related accident of a Maw and Meggins employee, the firm was applauded for offering money to the victim's family.

I am writing to say that Maw and Meggins should not be applauded for its actions in this matter. Instead, the firm should be forced to take responsibility for what went wrong with its machinery. Factories must be held accountable for the condition of their equipment. Factories must be held accountable for the safety of their workers. How else can job-related accidents be prevented? Money cannot replace someone's life.

The writer draws attention to the issue of responsibility by repeating the phrase *Factories must be held accountable* in two sentences. By asking the question *How else can job-related accidents be prevented?* the writer involves the reader in the argument by requiring an answer.

You might also try some of these other strategies for creating emphasis:

- Use short, simple, direct sentences.
- Use alliteration–that is, draw attention to important ideas by using words that begin with the same consonant sound.
- Use parallel construction, so that phrases or sentences with similar functions also have similar construction.
- Use inverted sentence order, placing the verb before the subject.

You don't need to use all of these strategies in one piece of writing. Choose the strategies that work best for your particular purpose and audience.

EXERCISES

1. Identify an issue that you believe in strongly. Then write an introductory paragraph for a letter to the editor about this topic. Ask a partner to read your paragraph and tell you which of your ideas come across most strongly. If these ideas aren't the ones that are most important to you, rewrite the paragraph.
2. Look through the letters to the editor sections of newspapers and magazines and notice when your attention is drawn to certain ideas. Make a list of at least four ways the letter writers have created emphasis. In your list, include examples from the letters.

Multimedia: Creating Hyperfiction

Hyperfiction is a fairly new kind of fiction made possible by the computer and hypertext software. Hyperfiction makes use of **hypertext** links–words, phrases, or buttons a reader can click on to display other documents. In hyperfiction, these hyperlinks lead to other parts of a story.

Hypertext and the Elements of a Short Story

Most short stories follow a pattern that can be diagrammed something like this:

Hypertext allows you to write a story that looks more like this:

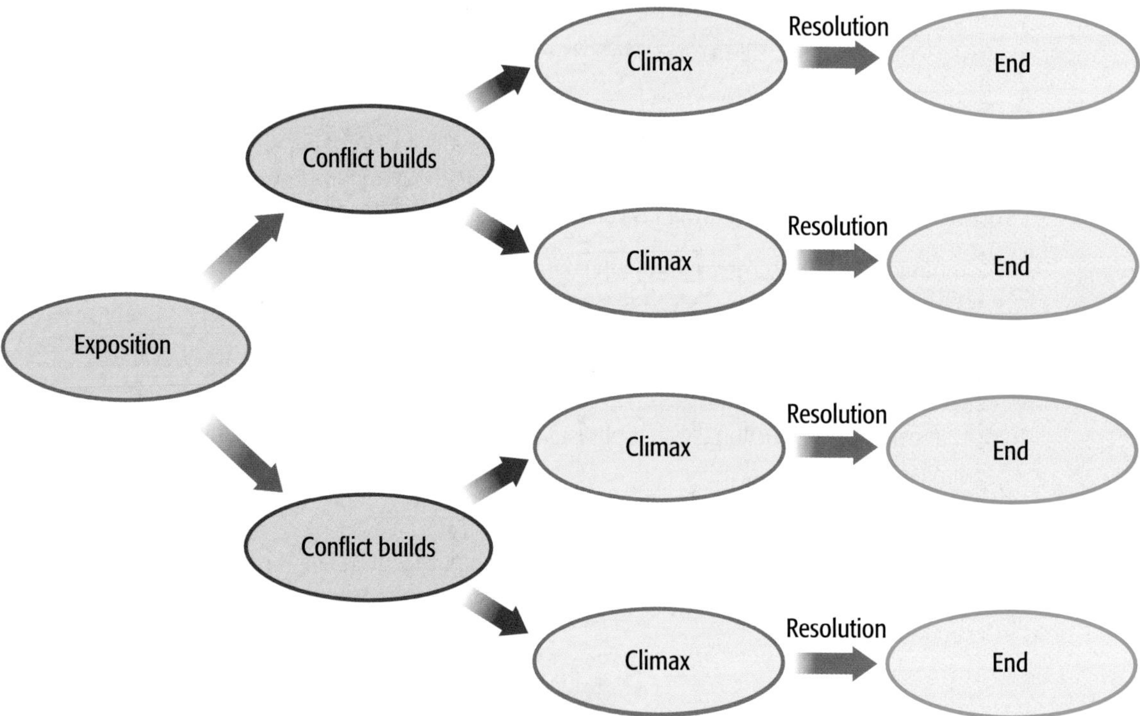

In the hypertext example above, the plot soon splits into two possible paths. As the conflict builds, each plot line splits again, leading to four different plot lines. The reader can follow any path he or she chooses to read one of four possible versions of the story.

This diagram is an extremely simple example of hyperfiction. There can be many more alternate paths, and paths can even lead back into one another. In addition, authors can include hyperlinks to flashbacks of earlier events, further descriptions of characters or scenes, changes in point of view, or any other variations. In really complex hyperfiction, it's possible that no two readers will ever read the exact same story.

Before You Get Started . . .

Think about what you did to get ready for school this morning. For each action, consider what you might have done differently and what effect each change could have had on your day. For instance, what if you hadn't eaten breakfast? Would you have stopped at a snack machine? If you had done so, might you have met someone there? How might that meeting have affected what you did next? Would that meeting have happened if you had eaten breakfast?

In your journal, write down possible scenarios for your day, including the results for all the alternate decisions that might have changed the course of your day. With a partner, share the scenarios you explored in your journals. Discuss how each decision might have led to a different unfolding of events.

ACTIVITIES

1. Work with a partner to create your own hyperfiction story.
   a. Together, decide on a title for an original short story.
   b. Create a plot line leading to four different conflicts, each one involving a personal decision. You may find it helpful to sketch out a diagram similar to the hypertext diagram on page 186 to show how the parts of your story will fit together.
   c. Using HyperCard, HyperStudio, or another hypertext program, create a card stack that takes readers on an interactive journey through your short story. Start with a title card and one or more cards that set the scene for the story. At the conclusion of your scene setting, include four buttons, each one leading the reader to a different conflict. Each conflict should lead to a climax, and each climax to a resolution.
   d. When you finish, ask another pair of students to read through your story and suggest ways the cards may be improved. Make changes as appropriate.
2. To further develop your hypertext skills, do one or more of the following:
   a. Write your own hypertext short story for inclusion in your electronic portfolio.
   b. Ask your teacher if you can complete your next creative assignment using a hypertext program.
   c. If you are comfortable with your hypertext program, explore other objects you can include in your card stack, such as movie clips, sound clips, pop-up objects, or animation.

TECHNOLOGY TIP

When you've completed your short-story project, save it on a disk or on the shared drive of your local area network. (Ask your lab instructor for directions on saving your work.)

Before You Read

Tuesday Siesta

Reading Focus

Have you ever experienced oppressively hot weather or become overheated while exercising or spending time in a hot, stuffy room?

Map It! Create a spider map to explore how oppressive heat made you feel. Surround the word HEAT with words and phrases that express your feelings. Continue branching out with additional details.

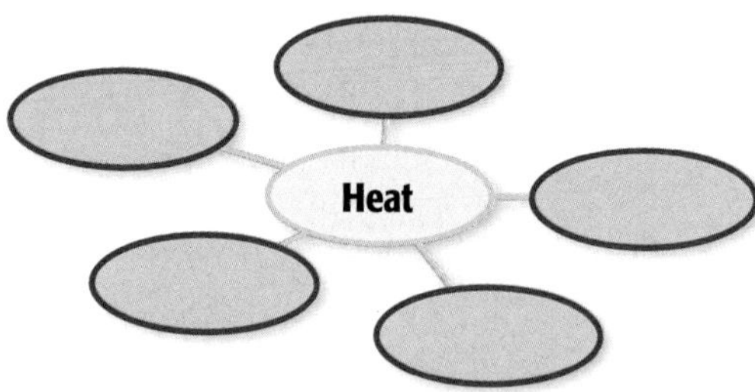

Setting a Purpose Read to learn the importance of time of day to the action in this story.

Building Background

The Time and Place

"Tuesday Siesta" takes place in a Latin American country, probably in the 1930s or 1940s.

Did You Know?

During the hottest part of the day in tropical or Mediterranean climates, people avoid heatstroke and sunstroke by taking a siesta. Siesta time usually begins around noon. Schools and shops close, and people enjoy a meal followed by several hours of resting. Later in the day, when the sun is not so hot, activities resume.

Vocabulary Preview

interminable (in tur′ mi nə bəl) *adj.* lasting, or seeming to last, forever; endless; p. 189

stifling (stī′ fling) *adj.* smothering; suffocating; p. 189

serenity (sə ren′ ə tē) *n.* calmness; peacefulness; p. 190

permeated (pur′ mē ā′ təd) *adj.* filled with; p. 191

scrutinize (skrōōt′ ən īz) *v.* to look at closely; inspect carefully; p. 192

inscrutable (in skrōō′ tə bəl) *adj.* mysterious; p. 193

skeptical (skep′ ti kəl) *adj.* having or showing doubt or suspicion; questioning; disbelieving; p. 193

Meet Gabriel García Márquez

"I had a fabulous childhood," García Márquez has said of his youth. He was raised by his grandparents, who "had an enormous house, full of ghosts. They were very superstitious. . . . It was a world of fantastic terrors." For García Márquez, the process of writing involves recovering experiences that are buried and then re-creating them in realistic and magical detail. He won the Nobel Prize for literature in 1982.

Gabriel García Márquez was born in Aracata, Colombia, in 1928 and has lived most of his life in Mexico City. This story was written in 1948.

Tuesday Siesta

Gabriel García Márquez
Translated by J. S. Bernstein

THE TRAIN EMERGED FROM THE QUIVERING tunnel of sandy rocks, began to cross the symmetrical, interminable banana plantations, and the air became humid and they couldn't feel the sea breeze any more.

A stifling blast of smoke came in the car window. On the narrow road parallel to the railway there were oxcarts loaded with green bunches of bananas. Beyond the road, in uncultivated spaces set at odd intervals there were offices with electric fans, red-brick buildings, and residences with chairs and little white tables on the terraces among dusty palm trees and rosebushes. It was eleven in the morning, and the heat had not yet begun.

"You'd better close the window," the woman said. "Your hair will get full of soot."

The girl tried to, but the shade wouldn't move because of the rust.

They were the only passengers in the lone third-class car. Since the smoke of the locomotive kept coming through the window, the girl left her seat and put down the only things they had with them: a plastic sack with some things to eat and a bouquet of flowers wrapped in newspaper. She sat on the opposite seat, away from the window, facing her mother. They were both in severe and poor mourning clothes.

The girl was twelve years old, and it was the first time she'd ever been on a train. The woman seemed too old to be her mother, because of the blue veins on her eyelids and

Vocabulary
interminable (in tur′ mi nə bəl) *adj.* lasting, or seeming to last, forever; endless
stifling (stī′ fling) *adj.* smothering; suffocating

Did You Know?
A *cassock* is the black, ankle-length garment traditionally worn by a Roman Catholic priest.

her small, soft, and shapeless body, in a dress cut like a cassock. She was riding with her spinal column braced firmly against the back of the seat, and held a peeling patent-leather handbag in her lap with both hands. She bore the conscientious serenity of someone accustomed to poverty.

By twelve the heat had begun. The train stopped for ten minutes to take on water at a station where there was no town. Outside, in the mysterious silence of the plantations, the shadows seemed clean. But the still air inside the car smelled like untanned leather. The train did not pick up speed. It stopped at two identical towns with wooden houses painted bright colors. The woman's head nodded and she sank into sleep. The girl took off her shoes. Then she went to the washroom to put the bouquet of flowers in some water.

When she came back to her seat, her mother was waiting to eat. She gave her a piece of cheese, half a corn-meal pancake, and a cookie, and took an equal portion out of the plastic sack for herself. While they ate, the train crossed an iron bridge very slowly and passed a town just like the ones before, except that in this one there was a crowd in the plaza. A band was playing a lively tune under the oppressive sun. At the other side of town the plantations ended in a plain which was cracked from the drought.

The woman stopped eating.

"Put on your shoes," she said.

The girl looked outside. She saw nothing but the deserted plain, where the train began to pick up speed again, but she put the last piece of cookie into the sack and quickly put on her shoes. The woman gave her a comb.

"Comb your hair," she said.

The train whistle began to blow while the girl was combing her hair. The woman dried the sweat from her neck and wiped the oil from her face with her fingers. When the girl stopped combing, the train was passing the outlying houses of a town larger but sadder than the earlier ones.

"If you feel like doing anything, do it now," said the woman. "Later, don't take a drink anywhere even if you're dying of thirst. Above all, no crying."

The girl nodded her head. A dry, burning wind came in the window, together with the locomotive's whistle and the clatter of the old cars. The woman folded the plastic bag with the rest of the food and put it in the handbag. For a moment a complete picture of the town, on that bright August Tuesday, shone in the window. The girl wrapped the flowers in the soaking-wet newspapers, moved a little farther away from the window, and stared at her mother. She received a pleasant expression in return. The train began to whistle and slowed down. A moment later it stopped.

There was no one at the station. On the other side of the street, on the sidewalk shaded by the almond trees, only the pool hall was open. The town was floating in the heat. The woman and the girl got off the train and crossed the abandoned station—the tiles split apart by the grass growing up between—and over to the shady side of the street.

It was almost two. At that hour, weighted down by drowsiness, the town was taking a siesta. The stores, the town offices, the public school were closed at eleven, and didn't reopen until a little before four, when the train went

Vocabulary
serenity (sə ren′ ə tē) *n.* calmness; peacefulness

back. Only the hotel across from the station, with its bar and pool hall, and the telegraph office at one side of the plaza stayed open. The houses, most of them built on the banana company's model, had their doors locked from inside and their blinds drawn. In some of them it was so hot that the residents ate lunch in the patio. Others leaned a chair against the wall, in the shade of the almond trees, and took their siesta right out in the street.

Keeping to the protective shade of the almond trees, the woman and the girl entered the town without disturbing the siesta. They went directly to the parish house.[1] The woman scratched the metal grating on the door with her fingernail, waited a moment, and scratched again. An electric fan was humming inside. They did not hear the steps. They hardly heard the slight creaking of a door, and immediately a cautious voice, right next to the metal grating: "Who is it?" The woman tried to see through the grating.

"I need the priest," she said.

"He's sleeping now."

"It's an emergency," the woman insisted.

Her voice showed a calm determination.

The door was opened a little way, noiselessly, and a plump, older woman appeared, with very pale skin and hair the color of iron. Her eyes seemed too small behind her thick eyeglasses.

"Come in," she said, and opened the door all the way.

They entered a room permeated with an old smell of flowers. The woman of the

1. A *parish house* is the home of the priest of a local church district.

Vocabulary

permeated (pur′ mē ā′ təd) *adj.* filled with

Campanario, c. 1947. Joaquín Torres-García. Oil on board laid down on panel, 13¼ x 16½ in. Private collection.

Viewing the painting: How does this scene help you envision the town during siesta?

house led them to a wooden bench and signaled them to sit down. The girl did so, but her mother remained standing, absentmindedly, with both hands clutching the handbag. No noise could be heard above the electric fan.

The woman of the house reappeared at the door at the far end of the room. "He says you should come back after three," she said in a very low voice. "He just lay down five minutes ago."

"The train leaves at three-thirty," said the woman.

It was a brief and self-assured reply, but her voice remained pleasant, full of undertones.[2] The woman of the house smiled for the first time.

"All right," she said.

When the far door closed again, the woman sat down next to her daughter. The narrow waiting room was poor, neat, and clean. On the other side of the wooden railing which divided the room, there was a worktable, a plain one with an oilcloth cover, and on top of the table a primitive typewriter next to a vase of flowers. The parish records were beyond. You could see that it was an office kept in order by a spinster.[3]

The far door opened and this time the priest appeared, cleaning his glasses with a handkerchief. Only when he put them on was it evident that he was the brother of the woman who had opened the door.

"How can I help you?" he asked.

"The keys to the cemetery," said the woman.

The girl was seated with the flowers in her lap and her feet crossed under the bench. The priest looked at her, then looked at the woman, and then through the wire mesh of the window at the bright, cloudless sky.

"In this heat," he said. "You could have waited until the sun went down."

The woman moved her head silently. The priest crossed to the other side of the railing, took out of the cabinet a notebook covered in oilcloth, a wooden penholder, and an inkwell, and sat down at the table. There was more than enough hair on his hands to account for what was missing on his head.

"Which grave are you going to visit?" he asked.

"Carlos Centeno's," said the woman.

"Who?"

"Carlos Centeno," the woman repeated.

The priest still did not understand.

"He's the thief who was killed here last week," said the woman in the same tone of voice. "I am his mother."

The priest scrutinized her. She stared at him with quiet self-control, and the Father blushed. He lowered his head and began to write. As he filled the page, he asked the woman to identify herself, and she replied unhesitatingly, with precise details, as if she were reading them. The Father began to sweat. The girl unhooked the buckle of her left shoe, slipped her heel out of it, and rested it on the bench rail. She did the same with the right one.

It had all started the Monday of the previous week, at three in the morning, a few blocks from there. Rebecca, a lonely widow who lived in a house full of odds and ends, heard above the sound of the drizzling rain someone trying to force the front door from outside. She got up, rummaged around in her closet for an ancient revolver that no one had fired since the

2. *Undertones* are underlying or implied meanings.
3. *Spinster* usually refers to an older woman who has never been married.

Vocabulary
scrutinize (skrōōt′ ən īz) *v.* to look at closely; inspect carefully

days of Colonel Aureliano Buendía,[4] and went into the living room without turning on the lights. Orienting herself not so much by the noise at the lock as by a terror developed in her by twenty-eight years of loneliness, she fixed in her imagination not only the spot where the door was but also the exact height of the lock. She clutched the weapon with both hands, closed her eyes, and squeezed the trigger. It was the first time in her life that she had fired a gun. Immediately after the explosion, she could hear nothing except the murmur of the drizzle on the galvanized roof. Then she heard a little metallic bump on the cement porch, and a very low voice, pleasant but terribly exhausted: "Ah, Mother." The man they found dead in front of the house in the morning, his nose blown to bits, wore a flannel shirt with colored stripes, everyday pants with a rope for a belt, and was barefoot. No one in town knew him.

"So his name was Carlos Centeno," murmured the Father when he finished writing.

"Centeno Ayala,"[5] said the woman. "He was my only boy."

The priest went back to the cabinet. Two big rusty keys hung on the inside of the door; the girl imagined, as her mother had when she was a girl and as the priest himself must have imagined at some time, that they were Saint Peter's keys.[6] He took them down, put them on the open notebook on the railing, and pointed with his forefinger to a place on the page he had just written, looking at the woman.

"Sign here."

The woman scribbled her name, holding the handbag under her arm. The girl picked up the flowers, came to the railing shuffling her feet, and watched her mother attentively.

The priest sighed.

"Didn't you ever try to get him on the right track?"

The woman answered when she finished signing.

"He was a very good man."

The priest looked first at the woman and then at the girl, and realized with a kind of pious[7] amazement that they were not about to cry. The woman continued in the same tone:

"I told him never to steal anything that anyone needed to eat, and he minded me. On the other hand, before, when he used to box, he used to spend three days in bed, exhausted from being punched."

"All his teeth had to be pulled out," interrupted the girl.

"That's right," the woman agreed. "Every mouthful I ate those days tasted of the beatings my son got on Saturday nights."

"God's will is inscrutable," said the Father.

But he said it without much conviction, partly because experience had made him a little skeptical and partly because of the heat. He suggested that they cover their heads to guard against sunstroke. Yawning, and now almost completely asleep, he gave them instructions about how to find Carlos Centeno's grave. When they came back, they didn't have to knock. They should put the key under the door; and in the same place, if they could, they should put an offering for the Church.

4. *Aureliano Buendía* (ou′ rā lyä′ nō bwān dē′ ä)

5. *[Ayala]* The young man's full name was Carlos *Centeno Ayala* (sen tā′ nō ä yä′ lə). In Spanish-speaking countries, one's first name and surname are, by custom, followed by the mother's maiden name.

6. *Saint Peter's keys* refers to the traditional belief of some Christians that Saint Peter is in charge of the keys to the gates of heaven.

7. The word *pious* (pī′ əs) may mean *either* having genuine reverence for God *or* having a false or hypocritical religious devotion.

Vocabulary

inscrutable (in skro͞o′ tə bəl) *adj.* mysterious

skeptical (skep′ ti kəl) *adj.* having or showing doubt or suspicion; questioning; disbelieving

Landscape with Figures (Paisaje con Figura). Arturo Gordon Vargas (1853–1933). Oil on canvas, 43 x 54 cm.

Viewing the painting: In your opinion, how are the characters in the painting similar to the woman and the girl in the story?

The woman listened to his directions with great attention, but thanked him without smiling.

The Father had noticed that there was someone looking inside, his nose pressed against the metal grating, even before he opened the door to the street. Outside was a group of children. When the door was opened wide, the children scattered. Ordinarily, at that hour there was no one in the street. Now there were not only children. There were groups of people under the almond trees. The Father scanned the street swimming in the heat and then he understood. Softly, he closed the door again.

"Wait a moment," he said without looking at the woman.

His sister appeared at the far door with a black jacket over her nightshirt and her hair down over her shoulders. She looked silently at the Father.

"What was it?" he asked.

"The people have noticed," murmured his sister.

"You'd better go out by the door to the patio," said the Father.

"It's the same there," said his sister. "Everybody is at the windows."

The woman seemed not to have understood until then. She tried to look into the street through the metal grating. Then she took the bouquet of flowers from the girl and began to move toward the door. The girl followed her.

"Wait until the sun goes down," said the Father.

"You'll melt," said his sister, motionless at the back of the room. "Wait and I'll lend you a parasol."

"Thank you," replied the woman. "We're all right this way."

She took the girl by the hand and went into the street.

Responding to Literature

Personal Response

Do you approve of the way the woman and the girl leave the parish house at the end of the story? Why or why not?

Analyzing Literature

Recall

1. How do the woman and the girl act on the train?
2. Describe what the woman and the girl see as they walk from the train station to the parish house.
3. Why do the girl and the woman go to the parish house?
4. What happened to Carlos Centeno?
5. What happens outside the parish house while the woman is inside?

Interpret

6. From the way the woman and the girl act, what can you infer about their relationship and about their journey?
7. Why might the woman have decided to arrive in town during the afternoon siesta?
8. How would you characterize the way the woman behaves when telling the priest who she is and why she is there? Do you find anything unusual about her behavior in those circumstances? Explain.
9. Carlos's mother refers to him as a thief but also tells the priest: "He was a very good man." What do you think she means by this? What details from the story support your opinion?
10. In your opinion, why do the woman and the girl leave the parish house right away, rather than waiting until later? What might happen to them after they leave?

Evaluate and Connect

11. Think about your response to the Reading Focus on page 186. Why do you think the author might have chosen such an oppressively hot day for the **setting** of the story?
12. How would you describe the relationship between Carlos, his mother, and his sister?
13. Do you have more sympathy for Carlos or Rebecca? Why?
14. Describe the moral code that Carlos's mother has taught him. Do you think her attitude is common in society today? Explain.
15. In your opinion, why might people hide their true feelings? Do you think any of those reasons apply to the woman in this story? Explain.

Tone

The **tone** of a story is the attitude the writer takes toward the story's subject. A writer selects language and details to create a desired tone. For example, a writer might describe a desert as "sunny, hot, filled with unexpected flowers" or as "scorching, arid, dangerous." In the first description, the tone is cheerful and appreciative; in the second, the tone is fearful.

1. Read the first four paragraphs that describe the initial setting of "Tuesday Siesta." Identify the tone and cite two or three phrases that seem to convey that tone.
2. List two phrases that introduce the woman and girl. Explain how these descriptions support or alter the tone of the story.
3. Examine the description on pages 192–193 of the night Carlos was killed. What details help convey the tone of this passage? Using specific details from the story, compare and contrast the tone of this passage with that of the rest of the story.

- See **Literary Terms Handbook,** p. R13.

Literature and Writing

Writing About Literature

Character Sketch Brainstorm a list of character traits that the mother in "Tuesday Siesta" exhibits. Next to each item, note a detail or incident from the story that illustrates this character trait. Use your notes to write a brief character sketch of the mother. Compare your sketch with those made by other students.

Creative Writing

Dear Father Imagine that you are the priest in this story. Write a letter to a fellow member of the clergy, describing the visit made by the mother and daughter. Be sure to describe not only what happened but also your reaction to the encounter.

Extending Your Response

Literature Groups

Evaluating a Character's Actions In your opinion, was it more honorable for Carlos to try to support his family by boxing or by stealing? Let each member of your group give an opinion about this question, and feel free to challenge your fellow group members to support their opinions with evidence from the story. Finally, tally up the group's responses and share the results with the class.

Interdisciplinary Activity

Art: Making an Illustration Imagine that you are riding the same train as the mother and daughter in this story. Illustrate something that you see as you look out of the window, or sketch a character or scene aboard the train.

Internet Connection

Location, Location, Location
Use the Internet to find which countries might be settings for this story. Find locations in Central or South America that have hot, dry climates and that supported a flourishing banana industry in the first half of the 1900s. Use other clues from the story to help focus your search.

Save your work for your portfolio.

Skill Minilesson

VOCABULARY • The Suffix *-ity*

Knowing how to use a single suffix can increase a person's vocabulary by a hundred words or so, all at once. For example, the suffix *-ity* means "state or condition." It turns adjectives into nouns.

The mother in "Tuesday Siesta" has *serenity*; therefore, she is *serene*. The weather is humid (an adjective); therefore, people feel the humidity (a noun). Just as with *-ing* endings, a final *e* drops off when *-ity* is added.

PRACTICE For each word shown below, write a sentence that uses the word correctly.

1. acidity
2. authenticity
3. durability
4. solemnity
5. continuity

For more about adding suffixes, see **Language Handbook,** Spelling, p. R55.

MEDIA connection

News Article

For some drivers, crossing a long bridge can be terrifying. In Michigan, acrophobic drivers have a helping hand.

Holiday Traffic Brings Out Fear on Suspension Bridge

by Thomas Bevier—*Gannett News Service*, May 28, 1994

DETROIT—Even an Upper Peninsula engineering professor can't look down when he drives above northern Michigan's Straits of Mackinac on the world's largest suspension bridge.

"I dread it," said Edward Fisher of Michigan Technological University in Houghton. "My feet tingle just thinking about it."

Panic attacks on the five-mile Mackinac Bridge can bring the truly frightened to a halt. Many people with acrophobia—fear of heights—can't drive from one Michigan peninsula to the other.

That's when a professional bridge-crosser slips behind the wheel. The Mackinac Bridge Authority provides free escort drivers.

"For some people, it's terrifying," said Operations Manager William Frazier. "Some of them put their heads between their legs and cry all the way across. Some try to grab you."

The span's peak season started this weekend, and even Frazier will take his turn helping dizzy drivers who request the service five to ten times a day.

"They keep us busy," he said. "We put on extra help in the summer."

Anyone needing a designated driver can call the Bridge Authority at or before driving onto the approach ramps. Patrol cars are on standby for dispatch to Mackinaw City or St. Ignace on the northern side. An employee will drive timid travelers across the span, which has a roadway rising nearly 200 feet above water.

Occasionally, motorists freeze and stop on the bridge—waiting until an escort arrives.

There is no stereotypical acrophobia victim.

"We get young people and old people," Frazier said. "Motorcyclists need help and so do even a few over-the-road truck drivers."

Dr. James R. Creps, a psychiatrist at the anxiety disorder center at Henry Ford Medical Center in Detroit, said the bridge is the toughest test for skittish sightseers.

Those who point at passing freighters as they drive across can't understand why anyone sees the trip as an ordeal, Creps said. But he stressed that the panic is vivid and real.

"They are overcome with fear of suffocation and of dying. They have trouble breathing. Something as awesome as the Mackinac Bridge can be overwhelming," Creps said.

"They may even realize that their fear is unreasonable, but they still can't control it."

Analyzing Media

1. What do you think it might be like to work as an escort driver on the Mackinac Bridge?
2. When faced with fear, how do you deal with it?

Before You Read

Contents of the Dead Man's Pocket

Reading Focus

What activity in your life gets your greatest effort, attention, and time? Is this activity also what matters most to you?

Chart It! Estimate how you spend your time over the course of an average day. Chart the time you spend on each activity. Which activity takes up the most time? Is this activity of great value to you?

Setting a Purpose Read to learn how a young man discovers what is most important in his life.

Building Background

The Time and Place
"Contents of the Dead Man's Pocket" takes place in New York City, probably sometime during the 1950s.

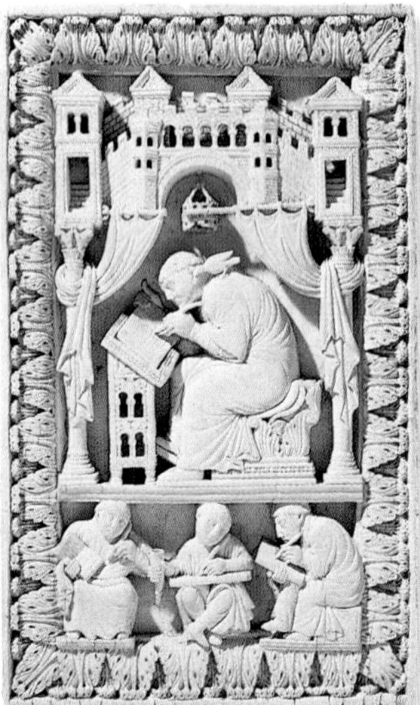

Did You Know?
At the time the story takes place, copies of documents typically were made by hand or with layers of carbon paper inserted between sheets of paper. Developments in copying and printing technology during the 1950s and 1960s led to photocopying as we now know it.

Vocabulary Preview

convoluted (kon′ və lo͞o′ təd) *adj.* turned in or wound up upon itself; coiled; twisted; p. 201
improvised (im′ prə vīzd′) *adj.* invented, composed, or done without preparing beforehand; p. 201
taut (tôt) *adj.* tense; tight; p. 204
spasmodic (spaz mod′ ik) *adj.* sudden, violent, and temporary; p. 204
deftness (deft′ nəs) *n.* the quality of being skillful and nimble; p. 205
pent-up (pent′ up) *adj.* not expressed or released; held in; p. 206
reveling (rev′ əl ing) *adj.* taking great pleasure; p. 207
unimpeded (un′ im pē′ dəd) *adj.* not obstructed; unblocked; p. 211

Meet Jack Finney

Although several of Finney's works have been made into movies, Finney himself shunned the limelight. Born in Milwaukee, Wisconsin, Walter Braden (Jack) Finney grew up in the Midwest. He did not begin writing fiction until he was thirty-five.

Although one of his best-known works is *Invasion of the Body Snatchers*, Finney did not consider himself a science fiction writer but rather a writer of fantasy who was most interested in ordinary people's responses to extraordinary situations. He developed this interest in the story you are about to read.

Jack Finney was born in 1911 and died in 1995. This story, from a collection called The Third Level, *was published in 1957.*

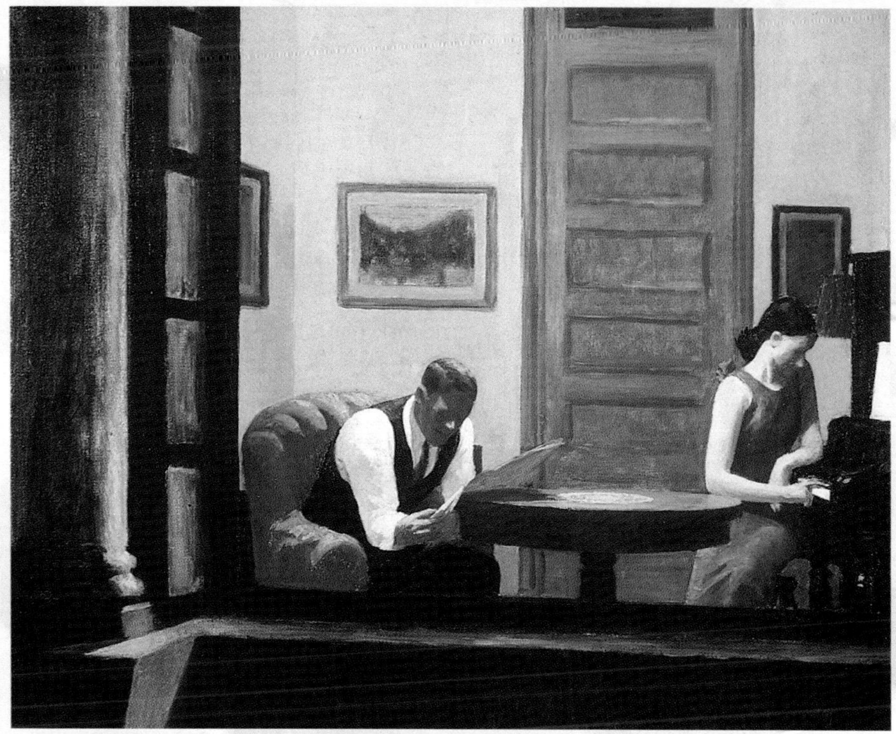

Room in New York, 1932. Edward Hopper. Oil on canvas, 29 x 36 in. Sheldon Memorial Art Gallery, University of Nebraska–Lincoln, F. M. Hall Collection. 1936.H-166.

Contents of the Dead Man's Pocket

Jack Finney

At the little living-room desk Tom Benecke rolled two sheets of flimsy and a heavier top sheet, carbon paper sandwiched between them, into his portable.[1] *Inter-office Memo*, the top sheet was headed, and he typed tomorrow's date just below this; then he glanced at a creased yellow sheet, covered with his own handwriting, beside the typewriter. "Hot in here," he muttered to himself. Then, from the short hallway at his back, he heard the muffled clang of wire coat hangers in the bedroom closet, and at this reminder of what his wife was doing he thought: Hot, hell—guilty conscience.

He got up, shoving his hands into the back pockets of his gray wash slacks,[2] stepped to the living-room window beside the desk and stood breathing on the glass, watching the expanding circlet of mist, staring down through the autumn night at Lexington Avenue, eleven stories below. He was a tall, lean, dark-haired young man in a pullover sweater, who looked as though he had played not football, probably, but basketball in college. Now he placed

1. Before the laptop computer, one might type on a compact, fairly lightweight typewriter called a *portable*.

2. *Wash slacks* are pants that, because they are cotton, can be washed instead of dry-cleaned.

the heels of his hands against the top edge of the lower window frame and shoved upward. But as usual the window didn't budge, and he had to lower his hands and then shoot them hard upward to jolt the window open a few inches. He dusted his hands, muttering.

But still he didn't begin his work. He crossed the room to the hallway entrance and, leaning against the doorjamb, hands shoved into his back pockets again, he called, "Clare?" When his wife answered, he said, "Sure you don't mind going alone?"

"No." Her voice was muffled, and he knew her head and shoulders were in the bedroom closet. Then the tap of her high heels sounded on the wood floor and she appeared at the end of the little hallway, wearing a slip, both hands raised to one ear, clipping on an earring. She smiled at him—a slender, very pretty girl with light brown, almost blonde, hair—her prettiness emphasized by the pleasant nature that showed in her face. "It's just that I hate you to miss this movie; you wanted to see it too."

"Yeah, I know." He ran his fingers through his hair. "Got to get this done though."

She nodded, accepting this. Then, glancing at the desk across the living room, she said, "You work too much, though, Tom—and too hard."

He smiled. "You won't mind though, will you, when the money comes rolling in and I'm known as the Boy Wizard of Wholesale Groceries?"

"I guess not." She smiled and turned back toward the bedroom.

At his desk again, Tom lighted a cigarette; then a few moments later as Clare appeared, dressed and ready to leave, he set it on the rim of the ash tray. "Just after seven," she said. "I can make the beginning of the first feature."

He walked to the front-door closet to help her on with her coat. He kissed her then and, for an instant, holding her close, smelling the perfume she had used, he was tempted to go with her; it was not actually true that he had to work tonight, though he very much wanted to. This was his own project, unannounced as yet in his office, and it could be postponed. But then they won't see it till Monday, he thought once again, and if I give it to the boss tomorrow he might read it over the weekend . . . "Have a good time," he said aloud. He gave his wife a little swat and opened the door for her, feeling the air from the building hallway, smelling faintly of floor wax, stream gently past his face.

He watched her walk down the hall, flicked a hand in response as she waved, and then he started to close the door, but it resisted for a moment. As the door opening narrowed, the current of warm air from the hallway, channeled through this smaller opening now, suddenly rushed past him with accelerated force. Behind him he heard the slap of the window curtains against the wall and the sound of paper fluttering from his desk, and he had to push to close the door.

Turning, he saw a sheet of white paper drifting to the floor in a series of arcs, and another sheet, yellow, moving toward the window, caught in the dying current flowing through the narrow opening. As he watched, the paper struck the bottom edge of the window and hung there for an instant, plastered against the glass and wood. Then as the moving air stilled completely the curtains swinging back from the wall to hang free again, he saw the yellow sheet drop to the window ledge and slide over out of sight.

He ran across the room, grasped the bottom edge of the window and tugged, staring through the glass. He saw the yellow sheet, dimly now in the darkness outside, lying on the ornamental ledge a yard below the window. Even as he watched, it was moving, scraping slowly along the ledge, pushed by the breeze that pressed steadily against the building wall. He heaved on the window with all his strength and it shot open with a bang, the window weight rattling in the casing. But the paper was past his reach and, leaning out into the night, he watched it scud[3] steadily along the ledge to the south, half plastered against the building wall. Above the muffled sound of the street traffic far below, he could hear the dry scrape of its movement, like a leaf on the pavement.

The living room of the next apartment to the south projected a yard or more farther out toward the street than this one; because of this the Beneckes paid seven and a half dollars less rent than their neighbors. And now the yellow sheet, sliding along the stone ledge, nearly invisible in the night, was stopped by the projecting blank wall of the next apartment. It lay motionless, then, in the corner formed by the two walls—a good five yards away, pressed firmly against the ornate corner ornament of the ledge, by the breeze that moved past Tom Benecke's face.

He knelt at the window and stared at the yellow paper for a full minute or more, waiting for it to move, to slide off the ledge and fall, hoping he could follow its course to the street, and then hurry down in the elevator and retrieve it. But it didn't move, and then he saw that the paper was caught firmly between a projection of the convoluted corner ornament and the ledge. He thought about the poker from the fireplace, then the broom, then the mop—discarding each thought as it occurred to him. There was nothing in the apartment long enough to reach that paper.

It was hard for him to understand that he actually had to abandon it—it was ridiculous—and he began to curse. Of all the papers on his desk, why did it have to be this one in particular! On four long Saturday afternoons he had stood in supermarkets counting the people who passed certain displays, and the results were scribbled on that yellow sheet. From stacks of trade publications, gone over page by page in snatched half hours at work and during evenings at home, he had copied facts, quotations and figures onto that sheet. And he had carried it with him to the Public Library on Fifth Avenue, where he'd spent a dozen lunch hours and early evenings adding more. All were needed to support and lend authority to his idea for a new grocery-store display method; without them his idea was a mere opinion. And there they all lay, in his own improvised shorthand—countless hours of work—out there on the ledge.

For many seconds he believed he was going to abandon the yellow sheet, that there was nothing else to do. The work could be duplicated. But it would take two months, and the time to present this idea, damn it, was *now*, for use in the spring displays. He struck his fist on the window ledge. Then he shrugged. Even though his plan were adopted, he told himself, it wouldn't bring him a raise in pay—not immediately, anyway, or as a direct result. It won't bring me a promotion either, he argued—not of itself.

But just the same, and he couldn't escape the thought, this and other independent projects, some already done and others planned for the future, would gradually mark him out from the score of other young men in

3. To *scud* is to run or move swiftly.

Vocabulary

convoluted (kon′ və lo͞o′ təd) *adj.* turned in or wound up upon itself; coiled; twisted

improvised (im′ prə vīzd′) *adj.* invented, composed, or done without preparing beforehand his company. They were the way to change from a name on the payroll to a name in the minds of the company officials. They were the beginning of the long, long climb to where he was determined to be, at the very top. And he knew he was going out there in the darkness, after the yellow sheet fifteen feet beyond his reach.

By a kind of instinct, he instantly began making his intention acceptable to himself by laughing at it. The mental picture of himself sidling along the ledge outside was absurd—it was actually comical—and he smiled. He imagined himself describing it; it would make a good story at the office and, it occurred to him, would add a special interest and importance to his memorandum, which would do it no harm at all.

To simply go out and get his paper was an easy task—he could be back here with it in less than two minutes—and he knew he wasn't deceiving himself. The ledge, he saw, measuring it with his eye, was about as wide as the length of his shoe, and perfectly flat. And every fifth row of brick in the face of the building, he remembered—leaning out, he verified this—was indented half an inch, enough for the tips of his fingers, enough to maintain balance easily. It occurred to him that if this ledge and wall were only a yard aboveground—as he knelt at the window staring out, this thought was the final confirmation of his intention—he could move along the ledge indefinitely.

On a sudden impulse, he got to his feet, walked to the front closet and took out an old tweed jacket, it would be cold outside. He put it on and buttoned it as he crossed the room rapidly toward the open window. In the back of his mind he knew he'd better hurry and get this over with before he thought too much, and at the window he didn't allow himself to hesitate.

He swung a leg over the sill, then felt for and found the ledge a yard below the window with his foot. Gripping the bottom of the window frame very tightly and carefully, he slowly ducked his head under it, feeling on his face the sudden change from the warm air of the room to the chill outside. With infinite care he brought out his other leg, his mind concentrating on what he was doing. Then he slowly stood erect. Most of the putty, dried out and brittle, had dropped off the bottom edging of the window frame, he found, and the flat wooden edging provided a good gripping surface, a half inch or more deep, for the tips of his fingers.

Now, balanced easily and firmly, he stood on the ledge outside in the slight, chill breeze, eleven stories above the street, staring into his own lighted apartment, odd and different-seeming now.

First his right hand, then his left, he carefully shifted his finger-tip grip from the puttyless window edging to an indented row of bricks directly to his right. It was hard to take the first shuffling sideways step then—to make himself move—and the fear stirred in his stomach, but he did it, again by not allowing himself time to think. And now—with his chest, stomach, and the left side of his face pressed against the rough cold brick—his lighted apartment was suddenly gone, and it was much darker out here than he had thought.

Without pause he continued—right foot, left foot, right foot, left—his shoe soles shuffling and scraping along the rough stone, never lifting from it, fingers sliding along the exposed edging of brick. He moved on the balls of his feet, heels lifted slightly; the ledge was not quite as wide as he'd expected. But leaning slightly inward toward the face of the building and pressed against it, he could feel his balance firm and secure, and moving

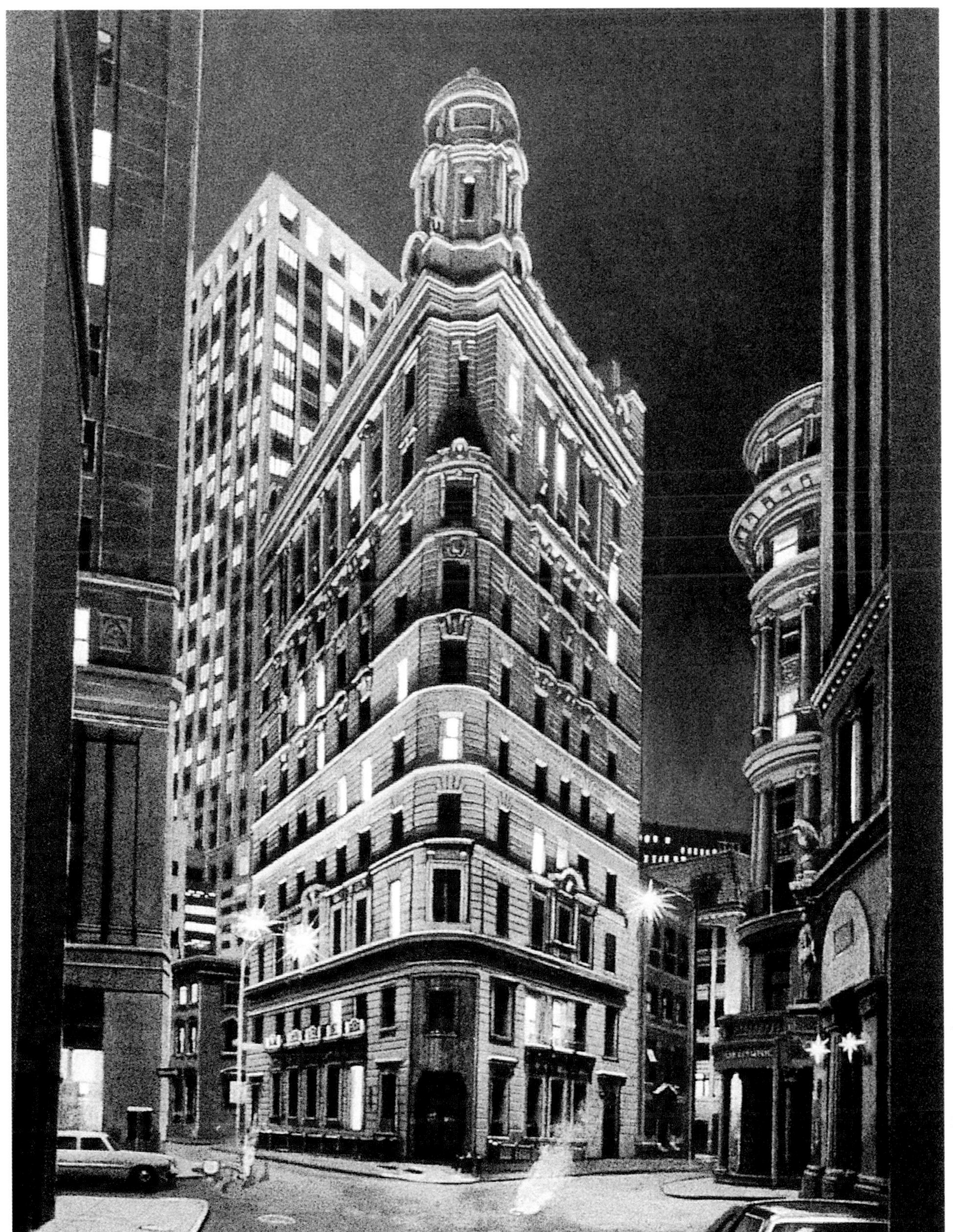

William Street at Night, 1981. Richard Haas. Watercolor, 33¼ x 23 in.

Viewing the painting: How does this painting affect your reaction to Tom's climbing out of his window? Explain.

along the ledge was quite as easy as he had thought it would be. He could hear the buttons of his jacket scraping steadily along the rough bricks and feel them catch momentarily, tugging a little, at each mortared crack. He simply did not permit himself to look down, though the compulsion to do so never left him; nor did he allow himself actually to think. Mechanically—right foot, left foot, over and again—he shuffled along crabwise, watching the projecting wall ahead loom steadily closer. . . .

Then he reached it and, at the corner—he'd decided how he was going to pick up the paper—he lifted his right foot and placed it carefully on the ledge that ran along the projecting wall at a right angle to the ledge on which his other foot rested. And now, facing the building, he stood in the corner formed by the two walls, one foot on the ledging of each, a hand on the shoulder-high indentation of each wall. His forehead was pressed directly into the corner against the cold bricks, and now he carefully lowered first one hand, then the other, perhaps a foot farther down, to the next indentation in the rows of bricks.

Very slowly, sliding his forehead down the trough of the brick corner and bending his knees, he lowered his body toward the paper lying between his outstretched feet. Again he lowered his fingerholds another foot and bent his knees still more, thigh muscles taut, his forehead sliding and bumping down the brick V. Half squatting now, he dropped his left hand to the next indentation and then slowly reached with his right hand toward the paper between his feet.

He couldn't quite touch it, and his knees now were pressed against the wall; he could bend them no farther. But by ducking his head another inch lower, the top of his head now pressed against the bricks, he lowered his right shoulder and his fingers had the paper by a corner, pulling it loose. At the same instant he saw, between his legs and far below, Lexington Avenue stretched out for miles ahead.

He saw, in that instant, the Loew's theater sign, blocks ahead past Fiftieth Street; the miles of traffic signals, all green now; the lights of cars and street lamps; countless neon signs; and the moving black dots of people. And a violent instantaneous explosion of absolute terror roared through him. For a motionless instant he saw himself externally—bent practically double, balanced on this narrow ledge, nearly half his body projecting out above the street far below—and he began to tremble violently, panic flaring through his mind and muscles, and he felt the blood rush from the surface of his skin.

In the fractional moment before horror paralyzed him, as he stared between his legs at that terrible length of street far beneath him, a fragment of his mind raised his body in a spasmodic jerk to an upright position again, but so violently that his head scraped hard against the wall, bouncing off it, and his body swayed outward to the knife edge of balance, and he very nearly plunged backward and fell. Then he was leaning far into the corner again, squeezing and pushing into it, not only his face but his chest and stomach, his back arching; and his fingertips clung with all the pressure of his pulling arms to the shoulder-high half-inch indentation in the bricks.

He was more than trembling now; his whole body was racked with a violent

Vocabulary

taut (tôt) *adj.* tense; tight

spasmodic (spaz mod′ ik) *adj.* sudden, violent, and temporary shuddering beyond control, his eyes squeezed so tightly shut it was painful, though he was past awareness of that. His teeth were exposed in a frozen grimace, the strength draining like water from his knees and calves. It was extremely likely, he knew, that he would faint, to slump down along the wall, his face scraping, and then drop backward, a limp weight, out into nothing. And to save his life he concentrated on holding onto consciousness, drawing deliberate deep breaths of cold air into his lungs, fighting to keep his senses aware.

Then he knew that he would not faint, but he could not stop shaking nor open his eyes. He stood where he was, breathing deeply, trying to hold back the terror of the glimpse he had of what lay below him; and he knew he had made a mistake in not making himself stare down at the street, getting used to it and accepting it, when he had first stepped out onto the ledge.

It was impossible to walk back. He simply could not do it. He couldn't bring himself to make the slightest movement. The strength was gone from his legs; his shivering hands—numb, cold and desperately rigid—had lost all deftness; his easy ability to move and balance was gone. Within a step or two, if he tried to move, he knew that he would stumble clumsily and fall.

Seconds passed, with the chill faint wind pressing the side of his face, and he could hear the toned-down volume of the street traffic far beneath him. Again and again he slowed and then stopped, almost to silence; then presently, even this high, he would hear the click of the traffic signals and the subdued roar of the cars starting up again. During a lull in the street sounds, he called out. Then he was shouting "*Help!*" so loudly it rasped his throat. But he felt the steady pressure of the wind, moving between his face and the blank wall, snatch up his cries as he uttered them, and he knew they must sound directionless and distant. And he remembered how habitually, here in New York, he himself heard and ignored shouts in the night. If anyone heard him, there was no sign of it, and presently Tom Benecke knew he had to try moving; there was nothing else he could do.

Eyes squeezed shut, he watched scenes in his mind like scraps of motion-picture film—he could not stop them. He saw himself stumbling suddenly sideways as he crept along the ledge and saw his upper body arc outward, arms flailing. He saw a dangling shoestring caught between the ledge and the sole of his other shoe, saw a foot start to move, to be stopped with a jerk, and felt his balance leaving him. He saw himself falling with a terrible speed as his body revolved in the air, knees clutched tight to his chest, eyes squeezed shut, moaning softly.

Out of utter necessity, knowing that any of these thoughts might be reality in the very next seconds, he was slowly able to shut his mind against every thought but what he now began to do. With fear-soaked slowness, he slid his left foot an inch or two toward his own impossibly distant window. Then he slid the fingers of his shivering left hand a corresponding distance. For a moment he could not bring himself to lift his right foot from one ledge to the other; then he did it, and became aware of the harsh exhalation of air from his throat and realized that he was panting. As his right hand, then, began to slide along the brick edging, he was astonished to feel the yellow paper pressed to the bricks underneath his stiff fingers, and he uttered a terrible, abrupt bark that might have been a laugh or a moan.

Vocabulary

deftness (deft′ nəs) *n.* the state or quality of being skillful and nimble

Flatiron Intersection, 1975. Yvonne Jacquette. Oil on canvas, 60 x 80 in. Courtesy DC Moore Gallery, New York.

Viewing the painting: What sensations does this painting portray? How might they be similar to Tom's feelings as he stepped along the ledge?

He opened his mouth and took the paper in his teeth, pulling it out from under his fingers.

By a kind of trick—by concentrating his entire mind on first his left foot, then his left hand, then the other foot, then the other hand—he was able to move, almost imperceptibly, trembling steadily, very nearly without thought. But he could feel the terrible strength of the pent-up horror on just the other side of the flimsy barrier he had erected in his mind; and he knew that if it broke through he would lose this thin artificial control of his body.

During one slow step he tried keeping his eyes closed; it made him feel safer, shutting him off a little from the fearful reality of where he was. Then a sudden rush of giddiness swept over him and he had to open his eyes wide, staring sideways at the cold rough brick and angled lines of mortar, his cheek tight against the building. He kept his eyes open then, knowing that if he once let them flick outward, to stare for an instant at the lighted windows across the street, he would be past help.

He didn't know how many dozens of tiny sidling steps he had taken, his chest, belly

Vocabulary

pent-up (pent′ up) *adj.* not expressed or released; held in and face pressed to the wall; but he knew the slender hold he was keeping on his mind and body was going to break. He had a sudden mental picture of his apartment on just the other side of this wall—warm, cheerful, incredibly spacious. And he saw himself striding through it, lying down on the floor on his back, arms spread wide, reveling in its unbelievable security. The impossible remoteness of this utter safety, the contrast between it and where he now stood, was more than he could bear. And the barrier broke then, and the fear of the awful height he stood on coursed through his nerves and muscles.

A fraction of his mind knew he was going to fall, and he began taking rapid blind steps with no feeling of what he was doing, sidling with a clumsy desperate swiftness, fingers scrabbling along the brick, almost hopelessly resigned to the sudden backward pull and swift motion outward and down. Then his moving left hand slid onto not brick but sheer emptiness, an impossible gap in the face of the wall, and he stumbled.

His right foot smashed into his left anklebone; he staggered sideways, began falling, and the claw of his hand cracked against glass and wood, slid down it, and his finger tips were pressed hard on the puttyless edging of his window. His right hand smacked gropingly beside it as he fell to his knees; and, under the full weight and direct downward pull of his sagging body, the open window dropped shudderingly in its frame till it closed and his wrists struck the sill and were jarred off.

For a single moment he knelt, knee bones against stone on the very edge of the ledge, body swaying and touching nowhere else, fighting for balance. Then he lost it, his shoulders plunging backward, and he flung his arms forward, his hands smashing against the window casing on either side; and—his body moving backward—his fingers clutched the narrow wood stripping of the upper pane.

For an instant he hung suspended between balance and falling, his finger tips pressed onto the quarter-inch wood strips. Then, with utmost delicacy, with a focused concentration of all his senses, he increased even further the strain on his finger tips hooked to these slim edgings of wood. Elbows slowly bending, he began to draw the full weight of his upper body forward, knowing that the instant his fingers slipped off these quarter-inch strips he'd plunge backward and be falling. Elbows imperceptibly bending, body shaking with the strain, the sweat starting from his forehead in great sudden drops, he pulled, his entire being and thought concentrated in his finger tips. Then suddenly, the strain slackened and ended, his chest touching the window sill, and he was kneeling on the ledge, his forehead pressed to the glass of the closed window.

Dropping his palms to the sill, he stared into his living room—at the red-brown davenport across the room, and a magazine he had left there; at the pictures on the walls and the gray rug; the entrance to the hallway; and at his papers, typewriter and desk, not two feet from his nose. A movement from his desk caught his eye and he saw that it was a thin curl of blue smoke; his cigarette, the ash long, was still burning in the ash tray where he'd left it—this was past all belief—only a few minutes before.

His head moved, and in faint reflection from the glass before him he saw the yellow paper clenched in his front teeth. Lifting a hand from the sill he took it from his mouth; the moistened corner parted from the paper, and he spat it out.

Vocabulary

reveling (rev′əl ing) *adj.* taking great pleasure

For a moment, in the light from the living room, he stared wonderingly at the yellow sheet in his hand and then crushed it into the side pocket of his jacket.

He couldn't open the window. It had been pulled not completely closed, but its lower edge was below the level of the outside sill; there was no room to get his fingers underneath it. Between the upper sash and the lower was a gap not wide enough—reaching up, he tried—to get his fingers into; he couldn't push it open. The upper window panel, he knew from long experience, was impossible to move, frozen tight with dried paint.

Very carefully observing his balance, the finger tips of his left hand again hooked to the narrow stripping of the window casing, he drew back his right hand, palm facing the glass, and then struck the glass with the heel of his hand.

His arm rebounded from the pane, his body tottering, and he knew he didn't dare strike a harder blow.

But in the security and relief of his new position, he simply smiled; with only a sheet of glass between him and the room just before him, it was not possible that there wasn't a way past it. Eyes narrowing, he thought for a few moments about what to do. Then his eyes widened, for nothing occurred to him. But still he felt calm: the trembling, he realized, had stopped. At the back of his mind there still lay the thought that once he was again in his home, he could give release to his feelings. He actually *would* lie on the floor, rolling, clenching tufts of the rug in his hands. He would literally run across the room, free to move as he liked, jumping on the floor, testing and reveling in its absolute security, letting the relief flood through him, draining the fear from his mind and body. His yearning for this was astonishingly intense, and somehow he understood that he had better keep this feeling at bay.

He took a half dollar from his pocket and struck it against the pane, but without any hope that the glass would break and with very little disappointment when it did not. After a few moments of thought he drew his leg up onto the ledge and picked loose the knot of his shoelace. He slipped off the shoe and, holding it across the instep, drew back his arm as far as he dared and struck the leather heel against the glass. The pane rattled, but he knew he'd been a long way from breaking it. His foot was cold and he slipped the shoe back on. He shouted again, experimentally, and then once more, but there was no answer.

The realization suddenly struck him that he might have to wait here till Clare came home, and for a moment the thought was funny. He could see Clare opening the front door, withdrawing her key from the lock, closing the door behind her and then glancing up to see him crouched on the other side of the window. He could see her rush across the room, face astounded and frightened, and hear himself shouting instructions: "Never mind how I got here! Just open the wind—" She couldn't open it, he remembered, she'd never been able to; she'd always had to call him. She'd have to get the building superintendent or a neighbor, and he pictured himself smiling and answering their questions as he climbed in. "I just wanted to get a breath of fresh air, so—"

He couldn't possibly wait here till Clare came home. It was the second feature she'd wanted to see, and she'd left in time to see the first. She'd be another three hours or—He glanced at his watch; Clare had been gone eight minutes. It wasn't possible, but only eight minutes ago he had kissed his wife good-by. She wasn't even at the theater yet!

It would be four hours before she could possibly be home, and he tried to picture himself kneeling out here, finger tips hooked to these narrow strippings, while first one movie, preceded by a slow listing of credits, began, developed, reached its climax and then finally ended. There'd be a newsreel next, maybe, and then an animated cartoon, and then interminable scenes from coming pictures. And then, once more, the beginning of a full-length picture—while all the time he hung out here in the night.

He might possibly get to his feet, but he was afraid to try. Already his legs were cramped, his thigh muscles tired; his knees hurt, his feet felt numb and his hands were stiff. He couldn't possibly stay out here for four hours, or anywhere near it. Long before that his legs and arms would give out; he would be forced to try changing his position often—stiffly, clumsily, his co-ordination and strength gone—and he would fall. Quite realistically, he knew that he would fall; no one could stay out here on this ledge for four hours.

A dozen windows in the apartment building across the street were lighted. Looking over his shoulder, he could see the top of a man's head behind the newspaper he was reading; in another window he saw the blue-gray flicker of a television screen. No more than twenty-odd yards from his back were scores of people, and if just one of them would walk idly to his window and glance out. . . . For some moments he stared over his shoulder at the lighted rectangles, waiting. But no one appeared. The man reading his paper turned a page and then continued his reading. A figure passed another of the windows and was immediately gone.

In the inside pocket of his jacket he found a little sheaf of papers, and he pulled one out and looked at it in the light from the living room. It was an old letter, an advertisement of some sort; his name and address, in purple ink, were on a label pasted to the envelope. Gripping one end of the envelope in his teeth, he twisted it into a tight curl. From his shirt pocket he brought out a book of matches. He didn't dare let go the casing with both hands but, with the twist of paper in his teeth, he opened the matchbook with his free hand; then he bent one of the matches in two without tearing it from the folder, its red-tipped end now touching the striking surface. With his thumb, he rubbed the red tip across the striking area.

He did it again, then again, and still again, pressing harder each time, and the match suddenly flared, burning his thumb. But he kept it alight, cupping the matchbook in his hand and shielding it with his body. He held the flame to the paper in his mouth till it caught. Then he snuffed out the match flame with his thumb and forefinger, careless of the burn, and replaced the book in his pocket. Taking the paper twist in his hand, he held it flame down, watching the flame crawl up the paper, till it flared bright. Then he held it behind him over the street, moving it from side to side, watching it over his shoulder, the flame flickering and guttering in the wind.

There were three letters in his pocket and he lighted each of them, holding each till the flame touched his hand and then dropping it to the street below. At one point, watching over his shoulder while the last of the letters burned, he saw the man across the street put down his paper and stand—even seeming, to Tom, to glance toward his window. But when he moved, it was only to walk across the room and disappear from sight.

There were a dozen coins in Tom Benecke's pocket and he dropped them, three or four at a time. But if they struck anyone, or if anyone noticed their falling, no one connected them with their source, and no one glanced upward.

His arms had begun to tremble from the steady strain of clinging to this narrow perch, and he did not know what to do now and was terribly frightened. Clinging to the window stripping with one hand, he again searched his pockets. But now—he had left his wallet on his dresser when he'd changed clothes—there was nothing left but the yellow sheet. It occurred to him irrelevantly that his death on the sidewalk below would be an eternal mystery; the window closed—why, how, and from where could he have fallen? No one would be able to identify his body for a time, either—the thought was somehow unbearable and increased his fear. All they'd find in his pockets would be the yellow sheet. *Contents of the dead man's pockets,* he thought, *one sheet of paper bearing penciled notations—incomprehensible.*

He understood fully that he might actually be going to die; his arms, maintaining his balance on the ledge, were trembling steadily now. And it occurred to him then with all the force of a revelation that, if he fell, all he was ever going to have out of life he would then, abruptly, have had. Nothing, then, could ever be changed; and nothing more—no least experience or pleasure—could ever be added to his life. He wished, then, that he had not allowed his wife to go off by herself tonight—and on similar nights. He thought of all the evenings he had spent away from her, working; and he regretted them. He thought wonderingly of his fierce ambition and of the direction his life had taken; he thought of the hours he'd spent by himself, filling the yellow sheet that had brought him out here. *Contents of the dead man's pockets*, he thought with sudden fierce anger, *a wasted life*.

He was simply not going to cling here till he slipped and fell; he told himself that now. There was one last thing he could try; he had been aware of it for some moments, refusing to think about it, but now he faced it. Kneeling here on the ledge, the finger tips of one hand pressed to the narrow strip of wood, he could, he knew, draw his other hand back a yard perhaps, fist clenched tight, doing it very slowly till he sensed the outer limit of balance, then, as hard as he was able from the distance, he could drive his fist forward against the glass. If it broke, his fist smashing through, he was safe; he might cut himself badly, and probably would, but with his arm inside the room, he would be secure. But if the glass did not break, the rebound, flinging his arm back, would topple him off the ledge. He was certain of that.

He tested his plan. The fingers of his left hand clawlike on the little stripping, he drew back his other fist until his body began teetering backward. But he had no leverage now—he could feel that there would be no force to his swing—and he moved his fist slowly forward till he rocked forward on his knees again and could sense that his swing would carry its greatest force. Glancing down, however, measuring the distance from his fist to the glass, he saw that it was less than two feet.

It occurred to him that he could raise his arm over his head, to bring it down against the glass. But, experimenting in slow motion, he knew it would be an awkward girl-like blow without the force of a driving punch, and not nearly enough to break the glass.

Facing the window, he had to drive a blow from the shoulder, he knew now, at a distance of less than two feet; and he did not know whether it would break through the heavy glass. It might; he could picture it happening, he could feel it in the nerves of his arm. And it might not; he could feel that too—feel his fist striking this glass and being instantaneously flung back by the unbreaking pane, feel the fingers of his other hand breaking loose, nails scraping along the casing as he fell.

He waited, arm drawn back, fist balled, but in no hurry to strike; this pause, he knew, might be an extension of his life. And to live even a few seconds longer, he felt, even out here on this ledge in the night, was infinitely better than to die a moment earlier than he had to. His arm grew tired, and he brought it down and rested it.

Then he knew that it was time to make the attempt. He could not kneel here hesitating indefinitely till he lost all courage to act, waiting till he slipped off the ledge. Again he drew back his arm, knowing this time that he would not bring it down till he struck. His elbow protruding over Lexington Avenue far below, the fingers of his other hand pressed down bloodlessly tight against the narrow stripping, he waited, feeling the sick tenseness and terrible excitement building. It grew and swelled toward the moment of action, his nerves tautening. He thought of Clare—just a wordless, yearning thought—and then drew his arm back just a bit more, fist so tight his fingers pained him, and knowing he was going to do it. Then with full power, with every last scrap of strength he could bring to bear, he shot his arm forward toward the glass, and he said, "*Clare!*"

He heard the sound, felt the blow, felt himself falling forward, and his hand closed on the living-room curtains, the shards and fragments of glass showering onto the floor. And then, kneeling there on the ledge, an arm thrust into the room up to the shoulder, he began picking away the protruding slivers and great wedges of glass from the window frame, tossing them in onto the rug. And, as he grasped the edges of the empty window frame and climbed into his home, he was grinning in triumph.

He did not lie down on the floor or run through the apartment, as he had promised himself; even in the first few moments it seemed to him natural and normal that he should be where he was. He simply turned to his desk, pulled the crumpled yellow sheet from his pocket and laid it down where it had been, smoothing it out; then he absently laid a pencil across it to weight it down. He shook his head wonderingly, and turned to walk toward the closet.

There he got out his topcoat and hat and, without waiting to put them on, opened the front door and stepped out, to go find his wife. He turned to pull the door closed and warm air from the hall rushed through the narrow opening again. As he saw the yellow paper, the pencil flying, scooped off the desk and, unimpeded by the glassless window, sail out into the night and out of his life, Tom Benecke burst into laughter and then closed the door behind him.

Vocabulary

unimpeded (un′ im pē′ dəd) *adj.* not obstructed; unblocked

Responding to Literature

Personal Response

Which part of the story did you react to most strongly? Discuss your reaction with a partner.

Analyzing Literature

Recall

1. Why does Tom decide not to go to the movies with Clare?
2. What happens to the yellow sheet of paper? What does Tom plan to do about it? Why?
3. At what moment does Tom's adventure change from risky to terrifying?
4. What is the revelation Tom has when looking into his living room?
5. What happens to the yellow sheet of paper at the end of the story? What is Tom's reaction then?

Interpret

6. What do you learn about Tom from his decision not to go with Clare?
7. What does the yellow paper represent to Tom? How might his feelings about the paper have influenced his decision to retrieve it?
8. In your opinion, why does terror suddenly seize Tom when he had been fairly calm up until that moment? What kinds of thoughts might he have had before and after he became terrified?
9. Before his revelation, Tom thinks, "Contents of the dead man's pockets, . . . one sheet of paper bearing penciled notations–incomprehensible." After the revelation, he thinks, "Contents of the dead man's pockets, . . . a wasted life." Why might he feel this way?
10. Why do you think Tom reacts as he does when he sees the yellow sheet of paper at the end of the story?

Evaluate and Connect

11. What is the significance of the title of the story?
12. Think about successful businesspeople and famous musicians, athletes, dancers, or artists. What might they have in common with Tom? Explain.
13. What is the author saying about priorities in life? Do you agree?
14. What examples of **foreshadowing** do you find in the story? (See page R5.) Did you notice the foreshadowing as you read, or did you recognize it after you had finished the story? Explain.
15. Tom was on the ledge for eight minutes, yet to the reader it seems much longer. How does Finney build suspense and hold our attention?

Literary ELEMENTS

Point of View

The **point of view** a fiction writer uses depends on which approach would tell the story in the most interesting and appealing way. The writer of "Contents of the Dead Man's Pocket" uses **limited third-person** point of view, in which the narrator stands outside the story and reveals the thoughts and feelings of only one character. The narrator refers to that character as "he" or "she."

1. Why might Finney have chosen to limit the reader's information to Tom's thoughts and observations?
2. In your opinion, would the story be stronger or more interesting if the narrator also included Clare's thoughts and feelings? Explain.
3. Imagine a third character in the story–perhaps a neighbor across the street who watches the action from a window. Retell one scene from that neighbor's point of view. How does the change in point of view change the story?

- See **Literary Terms Handbook,** p. R9.

Literature and Writing

Writing About Literature

Setting Write an analysis of the way Jack Finney uses the setting to help create suspense in this story. Consider not only the place where the action occurs but also the time of day, the weather conditions, and the contrast between where Tom is and where he wants to be.

Creative Writing

A Different Twist How might this story have ended if it were a comedy, a tragedy, a mystery, or a science fiction piece? Choose one of these types of fiction and rewrite the ending of the story to make it fit that type. Use your imagination, but try to keep your ending consistent with the first part of the story.

Extending Your Response

Literature Groups

Relating to the Character Discuss Tom Benecke's discovery about the way he spends his time. How does Tom's revelation compare with what you discovered when you created the chart for the Reading Focus on page 198? Compile the results of the Reading Focus from members in the group and develop some generalizations about how people your age spend their time. Do you come to the same conclusion Tom did? Share your findings with the class.

7–7:30	*get ready for school*
7:30–7:45	*travel to school*
7:45–8	*talk to friends at school*

Interdisciplinary Activity

Art: Illustrate the Highlights Choose a significant part of the story and retell it in a drawing. Use whatever style you like–cartoon, abstract, with captions or without–and present your drawing to the class. Explain why you chose the scene you did.

Performing

A Monologue Finney writes what Tom is thinking as he gropes his way along the ledge, but if this were a play, Tom would speak what he thinks. Write a first-person monologue for Tom based on part of the story. Deliver it to the class as if you were standing on a ledge!

Reading Further

If you would like to read more by Jack Finney, you might enjoy these works:

Novels: In *Time and Again* and its sequel, *From Time to Time,* the hero travels back in time to New York City of the 1800s and finds romance and mystery.

Invasion of the Body Snatchers is a science fiction thriller.

Short Story Collections: *Forgotten News: The Crime of the Century and Other Lost Stories*

About Time: Twelve Stories

Viewing: *Time and Again* has gained a loyal following of fans. Other popular films based on Finney's work include *Invasion of the Body Snatchers* and *Good Neighbor Sam.*

Save your work for your portfolio.

Skill Minilessons

GRAMMAR AND LANGUAGE • Introductory Phrases

Jack Finney uses many introductory prepositional and participial phrases to describe Tom's actions and emotions. For example:

Introductory Prepositional Phrase: *During a lull in the street sounds,* he called out.

Introductory Participial Phrases: *Glancing down,* however, *measuring the distance from his fist to the glass,* he saw that it was less than two feet.

PRACTICE On your paper, combine each pair of sentences by changing one of the sentences into an introductory prepositional or participial phrase.

1. Tom waved to Clare. He wished he could go with her.
2. Tom sidled across the ledge. His heart was in his mouth.
3. Tom took deep breaths. He was afraid he would faint.
4. Tom felt the rough bricks. He pressed his face to the wall.
5. A man was reading. He was in a nearby apartment.

APPLY Revise a response you wrote for "Contents of the Dead Man's Pocket" to include an introductory phrase.

● For more about phrases, see **Language Handbook,** p. R41.

READING AND THINKING • Problem Solving

Tom Benecke had a problem–an important paper blew out the window of his eleventh-story apartment. This was his first attempt to solve the problem: "He thought about the poker from the fireplace, then the broom, then the mop–discarding each thought as it occurred to him. There was nothing in the apartment long enough to reach that paper."

PRACTICE Make a chart like the one shown to list the steps that Tom eventually follows to solve his problem.

Problem:	An important paper blew out a window.
Steps Taken to Solve the Problem:	Tom thinks about tools to use to retrieve the paper.
The Outcome:	That solution is unsuccessful; the tools are all too short.

● For more about problem solving, see **Reading Handbook,** pp. R78–R107.

VOCABULARY • Analogies

An analogy is a type of comparison that is based on the relationships between things or ideas. Some analogies are of a type that could be called "defining characteristic." The characteristic given need not be the most important or most distinguishing trait, but it is part of what makes the person, object, idea, or animal what it is.

rabbit : furry :: bird : feathered

A rabbit is furry; a bird is feathered.

To finish an analogy, decide what relationship exists between the first two things or ideas. Then apply that relationship to another pair of words and see if it is the same.

● For more about analogies, see **Communications Skills Handbook,** p. R77.

PRACTICE Choose the word that best completes each analogy.

1. knot : convoluted :: noose :
   a. tight   b. looped   c. stretched
2. tightrope : taut :: net :
   a. safe   b. delicate   c. meshed
3. improvised : rehearsed :: temporary :
   a. skit   b. permanent   c. brief
4. sneeze : spasmodic :: waltz :
   a. rhythmic   b. irregular   c. natural
5. deftness : clumsiness :: honesty :
   a. deceit   b. skill   c. truth

INTERDISCIPLINARY CONNECTION

SPORTS AND FITNESS

Rock Climbing

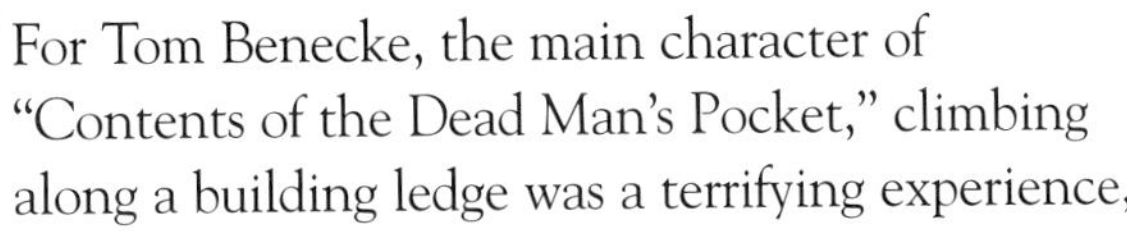

For Tom Benecke, the main character of "Contents of the Dead Man's Pocket," climbing along a building ledge was a terrifying experience, yet many men and women enthusiastically scale vertical surfaces to dizzying heights. They wedge their fingers and toes into cracks that may be no wider than a fingernail. Then they pull themselves up boulders, walls, and sheer mountain cliffs one step at a time.

While many people get dizzy looking down from high places, climbers actively seek out climbs that take them to new heights with vast, impressive views. Sometimes the final destinations are so high that after a full day of climbing, climbers must spend the night on a rock wall. They sleep on a narrow ledge or in a portable hammock-type device attached to a cliff, and at dawn they continue their ascent.

In addition to being physically fit and carefully trained, good climbers use special equipment designed to increase their climbing ability and protect them from accidents.

The Equipment

Perhaps the most important piece of rock climbing equipment is a strong, stretchable rope. The rope attaches to a harness the climber wears, which has a padded waistband and leg loops. Climbers either affix the rope to a fixture at their destination at the top before they begin their ascent—this is called top-roping, or they climb in groups or pairs with the rope attached to one another—which is called lead climbing. Sometimes, climbers rely on their ropes only for protection in case of a fall. Other times, they use the ropes to scale a cliff face or wall. In either case, they maintain their equipment carefully. A faulty harness or frayed rope could send the wearer crashing down to his or her death.

Climbers wear special shoes to enhance their ability. Much smaller, slimmer, and tighter than ordinary sneakers, they allow a climber greater control and balance. These shoes have sticky rubber soles to grip onto surfaces and tapered toes so that the wearer can jam them into cracks or crevices to get a toehold.

Rock climbers also give their hands special attention. Climbers sometimes coat their palms and fingers with powdered chalk to improve their grip and keep them from slipping. They may also wrap tape around their hands to prevent rocks from cutting or scraping their skin.

Activity

Find the rock climbing locations nearest you. Read nature guides, search the Internet, or conduct telephone research to locate one indoor and one outdoor location. Note the kind of surface on which the climbing is done and each location's levels of difficulty.

MEDIA connection

Comic Strip

How important is it to be able to express thoughts freely—without fear of censorship—even if other people don't like what they hear? Jason Fox, of the *Fox Trot* comic strip, believes it is a right that should not be squished or squashed.

Analyzing Media

1. What do you think was most disappointing to Jason about having his comic strip rejected by the school paper?
2. How might you react if your freedom of expression was being squashed?

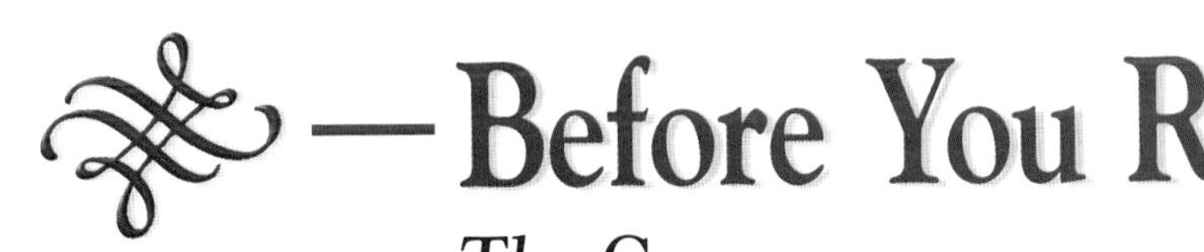

Before You Read

The Censors

Reading Focus

Have you ever heard the expression, "If you can't beat 'em, join 'em"? It refers to a strategy for dealing with strong opponents when other attempts at besting them have failed. Can you imagine a situation in which you might use this strategy?

List Ideas List the advantages and disadvantages of the strategy of joining up with opponents.

Setting a Purpose Read to learn how a careful strategy backfires.

Building Background

The Time and Place

Luisa Valenzuela doesn't name a specific city, country, or time in which "The Censors" takes place. The events most likely occur in Latin America during the middle of the 1900s. However, a story of censors and censorship could take place almost anywhere at any time.

Did You Know?

The job of a censor is to limit the kinds of information people have access to. Censors examine print materials or other media, such as films, and either remove objectionable parts or completely reject the material. For example, a censor might remove a book with crude language from a school library. A censor in the military might examine personal mail and delete information that would threaten national security. Some authoritarian governments control the news media, dictating what kinds of news can be reported.

People disagree over the issue of censorship. Some think there should be no censorship at all. Others believe that it is desirable to control the spread of information that might harm people. Still others use censorship as a form of power, to control people by controlling what they hear or read.

Meet Luisa Valenzuela

Luisa Valenzuela wrote her first short story, "City of the Unknown," when she was seventeen, claiming that she "slipped into mother's footsteps." (Her mother is also a writer.) Valenzuela writes about Argentinean politics as well as the fate of women in repressive societies. Many of her works combine the real and the fantastic, a Latin American style called "magical realism."

Luisa Valenzuela was born in 1938 in Buenos Aires, Argentina. "The Censors" was first published in 1976.

Vocabulary Preview

irreproachable (ir′ i prō′ chə bəl) *adj.* free from blame or criticism; faultless; p. 218

albeit (ôl bē′ it) *conj.* although; even if; p. 219

ulterior (ul tēr′ ē ər) *adj.* intentionally withheld or concealed; p. 219

staidness (stād′ nəs) *n.* the state or quality of being serious, steady, or conservative in character; p. 219

subversive (sub vur′ siv) *adj.* seeking to weaken, destroy, or overthrow; p. 220

THE CENSORS

Luisa Valenzuela

POOR JUAN! One day they caught him with his guard down before he could even realize that what he had taken as a stroke of luck was really one of fate's dirty tricks. These things happen the minute you're careless, as one often is. Juancito[1] let happiness—a feeling you can't trust—get the better of him when he received from a confidential source Mariana's new address in Paris and knew that she hadn't forgotten him. Without thinking twice, he sat down at his table and wrote her a letter. *The* letter that now keeps his mind off his job during the day and won't let him sleep at night (what had he scrawled, what had he put on that sheet of paper he sent to Mariana?).

Juan knows there won't be a problem with the letter's contents, that it's irreproachable, harmless. But what about the rest? He knows that they examine, sniff, feel, and read between the lines of each and every letter, and check its tiniest comma and most accidental stain. He knows that all letters pass from hand to hand and go through all sorts of tests in the huge censorship offices and that, in the end, very few continue on their way. Usually it takes months, even years, if there aren't any snags; all this time the freedom, maybe even the life, of both sender and receiver is in jeopardy. And that's why Juan's so troubled: thinking that something might happen to Mariana because of his letters. Of all people, Mariana, who must finally feel safe there where she always dreamt she'd live. But he knows that the *Censor's Secret Command* operates all over the world and cashes in on the discount in air fares; there's nothing to stop them from going as far as that hidden Paris neighborhood, kidnapping Mariana, and returning to their cozy homes, certain of having fulfilled their noble mission.

Well, you've got to beat them to the punch, do what everyone tries to do: sabotage the machinery, throw sand in its gears, get to the bottom of the problem so as to stop it.

This was Juan's sound plan when he, like many others, applied for a censor's job—not because he had a calling or needed a job: no,

1. *Juancito* (wän sē′ tō)

Vocabulary

irreproachable (ir′ i prō′ chə bəl) *adj.* free from blame or criticism; faultless

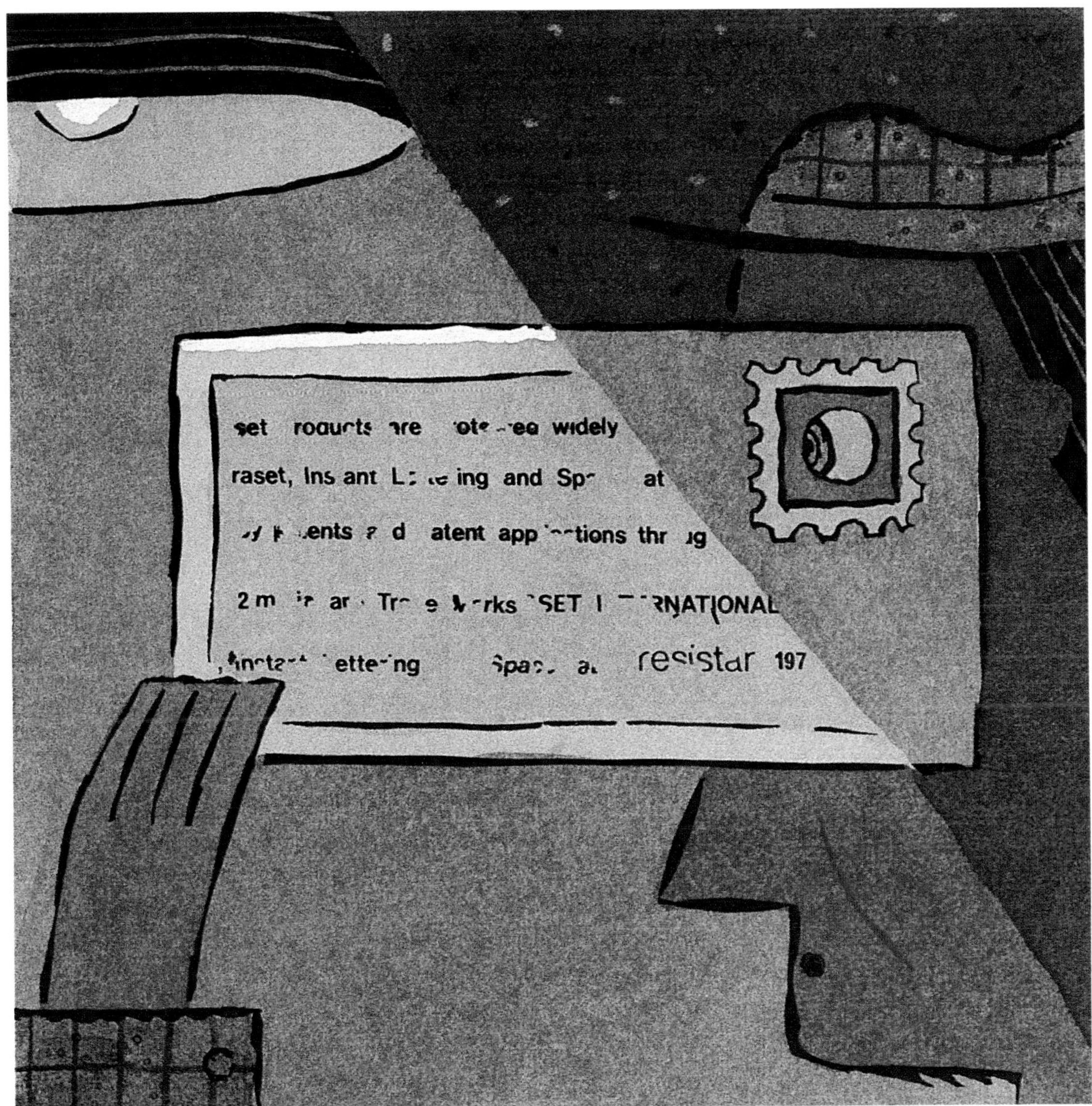

he applied simply to intercept his own letter, a consoling albeit unoriginal idea. He was hired immediately, for each day more and more censors are needed and no one would bother to check on his references.

Ulterior motives couldn't be overlooked by the *Censorship Division*, but they needn't be too strict with those who applied. They knew how hard it would be for the poor guys to find the letter they wanted and even if they did, what's a letter or two when the new censor would snap up so many others? That's how Juan managed to join the *Post Office's Censorship Division*, with a certain goal in mind.

The building had a festive air on the outside that contrasted with its inner staidness. Little by little, Juan was absorbed by his job, and he felt at peace since he was doing

---

Vocabulary

albeit (ôl bē′ it) *conj.* although; even if

ulterior (ul tēr′ ē ər) *adj.* intentionally withheld or concealed; hidden

staidness (stād′ nəs) *n.* the state or quality of being serious, steady, or conservative in character everything he could to get his letter for Mariana. He didn't even worry when, in his first month, he was sent to *Section K* where envelopes are very carefully screened for explosives.

It's true that on the third day, a fellow worker had his right hand blown off by a letter, but the division chief claimed it was sheer negligence on the victim's part. Juan and the other employees were allowed to go back to their work, though feeling less secure. After work, one of them tried to organize a strike to demand higher wages for unhealthy work, but Juan didn't join in; after thinking it over, he reported the man to his superiors and thus got promoted.

You don't form a habit by doing something once, he told himself as he left his boss's office. And when he was transferred to *Section J*, where letters are carefully checked for poison dust, he felt he had climbed a rung in the ladder.

By working hard, he quickly reached *Section E* where the job became more interesting, for he could now read and analyze the letters' contents. Here he could even hope to get hold of his letter, which, judging by the time that had elapsed, had gone through the other sections and was probably floating around in this one.

Soon his work became so absorbing that his noble mission blurred in his mind. Day after day he crossed out whole paragraphs in red ink, pitilessly chucking many letters into the censored basket. These were horrible days when he was shocked by the subtle and conniving ways employed by people to pass on subversive messages; his instincts were so sharp that he found behind a simple "the weather's unsettled" or "prices continue to soar" the wavering hand of someone secretly scheming to overthrow the Government.

His zeal brought him swift promotion. We don't know if this made him happy. Very few letters reached him in *Section B*—only a handful passed the other hurdles—so he read them over and over again, passed them under a magnifying glass, searched for microprint with an electronic microscope, and tuned his sense of smell so that he was beat by the time he made it home. He'd barely manage to warm up his soup, eat some fruit, and fall into bed, satisfied with having done his duty. Only his darling mother worried, but she couldn't get him back on the right track. She'd say, though it wasn't always true: Lola called, she's at the bar with the girls, they miss you, they're waiting for you. Or else she'd leave a bottle of red wine on the table. But Juan wouldn't overdo it: any distraction could make him lose his edge and the perfect censor had to be alert, keen, attentive, and sharp to nab cheats. He had a truly patriotic task, both self-denying and uplifting.

His basket for censored letters became the best fed as well as the most cunning basket in the whole *Censorship Division*. He was about to congratulate himself for having finally discovered his true mission, when his letter to Mariana reached his hands. Naturally, he censored it without regret. And just as naturally, he couldn't stop them from executing him the following morning, another victim of his devotion to his work.

Vocabulary

subversive (sub vur′ siv) *adj.* seeking to weaken, destroy, or overthrow

Responding to Literature

Personal Response

What feelings did you have about Juan at the end of the story? Did your feelings about him change during the course of the story? Explain.

Analyzing Literature

Recall

1. What does Juan do as soon as he gets Mariana's address? How does he feel?
2. What was Juan's plan in applying for a censor's job?
3. What accounts for Juan's promotion from *Section K*?
4. Briefly describe Juan's way of life by the time he's promoted to *Section B.*
5. What happens to Juan as a "natural" result of his censoring skills?

Interpret

6. Why, do you think, does Juan feel so strongly about what he has done?
7. At the beginning of the story, how does Juan feel about the *Censor's Secret Command* and the government of his country in general?
8. "'You don't form a habit by doing something once,' he told himself as he left his boss's office." What, do you think, is the "something," and what has it got to do with Juan's transfer from *Section K* to *Section J*?
9. In your opinion, what are the advantages and disadvantages of Juan's new way of life?
10. Valenzuela says of Juan, "Naturally, he couldn't stop them . . . ," but she doesn't say why. In your opinion, why can't Juan stop them?

Evaluate and Connect

11. Think back to the list you made for the Reading Focus on page 217. After reading this story, what other advantages and disadvantages would you add to your list?
12. What do you think accounts for the change in Juan over the course of the story?
13. What parts of this story seem logical and believable to you? Are there any parts that are unbelievable? Use details from the story to explain.
14. In your opinion, what does Valenzuela achieve by keeping the **tone** of the story so light and "natural"? (See page R13.)
15. Is there anything in this story that frightens you? Explain your answer.

Literary ELEMENTS

Satire

Satire is writing that uses humor or wit to ridicule institutions or humanity for the purpose of effecting change or improvement. Some satire uses gentle, accepting humor; other satire attacks with bitter and angry humor.

1. How does Valenzuela signal the reader in paragraph one that this story may be a satire?
2. How does Valenzuela use humor to satirize the censors?
3. What is the object of satire in this story? What is Valenzuela trying to illustrate by using satire?

- See **Literary Terms Handbook,** p. R11.

Literary Criticism

Throughout "The Censors," observes Amanda Hopkinson, "there is a notable sensitivity to the uses of language—particularly when it has been hijacked by unspecified rulers who, by alternatively appropriating and eliminating terminologies, seek to strip human beings of an essential characteristic." Find examples from the story of how language is used to "strip human beings of an essential characteristic." In a brief essay, discuss what the people in the story are losing.

Literature and Writing

Writing About Literature

Character Analysis Juan undergoes many changes during his attempt to intercept his letter to Mariana. Write a character analysis of Juan comparing the traits he exhibits at the beginning of the story with those he exhibits as the story unfolds. Discuss the reasons for the changes in his character.

Creative Writing

Juan, Juan, Juan A **ballad** is a narrative poem or song often about a folk hero. Write a ballad about Juan. For models, listen to folk songs of the 1960s and 1970s. Before writing your ballad, decide if Juan was a victim or a hero. Then decide on the message you want to deliver. Use the refrain, or repeated chorus, to stress your point.

Extending Your Response

Literature Groups

Uncensored Thoughts Imagine that you live in a country like Juan's where the government denies freedom to the citizens. How might government officials react to "The Censors"? How might you, the people, react to the story if you were allowed to read it? In your group, discuss whether Valenzuela's satire could be an effective tool for changing people's opinion. Share your groups' thoughts with the class.

Learning for Life

A Gentle Satire Think of something that you feel should be changed: bus routes in your town, the length of lunch break in your school, the voting age. Address the issue by writing a gentle satire for your school's literary magazine. Use humor and wit to make your point.

Internet Connection

Prizewinning Cartoons Creators of political cartoons for newspapers and newsmagazines often use satire to express their views. Political cartoons are so important that the Pulitzer Prize committee awards a prize each year in the category of Editorial Cartoons. Search the Internet for winners from the past five years.

Save your work for your portfolio.

VOCABULARY • Usage

Dictionaries rarely provide enough information about how words are used. Although one meaning for *ulterior* is "intentionally withheld or concealed; hidden," a person concealed in the closet during Hide and Seek is not ulterior. In "The Censors," *ulterior* is used to modify *motive,* or intentions, and this is its most common use.

A word used to describe one thing may not be appropriate to describe something else. For example, a painter's work habits may be irreproachable; a perfectly painted wall is not. Reading and listening are the best ways to discover how words are actually used.

PRACTICE Review how each of the following words is used in "The Censors." Then write your own sentence for each, using it in a similar way.

1. ulterior
2. irreproachable
3. subversive

Reading & Thinking Skills

Making Predictions

As you read "The Censors," did you suspect that Juan might be in danger? If so, you were **predicting,** or making an educated guess about what would happen next. Make predictions and check them as you read to add to your involvement in the story.

As you're making predictions, notice the author's use of foreshadowing, or signs about what's going to happen next. Small details, or even the author's expressions and tone, can signal big events or deeper meaning. In "The Censors," for example, the narrator says:

> **Little by little, Juan was absorbed by his job, and he felt at peace since he was doing everything he could to get his letter for Mariana. He didn't even worry when, in his first month, he was sent to *Section K* where envelopes are very carefully screened for explosives.**

The narrator's tone implies that perhaps Juan *should* have been worried and suggests that Juan really might be in danger. As you gather more information in the course of your reading, you may find that you want to change your predictions.

- For more about related reading strategies, see **Reading Handbook,** pp. R78–R107.

ACTIVITY

The following paragraphs are from "The False Gems," by Maupassant, a story that appears later in this unit. The passage describes a young middle-class couple in Paris in the 1800s. Read the passage and then, on a separate piece of paper, do the exercise that follows.

> **He found fault with only two of [his wife's] tastes: Her love for the theatre, and her taste for imitation jewelry. . . . Around her neck she wore strings of false pearls, on her arms bracelets of imitation gold. . . .**
>
> **Sometimes, . . . she would . . . examine the false gems with a passionate attention, as though they imparted some deep and secret joy; and she often persisted in passing a necklace around her husband's neck, and, laughing heartily, would exclaim: "How droll you look!" Then she would throw herself into his arms, and kiss him affectionately.**

- Predict two possible conflicts that might be central to "The False Gems." Then predict the outcome of each conflict. Note the information that helped you make your predictions.

Before You Read

The Ring

Reading Focus

Do you know anyone who has been happily married for a long time? In your opinion, what character traits are necessary for a long and successful marriage?

Sharing Ideas Discuss with a partner the character traits you would most value in a spouse. What traits might make a marriage difficult?

Setting a Purpose Read to learn how the choice a wife makes affects her relationship with her husband.

Building Background

The Time and Place

"The Ring" takes place in the Danish countryside, around 1800. At that time, most people in Denmark lived on farms.

Did You Know?

Gentle and submissive by nature, sheep make ideal farm animals. Domestic sheep provide a variety of valuable products, including meat, wool, pelts, and milk. Sheep live in flocks and are known as followers. When out grazing, they may separate slightly, but as soon as one sheep begins to move to a new location, the rest will follow, often in a single file. Domestic sheep are quite timid and virtually defenseless when attacked by predators. Thus, they must depend on humans to protect and care for them.

Vocabulary Preview

rustic (rus′ tik) *adj.* of, or relating to, the country; p. 226
void (void) *n.* an empty space; vacuum; p. 228
apparition (ap′ ə rish′ ən) *n.* something strange or unexpected that comes suddenly into view, as a ghost; p. 229
definitive (di fin′ ə tiv) *adj.* conclusive; final; decisive; p. 230
unconditional (un′ kən dish′ ən əl) *adj.* absolute; complete; p. 230
conceive (kən sēv′) *v.* to form a mental image or idea of; imagine; p. 230

Meet Isak Dinesen

Isak Dinesen (ē′ säk di′ nə sən) is the pen name of the Danish writer Karen Blixen, who spent seventeen years managing a coffee plantation in eastern Africa. Dinesen recorded the triumphs and sorrows of those years in her memoir *Out of Africa*, from which the Oscar-winning film of the same name was made in 1985. Dinesen returned to the family estate at Rungstedlund in 1931 and devoted herself to her writing. "As for me I have one ambition only: to invent stories, very beautiful stories," she said. Her short story collections include *Seven Gothic Tales* and *Winter's Tales*.

Isak Dinesen was born in 1885 in Rungsted, Denmark. She died there in 1962. This story was first published in 1953.

The Ring

Isak Dinesen

ON A SUMMER MORNING a hundred and fifty years ago a young Danish squire and his wife went out for a walk on their land. They had been married a week. It had not been easy for them to get married, for the wife's family was higher in rank and wealthier than the husband's. But the two young people, now twenty-four and nineteen years old, had been set on their purpose for ten years; and in the end her haughty parents had had to give in to them.

Summer Day near Thordager, Arrhus. Pauline Thomsen (1858–1931). Oil on canvas, 36½ x 50 in. Private collection.

They were wonderfully happy. The stolen meetings and secret, tearful love letters were now things of the past. To God and man they were one; they could walk arm in arm in broad daylight and drive in the same carriage, and they would walk and drive so till the end of their days. Their distant paradise had descended to earth and had proved, surprisingly, to be filled with the things of everyday life: with jesting and railleries,[1] with breakfasts and suppers, with dogs, haymaking and sheep. Sigismund, the young husband, had promised himself that from now there should be no stone in his bride's path, nor should any shadow fall across it. Lovisa, the wife, felt that now, every day and for the first time in her young life, she moved and breathed in perfect freedom because she could never have any secret from her husband.

To Lovisa—whom her husband called Lise—the rustic atmosphere of her new life was a matter of wonder and delight. Her husband's fear that the existence he could offer her might not be good enough for her filled her heart with laughter. It was not a long time since she had played with dolls; as now she dressed her own hair, looked over her linen press and arranged her flowers she again lived through an enchanting and cherished experience: one was doing everything gravely and solicitously, and all the time one knew one was playing.

It was a lovely July morning. Little woolly clouds drifted high up in the sky, the air was full of sweet scents. Lise had on a white muslin frock and a large Italian straw hat. She and her husband took a path through the park; it wound on across the meadows, between small groves and groups of trees, to the sheep field. Sigismund was going to show his wife his sheep. For this reason she had not brought her small white dog, Bijou, with her, for he would yap at the lambs and frighten them, or he would annoy the sheep dogs. Sigismund prided himself on his sheep; he had studied sheep-breeding in Mecklenburg[2] and England, and had brought back with him Cotswold rams by which to improve his Danish stock. While they walked he explained to Lise the great possibilities and difficulties of the plan.

Did You Know?
Cotswold is a breed of sheep with long, coarse hair, originally bred in the Cotswold Hills of southwestern England.

She thought: "How clever he is, what a lot of things he knows!" and at the same time: "What an absurd person he is, with his sheep! What a baby he is! I am a hundred years older than he."

But when they arrived at the sheepfold the old sheepmaster Mathias met them with the sad news that one of the English lambs was dead and two were sick. Lise saw that her husband was grieved by the tidings; while he questioned Mathias on the matter she kept silent and only gently pressed his arm. A couple of boys were sent off to fetch the sick lambs, while the master and servant went into the details of the case. It took some time.

Lise began to gaze about her and to think of other things. Twice her own thoughts made her blush deeply and happily, like a red rose, then slowly her blush died away, and the two men were still talking about sheep. A little while after their conversation caught her attention. It had turned to a sheep thief.

1. *Railleries* are instances of good-natured ridicule or teasing.

2. *Mecklenburg* is a farming region in northeastern Germany.

Vocabulary
rustic (rus′ tik) *adj.* of, or relating to, the country

This thief during the last months had broken into the sheepfolds of the neighborhood like a wolf, had killed and dragged away his prey like a wolf and like a wolf had left no trace after him. Three nights ago the shepherd and his son on an estate ten miles away had caught him in the act. The thief had killed the man and knocked the boy senseless, and had managed to escape. There were men sent out to all sides to catch him, but nobody had seen him.

Lise wanted to hear more about the horrible event, and for her benefit old Mathias went through it once more. There had been a long fight in the sheep house, in many places the earthen floor was soaked with blood. In the fight the thief's left arm was broken; all the same, he had climbed a tall fence with a lamb on his back. Mathias added that he would like to string up the murderer with these two hands of his, and Lise nodded her head at him gravely in approval. She remembered Red Ridinghood's wolf, and felt a pleasant little thrill running down her spine.

Sigismund had his own lambs in his mind, but he was too happy in himself to wish anything in the universe ill. After a minute he said: "Poor devil."

Lise said: "How can you pity such a terrible man? Indeed Grandmamma was right when she said that you were a revolutionary and a danger to society!" The thought of Grandmamma, and of the tears of past days, again turned her mind away from the gruesome tale she had just heard.

The boys brought the sick lambs and the men began to examine them carefully, lifting them up and trying to set them on their legs; they squeezed them here and there and made the little creatures whimper. Lise shrank from the show and her husband noticed her distress.

"You go home, my darling," he said, "this will take some time. But just walk ahead slowly, and I shall catch up with you."

So she was turned away by an impatient husband to whom his sheep meant more than his wife. If any experience could be sweeter than to be dragged out by him to look at those same sheep, it would be this. She dropped her large summer hat with its blue ribbons on the grass and told him to carry it back for her, for she wanted to feel the summer air on her forehead and in her hair. She walked on very slowly, as he had told her to do, for she wished to obey him in everything. As she walked she felt a great new happiness in being altogether alone, even without Bijou. She could not remember that she had ever before in all her life been altogether alone. The landscape around her was still, as if full of promise, and it was hers. Even the swallows cruising in the air were hers, for they belonged to him, and he was hers.

She followed the curving edge of the grove and after a minute or two found that she was out of sight to the men by the sheep house. What could now, she wondered, be sweeter than to walk along the path in the long flowering meadow grass, slowly, slowly, and to let her husband overtake her there? It would be sweeter still, she reflected, to steal into the grove and to be gone, to have vanished from the surface of the earth from him when, tired of the sheep and longing for her company, he should turn the bend of the path to catch up with her.

An idea struck her; she stood still to think it over.

A few days ago her husband had gone for a ride and she had not wanted to go with him, but had strolled about with Bijou in order to explore her domain. Bijou then, gamboling, had led her straight into the grove. As she had followed him, gently forcing her way into the shrubbery, she had suddenly come upon a glade in the midst of it, a narrow space like a small alcove with hangings of thick green and

Le Chemineau (The Hobo). Gustave Courbet (1819–1877). Municipal Museum, Dole, France.

Viewing the painting: What characteristics do you see in this man that the thief might share?

golden brocade, big enough to hold two or three people in it. She had felt at that moment that she had come into the very heart of her new home. If today she could find the spot again she would stand perfectly still there, hidden from all the world. Sigismund would look for her in all directions; he would be unable to understand what had become of her and for a minute, for a short minute—or, perhaps, if she was firm and cruel enough, for five—he would realize what a void, what an unendurably sad and horrible place the universe would be when she was no longer in it. She gravely scrutinized the grove to find the right entrance to her hiding-place, then went in.

She took great care to make no noise at all, therefore advanced exceedingly slowly. When a twig caught the flounces of her ample skirt she loosened it softly from the muslin, so as not to crack it. Once a branch took hold of one of her long golden curls; she stood still, with her arms lifted, to free it. A little way into the grove the soil became moist; her light steps no longer made any sound upon it. With one hand she held her small handkerchief to her lips, as if to emphasize the secretness of her course. She found the spot she sought and bent down to divide the foliage and make a door to her sylvan[3] closet. At this the hem of her dress caught her foot and she stopped to loosen it. As she rose she looked into the face of a man who was already in the shelter.

He stood up erect, two steps off. He must have watched her as she made her way straight toward him.

She took him in in one single glance. His face was bruised and scratched, his hands and wrists stained with dark filth. He was dressed in rags, barefooted, with tatters wound round his naked ankles. His arms hung down to his sides, his right hand clasped the hilt of a knife. He was about her own age. The man and the woman looked at each other.

3. *Sylvan* means "in or among woods, or formed by trees."

Vocabulary

void (void) *n.* an empty space; vacuum

This meeting in the wood from beginning to end passed without a word; what happened could only be rendered by pantomime. To the two actors in the pantomime it was timeless; according to a clock it lasted four minutes.

She had never in her life been exposed to danger. It did not occur to her to sum up her position, or to work out the length of time it would take to call her husband or Mathias, whom at this moment she could hear shouting to his dogs. She beheld the man before her as she would have beheld a forest ghost: the apparition itself, not the sequels[4] of it, changes the world to the human who faces it.

Although she did not take her eyes off the face before her she sensed that the alcove had been turned into a covert.[5] On the ground a couple of sacks formed a couch; there were some gnawed bones by it. A fire must have been made here in the night, for there were cinders strewn on the forest floor.

After a while she realized that he was observing her just as she was observing him. He was no longer just run to earth and crouching for a spring, but he was wondering, trying to know. At that she seemed to see herself with the eyes of the wild animal at bay[6] in his dark hiding-place; her silently approaching white figure, which might mean death.

He moved his right arm till it hung down straight before him between his legs. Without lifting the hand he bent the wrist and slowly raised the point of the knife till it pointed at her throat. The gesture was mad, unbelievable. He did not smile as he made it, but his nostrils distended,[7] the corners of his mouth quivered a little. Then slowly he put the knife back in the sheath by his belt.

She had no object of value about her, only the wedding ring which her husband had set on her finger in church, a week ago. She drew it off, and in this movement dropped her handkerchief. She reached out her hand with the ring toward him. She did not bargain for her life. She was fearless by nature, and the horror with which he inspired her was not fear of what he might do to her. She commanded him, she besought[8] him to vanish as he had come, to take a dreadful figure out of her life, so that it should never have been there. In the dumb[9] movement her young form had the grave authoritativeness[10] of a priestess conjuring down some monstrous being by a sacred sign.

He slowly reached out his hand to hers, his finger touched hers, and her hand was steady at the touch. But he did not take the ring. As she let it go it dropped to the ground as her handkerchief had done.

For a second the eyes of both followed it. It rolled a few inches toward him and stopped before his bare foot. In a hardly perceivable movement he kicked it away and again looked into her face. They remained like that, she knew not how long, but she felt that during that time something happened, things were changed.

He bent down and picked up her handkerchief. All the time gazing at her, he again drew his knife and wrapped the tiny bit of

4. Here, *sequels* refers to results or consequences.
5. As a noun, *covert* means "a hiding place." More often, you'll see the word used as an adjective to mean "secret, hidden, or concealed."
6. *At bay* refers to the position of a cornered animal that is forced to turn and confront its pursuers.
7. *Distended* means "enlarged or expanded."
8. *Besought* is the past tense of *beseech* and means "begged or asked earnestly."
9. Here, dumb means "silent; without words."
10. *Authoritativeness* is the quality of having and using the power to act or command.

Vocabulary

apparition (ap′ ə rish′ ən) *n.* something strange or unexpected that comes suddenly into view, as a ghost cambric[11] round the blade. This was difficult for him to do because his left arm was broken. While he did it his face under the dirt and sun-tan slowly grew whiter till it was almost phosphorescent.[12] Fumbling with both hands, he once more stuck the knife into the sheath. Either the sheath was too big and had never fitted the knife, or the blade was much worn—it went in. For two or three more seconds his gaze rested on her face; then he lifted his own face a little, the strange radiance still upon it, and closed his eyes.

The movement was definitive and unconditional. In this one motion he did what she had begged him to do: he vanished and was gone. She was free.

She took a step backward, the immovable, blind face before her, then bent as she had done to enter the hiding-place, and glided away as noiselessly as she had come. Once outside the grove she stood still and looked round for the meadow path, found it, and began to walk home.

Her husband had not yet rounded the edge of the grove. Now he saw her and helloed to her gaily; he came up quickly and joined her.

The path here was so narrow that he kept half behind her and did not touch her. He began to explain to her what had been the matter with the lambs. She walked a step before him and thought: All is over.

After a while he noticed her silence, came up beside her to look at her face and asked, "What is the matter?"

She searched her mind for something to say, and at last said: "I have lost my ring."

"What ring?" he asked her.

She answered, "My wedding ring."

As she heard her own voice pronounce the words she conceived their meaning.

Her wedding ring. "With this ring"—dropped by one and kicked away by another—"with this ring I thee wed." With this lost ring she had wedded herself to something. To what? To poverty, persecution, total loneliness. To the sorrows and the sinfulness of this earth. "And what therefore God has joined together let man not put asunder."[13]

"I will find you another ring," her husband said. "You and I are the same as we were on our wedding day; it will do as well. We are husband and wife today too, as much as yesterday, I suppose."

Her face was so still that he did not know if she had heard what he said. It touched him that she should take the loss of his ring so to heart. He took her hand and kissed it. It was cold, not quite the same hand as he had last kissed. He stopped to make her stop with him.

"Do you remember where you had the ring on last?" he asked.

"No," she answered.

"Have you any idea," he asked, "where you may have lost it?"

"No," she answered. "I have no idea at all."

11. *Cambric* is the soft, lightweight linen of which Lise's handkerchief is made.

12. Here, *phosphorescent* (fos′ fə res′ ənt) means "glowing."

13. *Asunder* (ə sun′ dər) means "in separate parts." These words of Jesus (Matthew 19:6) are often repeated at the end of a traditional Christian marriage ceremony.

Vocabulary

definitive (di fin′ ə tiv) *adj.* conclusive; final; decisive
unconditional (un′ kən dish′ ən əl) *adj.* absolute; complete
conceive (kən sēv′) *v.* to form a mental image or idea of; imagine

Responding to Literature

Personal Response

By the end of the story, Lise's feelings toward her husband have changed dramatically. How did this change make you feel? If you had been in Lise's situation, how might you have felt and acted?

Analyzing Literature

Recall

1. Summarize the information the author gives about Lise and Sigismund in the first three paragraphs of the story.
2. Describe the **setting** of the story, particularly the July morning on which the story takes place.
3. What idea strikes Lise as she walks home alone? What does she hope to accomplish with her plan?
4. Summarize what happens in the alcove.
5. How does Lise act when Sigismund rejoins her for the walk home? How does Sigismund interpret his wife's behavior?

Interpret

6. After reading the first three paragraphs of the story, what conclusions can you draw about the relationship between Lise and Sigismund?
7. What elements of the setting contrast with each other? What do you think the author's purpose might be in setting up these contrasts?
8. Consider the plan that Lise makes during her walk home. In your opinion, what does this plan reveal about her?
9. How does Lise feel when the thief closes his eyes? Explain.
10. After her encounter with the thief, Lise thinks, "All is over." In your opinion, what does Lise mean by this?

Evaluate and Connect

11. What do you think the author's attitude is toward Lise? How does the author reveal that attitude?
12. In your opinion, what is the importance of the sheep in this story? What might they **symbolize** (see page R13)?
13. Which of the characters most arouses your sympathy? Why?
14. **Theme Connections** Why, do you think, does Lise not tell Sigismund about the thief? Would you have made the same choice? Explain.
15. Think about the change in Lise's feelings toward her husband. Have you ever experienced such a dramatic change in your feelings toward another person? If so, what caused this change?

Literary ELEMENTS

Characterization

Authors use a variety of methods to reveal what their characters are like. They may describe their characters' appearance, actions, thoughts, feelings, and conversations. These methods are called **characterization.** In this story, for example, the author writes: "Lise wanted to hear more about the horrible event." This lets the reader know that Lise has an immature curiosity about such morbid things as the gruesome fight in the sheep house.

1. Choose Sigismund, Lise, or the thief. Go through the story and identify passages that help reveal what that character is like. Tell what you think each passage reveals about the character.
2. In your opinion, does Sigismund change over the course of the story? Explain your answers.

- See **Literary Terms Handbook,** p. R2.

Literary Criticism

Struthers Brut wonders why Dinesen's tales are so interesting "for the tales themselves, all of them symbolic, are not especially exciting in their plots. . . . But the final effect is unforgettable." Write a letter to this reviewer, explaining whether you found "The Ring" interesting and giving your interpretation of what the ring might symbolize.

Literature and Writing

Writing About Literature

Comparing Characters How are Lise and the thief alike? How are they different? Jot down notes about their appearance, behavior, values, and outlook on life. Use your notes to write two paragraphs about Lise and the thief. In the first paragraph, explain how they are different; in the second one, tell how they are alike.

Personal Writing

The Sequel What do you think might happen after this story ends? Will Lise tell anyone where the thief is hiding? Will the thief just go away, or will he kill again? Will Lise leave her husband? Write a sequel to "The Ring." Compare your sequel with those written by other students.

Extending Your Response

Literature Groups

Will This Marriage Last? Think back to your responses to the Reading Focus on page 224. In your group, share your ideas about the character traits you would value in a spouse. Then discuss whether you think the character traits shown by Sigismund and Lise will enable them to have a successful marriage. Let each group member give his or her opinion on this topic. Tally your group's responses and share the results with the rest of the class.

Internet Connection

Virtual Experience Even if you never get the chance to travel to Denmark to visit the Karen Blixen (Isak Dinesen) Museum, you can learn more about the author on the Internet. Share the information you find with the rest of the group. You may want to print out some of this information and post it on a bulletin board.

Performing

Dialogue Imagine that Lise is asking her parents' permission to marry Sigismund. With two partners, prepare a dialogue between Lise and her parents. Perform your dialogue for the class.

Save your work for your portfolio.

VOCABULARY • Antonyms

You already know that antonyms are words with opposite meanings and that many words don't have antonyms. Several of the vocabulary words in "The Ring" do not have antonyms. (What word could be the opposite of *apparition* or *conceive?*) Other words have many possible antonyms; therefore, you have to think carefully about what a word actually means to identify the word that best represents its opposite.

PRACTICE For each numbered word write the letter of the answer choice that is an antonym.

1. solicitously
   a. hesitantly b. heartlessly c. impatiently
2. unendurably
   a. pleasantly b. temporarily c. cruelly
3. rustic
   a. luxurious b. urban c. cheerful
4. unconditional
   a. limited b. lasting c. neutral
5. definitive
   a. unknown b. meaningful c. hesitant

Grammar Link

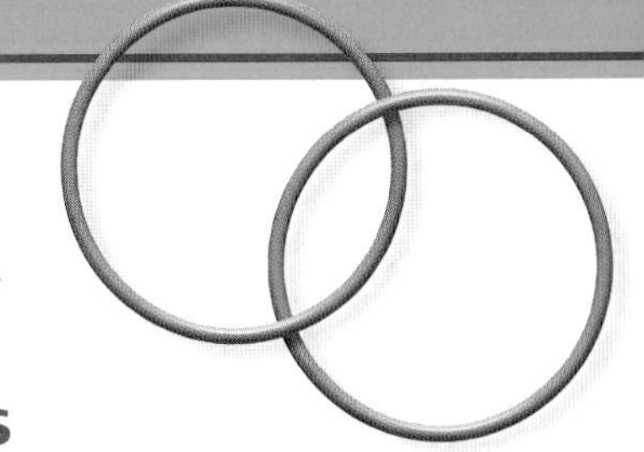

Avoiding Run-on Sentences

A clause is a group of words with a subject and a verb. If a clause can stand alone as a sentence, it is called a main, or independent, clause. Main clauses must be separated from each other by end punctuation, by a comma plus a conjunction, or by a semicolon. A **run-on sentence** is one that fails to obey this rule.

Problem 1 Some run-on sentences contain two main clauses with only a comma between them—an error called a comma splice. (To splice is to join together.)
Lise and Sigismund were happy, they had just been married.

Solution A Separate the main clauses into two sentences.
Lise and Sigismund were happy. They had just been married.

Solution B Add a conjunction with the comma.
Lise and Sigismund were happy, for they had just been married.

Solution C Replace the comma with a semicolon.
Lise and Sigismund were happy; they had just been married.
Beware! Use a semicolon only when the clauses are closely related.

Problem 2 Some run-on sentences contain two main clauses with only a conjunction between them. To hold two main clauses together in one sentence, both a comma and a conjunction are needed.
The couple walked through the meadow and her dog followed them.

Solution A Separate the main clauses into two sentences.
The couple walked through the meadow. Her dog followed them.

Solution B Add a comma before the conjunction.
The couple walked through the meadow, and her dog followed them.

Solution C Replace the conjunction with a semicolon.
The couple walked through the meadow; her dog followed them.

For more about run-on sentences, see **Language Handbook,** p. R15.

EXERCISE

If the sentence is correct, write an *S* on your paper. If it is a run-on sentence, write *R* and rewrite the sentence to correct it.

1. Lise's little dog is named Bijou, it follows her everywhere.
2. Since childhood, Lise has loved Sigismund and Sigismund has loved Lise.
3. Lise did not take Bijou to the field, because the dog would have frightened the sheep.
4. Lise and her husband meet up on the path, they begin to walk home.
5. Will Lise and Sigismund stay together or will their marriage fail?

Writing Workshop

Persuasive Writing:
Letter to the Editor

Everyone has opinions. In persuasive writing, you try to convince readers to agree with your opinion and, sometimes, to take a specific action. One way to bring your opinions to a wide audience is by writing a letter to the editor of a newspaper or magazine. **In this workshop, you will write a letter to the editor on an issue you feel strongly about.** To persuade your readers, you will use details and phrasing that appeal to reason and to emotion.

- As you write your persuasive letter, refer to the **Writing Handbook**, pp. R58–R71.

EVALUATION RUBRIC

By the time you complete this Writing Workshop, you will have

- clearly introduced your position on a specific issue
- presented concrete facts, reasons, and examples for support
- used persuasive techniques geared toward a particular audience
- concluded by restating your position and calling readers to action
- presented a letter that is free of errors in grammar, usage, and mechanics

The Writing Process

PREWRITING

PREWRITING TIP

From the beginning of the process, stay tightly focused on your opinion and use specific, relevant evidence to support it.

Explore ideas

The characters in the stories in Theme Two all had to make a choice–to take a stand about something and act on it. In exploring ideas for your letter to the editor, look for issues that are important to you. Then choose what stand you will take on that issue and what action you want other people to take.

You might write a letter to the editor stating your opinion of the choice made by a character in this theme. You could also look through current periodicals to find articles about issues that you care about. Then use the following questions to explore your opinions.

- What is the real issue here?
- What are the arguments on each side of the issue?
- What position do you choose to take on the issue? What facts support your choice?

Drawing a web can help you clarify your ideas and gather support for your position. Print a statement of the issue at the center of a piece of paper. Around the center show different opinions about the issue. Add ovals for facts and other evidence that support each position.

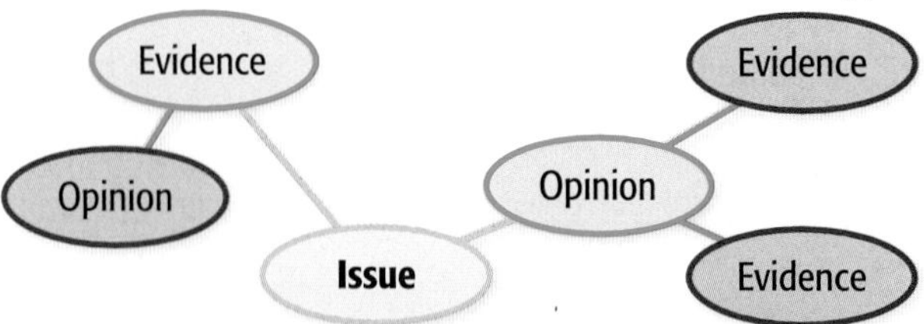

Consider your purpose

Your purpose is to state your opinion, to show that it is reasonable, to persuade your readers to agree with it, and, possibly, to persuade them to take action to support your position.

Choose an audience

In persuasive writing, it is important to know who your audience is and how best to convince them. For a letter to the editor, your audience will be the readers of the newspaper or magazine you write to. Read the letters in a few issues of that publication to get an idea of readers' concerns and attitudes. As you write your own letter, anticipate the readers' reactions.

Consider the conventions of a letter to the editor

You will have a better chance of seeing your letter published if you study the style and format of the letters to the editor in the publication where you intend to send it. Notice how people address the editor and what style of language is used. Many publications include a note somewhere on the letters page that indicates how long letters can be. For more on formatting a business letter, see the **Writing Handbook,** page R70.

Make a plan

Here is one way to organize a persuasive argument.

STUDENT MODEL

Identify the issue and your position	What news article or event inspired you to write? What issue is involved? What is your position? What are some reasons for your position?	An article that said the school board is considering adopting school uniforms in the high school. The freedom to express oneself Making students wear school uniforms would be wrong. The way a student dresses is a matter of individual expression, like free speech.
State and answer opposing views	What is an opposing viewpoint? Why is that viewpoint faulty? What evidence supports your position?	School uniforms decrease violence and improve test scores. (the Long Beach school district had 36% less crime after adopting school uniforms.) The school also assigned more hall monitors; these and other changes the school made, not school uniforms, might be why crime decreased.
Restate your position and call readers to action	What statement sums up your position? What action do you want your readers to take?	Clothing is a form of personal expression, and personal expression is the heart of a democracy. Readers should urge the School Board to vote against making students wear uniforms.

Complete Student Model on p. R110.

DRAFTING

DRAFTING TIP

Draft your letter as if you were trying to convince a friend to agree with you. Be honest, but be persuasive.

Is your argument sound?

In persuasive writing, an argument consists of your position and the support you provide for it. First, make sure your opinion is based on relevant facts and other reasonable evidence, not on rumor, hearsay, and prejudice. Next, use that evidence to support your argument. Include facts and statistics and quote expert opinions when you can.

Write your draft

As you write, refer to your plan to make sure that you are working within the basic structure of stating the issue and your opinion, anticipating and addressing opposing views, and finally summing up and calling readers to action. If, as you write, you discover that this structure isn't working for your argument, don't be afraid to try something new. Keep the ideas coming and keep writing; you may find that an important new idea comes to you as you draft.

STUDENT MODEL

One of the goals of a school is to prepare us for being citizens of a democracy. A democracy can exist only in an environment where everyone tolerates a diversity of opinions, ideas, and ways of life. I think school uniforms would create an atmosphere of intolerance of diversity at my high school. Therefore, adopting school uniforms would also jeopardize our future success as good citizens of the United States of America, a country founded on freedom and the belief that every individual has personal rights. The ACLU agrees with my position. On their Web site, the director of the New York Civil Liberties Union says, "A student's choice of dress is an expressive activity. It should be of no concern to the school."

Complete Student Model on p. R110.

Use this graphic to help you visualize the structure of your letter to the editor.

Issue → Your opinion and reasons → Opposing view and its weakness → Your opinion and call to action

REVISING

Take another look

If you have written about a strong opinion, you may have written an impassioned letter. Good. Now let it cool down for a bit. Put it away and return to it after a while. Look at it with the cold, hard eye of the editor who will receive it. Find the weak spots in your argument and strengthen them. Use the **Rubric for Revising** to guide you as you work.

Read your response aloud

Find a listener for a "field test" of your letter. The best listener is someone who disagrees with your opinion. From your listener's responses, you will get a good indication of how persuasive you have been. (Since your letter isn't polished, don't give the text to your listener, just read it aloud.) Use the listener's responses and the **Rubric for Revising** to help you revise.

REVISING TIP

To strengthen an emotional appeal, replace neutral words with words that have strong positive or negative connotations.

STUDENT MODEL

The article on school uniforms that appeared in Tuesday's issue of your newspaper ~~is typical of the adults around here and really makes me mad.~~ made me angry. ~~It~~ The article said that our ~~so-called concerned~~ school board is considering adopting school uniforms in the high school as a way to decrease violence in the schools and improv~~ing~~e test scores. ~~The way I dress is up to me.~~ As a tenth grader in one of our schools, I believe that adopting this policy would be wrong~~!~~. ~~I can dress however I want. It's like free~~ The way a person dresses is a matter of individual expression, which, like speech ~~and~~ is protected by the U. S. Constitution.

Complete Student Model on p. R110.

RUBRIC FOR REVISING

Your revised letter to the editor should have

- ☑ an attention-getting introduction that clearly identifies the issue and your position on it
- ☑ relevant facts, quotes from experts, and other evidence to support your position
- ☑ a logical and effective response to opposing views
- ☑ specific word choices and arguments that appeal to your particular audience
- ☑ a conclusion that summarizes your position and inspires readers to take a specific action

Your revised letter should be free of

- ☑ rumor, hearsay, and prejudice
- ☑ errors in grammar, usage, and mechanics

EDITING/PROOFREADING

EDITING TIP

Read your letter again. Have you varied the types of sentence structure?

Revise your letter until it says what you want it to say and does not include irrelevant information or unnecessary words. Then edit your letter to correct any errors. Make three editorial passes: one for grammar, one for spelling, and one for punctuation. Use the **Proofreading Checklist** on the inside back cover of this book.

Grammar Hint

Make sure that you have avoided comma splices, independent clauses joined by a comma alone. Make each independent clause a separate sentence, join the clauses with a semicolon, or add a conjunction with a comma.

School uniforms are not the only way to solve problems; schools have found other solutions that do not take away students' individual rights.

- For more about comma splices, see **Language Handbook,** pp. R15–R16.

Complete Student Model

For a complete version of the model developed in this workshop, refer to **Writing Workshop Models**, p. R110.

STUDENT MODEL

The school board is considering making students wear uniforms. I think this would violate student's constitutional right to freedom of expression.

Complete Student Model on p. R110.

PUBLISHING/PRESENTING

PRESENTING TIP

Neatness counts. Newspaper and magazine editors don't have time to decipher poorly written letters.

You will start by sending your letter to your target publication—the newspaper or magazine that you've had in mind all along as the ideal place for your letter to appear. However, you should make a list of back-ups, publications that would also be suitable. If your letter doesn't appear in your first choice after a reasonable time, send it to the next one on your list. You can also post it on an Internet bulletin board devoted to the topic or a related topic.

Reflecting

Think about the process you went through to develop your opinion and find the best evidence to support it. Did your evidence provide strong, relevant support for your argument? Were you able to appeal to your readers' emotions as well as to their intellect?

Save your work for your portfolio.

Twists

The journey of life is marked with unexpected twists and turns that surprise us and keep life interesting. The plots of the stories you will read in this theme all have twists that will intrigue and surprise you—and in some cases, even shock you.

THEME PROJECTS

Listening and Speaking

Where Are They Now? Imagine that you are a reporter interviewing characters from two or three of the stories in this theme, years after the events described in their stories.

1. Consider the twist or surprise that confronts each of the characters you have chosen.
2. Create a list of questions to ask the characters, along with responses they might give.
3. Prepare a report for the "Where Are They Now?" segment of a television newsmagazine, explaining what has happened to the characters since their stories were in the news. Present your report to the class.

Interdisciplinary Project

Art: Design Video Cases Working in a small group, design a video case for a movie version of one of the short stories in this theme.

1. Illustrate a scene from the story for the front cover of the case.
2. Decide how you will show the movie's title and the names of the actors. Experiment with different sizes and styles of type.
3. Create a design for the back cover of the case, as well as the spine. Display your finished video case for the class.

Before You Read

The Happy Man's Shirt

Reading Focus

Very little is needed to make a happy life.

–Marcus Aurelius

The two foes of human happiness are pain and boredom.

–Arthur Schopenhauer

To fill the hour–that is happiness.

–Ralph Waldo Emerson

Small Groups Which quote best describes your group's view of happiness? Explain your choice.

Setting a Purpose Read to learn what might interfere with happiness.

Building Background

The Time and Place

"The Happy Man's Shirt" takes place in Italy, in a time long ago.

Did You Know?

What is happiness? How can a person find happiness? People have been pondering these questions for thousands of years. The great Greek philosopher Aristotle (384–322 B.C.) thought that happiness came through the search for the good life, a life made up of virtuous actions. During the Enlightenment, the French philosopher Jean-Jacques Rousseau (1712–1778) believed that people could find happiness and fulfillment with other people in situations free of the falseness of society. Today, many people seem to think that fame or material wealth will lead to happiness.

Vocabulary Preview

hue (hū) *n.* a color; shade or tint; p. 241

decree (di krē′) *n.* an order or decision made by a judge, monarch, or other official; p. 241

slew (slo͞o) *n.* a large number or group; p. 242

refrain (ri frān′) *n.* in a song or poem, a phrase or verse that is repeated regularly, especially at the end of each stanza; p. 242

retinue (ret′ ən o͞o′) *n.* the group of attendants or servants accompanying a person of rank or authority; p. 242

Meet Italo Calvino

Italo Calvino (ē′ tä lō käl vē′ nō) began writing when he was a teenager in Italy, during the reign of dictator Benito Mussolini. Much of Calvino's early writings—which resemble fables or myths—were influenced by the oppressive political conditions of Mussolini's fascist regime. "When a man cannot give clear form to his thinking, he expresses it in fables." The spare, haunting quality of Calvino's work stems from this early period and continues into his later work. Calvino, who received many important literary awards, wrote novels, stories, essays, and translations.

Italo Calvino was born in Cuba in 1923. He died in 1985. The English translation of the collection in which this story appears was published in 1980.

The Happy Man's Shirt

Retold by Italo Calvino

Translated by George Martin

A king had an only son that he thought the world of. But this prince was always unhappy. He would spend days on end at his window staring into space.

"What on earth do you lack?" asked the king. "What's wrong with you?"

"I don't even know myself, Father."

"Are you in love? If there's a particular girl you fancy, tell me, and I'll arrange for you to marry her, no matter whether she's the daughter of the most powerful king on earth or the poorest peasant girl alive!"

"No, Father, I'm not in love."

The king tried in every way imaginable to cheer him up, but theaters, balls, concerts, and singing were all useless, and day by day the rosy hue drained from the prince's face.

The king issued a decree, and from every corner of the earth came the most learned philosophers, doctors, and professors. The king showed them the prince and asked for their advice. The wise men withdrew to think, then returned to the king. "Majesty, we have given the matter close thought and we have studied the stars. Here's what you must do. Look for a happy man, a man who's happy through and through, and exchange your son's shirt for his."

That same day the king sent ambassadors to all parts of the world in search of the happy man.

A priest was taken to the king. "Are you happy?" asked the king.

Vocabulary

hue (hū) *n.* a color; shade or tint

decree (di krē′) *n.* an order or decision made by a judge, monarch, or other official

"Yes, indeed, Majesty."

"Fine. How would you like to be my bishop?"

"Oh, Majesty, if only it were so!"

"Away with you! Get out of my sight! I'm seeking a man who's happy just as he is, not one who's trying to better his lot."

Thus the search resumed, and before long the king was told about a neighboring king, who everybody said was a truly happy man. He had a wife as good as she was beautiful and a whole slew of children. He had conquered all his enemies, and his country was at peace. Again hopeful, the king immediately sent ambassadors to him to ask for his shirt.

The neighboring king received the ambassadors and said, "Yes, indeed, I have everything anybody could possibly want. But at the same time I worry because I'll have to die one day and leave it all. I can't sleep at night for worrying about that!" The ambassadors thought it wiser to go home without this man's shirt.

At his wit's end, the king went hunting. He fired at a hare but only wounded it, and the hare scampered away on three legs. The king pursued it, leaving the hunting party far behind him. Out in the open field he heard a man singing a refrain. The king stopped in his tracks. "Whoever sings like that is bound to be happy!" The song led him into a vineyard, where he found a young man singing and pruning the vines.

"Good day, Majesty," said the youth. "So early and already out in the country?"

"Bless you! Would you like me to take you to the capital? You will be my friend."

"Much obliged, Majesty, but I wouldn't even consider it. I wouldn't even change places with the Pope."

"Why not? Such a fine young man like you . . ."

"No, no, I tell you. I'm content with just what I have and want nothing more."

"A happy man at last!" thought the king. "Listen, young man. Do me a favor."

"With all my heart, Majesty, if I can."

"Wait just a minute," said the king, who, unable to contain his joy any longer, ran to get his retinue. "Come with me! My son is saved! My son is saved!" And he took them to the young man. "My dear lad," he began, "I'll give you whatever you want! But give me . . . give me . . ."

"What, Majesty?"

"My son is dying! Only you can save him. Come here!"

The king grabbed him and started unbuttoning the youth's jacket. All of a sudden he stopped, and his arms fell to his sides.

The happy man wore no shirt.

Vocabulary

slew (slo͞o) *n.* a large number or group

refrain (ri frān′) *n.* in a song or poem, a phrase or verse that is repeated regularly, especially at the end of each stanza

retinue (ret′ ən o͞o′) *n.* the group of attendants or servants accompanying a person of rank or authority

Responding to Literature

Personal Response

How did you feel when you read the last line of the story? How do you think you would have reacted if you had been in the king's place?

Analyzing Literature

Recall

1. What is wrong with the king's son?
2. What does the king do to try to cure his son? What do the wise men recommend?
3. What does the king eventually discover about the priest and the neighboring king?
4. How does the king discover the happy man? Who is this man?
5. Is the happy man able to do the favor the king requests? Why or why not?

Interpret

6. What might be the real reason the prince is unhappy?
7. Why do you think the wise men make the suggestion they do? How might a shirt help the prince?
8. Do you think the neighboring king would have given his shirt to the ambassadors, had they asked for it? Explain.
9. What makes the king believe that the young man he has found is truly happy?
10. How do you think the king feels when he unbuttons the young man's jacket? Why might the young man be dressed as he is?

Evaluate and Connect

11. Do you think it is possible to have everything one might wish for and still be unhappy, like the prince in this story? Explain.
12. Do you think the king is a good father to his son? Why or why not?
13. In your opinion, does a person like the happy man really exist? Do you think anyone is truly satisfied with what he or she has? Explain your answer.
14. In your opinion, what is the lesson, or **moral,** of this story?
15. **Theme Connections** What makes the ending of this story so surprising? How is the surprise ending related to the moral of the story?

Literary ELEMENTS

Symbol

A **symbol** is a person, an object, or an act that means more than what it is. The symbol refers to or stands for someone or something else. Parables, fables, and folktales, such as "The Happy Man's Shirt," often contain symbols to help get the author's meaning across.

1. What kinds of people do the king and the son in "The Happy Man's Shirt" symbolize?
2. What does the king want for his son? What is the symbol for that quality?
3. What characteristics or qualities might the priest and the other king symbolize?

- See Literary Terms Handbook, p. R13.

Literary Criticism

Critic Franco Ricco observes that Calvino uses fables to explore "moral and social issues." As a class, discuss what moral and social issues Calvino is exploring in "The Happy Man's Shirt." Support your opinions with specific references to the story.

Literature and Writing

Writing About Literature

Performance Review Imagine that you are one of the "wise men" in this story. Write a paragraph in which you evaluate the advice you gave to the king. Explain how you might advise him differently on the matter of his son's unhappiness, should he ever consult you again.

Personal Writing

Happiness Is . . . Record your own thoughts about what happiness is. Consider questions like these: What does a person need in order to be truly happy? Can happiness be bought? Read the quotes in the Reading Focus on page 240. Which quote expresses your ideas about happiness?

Extending Your Response

Literature Groups

Brainstorming When this story ends, the king seems to have failed in his quest to find happiness for his son. Brainstorm ideas about what the king might do next. Will he give up, continue his quest, or ask his advisors for another plan of action? Share your ideas with another group, and discuss which scenarios are the most likely.

Performing

New Endings What might have happened if the happy man had been wearing a shirt? Work with a partner to create a new ending for the story based on this assumption. Share your ending with the rest of the class.

Interdisciplinary Activity

Art: A Picture Book With other students, create a picture-book retelling of this story. Look at several picture books for younger readers for models of how text and illustration interact to tell the story. You will need writers to retell the story, editors to read the story and suggest changes, illustrators to create the artwork, and designers to lay out the text and illustrations on the pages of the book. If you have access to desktop publishing software, it can help guide you through the process. Don't forget to create a cover for your book.

Save your work for your portfolio.

VOCABULARY • Analogies

An analogy is a type of comparison based on relationships between things or ideas. Some analogies are based on *part-to-whole* relationships.

horse : herd :: book : library

There are many horses in a herd; there are many books in a library.

To finish an analogy, decide what relationship exists between the first two things or ideas. Then apply that relationship to another pair of words.

PRACTICE Choose the word that best completes each analogy.

1. bee : swarm :: hue :
   a. color b. rainbow c. design
2. individual : slew :: tree :
   a. plant b. root c. forest
3. attendant : retinue :: bird :
   a. flock b. nest c. wing
4. hymn : refrain :: drama :
   a. scene b. audience c. playwright
5. decree : order :: verdict :
   a. court b. jury c. decision

For more about analogies, see **Communications Skills Handbook,** p. R77.

MEDIA connection

Newspaper Article

Have you ever gotten something that you wanted—a new game, a new pair of shoes, a sum of money—and found that you weren't happy after all? What is happiness, anyway? Read on for advice on how to find it.

What is the meaning of this? We ponder happiness.

by Amanda Vogt—*Chicago Tribune*, August 4, 1998

Happiness is so important to Americans that the right to pursue it is guaranteed in our Declaration of Independence.

Today, happiness often is more closely linked to fame and fortune than freedom. But many people who gain these things still don't find happiness. Think Kurt Cobain or Princess Diana. (It's kind of ironic that their freedom was actually limited by their fame and fortune.) So what is this happiness thing, anyway?

Happiness is a bit of a riddle. It's not a person, place or thing. You can't put a price tag on it.

OK, that tells us what happiness isn't. But what is it?

"Happiness has to do with things that can't be touched or measured," says Geri Piorkowski, director of the counseling center at University of Illinois at Chicago.

Like friendship? Absolutely, says Jeri B., 14, of Chicago, who says happiness

is "friends who love you enough [to] stay and comfort you" when you're down. How about achieving shared goals?

You bet, says Lawrence J., 15, of Wheaton. "Happiness is doing something you love, like building a treehouse or playing baseball, with a bunch of people who love to do it too."

In 1996, a study of more than 1,000 12- to 15-year-olds was conducted by Teenage Research Unlimited (TRU), a market research firm in Northbrook [Illinois]. The study found that 93 percent of kids in this age group see themselves as happy some or most of the time.

But TRU researchers found that as kids approach adulthood and start to worry about grades, appearance, dating and jobs, they report fewer happy times.

So must the happy times dwindle as we get bogged down in the weighty responsibilities of adulthood?

Of course not, counseling director Piorkowski says. "The people who are the most successful at finding happiness tend to be those who keep their lives simple."

So how do you do that? Figure out what you want out of life and go for it, she says. If you know what you want, someone else's ideas about success, happiness or popularity won't matter.

If you're true to yourself, chances are you'll discover a happiness that works for you.

Analyzing Media

1. Does the author think fame, fortune, or freedom is most likely to lead to happiness? Do you think the people she interviewed would agree with her opinion?
2. Which of the above definitions of happiness are most close to your own? What did the advice for finding happiness tell you that you didn't already know?

Vo•cab•u•lar•y Skills

Context Clues

When you come across an unfamiliar word, it's a good idea to check its meaning in a dictionary. But face it, you won't always have a dictionary handy. Besides, stopping to look up every unfamiliar word can really slow down your reading. That's why **context clues** can be so valuable.

The **context** of a word is the sentence or group of sentences in which the word appears. Luckily, the context often provides clues that can help you figure out what an unfamiliar word means. For example, "The Happy Man's Shirt" provides details to explain a happy king's happiness. One detail is that he has "a whole slew of children." The context helps you figure out that *slew* means a large number of something–in this case, children.

There are many different kinds of context clues. Here are some other examples.

Contrast: Grandma was a laconic woman. Grandpa, on the other hand, never stopped talking. (The clue phrase *on the other hand* helps you figure out that *laconic* means the opposite of "never stopped talking.")

Definition: The prince's countenance, or facial expression, was always sad. (The clue word *or* lets you know that *countenance* means "facial expression.")

As you read, look for context clues that can help you figure out the meanings of unfamiliar words. It's easier than lugging a dictionary with you wherever you go!

EXERCISE

Use context clues to figure out what the underlined words mean. On your paper, write a synonym or a short definition for each one.

1. Day by day, the prince's malaise became more serious, and it seemed as though nothing could lift his spirits.
2. What feelings of dread and foreboding must have tortured the king as he thought about the future!
3. The men who came to advise the king were erudite–that is, they were very learned and intelligent men.
4. It seemed like it would be a simple matter to follow the wise men's advice; instead, it turned out to be an arduous task.
5. The king kept trying and trying and trying to help his son–as assiduously as any loving parent would.

Before You Read

The Californian's Tale

Reading Focus

Imagine that you are going on a mission to a distant planet. You will be gone for twenty years and will have little, if any, contact with home.

Quickwrite List the items you would take with you as reminders of the life you are leaving behind.

Setting a Purpose Read to learn how furnishings from "home" affect a group of aging forty-niners.

Building Background

The Time and Place

This story takes place in California, probably during the 1860s or 1870s. What was once a bustling gold-mining area is now overrun with weeds, inhabited only by a few remaining pioneers who could not or would not leave.

Did You Know?

In the ten years following the discovery of gold at Sutter's Mill in 1848, nearly 400,000 people–mostly men–journeyed to California to prospect for gold. During the gold rush many of the forty-niners, as the gold seekers were called, were young. However, hardship, hard work, and poor diet caused them to age quickly. Some did strike it rich, but many more returned east or were forced to take low-paying jobs.

Vocabulary Preview

predecessor (pred′ ə ses′ ər) *n.* one who comes, or has come, before another in time; p. 249

sever (sev′ ər) *v.* to break off; p. 249

materialistic (mə tēr′ ē ə lis′ tik) *adj.* overly concerned with material matters and worldly possessions; p. 250

solace (sol′ is) *n.* relief from sorrow or disappointment; comfort; p. 250

sedate (si dāt′) *adj.* quiet and restrained in style or manner; calm; p. 252

imploring (im plôr′ ing) *adj.* asking earnestly; begging; p. 253

boding (bōd′ ing) *n.* a warning or indication, especially of evil; p. 253

apprehension (ap′ ri hen′ shən) *n.* fear of what may happen; anxiety; p. 253

Meet Mark Twain

Printer, riverboat pilot, miner, journalist, author, lecturer—Mark Twain worked at all of these jobs at various times in his life. Born Samuel Langhorne Clemens, he took the pen name Mark Twain, a nautical term meaning "two fathoms deep," when he wrote humorous pieces for a Nevada newspaper. As a writer, humorist, and lecturer, Twain became a popular American favorite. His most famous works are *The Adventures of Tom Sawyer* and *The Adventures of Huckleberry Finn*. The story you are about to read draws on Twain's experience in prospecting for gold and silver in the West.

Mark Twain was born in 1835 in Missouri and died in 1910.

The Californian's Tale

Mark Twain

Old House with Tree Shadows, 1916. Grant Wood. Oil on composition board, 13 x 15 in. Cedar Rapids Museum of Art, IA. Gift of Happy Young and John B. Turner II.

THIRTY-FIVE YEARS AGO I was out prospecting on the Stanislaus, tramping all day long with pick and pan and horn, and washing a hatful of dirt here and there, always expecting to make a rich strike, and never doing it. It was a lovely region, woodsy, balmy, delicious, and had once been populous, long years before, but now the people had vanished and the charming paradise was a solitude.[1]

They went away when the surface diggings gave out. In one place, where a busy little city with banks and newspapers and fire companies and a mayor and aldermen had been, was nothing but a wide expanse of emerald turf, with not even the faintest sign that human life had ever been present there. This was down toward Tuttletown.[2] In the country neighborhood thereabouts, along the dusty roads, one found at intervals the prettiest little cottage homes, snug and cozy, and so cobwebbed with vines snowed thick with roses that the doors and windows were wholly hidden from sight—sign that these were deserted homes, forsaken years ago by defeated and disappointed families who could neither sell them nor give them away. Now and then, half an hour apart, one came across solitary log cabins of the earliest mining days, built by the first gold-miners, the predecessors of the cottage-builders. In some few cases these cabins were still occupied; and when this was so, you could depend upon it that the occupant was the very pioneer who had built the cabin; and you could depend on another thing, too—that he was there because he had once had his opportunity to go home to the States rich, and had not done it; had rather lost his wealth, and had then in his humiliation resolved to sever all communication with his home relatives and friends, and be to them thenceforth as one dead. Round about California in that day were scattered a host of these living dead men—pride-smitten[3] poor fellows, grizzled[4] and old at forty, whose secret thoughts were made all of regrets and longings—regrets for their wasted lives, and longings to be out of the struggle and done with it all.

It was a lonesome land! Not a sound in all those peaceful expanses of grass and woods but the drowsy hum of insects; no glimpse of man or beast; nothing to keep up your spirits and make you glad to be alive. And so, at last, in the early part of the afternoon, when I caught sight of a human creature, I felt a most grateful uplift. This person was a man about forty-five years old, and he was standing at the gate of one of those cozy little rose-clad cottages of the sort already referred to. However, this one hadn't a deserted look; it had the look of being lived in and petted and cared for and looked after; and so had its front yard, which was a garden of flowers, abundant, gay, and flourishing. I was invited in, of course, and required to make myself at home—it was the custom of the country.

It was delightful to be in such a place, after long weeks of daily and nightly familiarity with miners' cabins—with all which this implies of dirt floor, never-made beds, tin plates and cups, bacon and beans and black coffee, and nothing of ornament but war pictures from the Eastern

1. The narrator was exploring for gold *(prospecting)* along the Stanislaus River in central California. Here, *solitude* refers to a lonely, isolated place.
2. *Tuttletown* was a mining town near the Stanislaus.
3. Someone who is *smitten* is strongly affected by some powerful feeling.
4. *Grizzled* means "gray or mixed with gray."

Vocabulary

predecessor (pred′ ə ses′ ər) *n.* one who comes, or has come, before another in time
sever (sev′ ər) *v.* to break off

illustrated papers tacked to the log walls. That was all hard, cheerless, materialistic desolation, but here was a nest which had aspects to rest the tired eye and refresh that something in one's nature which, after long fasting, recognizes, when confronted by the belongings of art, howsoever cheap and modest they may be, that it has unconsciously been famishing and now has found nourishment. I could not have believed that a rag carpet could feast me so, and so content me; or that there could be such solace to the soul in wall-paper and framed lithographs,[5] and bright-colored tidies[6] and lamp-mats, and Windsor chairs, and varnished what-nots,[7] with sea-shells and books and china vases on them, and the score of little unclassifiable tricks and touches that a woman's hand distributes about a home, which one sees without knowing he sees them, yet would miss in a moment if they were taken away. The delight that was in my heart showed in my face, and the man saw it and was pleased; saw it so plainly that he answered it as if it had been spoken.

Did You Know?
A *Windsor chair* has a high, spoked back, slanting legs, and a slightly curving seat. It is named for the city in England where this style of chair was first designed and built.

"All her work," he said, caressingly; "she did it all herself—every bit," and he took the room in with a glance which was full of affectionate worship. One of those soft Japanese fabrics with which women drape with careful negligence the upper part of a picture-frame was out of adjustment. He noticed it, and rearranged it with cautious pains, stepping back several times to gauge the effect before he got it to suit him. Then he gave it a light finishing pat or two with his hand, and said: "She always does that. You can't tell just what it lacks, but it does lack something until you've done that—you can see it yourself after it's done, but that is all you know; you can't find out the law of it. It's like the finishing pats a mother gives the child's hair after she's got it combed and brushed, I reckon. I've seen her fix all these things so much that I can do them all just her way, though I don't know the law of any of them. But she knows the law. She knows the why and the how both; but I don't know the why; I only know the how."

He took me into a bedroom so that I might wash my hands; such a bedroom as I had not seen for years: white counterpane,[8] white pillows, carpeted floor, papered walls, pictures, dressing-table, with mirror and pin-cushion and dainty toilet things; and in the corner a washstand, with real chinaware bowl and pitcher, and with soap in a china dish, and on a rack more than a dozen towels—towels too clean and white for one out of practice to use without some vague sense of profanation.[9] So my face spoke again, and he answered with gratified words:

"All her work; she did it all herself—every bit. Nothing here that hasn't felt the touch of her hand. Now you would think— But I mustn't talk so much."

5. *Lithographs* are pictures printed by a process in which a flat surface is treated either to retain or to repel ink.
6. *Tidies* are small, decorative coverings placed over the back or arms of a chair or sofa to keep them from being soiled or worn.
7. *What-nots* are open shelves for displaying objects.
8. A *counterpane* is a quilt or bedspread.
9. *Profanation* is the act of making something impure through unworthy use.

Vocabulary

materialistic (mə tēr′ ē ə lis′ tik) *adj.* overly concerned with material matters and worldly possessions

solace (sol′ is) *n.* relief from sorrow or disappointment; comfort

By this time I was wiping my hands and glancing from detail to detail of the room's belongings, as one is apt to do when he is in a new place, where everything he sees is a comfort to his eye and his spirit; and I became conscious, in one of those unaccountable ways, you know, that there was something there somewhere that the man wanted me to discover for myself. I knew it perfectly, and I knew he was trying to help me by furtive indications with his eye, so I tried hard to get on the right track, being eager to gratify him. I failed several times, as I could see out of the corner of my eye without being told; but at last I knew I must be looking straight at the thing—knew it from the pleasure issuing in invisible waves from him. He broke into a happy laugh, and rubbed his hands together, and cried out:

"That's it! You've found it. I knew you would. It's her picture."

I went to the little black-walnut bracket on the farther wall, and did find there what I had not yet noticed—a daguerreotype-case.[10] It contained the sweetest girlish face, and the most beautiful, as it seemed to me, that I had ever seen. The man drank the admiration from my face, and was fully satisfied.

Did You Know?
Here, *bracket* refers to a small shelf hung on the wall and supported by brackets.

"Nineteen her last birthday," he said, as he put the picture back; "and that was the day we were married. When you see her—ah, just wait till you see her!"

That second glimpse broke down my good resolution.

"Where is she? When will she be in?"

"Oh, she's away now. She's gone to see her people. They live forty or fifty miles from here. She's been gone two weeks today."

"When do you expect her back?"

"This is Wednesday. She'll be back Saturday, in the evening—about nine o'clock, likely."

I felt a sharp sense of disappointment.

"I'm sorry, because I'll be gone then," I said, regretfully.

"Gone? No—why should you go? Don't go. She'll be so disappointed."

She would be disappointed—that beautiful creature! If she had said the words herself they could hardly have blessed me more. I was feeling a deep, strong longing to see her—a longing so supplicating, so insistent, that it made me afraid. I said to myself: "I will go straight away from this place, for my peace of mind's sake."

"You see, she likes to have people come and stop with us—people who know things, and can talk—people like you. She delights in it; for she knows—oh, she knows nearly everything herself, and can talk, oh, like a bird—and the books she reads, why, you would be astonished. Don't go; it's only a little while, you know, and she'll be so disappointed."

I heard the words, but hardly noticed them, I was so deep in my thinkings and strugglings. He left me, but I didn't know. Presently he was back, with the picture-case in his hand, and he held it open before me and said:

"There, now, tell her to her face you could have stayed to see her, and you wouldn't."

That second glimpse broke down my good resolution. I would stay and take the risk.

10. A *daguerreotype* (də ger′ ə tīp′) is a photograph produced by exposing light to a silver-coated copper plate, a process invented by Louis Daguerre in France in the mid-1800s.

Portrait of Martha Pickman Rogers in Her Wedding Gown. Albert Sands Southworth (1811–1894) and Josiah Johnson Hawes (1801–1901). Daguerreotype. Courtesy, Museum of Fine Arts, Boston. Bequest of Maxim Karolik.

That night we smoked the tranquil pipe, and talked till late about various things, but mainly about her; and certainly I had had no such pleasant and restful time for many a day. The Thursday followed and slipped comfortably away. Toward twilight a big miner from three miles away came—one of the grizzled, stranded pioneers—and gave us warm salutation, clothed in grave and sober speech. Then he said:

"I only just dropped over to ask about the little madam, and when is she coming home. Any news from her?"

"Oh yes, a letter. Would you like to hear it, Tom?"

"Well, I should think I would, if you don't mind, Henry!"

Henry got the letter out of his wallet, and said he would skip some of the private phrases, if we were willing; then he went on and read the bulk of it—a loving, sedate, and altogether charming and gracious piece of handiwork, with a postscript full of affectionate regards and messages to Tom, and Joe, and Charley, and other close friends and neighbors.

As the reader finished, he glanced at Tom, and cried out:

"Oho, you're at it again! Take your hands away, and let me see your eyes. You always do that when I read a letter from her. I will write and tell her."

"Oh no, you mustn't, Henry. I'm getting old, you know, and any little disappointment makes me want to cry. I thought she'd be here herself, and now you've got only a letter."

"Well, now, what put that in your head? I thought everybody knew she wasn't coming till Saturday."

"Saturday! Why, come to think, I did know it. I wonder what's the matter with me lately? Certainly I knew it. Ain't we all getting ready for her? Well, I must be going now. But I'll be on hand when she comes, old man!"

Late Friday afternoon another gray veteran tramped over from his cabin a mile or so away, and said the boys wanted to have a little

Vocabulary

sedate (si dāt′) *adj.* quiet and restrained in style or manner; calm gaiety and a good time Saturday night, if Henry thought she wouldn't be too tired after her journey to be kept up.

"Tired? She tired! Oh, hear the man! Joe, *you* know she'd sit up six weeks to please any one of you!"

When Joe heard that there was a letter, he asked to have it read, and the loving messages in it for him broke the old fellow all up; but he said he was such an old wreck that *that* would happen to him if she only just mentioned his name. "Lord, we miss her so!" he said.

Saturday afternoon I found I was taking out my watch pretty often. Henry noticed it, and said, with a startled look:

"You don't think she ought to be here so soon, do you?"

I felt caught, and a little embarrassed; but I laughed, and said it was a habit of mine when I was in a state of expectancy. But he didn't seem quite satisfied; and from that time on he began to show uneasiness. Four times he walked me up the road to a point whence we could see a long distance; and there he would stand, shading his eyes with his hand, and looking. Several times he said:

"I'm getting worried, I'm getting right down worried. I know she's not due till about nine o'clock, and yet something seems to be trying to warn me that something's happened. You don't think anything has happened, do you?"

I began to get pretty thoroughly ashamed of him for his childishness; and at last, when he repeated that imploring question still another time, I lost my patience for the moment, and spoke pretty brutally to him. It seemed to shrivel him up and cow[11] him; and he looked so wounded and so humble after that, that I detested myself for having done the cruel and unnecessary thing. And so I was glad when Charley, another veteran, arrived toward the edge of the evening, and nestled up to Henry to hear the letter read, and talked over the preparations for the welcome. Charley fetched out one hearty speech after another, and did his best to drive away his friend's bodings and apprehensions.

"Anything *happened* to her? Henry, that's pure nonsense. There isn't anything going to happen to her; just make your mind easy as to that. What did the letter say? Said she was well, didn't it? And said she'd be here by nine o'clock, didn't it? Did you ever know her to fail of her word? Why, you know you never did. Well, then, don't you fret; she'll *be* here, and that's absolutely certain, and as sure as you are born. Come, now, let's get to decorating—not much time left."

Anything *happened* to her? Henry, that's pure nonsense.

Pretty soon Tom and Joe arrived, and then all hands set about adorning the house with flowers. Toward nine the three miners said that as they had brought their instruments they might as well tune up, for the boys and girls would soon be arriving now, and hungry for a good, old-fashioned breakdown.[12] A fiddle, a banjo, and a clarinet—these were the

11. To *cow* is to frighten with threats.
12. Here, *breakdown* refers to a fast, lively country dance.

Vocabulary

imploring (im plôr′ ing) *adj.* asking earnestly; begging
boding (bōd′ ing) *n.* a warning or indication, especially of evil
apprehension (ap′ ri hen′ shən) *n.* fear of what may happen; anxiety

instruments. The trio took their places side by side, and began to play some rattling dance-music, and beat time with their big boots.

It was getting very close to nine. Henry was standing in the door with his eyes directed up the road, his body swaying to the torture of his mental distress. He had been made to drink his wife's health and safety several times, and now Tom shouted:

"All hands stand by! One more drink, and she's here!"

Joe brought the glasses on a waiter,[13] and served the party. I reached for one of the two remaining glasses, but Joe growled, under his breath:

"Drop that! Take the other."

Which I did. Henry was served last. He had hardly swallowed his drink when the clock began to strike. He listened till it finished, his face growing pale and paler; then he said:

"Boys, I'm sick with fear. Help me—I want to lie down!"

They helped him to the sofa. He began to nestle and drowse, but presently spoke like one talking in his sleep, and said: "Did I hear horses' feet? Have they come?"

One of the veterans answered, close to his ear: "It was Jimmy Parrish come to say the party got delayed, but they're right up the road a piece, and coming along. Her horse is lame, but she'll be here in half an hour."

"Oh, I'm *so* thankful nothing has happened!"

13. The *waiter,* in this case, is a small tray.

He was asleep almost before the words were out of his mouth. In a moment those handy men had his clothes off, and had tucked him into his bed in the chamber where I had washed my hands. They closed the door and came back. Then they seemed preparing to leave; but I said: "Please don't go, gentlemen. She won't know me; I am a stranger."

They glanced at each other. Then Joe said:

"She? Poor thing, she's been dead nineteen years!"

"Dead?"

"That or worse. She went to see her folks half a year after she was married, and on her way back, on a Saturday evening, the Indians captured her within five miles of this place, and she's never been heard of since."

"And he lost his mind in consequence?"

"Never has been sane an hour since. But he only gets bad when that time of the year comes round. Then we begin to drop in here, three days before she's due, to encourage him up, and ask if he's heard from her, and Saturday we all come and fix up the house with flowers, and get everything ready for a dance. We've done it every year for nineteen years. The first Saturday there was twenty-seven of us, without counting the girls; there's only three of us now, and the girls are all gone. We drug him to sleep, or he would go wild; then he's all right for another year—thinks she's with him till the last three or four days come round; then he begins to look for her, and gets out his poor old letter, and we come and ask him to read it to us. Lord, she was a darling!"

Responding to Literature

Personal Response

Did the ending of the story surprise you? Explain why or why not.

Analyzing Literature

Recall

1. Describe the **setting** of the story. How does the narrator describe the men who still live in the log cabins?
2. How is the interior of the cottage different from the miners' cabins in which the narrator has been staying?
3. How does the narrator react to the woman's picture?
4. Summarize what happens at the cottage on Saturday evening before Henry falls asleep.
5. Summarize what the narrator learns about the woman from Henry's friend.

Interpret

6. What is the narrator's attitude toward the men who live in the log cabins? Support your answer with evidence from the story.
7. In your opinion, what do the furnishings, pictures, and other objects in the cottage **symbolize** for the narrator? Look at the list of items you made in the Reading Focus on page 247. What do these items symbolize for you?
8. In your opinion, how does the narrator feel about meeting the woman?
9. In your opinion, why do the miners encourage Henry in his delusion? Why don't they help him face the truth?
10. Why do Henry's friends wait so long to reveal the truth to the narrator?

Evaluate and Connect

11. Suggest possible reasons the author might have for not revealing the woman's name.
12. Identify three ways in which the author builds **suspense.**
13. Just as we celebrate happy anniversaries, we also commemorate sad ones. Give at least one example of a somber national event and describe how people choose to recognize it.
14. If a friend of yours were in a situation similar to Henry's, how would you handle the dilemma? Give reasons for your choice.
15. **Theme Connections** In what ways does the twist in the plot change the way you think about the characters?

Literary ELEMENTS

Style

Style is the author's choice and arrangement of words in a piece of writing. In "The Californian's Tale," Mark Twain uses an intimate, conversational style that helps draw the reader into the story.

1. Find at least two passages in the story that express the narrator's personal reactions and opinions.
2. How does the use of dialogue help prepare the reader for the surprise ending?
3. Twain uses specific details to re-create the geography, customs, and speech of the region in which the story takes place. Give at least two examples of such details.

- See **Literary Terms Handbook,** p. R12.

Literary Criticism

"As readers have generally agreed for more than 100 years," argues Henry B. Wonham, "Mark Twain is at his best at the level of village life, where regional peculiarities directly inform his conceptions of setting and character." How are the characters and setting in "The Californian's Tale" particular to the American West and its gold-mining lifestyle? Write several paragraphs examining the regionalism in the story.

Literature and Writing

Writing About Literature

Analyze a Literary Technique Although Henry's wife is absent from the story, a detailed image of her emerges. Analyze in two or three paragraphs how Twain is able to create such a clear image of a character who never appears in the story. Share your analysis with others in a small group.

Creative Writing

Double Twist Surprise readers one more time. Add a new twist to the ending, developing additional characters and details, as necessary.

Extending Your Response

Literature Groups

To Tell the Truth? Were Henry's friends right not to make him face the truth nineteen years ago? How might Henry's life have been different had he faced the truth? Debate these questions in your group, then share your ideas with the class.

Interdisciplinary Activity

Earth Science: Gold Fever Find out about the gold deposits that lured forty-niners to California in the mid-1800s. You might focus on what geological forces created such gold deposits or on how miners extracted the gold from the land. Make a model or a drawing to illustrate your findings and share it with the class.

Learning for Life

Community Support The characters in this story find ways to cope with isolation, tragedy, and disappointment. When people in your own community find themselves in similar circumstances, where can they turn for help? Research the community resources that are available. List several resources and the services that each one offers.

Reading Further

You might enjoy these works by and about Mark Twain:

Novel: *Roughing It,* a semiautobiographical novel, includes Twain's humorous description of his own stagecoach journey through the American West.

Short Story: "The Celebrated Jumping Frog of Calaveras County," published in 1865, made Twain an "overnight sensation."

Viewing: *The Incredible Rocky Mountain Race* tells the epic story of a cross-country race between Mark Twain and legendary character Mike Fink.

Save your work for your portfolio.

Skill Minilessons

GRAMMAR AND LANGUAGE • Dashes

Dashes are used to indicate an abrupt break or change in thought within a sentence or to set off and emphasize supplemental information:

"Now you would think–But I mustn't talk so much."

"All her work; she did it all herself–every bit."

PRACTICE Rewrite the following sentences, adding dashes where needed.

1. The narrator is a miner but that's irrelevant to the plot.
2. Henry's wife was charming so charming that all of Henry's miner friends loved her.
3. Henry's home showed a woman's touch lovely linens, wallpaper, framed artwork, and a variety of decorative objects.
4. Gold fever spread like wildfire everyone wanted to strike it rich.

For more about using dashes, see **Language Handbook,** p. R49.

READING AND THINKING • Scanning

Scanning is glancing over a piece of writing in search of specific information, such as the answer to a question, a detail to support a fact or opinion, or a quote from a character in a story. For example, you might have scanned "The Californian's Tale" after you had read it to find clues you missed about Henry's problem. To scan a story, quickly glance over the text, looking for key words or phrases that will help you find the information you need. Don't waste time reading every word.

For more about related reading strategies, see **Reading Handbook,** pp. R78–R107.

PRACTICE Use scanning to find the answers to these questions about "The Californian's Tale."

1. Who are the people that the narrator refers to as "living dead men"?
2. Where had Henry's wife gone?
3. How does Tom react when Henry reads aloud the letter from his wife?
4. What is "the cruel and unnecessary thing" that the narrator does?
5. What does Joe say when the narrator reaches for the wrong glass?

VOCABULARY • The Prefix *Pre-*

The English prefix *pre-* always means either "before" (prehistoric) or "leading up to" (preschool). However, *pre-* is also a Latin prefix (spelled *prae*) that was attached to many Latin words before they became part of the English language. For example, *preface* comes from the Latin *prae* plus *fari* ("to speak"), not from the English *pre-* plus *face*.

PRACTICE For each of the following words, write *English* if you think the prefix *pre-* is attached to an English base word. Write *Latin* if you think it is attached to a Latin root. Then use a dictionary to check your work.

1. preheat
2. predict
3. predecessor
4. premature
5. preview
6. presume
7. pretense
8. preliminary
9. predetermined
10. present

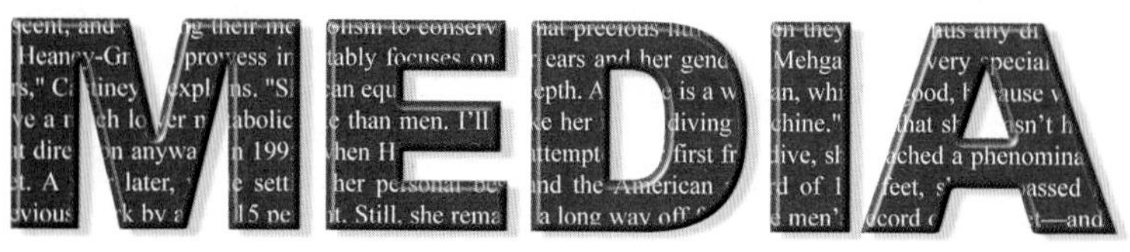

connection

Web Site

Do you have a dog—or know a dog—who might like to know what the future holds? Here's what a dog's horoscope might look like.

This Week's Horoscope for Your Dog

Address: www.purina.com

Aquarius Dog *(Jan. 20–Feb. 18)* Break your routine. Head to an out-of-the-way park for new trees and scents.

Pisces Dog *(Feb. 19–Mar. 20)* Shine as a leader. Start the nightly neighborhood bark-a-thon. Stop the minute it starts so you don't get blamed.

Aries Dog *(Mar. 21–Apr. 19)* Keep alert and you'll enjoy the unexpected. An extra treat tossed your way for no reason. The long-lost ball that appears out of nowhere.

Taurus Dog *(Apr. 20–May 20)* Focus on the written word. Get out and fetch a newspaper. Chew on a magazine left carelessly within reach. It's a good way to digest the news.

Gemini Dog *(May 21–June 21)* Attention revolves around you. Soak it up. You won't have to look far for a hand to pet you, a lap to cuddle in, or a scratch behind the ears.

Cancer Dog *(June 22–July 22)* Decisions, decisions. Chew the rubber toy or the rawhide? Doze on the couch or in the sunbeam? Fetch or roll over? It's a week of tough choices.

Leo Dog *(July 23–Aug. 22)* You were just trying to help, but Mom and Dad didn't see it that way, and now you're in the doghouse (or basement, or garage). Oh, well. Time for a nap.

Virgo Dog *(Aug. 23–Sept. 22)* Communication is essential this week. Rev up those vocal chords with a few good growls and wait for the moon to make its debut. When it does, howl away.

Libra Dog *(Sept. 23–Oct. 23)* Teamwork is in the offing. Joining forces with the Lab next door may help you scare off that pesky little squirrel in the far oak. Pairing up with the kids gets you in the pool on a hot afternoon.

Scorpio Dog *(Oct. 24–Nov. 22)* Investigation is needed this week. Tune up the ol' sniffer and head out into the yard. Track that smell to the back fence, then around to the hose and over to the edge of the patio. Track the scent again and again; it'll be dinnertime soon.

Sagittarius Dog *(Nov. 23–Dec. 21)* Security is the watchword of the day. Pay close attention to the front and back doors. Prick up your ears and keep that tail up; the integrity of the perimeter depends on you.

Capricorn Dog *(Dec. 22–Jan. 19)* Tend to financial matters. You need to tally your assets, so head to the yard and start digging. There's satisfaction in seeing your wealth piled in front of you. Now re-bury and invest for the future.

Analyzing Media

1. In your opinion, which dogs had the most fun this week?
2. Which horoscope reminds you of a pet you have known or read about? Explain.

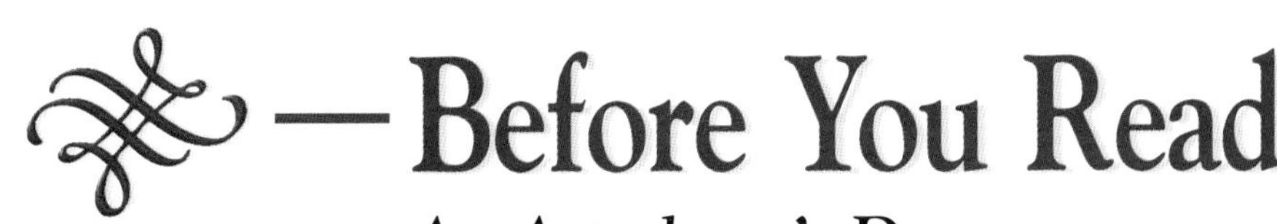

Before You Read

An Astrologer's Day

Reading Focus

What would it be like to look into your future and learn what will happen in your life?

List It! List three questions that you would like to have answered about your future.

Setting a Purpose Read to learn what is revealed when a man asks about his future.

Building Background

The Time and Place

"An Astrologer's Day" takes place in Malgudi, an imaginary town in southern India, probably in the 1940s.

Did You Know?

Some astrologers claim the ability to foretell an individual's future by drawing and studying a chart called a *horoscope.* A horoscope shows the configuration of the planets and stars at the moment of an individual's birth; this configuration supposedly influences that person's life. Those who believe in astrology may rely on their astrologers to counsel them on major decisions. Astronomers and other scientists, however, maintain that the configuration of heavenly bodies has nothing whatever to do with human destiny.

Vocabulary Preview

enhance (en hans′) *v.* to make greater, as in beauty or value; p. 260
dally (dal′ ē) *v.* to linger; delay; waste time; p. 260
impetuous (im pech′ o͞o əs) *adj.* rushing headlong into things; rash; p. 262
paraphernalia (par′ ə fər nāl′ yə) *n.* things used in a particular activity; equipment; p. 262
piqued (pēkt) *adj.* aroused to anger or resentment; offended; p. 262
incantation (in′ kan tā′ shən) *n.* words spoken in casting a spell; p. 262

Meet R. K. Narayan

After realizing that he did not want to be a teacher, civil servant, or journalist, R. K. Narayan (nä rä′ yan) turned to fiction writing as a career. His first novel, *Swami and Friends*, was published in 1935. Narayan has written ten novels and numerous short stories; he also has published nonfiction works. His tales of the fictional Indian village of Malgudi—the setting for the story you are about to read—have had a wide appeal. In fact, Narayan is probably best known as the creator of Malgudi, a place that has been called a "zany, eccentric and, at the same time, true-to-life world."

Rasipuram Krishnaswami Narayan was born in 1906 in Madras, India. "An Astrologer's Day" was published in 1947.

An Astrologer's

R. K. Narayan

PUNCTUALLY AT MIDDAY he opened his bag and spread out his professional equipment, which consisted of a dozen cowrie[1] shells, a square piece of cloth with obscure mystic charts on it, a notebook and a bundle of palmyra writing. His forehead was resplendent with sacred ash and vermilion,[2] and his eyes sparkled with a sharp abnormal gleam which was really an outcome of a continual searching look for customers, but which his simple clients took to be a prophetic light and felt comforted. The power of his eyes was considerably enhanced by their position—placed as they were between the painted forehead and the dark whiskers which streamed down his cheeks: even a half-wit's eyes would sparkle in such a setting. To crown the effect he wound a saffron-colored[3] turban around his head. This color scheme never failed. People were attracted to him as bees are attracted to cosmos or dahlia stalks. He sat under the boughs of a spreading tamarind tree which flanked a path running through the Town Hall Park. It was a remarkable place in many ways: a surging crowd was always moving up and down this narrow road morning till night. A variety of trades and occupations was represented all along its way: medicine-sellers, sellers of stolen hardware and junk, magicians and, above all, an auctioneer of cheap cloth, who created enough din all day to attract the whole town. Next to him in vociferousness[4] came a vendor of fried groundnuts, who gave his ware a fancy name each day, calling it Bombay Ice-Cream one day, and on the next Delhi Almond, and on the third Raja's Delicacy, and so on and so forth, and people flocked to him. A considerable portion of this crowd dallied before the astrologer too. The astrologer transacted his business by the light of a flare which crackled and smoked up above the groundnut heap nearby. Half the enchantment of the place was due to the fact that it did not have the benefit of municipal lighting. The place was lit up by shop lights. One or two had hissing gaslights, some had

1. The *cowrie* (kau′ rē) is a small snail commonly found in warm, shallow waters of the Pacific and Indian Oceans.
2. Here, *obscure* means "difficult to understand" and *mystic* means "having hidden or secret meanings." *Palmyra* (pal mī′ ra) refers to paper made from the leaves of the palmyra tree. The man's forehead is full of splendor *(resplendent)* in that it is painted with dark ash and a red pigment called *vermilion*.
3. *Saffron* is an orange-yellow color.
4. *Vociferousness* (vō sif′ ər əs nəs) means "noisy outcrying."

Vocabulary

enhance (en hans′) *v.* to make greater, as in beauty or value
dally (dal′ ē) *v.* to linger; delay; waste time

By permission of the British Library.

Day

naked flares stuck on poles, some were lit up by old cycle lamps and one or two, like the astrologer's, managed without lights of their own. It was a bewildering criss-cross of light rays and moving shadows. This suited the astrologer very well, for the simple reason that he had not in the least intended to be an astrologer when he began life; and he knew no more of what was going to happen to others than he knew what was going to happen to himself next minute. He was as much a stranger to the stars as were his innocent customers. Yet he said things which pleased and astonished everyone: that was more a matter of study, practice and shrewd guesswork. All the same, it was as much an honest man's labor as any other, and he deserved the wages he carried home at the end of a day.

He had left his village without any previous thought or plan. If he had continued there he would have carried on the work of his forefathers—namely, tilling the land, living, marrying and ripening in his cornfield and ancestral home. But that was not to be. He had to leave home without telling anyone, and he could not rest till he left it behind a couple of hundred miles. To a villager it is a great deal, as if an ocean flowed between.

He had a working analysis of mankind's troubles: marriage, money and the tangles of human ties. Long practice had sharpened his perception. Within five minutes he understood what was wrong. He charged three pice[5] per question and never opened his mouth till the other had spoken for at least ten minutes, which provided him enough stuff for a dozen answers and advices. When he told the person before him, gazing at his palm, "In many ways you are not getting the fullest results for your efforts," nine out of ten were disposed to agree with him. Or he questioned: "Is there any woman in your family, maybe even a distant relative, who is not well disposed[6] towards you?" Or he gave an analysis of character:

5. A *pice* is a coin of India of very small value.
6. In this paragraph, *disposed* is used twice with slightly different meanings. The first time, you might substitute *likely* or *inclined*. The second time, substitute *favorable* for the phrase "well disposed."

"Most of your troubles are due to your nature. How can you be otherwise with Saturn where he is? You have an impetuous nature and a rough exterior." This endeared him to their hearts immediately, for even the mildest of us loves to think that he has a forbidding exterior.

The nuts-vendor blew out his flare and rose to go home. This was a signal for the astrologer to bundle up too, since it left him in darkness except for a little shaft of green light which strayed in from somewhere and touched the ground before him. He picked up his cowrie shells and paraphernalia and was putting them back into his bag when the green shaft of light was blotted out; he looked up and saw a man standing before him. He sensed a possible client and said: "You look so careworn. It will do you good to sit down for a while and chat with me." The other grumbled some vague reply. The astrologer pressed his invitation; whereupon the other thrust his palm under his nose, saying: "You call yourself an astrologer?" The astrologer felt challenged and said, tilting the other's palm towards the green shaft of light: "Yours is a nature . . ." "Oh, stop that," the other said. "Tell me something worthwhile. . . ."

Our friend felt piqued. "I charge only three pice per question, and what you get ought to be good enough for your money. . . ." At this the other withdrew his arm, took out an anna and flung it out to him, saying, "I have some questions to ask. If I prove you are bluffing, you must return that anna to me with interest."

"If you find my answers satisfactory, will you give me five rupees?"[7]

"No."

"Or will you give me eight annas?"

"All right, provided you give me twice as much if you are wrong," said the stranger. This pact was accepted after a little further argument. The astrologer sent up a prayer to heaven as the other lit a cheroot.[8] The astrologer caught a glimpse of his face by the matchlight. There was a pause as cars hooted on the road, *jutka*[9] drivers swore at their horses and the babble of the crowd agitated the semi-darkness of the park. The other sat down, sucking his cheroot, puffing out, sat there ruthlessly. The astrologer felt very uncomfortable. "Here, take your anna back. I am not used to such challenges. It is late for me today. . . ." He made preparations to bundle up. The other held his wrist and said, "You can't get out of it now. You dragged me in while I was passing." The astrologer shivered in his grip; and his voice shook and became faint. "Leave me today. I will speak to you tomorrow." The other thrust his palm in his face and said, "Challenge is challenge. Go on." The astrologer proceeded with his throat drying up. "There is a woman . . ."

"Stop," said the other. "I don't want all that. Shall I succeed in my present search or not? Answer this and go. Otherwise I will not let you go till you disgorge[10] all your coins." The astrologer muttered a few incantations and replied, "All right. I will speak. But will you give me a rupee if what I say is convincing? Otherwise I will not open my mouth, and you may do what you like." After a

7. The *anna* is a former coin of India that was equal to four pice. The *rupee* is a coin of India (and other countries) equal to sixteen annas.

8. A *cheroot* (shə ro͞ot′) is a cigar cut square at both ends.

9. A *jutka* (jo͞ot′ kə) is a two-wheeled, horse-drawn vehicle.

10. Here, *disgorge* means "to give up or hand over."

Vocabulary

impetuous (im pech′ o͞o əs) *adj.* rushing headlong into things; rash

paraphernalia (par′ ə fər nāl′ yə) *n.* things used in a particular activity; equipment

piqued (pēkt) *adj.* aroused to anger or resentment; offended

incantation (in′ kan tā′ shən) *n.* words spoken in casting a spell good deal of haggling the other agreed. The astrologer said, "You were left for dead. Am I right?"

"Ah, tell me more."

"A knife has passed through you once?" said the astrologer.

"Good fellow!" He bared his chest to show the scar. "What else?"

"And then you were pushed into a well nearby in the field. You were left for dead."

"I should have been dead if some passerby had not chanced to peep into the well," exclaimed the other, overwhelmed by enthusiasm. "When shall I get at him?" he asked, clenching his fist.

"In the next world," answered the astrologer. "He died four months ago in a far-off town. You will never see any more of him." The other groaned on hearing it. The astrologer proceeded.

"Guru Nayak—"

"You know my name!" the other said, taken aback.[11]

"As I know all other things. Guru Nayak, listen carefully to what I have to say. Your village is two days' journey due north of this town. Take the next train and be gone. I see once again great danger to your life if you go from home." He took out a pinch of sacred ash and held it out to him. "Rub it on your forehead and go home. Never travel southward again, and you will live to be a hundred."

"Why should I leave home again?" the other said reflectively.[12] "I was only going away now and then to look for him and to choke out his life if I met him." He shook his head regretfully. "He has escaped my hands. I hope at least he died as he deserved." "Yes," said the astrologer. "He was crushed under a lorry."[13] The other looked gratified to hear it.

The place was deserted by the time the astrologer picked up his articles and put them into his bag. The green shaft was also gone, leaving the place in darkness and silence. The stranger had gone off into the night, after giving the astrologer a handful of coins.

It was nearly midnight when the astrologer reached home. His wife was waiting for him at the door and demanded an explanation. He flung the coins at her and said, "Count them. One man gave all that."

"Twelve and a half annas," she said, counting. She was overjoyed. "I can buy some *jaggery*[14] and coconut tomorrow. The child has been asking for sweets for so many days now. I will prepare some nice stuff for her."

"The swine has cheated me! He promised me a rupee," said the astrologer. She looked up at him. "You look worried. What is wrong?"

"Nothing."

After dinner, sitting on the *pyol*,[15] he told her, "Do you know a great load is gone from me today? I thought I had the blood of a man on my hands all these years. That was the reason why I ran away from home, settled here and married you. He is alive."

She gasped, "You tried to kill!"

"Yes, in our village, when I was a silly youngster. We drank, gambled and quarreled badly one day—why think of it now? Time to sleep," he said, yawning, and stretched himself on the *pyol*.

11. The expression *taken aback* means "suddenly surprised or startled."
12. Here, *reflectively* (ri flek′ tiv lē) means "in a way that shows serious and careful consideration."
13. Here, the *lorry* is a long, flat, horse-drawn wagon.
14. *Jaggery* is unrefined sugar made from palm tree sap.
15. A *pyol* (pī′ ôl) is a low bench.

Responding to Literature

Personal Response

Were you surprised by the outcome of the story, particularly the astrologer's conversation with his wife? Explain why or why not.

Analyzing Literature

Recall

1. According to the narrator, how does the astrologer's appearance help him attract customers?
2. Describe the astrologer's place of business.
3. Summarize the agreement the astrologer and the stranger make. What does the astrologer try to do after making the agreement?
4. What does the astrologer tell the stranger about his past? What advice does he give him about his future?
5. What does the astrologer finally reveal to his wife about his past?

Interpret

6. In your opinion, what service does the astrologer actually perform for his customers?
7. Compare the life the astrologer expected to live with the one he is actually living.
8. What details indicate that the astrologer is afraid of the stranger? What causes this fear, in your opinion?
9. Why does the astrologer know so much about the stranger's past? Why does he give him this particular advice about his future?
10. Do you think the astrologer feels remorseful about the incident he reveals to his wife? Support your answer with details from the story.

Evalaute and Connect

11. Look back at the questions you listed in the Reading Focus on page 259. How do you think the astrologer might answer your questions?
12. In your opinion, what is **ironic** about Guru Nayak's meeting with the astrologer? (See Literary Terms Handbook, page R6.)
13. What do you think might have happened if the stranger had arrived earlier in the day? Explain your answer.
14. You may have heard the expression, "The past has a way of coming back to haunt you." How does that expression apply to this story? To what real-life experiences might the expression be applied?
15. In your opinion, why do people seek advice about the future? From whom do people today seek such advice?

Literary ELEMENTS

Description

Description is writing that helps readers imagine what characters see, hear, feel, taste, or touch. Notice the vivid description in this passage from "An Astrologer's Day": "The astrologer caught a glimpse of [the stranger's] face by the matchlight. There was a pause as cars hooted on the road, *jutka* drivers swore at their horses and the babble of the crowd agitated the semidarkness of the park." Descriptive language can help bring a character to life. Description also can help build suspense or provide clues about what might happen next.

1. List descriptive details that help you visualize the marketplace in which the astrologer conducts his business.
2. What details and techniques does Narayan use to describe the astrologer?

- See **Literary Terms Handbook,** p. R3.

Literary Criticism

William Walsh writes about the Indian village where Narayan set many of his stories: "Whatever happens in India happens in Malgudi, and whatever happens in Malgudi happens everywhere." With a partner, consider how this quotation applies to "An Astrologer's Day." What story elements are universal? Which are unique to the time and place in which the story is set?

Literature and Writing

Writing About Literature

Changing Impressions The characters who live in or pass through the fictional town of Malgudi are not always what they first appear to be. In a paragraph, describe your first impression of either the astrologer or the stranger. Then write a second paragraph explaining how your impression may have changed as the story progressed. Support your first and later impressions with details from the story. Share your writing with others in a small group.

Creative Writing

Guru Nayak's Story Retell all or part of this story from the first-person point of view, with the stranger as the narrator. You may wish to begin the story at an earlier time, perhaps the day on which the stranger quarreled with the man who later became an astrologer. Feel free to invent details or conversations, as necessary.

Extending Your Response

Literature Groups

You Be the Judge Does the astrologer deserve to be punished for what he did to Guru Nayak? Does his apparent lack of remorse make his crime seem even worse? Do you think it's unfair that he seems to have gotten away with his crime? Does the fact that he was a "silly youngster" when he committed the crime make him any less responsible for his actions? Debate these issues in your group. Share your ideas with the class.

Interdisciplinary Activity

Art: An Astrologer's Portrait Create a portrait of the astrologer. Before you begin, carefully reread the description of the astrologer in the first paragraph of the story. Compare your portrait with those created by your classmates.

Performing

Dialogue With a partner, practice performing all or part of the dialogue between the astrologer and the stranger. Do your best to duplicate the actions and gestures described in the story. Simulate these actions when necessary—for example, the student portraying the stranger should pretend to light a cigar. Perform your dialogue for the class.

Reading Further

You might also enjoy these short stories by R. K. Narayan:

"Uncle" from *A Horse and Two Goats* tells how a young boy grows up under the guidance of his uncle.

"A Career" from *Under the Banyan Tree* recounts how a young man seems perfect in every way, except for one major flaw.

Save your work for your portfolio.

Skill Minilessons

GRAMMAR AND LANGUAGE • Concrete and Abstract Nouns

A **noun** is a word that names a person, place, thing, or idea. A **concrete noun** names something that occupies space, or that you can see, hear, taste, smell, or feel. "An Astrologer's Day" includes such concrete nouns as *magicians, shadows, din,* and *groundnuts.* An **abstract noun** names an idea, a quality, or a characteristic. Abstract nouns from the story include such words as *enchantment, danger,* and *guesswork.*

PRACTICE On your paper, make two columns. Label one column *Concrete Nouns* and the other *Abstract Nouns.* Write each of the following words in the correct column. Then write three or four sentences in which you use as many of the nouns as possible.

> astrologer, turban, flare, thought, money, palm, incantations, babble, enthusiasm, coins, coconut, silence, blood, challenge, perception

APPLY Review one or two pieces of your writing. List at least ten concrete nouns and five abstract nouns from your work.

● For more about nouns, see **Language Handbook,** pp. R40–R41.

READING AND THINKING • Making Inferences

The narrator of "An Astrologer's Day" reveals a great deal of information about the characters, especially the astrologer. Still, the reader must make **inferences**—reasonable judgments based on information in the story—in order to fully understand the characters and the plot. For example, the narrator doesn't directly state the astrologer's economic status. What can you infer about it from this passage describing the marketplace?

> The place was lit up by shop lights. One or two had hissing gaslights, some had naked flares stuck on poles, some were lit up by old cycle lamps and one or two, like the astrologer's, managed without lights of their own.

It would be reasonable to infer that the astrologer is poor, since he apparently cannot afford lighting for his place of business.

PRACTICE Reread the last seven paragraphs of the story. On your paper, list inferences you might make about the astrologer's wife, based on her words and actions.

APPLY What inference might you make about Guru Nayak's economic situation? List the information on which your inference is based.

● For more about inferences, see **Reading Handbook,** pp. R78–R107.

VOCABULARY • Etymology

Sometimes it is hard to recognize that two words are related in meaning because the spelling of one word has changed over time. For example, *incantation,* which means "words spoken in casting a spell," comes from the same root as *chant* and *enchant.* That connection would be clearer if the *h* hadn't been dropped. Still, learning the etymology, or history, of the word *incantation* makes the relationship clear and can help you remember what the word means.

PRACTICE Use a dictionary to look up the etymologies of each pair of words. (A word's etymology is usually given in brackets along with its definition.) Then briefly explain what their etymologies reveal about how the two words are related.

1. *impetuous* and *petulant*
2. *pique* and *piquant*
3. *enhance* and *haughty*

LISTENING, SPEAKING, and VIEWING

Storytelling

In "An Astrologer's Day," the astrologer is such a convincing storyteller that he makes the "stranger" believe a lie. Oral storytellers have played an important role in cultures around the world, from ancient times to the present day. Their stories have served not only to entertain people but also to pass on a culture's history, values, traditions, and customs from one generation to another. A storyteller brings a tale to life by making the telling of a story into a performance. The storyteller speaks dramatically, uses gestures, and sometimes includes sound effects and music. How would you like to step into the shoes of a storyteller? These guidelines can help you prepare and tell a story.

Practicing a Story

- Become familiar enough with your story that you remember all the important details in the correct order. Remember, you won't *read* the story, you'll *tell* it. So don't memorize the story word for word; just memorize what happens.
- Practice telling your story in front of a mirror. Speak clearly and distinctly. Vary the pitch and tone of your voice to convey excitement, surprise, and other emotions.
- If you wish, add sound effects or music to your performance. You can make your own sound effects using your voice, your hands, or simple tools.
- Use gestures and facial expressions to emphasize exciting parts of your story.
- Ask a friend or family members to watch your performance and give you tips on ways to make it more effective. You might even have someone videotape your performance so that you can critique it yourself.

Telling the Story

- Before you begin, take a deep breath and relax.
- Prepare your audience to listen to your story. If necessary, set the scene by telling where and when the story takes place, and what it is about.
- Enjoy your performance! Your listeners are likely to share your level of enthusiasm.

ACTIVITIES

1. Find and view a videotape of a master storyteller. Take notes on how the storyteller uses tone of voice, gestures, expressions, and sound effects to create a mood and "paint pictures" for the audience. Share your observations with the class.
2. Search through books of folktales and myths to find one you would like to tell, or choose one of the short stories in this book. Use the suggestions given in this lesson to prepare your performance. Then make your debut as a storyteller before the class.

Before You Read

The Interlopers

Reading Focus

Have you ever had an enemy you no longer disliked or a friend you no longer liked, and yet felt bound to maintain the relationship—just the way it was?

Quickwrite List reasons you might be unwilling or unable to break off with a friend, or to reconcile with a former enemy. Why is it sometimes so difficult to change an existing relationship with another person?

Setting a Purpose Read to learn about two men who are caught in an old relationship.

Building Background

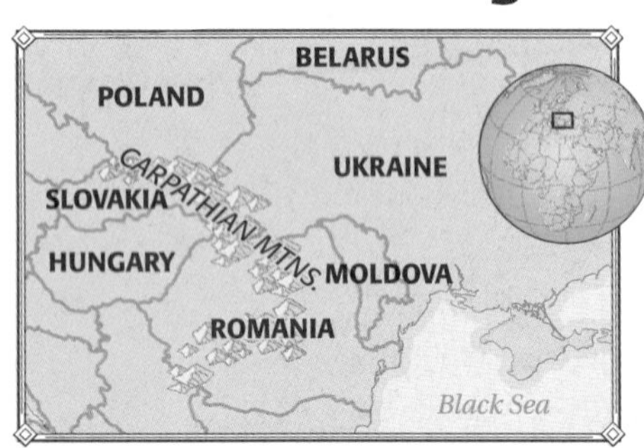

The Time and Place

"The Interlopers" takes place in the Carpathian Mountains in southeast Europe, probably in the early 1900s.

Did You Know?

Poaching—trespassing on another person's land to hunt or fish—has been a crime, sometimes punishable by death, for hundreds of years. In some parts of the world today, poachers illegally capture or kill wild animals to sell to collectors, or they kill the animals and then sell their skins or other body parts.

Vocabulary Preview

acquiesce (ak′ wē es′) *v.* to consent or agree to without protest; p. 270
wont (wōnt) *adj.* accustomed; used; p. 270
pious (pī′ əs) *adj.* having either genuine or pretended religious devotion; p. 272
endeavor (en dev′ ər) *n.* a serious or strenuous attempt to accomplish something; p. 272
languor (lang′ gər) *n.* weakness; fatigue; p. 273
reconciliation (rek′ ən sil′ ē ā′ shən) *n.* a settlement of a controversy or disagreement; p. 274
succor (suk′ ər) *n.* help; assistance; relief; p. 274
pestilential (pes′ tə len′ shəl) *adj.* harmful; destructive; p. 274

Meet H. H. Munro (Saki)

After his mother's early death, H. H. Munro, who was born in Burma (now Myanmar) to Scottish parents, was sent to England to live with relatives. As a young man, Munro had the opportunity to travel widely. Eventually he turned to journalism and short-story writing, using the name *Saki* (sä′ kē)—which he took from a twelfth-century Persian poem—as a pseudonym. During World War I, when he was forty-four, Munro felt compelled to enlist in the British army. Two years later he died on a battlefield in France.

Hector Hugh Munro was born in 1870 and died in 1916.

IN A FOREST of mixed growth somewhere on the eastern spurs of the Carpathians,[1] a man stood one winter night watching and listening, as though he waited for some beast of the woods to come within the range of his vision, and, later, of his rifle. But the game for whose presence he kept so keen an outlook was none that figured in the sportsman's calendar as lawful and proper for the chase; Ulrich von Gradwitz[2] patrolled the dark forest in quest of a human enemy.

1. The *Carpathians* are a mountain range in southeast Europe, and their *spurs* are ridges of mountains that extend from the main range.
2. *Ulrich von Gradwitz* (o͞ol′ rik fōn gräd′ vitz)

Poacher, 1894. Bruno Liljefors. Oil on canvas, 61 x 41 cm. Statens Konstmuseer, Stockholm.

The Interlopers

Saki

The forest lands of Gradwitz were of wide extent and well stocked with game; the narrow strip of precipitous woodland that lay on its outskirt was not remarkable for the game it harbored or the shooting it afforded, but it was the most jealously guarded of all its owner's territorial possessions. A famous lawsuit, in the days of his grandfather, had wrested it from the illegal possession of a neighboring family of petty landowners; the dispossessed party had never acquiesced in the judgment of the Courts, and a long series of poaching affrays[3] and similar scandals had embittered the relationships between the families for three generations. The neighbor feud had grown into a personal one since Ulrich had come to be head of his family; if there was a man in the world whom he detested and wished ill to it was Georg Znaeym,[4] the inheritor of the quarrel and the tireless game-snatcher and raider of the disputed border-forest. The feud might, perhaps, have died down or been compromised if the personal ill-will of the two men had not stood in the way; as boys they had thirsted for one another's blood, as men each prayed that misfortune might fall on the other, and this wind-scourged[5] winter night Ulrich had banded together his foresters to watch the dark forest, not in quest of four-footed quarry,[6] but to keep a look-out for the prowling thieves whom he suspected of being afoot from across the land boundary. The roebuck, which usually kept in the sheltered hollows during a storm-wind, were running like driven things tonight, and there was movement and unrest among the creatures that were wont to sleep through the dark hours. Assuredly there was a disturbing element in the forest, and Ulrich could guess the quarter from whence it came.

Did You Know?
A *roebuck* is the male of the roe deer, which reaches a height of about thirty inches at the shoulder.

He strayed away by himself from the watchers whom he had placed in ambush on the crest of the hill, and wandered far down the steep slopes amid the wild tangle of undergrowth, peering through the tree-trunks and listening through the whistling and skirling[7] of the wind and the restless beating of the branches for sight or sound of the marauders. If only on this wild night, in this dark, lone spot, he might come across Georg Znaeym, man to man, with none to witness—that was the wish that was uppermost in his thoughts. And as he stepped round the trunk of a huge beech he came face to face with the man he sought.

The two enemies stood glaring at one another for a long silent moment. Each had a rifle in his hand, each had hate in his heart and murder uppermost in his mind. The chance had come to give full play to the

3. The woods are on a very steep *(precipitous)* hillside. The court took the land, as if by force (*wrested* it), and returned it to Gradwitz's family. However, the two families continued their dispute with noisy public quarrels *(affrays)* in which each side accused the other of hunting illegally *(poaching)* on its land.
4. *Georg Znaeym* (gā′ ôrg znē′ əm)
5. *Wind-scourged* means "wind-whipped."
6. *Quarry* (kwôr′ ē) refers to an animal—or anything—that is being hunted or pursued.
7. *Skirling* is any long, shrill sound, but the word originally referred to the sound of a bagpipe.

Vocabulary
acquiesce (ak′ wē es′) *v.* to consent or agree to without protest
wont (wōnt) *adj.* accustomed; used

The Wood at Dusk. William Fraser Garden (1856–1921). Watercolor. Private collection.
Viewing the painting: How does this scene help you picture the setting of the story?

passions of a lifetime. But a man who has been brought up under the code of a restraining civilization cannot easily nerve himself to shoot down his neighbor in cold blood and without word spoken, except for an offense against his hearth[8] and honor. And before the moment of hesitation had given way to action a deed of Nature's own violence overwhelmed them both. A fierce shriek of the storm had been answered by a splitting crash over their heads, and ere[9] they could leap aside a mass of falling beech tree had thundered down on them. Ulrich von Gradwitz found himself stretched on the ground, one arm numb beneath him and the other held almost as helplessly in a tight tangle of forked branches, while both legs were pinned beneath the fallen mass. His heavy shooting-boots had saved his feet from being crushed to pieces, but if his fractures were not as serious as they might have been, at least it was evident that he could not move from his present position till some one came to release him. The descending twigs had slashed the skin of his face, and he had to wink away some drops of blood from his eyelashes before he could take in a general view

8. Here, *hearth* is used figuratively to mean "home and family."
9. *Ere* (âr) is an old word for *before.*

of the disaster. At his side, so near that under ordinary circumstances he could almost have touched him, lay Georg Znaeym, alive and struggling, but obviously as helplessly pinioned[10] down as himself. All round them lay a thick-strewn wreckage of splintered branches and broken twigs.

Relief at being alive and exasperation at his captive plight brought a strange medley of pious thank-offerings and sharp curses to Ulrich's lips. Georg, who was nearly blinded with the blood which trickled across his eyes, stopped his struggling for a moment to listen, and then gave a short, snarling laugh.

"So you're not killed, as you ought to be, but you're caught, anyway," he cried; "caught fast. Ho, what a jest, Ulrich von Gradwitz snared in his stolen forest. There's real justice for you!"

And he laughed again, mockingly and savagely.

"I'm caught in my own forest-land," retorted Ulrich. "When my men come to release us you will wish, perhaps, that you were in a better plight than caught poaching on a neighbor's land, shame on you."

Georg was silent for a moment; then he answered quietly:

"Are you sure that your men will find much to release? I have men, too, in the forest tonight, close behind me, and *they* will be here first and do the releasing. When they drag me out from under these damned branches it won't need much clumsiness on their part to roll this mass of trunk right over on the top of you. Your men will find you dead under a fallen beech tree. For form's sake I shall send my condolences to your family."

"It is a useful hint," said Ulrich fiercely. "My men had orders to follow in ten minutes' time, seven of which must have gone by already, and when they get me out—I will remember the hint. Only as you will have met your death poaching on my lands I don't think I can decently send any message of condolence to your family."

Both men spoke with the bitterness of possible defeat before them.

"Good," snarled Georg, "good. We fight this quarrel out to the death, you and I and our foresters, with no cursed interlopers[11] to come between us. Death and damnation to you, Ulrich von Gradwitz."

"The same to you, Georg Znaeym, forest-thief, game-snatcher."

Both men spoke with the bitterness of possible defeat before them, for each knew that it might be long before his men would seek him out or find him; it was a bare matter of chance which party would arrive first on the scene.

Both had now given up the useless struggle to free themselves from the mass of wood that held them down; Ulrich limited his endeavors to an effort to bring his one

10. To be *pinioned* is to be disabled by the binding of one's arms.

11. *Interlopers* are people who violate or interfere with the rights of another, such as by trespassing.

Vocabulary

pious (pī′ əs) *adj.* having either genuine or pretended religious devotion

endeavor (en dev′ ər) *n.* a serious or strenuous attempt to accomplish something partially free arm near enough to his outer coat-pocket to draw out his wine-flask. Even when he had accomplished that operation it was long before he could manage the unscrewing of the stopper or get any of the liquid down his throat. But what a Heaven-sent draught[12] it seemed! It was an open winter, and little snow had fallen as yet, hence the captives suffered less from the cold than might have been the case at that season of the year; nevertheless, the wine was warming and reviving to the wounded man, and he looked across with something like a throb of pity to where his enemy lay, just keeping the groans of pain and weariness from crossing his lips.

"Could you reach this flask if I threw it over to you?" asked Ulrich suddenly; "there is good wine in it, and one may as well be as comfortable as one can. Let us drink, even if tonight one of us dies."

"No, I can scarcely see anything; there is so much blood caked round my eyes," said Georg, "and in any case I don't drink wine with an enemy."

Ulrich was silent for a few minutes, and lay listening to the weary screeching of the wind. An idea was slowly forming and growing in his brain, an idea that gained strength every time that he looked across at the man who was fighting so grimly against pain and exhaustion. In the pain and languor that Ulrich himself was feeling the old fierce hatred seemed to be dying down.

"Neighbor," he said presently, "do as you please if your men come first. It was a fair compact. But as for me, I've changed my mind. If my men are the first to come you shall be the first to be helped, as though you were my guest. We have quarrelled like devils all our lives over this stupid strip of forest, where the trees can't even stand upright in a breath of wind. Lying here tonight, thinking, I've come to think we've been rather fools; there are better things in life than getting the better of a boundary dispute. Neighbor, if you will help me to bury the old quarrel I—I will ask you to be my friend."

Georg Znaeym was silent for so long that Ulrich thought, perhaps, he had fainted with the pain of his injuries. Then he spoke slowly and in jerks.

"How the whole region would stare and gabble[13] if we rode into the market-square together. No one living can remember seeing a Znaeym and a von Gradwitz talking to one another in friendship. And what peace there would be among the forester folk if we ended our feud tonight. And if we choose to make peace among our people there is none other to interfere, no interlopers from outside. . . . You would come and keep the Sylvester night beneath my roof, and I would come and feast on some high day[14] at your castle. . . . I would never fire a shot on your land, save when you invited me as a guest; and you should come and shoot with me down in the marshes where the wildfowl are. In all the countryside there are none that could hinder if we willed to make peace. I never thought to have wanted to do other than hate you all my life, but I think I have changed my mind about things too, this last half-hour. And you

12. *Draught* is the amount taken in one drink. The word is pronounced the same as, and is often spelled, *draft.*

13. *Gabble* means "to talk rapidly and foolishly; jabber."

14. *Sylvester night* refers to New Year's Eve festivities honoring Saint Sylvester who, according to legend, converted Constantine the Great to Christianity after curing him of leprosy. A *high day* is any holy day (or *holiday*) in the church calendar.

Vocabulary
languor (lang′ gər) *n.* weakness; fatigue

offered me your wine-flask. . . . Ulrich von Gradwitz, I will be your friend."

For a space both men were silent, turning over in their minds the wonderful changes that this dramatic reconciliation would bring about. In the cold, gloomy forest, with the wind tearing in fitful gusts through the naked branches and whistling round the tree-trunks, they lay and waited for the help that would now bring release and succor to both parties. And each prayed a private prayer that his men might be the first to arrive, so that he might be the first to show honorable attention to the enemy that had become a friend.

The two raised their voices in a prolonged hunting call.

Presently, as the wind dropped for a moment, Ulrich broke silence.

"Let's shout for help," he said; "in this lull our voices may carry a little way."

"They won't carry far through the trees and undergrowth," said Georg, "but we can try. Together, then."

The two raised their voices in a prolonged hunting call.

"Together again," said Ulrich a few minutes later, after listening in vain for an answering halloo.

"I heard something that time, I think," said Ulrich.

"I heard nothing but the pestilential wind," said Georg hoarsely.

There was silence again for some minutes, and then Ulrich gave a joyful cry.

"I can see figures coming through the wood. They are following in the way I came down the hillside."

Both men raised their voices in as loud a shout as they could muster.

"They hear us! They've stopped. Now they see us. They're running down the hill towards us," cried Ulrich.

"How many of them are there?" asked Georg.

"I can't see distinctly," said Ulrich; "nine or ten."

"Then they are yours," said Georg; "I had only seven out with me."

"They are making all the speed they can, brave lads," said Ulrich gladly.

"Are they your men?" asked Georg. "Are they your men?" he repeated impatiently as Ulrich did not answer.

"No," said Ulrich with a laugh, the idiotic chattering laugh of a man unstrung with hideous fear.

"Who are they?" asked Georg quickly, straining his eyes to see what the other would gladly not have seen.

"*Wolves.*"

Vocabulary

reconciliation (rek′ ən sil′ ē ā′ shən) *n.* a settlement of a controversy or disagreement
succor (suk′ ər) *n.* help; assistance; relief
pestilential (pes′ tə len′ shəl) *adj.* harmful; destructive

Responding to Literature

Personal Response

Were you surprised by the way the story ended? What thoughts went through your mind at the end of the story? Describe your reactions in your journal.

Analyzing Literature

Recall

1. What started the feud between Ulrich von Gradwitz and Georg Znaeym? What caused the feud to become personal?
2. Why are Ulrich and Georg out on such a "wind-scourged" night?
3. Describe what happens to Ulrich and Georg as a result of "a deed of Nature's own violence." How does the men's relationship gradually change after this event?
4. What events does Georg envision as coming from his new relationship with Ulrich?
5. Who are the figures that Ulrich sees coming through the forest?

Interpret

6. In your opinion, why do Ulrich and Georg hate each other so much?
7. Do Ulrich and Georg seem to meet by chance or by design? Explain your answer.
8. In your opinion, what causes the change in the men's relationship? Support your answer with evidence from the story.
9. Why do you think the feud between Ulrich and Georg has gone on for such a long time? As you consider this question, refer to the reasons you listed in the Reading Focus on page 268.
10. What is **ironic** about the way the story ends? (See page R6.)

Evaluate and Connect

11. Would you continue a family feud, as Ulrich and Georg have done? Give reasons for your answer.
12. Describe the **mood** of this story. How does the mood change as the story progresses?
13. To whom or what might the title of this story refer?
14. **Theme Connections** "The Interlopers," like many of Saki's stories, has a "trick ending." Why might Saki have chosen to end the story in this manner? What message might the author wish to convey?
15. Do you agree with Ulrich when he says that "there are better things in life than getting the better of a boundary dispute"? Explain your answer.

Literary ELEMENTS

Conflict

The two main characters in "The Interlopers" confront both **internal** and **external conflicts.** For example, when Ulrich and Georg come face to face in the forest, each struggles with an internal conflict–the desire to shoot down the other in cold blood. Before either man can resolve this internal conflict, a falling tree creates an external conflict that both men must confront.

1. Briefly describe another internal conflict faced by either or both of the main characters in this story. How is this conflict resolved?
2. Consider the bitter family feud that Ulrich and Georg have inherited. In your opinion, is this feud an internal or external conflict? Explain your answer.
3. What external conflict do both men face at the end of the story? How do you think this conflict is resolved? In your opinion, why doesn't the author describe the resolution of this conflict?

- See **Literary Terms Handbook,** p. R3.

Literature and Writing

Writing About Literature

Setting Saki uses many sensory details in describing the setting of "The Interlopers." Write a one-paragraph description of the story's setting, incorporating as many sensory details as possible. In a second paragraph, discuss how the setting of the story contributes to its mood, or atmosphere. Share your writing with others in a small group.

Creative Writing

The Sequel What happens after "The Interlopers" ends? Write a sequel to the story, in which you narrate the events that occur after Ulrich identifies the figures that are running toward him and Georg.

Extending Your Response

Literature Groups

In Cold Blood? What might have happened if the tree had not fallen on Ulrich and Georg? At the time of the accident, each man "had a rifle in his hand, each had hate in his heart and murder uppermost in his mind." In your group, discuss what you think might have happened, had not "a deed of Nature's own violence overwhelmed them both." Support your opinion with evidence from the story or from your own experience. Share your ideas with the class.

Interdisciplinary Activity

History: Famous Feuds A feud between two families plays an important role in "The Interlopers." Throughout history there have been many famous feuds. For example, in the 1860s, a feud began between two Appalachian families, the Hatfields and the McCoys. This feud lasted about thirty years and left at least twenty people dead. One of the most famous feuds in literature is the one between the Montagues and the Capulets in Shakespeare's *Romeo and Juliet.* Research a famous feud in history or in literature. Share your findings with the class.

Performing

Dialogue With a partner, practice all or part of the dialogue that Georg and Ulrich have while they are pinned under the fallen tree. Think about the emotions that each character is experiencing, and do your best to convey those emotions as you speak. Perform the dialogue for the class.

Reading Further

If you want to read more of Saki's short stories, you might consult these collections:

Surprising Stories by Saki: Twenty-Two Tales with Twists, a collection of fascinating stories, includes "Tobermory," a story about an unusual cat.

The Chronicles of Clovis includes "Sredni Vashtar," a story whose main character depicts Saki's Aunt Augusta.

Save your work for your portfolio.

Skill Minilessons

GRAMMAR AND LANGUAGE • Sentence Variety

Varying the length of sentences is one way to make a piece of writing more interesting. For example, in the third paragraph of "The Interlopers," Saki uses three sentences. The first sentence is quite long; the second sentence is about half as long as the first; and the third sentence is shorter still. By varying the length of his sentences, Saki holds the reader's attention. He avoids the monotony of too many long sentences in a row, as well as the choppy sound of too many short sentences.

For more about sentences, see **Language Handbook,** p. R43.

PRACTICE Rewrite the following passage so that it has sentences of varying lengths. Feel free to rearrange ideas and add words or phrases.

> Ulrich lay pinned under the tree. He was suffering great pain. He looked over at Georg. His enemy was in the same predicament. Ulrich's great hatred for Georg began to melt away. He realized how stupid their quarrel really was. Ulrich decided to ask Georg to be his friend.

APPLY Review a piece of your writing. Revise your sentences as needed to vary their length.

READING AND THINKING • Summarizing

When you summarize events in a short story, you briefly describe the main events, leaving out most of the details. For example, the following paragraph summarizes the first part of "The Interlopers."

> On a cold winter night, Ulrich von Gradwitz patrols a forest on the border of his property. He hopes to catch his neighbor, Georg Znaeym, in the act of trespassing. The two neighbors have inherited a bitter family feud over ownership of this forest. Soon Ulrich gets his wish: he and his enemy come face to face. But before either man can act, a falling tree pins both of them to the ground.

PRACTICE Write a summary of the events that occur from the moment Ulrich and Georg find themselves pinned under the tree, to the end of "The Interlopers."

For more about summarizing, see **Reading Handbook,** pp. R78–R107.

VOCABULARY • Analogies

An analogy is a type of comparison based on the relationships between things or ideas. Some analogies are based on a relationship that can be called "an action and its significance."

hug : affection :: wince : pain

A hug is a sign of affection; a wince is a sign of pain.

To finish an analogy, decide what relationship exists between the first two things or ideas. Then apply that relationship to another pair of words.

For more about analogies, see **Communications Skills Handbook,** p. R77.

PRACTICE Choose the word that best completes each analogy. Some of the analogies are based on a relationship of action and its significance.

1. nurse : succor :: teacher :
   a. education b. school c. homework
2. nod : acquiesce :: frown :
   a. agree b. disapprove c. displease
3. pestilential : beneficial :: studious :
   a. lazy b. diligent c. wealthy
4. handshake : reconciliation :: applause :
   a. explanation b. truce c. approval

Before You Read

As It Is with Strangers

Reading Focus

What might it be like to meet a relative you didn't know existed?

Draw the Line! With a partner, brainstorm to develop a list of feelings you might experience upon meeting a long-lost relative. Draw a line to show a continuum of feelings. Write "extremely uncomfortable" at one end of the line and "totally at ease" at the other. List a variety of feelings that might fall between the two extremes.

Extremely uncomfortable ———————————— Totally at ease

Setting a Purpose Read to learn how a surprise relative affects the narrator's relationship with her mother.

Building Background

The Time and Place

This story takes place in the recent past, in an unnamed city or town in the United States.

Did You Know?

The practice of adoption dates back to the time of ancient Greece and Rome. Today, the main purpose of adoption is to improve the lives of adoptive children. While adoption can be a joyful experience for adoptive parents, it is often difficult for birth parents to give up a child. Also, problems can arise when adopted children want information about their birth parents, or when birth parents want to find a child they have given up for adoption. Many agencies refuse to provide access to adoption records. One approach to solving this problem has been to establish registries that help adopted children and birth parents make contact.

Vocabulary Preview

presumably (pri zo͞o′ mə blē) *adv.* supposedly; probably; p. 279

prodigal (prod′ i gəl) *adj.* recklessly wasteful; p. 280

sanctity (sangk′ tə tē) *n.* the quality of deserving solemn respect as something not to be violated; p. 281

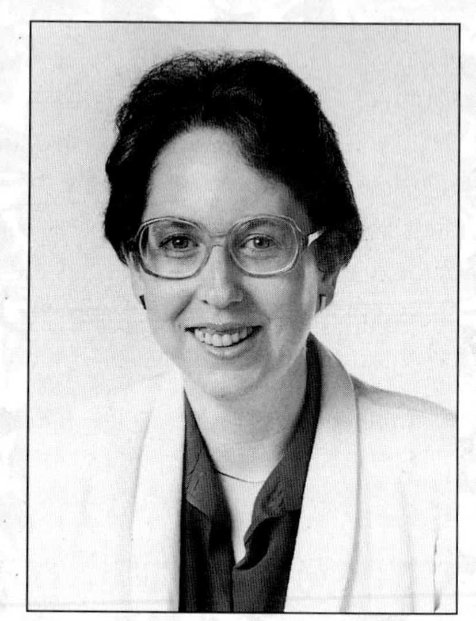

Meet Susan Beth Pfeffer

When she was six, Susan Pfeffer's father, a lawyer, published a book and dedicated it to her. She loved seeing her name in print and decided then and there to become a writer. Earlier, she had planned to become either a cowgirl or the Queen of England. Pfeffer wrote often throughout school and was a professional writer by the time she was twenty-one. She hasn't forgotten her childhood fantasies, however. ". . . Queen of England is a job I could handle . . . (I look wonderful in crowns)," she has written.

Susan Beth Pfeffer was born in 1948 in New York City. This story was first published in 1989.

As It Is with Strangers

Susan Beth Pfeffer

IT WASN'T UNTIL right before I went to bed on Thursday that Mom bothered to tell me the son she'd given up for adoption twenty years earlier was coming over for supper the next day.

"What son?" I asked.

"I'm sure I've told you about him," Mom said. "You must have forgotten."

I figured I probably had. I'm always forgetting little things like my homework assignments and being elected President of the United States. Having an older brother must have just slipped my mind. "How'd you two find each other?" I asked. Presumably Mom had never told me that.

"I registered with an agency," she said. "Put my name and address in a book, so if he ever wanted to find me, he could. I guess he did. Don't be late for supper tomorrow."

"I won't be," I promised. This was one reunion I had no intention of missing.

School the next day really dragged on. School never goes fast on Fridays, but when your mind is on some newly acquired half brother, it's real hard to care about Julius Caesar.[1] I didn't tell anybody, though. It seemed to me it was Mom's story, not mine, and besides, my friends all think she's crazy anyway. Probably from things I've said over the years.

I went straight home from school, and was surprised, first to find the place spotless, and then to see Mom in the kitchen cooking away.

"I took a sick day," she informed me. "So I could prepare better."

1. In referring to *Julius Caesar,* the narrator probably means the title character in the play by William Shakespeare. (This play begins on page 778 of this anthology.)

Vocabulary

presumably (pri zo͞o′ mə blē) *adv.* supposedly; probably

"Everything looks great," I told her. It was true. I hadn't seen the place look so good since Great-Aunt Trudy came with the goat, but that's another story. "You look very pretty too."

"I got my nails done," Mom said, showing them off for me. They were coral colored. "And my hair."

I nodded. Mom had taught me that nothing was unbearable if your hair looked nice.

"Is that what you're planning to wear tonight?" she asked.

"I thought I'd shower and change into my dress," I said. I own a grand total of one dress, but this seemed to be the right kind of occasion for it.

Mom gave me a smile like I'd just been canonized.[2] "Thank you," she said. "Tonight's kind of important for me."

I nodded. I wasn't sure just what to say anymore. Mom and I have been alone for eight years, and you'd figure by now I'd know how to handle her under any circumstances, but this one had me stumped. "What's for supper?" I finally asked.

"Southern fried chicken," Mom said. "At first I thought I'd make a roast, but then what if he doesn't like his meat rare? And turkey seemed too Thanksgivingish, if you know what I mean. Everybody likes fried chicken. And I made mashed potatoes and biscuits and a spinach salad."

"Spinach salad?" I asked. I could picture Mom pouring the spinach out of a can and dousing it with Wishbone.[3]

"From scratch," Mom informed me. "Everything's from scratch. And I baked an apple pie too. The ice cream is store bought, but I got one of those expensive brands. What do you think?"

I thought that there obviously was something to that Prodigal Son[4] story, since Mom never made anything more elaborate for me than scrambled eggs. "It smells great," I said. It did, too, the way you picture a house in a commercial smelling, all homey and warm. "I'm sure everything will go fine."

"I want it to," Mom said, as though I'd suggested that maybe she didn't.

There were a few things I knew I'd better clear up before Big Brother showed up. "What's his name?" I asked, for starters.

"Jack," Mom said. "That's not what I would have named him. I would have named him Ronald."

"You would have?" I asked. I personally am named Tiffany, and Ronald would not have been my first guess.

"That was my boyfriend's name," Mom said. "Ronny."

"Your boyfriend," I said. "You mean his father?"

Mom nodded. "You think of them as boyfriends, not fathers, when you're sixteen," she said.

Well that answered question number two. It had seemed unlikely to me that my father was responsible, but who knew? I wasn't there. Maybe he and Mom had decided they wanted a girl, and chucked out any boys that came along first.

Speaking of which. "There aren't any other brothers I've forgotten about?" I asked. "Is this going to be the first of many such dinners?"

2. In some Christian religions, to be *canonized* is to be declared a saint. Here, of course, the narrator is making a joke.

3. *Wishbone* is the brand name of a line of salad dressings.

4. In the *Prodigal Son* story from the Christian Bible, an older son is bitter when his younger brother, who had left home and wasted his inheritance, is warmly welcomed home by their father.

Vocabulary

prodigal (prod′ i gəl) *adj.* recklessly wasteful

"Jack's the only one," Mom replied. "I wanted to keep him, but Ronny wasn't about to get married, and Dad said if I gave him up for adoption then I could still go to college. I did the right thing, for him and for me. And I would have gone to college if I hadn't met your father. I don't know. Maybe because I gave up the baby, I was too eager to get married. I never really thought about it."

"Did Dad know?" I asked.

"I told him," Mom said. "He said it didn't matter to him. And it didn't. Whatever else was wrong in our marriage, he never threw the baby in my face."

I found myself picturing a baby being thrown in Mom's face, and decided I should take my shower fast. So I sniffed the kitchen appreciatively and scurried out. In the shower I tried to imagine what this Jack would look like, but he kept resembling Dad's high-school graduation picture, which made no sense biologically at all. So I stopped imagining.

When I went to my bedroom to change, though, I was really shocked. Mom had extended her cleaning ways to include my room. All my carefully laid out messes were gone. It would probably take me months to reassemble things. I considered screaming at Mom about the sanctity of one's bedroom, but I decided against it. Mom obviously wanted this guy to think she and I were the perfect American family, and if that meant even my room had to be clean, then nothing was going to stop her. I could live with it, at least for the evening.

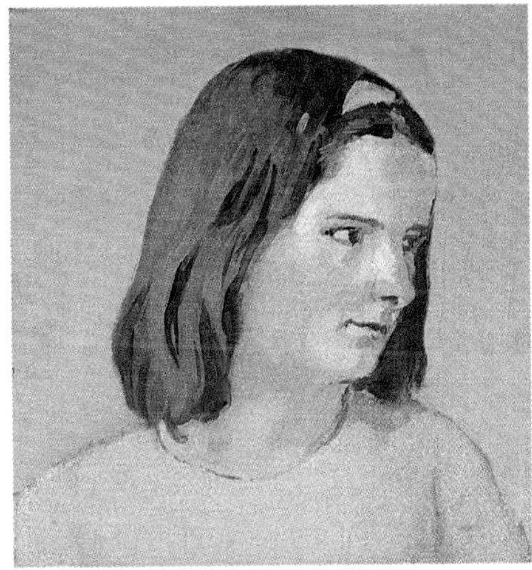

Katie, 1964. Fairfield Porter. Oil on canvas, 15 x 14½ in. Permanent collection of the Art Students League of New York.

Viewing the painting: Does the girl in this painting fit your image of Tiffany? Explain.

Mom and I set the table three times before the doorbell finally rang. When it did, neither one of us knew who should answer it, but Mom finally opened the door.

"Hello," this guy said. "I'm Jack."

"I'm Linda," Mom replied. "Come on in. It's nice to . . . well, it's good seeing you."

"Good to see you too," Jack said. He didn't look anything like my father.

"This is Tiffany," Mom said. "She, uh . . ."

"Her daughter," I said. "Your sister." I mean, those words were going to be used at some point during the evening. We might as well get them out of the way fast. Then when we got around to the big tricky words like *mother* and *son*, at least some groundwork would have been laid.

"It's nice to meet you," Jack said, and he gave me his hand to shake, so I shook it. They say you can tell a lot about a man from his handshake, but not when he's your long-lost brother. "I hope my coming like this isn't any kind of a brother. I mean bother."

"Not at all," Mom said. "I'm going to check on dinner. Tiffany, why don't you show Jack the living room? I'll join you in a moment."

Vocabulary

sanctity (sangk′ tə tē) *n.* the quality of deserving solemn respect as something not to be violated

"This is the living room," I said, which was pretty easy to show Jack, since we were already standing in it. "Want to sit down?"

"Yeah, sure," Jack said. "Have you lived here long?"

"Since the divorce," I said. "Eight years ago."

"That long," Jack said. "Where's your father?"

"He lives in Oak Ridge," I said. "That's a couple of hundred miles from here. I see him sometimes."

"Is he . . ." Jack began. "I mean, I don't suppose you'd know . . ."

"Is he your father too?" I said. "No. I kind of asked. Your father's name is Ronny. My father's name is Mike. I don't know much else about your father except he didn't want to marry Mom. They were both teenagers, I guess. Do you want to meet him too?"

"Sometime," Jack said. "Not tonight."

I could sure understand that one. "I've always wanted to have a big brother," I told him. "I always had crushes on my friends' big brothers. Did you want that—to have a kid sister, I mean?"

"I have one," Jack said. "No, I guess now I have two. I have a sister back home. Her name is Leigh Ann. She's adopted too. She's Korean."

"Oh," I said. "That's nice. I guess there isn't much of a family resemblance, then."

"Not much," Jack said, but he smiled. "She's twelve. How old are you?"

"Fifteen," I said. "Do you go to college?"

Jack nodded. "I'm a sophomore at Bucknell," he said. "Do you think you'll go to college?"

"I'd like to," I said. "I don't know if we'll have the money, though."

"It's rough," Jack said. "College costs a lot these days. My father's always griping about it. He owns a car dealership. New and used. I work there summers. My mom's a housewife."

I wanted to tell him how hard Mom had worked on supper, how messy the apartment usually was, how I never wore a dress, and Mom's nails were always a deep sinful scarlet. I wanted to tell him that maybe someday I'd be jealous that he'd been given away to a family that could afford to send him to college, but that it was too soon for me to feel much of anything about him. There was a lot I wanted to say, but I didn't say any of it.

"What's she like?" Jack asked me, and he gestured toward the kitchen, as though I might not otherwise know who he was talking about.

"Mom?" I said. "She's terrible. She drinks and she gambles and she beats me black and blue if I even think something wrong."

Jack looked horrified. I realized he had definitely not inherited Mom's sense of humor.

"I'm only kidding," I said. "I haven't even been spanked since I was five. She's fine. She's a good mother. It must have really hurt her to give you away like that."

"Have you known long?" Jack asked. "About me?"

"Not until recently," I said. It didn't seem right to tell him I'd learned less than twenty-four hours before. "I guess Mom was waiting until I was old enough to understand."

"I always knew I was adopted," Jack said. "And for years I've wanted to meet my biological parents. To see what they looked like. I love Mom and Dad, you understand. But I felt this need."

"I can imagine," I said, and I could too. I was starting to develop a real need to see what Jack's parents looked like, and we weren't even related.

"Tiffany, could you come in here for a minute?" Mom called from the kitchen.

"Coming, Mom," I said, and left the living room fast. It takes a lot out of you making small talk with a brother.

"What do you think?" Mom whispered as soon as she saw me. "Does he look like me?"

"He has your eyes," I said. "And I think he has your old hair color."

"I know," Mom said, patting her bottle red hair. "I almost asked them to dye me back to my original shade, but I wasn't sure I could remember it anymore. Do you like him? Does he seem nice?"

"Very nice," I said. "Very good manners."

"He sure didn't inherit those from Ronny," Mom declared. "Come on, let's start taking the food out."

So we did. We carried out platters of chicken and mashed potatoes and biscuits and salad. Jack came to the table as soon as he saw what we were doing.

"Oh, no," he said. "I mean, I'm sorry. I should have told you. I'm a vegetarian."

"You are?" Mom said. She looked as shocked as if he'd told her he was a vampire. Meat is very important to Mom. "You're not sick or anything, are you?"

"No, it's for moral reasons," Jack said. "It drives my mom, my mother, her name's Cathy, it drives Cathy crazy."

"Your mom," my mom said. "It would drive me crazy, too, if Tiffany stopped eating meat just for moral reasons."

"Don't worry about it," I told her. "I'll never be that moral."

"There's plenty for me to eat," Jack said. "Potatoes and biscuits and salad."

"The salad has bacon in it," Mom said. "I crumbled bacon in it."

"We can wash the bacon off, can't we Jack?" I said. "You'll eat it if we wash the bacon off, won't you?"

Jerry, 1964. Fairfield Porter. Oil on canvas, 14½ x 14½ in. Portland Art Museum, Oregon Art Institute. Gift of Mrs. Fairfield Porter.

Viewing the painting: What personal qualities or characteristics does this young man seem to possess? Which of these qualities might Jack have also?

I thought he hesitated for a moment, but then he said, "Of course I can," and for the first time since we'd met, I kind of liked him. I took the salad into the kitchen and washed it all. The salad dressing went the way of the bacon, but we weren't about to complain. At least there'd be something green on Jack's plate. All his other food was gray-white.

Mom hardly ate her chicken, which I figured was out of deference to the vegetarian, but I had two and a half pieces, figuring it might be years before Mom made it again. Jack ate more potatoes than I'd ever seen another human being eat. No gravy, but lots of potatoes. We talked polite stuff during dinner, what he was studying in college, where Mom worked, the adjustments Leigh Ann had had to make. The real things could only be discussed one on one, so after the pie and ice cream, I excused myself and went to Mom's room to watch TV. Only I couldn't make my eyes focus, so I crossed the hall to my room, and recreated my messes. Once I had everything in proper order, though, I put things back the way Mom had had them. I could hear them talking while I moved piles around, and then I turned on my radio, so I couldn't even hear the occasional stray word, like *father* and *high school* and *lawyer*. That was a trick I'd learned years ago, when Mom and Dad were in their fighting stage. The radio played a lot of old songs that night. It made me feel like I was seven all over again.

After a while Mom knocked on my door and said Jack was leaving, so I went to the living room and shook hands with him again. I still couldn't tell anything about his personality from his handshake, but he did have good manners, and he gave me a little pecking kiss on my check, which I thought was sweet of him. Mom kept the door open, and watched as he walked the length of the corridor to the stairs. She didn't close the door until he'd gotten into a car, his I assumed. Maybe it was a loaner from his father.

Big Table with Pomegranates, 1978. Nell Blaine. Oil on canvas, 22 x 26 in. Metropolitan Museum of Art. Gift of Arthur W. Cohen, 1985. 1985.36.1.

Viewing the painting: What adjectives might you use to describe the dinner scene pictured here? What adjectives could also be applied to the dinner scene in the story?

"You give away a baby," Mom said, "and twenty years later he turns up on your doorstep a vegetarian."

"He turns up a turnip," I said.

But Mom wasn't in the mood for those kinds of jokes. "Don't you ever make that mistake," she said.

"What mistake?" I asked, afraid she meant making jokes. If I couldn't make jokes with Mom, I wouldn't know how to talk with her.

"Don't you ever give up something so important to you that it breathes when you do," Mom said. "It doesn't have to be a kid. It can be a dream, an ambition, or a marriage, or a house. It can be anything you care about as deeply as you care about your own life. Don't ever just give it away, because you'll spend the rest of your life wondering about it, or pretending you don't wonder, which is the same thing, and you'll wake up one morning and realize it truly is gone and a big part of you is gone with it. Do you hear me, Tiffany?"

"I hear you," I said. I'd never seen Mom so intense, and I didn't like being around her. "I'm kind of tired now, Mom. Would you mind if I went to bed early?"

"I'll clean up tomorrow," Mom said. "You can go to bed."

So I did. I left her sitting in the living room and went to my bedroom and closed my door. But this time I didn't turn the radio on, and later, when I'd been lying on my bed for hours, not able to sleep, I could hear her in her room crying. I'd heard her cry in her room a hundred times before, and a hundred times before I'd gotten up and comforted her, and I knew she'd cry a hundred times again, and I'd comfort her then, too, but that night I just stayed in my room, on my bed, staring at the ceiling and listening to her cry. I think I did the right thing, not going in there. That's how it is with strangers. You can never really comfort them.

Responding to Literature

Personal Response

What are your thoughts about the relationship between Tiffany and her mother? Is it a "typical" mother-daughter relationship? Why or why not? Record your thoughts in your journal.

Analyzing Literature

Recall

1. How does Tiffany describe her mother to the reader? To Jack?
2. What does Tiffany's mother, Linda, do to prepare for Jack's visit?
3. What is Linda's explanation for why she gave up Jack for adoption? What did Linda do after the adoption?
4. What does Jack tell Tiffany and Linda about himself and his adopted family?
5. Describe how Tiffany behaves after dinner and then after Jack leaves.

Interpret

6. Based on Tiffany's descriptions of her mother, what can you infer about Tiffany's personality? About her feelings toward her mother?
7. What might Linda's feelings be about this reunion with her son? What kind of impression does she seem to want to create?
8. Consider the choices Linda made after giving up her son for adoption. In your opinion, what are some possible reasons for her choices?
9. What conclusions might you draw about Jack's situation in life?
10. How would you explain Tiffany's behavior after dinner and after Jack's departure? Give reasons for your answers.

Evaluate and Connect

11. Susan Pfeffer has chosen to tell this story from Tiffany's **point of view.** How do you think the story might be different if it were told from Jack's point of view? From Linda's point of view?
12. Consider the alternatives Linda had as an unwed, pregnant teenager. In your opinion, did she make a good decision by giving up her son for adoption? Why or why not?
13. Do you think this story is humorous or serious–or is it both? Explain.
14. Look back at the continuum of feelings you made in the Reading Focus on page 278. Where might you place Tiffany, Jack, and Linda along that line? Explain your decisions.
15. **Theme Connections** What do you think the theme of this story is? Explain how the story theme relates to the subunit theme of Twists.

Literary ELEMENTS

Understatement

When a writer intentionally represents something as less than it is, that writer is using **understatement.** Understatement may be used to insert humor into a story or to focus the reader's attention on something the author wants to emphasize. For example, in "As It Is with Strangers," Tiffany explains that "when your mind is on some newly acquired half brother, it's real hard to care about Julius Caesar." Her understatement creates humor, while also emphasizing the uncertainty she feels about meeting her "new" brother, Jack.

1. Find two examples in which Tiffany uses understatement.
2. Do you think Tiffany's understatements are anything other than attempts at humor? Explain your answer.

- See **Literary Terms Handbook,** p. R13.

Literature and Writing

Writing About Literature

Analyze the Story's Title Think about why the author may have chosen the title "As It Is with Strangers" for this story. Reread the last paragraph of the story, in which Tiffany refers to her mother as a stranger. In what ways might Tiffany and her mother be considered strangers? Which other character in the story might be considered a stranger? Use details from the selection to support your analysis of the story's title. Share your ideas with others in a small group.

Creative Writing

Yours Truly Imagine that you are Jack. Write a thank-you letter to Linda and Tiffany. Besides the dinner, what else might you be grateful for? What thoughts or feelings might you want to convey to your birth mother? What might you want to say to your newly discovered half sister? What are your hopes or plans for a future relationship with Linda and Tiffany? You may want to compare your letter with those written by several classmates.

Extending Your Response

Literature Groups

Too Late in the Game? Tiffany learns about Jack's existence less than twenty-four hours before she meets him. In your opinion, should Linda have told Tiffany about Jack long before she did? Was it right for Linda to conceal Jack's existence from Tiffany until Jack actually appeared in their lives? How do you think Tiffany feels about her mother's failure to tell her the truth much sooner? Debate these issues in your group. Share your ideas with the class.

Internet Connection

Where Are They Now? In this story, Jack was able to find his birth mother because Linda had registered with an agency that helped adopted children and their birth parents locate each other. Look for online resources that provide a similar service. Share with the class what you learn about these resources.

Performing

Role-Play Working with two other students, role-play a conversation that Jack and his adoptive parents might have after his visit with Linda and Tiffany. What might Jack say about his birth mother and half sister? What information or impressions might he choose *not* to convey? What questions might Jack's adoptive parents ask, or what concerns might they raise?

Reading Further

If you enjoyed reading this story, you might also enjoy these stories about teens and their families in Cynthia Rylant's collection, *Every Living Thing*:

"Shells" is a story about a boy and his aunt who are learning to live together after the death of the boy's parents.

"Stray" tells how a family adopts an abandoned puppy.

Save your work for your portfolio.

Literary Criticism

According to one reviewer, "Susan Beth Pfeffer has garnered praise for her handling of controversial subjects within the dramatic form." Do you think Pfeffer handles the subject of adoption with sensitivity and skill in this short story? Discuss your opinion with your classmates, providing examples to support your answer.

Skill Minilessons

GRAMMAR AND LANGUAGE • Vivid Verbs

"I could picture Mom pouring the spinach out of a can and *dousing* it with Wishbone."

Vivid verbs make an impact on readers. *Dousing* provides a mental picture of Linda *generously pouring* salad dressing on the spinach. In this example, one vivid verb conveys the same information that a verb and an adverb do.

PRACTICE Replace the underlined verb-adverb combination in each sentence with one vivid verb. Use a thesaurus for help.

1. Tiffany nervously moved around in her chair.
2. Jack ate the potatoes quickly.
3. Linda cried softly.
4. Tiffany quickly walked out of the kitchen.
5. Linda finally told her secret to Tiffany.

APPLY Review a piece of your writing. Try to improve it by adding a few vivid verbs. Consult a thesaurus, if necessary.

● For more about verbs, see **Language Handbook,** p. R44.

READING AND THINKING • Interpreting

In "As It Is with Strangers," Tiffany's words often do not mean what they literally say. As you read, you have to interpret what she really means in order to understand the story. Tiffany jokes around a lot; she creates humor using understatement, exaggeration, and sarcasm. For example, Tiffany is being sarcastic when she asks Linda, "Is this going to be the first of many such dinners?" Tiffany is really asking her mother if she has any other secrets to tell her–anything as important as the existence of a half brother.

PRACTICE Interpret each of these comments made by Tiffany. Explain what you think Tiffany really means.

1. "I'm always forgetting little things like my homework assignments and being elected President of the United States. Having an older brother must have just slipped my mind."
2. "There aren't any other brothers I've forgotten about?"
3. "Mom? She's terrible. She drinks and she gambles and she beats me black and blue if I even think something wrong."
4. "Don't worry about it. I'll never be that moral."
5. "He turns up a turnip."

● For more about related reading strategies, see **Reading Handbook,** pp. R78–R107.

VOCABULARY • Unlocking Meaning

Tiffany believes that the sanctity of her bedroom was violated. *Sanctity* comes from the Latin word *sanctus,* which means "holy." Although all words formed from *sanctus* originally had to do with holiness, they may or may not carry that specific meaning today. For example, in this story, Tiffany uses a broader meaning for *sanctity:* here, it means the quality of being regarded with respect.

Another useful word is *sanction.* Its most common meaning is "approval by a recognized authority." Originally, that authority was the Roman Catholic Church.

PRACTICE Briefly state what you'd guess is the meaning of each underlined word.

1. In some religions, it is a terrible fate to be buried in unsanctified ground.
2. The hunted fox searched desperately for a sanctuary.
3. There was a ceremony to sanctify the new altar.
4. Do not disturb me in my study, which I consider my sanctum.

Before You Read

The False Gems

Reading Focus

In what situations have you noticed that people and things are not what they seem?

Quickwrite Spend five minutes writing about people or things that turned out to be completely different from the way you first perceived them to be.

Setting a Purpose Read to learn what happens to one man who discovers that things are not as they seem.

Building Background

The Time and Place
"The False Gems" takes place in Paris, sometime in the 1870s or early 1880s.

Did You Know?
It's almost impossible to distinguish some false gems from real ones. Even the British Crown Jewels contain false gems, such as the Black Prince's Ruby and the Timur Ruby, which, despite their names, are not rubies at all. Synthetic gemstones made from the compound cubic zirconia can easily pass for diamonds in brilliance and color. To the naked eye, cultured pearls are virtually indistinguishable from natural ones.

Vocabulary Preview

remonstrate (ri mon′ strāt) *v.* to say or plead in protest; argue; p. 290
impart (im pärt′) *v.* to give or share; p. 290
droll (drōl) *adj.* amusingly odd or fanciful; p. 291
assuage (ə swāj′) *v.* to lessen in intensity; diminish; p. 291
incur (in kur′) *v.* to acquire (something undesirable); bring upon oneself; p. 291
rancor (rang′ kər) *n.* ill will; resentment; p. 291
perceive (pər sēv′) *v.* to be or become aware through the senses; p. 293
disdain (dis dān′) *n.* a feeling of contempt for something or someone; scorn; p. 294

Meet Guy de Maupassant

Few writers have achieved more than Guy de Maupassant (gē də mō pä san′), who died when he was only forty-two. Maupassant published more than three hundred short stories, each so finely crafted that he is renowned as one of the finest short-story writers in any language. An athletic and energetic person, the author loved the sport of rowing. Maupassant also had an active social life in Paris, where he worked as a government clerk as well as a writer. His stories reflect his views about the world. In fact, one French critic has claimed that it is "impossible to fully comprehend the France of 1850–90 without these stories."

Guy de Maupassant was born in 1850 in France and died in 1893. This story was first published in 1883.

Woman with a Pearl Necklace in a Loge, 1897. Mary Cassatt. Oil on canvas, 32 x 23½ in. Philadelphia Museum of Art. Bequest of Charlotte Dorrance Wright.

The False Gems

Guy de Maupassant

MONSIEUR LANTIN[1] had met the young girl at a reception at the house of the second head of his department, and had fallen head over heels in love with her.

She was the daughter of a provincial tax collector, who had been dead several years. She and her mother came to live in Paris, where the latter, who made the acquaintance of some of the families in her neighborhood, hoped to find a husband for her daughter.

They had very moderate means, and were honorable, gentle, and quiet.

The young girl was a perfect type of the virtuous woman in whose hands every sensible young man dreams of one day intrusting his happiness. Her simple beauty had the charm of angelic modesty, and the imperceptible smile which constantly hovered about the lips seemed to be the reflection of a pure and lovely soul.

---

1. ***Monsieur Lantin*** (mə syœ′ län taɴ′)

Her praises resounded on every side. People never tired of repeating: "Happy the man who wins her love! He could not find a better wife."

Monsieur Lantin, then chief clerk in the Department of the Interior, enjoyed a snug little salary of three thousand five hundred francs, and he proposed to this model young girl, and was accepted.

He was unspeakably happy with her. She governed his household with such clever economy that they seemed to live in luxury. She lavished the most delicate attentions on her husband, coaxed and fondled him; and so great was her charm that six years after their marriage, Monsieur Lantin discovered that he loved his wife even more than during the first days of their honeymoon.

He found fault with only two of her tastes: Her love for the theatre, and her taste for imitation jewelry. Her friends (the wives of some petty officials) frequently procured[2] for her a box at the theatre, often for the first representations of the new plays; and her husband was obliged to accompany her, whether he wished it or not, to these entertainments which bored him excessively after his day's work at the office.

After a time, Monsieur Lantin begged his wife to request some lady of her acquaintance to accompany her, and to bring her home after the theatre. She opposed this arrangement, at first; but, after much persuasion, finally consented, to the infinite delight of her husband.

Now, with her love for the theatre, came also the desire for ornaments. Her costumes remained as before, simple, in good taste, and always modest; but she soon began to adorn her ears with huge rhinestones, which glittered and sparkled like real diamonds. Around her neck she wore strings of false pearls, on her arms bracelets of imitation gold, and combs set with glass jewels.

Her husband frequently remonstrated with her, saying:

"My dear, as you cannot afford to buy real jewelry, you ought to appear adorned with your beauty and modesty alone, which are the rarest ornaments of your sex."

But she would smile sweetly, and say:

"What can I do? I am so fond of jewelry. It is my only weakness. We cannot change our nature."

Then she would wind the pearl necklace round her fingers, make the facets of the crystal gems sparkle, and say:

"Look! are they not lovely? One would swear they were real."

Did You Know?
Facets are the small, polished, plane surfaces of a cut gem.

Monsieur Lantin would then answer, smilingly:

"You have bohemian[3] tastes, my dear."

Sometimes, of an evening, when they were enjoying a *tête-à-tête*[4] by the fireside, she would place on the tea table the morocco leather box containing the "trash," as Monsieur Lantin called it. She would examine the false gems with a passionate attention, as though they imparted some deep and secret

2. The tickets were acquired or obtained *(procured)* for her.

3. *Bohemian* suggests following one's own sense of style rather than what is generally accepted as fashionable and proper.

4. A *tête-à-tête* (tet′ ə tet′) is a private or intimate conversation between two people. Directly translated from French, the phrase means "head to head."

Vocabulary
remonstrate (ri mon′ strāt) *v.* to say or plead in protest; argue
impart (im pärt′) *v.* to give or share

joy; and she often persisted in passing a necklace around her husband's neck, and, laughing heartily, would exclaim: "How droll you look!" Then she would throw herself into his arms, and kiss him affectionately.

One evening, in winter, she had been to the opera, and returned home chilled through and through. The next morning she coughed, and eight days later she died of inflammation of the lungs.

Monsieur Lantin's despair was so great that his hair became white in one month. He wept unceasingly; his heart was broken as he remembered her smile, her voice, every charm of his dead wife.

Time did not assuage his grief. Often, during office hours, while his colleagues were discussing the topics of the day, his eyes would suddenly fill with tears, and he would give vent to his grief in heart-rending sobs. Everything in his wife's room remained as it was during her lifetime; all her furniture, even her clothing, being left as it was on the day of her death. Here he was wont to seclude himself daily and think of her who had been his treasure—the joy of his existence.

But life soon became a struggle. His income, which, in the hands of his wife, covered all household expenses, was now no longer sufficient for his own immediate wants; and he wondered how she could have managed to buy such excellent wine and the rare delicacies which he could no longer procure with his modest resources.

He incurred some debts, and was soon reduced to absolute poverty. One morning, finding himself without a cent in his pocket, he resolved to sell something, and immediately the thought occurred to him of disposing of his wife's paste jewels,[5] for he cherished in his heart a sort of rancor against these "deceptions," which had always irritated him in the past. The very sight of them spoiled, somewhat, the memory of his lost darling.

To the last days of her life she had continued to make purchases, bringing home new gems almost every evening, and he turned them over some time before finally deciding to sell the heavy necklace, which she seemed to prefer, and which, he thought, ought to be worth about six or seven francs; for it was of very fine workmanship, though only imitation.

He put it in his pocket, and started out in search of what seemed a reliable jeweler's shop. At length he found one, and went in, feeling a little ashamed to expose his misery, and also to offer such a worthless article for sale.

"Sir," said he to the merchant, "I would like to know what this is worth."

The man took the necklace, examined it, called his clerk, and made some remarks in an undertone; he then put the ornament back on the counter, and looked at it from a distance to judge of the effect.

Monsieur Lantin, annoyed at all these ceremonies, was on the point of saying: "Oh! I know well enough it is not worth anything," when the jeweler said: "Sir, that necklace is worth from twelve to fifteen thousand francs; but I could not buy it, unless you can tell me exactly where it came from."

5. *Paste jewels* are artificial or imitation gems made of a hard, glasslike material.

Vocabulary

droll (drōl) *adj.* amusingly odd or fanciful
assuage (ə swāj′) *v.* to lessen in intensity; diminish
incur (in kur′) *v.* to acquire (something undesirable); bring upon oneself
rancor (rang′ kər) *n.* ill will; resentment

The widower opened his eyes wide and remained gaping, not comprehending the merchant's meaning. Finally he stammered: "You say—are you sure?" The other replied, drily: "You can try elsewhere, and see if any one will offer you more. I consider it worth fifteen thousand at the most. Come back here, if you cannot do better."

Monsieur Lantin, beside himself with astonishment, took up the necklace and left the store. He wished time for reflection.

Once outside, he felt inclined to laugh, and said to himself: "The fool! Oh, the fool! Had I only taken him at his word! That jeweler cannot distinguish real diamonds from the imitation article."

A few minutes after, he entered another store, in the Rue de la Paix.[6] As soon as the proprietor glanced at the necklace, he cried out:

"Ah, *parbleu!*[7] I know it well; it was bought here."

Monsieur Lantin, greatly disturbed, asked:

"How much is it worth?"

"Well, I sold it for twenty thousand francs. I am willing to take it back for eighteen thousand, when you inform me, according to our legal formality, how it came to be in your possession."

This time, Monsieur Lantin was dumbfounded. He replied:

"But—but—examine it well. Until this moment I was under the impression that it was imitation."

The jeweler asked:

"What is your name, sir?"

"Lantin—I am in the employ of the Minister of the Interior. I live at number sixteen Rue des Martyrs."[8]

The merchant looked through his books, found the entry, and said: "That necklace was sent to Madame Lantin's address, sixteen Rue des Martyrs, July 20, 1876."

The two men looked into each other's eyes—the widower speechless with astonishment; the jeweler scenting a thief. The latter broke the silence.

"Will you leave this necklace here for twenty-four hours?" said he; "I will give you a receipt."

Monsieur Lantin answered hastily: "Yes, certainly." Then, putting the ticket in his pocket, he left the store.

He wandered aimlessly through the streets, his mind in a state of dreadful confusion. He tried to reason, to understand. His wife could not afford to purchase such a costly ornament. Certainly not. But, then, it must have been a present!—a present!—a present, from whom? Why was it given her?

He stopped, and remained standing in the middle of the street. A horrible doubt entered his mind—She? Then, all the other jewels must have been presents, too! The earth seemed to tremble beneath him—the tree before him to be falling; he threw up his arms, and fell to the ground, unconscious. He recovered his senses in a pharmacy, into which the passers-by had borne him. He asked to be taken home, and, when he reached the house, he shut himself up in his room, and wept until nightfall. Finally, overcome with fatigue, he went to bed and fell into a heavy sleep.

The sun awoke him next morning, and he began to dress slowly to go to the office. It

6. *Rue de la Paix* (ru də lä pā′) translates as "Street of Peace."

7. *[parbleu]* (pär blœ′) In France in the 1200s, King Louis IX hated swear words, especially *pardieu* ("by God!"), *cordieu* ("God's heart!"), and *têtedieu* ("God's head!"). He punished swearers by branding their tongues with hot irons. Luckily, Louis had a pet dog named Bleu, and people began to substitute the dog's name for God's—*parbleu, corbleu, sacre bleu*, and so on.

8. *Rue des Martyrs* (ru dā mär tēr′) translates as "Street of Martyrs." A martyr is one who dies or suffers greatly for a belief or cause.

Portrait of Zacharie Astruc, 1863. Eduoard Manet. Oil on canvas, 35½ x 45¾ in. Kunsthalle, Bremen, Germany.
Viewing the painting: Which characteristics of Monsieur Lantin do you think are reflected in this painting?

was hard to work after such shocks. He sent a letter to his employer, requesting to be excused. Then he remembered that he had to return to the jeweler's. He did not like the idea; but he could not leave the necklace with that man. He dressed and went out.

It was a lovely day; a clear, blue sky smiled on the busy city below. Men of leisure were strolling about with their hands in their pockets.

Monsieur Lantin, observing them, said to himself: "The rich, indeed, are happy. With money it is possible to forget even the deepest sorrow. One can go where one pleases, and in travel find that distraction which is the surest cure for grief. Oh! if I were only rich!"

He perceived that he was hungry, but his pocket was empty. He again remembered the necklace. Eighteen thousand francs! Eighteen thousand francs! What a sum!

He soon arrived in the Rue de la Paix, opposite the jeweler's. Eighteen thousand francs! Twenty times he resolved to go in, but shame kept him back. He was hungry, however—very hungry—and not a cent in his pocket. He decided quickly, ran across the street, in order not to have time for reflection, and rushed into the store.

The proprietor immediately came forward, and politely offered him a chair; the clerks glanced at him knowingly.

Vocabulary
perceive (pər sēv′) *v.* to be or become aware through the senses

"I have made inquiries, Monsieur Lantin," said the jeweler, "and if you are still resolved to dispose of the gems, I am ready to pay you the price I offered."

"Certainly, sir," stammered Monsieur Lantin.

Whereupon the proprietor took from a drawer eighteen large bills, counted, and handed them to Monsieur Lantin, who signed a receipt; and, with trembling hand, put the money into his pocket.

As he was about to leave the store, he turned toward the merchant, who still wore the same knowing smile, and lowering his eyes, said:

"I have—I have other gems, which came from the same source. Will you buy them, also?"

The merchant bowed: "Certainly, sir."

Monsieur Lantin said gravely, "I will bring them to you." An hour later, he returned with the gems.

Did You Know?
A *solitaire pendant* is a single gem suspended from a chain and worn as a necklace or bracelet.

The large diamond earrings were worth twenty thousand francs; the bracelets, thirty-five thousand; the rings, sixteen thousand; a set of emeralds and sapphires, fourteen thousand; a gold chain with solitaire pendant, forty thousand—making the sum of one hundred and forty-three thousand francs.

The jeweler remarked, jokingly:

"There was a person who invested all her savings in precious stones."

Monsieur Lantin replied, seriously:

"It is only another way of investing one's money."

That day he lunched at Voisin's, and drank wine worth twenty francs a bottle. Then he hired a carriage and made a tour of the Bois.[9] He gazed at the various turnouts[10] with a kind of disdain, and could hardly refrain from crying out to the occupants:

"I, too, am rich!—I am worth two hundred thousand francs."

Suddenly he thought of his employer. He drove up to the bureau, and entered gaily, saying:

"Sir, I have come to resign my position. I have just inherited three hundred thousand francs."

He shook hands with his former colleagues, and confided to them some of his projects for the future; he then went off to dine at the Café Anglais.

He seated himself beside a gentleman of aristocratic bearing; and, during the meal, informed the latter confidentially that he had just inherited a fortune of four hundred thousand francs.

For the first time in his life, he was not bored at the theatre, and spent the remainder of the night in a gay frolic.

Six months afterward, he married again. His second wife was a very virtuous woman; but had a violent temper. She caused him much sorrow.

9. *The Bois* (bwä) refers to Bois de Boulogne, a forested park in Paris.
10. A *turnout* is a carriage complete with attendants, horses, and rigging.

Vocabulary
disdain (dis dān′) *n.* a feeling of contempt for something or someone; scorn

Responding to Literature

Personal Response

What aspect of the story surprised you the most? Explain your answer.

Analyzing Literature

Recall

1. What admirable qualities does Monsieur Lantin's wife seem to possess?
2. According to Monsieur Lantin, what are his wife's only two flaws?
3. Why does Monsieur Lantin assume that the gems are false?
4. What does Monsieur Lantin do with his wife's jewelry? Why?
5. In what way does Monsieur Lantin's life change after his final visit to the jeweler?

Interpret

6. Which clues early in the story **foreshadow** the unexpected twist in the plot? Explain what each clue seems to suggest.
7. In your opinion, how are Madame Lantin's two "flaws" related to each other? Explain.
8. To what, besides Madame Lantin's jewels, might the title of this story refer? Explain.
9. What do you think accounts for Monsieur Lantin's financial difficulties?
10. Does Monsieur Lantin's attitude toward himself and others seem to change as a result of the new circumstances of his life? Explain your answer.

Evaluate and Connect

11. In your opinion, does Madame Lantin's fondness for the gems have anything to do with their source? Explain.
12. In your opinion, what lessons for husbands and wives might this story contain?
13. If you had been in Monsieur Lantin's situation, what do you think you would have done with the jewels? Give reasons for your answer.
14. Reread the story's last paragraph. What is **ironic** about the situation in which Monsieur Lantin finds himself? (See Literary Terms Handbook, page R6.)
15. How do you feel about the two main characters in this story? With whom do you sympathize more? Explain your thinking.

Point of View

Point of view is the relationship of the narrator, or storyteller, to the story. When a story is told from a **first-person point of view,** the narrator is a character in the story, who refers to himself or herself as "I." In general, the reader sees everything through that character's eyes. In a story told from a **limited third-person point of view,** the narrator reveals the thoughts of only one character, through whose eyes the reader sees the story. The narrator refers to that character as "he" or "she." In a story with an **omniscient point of view,** the narrator–who is not a character in the story–reveals the thoughts of several characters.

1. What point of view does Maupassant use in "The False Gems"? How do you know?
2. Why do you think Maupassant chose to tell the story from this point of view?
3. How might the story be different if it were told from a different point of view? Give specific examples.

- See **Literary Terms Handbook,** p. R9.

Literature and Writing

Writing About Literature

Character Sketch Maupassant develops the character of Madame Lantin in a number of ways. He describes her appearance and family background. He also tells what she says and does, and shows how others react to her. Write a character sketch of Madame Lantin, using details from the story to support your description. Share your sketch with a group of your classmates.

Personal Writing

Clueless? Monsieur Lantin lived with his wife for at least six years. How could he be so naive about her character? How could he not know they were living beyond their means? Think back to the Reading Focus on page 288. Then write a response to these questions: When our perceptions of people or things turn out to be wrong, is it because sometimes we allow ourselves to be fooled? Do you think this was the case with Monsieur Lantin? Explain.

Extending Your Response

Literature Groups

Debate the Issue What do you think Monsieur Lantin would have preferred: false gems and a true wife, or real gems and a false wife? Debate this question in your group. Support your ideas with evidence from the story and your knowledge of human nature. Share your opinions with the class.

Interdisciplinary Activity

Art: The Passing Scene The scenes that Monsieur Lantin saw from the window of his hired carriage were those of a vibrant and colorful capital city. Do research to discover some of the scenes he might have viewed in late nineteenth-century Paris. Illustrate a scene as Monsieur Lantin might have viewed it from the carriage window.

Performing

Another View Imagine that Madame Lantin had a close friend, Madame LeClair, to whom she confided everything. Now that her friend is dead, Madame LeClair wants to tell what she knows about the young woman's secret life. Write a monologue for Madame LeClair in which she explains Madame Lantin's behavior and the source of the jewels. Add details that are consistent with the information given in the story. Practice the monologue and perform it for your classmates.

Reading Further

If you enjoyed this story by Guy de Maupassant, you might also enjoy the following stories from *Fifteen by Maupassant*:

"Simon's Papa" tells of a discouraged boy who faces life without a father.

"My Uncle Jule" describes a working-class family who never seems to get ahead.

"On the River" is narrated by a boatman who expresses his fears of the river environment at night.

Save your work for your portfolio.

Skill Minilessons

GRAMMAR AND LANGUAGE • Infinitives and Infinitive Phrases

An **infinitive** is a verb form that usually is preceded by the word *to.* An infinitive may have complements and modifiers, forming an **infinitive phrase.** Sometimes an infinitive or an infinitive phrase is used as a noun in a sentence.

Monsieur Lantin fell in love and decided to marry. (infinitive used as a noun)

Madame Lantin's goal was to deceive her husband. (infinitive phrase used as a noun)

PRACTICE In "The False Gems," find three examples of sentences containing an infinitive or infinitive phrase used as a noun. Copy the sentences and underline the infinitive or infinitive phrase in each one.

● For more about infinitives, see **Language Handbook,** p. R40.

READING AND THINKING • Drawing Conclusions

When people draw conclusions, they come up with logical explanations for events, using reasons and details from the information they have available to them at the time. For example, after the first jeweler appraised the necklace, Monsieur Lantin drew this conclusion: "That jeweler cannot distinguish real diamonds from the imitation article." Lantin based his conclusion on these facts: his wife could not afford to buy real gems, she had told him the jewels were imitation, and he had no reason to doubt her. It was a reasonable conclusion, although it turned out to be incorrect.

PRACTICE At the end of the story, what can you conclude about Madame Lantin's character? State your conclusion on your paper. List the facts from the text on which you base your conclusion.

● For more about related comprehension skills, see **Reading Handbook,** pp. R78–R107.

VOCABULARY • Analogies

An analogy is a type of comparison that is based on the relationships between things or ideas. Some analogies are based on a relationship that could be called "an action and its significance."

blush : embarrassment :: laugh : amusement

A blush is a sign of embarrassment; a laugh is a sign of amusement. Instead of saying "is a sign of," you could substitute the word "indicates" or "signifies."

To finish an analogy, decide what relationship exists between the first two things or ideas. Then apply that relationship to another pair of words and see if it is the same.

● For more about analogies, see **Communications Skills Handbook,** p. R77.

PRACTICE Choose the word pair that best completes each analogy.

1. sneer : disdain ::
   a. bow : respect
   b. crown : royalty
   c. smile : face
   d. introduction : stranger
   e. hug : squeeze

2. snarl : hostility ::
   a. dog : danger
   b. snap : bite
   c. purr : contentment
   d. warning : siren
   e. yawn : bed

Before You Read

The Saleswoman

Reading Focus

In your opinion, what qualities make a salesperson good at his or her job?

Map It! Create a character map by surrounding the word *salesperson* with words and phrases that describe the qualities of a successful salesperson.

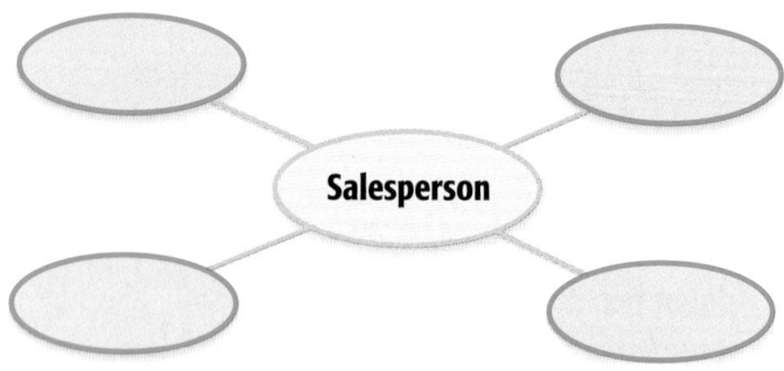

Setting a Purpose Read to assess the saleswoman's technique.

Building Background

The Time and Place

"The Saleswoman" takes place in a hat shop in Paris, probably in the 1920s.

Did You Know?

The French *cloche,* a popular hat style of the 1920s, was a tight-fitting, bell-shaped hat that concealed most or all of a woman's hair and part of her face. Along with raised hemlines and short hairstyles, the *cloche* became a fashion symbol of the 1920s.

Vocabulary Preview

indulge (in dulj′) *v.* to yield to a desire (by doing something); take pleasure (in); p. 299

chic (shēk) *adj.* attractive, tasteful, and fashionable in style; p. 301

mortify (môr′ tə fī′) *v.* to shame, humiliate, or embarrass; p. 301

clientele (klī′ ən tel′) *n.* clients or customers considered as a group; p. 301

Meet Colette

The French author Colette once said of her writing that her "great landscape was always the human face." She was well known for her sensitive observations of human character—particularly of women. Like many of her female characters, Colette was a dynamic, independent, intelligent woman. She wrote numerous novels and short stories, performed in French cabarets as an actress and a dancer, and even introduced her own line of cosmetics. Her novel *Gigi* was also made into a movie, which won an Academy Award in 1958.

Colette, whose full name was Sidonie-Gabrielle Colette, was born in the Burgundy region of France in 1873. She died in 1954.

The SALESWOMAN

Colette

AT THE HAT SHOP. With the arrival of a client, the saleswoman rushes up: twenty-five years old, with the eyes of a young tyrant, a tower of blond hair on the top of her head. Her hands, her figure, her mouth, her feet, all are thin to excess, witty, and aggressive.

"Ah, Madame! At last; you've come back to us! I had almost given up hope. I was saying to myself, 'That's it! She must have gone to Harry's to have some Berlin-style hats made for herself!' But . . . what is that you have on your head?"

". . . ?"

"Yes, that thing with the blue wing on the side and the velour[1] all around it?"

". . . ?"

"What, you made it yourself? All by yourself. Why, that's incredible, it's miraculous! If I may indulge in a little joke, you have a future in fashion. Would you do our *maison*[2] the honor of entering it as trimmer?"

". . . ?"

"The trimmer? She's . . . well, heavens, she's the one who puts the linings inside the hats, who . . . well . . . who does a lot of little things. Give me your lovely little 'creation'; oh, I'll give it back to you! Here, I'll give it back . . . let's see . . . tomorrow. Yes, tomorrow. Exactly, the car is making a delivery tomorrow in your suburb."

". . . ?"

"Yes, well, in your neighborhood, I meant. It's so far! I'm just a poor little Parisian girl who never has time to leave her post, you understand. The boulevard shop in winter, Deauville in the summer, the Biarritz shop in September, Monte Carlo in January . . . Oh, not everybody can live in Auteuil.[3] Quick, come with me, I have a nice corner in the little fitting room facing the street. It's poorly lit? You don't like being with your back to the light? But it's the best place for trying on hats! Your silhouette is projected on the window, and with hats, it's primarily a question of silhouette, this season; one disregards the details. And, you see, you're between Mademoiselle X, the 'little diva,'[4] who's trying on hats for her tour right now, and Princess Z, who's just back from the south."

1. *Velour* (vi loor′) is a soft, thick, velvety fabric.
2. The French word *maison* (mā zōn′) can mean a house, one's family, or a business. Here, the saleswoman is referring to the hat shop.
3. *[Deauville, Biarritz, Monte Carlo, Auteuil]* These are all high-class resort areas.
4. *Diva* (dē′ və), from the Italian, means "a famous female opera singer."

Vocabulary

indulge (in dulj′) *v.* to yield to a desire (by doing something); take pleasure (in)

She takes her with her everywhere, to her couturier's,[5] to her jeweler's; she stays here for hours trying on twenty-five different hats under her poor friend's nose—to distract her.

"Let's see now, how about if we talk a little more seriously now? I've gotten it into my head that I could really do a job on you today. It's days like this when my mind is set on business. Okay, for starters, pull this little cloche down over your beautiful hair for me! . . . You haven't changed color?"

". . ."

"Excuse me, it's a reflection from the outside light. I was saying to myself: it has more gold in it than usual. You might have gotten the urge to change, just for a change. And then there are some people who go gray very early. On the side, on the side, completely covering one ear! There! . . . What do you think of it?"

". . . !"

"I can see it's not a hit. Besides, you're right, it's not your style. On you, it looks a little . . . a little too ladylike. It's funny, I just sold the same hat to Mrs. W. She is ravishing in it, Mrs. W, with her long neck, and especially here, you see, her chin, her cheeks, so fresh and the ear . . . Let's say good-bye to this style here for a minute; one lost, ten found. Look at that, what was I telling you! This is what we're after. Way down, all right?"

". . ."

". . . ?"

"Yes, that one, the fat old lady. In the shop, we call her the 'Pink Pompon.'"

". . . ?"

"Because whenever she doesn't like a hat, she always says, 'I think it's missing something, here, in the hollow . . . a little nothing, a little flower . . . a bouquet of pompon roses!' Mademoiselle X, that one there, to your left, she's not what you'd normally call pretty, but she has such a good heart!"

". . . ?"

"Oh, a heart of gold. Look, the lady who's with her, yes, that sort of little shark in black, is a poor friend she's taken in.

5. A *couturier* (ko͞o toor′ ē ā′) is a dressmaker or designer who makes and sells highly fashionable, usually custom-made clothing for women.

"More than that, more than that! I can still see the hair on your temple, and on the back of your neck! I believe you're familiar with the 'great hat principle of the season,' as the owner herself says?"

". . . ?"

"The great hat principle is that when you meet a woman on the street and her hat allows you to see whether she's a brunette, a blond, or a redhead, the woman in question is not wearing a chic hat. There! . . . Notice I'm not saying anything, I'll let you make up your own mind. Well?"

". . ."

"You prefer the navy-blue one? That one there, on the mushroom?[6] Yes? . . . Well, really!"

". . ."

"No, no, it's not sold."

". . . ?"

"Why no, Madame, I don't want to keep you from buying it! I wasn't suggesting it to you because I didn't think I was talented enough to sell hats like that one. But it's true, it does seem to go with your face. Ah, you really know what it is you want! Like I always say: there are only two categories of clients whose minds can't be changed: artists and lower-middle-class women."

". . ."

"You're not an artist, but you still have a very independent sense of judgment. Try on this one here, just for me. It's not at all excessive, but I think it's both rich and discreet, because of this polished cotton fantasia which gives it all its cachet[7] . . . No? Ah, I'm not having any luck at all, you're just trying to mortify me. If your two sons have your personality, they'll be terrible men! Are those two big boys doing all right?"

". . ."

"Already? How time flies, my Lord! And still good-looking, I'm sure. Well, there's nothing surprising about that."

". . . !"

"No, Madame, there's no flattery intended at all; anyway, everybody in the shop agrees with me, it's just what everybody says about the presence, the charm, the intelligence of your husband . . . and everyone knows that your two gorgeous children also inherited your beautiful health! What a shame they're not daughters! I'd already be fitting them for hats, and spoiling them as much as you. So, nothing more today, except the little blue hat? Shall I have it sent down to you in your car?"

". . ."

"Yes, yes, don't worry, I give the description of the car to the messenger boy myself. You think I don't know the brown sedan you've had for six years? Good-bye, Madame, and thank you for your lovely visit, don't go so long without coming to see your faithful saleswoman; I enjoy seeing you so much . . . it gives me a rest from our American clientele: all I feel like telling those women are disagreeable things."

6. Here, the *mushroom* is a mushroom-shaped stand used to display a hat.

7. A *fantasia* is a fanciful musical composition. Here, the saleswoman uses the word figuratively to describe the hat's adornment of fancifully constructed, shiny cotton ribbon. And this adornment, she says, gives the hat its special distinction or individuality—its *cachet* (ka shā′).

Vocabulary

chic (shēk) *adj.* attractive, tasteful, and fashionable in style
mortify (môr′ tə fī′) *v.* to shame, humiliate, or embarrass
clientele (klī′ ən tel′) *n.* clients or customers considered as a group

Responding to Literature

Personal Response

How do you feel about the saleswoman? If she worked at your favorite store, would you seek her out? Explain in your journal.

Analyzing Literature

Recall

1. In the first paragraph, which words and phrases provide clues about the saleswoman's personality?
2. Summarize the comments the saleswoman makes about Princess Z, Mademoiselle X, and her friend.
3. What punctuation marks are used to indicate that the customer is responding to the saleswoman's comments?
4. What is the "great hat principle of the season"?
5. In choosing which hat to buy, does the client follow the salesperson's advice? Explain your answer.

Interpret

6. What words do you think the client might use to describe the saleswoman?
7. If the saleswoman's customers had overheard her descriptions of them, how might they have reacted?
8. How do the saleswoman's remarks help you infer what the client is saying? Give three examples.
9. In your opinion, what is the saleswoman's motive for mentioning the "great hat principle of the season"?
10. Identify two instances of the saleswoman's flattery. In your opinion, how does the flattery influence the client's purchase?

Evaluate and Connect

11. Compare and contrast the opening paragraph with the rest of the story.
12. What do you think the author's purpose is in revealing only the saleswoman's words?
13. Identify at least two sales techniques that the saleswoman uses on her client. How would you respond to similar techniques?
14. Many of the saleswoman's "compliments" are actually disguised insults. How might you respond to backhanded compliments?
15. Use the character map you made in the Reading Focus on page 298 to evaluate the saleswoman. Would you consider her a successful salesperson?

Literary ELEMENTS

Dialogue

A **dialogue** is a conversation carried on between two people. Writers use dialogue to reveal their characters' traits and motivations. They also use it to convey information about other characters or events in the story. In "The Saleswoman," readers only see the title character's side of a conversation.

1. Select two examples of dialogue that, in your opinion, help reveal the saleswoman's true character. Explain what each example reveals.
2. Even though the client's part of the dialogue does not appear in the story, the saleswoman's remarks reveal many facts about her client. Give three examples of such facts.
3. Select one or two paragraphs from the story. Complete the dialogue by supplying the words that the saleswoman's client might have spoken.

- See **Literary Terms Handbook,** p. R3.

Literary Criticism

Critics praise Colette's ". . . ability to evoke in a few brief pages a precise atmosphere, a moral lesson, or a psychological insight." In a brief summary, describe the atmosphere of "The Saleswoman," the lesson to be learned, and any insights you gained from the story.

Literature and Writing

Writing About Literature

Analyze Double Meanings Although the saleswoman seems to flatter her client, her compliments often are disguised insults. For example, she compliments the "beautiful health" that the client's children have inherited from her, while implying that they got their good looks from their father. In the story, find two other disguised insults and write an explanation of the double meaning of each one.

Creative Writing

The Beat Goes On Imagine that the client has left the shop after buying the blue hat, and the saleswoman begins telling a new client how glad she is to see her after the disagreeable experience she's just had with her last client. Write a paragraph or two of monologue for the saleswoman in which she describes what it was like to wait on her previous client.

Extending Your Response

Literature Groups

Examining an Author's Attitude What does this story suggest about the author's attitude toward salespeople? Is the author suggesting that salespeople are insincere and motivated only by the final sale? Or is she suggesting that good salespeople must know their customers and their tastes? Discuss these ideas in your group, and then share your ideas with the class.

Listening and Speaking

Interview Talk to several salespeople in your community to find out what they regard as the most rewarding and most difficult aspects of their jobs. Ask them to describe the sales techniques they use and to evaluate the effectiveness of each one. Report your findings to the class.

Learning for Life

Send a Résumé, Please Prepare a résumé that the saleswoman might write. Use your imagination to fill in the details not supplied by the story. To find a suitable résumé style, consult library or Internet resources.

Reading Further

You might also enjoy these works by Colette:

Autobiography: "Laughter" from *My Mother's House and Sido* features Colette's memories of how her mother found joy even during the worst situations.

Viewing: *Gigi,* the movie of Colette's novel, won an Academy Award for Best Picture in 1958.

Save your work for your portfolio.

Skill Minilesson

VOCABULARY • Borrowed Words

English words came from many languages. Most often, the English word developed from a root taken from another language. Words adopted into our language with no change whatsoever are called "borrowed words." *Chic* and *clientele,* for example, are French words that mean exactly the same thing in English as they do in French.

Borrowed English words can be hard to spell because they follow the spelling rules of the language from which they were borrowed.

PRACTICE The following words were "borrowed" from the French language without any spelling changes. Think about how you might pronounce each word in English, then look up the word in the dictionary to find the correct pronunciation and the definition. Write sentences or a paragraph that correctly uses all the words.

1. cliché
2. croquet
3. fiancée
4. boutique
5. champagne

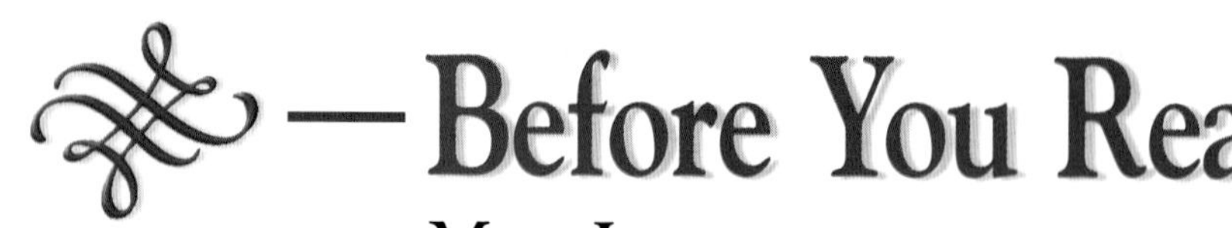

Before You Read

Mrs. James

Reading Focus

Have you ever had any kind of job? Perhaps you've worked as a babysitter, lifeguard, clerk, cashier, landscaper, or delivery person.

Sharing Ideas In a small group, briefly describe any kind of job you've had. Tell what type of relationship you had with the person for whom you worked. Were you treated with respect? How did you resolve any conflicts that arose?

Setting a Purpose Read to learn about the relationship between a woman and her employer.

Building Background

The Time and Place

This story takes place in New York City, probably sometime in the late 1940s or early 1950s, when the Great Depression, a period of great economic hardship for most Americans, was still a vivid memory.

Did You Know?

In the first half of the twentieth century, African American women had few employment opportunities. The majority of those who found work–like the character Mildred in this story, as well as the author herself–were employed as domestics. Domestics worked as maids, housekeepers, cooks, and nannies in the homes of families who could afford paid household help. At the time, most of these families were white.

Vocabulary Preview

pantry (pan′ trē) *n.* room or closet in which food and articles for preparing and serving food are kept; p. 305

sashay (sa shā′) *v.* to walk or move in a way that shows indifference or a lack of interest; p. 305

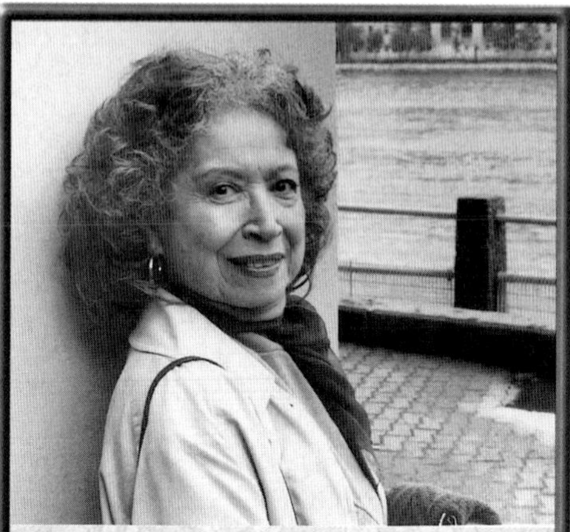

Meet Alice Childress

When Alice Childress was a girl, she lived with her grandmother in the Harlem section of New York City. Her grandmother encouraged Childress to believe that her ideas were valuable, and she urged her granddaughter to write them down. The young girl embraced this concept and dedicated herself to becoming a writer. She also became an accomplished actress and playwright and was the first African American woman to have a play produced on Broadway.

Alice Childress was born in Charleston, South Carolina, in 1920. She lived in Manhattan at the time of her death in 1994. This story appears in the short story collection Like One of the Family: Conversations from a Domestic's Life.

Mrs. James

Alice Childress

WELL MARGE, YOU HAVEN'T HEARD anything! You should hear the woman I work for . . . she's really something. Calls herself "Mrs. James!" All the time she says "Mrs. James."

The first day I was there she come into the kitchen and says, "Mildred, Mrs. James would like you to clean the pantry." Well I looked 'round to see if she meant her mother-in-law or somebody and then she adds, "If anyone calls, Mrs. James is out shopping." And with that she sashays out the door.

Now she keeps on talking that way all the time, the whole time I'm there. That woman wouldn't say "I" or "me" for nothing in the world. The way I look at it . . . I guess she thought it would be too personal.

Now Marge, you know I don't work Saturdays for nobody! Well sir! Last Friday she breezed in the kitchen and fussed around a little . . . movin' first the salt and then the pepper, I could feel something brewin' in the air. Next thing you know she speaks up. "Mildred," she says, "Mrs. James will need you this Saturday." I was polishin' silver at the time but I turned around and looked her dead in the eye and said, "Mildred does not work on Saturdays."

Well, for the rest of the day things went along kind of quiet-like but just before time for me to go home she drifted by the linen closet to check the ruffle on a guest towel and threw in her two cents more. "Mildred," she says, "a depression might do this country some good, then some people might work eight days a week and be glad for the chance to do it."

I didn't bat an eyelash, but about 15 minutes later when I was headin' for home, I stopped off at the living room and called to her, "That's very true, but on the other hand some folks might be doin' their own housework . . . don'tcha know." With that and a cool "goodnight" I gently went out the front door. . . .

Oh, but we get along fine now. . . . Just fine!

Vocabulary

pantry (pan′ trē) *n.* room or closet in which food and articles for preparing and serving food are kept

sashay (sa shā′) *v.* to walk or move in a way that shows indifference or a lack of interest

Responding to Literature

Personal Response

Were you surprised by the way Mrs. James spoke to Mildred? By the way Mildred spoke to Mrs. James? Explain in your journal.

Analyzing Literature

Recall and Interpret

1. What peculiar habit does Mrs. James have? What impression does this habit seem to make on Mildred? What impression does it make on you?
2. Describe the scene in which Mrs. James tells Mildred that she is needed on Saturday. What feelings do the two characters seem to have during this scene? Use details from the story to support your answer.
3. Summarize what happens by the linen closet. In your opinion, what does Mrs. James's remark reveal about her attitude toward Mildred?
4. In your own words, explain what Mildred says to Mrs. James as she departs. How do you think Mrs. James might have reacted? Explain.

Evaluate and Connect

5. Rather than slamming the front door, Mildred leaves "gently." Why do you think she does this? What would you have done?
6. Early in her career, the author worked as a domestic. What specific details in the story reveal this firsthand experience?
7. Do you think an economic depression would be more painful for Mildred or for Mrs. James? Give reasons for your answer.
8. Look back at the Reading Focus on page 304. How does the relationship between Mildred and Mrs. James compare with your own relationship with a current or past employer? Be as specific as possible.

Tone

Tone is the attitude of the author toward the subject of a work. The author's choice of details and language creates a particular tone. In "Mrs. James," Mildred explains that Mrs. James "drifted by the linen closet . . . and threw in her two cents more." Here, the narrator's tone is mocking and sarcastic. Note that a single piece of writing can convey more than one attitude, or tone.

1. What words would you use to describe Mildred's attitude toward Mrs. James? What specific details help to create this attitude, or tone?
2. Find two passages in the story that convey a particular tone, or attitude. Identify the tone of each passage.

- See **Literary Terms Handbook,** p. R13.

Extending Your Response

Literature Groups

Survival and Dignity Alice Childress once said that she focused on "portraying have-nots in a *have* society, those seldom singled out by the mass media, except as source material for derogatory humor. . . ." Compare the author's depiction of Mildred to ways that the "have-nots" in our society today are depicted in the mass media. Share your ideas with the class.

Creative Writing

Dear Mrs. James Write a letter to Mrs. James, giving her advice about how to treat household employees. You may wish to organize your advice into two lists, one titled *Do* and the other titled *Don't.* For example: *Don't refer to yourself as "Mrs. James." It sounds silly and pretentious.*

Save your work for your portfolio.

COMPARING selections

THE SALESWOMAN and *Mrs. James*

COMPARE **CHALLENGES**

DISCUSS The main characters in "The Saleswoman" and "Mrs. James" are working women whose occupations present very different challenges.

1. What must the saleswoman do to succeed at her job? What challenge does Mildred face in dealing with Mrs. James?
2. Compare the different ways in which the women deal with the challenges of their jobs.
3. In your opinion, which character is more successful in her job? Give reasons for your answer.

COMPARE **DRAMATIC EVENTS**

DRAMATIZE Both Colette and Alice Childress were playwrights, which perhaps explains why they told these stories through monologue–a dramatic technique in which a single character speaks.

- In a group, compare the two stories; decide which would make a better stage production.
- Develop a play script for "The Saleswoman" or "Mrs. James." Use the monologue from the story as the basis for your script. Include a set description and stage directions.
- Perform your play for the class.

COMPARE **RESPONSES**

GIVE ADVICE Imagine that the saleswoman and Mildred have a newspaper column called "Work It Out," in which they give advice to working people. Write a response from each character to the following letter, and then compare your responses to those written by several classmates.

Dear Work It Out,
I am a sales clerk in a jewelry store that caters to the wealthy. I like my job, but my supervisor is very demanding and does not think I have a life outside the store. Also, some of my customers treat me like a servant. How can I keep my job and my dignity at the same time?

Writing Workshop

Narrative Writing:
Short Story

Would you like to resolve an old conflict with a friend in a different way, journey to an exotic world, or get inside the mind of a person who's very different from you? **You can venture anywhere you wish by writing your own short story, using this workshop as a guide.** You may want to write a realistic story, a fantasy, science fiction, a fable, or a mystery–the choice is yours. Don't be afraid to unleash your imagination. You may surprise yourself!

- As you write your narrative, refer to the **Writing Handbook,** pp. R58–R71.

EVALUATION RUBRIC
By the time you complete this Writing Workshop, you will have
- written a short story with a plot that includes an engaging opening, rising action, climax, and resolution
- developed and maintained a consistent point of view
- used vivid details to describe the setting, characters, and events
- created natural-sounding dialogue
- presented a short story that is free of errors in grammar, usage, and mechanics

The Writing Process

PREWRITING

PREWRITING TIP
Remember that a short story typically focuses on a single incident and has a limited number of characters.

Explore ideas

Story ideas can be based on your own experiences and relationships, as well as those you have observed or read about. Your imagination is another rich source of story ideas. As you read the following questions and suggestions, jot down any story ideas that come to you.

- What **characters** would you like to write about? You can create characters based on people you've known or other characters you've read about, such as Monsieur Lantin in "The False Gems" or Mildred in "Mrs. James."
- Think about the **conflicts**–both internal and external–that confronted the characters in the stories in this theme. Could you write a story about a similar type of conflict? Another approach is to recall conflicts you've experienced, observed, dreamed about, or imagined.

Consider your audience and purpose

- Whom do you want to read your story? You might submit your story to a magazine or enter it in a contest. You might share it with your classmates, friends, and family.
- Why do you or your characters want to tell a particular story? Perhaps your purpose is to explore one of life's big questions, as Italo Calvino does in "The Happy Man's Shirt." If you're writing a humorous story, you might simply want to make your readers laugh. Think about your purpose before you begin your story, but don't be afraid to let your purpose change as your story develops.

Choose and develop an idea

Once you have a story idea you like, play around with it. Whether you start with a character, a conflict, or even a setting, start freewriting about your idea and see where it leads you. Or if you prefer, go ahead and work out the entire plot in your head before you write a single word. As you develop your idea, ask yourself questions about the basic elements of a short story. Jot down your answers.

		STUDENT MODEL
Characters	Who are the characters? What are they like? Which ones do you really need? (Too many characters in a short story can cause confusion.)	Tina: young girl who wants to study ballet. Ms. Ruzinsky: ballet instructor. Maria: Tina's best friend who doesn't want to study ballet. Giselle Turner: a spoiled girl who takes ballet classes and lives in Tina and Maria's neighborhood.
Plot	What happens in the story? What is the main problem, or conflict? How do events build to a climax, or high point? How is the conflict resolved?	Tina has always wanted to study ballet, but her mother can't afford the lessons. Maria talks Tina into taking her place at ballet class. Giselle tells the instructor Tina's real name, and Tina has to admit the truth to Ms. Ruzinsky. The instructor decides to award Tina a scholarship.
Setting	When and where does the story take place? What details will make the setting seem real to your readers?	Time: 4:30 on a summer afternoon. Place: a large, air-conditioned ballet studio, called Ruzinsky's Dance Studio, in the city.
Point of view	Will you tell the story from the **first-person point of view,** using one of the story's characters as the narrator? Or will you write from the **third-person point of view?**	I'll use the third-person limited point of view. Narrator is not a character in the story but describes events as Tina sees them.
Theme	What message do you want your story to convey? (Your theme may change as you write your story.)	Something about lying, telling the truth, and forgiveness.

Complete Student Model on p. R111.

DRAFTING

Drafting Tip

Skim your notes and your freewriting, and underline or highlight a few phrases or sentences to use as you start drafting your story.

Begin with the action

For many short-story writers, the hardest part is getting the story opening just right—so don't start with the opening unless you really want to do so. Just plunge right into the action of your story. Later, you can go back and write the opening.

Write your draft

Refer to your freewriting and your notes as you write, but let your ideas flow freely. If new ideas take your story in a different direction, go ahead and change the plot or other elements of the story. Rather than *telling* your readers what's happening, use details, description, and dialogue to help them *experience* your story. Don't forget that events should build to a climax and then end with a resolution. At some point, you'll need to write an opening that grabs readers' attention and draws them into your story.

Use this graphic to help shape your story.

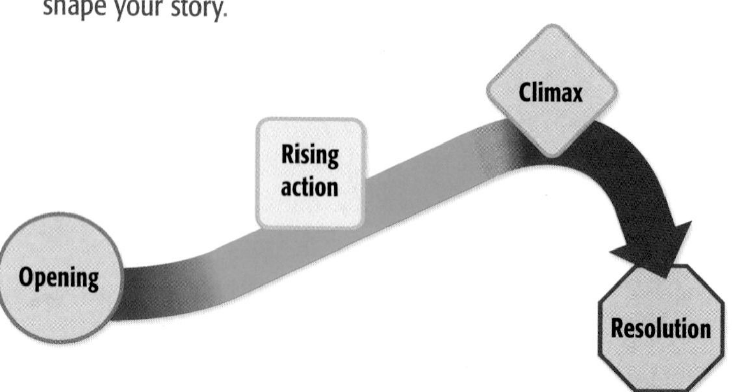

STUDENT MODEL

Ever since Tina could remember, she had had pictures of ballerinas hanging on the walls of her room. But her mother had never been able to afford for Tina to take lessons. Although Tina didn't feel totally right about lying, Tina was about to take her first ballet lesson ever by pretending that she was her best friend Maria. Maria's mother had decided to pay for her to study ballet, but Maria didn't want to go. She had convinced Tina that no one would care if she pretended to be Maria and showed up at the classes instead. Now Tina was at the studio, trying to work up her nerve to say she was Maria.

A little bell rang as she pushed the door open and stepped inside the studio. Tina was in a hot, empty office. Just then, a tall, pale lady with black hair came through the office door. Tina tried hard to look like she belonged there.

"Who are you?" asked the woman, smiling.

"Maria," said Tina. "I'm Maria Arsuga. I'm here for the 4:30 class."

Complete Student Model on p. R111.

REVISING

Evaluate your work

Let your draft sit for a few hours or days before you come back to it. Then imagine that you are reading it for the first time. Using the **Rubric for Revising** to guide you, mark the places where you could make improvements. Then revise your draft.

Have a writing conference

Read your story aloud to a friend. Ask your friend how well your story meets the criteria in the **Rubric for Revising**, and jot down the responses. Consider all responses, but make only the changes you feel are needed.

REVISING TIP

Read your story aloud to yourself. Put a check mark by any passages that sound confusing or awkward. Go back and rework those parts until they flow smoothly.

STUDENT MODEL

Ms. Ruzinsky started the class by lining them up at the barre, a wooden railing ^attached to the walls at about waist level. Ms. Ruzinsky told them to ~~put~~ rest their hands on the barre ^lightly, never to grab it. She told them to imagine an invisible thread ~~going~~ running from the top of their heads to the ceiling. Tina closed her eyes and imagined as hard as she could.

^Next, Ms. Ruzinsky taught them how to stand in first position ^with their feet turned out. She showed them how to point their feet and ~~put~~ extend a leg straight in front of them and then ~~move~~ draw it ~~back again~~ in quickly, all in time to a beat she clapped out. Tina was learning so much. She couldn't wait to tell Maria everything.

Suddenly Ms. Ruzinsky called out: "Maria! You are the only one who understands the exercise. Come to the center of the floor and demonstrate ~~this exercise for everyone else in the class~~."

Tina felt proud and scared at once. She went to the middle of the floor and stood in front of Ms. Ruzinsky. She turned her feet out into first position.

Just then, Giselle ran forward and ~~said~~ shouted, "She is not Maria! Her name is Tina. She ~~does not~~ doesn't belong here!"

Complete Student Model on p. R111.

RUBRIC FOR REVISING

Your revised short story should have

- ☑ a powerful opening that grabs the reader's interest
- ☑ active verbs, vivid language, and specific details to bring the setting, characters, and conflict to life
- ☑ realistic-sounding dialogue that helps to advance the plot and develop the characters
- ☑ a clear, believable plot that comes to a satisfying resolution
- ☑ a clear and consistent point of view

Your revised story should be free of

- ☑ clichés and vague, tired language
- ☑ errors in grammar, usage, and mechanics

EDITING/PROOFREADING

PROOFREADING TIP
Look for misspelled words by reading your story word by word. Or, if you're using a computer, use a spelling checker to help you find spelling errors.

When you are satisfied with your story's content, proofread it carefully for errors in grammar, usage, mechanics, and spelling. Use the **Proofreading Checklist** on the inside back cover of this book as a guide.

Grammar Hint

Use punctuation marks to seperate each part of a direct quotation from an explanatory phrase, such as *he said.*
Begin a new paragraph and use a new set of quotation marks each time the speaker changes.

"Is your name really Tina?" Ms. Ruzinsky asked her kindly.

"Yes," replied Tina. She nodded and began to cry. "I'm sorry that I lied. I just wanted to be here so badly."

STUDENT MODEL

Complete Student Model
For a complete version of the model developed in this workshop, refer to **Writing Workshop Models**, p. R111.

"Ms. Ruzinsky," Giselle said, "she's not Maria. She's Tina!" ¶ "Maria?" Ms. Ruzinsky asked. She raised her eyebrows and looked at Tina, puzzled. "What's going on here?"

Complete Student Model on p. R111.

PUBLISHING/PRESENTING

TECHNOLOGY TIP
If you're using a computer, choose a typeface and layout that suit your story.

Decide how you'll share your story with others. You might read it aloud to friends and classmates, or make copies for them to read. If you're submitting the story to a magazine, follow the submission guidelines. If you're entering a contest, follow the contest rules precisely.

Reflecting

Think about your story-writing experience. Do you like the result? Consider adding the piece to your portfolio. In your journal, comment on the most difficult part of the experience, the most enjoyable part, and what you learned as a writer. Set goals for your next adventure in story writing. What might you do differently the next time you write a short story?

Save your work for your portfolio.

Theme 4 Challenges and Consequences

How do you face challenges in your life? Do you consider all of the possible consequences of your actions, or do you rush headlong into situations? In every story in this theme, one or more characters face challenges. Not all of them are prepared for the consequences, which will alter the course of their lives and, in some cases, seal their fate.

THEME PROJECTS

Creative Writing

Epigraphs An epigraph is a quotation used at the beginning of a story to suggest its overall theme.

1. As you read the stories in this theme, write down what you believe is the overall meaning of each story.
2. With a partner, select a meaningful quote that would be an appropriate epigraph for each story. Look in *Bartlett's Familiar Quotations* or in other favorite literary works. Share the epigraphs with your class and be prepared to explain why you chose each quote.

Interdisciplinary Project

Science: Expert Advice Several of the characters in these stories might have benefited from scientific knowledge related to the challenges and conflicts they faced.

1. Imagine that you are a scientist and that one or two characters from stories in this theme have come to you for advice.
2. Look up your topic in your biology or life science textbook, speak to a science teacher, or consult appropriate reference works. Then write a brief explanation of the advice you would give to each character.

MEDIA connection

Comic Strip

Have you ever wondered what it might have been like to live in the time of the dinosaurs? For Calvin, the dinosaur era doesn't seem any farther away than the dinner table.

Calvin and Hobbes

by Bill Watterson

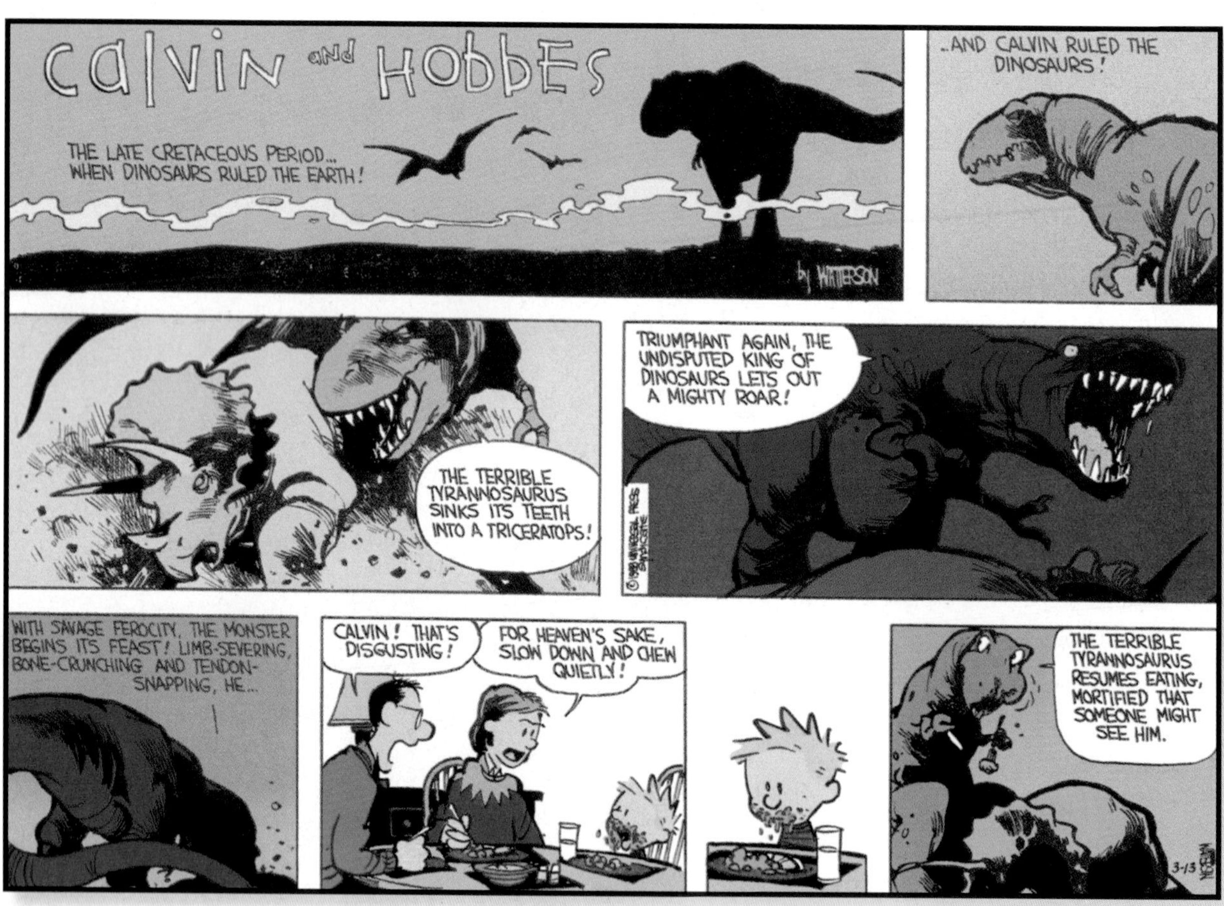

Analyzing Media

1. Do the drawings of Calvin at the dinner table make you think of a child you know–or worse yet, of yourself as a child? Explain.
2. What words might you use to describe the scene shown in the last frame of the cartoon?

Before You Read

A Sound of Thunder

Reading Focus

What happens if you line up a set of dominoes on end, one in front of the other, and knock down the first one?

Sharing Ideas The term "domino effect" is used to describe a series of events set into motion by a single event or cause. Discuss ways you may have seen a "domino effect" at work in the world around you.

Setting a Purpose Read to discover how one small action causes a complex chain of events.

Building Background

The Time and Place

This story begins in an unnamed part of the United States in A.D. 2055.

Did You Know?

Although the term *science fiction* was not used until about 1930, science fiction tales have been told since before the invention of writing. One of the earliest science fiction writers was Lucian of Samosata who, around A.D. 100, wrote a fantasy about a journey to the moon. Modern science fiction began to take shape in the 1800s. Landmarks of this period include Mary Shelley's *Frankenstein* (1818) and H. G. Wells's *The Time Machine* (1895).

Vocabulary Preview

expendable (iks pen′ də bəl) *adj.* not strictly necessary; capable of being sacrificed without negative effect; p. 319

correlate (kôr′ ə lāt′) *v.* to bring (one thing) into relation (with another thing); calculate; p. 320

paradox (par′ ə doks′) *n.* something that seems illogical, contradictory, or absurd, but that in fact may be true; p. 320

resilient (ri zil′ yənt) *adj.* capable of springing back into shape or position after being bent, stretched, or compressed; p. 321

primeval (prī mē′ vəl) *adj.* of or having to do with the first or earliest age; primitive; p. 324

Meet Ray Bradbury

"You have to know fear and apprehension in some form before you can write about it thoroughly."

Bradbury experienced fear and apprehension early in life. "Some of my first memories," he says, "concern going upstairs at night and finding an unpleasant beast waiting at the next to the last step." An early love of reading led Bradbury quite naturally to a love of writing. At the age of twelve, using a toy typewriter, he wrote a story about Martians. A master of science fiction, he has published more than five hundred works since the 1940s.

Ray Bradbury was born in Waukegan, Illinois, in 1920. This story was first published in 1952.

A Sound of Thunder

Ray Bradbury

THE SIGN ON THE WALL seemed to quaver under a film of sliding warm water. Eckels felt his eyelids blink over his stare, and the sign burned in this momentary darkness:

> TIME SAFARI, INC.
> SAFARIS TO ANY YEAR IN THE PAST.
> YOU NAME THE ANIMAL.
> WE TAKE YOU THERE.
> YOU SHOOT IT.

A warm phlegm gathered in Eckels' throat; he swallowed and pushed it down. The muscles around his mouth formed a smile as he put his hand slowly out upon the air, and in that hand waved a check for ten thousand dollars to the man behind the desk.

"Does this safari guarantee I come back alive?"

"We guarantee nothing," said the official, "except the dinosaurs." He turned. "This is Mr. Travis, your Safari Guide in the Past. He'll tell you what and where to shoot. If he says no shooting, no shooting. If you disobey instructions, there's a stiff penalty of another ten thousand dollars, plus possible government action, on your return."

Eckels glanced across the vast office at a mass and tangle, a snaking and humming of wires and steel boxes, at an aurora[1] that flickered now orange, now silver, now blue. There was a sound like a gigantic bonfire burning all of Time, all the years and all the parchment calendars, all the hours piled high and set aflame.

A touch of the hand and this burning would, on the instant, beautifully reverse itself. Eckels remembered the wording in the advertisements to the letter. Out of chars and ashes, out of dust and coals, like golden salamanders, the old years, the green years, might leap; roses sweeten the air, white hair turn Irish-black, wrinkles vanish; all, everything fly back to seed, flee death, rush down to their beginnings, suns rise in western skies and set in glorious easts, moons eat themselves opposite to the custom, all and everything cupping one in another like Chinese boxes, rabbits into hats, all and everything returning to the fresh death, the seed death, the green death, to the time before the beginning. A touch of a hand might do it, the merest touch of a hand.

---

1. Here, *aurora* refers to the shimmering lights that come off of the time machine.

"Unbelievable." Eckels breathed, the light of the Machine on his thin face. "A real Time Machine." He shook his head. "Makes you think. If the election had gone badly yesterday, I might be here now running away from the results. Thank God Keith won. He'll make a fine President of the United States."

"Yes," said the man behind the desk. "We're lucky. If Deutscher had gotten in, we'd have the worst kind of dictatorship. There's an anti-everything man for you, a militarist, anti-Christ, anti-human, anti-intellectual. People called us up, you know, joking but not joking. Said if Deutscher became President they wanted to go live in 1492. Of course it's not our business to conduct Escapes, but to form Safaris. Anyway, Keith's President now. All you got to worry about is—"

"Shooting my dinosaur," Eckels finished it for him.

"A *Tyrannosaurus rex*. The Tyrant Lizard, the most incredible monster in history. Sign this release. Anything happens to you, we're not responsible. Those dinosaurs are hungry."

Eckels flushed angrily. "Trying to scare me!"

"Frankly, yes. We don't want anyone going who'll panic at the first shot. Six Safari leaders were killed last year, and a dozen hunters. We're here to give you the severest thrill a *real* hunter ever asked for. Traveling you back sixty million years to bag the biggest game in all of Time. Your personal check's still there. Tear it up."

Mr. Eckels looked at the check for a long time. His fingers twitched.

"Good luck," said the man behind the desk. "Mr. Travis, he's all yours."

They moved silently across the room, taking their guns with them, toward the Machine, toward the silver metal and the roaring light.

First a day and then a night and then a day and then a night, then it was day-night-day-night-day. A week, a month, a year, a decade! A.D. 2055. A.D. 2019. 1999! 1957! Gone! The Machine roared.

They put on their oxygen helmets and tested the intercoms.

Eckels swayed on the padded seat, his face pale, his jaw stiff. He felt the trembling in his arms and he looked down and found his hands tight on the new rifle. There were four other men in the Machine. Travis, the Safari Leader, his assistant, Lesperance, and two other hunters, Billings and Kramer. They sat looking at each other, and the years blazed around them.

"Can these guns get a dinosaur cold?" Eckels felt his mouth saying.

"If you hit them right," said Travis on the helmet radio. "Some dinosaurs have two brains, one in the head, another far down the spinal column. We stay away from those. That's stretching luck. Put your first two shots into the eyes, if you can, blind them, and go back into the brain."

The Machine howled. Time was a film run backward. Suns fled and ten million moons fled after them. "Think," said Eckels. "Every hunter that ever lived would envy us today. This makes Africa seem like Illinois."

The Machine slowed; its scream fell to a murmur. The Machine stopped.

The sun stopped in the sky.

The fog that had enveloped the Machine blew away and they were in an old time, a very old time indeed, three hunters and two Safari Heads with their blue metal guns across their knees.

"Christ isn't born yet," said Travis. "Moses has not gone to the mountain to talk with God. The Pyramids are still in the earth, waiting to be cut out and put up. *Remember* that. Alexander, Caesar, Napoleon, Hitler—none of them exists."

The men nodded.

"That"—Mr. Travis pointed—"is the jungle of sixty million two thousand and fifty-five years before President Keith."

He indicated a metal path that struck off into green wilderness, over steaming swamp, among giant ferns and palms.

"And that," he said, "is the Path, laid by Time Safari for your use. It floats six inches above the earth. Doesn't touch so much as one grass blade, flower, or tree. It's an anti-gravity metal. Its purpose is to keep you from touching this world of the past in any way. Stay on the Path. Don't go off it. I repeat. *Don't go off.* For *any* reason! If you fall off, there's a penalty. And don't shoot any animal we don't okay."

"Why?" asked Eckels.

They sat in the ancient wilderness. Far birds' cries blew on a wind, and the smell of tar and an old salt sea, moist grasses, and flowers the color of blood.

"We don't want to change the Future. We don't belong here in the Past. The government doesn't *like* us here. We have to pay big graft to keep our franchise.[2] A Time Machine is finicky business. Not knowing it, we might kill an important animal, a small bird, a roach, a flower even, thus destroying an important link in a growing species."

"That's not clear," said Eckels.

"All right," Travis continued, "say we accidentally kill one mouse here. That means all the future families of this one particular mouse are destroyed, right?"

"Right."

"And all the families of the families of the families of that one mouse! With a stamp of your foot, you annihilate first one, then a dozen, then a thousand, a million, a *billion* possible mice!"

"So they're dead," said Eckels. "So what?"

"So what?" Travis snorted quietly. "Well, what about the foxes that'll need those mice to survive? For want of ten mice, a fox dies. For want of ten foxes, a lion starves. For want of a lion, all manner of insects, vultures, infinite billions of life forms are thrown into chaos and destruction. Eventually it all boils down to this: fifty-nine million years later, a cave man, one of a dozen on the *entire world,* goes hunting wild boar or saber-tooth tiger for food. But you, friend, have *stepped* on all the tigers in that region. By stepping on one single mouse. So the cave man starves. And the cave man, please note, is not just *any* expendable man, no! He is an *entire future nation.* From his loins would have sprung ten sons. From *their* loins one hundred sons, and thus onward to a civilization. Destroy this one man, and you destroy a race, a people, an entire history of life. It is comparable to slaying some of Adam's grandchildren. The stomp of your foot, on one mouse, could start an earthquake, the effects of which could shake our earth and destinies down through Time, to their very foundations. With the death of that one cave man, a billion others yet unborn are throttled in the womb. Perhaps Rome never rises on its seven hills. Perhaps Europe is forever a dark forest, and only Asia waxes healthy and teeming. Step on a mouse and you crush the Pyramids. Step on a mouse and you leave your print, like a Grand Canyon, across Eternity. Queen

2. *[graft to keep our franchise]* Time Safari, Inc., pays money as bribes to government officials in return for continued permission to run its business.

Vocabulary

expendable (iks pen′ də bəl) *adj.* not strictly necessary; capable of being sacrificed without negative effect

Elizabeth might never be born. Washington might not cross the Delaware, there might never be a United States at all. So be careful. Stay on the Path. *Never* step off!"

"I see," said Eckels. "Then it wouldn't pay for us even to touch the *grass?*"

"Correct. Crushing certain plants could add up infinitesimally.[3] A little error here would multiply in sixty million years, all out of proportion. Of course maybe our theory is wrong. Maybe Time *can't* be changed by us. Or maybe it can be changed only in little subtle ways. A dead mouse here makes an insect imbalance there, a population disproportion later, a bad harvest further on, a depression, mass starvation, and, finally, a change in *social* temperament in far-flung countries. Something much more subtle, like that. Perhaps only a soft breath, a whisper, a hair, pollen on the air, such a slight, slight change that unless you looked close you wouldn't see it. Who knows? Who really can say he knows? We don't know. We're guessing. But until we do know for certain whether our messing around in Time *can* make a big roar or a little rustle in history, we're being careful. This Machine, this Path, your clothing and bodies, were sterilized, as you know, before the journey. We wear these oxygen helmets so we can't introduce our bacteria into an ancient atmosphere."

"How do we know which animals to shoot?"

"They're marked with red paint," said Travis. "Today, before our journey, we sent Lesperance here back with the Machine. He came to this particular era and followed certain animals."

"Studying them?"

"Right," said Lesperance. "I track them through their entire existence, noting which of them lives longest. Very few. How many times they mate. Not often. Life's short. When I find one that's going to die when a tree falls on him, or one that drowns in a tar pit, I note the exact hour, minute, and second. I shoot a paint bomb. It leaves a red patch on his hide. We can't miss it. Then I correlate our arrival in the Past so that we meet the Monster not more than two minutes before he would have died anyway. This way, we kill only animals with no future, that are never going to mate again. You see how *careful* we are?"

"But if you came back this morning in Time," said Eckels eagerly, "you must've bumped into *us*, our Safari! How did it turn out? Was it successful? Did all of us get through—alive?"

Travis and Lesperance gave each other a look.

"That'd be a paradox," said the latter. "Time doesn't permit that sort of mess—a man meeting himself. When such occasions threaten, Time steps aside. Like an airplane hitting an air pocket. You felt the Machine jump just before we stopped? That was us passing ourselves on the way back to the Future. We saw nothing. There's no way of telling *if* this expedition was a success, *if we* got our monster, or whether all of us—meaning *you*, Mr. Eckels—got out alive."

Eckels smiled palely.

"Cut that," said Travis sharply. "Everyone on his feet!"

They were ready to leave the Machine.

3. *Infinitesimally* (in′ fi nə tes′ ə məl lē) describes something being done "in a way that is too small to be measured."

Vocabulary

correlate (kôr′ ə lāt′) *v.* to bring (one thing) into relation (with another thing); calculate

paradox (par′ ə doks′) *n.* something that seems illogical, contradictory, or absurd, but that in fact may be true

Did You Know?
Pterodactyls (ter′ ə dak′ tilz) are extinct flying reptiles with wingspans of up to forty feet.

The jungle was high and the jungle was broad and the jungle was the entire world forever and forever. Sounds like music and sounds like flying tents filled the sky, and those were pterodactyls soaring with cavernous gray wings, gigantic bats of delirium and night fever. Eckels, balanced on the narrow Path, aimed his rifle playfully.

"Stop that!" said Travis. "Don't even aim for fun, blast you! If your gun should go off—"

Eckels flushed. "Where's our *Tyrannosaurus?*"

Lesperance checked his wristwatch. "Up ahead. We'll bisect his trail in sixty seconds. Look for the red paint! Don't shoot till we give the word. Stay on the Path. *Stay on the Path!*"

They moved forward in the wind of morning.

"Strange," murmured Eckels. "Up ahead, sixty million years, Election Day over. Keith made President. Everyone celebrating. And here we are, a million years lost, and they don't exist. The things we worried about for months, a lifetime, not even born or thought about yet."

"Safety catches off, everyone!" ordered Travis. "You, first shot, Eckels. Second, Billings. Third, Kramer."

"I've hunted tiger, wild boar, buffalo, elephant, but now, this is *it*," said Eckels. "I'm shaking like a kid."

"Ah," said Travis.

Everyone stopped.

Travis raised his hand. "Ahead," he whispered. "In the mist. There he is. There's His Royal Majesty now."

The jungle was wide and full of twitterings, rustlings, murmurs, and sighs.

Suddenly it all ceased, as if someone had shut a door.

Silence.

A sound of thunder.

Out of the mist, one hundred yards away, came *Tyrannosaurus rex.*

"It," whispered Eckels. "It . . ."

"Sh!"

It came on great oiled, resilient, striding legs. It towered thirty feet above half of the trees, a great evil god, folding its delicate watchmaker's claws close to its oily reptilian[4] chest. Each lower leg was a piston, a thousand pounds of white bone, sunk in thick ropes of muscle, sheathed over in a gleam of pebbled skin like the mail of a terrible warrior. Each thigh was a ton of meat, ivory, and steel mesh. And from the great breathing cage of the upper body those two delicate arms dangled out front, arms with hands which might pick up and examine men like toys, while the snake neck coiled. And the head itself, a ton of sculptured stone, lifted easily upon the sky. Its mouth gaped, exposing a fence of teeth like daggers. Its eyes rolled, ostrich eggs, empty of all expression save hunger. It closed its mouth in a death grin. It ran, its pelvic bones crushing aside trees and bushes, its taloned feet clawing damp earth, leaving prints six inches deep wherever it settled its weight. It ran with a gliding ballet

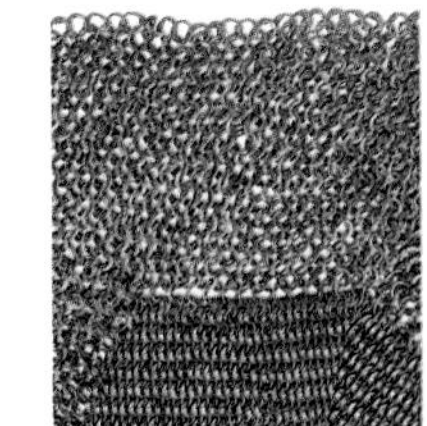

Did You Know?
Mail is a flexible body armor made of small, overlapping or interlinked metal plates or rings.

4. *Reptilian* (rep til′ ē ən) means "of or like a reptile."

Vocabulary

resilient (ri zil′ yənt) *adj.* capable of springing back into shape or position after being bent, stretched, or compressed step, far too poised and balanced for its ten tons. It moved into a sunlit arena warily, its beautifully reptilian hands feeling the air.

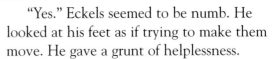

"Why, why," Eckels twitched his mouth. "It could reach up and grab the moon."

"Sh!" Travis jerked angrily. "He hasn't seen us yet."

"It can't be killed." Eckels pronounced this verdict quietly, as if there could be no argument. He had weighed the evidence and this was his considered opinion. The rifle in his hands seemed a cap gun. "We were fools to come. This is impossible."

"Shut up!" hissed Travis.

"Nightmare."

"Turn around," commanded Travis. "Walk quietly to the Machine. We'll remit one half your fee."

"I didn't realize it would be this *big*," said Eckels. "I miscalculated, that's all. And now I want out."

"It *sees* us!"

"There's the red paint on its chest!"

The Tyrant Lizard raised itself. Its armored flesh glittered like a thousand green coins. The coins, crusted with slime, steamed. In the slime, tiny insects wriggled, so that the entire body seemed to twitch and undulate,[5] even while the monster itself did not move. It exhaled. The stink of raw flesh blew down the wilderness.

"Get me out of here," said Eckels. "It was never like this before. I was always sure I'd come through alive. I had good guides, good safaris, and safety. This time, I figured wrong. I've met my match and admit it. This is too much for me to get hold of."

"Don't run," said Lesperance. "Turn around. Hide in the Machine."

"Yes." Eckels seemed to be numb. He looked at his feet as if trying to make them move. He gave a grunt of helplessness.

"Eckels!"

He took a few steps, blinking, shuffling.

"Not *that* way!"

The Monster, at the first motion, lunged forward with a terrible scream. It covered one hundred yards in four seconds. The rifles jerked up and blazed fire. A windstorm from the beast's mouth engulfed them in the stench of slime and old blood. The Monster roared, teeth glittering with sun.

Eckels, not looking back, walked blindly to the edge of the Path, his gun limp in his

5. ***Undulate*** (un′ jə lāt′) means "to move like a wave."

arms, stepped off the Path, and walked, not knowing it, in the jungle. His feet sank into green moss. His legs moved him, and he felt alone and remote from the events behind.

The rifles cracked again. Their sound was lost in shriek and lizard thunder. The great level of the reptile's tail swung up, lashed sideways. Trees exploded in clouds of leaf and branch. The Monster twitched its jeweler's hands down to fondle at the men, to twist them in half, to crush them like berries, to cram them into its teeth and its screaming throat. Its boulder-stone eyes leveled with the men. They saw themselves mirrored. They fired at the metallic eyelids and the blazing black iris.

Like a stone idol, like a mountain avalanche, *Tyrannosaurus* fell. Thundering, it clutched trees, pulled them with it. It wrenched and tore the metal Path. The men flung themselves back and away. The body hit, ten tons of cold flesh and stone. The guns fired. The Monster lashed its armored tail, twitched its snake jaws, and lay still. A fount of blood spurted from its throat. Somewhere inside, a sac of fluids burst. Sickening gushes drenched the hunters. They stood, red and glistening.

The thunder faded.

The jungle was silent. After the avalanche, a green peace. After the nightmare, morning.

Billings and Kramer sat on the pathway and threw up. Travis and Lesperance stood with smoking rifles, cursing steadily.

In the Time Machine, on his face, Eckels lay shivering. He had found his way back to the Path, climbed into the Machine.

Travis came walking, glanced at Eckels, took cotton gauze from a metal box, and returned to the others, who were sitting on the Path.

"Clean up."

They wiped the blood from their helmets. They began to curse too. The Monster lay, a hill of solid flesh. Within, you could hear the sighs and murmurs as the furthest chambers of it died, the organs malfunctioning, liquids running a final instant from pocket to sac to spleen, everything shutting off, closing up forever. It was like standing by a wrecked locomotive or a steam shovel at quitting time, all valves being released or levered tight. Bones cracked; the tonnage of its own flesh, off balance, dead weight, snapped the delicate forearms, caught underneath. The meat settled, quivering.

Another cracking sound. Overhead, a gigantic tree branch broke from its heavy mooring, fell. It crashed upon the dead beast with finality.

"There." Lesperance checked his watch. "Right on time. That's the giant tree that was scheduled to fall and kill this animal originally." He glanced at the two hunters. "You want the trophy picture?"

"What?"

"We can't take a trophy back to the Future. The body has to stay right here where it would have died originally, so the insects, birds, and bacteria can get at it, as they were intended to. Everything in balance. The body stays. But we *can* take a picture of you standing near it."

The two men tried to think, but gave up, shaking their heads.

They let themselves be led along the metal Path. They sank wearily into the Machine cushions. They gazed back at the ruined Monster, the stagnating mound, where already strange reptilian birds and golden insects were busy at the steaming armor.

A sound on the floor of the Time Machine stiffened them. Eckels sat there, shivering.

"I'm sorry," he said at last.

"Get up!" cried Travis.

Eckels got up.

"Go out on that Path alone," said Travis.

He had his rifle pointed. "You're not coming back in the Machine. We're leaving you here!"

Lesperance seized Travis' arm. "Wait—"

"Stay out of this!" Travis shook his hand away. "This fool nearly killed us. But it isn't *that* so much, no. It's his *shoes*! Look at them! He ran off the Path. That *ruins* us! We'll forfeit! Thousands of dollars of insurance! We guarantee no one leaves the Path. He left it. Oh, the fool! I'll have to report to the government. They might revoke[6] our license to travel. Who knows *what* he's done to Time, to History!"

"Take it easy, all he did was kick up some dirt."

"How do we *know?*" cried Travis. "We don't know anything! It's all a mystery! Get out there, Eckels!"

Eckels fumbled his shirt. "I'll pay anything. A hundred thousand dollars!"

Travis glared at Eckels' checkbook and spat. "Go out there. The Monster's next to the Path. Stick your arms up to your elbows in his mouth. Then you can come back with us."

"That's unreasonable!"

"The Monster's dead, you idiot. The bullets! The bullets can't be left behind. They don't belong in the Past; they might change anything. Here's my knife. Dig them out!"

The jungle was alive again, full of the old tremorings and bird cries. Eckels turned slowly to regard the primeval garbage dump, that hill of nightmares and terror. After a long time, like a sleepwalker, he shuffled out along the Path.

He returned, shuddering, five minutes later, his arms soaked and red to the elbows. He held out his hands. Each held a number of steel bullets. Then he fell. He lay where he fell, not moving.

"You didn't have to make him do that," said Lesperance.

"Didn't I? It's too early to tell." Travis nudged the still body. "He'll live. Next time he won't go hunting game like this. Okay." He jerked his thumb wearily at Lesperance. "Switch on. Let's go home."

1492. 1776. 1812.

They cleaned their hands and faces. They changed their caking shirts and pants. Eckels was up and around again, not speaking. Travis glared at him for a full ten minutes.

"Don't look at me," cried Eckels. "I haven't done anything."

"Who can tell?"

"Just ran off the Path, that's all, a little mud on my shoes—what do you want me to do—get down and pray?"

"We might need it. I'm warning you, Eckels, I might kill you yet. I've got my gun ready."

"I'm innocent. I've done nothing."

1999. 2000. 2055.

The Machine stopped.

"Get out," said Travis.

The room was there as they had left it. But not the same as they had left it. The same man sat behind the same desk. But the same man did not quite sit behind the same desk.

Travis looked around swiftly. "Everything okay here?" he snapped.

"Fine. Welcome home!"

Travis did not relax. He seemed to be looking at the very atoms of the air itself, at the way the sun poured through the one high window.

"Okay, Eckels, get out. Don't ever come back."

Eckels could not move.

6. *Revoke* means "to cancel or withdraw."

Vocabulary

primeval (prī mē′ vəl) *adj.* of or having to do with the first or earliest age; primitive

"You heard me," said Travis. "What're you *staring* at?"

Eckels stood smelling of the air, and there was a thing to the air, a chemical taint[7] so subtle, so slight, that only a faint cry of his subliminal[8] senses warned him it was there. The colors, white, gray, blue, orange, in the wall, in the furniture, in the sky beyond the window, were . . . were . . . And there was a *feel*. His flesh twitched. His hands twitched. He stood drinking the oddness with the pores of his body. Somewhere, someone must have been screaming one of those whistles that only a dog can hear. His body screamed silence in return. Beyond this room, beyond this wall, beyond this man who was not quite the same man seated at this desk that was not quite the same desk . . . lay an entire world of streets and people. What sort of world it was now, there was no telling. He could feel them moving there, beyond the walls, almost, like so many chess pieces blown in a dry wind. . . .

But the immediate thing was the sign painted on the office wall, the same sign he had read earlier today on first entering.

Somehow, the sign had changed:

TYME SEFARI INC.
SEFARIS TU ANY YEER EN THE PAST.
YU NAIM THE ANIMALL.
WEE TAEKYUTHAIR.
YU SHOOT ITT.

7. A *taint* is a trace of something that harms or spoils.
8. *Subliminal* (sub lim′ ən əl) means "existing below the limits of sensation or consciousness; subconscious."

Eckels felt himself fall into a chair. He fumbled crazily at the thick slime on his boots. He held up a clod of dirt, trembling, "No, it *can't* be. Not a *little* thing like that. No!"

Embedded in the mud, glistening green and gold and black, was a butterfly, very beautiful and very dead.

"Not a little thing like *that!* Not a butterfly!" cried Eckels.

It fell to the floor, an exquisite thing, a small thing that could upset balances and knock down a line of small dominoes and then big dominoes and then gigantic dominoes, all down the years across Time. Eckels' mind whirled. It *couldn't* change things. Killing one butterfly couldn't be *that* important! Could it?

His face was cold. His mouth trembled, asking: "Who— Who won the presidential election yesterday?"

The man behind the desk laughed. "You joking? You know very well. Deutscher, of course! Who else? Not that fool weakling Keith. We got an iron man now, a man with guts!" The official stopped. "What's wrong?"

Eckels moaned. He dropped to his knees. He scrabbled at the golden butterfly with shaking fingers. "Can't we," he pleaded to the world, to himself, to the officials, to the Machine, "can't we take it *back*, can't we *make* it alive again? Can't we start over? Can't we—"

He did not move. Eyes shut, he waited, shivering. He heard Travis breathe loud in the room; he heard Travis shift his rifle, click the safety catch, and raise the weapon.

There was a sound of thunder.

Responding to Literature

Personal Response

What was your reaction to the outcome of the story? Explain.

Analyzing Literature

Recall

1. Why has Eckels come to the Time Safari office? What does he plan to do?
2. Describe what happens after the party enters the Machine.
3. Summarize the rules the hunters are told to follow and the reasons Travis gives for those rules.
4. How does Eckels react when the *Tyrannosaurus rex* appears? Briefly describe what he and the other men do.
5. What do the men discover when they return from their trip?

Interpret

6. What do you think might be so appealing about the service Time Safari offers?
7. What feelings does Eckels experience during his first journey in the Machine? Use evidence from the story to support your answer.
8. Think back to the Reading Focus on page 315. How might the term "domino effect" be applied to Travis's explanation for Time Safari's rules?
9. In your opinion, why do Eckels and the other men react the way they do when the *Tyrannosaurus rex* appears?
10. Why do you think Eckels and Travis are so dismayed by the changes they find on their return? Explain your answer.

Evaluate and Connect

11. Within the fictional world that Bradbury has created, do events seem to occur in a logical, predictable way? Support your answer with specific examples from the story.
12. Considering how risky the activities of Time Safari are, what reasons might the company have for staying in business?
13. Identify at least three **metaphors** the author uses to describe the *Tyrannosaurus rex.* What two things are being compared in each metaphor? How do these metaphors help you visualize the Monster? (See Literary Terms Handbook, page R7.)
14. If it were possible to travel to the past in order to change the future, what might you want to change? Why?
15. **Theme Connections** In your opinion, which character in the story faced the greatest challenge? Explain your answer.

Literary ELEMENTS

Foreshadowing

Writers often give clues to prepare readers for events that will happen as a story develops. The use of such clues, called **foreshadowing,** also helps build suspense in a story. For example, when the official at the Time Safari office tells Eckels that the company doesn't guarantee his safe return, this creates suspense and helps prepare readers for the challenges the hunters will encounter.

1. What clues help prepare you for the way Eckels behaves in a crisis?
2. Reread the last section of the story, beginning with the words "1492. 1776. 1812." Identify two clues that foreshadow the outcome of the story.

- See **Literary Terms Handbook,** p. R5.

Literary Criticism

According to one critic, a major theme in Bradbury's stories is "the conflict between individual and social concerns." Write an analysis of "A Sound of Thunder," exploring how this theme is developed in the story.

Literature and Writing

Writing About Literature

Evaluate Imagery The world that Bradbury has created in this story comes alive through the use of sensory images. Find a passage in the story that contains vivid imagery. In a paragraph, explain how each image helps you to imagine what it's like to see, hear, smell, taste, or touch the thing that's being described. Share your paragraph with several classmates.

Creative Writing

Time Travel Imagine that, like the characters in this story, you can travel back to any year in the past. What year would you choose? What place on Earth would you want to visit at that time in history? Write your own time travel adventure. Add illustrations, if you wish.

Extending Your Response

Literature Groups

Size Up a Character What kind of man is Eckels? Is he a clumsy, cowardly person who simply makes a mistake, or is he an arrogant, thoughtless, self-centered man who deserves his fate? Or is he something else? Debate these questions in your group, using information from the story to support your opinions. Compare your group's responses with those of other groups.

Interdisciplinary Activity

Science: End of an Era *Tyrannosaurus rex,* along with all the other remaining dinosaurs, became extinct at the end of the Cretaceous period 65 million years ago. There are numerous theories about what happened and why dinosaurs did not survive into the modern world. Use the Internet or other resources to explore some of these theories. Discuss your findings with a group of classmates.

Learning for Life

Magazine Ad Work with a partner to create a magazine advertisement for Time Safari, Inc. Discuss these points: Who are your prospective clients? What hook, or main idea, will you use to sell your service? What techniques–such as slogans, headlines, and testimonials from customers–will you use? How will you illustrate your ad? Now create your ad. You might use a computer to design and produce it.

Save your work for your portfolio.

VOCABULARY • The Prefix *com-*

If you look up the prefix *cor-* in the dictionary, the entry will probably read: "See **com-**." The basic prefix *com-* changes its spelling to *cor-* in front of *r.* It is spelled *col-, con-,* or *co-* in front of other letters. These prefixes mean "together" or "very much." To *cooperate* is to operate (work) together; to *correlate* is to relate together or to bring one thing into relation with another.

PRACTICE Match each numbered word in the list with its Latin root (labeled with an uppercase letter) and its definition (labeled with a lowercase letter). Use the "together" meaning of the prefix *com-*.

1. colloquial
2. concoct
3. conjunction
4. compensate
5. constrict

A. *stringere* (to draw tight)
B. *loqui* (to speak)
C. *coquo* (to cook)
D. *jungere* (to join)
E. *pensare* (to weigh)

a. a union or combination
b. to hold in; limit; restrict
c. having to do with conversational speech
d. to make by combining ingredients
e. to balance in force or effect; make up for

MEDIA connection

Magazine Article

What traditions does your family have? How are they passed on? In the Navajo culture, girls learn about traditional ways of doing things by watching and talking to their female relatives.

Three Generations of Navajo Weavers

by Paul Zolbrod—*Indian Artist,* Fall 1997

"When my arm gets tired, she takes over," laughs Rondelle Benally, 18, motioning to Roxanne, who is two years younger. "And when hers does, it's my turn again." Once they get into the design, however, the two sisters weave together side by side. Their eyes sparkle with teenage enthusiasm while discussing this distinctive Navajo art with their mother, Bonnie, 41, and their grandmother Loretta, now in her late 70s, near their home in Crownpoint, New Mexico.

The two Benally sisters started learning the traditional way of weaving while they were still preschoolers. Much the way their grandmother had, they looked on as their mother wove. "We'd sit and watch her, and she'd tell us what she was doing and why she did it," Rondelle recalls.

Inevitable contrasts mark the experiences of the three generations of weavers. Loretta tells of growing up in a hogan with no electricity, traveling back and forth by horse, and never going to school. She remembers the shift from a pastoral way of life to a labor-based cash economy. Bonnie passed her childhood in a "square house," enjoyed the benefits of motor vehicles, and went to high school. Rondelle and Roxanne, of course, grew up with television and shopping malls and anticipate going to college.

Strong similarities underlie the differences, however. All four believe that the tradition of weaving must be maintained. All exhibit a deep love for sheep and the feel of raw wool. For them, the standing loom promises to perpetuate an art whose distinctiveness seems obvious and yet inexplicable.

"At first, I just wanted to learn because my grandmother knew and my mother knew," says Rondelle. "Now I realize that my pride as a weaver comes from the tradition I'm learning about."

Analyzing Media

1. How did Rondelle and Roxanne learn to weave? What skills have you learned in a similar manner?
2. If they had not grown up near their mother and grandmother, how might the lives of the Benally sisters be different today?

Before You Read

Lullaby

Reading Focus

When you're feeling troubled or discouraged, do you ever think back to a happier time in the past? How can memories lift your spirits?

Quickwrite Take five minutes to write about a memory that has helped lift your spirits in some way.

Setting a Purpose Read to share the painful and tender memories of one mother.

Building Background

The Time and Place

This story takes place in west central New Mexico, near the Cañoncito (Navajo) Reservation; parts of the story may actually take place on the reservation. The time of the story is probably the late 1960s or the 1970s.

Did You Know?

Pulmonary tuberculosis, also known as TB, is a contagious lung disease that can lead to death if left untreated. The first antibiotic treatment for TB was not discovered until 1943. By the mid-1950s, chest X rays were used to test millions of Americans for TB; infected people were then treated for the disease. But large numbers of infected people remained undiagnosed and thus continued to infect others. Included in this group were thousands of Navajo Indians, many of whom mistrusted white doctors. In the 1950s, U.S. government health agencies began testing Navajos for TB. Infected people were sent away—sometimes against their will—to special hospitals, called sanatoriums, for long-term care.

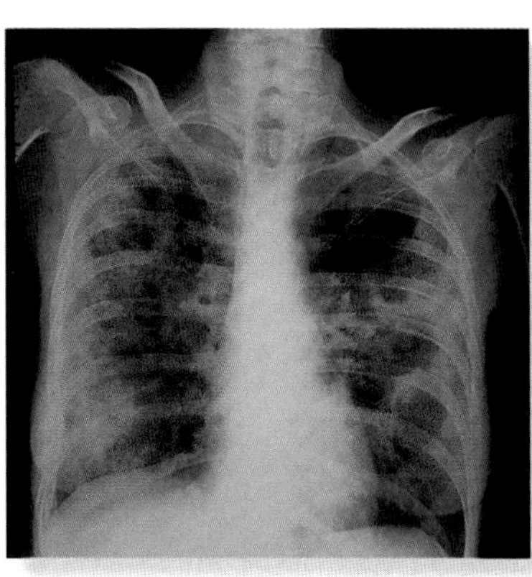

Vocabulary Preview

arroyo (ə roi′ ō) *n.* a dry gully or stream bed; p. 331
crevice (krev′ is) *n.* a narrow crack into or through something; p. 335
sparse (spärs) *adj.* thinly spread or distributed; p. 337
distortion (dis tôr′ shən) *n.* an appearance of being twisted or bent out of shape; p. 338

Meet Leslie Marmon Silko

"I suppose at the core of my writing is the attempt to identify what it is to be a half-breed, or mixed-blooded person; what it is to grow up neither white nor fully traditional Indian," Leslie Marmon Silko has written. Silko grew up in Laguna, New Mexico, where she spent much of her time with her great-grandmother, a Laguna Indian who had married a white man. From her great-grandmother, Silko heard stories about what life was like long ago. In her writing, Silko doesn't claim to represent Native Americans in general. "I am only one human being, one Laguna woman," she has written.

Leslie Marmon Silko was born in 1948 in Albuquerque, New Mexico. This story appears in Storyteller, *published in 1981.*

Lullaby

Leslie Marmon Silko

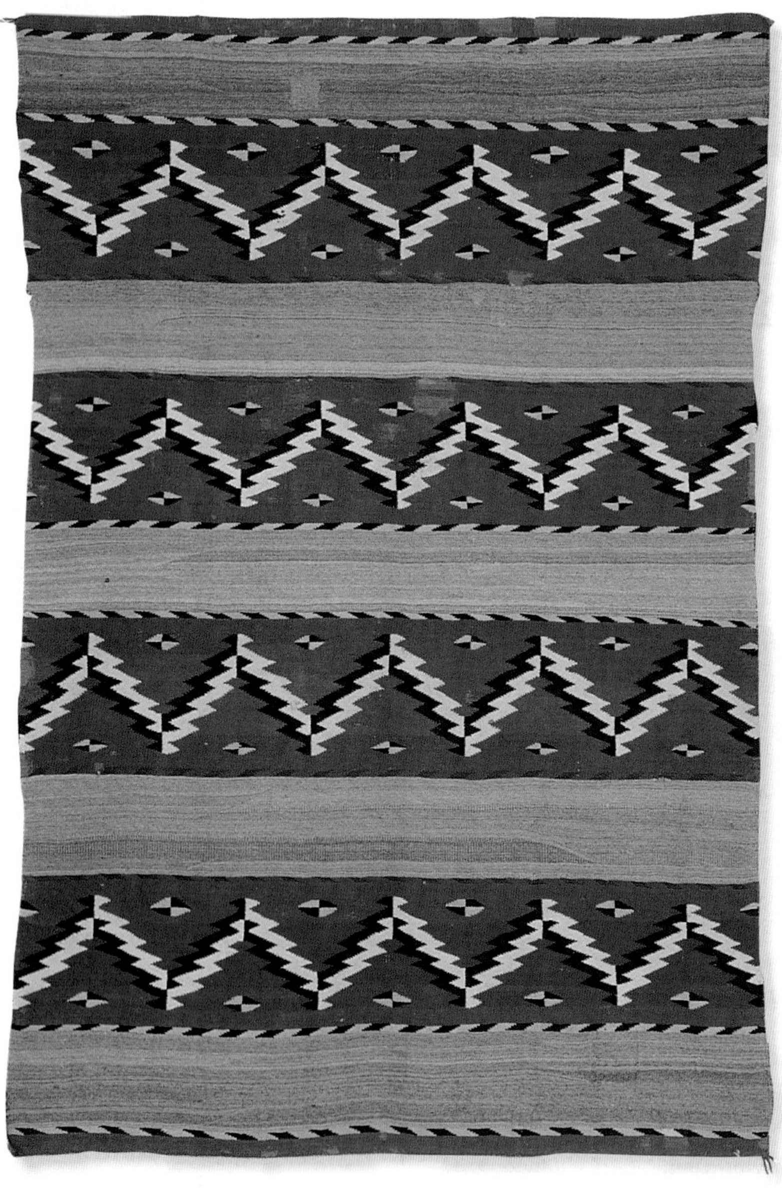

Navajo Zoned Blanket Design, c. 1870s. Wool, 72 x 51 in. The Lowe Art Museum, The University of Miami, Miami, FL.

THE SUN HAD GONE DOWN but the snow in the wind gave off its own light. It came in thick tufts like new wool—washed before the weaver spins it. Ayah[1] reached out for it like her own babies had, and she smiled when she remembered how she had laughed at them. She was an old woman now, and her life had become memories. She sat down with her back against the wide cottonwood tree, feeling the rough bark on her back bones; she faced east and listened to the wind and snow sing a high-pitched Yeibechei[2] song. Out of the wind she felt warmer, and she could watch the wide fluffy snow fill in her tracks, steadily, until the direction she had come from was gone. By the light of the snow she could see the dark outline of the big arroyo a few feet away. She was sitting on the edge of Cebolleta[3] Creek, where in the springtime the thin cows would graze on grass already chewed flat to the ground. In the wide deep creek bed where only a trickle of water flowed in the summer, the skinny cows would wander, looking for new grass along winding paths splashed with manure.

Ayah pulled the old Army blanket over her head like a shawl. Jimmie's blanket—the one he had sent to her. That was a long time ago and the green wool was faded, and it was unraveling on the edges. She did not want to think about Jimmie. So she thought about the weaving and the way her mother had done it. On the tall wooden loom set into the sand under a tamarack[4] tree for shade. She could see it clearly. She had been only a little girl when her grandma gave her the wooden combs to pull the twigs and burrs from the raw, freshly washed wool. And while she combed the wool, her grandma sat beside her, spinning a silvery strand of yarn around the smooth cedar spindle. Her mother worked at the loom with yarns dyed bright yellow and red and gold. She watched them dye the yarn in boiling black pots full of beeweed petals, juniper berries, and sage. The blankets her mother made were soft and woven so tight that rain rolled off them like birds' feathers. Ayah remembered sleeping warm on cold windy nights, wrapped in her mother's blankets on the hogan's[5] sandy floor.

Did You Know?
In yarn-making, the *spindle* is a round, tapered stick that is turned by hand to twist wool fibers into a thread of yarn.

The snow drifted now, with the northwest wind hurling it in gusts. It drifted up around her black overshoes—old ones with little metal buckles. She smiled at the snow which was trying to cover her little by little. She could remember when they had no black rubber overshoes; only the high buckskin leggings that they wrapped over their elkhide moccasins. If the snow was dry or frozen, a person could walk all day and not get wet; and in the evenings the beams of the ceiling would hang with lengths of pale buckskin leggings, drying out slowly.

She felt peaceful remembering. She didn't feel cold any more. Jimmie's blanket seemed warmer than it had ever been. And she could

1. *Ayah* (ä′ yə)
2. The *Yeibechei* (yā′ bə chā) are masked Navajo dancers who sing in high-pitched voices.
3. *Cebolleta* (se′ bō yā′ tä) is also the name of a town in the story.
4. *Tamarack* is another name for the larch, a tree in the pine family.
5. Traditionally, a *hogan* is a Navajo dwelling made of wood and covered with earth.

Vocabulary
arroyo (ə roi′ ō) *n.* a dry gully or stream bed

remember the morning he was born. She could remember whispering to her mother, who was sleeping on the other side of the hogan, to tell her it was time now. She did not want to wake the others. The second time she called to her, her mother stood up and pulled on her shoes; she knew. They walked to the old stone hogan together, Ayah walking a step behind her mother. She waited alone, learning the rhythms of the pains while her mother went to call the old woman to help them. The morning was already warm even before dawn and Ayah smelled the bee flowers blooming and the young willow growing at the springs. She could remember that so clearly, but his birth merged into the births of the other children and to her it became all the same birth. They named him for the summer morning and in English they called him Jimmie.

It wasn't like Jimmie died. He just never came back, and one day a dark blue sedan with white writing on its doors pulled up in front of the boxcar shack where the rancher let the Indians live. A man in a khaki uniform trimmed in gold gave them a yellow piece of paper and told them that Jimmie was dead. He said the Army would try to get the body back and then it would be shipped to them; but it wasn't likely because the helicopter had burned after it crashed. All of this was told to Chato[6] because he could understand English. She stood inside the doorway holding the baby while Chato listened. Chato spoke English like a white man and he spoke Spanish too. He was taller than the white man and he stood straighter too. Chato didn't explain why; he just told the military man they could keep the body if they found it. The white man looked bewildered; he nodded his head and he left. Then Chato looked at her and shook his head, and then he told her, "Jimmie isn't coming home anymore," and when he spoke, he used the words to speak of the dead. She didn't cry then, but she hurt inside with anger. And she mourned him as the years passed, when a horse fell with Chato and broke his leg, and the white rancher told them he wouldn't pay Chato until he could work again. She mourned Jimmie because he would have worked for his father then; he would have saddled the big bay[7] horse and ridden the fence lines each day, with wire cutters and heavy gloves, fixing the breaks in the barbed wire and putting the stray cattle back inside again.

She mourned him after the white doctors came to take Danny and Ella away. She was at the shack alone that day they came. It was back in the days before they hired Navajo women to go with them as interpreters. She recognized one of the doctors. She had seen him at the children's clinic at Cañoncito[8] about a month ago. They were wearing khaki uniforms and they waved papers at her and a black ball-point pen, trying to make her understand their English words. She was frightened by the way they looked at the children, like the lizard watches the fly. Danny was swinging on the tire swing on the elm tree behind the rancher's house, and Ella was toddling around the front door, dragging the broomstick horse Chato made for her. Ayah could see they wanted her to sign the papers, and Chato had taught her to sign her name. It was something she was proud of. She only wanted them to go, and to take their eyes away from her children.

She took the pen from the man without looking at his face and she signed the papers in three different places he pointed to. She stared at the ground by their feet and waited for them to leave. But they stood there and began to point and gesture at the children.

6. *Chato* (chä′ tō)

7. Here, *bay* is the horse's color—a reddish brown.

8. *Cañoncito* (kan′ yən sē′ tō) is the name of the Navajo reservation located in west central New Mexico.

Danny stopped swinging. Ayah could see his fear. She moved suddenly and grabbed Ella into her arms; the child squirmed, trying to get back to her toys. Ayah ran with the baby toward Danny; she screamed for him to run and then she grabbed him around his chest and carried him too. She ran south into the foothills of juniper trees and black lava rock. Behind her she heard the doctors running, but they had been taken by surprise, and as the hills became steeper and the cholla cactus were thicker, they stopped. When she reached the top of the hill, she stopped to listen in case they were circling around her. But in a few minutes she heard a car engine start and they drove away. The children had been too surprised to cry while she ran with them. Danny was shaking and Ella's little fingers were gripping Ayah's blouse.

Did You Know?
A *cholla* (choi′ ə) is a spiny, shrubby, or treelike cactus.

She stayed up in the hills for the rest of the day, sitting on a black lava boulder in the sunshine where she could see for miles all around her. The sky was light blue and cloudless, and it was warm for late April. The sun warmth relaxed her and took the fear and anger away. She lay back on the rock and watched the sky. It seemed to her that she could walk into the sky, stepping through clouds endlessly. Danny played with little pebbles and stones, pretending they were birds' eggs and then little rabbits. Ella sat at her feet and dropped fistfuls of dirt into the breeze, watching the dust and particles of sand intently. Ayah watched a hawk soar high above them, dark wings gliding; hunting or only watching, she did not know. The hawk was patient and he circled all afternoon before he disappeared around the high volcanic peak the Mexicans called Guadalupe.[9]

Late in the afternoon, Ayah looked down at the gray boxcar shack with the paint all peeled from the wood; the stove pipe on the roof was rusted and crooked. The fire she had built that morning in the oil drum stove had burned out. Ella was asleep in her lap now and Danny sat close to her, complaining that he was hungry; he asked when they would go to the house. "We will stay up here until your father comes," she told him, "because those white men were chasing us." The boy remembered then and he nodded at her silently.

If Jimmie had been there he could have read those papers and explained to her what they said. Ayah would have known then, never to sign them. The doctors came back the next day and they brought a BIA[10] policeman with them. They told Chato they had her signature and that was all they needed. Except for the kids. She listened to Chato sullenly; she hated him when he told her it was the old woman who died in the winter, spitting blood; it was her old grandma who had given the children this disease. "They don't spit blood," she said coldly. "The whites lie." She held Ella and Danny close to her, ready to run to the hills again. "I want a medicine man first," she said to Chato, not looking at him. He shook his head. "It's too late now. The policeman is with them. You signed the paper." His voice was gentle.

It was worse than if they had died: to lose the children and to know that somewhere, in a place called Colorado, in a place full of sick

9. *Guadalupe* (gwä′ də lo͞o′ pā)
10. The Bureau of Indian Affairs, or *BIA,* is the federal agency in charge of administering government policies toward Native Americans.

In Grandma's Care. Johnson J. Yazzi (b. 1957). Pastel, 22 x 18 in. Jesse Monongye Studios, Scottsdale, AZ.

Viewing the painting: How might the relationship of these two people compare with the relationship of Ayah and her children?

and dying strangers, her children were without her. There had been babies that died soon after they were born, and one that died before he could walk. She had carried them herself, up to the boulders and great pieces of the cliff that long ago crashed down from Long Mesa; she laid them in the crevices of sandstone and buried them in fine brown sand with round quartz pebbles that washed down the hills in the rain. She had endured it because they had been with her. But she could not bear this pain. She did not sleep for a long time after they took her children. She stayed on the hill where they had fled the first time, and she slept rolled up in the blanket Jimmie had sent her. She carried the pain in her belly and it was fed by everything she saw: the blue sky of their last day together and the dust and pebbles they played with; the swing in the elm tree and broomstick horse choked life from her. The pain filled her stomach and there was no room for food or for her lungs to fill with air. The air and the food would have been theirs.

She hated Chato, not because he let the policeman and doctors put the screaming children in the government car, but because he had taught her to sign her name. Because it was like the old ones always told her about learning their language or any of their ways: it endangered you. She slept alone on the hill until the middle of November when the first snows came. Then she made a bed for herself where the children had slept. She did not lie down beside Chato again until many years later, when he was sick and shivering and only her body could keep him warm. The illness came after the white rancher told Chato he was too old to work for him anymore, and Chato and his old woman should be out of the shack by the next afternoon because the rancher had hired new people to work there. That had satisfied her. To see how the white man repaid Chato's years of loyalty and work. All of Chato's fine-sounding English talk didn't change things.

It snowed steadily and the luminous light from the snow gradually diminished into the darkness. Somewhere in Cebolleta a dog barked and other village dogs joined with it. Ayah looked in the direction she had come, from the bar where Chato was buying the wine. Sometimes he told her to go on ahead and wait; and then he never came. And when she finally went back looking for him, she would find him passed out at the bottom of the wooden steps to Azzie's Bar. All the wine would be gone and most of the money too, from the pale blue check that came to them once a month in a government envelope. It was then that she would look at his face and his hands, scarred by ropes and the barbed wire of all those years, and she would think, this man is a stranger; for forty years she had smiled at him and cooked his food, but he remained a stranger. She stood up again, with the snow almost to her knees, and she walked back to find Chato.

It was hard to walk in the deep snow and she felt the air burn in her lungs. She stopped a short distance from the bar to rest and readjust the blanket. But this time he wasn't waiting for her on the bottom step with his old Stetson hat pulled down and his shoulders hunched up in his long wool overcoat.

She was careful not to slip on the wooden steps. When she pushed the door open, warm air and cigarette smoke hit her face. She looked around slowly and deliberately, in every corner, in every dark place that the old man might find to sleep. The bar owner didn't like Indians in there, especially Navajos, but he let Chato come in because he could talk Spanish like he was one of them. The men at the bar

Vocabulary
crevice (krev′ is) *n.* a narrow crack into or through something

stared at her, and the bartender saw that she left the door open wide. Snowflakes were flying inside like moths and melting into a puddle on the oiled wood floor. He motioned to her to close the door, but she did not see him. She held herself straight and walked across the room slowly, searching the room with every step. The snow in her hair melted and she could feel it on her forehead. At the far corner of the room, she saw red flames at the mica window of the old stove door; she looked behind the stove just to make sure. The bar got quiet except for the Spanish polka music playing on the jukebox. She stood by the stove and shook the snow from her blanket and held it near the stove to dry. The wet wool smell reminded her of new-born goats in early March, brought inside to warm near the fire. She felt calm.

Did You Know?
Mica is a mineral (abundant in New Mexico) that can be split into thin, strong, flexible sheets. A sheet of colorless mica makes a decent, inexpensive substitute for glass.

In past years they would have told her to get out. But her hair was white now and her face was wrinkled. They looked at her like she was a spider crawling slowly across the room. They were afraid; she could feel the fear. She looked at their faces steadily. They reminded her of the first time the white people brought her children back to her that winter. Danny had been shy and hid behind the thin white woman who brought them. And the baby had not known her until Ayah took her into her arms, and then Ella had nuzzled close to her as she had when she was nursing. The blonde woman was nervous and kept looking at a dainty gold watch on her wrist. She sat on the bench near the small window and watched the dark snow clouds gather around the mountains; she was worrying about the unpaved road. She was frightened by what she saw inside too: the strips of venison drying on a rope across the ceiling and the children jabbering excitedly in a language she did not know. So they stayed for only a few hours. Ayah watched the government car disappear down the road and she knew they were already being weaned from these lava hills and from this sky. The last time they came was in early June, and Ella stared at her the way the men in the bar were now staring. Ayah did not try to pick her up; she smiled at her instead and spoke cheerfully to Danny. When he tried to answer her, he could not seem to remember and he spoke English words with the Navajo. But he gave her a scrap of paper that he had found somewhere and carried in his pocket; it was folded in half, and he shyly looked up at her and said it was a bird. She asked Chato if they were home for good this time. He spoke to the white woman and she shook her head. "How much longer?" he asked, and she said she didn't know; but Chato saw how she stared at the boxcar shack. Ayah turned away then. She did not say good-bye.

She felt satisfied that the men in the bar feared her. Maybe it was her face and the way she held her mouth with teeth clenched tight, like there was nothing anyone could do to her now. She walked north down the road, searching for the old man. She did this because she had the blanket, and there would be no place for him except with her and the blanket in the old adobe barn near the arroyo. They always slept there when they came to Cebolleta. If the money and the wine were gone, she would be relieved because then they could go home again: back to the old hogan with a dirt roof and rock walls where she herself had been born. And the next day the old man could go back to the few sheep they still had, to follow along behind them, guiding them, into dry sandy arroyos where sparse grass grew. She knew he did not like walking behind old ewes when for so many years he rode big quarter horses and worked with cattle. But she wasn't sorry for him; he should have known all along what would happen.

There had not been enough rain for their garden in five years; and that was when Chato finally hitched a ride into the town and brought back brown boxes of rice and sugar and big tin cans of welfare[11] peaches. After that, at the first of the month they went to Cebolleta to ask the postmaster for the check; and then Chato would go to the bar and cash it. They did this as they planted the garden every May, not because anything would survive the summer dust, but because it was time to do this. The journey passed the days that smelled silent and dry like the caves above the canyon with yellow painted buffaloes on their walls.

Her Precious Time, c. 1987. Redwing T. Nez. Mixed media, 29½ x 22½ in. Museum of Northern Arizona, Flagstaff, AZ.

Viewing the painting: What personal qualities do you see in this woman that might be shared by Ayah? Explain.

He was walking along the pavement when she found him. He did not stop or turn around when he heard her behind him. She walked beside him and she noticed how slowly he moved now. He smelled strong of woodsmoke and urine. Lately he had been forgetting. Sometimes he called her by his sister's name and she had been gone for a long time. Once she had found him wandering on the road to the white man's ranch, and she asked him why he was going that way; he laughed at her and said, "You know they can't run that ranch without me," and he walked on determined, limping on the leg that had been crushed many years before. Now he looked at her curiously, as if for the first time, but he kept shuffling along, moving slowly along the side of the highway. His gray hair had grown long and spread out on the shoulders of the long overcoat. He wore the old felt hat pulled down over his ears. His boots were worn out at the toes and he had stuffed pieces of an old red shirt in the holes. The rags

11. The canned peaches came from a government *welfare* program to help needy people.

Vocabulary
sparse (spärs) *adj.* thinly spread or distributed

made his feet look like little animals up to their ears in snow. She laughed at his feet; the snow muffled the sound of her laugh. He stopped and looked at her again. The wind had quit blowing and the snow was falling straight down; the southeast sky was beginning to clear and Ayah could see a star.

"Let's rest awhile," she said to him. They walked away from the road and up the slope to the giant boulders that had tumbled down from the red sandrock mesa throughout the centuries of rainstorms and earth tremors. In a place where the boulders shut out the wind, they sat down with their backs against the rock. She offered half of the blanket to him and they sat wrapped together.

The storm passed swiftly. The clouds moved east. They were massive and full, crowding together across the sky. She watched them with the feeling of horses—steely blue-gray horses startled across the sky. The powerful haunches pushed into the distances and the tail hairs streamed white mist behind them. The sky cleared. Ayah saw that there was nothing between her and the stars. The light was crystalline.[12] There was no shimmer, no distortion through earth haze. She breathed the clarity of the night sky; she smelled the purity of the half moon and the stars. He was lying on his side with his knees pulled up near his belly for warmth. His eyes were closed now, and in the light from the stars and the moon, he looked young again.

She could see it descend out of the night sky: an icy stillness from the edge of the thin moon. She recognized the freezing. It came gradually, sinking snowflake by snowflake until the crust was heavy and deep. It had the strength of the stars in Orion, and its journey was endless. Ayah knew that with the wine he would sleep. He would not feel it. She tucked the blanket around him, remembering how it was when Ella had been with her; and she felt the rush so big inside her heart for the babies. And she sang the only song she knew to sing for babies. She could not remember if she had ever sung it to her children, but she knew that her grandmother had sung it and her mother had sung it:

The earth is your mother,
she holds you.
The sky is your father,
he protects you.
Sleep,
sleep.
Rainbow is your sister,
she loves you.
The winds are your brothers,
they sing to you.
Sleep,
sleep.
We are together always
We are together always
There never was a time
when this
was not so.

Did You Know?
The constellation *Orion* contains two of the brightest stars in the sky. In Greek mythology, Orion is traditionally depicted as a hunter wearing a belt with a sword at his side.

12. Here, *crystalline* means "clear and pure as a crystal."

Vocabulary
distortion (dis tôr′ shən) *n.* an appearance of being twisted or bent out of shape

Responding to Literature

Personal Response

For which character did you have more sympathy, Ayah or Chato? For whom did you have more respect or admiration? Give reasons.

Analyzing Literature

Recall

1. In the first three paragraphs of the story, what things around Ayah remind her of events in the past? What are those events?
2. What happened to Jimmie, to Danny and Ella, and to Ayah's other children?
3. Describe the type of life Ayah and Chato are living at the present time. Why have they come to Cebolleta?
4. How does Chato look and act when Ayah finally finds him?
5. Describe Ayah's thoughts and actions after she and Chato find shelter among the boulders.

Interpret

6. Why might Ayah's thoughts turn so often to the past?
7. How did Ayah react to what happened to Jimmie? To Danny and Ella? To her other children? Explain why you think Ayah reacted the way she did. Use details from the story to support your answers.
8. Why have Ayah's and Chato's lives changed so much now that they are older? Compare and contrast their ways of coping.
9. In your opinion, how does Ayah feel about her husband? Use evidence from the story to support your ideas.
10. What is the **mood** at the end the story, when Ayah and Chato are resting? What details help to create that mood? (See page R8.)

Evaluate and Connect

11. What do you think happens to Chato at the end of the story? Give reasons for your answer.
12. In your opinion, is "Lullaby" an appropriate title for this story? Explain.
13. Compare the ways Ayah and Chato reacted when the doctors came to take the children. What do you think you would have done?
14. Look back at your response to the Reading Focus on page 329. How do you think Ayah's response might compare to yours? Explain.
15. **Theme Connections** Think about the obstacles that Ayah and Chato have faced, as well as the tragedies they have endured. In your opinion, have they triumphed over adversity, or has it defeated them? Explain.

Literary ELEMENTS

Flashback

A **flashback** is a memory or account of an event that took place at an earlier time. Although a flashback interrupts the chronological sequence of story events, it usually reveals important information. In "Lullaby," for example, the narrator includes a flashback to the day Ayah and Chato found out that Jimmie had died. This flashback reveals not only a tragic event in the characters' lives, but also their reactions to that event. This information gives the reader a better context for understanding the story's events and the characters who experience those events.

1. Describe two other flashbacks from the story. Explain how they help you better understand the story's characters and events.
2. In your opinion, are flashbacks an effective means of presenting information about Ayah and Chato's past experiences? Explain.

- See **Literary Terms Handbook**, p. R5.

Literature and Writing

Writing About Literature

Analyze Setting and Mood The narrator of "Lullaby" describes a variety of settings in which present and past events take place. Choose one of those settings and identify details the narrator uses to describe the setting. Then write an analysis of how the setting helps to create a particular atmosphere, or mood, in that part of the story. Meet with a small group of classmates to share your analysis.

Creative Writing

Ayah's Song The song Ayah sings at the end of the story is a lullaby. Write the lyrics of a song for Ayah. It can be a lullaby, like the one in the story; a ballad that tells the story of Ayah's life; a rap, whose lyrics will be spoken or chanted; or any other type of song you choose to write. Share your song lyrics with the class. Set your lyrics to music, if you wish.

Extending Your Response

Literature Groups

The Power of Language Ayah has never learned to speak or read English, following the advice of older Navajos who "told her about learning [the white people's] language or any of their ways: it endangered you." Evaluate this advice in light of events that occur in "Lullaby." Discuss and debate such questions as: How did the white doctors get Ayah's permission to take Danny and Ella? How might this situation have been avoided? Was it a mistake for Chato to teach Ayah to sign her name? Why or why not? How did Chato benefit from knowing how to speak English? Did Chato's knowledge of English help him when he was unable to work? Why or why not? Share your ideas with the class.

Learning for Life

Letter of Inquiry Imagine that you are Ayah's friend and she has come to you, confused and frightened about what the doctors want and what they intend to do. Write a letter of inquiry, asking the doctors to explain the situation. Be polite and businesslike in your approach. Use the proper form for a business letter.

Reading Further

You might also enjoy these essays by Leslie Marmon Silko: "The People and the Land are Inseparable" and "Fifth World: The Return of Ma ah shra true ee, the Giant Serpent" are from *Yellow Woman and a Beauty of the Spirit,* a partially autobiographical collection of essays about Native American experiences.

Save your work for your portfolio.

VOCABULARY • The Latin Root *tort*

The word *distortion* comes from the Latin prefix *dis-*, meaning (in this case) "thoroughly," and the root *tort,* which comes from *torquere,* meaning "to twist."

A *retort* is a response of the same kind originally spoken. It is, in a sense, a remark that is twisted back upon the original speaker. To *extort* is to get money or goods by "twisting" them out of someone. *Torture* involves twisting a victim—physically, mentally, or emotionally.

Recognizing the root *tort* when you see it in an unfamiliar word can help you get at least a general sense of the word's meaning.

PRACTICE Briefly state what you think might be the meaning of each underlined word.

1. We followed a <u>tortuous</u> path down the mountain.
2. To do that exercise, you'd have to be a <u>contortionist</u>!
3. <u>Torsion</u> in the rope of a tire swing will cause it to spin.

INTERDISCIPLINARY HISTORY CONNECTION

Navajo Code Talkers in World War II

Like Ayah's son Jimmie in "Lullaby," many Navajos have served in the United States armed forces in times of war and in times of peace. In fact, during World War II, the Navajos made an invaluable contribution as *Code Talkers*—highly trained soldiers who relayed secret, oral coded messages.

A perpetual problem in military operations is how to send messages that the enemy cannot understand. In World War II, both sides intercepted and decoded each other's radio and telephone communications. New codes had to be continually developed as old ones were broken. But in the Pacific, the Navajos relayed messages using the only code that an enemy has never cracked.

A little-known and little-used language that had never been written down, Navajo was difficult to learn because of its intricate grammatical rules and tonal character. Other than the Navajo themselves, few people in the world had mastered its unusual and complicated sounds.

Originally, twenty-nine Navajo recruits, some as young as fifteen, developed and mastered a Navajo code for use in the Pacific war front. The system that resulted could relay messages more quickly, accurately—and securely—than any other then in use.

The Navajo had no words for many military terms and place names, so the Code Talkers used words with logical associations. This chart shows a few examples.

Term	Code word
Battleship	Whale
Fighter plane	Hummingbird
Germany	Iron hat
Grenade	Potato
Submarine	Iron fish

The program eventually involved hundreds of Navajos who participated in Marine actions in the Pacific from 1942 to 1945. The Code Talkers used field telephones and walkie-talkies to report enemy locations and to direct troop movements, air strikes, and artillery fire.

In the capture of the island of Iwo Jima in 1945, six Navajo Code Talkers worked tirelessly during the first two days of the campaign, while the Marines landed and took up their shore positions. The Code Talkers relayed more than eight hundred messages without a single error. A Marine officer later declared, "Were it not for the Navajos, the Marines never would have taken Iwo Jima."

Activity

What happened to the Code Talkers after the war? How did they readjust to reservation life? Were they ever recognized for their invaluable contribution? Search the Internet and skim such books as Margaret Bixler's *Winds of Freedom* to find the answers. Then prepare a brief oral report.

Before You Read

And of Clay Are We Created

Reading Focus

Would most people try to save the life of a total stranger? Would they do so even if it meant putting their own safety at risk?

Sharing Ideas Firefighters and police officers put their lives on the line for strangers all the time. To what extent are ordinary people obligated to help another person in a life-threatening situation? Discuss these issues in a small group.

Setting a Purpose Read to learn how one person responds to another's terrible situations.

Building Background

The Time and Place

This story is based on actual events that took place in November 1985, in the town of Armero, Colombia, not far from the capital city of Bogotá.

Did You Know?

According to geologists, the greatest danger at many volcanic sites comes not from lava, but from sudden, massive mud flows called *lahars.* When the previously dormant volcano Nevado del Ruiz erupted on November 13, 1985, a monstrous mudslide cascaded from the volcano's icy peak and crashed into the town of Armero, Colombia. Although the eruption was relatively small, the lahar that the eruption produced smothered more than 20,000 people under its blanket of mud and debris.

Vocabulary Preview

cataclysm (kat′ ə kliz′ əm) *n.* a disaster, usually one that causes sudden and violent change; p. 344

presentiment (pri zen′ tə mənt) *n.* a feeling that something is about to happen; p. 344

equanimity (ek′ wə nim′ ə tē) *n.* the ability to remain calm and assured; p. 345

fortitude (fôr′ tə tōōd′) *n.* firm courage or strength of mind in the face of pain or danger; p. 345

pandemonium (pan′ də mō′ nē əm) *n.* wild disorder and uproar; p. 347

tribulation (trib′ yə lā′ shən) *n.* great misery or distress; suffering; p. 350

Meet Isabel Allende

"I write to preserve memory. I write what should not be forgotten."

With these words, Chilean author Isabel Allende (ēs′ ä bel ä yen′ dā) defines her purpose for writing, a purpose she believes she shares with all writers. Allende grew up in her grandparents' home in Santiago, Chile, where she learned to read and love books at an early age. After living in Bolivia, Europe, and the Middle East, Allende returned to Chile as a journalist. She was forced to flee the country in 1973 when her uncle, President Salvador Allende, was killed in a bloody government coup.

Allende was born in Lima, Peru, in 1942. This story appears in The Stories of Eva Luna, *which was published in 1991.*

And of Clay Are We Created

Isabel Allende

Translated by Margaret Sayers Peden

They discovered the girl's head protruding from the mudpit, eyes wide open, calling soundlessly. She had a First Communion name, Azucena.[1] Lily. In that vast cemetery where the odor of death was already attracting vultures from far away, and where the weeping of orphans and wails of the injured filled the air, the little girl obstinately clinging to life became the symbol of the tragedy.

1. ***Azucena*** (ä zo͞o kē′ nä)

The television cameras transmitted so often the unbearable image of the head budding like a black squash from the clay that there was no one who did not recognize her and know her name. And every time we saw her on the screen, right behind her was Rolf Carlé,[2] who had gone there on assignment, never suspecting that he would find a fragment of his past, lost thirty years before.

First a subterranean[3] sob rocked the cotton fields, curling them like waves of foam. Geologists had set up their seismographs[4] weeks before and knew that the mountain had awakened again. For some time they had predicted that the heat of the eruption could detach the eternal ice from the slopes of the volcano, but no one heeded their warnings; they sounded like the tales of frightened old women. The towns in the valley went about their daily life, deaf to the moaning of the earth, until that fateful Wednesday night in November when a prolonged roar announced the end of the world, and walls of snow broke loose, rolling in an avalanche of clay, stones, and water that descended on the villages and buried them beneath unfathomable[5] meters of telluric[6] vomit. As soon as the survivors emerged from the paralysis of that first awful terror, they could see that houses, plazas, churches, white cotton plantations, dark coffee forests, cattle pastures—all had disappeared. Much later, after soldiers and volunteers had arrived to rescue the living and try to assess the magnitude of the cataclysm, it was calculated that beneath the mud lay more than twenty thousand human beings and an indefinite number of animals putrefying in a viscous soup. Forests and rivers had also been swept away, and there was nothing to be seen but an immense desert of mire.[7]

When the station called before dawn, Rolf Carlé and I were together. I crawled out of bed, dazed with sleep, and went to prepare coffee while he hurriedly dressed. He stuffed his gear in the green canvas backpack he always carried, and we said goodbye, as we had so many times before. I had no presentiments. I sat in the kitchen, sipping my coffee and planning the long hours without him, sure that he would be back the next day.

He was one of the first to reach the scene, because while other reporters were fighting their way to the edges of that morass[8] in jeeps, bicycles, or on foot, each getting there however he could, Rolf Carlé had the advantage of the television helicopter, which flew him over the avalanche. We watched on our screens the footage captured by his assistant's camera, in which he was up to his knees in muck, a microphone in his hand, in the midst of a bedlam[9] of lost children, wounded survivors, corpses, and devastation. The story came to us in his calm voice. For years he had been a familiar figure in newscasts, reporting live at the scene of battles and catastrophes with awesome

2. *Rolf Carlé* (rälf   cär lā′)
3. Something *subterranean* is beneath the earth's surface.
4. *Seismographs* are scientific instruments that record the intensity and duration of earthquakes.
5. Here, *unfathomable* (un fath′ əm ə bəl) means "immeasurable."
6. *Telluric* (te loor′ ik) means "coming or rising from the earth."
7. The decaying *(putrefying)* corpses are buried in the muddy slime, a thick, syrupy *(viscous)* soup; the landscape has become a wasteland of mud *(mire)*.
8. A *morass* (mə ras′) is any difficult, confused, or entangling condition or situation.
9. Here, *bedlam* refers to the noisy uproar and confusion of the situation.

Vocabulary

cataclysm (kat′ ə kliz′ əm) *n.* a disaster, usually one that causes sudden and violent change
presentiment (pri zen′ tə mənt) *n.* a feeling that something is about to happen

Tepetl, 1991. Baruj Salinas. Acrylic on canvas, 54 x 54 in. Private collection.
Viewing the painting: How well does this painting capture the mood of the story? Explain.

tenacity. Nothing could stop him, and I was always amazed at his equanimity in the face of danger and suffering; it seemed as if nothing could shake his fortitude or deter his curiosity. Fear seemed never to touch him, although he had confessed to me that he was not a courageous man, far from it. I believe that the lens of the camera had a strange effect on him; it was as if it transported him to a different time from which he could watch events without actually participating in them. When I knew him better, I came to realize that this fictive distance seemed to protect him from his own emotions.

Vocabulary
equanimity (ēk′ wə nim′ ə tē) *n.* the ability to remain calm and assured
fortitude (fôr′ tə to͞od′) *n.* firm courage or strength of mind in the face of pain or danger

Rolf Carlé was in on the story of Azucena from the beginning. He filmed the volunteers who discovered her, and the first persons who tried to reach her; his camera zoomed in on the girl, her dark face, her large desolate eyes, the plastered-down tangle of her hair. The mud was like quicksand around her, and anyone attempting to reach her was in danger of sinking. They threw a rope to her that she made no effort to grasp until they shouted to her to catch it; then she pulled a hand from the mire and tried to move, but immediately sank a little deeper. Rolf threw down his knapsack and the rest of his equipment and waded into the quagmire, commenting for his assistant's microphone that it was cold and that one could begin to smell the stench of corpses.

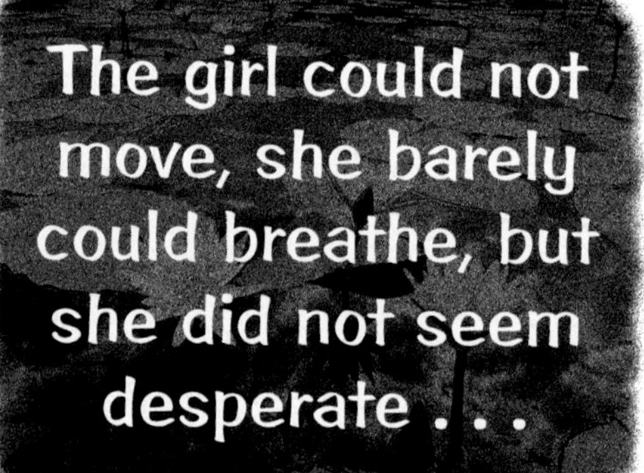
The girl could not move, she barely could breathe, but she did not seem desperate . . .

"What's your name?" he asked the girl, and she told him her flower name. "Don't move, Azucena," Rolf Carlé directed, and kept talking to her, without a thought for what he was saying, just to distract her, while slowly he worked his way forward in mud up to his waist. The air around him seemed as murky as the mud.

It was impossible to reach her from the approach he was attempting, so he retreated and circled around where there seemed to be firmer footing. When finally he was close enough, he took the rope and tied it beneath her arms, so they could pull her out. He smiled at her with that smile that crinkles his eyes and makes him look like a little boy; he told her that everything was fine, that he was here with her now, that soon they would have her out. He signaled the others to pull, but as soon as the cord tensed, the girl screamed. They tried again, and her shoulders and arms appeared, but they could move her no farther; she was trapped. Someone suggested that her legs might be caught in the collapsed walls of her house, but she said it was not just rubble, that she was also held by the bodies of her brothers and sisters clinging to her legs.

"Don't worry, we'll get you out of here," Rolf promised. Despite the quality of the transmission, I could hear his voice break, and I loved him more than ever. Azucena looked at him, but said nothing.

During those first hours Rolf Carlé exhausted all the resources of his ingenuity to rescue her. He struggled with poles and ropes, but every tug was an intolerable torture for the imprisoned girl. It occurred to him to use one of the poles as a lever but got no result and had to abandon the idea. He talked a couple of soldiers into working with him for a while, but they had to leave because so many other victims were calling for help. The girl could not move, she barely could breathe, but she did not seem desperate, as if an ancestral resignation allowed her to accept her fate. The reporter, on the other hand, was determined to snatch her from death. Someone brought him a tire, which he placed beneath her arms like a life buoy, and then laid a plank near the hole to hold his weight and allow him to stay closer to her. As it was impossible to remove the rubble blindly, he tried once or twice to dive toward her feet, but emerged frustrated, covered with mud, and spitting gravel. He concluded that he would have to have a pump to drain the water, and radioed a request for one, but received in return a message that there was no available transport and it could not be sent until the next morning.

"We can't wait that long!" Rolf Carlé shouted, but in the pandemonium no one stopped to commiserate.[10] Many more hours would go by before he accepted that time had stagnated and reality had been irreparably distorted.

A military doctor came to examine the girl, and observed that her heart was functioning well and that if she did not get too cold she could survive the night.

"Hang on, Azucena, we'll have the pump tomorrow," Rolf Carlé tried to console her.

"Don't leave me alone," she begged.

"No, of course I won't leave you."

Someone brought him coffee, and he helped the girl drink it, sip by sip. The warm liquid revived her and she began telling him about her small life, about her family and her school, about how things were in that little bit of world before the volcano had erupted. She was thirteen, and she had never been outside her village. Rolf Carlé, buoyed by a premature optimism, was convinced that everything would end well: the pump would arrive, they would drain the water, move the rubble, and Azucena would be transported by helicopter to a hospital where she would recover rapidly and where he could visit her and bring her gifts. He thought, She's already too old for dolls, and I don't know what would please her; maybe a dress. I don't know much about women, he concluded, amused, reflecting that although he had known many women in his lifetime, none had taught him these details. To pass the hours he began to tell Azucena about his travels and adventures as a newshound, and when he exhausted his memory, he called upon imagination, inventing things he thought might entertain her. From time to time she dozed, but he kept talking in the darkness, to assure her that he was still there and to overcome the menace of uncertainty.

That was a long night.

Many miles away, I watched Rolf Carlé and the girl on a television screen. I could not bear the wait at home, so I went to National Television, where I often spent entire nights with Rolf editing programs. There, I was near his world, and I could at least get a feeling of what he lived through during those three decisive days. I called all the important people in the city, senators, commanders of the armed forces, the North American ambassador, and the president of National Petroleum, begging them for a pump to remove the silt, but obtained only vague promises. I began to ask for urgent help on radio and television, to see if there wasn't *someone* who could help us. Between calls I would run to the newsroom to monitor the satellite transmissions that periodically brought new details of the catastrophe. While reporters selected scenes with most impact for the news report, I searched for footage that featured Azucena's mudpit. The screen reduced the disaster to a single plane and accentuated the tremendous distance that separated me from Rolf Carlé; nonetheless, I was there with him. The child's every suffering hurt me as it did him; I felt his frustration, his impotence. Faced with the impossibility of communicating with him, the fantastic idea came to me that if I tried, I could reach him by force of mind and in that

10. No one stopped to show or express sympathy—to *commiserate* (kə miz′ ə rāt′).

Vocabulary

pandemonium (pan′ də mō′ nē əm) *n.* wild disorder and uproar way give him encouragement. I concentrated until I was dizzy—a frenzied and futile activity. At times I would be overcome with compassion and burst out crying; at other times, I was so drained I felt as if I were staring through a telescope at the light of a star dead for a million years.

I watched that hell on the first morning broadcast, cadavers of people and animals awash in the current of new rivers formed overnight from the melted snow. Above the mud rose the tops of trees and the bell towers of a church where several people had taken refuge and were patiently awaiting rescue teams. Hundreds of soldiers and volunteers from the Civil Defense were clawing through rubble searching for survivors, while long rows of ragged specters awaited their turn for a cup of hot broth. Radio networks announced that their phones were jammed with calls from families offering shelter to orphaned children. Drinking water was in scarce supply, along with gasoline and food. Doctors, resigned to amputating arms and legs without anesthesia, pled that at least they be sent serum and painkillers and antibiotics; most of the roads, however, were impassable, and worse were the bureaucratic obstacles that stood in the way. To top it all, the clay contaminated by decomposing bodies threatened the living with an outbreak of epidemics.

"The sky
is weeping,"
Azucena
murmured . . .

Azucena was shivering inside the tire that held her above the surface. Immobility and tension had greatly weakened her, but she was conscious and could still be heard when a microphone was held out to her. Her tone was humble, as if apologizing for all the fuss. Rolf Carlé had a growth of beard, and dark circles beneath his eyes; he looked near exhaustion. Even from that enormous distance I could sense the quality of his weariness, so different from the fatigue of other adventures. He had completely forgotten the camera; he could not look at the girl through a lens any longer. The pictures we were receiving were not his assistant's but those of other reporters who had appropriated Azucena, bestowing on her the pathetic responsibility of embodying the horror[11] of what had happened in that place. With the first light Rolf tried again to dislodge the obstacles that held the girl in her tomb, but he had only his hands to work with; he did not dare use a tool for fear of injuring her. He fed Azucena a cup of the cornmeal mush and bananas the Army was distributing, but she immediately vomited it up. A doctor stated that she had a fever, but added that there was little he could do: antibiotics were being reserved for cases of gangrene. A priest also passed by and blessed her, hanging a medal of the Virgin around her neck. By evening a gentle, persistent drizzle began to fall.

"The sky is weeping," Azucena murmured, and she, too, began to cry.

"Don't be afraid," Rolf begged. "You have to keep your strength up and be calm. Everything will be fine. I'm with you, and I'll get you out somehow."

Reporters returned to photograph Azucena and ask her the same questions, which she no

11. *[appropriated . . . horror]* In other words, the reporters have begun to use TV images of Azucena's situation, making her a living symbol of the tragedy.

longer tried to answer. In the meanwhile, more television and movie teams arrived with spools of cable, tapes, film, videos, precision lenses, recorders, sound consoles, lights, reflecting screens, auxiliary motors, cartons of supplies, electricians, sound technicians, and cameramen: Azucena's face was beamed to millions of screens around the world. And all the while Rolf Carlé kept pleading for a pump. The improved technical facilities borc results, and National Television began receiving sharper pictures and clearer sound; the distance seemed suddenly compressed, and I had the horrible sensation that Azucena and Rolf were by my side, separated from me by impenetrable glass. I was able to follow events hour by hour; I knew everything my love did to wrest the girl from her prison and help her endure her suffering; I overheard fragments of what they said to one another and could guess the rest; I was present when she taught Rolf to pray, and when he distracted her with the stories I had told him in a thousand and one nights beneath the white mosquito netting of our bed.

When darkness came on the second day, Rolf tried to sing Azucena to sleep with old Austrian folk songs he had learned from his mother, but she was far beyond sleep. They spent most of the night talking, each in a stupor of exhaustion and hunger, and shaking with cold. That night, imperceptibly, the unyielding floodgates that had contained Rolf Carlé's past for so many years began to open, and the torrent of all that had lain hidden in the deepest and most secret layers of memory poured out, leveling before it the obstacles that had blocked his consciousness for so long. He could not tell it all to Azucena; she perhaps did not know there was a world beyond the sea or time previous to her own; she was not capable of imagining Europe in the years of the war. So he could not tell her of defeat, nor of the afternoon the Russians had led them to the concentration camp to bury prisoners dead from starvation. Why should he describe to her how the naked bodies piled like a mountain of firewood resembled fragile china? How could he tell this dying child about ovens and gallows? Nor did he mention the night that he had seen his mother naked, shod in stiletto-heeled red boots, sobbing with humiliation. There was much he did not tell, but in those hours he relived for the first time all the things his mind had tried to erase. Azucena had surrendered her fear to him and so, without wishing it, had obliged Rolf to confront his own. There, beside that hellhole of mud, it was impossible for Rolf to flee from himself any longer, and the visceral[12] terror he had lived as a boy suddenly invaded him. He reverted to the years when he was the age of Azucena, and younger, and, like her, found himself trapped in a pit without escape, buried in life, his head barely above ground; he saw before his eyes the boots and legs of his father, who had removed his belt and was whipping it in the air with the never-forgotten hiss of a viper coiled to strike. Sorrow flooded through him, intact and precise, as if it had lain always in his mind, waiting. He was once again in the armoire where his father locked him to punish him for imagined misbehavior, there where for eternal hours he had crouched with his eyes closed, not to see the darkness, with his hands over his ears, to shut out the beating of his

Did You Know?
An *armoire* (ärm wär′) is a large, moveable cupboard or wardrobe.

12. Here, *visceral* means "emotional or instinctive rather than intellectual."

heart, trembling, huddled like a cornered animal. Wandering in the mist of his memories he found his sister Katherina, a sweet, retarded child who spent her life hiding, with the hope that her father would forget the disgrace of her having been born. With Katherina, Rolf crawled beneath the dining room table, and with her hid there under the long white tablecloth, two children forever embraced, alert to footsteps and voices. Katherina's scent melded with his own sweat, with aromas of cooking, garlic, soup, freshly baked bread, and the unexpected odor of putrescent clay. His sister's hand in his, her frightened breathing, her silk hair against his cheek, the candid gaze of her eyes. Katherina . . . Katherina materialized before him, floating on the air like a flag, clothed in the white tablecloth, now a winding sheet, and at last he could weep for her death and for the guilt of having abandoned her. He understood then that all his exploits as a reporter, the feats that had won him such recognition and fame, were merely an attempt to keep his most ancient fears at bay, a stratagem[13] for taking refuge behind a lens to test whether reality was more tolerable from that perspective. He took excessive risks as an exercise of courage, training by day to conquer the monsters that tormented him by night. But he had come face to face with the moment of truth; he could not continue to escape his past. He *was* Azucena; he was buried in the clayey mud; his terror was not the distant emotion of an almost forgotten childhood, it was a claw sunk in his throat. In the flush of his tears he saw his mother, dressed in black and clutching her imitation-crocodile pocketbook to her bosom, just as he had last seen her on the dock when she had come to put him on the boat to South America. She had not come to dry his tears, but to tell him to pick up a shovel: the war was over and now they must bury the dead.

"Don't cry. I don't hurt anymore. I'm fine," Azucena said when dawn came.

"I'm not crying for you," Rolf Carlé smiled. "I'm crying for myself. I hurt all over."

The third day in the valley of the cataclysm began with a pale light filtering through storm clouds. The President of the Republic visited the area in his tailored safari jacket to confirm that this was the worst catastrophe of the century; the country was in mourning; sister nations had offered aid; he had ordered a state of siege; the Armed Forces would be merciless, anyone caught stealing or committing other offenses would be shot on sight. He added that it was impossible to remove all the corpses or count the thousands who had disappeared; the entire valley would be declared holy ground, and bishops would come to celebrate a solemn mass for the souls of the victims. He went to the Army field tents to offer relief in the form of vague promises to crowds of the rescued, then to the improvised hospital to offer a word of encouragement to doctors and nurses worn down from so many hours of tribulations. Then he asked to be taken to see Azucena, the little girl the whole world had seen. He waved to her with a limp statesman's hand, and microphones recorded his emotional voice and paternal[14] tone as he told her that her courage

13. A *stratagem* is a trick or scheme for achieving some purpose.

14. Here, *paternal* means "fatherly."

Vocabulary

tribulation (trib′ yə lā′ shən) *n.* great misery or distress; suffering had served as an example to the nation. Rolf Carlé interrupted to ask for a pump, and the President assured him that he personally would attend to the matter. I caught a glimpse of Rolf for a few seconds kneeling beside the mudpit. On the evening news broadcast, he was still in the same position; and I, glued to the screen like a fortuneteller to her crystal ball, could tell that something fundamental had changed in him. I knew somehow that during the night his defenses had crumbled and he had given in to grief; finally he was vulnerable. The girl had touched a part of him that he himself had no access to, a part he had never shared with me. Rolf had wanted to console her, but it was Azucena who had given him consolation.

I recognized the precise moment at which Rolf gave up the fight and surrendered to the torture of watching the girl die. I was with them, three days and two nights, spying on them from the other side of life. I was there when she told him that in all her thirteen years no boy had ever loved her and that it was a pity to leave this world without knowing love. Rolf assured her that he loved her more than he could ever love anyone, more than he loved his mother, more than his sister, more than all the women who had slept in his arms, more than he loved me, his life companion, who would have given anything to be trapped in that well in her place, who would have exchanged her life for Azucena's, and I watched as he leaned down to kiss her poor forehead, consumed by a sweet, sad emotion he could not name. I felt how in that instant both were saved from despair, how they were freed from the clay, how they rose above the vultures and helicopters, how together they flew above the vast swamp of corruption and laments. How, finally, they were able to accept death. Rolf Carlé prayed in silence that she would die quickly, because such pain cannot be borne.

By then I had obtained a pump and was in touch with a general who had agreed to ship it the next morning on a military cargo plane. But on the night of that third day, beneath the unblinking focus of quartz lamps and the lens of a hundred cameras, Azucena gave up, her eyes locked with those of the friend who had sustained her to the end. Rolf Carlé removed the life buoy, closed her eyelids, held her to his chest for a few moments, and then let her go. She sank slowly, a flower in the mud.

ou are back with me, but you are not the same man. I often accompany you to the station and we watch the videos of Azucena again; you study them intently, looking for something you could have done to save her, something you did not think of in time. Or maybe you study them to see yourself as if in a mirror, naked. Your cameras lie forgotten in a closet; you do not write or sing; you sit long hours before the window, staring at the mountains. Beside you, I wait for you to complete the voyage into yourself, for the old wounds to heal. I know that when you return from your nightmares, we shall again walk hand in hand, as before.

Responding to Literature

Personal Response

Which character in the story do you admire the most? Why?

Analyzing Literature

Recall

1. Describe the catastrophic event that occurs before the story begins. What is Azucena's predicament as a result of this event?
2. Why is Rolf Carlé sent to the disaster site?
3. Summarize the efforts Rolf makes to save Azucena.
4. What hidden memories flood into Rolf's mind during the second night he spends with Azucena?
5. What happens to Azucena at the end of the story? How does Rolf spend his time after this event?

Intrepret

6. In your opinion, why does Azucena quickly become the **symbol** of the tragedy?
7. According to the narrator, what qualities does Rolf exhibit while doing his job? In your opinion, do these qualities help him? Explain.
8. **Theme Connections** Why do you think Rolf tries so hard to save Azucena?
9. In your opinion, how does Azucena help Rolf? Use evidence from the story to support your answer.
10. What do you think the narrator means when she says that both Rolf and Azucena "were saved from despair" and "were freed from the clay"?

Evaluate and Connect

11. How does Rolf's attitude toward Azucena change as the story progresses? Support your answer with evidence from the story.
12. Look back at the issues raised in the Reading Focus on page 342. Do you think Rolf was obligated to help Azucena, even though it meant putting his own safety at risk? Give reasons for your answer.
13. In your opinion, do the news media sometimes exploit people, such as Azucena, who are the victims of tragedies? Explain your answer.
14. What conclusions can you draw about the narrator's opinion of the President of the Republic? How would you describe the **tone** of her description? (See Literary Terms Handbook, page R13.)
15. What do you think the title of this story means? In your opinion, is it an appropriate title? Why or why not?

Mood

Mood is the emotional quality, or atmosphere, that a writer creates in a story. The writer's language and choice of details contribute to a story's mood. Allende immediately establishes the somber, tragic mood of "And of Clay Are We Created" with the horrific image of "the girl's head protruding from the mudpit, eyes wide open, calling soundlessly."

1. How does the author's description of the setting contribute to the mood of the story? Support your ideas with specific details from the selection.
2. Find two examples of events that help to create the tragic mood of the story. Identify words or images that the author uses to convey the horror of the situation.
3. Besides *somber* and *tragic,* what other words would you choose to describe the mood of this story? Explain your choices.

- See **Literary Terms Handbook,** p. R8.

Literary Criticism

"In [her novel] *Eva Luna,*" writes Elizabeth Benedict, "Allende moves between the personal and the political, between realism and fantasy." In a brief critical review, explore how Benedict's observation applies to the story "And of Clay Are We Created."

Literature and Writing

Writing About Literature

Examine Characterization Reflecting on the actual televised images of Azucena, Allende has said: "I see the girl again . . . talking to me about patience, about endurance, about courage." Write several paragraphs explaining how Allende shows that Azucena possesses these character traits. Share your ideas with a classmate.

Personal Writing

My Dearest For some people, such as author Isabel Allende, writing letters is similar to keeping a diary. Imagine that you are Rolf. Write a letter to the narrator, giving your own account of some or all of the events described in the story.

Extending Your Response

Literature Groups

More than Meets the Eye A **symbol** is any object, person, place, or experience that means more than it is. Writers often use symbols to convey ideas and attitudes to the reader. In "And of Clay Are We Created," for example, the narrator says that Azucena became "the symbol of the tragedy" after the eruption. In your group, identify symbols that you think Allende uses in the story. Discuss and debate their possible meanings. Share your ideas with the class.

Learning for Life

Public Service Announcement Prepare a public service announcement to be broadcast on radio or television stations serving the areas near the disaster site described in this story. Include a brief update on conditions at the disaster site, as well as information about how volunteers can donate money, supplies, or services. Read your announcement to the class.

Reading Further

You might also enjoy this short story by Isabel Allende: "Phantom Palace" from *Eva Luna* tells how a foreign diplomat's wife becomes entangled in mystery.

Save your work for your portfolio.

VOCABULARY • Analogies

An analogy is a type of comparison based on the relationships between things or ideas. One type of analogy deals with pairs of words that represent different degrees of intensity.

stunned : surprised :: exhausted : tired

Someone who is *stunned* is *extremely surprised;* someone who is *exhausted* is *extremely tired.*

To finish an analogy, decide what relationship exists between the first two things or ideas. Then apply that relationship to another pair of words and see if it is the same.

- For more about analogies, see **Communications Skills Handbook,** p. R77.

PRACTICE Choose the word that best completes each analogy.

1. ecstasy : happiness :: tribulation :
   a. discomfort b. faith c. risk
2. hostility : unfriendliness :: pandemonium :
   a. peace b. insecurity c. confusion
3. cruel : kind :: candid :
   a. sneaky b. planned c. sympathetic
4. equanimity : calmness :: presentiment :
   a. insensitivity b. uneasiness c. anger
5. hurricane : wind :: cataclysm :
   a. effort b. misfortune c. luck

Before You Read

Colombia's Mortal Agony

Reading Focus

Why are most people interested in catastrophic events, even ones that have absolutely no effect on their own lives?

Discuss Think about a recent disaster or tragedy in the news. How did you respond? How did people around you and around the world respond? Discuss different ways people react when disaster strikes.

Setting a Purpose Read to appreciate the heroic efforts made in response to a natural disaster.

Building Background

The Time and Place

The events described in this selection took place in November 1985, near Bogotá, Colombia.

Did You Know?

Have you ever heard of the ancient Italian city of Pompeii? This city was totally destroyed in A.D. 79 when Mount Vesuvius erupted. Two thousand people lost their lives in the catastrophe. Ironically, the wet volcanic ash and cinders that buried Pompeii also preserved many of the city's dwellings and public buildings, along with invaluable artifacts from this ancient Italian culture. Excavations of the ruins of Pompeii have revealed a picture of city life for first-century Italians.

Vocabulary Preview

phenomena (fə nom′ ə nə′) *n.* facts, events, or conditions that can be known through the senses; p. 355

pall (pôl) *n.* a covering that darkens or conceals; atmosphere of gloom; p. 355

ferocity (fə ros′ ə tē) *n.* great fierceness; extreme intensity; p. 357

tentative (ten′ tə tiv) *adj.* not fully worked out; uncertain; p. 357

spawn (spôn) *v.* to bring forth; give birth; p. 358

Meet George Russell

George Russell was hired by *Time* magazine in 1974 as a staff writer for its Canadian edition. Working his way through the ranks as writer, associate editor, and South American bureau chief, Russell became senior editor for Time International in 1987. Since 1992 he has been chiefly responsible for *Time*'s Canadian, Asian, and Latin American editions.

George Russell was born and educated in Calgary, Alberta, Canada. He is coauthor of the book Eyewitness: 150 Years of Photojournalism, *published in 1990, and cowinner of the 1988 Hancock Award for business journalism.*

COLOMBIA'S MORTAL AGONY

George Russell

IT WAS SHORTLY AFTER 9 P.M. Wednesday, and Pilot Manuel Cervero was nearly home. Cervero was flying a DC-8 cargo jet from Miami to the Colombian capital, Bogotá, a sprawling city of 5 million in the Andes. The plane was cruising at 24,000 ft., 110 miles or ten minutes from El Dorado International Airport. Then, without warning, Cervero and his aircraft ran afoul of one of nature's most destructive phenomena.

"First came a reddish illumination that shot up to about 26,000 ft.," the pilot recalled. "Then came a shower of ash that covered us and left me without visibility. The cockpit filled with smoke and heat and the smell of sulfur."[1] The blast charred the nose of the DC-8 and turned the aircraft's windows white. Flying only on instruments, Cervero diverted the plane to the city of Cali, 20 minutes from Bogotá. Making his final approach, the pilot said, he had to push open one of the cockpit's side windows in order to catch a glimpse of the airport's runway lights. He landed safely.

Cervero did not at first know that he had been flying 7,000 ft. above a 17,716-ft.-high, long-dormant volcano known as Nevado del Ruiz at the exact moment when it came thunderously alive. Within hours, that rebirth had left upwards of 20,000 people dead or missing in a steaming, mile-wide avalanche of gray ash and mud. Thousands more were injured, orphaned and homeless. The Colombian town of Armero (pop. about 22,500) had virtually disappeared. At week's end a huge cloud of ash, rising as high as 45,000 ft., hung dramatically over the area. The pall obscured the sun and caused the normal afternoon temperature of 77°F to drop to about 55°F. As rescuers hunted

1. *Sulfur* is an abundant element that, by itself, has no taste or odor. As sulfur burns (in a volcano, for instance), it combines with oxygen to form *sulfur dioxide,* a colorless, poisonous gas that does have a sharp odor.

Vocabulary

phenomena (fə nom′ ə nə′) *n.* facts, events, or conditions that can be known through the senses

pall (pôl) *n.* a covering that darkens or conceals; atmosphere of gloom

Did You Know?
Mount Vesuvius (vi so͞o′ vē əs) is a still-active volcano in southern Italy.

frantically amid the soupy devastation for mud-covered survivors, it was soon clear that Nevado del Ruiz would rate as one of the deadliest volcanic eruptions in all of recorded history, roughly equivalent to the A.D. 79 explosion of Mount Vesuvius, which destroyed the cities of Pompeii and Herculaneum. . . .

The explosion in the snowy, rugged Andean peak came from a buildup of molten rock and trapped gases that was ultimately caused by the movement of two of the earth's huge tectonic plates.[2] Similar forces were responsible for the Mexico City earthquake (September 19, 1985), as well as the tremors that perennially shake California. But the eruption also bore an eerie similarity to the 1980 detonation[3] of Washington State's Mount St. Helens, which left an estimated 65 people dead and missing. The initial Nevado del Ruiz blast sent steam and millions of tons of ash into the Andean air, but the debris was followed by almost no lava. About 90 minutes after the initial detonation, there was a second. It was so forceful that it shook the air in Cali, 150 miles to the southwest. Said a civil defense worker in that city: "At first I thought it might be a terrorist bombing in our neighborhood."

The double eruption produced none of the spectacular lava displays that characterize such perennially active volcanoes as Hawaii's Kilauea. Instead, the superheated magma[4] within Nevado del Ruiz began to melt the thick blanket of snow and ice that caps the top 2,000 ft. of the peak. Filthy water started to flow down the sides of the mountain. The trickle swiftly turned into a torrent of viscous mud, stones, ashes and debris with a crest of 15 ft. to 50 ft. The liquid avalanche, known as a lahar, was soon hurtling down the steep slopes at speeds of up to 30 m.p.h. With irresistible force, it roared down the flanks of Nevado del Ruiz in the most natural of channels: the beds of the Guali, Azufrado and Lagunilla rivers, which flow east and south from the base of the volcano.

Some 30 miles from Nevado del Ruiz, in the Lagunilla River canyon, lay Armero. A thriving agricultural center of whitewashed, tile-roofed homes and pastel colonial churches, the town had taken little part in the more turbulent eras of modern Colombian history. The region's wealth is based on cotton and rice farming. The surrounding Lagunilla River canyon contains some of the country's finest agricultural land. . . .

The region's good life disappeared in a few minutes on Wednesday night. . . . "First there were earth tremors," remembered Rosa Maria Henao, 39, the mother of two, as she lay in the 30-bed hospital of Mariquita, a small town about 15 miles north of Armero. "The air suddenly seemed heavy. It smelled of sulfur. Then there was a horrible rumbling that seemed to come from deep inside the earth."

2. The earth's crust is composed of about a dozen gigantic slabs called *tectonic plates.* Volcanoes commonly develop where these plates meet.
3. A *detonation* is a loud explosion.
4. The hot, melted rock deep inside the earth is called *magma.*

base of the volcano a local emergency area, and Alzate planned to have the water buildup drained through an escape canal. Work on that project had not begun when death thundered down the mountainside.

As the avalanche poured down on Armero, it gained additional ferocity from several sources. Three days of torrential rains had greatly swollen the Lagunilla River, which was already choked with mudslides from the volcano's tentative stirrings in September. At that time geologists from the surrounding federal department[5] of Tolima had expressed concern about the dangers from the dammed-up river. At first the departmental governor, Eduardo Alzate García, said that "there are no immediate risks." Two days later he changed his mind. The geologists declared the region at the

The first word to the outside world came from Armero's mayor, Ramón Antonio Rodríguez, 34. A ham[6] operator, he was on the radio to a fellow ham in Ibagué, 60 miles to the south, when Nevado del Ruiz erupted, scattering rock and ashes across the Lagunilla Canyon. The mayor was calmly describing the event when suddenly he shouted, "Wait a minute. I think the town is getting flooded." Those words were his last.

The mudslide that entombed Rodríguez cut through Armero like a liquid scythe. Henao later recollected that the wave "rolled into town with a moaning sound, like some sort of monster." Luckily, her home was on a hill. "Houses below us started cracking under the advance of the river of mud," she recalled. She grabbed her children and climbed to the roof of her home. As they watched, more than 80% of the roughly 4,200 buildings in Armero simply vanished into the torrents of slime. Said she: "It seemed like the end of the world."

Those with the opportunity and the presence of mind, like Henao, rushed desperately

5. Colombia is divided into twenty-three *departments,* nine territories, and the Special District of Bogotá. Each department has an elected legislature.

6. Amateur, or *ham,* radio is a hobby in which an individual (also called a ham) operates his or her own radio station, sending messages by voice or Morse code.

Vocabulary

ferocity (fə ros′ ə tē) *n.* great fierceness; extreme intensity

tentative (ten′ tə tiv) *adj.* not fully worked out; uncertain onto rooftops, or clambered into the branches of nearby trees. Some ran for the city's highest ground, its hilltop cemetery, or found other spots above the flood crest. Survivors later testified that the first wave of mud to hit the town was ice cold, like the mountain snows that spawned it. As it rolled onward, the mud carried along more and more of the inner fire of Nevado del Ruiz, until finally the cascade was smoking hot. . . .

"It seemed like the end of the world."

The tidal wave rolled on, submerging the neighboring village of Santuario (pop. about 1,400) and two other small communities. To the west, on the opposite slope of Nevado del Ruiz, a second avalanche broke loose and headed for Chinchiná, a city of about 34,000. Some 200 families fled the area. Chinchiná, six miles from the base of the volcano, escaped major damage, but civil authorities estimate that 1,090 people died in the immediate area.

What was left behind in Armero, in Henao's words, was "one big beach of mud." A viscous gray layer, between 7 ft. and 15 ft. thick, covered most of the town. Thousands of bodies were buried in the sludge, their location sometimes marked by pools of blood on the surface. Other corpses lay half visible in miniature bogs that were as treacherous as quicksand. Some exhausted survivors lay on the surface of the mud in shallows, or staggered along in shock on drier ground. Many of the living were naked or only partly clothed; their garments had been torn from them by the swift-moving lahar. All were encrusted with ash-colored goo that quickly hardened under the next morning's sun into a gritty carapace.[7] Many of the survivors had suffered serious injuries. A sepulchral[8] silence reigned over the devastated town.

Most horrifying of all was the plight of those who were trapped, still living, in the mud. Many were buried up to their necks; some had their mouths stopped with filth, so they could not cry for help. Sometimes the buried survivors were still locked in gruesome embrace with the dead. One was Omaira Sanchez, 13, who remained up to her neck in ooze two days following the disaster. When the mudslide struck, Omaira was washed up against her aunt, who grabbed hold of her. The aunt died, but kept her grip, even after rigor mortis[9] had set in. Finally, after rescuers worked fruitlessly for 60 hours, Omaira died of a heart attack. In the days after the disaster, one doctor estimated that there were at least 1,000 living victims still trapped in the morass. . . .

At week's end the rescue squads working heroically in the shadow of the volcano were giving fear little thought. All their efforts were bent on saving the living. Only now and then did they have time to think of the thousands of dead who lay beneath their feet. Giving in fully to the release of grief was a luxury that Colombia could not yet afford.

7. A *carapace* (kar′ ə pās′) is a case or shell, such as a turtle's.
8. A *sepulchral* (si pul′ krəl) silence is deep and gloomy, like that at a burial.
9. *Rigor mortis* is the name for the stiffening of the muscles in the body after death.

Vocabulary
spawn (spôn) *v.* to bring forth; give birth

Responding to Literature

Personal Response

What fact or image disturbed you the most as you read this selection? Explain in your journal.

Analyzing Literature

Recall and Interpret

1. What does pilot Manuel Cervero experience as he flies over Nevado del Ruiz? What is **ironic** about the author's reference to the "rebirth" of the volcano? Use specific details to support your answer. (See page R6.)
2. Describe the initial and secondary eruptions of Nevado del Ruiz. How do they compare with the other historic disasters mentioned?
3. Summarize what happens after the double eruption. What does the author seem to suggest about the government officials' response?
4. Describe what Armero looks like after the mudslide. In your opinion, are the dead better off than some of the survivors? Give reasons for your answer.

Evaluate and Connect

5. Look back at the Reading Focus on page 354. As you read this selection, how did you respond to the tragedy the author describes? To the fact that the rescue workers risked their own lives to save others? Explain.
6. How does the writer's use of specific measurements (for example, "a 17,716-ft.-high . . . volcano") affect your understanding of what the disaster was like?
7. Why, do you think, did the author choose Omaira Sanchez to illustrate the plight of the trapped survivors?
8. Do you think that the title of this selection is appropriate? Explain.

Literary ELEMENTS

Description

To enliven an expository essay such as "Colombia's Mortal Agony," a writer may use vivid descriptions of an event. For example, George Russell begins his account of a disastrous volcanic eruption by describing what Manuel Cervero sees, smells, and feels as he pilots an airplane seven thousand feet above the exploding volcano.

1. Why do you think Russell describes the pilot's experiences rather than stating that Nevado del Ruiz has erupted? What effect does this have on the reader?
2. Identify at least two other vivid descriptions that add interest to the essay. How does Russell make these descriptions come alive?

- See **Literary Terms Handbook,** p. R3.

Extending Your Response

Literature Groups

Who's to Blame? Do you think that government officials could have done more to protect the people living near Nevado del Ruiz? What warnings did these officials have that a dangerous situation existed? How did they respond to these warnings? Do you think that the people living near the volcano should have been more aware of the dangers they faced? Discuss and debate these issues in your group. Share your ideas with the class.

Creative Writing

In Memoriam Imagine that a memorial is being built to commemorate the victims of the Nevado del Ruiz eruption. Write the text for a plaque that will be displayed at the memorial. Include the date of the disaster, the number of people killed, and the names of the towns where they lived. Add any additional information that you consider interesting and important.

Save your work for your portfolio.

COMPARING selections

And of Clay Are We Created

and COLOMBIA'S MORTAL AGONY

COMPARE DESCRIPTIONS

Both Allende and Russell describe the actual eruption of the volcano and the massive mudslide that followed.

1. How are these descriptions alike? How do the two descriptions differ?
2. In your opinion, which selection more effectively conveys the horror and terrible suffering caused by the volcano's eruption? Give reasons for your answer.

COMPARE VIEWPOINTS

Imagine that Rolf Carlé, Allende's fictional reporter, and Rosa Maria Henao, the survivor quoted by Russell, meet a week after the eruption.

- Write a dialogue in which Carlé and Henao compare their experiences and share their feelings about the catastrophe.
- Practice the dialogue with a classmate. Then present it to the class.

COMPARE FACT AND FICTION

Both selections are about the tragic plight of Omaira Sanchez.

- With a partner, reread Russell's account of what happens to Omaira Sanchez. Record the details in a chart like the one shown.
- Complete the chart by filling in the appropriate details from Allende's story.
- Compare the details in the Fact and Fiction columns of the chart. Discuss why you think Allende chose to change certain details.

	Fact: Russell	Fiction: Allende
Girl's name	Omaira Sanchez	Azucena
Age		
Predicament		
Attempted solution(s)		
Resolution		

Writing Skills

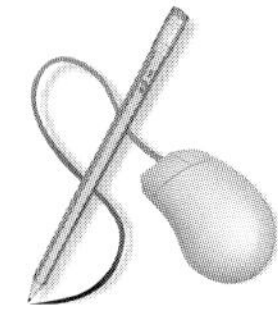

Writing Dialogue

Dialogue–conversation between characters in a literary work–can serve many purposes in a short story. Writers may use dialogue to move the plot along, to show characters' personalities or relationships, to provide a sense of time and place, or to foreshadow certain events. Dialogue also can be used to draw attention to important moments in a story. Notice how Isabel Allende uses dialogue in this passage from "And of Clay Are We Created."

> **A military doctor came to examine the girl, and observed that her heart was functioning well and that if she did not get too cold she could survive the night.**
>
> **"Hang on, Azucena, we'll have the pump tomorrow," Rolf Carlé tried to console her.**
>
> **"Don't leave me alone," she begged.**
>
> **"No, of course I won't leave you."**

Allende quotes the doctor indirectly; she tells the reader what he says but does not repeat his exact words. Then she uses dialogue to draw attention to Rolf and Azucena. These direct quotations provide information about the characters' relationship. They show that Rolf is doing his best to help Azucena survive and that she desperately wants him to stay with her.

The words used to identify each speaker are called **tag lines.** In the dialogue above, the tag line *she begged* not only tells the reader who said the words *"Don't leave me alone,"* it also gives information about Azucena's emotional state. Adding such information can make a scene more vivid. Sometimes, however, if the identity of the speaker is obvious, the tag line can be omitted.

Follow these guidelines when you write dialogue:

- Make sure your dialogue has a purpose.
- Make your dialogue sound natural. Have your characters use words and phrases that they'd be likely to use if they were real people.
- Make your dialogue sound like real conversation by including interruptions and pauses where they might naturally occur.
- Make your dialogue easy to follow by using correct paragraphing and punctuation.

EXERCISE

Write a dialogue between two characters who are unlike each other. For example, your characters might be an assertive girl and a timid one. Use the dialogue to reveal each character's personality.

Before You Read

Winter Night

Reading Focus

Think back to late winter afternoons when you were a child. How did you feel at the early approach of darkness? Fearful? Apprehensive? Calm?

Sketch It! Using any colors you choose, try to re-create your childhood impressions in an abstract or realistic drawing. Somewhere on your drawing, write several words that describe your memories.

Setting a Purpose Read to see what one child experiences on a winter evening.

Building Background

The Time and Place

This story takes place in New York City, probably around the mid-1940s near the end of World War II (1939–1945).

Did You Know?

- During World War II, American women played a key role in the war effort by working in defense plants and in other businesses, replacing the millions of men who had gone off to war.
- Near the end of the war, the horrors of Nazi concentration camps began to come to light. In these camps, Nazi dictator Adolf Hitler carried out his plan to "purify" Europe by killing millions of Jews, Gypsies, and members of other ethnic groups.

Vocabulary Preview

abeyance (ə bā′ əns) *n.* a state of temporary inactivity; p. 363
reprieve (ri prēv′) *v.* to give temporary relief, as from something unpleasant or difficult; p. 363
obscurity (əb skyo͞or′ ə tē) *n.* darkness; dimness; p. 364
derision (di rizh′ ən) *n.* mockery; ridicule; p. 364
singular (sing′ gyə lər) *adj.* unusual or remarkable; p. 366

Meet Kay Boyle

By the age of seventeen, Kay Boyle had already written a novel, short stories, and a great deal of poetry. Boyle, who lived in Europe during much of her childhood, returned there with her French husband in the early 1920s and stayed for almost twenty years. During the late 1930s, she and her family moved from one European country to another as they fled from the threat of Nazism. In keeping with her belief that writers should "write of their times and of the issues of their times," Boyle often portrayed people looking for love in a chaotic world.

Kay Boyle was born in St. Paul, Minnesota, in 1902 and died in 1992. This story was first published in The New Yorker *magazine in 1946.*

WINTER NIGHT

Kay Boyle

THERE IS A TIME OF APPREHENSION which begins with the beginning of darkness, and to which only the speech of love can lend security. It is there, in abeyance, at the end of every day, not urgent enough to be given the name of fear but rather of concern for how the hours are to be reprieved from fear, and those who have forgotten how it was when they were children can remember nothing of this. It may begin around five o'clock on a winter afternoon when the light outside is dying in the windows. At that hour the New York apartment in which Felicia lived was filled with shadows, and the little girl would wait alone in the living room, looking out at the winter-stripped trees that stood black in the park against the isolated ovals of unclean snow. Now it was January, and the day had been a cold one; the water of the artificial lake was frozen fast, but because of the cold and the coming darkness, the skaters had ceased to move across its surface. The street that lay between the park and the apartment house was wide, and the two-way streams of cars and busses, some with their headlamps already shining, advanced and halted, halted and poured swiftly on to the tempo of the traffic signals' altering lights. The time of apprehension had set in, and Felicia, who was seven, stood at the window in the evening and waited before she asked the question. When the signals below would change from red to green again,

Vocabulary

abeyance (ə bā′ əns) *n.* a state of temporary inactivity
reprieve (ri prēv′) *v.* to give temporary relief, as from something unpleasant or difficult

Did You Know?
A *double-decker bus* has two decks, or floors, each containing passenger seats. Often, the upper deck is roofless and has low walls.

or when the double-decker bus would turn the corner below, she would ask it. The words of it were already there, tentative in her mouth, when the answer came from the far end of the hall.

"Your mother," said the voice among the sound of kitchen things, "she telephoned up before you came in from nursery school. She won't be back in time for supper. I was to tell you a sitter was coming in from the sitting parents' place."[1]

Felicia turned back from the window into the obscurity of the living room, and she looked toward the open door, and into the hall beyond it where the light from the kitchen fell in a clear yellow angle across the wall and onto the strip of carpet. Her hands were cold, and she put them in her jacket pockets as she walked carefully across the living-room rug and stopped at the edge of light.

"Will she be home late?" she said.

For a moment there was the sound of water running in the kitchen, a long way away, and then the sound of the water ceased, and the high, Southern voice went on:

"She'll come home when she gets ready to come home. That's all I have to say. If she wants to spend two dollars and fifty cents and ten cents' carfare on top of that three or four nights out of the week for a sitting parent to come in here and sit, it's her own business. It certainly ain't nothing to do with you or me. She makes her money, just like the rest of us does. She works all day down there in the office, or whatever it is, just like the rest of us works, and she's entitled to spend her money like she wants to spend it. There's no law in the world against buying your own freedom. Your mother and me, we're just buying our own freedom, that's all we're doing. And we're not doing nobody no harm."

"Do you know who she's having supper with?" said Felicia from the edge of dark. There was one more step to take, and then she would be standing in the light that fell on the strip of carpet, but she did not take the step.

"Do I know who she's having supper with?" the voice cried out in what might have been derision, and there was the sound of dishes striking the metal ribs of the drainboard by the sink. "Maybe it's Mr. Van Johnson, or Mr. Frank Sinatra,[2] or maybe it's just the Duke of Wincers[3] for the evening. All I know is you're having soft-boiled egg and spinach and applesauce for supper, and you're going to have it quick now because the time is getting away."

The voice from the kitchen had no name. It was as variable as the faces and figures of the women who came and sat in the evenings. Month by month the voice in the kitchen altered to another voice, and the sitting parents were no more than lonely aunts of an evening or two who sometimes returned and sometimes did not to this apartment in which they had sat before. Nobody stayed

1. Today, a *sitting parents' place* would be called a "baby-sitters' agency" or "child-care agency."

2. *Van Johnson* and *Frank Sinatra* were popular movie stars in the 1940s.

3. *Wincers* is the character's pronunciation of "Windsor." In 1936, King Edward VIII gave up the British throne to marry an American divorcee. He was then given the title Duke of Windsor.

Vocabulary
obscurity (əb skyo͞or′ ə tē) *n.* darkness; dimness
derision (di rizh′ ən) *n.* mockery; ridicule

anywhere very long any more, Felicia's mother told her. It was part of the time in which you lived, and part of the life of the city, but when the fathers came back, all this would be miraculously changed. Perhaps you would live in a house again, a small one, with fir trees on either side of the short brick walk, and Father would drive up every night from the station just after darkness set in. When Felicia thought of this, she stepped quickly into the clear angle of light, and she left the dark of the living room behind her and ran softly down the hall.

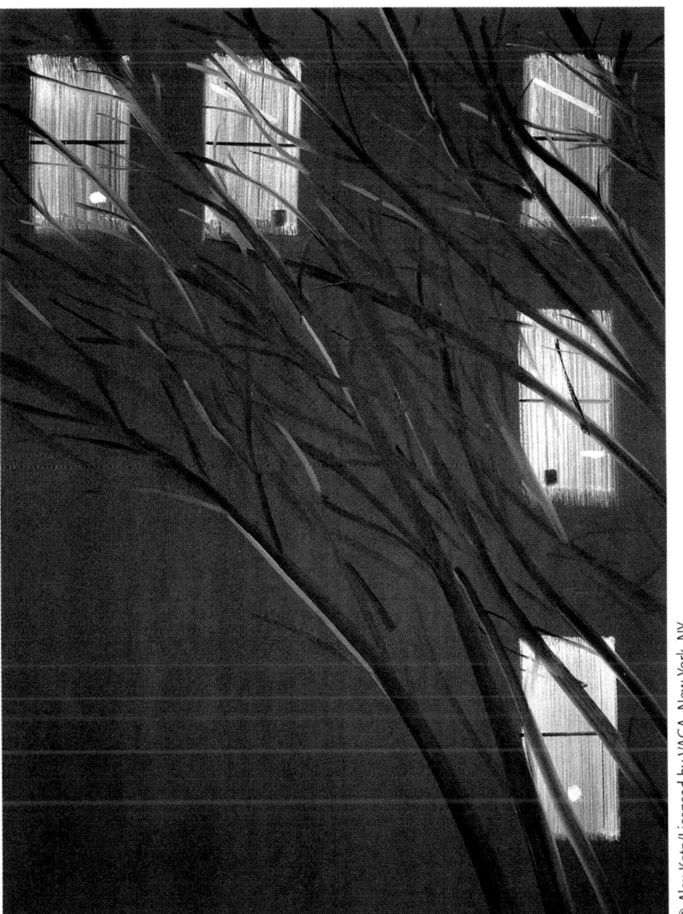

© Alex Katz/Licensed by VAGA, New York, NY.

Purple Wind, 1995. Alex Katz. Oil on canvas, 90 x 66 in. Courtesy, Marlborough Gallery, New York.

Viewing the painting: Do you think the mood of this scene reflects the mood of the story? Why or why not?

The drop-leaf table[4] stood in the kitchen between the refrigerator and the sink, and Felicia sat down at the place that was set. The voice at the sink was speaking still, and while Felicia ate it did not cease to speak until the bell of the front door rang abruptly. The girl walked around the table and went down the hall, wiping her dark palms in her apron, and, from the drop-leaf table, Felicia watched her step from the angle of light into darkness and open the door.

"You put in an early appearance," the girl said, and the woman who had rung the bell came into the hall. The door closed behind her, and the girl showed her into the living room, and lit the lamp on the bookcase, and the shadows were suddenly bleached away. But when the girl turned, the woman turned from the living room too and followed her, humbly and in silence, to the threshold of the kitchen. "Sometimes they keep me standing around waiting after it's time for me to be getting on home, the sitting parents do," the girl said, and she picked up the last two dishes from the table and put them in the sink. The woman who stood in the doorway was a small woman, and when she undid the white silk scarf from around her head, Felicia saw that her hair was black. She wore it parted in the middle, and it had not been cut, but was drawn back loosely into a knot behind her head. She had very clean white gloves on, and her face was pale, and there was a look of sorrow in her soft black eyes. "Sometimes I have to stand out there in the hall with my hat and coat on, waiting for the sitting parents to turn up," the girl said, and, as she turned on the water in the sink, the contempt

4. A *drop-leaf table* has hinged sections that can be folded down when not in use.

she had for them hung on the kitchen air. "But you're ahead of time," she said, and she held the dishes, first one and then the other, under the flow of steaming water.

The woman in the doorway wore a neat black coat, not a new-looking coat, and it had no fur on it, but it had a smooth velvet collar and velvet lapels. She did not move, or smile, and she gave no sign that she had heard the girl speaking above the sound of water at the sink. She simply stood looking at Felicia, who sat at the table with the milk in her glass not finished yet.

"Are you the child?" she said at last, and her voice was low, and the pronunciation of the words a little strange.

"Yes, this here's Felicia," the girl said, and the dark hands dried the dishes and put them away. "You drink up your milk quick now, Felicia, so's I can rinse your glass."

"I will wash the glass," said the woman. "I would like to wash the glass for her," and Felicia sat looking across the table at the face in the doorway that was filled with such unspoken grief. "I will wash the glass for her and clean off the table," the woman was saying quietly. "When the child is finished, she will show me where her night things are."

A Long Time Ago (Hace Mucho Tiempo), 1995. Alicia Carletti. Oil on canvas, 100 x 80 cm. Zurbaran Galeria, Buenos Aires.

Viewing the painting: How does the girl's expression reflect how Felicia felt when the sitting parents come?

"The others, they wouldn't do anything like that," the girl said, and she hung the dishcloth over the rack. "They wouldn't put their hand to housework, the sitting parents. That's where they got the name for them," she said.

Whenever the front door closed behind the girl in the evening, it would usually be that the sitting parent who was there would take up a book of fairy stories and read aloud for a while to Felicia; or else would settle herself in the big chair in the living room and begin to tell the words of a story in drowsiness to her, while Felicia took off her clothes in the bedroom, and folded them, and put her pajamas on, and brushed her teeth, and did her hair. But this time, that was not the way it happened. Instead, the woman sat down on the other chair at the kitchen table, and she began at once to speak, not of good fairies or bad, or of animals endowed with human speech, but to speak quietly, in spite of the eagerness behind her words, of a thing that seemed of singular importance to her.

"It is strange that I should have been sent here tonight," she said, her eyes moving slowly from feature to feature of Felicia's face,

Vocabulary

singular (sing′ gyə lər) *adj.* unusual or remarkable

"for you look like a child that I knew once, and this is the anniversary of that child."

"Did she have hair like mine?" Felicia asked quickly, and she did not keep her eyes fixed on the unfinished glass of milk in shyness any more.

"Yes, she did. She had hair like yours," said the woman, and her glance paused for a moment on the locks which fell straight and thick on the shoulders of Felicia's dress. It may have been that she thought to stretch out her hand and touch the ends of Felicia's hair, for her fingers stirred as they lay clasped together on the table, and then they relapsed into passivity again. "But it is not the hair alone, it is the delicacy of your face, too, and your eyes the same, filled with the same spring lilac color," the woman said, pronouncing the words carefully. "She had little coats of golden fur on her arms and legs," she said, "and when we were closed up there, the lot of us in the cold, I used to make her laugh when I told her that the fur that was so pretty, like a little fawn's skin on her arms, would always help to keep her warm."

"And did it keep her warm?" asked Felicia, and she gave a little jerk of laughter as she looked down at her own legs hanging under the table, with the bare calves thin and covered with a down of hair.

"It did not keep her warm enough," the woman said, and now the mask of grief had come back upon her face. "So we used to take everything we could spare from ourselves, and we would sew them into cloaks and other kinds of garments for her and for the other children. . . ."

"Was it a school?" said Felicia when the woman's voice had ceased to speak.

"No," said the woman softly, "it was not a school, but still there were a lot of children there. It was a camp—that was the name the place had; it was a camp. It was a place where they put people until they could decide what was to be done with them." She sat with her hands clasped, silent a moment, looking at Felicia. "That little dress you have on," she said, not saying the words to anybody, scarcely saying them aloud. "Oh, she would have liked that little dress, the little buttons shaped like hearts, and the white collar—"

> *"It is strange that I should have been sent here tonight."*

"I have four school dresses," Felicia said. "I'll show them to you. How many dresses did she have?"

"Well, there, you see, there in the camp," said the woman, "she did not have any dresses except the little skirt and the pullover. That was all she had. She had brought just a handkerchief of her belongings with her, like everybody else—just enough for three days away from home was what they told us, so she did not have enough to last the winter. But she had her ballet slippers," the woman said, and her clasped fingers did not move. "She had brought them because she thought during her three days away from home she would have the time to practice her ballet."

"I've been to the ballet," Felicia said suddenly, and she said it so eagerly that she stuttered a little as the words came out of her mouth. She slipped quickly down from the chair and went around the table to where the woman sat. Then she took one of the woman's hands away from the other that held it fast, and she pulled her toward the door. "Come into the living room and I'll do a pirouette[5] for you," she said, and then she

5. A *pirouette* (pir′ o͞o et′) is a rapid full turn done while standing on the toes of one foot.

stopped speaking, her eyes halted on the woman's face. "Did she—did the little girl—could she do a pirouette very well?" she said.

"Yes, she could. At first she could," said the woman, and Felicia felt uneasy now at the sound of sorrow in her words. "But after that she was hungry. She was hungry all winter," she said in a low voice. "We were all hungry, but the children were the hungriest. Even now," she said, and her voice went suddenly savage, "when I see milk like that, clean, fresh milk standing in a glass, I want to cry out loud, I want to beat my hands on the table, because it did not have to be . . ." She had drawn her fingers abruptly away from Felicia now, and Felicia stood before her, cast off, forlorn, alone again in the time of apprehension. "That was three years ago," the woman was saying, and one hand was lifted, as in weariness, to shade her face. "It was somewhere else, it was in another country," she said, and behind her hand her eyes were turned upon the substance of a world in which Felicia had played no part.

"Did—did the little girl cry when she was hungry?" Felicia asked, and the woman shook her head.

"Sometimes she cried," she said, "but not very much. She was very quiet. One night when she heard the other children crying, she said to me, 'You know, they are not crying because they want something to eat. They are crying because their mothers have gone away.'"

"Did the mothers have to go out to supper?" Felicia asked, and she watched the woman's face for the answer.

"No," said the woman. She stood up from her chair, and now that she put her hand on the little girl's shoulder, Felicia was taken into the sphere of love and intimacy again. "Shall we go into the other room, and you will do your pirouette for me?" the woman said, and they went from the kitchen and down the strip of carpet on which the clear light fell. In the front room, they paused hand in hand in the glow of the shaded lamp, and the woman looked about her, at the books, the low tables with the magazines and ash trays on them, the vase of roses on the piano, looking with dark, scarcely seeing eyes at these things that had no reality at all. It was only when she saw the little white clock on the mantelpiece that she gave any sign, and then she said quickly: "What time does your mother put you to bed?"

Felicia waited a moment, and in the interval of waiting the woman lifted one hand and, as if in reverence, touched Felicia's hair.

"What time did the little girl you knew in the other place go to bed?" Felicia asked.

"Ah, God, I do not know, I do not remember," the woman said.

"Was she your little girl?" said Felicia softly, stubbornly.

"No," said the woman. "She was not mine. At least, at first she was not mine. She had a mother, a real mother, but the mother had to go away."

"Did she come back late?" asked Felicia.

"No, ah, no, she could not come back, she never came back," the woman said, and now she turned, her arm around Felicia's shoulders, and she sat down in the low soft chair. "Why am I saying all this to you, why am I doing it?" she cried out in grief, and she held Felicia close against her. "I had thought to speak of the anniversary to you, and that was all, and now I am saying these other things to you. Three years ago today, exactly, the little girl became my little girl because her mother went away. That is all there is to it. There is nothing more."

Felicia waited another moment, held close against the woman, and listening to the swift, strong heartbeats in the woman's breast.

"But the mother," she said then in a small, persistent voice, "did she take a taxi when she went?"

"This is the way it used to happen," said the woman, speaking in hopelessness and bitterness in the softly lighted room. "Every week they used to come into the place where we were and they would read a list of names out. Sometimes it would be the names of children they would read out, and then a little later they would have to go away. And sometimes it would be the grown people's names, the names of the mothers or big sisters, or other women's names. The men were not with us. The fathers were somewhere else, in another place."

"Yes," Felicia said. "I know."

"We had been there only a little while, maybe ten days or maybe not so long," the woman went on, holding Felicia against her still, "when they read the name of the little girl's mother out, and that afternoon they took her away."

"What did the little girl do?" Felicia said.

"She wanted to think up the best way of getting out so that she could go find her mother," said the woman, "but she could not think of anything good enough until the third or fourth day. And then she tied her ballet slippers up in the handkerchief again, and she went up to the guard standing at the door." The woman's voice was gentle, controlled

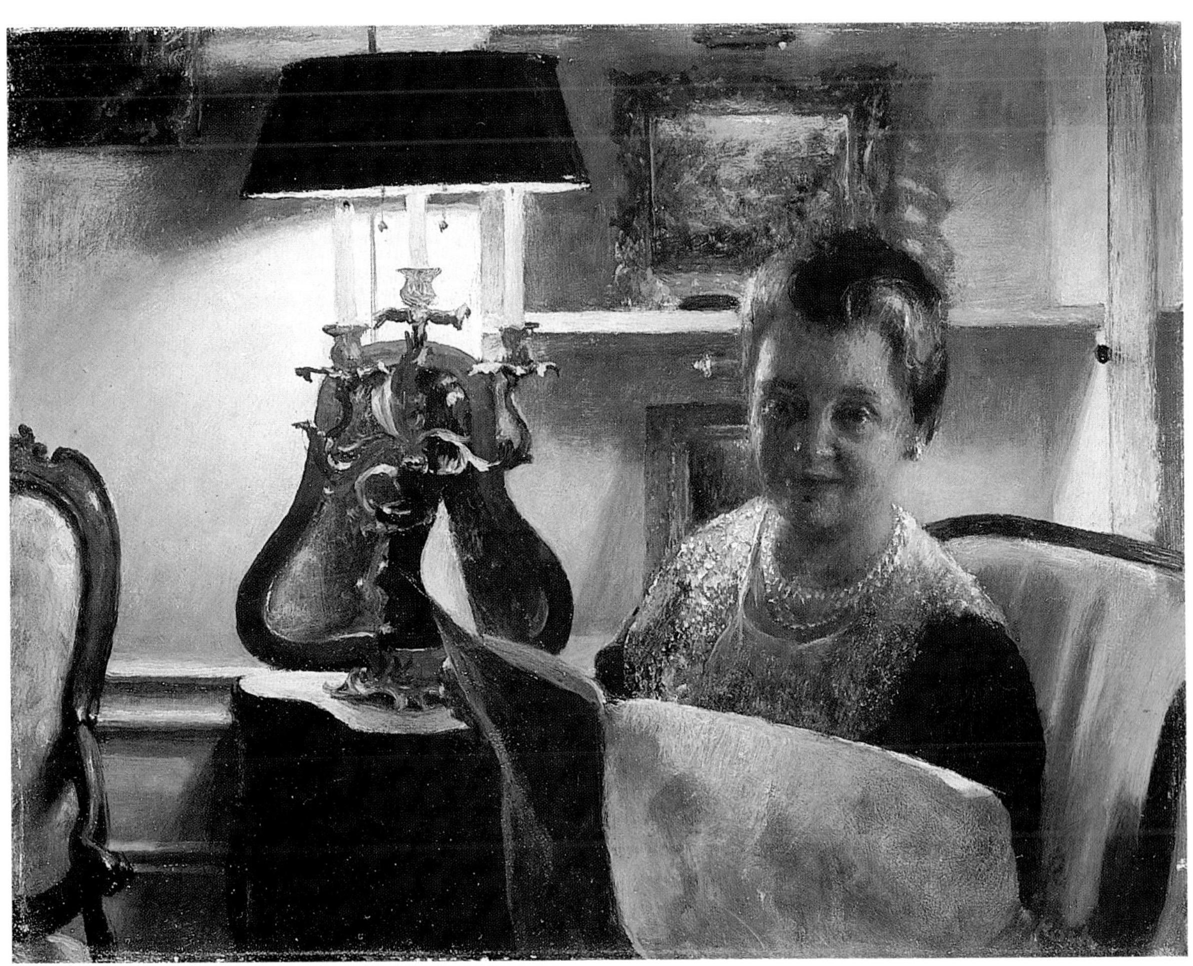

Lamplight with Dora, c. 1973. John Koch. Oil on Masonite, 7⅞ x 10 in. Private collection.

Viewing the painting: In your opinion, does the setting of this painting capture the setting of the story? Why or why not?

now. "She asked the guard please to open the door so that she could go out. 'This is Thursday,' she said, 'and every Tuesday and Thursday I have my ballet lessons. If I miss a ballet lesson, they do not count the money off, so my mother would be just paying for nothing, and she cannot afford to pay for nothing. I missed my ballet lesson on Tuesday,' she said to the guard, 'and I must not miss it again today.'"

Felicia lifted her head from the woman's shoulder, and she shook her hair back and looked in question and wonder at the woman's face.

"And did the man let her go?" she said.

"No, he did not. He could not do that," said the woman. "He was a soldier and he had to do what he was told. So every evening after her mother went, I used to brush the little girl's hair for her," the woman went on saying. "And while I brushed it, I used to tell her the stories of the ballets. Sometimes I would begin with *Narcissus*,"[6] the woman said, and she parted Felicia's locks with her fingers, "so if you will go and get your brush now, I will tell it while I brush your hair."

"Oh, yes," said Felicia, and she made two whirls as she went quickly to the bedroom. On the way back, she stopped and held on to the piano with the fingers of one hand while she went up on her toes. "Did you see me? Did you see me standing on my toes?" she called to the woman, and the woman sat smiling in love and contentment at her.

Felicia came spinning toward her, whirling in pirouette after pirouette.

"Yes, wonderful, really wonderful," she said. "I am sure I have never seen anyone do it so well." Felicia came spinning toward her, whirling in pirouette after pirouette, and she flung herself down in the chair close to her, with her thin bones pressed against the woman's soft, wide hip. The woman took the silver-backed, monogrammed brush and the tortoise-shell comb in her hands, and now she began to brush Felicia's hair. "We did not have any soap at all and not very much water to wash in, so I never could fix her as nicely and prettily as I wanted to," she said, and the brush stroked regularly, carefully down, caressing the shape of Felicia's head.

"If there wasn't very much water, then how did she do her teeth?" Felicia said.

"She did not do her teeth," said the woman, and she drew the comb through Felicia's hair. "There were not any toothbrushes or tooth paste, or anything like that."

Felicia waited a moment, constructing the unfamiliar scene of it in silence, and then she asked the tentative question.

"Do I have to do my teeth tonight?" she said.

"No," said the woman, and she was thinking of something else, "you do not have to do your teeth."

"If I am your little girl tonight, can I pretend there isn't enough water to wash?" said Felicia.

"Yes," said the woman, "you can pretend that if you like. You do not have to wash," she said, and the comb passed lightly through Felicia's hair.

"Will you tell me the story of the ballet?"

6. *Narcissus* is a ballet based on the Greek myth of Narcissus, who scorns all women, believing he is more beautiful than they. The goddess of love punishes him by making him fall in love with his own reflection in a pool.

said Felicia, and the rhythm of the brushing was like the soft, slow rocking of sleep.

"Yes," said the woman. "In the first one, the place is a forest glade with little pale birches growing in it, and they have green veils over their faces and green veils drifting from their fingers, because it is the springtime. There is the music of a flute," said the woman's voice softly, softly, "and creatures of the wood are dancing—"

"But the mother," Felicia said as suddenly as if she had been awaked from sleep. "What did the little girl's mother say when she didn't do her teeth and didn't wash at night?"

"The mother was not there, you remember," said the woman, and the brush moved steadily in her hand. "But she did send one little letter back. Sometimes the people who went away were able to do that. The mother wrote it in a train, standing up in a car that had no seats," she said, and she might have been telling the story of the ballet still, for her voice was gentle and the brush did not falter on Felicia's hair. "There were perhaps a great many other people standing up in the train with her, perhaps all trying to write their little letters on the bits of paper they had managed to hide on them, or that they had found in forgotten corners as they traveled. When they had written their letters, then they must try to slip them out through the boards of the car in which they journeyed, standing up," said the woman, "and these letters fell down on the tracks under the train, or they were blown into the fields or onto the country roads, and if it was a kind person who picked them up, he would seal them in envelopes and send them to where they were addressed to go. So a letter came back like this from the little girl's mother," the woman said, and the brush followed the comb, the comb the brush in steady pursuit through Felicia's hair. "It said good-by to the little girl, and it said please to take care of her. It said: 'Whoever reads this letter in the camp, please take good care of my little girl for me, and please have her tonsils looked at by a doctor if this is possible to do.'"

"And then," said Felicia softly, persistently, "what happened to the little girl?"

"I do not know. I cannot say," the woman said. But now the brush and comb had ceased to move, and in the silence Felicia turned her thin, small body on the chair, and she and the woman suddenly put their arms around each other. "They must all be asleep now, all of them," the woman said, and in the silence that fell on them again, they held each other closer. "They must be quietly asleep somewhere, and not crying all night because they are hungry and because they are cold. For three years I have been saying 'They must all be asleep, and the cold and the hunger and the seasons or night or day or nothing matters to them—'"

It was after midnight when Felicia's mother put her key in the lock of the front door, and pushed it open, and stepped into the hallway. She walked quickly to the living room, and just across the threshold she slipped the three blue foxskins from her shoulders and dropped them, with her little velvet bag, upon the chair. The room was quiet, so quiet that she could hear the sound of breathing in it, and no one spoke to her in greeting as she crossed toward the bedroom door. And then, as startling as a slap across her delicately tinted face, she saw the woman lying sleeping on the divan, and Felicia, in her school dress still, asleep within the woman's arms.

Responding to Literature

Personal Response

Do you approve of the way Felicia's mother is raising her daughter? Why or why not?

Analyzing Literature

Recall

1. Describe what Felicia sees as she looks out of the living room window.
2. Why is Felicia's mother gone so much of the time? Who takes care of Felicia when her mother is away?
3. Describe the woman who comes to take care of Felicia for the evening. How is she different from the other sitting parents?
4. Summarize what the woman tells Felicia about the camp and the little girl she met there.
5. How does the woman answer when Felicia asks what happened to the little girl?

Interpret

6. Why do you think Felicia feels so apprehensive as she stands at the window every evening?
7. How does Felicia seem to feel about her mother's frequent absences? Support your answer with evidence from the story.
8. How does Felicia react to the woman who has come to care for her? In your opinion, why does Felicia react this way?
9. Compare and contrast Felicia and the little girl in the camp. How are they alike? How are they different?
10. What do you think really happened to the little girl and to most of the others in the camp? Explain.

Evaluate and Connect

11. Look again at your response to the Reading Focus on page 362. Compare your feelings with the ones Felicia experiences at the start of the story.
12. Theme Connections What are some consequences of the ways in which Felicia's mother responds to the challenges of her time?
13. It has been said that Kay Boyle's stories provide a catalog of the ways in which love can fail. Do you think this story demonstrates the failure of love? Explain your answer.
14. Reread the Did You Know? section on page 362. How does this information help you better understand this story?
15. What advice would you like to give to Felicia's mother?

Literary ELEMENTS

Irony

Irony is a contrast between reality and what seems to be real. There are several types of irony. **Verbal irony** exists when a person says one thing and means another. Calling a very slow person a "speed demon" is an example of verbal irony. **Dramatic irony** occurs when the reader has important information that characters in a literary work do not have. For example, Felicia knows nothing about the type of camp the woman is describing, but the author assumes that the reader knows the woman is talking about a Nazi concentration camp.

1. Find two examples of dramatic irony in the conversation Felicia has with her baby-sitter. How does the author's use of irony affect your reaction to the story?
2. "Your mother and me, we're just buying our own freedom, that's all we're doing. And we're not doing nobody no harm." Explain the irony in this statement made by the housekeeper.

- See **Literary Terms Handbook,** p. R6.

Literature and Writing

Writing About Literature

Identifying a Foil A **foil** is a character who is used as a contrast to another character. For example, a handsome but dull character might be a foil for one who is unattractive but dynamic. Authors sometimes use a foil to underscore the distinctive qualities of a character. Find a character in "Winter Night" who functions as a foil to another character. In a paragraph, explain your choice, identifying the distinctive qualities of each character.

Creative Writing

I Can Explain, Mother What do you think happens when Felicia's mother wakes up her daughter and the baby-sitter? How do Felicia and the woman explain the situation? How does the mother react? Write a continuation to "Winter Night," in which you tell what happens next. Include a dialogue that the three characters might have.

Extending Your Response

Literature Groups

Lasting Impressions On the front of an index card, copy a brief passage from "Winter Night" that impressed you—for example, a passage that surprised you, made you angry, touched your heart, or caused you to think. On the back of the card, explain why you chose this passage. In your group, take turns reading your passages and discussing their meanings. After each passage has been discussed, the person who chose it should read the reason he or she wrote on the back of the card. Share your cards with another group in your class.

Internet Connection

Recalling the Horror Like the baby-sitter in "Winter Night," many survivors of Nazi concentration camps have told about their experiences in these camps. Search the Internet to find one or two such accounts to share with the class.

Listening and Speaking

Interviewing Interview someone who served in the armed forces during World War II, or someone who was left behind when a family member or close friend went off to war. Find out what life was like on the war front or on the home front. Tape-record your interview and select highlights to play for the class.

Reading Further

You might also enjoy these works by Kay Boyle:

Short Story Collections: *Fifty Stories* is set in Europe and the United States between 1927 and 1966.

Life Being the Best and Other Stories, thirteen of Boyle's earliest stories, was written in Paris in the 1920s.

Autobiography: *Being Geniuses Together* is a collaborative work by Kay Boyle and Robert McAlmon about their lives in the 1920s.

Save your work for your portfolio.

Skill Minilessons

GRAMMAR AND LANGUAGE • Coordinate Adjectives

Coordinate adjectives modify the same noun to an equal degree. If a sentence sounds correct when you reverse the adjectives or put *and* between them, the adjectives are coordinate. Place a comma between coordinate adjectives that precede a noun, as in this example: "The woman took the *silver-backed, monogrammed* brush. . . ."

PRACTICE Rewrite the sentences that have coordinate adjectives, adding a comma between coordinate adjectives that precede a noun.

1. Felicia looks out of the window on a dark cold evening and sees black winter-stripped trees.
2. The housekeeper prepares a quick unappetizing supper.
3. The baby-sitter is a pale dark-haired woman.
4. The girl's eyes were a beautiful lilac color.
5. Felicia's mother wears three blue foxskins.

APPLY Review a piece of your writing, adding coordinate adjectives where appropriate.

For more about adjectives, see **Language Handbook,** p. R38.

READING AND THINKING • Activating Prior Knowledge

Reading is an interactive process between a reader and a piece of writing. When you read, you bring your prior knowledge and past experiences to the task. You derive meaning by combining what you already know with the words on the page. For example, to fully understand "Winter Night," you must use your prior knowledge about conditions in the United States and in Europe during World War II. You must also draw on your personal experiences to understand Felicia's relationships with her mother and with others.

PRACTICE On your paper, list the prior knowledge or personal experiences that help you understand each event or statement.

1. Felicia feels lonely and apprehensive each evening as darkness begins to fall.
2. Felicia's father is away from home, but she expects him to return one day.
3. The baby-sitter spent time in a camp where people were kept until a decision could be made about what to do with them.
4. The little girl's mother was taken away. She never came back.
5. The baby-sitter says the little girl and all the others must be "asleep" and are no longer hungry or cold.

For more about related comprehension skills, see **Reading Handbook,** p. R83.

VOCABULARY • Etymology

Studying the etymology, or history, of a word can help you better understand its meaning. For example, *derision* is a noun formed from the verb *deride,* which comes from the Latin words *de-*, meaning "down," and *ridere,* meaning "to laugh." Thus, if you put someone down by laughing at him or her, you *deride* that person. The noun *derision,* which comes from *deride,* means "mockery" or "ridicule."

PRACTICE Use a dictionary to look up the etymologies of *reprieve, obscurity,* and *singular.* Explain the connection between the origin of each word and its current meaning.

Vo•cab•u•lar•y Skills

Roots

The **root** of a word can be a whole word, such as *self.* Word parts can be attached to the root to form new words, such as *unselfish* and *selfless.* A root that is a whole word is called a **base word.** Some words, such as *self-help,* are formed by combining two base words.

Most words, however, are formed from roots that are not whole words. These roots come from many languages; thus, their meanings may not be obvious at first glance. For example, the root of *magnify* is *magni.* It comes from a Latin word that means "great." From the same root grew such words as *magnificent, magnitude,* and *magnification.*

Because a number of words may come from the same root, recognizing commonplace roots can help you to unlock the meanings of many words. Here are a few roots.

Root	Meaning	Examples
anim	life; spirit	animal
cogn	know	recognize
miss	send	dismiss
mut	change	mutation, commute
sect	cut	section
sens	feel	sensation
ver	truth	verify, verdict
vol	wish; will	volunteer

You may not know what a new word means, even if you recognize its root. However, looking at its root is often a good place to start when trying to figure out its meaning.

EXERCISE

Use the list of roots above to decide which word is the best substitute for the underlined word in each sentence.

1. Felicia is not cognizant of the tragedy behind the baby-sitter's story.
   a. aware b. part c. doubtful
2. The past, as the baby-sitter knows too well, is immutable.
   a. horrifying b. senseless c. unchangeable
3. Felicia's mother, unlike the mother in the camp, is absent of her own volition.
   a. choice b. selfishness c. insensitivity
4. Although Felicia does not really understand the story she is told, she does not doubt its veracity.
   a. motivation b. truthfulness c. sadness
5. Felicia becomes quite animated when she learns that the little girl studied ballet.
   a. noticeable b. lively c. graceful

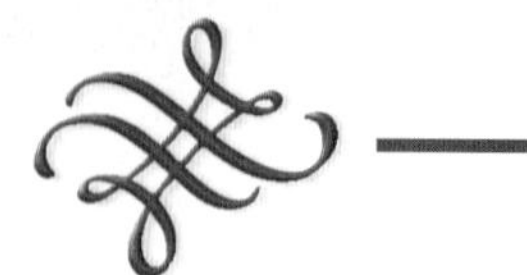

Before You Read

Waltz of the Fat Man

Reading Focus

Think about a situation in which you felt like an outsider.

Quickwrite Jot down a brief description of a situation in which you felt like an outsider. How did you deal with the situation? What emotions did you experience?

Setting a Purpose Read to see how the main character in this story deals with feelings of being an outsider.

Building Background

The Time and Place

The setting of "Waltz of the Fat Man" is not clearly identified, but details in the story suggest that it takes place in a small village in northern Mexico in the early 1900s.

Did You Know?

In traditional Mexican culture, the belief in ghosts, magic, and superstition can be very strong. For example, the Mexican celebration *El Día de los Muertos* (the Day of the Dead) recognizes the return of the spirits of the dead to visit the living. Such traditions and celebrations reflect an acceptance of the idea that fantastic or magical events are a natural part of life.

Vocabulary Preview

patronize (pā′ trə nīz) *v.* to be a customer of (a business), especially on a regular basis; p. 378

consequent (kon′ sə kwent′) *adj.* following as a result or effect; p. 378

manifest (man′ ə fest′) *v.* to make obvious or clear; show plainly; p. 378

bereaved (bi rēvd′) *adj.* sad and forlorn due to a loss, such as the death of a loved one; p. 379

propriety (prə prī′ ə tē) *n.* the quality of being proper or appropriate; suitability; p. 379

theorize (thē′ ə rīz′) *v.* to form an idea that explains a group of facts; p. 380

gingerly (jin′ jər lē) *adv.* with extreme caution; carefully; p. 383

intricacy (in′ tri kə sē) *n.* something that is complicated, involved, or confusing; p. 383

Meet Alberto Alvaro Ríos

"In working with poems and stories I have in the past found myself either filling out a poem to make a story, or paring down a story to find a poem," says poet and short story writer Alberto Alvaro Ríos. Of his work, Ríos also explains that "obsessions, characters, and places reappear from time to time. . . ."

Ríos was born in Nogales, Arizona, a town located on the Mexican border. His mother was born in England and his father in Mexico. He speaks Spanish fluently but chooses to write in English.

Alberto Alvaro Ríos was born in 1952. This story was first published in 1991.

Waltz of the Fat Man

Alberto Alvaro Ríos

Dancers, 1980. Fernando Botero. Watercolor. Courtesy, Marlborough Gallery, New York.

Noé's house trim was painted blue, good blue, deep and neat, with particular attention to the front door, that it should stand against spirits. He kept the house in repair, and hired a gardener in the three seasons, spring and summer, a little in autumn. In this place it was a gray wind after that, a time for planting things in the ground to save them, or to hide them.

His personal appearance suffered nothing from the attentions to his house, as Noé kept on himself a trim mustache and a clean face, neat clothes for which he thanked Mrs. Martínez, patronizing her for a quarter of a century. From ironing his clothing, she knew the shape of his body more than he did, and for her consequent attention to detail in that regard he was appreciative—just the right fold in the collars, a crease moving a little to the left along his right leg, the minor irregularities and embarrassments. And he was doubly thankful as she never said a word to him about it.

His was a body full of slow bones, after all, and Noé moved as if long fish swam in a small place.

He did not think himself fat, but he felt himself heavy, in a manner he could not explain to anyone. His body to be sure was overweight, but he did not feel it to be something of the stomach or thighs; rather, it was a heaviness that came from the inside out, manifesting itself to the world as the body of a fat man.

On his best days, Noé could make that weight look like muscles. On his best days he could make his stomach go into his chest and his shoulders, and people would believe anything he had to say.

Noé had a business as a butcher, but it was too much for him, a sadness cutting the meats. He had become a butcher, after all, purely for social reasons. It was a civic service, and he wanted to do good things. But it was not a good choice, given what he desired, which was simply to be part of the town.

To be sure, people patronized his shop, and took him up on his offer of extra services and niceties, but they did not finally stay very long to talk, not in the way they stayed for coffee and to warm themselves at the baker's. He could see them in there, with their mouths open and their eyes rolling along a line of laughter.

He could not say why the townspeople were like this, exactly. Perhaps it was his full size, or something about his looks, or about being the butcher in a town and being too good at his trade. But, the whole of his life was that no one cared much for him, or even spoke to him very much, and when he attended wakes,[1] which he did because he was a courteous man, he left indentations in the kitchen linoleum, which would not go away.

Noé knew that, though he tried not to be, in the people's minds he was simply an irritation.

In whatever part of the town he walked, people spoke behind their hands, and pointed when they didn't think Noé could see them. But his eyes were fat as well, and because of that he could see more.

When Noé danced, he wore a blue suit, and was always alone, always at the same place outside of town, by the river reeds.

He danced with the wind, which was also cruel like the women of the town, but the wind at least did not have a face. He locked the trunks of his arms with the branch arms of the black walnut trees, which also like the women of the town did not bend around to hold him, did not invite him to another, softer room.

But neither could these arms of a tree leave Noé so easily. They could not so quickly

1. A *wake* is a gathering of people to watch over the body of a dead person before burial.

Vocabulary

patronize (pā′ trə nīz) *v.* to be a customer of (a business), especially on a regular basis
consequent (kon′ sə kwent′) *adj.* following as a result or effect
manifest (man′ ə fest′) *v.* to make obvious or clear; show plainly

give him over cruelly to the half-hot tongues of the weeds so that they might talk about him, and make their disapproving sounds.

When he danced this dance he let out with a small noise his thin girl, which he kept inside himself. This is what had made him look fat, the holding in, the keeping in of the noise inside himself, his desire to freely speak his needs as a human being in the company of other human beings. This was his thin girl.

And Noé would let her out and they would dance the dance of weddings into the night.

Noé took to wearing his blue suit to the shop, because he thought he looked better. He did this in case someone would look at him, and think the better of him, think him something of a fine man after all.

Then his plan of the blue suit grew into a great deal more, taking as he did the wearing of his suit as some small license. It was the license, he thought, of a regular man. And he tried what he imagined to be the secret work of a regular man in the company of a regular woman.

When he shook the hands of women, he did so vigorously, hoping to see movement on their bodies, some small adventure to take his breath, some nodding yes, some quiet dance of the upper body. This first adventure of a man.

His was a modest plan, and worked a little. The shaking of the hands was, however, the most Noé did. It gave to him so much, and he thought the intimate movements of a woman to be so loud, there in front of everybody, that he could go no further.

But it is why Noé attended wakes so faithfully as well, sometimes as if they were the whole of his social life: how in comforting a bereaved wife he could—properly and in front of everyone so that there was no question of propriety—kiss her on the cheek.

Even then, after the hour of praying for the deceased and thinking about what he would do, by the time his moment was at hand, his attempt at kissing was a dizzied missing of the mark. His lips to the cheek were so clumsy and so fast that the kiss was more of something else, something not quite anything, something in keeping with his life after all.

The butcher shop through the slow years began to change, as did Noé himself. He had taken up in his house the collection and caring of clocks, because, he said to himself, they had hands, and in so many clocks was a kind of heaven, a dream of sounds to make the hours pass in a manner that would allow him to open up shop again the next day.

His nighttime dream became a daytime dream as well. He did not keep them, could not keep the clocks, finally, only at home. Along with Noé in his blue suit, the shop also began to find itself dressed differently, hung with clocks, first one, a plain dark wood, and then two, and then a hundred. Each of them with two hands for him.

There was a blue clock. Cuckoos and 28-day, anniversary clocks to the side of the scale, large-faced numbers where once there had been letters in the sections of an illustrated cow.

What Noé knew and did not say was that here was the anniversary Mariquita, the schoolhouse Mariette, Marina the singular blue, Caras with her bird tongue. Armida had hands that sometimes rose outstretched to the two and ten like the blessing arms of Christ, and sometimes lowered to the five and seven of desire, one hand shorter, in the act of

Vocabulary

bereaved (bi rēvd′) *adj.* sad and forlorn due to a loss, such as the death of a loved one

propriety (prə prī′ ə tē) *n.* the quality of being proper or appropriate; suitability beckoning him, a come here, Noé. A come here, I've got something to tell you, Noé, come on, don't be afraid.

This was no butcher shop, the townspeople would say to themselves, not with clocks. One or two clocks maybe, but not so many as this. It would not have been so bad, except that he was the only butcher in town, and people had to make use of his services. An unofficial inquiry was opened as to whether or not there was perhaps a law, some ordinance, prohibiting such abuses of the known world, but no one could find any reference that applied to the walls of a butcher shop, other than cleanliness. And of that, there could be no discussion. Noé did not neglect the clocks, and therefore did not neglect the white-sheeted bed of his walls.

One evening in winter as Noé was closing up his shop, having wound the clocks for the night and having left just enough heat in the stove that they would not suffer, he heard the blue clock falter. So much like a heartbeat had the sounds of the clocks come to be for him, that he was alarmed and stumbled in his quickness to reach the clock, though it could not move and was not falling. It called to him nonetheless as a wife in pain might call to her husband: honey, it said, please.

He reached it too late, he thought, though it was simply a clock, and he laughed at himself.

He tried winding the clock again, thinking the unthinkable, that perhaps he had missed its turn in his haste to leave. But that was not it: the spring was taut, and there was no play.

He took it down from its nail, and looked at it from different angles in his hands, but he could see nothing extraordinary. There was no obvious damage, no one had dropped it without telling him and rehung it, no insect had been boring into its side. Its blue was still blue, without blemish.

He took it to the counter and measured out some butcher's paper in which to wrap it, deciding that he would take it home to see to its difficulty. He put string around it and made a good blanket of the paper, which should comfort, he always said, what was inside. As he picked it up he could hear the workings move, and he resolved to be wary of its delicacy.

He need not have done it, but he warned himself, as if he were his own mother. He put the clock in the crook of his arm, closed and locked his door, took a deep breath in the cold air, hunched his shoulders and began his walk toward home.

He had errands, but they could wait. And he was, in any event, the last of the merchants to close for the evening, so he would have been out of luck anyway. Save for the clock, this was how his evenings most often came to an end, the closing of the door and the walk toward home.

An occasional voice greeted him, and he returned the hello, but it was the conversation of single words, friendly enough, and that was all.

Some theorized later it was the soldiers who were common in those days and who hung around with nothing better to do, that it was they who had been paid, because they never did anything for nothing, but would do anything for something, those soldiers from that kind of army.

There was nothing tragic, of course, nothing for which any charges could be drawn, in much the same manner that nothing could be legally said about what Noé had done to his butcher's shop. You get back what you give,

Vocabulary

theorize (thē′ ə rīz′) *v.* to form an idea that explains a group of facts

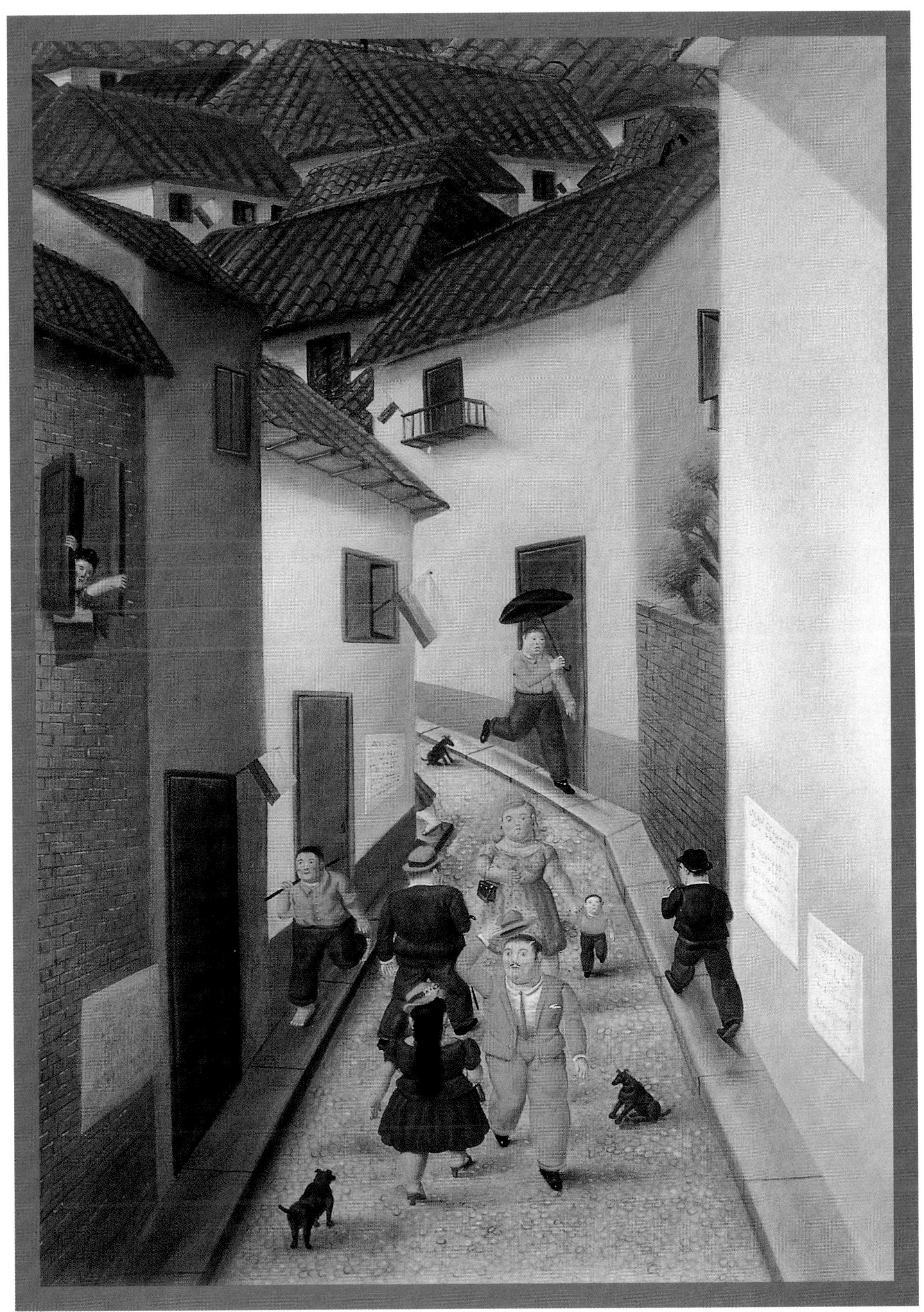

The Street, 1988. Fernando Botero. Oil on canvas, 74 x 52 in. Courtesy, Marlborough Gallery, New York.

Viewing the painting: In what ways does this scene compare with the atmosphere of Noé's town?

someone was later reported as having said, someone but not anyone in particular. That's how it was told to the captain of the police.

Noé was walking home with his package, which no one could have known was the blue clock. No one but perhaps the soldiers, and only then if they had been nosy enough to have been watching through his window, which had been recently broken and was full of cardboard patches, easy enough to hide behind.

The package's aspect was of a ham or a roast of some sort, a good rabbit, something simple and natural in the arm of a big man walking home to dinner.

Darkness had set and the moon was new. He cast no shadow and made his way quickly as he left the last of the downtown buildings. The ground was neither muddy nor dry, resembling something closer to a woody mulch,[2] and through him passed a moment of gardens from sometime in his life, gardens he had passed through, or that his mother had kept. It was a simple feeling, and brought a prickling to his skin.

Did You Know?
Oleander is a poisonous evergreen shrub that has fragrant white, pink, or purple flowers.

He next passed by the stand of walnut trees and wild oleander which was white-flowered in the summer.

The oleander called to him, *Noé*.

At first it was so quiet he said to himself he did not hear it, *Noé*.

Noé, the oleanders said, louder this time, and he stopped to look. Though it was dark and the moon was hidden, he was not afraid.

His size was such that he had never been made to be afraid, not at a moment like this. It was, if one could read his face, a curiosity, this sound which was reminiscent of his name. It was like the mulch and his mother's garden, and it gave him a prickling of the skin once more.

Noé. He heard it again, and stopped, and turned to it, saying who was there, what did they want, that perhaps he could be of some service.

No one answered, so he reached his free hand into the leaves and moved them around. He heard the sound and then saw what seemed like, in the dimness, a rabbit, running into the underbrush.

Ha, he said, and let it go. He turned again to walk, pulling his coat back up onto his neck.

Noé. It was a whisper, this time he was sure. Not a voice, but more of a breath. A half-breath, but unmistakable in its enunciation.[3]

As a child, Noé might have crossed himself, and as he was sometimes his own mother, he had the impulse, but he just stood there, once more.

He put down the clock in order to enter the oleander more fully, and see what was what, but he found nothing, only branches and the small noises of startled birds and lizards.

When he came out he could not find his package, though he concentrated with his eyes and with his hands. It was not there.

A voice whispered once more, *Noé. You know me*, it said, *you know who I am*.

Noé no longer moved around. He listened, and he waited.

Noé. He did know the whisper. He had in fact heard it many times. He knew the whisper more than the voice of his neighbor, whom he had seen a thousand times.

He would not have believed any of it had this not been the blue clock. Marina his blue, who had made so many places for herself in

2. *Mulch* is straw, wood chips, or other similar material that is spread around plants to protect them from cold, to hold in moisture, and to prevent weed growth.

3. Here, *enunciation* refers to the whispered pronunciation of the name *Noé*.

his life. Not big places, but so many, her hair color on the trim of his house, the color of her eyes in his suit, and so on. She was the blueness inside him, the color of his appetite, the color both of what filled him and what he needed more of.

Marina, he said.

Noé.

He stood there and waited.

Do you love me?

Noé did not answer.

You can love me if you love me like a horse, said the whisper. *Can you be a horse, Noé? Can you show me how you are a horse?*

Noé stood there, quietly.

He stamped his foot, gingerly at first, unsure and sure at the same time.

Is that it, Noé, is that all the horse you are?

Noé stamped his foot harder, and made a noise with his nose, and partway through his mouth.

Yes, Noé. And are you more of a horse still?

If this were anything but his blue clock, Marina, he would have gone, and given the moment up as the ghosts of this place. Or children, or who knew what. But he could not.

And then he heard the laughter of the soldiers as they could no longer contain themselves camouflaged so well otherwise in the oleanders. He heard the laughter, but did not bother with it. He turned and went home, without the clock.

He had gone away from home once before, from his family. He had to. One thing and another, right or wrong, these things didn't matter. It was simply too much to stay.

He had in some manner become an exponent to a regular number. He was ordinary times ten or times twenty, always too much. And his desire carried an exponent as well. He wanted everything to be nice, to be only the Golden Rule,[4] but times ten, and that is too much. He had no sense of himself, and yet he was everything. In that sea of mathematics he had drowned a sailor's death.

And now he had to go away again. The tide had come up, and caught him once more. He sold what was left of his business at a loss finally to Mr. Molina, who had a scarred face and who wanted to do the work. There was an art in the cutting, and it took Noé, because he was a courteous man, the afternoon to teach the profession's immediate intricacies to Mr. Molina, who had no idea there was so much.

And that same night Noé bought a brown horse and rode it as far into the following days and weeks, as far into the future as he could because he could not wait to see what was there. He arrived at the circus, and in it he made his life again.

But he almost did not make it. A man and a sparrow—each puts a shoulder to the wind, each to his own intention: a sparrow to fly, a man to run. Noé on this night was in between, and even with his weight he felt himself lifted, as if he were in league with angels at the edge of heaven, not quite deserving, but sneaking in with some help through a back door, hoping to go unnoticed again, as he had felt when he had come to this town. But it was not heaven, these places.

He stopped because the circus people were the first to wave him down, all of them standing near the road, as if this were the place, and they knew him, and they had

4. The *Golden Rule* is the rule of conduct that one should treat others as one wishes to be treated.

Vocabulary

gingerly (jin′ jər lē) *adv.* with extreme caution; carefully

intricacy (in′ tri kə sē) *n.* something that is complicated, involved, or confusing

Man on a Horse, 1981. Fernando Botero. Watercolor, 22 x 37.5 cm. Courtesy, Marlborough Gallery, New York.

Viewing the painting: How does this painting reflect the changes in Noé at the end of the story? Explain.

been waiting, and what took him so long, had he not heard them calling into the night for him.

But they had called him without telegraph or telephone. Something stronger.

His mustache curled up from the wind and his body, which had sometimes seemed fat, was hardened, tense in that moment from the cold which had made him hold his breath and flex his muscles for the whole distance of the ride.

He arrived as a beast, almost, something crazed and unshaven, out of breath.

Or as a beast on top of a man, as if the horse itself was more human, and asking for help.

His was a body full of slow bones still, but if it had taken his lifetime up to now to be slow, now the other foot was coming down, and it was fast.

It was the other half of himself now, for the rest of his years.

This was, after all, the place. And in that moment of dust kicked up and of noise, he began his real career, this life with a whole company of half-size men, two-bodied women, and all the rest of the animals who danced.

Responding to Literature

Personal Response

Which images from the story have lingered in your mind? In your journal, describe these images and any thoughts and feelings they bring to mind.

Analyzing Literature

Recall

1. Describe Noé's appearance and his business. Why did he choose this line of work?
2. How do the townspeople treat Noé? How does Noé account for their behavior toward him?
3. Who is Noé's "thin girl"? What does she represent?
4. Describe how Noé treats his clocks.
5. Summarize the incident with the blue clock. What changes does Noé make in his life after this incident?

Interpret

6. What do you think the narrator means when he says that Noé felt "a heaviness that came from the inside out"? What do you think this "heaviness" represents?
7. In your opinion, why might the townspeople treat Noé as they do?
8. Compare Noé's relationship with his "thin girl" to his relationships with women in general.
9. In your opinion, why are the clocks so important to Noé? What role do they seem to play in his life?
10. What does the last line of the story suggest to you about Noé's new life? Do you think he will find happiness in this new life? Why or why not?

Evaluate and Connect

11. Reread the description you wrote in the Reading Focus on page 376. Does your experience help you understand Noé's situation? Explain.
12. In your opinion, what lesson or lessons about human nature might this story suggest?
13. Suppose that you met a person like Noé. How might you respond to him or her? Why?
14. Do you think a person like Noé would find greater acceptance in your community than he found in his own? Why or why not?
15. In your opinion, is "Waltz of the Fat Man" a good title for this story? Explain your answer.

Literary ELEMENTS

Magical Realism

Magical realism is a style of writing in which realistic details, events, settings, characters, and dialogue are interwoven with elements of the magical, supernatural, fantastic, or bizarre. For example, Noé's occupation as a shop owner in a small town is realistic, but his relationship with his clocks is fantastic and bizarre. When the blue clock malfunctions, the narrator says the clock called to Noé "as a wife in pain might call to her husband: honey, it said, please." Clearly, the author is describing events that could happen only in the realm of the imagination.

1. Find one or two passages in the story in which realistic elements are interwoven with elements that are magical, fantastic, or bizarre.
2. What effect does the use of magical realism have on your experience of the story or your reaction to it? Support your answer using specific details from the story.

- See **Literary Terms Handbook,** p. R7.

Literature and Writing

Writing About Literature

Analyzing Personification In "Waltz of the Fat Man" Alberto Alvaro Ríos uses personification–the giving of human form or characteristics to an animal, object, or idea. For example, the author portrays the wind as Noé's dancing partner and describes the wind as, "cruel like the women of the town." This conveys to readers a sense of Noé's loneliness and isolation from other people. List three other examples of personification in the story. Then write an analysis of how the author's use of this technique contributes to the atmosphere of the story and your impressions of Noé.

Creative Writing

In the Psychologist's Chair Why do you think Noé is the way he is? What lies at the root of his unhappiness? Look for clues in the story. Then, imagine that you are a psychologist analyzing Noé's mental state. Write a brief case study of Noé in which you describe his problem and analyze its cause or causes.

Extending Your Response

Literature Groups

Puzzling Passages What lingering questions do you have about this story? What passages do you find confusing? Skim the story and use stick-on notes to mark one or two passages that you find puzzling. In your group, discuss possible interpretations of these passages. Then share your ideas with the class.

Interdisciplinary Activity

Art History: Mexican Muralists Working in a small group, do library or Internet research to find out about a Mexican muralist, such as José Orozco or Diego Rivera, or another Mexican artist. Find examples of your artist's work, then refer to these examples to suggest how he or she might have depicted a scene from "Waltz of the Fat Man." Prepare an oral presentation about your artist for the class and conclude with a description of the work he or she might have painted for this story.

Performing

Dramatic Presentation The language of "Waltz of the Fat Man" is rhythmic and musical. In a group, prepare a dramatic reading of a scene from the story. If you wish, you might also act out the scene. For example, you might perform Noé's dance with the wind and trees or his impression of a horse. After rehearsing, give your performance for the class.

Reading Further

If you enjoyed "Waltz of the Fat Man," you might also like these other works by Alberto Alvaro Ríos:

Short Story Collection: *Pig Cookies and Other Stories,* continues the tradition of magical realism in Ríos's work.

Poetry: *Whispering to Fool the Wind,* won the Walt Whitman Prize of the Poetry Society of America.

Save your work for your portfolio.

Skill Minilessons

GRAMMAR AND LANGUAGE • Denotations and Connotations

A word's **denotations** are its definitions; its **connotations** are the feelings and values usually associated with the word. Although words may have similar denotations, their connotations may be quite different. For example, consider this description of Noé: "He did not think himself fat, but he felt himself heavy. . . . His body to be sure was overweight. . . ." *Fat, heavy,* and *overweight* all have similar definitions, or denotations; however, their connotations differ. Most people with a weight problem would prefer to be called *heavy* or *overweight* rather than *fat,* because of the negative connotations associated with the word *fat.*

PRACTICE For each word below that Noé might use to describe himself, write a word with a similar denotation, but a different connotation, that the townspeople might use to describe him.

1. confused
2. ingratiating
3. lonely
4. awkward
5. trusting

● For more about denotation and connotation, see **Literary Terms Handbook,** p. R3.

READING AND THINKING • Inferring Characters' Motivations

When you make inferences, you make reasonable judgments based on the information available to you. In "Waltz of the Fat Man," you can use details from the story, as well as your own knowledge of human nature, to make inferences about why the characters do certain things. For example, when the narrator says that people lingered to socialize at the baker's but never stayed long at Noé's shop, you might infer that people don't particularly like Noé.

PRACTICE Use details from the story, as well as your own knowledge and experience, to infer why the characters do each thing listed below.

1. Noé dances with the wind and the black walnut trees.
2. The townspeople investigate whether it's legal to hang a hundred clocks on the walls of a butcher shop.
3. Noé leaves town.
4. The circus people call out to Noé.

● For more about inference, see **Reading Handbook,** p. R92.

VOCABULARY • Analogies

An analogy is a type of comparison based on the relationships between things or ideas. Some analogies are based on antonyms, as in this example.

enormous : diminutive :: thoroughly : partially

Enormous and *diminutive* have opposite meanings; *thoroughly* is an antonym of *partially.*

To complete an analogy, determine what relationship exists between the first two things or ideas. Then apply the same relationship to another pair of words.

● For more about analogies, see **Communications Skills Handbook,** p. R77.

PRACTICE Choose the word that best completes each analogy.

1. elevate : lower :: patronize :
   a. lift b. boycott c. select
2. gloom : radiance :: intricacy :
   a. variety b. confusion c. simplicity
3. steady : wavering :: bereaved :
   a. unlucky b. joyous c. prompt
4. professionally : amateurishly :: gingerly :
   a. carelessly b. angrily c. properly

Before You Read

The Masque of the Red Death

Reading Focus

How much control do you think you have over the events in your life?

Discuss In a small group, discuss these questions: What events in your life do you feel you can control? What events do you feel are beyond your control? Share your ideas with the members of another group.

Setting a Purpose Read to learn about events that are beyond the control of some party goers.

Building Background

The Time and Place
"The Masque of the Red Death" takes place long ago, in an unnamed kingdom somewhere in Europe.

Did You Know?
A *pestilence,* also called an epidemic, is any contagious disease that spreads quickly and has a high death rate. An epidemic of a disease called plague caused an estimated twenty-five million deaths when it swept across Europe in the 1300s; at that time, the disease was called the Black Death. Between 1664 and 1665, an outbreak of plague in London killed more than 70,000 people. In modern times, improved sanitation and advances in medical science have all but eliminated many deadly diseases.

Vocabulary Preview

profuse (prə fūs′) *adj.* great in amount; plentiful; p. 389
dauntless (dônt′ lis) *adj.* fearless; courageous; daring; p. 390
sagacious (sə gā′ shəs) *adj.* having or showing wisdom and good judgment; p. 390
countenance (koun′ tə nəns) *n.* the face; p. 391
wanton (wont′ ən) *adj.* shamelessly unrestrained; immoral; p. 392
appal (ə pôl′) *v.* to fill with horror or dismay; shock; p. 393
spectral (spek′ trəl) *adj.* ghostlike; p. 393
blasphemous (blas′ fə məs) *adj.* showing disrespect or scorn for God or anything sacred; p. 394

Meet Edgar Allan Poe

"I asked myself—'Of all melancholy topics, what, according to the universal understanding of mankind, is the most melancholy?' Death—was the obvious reply."

The melancholy associated with death was well known to Poe, who lost both his parents at an early age and watched his cherished young wife succumb to tuberculosis. But despite personal tragedies and frustrations, Poe was able to create some of the most astonishing and terrifying work of his age. Poe is credited with writing the world's first detective story, "The Murders in the Rue Morgue."

Poe was born in Boston, Massachusetts, in 1809 and died in 1849. This story was first published in 1842.

The Masque of the Red Death

Edgar Allan Poe

THE "RED DEATH" had long devastated the country. No pestilence had ever been so fatal, or so hideous. Blood was its Avatar[1] and its seal—the redness and the horror of blood. There were sharp pains, and sudden dizziness, and then profuse bleeding at the pores, with dissolution.[2] The scarlet stains upon the body and especially upon the face of the victim, were the pest ban[3] which shut him out from the aid and from the sympathy of his fellow-men. And the whole seizure, progress, and termination of the disease, were the incidents of half an hour.

1. In Hinduism, an *Avatar* is a god that takes on human form. Here, the word means a visible form, or embodiment, of the disease.
2. Here, *dissolution* is death.
3. A *pest ban* is an official declaration that a person has been stricken with plague. Here, the blood stains on the victim's body became their own pest ban.

Vocabulary
profuse (prə fūs′) *adj.* great in amount; plentiful

But the Prince Prospero was happy and dauntless and sagacious. When his dominions[4] were half depopulated, he summoned to his presence a thousand hale and light-hearted friends from among the knights and dames of his court, and with these retired to the deep seclusion of one of his castellated abbeys.[5] This was an extensive and magnificent structure, the creation of the prince's own eccentric yet august taste. A strong and lofty wall girdled it in. This wall had gates of iron. The courtiers, having entered, brought furnaces and massy hammers and welded the bolts. They resolved to leave means neither of ingress nor egress[6] to the sudden impulses of despair or of frenzy from within. The abbey was amply provisioned. With such precautions the courtiers might bid defiance to contagion. The external world could take care of itself. In the meantime it was folly to grieve, or to think. The prince had provided all the appliances of pleasure. There were buffoons, there were improvisatori,[7] there were ballet-dancers, there were musicians, there was Beauty, there was wine. All these and security were within. Without was the "Red Death."

It was toward the close of the fifth or sixth month of his seclusion, and while the pestilence raged most furiously abroad, that the Prince Prospero entertained his thousand friends at a masked ball of the most unusual magnificence.

It was a voluptuous[8] scene, that masquerade. But first let me tell of the rooms in which it was held. There were seven—an imperial suite. In many palaces, however, such suites form a long and straight vista, while the folding doors slide back nearly to the walls on either hand, so that the view of the whole extent is scarcely impeded. Here the case was very different; as might have been expected from the duke's love of the *bizarre*. The apartments were so irregularly disposed[9] that the vision embraced but little more than one at a time. There was a sharp turn at every twenty or thirty yards, and at each turn a novel effect. To the right and left, in the middle of each wall, a tall and narrow Gothic window looked out upon a closed corridor which pursued the windings of the suite. These windows were of stained glass whose color varied in accordance with the prevailing hue of the decorations of the chamber into which it opened. That at the eastern extremity was hung, for example, in blue—and vividly blue were its windows. The second chamber was purple in its ornaments and tapestries, and

Did You Know?
Gothic architecture developed in Europe between the twelfth and sixteenth centuries. A Gothic window has a pointed arch and many small panes of stained or clear glass.

4. The prince's *dominions* are the territories he rules.
5. A *castellated abbey* is a fortified structure originally built as a monastery or intended, as the prince's was, to resemble one.
6. With *means neither of ingress nor egress*, there's no way in and no way out.
7. *Buffoons* are clowns or comedians, and *improvisatori* (im prov′ ə zə tôr′ ē) are poets who improvise, or make up, verses as they perform.
8. Here, *voluptuous* (və lup′ cho͞o əs) means "giving great pleasure to the senses."
9. *Bizarre* means "that which is extremely strange or odd." A bizarre feature of Prospero's abbey is the way the rooms *(apartments)* are arranged *(disposed)* so that only one is visible at a time.

Vocabulary
dauntless (dônt′ lis) *adj.* fearless; courageous; daring
sagacious (sə gā′ shəs) *adj.* having or showing wisdom and good judgment

here the panes were purple. The third was green throughout, and so were the casements.[10] The fourth was furnished and lighted with orange—the fifth with white—the sixth with violet. The seventh apartment was closely shrouded in black velvet tapestries that hung all over the ceiling and down the walls, falling in heavy folds upon a carpet of the same material and hue. But in this chamber only, the color of the windows failed to correspond with the decorations. The panes here were scarlet—a deep blood color. Now in no one of the seven apartments was there any lamp or candelabrum, amid the profusion of golden ornaments that lay scattered to and fro or depended from the roof. There was no light of any kind emanating from lamp or candle within the suite of chambers. But in the corridors that followed the suite, there stood, opposite to each window, a heavy tripod, bearing a brazier[11] of fire, that projected its rays through the tinted glass and so glaringly illumined the room. And thus were produced a multitude of gaudy and fantastic appearances. But in the western or black chamber the effect of the fire-light that streamed upon the dark hangings through the blood-tinted panes was ghastly in the extreme, and produced so wild a look upon the countenances of those who entered, that there were few of the company bold enough to set foot within its precincts at all.

Costume Ball in the Tuileries: Napoleon III and the Countess Castiglione, 1867. Jean Baptiste Carpeaux. Oil on canvas. Musee d'Orsay, Paris.

Viewing the painting: In what ways does this painting reflect the party in the story?

It was in this apartment, also, that there stood against the western wall, a gigantic clock of ebony. Its pendulum swung to and fro with a dull, heavy, monotonous clang; and

10. *Casements* are windows.
11. A *brazier* (brā′ zhər) is a metal pan used to hold burning coal or charcoal, as a source of heat and light.

Vocabulary

countenance (koun′ tə nəns) *n.* the face

when the minute-hand made the circuit of the face, and the hour was to be stricken, there came from the brazen[12] lungs of the clock a sound which was clear and loud and deep and exceedingly musical, but of so peculiar a note and emphasis that, at each lapse of an hour, the musicians of the orchestra were constrained to pause, momentarily, in their performance, to hearken to the sound; and thus the waltzers perforce ceased their evolutions; and there was a brief disconcert[13] of the whole gay company; and, while the chimes of the clock yet rang, it was observed that the giddiest grew pale, and the more aged and sedate passed their hands over their brows as if in confused revery or meditation. But when the echoes had fully ceased, a light laughter at once pervaded the assembly; the musicians looked at each other and smiled as if at their own nervousness and folly, and made whispering vows, each to the other, that the next chiming of the clock should produce in them no similar emotion; and then, after the lapse of sixty minutes (which embrace three thousand and six hundred seconds of the Time that flies), there came yet another chiming of the clock, and then were the same disconcert and tremulousness and meditation as before.

But, in spite of these things, it was a gay and magnificent revel. The tastes of the duke were peculiar. He had a fine eye for colors and effects. He disregarded the *decora* of mere fashion. His plans were bold and fiery, and his conceptions glowed with barbaric lustre. There are some who would have thought him mad. His followers felt that he was not. It was necessary to hear and see and touch him to be *sure* that he was not.

He had directed, in great part, the movable embellishments of the seven chambers, upon occasion of this great *fête;*[14] and it was his own guiding taste which had given character to the masqueraders. Be sure they were grotesque. There were much glare and glitter and piquancy and phantasm—much of what has been since seen in "Hernani."[15] There were arabesque figures with unsuited limbs and appointments. There were delirious fancies such as the madman fashions. There were much of the beautiful, much of the wanton, much of the *bizarre*, something of the terrible, and not a little of that which might have excited disgust. To and fro in the seven chambers there stalked, in fact, a multitude of dreams. And these—the dreams—writhed in and about, taking hue from the rooms, and causing the wild music of the orchestra to seem as the echo of their steps. And, anon, there strikes the ebony clock which stands in the hall of the velvet. And then, for a moment, all is still, and all is silent save the voice of the clock. The dreams are stiff-frozen as they stand. But the echoes of the chime die away—they have endured but an instant—and a light, half-subdued laughter floats after them as they depart. And now again the music swells, and the dreams live, and writhe to and fro more merrily than ever, taking hue from the many-tinted windows through which stream the rays from the tripods. But

12. The clock's outer parts are *ebony*, a black wood; its inner workings are brass *(brazen)*.

13. The musicians feel obliged *(constrained)* to stop playing, the waltzers halt their complex patterns of movement *(evolutions)*, and everyone experiences temporary confusion and disorder *(disconcert)*.

14. A *fête* (fāt) is a large, elaborate party.

15. Here, *piquancy* (pē′ kən sē) refers to what is charming, and *phantasm* to what is fantastic and unreal. *"Hernani,"* an 1830 drama and, especially, an opera based on the drama, is notable for the use of colorful, imaginative spectacle.

Vocabulary

wanton (wont′ ən) *adj.* shamelessly unrestrained; immoral to the chamber which lies most westwardly of the seven there are now none of the maskers who venture; for the night is waning away; and there flows a ruddier light through the blood-colored panes; and the blackness of the sable drapery appals; and to him whose foot falls upon the sable carpet, there comes from the near clock of ebony a muffled peal more solemnly emphatic than any which reaches *their* ears who indulge in the more remote gaieties of the other apartments.

But these other apartments were densely crowded, and in them beat feverishly the heart of life. And the revel went whirlingly on, until at length there commenced the sounding of midnight upon the clock. And then the music ceased, as I have told; and the evolutions of the waltzers were quieted; and there was an uneasy cessation of all things as before. But now there were twelve strokes to be sounded by the bell of the clock; and thus it happened, perhaps that more of thought crept, with more of time, into the meditations of the thoughtful among those who revelled. And thus too, it happened, perhaps, that before the last echoes of the last chime had utterly sunk into silence, there were many individuals in the crowd who had found leisure to become aware of the presence of a masked figure which had arrested the attention of no single individual before. And the rumor of this new presence having spread itself whisperingly around, there arose at length from the whole company a buzz, or murmur, expressive of disapprobation[16] and surprise—then, finally, of terror, of horror, and of disgust.

In an assembly of phantasms such as I have painted, it may well be supposed that no ordinary appearance could have excited such sensation. In truth the masquerade license of the night was nearly unlimited; but the figure in question had out-Heroded Herod,[17] and gone beyond the bounds of even the prince's indefinite decorum. There are chords in the hearts of the most reckless which cannot be touched without emotion. Even with the utterly lost, to whom life and death are equally jests, there are matters of which no jest can be made. The whole company, indeed, seemed now deeply to feel that in the costume and bearing of the stranger neither wit nor propriety existed. The figure was tall and gaunt, and shrouded from head to foot in the habiliments[18] of the grave. The mask which concealed the visage was made so nearly to resemble the countenance of a stiffened corpse that the closest scrutiny must have had difficulty in detecting the cheat. And yet all this might have been endured, if not approved, by the mad revellers around. But the mummer had gone so far as to assume the type of the Red Death. His vesture[19] was dabbled in *blood*—and his broad brow, with all the features of the face, was besprinkled with the scarlet horror.

When the eyes of Prince Prospero fell upon this spectral image (which, with a slow and solemn movement, as if more fully to sustain its *rôle*, stalked to and fro among the waltzers) he was seen to be convulsed, in the first moment with a strong shudder either of

16. *Disapprobation* means "disapproval."

17. To have *out-Heroded Herod,* the mysterious figure has done something even more outrageous than Herod the Great, the tyrant who, in an effort to kill the baby Jesus, ordered the murder of all male infants in Bethlehem.

18. *Habiliments* are clothes.

19. A *mummer* is a person dressed in a mask and costume for a party or play, and *vesture* is clothing.

Vocabulary

appal (ə pôl′) *v.* to fill with horror or dismay; shock
spectral (spek′ trəl) *adj.* ghostlike

terror or distaste; but, in the next, his brow reddened with rage.

"Who dares"—he demanded hoarsely of the courtiers who stood near him—"who dares insult us with this blasphemous mockery? Seize him and unmask him—that we may know whom we have to hang, at sunrise, from the battlements!"

It was in the eastern or blue chamber in which stood the Prince Prospero as he uttered these words. They rang throughout the seven rooms loudly and clearly, for the prince was a bold and robust man, and the music had become hushed at the waving of his hand.

It was in the blue room where stood the prince, with a group of pale courtiers by his side. At first, as he spoke, there was a slight rushing movement of this group in the direction of the intruder, who, at the moment was also near at hand, and now, with deliberate and stately step, made closer approach to the speaker. But from a certain nameless awe with which the mad assumptions of the mummer had inspired the whole party, there were found none who put forth hand to seize him; so that, unimpeded, he passed within a yard of the prince's person; and, while the vast assembly, as if with one impulse, shrank from the centres of the rooms to the walls, he made his way uninterruptedly, but with the same solemn and measured step which had distinguished him from the first, through the blue chamber to the purple—through the purple to the green—through the green to the orange—through this again to the white—and even thence to the violet, ere a decided movement had been made to arrest him. It was then, however, that the Prince Prospero, maddening with rage and the shame of his own momentary cowardice, rushed hurriedly through the six chambers, while none followed him on account of a deadly terror that had seized upon all. He bore aloft a drawn dagger, and had approached, in rapid impetuosity, to within three or four feet of the retreating figure, when the latter, having attained the extremity of the velvet apartment, turned suddenly and confronted his pursuer. There was a sharp cry—and the dagger dropped gleaming upon the sable carpet, upon which, instantly afterward, fell prostrate in death the Prince Prospero. Then, summoning the wild courage of despair, a throng of the revellers at once threw themselves into the black apartment, and, seizing the mummer, whose tall figure stood erect and motionless within the shadow of the ebony clock, gasped in unutterable horror at finding the grave cerements[20] and corpse-like mask, which they handled with so violent a rudeness, untenanted[21] by any tangible form.

And now was acknowledged the presence of the Red Death. He had come like a thief in the night. And one by one dropped the revellers in the blood-bedewed halls of their revel, and died each in the despairing posture of his fall. And the life of the ebony clock went out with that of the last of the gay. And the flames of the tripods expired. And Darkness and Decay and the Red Death held illimitable dominion over all.

20. *Cerements* are strips of cloth used to wrap a dead body.
21. *Untenanted* means "unoccupied or uninhabited."

Vocabulary
blasphemous (blas′ fə məs) *adj.* showing disrespect or scorn for God or anything sacred

Responding to Literature

Personal Response

If you had been a guest at the ball, what do you think you would have done when you saw the masked stranger? Why?

Analyzing Literature

Recall

1. What is the "Red Death"? Explain how it affects its victims.
2. Briefly describe the seven rooms in which the masked ball is held.
3. Describe the clock that stands in the seventh room. What happens each time the clock chimes?
4. How are the guests dressed for the ball? What are some words Poe uses to describe their appearance?
5. How does Prince Prospero react to the midnight guest? What happens to the prince? To his guests?

Interpret

6. In your opinion, what does Prince Prospero's response to the "Red Death" reveal about his character?
7. Why do you think Prospero decorated the rooms the way he did?
8. What do you think the clock **symbolizes?**
9. How is the appearance of the "midnight guest" similar to that of the other guests? How is it different?
10. At the end of the story, Poe alludes to a biblical prophecy that the day of judgment will come "as a thief in the night." Why do you think Poe makes this **allusion?**

Evaluate and Connect

11. Do you think Poe is using **irony** when he says that Prince Prospero is brave and wise? Explain your answer.
12. In your opinion, what is the **moral,** or lesson, of this story? Explain.
13. How might people react today if their political leaders responded to a crisis as Prince Prospero did? Explain.
14. Think back to the discussion you had in response to the Reading Focus on page 388. Has this story changed your ideas about the level of control you feel you have over events in your life? Explain.
15. **Theme Connections** Consider Prince Prospero's response to the challenge he faces at the beginning of the story. If his response had been different, do you think it might have altered his fate? Explain.

Literary ELEMENTS

Setting and Mood

Setting refers to the time and place in which a story occurs. A writer's use of sensory details can make the setting come alive for readers and can affect the **mood,** or atmosphere, of the story. In a horror story, the setting often helps create a growing sense of terror. For example, Poe sets "The Masque of the Red Death" in Prince Prospero's extensive and magnificent abbey. The people within believe that nothing and no one can penetrate its gates of iron.

1. Contrast the mood outside the prince's abbey to that within. What details does Poe use at the beginning of the story to create these contrasting moods?
2. What sensory details used to describe the setting help to create a mood of horror? Find two examples each of details that appeal to the senses of sight, hearing, and touch. Explain how each detail contributes to the mood of horror.

- See **Literary Terms Handbook,** p. R8.

Literature and Writing

Writing About Literature

Analyze Allegorical Symbols In an **allegory**–a literary work whose underlying meaning differs from the literal meaning–the writer often uses characters, objects, or events as symbols. In this story, for example, Prince Prospero might represent selfishness. Identify other allegorical symbols in the story. Explain what you think each symbol represents, how the symbols are connected, and how they contribute to the lesson, or moral, of the story. Share your ideas with a small group of classmates.

Personal Writing

R.S.V.P. Imagine that you have received an invitation from Prince Prospero to be sealed up in the abbey with the one thousand knights and ladies. Write a note responding to the invitation. Explain why you will or will not come.

Extending Your Response

Literature Groups

What Makes a Good Horror Story? Create a horror story web using words and phrases that, in your opinion, describe essential elements of a good horror story. Use "The Masque of the Red Death" and other horror stories you know as a guide. Refer to your web as you debate this question in your group: *What are the essential elements of a good horror story?* Share your ideas with the class.

Interdisciplinary Activity

Art: Party Decor Poe gives a detailed description of how Prince Prospero decorated the seven rooms in which the masked ball was held. Reread the description, and then draw a picture of one or more of the rooms. You may wish to include in your drawing the corridors that stand outside each room.

Listening and Speaking

Interview With a partner, prepare questions for an interview with a servant who survived Prince Prospero's masked ball. Conduct the interview, with one person playing the role of the servant and the other the role of the interviewer. Tape-record the interview and play it for the class, or do a live performance.

Reading Further

Edgar Allan Poe's best-known stories can be found in this collection:

Short Story Collection: *The Essential Poe Tales of Mystery and Horror* presents twenty-six thrilling tales including "The Tell-Tale Heart" and "The Murder in the Rue Morgue."

Viewing: *Masque of the Red Death,* stars Vincent Price as Prince Prospero.

Save your work for your portfolio.

Skill Minilessons

GRAMMAR AND LANGUAGE • Subject Complements

The two kinds of **subject complements** are predicate nominatives and predicate adjectives. A **predicate nominative** is a noun or pronoun that follows a linking verb and points back to the subject to identify or rename it.

Prospero is a *prince* who tries to escape the Red Death.

A **predicate adjective** follows a linking verb and points back to the subject to further describe it.

The disease is *hideous* and *fatal.*

PRACTICE Complete each sentence by adding one or more nouns, pronouns, or adjectives. (You may also add other words.) Write *PN* or *PA* to identify each predicate nominative or predicate adjective.

1. Prince Prospero seems ________________ .
2. The prince's abbey is ________________ .
3. The guests at the abbey are ________________ .
4. In the black room, people's faces look ___________ .
5. The mysterious guest is________________ .

● For more about complements, see **Language Handbook,** p. R39.

READING AND THINKING • Visualizing

Using story details, you can create a mental picture of the setting, characters, and events. Reread Poe's description of the "Red Death" at the beginning of the story. Feel the horror as you visualize its victims racked with dizziness, sharp pains, and bleeding at the pores.

PRACTICE Find a passage in the story that helps you visualize a particular character, event, or element of the setting. Explain to a classmate the mental picture that you "see" after reading this passage. Discuss how visualizing the passage adds to your understanding of the story.

APPLY Visualize the final events of the story, starting with the moment when Prince Prospero first notices the ghastly guest. Then draw a picture that you think captures the horror of the final moments of the masked ball.

● For more about reading strategies, see **Reading Handbook,** p. R84.

VOCABULARY • Analogies

An analogy is a type of comparison that is based on the relationships between things or ideas. This relationship can be expressed in a statement:

owl : sagacious :: lion : dauntless

The **owl** often represents the quality of being **sagacious.** Replacing the boldface words with the second pair of words in the analogy results in another statement: *The* ***lion*** *often represents the quality of being* ***dauntless.***

To finish an analogy, decide what relationship exists between the first two things or ideas. Then apply that relationship to another pair of words and see if it is the same.

● For more about analogies, see **Communications Skills Handbook,** p. R77.

PRACTICE Choose the word that best completes each analogy.

1. nose : countenance :: finger :
   a. thumb b. knuckle c. hand
2. please : delight :: appal :
   a. interest b. horrify c. bore
3. spectral : tangible :: sagacious :
   a. wise b. practical c. ignorant
4. generous : stingy :: profuse :
   a. sufficient b. meager c. abundant
5. blasphemous : reverence :: wanton :
   a. evil b. restraint c. desire

Before You Read

To Da-duh, in Memoriam

Reading Focus

Have you ever heard the following sayings?

Opposites attract.

Birds of a feather flock together.

Journal Think about the two sayings in terms of your own relationships with family members. With whom do you get along the best–relatives whose personalities are similar to yours, or those with personalities that are different from your own? Record your thoughts in your journal.

Setting a Purpose Read to find out about the relationship between a child from the city and her Barbadian grandmother.

Building Background

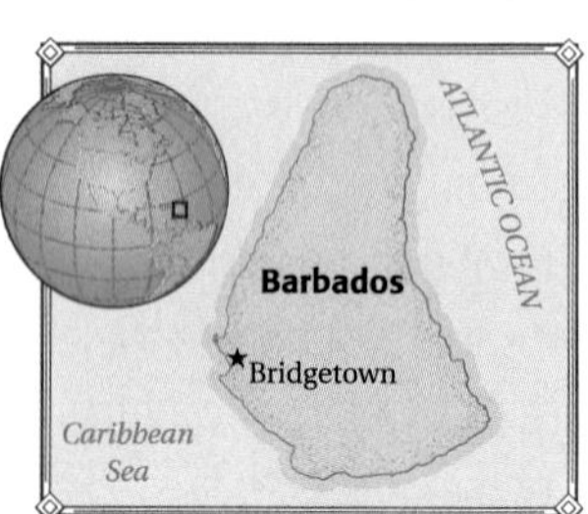

The Time and Place

"To Da-duh, in Memoriam" takes place in Barbados, in the 1930s.

Did You Know?

Barbados is a tiny Caribbean island, with mostly flat terrain. Its highest point, Mount Hillaby, is shorter than New York City's Empire State Building. The island became an independent state in 1966, after being under British colonial rule for more than three centuries. Although the people of Barbados speak English, the folk culture is of African origin. From 1937 to 1938, the island experienced violent unrest as a result of economic depression and other stresses.

Vocabulary Preview

formidable (fôr′ mi də bəl) *adj.* causing fear, dread, or awe by reason of size, strength, or power; p. 400

decrepit (di krep′ it) *adj.* broken down by long use or old age; p. 401

hurtle (hurt′ əl) *v.* to move rapidly, especially with much force or noise; p. 403

arrogant (ar′ ə gənt) *adj.* full of self-importance; haughty; p. 403

malicious (mə lish′ əs) *adj.* having or showing a desire to harm another; p. 407

Meet Paule Marshall

Paule Marshall grew up in a Barbadian community in New York City, where, she says, she learned all about writing in her mother's kitchen. In this "word-shop," her mother and her mother's friends passed on to her "the rich legacy of language and culture" that they shared after their workdays of "scrubbing floor." Marshall went on to write many award-winning novels, short stories, and articles, including her most famous work, *Praisesong for the Widow*.

The story you are about to read is "the most autobiographical of the stories."

Paule Marshall was born in Brooklyn, New York, in 1929. This story was first published in 1967 in New World Magazine.

To Da-duh, in Memoriam

Paule Marshall

Peaceful Day, 1994. Shakito. 24 x 18 in.
Private collection.

"... Oh Nana! all of you
is not involved in this evil
business Death,
Nor all of us in life."

—*from* "At My
Grandmother's Grave,"
by Lebert Bethune

I did not see her at first I remember. For not only was it dark inside the crowded disembarkation[1] shed in spite of the daylight flooding in from outside, but standing there waiting for her with my mother and sister I was still somewhat blinded from the sheen of tropical sunlight on the water of the bay which we had just crossed in the landing boat, leaving behind us the ship that had brought us from New York lying in the offing.[2] Besides, being only nine years of age at the time and knowing nothing of islands I was busy attending to the alien sights and sounds of Barbados, the unfamiliar smells.

I did not see her, but I was alerted to her approach by my mother's hand which suddenly tightened around mine, and looking up I traced her gaze through the gloom in the shed until I finally made out the small, purposeful, painfully erect figure of the old woman headed our way.

Her face was drowned in the shadow of an ugly rolled-brim brown felt hat, but the details of her slight body and of the struggle taking place within it were clear enough—an intense, unrelenting[3] struggle between her back which was beginning to bend ever so slightly under the weight of her eighty-odd years and the rest of her which sought to deny those years and hold that back straight, keep it in line. Moving swiftly toward us (so swiftly it seemed she did not intend stopping when she reached us but would sweep past us out the doorway which opened onto the sea and like Christ walk upon the water!), she was caught between the sunlight at her end of the building and the darkness inside—and for a moment she appeared to contain them both: the light in the long severe old-fashioned white dress she wore which brought the sense of a past that was still alive into our bustling present and in the snatch of white at her eye; the darkness in her black high-top shoes and in her face which was visible now that she was closer.

It was as stark and fleshless as a death mask, that face. The maggots might have already done their work, leaving only the framework of bone beneath the ruined skin and deep wells at the temple and jaw. But her eyes were alive, unnervingly so for one so old, with a sharp light that flicked out of the dim clouded depths like a lizard's tongue to snap up all in her view. Those eyes betrayed a child's curiosity about the world, and I wondered vaguely seeing them, and seeing the way the bodice of her ancient dress had collapsed in on her flat chest (what had happened to her breasts?), whether she might not be some kind of child at the same time that she was a woman, with fourteen children, my mother included, to prove it. Perhaps she was both, both child and woman, darkness and light, past and present, life and death—all the opposites contained and reconciled in her.

"My Da-duh," my mother said formally and stepped forward. The name sounded like thunder fading softly in the distance.

"Child," Da-duh said, and her tone, her quick scrutiny of my mother, the brief embrace in which they appeared to shy from each other rather than touch, wiped out the fifteen years my mother had been away and restored the old relationship. My mother, who was such a formidable figure in my eyes, had suddenly with a word been reduced to my status.

1. To *disembark* is to get off a ship or plane.
2. In this context, *in the offing* means "just in view from the shore."
3. An *unrelenting* (un′ ri len′ ting) struggle is one that does not ease or lessen in intensity.

Vocabulary

formidable (fôr′ mi də bəl) *adj.* causing fear, dread, or awe by reason of size, strength, or power

"Yes, God is good," Da-duh said with a nod that was like a tic.[4] "He has spared me to see my child again."

We were led forward then, apologetically because not only did Da-duh prefer boys but she also liked her grandchildren to be "white," that is, fair-skinned; and we had, I was to discover, a number of cousins, the outside children of white estate managers and the like, who qualified. We, though, were as black as she.

My sister being the oldest was presented first. "This one takes after the father," my mother said and waited to be reproved.

Frowning, Da-duh tilted my sister's face toward the light. But her frown soon gave way to a grudging smile, for my sister with her large mild eyes and little broad winged nose, with our father's high-cheeked Barbadian cast to her face, was pretty.

"She's goin' be lucky," Da-duh said and patted her once on the cheek. "Any girl child that takes after the father does be lucky."

She turned then to me. But oddly enough she did not touch me. Instead leaning close, she peered hard at me, and then quickly drew back. I thought I saw her hand start up as though to shield her eyes. It was almost as if she saw not only me, a thin truculent[5] child who it was said took after no one but myself, but something in me which for some reason she found disturbing, even threatening. We looked silently at each other for a long time there in the noisy shed, our gaze locked. She was the first to look away.

"But Adry," she said to my mother and her laugh was cracked, thin, apprehensive. "Where did you get this one here with this fierce look?"

"We don't know where she came out of, my Da-duh," my mother said, laughing also. Even I smiled to myself. After all I had won the encounter. Da-duh had recognized my small strength—and this was all I ever asked of the adults in my life then.

"Come, soul," Da-duh said and took my hand. "You must be one of those New York terrors you hear so much about."

She led us, me at her side and my sister and mother behind, out of the shed into the sunlight that was like a bright driving summer rain and over to a group of people clustered beside a decrepit lorry. They were our relatives, most of them from St. Andrews although Da-duh herself lived in St. Thomas, the women wearing bright print dresses, the colors vivid against their darkness, the men rusty black suits that encased them like strait-jackets. Da-duh, holding fast to my hand, became my anchor as they circled round us like a nervous sea, exclaiming, touching us with their calloused hands, embracing us shyly. They laughed in awed bursts: "But look Adry got big-big children!" / "And see the nice things they wearing, wrist-watch and all!" / "I tell you, Adry has done all right for sheself in New York. . . ."

Did You Know?
Lorry is what the British call a truck.

Da-duh, ashamed at their wonder, embarrassed for them, admonished them the while. . . . "Why you all got to get on like you never saw people from 'Away' before? You would think New York is the only place in the world to hear wunna.[6] That's why I don't like

4. Here, a *tic* is an involuntary twitching.
5. To be *truculent* is to be fierce and ready to fight.
6. *To hear wunna* may be Da-duh's way of saying "to have wonders."

Vocabulary
decrepit (di krep′ it) *adj.* broken down by long use or old age

Good Old Days, 1993. Shakito. Private collection.

Viewing the painting: How is this house similar to Da-duh's? How do the grounds reflect the island in the story?

to go anyplace with you St. Andrews people, you know. You all ain't been colonized."

We were in the back of the lorry finally, packed in among the barrels of ham, flour, cornmeal and rice and the trunks of clothes that my mother had brought as gifts. We made our way slowly through Bridgetown's clogged streets, part of a funereal[7] procession of cars and open-sided buses, bicycles and donkey carts. The dim little limestone shops and offices along the way marched with us, at the same mournful pace, toward the same grave ceremony—as did the people, the women balancing huge baskets on top their heads as if they were no more than hats they wore to shade them from the sun. Looking over the edge of the lorry I watched as their feet slurred the dust. I listened, and their voices, raw and loud and dissonant in the heat, seemed to be grappling with each other high overhead.

Da-duh sat on a trunk in our midst, a monarch amid her court. She still held my hand, but it was different now. I had suddenly become her anchor, for I felt her fear of the lorry with its asthmatic motor (a fear and distrust, I later learned, she held of all machines) beating like a pulse in her rough palm.

As soon as we left Bridgetown behind though, she relaxed, and while the others around us talked she gazed at the canes standing tall on either side of the winding marl[8] road. "C'dear," she said softly to herself after a time. "The canes this side are pretty enough."

They were too much for me. I thought of them as giant weeds that had overrun the

7. *Funereal* means "like, or suitable to, a funeral."

8. A *marl* road is paved with a crumbly clay of the sort used to make cement.

island, leaving scarcely any room for the small tottering houses of sunbleached pine we passed or the people, dark streaks as our lorry hurtled by. I suddenly feared that we were journeying, unaware that we were, toward some dangerous place where the canes, grown as high and thick as a forest, would close in on us and run us through with their stiletto blades. I longed then for the familiar: for the street in Brooklyn[9] where I lived, for my father who had refused to accompany us ("Blowing out good money on foolishness," he had said of the trip), for a game of tag with my friends under the chestnut tree outside our aging brownstone house.

"Yes, but wait till you see St. Thomas canes," Da-duh was saying to me. "They's canes father, bo," she gave a proud arrogant nod. "Tomorrow, God willing, I goin' take you out in the ground and show them to you."

True to her word Da-duh took me with her the following day out into the ground. It was a fairly large plot adjoining her weathered board and shingle house and consisting of a small orchard, a good-sized canepiece and behind the canes, where the land sloped abruptly down, a gully. She had purchased it with Panama money sent her by her eldest son, my uncle Joseph, who had died working on the canal. We entered the ground along a trail no wider than her body and as devious and complex as her reasons for showing me her land. Da-duh strode briskly ahead, her slight form filled out this morning by the layers of sacking petticoats she wore under her working dress to protect her against the damp. A fresh white cloth, elaborately arranged around her head, added to her height, and lent her a vain, almost roguish air.

9. *Brooklyn* is one of New York City's five boroughs, or districts.

Her pace slowed once we reached the orchard, and glancing back at me occasionally over her shoulder, she pointed out the various trees.

"This here is a breadfruit," she said. "That one yonder is a papaw. Here's a guava. This is a mango. I know you don't have anything like these in New York. Here's a sugar apple." (The fruit looked more like artichokes than apples to me.) "This one bears limes. . . ." She went on for some time, intoning the names of the trees as though they were those of her gods. Finally, turning to me, she said, "I know you don't have anything this nice where you come from." Then, as I hesitated: "I said I know you don't have anything this nice where you come from. . . ."

"No," I said and my world did seem suddenly lacking.

Da-duh nodded and passed on. The orchard ended and we were on the narrow cart road that led through the canepiece, the canes clashing like swords above my cowering head. Again she turned and her thin muscular arms spread wide, her dim gaze embracing the small field of canes, she said—and her voice almost broke under the weight of her pride, "Tell me, have you got anything like these in that place where you were born?"

"No."

"I din' think so. I bet you don't even know that these canes here and the sugar you eat is one and the same thing. That they does throw the canes into some damn machine at the factory and squeeze out all the little life in them to make sugar for you all so in New York to eat. I bet you don't know that."

"I've got two cavities and I'm not allowed to eat a lot of sugar."

Vocabulary

hurtle (hurt′ əl) *v.* to move rapidly, especially with much force or noise
arrogant (ar′ ə gənt) *adj.* full of self-importance; haughty

But Da-duh didn't hear me. She had turned with an inexplicably angry motion and was making her way rapidly out of the canes and down the slope at the edge of the field which led to the gully below. Following her apprehensively down the incline amid a stand of banana plants whose leaves flapped like elephants' ears in the wind, I found myself in the middle of a small tropical wood—a place dense and damp and gloomy and tremulous with the fitful play of light and shadow as the leaves high above moved against the sun that was almost hidden from view. It was a violent place, the tangled foliage fighting each other for a chance at the sunlight, the branches of the trees locked in what seemed an immemorial[10] struggle, one both necessary and inevitable. But despite the violence, it was pleasant, almost peaceful in the gully, and beneath the thick undergrowth the earth smelled like spring.

This time Da-duh didn't even bother to ask her usual question, but simply turned and waited for me to speak.

"No," I said, my head bowed. "We don't have anything like this in New York."

"Ah," she cried, her triumph complete. "I din' think so. Why, I've heard that's a place where you can walk till you near drop and never see a tree."

"We've got a chestnut tree in front of our house," I said.

"Does it bear?" She waited. "I ask you, does it bear?"

"Not anymore," I muttered. "It used to, but not anymore."

She gave the nod that was like a nervous twitch. "You see," she said. "Nothing can bear there." Then, secure behind her scorn, she added, "But tell me, what's this snow like that you hear so much about?"

Looking up, I studied her closely, sensing my chance, and then I told her, describing at length and with as much drama as I could summon not only what snow in the city was like, but what it would be like here, in her perennial summer kingdom.

It was a violent place, the tangled foliage fighting each other for a chance at the sunlight . . .

". . . And you see all these trees you got here," I said. "Well, they'd be bare. No leaves, no fruit, nothing. They'd be covered in snow. You see your canes. They'd be buried under tons of snow. The snow would be higher than your head, higher than your house, and you wouldn't be able to come down into this here gully because it would be snowed under. . . ."

She searched my face for the lie, still scornful but intrigued. "What a thing, huh?" she said finally, whispering it softly to herself.

"And when it snows you couldn't dress like you are now," I said. "Oh no, you'd freeze to death. You'd have to wear a hat and gloves and galoshes and ear muffs so your ears wouldn't freeze and drop off, and a heavy coat. I've got a Shirley Temple[11] coat with fur on the collar. I can dance. You wanna see?"

Before she could answer I began, with a dance called the Truck which was popular back then in the 1930s. My right forefinger waving, I trucked around the nearby trees and

10. An *immemorial* struggle would be one that extended back beyond memory or record.

11. *Shirley Temple* was a popular child movie star of the 1930s.

around Da-duh's awed and rigid form. After the Truck I did the Suzy-Q, my lean hips swishing, my sneakers sidling zigzag over the ground. "I can sing," I said and did so, starting with "I'm Gonna Sit Right Down and Write Myself a Letter," then without pausing, "Tea For Two," and ending with "I Found a Million Dollar Baby in a Five and Ten Cent Store."

For long moments afterwards Da-duh stared at me as if I were a creature from Mars, an emissary from some world she did not know but which intrigued her and whose power she both felt and feared. Yet something about my performance must have pleased her, because bending down she slowly lifted her long skirt and then, one by one, the layers of petticoats until she came to a drawstring purse dangling at the end of a long strip of cloth tied round her waist. Opening the purse she handed me a penny. "Here," she said half-smiling against her will. "Take this to buy yourself a sweet at the shop up the road. There's nothing to be done with you, soul."

From then on, whenever I wasn't taken to visit relatives, I accompanied Da-duh out into the ground, and alone with her amid the canes or down in the gully I told her about New York. It always began with some slighting remark on her part: "I know they don't have anything this nice where you come from," or "Tell me, I hear those foolish people in New York does do such and such. . . ." But as I answered, recreating my towering world of steel and concrete and machines for her, building the city out of words, I would feel her give way. I came to know the signs of her surrender: the total stillness that would come over the little hard dry form, the probing gaze that like a surgeon's knife sought to cut through my skull to get at the images there, to see if I were lying; above all, her fear, a fear nameless and profound, the same one I had felt beating in the palm of her hand that day in the lorry.

Over the weeks I told her about refrigerators, radios, gas stoves, elevators, trolley cars, wringer washing machines, movies, airplanes, the cyclone at Coney Island,[12] subways, toasters, electric lights: "At night, see, all you have to do is flip this little switch on the wall and all the lights in the house go on. Just like that. Like magic. It's like turning on the sun at night."

"But tell me," she said to me once with a faint mocking smile, "do the white people have all these things too or it's only the people looking like us?"

I laughed. "What d'ya mean," I said. "The white people have even better." Then: "I beat up a white girl in my class last term."

"Beating up white people!" Her tone was incredulous.

"How you mean!" I said, using an expression of hers. "She called me a name."

For some reason Da-duh could not quite get over this and repeated in the same hushed, shocked voice, "Beating up white people now! Oh, the lord, the world's changing up so I can scarce recognize it anymore."

One morning toward the end of our stay, Da-duh led me into a part of the gully that we had never visited before, an area darker and more thickly overgrown than the rest, almost impenetrable. There in a small clearing amid the dense bush, she stopped before an incredibly tall royal palm which rose cleanly out of the ground, and drawing the eye up with it, soared high above the trees around it into the sky. It appeared to be touching the blue dome of sky, to be flaunting its dark crown of fronds right in the blinding white face of the late morning sun.

12. *Coney Island* is an amusement park and beach in Brooklyn, and the *cyclone* was a popular thrill ride.

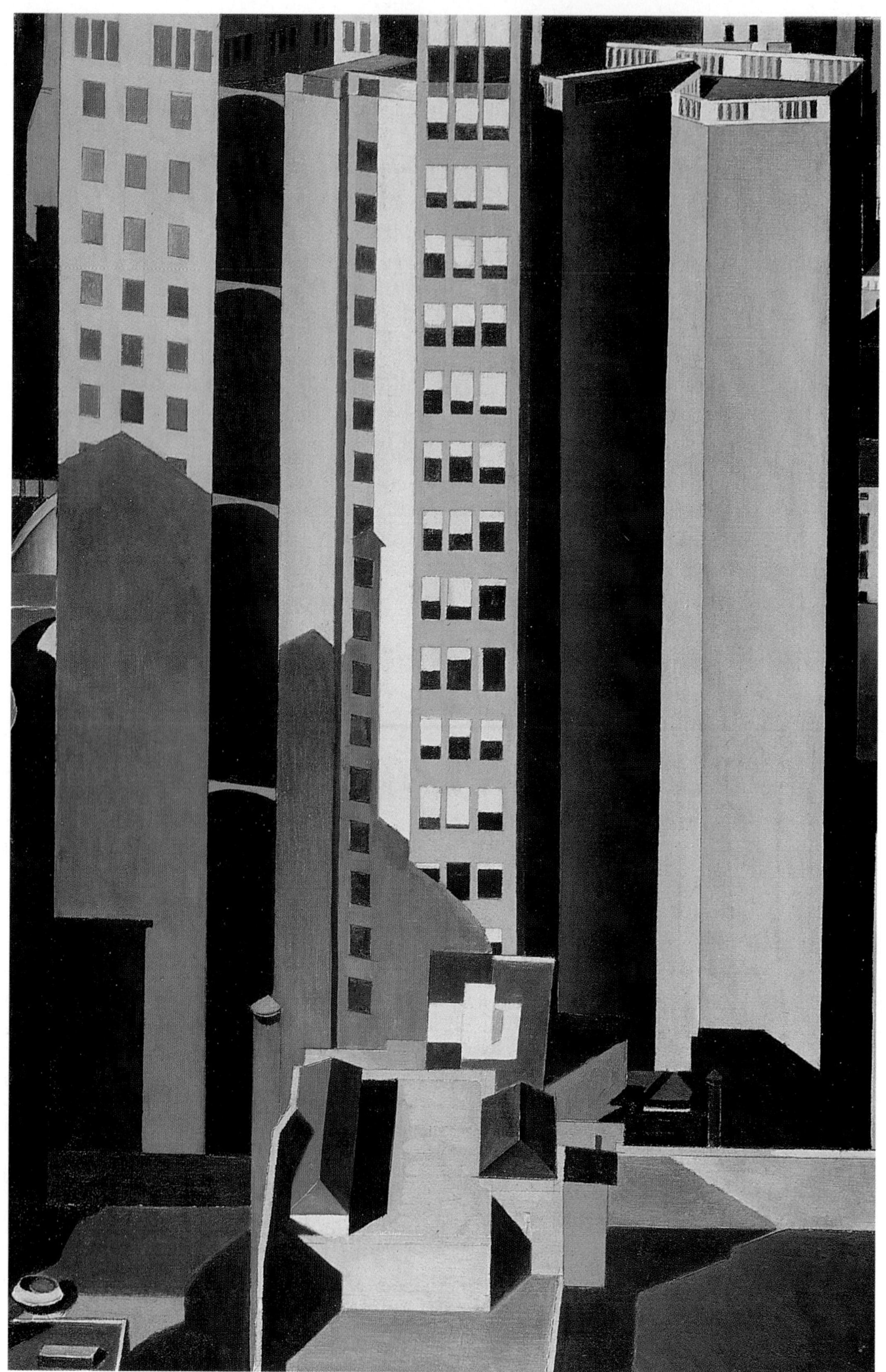

Skyscrapers (Offices), 1922. Charles Sheeler. Oil on canvas, 20 x 13 in. The Phillips Collection, Washington, DC.

Viewing the painting: Contrast the setting in this painting with *Peaceful Day* on page 399. How does this contrast relate to a conflict in the story?

Da-duh watched me a long time before she spoke, and then she said, very quietly, "All right, now, tell me if you've got anything this tall in that place you're from."

I almost wished, seeing her face, that I could have said no. "Yes," I said. "We've got buildings hundreds of times this tall in New York. There's one called the Empire State Building that's the tallest in the world. My class visited it last year and I went all the way to the top. It's got over a hundred floors. I can't describe how tall it is. Wait a minute. What's the name of that hill I went to visit the other day, where they have the police station?"

"You mean Bissex?"

"Yes, Bissex. Well, the Empire State Building is way taller than that."

"You're lying now!" she shouted, trembling with rage. Her hand lifted to strike me.

"No, I'm not," I said. "It really is, if you don't believe me I'll send you a picture postcard of it soon as I get back home so you can see for yourself. But it's way taller than Bissex."

All the fight went out of her at that. The hand poised to strike me fell limp to her side, and as she stared at me, seeing not me but the building that was taller than the highest hill she knew, the small stubborn light in her eyes (it was the same amber as the flame in the kerosene lamp she lit at dusk) began to fail. Finally, with a vague gesture that even in the midst of her defeat still tried to dismiss me and my world, she turned and started back through the gully, walking slowly, her steps groping and uncertain, as if she were suddenly no longer sure of the way, while I followed triumphant yet strangely saddened behind.

The next morning I found her dressed for our morning walk but stretched out on the Berbice chair in the tiny drawing room where she sometimes napped during the afternoon heat, her face turned to the window beside her. She appeared thinner and suddenly indescribably old.

"My Da-duh," I said.

"Yes, nuh," she said. Her voice was listless and the face she slowly turned my way was, now that I think back on it, like a Benin mask, the features drawn and almost distorted by an ancient abstract sorrow.

"Don't you feel well?" I asked.

"Girl, I don't know."

"My Da-duh, I goin' boil you some bush tea," my aunt, Da-duh's youngest child, who lived with her, called from the shed roof kitchen.

"Who tell you I need bush tea?" she cried, her voice assuming for a moment its old authority. "You can't even rest nowadays without some malicious person looking for you to be dead. Come girl," she motioned me to a place beside her on the old-fashioned lounge chair, "give us a tune."

I sang for her until breakfast at eleven, all my brash irreverent Tin Pan Alley[13] songs, and then just before noon we went out into the ground. But it was a short, dispirited walk. Da-duh didn't even notice that the mangoes were beginning to ripen and would have to be picked before the village boys got to them. And when she paused occasionally and looked out across the canes or up at her trees it wasn't as if she were seeing them but something else. Some huge, monolithic[14] shape had imposed itself, it seemed, between her and the land, obstructing her vision.

13. *Tin Pan Alley* was a district in New York City associated with composers and publishers of popular music. These pop songs were bright and lively, often treating their subjects with rude and disrespectful *(brash, irreverent)* mockery.
14. A *monolithic* shape would resemble a monument or other structure formed from a single, giant block of stone.

Vocabulary
malicious (mə lish′ əs) *adj.* having or showing a desire to harm another

Returning to the house she slept the entire afternoon on the Berbice chair.

She remained like this until we left, languishing away the mornings on the chair at the window gazing out at the land as if it were already doomed; then, at noon, taking the brief stroll with me through the ground during which she seldom spoke, and afterwards returning home to sleep till almost dusk sometimes.

On the day of our departure she put on the austere, ankle length white dress, the black shoes and brown felt hat (her town clothes she called them), but she did not go with us to town. She saw us off on the road outside her house and in the midst of my mother's tearful protracted[15] farewell, she leaned down and whispered in my ear, "Girl, you're not to forget now to send me the picture of that building, you hear."

By the time I mailed her the large colored picture postcard of the Empire State Building she was dead. She died during the famous '37 strike which began shortly after we left. On the day of her death England sent planes flying low over the island in a show of force—so low, according to my aunt's letter, that the downdraft from them shook the ripened mangoes from the trees in Da-duh's orchard. Frightened, everyone in the village fled into the canes. Except Da-duh. She remained in the house at the window so my aunt said, watching as the planes came swooping and screaming like monstrous birds down over the village, over her house, rattling her trees and flattening the young canes in her field. It must have seemed to her lying there that they did not intend pulling out of their dive, but like the hardback beetles which hurled themselves with suicidal force against the walls of the house at night, those menacing silver shapes would hurl themselves in an ecstasy of self-immolation[16] onto the land, destroying it utterly.

When the planes finally left and the villagers returned they found her dead on the Berbice chair at the window.

She died and I lived, but always, to this day even, within the shadow of her death. For a brief period after I was grown I went to live alone, like one doing penance,[17] in a loft above a noisy factory in downtown New York and there painted seas of sugarcane and huge swirling Van Gogh[18] suns and palm trees striding like brightly-plumed Tutsi[19] warriors across a tropical landscape, while the thunderous tread of the machines downstairs jarred the floor beneath my easel, mocking my efforts.

15. A *protracted* (prō trak′ təd) farewell would be one that takes a lot of time.

16. *Self-immolation* is the act of setting oneself on fire.

17. *Penance* (pen′ əns) is a punishment one undergoes, usually voluntarily, to show sorrow for having committed a sin or offense.

18. *Van Gogh* was a nineteenth-century Dutch painter famous for his swirling brush strokes and for the dramatic effects they produced.

19. The *Tutsi* are a people in central Africa.

Responding to Literature

Personal Response

Do you approve of the way the narrator treated Da-duh? Explain.

Analyzing Literature

Recall

1. Describe the narrator's initial impression of Da-duh.
2. Summarize what happens the first time Da-duh takes her granddaughter "out into the ground."
3. Describe how the girl re-creates New York for her grandmother.
4. At what point in the story do Da-duh's appearance and behavior abruptly change? Describe this change.
5. What happens to Da-duh shortly after the narrator leaves? Under what circumstances does this event occur?

Interpret

6. Why do you think the narrator tries to "win" the initial encounter between Da-duh and herself?
7. In your opinion, why does Da-duh compare Barbados with New York?
8. What conclusions can you draw about Da-duh, based on her reactions to the girl's descriptions of New York?
9. In your opinion, what causes the abrupt change in the way Da-duh looks and acts? Explain.
10. In what **setting** does the narrator later live and paint? How does this setting reflect the **conflict** between Da-duh and the narrator? (See Literary Terms Handbook, page R11.)

Evaluate and Connect

11. Da-duh and her granddaughter seem to be playing a game that might be called, "Can You Top This?" Describe a time when you played a game of one-upmanship. Did you win or lose?
12. In your opinion, what does the Empire State Building **symbolize** in this story?
13. Look back at the Reading Focus on page 398. Which saying, do you think, describes the relationship between the narrator and Da-duh? Explain.
14. **Theme Connections** In your opinion, what are the consequences of the narrator's triumph over the challenges she faces?
15. The narrator finds herself in unfamiliar surroundings. Describe a similar experience you have had. How did you cope with it?

Literary ELEMENTS

Local Color

Local color is a technique of writing that uses specific details to evoke a particular region. In "To Da-duh, in Memoriam," Paule Marshall re-creates Barbados in the 1930s by describing the characters' habits and customs, their clothing, and the land they inhabit. For example, Marshall writes about "the women balancing huge baskets on top their heads" and "the small tottering houses of sunbleached pine." The characters use distinctively Barbadian expressions and dialect, such as, "I tell you, Adry has done all right for sheself in New York." All of these details help to re-create the region in which the story takes place.

1. Find five details the author uses to evoke the landscape of Barbados.
2. Give three examples of Barbadian expressions or dialect used in the story. What other words might the narrator use to express the same ideas?
3. What are three other examples of specific details that evoke the region in which this story takes place?

- See **Literary Terms Handbook,** p. R7.

Literature and Writing

Writing About Literature

Explore Character Development A character who grows or changes during a story is called a **dynamic character.** Write a paragraph in which you explain how the narrator of "To Da-duh, in Memoriam" grows and changes as a result of her visit to Barbados. Use specific details from the story to support your ideas. Share your writing with others in a small group.

Creative Writing

What's It Like, Da-duh? Use the characters of Da-duh and the narrator to create a picture storybook for young children, in which an old woman named Da-duh tells her American granddaughter about Barbados. Illustrate your story with your own drawings, with photocopies of pictures from books or magazines, or with images you have downloaded from the Internet. Display your book in the classroom.

Extending Your Response

Literature Groups

Two Worlds Colliding Paule Marshall has said that she wanted this story to tell more than just the story of a grandmother and granddaughter. She also wanted it to be about the "relationship of Western civilization and the Third World." Find examples from the story that explore the relationship of western civilization–represented by the United States, a highly developed and industrialized nation–and the Third World, represented by Barbados, which in the 1930s was still under British colonial rule. Do you think Marshall achieved the goal stated above? Compare your group's findings and opinions with those of other groups.

Internet Connection

Fun-in-the-Sun Brochure Work with a partner to create a tourist brochure about Barbados. Use the Internet to locate information about the sights, sounds, and tastes of this West Indian island. Create a brochure that lists key attractions, gives up-to-date travel information, and offers brief advice on what to do, where to eat, and where to stay. Illustrate your brochure, if you wish.

Interdisciplinary Activity

Music: Pop Songs from the Past Find sheet music or a recording of one of the songs the narrator sings in this story. Then look for an example of a Caribbean song–if possible, a song that was popular around the time of the story (the 1930s). Play a recording of each song, or sing it to the class. Discuss the similarities and differences between the two songs. Which one do you prefer? Explain your preference.

Reading Further

If you'd like to read more of Paule Marshall's writing, you might enjoy this short story:

"The Valley Between" from *Reena and Other Stories* tells about a young woman who juggles the roles of wife and mother while striving to reach her educational goals.

Save your work for your portfolio.

Skill Minilessons

GRAMMAR AND LANGUAGE • Concrete and Abstract Nouns

A **concrete noun,** such as the word *ship,* names an object that occupies space or that can be recognized by any of the senses. An **abstract noun,** such as the word *foolishness,* names an idea, a quality, or a characteristic. Notice how the narrator uses a string of concrete nouns as she tries to re-create her world for Da-duh: ". . . I told her about refrigerators, radios, gas stoves, elevators, trolley cars, wringer washing machines, movies, airplanes, the cyclone at Coney Island, subways, toasters, electric lights. . . ." In the same paragraph, she uses an abstract noun–*magic*–to help Da-duh understand how wonderful electric lights really are.

PRACTICE Find a passage in the story that includes both concrete and abstract nouns. Copy the passage and label each noun as *concrete* or *abstract.* Then explain how the use of both types of nouns helps the author convey her intended meaning.

APPLY Review your use of concrete and abstract nouns in a piece of your writing. Have you used both types of nouns effectively in order to convey your intended meaning? Make any necessary revisions to your work.

● For more about nouns, see **Language Handbook,** p. R40.

READING AND THINKING • Activating Prior Knowledge

Prior knowledge–what you already know from your own experience–often helps you better understand a piece of writing. For example, have you ever felt almost blinded by the reflection of bright sunlight on a body of water? If so, you understand what the narrator means when she says that she "was still somewhat blinded from the sheen of tropical sunlight on the water." Have you ever won an argument with someone but felt bad about it? This prior knowledge helps you understand how the narrator could feel "triumphant yet strangely saddened" after telling Da-duh about the Empire State Building.

PRACTICE On your paper, create a chart listing three story events or details and explain how your prior knowledge adds to your understanding of each one.

● For more about reading strategies, see **Reading Handbook,** p. R82.

VOCABULARY • Synonyms: Shades of Meaning

A thesaurus (a book of words and their synonyms) is a very useful tool for writers, but every thesaurus should begin with the warning, "Use with caution!" If you aren't completely sure what a listed synonym means and you plug it into your essay or report anyway, you may say something you didn't mean to say at all and may look quite foolish while doing so. Even if that doesn't happen, you may fail to communicate precisely what you mean.

Good speakers and good writers choose words carefully. When they want to emphasize the feeling of awe (perhaps tinged with some fear) that a particular person inspires, they might choose *formidable* to describe that person, not just *impressive,* even though *impressive* is a synonym for *formidable.*

PRACTICE Each word on the left is a vocabulary word from "To Da-duh, in Memoriam." Briefly explain how each word differs in meaning from the synonym that follows it.

1. *malicious* synonym: *unkind*
2. *decrepit* synonym: *weak*
3. *arrogant* synonym: *proud*
4. *hurtle* synonym: *hurry*

Writing Workshop

Expository Writing:
Critical Response

When you look at a full moon on a clear night, what do you see? A white circle with a few dark splotches on it? If you examine the moon carefully through a telescope, you'll see much more. A short story is much the same: the closer you look, the more you'll see—deeper meanings, additional ideas, details that show the author's craftsmanship, maybe even some flaws. Writing a critical response is a good way to closely inspect and evaluate a literary work. **Write a critical response to a short story, using this workshop as a guide.**

- As you write your critical response, refer to **Writing Handbook,** pp. R58–R71.

EVALUATION RUBRIC

By the time you complete this Writing Workshop, you will have

- identified the story to which you are responding and provided the title, the author's name, and a brief plot summary
- presented a thesis statement telling which element of the story you will critique and stating your evaluation of the author's handling of this element
- elaborated on your thesis using specific passages from the story
- developed a conclusion that restates the thesis
- presented an essay that is free of errors in grammar, usage, and mechanics

The Writing Process

PREWRITING

PREWRITING TIP

Choose a story that made a strong impression on you—even if it was a negative one. When you have definite opinions and strong feelings about something, it's usually easier to write about it.

Explore ideas

Skim the Table of Contents to recall the titles of all the short stories you've read in this unit. Choose a story that particularly impressed or intrigued you. As you reread the story, jot down notes on the elements that made the strongest impression on you.

- Is the plot clever? Believable? Suspenseful? Explain in your notes.
- How are the characters developed? Do they seem true to life? Why or why not?
- How does the author establish the story's setting?
- How does the setting contribute to the story's mood?
- How does the point of view affect your understanding of the plot or the characters?
- What is the theme of the story, and how is it conveyed? What is your reaction to the theme?

Consider your purpose and audience

Your purpose is to evaluate some element of a short story and to explain and support your evaluation. Who will read your critical response? Will other students read it, as well as your teacher? Will you submit it to a student literary journal or post it on the Internet? Identify your readers and keep their understanding of the subject in mind as you prepare your critical response.

Make a plan

Review your prewriting notes and circle the element of the story that most intrigues you. Develop a **thesis**—a one- or two-sentence statement that sums up your opinion on this element. Then plan your critical response using the basic essay structure of **introduction, body,** and **conclusion.** Write notes on how you will develop each section.

STUDENT MODEL

Introduction	Set the stage for your readers: What is the title of the story, who is the author, and what is the story about? On what element of the story are you focusing? What is your evaluation of this element? (Your evaluation is your **thesis statement.**)	Lullaby" by Leslie Marmon Silko. About Ayah, an aging Navajo woman who lives with her husband, Chato. Ayah, in a snowstorm with Chato, recalls memories from her life. Focus on similes and description. **Thesis statement:** Silko reflects Navajo culture in her story through unusual similes and through beautifully crafted descriptions.
Body	Elaborate on your thesis: Define or explain the element you're focusing on. How is this element developed in the story? Use passages from the story as examples. Evaluate the author's effectiveness in handling this element of the story.	**Simile:** A figure of speech that uses *like* or *as* to compare two things. Silko uses a simile to compare the snow and weaving and to show how Ayah sees the world symbolically through her culture's traditions. The author also uses descriptive details about the natural world to give insights into Ayah's life. The use of similes and description emphasizes Ayah's connection to nature, family, and tradition and shows how these elements affect her.
Conclusion	Restate your thesis and leave the reader with a final thought or two.	Through the use of similes and description, Silko shows that Ayah has a strong sense of connection to her culture, and through this connection, Ayah finds peace.

Complete Student Model on p. R113.

DRAFTING

Drafting Tip

If you get stuck while drafting, turn to the story and copy a passage that you want to use as an example. Explain how this passage illustrates the element of the story you're focusing on.

Begin at the beginning

In your introductory paragraph, briefly tell what the story is about. Identify the element of the story that will be your focus. End with your thesis statement.

Write your draft

Refer to your plan as you write. Don't worry too much about form. Just get your ideas down.

STUDENT MODEL

Leslie Marmon Silko's short story, "Lullaby," takes place in the wintertime New Mexico. In this story, the main character, Ayah, recalls her life and her happy and painful memories. She remembers her own childhood, her children and how she lost three of them, and the difficulties that her husband, Chato, experienced while working for white ranchers. The story shows aspects of Navajo culture—a deep connection to nature, strong family ties, and reliance on tradition—and shows how these elements affect Ayah. Silko reflects Navajo culture in her story through unusual similes and through beautifully crafted descriptions.

Complete Student Model on p. R113.

REVISING

Revising Tip

As you revise, cross out phrases like "I think that," "It seems to me that," or "It appears to be true that." Just go ahead and state your opinions.

Take another look

Set your work aside for a few hours or days so you can look at your essay with a fresh eye.

Read your work aloud

Invite a friend to listen as you read your critical response aloud. Ask for feedback, using the **Rubric for Revising**.

STUDENT MODEL

~~I think that~~ the [vivid] details that Silko uses to describe [Ayah's] memories reflect ~~the~~ [Ayah's] connection to nature and tradition. ~~For instance, Ayah has many memories.~~ Ayah remembers the ["high buckskin"] leggings that they wrapped over their [elkhide] moccasins when she was young ~~for one thing~~. She recalls how she walked ~~when she was with~~ ["a step behind"] her mother [when Ayah was] about to give birth.

Complete Student Model on p. R113.

Rubric for Revising

Your revised critical response should have

- ☑ an introduction that gives the title, author's name, and a summary of the story
- ☑ a strong thesis statement that focuses on the story element being critiqued and on the author's handling of it
- ☑ details and passages from the story to support your main points
- ☑ a conclusion that restates your thesis and leaves readers with a final thought

Your revised critical response should be free of

- ☑ any words or passages that do not support your thesis and main points
- ☑ errors in grammar, usage, and mechanics

EDITING/PROOFREADING

Once you're satisfied with the content of your critical response, edit and proofread it to correct errors in grammar, usage, mechanics, and spelling. Use the **Proofreading Checklist** on the inside back cover of this book as a guide. When necessary, consult a dictionary and the Language Handbook.

PROOFREADING TIP

What types of mistakes do you make most often in your writing? Keep this "hit list" in mind as you proofread your critical response.

Grammar Hint

A verb must agree with its subject. Be careful not to mistake words in a prepositional phrase for the subject of a sentence. The subject of the following is *memories;* it takes a plural verb.

Ayha's memories of her eldest son, Jimmie, make her feel both comforted and sad.

- For more about subject-verb agreement, see **Language Handbook,** p. R17.

STUDENT MODEL

Details about the natural world gives insights into Ayah's life. For example the yarn for weaving is dyed in, "boiling black pots full of beesweed petals, juniper berries, and sage." This detail is followed by a beautiful haunting simile. "The blankets . . . were soft and woven so tight that rain rolled off them like birds' feathers."

Complete Student Model on p. R113.

Complete Student Model

For a complete version of the model developed in this workshop, see **Writing Workshop Models**, p. R113.

PUBLISHING/PRESENTING

If you're submitting your critical response to a student literary journal, make sure you have met all the journal's requirements. If your classmates are your audience, you might distribute copies of your essay or post one copy on a bulletin board in your classroom.

PRESENTING TIP

Are you planning to read your critical response aloud in class? If so, you might want to begin with a dramatic reading of an excerpt from the story.

Reflecting

How did writing this critical response affect your appreciation of the short story you chose? Jot down your response in your journal. Then evaluate your own writing.

Save your work for your portfolio.

Unit Assessment

Personal Response

1. Which of the stories in this unit would you recommend to a friend? Explain your reasons.
2. How did your work in this unit enhance your skills in these areas?
   - reading for enjoyment and enrichment
   - discussing short stories in ways that lead to a deeper understanding of their meanings
   - understanding various literary techniques
   - working cooperatively with your classmates

Analyzing Literature

Comparing Two Elements Choose two stories from this unit and compare them, using the short story elements you have studied. (See the Genre Focus on short stories on pages 2 and 3.) Avoid choosing elements of stories that were already compared in the unit. You might, for example, choose to compare and contrast the character traits of Eckels in "A Sound of Thunder" and Prince Prospero in "The Masque of the Red Death," explaining how the traits of these two characters influence the final outcome of their stories.

Evaluate and Set Goals

Evaluate

1. What was your most valuable contribution to the class as you worked through this unit?
2. What assigned task in this unit did you find most challenging?
   - How did you approach this task?
   - What was the outcome?
3. How would you assess your work in this unit, using the following scale? Give at least two reasons for your assessment.
   4 = outstanding **3** = good **2** = fair **1** = weak

Set Goals

1. Choose a goal to work toward in Unit 2. Concentrate on any skill you wish to improve, such as reading, writing, speaking, or working in a group.
2. Discuss your goal with your teacher.
3. Write down three steps you will take to help you achieve your goal.
4. Plan checkpoints at specific intervals in the unit to assess your progress toward your goal.
5. Include a self-evaluation plan to determine whether you have reached your goal.

Build Your Portfolio

Select Choose two pieces of writing you did in this unit and include them in your portfolio. Use these questions to help you make your selection.

- Which pieces represent your best work?
- Which challenged you the most?
- Which pieces expanded your mind in unexpected ways?
- Which gave you the greatest sense of accomplishment?

Reflect Write some notes to accompany the pieces you selected. Use these questions to guide you.

- What do you like best about the piece?
- How did you grow as a writer because of the work you did on it?
- How else might you have approached this piece?

Reading on Your Own

You might also be interested in the following books.

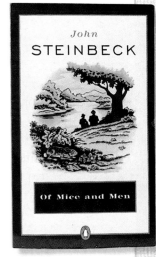

Fahrenheit 451
by Ray Bradbury Can you envision a future in which all books are not only banned, but burned? Firefighter Guy Montag goes about his job of burning books until he encounters a young woman who introduces him to the adventure that books can offer. Guy makes a decision that sets him on the adventure of his life.

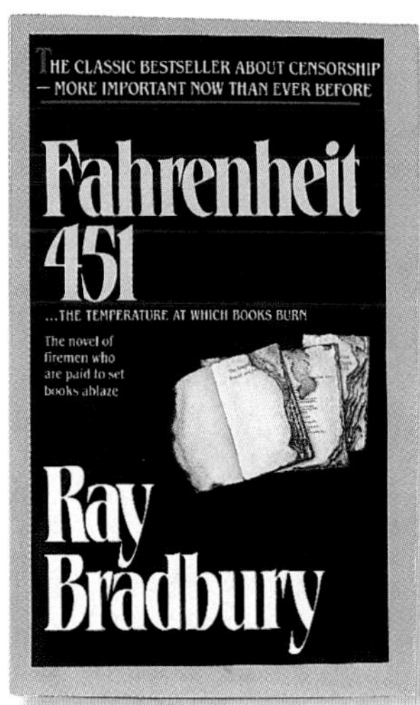

Of Mice and Men
by John Steinbeck Their dreams of someday owning a small farm are all that sustain ranch hands George and Lennie as they go from one difficult job and disheartening experience to the next. When Lennie inadvertently causes a tragedy, George must make a painful decision about how best to help his friend.

My Ántonia
by Willa Cather The courage, joys, and suffering of immigrant farmers who settled the Nebraska frontier are realistically portrayed in this classic novel. Narrator Jim Burden remembers his innocent childhood on the prairie and recounts the triumphs of his strong and capable lifelong friend Antonia.

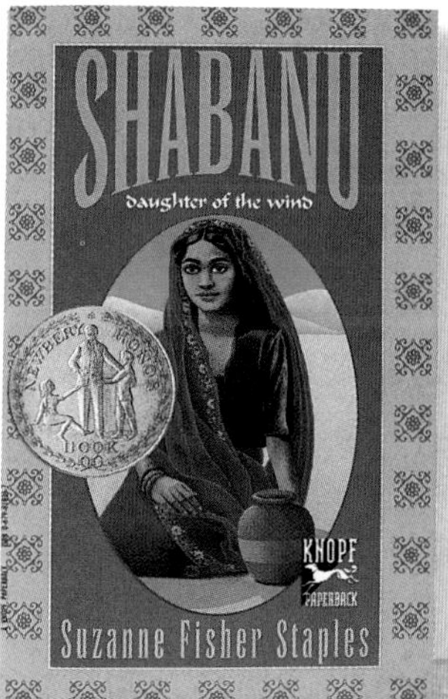

Shabanu, Daughter of the Wind
by Suzanne Fisher Staples Shabanu is a Pakistani girl with a fierce sense of self. She loves her family and their life as camel herders in the desert, but her world is shattered when her parents arrange for her to marry a wealthy, older man. Shabanu is torn between accepting the marriage or suffering the consequences of going against tradition.

Reading and Analyzing Test Questions

Read the following passage. Then read each question on page 419. Decide which is the best answer to each question. Mark the letter for that answer on your paper.

Across the Water

Brian had been boating with his grandfather since he was five years old, and he had quickly graduated from a novice to a proficient sailor. At eighteen, he was well prepared for the sojourn he had planned, and he waited anxiously for the day when he could realize his dream: to sail from Harrisville, Michigan, to Port Elgin, Canada. It would be the first long trip he would take alone. Pop had prepared him well for this challenge. The most difficult part would be telling Pop that the time had come.

At dinner that evening, Brian and Pop sat facing each other as they did every evening. Pop noticed that Brian was unusually quiet.

"What's on your mind, Bri?"

Pop knew Brian well. Usually talkative, Brian had been almost silent. He tried to think up a reply that sounded believable, but he knew in his heart he could never lie to Pop.

"Well, Pop, I've been thinking. Thinking about taking the boat out by myself for a trip."

"Oh, is that all? From the look on your face it seemed to be more serious than that. You've been out alone many times. Go on."

"Well, it's more than just any kind of trip. I want to go from Harrisville and sail to Port Elgin, Canada."

The room was silent. Pop was not prepared for this request. Although he knew Brian was an excellent sailor, he was not certain that his grandson could handle the challenges that Lake Huron might offer. He weighed his words carefully because he didn't want to discourage Brian. Pop had always prided himself on being supportive and encouraging of his grandson.

"Here's what I think, Bri. I want you to go, but I would like to go with you. Don't get me wrong—I am very confident in your abilities. However, I would feel better if I could go with you and be your first mate."

Brian's face fell, and he stared at the kitchen floor. He didn't quite know what to say in response. Finally, he offered, "Pop, you know how much I've learned from you and how I appreciate all you've taught me. But I really feel that I should do this on my own. Please let me go alone."

Brian didn't ask for much, so Pop knew how important this was to him. Brian needed to prove he could be self-reliant. Pop decided to let Brian go.

Over the next week, Brian gathered all the supplies that he would need and prepared the boat. Before Pop could change his mind, Brian was ready to leave.

On the morning he was to set sail, Brian was up and ready before the sun rose. Pop saw him off with a thermos full of hot coffee. He gave Brian a firm hug and wished him luck.

"Now, you just do as you've been taught and you'll be just fine. Good luck to you. You learned from the best." Pop gave Brian a wink, and Brian was off to pursue his dream. He had no idea what he would encounter, but he knew he had Pop's lessons and love to support him.

1 At the end of the passage, we can tell that Brian —

A is afraid he might have to turn around and come home

B plans to do everything he can to sail across Lake Huron to Canada

C has too much confidence in his ability to sail

D wishes his grandfather was coming with him

2 Pop's thoughts as Brian asks for permission to sail by himself indicate that Pop is —

F torn between his desire to let Brian go and his fear of what may happen

G curious about why Brian would want to go that far

H getting too old to want to make the trip himself

J concerned about the condition of the boat

3 The main idea of this passage is that —

A people need to be given opportunities to prove themselves

B it is important to be well prepared for a big trip

C children always want to attempt more than they can accomplish

D attempts to cross Lake Huron can be challenging

4 Which is an OPINION held by Pop and Brian about crossing Lake Huron alone?

F Pop will probably follow Brian for safety reasons.

G Brian isn't strong enough to make the trip alone.

H The best way to succeed on the trip is to fish for your food.

J Making the trip alone is potentially dangerous for many reasons.

5 The author sees the request to sail alone as evidence of Brian's —

A developing independence from Pop

B disregard for Pop's feelings of love and support

C dangerous quest for glory and recognition

D love of the water

6 The word proficient in this passage means —

F capable and skilled

G gruff and old

H new and unskilled

J tentative and sensitive

STOP

DAILY NEW
NUCLEAR
ARMS
BUILDUP
DAILY NEWS
Isles breeze, 5-0
lead Rangers, 3-0

UNIT TWO

Nonfiction

"When you write, you lay out a line of words. The line of words is a miner's pick, a woodcarver's gouge, a surgeon's probe. You wield it, and it digs a path you follow."

—Annie Dillard

Daily News, 1983. Dona Nelson. 84 x 60 in. Metropolitan Museum of Art, New York. Museum purchase, Emman P. Ziprik Memorial Fund Gift, in memory of Fred and Emma P. Ziprik, 1984.

Genre Focus

Nonfiction

Nonfiction—writing about real people, events, and ideas—is the broadest category of literature. Under this huge umbrella come autobiographies, biographies, memoirs, diaries, letters, essays, speeches, travelogues, news articles, and many more types of writing. Like works of fiction, all these types of writing can be inventive and creative, even though they deal with real, rather than imaginary, subjects.

Narrative Nonfiction

Some works of nonfiction tell a story, just as works of fiction do. Autobiographies, memoirs, biographies, and narrative essays are types of narrative nonfiction.

- An **autobiography** presents the story of a person's life written by that person. Most autobiographies are told from the first-person point of view, using the pronoun *I*. Writers of autobiographies typically focus on themselves and events in their own lives.
- A **memoir** is also a first-person account of events in the author's life. Memoirs, however, tend to emphasize subjects outside the writer's personal life, such as significant historical events the writer has been a part of or has witnessed, or other people the writer has known.
- A **biography** is an account of a person's life written by someone else. It is presented from the third-person point of view.
- A **narrative essay** is a short composition that relates a true story from either the first- or the third-person point of view.

Because they tell stories, autobiographies, memoirs, biographies, and narrative essays share many characteristics of fiction. Like fictional stories, they may include such elements as setting, characters, theme, plot, and conflict. They also are organized like fictional stories. A writer might choose to present events in **chronological order,** or the order in which they occurred. Or the writer might use a **flashback,** going back in time to present incidents that happened before the beginning of the story.

Informative Nonfiction

While narrative nonfiction tells a story, informative nonfiction explains a topic or promotes an opinion. Examples of informative nonfiction include essays, speeches, letters, and news articles. The differences between narrative and informative nonfiction are not always clear, however, because writers of informative works sometimes weave stories into their writing, and writers of narratives sometimes explain topics and promote opinions.

Essays are one of the most common types of literary nonfiction. An essay is a short piece of writing devoted to a single topic. Two main kinds of informative essays are expository and persuasive.

- **Expository essays** offer information about a topic, from explaining how a process works, to analyzing or commenting on a political or historical event, to reviewing a theatrical production.
- **Persuasive essays** promote an opinion or position. Commonly, persuasive essays describe a situation and then offer reasons that the reader should believe or act in a certain way regarding the issue.

Many expository and persuasive essays follow a general structure of lead, body, and conclusion. This diagram shows the structure of a typical informative essay.

- The **lead,** or introduction, serves to pique the reader's interest. It also often includes the **thesis,** or main idea, of the essay. Sometimes, though, a writer saves the thesis statement for the end of the work.
- The **body** develops or attempts to prove the thesis with **supporting details,** such as facts, reasons, statistics, sensory details, examples, observations, and personal experiences. This part of the work might also include quotations from expert sources and graphics, such as diagrams, graphs, and illustrations.
- The **conclusion** typically restates the thesis and provides the reader with a final or summarizing thought. It might also call on readers to accept a new idea or to take a specific action.

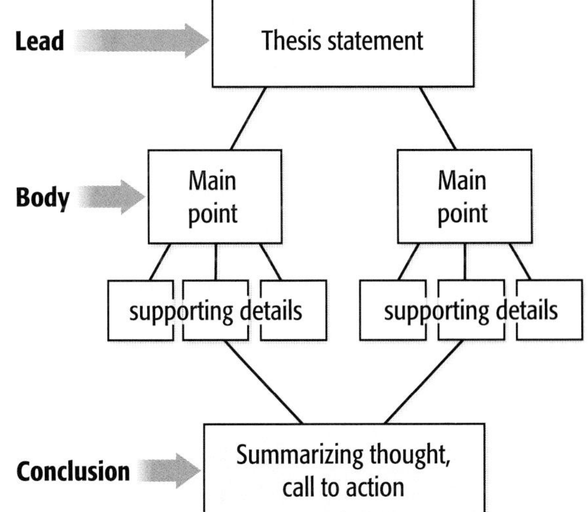

Analyzing Nonfiction

The first step in analyzing nonfiction is to identify the type of work you are reading. By looking at the title and skimming the first few paragraphs, you can usually tell whether the work is an autobiography or a memoir, a biography, an essay, or another type of nonfiction.

As you read, you might further classify the type of work by identifying the **author's purpose,** or reason for writing. Ask yourself what the writer is trying to achieve. Is the writer's purpose to entertain, to inform, or to persuade the reader? The answer to that question will help you classify the work you are reading.

Once you know the type of work you are reading, you will know what to look for, such as elements of fiction, a thesis and supporting details, or persuasive techniques. Be aware, however, that writers may combine various elements, and purposes, in a single work. For example, you might read a persuasive essay that is not only entertaining but also tells a story. Perhaps the best approach is to think of each work of nonfiction as a unique combination of familiar elements.

Active Reading Strategies

Nonfiction

To get the most from reading nonfiction, active readers use strategies similar to those used in reading short stories. As an active reader, however, you will need to adapt the strategies to the particular type of nonfiction you are reading.

● For more about related reading strategies, see **Reading Handbook,** pp. R78–R107.

PREDICT Make educated guesses about what you are reading. Preview the work by looking at the title, skimming the text, and examining photographs, illustrations, charts, and other graphics. Make predictions before beginning to read and also as you read.

Ask yourself . . .
- What will this work be about?
- What might the writer's main idea about this topic be?
- What supporting evidence might the writer use?
- What point will the writer make next?

CONNECT Make connections with what you already know and with your own life.

Ask yourself . . .
- What people, events, and experiences in my own life are similar to those written about here?
- What have I heard or read about the subject?
- How does this subject relate to other subjects I know about?

QUESTION Question anything you do not understand. Reread any part that confuses you, and then read on to see if your questions are answered.

Ask yourself . . .
- What is the writer really saying here?
- Why is the writer giving me these facts?
- What does this concept have to do with what I just read?

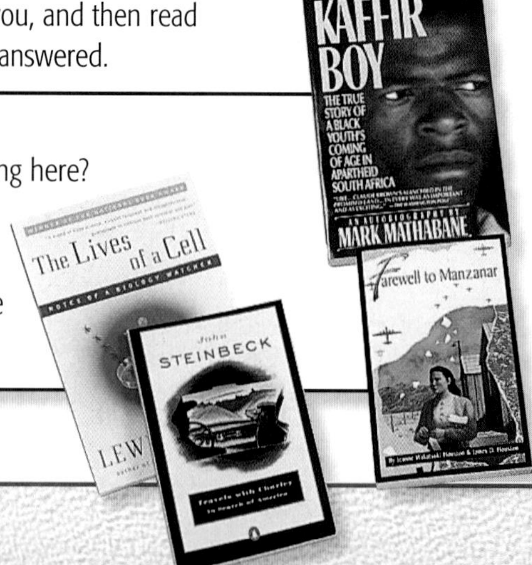

VISUALIZE Use details the writer gives you to form mental pictures of people, places, and objects, and to see the steps in a process or how something works.

Ask yourself . . .

- What does this person look like?
- How does this scene or object look?
- Where does this part fit with the others?
- How does this step relate to the next one? the one before?

EVALUATE Make judgments about what you read.

Ask yourself . . .

- Is this statement a fact or an opinion?
- Does this information really support the thesis?
- Do I agree with the writer's opinions and interpretations?
- What does this action reveal about this person?

REVIEW Pause often to think about what you have read.

Say to yourself . . .

- The main idea is . . .
- Details supporting this thesis include . . .
- The steps in this process are . . .
- The writer's purpose is to . . .

RESPOND React to what you are reading. Identify and consider your spontaneous thoughts about what the writer is saying. Decide what you like or dislike about the work.

Say to yourself . . .

- I'd like to ask the writer why . . .
- I think this thesis is . . .
- That's pretty interesting. I'd like to know more about . . .
- Who else might benefit from learning this information?

Applying the Strategies

Read the next selection from *Travels with Charley* by John Steinbeck using the Active Reading Model in the margins. Then practice the strategies as you read another work of nonfiction.

Before You Read

from *Travels with Charley*

Reading Focus

When you make important decisions, does your intellect sometimes tell you to do one thing while your emotions urge you to do something different?

Journal Write about a time when your head told you to do one thing, and your heart told you to do the opposite.

Setting a Purpose Read to learn how the author resolved a conflict between his head and his heart.

Building Background

The Time and Place

In the early 1960s, author John Steinbeck traveled across the United States with his dog, Charley, in a truck outfitted as a camper. This selection recounts an encounter they had as they crossed the Mojave Desert in southeastern California.

Did You Know?

Coyotes are members of the wild dog family and are related to foxes, wolves, and jackals. Intelligent and extremely adaptable, they live almost everywhere in the United States, including deserts, farmland, and even cities and suburbs. Because many people consider them nuisances and blame them for killing farm animals, about 100,000 coyotes are hunted and killed each year. Recent studies, however, show that coyotes account for only a fraction of the deaths of domestic animals.

Vocabulary Preview

constancy (kon′ stən sē) *n.* the quality of being unchanging; faithfulness; loyalty; p. 427

loll (lol) *v.* to hang down loosely; droop; p. 427

temper (tem′ pər) *v.* to moderate by mingling with another thing; p. 427

vermin (vur′ min) *n.* any animals that are harmful, destructive, or troublesome; p. 428

token (tō′ kən) *adj.* symbolic; p. 428

Meet John Steinbeck

John Steinbeck is best known for his sympathetic portrayals of people living on the fringes of society: the poor, the socially outcast, the dispossessed. In *The Grapes of Wrath*, Steinbeck's most famous novel, the author chronicled the struggles of an Oklahoma farm family who lost their land during the Great Depression. Although much of Steinbeck's work is serious, even grim, the author also wrote a number of humorous works and often showed a sense of humor in dealing with critics' reactions to his work. Steinbeck was awarded the Nobel Prize for Literature in 1962.

John Steinbeck was born in 1902 in Salinas, California, and died in 1968. Travels with Charley *was published in 1962.*

from Travels with Charley

John Steinbeck

Active Reading Model

THE MOJAVE IS A BIG DESERT AND A FRIGHTENING ONE. It's as though nature tested a man for endurance and constancy to prove whether he was good enough to get to California. The shimmering dry heat made visions of water on the flat plain. And even when you drive at high speed, the hills that mark the boundaries recede before you. Charley, always a dog for water, panted asthmatically, jarring his whole body with the effort, and a good eight inches of his tongue hung out flat as a leaf and dripping. I pulled off the road into a small gulley to give him water from my thirty-gallon tank. But before I let him drink I poured water all over him and on my hair and shoulders and shirt. The air is so dry that evaporation makes you feel suddenly cold.

PREDICT

Based on the title and the first paragraph, what type of nonfiction is this?

I opened a can of beer from my refrigerator and sat well inside the shade of Rocinante,[1] looking out at the sunpounded plain, dotted here and there with clumps of sagebrush.

About fifty yards away two coyotes stood watching me, their tawny coats blending with sand and sun. I knew that with any quick or suspicious movement of mine they could drift into invisibility. With the most casual slowness I reached down my new rifle from its sling over my bed—the .222 with its bitter little high-speed, long-range stings. Very slowly I brought the rifle up. Perhaps in the shade of my house I was half hidden by the blinding light outside. The little rifle has a beautiful telescope sight with a wide field. The coyotes had not moved.

QUESTION

Why is Steinbeck getting his rifle?

I got both of them in the field of my telescope, and the glass brought them very close. Their tongues lolled out so that they seemed to smile mockingly. They were favored animals, not starved, but well furred, the golden hair tempered with black guard hairs.[2] Their little lemon-yellow eyes were plainly visible in the glass. I moved the cross hairs to the breast of the right-hand animal, and pushed the safety. My elbows on the table steadied the gun. The cross hairs lay unmoving on

VISUALIZE

Picture the view of the two coyotes through the telescope sight.

1. Steinbeck named his truck *Rocinante* (rō′ sə nän′ tā) in honor of the broken-down old horse that carries a broken-down old knight into his romantic and crazy adventures in *Don Quixote,* a novel by Miguel de Cervantes.
2. A coyote's *guard hairs* are the long, coarse outer hairs that protect its soft undercoat.

Vocabulary

constancy (kon′ stən sē) *n.* the quality of being unchanging; faithfulness; loyalty
loll (lol) *v.* to hang down loosely; droop
temper (tem′ pər) *v.* to moderate by mingling with another thing

Active Reading Model

the brisket.[3] And then the coyote sat down like a dog and its right rear paw came up to scratch the right shoulder.

My finger was reluctant to touch the trigger. I must be getting very old and my ancient conditioning worn thin. Coyotes are vermin. They steal chickens. They thin the ranks of quail and all other game birds. They must be killed. They are the enemy. My first shot would drop the sitting beast, and the other would whirl to fade away. I might very well pull him down with a running shot because I am a good rifleman.

CONNECT

How would you react in this situation?

And I did not fire. My training said, "Shoot!" and my age replied, "There isn't a chicken within thirty miles, and if there are any they aren't my chickens. And this waterless place is not quail country. No, these boys are keeping their figures with kangaroo rats and jackrabbits, and that's vermin eat vermin. Why should I interfere?"

"Kill them," my training said. "Everyone kills them. It's a public service." My finger moved to the trigger. The cross was steady on the breast just below the panting tongue. I could imagine the splash and jar of angry steel, the leap and struggle until the torn heart failed, and then, not too long later, the shadow of a buzzard, and another. By that time I would be long gone—out of the desert and across the Colorado River. And beside the sagebush there would be a naked, eyeless skull, a few picked bones, a spot of black dried blood and a few rags of golden fur.

RESPOND

Do you like Steinbeck's character as it is portrayed here?

I guess I'm too old and too lazy to be a good citizen. The second coyote stood sidewise to my rifle. I moved the cross hairs to his shoulder and held steady. There was no question of missing with that rifle at that range. I owned both animals. Their lives were mine. I put the safety on and laid the rifle on the table. Without the telescope they were not so intimately close. The hot blast of light tousled the air to shimmering.

EVALUATE

Do you think Steinbeck made the right decision? Why or why not?

Then I remembered something I heard long ago that I hope is true. It was unwritten law in China, so my informant told me, that when one man saved another's life he became responsible for that life to the end of its existence. For, having interfered with a course of events, the savior could not escape his responsibility. And that has always made good sense to me.

REVIEW

What is Steinbeck's purpose and thesis?

Now I had a token responsibility for two live and healthy coyotes. In the delicate world of relationships, we are tied together for all time. I opened two cans of dog food and left them as a votive.[4]

3. The coyote's *brisket* is its chest or breast.
4. In this context, *votive* means "an offering."

Vocabulary

vermin (vur′ min) *n.* any animals that are harmful, destructive, or troublesome
token (tō′ kən) *adj.* symbolic

Responding to Literature

Personal Response

Did the outcome of this selection surprise you? Why or why not?

Active Reading Response

Review the Active Reading Strategies described on pages 424–425. Which of these strategies did you use when reading this selection? Which other strategies might you apply to it? Give two specific examples.

Analyzing Literature

Recall

1. Summarize Steinbeck's description of the Mojave in the first two paragraphs.
2. Describe the appearance and actions of the coyotes.
3. Summarize the thoughts that go through Steinbeck's mind as he watches the coyotes.
4. What "unwritten law" does Steinbeck remember?
5. What does Steinbeck do at the end of the selection?

Interpret

6. What might you infer about Steinbeck's attitude toward the Mojave from the way he describes it in the first two paragraphs?
7. How might the coyotes' appearance and actions influence Steinbeck's behavior? Explain.
8. What do Steinbeck's thoughts and actions seem to suggest about his character? Support your answer with evidence from the selection.
9. Why do you think Steinbeck feels that the "unwritten law" applies to him?
10. Do you think this experience has changed Steinbeck in any way? Use evidence from the selection to support your answer.

Evaluate and Connect

11. Do you think owning pets makes people more responsive to animals in the wild? Give reasons for your answer.
12. Review your response to the Reading Focus on page 426. Compare and contrast your experience with the one Steinbeck describes.
13. Steinbeck says, "I guess I'm too old and too lazy to be a good citizen." Is being old and lazy the real reason he acts as he does? Explain.
14. Identify at least two **sensory details** (see page R11) from the selection. Explain how each one helps you understand what is being described.
15. According to Steinbeck, "In the delicate world of relationships, we are tied together for all time." Do you agree? Why or why not?

Conflict

Conflict is a struggle between two opposing forces. An **external conflict** exists when a character struggles against an outside force, such as another person, nature, or society. In this excerpt from *Travels with Charley,* Steinbeck's dog "panted asthmatically, jarring his whole body with the effort," as he struggles against the searing heat of the desert. Steinbeck also suffers from the intense heat of the "sun-pounded plain." In addition, he faces an **internal conflict**–a struggle that takes place within the mind of a character. Usually, the character is torn between two opposing feelings or courses of action. In this selection, Steinbeck wrestles with a decision he has to make about the coyotes.

1. What external conflicts do the coyotes face in their daily lives in the desert? What new conflict might develop for them when Steinbeck stops his truck?
2. What internal conflict does Steinbeck face in this selection? How does he resolve this conflict? What details make the outcome uncertain?

- See **Literary Terms Handbook,** p. R3.

Literature and Writing

Writing About Literature

Explore Double Meanings When Steinbeck is looking at the coyotes through his telescope sight, he says, "I owned both animals. Their lives were mine." This statement has two different meanings: one in the context of the paragraph in which it appears, and another in the context of the two paragraphs that follow. In two or three paragraphs, analyze the two meanings of the statement. Share your analysis with a classmate.

Creative Writing

It's a Dog's Life Try to imagine how Charley might have viewed the encounter described in the selection. What thoughts might have gone through his mind as he watched his master aiming the rifle at the coyotes or opening the cans of dog food and leaving them in the desert? Imagine that after Charley returns home, he tells the dog next door about this incident. Write a brief humorous monologue giving Charley's view of the encounter.

Extending Your Response

Literature Groups

What If? Steinbeck finds the coyotes in a desert, where "There isn't a chicken within thirty miles. . . . And this waterless place is not quail country." What if he had found the coyotes in a farming area or in a place where quail do live? Would he have made the same decision? Debate this question in your group. Use evidence from the story to support your opinion. Share your ideas with the class.

Interdisciplinary Activity

Biology: Desert Animals Steinbeck mentions four animals that live in the Mojave Desert: the coyote, kangaroo rat, jackrabbit, and buzzard. Generate research questions about how these and other animals survive in an inhospitable environment. Then, research the answers and create a poster summarizing your conclusions from information gathered.

Listening and Speaking

Where Do You Stand? Consider whether humans ever have the right to control animal populations. If so, under what circumstances should this right be exercised? Decide where you stand on this issue. Then research and write a speech aimed at persuading your classmates to accept your point of view. Practice your speech with a friend or family member. Then present your speech to the class.

Reading Further

You may enjoy these other works by John Steinbeck:

Novel: *The Pearl,* about a fisherman who finds a valuable pearl but discovers that it does not bring him happiness.

Short Story: "The Red Pony," a coming-of-age story about a boy living on a California ranch.

Save your work for your portfolio.

VOCABULARY • Multiple-Meaning Words

Most words have more than one meaning. *Temper* is an example. When a coyote's golden coat is *tempered* with black, the basic color is moderated and made less intense. Steel, on the other hand, is *tempered* to make it harder and stronger. And when you lose your *temper,* you get angry.

PRACTICE For each pair, write two sentences, one with each meaning. Use a dictionary as needed.

1. a. a **tenor** voice   b. the **tenor** of the times
2. a. to build on a **lot**   b. her **lot** in life
3. a. to **pluck** a chicken   b. to demonstrate **pluck**

Theme 5 Remembering

Memories are one of the treasures of life. They help define who we are and who we might become. Memories link us to loved ones and help shape the way we look at our lives. Each author in this theme shares the memory of a unique experience that left an impression for a lifetime. How do your own memories enrich your understanding of the past and present?

THEME PROJECTS

Learning for Life

Journeys Unlimited Work with a partner to create a travel brochure for one of the places you "visit" in this theme.

1. Make a list of the settings in this theme. Choose one for your brochure.
2. Using the Internet, library resources, and materials from a travel agency, write and research a list of questions about the land, climate, people, customs, language, and foods of the place you have chosen.
3. With your partner, design and write a travel brochure that summarizes your findings and presents this place in an interesting way. Illustrate your brochure with photographs, maps, or drawings. Think of a captivating title for your brochure.

Interdisciplinary Project

Music: A Medley of Memories Create an audiotape of musical pieces that convey the subjects or moods of selections in this theme.

1. Investigate music from the various cultures represented in this theme. For three or four selections, choose music that fits the subject or mood of the selection.
2. Prepare a brief introduction that gives information about each piece. Tell which selection the music goes with and why you chose it.
3. Make an audiotape of the selections and introductions. Play the tape for your classmates, and discuss their reactions.

Before You Read

A Child's Christmas in Wales

Reading Focus

What are your strongest holiday memories from your childhood?

Web It! Recall a holiday from your childhood. Try to remember what you saw, heard, smelled, tasted, and touched. Record your sensory memories in a web like this one.

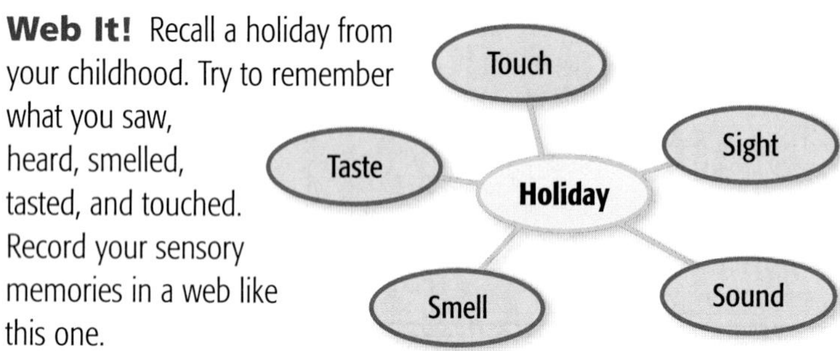

Setting a Purpose Read to share the author's childhood Christmas memories.

Building Background

The Time and Place

The events described in this selection take place in Swansea, Wales, in the early 1900s.

Did You Know?

Although Wales has been part of Great Britain for four hundred years, the Welsh have maintained their own traditions, literature, and language. The people of Wales primarily speak English, although about one-fifth of them speak Welsh, an ancient Celtic language. The Welsh people have always loved poetry and music, and each year they hold a national singing and poetry competition, the Royal National Eisteddfod. This celebration dates back to the 1700s.

Vocabulary Preview

daft (daft) *adj.* without sense or reason; crazy; silly; p. 435
judiciously (jo͞o dish′ əs lē) *adv.* in a way that shows good judgment; sensibly; p. 437
hale (hāl) *adj.* in good physical condition; healthy; p. 437
stridently (strīd′ ənt lē) *adv.* in a loud, harsh manner; shrilly; p. 437
loom (lo͞om) *v.* to appear to the mind as large; to stand out prominently; p. 438
lurk (lurk) *v.* to stay hidden, ready to attack; p. 438

Meet Dylan Thomas

From the time he first listened to childhood nursery rhymes, Dylan Thomas loved language. "What the words stood for, symbolized, or meant was of very secondary importance," he said. "What mattered was the *sound* of them." Thomas published his first poem when he was seventeen and his first volume of poetry, *18 Poems*, when he was twenty. He achieved fame not only for his poetry and other writing but also for his personal charm and passionate poetry readings. Thomas made three poetry-reading tours of the United States; he died in New York during the last tour, at the age of thirty-nine.

Dylan Thomas was born in 1914 and died in 1953. "A Child's Christmas in Wales" was first published in 1955.

A Child's Christmas in Wales

Dylan Thomas

Winter in Wales, c. 1954. Fred Uhlman. Oil on canvas, 46 x 61 cm. Private collection.

One Christmas was so much like another, in those years around the sea-town corner[1] now and out of all sound except the distant speaking of the voices I sometimes hear a moment before sleep, that I can never remember whether it snowed for six days and six nights when I was twelve or whether it snowed for twelve days and twelve nights when I was six.

All the Christmases roll down toward the two-tongued sea, like a cold and headlong moon bundling down the sky that was our street; and they stop at the rim of the ice-edged, fish-freezing waves, and I plunge my hands in the snow and bring out whatever I can find. In goes my hand into that wool-white bell-tongued ball of holidays resting at the rim of the carol-singing sea, and out come Mrs. Prothero and the firemen.

It was on the afternoon of the day of Christmas Eve, and I was in Mrs. Prothero's

1. The expression *around the sea-town corner* means "out of sight" or "long gone."

Snowballing, c. 1917. Dame Laura Knight. Watercolor heightened with bodycolor over pencil, 52 x 75 cm. Private collection.

Viewing the painting: What similarities do you find between the scene in this painting and the winter memories that Thomas describes?

garden, waiting for cats, with her son Jim. It was snowing. It was always snowing at Christmas. December, in my memory, is white as Lapland, though there were no reindeers. But there were cats. Patient, cold, and callous, our hands wrapped in socks, we waited to snowball the cats. Sleek and long as jaguars and horrible-whiskered, spitting and snarling, they would slink and sidle over the white back-garden walls, and the lynx-eyed[2] hunters, Jim and I, fur-capped and moccasined trappers from Hudson Bay, off Mumbles Road, would hurl our deadly snowballs at the green of their eyes.

The wise cats never appeared. We were so still, Eskimo-footed arctic marksmen in the muffling silence of the eternal snows—eternal, ever since Wednesday—that we never heard Mrs. Prothero's first cry from her igloo at the bottom of the garden. Or, if we heard it at all, it was, to us, like the far-off challenge of our enemy and prey, the neighbour's polar cat. But soon the voice grew louder. "Fire!" cried Mrs. Prothero, and she beat the dinner-gong.

And we ran down the garden, with the snowballs in our arms, toward the house; and smoke, indeed, was pouring out of the dining-room, and the gong was bombilating, and Mrs. Prothero was announcing ruin like a town crier in Pompeii.[3] This was better than all the cats in Wales standing on the wall in a row. We bounded into the house, laden with snowballs, and stopped at the open door of the smoke-filled room.

Something was burning all right; perhaps it was Mr. Prothero, who always slept there after midday dinner with a newspaper over his face. But he was standing in the middle of the room, saying, "A fine Christmas!" and smacking at the smoke with a slipper. "Call the fire brigade," cried Mrs. Prothero as she beat the gong.

"They won't be there," said Mr. Prothero, "it's Christmas."

There was no fire to be seen, only clouds of smoke and Mr. Prothero standing in the middle of them, waving his slipper as though he were conducting.

"Do something," he said.

And we threw all our snowballs into the smoke—I think we missed Mr. Prothero—and ran out of the house to the telephone box.

"Let's call the police as well," Jim said.

"And the ambulance."

2. The *lynx-eyed* hunters have sharp vision like the lynx, a wildcat of Europe and Asia.

3. *Pompeii* (pom pā′) was a Roman city destroyed and buried by a volcanic eruption in A.D. 79.

"And Ernie Jenkins, he likes fires."

But we only called the fire brigade, and soon the fire engine came and three tall men in helmets brought a hose into the house and Mr. Prothero got out just in time before they turned it on. Nobody could have had a noisier Christmas Eve. And when the firemen turned off the hose and were standing in the wet, smoky room, Jim's aunt, Miss Prothero, came downstairs and peered in at them. Jim and I waited, very quietly, to hear what she would say to them. She said the right thing, always. She looked at the three tall firemen in their shining helmets, standing among the smoke and cinders and dissolving snowballs, and she said: "Would you like anything to read?"

Years and years and years ago, when I was a boy, when there were wolves in Wales, and birds the color of red-flannel petticoats whisked past the harp-shaped hills, when we sang and wallowed all night and day in caves that smelt like Sunday afternoons in damp front farmhouse parlors, and we chased, with the jawbones of deacons, the English and the bears, before the motor-car, before the wheel, before the duchess-faced horse, when we rode the daft and happy hills bareback, it snowed and it snowed. But here a small boy says: "It snowed last year, too. I made a snowman and my brother knocked it down and I knocked my brother down and then we had tea."

"But that was not the same snow," I say. "Our snow was not only shaken from whitewash buckets down the sky, it came shawling[4] out of the ground and swam and drifted out of the arms and hands and bodies of the trees; snow grew overnight on the roofs of the houses like a pure and grandfather moss, minutely white-ivied the walls and settled on the postman, opening the gate, like a dumb, numb thunderstorm of white, torn Christmas cards."

"Were there postmen then, too?"

"With sprinkling eyes and wind-cherried noses, on spread, frozen feet they crunched up to the doors and mittened on them manfully. But all that the children could hear was a ringing of bells."

"You mean that the postman went rat-a-tat-tat and the doors rang?"

"I mean that the bells that the children could hear were inside them."

"I only hear thunder sometimes, never bells."

"There were church bells, too."

"Inside them?"

"No, no, no, in the bat-black, snow-white belfries, tugged by bishops and storks. And they rang their tidings over the bandaged town, over the frozen foam of the powder and ice-cream hills, over the crackling sea. It seemed that all the churches boomed for joy under my window; and the weathercocks crew for Christmas, on our fence."

"Get back to the postmen."

"They were just ordinary postmen, fond of walking and dogs and Christmas and the snow. They knocked on the doors with blue knuckles. . . ."

"Ours has got a black knocker. . . ."

"And then they stood on the white Welcome mat in the little, drifted porches and huffed and puffed, making ghosts with their breath, and jogged from foot to foot like small boys wanting to go out."

"And then the Presents?"

"And then the Presents, after the Christmas box.[5] And the cold postman, with a rose on his

4. Snow that is *shawling* is rising up like a shawl that is pulled up over the shoulders.

5. A *Christmas box* is a present for the postman.

Vocabulary

daft (daft) *adj.* without sense or reason; crazy; silly

Did You Know?
Sloths are shaggy-haired, tree-dwelling mammals native to the tropical forests of Central and South America. They have long limbs with long, curved claws.

button-nose, tingled down the tea-tray-slithered run of the chilly glinting hill. He went in his ice-bound boots like a man on fishmonger's slabs.[6] He wagged his bag like a frozen camel's hump, dizzily turned the corner on one foot, and, by God, he was gone."

"Get back to the Presents."

"There were the Useful Presents: engulfing mufflers of the old coach days, and mittens made for giant sloths; zebra scarfs of a substance like silky gum that could be tug-o'-warred down to the galoshes; blinding tam-o'-shanters like patchwork tea cosies and bunny-suited busbies and balaclavas[7] for victims of headshrinking tribes; from aunts who always wore wool next to the skin there were moustached and rasping vests that made you wonder why the aunts had any skin left at all; and once I had a little crocheted nose bag from an aunt now, alas, no longer whinnying with us. And pictureless books in which small boys, though warned with quotations not to, *would* skate on Farmer Giles' pond and did and drowned; and books that told me everything about the wasp, except why."

Did You Know?
A *tam-o'-shanter* is a round, flat hat that often has a pom-pom in the center.

"Go on to the Useless Presents."

"Bags of moist and many-coloured jelly babies and a folded flag and a false nose and a tram[8] conductor's cap and a machine that punched tickets and rang a bell; never a catapult; once, by mistake that no one could explain, a little hatchet; and a celluloid[9] duck that made, when you pressed it, a most unducklike sound, a mewing moo that an ambitious cat might make who wished to be a cow; and a painting book in which I could make the grass, the trees, the sea and the animals any color I pleased, and still the dazzling sky-blue sheep are grazing in the red field under the rainbow-billed and pea-green birds.

Hardboileds, toffee, fudge and allsorts, crunches, cracknels, humbugs, glaciers, marzipan, and butterwelsh for the Welsh. And troops of bright tin soldiers who, if they could not fight, could always run. And Snakes-and-Families and Happy Ladders. And Easy Hobbi-Games for Little Engineers, complete with instructions.

Oh, easy for Leonardo! And a whistle to make the dogs bark to wake up the old man next door to make him beat on the wall with his stick to shake our picture off the wall.

And a packet of cigarettes: you put one in your mouth and you stood at the corner of the street and you waited for hours, in vain, for an old lady to scold you for smoking a cigarette, and then with a smirk you ate it. And then it was breakfast under the balloons."

"Were there Uncles, like in our house?"

"There are always Uncles at Christmas.

The same Uncles. And on Christmas mornings, with dog-disturbing whistle and sugar fags[10] I would scour the swatched[11]

6. The blocks or trays of ice on which fish are displayed at a market are *fishmonger's slabs*.
7. *Busbies* and *balaclavas* are different types of hats made of wool or fur.
8. In Britain, a streetcar is called a *tram*.
9. *Celluloid* is a kind of plastic.
10. *Sugar fags* are candy cigarettes.
11. *Swatched* is a variation of the word *swathed* and means "bound" or "wrapped."

town for the news of the little world, and find always a dead bird by the white Post Office or by the deserted swings; perhaps a robin, all but one of his fires out. Men and women wading or scooping back from chapel, with taproom noses and wind-bussed cheeks, all albinos, huddled their stiff black jarring feathers against the irreligious snow. Mistletoe hung from the gas brackets[12] in all the front parlours; there was sherry and walnuts and bottled beer and crackers by the dessertspoons; and cats in their fur-abouts watched the fires; and the high-heaped fire spat, all ready for the chestnuts and the mulling pokers.[13]

Did You Know?
Here, *crackers* are small, decorated tubes that hold candy or party favors and, when opened, make a popping sound.

Some few large men sat in the front parlours, without their collars, Uncles almost certainly, trying their new cigars, holding them out judiciously at arms' length, returning them to their mouths, coughing, then holding them out again as though waiting for the explosion; and some few small Aunts, not wanted in the kitchen, nor anywhere else for that matter, sat on the very edges of their chairs, poised and brittle, afraid to break, like faded cups and saucers."

Not many those mornings trod the piling streets: an old man always, fawn-bowlered,[14] yellow-gloved and, at this time of year, with spats[15] of snow, would take his constitutional to the white bowling green[16] and back, as he would take it wet or fine on Christmas Day or Doomsday; sometimes two hale young men, with big pipes blazing, no overcoats and wind-blown scarfs, would trudge, unspeaking, down to the forlorn sea, to work up an appetite, to blow away the fumes, who knows, to walk into the waves until nothing of them was left but the two curling smoke clouds of their inextinguishable briars. Then I would be slap-dashing home, the gravy smell of the dinners of others, the bird smell, the brandy, the pudding and mince, coiling up to my nostrils, when out of a snow-clogged side lane would come a boy the spit of myself, with a pink-tipped cigarette and the violet past of a black eye, cocky as a bullfinch, leering all to himself.

I hated him on sight and sound, and would be about to put my dog whistle to my lips and blow him off the face of Christmas when suddenly he, with a violet wink, put *his* whistle to *his* lips and blew so stridently, so high, so exquisitely loud, that gobbling faces, their cheeks bulged with goose, would press against their tinselled windows, the whole length of the white echoing street. For dinner we had turkey and blazing pudding,[17] and after dinner the Uncles sat in front of the fire, loosened all buttons, put

12. *Gas brackets* are wall-mounted gas lamps that are fed by gas piped through the walls.
13. *Mulling pokers* are fireplace pokers used to heat and stir *mull,* a hot, spiced wine.
14. The man who is *fawn-bowlered* is wearing a fawn-colored *bowler,* a round, narrow-brimmed hat.
15. *Spats* are short coverings made of cloth or leather, worn over the tops of the shoes and around the ankles.
16. The old man took his *constitutional,* or walk, every day, regardless of the weather. A *bowling green* is the lawn used in a bowling game.
17. *Blazing pudding* is a fancy pudding that's doused with brandy and served flaming.

Vocabulary
judiciously (jo͞o dish′ əs lē) *adv.* in a way that shows good judgment; sensibly
hale (hāl) *adj.* in good physical condition; healthy
stridently (strīd′ ənt lē) *adv.* in a loud, harsh manner; shrilly

Did You Know?
Tureens are deep dishes used for serving food at the table.

their large moist hands over their watch chains, groaned a little and slept. Mothers, aunts and sisters scuttled to and fro, bearing tureens. Auntie Bessie, who had already been frightened, twice, by a clock-work mouse, whimpered at the sideboard and had some elderberry wine. The dog was sick. Auntie Dosie had to have three aspirins, but Auntie Hannah, who liked port, stood in the middle of the snowbound backyard, singing like a big-bosomed thrush. I would blow up balloons to see how big they would blow up to; and, when they burst, which they all did, the Uncles jumped and rumbled. In the rich and heavy afternoon, the Uncles breathing like dolphins and the snow descending, I would sit among festoons and Chinese lanterns and nibble dates and try to make a model man-o'-war, following the Instructions for Little Engineers, and produce what might be mistaken for a sea-going tramcar.

Did You Know?
Festoons are decorations that hang in loops or curves.

Or I would go out, my bright new boots squeaking, in to the white world, on to the seaward hill, to call on Jim and Dan and Jack and to pad through the still streets, leaving huge deep footprints on the hidden pavements.

"I bet people will think there's been hippos."

"What would you do if you saw a hippo coming down our street?"

"I'd go like this, bang! I'd throw him over the railings and roll him down the hill and then I'd tickle him under the ear and he'd wag his tail."

"What would you do if you saw *two* hippos?"

Iron-flanked and bellowing he-hippos clanked and battered through the scudding snow toward us as we passed Mr. Daniel's house.

"Let's post Mr. Daniel a snowball through his letter box."

"Let's write things in the snow."

"Let's write, 'Mr. Daniel looks like a spaniel' all over his lawn."

Or we walked on the white shore.

"Can the fishes see it's snowing?"

The silent one-clouded heavens drifted on to the sea. Now we were snow-blind travellers lost on the north hills, and vast dewlapped[18] dogs, with flasks round their necks, ambled and shambled up to us, baying "Excelsior."[19] We returned home through the poor streets where only a few children fumbled with bare red fingers in the wheel-rutted snow and catcalled after us, their voices fading away, as we trudged uphill, into the cries of the dock birds and the hooting of ships out in the whirling bay. And then, at tea the recovered Uncles would be jolly; and the ice cake loomed in the center of the table like a marble grave. Auntie Hannah laced her tea with rum, because it was only once a year.

Bring out the tall tales now that we told by the fire as the gaslight bubbled like a diver. Ghosts whooed like owls in the long nights when I dared not look over my shoulder; animals lurked in the cubbyhole under the stairs where the gas meter ticked. And I remember that we went singing carols once, when there

18. *Dewlapped* dogs have a loose fold of skin under the throat.
19. *Baying* means "howling." *Excelsior* is a Latin word meaning "still higher; ever upward." It is often used as an inspirational motto.

Vocabulary

loom (lo͞om) *v.* to appear to the mind as large; to stand out prominently
lurk (lurk) *v.* to stay hidden, ready to attack

wasn't the shaving of a moon to light the flying streets. At the end of a long road was a drive that led to a large house, and we stumbled up the darkness of the drive that night, each one of us afraid, each one holding a stone in his hand in case, and all of us too brave to say a word. The wind through the trees made noises as of old and unpleasant and maybe webfooted men wheezing in caves. We reached the black bulk of the house.

"What shall we give them? 'Hark the Herald'?"

"No," Jack said, " 'Good King Wenceslas.' I'll count three."

One, two, three, and we began to sing, our voices high and seemingly distant in the snow-felted darkness round the house that was occupied by nobody we knew. We stood close together, near the dark door.

Good King Wenceslas looked out
On the Feast of Stephen . . .

Ennui, c. 1914. Walter Richard Sickert. Oil on canvas, 152.4 x 112.4 cm. Tate Gallery, London.

Viewing the painting: How might the mood of this painting reflect the after-dinner mood in the selection?

And then a small, dry voice, like the voice of someone who has not spoken for a long time, joined our singing: a small dry, eggshell voice from the other side of the door: a small dry voice through the keyhole. And when we stopped running we were outside *our* house; the front room was lovely; balloons floated under the hot-water-bottle-gulping gas; everything was good again and shone over the town.

"Perhaps it was a ghost," Jim said.

"Perhaps it was trolls," Dan said, who was always reading.

"Let's go in and see if there's any jelly left," Jack said. And we did that.

Always on Christmas night there was music. An uncle played the fiddle, a cousin sang "Cherry Ripe," and another uncle sang "Drake's Drum." It was very warm in the little house.

Auntie Hannah, who had got on to the parsnip wine, sang a song about Bleeding Hearts and Death, and then another in which she said her heart was like a Bird's Nest; and then everybody laughed again; and then I went to bed. Looking through my bedroom window, out into the moonlight and the unending smoke-coloured snow, I could see the lights in the windows of all the other houses on our hill and hear the music rising from them up the long, steadily falling night. I turned the gas down, I got into bed. I said some words to the close and holy darkness, and then I slept.

Responding to Literature

Personal Response

What images or events from the story made the strongest impression on you? Why? Share your reactions with your classmates.

Analyzing Literature

Recall

1. Summarize what happens at the Prothero home.
2. What categories of presents does the narrator describe? Give at least three examples from each category.
3. How does the narrator spend Christmas morning?
4. What do the adults and children do after Christmas dinner?
5. How does Christmas day end?

Interpret

6. How does the narrator seem to feel about the incident at the Prothero home? Support your answer with evidence from the selection.
7. What might you infer about the narrator's childhood from the presents he describes?
8. What do the sights, sounds, smells, and feelings described by the narrator tell you about his experiences?
9. How does the narrator mix reality and fantasy in his description of the children's activities on Christmas afternoon? Give specific examples.
10. What do the last two sentences of the selection seem to suggest about the narrator's attitude toward Christmas?

Evaluate and Connect

11. Although this selection is nonfiction, Thomas embellished it with imaginary incidents. Why do you think he did this?
12. What conclusions might you draw about the culture in which Thomas grew up? Support your conclusions using evidence from the selection.
13. Find at least two examples of **imagery.** (See page R6.) Evaluate how effectively each image helps you imagine what it's like to see, hear, touch, smell, or taste what is being described.
14. Thomas relates only the pleasant memories from his childhood Christmases. Do you do the same thing when you recall your childhood holidays? Explain.
15. **Theme Connections** Why do you think people record their memories of past experiences? In your opinion, why do other people enjoy reading about such memories?

Literary ELEMENTS

Memoir

A **memoir** is a personal account of events from the author's past. It is usually written from the first-person point of view, using the pronoun *I;* this point of view allows the reader to see events as the author did. While an autobiography usually tells the story of a person's entire life, a memoir–such as "A Child's Christmas in Wales"–typically focuses on a single incident or a particular period in a person's life. Unlike a historical account, which is objective and emphasizes facts, a memoir usually includes the author's personal observations and responses to people and events.

1. Choose a favorite passage from Thomas's memoir. Explain how the author's personal responses and observations add to your understanding and appreciation of the passage.
2. Imagine reading a historical account of Christmas in Wales in the early 1900s. How might such an account differ from Thomas's memoir? Cite specific details from the text to support your response.

- See **Literary Terms Handbook,** p. R7.

Literature and Writing

Writing About Literature

Evaluate the Author's Approach In this memoir, Thomas merged his recollections of many Christmases. In a paragraph, evaluate this approach. Consider these questions: What are the advantages and disadvantages of such an approach? Why do you think Thomas chose this approach? Share your ideas with your classmates.

Personal Writing

Childhood Memory Review your response to the Reading Focus on page 432. Try to add more **sensory details** to your web. Then write a description of this holiday from your childhood. Include **images** to help the reader imagine what you saw, heard, smelled, tasted, and touched.

Extending Your Response

Literature Groups

Clarifying Meaning What passages from the selection did group members find difficult or confusing? Write down each difficult passage on one side of a note card; then discuss each passage in your group, with the goal of better understanding and appreciating the passage. Finally, on the back of each card, paraphrase the passage according to the meaning the group develops. Share your insights with the members of another group.

Interdisciplinary Activity

Social Studies: Winter Holidays Many cultures observe winter holidays, such as Chanukah, Christmas, Kwanzaa, and New Year's Day. Interview a friend, relative, or acquaintance who celebrates one of these holidays. Ask the person to describe the significance of the holiday and to recall his or her favorite childhood memories of it. In a small group, share the information you have gathered.

Family celebrating Kwanzaa.

Listening and Speaking

Sound of Wales In addition to being a writer, Dylan Thomas was a gifted and popular speaker who read from his works with a forceful, distinctive voice. Find and listen to a recording of Dylan Thomas reading his work. You can find recordings on the Internet as well as in many libraries. After listening, try reading some of Thomas's poetry or prose aloud, modeling his speaking style.

Reading Further

If you have enjoyed this memoir, you might also enjoy these works:

Poetry: *Collected Poems of Dylan Thomas 1934–1952* includes some of Thomas's most famous poems.

Memoirs: *An American Childhood,* by Annie Dillard, a best-selling collection of the author's experiences growing up in Pittsburgh in the 1950s.

Boy: Tales of Childhood, by Roald Dahl, includes stories about Dahl's childhood in Wales, England, and Norway.

Viewing: *A Child's Christmas in Wales* is a video adaptation of Thomas's memoir.

Literary Criticism

"Sound," argues one critic, "was as important as sense in [Thomas's] poems—some would even say more important." On the basis of the selection that you have just read, do you think this statement could also apply to Thomas's prose? Write an analysis of Thomas's use of sound devices in "A Child's Christmas in Wales." What effect does the use of these devices have on your appreciation of this piece?

Save your work for your portfolio.

Skill Minilessons

GRAMMAR AND LANGUAGE • Compound Adjectives

Dylan Thomas commonly creates evocative, condensed descriptions by using compound adjectives–two words connected by a hyphen and used as an adjective before a noun. For example, instead of "the sea that sounds like it's singing carols," Thomas says "the carol-singing sea." "Carol-singing" is a compound adjective.

- For more about adjectives, see **Language Handbook,** p. R38.

PRACTICE Rewrite the following phrases so they contain compound adjectives:

1. snow that has been rutted by wheels
2. snow that is colored by smoke
3. a lane clogged by snow
4. hills that are shaped like a harp
5. noses that were cherried by the wind

READING AND THINKING • Clarifying

One outstanding feature of "A Child's Christmas in Wales" is the long complicated sentences that Thomas sometimes includes. If such sentences confuse you as you read, you might find it helpful to stop from time to time and clarify, or check your understanding of the text. One way to work through a difficult sentence is to find the subject of the sentence and then examine sentence parts set off by commas to see if they contain extra, nonessential information that you can overlook. Next, find the verb that goes with the subject and see how the main parts of the sentence fit together. Finally, try restating the meaning of the sentence in your own words. For example, after working through the first sentence of this selection, you might say, "The Christmases were so much alike that I can't remember whether I was twelve or six when we got the big snow."

PRACTICE Review "A Child's Christmas in Wales," looking for three sentences that are complicated or confusing. Work through each sentence to clarify the meaning for yourself, and then restate that meaning on your paper.

- For more about related comprehension skills, see **Reading Handbook,** pp. R82–R94.

VOCABULARY • Analogies

An **analogy** is a type of comparison that is based on the relationships between things or ideas. To complete an analogy, look for the relationship that exists between the first pair of ideas and describe it in a sentence. Then substitute the ideas in the second pair and see if the same relationship exists. If more than one of the answer choices fits your sentence, construct a more specific sentence.

- For more about analogies, see **Communications Skills Handbook,** p. R77.

PRACTICE Choose the word pair that best completes each analogy.

1. screech : stridently ::
   a. murmur : quietly
   b. look : sneakily
   c. scold : unfairly
   d. giggle : uncontrollably
2. hale : disease ::
   a. tall : strength
   b. wise : mistake
   c. jealous : love
   d. fair : bias

MEDIA connection

On-line Travel Guide

Did Dylan Thomas's lavish descriptions of his boyhood in Wales capture your imagination? If so, you might want to visit Wales one day. One of the highlights of your trip could be an excursion to a 700-year old castle.

Destination Wales

Address: http://www.lonelyplanet.com

PEMBROKESHIRE COAST NATIONAL PARK Most famous for the 167-mile Pembrokeshire Coast Path, the park runs along a coastline riddled with rugged cliffs, superb sandy beaches, rocky coves, and tiny fishing villages – there's some gorgeous scenery and spectacular coastal walks. Inland, the historic Preseli Hills hide ancient trade routes, hill forts, standing stones, and burial chambers. Offshore, the islands of Skomer, Skokholm, and Grassholm are inhabited by colonies of puffins, guillemots, razorbills, gannets, and grey seals. The area is an activity-lover's paradise, with a choice of hiking, pony trekking, surfing, windsurfing, kayaking, and fishing opportunities.

GOWER PENINSULA This area was the first part of Britain to be officially designated an Area of Outstanding Beauty—for good reason. A favorite haunt of Dylan Thomas, the predominantly National Trust–owned peninsula has superb sandy beaches, beautiful cliff scenery, smugglers' coves, and some great walks. Points of interest include Worm's Head and the village of Rhossili.

CASTLES Edward I's superb castles are one of Wales' biggest drawcards. His legacy includes the classically geometric Beaumaris, Caernarfon with its Prince of Wales affiliations, crenellated Conwy, and the sturdy ruins of Harlech. Wales' other castles include fairy-tale Caerphilly (9 miles (14 km) north of Cardiff), Victorian Gothic Cardiff, the rambling ruins of 12th-century Carew, the cliff-top drama of Chepstow, Swansea's Oystermouth, and tower-topped Pembroke.

Analyzing Media

1. Why, do you think, was the Gower Peninsula a "favorite haunt" of Dylan Thomas?
2. Which of these places would you enjoy visiting most? least? Give reasons for your answers.

Before You Read

from *Kaffir Boy*

Reading Focus

Henry Peter Brougham said, "Education makes a people easy to lead, but difficult to drive; easy to govern but impossible to enslave."

Discuss Do you agree with the ideas expressed in this quote? Why or why not?

Setting a Purpose Read about a boy who is forming his own ideas about education.

Building Background

The Time and Place
The events described in this selection take place in Johannesburg, South Africa, in the 1960s.

Did You Know?
Apartheid, which means "separateness," was a policy of racial discrimination that was officially adopted in 1948 by South Africa's white government. Under apartheid, black South Africans, who made up more than seventy-five percent of the population, were forced to live and work under a system of strict racial segregation. The separate and unequal conditions under which blacks lived extended to every facet of life, including education.

Apartheid sparked strong opposition in South Africa and in many other parts of the world and came to a definitive end in 1994, with the electoral victory of Nelson Mandela's African National Congress. Mandela then became the first black president of South Africa.

Vocabulary Preview

coterie (kō′ tər ē) *n.* a small group of people who share a particular interest and often meet socially; p. 448
admonish (ad mon′ ish) *v.* to warn, as against a specific action; p. 448
peruse (pə ro͞oz′) *v.* to read through or examine carefully; p. 450
credence (krēd′ əns) *n.* belief, especially in the reports or statements of others; p. 451
tirade (tī rād′) *n.* a long, angry or scolding speech; p. 453
vehemently (vē′ə mənt lē) *adv.* strongly; intensely; passionately; p. 454

Meet Mark Mathabane

What was it like to grow up in South Africa under the system of apartheid? For Mark Mathabane (mä tä bä′ ne) "it meant hate, bitterness, hunger, pain, terror, violence, fear, dashed hopes and dreams." Although illiterate, his mother understood the importance of education and insisted that her son attend school. Mathabane made up his mind to master English, which black South Africans were forbidden to learn. At the age of thirteen, he took up tennis and eventually won a tennis scholarship to an American college; he later called this scholarship "my passport to freedom."

Mark Mathabane was born in Johannesburg, South Africa, in 1960. Kaffir Boy *was published in 1986.*

from Kaffir Boy

Mark Mathabane

"EDUCATION WILL OPEN DOORS WHERE NONE SEEM TO EXIST."

When my mother began dropping hints that I would soon be going to school, I vowed never to go because school was a waste of time. She laughed and said, "We'll see. You don't know what you're talking about." My philosophy on school was that of a gang of ten-, eleven-, and twelve-year-olds whom I so revered that their every word seemed that of an oracle.[1]

---

1. In Greek mythology, the gods sometimes spoke through an *oracle*.

These boys had long left their homes and were now living in various neighborhood junkyards, making it on their own. They slept in abandoned cars, smoked glue and benzene,[2] ate pilchards and brown bread, sneaked into the white world to caddy and, if unsuccessful, came back to the township to steal beer and soda bottles from shebeens,[3] or goods from the Indian traders on First Avenue. Their life style was exciting, adventurous, and full of surprises; and I was attracted to it. My mother told me that they were no-gooders, that they would amount to nothing, that I should not associate with them, but I paid no heed. What does she know? I used to tell myself. One thing she did not know was that the gang's way of life had captivated me wholly, particularly their philosophy on school: they hated it and considered an education a waste of time.

They, like myself, had grown up in an environment where the value of an education was never emphasized, where the first thing a child learned was not how to read and write and spell, but how to fight and steal and rebel; where the money to send children to school was grossly[4] lacking, for survival was first priority. I kept my membership in the gang, knowing that for as long as I was under its influence, I would never go to school.

One day my mother woke me up at four in the morning.

"Are they here? I didn't hear any noises," I asked in the usual way.

"No," my mother said. "I want you to get into that washtub over there."

"What!" I balked, upon hearing the word *washtub.* I feared taking baths like one feared the plague. Throughout seven years of hectic living the number of baths I had taken could be counted on one hand with several fingers missing. I simply had no natural inclination for water; cleanliness was a trait I still had to acquire. Besides, we had only one bathtub in the house, and it constantly sprung a leak.

"I said get into that tub!" My mother shook a finger in my face.

Reluctantly, I obeyed, yet wondered why all of a sudden I had to take a bath. My mother, armed with a scropbrush and a piece of Lifebuoy soap, purged[5] me of years and years of grime till I ached and bled. As I howled, feeling pain shoot through my limbs as the thistles of the brush encountered stubborn calluses, there was a loud knock at the door.

Instantly my mother leaped away from the tub and headed, on tiptoe, toward the bedroom. Fear seized me as I, too, thought of the police. I sat frozen in the bathtub, not knowing what to do.

"Open up, Mujaji [my mother's maiden name]," Granny's voice came shrilling through the door. "It's me."

My mother heaved a sigh of relief; her tense limbs relaxed. She turned and headed to the kitchen door, unlatched it, and in came Granny and Aunt Bushy.

"You scared me half to death," my mother said to Granny. "I had forgotten all about your coming."

"Are you ready?" Granny asked my mother.

"Yes—just about," my mother said, beckoning me to get out of the washtub.

She handed me a piece of cloth to dry myself. As I dried myself, questions raced through my mind: What's going on? What's Granny doing at our house this ungodly[6] hour of the morning? And why did she ask my

2. The boys are taking a risk with *benzene,* a poisonous liquid obtained from coal.
3. *Shebeens* are taverns operating without government license or approval.
4. Here, *grossly* means "totally; entirely."
5. To *purge* is to cleanse or get rid of whatever is unclean or undesirable.
6. In this context, *ungodly* means "outrageous; shocking."

mother, "Are you ready?" While I stood debating, my mother went into the bedroom and came out with a stained white shirt and a pair of faded black shorts.

"Here," she said, handing me the togs, "put these on."

"Why?" I asked.

"Put them on I said!"

I put the shirt on; it was grossly loose-fitting. It reached all the way down to my ankles. Then I saw the reason why: it was my father's shirt!

"But this is Papa's shirt," I complained. "It don't fit me."

"Put it on," my mother insisted. "I'll make it fit."

"The pants don't fit me either," I said. "Whose are they anyway?"

"Put them on," my mother said. "I'll make them fit."

Moments later I had the garments on; I looked ridiculous. My mother started working on the pants and shirt to make them fit. She folded the shirt in so many intricate ways and stashed it inside the pants, they too having been folded several times at the waist. She then choked the pants at the waist with a piece of sisal rope to hold them up. She then lavishly smeared my face, arms, and legs with a mixture of pig's fat and vaseline. "This will insulate you from the cold," she said. My skin gleamed like the morning star, and I felt as hot as the center of the sun, and I smelled God knows like what. After embalming me, she headed to the bedroom.

Did You Know?
Sisal is a coarse, strong fiber obtained from the leaves of a tropical plant.

"Where are we going, Gran'ma?" I said, hoping that she would tell me what my mother refused to tell me. I still had no idea I was about to be taken to school.

"Didn't your mother tell you?" Granny said with a smile. "You're going to start school."

"What!" I gasped, leaping from the chair where I was sitting as if it were made of hot lead. "I am not going to school!" I blurted out and raced toward the kitchen door.

My mother had just reappeared from the bedroom and guessing what I was up to, she yelled, "Someone get the door!"

Aunt Bushy immediately barred the door. I turned and headed for the window. As I leaped for the windowsill, my mother lunged at me and brought me down. I tussled, "Let go of me! I don't want to go to school! Let me go!" but my mother held fast onto me.

"It's no use now," she said, grinning triumphantly as she pinned me down. Turning her head in Granny's direction, she shouted, "Granny! Get a rope quickly!"

Granny grabbed a piece of rope nearby and came to my mother's aid. I bit and clawed every hand that grabbed me, and howled protestations against going to school; however, I was no match for the two determined matriarchs.[7] In a jiffy they had me bound, hands and feet.

"What's the matter with him?" Granny, bewildered, asked my mother. "Why did he suddenly turn into an imp[8] when I told him you're taking him to school?"

"You shouldn't have told him that he's being taken to school," my mother said. "He doesn't want to go there. That's why I requested you come today, to help me take him there. Those boys in the streets have been a bad influence on him."

---

7. *Matriarchs* (mā′ trē ärks′) are women who head families or who have great authority in other groups.
8. Here, *imp* means "a mischievous child."

Small boys waiting by snack shop in Alexandra Township. Jason Lauré, photographer.

Viewing the photograph: How would you describe the expressions of the boys in the photograph? What might they say to Mathabane as he was being dragged off to school?

As the two matriarchs hauled me through the door, they told Aunt Bushy not to go to school but stay behind and mind the house and the children.

The sun was beginning to rise from beyond the veld[9] when Granny and my mother dragged me to school. The streets were beginning to fill with their everyday traffic: old men and women, wizened,[10] bent, and ragged, were beginning their rambling; workless men and women were beginning to assemble in their usual coteries and head for shebeens in the backyards where they discussed how they escaped the morning pass raids[11] and contemplated the conditions of life amidst intense beer drinking and vacant, uneasy laughter; young boys and girls, some as young as myself, were beginning their aimless wanderings along the narrow, dusty streets in search of food, carrying bawling infants piggyback.

As we went along some of the streets, boys and girls who shared the same fears about school as I were making their feelings known in a variety of ways. They were howling their protests and trying to escape. A few managed to break loose and make a mad dash for freedom, only to be recaptured in no time, admonished or whipped, or both, and ordered to march again.

As we made a turn into Sixteenth Avenue, the street leading to the tribal school I was being taken to, a short, chubby black woman came along from the opposite direction. She had a scuttle[12] overflowing with coal on her *doek*-covered (cloth-covered) head. An infant, bawling deafeningly, was loosely swathed with a piece of sheepskin onto her back. Following closely behind the woman, and picking up

9. In South Africa, the *veld* (velt) is a rolling grassland with scattered trees or bushes.
10. When old people become *wizened* (wiz′ənd), they are shriveled or withered due to age.
11. *Pass raids* refers to the practice whereby police periodically stopped black South Africans to see that they had the proper papers authorizing them to be in specific areas.
12. Here, a *scuttle* is a coal container.

Vocabulary

coterie (kō′ tər ē) *n.* a small group of people who share a particular interest and often meet socially

admonish (ad mon′ ish) *v.* to warn, as against a specific action pieces of coal as they fell from the scuttle and placing them in a small plastic bag, was a half-naked, potbellied, and thumb-sucking boy of about four. The woman stopped abreast.[13] For some reason we stopped too.

"I wish I had done the same to my oldest son," the strange woman said in a regretful voice, gazing at me. I was confounded[14] by her stopping and offering her unsolicited opinion.

"I wish I had done that to my oldest son," she repeated, and suddenly burst into tears; amidst sobs, she continued, "before . . . the street claimed him . . . and . . . turned him into a *tsotsi*."[15]

Granny and my mother offered consolatory remarks to the strange woman.

"But it's too late now," the strange woman continued, tears now streaming freely down her puffy cheeks. She made no attempt to dry them. "It's too late now," she said for the second time, "he's beyond any help. I can't help him even if I wanted to. *Uswile*[16] [He is dead]."

"How did he die?" my mother asked in a sympathetic voice.

"He shunned school and, instead, grew up to live by the knife. And the same knife he lived by ended his life. That's why whenever I see a boy-child refuse to go to school, I stop and tell the story of my dear little *mbitsini*[17] [heartbreak]."

Having said that, the strange woman left as mysteriously as she had arrived.

"Did you hear what that woman said!" my mother screamed into my ears. "Do you want the same to happen to you?"

I dropped my eyes. I was confused.

13. *Abreast* means "alongside the others."
14. To be *confounded* is to be confused or bewildered.
15. A *tsotsi* (tsot′ sē) is an armed street hoodlum or gangster.
16. *Uswile* (o͞o swē′ lā)
17. *mbitsini* (əm bit sē′ nē)

"Poor woman," Granny said ruefully. "She must have truly loved her son."

Finally, we reached the school and I was ushered into the principal's office, a tiny cubicle facing a row of privies[18] and a patch of yellowed grass.

"So this is the rascal we'd been talking about," the principal, a tall, wiry man, foppishly[19] dressed in a black pin-striped suit, said to my mother as we entered. His austere,[20] shiny face, inscrutable and imposing, reminded me of my father. He was sitting behind a brown table upon which stood piles of dust and cobweb-covered books and papers. In one upper pocket of his jacket was arrayed a variety of pens and pencils; in the other nestled a lily-white handkerchief whose presence was more decorative than utilitarian.[21] Alongside him stood a disproportionately portly[22] black woman, fashionably dressed in a black skirt and a white blouse. She had but one pen, and this she held in her hand. The room was hot and stuffy and buzzing with flies.

"Yes, Principal," my mother answered, "this is he."

"I see he's living up to his notoriety," remarked the principal, noticing that I had been bound. "Did he give you too much trouble?"

"Trouble, Principal," my mother sighed. "He was like an imp."

"He's just like the rest of them, Principal," Granny sighed. "Once they get out into the streets, they become wild. They take to the many vices of the streets like an infant takes to its mother's milk. They begin to think that there's no other life but the one shown them

18. *Privies* (priv′ ēz) are outhouses, or toilets.
19. The man surely wouldn't think that he dressed *foppishly*—in the style of one who pays too much attention to his clothes.
20. *Austere* means "serious, strict, or severe."
21. Something that is *utilitarian* is functional or practical.
22. A *portly* person has a heavy or stout but dignified appearance.

by the *tsotsis*. They come to hate school and forget about the future."

"Well," the principal said. "We'll soon remedy all that. Untie him."

"He'll run away," my mother cried.

"I don't think he's that foolish to attempt that with all of us here."

"He *is* that foolish, Principal," my mother said as she and Granny began untying me. "He's tried it before. Getting him here was an ordeal in itself."

The principal rose from his seat, took two steps to the door and closed it. As the door swung closed, I spotted a row of canes of different lengths and thicknesses hanging behind it. The principal, seeing me staring at the canes, grinned and said, in a manner suggesting that he had wanted me to see them, "As long as you behave, I won't have to use any of those on you."

Use those canes on me? I gasped. I stared at my mother—she smiled; at Granny—she smiled too. That made me abandon any inkling of escaping.

"So they finally gave you the birth certificate and the papers," the principal addressed my mother as he returned to his chair.

"Yes, Principal," my mother said, "they finally did. But what a battle it was. It took me nearly a year to get all them papers together." She took out of her handbag a neatly wrapped package and handed it to the principal. "They've been running us around for so long that there were times when I thought he would never attend school, Principal," she said.

"That's pretty much standard procedure, Mrs. Mathabane," the principal said, unwrapping the package. "But you now have the papers and that's what's important.

"As long as we have the papers," he continued, minutely perusing the contents of the package, "we won't be breaking the law in admitting your son to this school, for we'll be in full compliance with the requirements set by the authorities in Pretoria."[23]

"Sometimes I don't understand the laws from Pitori,"[24] Granny said. "They did the same to me with my Piet and Bushy. Why, Principal, should our children not be allowed to learn because of some piece of paper?"

"The piece of paper you're referring to, Mrs. Mabaso [Granny's maiden name]," the principal said to Granny, "is as important to our children as a pass is to us adults. We all hate passes; therefore, it's only natural we should hate the regulations our children are subjected to. But as we have to live with passes, so our children have to live with the regulations, Mrs. Mabaso. I hope you understand, that is the law of the country. We would have admitted your grandson a long time ago, as you well know, had it not been for the papers. I hope you understand."

"I understand, Principal," Granny said, "but I don't understand," she added paradoxically.

One of the papers caught the principal's eye and he turned to my mother and asked, "Is your husband a Shangaan, Mrs. Mathabane?"

"No, he's not Principal," my mother said. "Is there anything wrong? He's Venda and I'm Shangaan."[25]

The principal reflected for a moment or so and then said, concernedly, "No, there's nothing seriously wrong. Nothing that we can't take care of. You see, Mrs. Mathabane, technically,

23. The rules come from South Africa's capital, *Pretoria.*
24. *Pitori* is Granny's pronunciation of "Pretoria."
25. The people of South Africa belong to many different ethnic groups, including *Venda* and *Shangaan,* each with its own language.

Vocabulary

peruse (pə ro͞oz′) *v.* to read through or examine carefully the fact that your child's father is a Venda makes him ineligible to attend this tribal school because it is only for children whose parents are of the Shangaan tribe. May I ask what language the children speak at home?"

"Both languages," my mother said worriedly, "Venda and Shangaan. Is there anything wrong?"

The principal coughed, clearing his throat, then said, "I mean which language do they speak more?"

"It depends, Principal," my mother said, swallowing hard. "When their father is around, he wants them to speak only Venda. And when he's not, they speak Shangaan. And when they are out at play, they speak Zulu and Sisotho."[26]

"Well," the principal said, heaving a sigh of relief. "In that case, I think an exception can be made. The reason for such an exception is that there's currently no school for Vendas in Alexandra. And should the authorities come asking why we took in your son, we can tell them that. Anyway, your child is half-half."

Everyone broke into a nervous laugh, except me. I was bewildered by the whole thing. I looked at my mother, and she seemed greatly relieved as she watched the principal register me; a broad smile broke across her face. It was as if some enormously heavy burden had finally been lifted from her shoulders and her conscience.

"Bring him back two weeks from today," the principal said as he saw us to the door. "There're so many children registering today that classes won't begin until two weeks hence. Also, the school needs repair and cleaning up after the holidays. If he refuses to come, simply notify us, and we'll send a couple of big boys to come fetch him, and he'll be very sorry if it ever comes to that."

As we left the principal's office and headed home, my mind was still against going to school. I was thinking of running away from home and joining my friends in the junkyard.

I didn't want to go to school for three reasons: I was reluctant to surrender my freedom and independence over to what I heard every school-going child call "tyrannous discipline." I had heard many bad things about life in tribal school—from daily beatings by teachers and mistresses who worked you like a mule to long school hours—and the sight of those canes in the principal's office gave ample credence to rumors that school was nothing but a torture chamber. And there was my allegiance to the gang.

But the thought of the strange woman's lamentations over her dead son presented a

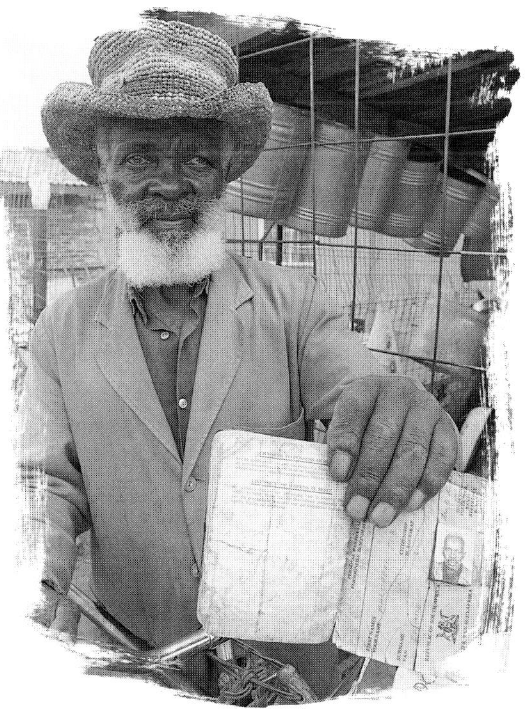

Man displaying passbook.

26. *Zulu* and *Sisotho* are ethnic groups as well as languages.

Vocabulary

credence (krēd′ əns) *n.* belief, especially in the reports or statements of others

Children in Alexandra Township.

Viewing the photograph: What does the background in this photograph tell you about these children's daily lives? How might the older three react to being enrolled in school like the author?

somewhat strong case for going to school: I didn't want to end up dead in the streets. A more compelling argument for going to school, however, was the vivid recollection of all that humiliation and pain my mother had gone through to get me the papers and the birth certificate so I could enroll in school. What should I do? I was torn between two worlds.

But later that evening something happened to force me to go to school.

I was returning home from playing soccer when a neighbor accosted[27] me by the gate and told me that there had been a bloody fight at my home.

"Your mother and father have been at it again," the neighbor, a woman, said.

"And your mother left."

I was stunned.

"Was she hurt badly?"

"A little bit," the woman said. "But she'll be all right. We took her to your grandma's place."

I became hot with anger.

"Is anyone in the house?" I stammered, trying to control my rage.

"Yes, your father is. But I don't think you should go near the house. He's raving mad. He's armed with a meat cleaver. He's chased out your brother and sisters, also. And some of the neighbors who tried to intervene he's threatened to carve them to pieces. I have never seen him this mad before."

I brushed aside the woman's warnings and went. Shattered windows convinced me that there had indeed been a skirmish of some sort. Several pieces of broken bricks, evidently broken after being thrown at the door, were lying about the door. I tried opening the door; it was locked from the inside. I knocked. No one answered. I knocked again. Still no one answered, until, as I turned to leave:

"Who's out there?" my father's voice came growling from inside.

"It's me, Johannes,"[28] I said.

27. In this case, to *accost* is to approach and speak to, often in a pushy way.

28. The author's name was *Johannes* (yō hä′ nis) before he changed it to Mark.

"Go away, . . . !" he bellowed. "I don't want you or that . . . mother of yours setting foot in this house. Go away before I come out there and kill you!"

"Let me in!" I cried. "Dammit, let me in! I want my things!"

"What things? Go away, you black swine!"

I went to the broken window and screamed obscenities at my father, daring him to come out, hoping that if he as much as ever stuck his black face out, I would pelt him with the half-a-loaf brick in my hand. He didn't come out. He continued launching a tirade of obscenities at my mother and her mother. . . . He was drunk, but I wondered where he had gotten the money to buy beer because it was still the middle of the week and he was dead broke. He had lost his entire wage for the past week in dice and had had to borrow bus fare.

"I'll kill you someday for all you're doing to my mother," I threatened him, overwhelmed with rage. Several nosey neighbors were beginning to congregate by open windows and doors. Not wanting to make a spectacle of myself, which was something many of our neighbors seemed to always expect from our family, I backtracked away from the door and vanished into the dark street. I ran, without stopping, all the way to the other end of the township where Granny lived. There I found my mother, her face swollen and bruised and her eyes puffed up to the point where she could scarcely see.

"What happened, Mama?" I asked, fighting to hold back the tears at the sight of her disfigured face.

"Nothing, child, nothing," she mumbled, almost apologetically, between swollen lips. "Your papa simply lost his temper, that's all."

"But why did he beat you up like this, Mama?" Tears came down my face. "He's never beaten you like this before."

My mother appeared reluctant to answer me. She looked searchingly at Granny, who was pounding millet with pestle and mortar and mixing it with sorghum[29] and nuts for an African delicacy. Granny said, "Tell him, child, tell him. He's got a right to know. Anyway, he's the cause of it all."

Did You Know?
The *pestle* is a blunt tool used to pound or grind substances in a mortar, a thick, hard bowl, often made of wood or stone.

"Your father and I fought because I took you to school this morning," my mother began. "He had told me not to, and when I told him that I had, he became very upset. He was drunk. We started arguing, and one thing led to another."

"Why doesn't he want me to go to school?"

"He says he doesn't have money to waste paying for you to get what he calls a useless white man's education," my mother replied. "But I told him that if he won't pay for your schooling, I would try and look for a job and pay, but he didn't want to hear that, also. 'There are better things for you to work for,' he said. 'Besides, I don't want you to work. How would I look to other men if you, a woman I owned, were to start working?' When I asked him why shouldn't I take you to school, seeing that you were now of age, he replied that he doesn't believe in schools. I told him that school would keep you off the streets and out of trouble, but still he was belligerent."

"Is that why he beat you up?"

"Yes, he said I disobeyed his orders."

29. *Millet* is a grain similar to wheat, and *sorghum* is a syrup made from a tropical grass.

Vocabulary
tirade (tī rād′) *n.* a long, angry or scolding speech

"He's right, child," Granny interjected. "He paid *lobola* [bride price] for you. And your father ate it all up before he left me."

To which my mother replied, "But I desperately want to leave this beast of a man. But with his *lobola* gone I can't do it. That worthless thing you call your husband shouldn't have sold Jackson's scrawny cattle and left you penniless."

"Don't talk like that about your father, child," Granny said. "Despite all, he's still your father, you know. Anyway, he asked for *lobola* only because he had to get back what he spent raising you. And you know it would have been taboo for him to let you or any of your sisters go without asking for *lobola*."

"You and Papa seemed to forget that my sisters and I have minds of our own," my mother said. "We didn't need you to tell us whom to marry, and why, and how. If it hadn't been for your interference, I could have married that schoolteacher."

Granny did not reply; she knew well not to. When it came to the act of "selling" women as marriage partners, my mother was vehemently opposed to it. Not only was she opposed to this one aspect of tribal culture, but to others as well, particularly those involving relations between men and women and the upbringing of children. But my mother's sharply differing opinion was an exception rather than the rule among tribal women. Most times, many tribal women questioned her sanity in daring to question well-established mores.[30] But my mother did not seem to care; she would always scoff at her opponents and call them fools in letting their husbands enslave them completely.

Though I disliked school, largely because I knew nothing about what actually went on there, and the little I knew had painted a dreadful picture, the fact that a father would not want his son to go to school, especially a father who didn't go to school, seemed hard to understand.

"Why do you want me to go to school, Mama?" I asked, hoping that she might, somehow, clear up some of the confusion that was building in my mind.

"I want you to have a future, child," my mother said. "And, contrary to what your father says, school is the only means to a future. I don't want you growing up to be like your father."

The latter statement hit me like a bolt of lightning. It just about shattered every defense mechanism[31] and every pretext[32] I had against going to school.

"Your father didn't go to school," she continued, dabbing her puffed eyes to reduce the swelling with a piece of cloth dipped in warm water, "that's why he's doing some of the bad things he's doing. Things like drinking, gambling, and neglecting his family. He didn't learn how to read and write; therefore, he can't find a decent job. Lack of any education has narrowly focused his life. He sees nothing beyond himself. He still thinks in the old, tribal way, and still believes that things should be as they were back in the old days when he was growing up as a tribal boy in Louis Trichardt. Though he's my husband, and your father, he doesn't see any of that."

"Why didn't he go to school, Mama?"

"He refused to go to school because his father led him to believe that an education was a tool through which white people were

30. The customs and moral standards followed by most people in a given society are called *mores* (môr′ āz).

31. A *defense mechanism* is an attitude or behavior a person unconsciously adopts to help block out painful or unpleasant feelings.

32. A *pretext* is a false reason or excuse one gives to hide a true reason or motive.

Vocabulary

vehemently (vē′ ə mənt lē) *adv.* strongly; intensely; passionately going to take things away from him, like they did black people in the old days. And that a white man's education was worthless insofar as black people were concerned because it prepared them for jobs they can't have. But I know it isn't totally so, child, because times have changed somewhat. Though our lot isn't any better today, an education will get you a decent job. If you can read or write you'll be better off than those of us who can't. Take my situation: I can't find a job because I don't have papers, and I can't get papers because white people mainly want to register people who can read and write. But I want things to be different for you, child. For you and your brother and sisters. I want you to go to school, because I believe that an education is the key you need to open up a new world and a new life for yourself, a world and life different from that of either your father's or mine. It is the only key that can do that, and only those who seek it earnestly and perseveringly will get anywhere in the white man's world. Education will open doors where none seem to exist. It'll make people talk to you, listen to you, and help you; people who otherwise wouldn't bother. It will make you soar, like a bird lifting up into the endless blue sky, and leave poverty, hunger, and suffering behind. It'll teach you to learn to embrace what's good and shun what's bad and evil. Above all, it'll make you a somebody in this world. It'll make you grow up to be a good and proud person. That's why I want you to go to school, child, so that education can do all that, and more, for you."

A long, awkward silence followed, during which I reflected upon the significance of my mother's lengthy speech. I looked at my mother; she looked at me.

Finally, I asked, "How come you know so much about school, Mama? You didn't go to school, did you?"

"No, child," my mother replied. "Just like your father, I never went to school." For the second time that evening, a mere statement of fact had a thunderous impact on me. All the confusion I had about school seemed to leave my mind, like darkness giving way to light. And what had previously been a dark, yawning void in my mind was suddenly transformed into a beacon of light that began to grow larger and larger, until it had swallowed up, blotted out, all the blackness. That beacon of light seemed to reveal things and facts, which, though they must have always existed in me, I hadn't been aware of up until now.

"But unlike your father," my mother went on, "I've always wanted to go to school, but couldn't because my father, under the sway of tribal traditions, thought it unnecessary to educate females. That's why I so much want you to go, child, for if you do, I know that someday I too would come to go, old as I would be then. Promise me, therefore, that no matter what, you'll go back to school. And I, in turn, promise that I'll do everything in my power to keep you there."

With tears streaming down my cheeks and falling upon my mother's bosom, I promised her that I would go to school "forever." That night, at seven and a half years of my life, the battlelines in the family were drawn. My mother on the one side, illiterate but determined to have me drink, for better or for worse, from the well of knowledge. On the other side, my father, he too illiterate, yet determined to have me drink from the well of ignorance. Scarcely aware of the magnitude of the decision I was making or, rather, the decision which was being emotionally thrust upon me, I chose to fight on my mother's side, and thus my destiny was forever altered.

Responding to Literature

Personal Response

What scene from this selection lingers in your mind? Why?

Analyzing Literature

Recall

1. As this account begins, what is Mathabane's opinion of school? What are his goals?
2. Describe the encounter with the woman on the street.
3. Summarize what happens in the principal's office.
4. How does Mathabane's father react to the day's events? According to his mother, what accounts for his father's behavior and outlook on life?
5. What goal does Mathabane's mother have for him? Why? How does he react to this goal?

Interpret

6. What do you think accounts for Mathabane's outlook on life at the beginning of the selection?
7. What might cause Mathabane to be confused after the encounter with the "strange woman"?
8. What conclusions can you draw about what life is like for blacks in South Africa, based on what happens in the principal's office?
9. How does the **conflict** between Mathabane's parents reflect their different outlooks on life?
10. Compare Mathabane's attitude toward school at the beginning of the selection with his attitude at the end. What factors account for this change?

Evaluate and Connect

11. Under apartheid, blacks in South Africa had limited access to education. What does this suggest about the relationship between education and power?
12. Do you agree that "Education will open doors where none seem to exist"? Explain.
13. In this account, what aspects of tribal culture serve to oppress women and limit their freedom?
14. Evaluate the importance of **setting** (see page R11) in this true story. How do the time and place influence the events that occur?
15. Why do you think Mathabane chose to write about this experience?

Literary **ELEMENTS**

Monologue

A **monologue** is a long speech made by a character in a literary work. In this excerpt from *Kaffir Boy,* Mark Mathabane asks Mama why his father didn't go to school. Mama responds with a monologue. In this lengthy speech, Mathabane's mother not only answers her son's question but also gives him compelling information about her own life. In addition, she expresses her views about an important topic: education. Throughout the monologue, Mama's words reveal a great deal about her own character.

1. In this monologue, what do you learn about Mathabane's parents? About social and economic conditions for blacks in South Africa?
2. What views about education does Mama express in this monologue?
3. What does the monologue seem to suggest about Mama's character? Use specific details from the monologue to support your answer.

- See **Literary Terms Handbook,** p. R8.

Literature and Writing

Writing About Literature

Analyze Mood **Mood** is the emotional quality, or atmosphere, of a literary work. Sometimes the mood of a piece changes as the setting shifts. In the selection, find several passages that have different moods. Write a paragraph about each passage, identifying the mood, as well as the specific details that help to create that mood. Share your analysis with a group of classmates.

Creative Writing

Double Trouble Mathabane's mother must struggle not only against the racist policies of apartheid but against a tribal culture that treats women as their husband's "possessions." Imagine that Mama—who can neither read nor write—asks you to record her thoughts about her own desire for freedom. In a paragraph or two, write down the ideas you think Mama would express.

Extending Your Response

Literature Groups

Compare Reactions Think back to the discussion you had about the quote in the Reading Focus on page 444. In your group, discuss and compare possible responses that different characters in this selection might have.

Performing

Dramatic Presentation With a small group, reenact the encounter that Mathabane, Mama, and Granny have with the "strange woman" on the street. Practice the scene and present it to the class. Justify your choice of performance techniques with details from the selection.

Internet Connection

South Africa Today Use the Internet to learn about the political situation in South Africa today. Make a list of research questions such as the following: What form of government does South Africa have? Who is the head of state? What are the most pressing political and social issues? What is the state of racial relations in South Africa? What progress has been made in healing the wounds caused by decades of apartheid? Share your findings with the class.

Save your work for your portfolio.

VOCABULARY • Analogies

An analogy is a type of comparison that is based on the relationships between things or ideas. One type of analogy deals with pairs of words that represent different degrees of intensity.

hilarious : amusing :: tragic : unfortunate

Something that is *hilarious* is extremely *amusing;* something that is *tragic* is extremely *unfortunate*.

To complete an analogy, decide what relationship exists between the first two things or ideas. Then apply that relationship to another pair of words.

For more about analogies, see **Communications Skills Handbook,** p. R77.

PRACTICE Choose the word that best completes each analogy.

1. terror : fear :: tirade :
   a. apology b. sensation c. criticism
2. hate : dislike :: revere :
   a. admire b. worship c. ignore
3. vehemently : strongly :: amazingly :
   a. surprisingly b. soothingly c. generally
4. forbid : discourage :: captivate :
   a. coax b. interest c. chase

Reading & Thinking Skills

Identifying Cause and Effect

Suppose you go to an out-of-town hockey game on a school night. You get home very late. The next day you feel so tired that you doze off in English class. The hockey game is the **cause** of your not getting enough sleep. Your dozing off is an **effect** of getting home late. When one event causes another one to happen, a **cause-and-effect relationship** exists.

If you can answer *why* something happened, you know its cause. If you can answer *what happened as a result* of something, you know the effect. Words and phrases such as *because, as a result,* and *consequently* often signal cause-and-effect relationships.

In written accounts of events, just as in real life, a single cause may have several effects, and one effect may have multiple causes. In *Kaffir Boy,* for example, Mark Mathabane explains how he came to side with his mother in the battle over education: "I chose to fight on my mother's side, and thus my destiny was forever altered." His decision is an *effect.* It is also the *cause* of events in his future. Here are three causes of Mathabane's decision to go to school.

- He is moved by his mother's speech about education.
- He does not want to be like his father.
- He does not want to die in the streets, like the son of the "strange woman" he encounters on the way to school.

● For more about related comprehension skills, see **Reading Handbook,** pp. R82–R94.

ACTIVITY

Read the following excerpt from *Kaffir Boy.* Complete the exercises.

> **"[Your father] refused to go to school because his father led him to believe that an education was a tool through which white people were going to take things away from him. . . . And that a white man's education was worthless insofar as black people were concerned because it prepared them for jobs they can't have. But I know it isn't totally so, child, because times have changed somewhat. . . . If you can read or write you'll be better off than those of us who can't. Take my situation: I can't find a job because I don't have papers, and I can't get papers because white people mainly want to register people who can read and write."**

1. Identify an effect of each of the following causes:
   a. Mathabane's mother does not have papers.
   b. White people mainly want to register people who can read and write.
2. Identify two causes for this effect: Mathabane's father refused to go to school.

Before You Read

from *Farewell to Manzanar*

Reading Focus

How might you react if you and your family were forced to pack up and move on very short notice?

Freewrite Imagine that you and your family have forty-eight hours to pack your belongings and move to a new and unfamiliar place. Spend five minutes writing about how you might feel and what you might do in such a situation.

Setting a Purpose Read to find out what life was like for many Japanese Americans who were forced to move during World War II.

Building Background

The Time and Place

The events described in this selection take place in California in 1941 and 1942, after Japan's surprise attack on the U.S. Pacific Fleet in Pearl Harbor, Hawaii, on December 7, 1941. After this attack, the United States entered World War II, declaring war on Japan on December 8, 1941.

Did You Know?

After the Japanese attack on Pearl Harbor, many Americans were suspicious of people of Japanese ancestry living in the United States. In February 1942, President Franklin D. Roosevelt issued Executive Order 9066, which essentially gave the U.S. War Department the authority to remove Japanese Americans from their homes on the West Coast and confine them to special camps for the duration of the war. Some 110,000 Japanese Americans, two-thirds of them U.S. citizens, were relocated by the military to ten remotely situated, prison-like camps.

Vocabulary Preview

exclusively (iks klo͞o′ siv lē) *adv.* only; excluding any other; p. 462
internment (in turn′ mənt) *n.* the act of restricting or being restricted to a particular place, especially during a war; p. 463
patriarch (pā′ trē ärk′) *n.* the male head of a family or group; p. 463
irrational (i rash′ ən əl) *adj.* contrary to reason; illogical; p. 464
designation (dez′ ig nā′ shən) *n.* a distinguishing name or mark; p. 464
alleviate (ə lē′ vē āt′) *v.* to make easier to bear; relieve; lessen; p. 467
whimsical (hwim′ zi kəl) *adj.* fanciful; curiously humorous; p. 467
subordinate (sə bôr′ də nāt′) *v.* to cause to be, or treat as, secondary, inferior, or less important; p. 471

Meet Jeanne Wakatsuki Houston and James D. Houston

"Everybody knows an injustice was done," James Houston has said about the internment of Japanese Americans in relocation camps during World War II. Houston's wife, Jeanne Wakatsuki Houston, spent more than three years of her childhood at the Manzanar Relocation Center in California. The Houstons wrote about that experience in *Farewell to Manzanar*, a book that she refers to as "a true story, involving an extraordinary episode in American history."

Jeanne Wakatsuki Houston was born in 1934; James D. Houston was born in 1933. Both are natives of California. Farewell to Manzanar *was first published in 1973.*

from Farewell to Manzanar

Jeanne Wakatsuki Houston
and James D. Houston

IN DECEMBER OF 1941 Papa's disappearance didn't bother me nearly so much as the world I soon found myself in.

He had been a jack-of-all-trades. When I was born he was farming near Inglewood. Later, when he started fishing, we moved to Ocean Park, near Santa Monica, and until they picked him up, that's where we lived, in a big frame house with a brick fireplace, a block back from the beach. We were the only Japanese family in the neighborhood. Papa liked it that way. He didn't want to be labeled or grouped by anyone. But with him gone and no way of knowing what to expect, my mother moved all of us down to Terminal Island.[1]

Woody already lived there, and one of my older sisters had married a Terminal Island boy. Mama's first concern now was to keep the family together; and once the war began, she felt safer there than isolated racially in Ocean Park. But for me, at age seven, the island was a country as foreign as India or Arabia would have been. It was the first time I had lived among other Japanese, or gone to school with them, and I was terrified all the time.

This was partly Papa's fault. One of his threats to keep us younger kids in line was "I'm going to sell you to the Chinaman." When I had entered kindergarten two years earlier, I was the only Oriental in the class. They sat me next to a Caucasian girl who happened to have very slanted eyes. I looked at her and began to scream, certain Papa had sold me out at last. My fear of her ran so deep I could not speak of

1. *Terminal Island,* part of the Port of Los Angeles, is at the city's southern tip.

it, even to Mama, couldn't explain why I was screaming. For two weeks I had nightmares about this girl, until the teachers finally moved me to the other side of the room. And it was still with me, this fear of Oriental faces, when we moved to Terminal Island.

In those days it was a company town, a ghetto owned and controlled by the canneries. The men went after fish, and whenever the boats came back—day or night—the women would be called to process the catch while it was fresh. One in the afternoon or four in the morning, it made no difference. My mother had to go to work right after we moved there. I can still hear the whistle—two toots for French's, three for Van Camp's—and she and Chizu would be out of bed in the middle of the night, heading for the cannery.

The house we lived in was nothing more than a shack, a barracks with single plank walls and rough wooden floors, like the cheapest kind of migrant workers' housing. The people around us were hardworking, boisterous, a little proud of their nickname, *yo-go-re,* which meant literally *uncouth one,* or roughneck, or dead-end kid. They not only spoke Japanese exclusively, they spoke a dialect peculiar to Kyushu,[2] where their families had come from in Japan, a rough, fisherman's language, full of oaths and insults. Instead of saying *ba-ka-ta-re,* a common insult meaning *stupid,* Terminal Islanders would say *ba-ka-ya-ro,* a coarser and exclusively masculine use of the word, which implies gross stupidity. They would swagger and pick on outsiders and persecute anyone who didn't speak as they did. That was what made my own time there so hateful. I had never spoken anything but English, and the other kids in the second grade despised me for it. They were tough and mean, like ghetto kids anywhere. Each day after school I dreaded their ambush. My brother Kiyo, three years older, would wait for me at the door, where we would decide whether to run straight home together, or split up, or try a new and unexpected route.

None of these kids ever actually attacked. It was the threat that frightened us, their fearful looks, and the noises they would make, like miniature Samurai, in a language we couldn't understand.

Did You Know?
For centuries, the *Samurai* (sam′ oo rī′) were a class of fearsome warriors. Japan abolished its class system in the 1860s.

At the time it seemed we had been living under this reign of fear for years. In fact, we lived there about two months. Late in February the navy decided to clear Terminal Island completely. Even though most of us were American-born, it was dangerous having that many Orientals so close to the Long Beach Naval Station, on the opposite end of the island. We had known something like this was coming. But, like Papa's arrest, not much could be done ahead of time. There were four of us kids still young enough to be living with Mama, plus Granny, her mother, sixty-five then, speaking no English, and nearly blind. Mama didn't know where else she could get work, and we had nowhere else to move *to.* On February 25 the choice was made for us. We were given forty-eight hours to clear out.

The secondhand dealers had been prowling around for weeks, like wolves, offering humiliating prices for goods and furniture they knew many of us would have to sell sooner or later. Mama had left all but her most valuable possessions in Ocean Park, simply because she had nowhere to put them. She had brought along her pottery, her silver, heirlooms like the kimonos Granny had brought from Japan, tea sets, lacquered tables, and one fine old set of china, blue and white porcelain, almost translucent.[3] On the day we were leaving, Woody's car was so crammed with boxes and luggage and kids we had just run out of room. Mama had to sell this china.

Did You Know?
A *kimono* (ki mō′ nə) is a loose robe or gown tied with a sash, traditionally worn as an outer garment by Japanese men and women.

2. *Kyushu* is the southernmost of Japan's four main islands.

3. A material that is *translucent,* such as frosted glass, allows light to pass through but doesn't permit objects on the other side to be clearly distinguished.

Vocabulary

exclusively (iks klo͞o′ siv lē) *adv.* only; excluding any other

One of the dealers offered her fifteen dollars for it. She said it was a full setting for twelve and worth at least two hundred. He said fifteen was his top price. Mama started to quiver. Her eyes blazed up at him. She had been packing all night and trying to calm down Granny, who didn't understand why we were moving again and what all the rush was about. Mama's nerves were shot, and now navy jeeps were patrolling the streets. She didn't say another word. She just glared at this man, all the rage and frustration channeled at him through her eyes.

He watched her for a moment and said he was sure he couldn't pay more than seventeen fifty for that china. She reached into the red velvet case, took out a dinner plate and hurled it at the floor right in front of his feet.

The man leaped back shouting, "Hey! Hey, don't do that! Those are valuable dishes!"

Mama took out another dinner plate and hurled it at the floor, then another and another, never moving, never opening her mouth, just quivering and glaring at the retreating dealer, with tears streaming down her cheeks. He finally turned and scuttled out the door, heading for the next house. When he was gone she stood there smashing cups and bowls and platters until the whole set lay in scattered blue and white fragments across the wooden floor.

The American Friends Service[4] helped us find a small house in Boyle Heights, another minority ghetto, in downtown Los Angeles, now inhabited briefly by a few hundred Terminal Island refugees. Executive Order 9066 had been signed by President Roosevelt, giving the War Department authority to define military areas in the western states and to exclude from them anyone who might threaten the war effort. There was a lot of talk about internment, or moving inland, or something like that in store for all Japanese Americans. I remember my brothers sitting around the table talking very intently about what we were going to do, how we would keep the family together. They had seen how quickly Papa was removed, and they knew now that he would not be back for quite a while. Just before leaving Terminal Island Mama had received her first letter, from Bismarck, North Dakota. He had been imprisoned at Fort Lincoln, in an all-male camp for enemy aliens.

Papa had been the patriarch. He had always decided everything in the family. With him gone, my brothers, like councilors in the absence of a chief, worried about what should be done. The ironic thing is, there wasn't much left to decide. These were mainly days of quiet, desperate waiting for what seemed at the time to be inevitable. There is a phrase the Japanese use in such situations, when something difficult must be endured. You would hear the older heads, the Issei,[5] telling others very quietly, "*Shikata ga nai*" (It cannot be helped). "*Shikata ga nai*" (It must be done).

Mama and Woody went to work packing celery for a Japanese produce dealer. Kiyo and my sister May and I enrolled in the local school, and what sticks in my memory from those few weeks is the teacher—not her

4. The *American Friends Service* is a Quaker charity that provides assistance to political and religious refugees and other displaced persons.

5. *Issei* (ēs′ sā′) literally means "first generation" and refers to Japanese natives who immigrated to the United States.

Vocabulary

internment (in turn′ mənt) *n.* the act of restricting or being restricted to a particular place, especially during a war

patriarch (pā′ trē ärk′) *n.* the male head of a family or group looks, her remoteness. In Ocean Park my teacher had been a kind, grandmotherly woman who used to sail with us in Papa's boat from time to time and who wept the day we had to leave. In Boyle Heights the teacher felt cold and distant. I was confused by all the moving and was having trouble with the classwork, but she would never help me out. She would have nothing to do with me.

This was the first time I had felt outright hostility from a Caucasian. Looking back, it is easy enough to explain. Public attitudes toward the Japanese in California were shifting rapidly. In the first few months of the Pacific war, America was on the run. Tolerance had turned to distrust and irrational fear. The hundred-year-old tradition of anti-Orientalism on the west coast soon resurfaced, more vicious than ever. Its result became clear about a month later, when we were told to make our third and final move.

The name Manzanar meant nothing to us when we left Boyle Heights. We didn't know where it was or what it was. We went because the government ordered us to. And, in the case of my older brothers and sisters, we went with a certain amount of relief. They had all heard stories of Japanese homes being attacked, of beatings in the streets of California towns. They were as frightened of the Caucasians as Caucasians were of us. Moving, under what appeared to be government protection, to an area less directly threatened by the war seemed not such a bad idea at all. For some it actually sounded like a fine adventure.

Our pickup point was a Buddhist church in Los Angeles. It was very early, and misty, when we got there with our luggage. Mama had bought heavy coats for all of us. She grew up in eastern Washington and knew that anywhere inland in early April would be cold. I was proud of my new coat, and I remember sitting on a duffel bag trying to be friendly with the Greyhound driver. I smiled at him. He didn't smile back. He was befriending no one. Someone tied a numbered tag to my collar and to the duffel bag (each family was given a number, and that became our official designation until the camps were closed), someone else passed out box lunches for the trip, and we climbed aboard.

I had never been outside Los Angeles County, never traveled more than ten miles from the coast, had never even ridden on a bus. I was full of excitement, the way any kid would be, and wanted to look out the window. But for the first few hours the shades were drawn. Around me other people played cards, read magazines, dozed, waiting. I settled back, waiting too, and finally fell asleep. The bus felt very secure to me. Almost half its passengers were immediate relatives. Mama and my older brothers had succeeded in keeping most of us together, on the same bus, headed for the same camp. I didn't realize until much later what a job that was. The strategy had been, first, to have everyone living in the same district when the evacuation began, and then to get all of us included under the same family number, even though names had been changed by marriage. Many families weren't as lucky as ours and suffered months of anguish while trying to arrange transfers from one camp to another.

We rode all day. By the time we reached our destination, the shades were up. It was late afternoon. The first thing I saw was a

Vocabulary

irrational (i rash′ ən əl) *adj.* contrary to reason; illogical

designation (dez′ ig nā′ shən) *n.* a distinguishing name or mark yellow swirl across a blurred, reddish setting sun. The bus was being pelted by what sounded like splattering rain. It wasn't rain. This was my first look at something I would soon know very well, a billowing flurry of dust and sand churned up by the wind through Owens Valley.[6]

We drove past a barbed-wire fence, through a gate, and into an open space where trunks and sacks and packages had been dumped from the baggage trucks that drove out ahead of us. I could see a few tents set up, the first rows of black barracks, and beyond them, blurred by sand, rows of barracks that seemed to spread for miles across this plain. People were sitting on cartons or milling around, with their backs to the wind, waiting to see which friends or relatives might be on this bus. As we approached, they turned or stood up, and some moved toward us expectantly. But inside the bus no one stirred. No one waved or spoke. They just stared out the windows, ominously silent. I didn't understand this. Hadn't we finally arrived, our whole family intact? I opened a window, leaned out, and yelled happily. "Hey! This whole bus is full of Wakatsukis!"

Outside, the greeters smiled. Inside there was an explosion of laughter, hysterical, tension-breaking laughter that left my brothers choking and whacking each other across the shoulders.

We had pulled up just in time for dinner. The mess halls[7] weren't completed yet. An outdoor chow line snaked around a half-finished building that broke a good part of the wind. They issued us army mess kits, the round metal kind that fold over, and plopped in scoops of canned Vienna sausage, canned string beans, steamed rice that had been cooked too long, and on top of the rice a serving of canned apricots. The Caucasian servers were thinking that the fruit poured over rice would make a good dessert. Among the Japanese, of course, rice is never eaten with sweet foods, only with salty or savory foods. Few of us could eat such a mixture. But at this point no one dared protest. It would have been impolite. I was horrified when I saw the apricot syrup seeping through my little mound of rice. I opened my mouth to complain. My mother jabbed me in the back to keep quiet. We moved on through the line and joined the others squatting in the lee[8] of half-raised walls, dabbing courteously at what was, for almost everyone there, an inedible concoction.

Did You Know?
A soldier in the field eats from a *mess kit,* which is a metal container that holds eating utensils and opens into a plate with two compartments.

After dinner we were taken to Block 16, a cluster of fifteen barracks that had just been finished a day or so earlier—although finished was hardly the word for it. The shacks were built of one thickness of pine planking covered with tarpaper. They sat on concrete footings, with about two feet of open space between the floorboards and the ground. Gaps showed between the planks, and as the weeks passed and the green wood dried out, the gaps widened. Knotholes gaped in the uncovered floor.

Each barracks was divided into six units, sixteen by twenty feet, about the size of a living room, with one bare bulb hanging from

6. Manzanar was built in *Owens Valley,* near Death Valley, about two hundred miles north of Los Angeles.
7. In the army, a *mess hall* is the place where meals are eaten.
8. *Lee* is shelter or protection, especially on the side of something facing away from the wind.

Japanese Americans en route to internment camp. Library of Congress.

Viewing the photograph: What atmosphere does the photograph convey? What word would you use to describe these children's and adults' reactions upon arriving at the camp?

the ceiling and an oil stove for heat. We were assigned two of these for the twelve people in our family group; and our official family "number" was enlarged by three digits—16 plus the number of this barracks. We were issued steel army cots, two brown army blankets each, and some mattress covers, which my brothers stuffed with straw.

The first task was to divide up what space we had for sleeping. Bill and Woody contributed a blanket each and partitioned off the first room: one side for Bill and Tomi, one side for Woody and Chizu and their baby girl. Woody also got the stove, for heating formulas.

The people who had it hardest during the first few months were young couples like these, many of whom had married just before the evacuation began, in order not to be separated and sent to different camps. Our two rooms were crowded, but at least it was all in the family. My oldest sister and her husband were shoved into one of those sixteen-by-twenty-foot compartments with six people they had never seen before—two other couples, one recently married like themselves, the other with two teenage boys. Partitioning off a room like that wasn't easy. It was bitter cold when we arrived, and the wind did not abate.[9] All they had to use for room dividers were those army blankets, two of which were barely enough to keep one person warm. They argued over whose blanket should be sacrificed and later argued about noise at night—the parents wanted their boys asleep by 9:00 P.M.—and they continued arguing over matters like that

9. The fact that the wind did not *abate* means that it did not lessen in force or intensity.

for six months, until my sister and her husband left to harvest sugar beets in Idaho. It was grueling[10] work up there, and wages were pitiful, but when the call came through camp for workers to alleviate the wartime labor shortage, it sounded better than their life at Manzanar. They knew they'd have, if nothing else, a room, perhaps a cabin of their own.

That first night in Block 16, the rest of us squeezed into the second room—Granny, Lillian, age fourteen, Ray, thirteen, May, eleven, Kiyo, ten, Mama, and me. I didn't mind this at all at the time. Being youngest meant I got to sleep with Mama. And before we went to bed I had a great time jumping up and down on the mattress. The boys had stuffed so much straw into hers, we had to flatten it some so we wouldn't slide off. I slept with her every night after that until Papa came back.

We woke early, shivering and coated with dust that had blown up through the knotholes and in through the slits around the doorway. During the night Mama had unpacked all our clothes and heaped them on our beds for warmth. Now our cubicle looked as if a great laundry bag had exploded and then been sprayed with fine dust. A skin of sand covered the floor. I looked over Mama's shoulder at Kiyo, on top of his fat mattress, buried under jeans and overcoats and sweaters. His eyebrows were gray, and he was starting to giggle. He was looking at me, at my gray eyebrows and coated hair, and pretty soon we were both giggling. I looked at Mama's face to see if she thought Kiyo was funny. She lay very still next to me on our mattress, her eyes scanning everything—bare rafters, walls, dusty kids—scanning slowly, and I think the mask of her face would have cracked had not Woody's voice just then come at us through the wall. He was rapping on the planks as if testing to see if they were hollow.

"Hey!" he yelled. "You guys fall into the same flour barrel as us?"

"No," Kiyo yelled back. "Ours is full of Japs."

All of us laughed at this.

"Well, tell 'em it's time to get up," Woody said. "If we're gonna live in this place, we better get to work."

He gave us ten minutes to dress, then he came in carrying a broom, a hammer, and a sack full of tin can lids he had scrounged somewhere. Woody would be our leader for a while now, short, stocky, grinning behind his mustache. He had just turned twenty-four. In later years he would tour the country with Mr. Moto, the Japanese tag-team wrestler, as his sinister assistant Suki—karate chops through the ropes from outside the ring, a chunky leg reaching from under his kimono to trip up Mr. Moto's foe. In the ring Woody's smile looked sly and crafty; he hammed it up. Offstage it was whimsical, as if some joke were bursting to be told.

"Hey, brother Ray, Kiyo," he said. "You see these tin can lids?"

"Yeah, yeah," the boys said drowsily, as if going back to sleep. They were both young versions of Woody.

"You see all them knotholes in the floor and in the walls?"

They looked around. You could see about a dozen.

Woody said, "You get those covered up before breakfast time. Any more sand comes in here through one of them knotholes, you have to eat it off the floor with ketchup."

10. *Grueling* work is very difficult, exhausting work.

Vocabulary

alleviate (ə lē′ vē āt′) *v.* to make easier to bear; relieve; lessen
whimsical (hwim′ zi kəl) *adj.* fanciful; curiously humorous

"What about sand that comes in through the cracks?" Kiyo said.

Woody stood up very straight, which in itself was funny, since he was only about five-foot-six.

"Don't worry about the cracks," he said. "Different kind of sand comes in through the cracks."

He put his hands on his hips and gave Kiyo a sternly comic look, squinting at him through one eye the way Papa would when he was asserting his authority. Woody mimicked Papa's voice: "And I can tell the difference. So be careful."

The boys laughed and went to work nailing down lids. May started sweeping out the sand. I was helping Mama fold the clothes we'd used for cover, when Woody came over and put his arm around her shoulder. He was short; she was even shorter, under five feet.

He said softly, "You okay, Mama?"

She didn't look at him, she just kept folding clothes and said, "Can we get the cracks covered too, Woody?"

Outside the sky was clear, but icy gusts of wind were buffeting our barracks every few minutes, sending fresh dust puffs up through the floorboards. May's broom could barely keep up with it, and our oil heater could scarcely hold its own against the drafts.

"We'll get this whole place as tight as a barrel, Mama. I already met a guy who told me where they pile all the scrap lumber."

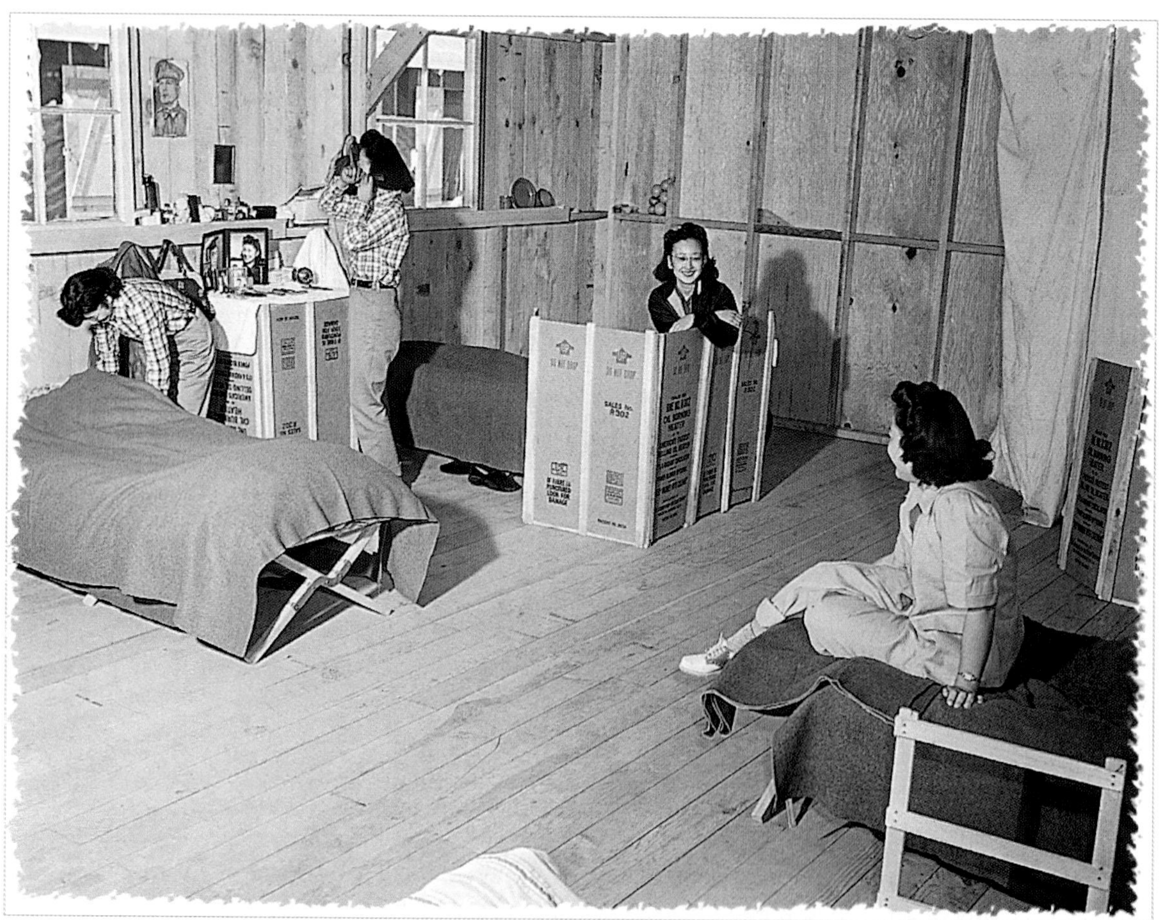

Viewing the photograph: What does this photograph say about life in the internment camp?

"Scrap?"

"That's all they got. I mean, they're still building the camp, you know. Sixteen blocks left to go. After that, they say maybe we'll get some stuff to fix the insides a little bit."

Her eyes blazed then, her voice quietly furious. "Woody, we can't live like this. Animals live like this."

It was hard to get Woody down. He'd keep smiling when everybody else was ready to explode. Grief flickered in his eyes. He blinked it away and hugged her tighter. "We'll make it better, Mama. You watch."

We could hear voices in other cubicles now. Beyond the wall Woody's baby girl started to cry.

"I have to go over to the kitchen," he said, "see if those guys got a pot for heating bottles. That oil stove takes too long—something wrong with the fuel line. I'll find out what they're giving us for breakfast."

"Probably hotcakes with soy sauce," Kiyo said, on his hands and knees between the bunks.

"No." Woody grinned, heading out the door. "Rice. With Log Cabin Syrup and melted butter."

I don't remember what we ate that first morning. I know we stood for half an hour in cutting wind waiting to get our food. Then we took it back to the cubicle and ate huddled around the stove. Inside, it was warmer than when we left, because Woody was already making good his promise to Mama, tacking up some ends of lath[11] he'd found, stuffing rolled paper around the door frame.

Trouble was, he had almost nothing to work with. Beyond this temporary weather stripping, there was little else he could do. Months went by, in fact, before our "home" changed much at all from what it was the day we moved in—bare floors, blanket partitions, one bulb in each compartment dangling from a roof beam, and open ceilings overhead so that mischievous boys like Ray and Kiyo could climb up into the rafters and peek into anyone's life.

The simple truth is the camp was no more ready for us when we got there than we were ready for it. We had only the dimmest ideas of what to expect. Most of the families, like us, had moved out from southern California with as much luggage as each person could carry. Some old men left Los Angeles wearing Hawaiian shirts and Panama hats and stepped off the bus at an altitude of 4000 feet, with nothing available but sagebrush and tarpaper to stop the April winds pouring down off the back side of the Sierras.[12]

The War Department was in charge of all the camps at this point. They began to issue military surplus from the First World War—olive-drab knit caps, earmuffs, peacoats, canvas leggings. Later on, sewing machines were shipped in, and one barracks was turned into a clothing factory. An old seamstress took a peacoat of mine, tore the lining out, opened and flattened the sleeves, added a collar, put arm holes in and handed me back a beautiful cape. By fall dozens of seamstresses were working full-time transforming thousands of these old army clothes into capes, slacks and

Did You Know?
A *peacoat* is a double-breasted jacket of thick woolen cloth, worn especially by sailors.

11. In construction, *lath* is any of the thin, narrow strips of wood used as a foundation for plaster or tiles.

12. The *Sierras,* or Sierra Nevada Mountains, run through eastern California. Manzanar was between these mountains and Death Valley.

stylish coats. But until that factory got going and packages from friends outside began to fill out our wardrobes, warmth was more important than style. I couldn't help laughing at Mama walking around in army earmuffs and a pair of wide-cuffed, khaki-colored wool trousers several sizes too big for her. Japanese are generally smaller than Caucasians, and almost all these clothes were oversize. They flopped, they dangled, they hung.

Did You Know?
The great actor and director *Charlie Chaplin* gained fame for his role as a tramp in baggy pants in a series of movies in the 1920s.

It seems comical, looking back; we were a band of Charlie Chaplins marooned in the California desert. But at the time, it was pure chaos. That's the only way to describe it. The evacuation had been so hurriedly planned, the camps so hastily thrown together, nothing was completed when we got there, and almost nothing worked.

I was sick continually, with stomach cramps and diarrhea. At first it was from the shots they gave us for typhoid, in very heavy doses and in assembly-line fashion: swab, jab, swab, *Move along now,* swab, jab, swab, *Keep it moving.* That knocked all of us younger kids down at once, with fevers and vomiting. Later, it was the food that made us sick, young and old alike. The kitchens were too small and badly ventilated. Food would spoil from being left out too long. That summer, when the heat got fierce, it would spoil faster. The refrigeration kept breaking down. The cooks, in many cases, had never cooked before. Each block had to provide its own volunteers. Some were lucky and had a professional or two in their midst. But the first chef in our block had been a gardener all his life and suddenly found himself preparing three meals a day for 250 people.

"The Manzanar runs" became a condition of life, and you only hoped that when you rushed to the latrine, one would be in working order.

That first morning, on our way to the chow line, Mama and I tried to use the women's latrine in our block. The smell of it spoiled what little appetite we had. Outside, men were working in an open trench, up to their knees in muck—a common sight in the months to come. Inside, the floor was covered with excrement, and all twelve bowls were erupting like a row of tiny volcanoes.

Mama stopped a kimono-wrapped woman stepping past us with her sleeve pushed up against her nose and asked, "What do you do?"

"Try Block Twelve," the woman said, grimacing. "They have just finished repairing the pipes."

It was about two city blocks away. We followed her over there and found a line of women waiting in the wind outside the latrine. We had no choice but to join the line and wait with them.

Inside it was like all the other latrines. Each block was built to the same design, just as each of the ten camps, from California to Arkansas, was built to a common master plan. It was an open room, over a concrete slab. The sink was a long metal trough against one wall, with a row of spigots for hot and cold water. Down the center of the room twelve toilet bowls were arranged in six pairs, back to back, with no partitions. My mother was a very modest person, and this was going to be agony for her, sitting down in public, among strangers.

One old woman had already solved the problem for herself by dragging in a large cardboard carton. She set it up around one of the bowls, like a three-sided screen. OXYDOL was printed in large black letters down the front. I remember this well, because that was the soap we were issued for laundry; later on, the smell of it would permeate these rooms. The upended carton was about four feet high. The old woman behind it wasn't much taller. When she stood, only her head showed over the top.

She was about Granny's age. With great effort she was trying to fold the sides of the screen together. Mama happened to be at the head of the line now. As she approached the vacant bowl, she and the old woman bowed to each other from the waist. Mama then moved to help her with the carton, and the old woman said very graciously, in Japanese, "Would you like to use it?"

Happily, gratefully, Mama bowed again and said, "*Arigato*" (Thank you). "*Arigato gozaimas*" (Thank you very much). "I will return it to your barracks."

"Oh, no. It is not necessary. I will be glad to wait."

The old woman unfolded one side of the cardboard, while Mama opened the other; then she bowed again and scurried out the door.

Those big cartons were a common sight in the spring of 1942. Eventually sturdier partitions appeared, one or two at a time. The first were built of scrap lumber. Word would get around that Block such and such had partitions now, and Mama and my older sisters would walk halfway across the camp to use them. Even after every latrine in camp was screened, this quest for privacy continued. Many would wait until late at night. Ironically, because of this, midnight was often the most crowded time of all.

shikata ga nai,
this cannot be helped

Like so many of the women there, Mama never did get used to the latrines. It was a humiliation she just learned to endure: *shikata ga nai*, this cannot be helped. She would quickly subordinate her own desires to those of the family or the community, because she knew cooperation was the only way to survive. At the same time she placed a high premium on personal privacy, respected it in others and insisted upon it for herself. Almost everyone at Manzanar had inherited this pair of traits from the generations before them who had learned to live in a small, crowded country like Japan. Because of the first they were able to take a desolate stretch of wasteland and gradually make it livable. But the entire situation there, especially in the beginning—the packed sleeping quarters, the communal mess halls, the open toilets—all this was an open insult to that other, private self, a slap in the face you were powerless to challenge.

Vocabulary

subordinate (sə bôr′ də nāt′) *v.* to cause to be, or treat as, secondary, inferior, or less important

Responding to Literature

Personal Response

Did this account of the treatment of Japanese Americans during World War II shock or surprise you? Share your reactions with your classmates.

Analyzing Literature

Recall

1. Describe what life on Terminal Island is like for the narrator and her family.
2. How do public attitudes toward the Japanese change during the family's stay in Boyle Heights? Where does the family go next? Why?
3. Describe the living conditions the Wakatsukis encounter when they first arrive at the camp.
4. How do the people interned at Manzanar make it more livable?
5. According to the narrator, why is privacy so important to the people living at the camp?

Interpret

6. Why do you think the Terminal Islanders treat "outsiders" as they do?
7. How does the narrator's attitude during the bus trip differ from that of her adult relatives? What do you think accounts for this difference?
8. What do the living conditions at the camp seem to suggest about the attitudes of the people who are in charge of the facility? Explain.
9. How does humor help the Wakatsukis cope with their situation? Give specific examples.
10. What might the old woman's cardboard carton **symbolize,** or stand for? Explain your response.

Evaluate and Connect

11. **Theme Connections** Reread the biography of the Houstons on page 459. How has remembering Manzanar helped Jeanne Wakatsuki Houston? How might others benefit from sharing her memories?
12. Which character in the selection do you admire the most? The least? Give reasons for your answer.
13. *Shikata ga nai* means "It cannot be helped. It must be done." To what situations in your own life might this expression apply? Explain.
14. What lesson or lessons about prejudice do you think this selection teaches? Explain.
15. The U.S. government has acknowledged that the internment of Japanese Americans was a mistake. Do you think this kind of mistake could happen again? Why or why not?

Literary ELEMENTS

Autobiography

An **autobiography** is a person's account of his or her own life. In most autobiographies, the writer tells the story from the first-person point of view, using the pronoun *I.* The use of this point of view makes most autobiographies very personal and subjective. In *Farewell to Manzanar,* for example, Jeanne Wakatsuki Houston gives a personal account of her experiences at an internment camp. She describes not only the events that occurred, but also her reactions to those events. For example, she describes the apricot and rice dessert served at the camp as "an inedible concoction." This description helps the reader understand the cultural gap that seems to exist between the Caucasians running the camp and the Japanese Americans who are interned there.

1. List some details from the selection that you would not find in a more objective source, such as an encyclopedia. How do these details help you better understand this episode in U.S. history?
2. How might this account be different if it were written from the point of view of one of the Caucasians working at the camp? Explain.

- See **Literary Terms Handbook,** p. R2.

Literature and Writing

Writing About Literature

Analyze Setting In *Farewell to Manzanar,* the narrator describes the different settings in which the events of the selection occur. Briefly describe each setting, and then compare and contrast the different places in which the narrator's family lived in 1941 and 1942. Which place does the narrator seem to like best? least? Why? Share your analysis with several classmates.

Creative Writing

It's Not Fair! Reread your response to the Reading Focus on page 459. Now imagine that you and your family, like the Wakatsukis, are being forced to move because of your ethnic background. Write a letter to your congressional representative in which you protest the injustice of this situation. Explain your position clearly, but avoid abusive language. Be sure to use the proper form for a business letter.

Extending Your Response

Literature Groups

Compare Passages Identify a passage in the selection that you found particularly powerful or moving. Share the passage with your group, as well as your reasons for choosing it. Discuss how each passage chosen helps to illuminate what Jeanne Wakatsuki Houston has called "an extraordinary episode in American history." Compare your group's choices with those of another group.

Interdisciplinary Activity

Music: Song Lyrics Protest songs are a traditional vehicle for responding to injustice. Write the lyrics of a song protesting the unjust treatment of Japanese Americans during World War II. Set your lyrics to music, if you wish, and perform your song for the class.

Internet Connection

Manzanar Today Manzanar is now a National Historic Site under the administration of the National Park Service. Create a list of questions about Manzanar. For example, you might ask what is being done to preserve this camp and to honor the people once interned there? Use the Internet to find answers to these questions. Then, with a group, create a multimedia display that presents what you have discovered.

Reading Further

If you'd like to read more about Japanese Americans during World War II, you might enjoy these works:

Nonfiction: *Behind Barbed Wire: The Imprisonment of Japanese Americans During World War II,* by Daniel S. Davis, looks at the factors that led to the internment of Japanese Americans.

Interviews: *And Justice for All,* by John Tateishi, contains Japanese Americans' accounts of their experiences in relocation camps.

Save your work for your portfolio.

Memorial at the Manzanar National Historic Site.

GRAMMAR AND LANGUAGE • Intervening Prepositional Phrases

A verb must agree with its subject in person and number. Sometimes, however, prepositional phrases intervene between the subject and verb. Make sure you don't mistake a word in the prepositional phrase for the subject. The object of a preposition is never the subject of a sentence.

Look at these examples. The subjects and verbs have been underlined.

The food from the kitchens makes the children sick.

Knotholes in the wall let the wind blow through the cabin.

● For information about similar usage problems, see **Language Handbook,** pp. R17–R19.

PRACTICE Some of the following sentences lack subject-verb agreement. Rewrite those sentences correctly on your paper. Write *OK* if a sentence is correct.

1. The plates in the velvet-lined box is valuable.
2. The aroma from the many foods on the table make my mouth water.
3. Only one of the spigots works.
4. The noises in our barrack sounds strange to us.
5. The people from that bus lives in this barrack.

APPLY Review a piece of your recent writing, looking for a lack of subject-verb agreement. Revise if necessary.

READING AND THINKING • Summarizing

You can track the plot and understand how events in a story relate to each other by stopping every so often and **summarizing.** When you summarize, you briefly state in your own words the important points of what you've read. For example, the following sentences summarize the first part of the excerpt from *Farewell to Manzanar.*

When Papa disappeared in December of 1941, Mama moved the family from Ocean Park to Terminal Island, a company town where everyone worked for the canneries. Their house was a shack in a ghetto. Every day the speaker and her brother lived in fear of encounters with the mean, threatening kids who lived there.

PRACTICE Write a summary of the events that occur from that first morning when Mama and the speaker try to use the women's latrine in their block to the end of the excerpt from *Farewell to Manzanar.* Ask yourself who, what, where, why, and when questions to come up with a good summary.

● For more about related comprehension skills, see **Reading Handbook,** pp. R82–R84.

VOCABULARY • Parts of Speech

When one word is modified to serve as a different part of speech, it still carries the central part of its meaning with it. So, when you learn one new word, you usually have a significant head start on understanding all the other forms of that word. For example, as a modified version of the word *patriarch,* the adjective *patriarchal* has much the same meaning.

PRACTICE Use your knowledge of the vocabulary words in *Farewell to Manzanar* to figure out the meanings of the underlined words below. For each, write either a synonym or a brief explanation of what the word means.

1. an exclusive club
2. alleviation of pain
3. a dislike of whimsy
4. organized as a patriarchy
5. to intern during wartime
6. her subordination of her own wishes

Government Document

In 1976 President Gerald Ford officially terminated Executive Order 9066, which had permitted the U.S. government to force more than one hundred thousand Japanese Americans to live in internment camps during World War II.

Termination of Executive Order 9066

An American Promise

In this Bicentennial Year, we are commemorating the anniversary dates of many of the great events in American history. An honest reckoning, however, must include a recognition of our national mistakes as well as our national achievements. Learning from our mistakes is not pleasant, but as a great philosopher once admonished, we must do so if we want to avoid repeating them.

February 19th is the anniversary of a sad day in American history. It was on that date in 1942, in the midst of the response to the hostilities that began on December 7, 1941, that Executive Order No. 9066 was issued, subsequently enforced by the criminal penalties of a statute enacted March 21, 1942, resulting in the uprooting of loyal Americans. Over one hundred thousand persons of Japanese ancestry were removed from their homes, detained in special camps, and eventually relocated. . . .

We now know what we should have known then—not only was that evacuation wrong, but Japanese Americans were and are loyal Americans. . . . The Executive Order that was issued on February 19, 1942, was for the sole purpose of prosecuting the war with the Axis Powers, and ceased to be effective with the end of those hostilities. Because there was no formal statement of its termination, however, there is concern among many Japanese Americans that there may yet be some life in that obsolete document. I think it appropriate, in this our Bicentennial Year, to remove all doubt on that matter, and to make clear our commitment in the future.

Now, therefore, I, Gerald R. Ford, President of the United States of America, do hereby proclaim that all the authority conferred by Executive Order No. 9066 terminated upon the issuance of Proclamation No. 2714, which formally proclaimed cessation of the hostilities of World War II on December 31, 1946.

I call upon the American people to affirm with me this American Promise—that we have learned from the tragedy of that long-ago experience forever to treasure liberty and justice for each individual American, and resolve that this kind of action shall never again be repeated.

Gerald R. Ford
The White House, 1976

Analyzing Media

1. What is the "American Promise" that President Ford made?
2. If you had spent time in an internment camp for Japanese Americans, how do you think you might react to this document?

Grammar Link

Making Sure Subjects and Verbs Agree

In every sentence, the subject and verb must agree; that is, if the subject–the who or what that is doing something–is singular, so is the verb. If the subject is plural, so is the verb. No matter how many words there are in a sentence, a verb agrees *only* with its subject.

Problem 1 A compound subject that is joined by *and*
Rice and canned apricots is not an agreeable dish.
The weather and the food are unfamiliar.

Solution If the parts of the compound subject belong to one unit, or if both parts refer to the same person or thing, use a singular verb. For example, *rice* and *canned apricots* belong to one unit: the dinner that was served. If the parts of the compound subject do not belong to one unit, use a plural verb. In this sentence *weather* and *food* refer to different things.

Problem 2 A compound subject that is joined by *or* or *nor*
Neither the living conditions nor the lack of privacy is acceptable to Mama.
Either chilling cold, blazing sun, or dusty winds keep us inside.

Solution Make the verb agree with the subject that is closest to it.

Problem 3 A collective noun as the subject
The number of Japanese Americans sent to camps is horrifying.
A number of the residents find ways to deal with various problems.

Solution If the collective noun refers to a group as a whole *(the number),* use a singular verb. If the collective noun refers to individuals *(a number),* use a plural verb.

Problem 4 A predicate nominative that differs in number from the subject
The floor is slats of scrap lumber.
Army blankets become a room divider.

Solution If the subject is singular, use a singular verb, even if the predicate nominative is plural. If the subject is plural, but the predicate nominative is singular, use a plural verb.

● For more about subject-verb agreement, see **Language Handbook,** pp. R17–R19.

ACTIVITY

For each sentence, write the correct form of the verb.

1. Boxes and luggage (fills, fill) the car.
2. At Manzanar the family (settles, settle) into two different shacks.
3. Neither Jeanne Wakatsuki nor her brothers (knows, know) what to expect.
4. Clear writing and a child's viewpoint (makes, make) *Farewell to Manzanar* interesting.

Vo•cab•u•lar•y Skills

Dictionary Skills: Pronunciation

All vowels and some consonants can be pronounced in different ways. Dictionaries get around this problem by "respelling" words. For example, *gigantic* would appear like this: jī gan′ tik. The first *g* has the "soft" *g* sound, the same sound that *j* has, so it is respelled as *j*. The second one has the "hard" *g* sound, which is represented by *g*.

Another consonant that can be pronounced two ways is *c*. Since both pronunciations can be represented by other letters, *c* never appears in a dictionary respelling. Instead, *s* or *k* is used, depending on which sound *c* has. Therefore, *circuit* is shown as: sur′ kit.

In a dictionary pronunciation guide, a vowel without any symbol represents the normal "short" sound, like the vowels in *sat, set, sit, cot,* and *cut.* Other vowel sounds are shown by symbols, such as a straight line above the vowel to show that it is "long." (Long vowels "say their own names.")

Symbol	Pronunciation
ä	the **ah** sound in **father**
ô	the **aw** sound in **coffee**
oo	the vowel sound in **wood**
o͞o	the vowel sound in **fool**
oi	the vowel sound in **toy**
ou	the **ow** sound in **out**
ə	the vowel sound in the second syllable of **pencil** and **lemon**
hw	**wh** as in **white**
th	**th** as in **thin**
t͟h	**th** as in **this**
zh	the sound made by the ***s*** in **treasure**

EXERCISE

The words shown below are vocabulary words you have recently studied. Use the pronunciation given for each word to answer the question that follows it.

1. *loll* (lol) Does this word rhyme with *bowl* or *parasol?*
2. *token* (tō′ kən) Does this word rhyme with *broken, soaking,* or *rockin'?*
3. *prodigious* (prə dij′ əs) Does the second syllable of this word rhyme with *ridge* or *big?*
4. *crucial* (kro͞o′ shəl) Is the first syllable of this word pronounced like *crook, crush,* or *crew?*
5. *judiciously* (jo͞o dish′ əs lē) Does the second syllable of this word rhyme with *sick, wish,* or *bike?*

Before You Read

By Any Other Name

Reading Focus

In *Romeo and Juliet,* William Shakespeare wrote, "What's in a name? that which we call a rose / By any other name would smell as sweet."

Discuss Do you agree with Shakespeare? Is your name just a name and nothing more? Discuss these questions in a small group.

Setting a Purpose Read to find out what's in a name for Santha Rama Rau.

Building Background

The Time and Place

The events described in this selection occur in the late 1920s, in Zorinabad, India, near the city of Allahabad in north central India.

Did You Know?

Between 1858 and 1947, India was a colony of Great Britain. During this time, British culture exerted a strong influence on Indian life. Some Indians adapted to British customs; others struggled to maintain their own traditions and cultural identity.

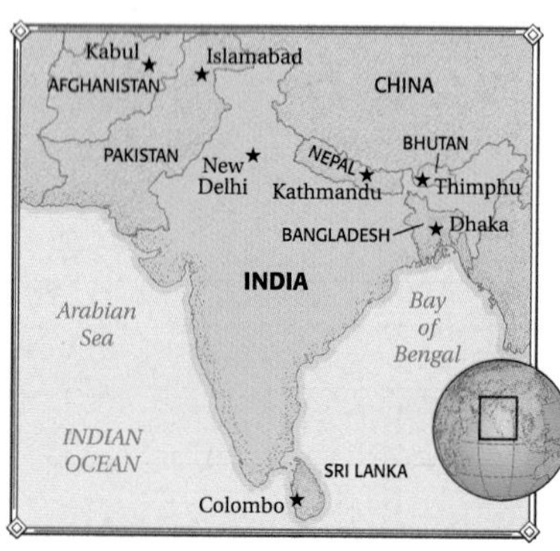

In 1920 Mohandas Gandhi organized a nonviolent resistance movement aimed at winning India's independence. As a result, tensions between India and Britain were high during the 1920s, when the events in this selection take place. Resistance continued until 1947, when Great Britain granted India independence.

Vocabulary Preview

intimidate (in tim′ə dāt′) *v.* to make timid or fearful; bully; p. 480
insular (in′ sə lər) *adj.* showing a limited point of view; p. 481
valid (val′ id) *adj.* acceptable; legitimate; p. 481
detached (di tacht′) *adj.* not involved emotionally; neutral; p. 481
palpitating (pal′ pə tāt′ ing) *adj.* quivering; trembling; vibrating; p. 482
incomprehensible (in′ kom pri hen′ sə bəl) *adj.* not understandable; p. 482
tepid (tep′ id) *adj.* moderately or slightly warm; lukewarm; p. 483

Meet Santha Rama Rau

Santha Rama Rau (sän′ thä rä′ mä rou) was raised in a traditional Indian family that she once referred to as an "unshakable little universe." She attended college in the United States and has lived in other parts of the world as well. Through all her journeys, however, Rama Rau has clung to her family and to her sense of national identity. In the 1940s, Rama Rau described herself as "a part of the great Indian struggle for independence." Her novels and nonfiction reflect her deep-seated love for her native land.

Santha Rama Rau was born in Madras, India, in 1923. This piece first appeared in the New Yorker *magazine and is included in the author's autobiography,* Gifts of Passage, *published in 1961.*

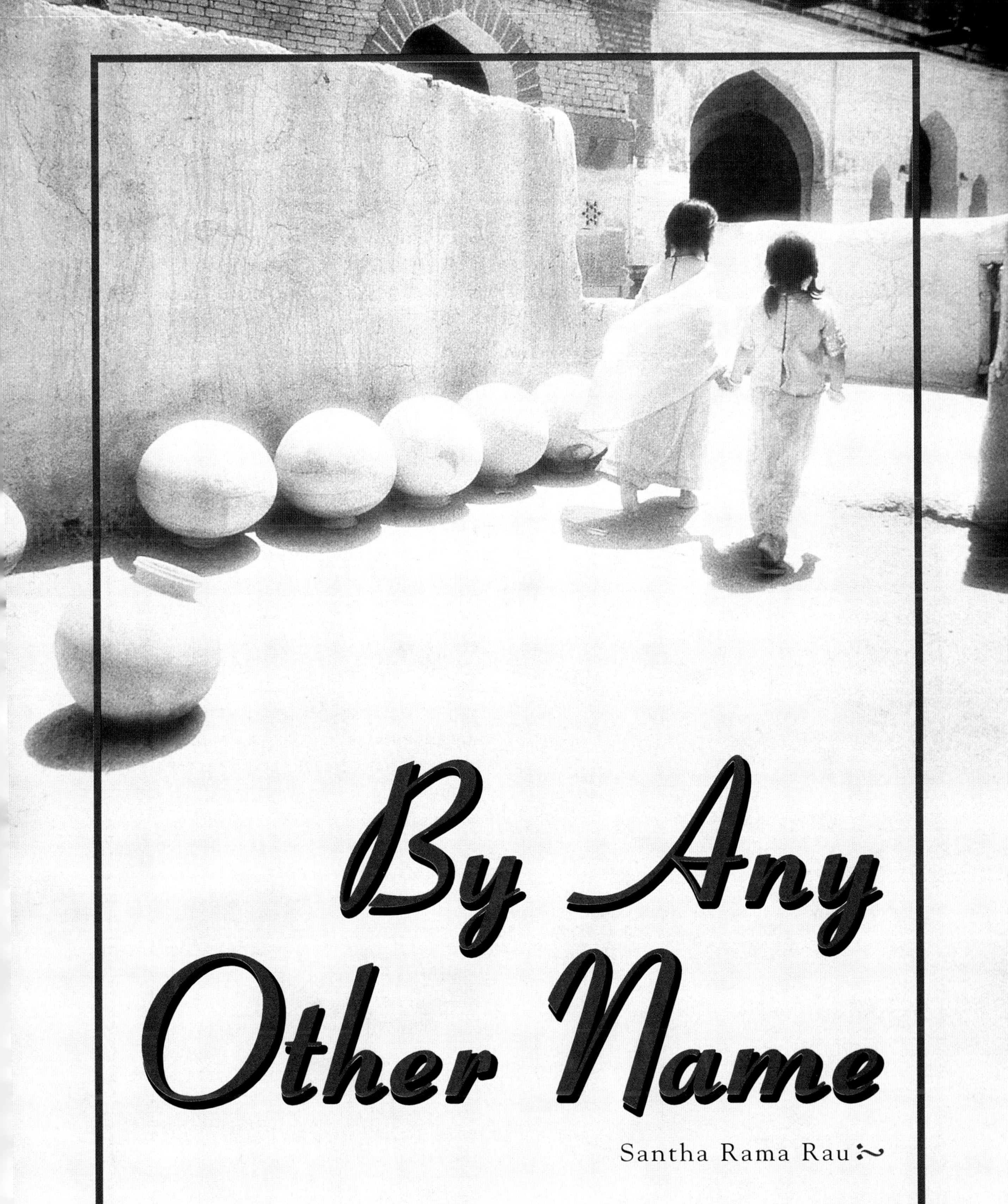

By Any Other Name

Santha Rama Rau

At the Anglo-Indian[1] day school in Zorinabad to which my sister and I were sent when she was eight and I was five and a half, they changed our names. On the first day of school, a hot, windless morning of a north Indian September, we stood in the headmistress's study and she said, "Now you're the new girls. What are your names?"

My sister answered for us. "I am Premila, and she"—nodding in my direction—"is Santha."[2]

The headmistress had been in India, I suppose, fifteen years or so, but she still smiled her helpless inability to cope with Indian names. Her rimless half-glasses glittered, and the precarious[3] bun on the top of her head trembled as she shook her head. "Oh, my dears, those are much too hard for me. Suppose we give you pretty English names. Wouldn't that be more jolly? Let's see, now—Pamela for you, I think." She shrugged in a baffled way at my sister. "That's as close as I can get. And for you," she said to me, "how about Cynthia? Isn't that nice?"

My sister was always less easily intimidated than I was, and while she kept a stubborn silence, I said, "Thank you," in a very tiny voice.

We had been sent to that school because my father, among his responsibilities as an officer of the civil service, had a tour of duty to perform in the villages around that steamy little provincial town, where he had his

1. *Anglo-* is a combining form that means "English" or "English and." Here, the Anglo-Indian school belongs to British colonists in India but accepts both English and Indian students.
2. *Premila* (prem′ il ə), *Santha* (san′ thä)
3. Here, a *precarious* bun is one that seems in danger of coming loose if the headmistress moves her head too vigorously.

Vocabulary

intimidate (in tim′ə dāt′) *v.* to make timid or fearful; bully headquarters at that time. He used to make his shorter inspection tours on horseback, and a week before, in the stale heat of a typically postmonsoon[4] day, we had waved good-bye to him and a little procession—an assistant, a secretary, two bearers, and the man to look after the bedding rolls and luggage. They rode away through our large garden, still bright green from the rains, and we turned back into the twilight of the house and the sound of fans whispering in every room.

Up to then, my mother had refused to send Premila to school in the British-run establishments of that time, because, she used to say, "you can bury a dog's tail for seven years and it still comes out curly, and you can take a Britisher away from his home for a lifetime and he still remains insular." The examinations and degrees from entirely Indian schools were not, in those days, considered valid. In my case, the question had never come up, and probably never would have come up if Mother's extraordinary good health had not broken down. For the first time in my life, she was not able to continue the lessons she had been giving us every morning. So our Hindi books were put away, the stories of the Lord Krishna[5] as a little boy were left in midair, and we were sent to the Anglo-Indian school.

That first day at school is still, when I think of it, a remarkable one. At that age, if one's name is changed, one develops a curious form of dual personality. I remember having a certain detached and disbelieving concern in the actions of "Cynthia," but certainly no responsibility. Accordingly, I followed the thin, erect back of the headmistress down the veranda to my classroom feeling, at most, a passing interest in what was going to happen to me in this strange, new atmosphere of School.

The building was Indian in design, with wide verandas opening onto a central courtyard, but Indian verandas are usually whitewashed, with stone floors. These, in the tradition of British schools, were painted dark brown and had matting on the floors. It gave a feeling of extra intensity to the heat.

I suppose there were about a dozen Indian children in the school—which contained perhaps forty children in all—and four of them were in my class. They were all sitting at the back of the room, and I went to join them. I sat next to a small, solemn girl who didn't smile at me. She had long, glossy-black braids and wore a cotton dress, but she still kept on her Indian jewelry—a gold chain around her neck, thin gold bracelets, and tiny ruby studs in her ears. Like most Indian children, she had a rim of black kohl around her eyes. The cotton dress should have looked strange, but all I could think of was that I should ask my mother if I couldn't wear a dress to school, too, instead of my Indian clothes.

Did You Know?
Kohl is a powder used to darken the eyelids and eyelashes.

4. In southern Asia, the *monsoon* is a seasonal wind that brings heavy rains from the Indian Ocean in the summer. Here, *postmonsoon* refers to the time following the rainy season.
5. India's official language is Hindustani, also called *Hindi.* Most Indians practice Hinduism, a religion in which *Lord Krishna* is one of the most important gods.

Vocabulary

insular (in′ sə lər) *adj.* showing a limited point of view
valid (val′ id) *adj.* acceptable; legitimate
detached (di tacht′) *adj.* not involved emotionally; neutral

I can't remember too much about the proceedings in class that day, except for the beginning. The teacher pointed to me and asked me to stand up. "Now, dear, tell the class your name."

I said nothing.

"Come along," she said, frowning slightly. "What's your name, dear?"

"I don't know," I said, finally.

The English children in the front of the class—there were about eight or ten of them—giggled and twisted around in their chairs to look at me. I sat down quickly and opened my eyes very wide, hoping in that way to dry them off. The little girl with the braids put out her hand and very lightly touched my arm. She still didn't smile.

"Come along," she said, frowning slightly. "What's your name, dear?"

"I don't know," I said, finally.

Most of that morning I was rather bored. I looked briefly at the children's drawings pinned to the wall, and then concentrated on a lizard clinging to the ledge of the high, barred window behind the teacher's head. Occasionally it would shoot out its long yellow tongue for a fly, and then it would rest, with its eyes closed and its belly palpitating, as though it were swallowing several times quickly. The lessons were mostly concerned with reading and writing and simple numbers—things that my mother had already taught me—and I paid very little attention. The teacher wrote on the easel blackboard words like "bat" and "cat," which seemed babyish to me; only "apple" was new and incomprehensible.

When it was time for the lunch recess, I followed the girl with braids out onto the veranda. There the children from the other classes were assembled. I saw Premila at once and ran over to her, as she had charge of our lunchbox. The children were all opening packages and sitting down to eat sandwiches. Premila and I were the only ones who had Indian food—thin wheat chapatties, some vegetable curry,[6] and a bottle of buttermilk. Premila thrust half of it into my hand and whispered fiercely that I should go and sit with my class, because that was what the others seemed to be doing.

The enormous black eyes of the little Indian girl from my class looked at my food longingly, so I offered her some. But she only shook her head and plowed her way solemnly through her sandwiches.

I was very sleepy after lunch, because at home we always took a siesta. It was usually a pleasant time of day, with the bedroom darkened against the harsh afternoon sun, the drifting off into sleep with the sound of Mother's voice reading a story in one's mind, and, finally, the shrill, fussy voice of the ayah[7] waking one for tea.

At school, we rested for a short time on low, folding cots on the veranda, and then we were expected to play games. During the hot part of the afternoon we played indoors, and after the shadows had begun to lengthen and the slight breeze of the evening had come up we moved outside to the wide courtyard.

6. *Chapatties* (chə pä′ tēz) are small, flat, disk-shaped loaves of bread, and *curry* is a stew seasoned with a combination of dried spices.

7. In India, an *ayah* (ä′ yə) is a governess or nursemaid.

Vocabulary

palpitating (pal′ pə tāt′ ing) *adj.* quivering; trembling; vibrating

incomprehensible (in′ kom pri hen′ sə bəl) *adj.* not understandable

I had never really grasped the system of competitive games. At home, whenever we played tag or guessing games, I was always allowed to "win"—"because," Mother used to tell Premila, "she is the youngest, and we have to allow for that." I had often heard her say it, and it seemed quite reasonable to me, but the result was that I had no clear idea of what "winning" meant.

When we played twos-and-threes that afternoon at school, in accordance with my training, I let one of the small English boys catch me, but was naturally rather puzzled when the other children did not return the courtesy. I ran about for what seemed like hours without ever catching anyone, until it was time for school to close. Much later I learned that my attitude was called "not being a good sport," and I stopped allowing myself to be caught, but it was not for years that I really learned the spirit of the thing.

When I saw our car come up to the school gate, I broke away from my classmates and rushed toward it yelling, "Ayah! Ayah!" It seemed like an eternity since I had seen her that morning—a wizened,[8] affectionate figure in her white cotton sari, giving me dozens of urgent and useless instructions on how to be a good girl at school. Premila followed more sedately, and she told me on the way home never to do that again in front of the other children.

Did You Know?
The *sari* (sär′ ē) is an outer garment worn chiefly by women of India and Pakistan.

When we got home we went straight to Mother's high, white room to have tea with her, and I immediately climbed onto the bed and bounced gently up and down on the springs. Mother asked how we had liked our first day in school. I was so pleased to be home and to have left that peculiar Cynthia behind that I had nothing whatever to say about school, except to ask what "apple" meant. But Premila told Mother about the classes, and added that in her class they had weekly tests to see if they had learned their lessons well.

I asked, "What's a test?"

Premila said, "You're too small to have them. You won't have them in your class for donkey's years."[9] She had learned the expression that day and was using it for the first time. We all laughed enormously at her wit. She also told Mother, in an aside,[10] that we should take sandwiches to school the next day. Not, she said, that *she* minded. But they would be simpler for me to handle.

That whole lovely evening I didn't think about school at all. I sprinted barefoot across the lawns with my favorite playmate, the cook's son, to the stream at the end of the garden. We quarreled in our usual way, waded in the tepid water under the lime trees, and waited for the night to bring out the smell of the jasmine. I listened with

Did You Know?
The *jasmine* (jaz′ min) is a sweet-smelling flower of a plant in the olive family.

8. The ayah is *wizened* (wiz′ ənd), which means she is shriveled and withered, probably from old age.

9. The expression *donkey's years* means "an indefinitely long time."
10. A remark not meant to be heard by everyone is an *aside.*

Vocabulary
tepid (tep′ id) *adj.* moderately or slightly warm; lukewarm

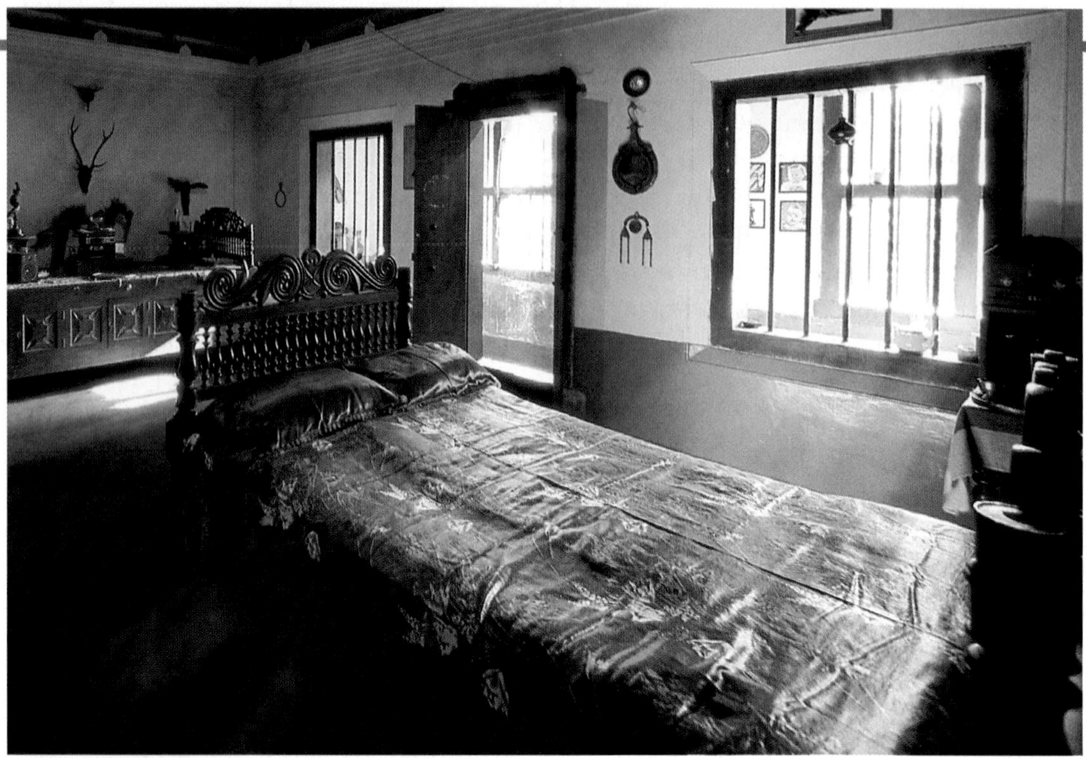

Interior of an Indic house. Anil A. Dave, photographer.

Viewing the photograph: Compare and contrast the mood of this photograph with Santha's thoughts and feelings after she comes home with Premila.

fascination to his stories of ghosts and demons, until I was too frightened to cross the garden alone in the semidarkness. The ayah found me, shouted at the cook's son, scolded me, hurried me in to supper—it was an entirely usual, wonderful evening.

It was a week later, the day of Premila's first test, that our lives changed rather abruptly. I was sitting at the back of my class, in my usual inattentive[11] way, only half listening to the teacher. I had started a rather guarded friendship with the girl with the braids, whose name turned out to be Nalini (Nancy, in school). The three other Indian children were already fast friends. Even at that age it was apparent to all of us that friendship with the English or Anglo-Indian children was out of the question. Occasionally, during the class, my new friend and I would draw pictures and show them to each other secretly.

The door opened sharply and Premila marched in. At first, the teacher smiled at her in a kindly and encouraging way and said, "Now, you're little Cynthia's sister?"

Premila didn't even look at her. She stood with her feet planted firmly apart and her shoulders rigid, and addressed herself directly to me. "Get up," she said. "We're going home."

I didn't know what had happened, but I was aware that it was a crisis of some sort. I rose obediently and started to walk toward my sister.

"Bring your pencils and your notebook," she said.

I went back for them, and together we left the room. The teacher started to say something just as Premila closed the door, but we didn't wait to hear what it was.

11. To be *inattentive* is to be unmindful or neglectful.

In complete silence we left the school grounds and started to walk home. Then I asked Premila what the matter was. All she would say was "We're going home for good."

It was a very tiring walk for a child of five and a half, and I dragged along behind Premila with my pencils growing sticky in my hand. I can still remember looking at the dusty hedges, and the tangles of thorns in the ditches by the side of the road, smelling the faint fragrance from the eucalyptus trees and wondering whether we would ever reach home. Occasionally a horse-drawn tonga[12] passed us, and the women, in their pink or green silks, stared at Premila and me trudging along on the side of the road. A few coolies[13] and a line of women carrying baskets of vegetables on their heads smiled at us. But it was nearing the hottest time of day, and the road was almost deserted. I walked more and more slowly, and shouted to Premila, from time to time, "Wait for me!" with increasing peevishness. She spoke to me only once, and that was to tell me to carry my notebook on my head, because of the sun.

When we got to our house the ayah was just taking a tray of lunch into Mother's room. She immediately started a long, worried questioning about what are you children doing back here at this hour of the day.

Mother looked very startled and very concerned, and asked Premila what had happened.

12. In India, a *tonga* is a small, two-wheeled carriage.
13. *Coolies* are unskilled, poorly paid laborers who often do hard work that no one else is willing to do.

Premila said, "We had our test today, and she made me and the other Indians sit at the back of the room, with a desk between each one."

Mother said, "Why was that, darling?"

"She said it was because Indians cheat," Premila added. "So I don't think we should go back to that school."

Mother looked very distant, and was silent a long time. At last she said, "Of course not, darling." She sounded displeased.

We all shared the curry she was having for lunch, and afterward I was sent off to the beautifully familiar bedroom for my siesta. I could hear Mother and Premila talking through the open door.

Mother said, "Do you suppose she understood all that?"

Premila said, "I shouldn't think so. She's a baby."

Mother said, "Well, I hope it won't bother her."

Of course, they were both wrong. I understood it perfectly, and I remember it all very clearly. But I put it happily away, because it had all happened to a girl called Cynthia, and I never was really particularly interested in her.

Responding to Literature

Personal Response

What is your reaction to the way in which the Indian children were treated at the school? Explain in your journal.

Analyzing Literature

Recall

1. Describe what happens in the headmistress's study.
2. Summarize the events and activities of Santha's first day at school.
3. What happens on the day of Premila's test?
4. How does Santha react to the incident that occurs on the day of Premila's test?
5. Why had the girls' mother been reluctant to send her daughters to a British-run school?

Interpret

6. How do Premila and Santha seem to feel about the headmistress? Support your answer with evidence from the selection.
7. For Santha, how does learning at school differ from learning at home? Compare and contrast the two environments.
8. In your opinion, what do Premila's actions on the day of the test reveal about her character?
9. Do you think Santha's self-esteem has been damaged by her school experience? Explain.
10. Do the actions of the headmistress and teachers seem to confirm or contradict the mother's opinion of British-run schools? Explain.

Evaluate and Connect

11. How does the information in the Did You Know? section on page 478 help you to better understand this selection?
12. **Theme Connections** Why do you think the author chose to write about this particular incident from her childhood?
13. If you had been in Premila's situation, how do you think you might have responded? Explain.
14. Look back at the questions you discussed in the Reading Focus on page 478. Evaluate how well the author addresses those questions in this selection.
15. Which character did you admire most? least? Give reasons for your choices.

Atmosphere

Atmosphere is the emotional quality, or mood, of a piece of writing. For example, a piece may have a romantic, light mood; an atmosphere of doom; or one of confusion and discomfort. The use of descriptive details is one way writers create a particular atmosphere. A writer's description of characters' words and actions also helps to convey the atmosphere. In "By Any Other Name," Santha Rama Rau re-creates two distinct atmospheres—one at her home and one at the Anglo-Indian school.

1. Describe the atmosphere at the school. How does the writer re-create this atmosphere? Use examples from the selection to support your answer.
2. Describe the atmosphere at the author's home. How does Rama Rau convey the special mood of this place? Give specific examples from the selection.
3. Based on the atmospheres in these two settings, what can you tell about the author's feelings about the events in this selection?

- See **Literary Terms Handbook,** p. R1.

Literature and Writing

Writing About Literature

Evaluate the Author's Attitude In a biography of Santha Rama Rau, S. K. Desai writes that in "By Any Other Name," Rama Rau shows "a remarkable power of observation and an equally remarkable attitude of detachment." Do you agree? Write a paragraph or two in which you respond to this question. Support your opinion with evidence from the selection. Meet with a small group of classmates to share your evaluation.

Creative Writing

Dear Diary Imagine that both Premila and Santha kept diaries. Write brief entries for both girls in which they record their feelings about the events that occur on the first day of school and on the day of Premila's test. As you write your diary entries, keep in mind the different ages and personalities of the two sisters.

Extending Your Response

Literature Groups

Actions and Reactions Do you think Premila was right to pull Santha out of class and take her home on the day of the test? Why or why not? Do you think their mother made a good decision in allowing them to stop attending school? What if the girls had stayed? Discuss these issues in your group. Share your ideas with the class.

Performing

Dramatize Imagine that Santha, Premila, and the headmistress have been invited to appear on a talk show to discuss the treatment of Indian students in the Anglo-Indian school. Work with a group to plan the interview. Do research as necessary to learn more about Anglo-Indian relations in the 1920s. Then assign roles, rehearse the interview, and perform it for the class.

Interdisciplinary Activity

Social Studies: What's in Your Name? Work with a small group to research the first names of group members. Explore the history of the names, including their origin, meaning, and changes in spelling. Decide as a group how you will present the information you have gathered. For example, you might display it in a chart or on a bulletin board, or you might want to create your own booklet.

Save your work for your portfolio.

VOCABULARY • Etymology

The etymology, or history, of *intimidate* isn't very surprising, especially if you noticed the word *timid* in it. *Intimidate* is made up of the Latin prefix *in-*, meaning "in," plus *timidus,* "to be afraid." The history of *tepid* is even more straightforward. It comes from *tepere,* which means "to be slightly warm."

PRACTICE Use the information provided about each word's etymology to answer these questions.

1. *Palpitating* comes from the Latin *palpare,* "to feel." What does a doctor do when he or she palpates a patient's spine?
2. *Incomprehensible* combines the English prefix *in-* ("not") with *comprehensible,* which comes from the Latin *comprehendere* ("to seize or grasp mentally"). What is an incomprehensible idea?
3. *Valid* comes from the Latin *validus* ("strong"). What does this tell you about a person who is described as an invalid?

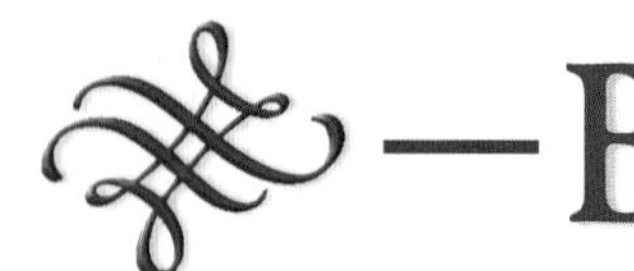

Before You Read

Living Well. Living Good.

Reading Focus

What do you need in order to live well and be happy?

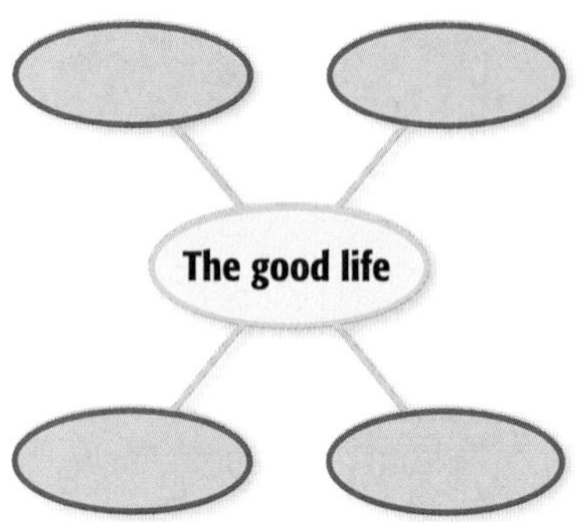

Explore It! Explore your ideas about living well. Make a web like the one shown, and write in words and phrases that describe your concept of "the good life."

Setting a Purpose
Read to learn some important lessons about the art of living.

Building Background

The Time and Place
The events described in this selection take place in Bel Air, California, in the mid-1900s, not long after World War II.

Did You Know?
In this selection, Maya Angelou's aunt recalls the pigs' feet, greens, fried chicken, and other foods that she and her friends shared on Saturday evenings. These dishes are part of the traditional African American cuisine that today is called soul food. Soul food has its roots in Southern cooking. On plantations of the Deep South before the Civil War, the enslaved people ate mainly cornmeal, which was most often eaten as mush, and poorer cuts of pork, such as chitlins (pig intestines). Occasionally, this diet was supplemented with hominy (made from corn), sweet potatoes, vegetables, and wild game and fish.

Vocabulary Preview

meticulous (mi tik′ yə ləs) *adj.* characterized by great or excessive concern about details; p. 490

commodious (kə mō′ dē əs) *adj.* having or containing ample room; spacious; p. 490

convivial (kən viv′ ē əl) *adj.* fond of merriment and parties with good company; sociable; p. 491

scenario (si nār′ ē ō′) *n.* an outline or model of an expected or imagined series of events; p. 491

inhibit (in hib′ it) *v.* to hold back one's natural impulses; restrain; p. 491

Meet Maya Angelou

"Somehow, we have come to the erroneous belief that we are all but flesh, blood, and bones, and that's all. . . . There is something more—the spirit, or the soul. I think that that quality encourages our courtesy and care and our minds."

With these words, author, poet, playwright, and songwriter Maya Angelou (mī′ yə an′ jəl ō) identifies the source of the optimism that infuses this selection and her work as a whole. Angelou gained national prominence with the publication in 1969 of her autobiography *I Know Why the Caged Bird Sings*.

Maya Angelou was born in St. Louis in 1928. This selection appears in Wouldn't Take Nothing for My Journey Now, *published in 1993.*

Living Well. Living Good.

Maya Angelou

Victorian Parlor II, 1945. Horace Pippin. Oil on canvas, 25¼ x 30 in. Metropolitan Museum of Art, New York. Arthur Hoppock Hearn Fund, 1958.

Living Well. Living Good.

AUNT TEE was a Los Angeles member of our extended family.[1] She was seventy-nine when I met her, sinewy,[2] strong, and the color of old lemons. She wore her coarse, straight hair, which was slightly streaked with gray, in a long braided rope across the top of her head. With her high cheekbones, old gold skin, and almond eyes, she looked more like an Indian chief than an old black woman. (Aunt Tee described herself and any favored member of her race as Negroes. *Black* was saved for those who had incurred her disapproval.)

She had retired and lived alone in a dead, neat ground-floor apartment. Wax flowers and china figurines sat on elaborately embroidered and heavily starched doilies. Sofas and chairs were tautly upholstered. The only thing at ease in Aunt Tee's apartment was Aunt Tee.

I used to visit her often and perch on her uncomfortable sofa just to hear her stories. She was proud that after working thirty years as a maid, she spent the next thirty years as a live-in housekeeper, carrying the keys to rich houses and keeping meticulous accounts.

"Living in lets the white folks know Negroes are as neat and clean as they are, sometimes more so. And it gives the Negro maid a chance to see white folks ain't no smarter than Negroes. Just luckier. Sometimes."

Aunt Tee told me that once she was housekeeper for a couple in Bel Air,[3] California, lived with them in a fourteen-room ranch house. There was a day maid who cleaned, and a gardener who daily tended the lush gardens. Aunt Tee oversaw the workers. When she had begun the job, she had cooked and served a light breakfast, a good lunch, and a full three- or four-course dinner to her employers and their guests. Aunt Tee said she watched them grow older and leaner. After a few years they stopped entertaining and ate dinner hardly seeing each other at the table. Finally, they sat in a dry silence as they ate evening meals of soft scrambled eggs, melba toast, and weak tea. Aunt Tee said she saw them growing old but didn't see herself aging at all.

She became the social maven.[4] She started "keeping company" (her phrase) with a chauffeur down the street. Her best friend and her friend's husband worked in service[5] only a few blocks away.

On Saturdays Aunt Tee would cook a pot of pigs' feet, a pot of greens, fry chicken, make potato salad, and bake a banana pudding. Then, that evening, her friends—the chauffeur, the other housekeeper, and her husband—would come to Aunt Tee's commodious live-in quarters. There the four would eat and drink, play records and dance. As the evening wore on, they would settle down to a serious game of bid whist.[6]

Naturally, during this revelry jokes were told, fingers snapped, feet were patted, and there was a great deal of laughter.

Aunt Tee said that what occurred during every Saturday party startled her and her friends the first time it happened. They had been playing cards, and Aunt Tee, who had just

1. Parents and their children make up what is called the nuclear family. One's *extended family* includes other relatives who are related by blood or marriage.
2. Here, *sinewy* (sin′ ū ē) could mean "tough and stringy," "physically powerful," or "vigorously healthy."
3. *Bel Air* is one of the wealthiest, most fashionable communities in Los Angeles.
4. A *maven* is one whose special knowledge or experience makes him or her an expert in a given field.
5. Aunt Tee's two friends *in service* were servants in another household.
6. *Bid whist* is a card game, somewhat like bridge, for two players or two teams of two players.

Vocabulary

meticulous (mi tik′ yə ləs) *adj.* characterized by great or excessive concern about details

commodious (kə mō′ dē əs) *adj.* having or containing ample room; spacious won the bid, held a handful of trumps. She felt a cool breeze on her back and sat upright and turned around. Her employers had cracked her door open and beckoned to her. Aunt Tee, a little peeved, laid down her cards and went to the door. The couple backed away and asked her to come into the hall, and there they both spoke and won Aunt Tee's sympathy forever.

"Theresa, we don't mean to disturb you . . ." the man whispered, "but you all seem to be having such a good time . . ."

The woman added, "We hear you and your friends laughing every Saturday night, and we'd just like to watch you. We don't want to bother you. We'll be quiet and just watch."

The man said, "If you'll just leave your door ajar, your friends don't need to know. We'll never make a sound." Aunt Tee said she saw no harm in agreeing, and she talked it over with her company. They said it was OK with them, but it was sad that the employers owned the gracious house, the swimming pool, three cars, and numberless palm trees, but had no joy. Aunt Tee told me that laughter and relaxation had left the house; she agreed it was sad.

That story has stayed with me for nearly thirty years, and when a tale remains fresh in my mind, it almost always contains a lesson which will benefit me.

My dears, I draw the picture of the wealthy couple standing in a darkened hallway, peering into a lighted room where black servants were lifting their voices in merriment and comradery, and I realize that living well is an art which can be developed. Of course, you will need the basic talents to build upon: They are a love of life and ability to take great pleasure from small offerings, an assurance that the world owes you nothing and that every gift is exactly that, a gift. That people who may differ from you in political stance, sexual persuasion, and racial inheritance can be founts of fun, and if you are lucky, they can become even convivial comrades.

Living life as art requires a readiness to forgive. I do not mean that you should suffer fools gladly, but rather remember your own shortcomings, and when you encounter another with flaws, don't be eager to righteously seal yourself away from the offender forever. Take a few breaths and imagine yourself having just committed the action which has set you at odds.

Because of the routines we follow, we often forget that life is an ongoing adventure. We leave our homes for work, acting and even believing that we will reach our destinations with no unusual event startling us out of our set expectations. The truth is we know nothing, not where our cars will fail or when our buses will stall, whether our places of employment will be there when we arrive, or whether, in fact, we ourselves will arrive whole and alive at the end of our journeys. Life is pure adventure, and the sooner we realize that, the quicker we will be able to treat life as art: to bring all our energies to each encounter, to remain flexible enough to notice and admit when what we expected to happen did not happen. We need to remember that we are created creative and can invent new scenarios as frequently as they are needed.

Life seems to love the liver of it. Money and power can liberate only if they are used to do so. They can imprison and inhibit more finally than barred windows and iron chains.

Vocabulary

convivial (kən viv′ ē əl) *adj.* fond of merriment and parties with good company; sociable
scenario (si nār′ ē ō′) *n.* an outline or model of an expected or imagined series of events
inhibit (in hib′ it) *v.* to hold back one's natural impulses; restrain

Responding to Literature

Personal Response

Does Aunt Tee remind you of someone you know or have known? If not, do you think you would enjoy meeting someone like her? Explain.

Analyzing Literature

Recall

1. Describe Aunt Tee's appearance and personality.
2. According to Aunt Tee, what benefits come from Negroes "living in"?
3. Describe a typical Saturday evening for Aunt Tee and her friends. What request do Aunt Tee's employers make one Saturday?
4. According to Angelou, what are the "basic talents" that one needs in order to live well?
5. What advice about the art of living does Angelou offer?

Interpret

6. Does Aunt Tee's apartment seem to match her personality? Explain.
7. In your opinion, does Aunt Tee resent having worked as a maid and housekeeper? Give reasons for your response.
8. Why do you think Aunt Tee and her friends respond as they do to the employers' request?
9. Do you think Aunt Tee has the "basic talents" that Angelou says are required for living well? Explain.
10. Do Aunt Tee's employers seem to understand the art of living, as described by Angelou? Explain.

Evaluate and Connect

11. Do you think it is possible to live life as art in the way that Angelou describes? Why or why not?
12. In literature, **pathos** is an element that evokes compassion or pity. How does Angelou create pathos in this selection?
13. Theme Connections Angelou says that "when a tale remains fresh in my mind, it almost always contains a lesson which will benefit me." What kinds of stories remain fresh in your mind? Why?
14. In the final paragraph, Angelou writes: "Life seems to love the liver of it." How might Aunt Tee's story be used to illustrate this statement?
15. After reading this selection, what changes or additions would you make to the web you created in the Reading Focus on page 488?

Literary ELEMENTS

Using Character to Understand Theme

The **theme** of a literary work is the main idea, or message, that the writer wishes to convey. Writers sometimes reveal the theme of a work through the experiences of one or more characters. In "Living Well. Living Good." Maya Angelou uses the character of Aunt Tee to help convey the theme of the selection. The other characters in Aunt Tee's story–her employers and her friends–also help to reveal the theme.

1. When Aunt Tee begins working for the couple in Bel Air, who seems to have a better life, Aunt Tee or her employers? Explain.
2. How does Aunt Tee's view of her employers change over time? What causes this change?
3. What message, or theme, does Angelou convey through the experiences of Aunt Tee, her friends, and her employers?

- See **Literary Terms Handbook,** p. R13.

Literature and Writing

Writing About Literature

Critique the Selection After telling Aunt Tee's story, Angelou concludes the selection with an "essay" about how to live life as art. What is your opinion of this "essay"? Does it add to your understanding and appreciation of the selection, or does it simply repeat the ideas expressed in Aunt Tee's story? Write a critique in which you answer these questions. Support your ideas using specific details from the selection.

Personal Writing

Reflections Choose someone you admire. Then close your eyes and reflect on the qualities that make that individual unique and admirable. Write a description of the person, modeling the style that Angelou uses to describe Aunt Tee in "Living Well. Living Good."

Extending Your Response

Literature Groups

Stepping Over the Line? Do you think Aunt Tee's employers invaded her privacy? Did they have a right to ask if they could watch her and her friends? Did Aunt Tee have a choice in her response? How might an employee react to such a request today? Debate these issues in your group. Share your ideas with the class.

Learning for Life

Bumper Sticker Wisdom Bumper stickers sometimes offer bits of wisdom drawn from everyday experiences. With a partner, create several bumper stickers that express kernels of wisdom drawn from this selection–for example, "Life loves those who love life." Write your sayings on poster board cut to the size of bumper stickers. Work with other pairs of students to create a bumper sticker display in the classroom.

Reading Further

You might also enjoy reading the following poems on the theme of remembering by Maya Angelou:

"In a Time" from *Just Give Me a Cool Drink of Water 'fore I Diiie,* "In Retrospect" from *And Still I Rise,* and "Caged Bird" from *Shaker, Why Don't You Sing?*

Save your work for your portfolio.

VOCABULARY • Analogies

An analogy is a type of comparison that is based on the relationships between things or ideas. In one type of relationship called "synonym variant," the paired words would be synonyms if they were the same part of speech.

spent : exhaustion :: shy : bashfulness

One who is *spent* feels *exhaustion;* one who is *shy* feels *bashfulness.* Once you have determined a relationship between the first two things or ideas, apply that relationship to the second pair of words.

PRACTICE Choose the word pair that best completes each analogy.

1. meticulous : perfectionist ::
   - a. tidy : housekeeper
   - b. strong : athletic
   - c. irritable : grouch
   - d. demanding : boss
2. commodious : space
   - a. large : gigantic
   - b. cramped : crowd
   - c. luxurious : comfort
   - d. picturesque : view

For more information on analogies, see **Communications Skills Handbook,** p. R77.

Before You Read

A Swimming Lesson

Reading Focus

Do you recall when you first learned to swim, skate, ride a bike, read, or do any activity you still enjoy today?

Freewrite Spend five minutes writing about a significant learning experience in your life. Think about questions like these as you write: Who taught you the skill? What teaching methods were used? How did you feel when you began to master the skill? How has this skill affected your life?

Setting a Purpose Read to share an important learning experience with the author.

Building Background

The Time and Place

This story takes place in the summer of 1957, at Revere Beach in Revere, Massachusetts, five miles north of Boston.

Did You Know?

Revere Beach, America's first public beach, was established in 1896. Revere is a city beach that is accessible by public transportation, which places it within reach of people from the entire Boston metropolitan area. Until the late 1980s, the sandy, crescent-shaped beach was flanked by amusement rides, restaurants and food stands, dance pavilions, and arcades. Today, only a few eating establishments remain.

Vocabulary Preview

torturous (tôr′ chər əs) *adj.* causing pain or suffering; p. 496
benevolence (bə nev′ ə ləns) *n.* kindness; generosity; p. 496
vulnerable (vul′ nər ə bəl) *adj.* easily damaged or hurt; p. 496
mainstream (mān′ strēm′) *adj.* representing the most widespread attitudes and values of a society or group; p. 496
superfluous (soo pur′ flo͞o əs) *adj.* not needed; unnecessary; p. 496
invaluable (in val′ ū ə bəl) *adj.* very great in value; p. 497

Meet Jewelle L. Gomez

"What do I hope to achieve by writing? Changing the world!"

Award-winning writer and social activist Jewelle Gomez attributes much of her success to her great-grandmother. "My great-grandmother, with whom I lived until I was twenty-two years old, was born on an Indian reservation in Iowa and had been a widow for fifty years. She maintained an intellectual curiosity and graciousness that no amount of education could have created. She formed the basis of much of my intellectual yearnings." Gomez has written poetry, essays, and award-winning fiction.

Jewelle L. Gomez was born in Boston in 1948. "A Swimming Lesson" appears in Forty-three Septembers, *a collection of essays published in 1993.*

A Swimming Lesson

Jewelle L. Gomez

At nine years old I didn't realize my grandmother, Lydia, and I were doing an extraordinary thing by packing a picnic lunch and riding the elevated train from Roxbury[1] to Revere Beach. It seemed part of the natural rhythm of summer to me. I didn't notice how the subway cars slowly emptied of most of their Black passengers as the train left Boston's urban center and made its way into the Italian and Irish suburban neighborhoods to the north. It didn't seem odd that all of the Black families stayed in one section of the beach and never ventured onto the boardwalk to the concession stands or the rides except in groups.

1. Boston's *Roxbury* neighborhood is southwest of downtown.

Sea and Tidal River, 1916. Alice Schille. Watercolor, gouache, and conte crayon on paper, 11½ x 13⅝ in. Columbus Museum of Art, Columbus, OH. Gift of Ferdinand Howald.

I do remember Black women perched cautiously on their blankets, tugging desperately at bathing suits rising too high in the rear and complaining about their hair "going back." Not my grandmother, though. She glowed with unashamed athleticism as she waded out, just inside the reach of the waves, and moved along the riptide[2] parallel to the shore. Once submerged, she would load me onto her back and begin her long, tireless strokes. With the waves partially covering us, I followed her rhythm with my short, chubby arms, taking my cues from the powerful movement of her back muscles. We did this again and again until I'd fall off, and she'd catch me and set me upright in the strong New England surf. I was thrilled by the wildness of the ocean and my grandmother's fearless relationship to it. I loved the way she never consulted her mirror after her swim, but always looked as if she had been born to the sea, a kind of aquatic heiress.

Sea and Tidal River, 1916 (detail).

None of the social issues of 1957 had a chance of catching my attention that year. All that existed for me was my grandmother, rising from the surf like a Dahomean[3] queen, shaking her head free of her torturous rubber cap, beaming down at me when I finally took the first strokes on my own. She towered above me in the sun with a benevolence that made simply dwelling in her presence a reward in itself. Under her gaze I felt part of a long line of royalty. I was certain that everyone around us—Black and white—saw and respected her magnificence.

Although I sensed her power, I didn't know the real significance of our summers together as Black females in a white part of town. Unlike winter, when we were protected by the cover of coats, boots and hats, summer left us vulnerable and at odds with the expectations for women's bodies—the narrow hips, straight hair, flat stomachs, small feet—handed down from the mainstream culture and media. But Lydia never noticed. Her long chorus-girl legs ended in size-nine shoes, and she dared to make herself even bigger as she stretched her broad back and became a woman with a purpose: teaching her granddaughter to swim.

My swimming may have seemed a superfluous skill to those who watched our lessons. After all, it was obvious that I wouldn't be doing the backstroke on the Riviera[4] or in

2. The *riptide* is the strong surface current that flows rapidly away from shore, returning the water carried landward by waves.

3. *Dahomean* (də hō′ mā ən) refers to Dahomey, a country in western Africa now called Benin (ben in′). Several kingdoms flourished in this region from the 1300s to the 1600s.

4. A popular resort area, the *Riviera* lies along the Mediterranean coasts of Italy and France.

Vocabulary

torturous (tôr′ chər əs) *adj.* causing pain or suffering
benevolence (bə nev′ ə ləns) *n.* kindness; generosity
vulnerable (vul′ nər ə bəl) *adj.* easily damaged or hurt
mainstream (mān′ strēm′) *adj.* representing the most widespread attitudes and values of a society or group
superfluous (soo pur′ flo͞o əs) *adj.* not needed; unnecessary

the pool of a penthouse spa. Certainly nothing in the popular media at that time made the "great outdoors" seem a hospitable place for Black people. It was a place in which we were meant to feel comfortable at best and hunted at worst. But my prospects for utilizing my skill were irrelevant to me, and when I finally got it right I felt as if I had learned some invaluable life secret.

When I reached college and learned the specifics of slavery and the Middle Passage,[5] the magnitude of that "peculiar institution"[6] was almost beyond my comprehension; it was like nothing I'd learned before about the history of my people. It was difficult making a connection with those Africans who had been set adrift from their own land. My initial reaction was "Why didn't the slaves simply jump from the ships while they were still close to shore, and swim home?" The child in me who had learned to survive in water was crushed to find that my ancestors had not necessarily shared this skill. Years later when I visited West Africa and learned of the poisonous, spiny fish that inhabit most of the coastal waters, I understood why swimming was not the local sport there that it was in New England. And now when I take to the surf, I think of those ancestors and of Lydia.

The sea has been a fearful place for us. It swallowed us whole when there was no escape from the holds of slave ships. For me, to whom the dark fathoms of a tenement hallway were the most unknowable thing so far encountered in my nine years, the ocean was a mystery of terrifying proportions. In teaching me to swim, my grandmother took away my fear. I began to understand something outside myself—the sea—and consequently something about myself as well. I was no longer simply a fat little girl: My body had become a sea vessel—sturdy, enduring, graceful. I had the means to be safe.

Before she died last summer I learned that Lydia herself couldn't really swim that well. As I was splashing, desperately trying to learn the right rhythm—face down, eyes closed, air out, reach, face up, eyes open, air in, reach—Lydia was brushing the ocean's floor with her feet, keeping us both afloat. When she told me, I was stunned. I reached into my memory trying to combine this new information with the Olympic vision I'd always kept of her. At first I'd felt disappointed, tricked, the way I used to feel when I'd learn that a favorite movie star was only five feet tall. But then I quickly realized what an incredible act of bravery it was for her to pass on to me a skill she herself had not quite mastered—a skill that she knew would always bring me a sense of accomplishment. And it was more than just the swimming. It was the ability to stand on any beach anywhere and be proud of my large body, my African hair. It was *not* fearing the strong muscles in my own back; it was gaining control over my own life.

5. The *Middle Passage* was the route followed by slave traders from Africa to the Americas. Through the months-long voyage, slaves suffered filth, disease, abuse, and death.
6. Prior to the Civil War, Southerners referred to slavery as their *peculiar institution,* meaning that they considered it to be vital to their economy and way of life.

Vocabulary

invaluable (in val′ ū ə bəl) *adj.* very great in value

Responding to Literature

Personal Response

What was your reaction to Lydia? Do you have–or would you like to have–a relative with a similar personality and outlook? Explain.

Analyzing Literature

Recall and Interpret

1. What is Lydia's attitude toward the sea and toward her own body? How does this attitude seem to affect the author's feelings for her grandmother?
2. According to Gomez, why might observers have considered her lessons a waste of time? Why do you think Gomez did not view them in this light?
3. What historical information has helped Gomez understand her ancestors' attitude toward the sea? Compare her own attitude with that of her ancestors.
4. How does Gomez react when she learns the truth about her swimming lessons? What might the author's reaction suggest about her character?

Evaluate and Connect

5. Evaluate Lydia as a role model for her granddaughter. In your opinion, are role models important to young people? Why or why not?
6. What "social issues of 1957" does Gomez refer to in this essay? How does her adult view of these issues differ from her childhood view of them?
7. Have you ever conquered a fear, as Gomez did with Lydia's help? Describe your experience.
8. In your opinion, what is the **theme,** or main idea, of this essay? Explain.

Literary **ELEMENTS**

Motif

A **motif** (mō tēf′) is a significant word, description, idea, or image that is repeated throughout a literary work and is related to its theme. "A Swimming Lesson" contains several motifs related to the theme of life lessons. For example, the author repeats the word *rhythm* as she describes the natural rhythm of summers with her grandmother, the rhythm she imitated while learning to swim, the rhythm her grandmother followed to become a woman with a purpose, and the rhythm required to gain control over her life.

1. Find other motifs in "A Swimming Lesson."
2. Choose one, and explain how it relates to the selection's theme.

- See **Literary Terms Handbook,** p. R8.

Extending Your Response

Writing About Literature

Analyze the Author's Purpose "A Swimming Lesson" appears in a collection of autobiographical essays written by Jewelle Gomez. Write a paragraph explaining why you think Gomez included this piece in the collection. Use evidence from the selection to support your ideas. Share your analysis with several classmates.

Creative Writing

Thanks a Million Choose one of the skills you listed in the Reading Focus on page 494. Write a thank-you letter to the person or persons who helped you master this skill. Explain why learning the skill was important to you and why you still enjoy the activity today. Be sure to express your appreciation for the time and effort spent in teaching the skill to you.

Save your work for your portfolio.

COMPARING selections

Living Well. Living Good. and A Swimming Lesson

COMPARE **LESSONS**

Both Aunt Tee and Lydia serve as teachers, not only for Angelou and Gomez but also for other people.

- What life lessons do Aunt Tee and Lydia teach? Compare and contrast these lessons.
- Do you think Angelou and Gomez are changed by the lessons they learn from Aunt Tee and Lydia? Give reasons for your answer.

COMPARE **DESCRIPTIONS**

Maya Angelou creates a memorable description of Aunt Tee, who has taught the author an important lesson. Gomez does the same thing with Lydia.

- Identify passages that describe the physical characteristics of Aunt Tee and Lydia. Record the details in a chart like the one shown.
- Look for clues to each woman's personality and character. Record these details.
- Compare the details to determine what the two women have in common. Which traits and characteristics make these women so impressive and so influential?

	Aunt Tee	Lydia
Physical characteristics		
Character traits		

COMPARE **ATTITUDES**

Imagine that Aunt Tee and Lydia have been asked to speak about the positive influence that older people can have on the lives of young people.

- With a partner, discuss the ideas and attitudes that the two women would be likely to express–how they might agree and disagree with each other.
- One partner should prepare Aunt Tee's remarks; the other, Lydia's.
- Practice your dialogue and then present it to the class. Compare the attitudes and ideas expressed in each woman's comments.

Writing Workshop

Narrative Writing: Autobiographical Incident

When asked if he knew Mark Twain as a young boy, an elderly resident of Hannibal, Missouri, replied: "Sure, I knew him. And I know just as many stories as he did, too. Only difference is, he writ 'em down." You too know many stories—episodes and incidents that have helped shape the person you are. **In this workshop, you will focus on one such story in your life and write an autobiographical incident.**

- As you write your narrative, refer to the **Writing Handbook,** pp. R58–R71.

EVALUATION RUBRIC

By the time you complete this Writing Workshop, you will have

- focused on a particular incident
- provided readers with necessary background information
- included characters, setting, and plot
- presented the event in first person in chronological order
- used vivid imagery, specific details, and lifelike dialogue
- presented an autobiographical incident that is free of errors in grammar, usage, and mechanics

The Writing Process

PREWRITING

PREWRITING TIP

To jog your memory about significant incidents in your life, watch family videotapes and browse through photo albums, scrapbooks, and diaries or journals you may have kept.

Explore ideas

Make a time line of significant incidents in your life. As a starting point, you can use your birth or the beginning of a new phase in your life, such as a move to a new house or city. Along your time line, note important incidents. For example, perhaps a grandparent died, or you won a sports competition. List as many incidents as you can think of, even if your time line becomes cluttered and you have to continue it on another sheet of paper.

Age 9
Moved to new house on Center Street.
Age 10
Met Jenna, became best friends.
Age 10 1/2
Learned to fish and canoe at summer camp.
Age 12
Won second place in citywide science fair.
Age 13
Tree fell on our house. We were on TV news!
Age 14
Played lead role in school musical.
Age 15 1/2
Worked as counselor at summer camp.

Consider your audience and purpose

Before you choose an incident to write about, think about your audience and purpose. Perhaps you'll want to limit your audience to your teacher because you consider your story too personal to share with classmates or with strangers. Or perhaps you *do* want to reach a wider audience, and so you'll select an incident that you don't mind sharing.

What is your purpose in writing an autobiographical incident? You might want to make your readers laugh by telling a humorous story. Perhaps you want to share a lesson you've learned, or maybe you want to figure out the meaning of an experience by writing about it. These, and other purposes, are all valid reasons for writing an autobiographical incident.

Choose an incident

Look at the incidents on your time line and choose one to write about. Pick one that is particularly vivid or meaningful to you, perhaps because it strongly influenced you or caused you to grow or change. Such incidents often involve some type of conflict. You might choose to write about:

- a moral or ethical choice, such as the one John Steinbeck faces in the excerpt from *Travels with Charley*
- an encounter with prejudice, such as the one Santha Rama Rau describes in "By Any Other Name"
- an important life lesson that someone has taught you, such as the lesson that Jewelle L. Gomez learns in "A Swimming Lesson"
- a particular time and place that you want to bring to life for the reader, as Dylan Thomas does in "A Child's Christmas in Wales"

Audience: Family members and classmates

Purpose: To share a meaningful personal experience that might entertain and inspire others

Incident: By taking care of a duckling my dad brought home, I earned my parents' trust to have other pets

Identify basic story elements

A true story has many of the same elements as a fictional story—it occurs in a particular time and place, it usually involves people and sometimes animals, and it contains a sequence of events. You don't have to invent the elements of your story, but you do need to bring that story to life for your readers. So to develop your idea, you'll have to identify the basic elements of your story. You might want to use a story map like this one.

Develop your autobiographical incident

After you have identified the basic elements of your story, it's a good idea to make notes about those elements. You will use these notes later, as you draft your autobiographical incident. Here are the notes one student made.

Characters

Myself at age eight: Loved animals but never had a family pet. A few friends had dogs and cats. My mom wasn't sure I was old enough to take care of one.

Dad: Loves animals too. Usually talks over decisions with my mom, but sometimes does something to surprise her.

Mom: Has a good sense of humor, but doesn't like to rush into big decisions. Wasn't sure she wanted a pet at first. Gets along well with my dad.

Daffy: A duckling that loved to swim anywhere she could and to rest under my grandmother's lawn chair

Setting

Time: Spring, about eight years ago

Place: At our house in the suburbs

Events

After months of my begging for a pet, one day Dad came home from the garden store with a duckling. I got to name and take care of the duckling. My dad built a cage for her. I found places for her to swim and walked her on a leash. Four months later, Daffy was too big to keep, so we gave her to a farm. My parents saw how responsible I had been for Daffy and let me have other pets.

DRAFTING

DRAFTING TIP

As you draft your autobiographical incident, imagine that you are telling the story to a friend. Let the words flow. Write the way you would talk.

Set the stage

Begin by giving your readers any background information they need in order to understand your story. When and where did the incident happen? Who was involved? As you write, refer to your story map and prewriting notes.

Tell your story

After setting the stage, continue to refer to your story map and prewriting notes as you tell your story. During the drafting process, try to put yourself right back into the incident and lose yourself in the memory of events. Give yourself up to the rush of the experience. What do you see, hear, feel? Describe it all.

STUDENT MODEL

My mom was setting the table when I heard my dad pull into the driveway. He had gone to buy some mulch for our garden. As he walked up the stairs, I noticed he had a little box in his hands. A peeping sound was coming from inside the box. I opened it and saw a fluffy, yellow duckling that was trying to huddle into a little ball.

My mom gave my dad one of her looks, but my dad just laughed and shrugged his shoulders.

Complete Student Model on p. R114.

Write your ending

At the end of your story, explain what the incident meant to you. Ask yourself: What is the point of my story? What did I learn, or how did I change as a result of what happened?

STUDENT MODEL

The best part about Daffy, though, was what happened *after* Daffy. Once my mom and dad saw that I could take care of a pet responsibly, we always had a houseful. Normal pets—goldfish, a cat, two gerbils. And just last week, Dad, who always did have an eye for the unique and exotic, brought home an iguana. The adventures continue.

Complete Student Model on p. R114.

REVISING

Take another look

Put your draft aside for a while so that you can come back to it with a reader's viewpoint. Then look at it with a fresh eye. Ask yourself: Have I made the incident come to life? Will the reader want to laugh, cry, or nod in understanding? Use the **Rubric for Revising** to guide you in marking the places that need improvement. Then revise your draft.

Read your work aloud

Ask someone to listen to your autobiographical incident as you read it aloud. Ask your listener to review the **Rubric for Revising** and note his or her comments directly on your copy. If you agree with any of the comments, make additional changes.

REVISING TIP

As you revise your autobiographical incident, remember that your readers were not there when the incident occurred. Ask yourself: What do I need to add so that the experience will seem as real for them as it was for me?

STUDENT MODEL

One neighbor had a ~~place~~ [little pond] where Daffy often ~~swam~~ [took a dip]. Or we would take walks around the block~~,~~; she wore a [tiny kitten] collar and leash. At times she would free herself and go [quacking madly] in the opposite direction, while I frantically tried to catch her.

[My favorite memory of] ~~I'll never forget this one thing that~~ Daffy ~~did~~. ~~It especially made me laugh. It~~ is when my great-grandmother visited us during the summer. Gramma loved to fall asleep [in a lounge chair] in our backyard—and Daffy would sit on the grass underneath her [lounge chair, enjoying the cool shade].

Complete Student Model on p. R114.

RUBRIC FOR REVISING

Your revised autobiographical incident should have

- ☑ a strong, interesting introduction
- ☑ enough relevant background information for readers
- ☑ lively accounts of the people, setting, and events involved in the incident
- ☑ vivid sensory details and dialogue
- ☑ a clear chronological order presented in the first-person point of view
- ☑ a consistent tone suited to your specific audience and purpose
- ☑ a conclusion that effectively explains the incident's significance

Your revised autobiographical incident should be free of

- ☑ irrelevant and confusing details
- ☑ errors in grammar, usage, and mechanics

EDITING/PROOFREADING

PROOFREADING TIP

In real speech, people sometimes break the rules of grammar. You may do so in written dialogue to make it sound like real speech. In the rest of your writing, however, be sure to correct any grammatical errors.

Go over your writing again, checking for errors in grammar, usage, mechanics, and spelling. As a guide, use the **Proofreading Checklist** on the inside back cover.

Grammar Hint

A pronoun must agree with its antecedent in number (singular or plural) and gender (masculine, feminine, or neuter). Notice how the sentence below has been corrected so that the pronoun *them* agrees with its plural, neutral antecedent *(pets).*

Since Daffy, I've had a number of other pets; I've always enjoyed taking care of ~~it~~. them

- For more on pronoun agreement, see **Language Handbook,** pp. R19–R20.

Complete Student Model

For a complete version of the model developed in this workshop, refer to **Writing Workshop Models**, p. R114.

STUDENT MODEL

I went crazy: Wow, a pet! I had been pleading for one ~~them~~ for ages! Now I'm embarrassed to admit that I gave the duckling a very corny name, but I guess you do things like that when you're eight. She looked as yellow as daffodils, so I called her ~~it~~ "Daffy."

Complete Student Model on p. R114.

PUBLISHING/PRESENTING

PRESENTING TIP

Include a photograph that relates to your autobiographical incident.

Share your autobiographical incident with your intended audience. As a class, you might consider compiling autobiographical incidents and creating an anthology with a title such as "Remembering" or "The Power of Memories."

Reflecting

Think about what you've learned about yourself from this writing experience. Jot down your thoughts in your journal. What did you find the hardest? What did you enjoy the most? What other incidents in your life would you like to write about?

Save your work for your portfolio.

Theme 6 Quests and Encounters

Think about a time when you worked hard to reach a goal or when an ordinary day turned extraordinary because of an unexpected event. Some of the people you will read about in this theme are on quests—seeking knowledge or striving for justice. Others have more chance encounters—with forces of nature or with themselves.

THEME PROJECTS

Listening, Speaking, and Viewing

Dog-Training Infomercial You and a few friends are opening a dog-training school. Prepare a ten-minute infomercial to advertise your school.

1. Choose three or four characters from this theme who are knowledgeable about animal behavior to be the experts in your infomercial.
2. Choose members of your group to be the host and the experts.
3. Prepare a list of research questions about dog behavior and the training of dogs. Then use the Internet or other resources to find information.
4. As a group, plan the interview between the host and the experts. Include topics such as the essentials of dog training and ownership, dog behavior, and the bond between dogs and humans.
5. Present your infomercial to your class.

Learning for Life

A Class Expedition Your school is planning two week-long excursions. One is a nature expedition to a wilderness area. The other is a cultural-exchange trip to a European city.

1. Decide which excursion you will join. Then, determine which characters from the selections you would like to have with you on the trip.
2. Write letters to the characters you have chosen. In each letter, explain the purpose of the trip and why you would like him or her to come along.

Jungfrau. John Cooke. Private collection.

Before You Read

Pizza in Warsaw, Torte in Prague

Reading Focus

Imagine that one day all the grocery stores in your neighborhood put up a sign reading: "No Milk, No Fresh Fruit or Vegetables, No Meat."

Discuss How might you react to the situation described above? What foods would you miss the most? Why?

Setting a Purpose Read to find out how one writer learns about food shortages in Eastern Europe.

Building Background

The Time and Place

The author describes her observations of daily life in Eastern Europe during a trip made in 1990.

Did You Know?

After World War II (1939–1945), the Soviet Union set up communist governments in nearly all the countries of Eastern Europe. Along with a loss of political freedom, most of the people of the region also endured such economic hardships as severe food and housing shortages. In 1989–1990, Soviet domination over Eastern Europe ended, and communist governments across the region crumbled. The Soviet Union collapsed in 1991.

Vocabulary Preview

impeccable (im pek′ ə bəl) *adj.* free from error; flawless; p. 507
affluent (af′ lo͞o ənt) *adj.* wealthy; prosperous; p. 509
totalitarian (tō tal′ ə tār′ ē ən) *adj.* characteristic of a government in which one political party has total control; p. 510
abstract (ab′ strakt) *adj.* thought of apart from any specific example or case; theoretical; p. 510
palpable (pal′ pə bəl) *adj.* capable of being touched or felt; p. 510
banality (bə nal′ ə tē) *n.* something that is trite; p. 511
ideology (ī′ dē ol′ə jē) *n.* the ideas on which a political, economic, or social system is based; p. 511

Meet Slavenka Drakulić

"Growing up in Eastern Europe you learn very young that politics is not an abstract concept, but a powerful force influencing people's everyday lives."

In early 1990, Croatian journalist Slavenka Drakulić (slä ven′ kä drä kū′ lich) traveled to five East European countries to learn how the collapse of communism affected women. "I sat in their kitchens—because that was always the warmest room in their poorly heated apartments—listening to their life stories."

Slavenka Drakulić was born in 1949 in Rijeka, Yugoslavia, now part of Croatia. This essay appears in How We Survived Communism and Even Laughed, *published in 1991.*

Pizza in Warsaw, Torte in Prague

Slavenka Drakulić

WE WERE HUNGRY, so I said "Let's have a pizza!" in the way you would think of it in, say, New York, or any West European city—meaning, "Let's go to a fast-food place and grab something to eat." Jolanta,[1] a small, blond, Polish translator of English, looked at me thoughtfully, as if I were confronting her with quite a serious task. "There are only two such places," she said in an apologetic tone of voice. Instantly, I was overwhelmed by the guilt of taking pizza in Poland for granted. "Drop it," I said. But she insisted on this pizza place. "You must see it," she said. "It's so different from the other restaurants in Warsaw."

We were lucky because we were admitted without reservations. This is a privately owned restaurant, one of the very few. We were also lucky because we could afford a pizza and beer here, which cost as much as dinner in a fancy hotel. The restaurant was a small, cozy place, with just two wooden tables and a few high stools at the bar—you couldn't squeeze more than twenty people in, even if you wanted to.

It was raining outside, a cold winter afternoon in Warsaw. Once inside, everything was different: two waiters dressed in impeccable white shirts, with bow ties and red aprons, a bowl of fresh tropical fruit on the bar, linen napkins and the smell of pizza baked in a real charcoal-fired oven. Jolanta and I were listening to disco music, eating pizza, and drinking Tuborg beer from long, elegant glasses. Perhaps this is what you pay for, the feeling that you are somewhere else, in a different Warsaw, in a dreamland where there is everything—pizza, fruit juice, thick grilled steaks, salads—and the everyday life of shortages and poverty can't seep in, at least, for the moment.

1. *Jolanta* (yō län′ tə)

Vocabulary

impeccable (im pek′ ə bəl) *adj.* free from error; flawless

Yet to understand just how different this place is, one has to see a "normal" coffee shop, such as the one in the modernistic building of concrete and glass that we visited the same day. Inside neon lights flicker, casting a ghostly light on the aluminum tables and chairs covered with plastic. This place looks more like a bus terminal than like a *kawiarnia.*[2] It's almost empty and the air is thick with cigarette smoke. A bleached blond waitress slowly approaches us with a very limited menu: tea, some alcoholic beverages, Coke, coffee. "With milk?" I ask.

"No milk," she shakes her head.

"Then, can I get a fruit juice perhaps?" I say, in the hopes of drinking just one in a Polish state-owned restaurant.

"No juice." She shakes her head impatiently (at this point, of course, there is no "sophisticated" question about the kind of juice one would perhaps prefer). I give up and get a cup of coffee. It's too sweet. Jolanta is drinking Coke, because there is Coke everywhere—in the middle of Warsaw as, I believe, in the middle of the desert. There may be neither milk nor water, but there is sure to be a bottle of Coke around. Nobody seems to mind the paradox that even though fruit grows throughout Poland, there is no fruit juice yet Coke is everywhere. But here Coke, like everything coming from America, is more of a symbol than a beverage.

To be reduced to having Coke and pizza offered not only as fancy food, but, what's more, as the idea of choice, strikes me as a form of imperialism, possible only where there is really very little choice. Just across the street from the private restaurant, where Jolanta parked her tiny Polski Fiat, is a grocery store. It is closed in the afternoon, so says a handwritten note on the door. Through the dusty shop window we can see the half-empty shelves, with a few cans of beans, pasta, rice, cabbage, vinegar. A friend, a Yugoslav living in Warsaw, told me that some years ago vinegar and mustard were almost all you could find in the stores. At another point, my friend noticed that shelves were stocked with prune compote. One might easily conclude that this is what Poles probably like the best or why else would it be in stores in such quantities? But the reason was just the opposite: Prune compote was what they had, not what they liked. However, the word "like" is not the best way to explain the food situation (or any situation) in Poland. Looking at a shop window where onions and garlic are two of the very few items on display, what meaning could the word "like" possibly have?

Slowly, one realizes that not only is this a different reality, but that words have a different meaning here, too. It makes you understand that the word "like" implies not only choice but refinement, even indulgence, *savoir-vivre*[3]—in fact, a whole different attitude toward food. It certainly doesn't imply that you stuff yourself with whatever you find at the farmer's market or in a grocery that day. Instead, it suggests a certain experience, a knowledge, a possibility of comparing quality and taste. Right after the overthrow of the Ceausescu government in Romania in December 1989, I read a report in

Did You Know?
Romania's dictator for thirty-four years, *Ceausescu* (chou shes′ ko͞o) was executed in 1989 for crimes against the state.

2. The Polish word *kawiarnia* (kä′ vē är′ nē ə) means "restaurant."

3. *Savoir-vivre* (sa′ vwär vēvr′) is a French term that refers to the ability to live elegantly, showing the tastes and social graces of fashionable society.

the newspaper about life in Bucharest.[4] There was a story about a man who ate the first banana in his life. He was an older man, a worker, and he said to a reporter shyly that he ate a whole banana, together with the skin, because he didn't know that he had to peel it. At first, I was moved by the isolation this man was forced to live in, by the fact that he never read or even heard what to do with a banana. But then something else caught my attention: "*It tasted good,*" he said. I can imagine this man, holding a sweet-smelling, ripe banana in his hand, curious and excited by it, as by a forbidden fruit. He holds it for a moment, then bites. It tastes strange but "good." It must have been good, even together with a bitter, tough skin, because it was something unachievable, an object of desire. It was not a banana that he was eating, but the promise, the hope of the future. So, he liked it no matter what its taste.

One of the things one is constantly reminded of in these parts is not to be thoughtless with food. I remember my mother telling me that I had to eat everything in front of me, because to throw away food would be a sin. Perhaps she had God on her mind, perhaps not. She experienced World War II and ever since, like most of the people in Eastern Europe, she behaves as if it never ended. Maybe this is why they are never really surprised that even forty years afterwards there is a lack of sugar, oil, coffee, or flour. To be heedless—to behave as if you are somewhere else, where everything is easy to get—is a sin not against God, but against people. Here you have to think of food, because it has entirely diverse social meanings. To bring a cake for dessert when you are invited for a dinner—a common gesture in another, more affluent country—means you invested a great deal of energy to find it if you didn't make it yourself. And even if you did, finding eggs, milk, sugar, and butter took time and energy. That makes it precious in a very different way from if you had bought it in the pastry shop next door.

When Jaroslav[5] picked me up at Prague airport, I wanted to buy a torte[6] before we went to his house for dinner. It was seven o'clock in the evening and shops were already closed. Czechs work until five or six, which doesn't leave much time to shop. "The old government didn't like people walking in the streets. It might cause them trouble," said Jaroslav, half joking. "Besides, there isn't much to buy anyway." My desire to buy a torte after six o'clock appeared to be quite an extravagance, and it was clear that one couldn't make a habit of bringing a cake for dessert. In the Slavia Café there were no pastries at all, not to mention a torte. The best confectioner[7] in Prague was closed, and in the Hotel Zlatá Husa[8] restaurant a waitress repeated "Torte?" after us as if we were in the wrong place. Then she shook her head. With every new place, my desire to buy a torte diminished. Perhaps it is not that there are no tortes—it's just hard to find them at that hour. At the end, we went to the only shop open until eight-thirty and bought ice cream. There were three kinds and Jaroslav picked vanilla, which is what his boys like the best.

4. *Bucharest* (bo͞o′ kə rest′) is Romania's capital and largest city.

5. *Jaroslav* (yär′ ə släv)

6. A *torte* (tôrt) is a rich cake.

7. A *confectioner* is a person who makes or sells candies and pastries.

8. *Zlatá Husa* (zlät′ yə ho͞o′ zə)

Vocabulary

affluent (af′ lo͞o ənt) *adj.* wealthy; prosperous

On another occasion, in the Bulgarian capital Sofia, Evelina is preparing a party. I am helping her in the small kitchen of the decaying apartment that she shares with a student friend, because as an assistant professor at the university, she cannot afford to rent an apartment alone. I peel potatoes, perhaps six pounds of them. She will make a potato salad with onions. Then she will bake the rest of them in the oven and serve them with . . . actually nothing. She calls it "a hundred-ways potato party"—sometimes humor is the only way to overcome depression. There are also four eggs for an omelet and two cans of sardines (imported from Yugoslavia), plus vodka and wine, and that's it, for the eight people she has invited.

We sit around her table: a Bulgarian theater director who lives in exile in Germany, three of Evelina's colleagues from the university, a historian friend and her husband, and the two of us. We eat potatoes with potatoes, drink vodka, discuss the first issue of the opposition paper *Demokratia,* the round-table talks between the Union of Democratic Forces and the communist government, and calculate how many votes the opposition will get in the forthcoming free elections—the first. Nobody seems to mind that there is no more food on the table—at least not as long as a passionate political discussion is going on. "*This* is our food," says Evelina. "We are used to swallowing politics with our meals. For breakfast you eat elections, a parliament discussion comes for lunch, and at dinner you laugh at the evening news or get mad at the lies that the Communist Party is trying to sell, in spite of everything." Perhaps these people can live almost without food—either because it's too expensive or because there is nothing to buy, or both—without books and information, but not without politics.

One might think that this is happening only now, when they have the first real chance to change something. Not so. This intimacy with political issues was a part of everyday life whether on the level of hatred, or mistrust, or gossip, or just plain resignation during Todor Živkov's communist government. In a totalitarian society, one *has* to relate to the power directly; there is no escape. Therefore, politics never becomes abstract. It remains a palpable, brutal force directing every aspect of our lives, from what we eat to how we live and where we work. Like a disease, a plague, an epidemic, it doesn't spare anybody. Paradoxically, this is precisely how a totalitarian state produces its enemies: politicized citizens. The "velvet revolution"[9] is the product not only of high politics, but of the consciousness of ordinary citizens, infected by politics.

Did You Know?
Todor Živkov (tō′ dôr ziv′ köv) was Bulgaria's head of state from 1962 until his forced resignation in 1989, after the people held mass demonstrations to demand democracy and greater freedom.

Before you get here, you tend to forget newspaper pictures of people standing in line in front of shops. You think they serve as proof in the ideological battle, the proof that

9. In 1989 communist rule in Czechoslovakia was replaced by a new, noncommunist government in a process so smooth it became known as the *velvet revolution.*

Vocabulary

totalitarian (tō tal′ ə tār′ ē ən) *adj.* characteristic of a government in which one political party has total control

abstract (ab′ strakt) *adj.* thought of apart from any specific example or case; theoretical

palpable (pal′ pə bəl) *adj.* capable of being touched or felt

People queuing for bread, Prague. Geoff Johnson, photographer.

Viewing the photograph: What would it be like to stand in a line this long every time you needed groceries?

communism is failing. Or you take them as mere pictures, not reality. But once here, you cannot escape the *feeling* of shortages, even if you are not standing in line, even if you don't see them. In Prague, where people line up only for fruit, there was enough of all necessities, except for oranges or lemons, which were considered a "luxury." It is hard to predict what will be considered a luxury item because this depends on planning, production, and shortages. One time it might be fruit, as in Prague, or milk, as in Sofia. People get used to less and less of everything. In Albania, the monthly ration for a whole family is two pounds of meat, two pounds of cheese, ten pounds of flour, less than half a pound each of coffee and butter. Everywhere, the bottom line is bread. It means safety—because the lack of bread is where real fear begins. Whenever I read a headline "No Bread" in the newspaper, I see a small, dark, almost empty bakery on Vladimir Zaimov Boulevard in Sofia, and I myself, even without reason, experience a genuine fear. It makes my bread unreal, too, and I feel as if I should grab it and eat it while it lasts.

Every mother in Bulgaria can point to where communism failed, from the failures of the planned economy (and the consequent lack of food, milk), to the lack of apartments, child-care facilities, clothes, disposable diapers, or toilet paper. The banality of everyday life is where it has really failed, rather than on the level of ideology. In another kitchen in Sofia, Ana, Katarine and I sit. Her one-year-old daughter is trying to grab our cups from the table. She looks healthy. "She is fine now," says Ana, "but you should have seen her six months ago. There was no formula to buy and normal milk you hardly get as it is. At one point our shops started to sell Humana, imported powdered milk from the dollar shops, because its shelf life was over. I didn't have a choice. I had to feed my baby with that milk, and she got very, very sick. By allowing this milk to be sold, our own government poisoned

Vocabulary

banality (bə nal′ ə tē) *n.* something that is trite

ideology (ī′ dē ol′ ə jē) *n.* the ideas on which a political, economic, or social system is based babies. It was even on TV; they had to put it on because so many babies in Sofia got sick. We are the Third World[10] here."

If communism didn't fail on bread or milk, it certainly failed on strawberries. When I flew to Warsaw from West Berlin, I bought cosmetics, oranges, chocolates, Nescafé, as a present for my friend Zofia—as if I were going home. I also bought a small basket of strawberries. I knew that by now she could buy oranges or even Nescafé from street vendors at a good price—but not strawberries. I bought them also because I remembered when we were together in New York for the first time, back in the eighties, and we went shopping. In a downtown Manhattan supermarket, we stood in front of a fruit counter and just stared. It was full of fruits we didn't know the names of—or if we did, like the man with the banana in Bucharest, we didn't know how they would taste. But this sight was not a miracle; we somehow expected it. What came as a real surprise was fresh strawberries, even though it was December and decorated Christmas trees were in the windows already. In Poland or Yugoslavia, you could see strawberries only in spring. We would buy them for children or when we were visiting a sick relative, so expensive were they. And here, all of a sudden—strawberries. At that moment, they represented all the difference between the world we lived in and this one, so strange and uncomfortably rich. It was not so much that you could see them in the middle of winter, but because you could afford them. When I handed her the strawberries in Warsaw, Zofia said: "How wonderful! I'll save them for my son." The fact that she used the word "save" told me everything: that almost ten years after we saw each other in New York, after the victory of Solidarity,[11] and private initiatives in the economy, there are still no strawberries and perhaps there won't be for another ten years. She was closer to me then, that evening, in the apartment where she lives with her sick, elderly, mother (because there is nobody else to take care of her and to put your parent in a state-run institution would be more than cruelty, it would be a crime). Both of them took just one strawberry each, then put the rest in the refrigerator "for Grzegorz."[12] This is how we tell our kids we love them, because food is love, if you don't have it, or if you have to wait in lines, get what you can, and then prepare a decent meal. Maybe this is why the chicken soup, cabbage stew, and mashed potatoes that evening tasted so good.

All this stays with me forever. When I come to New York and go shopping at Grace Balducci's Marketplace on Third Avenue and 71st Street, I think of Zofia, my mother, my friend Jasmina[13] who loves Swiss chocolates, my daughter's desire for Brooklyn chewing gum, and my own hungry self, still confused by the thirty kinds of cheese displayed in front of me. In an article in *Literaturnaya Gazeta* May 1989 the Soviet poet Yevgenii Yevtushenko tells of a *kolkhoz*[14] woman who fainted in an East Berlin shop, just because she saw twenty kinds of sausages. When she came back to her senses, she repeated in despair: "Why, but why?" How well I understand her question—but knowing the answer doesn't really help.

10. *Third World* generally refers to underdeveloped countries, mainly in Latin America, Africa, and Asia.

11. In the 1980s, *Solidarity,* an organization of trade unions, pushed for changes in the Polish economy and government. In 1990 Poland's Communist Party was dissolved, and Solidarity's leader was elected president.
12. *Grzegorz* (grzhe′ gôrzh)
13. *Jasmina* (yäz mē′ nə)
14. In the Soviet Union, a *kolkhoz* (kôl kôz′) was a collective farm, on which a group of laborers under state supervision shared the work and the management decisions.

Responding to Literature

Personal Response

How did reading this essay change your attitude about the things available to you in your own life? Give reasons for your answer.

Analyzing Literature

Recall

1. Describe Drakulić's visits to the pizza restaurant, the coffee shop, and the grocery store.
2. According to the author, how do most Eastern Europeans regard food? Why?
3. Summarize what happens during Drakulić's visit to Evelina's apartment.
4. What story does Ana relate to the author?
5. Why does Drakulić bring strawberries to Zofia? How does the author explain the way Zofia and her mother react to the gift?

Interpret

6. What can you infer about the food situation in Warsaw from Drakulić's visits to the two restaurants and the grocery store? Explain.
7. What do you think the author means when she says that in Eastern Europe, food has "entirely diverse social meanings"? Support your answer using details from the essay.
8. What do you think is **paradoxical,** or contradictory, about "politicized citizens" in a totalitarian state?
9. What do you think Drakulić means when she says, "The banality of everyday life is where [communism] has really failed"? Explain.
10. How do Drakulić's background and experiences seem to affect her own attitudes toward food?

Evaluate and Connect

11. Look back at the Reading Focus on page 506. Compare the way Eastern Europeans seem to react to shortages with the way you might react.
12. **Theme Connections** How do Drakulić's encounters help you better understand people's quest for freedom and self-determination?
13. In your opinion, do many Americans take prosperity for granted? Explain your answer.
14. If communist governments in Eastern Europe had met people's basic needs, do you think they would have survived? Why or why not?
15. Imagine living in Eastern Europe before the fall of communism. What aspects of daily life do you think you would dislike the most? Why?

Literary ELEMENTS

Thesis

A **thesis** is the main idea of a work of nonfiction. Sometimes, the thesis is implied rather than stated. In such cases, you have to use details from the selection to figure out the point you think the writer is trying to make. In other cases, the writer states the thesis directly. For example, in "Pizza in Warsaw, Torte in Prague," Slavenka Drakulić states her thesis in this passage: "Every mother in Bulgaria can point to where communism failed, from the failures of the planned economy (and the consequent lack of food, milk), to the lack of apartments, child-care facilities, clothes, disposable diapers, or toilet paper. The banality of everyday life is where it has really failed, rather than on the level of ideology."

1. Briefly restate the thesis of this essay in your own words.
2. Choose two of the following anecdotes, and explain how Drakulić uses them to develop her thesis: going out for pizza in Warsaw, trying to buy torte in Prague, Evelina's dinner party, Ana's milk story, a gift of strawberries for Zofia.

- See **Literary Terms Handbook,** p. R13.

Literature and Writing

Writing About Literature

Drawing Conclusions List details from Drakulić's essay that show how communism affected the daily lives of Eastern Europeans. What conclusions can you draw about communism's effect on people's hopes, dreams, and expectations? State your conclusions in one or two paragraphs, using details from the essay to support your ideas.

Creative Writing

Dear American Friend Put yourself in the place of one of the people Drakulić mentions in her essay. Write a letter to a friend in the United States explaining the food shortages in your country. What special food would you like your friend to bring on his or her upcoming visit? Explain why you would like to have this particular food.

Extending Your Response

Literature Groups

Count Your Blessings Discuss Eastern European attitudes toward food, family, and politics, as described in this essay. How do these attitudes compare with your own? Do you think the author is implying that most Americans take the ease of their daily lives for granted? Do you think they do? Discuss and debate these questions in your group. Share your ideas with the class.

Interdisciplinary Activity

Social Studies: Before and After Find maps that show Eastern Europe before and after the collapse of the Soviet Union. Select a country that did not exist as an independent nation in 1988. Using the Internet and other sources, find out what system of government the country has, what daily life is like there, as well as what major problems the country has. Prepare a poster display listing the information you have found. Add copies of maps and photographs, if you wish.

Learning for Life

Organize a Food Drive Drakulić says that "the lack of bread is where real fear begins." Unfortunately, many people in our own prosperous country do not have enough bread and other food to eat. Contact a local food bank to learn about its work and its current needs. Organize a food drive in your classroom and donate the food you collect to the food bank.

Save your work for your portfolio.

VOCABULARY • Analogies

An analogy is a type of comparison that is based on the relationships between things or ideas. To complete an analogy, you must figure out the relationship represented by the first pair of words. Then apply that relationship to another pair of words and see if it is the same.

- For more about analogies, see **Communications Skills Handbook,** p. R77.

PRACTICE Choose the word that best completes each analogy.

1. affluent : money :: brilliant :
   a. wealth b. luck c. intelligence
2. banality : original :: cruelty :
   a. merciful b. weak c. unfortunate
3. dictator : totalitarian :: president :
   a. powerful b. republican c. governmental

MEDIA connection

Television Transcript

What qualities do employers look for in their job applicants? Dr. Martin Luther King once applied to another church before coming to the Dexter Avenue Baptist Church in Montgomery, Alabama.

Dr. Martin Luther King's Early Days

CBS Saturday Morning, January 17, 1998

RUSS MITCHELL, co-host

The official holiday is Monday, but this week marked the 69th anniversary of the birth of the Reverend Martin Luther King Jr. Langston University historian Currie Ballard has been studying Dr. King for some 20 years and came across an early chapter in the life of the civil rights leader. It happened in 1954 when the young King passed through Oklahoma City.

[*film clip*]

DR. MARTIN LUTHER KING JR.

I accept this prize on behalf of all men who love peace and brotherhood.

MR. CURRIE BALLARD, Langston University Historian

Before Dr. King won the Nobel Peace Prize, before he led the march to Montgomery, and even before the Montgomery bus boycott, he applied for the pastor's position here at Calvary Baptist Church in Oklahoma City. The real story is that he was turned down.

DR. A. L. DOWELL, member, Calvary Baptist Church

When he came to Calvary, he preached, and some members liked him and others didn't. The membership was looking for a man who was older. They thought that Dr. King was too young. They were looking for someone who would preach somewhat on an emotional scale. In black churches they call that gravy. And they said that Dr. King didn't have enough gravy.

MR. BALLARD

What was a missed opportunity by Calvary Baptist Church and the people of Oklahoma City turned out to be a golden opportunity for Dexter Avenue Baptist Church and the people of Montgomery. Dr. King went on to lead the Montgomery bus boycott after the arrest of Mrs. Rosa Parks.

DR. A. L. DOWELL

This is what God had a calling for him to do. Come here and be denied and be accepted to go down there to help Miss Rosa Parks in Montgomery, Alabama. And that's the way God works.

MITCHELL

A fascinating story. Ballard says Dr. King did return to Calvary Baptist Church in 1960. He was the keynote speaker at a freedom rally there. And Dr. Dowell got to shake his hand. Hmm.

Analyzing Media

What do you find most ironic about the membership's first impression of Dr. King? Why?

Before You Read

I've Seen the Promised Land

Reading Focus

Would you be willing to dedicate your life to a cause in which you believed strongly? Why or why not?

Journal Record your responses to these questions in your journal. Consider what personal sacrifices you might be willing to make to further a cause you believed in.

Setting a Purpose Read to learn the views of a man who dedicated his life to a cause.

Building Background

The Time and Place

Martin Luther King Jr. delivered this speech at the Mason Temple in Memphis, Tennessee, on April 3, 1968.

Did You Know?

In April 1968, Martin Luther King Jr. traveled to Memphis, Tennessee, to lend his support to black sanitation workers who were on strike against the city. Memphis Mayor Henry Loeb had refused to recognize and negotiate with the nearly all-black union organization that had called the strike. King had led one march and planned to lead another to dramatize the workers' plight. On the evening of April 3, he spoke to a crowd of about 2,000; the speech he gave is the one you are about to read. The next evening, King was assassinated as he stood on the balcony outside his motel room.

Vocabulary Preview

grapple (grap′ əl) *v.* to attempt to deal with; struggle; p. 519
articulate (är tik′ yə lāt) *v.* to put into words; express clearly and effectively; p. 521
relevant (rel′ ə vənt) *adj.* connected with the matter at hand; pertinent; meaningful; p. 521
agenda (ə jen′ də) *n.* a program or schedule of things to be done; p. 522
compassionate (kəm pash′ ə nit) *adj.* having or showing sympathy for another's suffering or misfortune, combined with a desire to help; p. 522
speculate (spek′ yə lāt′) *v.* to guess; p. 523

Meet Martin Luther King Jr.

"I have a dream my four little children will one day live in a nation where they will not be judged by the color of their skin but by the content of their character. I have a dream today!"

With his famous "I Have a Dream" speech, Martin Luther King Jr. set the moral tone for the civil rights movement during his historic March on Washington in 1963. In 1964 he was awarded the Nobel Peace Prize for leading nonviolent demonstrations to help black Americans gain their civil rights.

Martin Luther King Jr. was born in 1929 in Atlanta, Georgia. He died in 1968, at the age of thirty-nine.

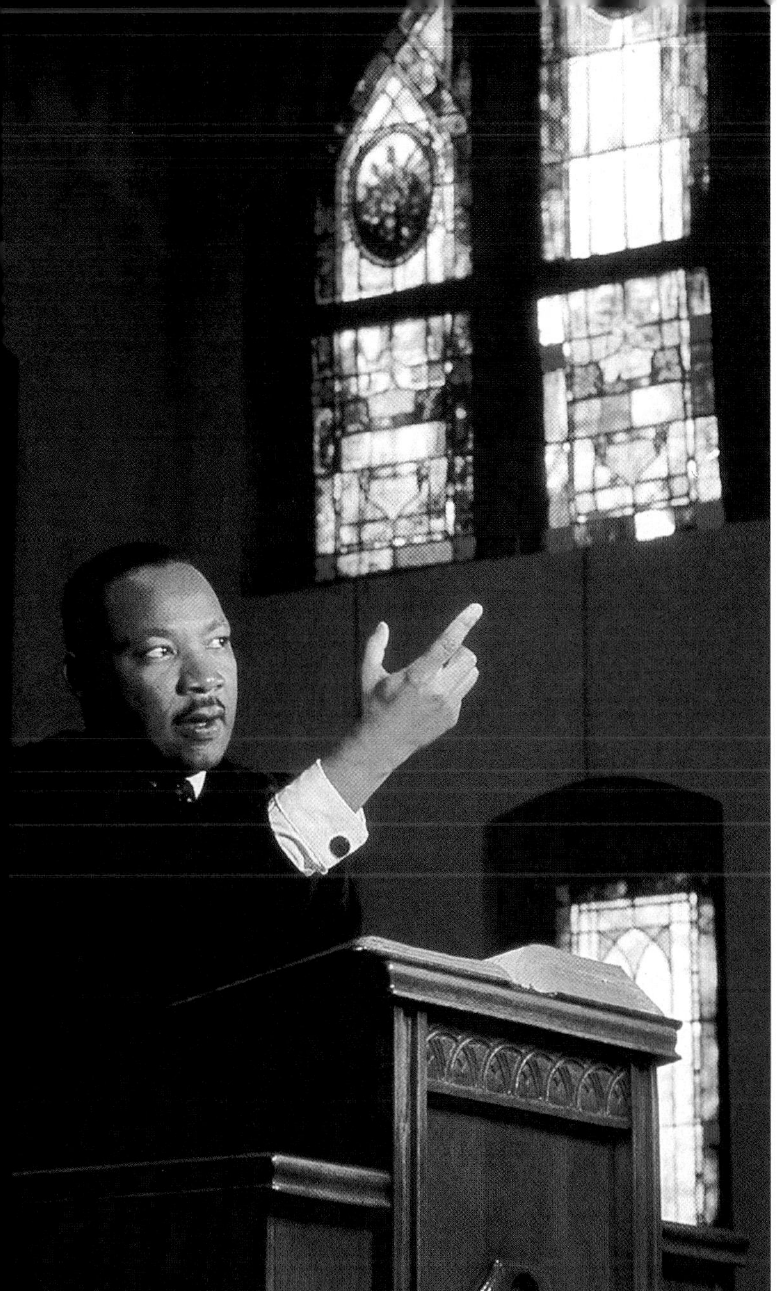

I've Seen the Promised Land

Martin Luther King Jr.

Portrait of Martin Luther King Jr.
Flip Schulke, photographer.

THANK YOU VERY KINDLY, MY FRIENDS. As I listened to Ralph Abernathy[1] in his eloquent and generous introduction and then thought about myself, I wondered who he was talking about. It's always good to have your closest friend and associate say something good about you. And Ralph is the best friend that I have in the world.

1. With King and other black ministers, *Ralph Abernathy* founded the Southern Christian Leadership Conference (SCLC), an organization devoted to the nonviolent struggle against racism and discrimination.

I've Seen the Promised Land

I'm delighted to see each of you here tonight in spite of a storm warning. You reveal that you are determined to go on anyhow. Something is happening in Memphis, something is happening in our world.

As you know, if I were standing at the beginning of time, with the possibility of general and panoramic view of the whole human history up to now, and the Almighty said to me, "Martin Luther King, which age would you like to live in?"—I would take my mental flight by Egypt through, or rather across the Red Sea, through the wilderness on toward the promised land. And in spite of its magnificence, I wouldn't stop there. I would move on by Greece, and take my mind to Mount Olympus. And I would see Plato, Aristotle, Socrates, Euripides and Aristophanes[2] assembled around the Parthenon as they discussed the great and eternal issues of reality.

Did You Know?
The *Parthenon,* a temple built in the fifth century B.C., still stands in Athens, Greece.

But I wouldn't stop there. I would go on, even to the great heyday of the Roman Empire. And I would see developments around there, through various emperors and leaders. But I wouldn't stop there. I would even come up to the day of the Renaissance, and get a quick picture of all that the Renaissance did for the cultural and esthetic life of man. But I wouldn't stop there. I would even go by the way that the man for whom I'm named had his habitat. And I would watch Martin Luther as he tacked his ninety-five theses[3] on the door at the church in Wittenberg.

Did You Know?
Martin Luther (1483–1546) was a German theologian whose arguments challenging certain teachings of the Roman Catholic Church led to the Protestant Reformation.

But I wouldn't stop there. I would come on up even to 1863, and watch a vacillating president by the name of Abraham Lincoln finally come to the conclusion that he had to sign the Emancipation Proclamation. But I wouldn't stop there. I would even come up to the early thirties, and see a man grappling with the problems of the bankruptcy of his nation. And come with an eloquent cry that we have nothing to fear but fear itself.[4]

But I wouldn't stop there. Strangely enough, I would turn to the Almighty, and say, "If you allow me to live just a few years in the second half of the twentieth century, I will be happy." Now that's a strange statement to make, because the world is all messed up. The nation is sick. Trouble is in the land. Confusion all around. That's a strange statement. But I know, somehow, that only when it is dark enough, can you see the stars. And I see God working in this period of the twentieth century in a way that men, in some strange way, are responding—something is happening in our world. The masses of people are rising up. And wherever they are assembled today, whether they are in Johannesburg, South Africa; Nairobi, Kenya; Accra, Ghana; New York City; Atlanta, Georgia; Jackson, Mississippi;

2. The lives of these five Greek teachers and writers spanned a 160-year period ending with Aristotle's death in 322 B.C. Their ideas greatly influenced modern Western civilization.

3. Here, *theses* means "arguments."

4. In these two sentences, King is referring to President Franklin D. Roosevelt, who led the United States during the Great Depression of the 1930s.

or Memphis, Tennessee—the cry is always the same—"We want to be free."

And another reason that I'm happy to live in this period is that we have been forced to a point where we're going to have to grapple with the problems that men have been trying to grapple with through history, but the demands didn't force them to do it. Survival demands that we grapple with them. Men, for years now, have been talking about war and peace. But now, no longer can they just talk about it. It is no longer a choice between violence and nonviolence in this world; it's nonviolence or nonexistence.

That is where we are today. And also in the human rights revolution, if something isn't done, and in a hurry, to bring the colored peoples of the world out of their long years of poverty, their long years of hurt and neglect, the whole world is doomed. Now, I'm just happy that God has allowed me to live in this period, to see what is unfolding. And I'm happy that he's allowed me to be in Memphis.

I can remember, I can remember when Negroes were just going around as Ralph has said, so often, scratching where they didn't itch, and laughing when they were not tickled. But that day is all over. We mean business now, and we are determined to gain our rightful place in God's world.

And that's all this whole thing is about. We aren't engaged in any negative protest and in any negative arguments with anybody. We are saying that we are determined to be men. We are determined to be people. We are saying that we are God's children. And that we don't have to live like we are forced to live.

Now, what does all of this mean in this great period of history? It means that we've got to stay together. We've got to stay together and maintain unity. You know, whenever Pharaoh[5] wanted to prolong the period of slavery in Egypt, he had a favorite, favorite formula for doing it. What was that? He kept the slaves fighting among themselves. But whenever the slaves get together, something happens in Pharaoh's court, and he cannot hold the slaves in slavery. When the slaves get together, that's the beginning of getting out of slavery. Now let us maintain unity.

Secondly, let us keep the issues where they are. The issue is injustice. The issue is the refusal of Memphis to be fair and honest in its dealings with its public servants, who happen to be sanitation workers. Now, we've got to keep attention on that. That's always the problem with a little violence. You know what happened the other day, and the press dealt only with the window-breaking. I read the articles. They very seldom got around to mentioning the fact that one thousand, three hundred sanitation workers were on strike, and that Memphis is not being fair to them, and that Mayor Loeb is in dire[6] need of a doctor. They didn't get around to that.

Now we're going to march again, and we've got to march again, in order to put the issue where it is supposed to be. And force everybody to see that there are thirteen hundred of God's children here suffering, sometimes going hungry, going through dark and dreary nights wondering how this thing is going to come out. That's the issue. And we've got to say to the nation: we know it's coming out. For when people get caught up with that which is right and they are willing to sacrifice for it, there is no stopping point short of victory.

5. In the Bible, the *Pharaoh* (ruler) of ancient Egypt enslaved the Israelites until Moses led them out of Egypt and into Canaan, which they called the "promised land."

6. *Dire* means "dreadful" or "terrible."

Vocabulary

grapple (grap′ əl) *v.* to attempt to deal with; struggle

We aren't going to let any mace stop us. We are masters in our nonviolent movement in disarming police forces; they don't know what to do. I've seen them so often. I remember in Birmingham, Alabama, when we were in that majestic struggle there we would move out of the 16th Street Baptist Church day after day; by the hundreds we would move out. And Bull Connor[7] would tell them to send the dogs forth and they did come; but we just went before the dogs singing, "Ain't gonna let nobody turn me round." Bull Connor next would say, "Turn the fire hoses on." And as I said to you the other night, Bull Connor didn't know history. He knew a kind of physics that somehow didn't relate to the transphysics[8] that we knew about. And that was the fact that there was a certain kind of fire that no water could put out. And we went before the fire hoses; we had known water. If we were Baptist or some other denomination, we had been immersed. If we were Methodist, and some others, we had been sprinkled, but we knew water.[9]

That couldn't stop us. And we just went on before the dogs and we would look at them; and we'd go on before the water hoses and we would look at it, and we'd just go on singing "Over my head I see freedom in the air." And then we would be thrown in the paddy wagons, and sometimes we were stacked in there like sardines in a can. And they would throw us in, and old Bull would say, "Take them off," and they did; and we would just go in the paddy wagon singing, "We Shall Overcome." And every now and

7. *Bull Connor,* whose given name was Eugene, was Birmingham's Commissioner of Public Safety and a candidate for mayor in the 1964 election.

8. *Physics* is the study of the physical properties of light, heat, electricity, magnetism, and so on. With the invented word *transphysics,* King refers to things that transcend, or go beyond, the physical, such as morality and philosophy.

9. King is referring to the Christian ritual of baptism, which may involve immersion in water or the sprinkling or pouring of water over a person's head.

Corner of 5th Avenue North and 17th Street, May 3, 1963. Charles Moore, photographer.

Viewing the photograph: This photograph was taken in Birmingham, Alabama. Describe what is happening.

then we'd get in the jail, and we'd see the jailers looking through the windows being moved by our prayers, and being moved by our words and our songs. And there was a power there which Bull Connor couldn't adjust to; and so we ended up transforming Bull into a steer, and we won our struggle in Birmingham.

Now we've got to go on to Memphis just like that. I call upon you to be with us Monday. Now about injunctions: We have an injunction[10] and we're going into court tomorrow morning to fight this illegal, unconstitutional injunction. All we say to America is, "Be true to what you said on paper." If I lived in China or even Russia, or any totalitarian country, maybe I could understand the denial of certain basic First Amendment privileges, because they hadn't committed themselves to that over there. But somewhere I read of the freedom of assembly. Somewhere I read of the freedom of speech. Somewhere I read of the freedom of the press. Somewhere I read that the greatness of America is the right to protest for right. And so just as I say, we aren't going to let any injunction turn us around. We are going on.

We need all of you. And you know what's beautiful to me, is to see all of these ministers of the Gospel. It's a marvelous picture. Who is it that is supposed to articulate the longings and aspirations of the people more than the preacher? Somehow the preacher must be an Amos,[11] and say, "Let justice roll down like waters and righteousness like a mighty stream." Somehow, the preacher must say with Jesus, "The spirit of the Lord is upon me, because he hath anointed me to deal with the problems of the poor."[12]

And I want to commend the preachers, under the leadership of these noble men: James Lawson, one who has been in this struggle for many years; he's been to jail for struggling; but he's still going on, fighting for the rights of his people. Rev. Ralph Jackson, Billy Kiles; I could just go right on down the list, but time will not permit. But I want to thank them all. And I want you to thank them, because so often, preachers aren't concerned about anything but themselves. And I'm always happy to see a relevant ministry.

It's alright to talk about "long white robes over yonder," in all of its symbolism. But ultimately people want some suits and dresses and shoes to wear down here. It's alright to talk about "streets flowing with milk and honey," but God has commanded us to be concerned about the slums down here, and his children who can't eat three square meals a day. It's alright to talk about the new Jerusalem, but one day, God's preacher must talk about the New York, the new Atlanta, the new Philadelphia, the new Los Angeles, the new Memphis, Tennessee. This is what we have to do.

Now the other thing we'll have to do is this: Always anchor our external direct action with the power of economic withdrawal. Now, we are poor people, individually, we are poor when you compare us with white society in America. We are poor. Never stop and forget that collectively, that means all of us together, collectively we are richer than all the nations in the world, with the exception of nine. Did

10. An *injunction* is a court order barring a specific action, such as a march, demonstration, or strike.
11. The Hebrew prophet *Amos* lived in the eighth century B.C.
12. Here, King has freely paraphrased the words that Jesus was reading from the prophet Isaiah.

Vocabulary

articulate (är tik′ yə lāt) *v.* to put into words; express clearly and effectively
relevant (rel′ ə vənt) *adj.* connected with the matter at hand; pertinent; meaningful

you ever think about that? After you leave[13] the United States, Soviet Russia, Great Britain, West Germany, France, and I could name the others, the Negro collectively is richer than most nations of the world. We have an annual income of more than thirty billion dollars a year, which is more than all of the exports of the United States, and more than the national budget of Canada. Did you know that? That's power right there, if we know how to pool it.

We don't have to argue with anybody. We don't have to curse and go around acting bad with our words. We don't need any bricks and bottles, we don't need any Molotov cocktails, we just need to go around to these stores, and to these massive industries in our country, and say, "God sent us by here, to say to you that you're not treating his children right. And we've come by here to ask you to make the first item on your agenda—fair treatment, where God's children are concerned. Now, if you are not prepared to do that, we do have an agenda that we must follow. And our agenda calls for withdrawing economic support from you . . ."

But not only that, we've got to strengthen black institutions. I call upon you to take your money out of the banks downtown and deposit your money in Tri-State Bank—we want a "bank-in" movement in Memphis. So go by the savings and loan association. I'm not asking you something that we don't do ourselves at SCLC. Judge Hooks and others will tell you that we have an account here in the savings and loan association from the Southern Christian Leadership Conference. We're just telling you to follow what we're doing. Put your money there. You have six or seven black insurance companies in Memphis. Take out your insurance there. We want to have an "insurance-in."

Now these are some practical things we can do. We begin the process of building a greater economic base. And at the same time, we are putting pressure where it really hurts. I ask you to follow through here.

Now, let me say as I move to my conclusion that we've got to give ourselves to this struggle until the end. Nothing would be more tragic than to stop at this point, in Memphis. We've got to see it through. And when we have our march, you need to be there. Be concerned about your brother. You may not be on strike. But either we go up together, or we go down together.

Let us develop a kind of dangerous unselfishness. One day a man came to Jesus; and he wanted to raise some questions about some vital matters in life. At points, he wanted to trick Jesus, and show him that he knew a little more than Jesus knew, and through this, throw him off base. Now that question could have easily ended up in a philosophical and theological debate. But Jesus immediately pulled that question from mid-air, and placed it on a dangerous curve between Jerusalem and Jericho. And he talked about a certain man, who fell among thieves. You remember that a Levite and a priest passed by on the other side. They didn't stop to help him. And finally a man of another race came by. He got down from his beast, decided not to be compassionate by proxy.[14] But

13. Here, the expression *after you leave* means "not counting" or "apart from."

14. In ancient Israel, men of the *Levite* tribe were temple priests or assistants. One might expect the two religious men to help, especially since the victim is also Jewish. Instead, it is *a man of another race* who decides not to leave it to someone else–a *proxy,* or substitute–to help.

Vocabulary

agenda (ə jen′ də) *n.* a program or schedule of things to be done

compassionate (kəm pash′ ə nit) *adj.* having or showing sympathy for another's suffering or misfortune, combined with a desire to help

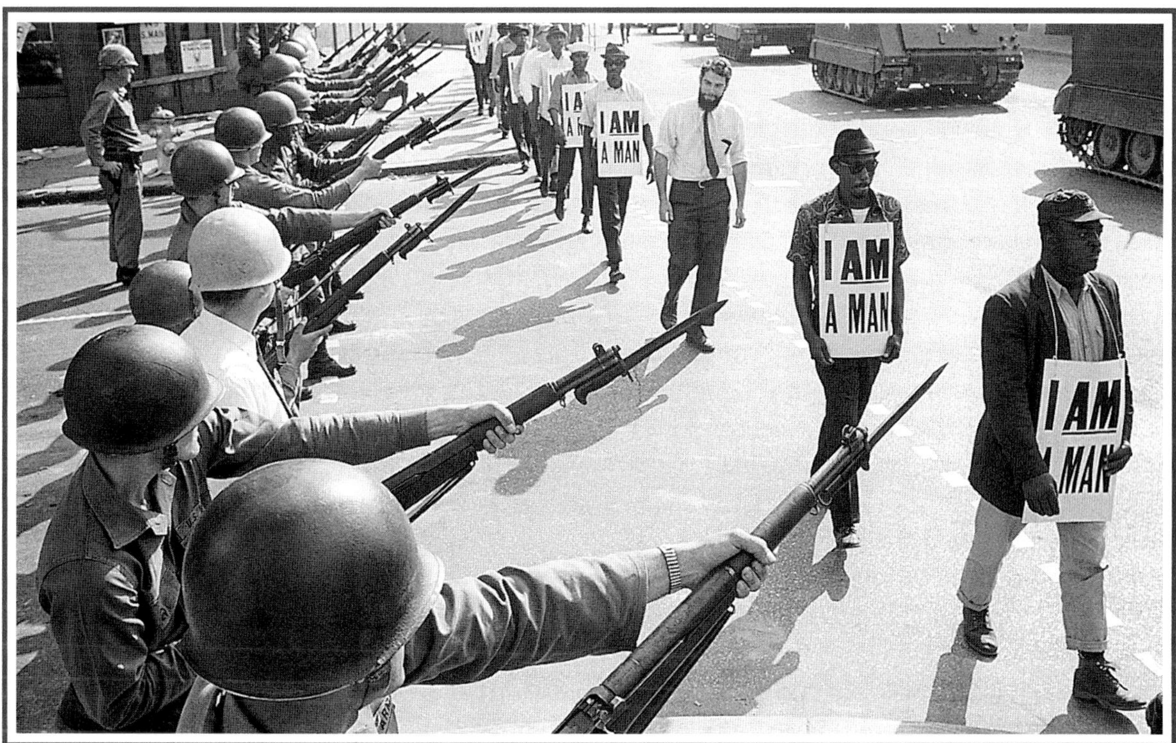

"I AM A MAN" march in Memphis, TN. United Press International.

Viewing the photograph: This photograph was taken in Memphis, Tennessee, the day after Martin Luther King Jr. led a march. Describe the action and mood that is depicted. What stands out the most?

with him, administered first aid, and helped the man in need. Jesus ended up saying, this was the good man, this was the great man, because he had the capacity to project the "I" into the "thou," and to be concerned about his brother. Now you know, we use our imagination a great deal to try to determine why the priest and the Levite didn't stop. At times we say they were busy going to church meetings—an ecclesiastical gathering—and they had to get on down to Jerusalem so they wouldn't be late for their meeting. At other times we would speculate that there was a religious law that "One who was engaged in religious ceremonials was not to touch a human body twenty-four hours before the ceremony." And every now and then we begin to wonder whether maybe they were not going down to Jerusalem, or down to Jericho, rather to organize a "Jericho Road Improvement Association." That's a possibility. Maybe they felt that it was better to deal with the problem from the causal root, rather than to get bogged down with an individual effort.

But I'm going to tell you what my imagination tells me. It's possible that these men were afraid. You see, the Jericho road is a dangerous road. I remember when Mrs. King and I were first in Jerusalem. We rented a car and drove from Jerusalem down to Jericho. And as soon as we got on that road, I said to my wife, "I can see why Jesus used this as a setting for his parable."[15] It's a winding, meandering road. It's really conducive for ambushing. You start out in Jerusalem, which is about 1200 miles, or rather 1200 feet above sea level.

15. A *parable* is a brief story intended to illustrate some truth or moral lesson.

Vocabulary
speculate (spek′ yə lāt′) *v.* to guess

And by the time you get down to Jericho, fifteen or twenty minutes later, you're about 2200 feet below sea level. That's a dangerous road. In the days of Jesus it came to be known as the "Bloody Pass." And you know, it's possible that the priest and the Levite looked over that man on the ground and wondered if the robbers were still around. Or it's possible that they felt that the man on the ground was merely faking. And he was acting like he had been robbed and hurt, in order to seize them over there, lure them there for quick and easy seizure. And so the first question that the Levite asked was, "If I stop to help this man, what will happen to me?" But then the Good Samaritan came by. And he reversed the question: "If I do not stop to help this man, what will happen to him?"

That's the question before you tonight. Not, "If I stop to help the sanitation workers, what will happen to all of the hours that I usually spend in my office every day and every week as a pastor?" The question is not, "If I stop to help this man in need, what will happen to me?" "If I do not stop to help the sanitation workers, what will happen to them?" That's the question.

Dr. Martin Luther King Jr. hugs his wife Coretta after learning he had been awarded the Nobel Prize for Peace. United Press International.

Let us rise up tonight with a greater readiness. Let us stand with a greater determination. And let us move on in these powerful days, these days of challenge to make America what it ought to be. We have an opportunity to make America a better nation. And I want to thank God, once more, for allowing me to be here with you.

You know, several years ago, I was in New York City autographing the first book that I had written. And while sitting there autographing books, a demented[16] black woman came up. The only question I heard from her was, "Are you Martin Luther King?"

And I was looking down writing, and I said yes. And the next minute I felt something beating on my chest. Before I knew it I had been stabbed by this demented woman. I was rushed to Harlem Hospital. It was a dark Saturday afternoon. And that blade had gone through, and the X rays revealed that the tip of the blade was on the edge of my aorta, the main artery. And once that's punctured, you drown in your own blood—that's the end of you.

It came out in the *New York Times* the next morning, that if I had sneezed, I would have died. Well, about four days later, they allowed me, after the operation, after my chest had been opened, and the blade had been taken out, to move around in the wheel chair in the hospital. They allowed me to read some of the mail that came in, and from all over the states, and the world, kind letters came in. I read a few, but one of them I will never forget. I had received one from the President and the Vice-President. I've forgotten what those telegrams

16. ***Demented*** **means "insane."**

said. I'd received a visit and a letter from the Governor of New York, but I've forgotten what the letter said. But there was another letter that came from a little girl, a young girl who was a student at the White Plains High School. And I looked at that letter, and I'll never forget it. It said simply, "Dear Dr. King: I am a ninth-grade student at the White Plains High School." She said, "While it should not matter, I would like to mention that I am a white girl. I read in the paper of your misfortune, and of your suffering. And I read that if you had sneezed, you would have died. And I'm simply writing you to say that I'm so happy that you didn't sneeze."

And I want to say tonight, I want to say that I am happy that I didn't sneeze. Because if I had sneezed, I wouldn't have been around here in 1960, when students all over the South started sitting in at lunch counters. And I knew that as they were sitting in, they were really standing up for the best in the American dream. And taking the whole nation back to those great walls of democracy which were dug deep by the Founding Fathers in the Declaration of Independence and the Constitution. If I had sneezed, I wouldn't have been around in 1962, when Negroes in Albany, Georgia,[17] decided to straighten their backs up. And whenever men and women straighten their backs up, they are going somewhere, because a man can't ride your back unless it is bent. If I had sneezed, I wouldn't have been here in 1963, when the black people of Birmingham, Alabama, aroused the conscience of this nation, and brought into being the Civil Rights Bill. If I had sneezed, I wouldn't have had a chance later that year, in August, to try to tell America about a dream that I had had. If I had sneezed, I wouldn't have been down in Selma, Alabama,[18] to see the great movement there. If I had sneezed, I wouldn't have been in Memphis to see a community rally around those brothers and sisters who are suffering. I'm so happy that I didn't sneeze.

And they were telling me, now it doesn't matter now. It really doesn't matter what happens now. I left Atlanta this morning, and as we got started on the plane, there were six of us, the pilot said over the public address system, "We are sorry for the delay, but we have Dr. Martin Luther King on the plane. And to be sure that all of the bags were checked, and to be sure that nothing would be wrong with the plane, we had to check out everything carefully. And we've had the plane protected and guarded all night."

And then I got into Memphis. And some began to say the threats, or talk about the threats that were out. What would happen to me from some of our sick white brothers?

Well, I don't know what will happen now. We've got some difficult days ahead. But it doesn't matter with me now. Because I've been to the mountaintop. And I don't mind. Like anybody, I would like to live a long life. Longevity has its place. But I'm not concerned about that now. I just want to do God's will. And He's allowed me to go up to the mountain. And I've looked over. And I've seen the promised land. I may not get there with you. But I want you to know tonight, that we, as a people will get to the promised land. And I'm happy, tonight. I'm not worried about anything. I'm not fearing any man. Mine eyes have seen the glory of the coming of the Lord.

17. In 1962 King took part in demonstrations in *Albany, Georgia,* protesting the segregation of public facilities.

18. In *Selma, Alabama,* in 1965, King led a march to protest restrictions on black voting rights. Soon afterward, the Voting Rights Act of 1965 was passed.

Responding to Literature

Personal Response

Which sentence or passage made the greatest impression on you? Why?

Analyzing Literature

Recall

1. Summarize King's mental journey through history. In which age does he want to live? Why?
2. According to King, what general goal are African Americans striving for? What specific issue faces them in Memphis?
3. What plan of action does King outline for black people in Memphis?
4. What reasons does King give for being happy he didn't sneeze after he was stabbed?
5. What feelings does King express about the dangers he faces? What reasons does he give for his feelings?

Interpret

6. What might you infer about King's character and beliefs on the basis of his mental journey through history?
7. What do you think King means when he tells Americans to "be true to what you said on paper"? Support your answer using details from the speech.
8. What is the purpose of King's plan of action? What results do you think he expects?
9. What message do you think King wants to convey by telling why he is glad he didn't sneeze?
10. At the end of his speech, King refers to the "promised land." What do you think this is?

Evaluate and Connect

11. How does King use **repetition** to emphasize important ideas? Find two examples and explain what ideas King is emphasizing in each example.
12. What is your opinion of King's nonviolent approach to instituting political and social change? Give reasons for your opinion.
13. If King were alive today, what issues do you think he might be addressing? Why?
14. How did the prophetic aspects of this speech affect your reaction to it? Explain.
15. Theme Connections Look back at the Reading Focus on page 516. Evaluate the level of dedication that King brought to his quest for justice and equality. What sacrifices did he make?

Literary ELEMENTS

Allusion

An **allusion** is a reference to a well-known character, place, or situation from history or from a work of literature, music, or art. In this speech, King uses both historical and biblical allusions. For example, King says, "I would take my mental flight by Egypt through, or rather across the Red Sea, through the wilderness on toward the promised land." He is alluding to the biblical story in which Moses leads the Israelites out of slavery in Egypt to the promised land of Canaan. An example of a historical allusion is King's reference to President Franklin D. Roosevelt's struggles during the Great Depression: "I would even come up to the early thirties, and see a man grappling with the problems of the bankruptcy of his nation."

1. Why do you think King alludes to the Israelites' flight from Egypt? To what might this journey be compared?
2. Locate two more examples of historical allusions, and explain why you think King included them.

- See **Literary Terms Handbook,** p. R1.

Literature and Writing

Writing About Literature

Character Sketch Think about what this speech reveals about King's character, beliefs, personality, and outlook on life. Go back to page 516 and reread the Did You Know? section and the author biography. Then write a character sketch of Martin Luther King Jr., using details from the speech and from page 516 to support your ideas. Share your character sketch in a small group.

Creative Writing

With Deepest Sympathy Imagine that you were in the audience the night King delivered this speech. The next evening, you turn on the television and learn that King has been assassinated. Write a letter of sympathy to King's widow and children in which you reflect on how you felt as you listened to his speech and how you feel now in light of King's violent and untimely death.

Extending Your Response

Literature Groups

Define a Term King challenges his audience by saying, "Let us develop a kind of dangerous unselfishness." He uses the biblical story of the Good Samaritan to illustrate the concept of "dangerous unselfishness." Discuss what you think King means by that term. As a group, write a definition of dangerous unselfishness. Compare your definition with those written by other groups.

Listening and Speaking

The Spoken Word With a partner, listen to recordings of this speech and others given by King. (King's speeches are available on video and audiocassettes, and you can find excerpts on the Internet.) Listen carefully to the cadence, or rhythmic flow, of King's delivery. Notice how King raises and lowers his voice to emphasize an idea. Make notes on how King's delivery affects his message. Share your ideas with the class.

Internet Connection

Notable People Use the Internet to gather information about another important figure in the civil rights movement, such as Ralph Abernathy, Rosa Parks, A. Philip Randolph, or Roy Wilkins. Share your findings with the class.

Rosa Parks

Save your work for your portfolio.

Skill Minilesson

GRAMMAR AND LANGUAGE • Parallelism

The use of a series of words, phrases, clauses, or sentences that have a similar grammatical structure is called **parallelism.** Skillful speakers and writers often use parallelism to emphasize an idea and to create a rhythmic flow to the language. King's speech "I've Seen the Promised Land" includes many examples of parallelism, such as this one: "But either we go up together, or we go down together." The two clauses repeat the pattern of subject *(we)*, verb *(go)*, and two adverbs *(up/down, together)*. Because of the repetition of specific words, the emphasis falls on the two adverbs *up* and *down.*

PRACTICE On your paper, write two more examples of parallelism you find in "I've Seen the Promised Land." Explain what grammatical elements are parallel and describe the effect of this parallelism.

- For more about parallelism, see **Literary Terms Handbook,** p. R9.

Writing Skills

Organizing Details

Good descriptive writing must contain vivid details. It must also organize those details into meaningful patterns. There are several ways to organize details in your writing.

- **Chronological order** presents events in the order in which they occur.
- **Spatial order** presents details according to their physical placement. For example, details might be described from left to right, from front to back, from top to bottom, clockwise or counterclockwise, or from near to far.
- **Order of importance** presents the least important details first and builds to the most important ones.

Since each of these strategies creates a different effect, your purpose for writing will help you determine which to use. For example, if you want to create a vivid image of your best friend's bedroom, you'll probably want to describe the details in spatial order. If you want to emphasize an important idea, you'll probably want to describe details in the order of their importance. Sometimes, you may combine strategies. For example, you might describe your friend's bedroom from right to left because the most important detail–a six-foot-tall terrarium–is on the left side of the room.

Notice the way Martin Luther King Jr. organizes details in this excerpt from "I've Seen the Promised Land":

> **I remember in Birmingham, Alabama, when we were in that majestic struggle there we would move out of the 16th Street Baptist Church day after day; by the hundreds we would move out. And Bull Connor would tell them to send the dogs forth and they did come; but we just went before the dogs singing, "Ain't gonna let nobody turn me round." Bull Connor next would say, "Turn the fire hoses on."**

King presents the details of this scene in **chronological order.** He provides a detail about what happened first: the marchers moved out from the church. Then Bull Connor called on the dogs, and the dogs came, but the people "just went before the dogs singing," and so forth. King uses transitional words, such as *and, but,* and *next,* to show sequence in time. By organizing the details about this incident in chronological order, King can describe the event as it unfolded.

EXERCISE

Using concrete, vivid details, write a paragraph describing one of your favorite places, a daily routine, or a holiday celebration you enjoy. Organize your details in the way that will most effectively convey what you are trying to describe.

MEDIA connection

Journal Entries

What draws explorers to the icy wilderness landscape of Antarctica? British naval officer R. F. Scott bravely undertook the Antarctic Expedition in 1910 mainly to achieve scientific results, but Scott and his crew died from exposure to the bitter cold.

Return from First Summit Depot

by R. F. Scott—*Scott's Last Expedition*

Thursday, February 8.

R. 22. Height 6260. Start Temp. −11°. . . . Had a beastly morning. Wind very strong and cold. Steered in for Mt. Darwin to visit rock. Sent Bowers on, on ski, as Wilson can't wear his at present. He obtained several specimens, all of much the same type, a close-grained granite rock which weathers red. Hence the pink limestone. After he rejoined we skidded downhill pretty fast, leaders on ski, Oates and Wilson on foot alongside sledge—Evans detached. We lunched at 2 well down towards Mt. Buckley, the wind half a gale and everybody very cold and cheerless. However better things were to follow. . . . We found ourselves under perpendicular cliffs of Beacon sandstone, weathering rapidly and carrying veritable coal seams. From the last Wilson, with his sharp eyes, has picked several plant impressions, the last a piece of coal with beautifully traced leaves in layers. . . . Altogether we have had a most interesting afternoon, and the relief of being out of the wind and in a warmer temperature is inexpressible. . . . A lot could be written on the delight of setting foot on rock after 14 weeks of snow and ice and nearly 7 out of sight of aught else. It is like going ashore after a sea voyage. We deserve a little good bright weather after all our trials. . . .

Friday, February 9.

R. 23. Height 5210 ft. Lunch Temp. +10°. . . . Kept along the edge of moraine to the end of Mt. Buckley. Stopped and geologized. Wilson got great find of vegetable impression in piece of limestone. Too tired to write geological notes. We all felt very slack this morning, partly rise of temperature, partly reaction, no doubt. . . . Did pretty well in the afternoon, marching 3¾ hours; the sledgemeter is

unshipped, so cannot tell distance traversed. Very warm on march and we are all pretty tired. Tonight it is wonderfully calm and warm, though it has been overcast all the afternoon. It is remarkable to be able to stand outside the tent and sun oneself. Our food satisfies now, but we must march to keep on the full ration, and we want rest, yet we shall pull through all right, D.V. We are by no means worn out.

Monday, March 19.
Lunch. . . . Sledge dreadfully heavy. We are 15½ miles from the depot and ought to get there in three days. What progress! We have two days' food but barely a day's fuel. All our feet are getting bad—Wilson's best, my right foot worst, left all right. There is no chance to nurse one's feet till we can get hot food into us. Amputation is the least I can hope for now, but will the trouble spread? That is the serious question. The weather doesn't give us a chance—the wind from N. to N.W. and −40° temp. today. . . .

Thursday, March 22 and 23.
Blizzard bad as ever—Wilson and Bowers unable to start—tomorrow last chance—no fuel and only one or two of food left—must be near the end. . . .

Thursday, March 29.
Since the 21st we have had a continuous gale from W.S.W. and S.W. We had fuel to make two cups of tea apiece and bare food for two days on the 20th. Every day we have been ready to start for our depot 11 miles away, but outside the door of the tent it remains a scene of whirling drift. I do not think we can hope for any better things now. We shall stick it out to the end, but we are getting weaker, of course, and the end cannot be far.

It seems a pity, but I do not think I can write more.

Interior view of living quarters.

Analyzing Media

1. What do you find most remarkable about the experiences that Scott recorded here in his journal? Why?
2. What does his account tell you about him as a person? Explain.

Before You Read

Exploring Antarctic Ice

Reading Focus

What might it be like to visit Antarctica?

Quickwrite Imagine that you have been invited to participate in a scientific expedition to Antarctica. Spend five minutes writing about what you think the trip might be like. What might you and your fellow scientists explore and study? What dangers or discomforts might you face? What wonders might you observe?

Setting a Purpose Read to learn about one author's experiences during a scientific expedition to Antarctica.

Building Background

The Time and Place

The events described in this selection take place in August and September 1995 on the winter sea ice surrounding Antarctica.

Did You Know?

Under extremely cold conditions, ice forms on the surface of the sea. Sea ice exists year-round on the waters surrounding Antarctica; during winter, the ice expands to cover an area that is almost twice as big as the United States. Scientists believe they can learn much about global warming and climate change by studying Antarctic ice, the sea beneath it, and the living things that inhabit this environment.

Vocabulary Preview

ephemeral (i fem′ ər əl) *adj.* short-lived; temporary; p. 534

ecosystem (e′ kō sis′ təm) *n.* a community of organisms together with their environment, functioning as a unit; p. 534

proliferation (prō lif′ ə rā′ shən) *n.* growth by rapidly producing new cells or offspring; p. 534

tedious (tē′ dē əs) *adj.* boring; tiresome; p. 534

disconcerting (dis′ kən surt′ ing) *adj.* disturbing, confusing, or frustrating; p. 536

devoid (di void′) *adj.* not possessing; lacking (with *of*); p. 536

transient (tran′ shənt) *adj.* of temporary or brief duration; not lasting; p. 537

Meet Jane Ellen Stevens

"I was always very curious about how the world worked, how people designed ways to solve problems."

When Jane Stevens was asked what she likes best about her work as a science and technology writer, she replied, "Asking people about what they do and how they think and discover, learning incredible things about this world, traveling to fascinating places." Indeed, Stevens is no armchair adventurer: She has traveled the world researching science, technology, and medical topics for newspaper and magazine articles.

Jane E. Stevens was born in 1948 in East Orange, New Jersey. This article first appeared in the May 1996 issue of National Geographic.

The temperature is 1°F, not very cold for this part of the world, and a moderate breeze ruffles the fur around the hoods of our regulation-issue bloodred parkas. It's our first day out on the ice, and with a dozen other people I am shoveling snow from a frozen ocean that stretches to the horizon like a white desert.

I hear a radio crackle with the voice of second officer Michael Watson. Like a plantation manager supervising his field hands, Watson eyes us through binoculars from the bridge of the *Nathaniel B. Palmer*. "Greg, be advised that there's a crack from the bow that's crossing the end of your line." Watson refers to the marker line along which we are digging holes to measure the snow and ice thickness.

"Roger that," says Greg Packard, the marine projects coordinator. "We'll keep an eye on it."

The skies, which dawned a clear, blazing blue, have grayed. Watson's disembodied voice emerges again from Packard's radio: "Greg, be advised, a section of ice under the ship's starboard wing just buckled and it's filling with water."

Exploring Antarctic Ice

Jane Ellen Stevens

"Roger that."

As I push the shovel into the snow, a hairline crack streaks from the ship's bow a hundred yards away right past the tips of my boots. I point it out to Martin Jeffries, our chief scientist. Jeffries, a 37-year-old glaciologist[1] from the Geophysical Institute of the University of Alaska Fairbanks, has 14 years' experience with Arctic and Antarctic sea ice.

"Watch it," he advises.

The icy landscape looks solid enough, but just two feet below my white rubber boots lies 12,000 feet of frigid water. Padded with 20 pounds of clothes, I might survive in the water a few minutes—if I had the presence of mind to inflate my life vest.

Suddenly Packard shouts a warning. The crack at the end of the line is widening. We stop digging and, in the silence, hear Watson's calm voice: "Greg, the pool under the wing is getting deeper."

Jeffries doesn't hesitate. "Get back to the ship!" he yells.

1. A scientist who studies glaciers is a *glaciologist.*

Did You Know?
A *floe* is a large sheet of floating ice.

We seize shovels, tape measures, ice corers, and sledges and shuffle across the floe as fast as we can. The buckled section of ice is now a large pond from which seawater pours onto the rest of the floe like a mountain stream. As we gather inside the ship, the flat ice we stood on with all the confidence of explorers on newly conquered land begins disintegrating.

"Rats!" Jeffries says. Then relief swells his voice: "Thanks to all for coming in alive."

We're at day seven of a fifty-day international scientific expedition that will take us 8,400 miles through the winter sea ice encircling Antarctica. It is early August, and a little more than a month from now the ice will reach its greatest expanse—twice the area of the entire United States. The ice appears and disappears every year. Beginning in March, the Antarctic autumn, it grows rapidly—at a rate of 22 square miles a minute—to an average thickness of three feet. By October, the middle of spring, it is melting twice as fast.

With me on the *Palmer*, a privately owned research icebreaker under contract to the National Science Foundation (NSF), are 35 men and 7 other women. It's my second voyage on the ship; this year, as a science journalist with an NSF fellowship,[2] I've signed on as a working member of Jeffries's group of ten researchers. We're as zealous as Nathaniel B. Palmer himself, the American seal hunter who in 1820 was one of the first people to see Antarctica. . . .

Martin Jeffries and his fellow scientists call this ephemeral frontier the "Antarctic winter sea-ice ecosystem" —a dull name that doesn't even hint at the dangers and mysteries that kept all but a handful of humans away until a decade ago. Science began nibbling at the winter sea ice in 1974, but it was not until 1986 that the first research ship, the German icebreaker *Polarstern*, ventured deep into it. People criticized that expedition as foolhardy[3] and unnecessary: The ice had trapped or crushed every ship that had gone in, and everyone assumed the place was a wasteland.

Yet the researchers on the *Polarstern* found life in abundance. Penguins, seals, and seabirds appeared out of nowhere on their way to no known place. They were fatter than those observed in summer. Even the sea ice itself seemed to breathe, opening into what looked like rivers meandering through a snowy prairie and then, without warning, closing again.

Since that pioneering voyage, only ten other scientific expeditions have explored the winter sea ice, seven of them on the *Nathaniel B. Palmer*. The information collected so far shows that the ice is vital for the proliferation of life throughout the southern oceans. In winter, algae living in the ice provide a rich pasture for krill, tiny shrimp-like creatures that are a staple food of larger animals such as whales. Dust particles blown in from distant landmasses are trapped in the ice. In spring when the ice melts, algae—perhaps fertilized by iron in the dust—bloom in the meltwater.

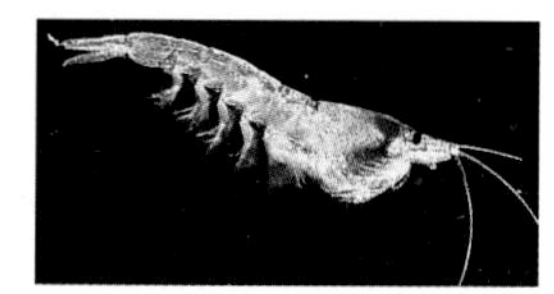

Did You Know?
Krill are tiny marine animals belonging to the same family as lobsters, crabs, and shrimp.

But we don't yet know, for instance, why the sea ice varies in thickness, structure, and distribution from one area to another or how changes in its mass affect ocean currents and climate. We don't know exactly how algae in the ice survive the winter, and we know hardly anything about the winter lives of the millions of Adélie and emperor penguins, Antarctic and snow petrels, and Weddell, crabeater, and leopard seals.

Solving these "whys" requires hours of tedious work, observing and measuring to first sort out the "whats" and "hows." How thick is the sea ice? How much snow covers it? How much of the ice is flooded with seawater? What is the temperature of the snow and ice?

2. A *fellowship* is a sum of money granted to allow work or advanced study in one's chosen field.
3. *Foolhardy* means "bold or daring in a foolish or unthinking way."

Vocabulary

ephemeral (i fem′ ər əl) *adj.* short-lived; temporary
ecosystem (e′ kō sis′ təm) *n.* a community of organisms together with their environment, functioning as a unit
proliferation (prō lif′ ə rā′ shən) *n.* growth by rapidly producing new cells or offspring
tedious (tē′ dē əs) *adj.* boring; tiresome

What kinds of crystals are present? Our expedition will help answer these questions.

After the ominous[4] incident our first day on the ice, we push south in the Ross Sea along longitude 180°, the date line,[5] meandering between yesterday and today through a world that will disappear two months from now. The *Palmer* makes 60 nautical miles—one degree of latitude—every 24 hours, and four days later, on Julian day 220,[6] we reach 69° south. At 9:30 A.M., as a neon orange rim appears along the horizon, we make a stop to collect atmospheric and oceanographic data. . . .

I consider myself lucky to be part of the snow and ice thickness team: Our time is vigorously spent. With shovels, four of us begin digging holes a yard apart along the 164-yard (150-meter) line. Even though the snow is fluffy and only about a foot deep, I soon work up a sweat. Five emperor penguins slide toward us on their white-pillowed bellies, push themselves up with their beaks, and spend the rest of the afternoon studying us.

The next job is to drill small holes through the ice itself. Each time I haul out the gas-powered drill, seawater spouts through the hole like a geyser. (We employ gas-powered machinery as little as possible to keep pollution to a minimum.) We then use a measuring stick to record the depth of the snow and tailor's tape attached to a weighted piece of string to measure the thickness of the ice. There's an irony in sailing to the Antarctic in a ship that costs more than $25,000 a day to run so we can work with a wooden stick and a piece of string.

At 3 P.M., three hours after we began shoveling, we trudge back to our warm metal

4. Here, *ominous* means "unfavorable" or "threatening."
5. The *date line* is the imaginary north-south line on the earth that marks the time boundary between one day and the next.
6. *Julian day 220* is August 8. The Julian calendar numbers the days of the year from 1 to 365 (or 366 in a leap year).

cocoon—a daily routine that hardly ever varies. This evening, though, I pause at the gangway. The sun, huge and vermilion[7] as it drops toward the western horizon, is framed by sun dogs, rainbows of brilliant color that appear when ice crystals are thick in the sunlit air. In the east a stark white moon rises against a cerulean[8] sky. The penguins, their white necks streaked with the colors of the sun, are standing on their heels, the tops of their feet tucked under their bellies for warmth.

If day 220 was tolerably comfortable, there are times on the ice when the windchill drops to minus 50°F, and the wind, blinding us with snow that turns the *Palmer* into a dim ghost ship, sucks the life heat from our fingers and toes so they ache and grow numb. Sometimes the floes are partly submerged under a burden of several feet of snow, and I find myself sloshing ankle-deep in water—a disconcerting reminder of the thinness of the skin between me and eternity. . . .

The ship rams the ice, stops, slides back, and rams again. Back and ram. Back and ram. It's day 224, and for the past three days we've been stopped at 70° south. Jeffries faces a dilemma. If he pushes on toward the Ross Ice Shelf as he had planned, he risks wasting fuel and precious time. However long it takes to get in, it will take that long to get out. The ice here is four to five feet thick, with ridges of nine feet, and the weather changes so quickly we also risk being trapped without warning. Jeffries decides to change course. You can't fight Antarctic sea ice, he says. "You've got to go with the flow." We will retrace the route he took the year before, northeast through the frozen Amundsen and Bellingshausen Seas.

Minke[9] whales off the bow! The word goes out at dawn on day 227, a morning so gray no horizon divides sky from ice. I run to the bridge and see two minkes, gray-black and about 30 feet long, break a hole in the thin, frozen sheet, then submerge. Out of the mist a dozen or so Adélie penguins scuttle single file across the ice to the hole and, like kids at a swimming hole, mill around before jumping in. They pop back out and spy another hole made by the minkes farther on. Again they rush over, inspect the hole, and plunge in.

Most likely the whales are feeding on krill, and the Adélies are probably tagging along to exploit the ready-made fishing holes. Penguins, seals, and birds such as snow petrels also use natural cracks in the ice to feed and, in the case of minke whales, to breathe.

That the great, shifting expanses of ice around us, utterly devoid of soil and rooted plants, support any life at all—let alone in such profusion—seems impossible. André Belém, a

Did You Know?
In 1911 Roald *Amundsen,* a Norwegian, became the first person to reach the South Pole. The Amundsen Sea is named after him.

Did You Know?
From 1819 to 1821, Fabian *Bellingshausen,* a Russian, led an expedition that sailed completely around Antarctica. The Bellingshausen Sea is named after him.

7. *Vermilion* is a bright red color.
8. *Cerulean* (sə ro͞o′ lē ən) is a bright blue color, often described as sky-blue.

9. *Minke* (ming′ kē)

Vocabulary

disconcerting (dis′ kən surt′ ing) *adj.* disturbing, confusing, or frustrating
devoid (di void′) *adj.* not possessing; lacking (with *of*)

graduate student from the University of Rio Grande in Brazil, offers me a dramatic insight when he shows me a test tube in which he has melted a small chunk of sea ice. "Look," he says in amazement. A thick yellowish sludge of algae floats in the bottom. "There's more life in there than in the water of an estuary."[10]

Indeed algal concentrations in the sea ice are among the highest ever recorded in any ocean. As the ice grows, the crystals snag algae. Channels winding among the crystals bring seawater—and nutrients—to the algae, which lure krill and krill larvae to the bottom of the ice floes, where they graze like tiny cows.

One day during our last week I climb with Jim Cooper, the electronics technician, to the top of the science mast, 130 feet above the ice. As he rubs the frost off the satellite receivers and meteorological sensors, I look down at a quilt of ice floes spreading to the horizon under the clear blue sky. Smoky wisps curl up around the ship like genies—ice crystals forming as water vapor from the lead we're gliding through encounters the colder air.

This transfer of heat from water to air is expressive of a much grander redistribution triggered by the sea ice: the streaming of cold water from the Antarctic toward the Equator. As seawater around Antarctica freezes, it squeezes out cold, dense brine,[11] some of which sinks to deeper water then moves north. It eventually mixes with warmer water, rises, and begins flowing back toward Antarctica.

One place where this warmer water comes to the surface is the Weddell Sea. On a *Palmer* expedition there two years ago, scientists measured the heat flow from a 38,000-square-mile area at 20 watts per square yard—enough energy during the austral[12] winter to power every U.S. household more than 20 times over.

What disruptions would occur if a warming or cooling trend were to shrink or expand the winter sea ice? Presumably ocean currents would shift, perhaps causing drastic shifts in climate. The *Palmer's* next two winter voyages will look into such questions.

Our last working day, Julian day 254—Monday, September 11—is typically dreary and windy. After watching the crew hoist the gangway for the last time, I stroll to the stern deck and stare at the ice around me as the *Palmer's* engines rumble to life.

I have grown to love this cold, strange place with an intensity that I could never have anticipated. Such a reaction may seem odd to those who have never heard the sigh of ice floes jostling on the swells or watched the vapors curling up out of a lead or felt the knife blade of an Antarctic gale. Alighting here briefly, like a bird of passage, I have come to see this transient frontier not as a harsh place but as a living creature that nurtures a multitude of other lives. Yet no humans can ever live here. We can't conquer it, settle it, even own it. The winter ice belongs only to itself.

10. An *estuary* is the wide mouth of a river where the ocean's tide meets the river's current. Estuaries are very fertile ecosystems that are believed to account for more than half of the life in all oceans.

11. Here, the *brine* is water that has a much higher salt content than ordinary sea water, which is also sometimes called brine.

12. *Austral* means "southern." It comes from the same Latin word that gives Australia its name.

Vocabulary

transient (tran′ shənt) *adj.* of temporary or brief duration; not lasting

Responding to Literature

Personal Response

What visual image was most striking to you as you read the selection? What made it so striking?

Analyzing Literature

Recall

1. Describe what happens during the researchers' first day out on the ice.
2. Summarize what scientists on previous expeditions had learned about the Antarctic winter sea-ice ecosystem.
3. How does Stevens spend Julian day 220?
4. Describe the relationship among the whales, penguins, krill, algae, and winter sea ice.
5. In the article's last paragraph, how does Stevens describe her attitude toward the winter sea ice?

Interpret

6. What can you infer about the work that the researchers are doing from the author's description of their first day on the ice?
7. How did previous expeditions change scientists' attitudes about studying the winter sea-ice ecosystem in Antarctica? Explain.
8. What feelings do you think Stevens might experience as she views the scene from the gangway on day 220?
9. What conclusions might you draw from Stevens's description of the relationship among the animals and the winter sea ice?
10. What do you think accounts for Stevens's attitude toward the winter sea ice in Antarctica?

Evaluate and Connect

11. Look back at your response to the Reading Focus on page 531. Compare your response with what Stevens actually experiences on this expedition.
12. Do you think the benefits of expeditions like this one outweigh the risks and expense? Explain.
13. Find three examples of **figurative language** in the selection. Explain how each example helps you better understand or appreciate what is being described. (See Literary Terms Handbook, page R5.)
14. How does this selection help you better understand the "balance of nature"? Explain.
15. Would you like to participate in a research expedition like this one? Why or why not?

Literary ELEMENTS

Author's Purpose

When you read a piece of nonfiction, think about the **author's purpose,** or reason, for writing. For example, the author may want to inform, entertain, tell a story, or persuade the reader. Keep in mind that in any work of nonfiction, the author may have more than one purpose. For example, in a piece of narrative nonfiction, the author may want to not only tell a story, but also persuade the reader to agree with a particular point of view. In informative nonfiction, the author may want to entertain the reader while providing information about a particular topic. In "Exploring Antarctic Ice," Jane Ellen Stevens uses elements of both narrative and informative nonfiction to achieve several purposes.

1. Do you think Stevens wrote this article to inform, to entertain, to tell a story, or to persuade the reader? Give reasons for your answers.
2. Evaluate how well you think Stevens achieved each of her purposes in writing this article.
3. Which purpose do you think was most important to Stevens? Explain.

- See **Literary Terms Handbook,** p. R1.

Literature and Writing

Writing About Literature

Evaluate a Concluding Statement Jane Stevens concludes her article with this statement: "The winter ice belongs only to itself." In a paragraph, explain what you think the author means by this statement, using details from the article to support your explanation. Then write another paragraph in which you tell whether you agree or disagree with this statement. Support your position using evidence from the article or from your own knowledge or experience. Compare your ideas with those of other students.

Creative Writing

Expedition Application Imagine that you are a science writer and want to join a research expedition to gain first-hand field experience. You have learned of an expedition to the region of the world that interests you the most. Write a letter of application to the expedition leader, explaining why you are interested in the research and what qualifications you would bring to the team.

Extending Your Response

Literature Groups

Intriguing Information Write the answer to this question on a note card: What fact about the Antarctic exploration intrigued you the most? On the back of the card, describe why this fact made such an impression on you. Then take turns in your group reading your answer to the question. After everyone has read his or her response, go around the group again, taking turns explaining why you chose the fact you did. Using specific details from the selection, try to convince other group members that your fact is much more intriguing than theirs are.

Learning for Life

Pack Your Bags Imagine that you have been invited to join a scientific expedition to a remote region of the world. Research the location, as well as the scientific field in which you'll be working. Then make a list of equipment and personal belongings that you and your team members will need for your expedition.

Internet Connection

Cold Enough for You? If you had been in the Antarctic on July 21, 1983, you could have experienced the coldest temperature on record: −128.6°F (−89.2°C). Generate a list of research questions about extremes in weather or climate. Then use the Internet to discover the answers to your questions. Summarize the information using a graphic such as a chart, graph, or map.

Reading Further

You may enjoy reading more articles about the Antarctic:

"Journey Into the Cold Unknown," by Jane E. Stevens (*International Wildlife,* January 1996).

"The Antarctic Pack-ice Ecosystem," by Jane E. Stevens (*BioScience,* March 1995).

"Lessons on the Ice," by Robert Lee Hotz (*Technology Review,* October 1996).

Save your work for your portfolio.

Skill Minilessons

GRAMMAR AND LANGUAGE • Capitalization

Capitalize the first word of every sentence, the first word of a direct quotation that is a complete sentence, and all proper nouns. Note the capitalization in these sentences from the article.

André Belém, a graduate student from the University of Rio Grande in Brazil, offers me a dramatic insight when he shows me a test tube. . . . "There's more life in there than in the water of an estuary."

PRACTICE On your paper, rewrite the following paragraph. Correct any mistakes in capitalization that you find.

journalist jane stevens participated in two expeditions to antarctica aboard the *nathaniel b. palmer.* they were sponsored by the national science foundation. in an article that stevens wrote for *International Wildlife,* she stated, "this is a coveted scientific odyssey."

For more on capitalization, see **Language Handbook,** p. R45.

READING AND THINKING • Recognizing Cause and Effect

Science writers, such as Stevens, use cause-and-effect relationships to explain the connection between a specific event (the cause) and the results of that event (effects). The cause is what makes something happen. The effect is what happens. Sometimes, one event begins a chain reaction of causes and effects. For example, Stevens points out that when wind blows dust particles from distant landmasses (cause), the particles become trapped in the winter sea ice (effect). This cause-and-effect relationship is the first in a chain of events that have a major effect on the Antarctic ecosystem.

PRACTICE Reread the part of the selection that discusses dust particles in the sea ice, and list other cause-and-effect relationships that result from the trapping of the particles in the ice.

For more on text structures, see **Reading Handbook,** pp. R86–R87.

VOCABULARY • Analogies

An analogy is a type of comparison that is based on the relationships between things or ideas. To complete an analogy, decide what relationship exists between the first two things or ideas. Then apply that relationship to another pair of words and see if it is the same. Many analogies are based on description. In this type of analogy, one word in a pair could be used as part of an accurate description of the other:

skywriting : ephemeral :: engraving : lasting

Skywriting is a method of writing that is *ephemeral; engraving* is a method of writing that is *lasting.* In identifying the relationship illustrated by the first pair of words, it is important to be as specific as possible.

PRACTICE Choose the word pair that best completes each analogy.

1. daredevil : foolhardy ::
   a. tattletale : disloyal
   b. cousin : related
   c. athlete : muscular
   d. neighbor : nearby
   e. soldier : drafted
2. tourist : transient ::
   a. traveler : tired
   b. hotel : urban
   c. host : gracious
   d. souvenir : memorable
   e. resident : permanent

For more on analogies, see **Communications Skills Handbook,** p. R77.

Listening, Speaking, and Viewing

Interviewing

When the journalist Slavenka Drakulić, author of "Pizza in Warsaw, Torte in Prague," wanted to find out how the collapse of communism was affecting the everyday lives of women in Eastern Europe, she interviewed a number of women there. Interviewing is a skill that all good journalists must master, but even if you're not a journalist, you'll find that your interviewing skills will come in handy in many situations, both inside and outside of school. For example, if you want to learn about a particular career, you might interview someone who's pursuing that career. If a class assignment requires you to find out about community resources for homeless people, you might interview the director of a local shelter for the homeless.

Preparing for an Interview

- Request an interview, explain your purpose, and make an appointment. If you have a tape recorder, ask permission to tape the interview.
- Research the background of the person and the topic.
- Write interview questions that are clear and tightly focused.

Conducting an Interview

- Arrive on time. Be polite, friendly, and businesslike.
- Ask a question, and listen to the answer. Don't interrupt. Ask follow-up questions.
- If you're taking notes rather than taping the interview, summarize the main points. Write down, word for word, any quotations you want to use.

Writing Up an Interview

Decide how you will present the information you have gathered–a script, a report, or another piece of writing.

ACTIVITIES

1. Learn from the experts by reading interviews in newspapers and magazines and on the Internet or by watching or listening to interviews on television and radio. Evaluate the techniques used by each interviewer. Share your observations with the class.
2. Polish your own skills by conducting an interview. You might interview someone to fulfill a class assignment, or simply to learn about a topic that interests you. Follow the steps described in this lesson as you prepare, conduct, and write up your interview. Then share the interview with your classmates.

INTERDISCIPLINARY CONNECTION

PHYSICAL SCIENCE

Lightning

Where there's smoke, there's fire—and where there's thunder, there's lightning, as Gretel Ehrlich's experience shows. But what about rain? Ehrlich was hit by lightning during what she describes as "a dry storm with only sputtering rain." Not only are there such things as dry thunderstorms, there are also many forms of lightning.

Common Forms of Lightning	
Streak	A single jagged flash
Forked	A flash with multiple branches
Ribbon	Separate side-by-side flashes of light
Bead or chain	A flash that fades into a dotted line

Thunderstorms develop within high, puffy clouds that can reach more than 75,000 feet in altitude. Within the clouds, air currents move rapidly up and down, producing electrical charges. A single flash of lightning may transmit from 100 million to a billion volts of electricity. In comparison, the typical current in a household electrical outlet, which is enough to kill a person, is 110 volts.

Lightning greatly heats up the air along its path—to more than 50,000°F—and causes the air to expand explosively. The hot expanding air generates shock waves, which become sound waves—or thunder. Thus, lightning causes thunder. Because sound travels more slowly than light, you hear thunder a number of seconds after you see the flash of lightning.

Lightning is not always visible, and it's not always accompanied by heavy rain. *Invisible lightning* occurs when an electric current continues to flow along the path set up by a visible strike. *Dry thunderstorms,* which bring lightning without rain, are common in arid regions of the western United States. In those areas, low humidity often causes the rain to evaporate before it ever hits the ground. Such conditions may have prevailed when lightning struck Gretel Ehrlich as she was walking with her dogs.

Other unusual and interesting forms of lightning exist, such as *ball lightning,* which consists of a glowing red, yellow, or orange ball seen for a few seconds after ordinary lightning. People have reported seeing these grapefruit-size balls floating along the ground and in houses, barns, and even airplanes. Other forms, called *red sprites, blue jets,* and *green elves* are colored lights flashing in the upper atmosphere above a thunderstorm. Like other aspects of thunderstorms, these lights have proven difficult for scientists to explain.

Activity

The Internet has a host of facts and figures about thunderstorms and lightning. Collect information that you find interesting and use it to create a pamphlet of thunderstorm facts. For example, you might discover which state has the most thunderstorms and which has hardly any. (And see if you can find out more about red sprites, blue jets, and green elves!)

Before You Read

from *A Match to the Heart*

Reading Focus

What have been your experiences with electrical storms? How do these storms make you feel?

List Ideas List words and phrases that describe what you experienced during a specific electrical storm. Include your emotional responses, your sensory responses (sight, sound, touch, smell), the time, and the place.

Setting a Purpose Read to learn about one person's experience with lightning.

Building Background

The Time and Place

This story takes place in Wyoming in 1991 on the ranch where the author was living and in nearby towns.

Did You Know?

Lightning occurs when the rising and falling air currents in a cloud cause positive and negative electrical charges in the air to separate. When accumulated positive and negative charges recombine, intense energy is released as lightning.

The lightning can occur within a cloud or between the air and the ground. Lightning that strikes the earth begins as an invisible channel of electrically charged air reaching toward the ground. When it nears the earth, an opposite charge of electricity surges upward toward the cloud, producing the visible bolt of lightning.

Vocabulary Preview

muse (mūz) *v.* to think or reflect, especially in an idle manner; p. 546

expend (iks pend′) *v.* to use up; consume; spend; p. 546

inert (i nurt′) *adj.* without power to move or act; lifeless; p. 546

incoherently (in′ kō hēr′ ənt lē) *adv.* in a confused, disconnected manner; unintelligibly; p. 547

abyss (ə bis′) *n.* an immeasurably deep hole; vast emptiness; nothingness; p. 547

fortuitous (fôr to͞o′ ə təs) *adj.* fortunate; lucky; p. 549

equilibrium (ēk′ wə lib′ rē əm) *n.* mental, emotional, or physical balance; p. 550

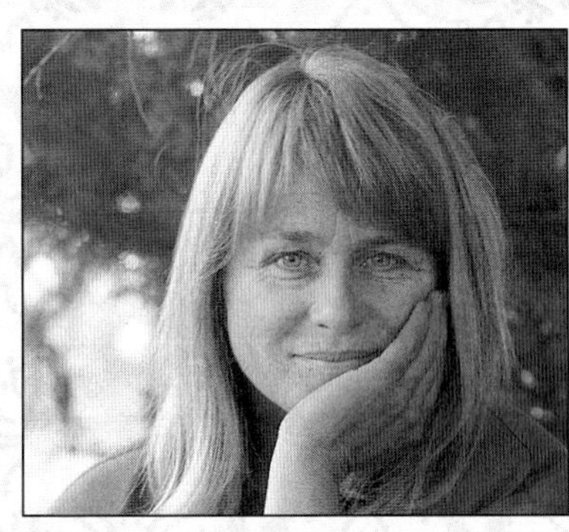

Meet Gretel Ehrlich

"Physical work has a spiritual equivalent: the ax cuts away self-delusion and the hoe turns mental compost into insight and understanding."

Gretel Ehrlich (ār′ likh) is a novelist and essayist who has honed her writing skills while living and working on ranches in California and Wyoming. She has "built and maintained fence, irrigated alfalfa, worked livestock, run a baler, stacked hay, pulled calves." She sees the writing and the ranch work as complementary endeavors that help her achieve mental and spiritual balance. "Whole books," she says, "came into my mind as I shoveled out ditches. . . ."

Gretel Ehrlich was born in Santa Barbara, California, in 1946. A Match to the Heart *was published in 1994.*

from

A Match to the Heart

Gretel Ehrlich

Before electricity carved its blue path toward me, before the negative charge shot down from cloud to ground, before "streamers" jumped the positive charge back up from ground to cloud, before air expanded and contracted producing loud pressure pulses I could not hear because I was already dead, I had been walking.

When I started out on foot that August afternoon, the thunderstorm was blowing in fast. On the face of the mountain, a mile ahead, hard westerly gusts and sudden updrafts collided, pulling black clouds apart. Yet the storm looked harmless. When a distant thunderclap scared the dogs, I called them to my side and rubbed their ears: "Don't worry, you're okay as long as you're with me."

I woke in a pool of blood, lying on my stomach some distance from where I should have been, flung at an odd angle to one side of the dirt path. The whole sky had grown dark. Was it evening, and if so, which one? How many minutes or hours had elapsed since I lost consciousness, and where were the dogs? I tried to call out to them but my voice didn't work. The muscles in my throat were paralyzed and I couldn't swallow. Were the dogs dead? Everything was terribly wrong: I had trouble seeing, talking, breathing, and I couldn't move my legs or right arm. Nothing remained in my memory—no sounds, flashes, smells, no warnings of any kind. Had I been shot in the back? Had I suffered a stroke or heart attack? These thoughts were dark pools in sand.

The sky was black. Was this a storm in the middle of the day or was it night with a storm traveling through? When thunder exploded over me, I knew I had been hit by lightning.

The pain in my chest intensified and every muscle in my body ached. I was quite sure I was dying. What was it one should do or think or know? I tried to recall the Buddhist instruction regarding dying—which position to lie in, which direction to face. Did the "Lion's position" taken by the Buddha mean lying on the left or the right? And which sutra to sing? Oh yes, the Heart Sutra . . . gaté, gaté, paragaté . . .[1] form and formlessness. Paradox and cosmic jokes. Surviving after trying to die "properly" would be truly funny, but the chances of that seemed slim.

---

1. A *sutra* (so͞o′ trə) is a passage from Buddha's writings, and the words *gaté, gaté, paragaté* (pär′ ə gä′ tā) are part of a meditative chant recited at the end of the passage known as the *Heart Sutra.*

Other words drifted in: how the "gateless barrier" was the gate through which one passes to reach enlightenment. Yet if there was no gate, how did one pass through? Above me, high on the hill, was the gate on the ranch that lead nowhere, a gate I had mused about often. Now its presence made me smile. Even when I thought I had no aspirations for enlightenment, too much effort in that direction was being expended. How could I learn to slide, yet remain aware?

. . . what a way to get enlightened.

To be struck by lightning: what a way to get enlightened. That would be the joke if I survived. It seemed important to remember jokes. My thinking did not seem connected to the inert body that was in such terrible pain. Sweep the mind of weeds, I kept telling myself—that's what years of Buddhist practice had taught me. . . . But where were the dogs, the two precious ones I had watched being born and had raised in such intimacy and trust? I wanted them with me. I wanted them to save me again.

It started to rain. Every time a drop hit bare skin there was an explosion of pain. Blood crusted my left eye. I touched my good hand to my heart, which was beating wildly, erratically. My chest was numb, as if it had been sprayed with novocaine. No feeling of peace filled me. Death was a bleakness,[2] a grayness about which it was impossible to be curious or relieved. I loved those dogs and hoped they weren't badly hurt. If I didn't die soon, how many days would pass before we were found, and when would the scavengers come? The sky was dark, or was that the way life flew out of the body, in a long tube with no light at the end? I lay on the cold ground waiting. The mountain was purple, and sage stirred against my face. I knew I had to give up all this, then my own body and all my thinking. Once more I lifted my head to look for the dogs but, unable to see them, I twisted myself until I faced east and tried to let go of all desire.

When my eyes opened again I knew I wasn't dead. Images from World War II movies filled my head: of wounded soldiers dragging themselves across a field, and if I could have laughed—that is, made my face work into a smile and get sounds to discharge from my throat—I would have. It would have been good to laugh. Instead, I considered my options: either lie there and wait for someone to find me—how many days or weeks would that take?—or somehow get back to the house. I calmly assessed what might be wrong with me—stroke, cerebral hemorrhage, gunshot wound—but it was bigger than I could understand. The instinct to survive does not rise from particulars; a deep but general misery rollercoasted me into

2. *Bleakness* is a condition of cold and dreary gloom.

Vocabulary

muse (mūz) *v.* to think or reflect, especially in an idle manner
expend (iks pend′) *v.* to use up; consume; spend
inert (i nurt′) *adj.* without power to move or act; lifeless

action. I tried to propel myself on my elbows but my right arm didn't work. The wind had swung around and was blowing in from the east. It was still a dry storm with only sputtering rain, but when I raised myself up, lightning fingered the entire sky.

It is not true that lightning never strikes the same place twice. I had entered a shower of sparks and furious brightness and, worried that I might be struck again, watched as lightning touched down all around me. Years before, in the high country, I'd been hit by lightning: an electrical charge had rolled down an open meadow during a fearsome thunderstorm, surged up the legs of my horse, coursed through me, and bounced a big spark off the top of my head. To be struck again—and this time it was a direct hit—what did it mean?

The feeling had begun to come back into my legs and after many awkward attempts, I stood. To walk meant lifting each leg up by the thigh, moving it forward with my hands, setting it down. The earth felt like a peach that had split open in the middle; one side moved up while the other side moved down and my legs were out of rhythm. The ground rolled the way it does during an earthquake and the sky was tattered book pages waving in different directions. Was the ground liquifying under me, or had the molecular composition of my body deliquesced?[3] I struggled to piece together fragments. Then it occurred to me that my brain was torn and that's where the blood had come from.

I walked. Sometimes my limbs held me, sometimes they didn't. I don't know how many times I fell but it didn't matter because I was making slow progress toward home.

Home—the ranch house—was about a quarter of a mile away. I don't remember much about getting there. My concentration went into making my legs work. The storm was strong. All the way across the basin, lightning lifted parts of mountains and sky into yellow refulgence[4] and dropped them again, only to lift others. The inside of my eyelids turned gold and I could see the dark outlines of things through them. At the bottom of the hill I opened the door to my pickup and blew the horn with the idea that someone might hear me. No one came. My head had swollen to an indelicate shape. I tried to swallow—I was so thirsty—but the muscles in my throat were still paralyzed and I wondered when I would no longer be able to breathe.

Inside the house, sounds began to come out of me. I was doing crazy things, ripping my hiking boots off because the bottoms of my feet were burning, picking up the phone when I was finally able to scream. One of those times, someone happened to be on the line. I was screaming incoherently for help. My last conscious act was to dial 911.

Dark again. Pressing against sore ribs, my dogs pulled me out of the abyss, pulled and pulled. I smelled straw. My face was on tatami.[5] I opened my eyes, looked up, and saw neighbors. Had they come for my funeral? The phone rang and I heard someone give directions to the ambulance driver, who was lost. . . .

3. *Deliquesced* means to have dissolved and become liquid.

4. *Refulgence* means "brightness; radiance."

5. The *tatami* (tä tä′ mē) is a mat woven from rice straw or a similar material.

Vocabulary

incoherently (in′ kō hēr′ ənt lē) *adv.* in a confused, disconnected manner; unintelligibly

abyss (ə bis′) *n.* an immeasurably deep hole; vast emptiness; nothingness

from A Match to the Heart

I slipped back into unconsciousness and when I woke again two EMTs[6] were listening to my heart. I asked them to look for my dogs but they wouldn't leave me. Someone else in the room went outside and found Sam and Yaki curled up on the porch, frightened but alive. Now I could rest. I felt the medics jabbing needles into the top of my hands, trying unsuccessfully to get IVs[7] started, then strapping me onto a backboard and carrying me out the front door of the house, down steps, into lightning and rain, into what was now a full-blown storm.

The ambulance rocked and slid, slamming my bruised body against the metal rails of the gurney. Every muscle was in violent spasm and there was a place on my back near the heart that burned. I heard myself yell in pain. Finally the EMTs rolled up towels and blankets and wedged them against my arms, shoulders, hips, and knees so the jolting of the vehicle wouldn't dislodge me. The ambulance slid down into ditches, struggled out, bumped from one deep rut to another. I asked to be taken to the hospital in Cody, but they said they were afraid my heart might stop again. As it was, the local hospital was thirty-five miles away, ten of them dirt, and the trip took more than an hour.

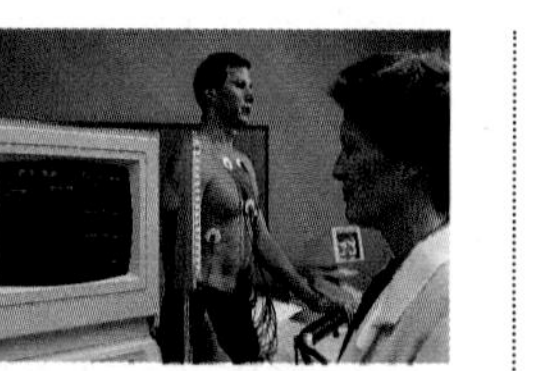

Did You Know?
An electrocardiograph, or *EKG machine,* is used to detect heart problems.

Our arrival seemed a portent[8] of disaster—and an occasion for comedy. I had been struck by lightning around five in the afternoon. It was now 9:00 P.M. Nothing at the hospital worked. Their one EKG machine was nonfunctional, and jokingly the nurses blamed it on me. "Honey, you've got too much electricity in your body," one of them told me. Needles were jammed into my hand—no one had gotten an IV going yet—and the doctor on call hadn't arrived, though half an hour had elapsed. The EMTs kept assuring me: "Don't worry, we won't leave you here." When another nurse, who was filling out an admission form, asked me how tall I was, I answered: "Too short to be struck by lightning."

"Electrical injury often results in ventricular fibrillation[9] *and injury to the medullary centers of the brain. Immediately after electric shock patients are usually comatose, apneic, and in circulatory collapse. . . ."*

When the doctor on call—the only doctor in town, waddled into what they called the emergency room, my aura,[10] he said, was yellow and gray—a soul in transition. I knew that he had gone to medical school but had never completed a residency and had been barred from ER or ICU[11] work in the hospitals of Florida, where he had lived previously. Yet I was lucky. Florida has many lightning victims, and unlike the doctors I would see later, he at least recognized the symptoms of a lightning strike. The tally sheet read this way: I had suffered a hit by lightning which caused ventricular

6. Emergency medical technicians, or *EMTs,* carry out basic lifesaving procedures before and during transport of a victim to a hospital via ambulance.
7. The *IVs* are medical equipment that allow drugs and fluids to be injected intravenously, or directly into a vein.
8. A *portent* is a warning or indication of something significant or disastrous that is about to happen.
9. This is the first of three paragraphs that describe the diagnosis and treatment of electrical injuries such as lightning strikes. *Ventricular fibrillation* is a series of rapid, irregular heart contractions. The last three terms in the paragraph refer to unconsciousness, a temporary suspension of breathing, and a rapid drop in blood pressure.
10. Here, the *aura* is a halo or glow said to surround the body, reflecting one's personal qualities and emotional, spiritual, and physical state. This concept is not endorsed by most traditional physicians.
11. A *residency* is a period during which a physician receives specialized training in, for example, the emergency room *(ER)* or intensive care unit *(ICU).*

fibrillation—cardiac arrest—though luckily my heart started beating again. Violent contractions of muscles when one is hit often causes the body to fly through the air: I was flung far and hit hard on my left side, which may have caused my heart to start again, but along with that fortuitous side effect, I sustained a concussion, broken ribs, a possible broken jaw, and lacerations above the eye. The paralysis below my waist and up through the chest and throat—called kerauno-paralysis—is common in lightning strikes and almost always temporary, but my right arm continued to be almost useless. Fernlike burns—arborescent erythema—covered my entire body. These occur when the electrical charge follows tracings of moisture on the skin—rain or sweat—thus the spidery red lines.

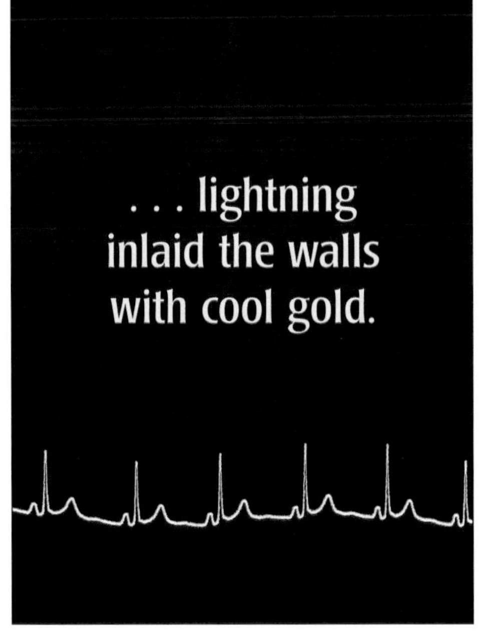
. . . lightning inlaid the walls with cool gold.

"Rapid institution of fluid and electrolyte therapy is essential with guidelines being the patient's urine output, hematocrit, osmolality, central venous pressure, and arterial blood gases. . . ."[12]

The nurses loaded me onto a gurney. As they wheeled me down the hall to my room, a front wheel fell off and I was slammed into the wall. Once I was in bed, the deep muscle aches continued, as did the chest pains. Later, friends came to visit. Neither doctor nor nurse had cleaned the cuts on my head, so Laura, who had herded sheep and cowboyed on all the ranches where I had lived and whose wounds I had cleaned when my saddle horse dragged her across a high mountain pasture, wiped blood and dirt from my face, arms, and hands with a cool towel and spooned yogurt into my mouth.

I was the only patient in the hospital. During the night, sheet lightning inlaid the walls with cool gold. I felt like an ancient, mummified child who had been found on a rock ledge near our ranch: bound tightly, unable to move, my dead face tipped backwards toward the moon.

In the morning, my regular doctor, Ben, called from Massachusetts, where he was vacationing, with this advice: "Get yourself out of that hospital and go somewhere else, anywhere." I was too weak to sign myself out, but Julie, the young woman who had a summer job on our ranch, retrieved me in the afternoon. She helped me get dressed in the cutoffs and torn T-shirt I had been wearing, but there were no shoes, so, barefoot, I staggered into Ben's office, where a physician's assistant kindly cleansed the gashes in my head. Then I was taken home.

Another thunderstorm slammed against the mountains as I limped up the path to the house. Sam and Yaki took one look at me and ran. These dogs lived with me, slept with me, understood every word I said, and I was too sick to find them, console them—even if they would have let me.

12. *[Rapid institution . . . blood gases]* This paragraph suggests administering fluids (by IV), based on urine output and various blood tests.

Vocabulary

fortuitous (fôr tōō′ ə təs) *adj.* fortunate; lucky

The next day my husband, who had just come down from the mountains where he worked in the summer, took me to another hospital. I passed out in the admissions office, was loaded onto a gurney, and taken for a CAT scan. No one bothered to find out why I had lost consciousness. Later, in the emergency unit, the doctor argued that I might not have been struck by lightning at all, as if I had imagined the incident. "Maybe a meteor hit me," I said, a suggestion he pondered seriously. After a blood panel and a brief neurological exam,[13] which I failed—I couldn't follow his finger with my eyes or walk a straight line—he promptly released me.

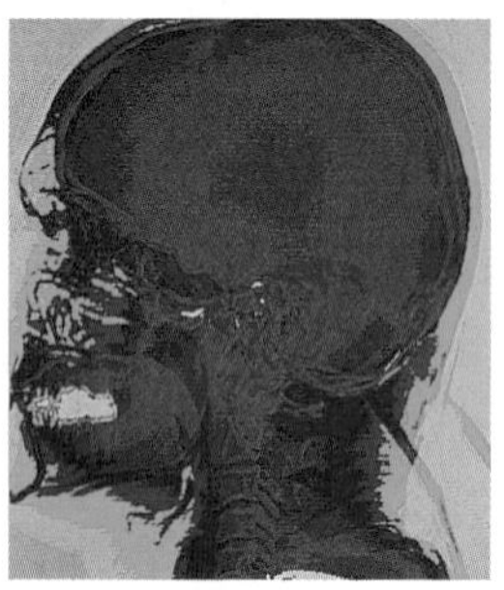

Did You Know?
A *CAT scan* is a sort of three-dimensional X ray. (*CAT* stands for "computerized axial tomography.")

"Patients should be monitored electrocardiographically for at least 24 hours for significant arrhythmias which often have delayed onset. . . ."[14]

It was difficult to know what was worse: being in a hospital where nothing worked and nobody cared, or being alone on an isolated ranch hundreds of miles from decent medical care.

In the morning I staggered into the kitchen. My husband, from whom I had been separated for three months, had left at 4:00 A.M. to buy cattle in another part of the state and would not be back for a month. Alone again, it was impossible to do much for myself. In the past I'd been bucked off, stiff and sore plenty of times but this felt different: I had no sense of equilibrium. My head hurt, every muscle in my body ached as if I had a triple dose of the flu, and my left eye was swollen shut and turning black and blue. Something moved in the middle of the kitchen floor. I was having difficulty seeing, but then I did see: a rattlesnake lay coiled in front of the stove. I reeled around and dove back into bed. Enough tests of character. I closed my eyes and half-slept. Later, when Julie came to the house, she found the snake and cut off its head with a shovel.

My only consolation was that the dogs came back. I had chest pains and all day Sam lay with his head against my heart. I cleaned a deep cut over Yaki's eye. It was half an inch deep but already healing. I couldn't tell if the dogs were sick or well, I was too miserable to know anything except that Death resided in the room: not as a human figure but as a dark fog rolling in, threatening to cover me; but the dogs stayed close and while my promise to keep them safe during a thunderstorm had proven fraudulent, their promise to keep me alive held good.

13. A *blood panel* is a series of blood tests, and a *neurological exam* checks the nervous system.
14. *[Patients should . . . delayed onset]* In other words, an EKG machine should be used to watch for the possible development of irregularities in the heartbeat.

Vocabulary
equilibrium (ēk′ wə lib′ rē əm) *n.* mental, emotional, or physical balance

Responding to Literature

Personal Response

What is your strongest or most immediate reaction to this selection? What is the basis for your response?

Analyzing Literature

Recall

1. Why does Ehrlich tell her dogs: "Don't worry, you're okay as long as you're with me"?
2. Describe Ehrlich's physical condition and state of mind immediately following the accident.
3. What does Ehrlich do to help herself?
4. Briefly summarize the medical treatment Ehrlich receives.
5. What happens that provokes Ehrlich to say that she has had enough "tests of character"?

Interpret

6. What is **ironic** about the comment Ehrlich makes to her dogs that they will be safe with her?
7. What do you think might account for the kinds of thoughts that come to Ehrlich right after the accident?
8. Why do you think Ehrlich's attitude changes when she awakens the second time?
9. How might Ehrlich describe her opinion of the medical care she received?
10. At the end of the selection, what does the incident in the kitchen reveal about Ehrlich's character?

Evaluate and Connect

11. Analyze the author's use of **humor** in the narrative. In your opinion, why does she use humor and what does it add to this account?
12. How important are the medical facts Ehrlich provides? Why do you think Ehrlich includes so many medical facts in her narrative? In what ways are they important to the selection?
13. Considering Ehrlich's experience, how would you respond to a person who belittles someone else's fear of lightning?
14. Has your attitude toward lightning changed as a result of reading this selection? Explain.
15. A Buddhist monk told Ehrlich, "You know how to be strong; now you must learn how to be weak." Do you think Ehrlich has learned this lesson? Explain.

Exposition

The **exposition** provides important background information about the plot, the characters, and the setting in a literary work. The details a writer chooses to include in the exposition set the tone for the rest of the work. In the excerpt from *A Match to the Heart,* the exposition appears in the first two paragraphs. Ehrlich's first sentence, "before electricity carved its blue path toward me . . . ," immediately draws readers into the plot.

1. What do you learn about the plot, the setting, and the narrator in the first two paragraphs of the excerpt?
2. What tone does the exposition set for the rest of the story?

- See **Literary Terms Handbook,** p. R4.

Literary Criticism

Susie Boyt makes the following statement about *A Match to the Heart:* "[It] is a tale of solitude. There is no one to share Ehrlich's ordeal intimately, to shoulder half the anxiety, half the danger. . . . Her solitude is almost never commented on; it is just a truth about her." With a partner, note the ways in which Ehrlich is both physically and mentally isolated. Discuss how she must have felt to be so alone and how you would respond in her situation.

Literature and Writing

Writing About Literature

Analyzing Supporting Characters Several people have an opportunity to help Gretel Ehrlich through her ordeal. Some do; others don't. Create a three-column chart to examine these people and your reaction to them. In the first column, list the people referred to in the narrative. In the second column, describe the role these people play. In the last column, write your reaction to how these people treat Ehrlich. Compare your chart to classmates' charts.

Creative Writing

Lightning Verse Skim the selection for the words and phrases Ehrlich uses to describe lightning and thunderstorms. Then review the list you prepared for the Reading Focus on page 543. Draw upon these ideas to write a poem about a thunderstorm you've witnessed. Illustrate your poem if you wish.

Extending Your Response

Literature Groups

Identifying with a Character After being struck by lightning, Gretel Ehrlich is convinced she is going to die. How does she try to prepare herself for death? What observation does she make about death? Do you think that she is afraid of dying? Would you have been? What images and thoughts might flash through your mind in similar circumstances? In your group, discuss these questions and jot down the group's responses. Then compare your responses with those of other groups.

Learning for Life

Learning About Lightning Work with a partner to prepare a lesson about lightning for younger students. Include a description of lightning, its causes, the risks to humans and property, and safety precautions. Include statistics and graphics appropriate to the age of your audience. The Internet is an excellent source of information.

Interdisciplinary Activity

Biology: The Brain Gretel Ehrlich suffered a serious brain injury when she was struck by lightning. Do research to learn how electrical impulses in the brain work, how electrical shock injures the brain, and what the typical aftereffects of electrical shock are. Summarize your findings in an oral report to the class. Include diagrams and illustrations to help your audience understand your presentation.

Reading Further

You might enjoy this essay by Gretel Ehrlich:

"The Smooth Skull of Winter" from *The Solace of Open Spaces* presents Ehrlich's winter experiences in Wyoming.

Save your work for your portfolio.

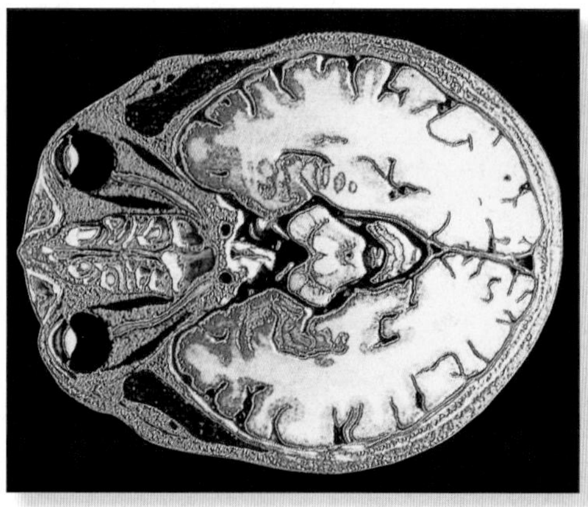

MRI of the human brain.

Skill Minilessons

GRAMMAR AND LANGUAGE • Abbreviations

Abbreviations are shortened forms of words or groups of words. Writers use abbreviations to save space and avoid wordiness. Abbreviations for proper nouns and for those related to dates and time are capitalized and usually followed by periods. *(Dr., U.S., P.M.)* Many abbreviations that stand for the names of organizations and agencies, as well as those used in medical and scientific writing, are written without periods. Ehrlich uses several medical abbreviations in her narrative, including *EMT* for "emergency medical technician" and *ICU* for "intensive care unit."

PRACTICE Write the abbreviation for each of the following terms. If in doubt about the correct form of an abbreviation, check a dictionary.

National Transportation Safety Board
Central Intelligence Agency
Veterans of Foreign Wars
National Aeronautics and Space Administration

For more on abbreviations, see **Language Handbook,** p. R52.

READING AND THINKING • Using Comparisons to Clarify

Writers use comparisons to help readers understand concepts and images that may be unclear to them. Comparisons can also serve to make the images and concepts more emphatic. For example, to explain the numbness in her chest, Ehrlich says it was "as if it had been sprayed with novocaine." Anyone who has been given novocaine at a doctor's or dentist's office can understand the feeling Ehrlich had in her chest.

PRACTICE Review Ehrlich's narrative and identify three comparisons. On your paper, explain what is being compared and how the comparison helps you better understand the concept or image.

For more on comprehension skills, see **Reading Handbook,** pp. R82–R94.

VOCABULARY • Etymology

A muse is a spirit that inspires an artist or writer. So what does the verb *muse* have to do with thinking in an idle manner? That question is just one of many that can be answered by etymology. By checking a dictionary, you'll learn that the noun *muse* comes from the Greek word for the nine goddesses of art and literature. The verb *muse* is not related; it comes from a French word that means "to loiter."

The *aura* that surrounds the narrator in the selection comes from a Greek word meaning "air." An *aural* signal, however, is one you can hear; *aural* comes from a Latin word meaning "ear." Most words that seem to be connected actually are related; however, some are not. Check a dictionary if you are not sure.

PRACTICE Use a dictionary to look up the etymologies of *incoherently, abyss,* and *equilibrium.* (A word's etymology is usually given with its definition.) For each, explain the connection between the origin of the word and its current meaning.

E-mail: Research Using E-mail

Much research is done through the World Wide Web. However, you can also conduct a scholarly investigation via e-mail. With a group, brainstorm ways in which you might use e-mail to research a topic.

Research Through E-mail

Your e-mail inbox can be similar to your mailbox. Companies that discover your e-mail address can fill your electronic mailboxes with ads, leaving you to sift through subject lines looking for legitimate messages. In addition, you can't see who's sending you e-mail. Just because someone says she or he is an expert doesn't make it so. When doing research, you must determine the accuracy of your e-mail information.

Getting Started

1. To begin, conduct a keyword search on the Net for electronic mailing lists that pertain to your research topic. Just add *+mailing list* following your topic keyword on the search engine.
2. Subscribing to a mailing list involves sending an e-mail to the electronic administrator of the list. When you find a list that interests you, click on "Subscribe" and follow the on-screen instructions. Generally, you will be asked to send the message "subscribe [list name] [your name]" to the list administrator.
3. The next time you log in to check your mail, you should receive a welcome message in your e-mail box. Be sure to save this message! It includes instructions for posting to the list and for unsubscribing.
4. After you've subscribed to the list, you can post questions that relate to your research. Other subscribers may answer your questions or point you to WWW sites that can help.
5. When you participate on a mailing list, it is considered polite to respond to e-mail directly rather than posting a response to the list. Be sure to always respond quickly when someone has taken the time to help you with your research.
6. One way to determine the accuracy of the information you've gathered through e-mail is to do what good journalists do: Get confirmation. In other words, never trust what you get from only one source. Locate other experts who can confirm the information.

TECHNOLOGY TIP

The short code following a period in an e-mail address (and in a home page address as well) tells you the domain's type of organization. *Com* (the "dot com" you often hear when someone gives a Net address in a TV ad) indicates a commercial organization. Some other codes are

- **edu** educational institution
- **gov** nonmilitary government organization
- **net** network (usually an internet service provider)
- **org** nonprofit organization

WHO'S WHO?

Just because someone says in an e-mail that he or she is an expert doesn't make it so. When doing research, you must discover how accurate the information you receive is. A clue to determining whether e-mail correspondents are who they claim to be is found in the e-mail address itself. All e-mail addresses include a domain name, a unique name that identifies a single Internet site. If you received an e-mail message from a Dr. Karen Veracruz, who says she is a professor of English, you should find a college name or abbreviation in her e-mail address. Her e-mail address would look something like: kveracruz@purdue.edu. Now you know she sends and receives e-mail through Purdue University. To find out whether she's really an English professor (she could be a student), find the Web site for Purdue University. Then look for her name in the faculty directory. Alternatively, find the subdirectory for the English department and send the department head an e-mail inquiring as to whether Karen Veracruz is on the faculty. Similarly, if someone claims to be an executive with IBM and he has an e-mail account from ibm.com, then there's a good chance he is who he claims to be.

E-mail and List Server Citations

When you turn your research into a written presentation, be sure to always cite the sources of your information. To find guidelines for documenting electronic sources, type "MLA guidelines + electronic" into your search engine. (See also the Writing Handbook, pp. R72–R73.) Here's a model for an e-mail or mailing list citation:

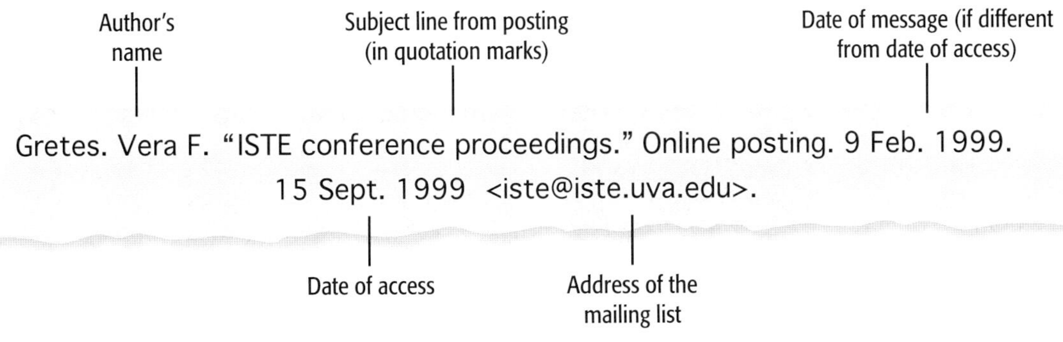

ACTIVITIES

1. Search for a "list of lists" on the Internet. These sites include directories of mailing lists divided by subject. Subscribe to one or two that can help you with your schoolwork. Save any messages you exchange on a mailing list in your electronic portfolio.
2. Look for lists that are applicable to topics you are studying in other classes. Ask your teachers if active participation on these lists can count toward fulfilling a technology requirement.
3. On your school's Web site, create a page of links to mailing lists that would be of interest to the school community.

Before You Read

The Angry Winter

Reading Focus

Are you affected today by what happened in the past? How might past events—either from the recent past or long ago—influence your behavior in the present?

Chart It! In a chart like the one shown, list events from the past, either from history or from your own life and note their influence in the present.

Past Events	Influence in the Present

Setting a Purpose Read to discover how two characters are influenced by the past.

Building Background

The Time and Place

The events in this essay take place on a snowy winter night at an unspecified time and place.

Did You Know?

Dogs belong to the animal family known as *Canidae,* along with wolves, coyotes, jackals, and foxes. Scientists think that canines have been a part of people's lives for thousands of years. Anthropologists have discovered the fossilized bones of wolves with human bones at sites dating back 400,000 years. Scientists speculate that some wolves may have ventured into campsites looking for food scraps. When humans realized that the wolves could be useful in warning of approaching danger, they accepted the wolves into their communities. Domesticated dogs, the descendants of those wolves, were first kept as pets about 14,000 years ago.

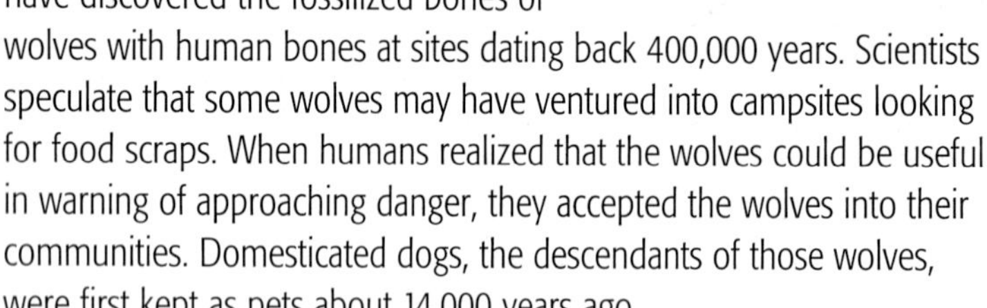

Vocabulary Preview

divert (di vurt′) *v.* to draw attention away; distract; p. 558

indifferently (in dif′ ər ənt lē) *adv.* in a way that shows a lack of feeling, concern, or care; p. 558

augment (ôg ment′) *v.* to make greater; increase; p. 559

Meet Loren Eiseley

Loren Eiseley once compared the brain of a writer to an attic in which pictures of the past are collected. The writer draws upon these pictures, expanding and reducing them, to create a pattern, he wrote. An avid reader and naturalist, Eiseley filled his "attic" with pictures from books, from the Nebraska prairie land of his youth, from his observations of nature, and from his work with fossils. In his lifetime he pursued many careers: anthropologist, university professor, philosopher, essayist, and poet.

Loren Eiseley was born in Nebraska in 1907 and died in 1977. "The Angry Winter" appears in The Unexpected Universe, *a collection of Eiseley's essays published in 1969.*

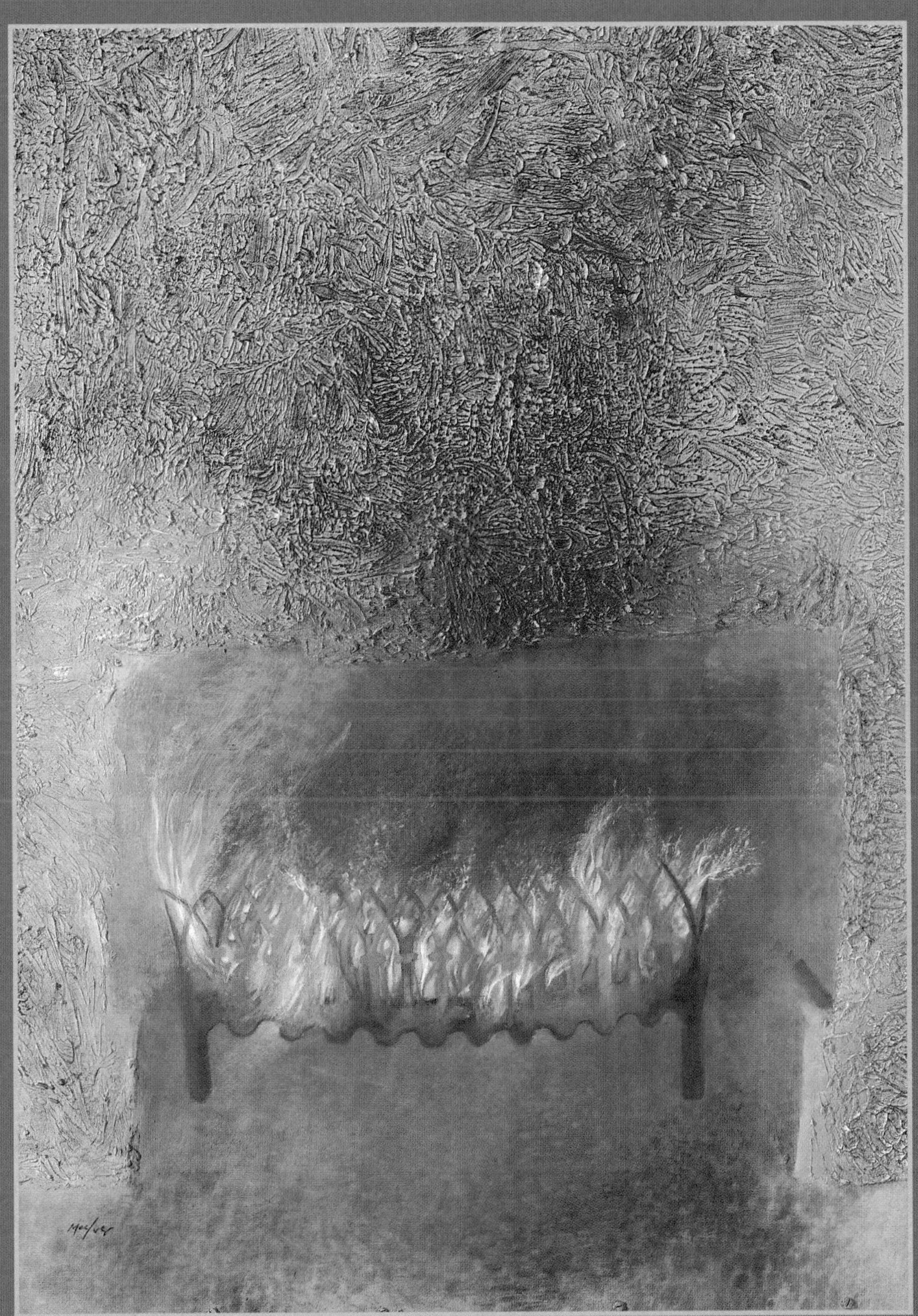

Hearth, 1957. Loren McIver. Oil on plaster on Masonite, 49⅝ x 34⅝ in. Metropolitan Museum of Art, New York. Museum purchase, Marie-Gaetana Matisse Gift, 1993. 1993.280.

The Angry Winter

Loren Eiseley

A time comes when creatures whose destinies have crossed somewhere in the remote past are forced to appraise each other as though they were total strangers. I had been huddled beside the fire one winter night, with the wind prowling outside and shaking the windows. The big shepherd dog on the hearth before me occasionally glanced up affectionately, sighed, and slept. I was working, actually, amidst the debris of a far greater winter. On my desk lay the lance points of ice age hunters and the heavy leg bone of a fossil bison. No remnants of flesh attached to these relics. The deed lay more than ten thousand years remote. It was represented here by naked flint and by bone so mineralized it rang when struck. As I worked on in my little circle of light, I absently laid the bone beside me on the floor. The hour had crept toward midnight. A grating noise, a heavy rasping of big teeth diverted me. I looked down.

The dog had risen. That rock-hard fragment of a vanished beast was in his jaws and he was mouthing it with a fierce intensity I had never seen exhibited by him before.

"Wolf," I exclaimed, and stretched out my hand. The dog backed up but did not yield. A low and steady rumbling began to rise in his chest, something out of a long-gone midnight. There was nothing in that bone to taste, but ancient shapes were moving in his mind and determining his utterance. Only fools gave up bones. He was warning me.

"Wolf," I chided again.

As I advanced, his teeth showed and his mouth wrinkled to strike. The rumbling rose to a direct snarl. His flat head swayed low and wickedly as a reptile's above the floor. I was the most loved object in his universe, but the past was fully alive in him now. Its shadows were whispering in his mind. I knew he was not bluffing. If I made another step he would strike.

Yet his eyes were strained and desperate. "Do not," something pleaded in the back of them, some affectionate thing that had followed at my heel all the days of his mortal life, "do not force me. I am what I am and cannot be otherwise because of the shadows. Do not reach out. You are a man, and my very god. I love you, but do not put out your hand. It is midnight. We are in another time, in the snow."

"The *other* time," the steady rumbling continued while I paused, "the other time in the snow, the big, the final, the terrible snow, when the shape of this thing I hold spelled life. I will not give it up. I cannot. The shadows will not permit me. Do not put out your hand."

I stood silent, looking into his eyes, and heard his whisper through. Slowly I drew back in understanding. The snarl diminished, ceased. As I retreated, the bone slumped to the floor. He placed a paw upon it, warningly.

And were there no shadows in my own mind, I wondered. Had I not for a moment, in the grip of that savage utterance, been about to respond, to hurl myself upon him over an invisible haunch ten thousand years removed? Even to me the shadows had whispered—to me, the scholar in his study.

"Wolf," I said, but this time, holding a familiar leash, I spoke from the door indifferently. "A walk in the snow." Instantly from his eyes that other visitant[1] receded. The bone was left lying. He came eagerly to my side, accepting the leash and taking it in his mouth as always.

1. A *visitant* is a visitor, especially one that seems to be supernatural.

Vocabulary

divert (di vurt′) *v.* to draw attention away; distract

indifferently (in dif′ ər ənt lē) *adv.* in a way that shows a lack of feeling, concern, or care

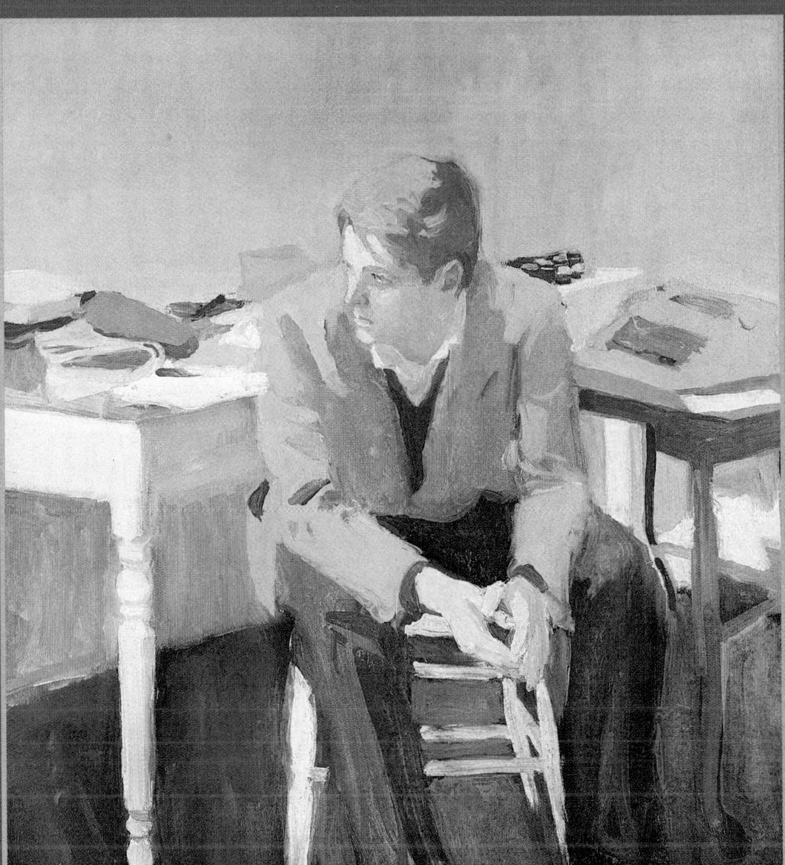

Portrait of Donald Schrader, 1962. Fairfield Porter. Oil on canvas, 30 x 28 in. Metropolitan Museum of Art. Bequest of Arthur M. Bullowa, 1993. 1993.406.12.

Viewing the painting: What mood do this man's expression and posture convey? How might that mood apply to the narrator?

A blizzard was raging when we went out, but he paid no heed. On his thick fur the driving snow was soon clinging heavily. He frolicked a little—though usually he was a grave dog—making up to me for something still receding in his mind. I felt the snowflakes fall upon my face, and stood thinking of another time, and another time still, until I was moving from midnight to midnight under ever more remote and vaster snows. Wolf came to my side with a little whimper. It was he who was civilized now. "Come back to the fire," he nudged gently, "or you will be lost." Automatically I took the leash he offered. He led me safely home and into the house.

"We have been very far away," I told him solemnly. "I think there is something in us that we had both better try to forget." Sprawled on the rug, Wolf made no response except to thump his tail feebly out of courtesy. Already he was mostly asleep and dreaming. By the movement of his feet I could see he was running far upon some errand in which I played no part.

Softly I picked up his bone—our bone, rather—and replaced it high on a shelf in my cabinet. As I snapped off the light the white glow from the window seemed to augment itself and shine with a deep, glacial blue. As far as I could see, nothing moved in the long aisles of my neighbor's woods. There was no visible track, and certainly no sound from the living. The snow continued to fall steadily, but the wind, and the shadows it had brought, had vanished.

Vocabulary

augment (ôg ment′) *v.* to make greater; increase

Responding to Literature

Personal Response

How did you react to the confrontation between Wolf and the narrator?

Analyzing Literature

Recall

1. Describe where the narrator and Wolf are and what they are doing as the essay begins.
2. What sound distracts the narrator? What is making this sound?
3. Recount the confrontation between Wolf and the narrator.
4. How did the narrator momentarily want to respond to Wolf during the confrontation?
5. Summarize what happens between the narrator and Wolf on their walk.

Interpret

6. In the opening paragraph, Eiseley describes "the wind prowling outside and shaking the windows." What is the **metaphor** in this description? Why is it an apt one? (See Literary Terms Handbook, page R7.)
7. When Wolf growls, Eiseley says, "Ancient shapes were moving in his mind and determining his utterance." What does Eiseley mean?
8. Eiseley uses the word *shadows* several times in explaining Wolf's behavior. What might the shadows represent?
9. In reflecting on the confrontation, what similarity does the narrator see between himself and Wolf?
10. The narrator says to Wolf, "We have been very far away." Where do you think Eiseley is suggesting they've been? What details help you draw this conclusion?

Evaluate and Connect

11. Describe the **mood,** or atmosphere, of this essay. What details help establish this mood? Explain.
12. Do you agree with Eiseley's explanation for Wolf's behavior? Why or why not? If not, what explanation would you give?
13. From this essay, what are your impressions of Loren Eiseley?
14. Look at the chart you completed for the Reading Focus on page 556. After reading this essay, have your thoughts about links to the past changed? Identify behaviors or reactions you may have inherited from people in your distant past.
15. This essay also appeared in *Reader's Digest* under the title, "The Night the Shadows Whispered." Suggest another title for the essay.

Literary ELEMENTS

Creative Nonfiction

"The Angry Winter" belongs to a literary genre known as creative nonfiction. In **creative nonfiction**, writers apply their own point of view to factual details about real people, settings, or events. The facts, however, aren't as important as the writer's larger ideas about real issues. Creative nonfiction writers typically start with an actual event or character and then creatively expand or dress up the details to make their overall message more engaging and lively. For example, Loren Eiseley never had a German shepherd named Wolf. He probably based Wolf's character on two actual dogs that he had known. Wolf was a literary vehicle that Eiseley used to help convey his message.

1. What, do you think, is the main idea of Eiseley's essay? Summarize it in a few sentences.
2. What references and details does Eiseley use to convey this idea? Cite specific examples from the selection.

- See **Literary Terms Handbook,** p. R3.

Literature and Writing

Writing About Literature

Analyze Characterization Eiseley portrays two sides of Wolf's personality. What labels would you apply to each? In a two-column chart, list the details that Eiseley provides to reveal these two sides of Wolf's personality. Then use the details to write a one-paragraph analysis of Eiseley's portrayal of Wolf.

Creative Writing

If Dogs Could Talk Imagine that Wolf could verbalize his thoughts and feelings. How might his glances and growls be interpreted? What might he be thinking when the narrator tries to get the bone? Write a dialogue that might take place between Wolf and the narrator during the confrontation. Share your dialogue with the class.

Extending Your Response

Literature Groups

The Marriage of Literature and Science Loren Eiseley believed that the literary and the scientific acts of creation had much in common because both were products of the human imagination. Do you think that science and the arts differ greatly, or do you agree with Eiseley that they have many similarities? In this essay, what evidence do you see of both scientific imagination and literary creativity? Share your ideas in your group.

Interdisciplinary Activity

Anthropology: Ice-Age Hunters and Beasts Investigate what anthropologists have pieced together about the lives of Ice Age people. Where and how did they live? What did they wear? What did they eat? What kinds of plants and animals shared their world? Use your findings to create a diorama of life in the Ice Age.

Internet Connection

Nature's Voices Use the Internet to find out more about Loren Eiseley and other naturalist writers, such as Rachel Carson, Gretel Ehrlich, Annie Dillard, Aldo Leopold, and John Muir. Create a bibliography of recommended books or essays about the natural world.

Save your work for your portfolio.

VOCABULARY • The Latin Root *vert*

The word *divert* comes from the Latin root *vert,* which means "to turn," and the Latin prefix *dis-,* meaning "away." If you *divert* someone, you turn his or her attention away from something. You could *divert* a stream by digging a channel to carry the water in a different direction.

PRACTICE Use your knowledge of the root *vert* to help you answer the following questions.

1. Does a *versatile* person turn easily from one task to another, or is he or she limited to one skill?
2. Is *vertigo* a feeling of itchiness or dizziness?
3. If a four-year-old's behavior *reverts,* does the child begin acting like a younger child or continue to act normally?
4. Is a *convert* a person who sticks to one belief or one who changes to another belief?
5. If you *avert* your eyes, do you look away or stare?

Before You Read

The Tucson Zoo

Reading Focus

How do you respond to new people or situations? Do you react instinctively? Or do you stand back, analyze the situation, and then make a decision about what to do?

Freewrite In your journal, describe your typical response to new people or situations.

Setting a Purpose Read to find out how the author responds to a new experience and what he discovers about himself.

Building Background

The Time and Place

The author reflects upon an experience he had at the Tucson Zoo in Arizona.

Did You Know?

The cortex of the brain has two cerebral hemispheres, or sides. The left side is analytical; it allows you to recognize the parts, or details, of a whole; it cannot, however, combine the parts to let you see the whole. The right hemisphere is creative. It allows you to see the whole of something from its parts. The right side also allows you to be in a good mood while the left side controls your darker moods. The *corpus callosum*, which Lewis Thomas refers to in this essay, is an arch of nervous tissue that bridges the two hemispheres and allows them to communicate with each other.

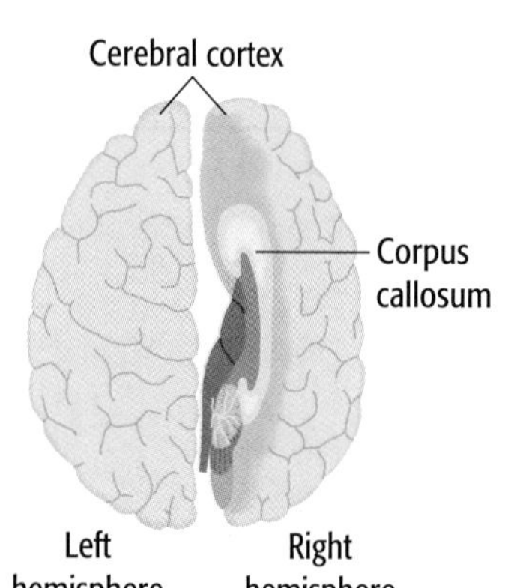

Vocabulary Preview

elation (i lā′ shən) *n.* a feeling of great joy; ecstasy; p. 564
intact (in takt′) *adj.* entire; untouched, uninjured, and having all parts; p. 564
exultation (eg′ zul tā′ shən) *n.* joy; jubilation; p. 564
debasement (di bās′ mənt) *n.* the state of being lowered in quality, value, or character; degradation; p. 565
attribute (at′ rə būt) *n.* a quality or characteristic of a person or thing; p. 565

Meet Lewis Thomas

"There is a tendency for living things to join up, establish linkages, . . . get along whenever possible. This is the way of the world."

Award-winning author Lewis Thomas was a renowned physician and research biologist who taught at some of the top medical schools in the United States. With the publication of his first book, *The Lives of a Cell*, Thomas established a reputation as a master writer of the short essay. In his inquisitive musings on nature, science, technology, and other subjects, he celebrated the mystery and marvel of life.

Lewis Thomas was born in 1913 in Flushing, New York. He died in 1993. This essay appeared in The Medusa and the Snail *in 1979.*

The Tucson Zoo

Lewis Thomas

SCIENCE GETS MOST of its information by the process of reductionism,[1] exploring the details, then the details of the details, until all the smallest bits of the structure, or the smallest parts of the mechanism, are laid out for counting and scrutiny. Only when this is done can the investigation be extended to encompass the whole organism or the entire system. So we say.

Sometimes it seems that we take a loss, working this way. Much of today's public anxiety about science is the apprehension that we may forever be overlooking the whole by an endless, obsessive preoccupation with the parts. I had a brief, personal experience of this misgiving one afternoon in Tucson, where I had time on my hands and visited the zoo, just outside the city. The designers there have cut a deep pathway between two small artificial ponds, walled by clear glass, so when you stand in the center of the path you can

1. *Reductionism* is a method of explaining complex processes or structures by reducing them to more basic principles or units.

look into the depths of each pool, and at the same time you can regard the surface. In one pool, on the right side of the path, is a family of otters; on the other side, a family of beavers. Within just a few feet from your face, on either side, beavers and otters are at play, underwater and on the surface, swimming toward your face and then away, more filled with life than any creatures I have ever seen before, in all my days. Except for the glass, you could reach across and touch them.

I was transfixed. As I now recall it, there was only one sensation in my head: pure elation mixed with amazement at such perfection. Swept off my feet, I floated from one side to the other, swiveling my brain, staring astounded at the beavers, then at the otters. I could hear shouts across my corpus callosum, from one hemisphere to the other. I remember thinking, with what was left in charge of my consciousness, that I wanted no part of the science of beavers and otters; I wanted never to know how they performed their marvels; I wished for no news about the physiology[2] of their breathing, the coordination of their muscles, their vision, their endocrine systems,[3] their digestive tracts. I hoped never to have to think of them as collections of cells. All I asked for was the full hairy complexity, then in front of my eyes, of whole, intact beavers and otters in motion.

It lasted, I regret to say, for only a few minutes, and then I was back in the late twentieth century, reductionist as ever, wondering about the details by force of habit, but not, this time, the details of otters and beavers. Instead, me. Something worth remembering had happened in my mind, I was certain of that; I would have put it somewhere in the brain stem; maybe this was my limbic system[4] at work. I became a behavioral scientist, an experimental psychologist, an ethologist, and in the instant I lost all the wonder and the sense of being overwhelmed. I was flattened.

But I came away from the zoo with something, a piece of news about myself: I am coded, somehow, for otters and beavers. I exhibit instinctive behavior in their presence, when they are displayed close at hand behind glass, simultaneously below water and at the surface. I have receptors for this display. Beavers and otters possess a "releaser" for me, in the terminology of ethology,[5] and the releasing was my experience. What was released? Behavior. What behavior? Standing, swiveling flabbergasted, feeling exultation and a rush of friendship. I could not, as the result of the transaction, tell you anything more about beavers and otters than you already know. I learned nothing new about them. Only about me, and I suspect also about you, maybe about human beings at large: we are endowed with genes which code out our reaction to beavers and otters, maybe our reaction to each other as well. We are stamped with stereotyped, unalterable patterns of response, ready to be released. And the behavior

2. *Physiology* is the branch of biology that studies the functions of living organisms and their parts.
3. The *endocrine system* consists of glands that secrete hormones into the bloodstream, affecting such bodily processes as growth and sexual development.
4. The *limbic system* is a region of the brain involved in the control of emotions and some types of behavior.
5. *Receptor* refers to a sensory nerve cell that responds to a stimulus in the environment and sends a message to the brain. *Ethology* (eth ol′ ə jē) is the study of animal behavior, including instinctive, or inherited, behavior.

Vocabulary

elation (i lā′ shən) *n.* a feeling of great joy; ecstasy
intact (in takt′) *adj.* entire; untouched, uninjured, and having all parts
exultation (eg′ zul tā′ shən) *n.* joy; jubilation

released in us, by such confrontations, is, essentially, a surprised affection. It is compulsory behavior and we can avoid it only by straining with the full power of our conscious minds, making up conscious excuses all the way. Left to ourselves, mechanistic and autonomic,[6] we hanker for friends.

Everyone says, stay away from ants. They have no lessons for us; they are crazy little instruments, inhuman, incapable of controlling themselves, lacking manners, lacking souls. When they are massed together, all touching, exchanging bits of information held in their jaws like memoranda, they become a single animal. Look out for that. It is a debasement, a loss of individuality, a violation of human nature, an unnatural act.

Sometimes people argue this point of view seriously and with deep thought. Be individuals, solitary and selfish, is the message. Altruism,[7] a jargon word for what used to be called love, is worse than weakness, it is sin, a violation of nature. Be separate. Do not be a social animal. But this is a hard argument to make convincingly when you have to depend on language to make it. You have to print up leaflets or publish books and get them bought and sent around, you have to turn up on television and catch the attention of millions of other human beings all at once, and then you have to say to all of them, all at once, all collected and paying attention: be solitary; do not depend on each other. You can't do this and keep a straight face.

Maybe altruism is our most primitive attribute, out of reach, beyond our control. Or perhaps it is immediately at hand, waiting to be released, disguised now, in our kind of civilization, as affection or friendship or attachment. I don't see why it should be unreasonable for all human beings to have strands of DNA coiled up in chromosomes, coding out instincts for usefulness and helpfulness. Usefulness may turn out to be the hardest test of fitness for survival, more important than aggression, more effective, in the long run, than grabbiness. If this is the sort of information biological science holds for the future, applying to us as well as to ants, then I am all for science.

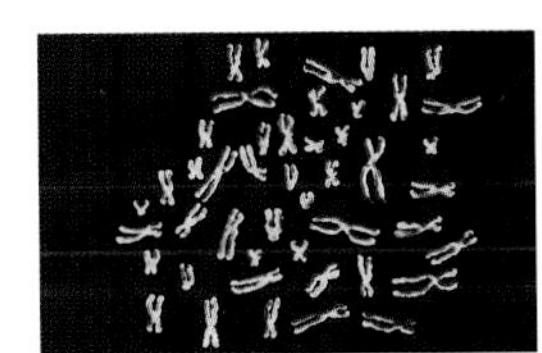

Did You Know?
Chromosomes are strands of DNA and proteins in the nucleus of cells. DNA carries the genes that pass on hereditary information from parent to child.

One thing I'd like to know most of all: when those ants have made the Hill, and are all there, touching and exchanging, and the whole mass begins to behave like a single huge creature, and *thinks*, what on earth is that thought? And while you're at it, I'd like to know a second thing: when it happens, does any single ant know about it? Does his hair stand on end?

6. In psychology, *compulsory* means "arising from an irresistible, illogical urge." Here, *mechanistic* means physically or biologically determined, and *autonomic* means involuntary and spontaneous.
7. In ethology, *altruism* is an animal's self-sacrificing behavior that benefits another animal or group of animals. Similarly, in humans, the term means "unselfish concern for others."

Vocabulary

debasement (di bās′ mənt) *n.* the state of being lowered in quality, value, or character; degradation

attribute (at′ rə būt) *n.* a quality or characteristic of a person or thing

Responding to Literature

Personal Response

What questions would you like to ask the author of this essay?

Analyzing Literature

Recall and Interpret

1. According to the process of reductionism, when can an entire organism be investigated? What does Thomas say is a drawback of reductionism?
2. **Theme Connections** What reaction does Thomas have to his encounter with the beavers and otters? What scientific explanation does he give for his reaction? What conclusions about himself and other people does he draw from his encounter?
3. According to Thomas, why does everyone say to "stay away from ants"? What is the message some people learn from ants? Does Thomas agree with this point of view?
4. What ideas does Thomas present about altruism? What do you think Thomas means in his final reference to ants?

Evaluate and Connect

5. In your opinion, what was Thomas's purpose in writing this essay? Support your answer with details from the selection.
6. Do you agree with the conclusions that Thomas draws about instinctive behavior in people? Why or why not?
7. Look at the freewriting you did for the Reading Focus on page 562. How does your typical response to new encounters compare with Thomas's response to the beavers and otters?
8. In your opinion, is Thomas a reductionist? Explain and support your answer.

Literary ELEMENTS

Voice

Voice is a writer's particular use of language to convey the writer's or the narrator's personality to the reader. Various elements of style determine a writer's voice. These elements include sentence structure, word choice, and tone. For example, when Thomas uses such words as "I am," "only about me," and "you," he shows a friendly voice.

1. Find other examples of Thomas's sentence structure, word choice, and tone that contribute to his voice.
2. What does Thomas's writing voice tell you about his personality, attitudes, and emotions? In what ways does his voice affect your appreciation of the subject of his essay?

- See **Literary Terms Handbook,** p. R13.

Extending Your Response

Literature Groups

Analyzing Meaning Thomas once explained a state of mind in which the mind empties itself of all acquired knowledge and shuts itself off from interior and exterior messages. This state, called "no-knowledge," provides a different or enlightened look at the world. With your group, discuss whether or not you think Thomas realizes this state of mind in "The Tucson Zoo." Compare your findings with other groups' results.

Interdisciplinary Activity

Performing: Lowly Creatures Speak Out At the end of the essay, Thomas expresses a desire to know what the ants who have made the Hill think and know. In a small group, brainstorm and then write a scene in which ants discuss their thoughts and feelings. Try to incorporate some of the ideas about ants that Thomas includes in the essay. Perform the scene for the class.

Save your work for your portfolio.

COMPARING *selections*

The Angry Winter and The Tucson Zoo

COMPARE **EXPERIENCES**

In both "The Angry Winter" and "The Tucson Zoo," ordinary events become extraordinary when the author-narrator of each essay experiences startling and unexpected insights.

- How are the experiences similar? How do they differ?
- Which author's experiences and comments, do you think, provide a more positive view of the human condition? Use evidence from the essays to support your opinion.

COMPARE **SCIENTIFIC FIELDS**

Loren Eiseley was an anthropologist. Lewis Thomas was a biologist. Their different scientific fields led them to explore different issues and concepts. Create a chart like that shown to compare anthropology and biology. In the third column, show how the characteristics and goals of each author's particular field are illustrated in the essay.

Field	Definition	Characteristics/Goals
Anthropology		
Biology		

COMPARE **VIEWPOINTS**

These two essays present opposing viewpoints on instincts and survival. Eiseley writes, ". . . ancient shapes were moving in his mind and determining his utterance. Only fools gave up bones." But Thomas says, "Maybe altruism is our most primitive attribute. . . . Usefulness may turn out to be the hardest test of fitness for survival, more important than aggression, more effective, in the long run, than grabbiness."

- With a partner, list examples and evidence to support each viewpoint.
- Role-play a debate between Eiseley and Thomas, arguing each viewpoint and providing evidence to support your argument.

Writing Workshop

Descriptive Writing:
Observational Report

Pick up any newspaper or magazine and you'll probably find a nonfiction article that is an observational report. An observational report is just what it sounds like–a report that describes a person, a place, a thing, an event, or a process that the writer has observed. Have you closely observed birds in the wild or fish swimming in a creek? Could you describe a pitcher's throwing technique? Do you pay special attention to changes in fashion or music? **In this workshop, you will write an observational report that describes something you have observed.**

- As you write your observational report, refer to the **Writing Handbook,** pp. R58–R71.

EVALUATION RUBRIC

By the time you complete this Writing Workshop, you will have

- provided sufficient background information for readers to understand your particular subject
- organized your observations effectively, using transitions
- used precise language and sensory details to elaborate
- stated the conclusions you've drawn from your observations
- presented an observational report that is free of errors in grammar, usage, and mechanics

The Writing Process

PREWRITING

PREWRITING TIP

If your memories are vivid, you can base your report on something that you have observed in the past. If not, choose a subject that you can observe now.

Explore ideas

With a partner or a small group, brainstorm for a list of subjects that you could observe and write about. Think about your everyday life, interests, activities, and travels. Almost anything and everything around you could be a possible topic. Like Slavenka Drakulić in "Pizza in Warsaw, Torte in Prague," you might focus on an aspect of everyday life in a city. Or, like Jane Ellen Stevens in "Exploring Antarctic Ice," you might make scientific observations, perhaps of the plant life in a vacant lot or of the wildlife in your backyard.

Consider your purpose and audience

Your main purpose in writing an observational report is to inform your readers about a subject you have observed and reflected upon. Decide whom you want to read your report. Then think about what your readers already know about your subject and be prepared to provide any background information they need to understand it.

Observe and take notes

Set aside time to make your observations. As you watch, use all your senses to observe your subject. Use an idea web like the one shown and jot down specific sensory details that strike you. Be as specific and thorough as possible when you record what you observe.

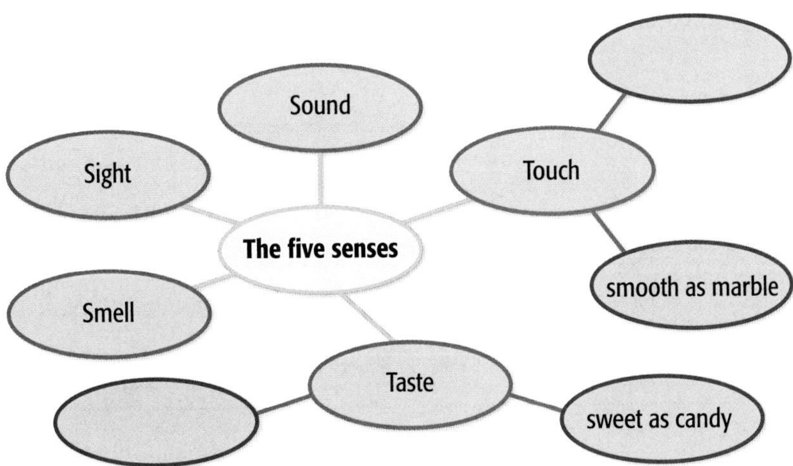

Make a plan

Review your notes and circle those that are necessary to give a complete picture of what you have observed. Think about the conclusions you can draw from these observations. To what main point do your observations lead? For example, in "Exploring Antarctic Ice," the author comes to the conclusion that the winter sea ice encircling Antarctica is an untamed, beautiful world teeming with life. Once you know your main point, use the basic essay structure of **introduction, body,** and **conclusion** to plan your report.

		STUDENT MODEL
Introduction	Tell what your subject is and provide any background information your readers need to understand your subject.	My father was born in Czechoslovakia, so each summer we visit Prague. The Charles Bridge in Prague links one side of the city to the other. Last summer, I sat on the bridge all afternoon and watched the bustle of commerce there.
Body	Present your observations.	Musicians and artists, tourists and locals, many different languages—a carnival atmosphere
Conclusion	State the conclusions you draw from your observations.	No longer the quiet, romantic place that my father recalls from his childhood, the Charles Bridge is now a busy tourist spot.

Complete Student Model on p. R115.

DRAFTING

Drafting Tip

Think about your subject as if you were painting a picture of it for your readers.

Refer to your notes and your plan as you draft your report. If you have trouble getting started, just copy one of your notes and begin with your observations. You can go back and write your introduction later.

STUDENT MODEL

Everything around me seemed hot and smelled sticky and sweet. I heard all sorts of languages but couldn't make out most of them, except for recognizing some English, Czech, and German. I could see the castle and Kampa Island.

Complete Student Model on p. R115.

REVISING

Revising Tip

Revise your draft sentence by sentence, making sure each sentence follows logically from the one before.

Evaluate your work

Wait a few hours or days before you begin revising so you can approach your report with a clear mind. Use the **Rubric for Revising** as a guide in making improvements in your draft.

Have a writing conference

Read your observational report aloud to a friend or classmate. Ask your listener to go through the **Rubric for Revising** and suggest changes to improve your report. Make any further changes you think are necessary.

STUDENT MODEL

My father was born in Prague, Czechoslavakia. He had escaped the Communist regime and came to the United States. Until the Communist government fell he couldn't return to his homeland. But we visit our relatives every year. Last summer I sat on the Charles Bridge and watched all the busy activity. I love it there and wish I could take my friends to see it, even though it's so touristy in some ways now. New hotels and restaurants are opening each year.

Complete Student Model on p. R115.

Rubric for Revising

Your revised observational report should have

- an introduction that provides needed background information
- precise language and sensory details
- effective transitions that clearly organize your ideas and observations
- a consistent tone suited to your specific audience and purpose
- a conclusion that reinforces the main idea drawn from your observations

Your observational report should be free of

- irrelevant details that may confuse the focus of your report
- errors in grammar, usage, and mechanics

EDITING/PROOFREADING

Edit and proofread your observational report to find and correct errors in grammar, usage, mechanics, and spelling. Use the **Proofreading Checklist** on the inside back cover as a guide.

Grammar Hint

To avoid confusion, place modifying phrases and clauses as close as possible to the word they modify. In the sentence below, the modifying phrase *speaking Czech* should be placed near *lady,* the word it modifies.

An old lady sat next to me speaking Czech on the park bench.

- For more about modifiers, see **Language Handbook,** pp. R24–R25.

PROOFREADING TIP

Look for errors by reading through your report word by word, using a pencil to point to each word and punctuation mark.

STUDENT MODEL

```
When he was growing up, my father told me that
the Charles bridge was known as a rommantic
place. From my observations, I can say that the
Charles bridge was no longer a place for lovers,
but only a place for tourists—buying and selling.
```

Complete Student Model on p. R115.

Complete Student Model

For a complete version of the model developed in this workshop, refer to **Writing Workshop Models**, p. R115.

PUBLISHING/PRESENTING

Share your observational report with your chosen audience. Also, consider compiling your report with those of your classmates and making a magazine to share with the rest of the school.

PRESENTING TIP

If you prepared your report on a computer, you might style it to look like a feature article in a magazine and add photographs or illustrations.

Reflecting

How did observing your subject and writing this report enhance your appreciation or understanding of the subject? Note your response in your journal. Then evaluate the strengths and weaknesses of your writing.

Save your work for your portfolio.

Unit Assessment

Personal Response

1. Which of the readings in this unit did you find the most exciting?
2. Which readings did you find the most moving or inspiring?
3. As a result of the work you have done in this unit, what new ideas do you have about the following?
   - how to classify the type of material you are reading
   - how to understand the author's purpose
   - how to work with other students in pairs or in groups

Analyzing Literature

Classifying Nonfiction Write a few paragraphs defining the terms *narrative nonfiction* and *informative nonfiction.* Cite examples from the selections in this unit to support your definitions. (For help in identifying these types of nonfiction, see the Genre Focus on Nonfiction on pages 422–423.) Focus on the differences between these types of nonfiction by contrasting the content, author's purpose, and writing style of the selections you cite.

Evaluate and Set Goals

Evaluate

1. What was your strongest contribution to group activities as you worked through this unit?
2. What was your most challenging task in this unit?
   - How did you approach this task?
   - What was the result?
3. How would you assess your work in this unit, using the following scale? Give at least two reasons for your assessment.
   4 = outstanding **3** = good **2** = fair **1** = weak

Set Goals

1. Choose a goal to work toward in the next unit. It could involve reading, writing, speaking, researching, or working in a group.
2. Discuss your goal with your teacher.
3. Jot down three or four steps that you will take to achieve your goal.
4. Decide at which points in the next unit you will stop and assess your progress toward your goal.

Build Your Portfolio

Select Choose two pieces of writing that you did in this unit and include them in your portfolio. Use these questions to help you make your selection.

- Which piece are you most satisfied with?
- Which one did you find most challenging to write?
- Which piece are you most likely to share?
- Which one led you to new discoveries as you wrote?

Reflect Write some notes to accompany the pieces you selected. Use these questions to guide you.

- What do you like best about each piece?
- What did you learn from the process of writing each one?
- What might you do or try if you were writing one or both of these pieces now?

Reading on Your Own

You might also be interested in the following books.

Night
by Elie Wiesel During World War II, the Nazis sent sixteen-year-old Elie Wiesel and his family to concentration camps. This memoir presents an account of young Wiesel's experiences of the horrors of the death camp. Wiesel's memories of that nightmare world force him to confront harsh realities about human nature.

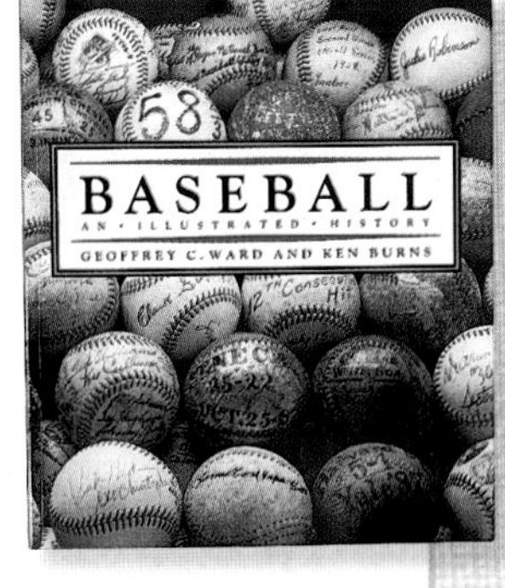

Baseball: An Illustrated History
by Geoffrey C. Ward and Ken Burns
The authors use photographs and narrative to document baseball's evolution since the mid-nineteenth century and bring to life baseball's most memorable players, such as Ty Cobb, Satchel Paige, Babe Ruth, Jackie Robinson, and Joe DiMaggio. This book also shows baseball's connection to American history and its influence on our national life.

The Edge of the Sea
by Rachel Carson How do small sea creatures hold on to rocks while strong waves wash over them? How does the arctic jellyfish survive "being solidly frozen for hours"? Carson reveals the dramatic and varied communities of plant and animal life along the rocky shores, sandy beaches, and coral reefs of the Atlantic Ocean. Delicate drawings depict the rich variety of life forms.

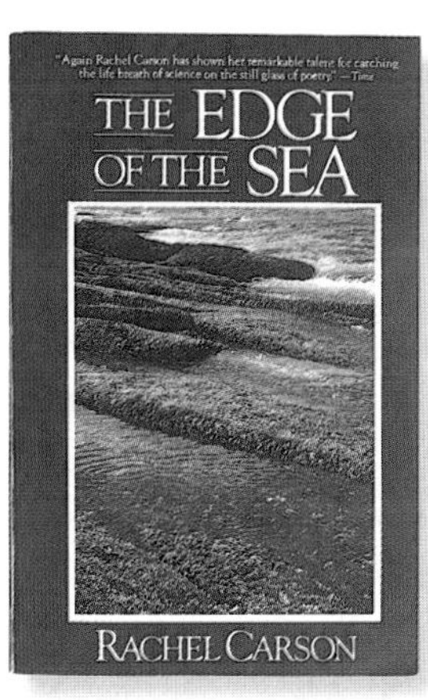

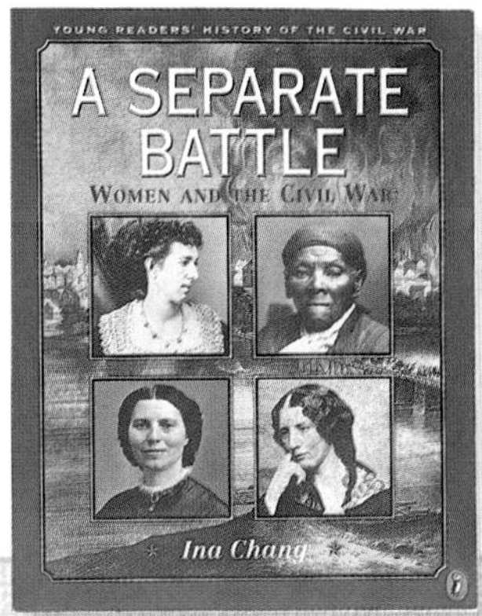

A Separate Battle: Women and the Civil War
by Ina Chang In both the North and South, women during the Civil War served vital roles. Some were doctors, nurses, and spies; others donned trousers and fought on the battlefront. This enlightening book reveals the wartime heroics of famous women like Louisa May Alcott and Harriet Beecher Stowe and of women such as Loreta Velazquez and Sarah Edmonds.

Reading and Analyzing Test Questions

Read the following passage. Then read each question on page 575. Decide which is the best answer to each question. Mark the letter for that answer on your paper.

Why Is Texas the Lone Star State?

The United States flag received its twenty-eighth star in 1845, when Texas became a state. If Texas is one of so many states, why do we call it the Lone Star State?

Colonizing Texas

In the early 1800s, Texas was a Spanish colony. Only a handful of people from the United States lived in Texas at the time. Most residents were Tejanos, or Mexicans who claimed Texas as their home. The Spaniards were afraid of losing control of the area, so they offered large tracts of land to *empresarios* (people who promised to recruit settlers to the region), in the hope that the *empresario system* would help ensure loyalty.

After Mexico gained its independence from Spain in 1821, the Mexican government granted these tracts of land only under the conditions that the settlers become citizens of Mexico, obey Mexican law, and accept the Roman Catholic faith. Despite these efforts to limit land ownership, thousands came into Texas without Mexico's permission. These settlers never formally agreed to the Mexicans' conditions. By 1830 there were far more United States settlers than Tejanos living in Texas, and the Mexican government took note. They banned any further U.S. immigration and ordered the construction of five new army posts in Texas.

The Fight for Independence

In 1833 Stephen Austin traveled to Mexico City with a petition demanding that Mexico repeal the ban against immigration and create a separate Texas state. General Antonio López de Santa Anna, the head of the Mexican government, agreed to the first demand but insisted Texas remain a part of Mexico. In response, Austin wrote a letter urging Texas to go ahead with plans for independence. When the letter fell into the Mexican government's hands, Austin was thrown in jail.

By the time Austin was released eight months later, Santa Anna had assumed the powers of a dictator. Many Texans believed that the time had finally come to break away from Mexican rule. On March 2, 1836, Texas announced its independence, creating an autonomous Republic of Texas and putting former Tennessee Governor Sam Houston in command of the army.

In April 1836, after several brutal skirmishes with the Mexican Army, Sam Houston decided to take the offensive. The perfect opportunity arose when he found the Mexican soldiers settled down near the San Jacinto River. The Texans launched a surprise attack, killing more than 600 Mexican soldiers and capturing hundreds more. This 18-minute Battle of San Jacinto ended the war.

On May 14, Santa Anna was forced to sign a peace treaty as well as a secret treaty endorsing Texan independence. Five months later, Sam Houston was elected president of the newly formed Republic of Texas. In 1839 the red, white, and blue Lone Star flag first flew over Texas.

From Sea to Shining Sea

The United States officially recognized Texas as an independent nation in 1837, but the peace between Texas and Mexico rested on shaky ground. Mexico never officially recognized Texas as independent, and twice in 1842 Mexican troops recaptured San Antonio. Tensions were only exacerbated when Texas passed a resolution claiming land reaching far west, to present-day California. Meanwhile, "manifest destiny," a theory arguing that America was meant to stretch across the continent, had caught on in the United States. For its own security, Texas sought admission to the United States, and in early 1845, Congress voted to annex Texas. By the end of the year, Texas became our twenty-eighth state.

---

1 What is the main idea of the third paragraph?

A The settlers had to accept the Roman Catholic faith.

B The Mexican government did not want settlers coming to Texas without their permission.

C The settlers did not like the Mexican form of government.

D The Mexican government built five new army posts in Texas.

2 Which is a FACT from the passage?

F Texas was a fertile place to farm.

G Stephen Austin was jailed for urging Texas to become independent.

H The settlers were looking for a new way of life.

J California became a state soon after Texas.

3 The word exacerbated means —

A worsened

B regulated

C eased

D reduced

4 Why did the Spaniards employ the *empresario* system?

F They wanted someone to farm their land.

G The Tejanos were threatening to go to war.

H They wanted to make sure settlers were loyal to their government.

J They wanted to improve relations with the United States government.

5 Which is the best summary of the passage?

A The Texans suffered greatly under the Mexican government.

B It was manifest destiny for the United States to annex Texas.

C Before 1845, Texas was an independent nation.

D There were many obstacles in the way of Texas becoming a state.

6 What conditions were set by the Mexican government to limit early land settlement?

F Settlers had to learn Spanish.

G Settlers had to obey Mexican law, become Mexican citizens, and accept the Roman Catholic faith.

H Settlers had to join the Mexican Army.

J Settlers had to accept their manifest destiny.

7 Why did Sam Houston decide to fight the Mexicans at San Jacinto?

A Because he was trapped

B Because the river was of tactical importance

C Because he wanted to capture General Santa Anna

D Because he had the element of surprise on his side

STOP

L'eté, 1964. Marc Chagall. Gouache, watercolor, pastel, and brush and black ink on paper, 27 x 19¾ in. Private collection.

UNIT THREE

Poetry

"The poem on the page is only a shadow of the poem in the mind. And the poem in the mind is only a shadow of the poetry and the mystery of the things of this world."

—Stanley Kunitz

Genre Focus

Poetry

Mexican poet Octavio Paz believes that the purpose of poetry is "to create among people the possibility of wonder, admiration, enthusiasm, mystery, the sense that life is marvelous . . . to *make* life a marvel—that is the role of poetry." How does poetry give us a sense of the mystery and marvel of life? It does so through what African American poet Quincy Troupe calls "the music of language." Says Troupe, "I want the words to sing." Understanding the basic elements of poetry will help you hear the singing and sense the marvel in the poems you read and hear.

ELEMENTS OF POETRY

MODELS:

Speaker

The **speaker** is the voice that communicates with the reader of a poem. A poem's speaker can be the voice of a person, an animal, or even a thing.

> Lie back, daughter, let your
> head / be tipped back in the
> cup of my hand.
>
> *from "First Lesson" by Philip Booth*

speaker = a parent

Lines and Stanzas

A **line** is a horizontal row of words, which may or may not form a complete sentence. A **stanza** is a group of lines forming a unit. The stanzas in a poem are separated by a line of space.

> Drum on your drums,
> batter on your banjoes,
> sob on the long cool
> winding saxophones.
> Go to it, O jazzmen.
>
> *from "Jazz Fantasia" by Carl Sandburg*

line

stanza

Rhythm and Meter

Rhythm is the pattern of sound created by the arrangement of stressed and unstressed syllables in a line. Rhythm can be regular or irregular. **Meter** is a regular pattern of stressed and unstressed syllables that sets the overall rhythm of certain poems. The basic unit in measuring rhythm is the **foot,** which usually contains one stressed syllable marked with (′) and one or more unstressed syllables marked with (˘).

> If I / had loved / you less / or played / you
> slyly
> I might / have held / you for / a sum / mer
> more,
>
> *from "Well, I Have Lost You; and I Lost You Fairly" by Edna St. Vincent Millay*

Rhyme

Rhyme is the repetition of the same stressed vowel sound and any succeeding sounds in two or more words. **Internal rhyme** occurs within lines of poetry. **End rhyme** occurs at the ends of lines. **Rhyme scheme,** the pattern of rhyme formed by the end rhyme, may be designated by assigning a different letter of the alphabet to each new rhyme.

The glory of the day was in her face, a
The beauty of the night was in her eyes. b
And over all her loveliness, the grace a
Of Morning blushing in the early skies. b

from "The Glory of the Day Was in Her Face" by James Weldon Johnson

Other Sound Devices

- **Alliteration** is the repetition of consonant sounds at the beginnings of words.
- **Consonance** is the repetition of consonant sounds within words or at the ends of words.
- **Assonance** is the repetition of vowel sounds within non-rhyming words.
- **Onomatopoeia** is the use of a word or phrase, such as *swoosh* or *clank,* that imitates or suggests the sound of what it describes.

a drum in the desert, harder
and harder to hear — alliteration

from "Making a Fist" by Naomi Shihab Nye

harder and harder to hear — consonance

The setting sun is watching
from a distance. — assonance

from "Missing You" by Shu Ting

Imagery

Imagery is descriptive language used to represent objects, feelings, and thoughts. It often appeals to one or more of the five senses: sight, hearing, touch, taste, and smell.

Black horses drive a mower
through the weeds,
And there, a field rat, startled,
squealing bleeds. — appeals to senses of sight, smell, and hearing

from "Reapers" by Jean Toomer

Figures of Speech

A **figure of speech** is a word or expression that is not meant to be taken literally.

- A **simile** uses the word *like* or *as* to compare two seemingly unlike things.
- A **metaphor** compares two or more different things by stating or implying that one thing *is* another.
- **Personification** involves giving human characteristics to an animal, object, or idea.

the poet like an acrobat /
climbs on rime — simile

from "Constantly Risking Absurdity" by Lawrence Ferlinghetti

the spring rain / is a / thread
of pearls — metaphor

from a tanka by Lady Ise

Sometime too hot the eye of
heaven shines, / And often is
his gold complexion dimmed; — personification

from "Shall I Compare Thee to a Summer's Day?" by William Shakespeare

Active Reading Strategies

Poetry

Use the following strategies to help you fully understand and appreciate each poem you read.

● For more about related reading strategies, see **Reading Handbook,** pp. R78–R107.

LISTEN

Read a poem aloud, listening to the way it sounds. Read without stopping until you come to a punctuation mark or a natural pause. Notice how the poem is formed and the lines are grouped. Are there sound patterns within these groups?

Ask yourself . . .

- What kind of rhythm does this poem have? Is it slow, fast, regular, irregular?
- Does the poem use rhyme? If so, what is the pattern of rhyme?
- What other sound devices does the poet use? How do these devices affect me? How do they affect the mood of the poem?

IMAGINE

Conjure up the sights, sounds, smells, tastes, and tactile sensations the poem describes or evokes.

Ask yourself . . .

- How does this scene or subject look?
- What details appeal to my different senses? How would they sound, smell, taste, or feel?
- What overall feeling does the poem convey?

RESPOND

Think about your spontaneous reaction to the poem.

Say to yourself . . .

- This poem makes me think . . .
- This poem reminds me of . . .
- That's pretty funny!
- What I really like about this poem is . . .
- I didn't expect that this poem would . . .

QUESTION Ask yourself questions to help you understand and interpret the poem. Write down or mentally note questions you can't answer.

Ask yourself . . .

- Do I understand what this poem is about?
- What does this image mean or represent? Why does the poet use figurative language in this way?
- What allusions or references does the poet use and how do they help me understand the poem's message?

CLARIFY Put the poem into your own words. Then summarize the poem, and think about what it might mean on a deeper level.

Say to yourself . . .

- These lines can be restated like this: . . .
- This stanza is about . . .
- This image brings to mind or symbolizes . . .
- Rereading this stanza helps me understand that . . .

INTERPRET Read the poem several times, focusing on interpreting its overall meaning.

Ask yourself . . .

- Does the title give a clue to the meaning of the poem?
- What main theme, or message, is the poet trying to convey?
- Does the poem have more than one meaning?
- How do the symbols and language support the meaning of this poem?

Applying the Strategies

1. Practice the strategies again as you read the poem "Eldorado" on page 583, using the Active Reading Model in the margins.
2. Choose another poem and practice using these strategies.

Before You Read

Eldorado

Reading Focus

Do you know anyone who has wanted to become rich quickly?

Share Ideas What methods do people often use to acquire money in a short period of time? Are their methods usually successful? Share your ideas with a partner.

Setting a Purpose Read about a knight's search for wealth.

Building Background

- The name *El Dorado*, meaning "the golden one," originally comes from a legendary region in northern South America where the ruler would cover his body with gold dust during festivals. At the end of the ceremonies, he would wash off the gold dust in a lake while his subjects threw jewels and golden objects into the water. In the early 1530s, explorers from Spain and Germany heard the tale and set off in search of the "gilded man." As the tale spread, the search for El Dorado came to mean the search for an entire region of gold, and explorers from around the world joined in the quest for the fabled golden city. El Dorado was never found (neither the man nor the place), but the name endured and is applied to any place of great wealth or to the dream of acquiring it.

Hernán Cortés

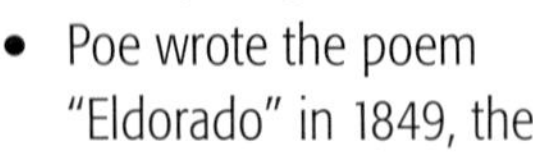

- Poe wrote the poem "Eldorado" in 1849, the year gold was discovered in California. That discovery brought many fortune seekers to the area in what later was called the "gold rush."

Meet Edgar Allan Poe

Edgar Allan Poe experienced loss at a young age, and throughout his lifetime he endured loneliness and suffering. Poe was orphaned before he was three and was then taken in by the Allans, a wealthy family in Richmond, Virginia. The Allans sent Poe to one of England's best boarding schools. There, when he was twelve years old, he wrote the poem "The Lake," which expressed his fears and his feelings of loss. While later poems such as "The Raven" and stories such as "The Gold-Bug" brought Poe admiration from critics, his writing never earned him much money, and he struggled with poverty until he died of unknown causes at forty.

Edgar Allan Poe was born in 1809 and died in 1849.

War memorial window. St. Mary's, Aldworth, Berkshire, UK.

Eldorado

Edgar Allan Poe

Gaily bedight,°
A gallant knight,
In sunshine and in shadow,
Had journeyed long,
Singing a song,
In search of Eldorado.

But he grew old—
This knight so bold—
And o'er his heart a shadow
Fell as he found
No spot of ground
That looked like Eldorado.

And, as his strength
Failed him at length,
He met a pilgrim shadow°—
"Shadow," said he,
"Where can it be—
This land of Eldorado?"

"Over the Mountains
Of the Moon,
Down the Valley of the Shadow,°
Ride, boldly ride,"
The shade° replied,—
"If you seek for Eldorado!"

El is a Spanish article meaning "the"; *Dorado* is Spanish for "golden."

1 The knight is dressed or equipped *(bedight)* in a bright, showy way *(gaily)*.

15 Here, *pilgrim* means "a traveler or wanderer," and the *shadow* is a spirit or ghost. In line 23, the shadow is called a *shade,* meaning the same thing.

21 In the Bible, a line in Psalm 23 reads, "Yea, though I walk through the *valley of the shadow* of death . . ."

Active Reading Model

IMAGINE

Picture a knight dressed in bright colors. Imagine his physical characteristics.

LISTEN

Hear how the rhythm of the first stanza is very regular, with a songlike quality.

QUESTION

Who is the pilgrim shadow?

INTERPRET

What do you think Poe is really saying about the search for wealth?

Responding to Literature

Personal Response

What images remain in your mind after reading the poem? List them.

Active Reading Response

Look back at the strategies described in the Active Reading Model notes on pages 580–581. Which Active Reading Strategy was most helpful to you in understanding the poem?

Analyzing Literature

Recall and Interpret

1. What is the knight doing in the first two stanzas? How does the knight change in the second stanza? What might account for those changes?
2. Whom does the knight meet in the third stanza? Whom or what do you think this person represents?
3. What advice does the knight receive in the last stanza? What, in your opinion, does this advice mean?
4. How often does Poe use the word *shadow?* What do you think the word means in each case? Based on the meanings for *shadow,* what would you say is the main message of this poem?

Evaluate and Connect

5. What might have happened to the knight after his encounter? Explain and support your response with evidence from the poem.
6. Have you read or heard about other quests of explorers or knights? What was the outcome of those quests?
7. What advice might the speaker give to fortune seekers today? In your opinion, why would he give this advice?
8. Think about your response to the Reading Focus on page 582. What insights have you gained after reading this selection? Explain.

Literary ELEMENTS

Narrative Poetry

Narrative poetry is poetry that tells a story. Narrative poetry has one or more characters and includes setting, plot, and point of view. In some narrative poems, such as "Eldorado," long periods of time may pass in a few lines. "Eldorado" tells the story of a knight's lifelong search in just four stanzas.

1. What events in the knight's life does the poem cover?
2. In your opinion, what does the brevity of the poem highlight?

- See **Literary Terms Handbook,** p. R8.

Extending Your Response

Interdisciplinary Activity

Geography: Map a Story Elaborate and expand on the story presented in the poem. Place the characters in the poem in a particular time and place, and map the region where the knight travels. Put captions at each place the knight visits, and explain whom he met or what he did there.

Writing About Literature

Analyzing Stanzas Each stanza, or group of lines, in Poe's poem presents one main idea and helps move the story along. In a few paragraphs, tell the key idea each stanza expresses. Then explain how the stanzas combine to tell a story.

Save your work for your portfolio.

Theme 7 Loves and Losses

What role does love play in life? Because love is such an important part of human life, its loss can be a painful experience. In this theme you will find poems about the joys and insights love can bring as well as the emptiness and pain of its loss.

THEME PROJECTS

Performing

Coffeehouse Poetry Poetry comes alive when it is read aloud. With a small group, choose three or four poems from this theme to present at a "coffeehouse" poetry reading.

1. Look carefully at each poem and decide how you can best convey the speaker's message. Assign poems or parts of poems to different members of the group.
2. Decide on appropriate music to accompany your readings of the poems. Choose from recorded music or ask a group member who is also a musician to play or sing.
3. With other groups, create the coffeehouse atmosphere and take turns presenting your performance.

Multimedia Project

Picturing Poetry With a partner, choose words and images from three or four of the poems, and create a multimedia presentation.

1. Decide which words or images from the poem represent the speaker's main idea.
2. Use a still camera or a video camera to create slides or a videotape of these images.
3. Then, using a tape recorder or video camera, create a voiceover for your presentation.
4. Present your mixed-media show to the class.

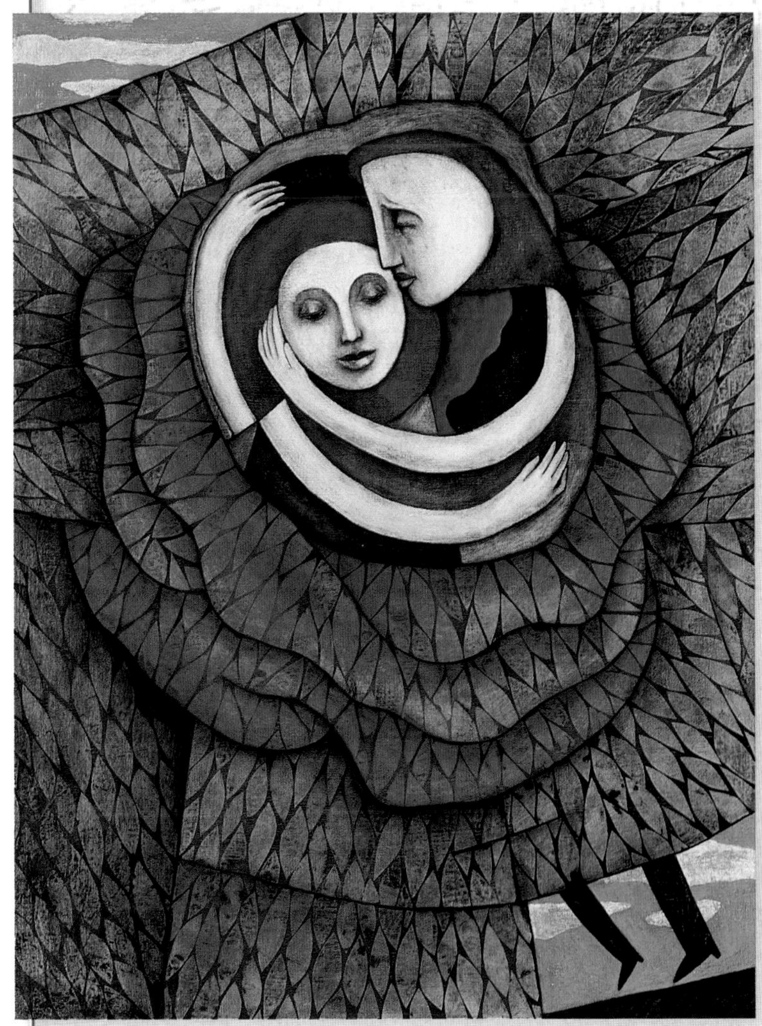

In Our Nature, 1996. Daniel Nevins. Oil, acrylic, and collage on wood, 37 x 29 in. Private collection.

Before You Read

One Perfect Rose and *Shall I Compare Thee . . .*

Reading Focus

Why do people write about love? What kinds of things do they say?

Map It! Create a word web to show some of the reasons people write about love. Write *love poem* in the middle of your map and connect it to at least four different reasons.

Setting a Purpose Read to find out what the speakers of two poems say about love and why they say it.

Building Background

- Throughout history, people in love have expressed their feelings by giving tokens of their affection, such as flowers, poems, candy, jewelry, locks of hair, and rings. Many of these items have symbolic meaning. A ring is a circle that may represent endless love. A lock of hair may be a cherished reminder of a beloved person. Flowers often symbolize ardent love.
- Dorothy Parker had a reputation for being clever and amusing, but she was also sensitive to matters of the heart and suffered her share of disappointments in love. In difficult times her humor sustained her. Once, after the death of her husband, someone asked if there was anything she needed, and she replied, "Get me a new husband." When her remark was considered unfeeling, she said, "So sorry. Then run down to the corner and get me a ham and cheese on rye and tell them to hold the mayo."
- To make his sonnets believable to the reader, Shakespeare uses the voice of a speaker that, as critic Helen Vendler explains, is like "a 'real voice' coming from a 'real mind' like our own." In each sonnet the speaker presents his inner thoughts and feelings. Although each sonnet is a complete poem that stands on its own, all 154 of Shakespeare's sonnets together form a sonnet sequence—a series of sonnets on the same subject.

Meet Dorothy Parker

Dorothy Parker wrote light verse for magazines such as the *Saturday Evening Post* and *Vogue*. Parker, one of the first writers to publish in the *New Yorker*, helped establish the style that became known as the *New Yorker* short story. Known for her biting wit, Parker said that genuine humor required courage and criticism, as well as "a disciplined eye and a wild mind."

Dorothy Parker was born in 1893 in West End, New Jersey. She died in 1967.

Meet William Shakespeare

English poet and playwright William Shakespeare wrote during the Elizabethan Age in England. Some historians believe that by the age of twenty, Shakespeare was known in London as a rising playwright. In addition to sonnets and numerous plays, Shakespeare wrote two long narrative poems.

William Shakespeare was born in 1564 in Stratford-upon-Avon, England, and died there in 1616.

One Perfect Rose

Dorothy Parker

A single flow'r he sent me, since we met.
   All tenderly his messenger he chose;
Deep-hearted, pure, with scented dew still wet—
   One perfect rose.

I knew the language of the floweret;
   "My fragile leaves," it said, "his heart enclose."
Love long has taken for his amulet°
   One perfect rose.

Why is it no one ever sent me yet
   One perfect limousine, do you suppose?
Ah no, it's always just my luck to get
   One perfect rose.

---

7 An *amulet* (am′ yə lit) is an object thought to bring good fortune or to protect against bad luck.

Shall I Compare Thee to a Summer's Day?

William Shakespeare

Shall I compare thee to a summer's day?
Thou art more lovely and more temperate.°
Rough winds do shake the darling buds of May,
And summer's lease hath all too short a date.
Sometime too hot the eye of heaven shines,
And often is his gold complexion dimmed;
And every fair° from fair sometime declines,
By chance, or nature's changing course untrimmed:°
But thy eternal summer shall not fade
Nor lose possession of that fair thou ow'st,°
Nor shall Death brag thou wand'rest in his shade,
When in eternal lines to time thou grow'st.
   So long as men can breathe or eyes can see,
   So long lives this, and this gives life to thee.

---

2 In terms of the weather, a *temperate* day is calm and free from extremes of temperature.

7 *Fair,* in this context, is a synonym for *beauty.*

8 Here, *untrimmed* means "stripped of beauty."

10 *[thou ow'st]* Read this poetic phrase as "you own" or "you possess."

Responding to Literature

Personal Response

Which poem better reflects your own attitude toward love? Explain in your journal.

Analyzing Literature

One Perfect Rose

Recall and Interpret

1. What words does the speaker use to describe the gift she receives? Who do you think has sent the gift?
2. According to the speaker, what does the gift **symbolize,** or stand for? Use evidence from the poem to support your answer.
3. How does the speaker react to the gift? Why do you think she reacts in this manner?
4. After reading this poem, what might you infer about the speaker's personality and character?

Evaluate and Connect

5. How does the speaker's **tone,** or attitude, toward her subject, change in the last stanza of the poem? What is the effect of this shift in tone?
6. How might you react if you received a token gift similar to the one the speaker receives? Give reasons for your answer.
7. Look again at the word web you made for the Reading Focus on page 586. In your opinion, why did Parker write this love poem? Add your suggested reason to the web, if it doesn't already appear there.

Shall I Compare Thee to a Summer's Day?

Recall and Interpret

8. Who might the speaker of this poem be? In your opinion, who is the speaker addressing? Use details from the poem to support your answers.
9. What two things is the speaker comparing? Which one does the speaker consider to be superior? Why? Support your answer with specific details from the poem.
10. According to the speaker, why will the subject of the poem have a summer that is eternal? What might this tell you about the poet's reason for writing the poem?

Evaluate and Connect

11. Find three examples of **personification.** (See Literary Terms Handbook, page R9.) Why might Shakespeare have chosen to give human characteristics to these things?
12. Think about the extended comparison Shakespeare uses in this poem. Why might he have chosen this particular comparison?
13. **Theme Connections** How is this poem related to the theme of "Loves and Losses"? Explain.
14. Reread critic Helen Vendler's comment in the Background section on page 586. Do you agree with Vendler about the speaker in Shakespeare's sonnet? Why or why not?

Literary ELEMENTS

Sonnet

Shakespeare used a poetic form known as a **sonnet.** Sonnets have fourteen lines that are almost always written in iambic pentameter–a meter in which the predominant foot, or unit of rhythm, is the *iamb*–that is, an unstressed syllable followed by a stressed syllable. There are five feet in each line of iambic pentameter. The Shakespearean sonnet contains three groups of four lines, called *quatrains.* Typically, the quatrains have a rhyme scheme of *abab cdcd efef.* A rhymed couplet ends the sonnet. The following lines from "Shall I Compare Thee . . ." are an example of iambic pentameter and the sonnet's *abab* rhyme scheme:

Shăll Í cŏmpáre thĕe tó ă súmmĕr's dáy? *(a)*
Thŏu árt mŏre lóvelÿ ănd mŏre témpĕráte. *(b)*
Rŏugh wínds dŏ sháke thĕ dárlĭng búds ŏf Máy, *(a)*
Ănd súmmĕr's léase hăth áll tŏo shórt ă dáte. *(b)*

1. Copy a different quatrain from the sonnet and mark the meter and rhyme scheme as modeled above.
2. The rhymed couplet of a sonnet often presents a conclusion to the issues or questions presented in the three quatrains. What is the effect of the couplet in the Shakespearean sonnet you have just read?

- See **Literary Terms Handbook,** p. R12.

Literature and Writing

Writing About Literature

Comparing the Poems How does the **tone** in "Shall I Compare Thee . . ." compare to the tone in "One Perfect Rose"? What words or other techniques does each poet use to create the tone? In a two-column chart, jot down specific information from each poem that relates to its tone. Then write a few paragraphs comparing the tone in the two poems. Share your comparison with the class.

Creative Writing

Shall I Compare Thee . . . ? Write a poem about a beloved friend or family member, in which you compare him or her to something else. You might start by listing some of the person's qualities and then identifying things that have similar qualities. For example, if your beloved is moody, you might compare him or her to unpredictable spring weather. Try writing your poem in sonnet form.

Extending Your Response

Literature Groups

Designing a Visual Representation Choose one or two pairs of lines that your group especially likes from the two poems. Then design a visual representation of the lines. You may want to use a cartoon approach or a more serious fine art style. Display your work in your classroom.

Interdisciplinary Activity

Mathematics: What's the Difference? Should you send roses or a limousine? Research the cost of an individual rose, a dozen roses, and the price of a rented limousine per hour and day. How many roses could be sent for the price of a rented limousine? Present your findings in a chart. Share your discoveries with the class.

Reading Further

You might also enjoy the following collection:

Committed to Memory: 100 Best Poems to Memorize, edited by John Hollander. The work contains sonnets and songs by Shakespeare as well as other types of poems by many poets.

Save your work for your portfolio.

Song Lyrics

Romantic love has inspired not only countless poems but also innumerable songs. Here's a version of one well-known love song from the 1960s performed by the soul singer Percy Sledge.

When a Man Loves a Woman

by C. Lewis and A. Wright

When a man loves a woman,
Can't keep his mind on nothin'
else,
He'd trade the world
For the good thing he's found.
If she's bad, he can't see it,
She can do no wrong,
Turn his back on his best friend
If he put her down.

When a man loves a woman,
Spend his very last dime
Trying to hold on to what he
needs.
He'd give up all his comforts
And sleep out in the rain,
If she said that's the way it
ought to be.
Well, this man loves you,
woman.
I gave you everything I had,
Trying to hold on to your
precious love.
Baby, please don't treat me bad.

When a man loves a woman,
Down deep in his soul,
She can bring him such misery.
If she plays him for a fool,
He's the last one to know.
Loving eyes can never see.

When a man loves a woman,
He can do her no wrong.
He can never hold her love
again.
Yes, when a man loves a
woman,
I know exactly how he feels.
Oh, baby, baby, baby, I know
so well.

When a man loves a woman,
I know exactly how he feels.
Oh, baby, baby, baby, I know
so well.
When a man loves a woman . . .

Analyzing Media

1. What do you like or dislike about these lyrics?
2. What is your favorite love song? How do its lyrics compare with these?

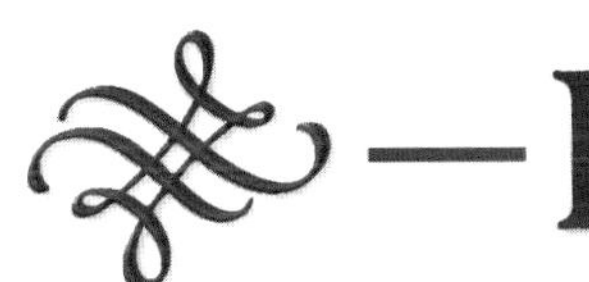

Before You Read

Simile and *Well, I Have Lost You; and I Lost You Fairly*

Reading Focus

What happens when two people who were in love find out that their feelings have changed?

List Ideas Think about the possible consequences of falling out of love. Do such couples always break up? Should they? Can they remain friends? List your ideas, and then share them with a partner.

Setting a Purpose Read the poems to learn how falling out of love affects two speakers.

Building Background

- Much of N. Scott Momaday's writing reflects the Native American world view that there is, as he puts it, "harmony in the universe." Momaday has said, "I believe that the Indian has an understanding of the physical world and of the earth as a spiritual entity that is his, very much his own. The non-Indian can benefit a good deal by having that perception revealed to him."

Kiowa woman in traditional dress.

- Edna St. Vincent Millay wrote "Well, I Have Lost You; and I Lost You Fairly" in the form of the **English sonnet.** The English sonnet is also called the **Shakespearean sonnet** because Shakespeare was the master of this sonnet form. English sonnets are divided into three quatrains, or groups of four lines, and one couplet, or group of two lines. The rhyme scheme is usually *abab cdcd efef gg.* The English sonnet form allows for the presentation and development of a problem or question in the three quatrains, and a solution in the couplet.

Meet N. Scott Momaday

N. Scott Momaday (mə mä′ dā) grew up on Southwestern reservations, where he was influenced by his Kiowa Indian heritage. When a small journal published one of Momaday's early poems, he wrote, "There was something about seeing my words in print that mattered to me greatly." His first novel, *House Made of Dawn*, won the Pulitzer Prize for Fiction in 1969.

N. Scott Momaday was born in 1934 in Lawton, Oklahoma.

Meet Edna St. Vincent Millay

Edna St. Vincent Millay wrote her first poem at age five, and in 1917 she published her first volume of poetry. Millay then moved to New York City's Greenwich Village, where she found the writers and artists to be "very, very poor and very, very merry." At age thirty-one, Millay won the Pulitzer Prize for Poetry.

Edna St. Vincent Millay was born in 1892 in Rockland, Maine, and died in 1950.

Simile

N. Scott Momaday

What did we say to each other
that now we are as the deer
who walk in single file
with heads high
with ears forward
with eyes watchful
with hooves always placed on firm ground
in whose limbs there is latent° flight

---

8 Something that is *latent* (lā′ tənt) is unseen or undeveloped but capable of bursting into full activity under certain conditions.

Woman and the Sea, 1972. Will Barnet. Oil on canvas, 51¾ x 41 in. Private collection.

Well, I Have Lost You; and I Lost You Fairly

Edna St. Vincent Millay

Well, I have lost you; and I lost you fairly;
In my own way, and with my full consent.
Say what you will, kings in a tumbrel° rarely
Went to their deaths more proud than this one went.
Some nights of apprehension and hot weeping
I will confess; but that's permitted me;
Day dried my eyes; I was not one for keeping
Rubbed in a cage a wing that would be free.
If I had loved you less or played you slyly
I might have held you for a summer more,
But at the cost of words I value highly,
And no such summer as the one before.
Should I outlive this anguish—and men do—
I shall have only good to say of you.

---

3 A *tumbrel* is a farmer's two-wheeled cart. During the French Revolution, such carts were used to carry condemned people–including King Louis XVI–to their execution.

Responding to Literature

Personal Response

Describe the mental image you formed after reading one of the poems.

Analyzing Literature

Simile

Recall and Interpret

1. Whom do you think the speaker is addressing? Give reasons for your answer.
2. Summarize in your own words the question the speaker is asking. What impression of the speaker does this question give you?
3. According to the speaker, how do deer behave? What might the comparison to deer suggest?
4. How would you describe the current relationship between the speaker and the person being addressed?

Evaluate and Connect

5. Do you think the comparison to deer is effective? Why or why not?
6. **Theme Connections** Explain how this poem is related to the theme of "Loves and Losses."
7. Have you experienced or observed a situation like the one described in this poem? Explain.

Well, I Have Lost You; and I Lost You Fairly

Recall and Interpret

8. Summarize the speaker's reaction and attitude toward the loss in lines 1–2. What does the speaker mean by losing "fairly" and "with my full consent"?
9. How does the speaker describe his or her reaction to the loss in lines 5–7? What does the tone of this description tell you about the speaker?
10. What **metaphor** does the speaker use in lines 7–8? What feeling does this comparison convey to you? (See Literary Terms Handbook, page R7.)
11. In your opinion, what does the speaker mean in lines 9–12? What does this tell you about the speaker's values?

Evaluate and Connect

12. Do you think the speaker will "outlive this anguish"? Give reasons for your answer.
13. Millay wrote this poem in the form of an English **sonnet** (see Literary Terms Handbook, page R12). Reread the background information on page 591 and explain how the content of the poem suits the English sonnet form.
14. Do you think the speaker acted wisely in the relationship described here? Would you have acted the same way? Why or why not?

Literary ELEMENTS

Simile

Poets often make comparisons in order to convey ideas and feelings. One kind of comparison is called a **simile**–a direct comparison that uses *like* or *as*. By comparing an experience, idea, or image to something that is familiar, a writer may reveal new insights about his or her subject. For example, in "Simile," Momaday reveals something about people in a relationship by comparing them to deer.

1. When you picture deer, what qualities do you think of that the poem does not specifically mention? Which of these qualities might also apply to the people?
2. What does this simile convey about the people that an ordinary description of them would not convey?

- See **Literary Terms Handbook**, p. R12.

Literature and Writing

Writing About Literature

Analyze Mood The emotional quality or atmosphere of a literary work is its **mood.** List words and phrases that describe the mood of each poem. Then write a paragraph about each poem, in which you describe its mood and explain how the mood reinforces the message each speaker is trying to convey. Share your analysis in a small group.

Creative Writing

Advice Column Imagine that you are an advice columnist and the two speakers have submitted their poems to you and asked you to advise them about their romantic dilemmas. Write a response to the speakers in which you evaluate what they've already done and also give them advice for the future.

Extending Your Response

Literature Groups

Breaking Up Is Hard to Do Review the ideas you listed in response to the Reading Focus on page 591. Which speaker in the two poems do you think is better off? Why? Are there "good" or "bad" ways to end a relationship? Is it possible to remain friendly with someone after splitting up? Use details from the selections to support or refute your arguments. Share your ideas with another group.

Interdisciplinary Activity

Geography: The Influence of Place Often physical environment influences a writer's work. Momaday grew up on Indian reservations in the southwestern United States, where he observed the natural world. Millay grew up in Maine and came to know its coast and countryside. Use the library or the Internet to research these places. How might the poets' different backgrounds have affected their poetry? Present your conclusions to the class.

Performing

Dialogue Work with a partner to create a dialogue that the speaker of either poem might have with the person to whom the poem is addressed. The speaker's part of the dialogue may include lines from the poem; you will need to supply the other person's response. Practice your dialogue and then perform it for the class.

Reading Further

You might enjoy these poems by Momaday and Millay:

"Earth and I Gave You Turquoise" by N. Scott Momaday from *Harper's Anthology of 20th Century Native American Poetry.*

"Love is not blind. I see with single eye" from *Collected Poems* by Edna St. Vincent Millay.

Save your work for your portfolio.

Grammar Link

Making Sure Pronouns and Antecedents Agree

Using pronouns correctly is not difficult or complicated; it's quite logical. Still, using pronouns incorrectly is a common grammatical error.

Every **pronoun** gets its meaning from a noun or another pronoun, called its **antecedent.** This is the word to which the pronoun refers. In order for your writing to be clear, each pronoun must agree with its antecedent in number, gender, and person.

Problem 1 A singular antecedent that can be either male or female
A poet may express deep and personal feelings in their poetry. [*Their* is plural; its antecedent, *poet,* is singular.]

Solution A Change the pronoun to agree with its antecedent. Although the pronoun *his* is grammatically correct in this example, *his or her* is preferable.
A poet may express deep and personal feelings in his or her poetry.

Solution B Reword the sentence so that both the antecedent and pronoun are plural.
Poets may express deep and personal feelings in their poetry.

Problem 2 A singular indefinite pronoun as an antecedent
Neither poet used rhyme in their poems. [The pronoun *their* is plural; its antecedent, *neither,* is singular.]

Solution A Change the antecedent to agree with the pronoun.
These poets did not use rhyme in their poems.

Solution B Change the pronoun to agree with its antecedent.
Neither poet used rhyme in his or her poem.

Problem 3 A second-person pronoun that refers to a third-person antecedent
Jo is going to a workshop that teaches you how to write poetry.

Solution A Replace the second-person pronoun with a third-person pronoun.
Jo is going to a workshop that teaches her to write poetry.

Solution B Replace the pronoun with the appropriate noun.
Jo is going to a workshop that teaches students to write poetry.

For more about pronouns and antecedents, see **Language Handbook,** p. R19.

EXERCISE

Revise the sentences to correct problems in pronoun use.

1. Jo and Amy like the bookstore that sells you snacks as well as books.
2. However, a poet may write such personal work that they do not want it published.
3. Each of the girls writes in their journal regularly.
4. Each poet who wrote about love dealt with romance in their own way.

Before You Read

The Glory of the Day Was in Her Face and *Missing You*

Reading Focus

How might you react if you lost the friendship or affection of someone you care about deeply?

Freewrite Spend five minutes writing an answer to the question above. If you have actually experienced such a loss, you might want to write about it.

Setting a Purpose Read the poems to learn how two speakers feel about losing love.

Building Background

The Time and Place

- During the 1920s, a New York City neighborhood called Harlem became a gathering place for African American writers, musicians, and other artists. Harlem writers such as Langston Hughes, Zora Neale Hurston, and James Weldon Johnson emerged as strong voices against racism and helped shape the important intellectual and artistic movement that became known as the Harlem Renaissance.
- The work of Chinese writers has long been tightly controlled by the Chinese communist government. One of the worst times for Chinese writers was during the Cultural Revolution, from 1966 to 1976, when educated people in China were systematically persecuted under the brutal rule of Mao Tse-tung. Mao and his Red Guard drove hundreds of thousands of Chinese citizens out of cities and forced them to work in the countryside as farm and factory laborers.

Meet James Weldon Johnson

Raised in a home where education was highly prized, Johnson refused to allow racial discrimination to limit his aspirations. "I will not allow one prejudiced person or one million or one hundred million to blight my life," he wrote. Johnson's outlook empowered him to express his diverse talents in a variety of careers, including writer, teacher, lawyer, diplomat, and civil rights leader.

James Weldon Johnson was born in 1871 in Jacksonville, Florida, and died after a car accident in 1938.

Meet Shu Ting

As a teenager, Shu Ting was driven from her Beijing home during China's Cultural Revolution and was forced to work in a factory. She began reading Western poets and writing poetry, and during the 1980s, Shu Ting became one of the Misty Poets, known for their powerful imagery, emotional expression, and belief in individual experience.

Shu Ting was born in Fujian, China, in 1952.

The Glory of the Day Was in Her Face

James Weldon Johnson

The glory of the day was in her face,
The beauty of the night was in her eyes.
And over all her loveliness, the grace
Of Morning blushing in the early skies.

And in her voice, the calling of the dove;
Like music of a sweet, melodious part.
And in her smile, the breaking light of love;
And all the gentle virtues° in her heart.

And now the glorious day, the beauteous night,
The birds that signal to their mates at dawn,
To my dull ears, to my tear-blinded sight
Are one with all the dead, since she is gone.

8 Her *virtues* are her good or admirable qualities.

Missing You

Shu Ting

Translated by Carolyn Kizer

A multi-colored chart without a boundary;
An equation chalked on the board, with no solution;
A one-stringed lyre° that tells the beads of rain;
A pair of useless oars that never cross the water.

Waiting buds in suspended animation;°
The setting sun is watching from a distance.
Though in my mind there may be an enormous ocean,
What emerges is the sum: a pair of tears.

Yes, from these vistas,° from these depths,
Only this.

3 The harplike *lyre* normally has four to ten strings.
5 In a state of *suspended animation,* a living thing shows no signs of life or appears to be frozen in time.
9 *Vista* can mean "a view of a landscape" or "an overall mental view of something."

Responding to Literature

Personal Response

Which line or lines from either poem affected you most strongly? Why?

Analyzing Literature

The Glory of the Day Was in Her Face

Recall and Interpret

1. Whom might the speaker be describing? In the first stanza, to what does the speaker compare this person?
2. What **images** does the speaker use to describe the person in the second stanza? What do these images and the ones in the first stanza suggest about his feelings for the person he is describing? (See Literary Terms Handbook, page R6.)
3. How does the speaker's **tone,** or attitude toward the subject, change in the third stanza? How does this shift in tone help you better understand the poem?

Evaluate and Connect

4. Identify an image from the poem that appeals to sight and one that appeals to sound. Evaluate the effect each image creates.
5. If you were writing a poem on a similar subject, what types of images might you use to describe the person? Give reasons for your choices.

Missing You

Recall and Interpret

6. What does the title suggest to you about the subject of this poem?
7. Explain what the images in lines 1–4 have in common. What do these images reveal about the speaker's feelings?
8. Explain the meaning of lines 7–10. What **irony** is the speaker pointing out? (See Literary Terms Handbook, page R6.)

Evaluate and Connect

9. **Theme Connections** Review the freewriting you did for the Reading Focus on page 596. How does your response to loss compare with the speaker's response in "Missing You"?
10. Reread Shu Ting's biography on page 596. Based on this poem, evaluate whether you think she has been properly classified as a member of the group called the Misty Poets.

Literary ELEMENTS

Metaphor

A **metaphor** is a type of figurative, or nonliteral, language that compares two or more things that have something in common. Metaphors create fresh insights and provide new understandings of familiar things. For example, in "The Glory of the Day Was in Her Face," Johnson compares a woman's eyes to the night: both are dark, beautiful, and perhaps mysterious.

1. Identify another metaphor in each of the poems. What things are compared, and what do they have in common?
2. How does the use of metaphor enhance your understanding and appreciation of these poems? Give specific examples.

- See **Literary Terms Handbook,** p. R7.

Literature and Writing

Writing About Literature

Message to the Speaker Choose one of the poems, and write a two-paragraph letter to the speaker. Explain what you particularly like about the poem and what your favorite metaphor is. Tell the speaker what overall impact the poem had on you. Explain what you wish for the speaker in the future.

Creative Writing

Missing Someone Think of a time when you were separated from a close friend or relative. Write a poem expressing your thoughts and feelings about missing that person. You may want to use sensory details in your poem, as well as figurative language (such as metaphors and symbols) in order to better convey your ideas and emotions.

Extending Your Response

Literature Groups

Analyze Metaphors As a group, choose three or four metaphors from the poems you have just read and analyze them in detail. What do you think each one represents? How effectively do the metaphors help convey the speaker's message? What fresh insights does each metaphor contribute to your reading of the poem? What would be lacking if more literal words were substituted? After discussing these questions with your group, compare your ideas with those of other groups.

Internet Connection

Social Context Both James Weldon Johnson and Shu Ting were shaped by the social and political conditions of their time. Generate a list of research questions about the Harlem Renaissance or China's Cultural Revolution. Research them on the Internet and share your findings with the class.

Interdisciplinary Activity

Science: The Language of Loss How is a person's body affected by sadness and grief? Are tears, sleeplessness, or a lack of appetite typical human reactions to the loss of a loved one? Research current scientific data on the ways a person's body can react to the loss of a loved one. Present your findings in a short report to your class. Consider including diagrams or other visual aids.

Reading Further

These works can help you understand Johnson and Shu Ting in historical context:

One More River to Cross, An African American Photograph Album documents the African American experience.

A Splintered Mirror, a collection of poetry from China's democracy movement.

Save your work for your portfolio.

Technology Skills

Internet: Publishing Your Writing on the Web

Much of the writing done in school is written for one particular person: your teacher. The World Wide Web provides a place where you can share your creativity and opinions with the rest of the world. Sites that publish teen 'zines often accept submissions of student writing, as do many other sites. For example, if you have an interest in in-line skating, you may want to submit a poem on the joys of the sport to a site dedicated to in-line skating. Similarly, if there's a band or musical group you really like, you could write a tribute article for submission.

Before You Get Started . . .

What interests you? Do you like to watch TV? go to movies? play video games? feed on baseball statistics? Choose one topic, and use a search engine to look for sites on the World Wide Web that relate to your interest. Try to be as specific as possible in your quest. For example, don't do a keyword search for sports. Instead, key in *baseball, field hockey,* or *figure skating.* In your journal, write the topic you've chosen and list the URLs (Uniform Resource Locators, or Web addresses) of sites you find interesting and relevant.

But What Do I Write?

Often writers have plenty of good ideas about interesting subjects, but when it comes to putting everything down in writing, they freeze up. If you're having trouble thinking of a format to write in, glance through the list below. Perhaps it will spark some new ideas. Looking at what others have written and placed on a site might also suggest something.

song	letter	newspaper article
rap	preview	opinion column
joke	review	script
riddle	critique	play
top ten list	summary	poem
recipe	proposal	haiku
menu	reasons for	character sketch
description	reasons against	short story
application	endorsement	essay

TECHNOLOGY TIP

Use the grammar-check that comes with your word processing program cautiously. Grammar-checks can't think; they just look for patterns. You must do the thinking. Consider each suggested change carefully before accepting or rejecting it.

1. Using one of the formats above, write about your chosen topic using the word processing software on your computer. Don't forget to save your work often.
2. When you finish, run the spell-check and, if you wish, the grammar-check. Then proofread it yourself.

3. Share your writing with a classmate. Ask her or him to suggest ways your message can be made clearer.
4. Make the appropriate changes, and share your work with your teacher. (Ask whether to submit hard copy or a floppy disk.)
5. Once you've gotten approval from your teacher, submit your piece to one of the Web sites you listed in your journal. Be sure to read through the site's submission guidelines before sending in your work.
6. If you would like to include your writing on your school's Web site, convert your work to HyperText Markup Language (HTML) using HTML editing software. If you don't have access to HTML software, you may convert your document using some basic codes:

Style	**Type as . . .**
headline	<H3> headline </H3>
bold text	<B> bold text </B>
italicized text	<I> italicized text </I>
underlined text	<U> underlined text </U>
end paragraph	paragraph<P>
link to another Web site	<A HREF = "http://www.sitename.edu">Click here</A>

For instance, the following piece can be converted just by adding a few codes.

Original Text:

It's Great to Skate

I **love** in-line skating. When I get my
skates on,
I know I'm ready to *fly.*
I used to fall a lot,
but now I know what I'm doing.

To find out more about in-line skating,
Click Here!

HyperText Markup Language:

<H3>It's Great to Skate</H3>
I <B>love</B> in-line skating. When I get my
skates on,
I know I'm ready to <I>fly.</I>
I used to fall <U>a lot,</U>
but now I know what I'm doing.<P>

To find out more about in-line skating, <A HREF =
"http://www.sitename.com">Click here!</A>

EXERCISES

1. Look through your portfolio and choose a piece you would like to share on the World Wide Web. Convert it to HTML, and submit it to relevant sites. If your submission is turned down, ask the editors to offer feedback so you can make your work better.
2. Create a subdirectory for your class on your school's Web site. Ask the computer lab instructor to help you with the programming.
3. Once you've practiced with HTML editors, consider creating a Web site for your class, a school club, or yourself.

Before You Read

First Lesson and *Those Winter Sundays*

Reading Focus

What important lessons about life have you learned?

Journal Think of an important life lesson that a parent or other family member has taught you. How have you benefited from this lesson? Describe your experience in your journal.

Setting a Purpose Read poems that share life lessons taught and learned by others.

Building Background

- Philip Booth sets many of his poems in New England, where he was born and has lived for most of his life. In particular, he focuses on the New England seacoast, incorporating the motions and rhythms of the tides into tight, spare poems about life, loss, love, and other affairs of the human heart. Booth explained that his love of words goes back to his parents. "If my father taught me respect for words, my mother's imagination intuitively made real to me the world that words reach for."

- Poet and teacher Robert Hayden dedicated his life to his craft and to working "closely with young people" in order "to encourage creative writing." Hayden researched and celebrated his heritage and wrote poetry that appealed to many audiences. Hayden said, "I believe in the essential oneness of all people," and his poems portray universal human concerns of loss and love. Hayden won many awards for his poetry and was the first African American to be named as the Library of Congress consultant in poetry, a position now called poet laureate.

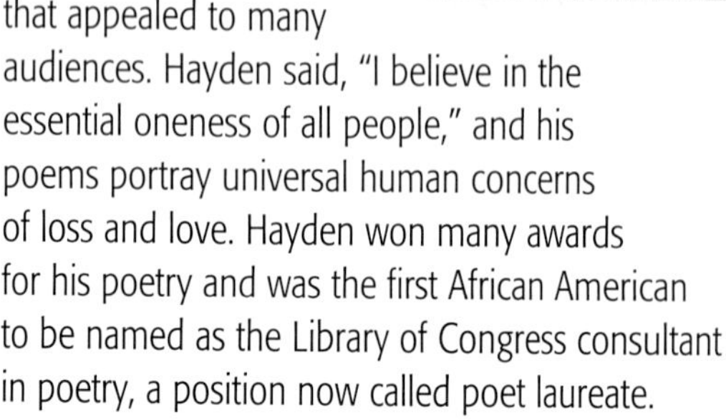

Meet Philip Booth

"Save for long Maine summers . . . where I hung around wharf-talk, . . . my boyhood was sheltered and lonely," says Philip Booth. He emerged from that boyhood to become a respected poet whose work reflects a strong identification with his native New England. More than a regional poet, Booth imparts in his poems truths relevant to all people.

Philip Booth was born in 1925 in Hanover, New Hampshire.

Meet Robert Hayden

Too nearsighted to play sports with his friends, Robert Hayden found companionship in books. After high school, Hayden read many contemporary poets, including those of the Harlem Renaissance, and won a scholarship to college. In graduate school he studied under the poet W. H. Auden, who greatly influenced him. Regarding civil rights, Hayden said, "I have the right to deal with these matters . . . as an artist."

Robert Hayden was born in 1913 in Detroit, Michigan, and died in 1980.

First Lesson

Philip Booth

Lie back, daughter, let your head
be tipped back in the cup of my hand.
Gently, and I will hold you. Spread
your arms wide, lie out on the stream
and look high at the gulls. A dead-
man's-float is face down. You will dive
and swim soon enough where this tidewater
ebbs° to the sea. Daughter, believe
me, when you tire on the long thrash°
to your island, lie up, and survive.
As you float now, where I held you
and let go, remember when fear
cramps your heart what I told you:
lie gently and wide to the light-year
stars, lie back, and the sea will hold you.

---

8 When the tide flows out to sea, it *ebbs* and is called the "ebb tide."

9 In this context, *thrash* means "a swim," from the idea that a swimmer beats, or thrashes, the water with the arms.

Father and Kids, 1997. Patti Mollica. Oil on canvas, 10 x 7¾ in.

Viewing the painting: What images from the poem does this painting reflect? Do you find the tone of the painting similar to the tone of the poem? Explain.

Those Winter Sundays

Robert Hayden

Sundays too my father got up early
and put his clothes on in the blueblack cold,
then with cracked hands that ached
from labor in the weekday weather made
banked fires° blaze. No one ever thanked him.

I'd wake and hear the cold splintering, breaking.
When the rooms were warm, he'd call,
and slowly I would rise and dress,
fearing the chronic angers of that house,

Speaking indifferently to him,
who had driven out the cold
and polished my good shoes as well.
What did I know, what did I know
of love's austere° and lonely offices?°

---

5 *Banked fires* are ones that have been covered with ashes to keep them burning at a very low level.

14 The word *austere* has a number of meanings: "severe; stern; strict; serious; simple." Similarly, *offices* can mean either "duties and responsibilities" or "favors and kindnesses."

Lynford, 1969. Karen Armitage. Oil on canvas. Private collection.

Viewing the painting: What words would you use to describe this man's expression and mood? Compare and contrast these traits to the personal qualities the speaker of the poem conveys to you.

Responding to Literature

Personal Response

What people or events in your own life do either or both of these poems bring to mind? Explain in your journal.

Analyzing Literature

First Lesson

Recall and Interpret

1. Who might the speaker be? Who is the speaker addressing? What activity is the speaker describing?
2. Summarize the advice the speaker gives in lines 1–8. What can you infer about the speaker's feelings from these lines?
3. The speaker tells the daughter she will "tire on the long thrash to your island." What do you think the long thrash to the island might **symbolize** or represent?
4. What is the literal meaning of the advice the speaker gives in lines 11–15? What broader meaning do you think the speaker might wish to convey? Explain.

Evaluate and Connect

5. Evaluate how the speaker's **tone,** or attitude toward the subject, contributes to the meaning and overall effect of the poem.
6. Do you think "First Lesson" is a good title for this poem? Why or why not? What lesson do you think it refers to? Explain.
7. Theme Connections How does this poem help you better understand the conflict that parents face between loving and protecting their children and helping them achieve independence?

Those Winter Sundays

Recall and Interpret

8. What did the speaker's father do on Sunday mornings in winter? As a child, did the speaker appreciate his father's efforts? How do you know?
9. Based on what the speaker says, what kind of life did the father live? What might you infer about the father's character, based on the information given?
10. What type of relationship did the speaker and his father seem to have? Support your response with details from the poem.
11. What does the speaker mean by "love's austere and lonely offices"? What has the speaker learned about his father since those winter Sundays?

Evaluate and Connect

12. Evaluate how the **mood,** or atmosphere, of the poem helps to reinforce its message.
13. Do you think that most people take for granted the many things that their parents or other family members do for them? Give specific examples to support your answer.
14. One critic said that this poem causes readers to "reevaluate their lives." Explain.

Literary ELEMENTS

Alliteration

Alliteration is the repetition of consonant sounds at the beginnings of words. In poetry, alliteration may be used to create a musical effect, to emphasize meaning, or to draw attention to particular words. Poets also use alliteration to help create a particular mood, or atmosphere, in a poem. Notice the alliteration in these lines from "First Lesson."

> *L*ie *b*ack, daughter, *l*et your *h*ead
> *b*e tipped *b*ack in the cup of my *h*and.

The repetition of the initial consonants *l, b,* and *h* produces a musical effect and helps create a mood of peace and tranquility. The alliteration also reinforces the speaker's meaning by drawing attention to the words the poet wants to emphasize. As you read poetry, pay attention to the way alliteration contributes to the overall meaning and effect of a particular poem.

1. Find several examples of alliteration in "First Lesson" and in "Those Winter Sundays." What words does the alliteration emphasize in each example?
2. What effects are created by each example of alliteration?

• See **Literary Terms Handbook,** p. R1.

Literature and Writing

Writing About Literature

Character Sketch Use the information in "Those Winter Sundays" to write a character sketch of the speaker's father. As you write your sketch, think about what is directly stated in the poem, as well as what can be inferred. Compare your character sketch with those created by other students.

Personal Writing

I Just Wanted to Say . . . Reread the journal entry you wrote in response to the Reading Focus on page 602. Then write a letter of thanks to the person who taught you an important life lesson. Explain how you have benefited from learning this lesson.

Extending Your Response

Literature Groups

Hidden Meaning A **metaphor** is a figure of speech that compares two things. Poets often use metaphors to help convey the poem's message. In your group, look for possible metaphors in "First Lesson" and "Those Winter Sundays." Create a list for each poem and jot down the group's ideas about what each metaphor is comparing. What impact do the metaphors have on the meaning of the poem? How do they affect your appreciation of the poem? Share your insights with the class.

Learning for Life

Survival Floating Imagine that you are reading "First Lesson" from a completely literal point of view, hoping to get advice on survival floating. Do research to find out what survival floating is, and when and how it should be done. Then evaluate the advice given in the poem. Create an illustrated poster that summarizes this information.

Listening and Speaking

Compare Oral Effects With a partner, take turns reading "First Lesson" and "Those Winter Sundays" out loud. Compare and contrast the **sound devices,** or techniques used to emphasize particular sounds in the poems. After hearing each other recite the poems, do you feel that you have a deeper understanding and appreciation of the poems and their meaning? Discuss these issues with your partner. Share and compare your conclusions with your classmates.

Save your work for your portfolio.

Vo•cab•u•lar•y Skills

Multiple-Meaning Words

Words with the same spelling but different meanings can sometimes be a source of confusion. Robert Hayden speaks of "love's austere and lonely *offices,*" and the reader who thinks he means "places where work is done" will fail to understand what Hayden is saying.

Some words happen to have the same spelling but do not share a history. *Bank* as Hayden uses it in "*banked* fires" and *bank* in a phrase such as "*banked* earnings" are two different words with completely different meanings. Dictionaries provide separate entries for these two words.

Confusion is more likely to occur when a reader must deal with the multiple meanings of a single word. The varied meanings of a word can range from extremely to only slightly different. Both *bank* and *office* have several related but different meanings.

Here are typical dictionary definitions for the transitive verb form of *bank* and for *office.*

bank *v.t.* **1.** to form into a bank; pile up; heap up: *Bank soil around the roses before the first frost.* **2.** to cause to slope up from an inside edge: *Bank the race track's curves to help cars hold the road.* **3.** to tilt or cause to slope to one side, especially while making a turn: *The pilot banked the plane.* **4.** to pile ashes on [a fire] or lessen a draft to cause slower burning: *Bank the fire before turning in for the night.*

office *n.* **1.** something done for another; an act of kindness; service: *to obtain a job through the good offices of a friend.* **2.** the duty, function, or role of a particular position: *to act in the office of advisor to the king.* **3.** a position of duty, trust, or authority: *named to the office of treasurer.* **4.** a place where work is done or business is carried out: *Go to the doctor's office.* **5.** a room assigned to a specific person or group in an organization: *His secretary works right outside his office.* **6.** those who carry on work in an office: *Inform the office regarding absences.*

EXERCISE

Use context clues to decide which definition of *bank* or *office* is used in each sentence below and write the number of that definition on your paper.

1. Her sharp turn *banked* the bicycle, but speed kept it upright.
2. Just *bank* the laundry up against the washing machine.
3. Absence from his beloved only *banked* his passion; nothing could extinguish it.
4. Base runners *bank* their bodies as they pass first, trying to stretch a single into a double.
5. Nearly half of the *office* is out with the flu.
6. Please stop by our main *office* and pick up a brochure.
7. I have lost respect for the man but not for the *office* he holds.
8. Sergio will faithfully carry out the *office* of classroom monitor.

MEDIA connection

Magazine Article

Many people feel a special connection to horses. A few have given back to wild horses in the West something they had lost—the freedom to run.

Halfway House for Horses

by Melanie L. Stephens, *Time,* January 1, 1990

Their high-pitched whinnies roll across the plains like a tumble-weed-scattering wind. At dusk one of them rears and paws the air, casting a silhouette that is the very image of freedom. These are mustangs, the legendary wild horses of the American West. Two decades ago, mustangs were headed for extinction. Now, at Mustang Meadows Ranch, a 32,000-acre spread near St. Francis, S. Dak., 1,500 of them have found sanctuary and a managed independence that may help assure their survival.

Descended from horses that escaped from Spanish herds, millions of mustangs roamed the prairie at the start of the 19th century. But as the wildness went out of the West and more and more rangeland was plowed for crops or fenced off for cattle, the number of mustangs dwindled. By 1970 only 17,000 were left, despite the passage of federal laws that banned the use of airplanes and motor vehicles to round them up for slaughter. In 1971 Congress responded to a massive letter-writing campaign by enacting the Wild Free-Roaming Horses and Burros Act, which assigned the federal Bureau of Land

Management [BLM] the responsibility for protecting these "living symbols of the historic and pioneer spirit of the West."

Under BLM, the mustangs have recovered: 42,000 horses now run free on the range. But their numbers have greatly surpassed the ability of the land to support them. To ease the overpopulation, BLM in 1976 inaugurated a national Adopt-a-Horse program, under which 90,000 wild horses have been sold to private owners. But the mustangs taken off the range annually include many that are too old, crippled, ugly or mean to make good pets. Until two years ago, thousands of unadoptable mustangs were crowded into dusty feeding pens in Nebraska, Nevada and Texas at a cost to taxpayers of $13 million a year.

Enter Dayton Hyde, an Oregon rancher with a reputation for unorthodox management and a deep interest in conservation. "In my travels I kept going by feedlots, seeing these poor creatures cooped up," says Hyde, 64. "I thought, 'That's no way to treat a wild horse.' My dream was to get these horses out of the feedlots and running free again."

In 1988 Hyde founded the nonprofit Institute for Range and the American Mustang [IRAM] in order to create sanctuaries—retirement homes of sorts—where unadoptable wild horses could once again roam freely. He convinced BLM that with foundation and public funds he could establish a self-sustaining sanctuary within three years. IRAM's first project was a 12,600-acre sanctuary in the Black Hills of South Dakota. . . . The project makes Hyde smile. "The horses are finally getting over their depression," he says. "They got so bored in the feedlots that they didn't know how to run anymore."

Hyde's ambition went beyond his successes at the Black Hills sanctuary. He next sought to establish a larger range that could accommodate thousands of horses. But since IRAM lacked both money and land, Hyde needed the help of a private investor. He turned out to be Alan Day, an owner of cattle ranches in Arizona and Nebraska. Day, says Hyde, "knew how to manage grass and was not afraid of the immensity of my dream."

The first mustangs arrived in August 1988. After being cooped up in corrals anywhere from one month to several years, they needed to readjust psychologically to the comparative freedom of the ranch's open pastures. By gradually approaching the wary mustangs in corrals, Day and his wranglers taught them to become comfortable around people. "They have had so much negative training before they get here, they think they are going to suffer if they see a man on horseback," says Day. "We want to show them that we are not the enemy."

Analyzing Media

1. What do you think—are people the enemy of wild animals? Explain your answer.
2. What actions can you take in your everyday life to improve the lives of wild animals?

Before You Read

Horses Graze and *A Blessing*

Reading Focus

Some people believe that animals have much to teach us if we pay attention. What have you learned from observing, interacting with, or reading about an animal?

Quickwrite Spend five minutes writing about what you learned and what it meant to you.

Setting a Purpose Read to see how two poets describe lessons that animals can teach.

Building Background

- Horses are hooved, herbivorous (plant-eating) mammals related to the zebra. They are herd animals well-adapted for living on the plains. Horses have wide, flat teeth designed for grinding grasses and other plants, and long foot bones designed for swift running. For centuries, people used horses extensively in warfare, agriculture, and transportation. Today, most horses are kept for sport and show.
- Horses have played an important role in literature and art. In cave paintings from the Ice Age, wild horses and cattle were the most prominent images. Because of their speed and vitality, horses in ancient Greek and Roman mythology, like the winged horse Pegasus, were associated with the sun and heavenly chariots. Today, the winged horse is a symbol for poetic inspiration.

Meet Gwendolyn Brooks

Gwendolyn Brooks recalled her youth as a "sparkly childhood, with two fine parents and one brother, in a plain but warmly enclosing two-story gray house." Her best times were at home with her family, where she wrote and read every day, dreaming of being a poet. Brooks's poetry, which she called "wild, raw, ragged free verse," earned her the Pulitzer Prize in 1950.

Gwendolyn Brooks was born in Kansas in 1917. She lived most of her life in Chicago, Illinois, where she died in 2000.

Meet James Wright

Referring to the small working-class town where he grew up, James Wright said, "I love the variety of Martins Ferry, a skinny place stretched out along the river between the railroad and the abrupt hills." Influenced by his childhood experiences, Wright wrote about poor people and social outcasts, and found dignity in the pain and sadness of living.

James Wright was born in Ohio in 1927 and died in 1980.

Horses Graze

Gwendolyn Brooks

Cows graze.
Horses graze.
They
eat
eat
eat.
Their graceful heads
are bowed
bowed
bowed
in majestic° oblivion.°
They are nobly oblivious
to your follies,°
your inflation,°
the knocks° and nettles° of administration.
They
eat
eat
eat.
And at the crest° of their brute satisfaction,
with wonderful gentleness, in affirmation,°
they lift their clean calm eyes and they lie down
and love the world.
They speak with their companions.
They do not wish that they were otherwhere.
Perhaps they know that creature feet may press
only a few earth inches at a time,
that earth is anywhere earth,
that an eye may see,
wherever it may be,
the Immediate arc, alone, of life, of love.
In Sweden,
China,
Afrika,
in India or Maine
the animals are sane;
they know and know and know
there's ground below
and sky
up high.

11 **majestic:** a quality of dignified greatness. **oblivion:** a lack of awareness or memory.

13 **folly:** a lack of good sense or a tragically foolish or wicked action.

14 **inflation:** an economic condition that occurs when consumer prices continuously rise or the purchasing power of money continuously declines; also, pomposity or empty pretentiousness.

15 **knock:** a sharp blow or hit. **nettle:** a weedy plant that releases a substance irritating to skin; metaphorically, nettle can be anything that irritates.

20 **crest:** a peak, high point, or climax.

21 **affirmation:** a positive judgment or an act or statement supporting the truth.

Earthenware Horse. Tang dynasty, China.

A Blessing

James Wright

Two Blue Horses (Zwei blaue Pferde), 1913. Franz Marc. Watercolor and india ink on paper, 7⅞ x 5¼ in. Solomon R. Guggenheim Museum, New York.

Just off the highway to Rochester, Minnesota,
Twilight bounds° softly forth on the grass.
And the eyes of those two Indian ponies
Darken with kindness.
They have come gladly out of the willows
To welcome my friend and me.
We step over the barbed wire into the pasture
Where they have been grazing all day, alone.
They ripple tensely, they can hardly contain their happiness
That we have come.
They bow shyly as wet swans. They love each other.
There is no loneliness like theirs.
At home once more,
They begin munching the young tufts of spring in the darkness.
I would like to hold the slenderer one in my arms,
For she has walked over to me
And nuzzled my left hand.
She is black and white,
Her mane falls wild on her forehead,
And the light breeze moves me to caress her long ear
That is delicate as the skin over a girl's wrist.
Suddenly I realize
That if I stepped out of my body I would break
Into blossom.

---

2 To *bound* is to move by leaping.

Responding to Literature

Personal Response

What images or descriptions in the poems did you find most striking?

Analyzing Literature

Horses Graze

Recall and Interpret

1. What animals does the speaker describe in this poem? To whom or what does the speaker compare them?
2. How does the speaker describe the animals in lines 7–11? Explain in your own words what the speaker means by "bowed in majestic oblivion."
3. How do the animals show their gentleness in lines 21–23? What might the animals be affirming?
4. According to the speaker, what do animals "know," and in what way are they "sane"? What might the poet be implying here about people?

Evaluate and Connect

5. Brooks uses only a few words to describe people. Why, in your view, might she have chosen the word *inflation?* Explain its meaning in the context of the poem.
6. What does the speaker think people could learn from animals? Review your response to the Reading Focus on page 610. How do the speaker's ideas compare to what you wrote?
7. How has this poem changed the way you see horses and cows? How has it changed the way you see people? Explain.

Recall and Interpret

8. What words does the speaker use in lines 1–10 to describe the ponies? What might this description convey about the speaker? Why?
9. According to the speaker, what feelings do the ponies express in lines 11–13? Why might they feel this way? Support your answer with evidence from the poem.
10. How does the speaker describe the slenderer animal? How do you think the speaker feels about that animal? Why?
11. Describe in your own words what the speaker experiences at the end of the poem. What message do you think the poet is communicating by describing this experience?

Evaluate and Connect

12. Which of Wright's **images** appeal to the sense of touch? Choose an image that you think is especially effective and explain why it is effective. (See page R6).
13. What, do you think, is the "blessing" referred to in the title of the poem?
14. What animals that you have known or read about seem similar to the animals described in the poem? Describe the similarities.

Literary ELEMENTS

Personification

Personification is a figure of speech that describes an animal as if it has human qualities, or an inanimate object, an idea, or force of nature as if it is alive or has human traits or feelings. Wright uses personification in "A Blessing" when he writes that the twilight "bounds." By personifying the twilight, Wright creates a strong visual image and communicates the sense that the natural world is alive. He also associates the twilight with the movement of the ponies, who actually do bound.

1. Give an example of the ponies being personified in "A Blessing" and tell what effect you think Wright was trying to achieve.
2. Give an example of the animals in "Horses Graze" being personified. What effect does this personification create?

- See **Literary Terms Handbook,** p. R9.

Literature and Writing

Writing About Literature

Analyzing Mood The **mood** of a poem is its general feeling or atmosphere. In a few paragraphs, write about the mood of each poem. Using details from the poem, tell how the mood is conveyed, what its effects are, and how it relates to the poem's message. Support your interpretation with evidence from the poems.

Personal Writing

Animal Understanding Using your response to the Reading Focus on page 610 as a starting point, write about a memorable relationship or encounter you've had with an animal. What was the relationship or encounter like? How did it affect you and why? Share your writing with a classmate.

Extending Your Response

Literature Groups

Animal Madness or Method? Both Wright and Brooks admire qualities they see in animals and seem to share a longing for the lost animal in themselves. Do you think people have lost their connection with animals and their own animal nature? Do you agree with Brooks' implication that animals are more "sane" than people? Debate these questions within your group and use details from each poem to support or refute each other's ideas. Share your conclusions with the class.

Listening and Speaking

Wild and Woolly Animal Stories Using a tape recorder or taking notes, interview several friends and/or relatives about enlightening or unusual experiences they've had with animals, including pets, domestic animals, and wildlife. Share your best stories with the class.

Learning for Life

Naturalist's Log Brooks and Wright paid close attention to the behavior and habits of the animals they wrote about. Making sure not to frighten or disturb it, observe a wild animal, a pet, or another domestic animal. Take notes about what it eats, when it is active and when it sleeps, what dangers it faces, and so on. Summarize your information in a report to share with the class.

Reading Further

You might enjoy these poems:

"The Bean Eaters" from *The Bean Eaters* and "Medgar Evers" from *After Mecca* by Gwendolyn Brooks. "Sitting in a Small Screenhouse on a Summer Morning" and "Autumnal" from *Above the River: The Complete Poems* by James Wright.

Save your work for your portfolio.

Reading & Thinking Skills

Understanding Denotation and Connotation

How would you react if someone called you "slender"? How might you react to being called "scrawny"? You would probably respond differently. *Slender* and *scrawny* have the same **denotation,** or explicit meaning. They both describe something that is lean or thin. However, the words have very different **connotations,** or meanings that go beyond the simple literal definition. Connotations are the feelings and values commonly associated with a word. The word *slender,* for example, has a positive connotation. It implies a pleasing slimness. The word *scrawny,* on the other hand, has a negative connotation. It suggests a malnourished appearance.

In his poem "A Blessing," James Wright uses the connotations of words to create a gentle, loving image of two horses. Words such as *nuzzled* and *delicate* suggest tenderness, gentleness, and gracefulness. Even the word *munching* has a connotation of gentleness. Imagine the difference in effect if the poet had used the word *chomping* instead.

In this poem, Wright also purposefully pairs words that have negative connotations with words that have positive ones. For example, at the end of the poem, the narrator says, "I would break / Into blossom." While the word *break* usually has a connotation of destruction, it is paired with *blossom,* which suggests springtime. The phrase thus brings to mind an image of joyous rebirth.

- For more about denotation and connotation, see **Reading Handbook,** p. R81.

EXERCISE

Read the following passage from Gwendolyn Brooks's poem "Horses Graze." Then answer the questions below.

> **Their graceful heads**
> **are bowed**
> **bowed**
> **bowed**
> **in majestic oblivion.**
> **They are nobly oblivious**
> **to your follies,**
> **your inflation,**
> **the knocks and nettles of administration.**

1. Which words have a positive connotation? Which words have a negative connotation?
2. How does Brooks use connotation in this passage to compare "you" to "them"?

Writing Workshop

Business Writing: Interview

An interview is a focused conversation in which an interviewer questions another person—the subject—on a topic. You will be interviewed when you apply for college or for a job, and you might interview potential employees or clients as part of your job. Interviewing is also a great way to get material for your writing. For example, direct comments from an interview can enliven nonfiction writing. **In this workshop, you will conduct an interview and write it so that it can stand on its own as an informative written piece.**

- As you write your interview, refer to the **Writing Handbook,** pp. R58–R71.

EVALUATION RUBRIC

By the time you complete this Writing Workshop, you will have

- prepared clear, open-ended questions
- effectively organized the interview
- begun the write-up of the interview with an attention-getting hook
- provided necessary background information
- used exact quotations from the person you have interviewed
- presented a write-up of the interview that is free of errors in grammar, usage, and mechanics

The Writing Process

PREWRITING

PREWRITING TIP

"Do your homework." Good interviewers learn as much as they can about their subject before asking questions.

When you request an interview, explain your purpose and make an appointment. Be polite, friendly, and businesslike.

Consider your purpose

The way you conduct and write your interview will depend on your purpose. If the interview is for business, you will ask questions designed to get specific information. For example, you might ask a potential employee about his or her work experience. If your interview is for a magazine article or to gain material for another piece of writing, you would probably ask other kinds of questions. For instance, you might want general information about the subject's life, or you might need to have a conversation focused on a more specific topic, such as your subject's views of love.

After the interview, your purpose will be to present that information to your readers. Your presentation will suffer if you don't get all the information you need from the interview, so be sure to ask the right questions.

Choose an audience

Before you start the interview, think about how much your audience knows about the topic you will explore with your subject. Try to put yourself into the minds of your readers and think of the questions they would want answered if they were interviewing your subject. You may need to ask some simple questions just to get background information that your audience will need.

Explore ideas

Your interview will be most productive if you focus your topic and plan your questions in advance. For example, in an interview on love and loss, you might explore topics that touch on

- the reasons for love lost, as in "Well, I Have Lost You; and I Lost You Fairly."
- the way love affects a lover's views, as in "Shall I Compare Thee to a Summer's Day?"
- a child's coming to understand a parent's love, as in "Those Winter Sundays."
- the distance that can come between friends, as in "Simile."
- the love of a pet or other animal, as in "A Blessing."

Clustering is a good way to focus your ideas for an interview. Start by writing down the general topic you want to cover. Circle it. Then surround that circle with related ideas. Connect each of those ideas with others, creating groups, or clusters, of ideas. For example, a student who wanted to write about an elderly aunt's views of love and loss began a cluster like this one.

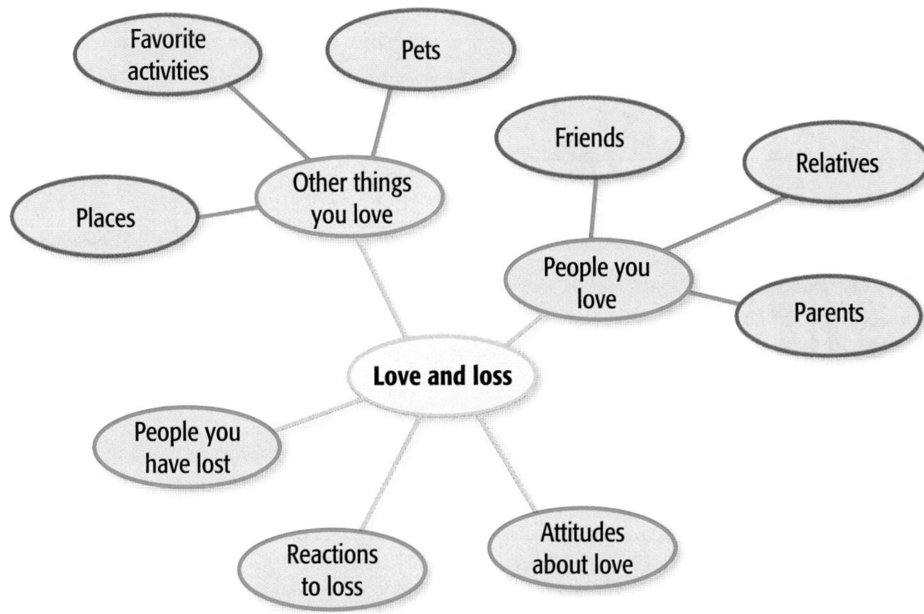

Prepare questions

Choose the ideas in the clusters that seem most appropriate for your purpose. Then compose questions around those ideas.

The success of an interview depends on asking good questions. Prepare questions that

- require more than yes or no answers.
- are clearly worded and easily understood.
- are related directly to your topic and purpose.

Ask on-the-spot questions

Be flexible during the interview. Listen closely to the subject's answers and be aware of opportunities to ask follow-up questions. This diagram shows how an insight would have been lost if the interviewer had plowed ahead with a prepared question instead of considering a follow-up question.

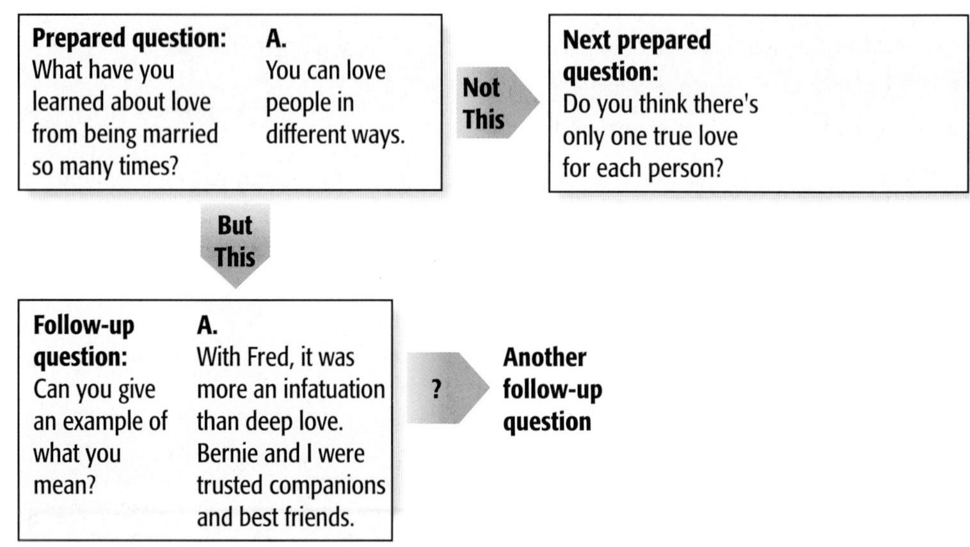

During the interview: Take notes

Even if you use a tape recorder, written notes will help you organize the information you get on tape. Listen carefully. Write words and phrases that summarize your subject's ideas. When a remark stands out, write the exact words and enclose them in quotation marks.

Make a plan

After the interview, plan to present the information you have gathered in a way that will make it understandable and interesting. You can use **chronological order** to present a narrative of the interview itself. However, many written interviews are more effective with the points arranged in **order of importance.** If you decide to use order of importance, take a tip from retailers. When they have a sale, they put the sale items at the back of the store, so that shoppers have to pass everything else to get to them. Put your most important or most interesting items at the end.

Use this order-of-importance organizer to help you put the sections of your interview into the most effective order.

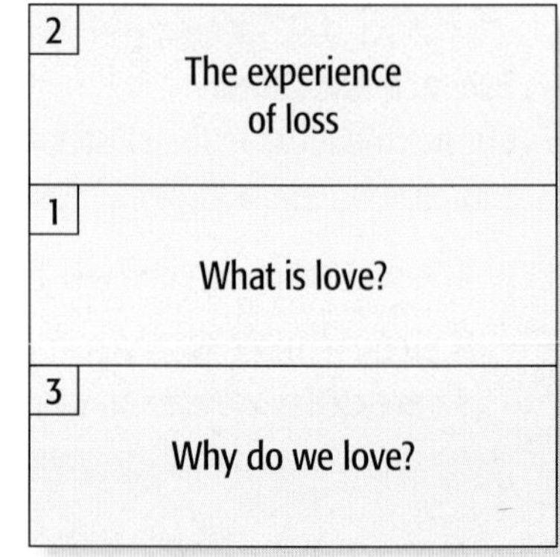

If you haven't already done so, gather your questions into related groups. Choose the three most important groups. Give each one a title. Write the titles of the groups in the blocks in any order. Then jot the key questions and their answers in the block, too. Finally, number the blocks in the order you will write about them. Review

DRAFTING

Drafting Tip

Adding details about the setting of the interview will make readers feel that they were there.

Start by selecting from your notes. Just write down the best of what you have in your notepad or on tape.

Hooks and previews

To catch your readers' attention, use a hook. Pick something interesting that your subject said and use it in your introduction. To hold your readers' attention, use a preview. Tease readers in the introduction with an intriguing piece of information that will be developed later in the interview.

Write your draft

Check your notes and plan. Keep the writing flowing. Alter your plan if new ideas come.

STUDENT MODEL

HOOK

It's not only movie stars who get married multiple times. At 92 my Great Aunt Lucille gives the actress Elizabeth Taylor a run for her money.

PREVIEW

I talked to Lucille about love and loss since she obviously has experienced a lot of each.

Complete Student Model on p. R116.

REVISING

Revising Tip

Don't change your subject's words. Check your notes carefully.

Evaluate your work

Let your draft "rest." Then use the **Rubric for Revising** to help you make revisions.

Have a writing conference

Read your written interview to a writing partner and discuss the **Rubric for Revising.**

STUDENT MODEL

I visited Lucille in her comfortable room [in a nursing home] in Riverdale, New York, where she [has] lived since her last husband died several years ago. I asked her if she [had] always wanted to be married. "It was wonderful growing up with so many sisters," she said. "But we were competitive. We made bets about which one of us would get married first." [In reply,] Lucille told me she grew up in a family of five girls.

Complete Student Model on p. R116.

Rubrics For Revising

Your revised interview should have

- ☑ a hook to grab your readers' attention
- ☑ sufficient background information
- ☑ direct, exact quotations of your subject's responses to your questions
- ☑ a clear focus with main points presented in a logical order
- ☑ a conclusion that effectively summarizes the subject's main points

Your revised interview should be free of

- ☑ inaccurate quotations or other details that might misrepresent your subject
- ☑ errors in grammar, usage, and mechanics

EDITING/PROOFREADING

When your interview has the form and content you want, edit it carefully for errors in grammar, usage, mechanics, and spelling. Use the **Proofreading Checklist** on the inside back cover for help. Work through your manuscript several times, looking for only one kind of error at a time. Give your subject a copy of the interview to check and correct.

Grammar Hint

The possessive of *it* is *its.*

The contraction of *it is* is *it's.*

Do you think that the word love *has lost so much of it's meaning now that its equal to the word* like?

- For more about possessives, see **Language Handbook,** p. R25.

STUDENT MODEL

Complete Student Model

For a complete version of the model developed in this workshop, refer to **Writing Workshop Models**, p. R116.

Its inspiring to talk to my Great Aunt Lucille. She's found love so many times in her life. She says that despite her three marriages, she believes people shouldn't worry too much about falling in love, instead they should find peace with themselves and letting life take it's own course.

Complete Student Model on p. R116.

PUBLISHING/PRESENTING

Presenting Tip

Photos of your subject are ideal illustrations. Portions of a taped interview can provide audio "illustrations" for a live presentation.

You might want to use your interview as a script to perform for the class. For a written presentation, you might submit the interview to a magazine that specializes in your subject's field of work. Interviews are often welcome as articles for school newspapers or magazines. Be sure that your work meets the requirements of the publication. Be sure to get your subject's approval of your plans before you go ahead with them.

Reflecting

Now that you've interviewed someone else, interview yourself. In your journal, conduct an interview about the interview experience. Be sure to ask yourself what you learned as a writer and how that will influence your goals for your next piece of writing.

Save your work for your portfolio.

Theme 8 Issues of Identity

What determines who you really are? Is it your background and experiences? The way you think and respond? What other people say about you? The poems in this theme examine several aspects of identity.

THEME PROJECTS

Listening and Speaking

Casting Call   Play the part of a casting agent.

1. With a group, choose at least three poems from this theme that you think could be turned into films.
2. Brainstorm a list of actors or other public figures who could portray the main characters of the poems.
3. Plan speeches that will convince the director to cast the actors you've chosen. Each member of the group should take a turn explaining to the class why your choices are best.

Performing

Each poem has a rhythm that affects the mood of the piece.

1. With a small group, choose three poems that have strong and different rhythms.
2. Think about how you could use performance to stress these poems' rhythms. For example, one person could read the poem while others play percussive instruments. Or you could do a choral reading, with members expressing rhythm by echoing, whispering, or shouting.
3. Perform your pieces live or record them ahead of time and play them for the class.

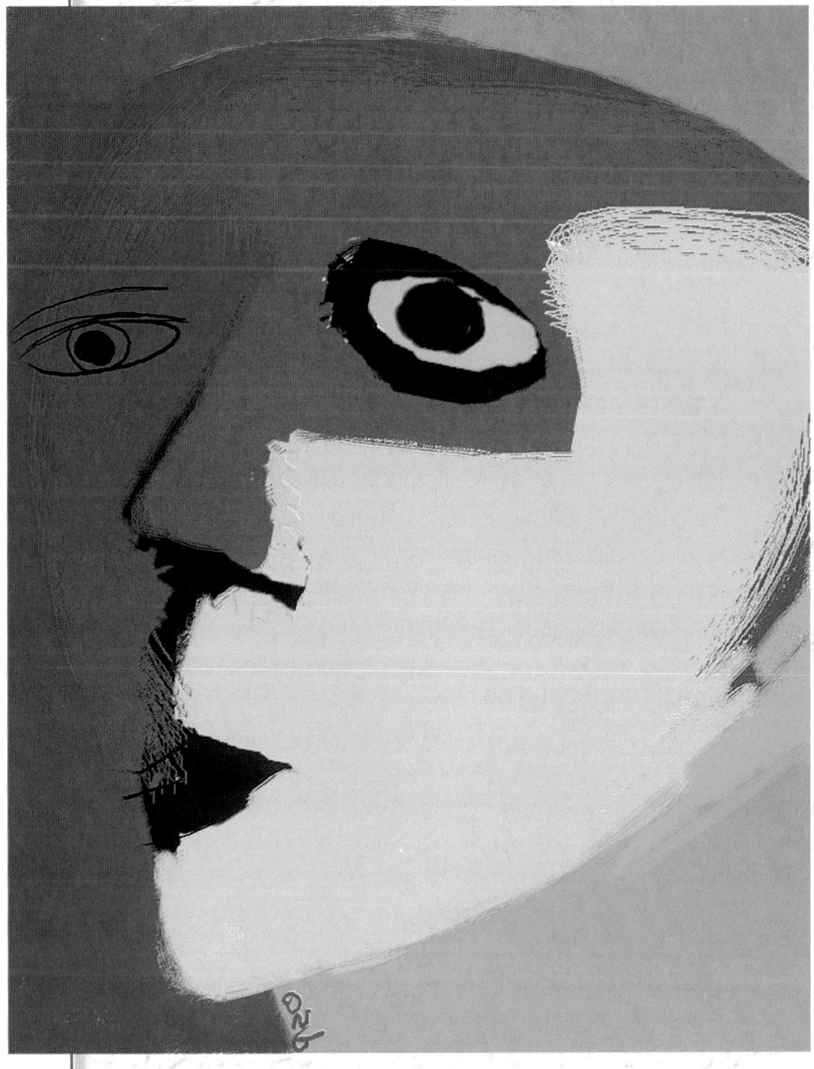

Electra #1, 1996. Diana Ong. Computer illustration.

Before You Read

Afro-American Fragment and *Heaven*

Reading Focus

Why do you think so many people are interested in their cultural heritage, or their family's history, customs, beliefs, and values?

List Ideas Make a list of reasons you might have for studying your cultural heritage.

Setting a Purpose Read to learn how the speakers are influenced by their cultural heritage.

Building Background

Did You Know?

- After visiting Africa, Langston Hughes realized that his primary cultural influences were not African but African American: "I . . . loved the surface of Africa and the rhythms of Africa—but I was not Africa," said Hughes. "I was Chicago and Kansas City and Broadway and Harlem." Indeed, Hughes was an important figure in the Harlem Renaissance—the intellectual and artistic movement that African Americans created in the New York City neighborhood of Harlem during the 1920s.
- The discovery of gold in California in 1848 sparked a worldwide "gold rush" of fortune seekers. Driven by poverty at home, thousands of Chinese men migrated to California, hoping to return home rich. By the 1860s, however, much of California's gold was gone, and many immigrants turned to railroad work for money. Enduring arduous, sometimes deadly working conditions, at one point as many as 12,000 Chinese worked for the Central Pacific Railroad, helping to complete the first transcontinental railway.

Building the Union Pacific, Wyoming, 1868.

Meet Langston Hughes

Langston Hughes won "instant" fame in 1925 when poet Vachel Lindsay dined at the hotel where Hughes was working. Hughes left three of his poems next to Lindsay's plate; Lindsay liked the poems, and when Hughes arrived at work the next day, reporters were waiting to interview the "bus boy poet."

Langston Hughes was born in Joplin, Missouri, in 1902 and died in 1967.

Meet Cathy Song

Cathy Song prefers to be classified not as an Asian American writer, but as simply a writer. Song often writes about women's experiences and family relationships. One of her best-known poems, "Picture Bride," describes her Korean grandmother coming to the United States at twenty-three as a mail-order bride. Song now teaches writing and has published three books of poetry.

Cathy Song was born in 1955 in Honolulu, Hawaii.

Afro-American Fragment

Langston Hughes

So long,
So far away
Is Africa.
Not even memories alive
Save those that history books create,
Save those that songs
Beat back into the blood—
Beat out of blood with words sad-sung
In strange un-Negro tongue—
So long,
So far away
Is Africa.

Subdued° and time-lost
Are the drums—and yet
Through some vast mist of race
There comes this song
I do not understand,
This song of atavistic° land,
Of bitter yearnings lost
Without a place—
So long,
So far away
Is Africa's
Dark face.

---

13 Here, *subdued* means "toned down; softened."

18 In this context, *atavistic* means "showing ancestral characteristics that have reappeared after being absent for many generations."

Heaven

Cathy Song

He thinks when we die we'll go to China.
Think of it—a Chinese heaven
where, except for his blond hair,
the part that belongs to his father,
everyone will look like him.
China, that blue flower on the map,
bluer than the sea
his hand must span like a bridge
to reach it.
An octave° away.

I've never seen it.
It's as if I can't sing that far.
But look—
on the map, this black dot.
Here is where we live,
on the pancake plains
just east of the Rockies,
on the other side of the clouds.
A mile above the sea,
the air is so thin, you can starve on it.
No bamboo trees
but the alpine equivalent,
reedy aspen with light, fluttering leaves.
Did a boy in Guangzhou° dream of this
as his last stop?

---

10 In music, an *octave* (ok′ tiv) refers to eight notes in a scale. On a piano keyboard, an octave is any group of eight white keys in a row, a distance of seven to eight inches.

24 Formerly called Canton, *Guangzhou* (gwäng′ jō′) is a large city in southern China.

I've heard the trains at night
whistling past our yards,
what we've come to own,
the broken fences, the whiny dog, the
rattletrap cars.
It's still the wild west,
mean and grubby,
the shootouts and fistfights in the back
alley.
With my son the dreamer
and my daughter, who is too young
to walk,
I've sat in this spot
and wondered why here?
Why in this short life,
this town, this creek they call a river?

He had never planned to stay,
the boy who helped to build
the railroads for a dollar a day.
He had always meant to go back.
When did he finally know
that each mile of track led him further
away,
that he would die in his sleep,
dispossessed,°
having seen Gold Mountain,°
the icy wind tunneling through it,
these landlocked, makeshift ghost towns?

46 *Dispossessed* means "deprived of possessions or homes."

47 Enthralled by tales of California's gold, the Chinese began referring to California, and the United States more generally, as *Gam Saan,* or *Gold Mountain.*

It must be in the blood,
this notion of returning.
It skipped two generations, lay
fallow,°
the garden an unmarked grave.
On a spring sweater day
it's as if we remember him.
I call to the children.
We can see the mountains
shimmering blue above the air.
If you look really hard
says my son the dreamer,
leaning out from the laundry's
rigging,
the work shirts fluttering like sails,
you can see all the way to heaven.

52 *Fallow* land has been left unplanted or unfarmed for at least one growing season.

Responding to Literature

Personal Response

What questions would you like to ask each poet? Why?

Analyzing Literature

Afro-American Fragment

Recall and Interpret

1. What is the speaker's relationship to Africa? How do you think the speaker feels about that relationship? Cite details from the poem.
2. In the first stanza, to what songs do you think the speaker is referring? Explain what you think the speaker is talking about in lines 6–9.
3. What is the "song" the speaker refers to in the second stanza? What does this "song" seem to **symbolize,** or stand for? Explain.

Evaluate and Connect

4. Evaluate how **repetition** and **rhyme** help to convey the poem's meaning and message. (See Literary Terms Handbook, page R10.)
5. Theme Connections What does the poem's title seem to imply about the speaker's sense of identity?
6. What place or places have helped shape your own sense of identity? Explain.

Heaven

Recall and Interpret

7. Who is the boy the speaker describes in the first stanza? What is his dream?
8. Where does the speaker live? What seems to be her attitude toward this place? Explain.
9. Who is the "boy" introduced in line 24? What did he do, and what happened to him? What does the speaker's description of him imply about her feelings toward him?
10. What does China seem to represent to the speaker's son? According to the speaker, why does her son have this attitude toward China? How do you think the speaker feels about his attitude?

Evaluate and Connect

11. What place do you think about or dream of visiting like the speaker's son thinks about China? Explain.
12. What is your reaction to the conversational tone of this poem? How does it affect your attitude toward the speaker and the message of the poem?

Literary Criticism

Du Bose Heyward describes Langston Hughes as "possessed of an unfaltering musical sense." Write a brief essay exploring how Hughes's use of literary elements and sound devices in "Afro-American Fragment" reflects his keen musical sense. Use specific examples from the poem to support your opinions.

Literary ELEMENTS

Free Verse

Free verse is poetry that has no fixed meter–that is, it does not have a regular pattern of stressed and unstressed syllables. Most free verse has irregular line lengths and lacks a regular rhyme scheme. For example, these lines from "Heaven" are written in free verse: "It's still the wild west, / mean and grubby, / the shootouts and fistfights in the back alley." Many poets of the 1900s have chosen to explore the looser, more subtle effects of free verse.

1. Why might Song have chosen to write "Heaven" in free verse? Do you think it is an effective form for the ideas and emotions she expresses? Why or why not?
2. Is "Afro-American Fragment" written in free verse? How do you know? Do you think the chosen style matches the poem's subject matter? Explain.

- See **Literary Terms Handbook,** p. R5.

Literature and Writing

Writing About Literature

Analyze Diction Because poetry is a concentrated form of writing, poets choose words carefully to get the most meaning from each word. Write two or three paragraphs analyzing the word choice, or **diction,** in "Afro-American Fragment" or "Heaven." What words and phrases are especially effective in conveying the poet's intended meaning? Explain how the poet's choice of words affects your understanding and appreciation of the poem.

Personal Writing

Home Sweet Home What might it be like to live in a different country? What would you miss most about your current life? What would you miss least? What difficulties might you face in adjusting to life in another culture? As you record your ideas about this topic in your journal, consider how the culture in which you grew up has helped to shape your own identity.

Extending Your Response

Literature Groups

Past and Present In your group, identify the ways the speakers in these poems, as well as the son and grandfather in "Heaven," seems to feel about their family history and cultural heritage. Then, using information from your discussion and the ideas you listed for the Reading Focus on page 622, debate this question: Is it important for people to appreciate and preserve their cultural heritage? Why or why not? As a group, decide which side has the stronger argument, and then share your ideas with other groups.

Listening and Speaking

Cultural Traditions Interview an older family member or a family friend to learn about cultural traditions that have been preserved over the years. Ask the person to explain the significance and importance of each tradition. Share what you have learned with the class.

Internet Connection

Virtual Visits One way to learn about other cultures is to "visit" them on the Internet. Choose a culture that interests you and use a search engine to locate Web sites about it. Share your findings with the class.

Save your work for your portfolio.

Before You Read

The Base Stealer and *To Satch*

Reading Focus

Think about a time when you felt full of energy and confidence.

Freewrite Spend about three minutes freewriting about that time. What were the circumstances? What did you accomplish?

Setting a Purpose Read to learn about two athletes who display great energy and confidence.

Building Background

Did You Know?

- In baseball, base stealing is a battle of wits between pitcher and base runner. The base runner's goal is to advance to the next base or to so rattle the pitcher that he or she makes a mistake. The pitcher's goal is to stop the runner.

  The runner takes a leadoff, or stands a few feet from the base ready to steal. Timing and a quick eye are crucial. The pitcher might throw to the batter or to the base to "pick off" the runner. The runner is thus pulled in both directions–forward to the next base and back to the base he or she is straying from.

- Leroy "Satchel" Paige, also known as "Satch," was a Baseball Hall of Famer whose legendary pitching career lasted almost thirty years. Although Paige began pitching in the Negro leagues in the 1920s, his major-league career did not begin until 1948, a year after Jackie Robinson became the first African American player in modern major-league baseball. Paige, who stood over six feet three inches tall, had long, lean legs and was known for kicking out his left leg to an almost impossible height during his windup, a move he referred to as "blacking out the sky." The title of his autobiography, *Maybe I'll Pitch Forever,* refers to the extraordinary length of his career.
- Although Samuel Allen never got to see Paige pitch, he met him one day after a sporting event in Washington, D.C. Allen introduced himself and handed Paige his poem "To Satch." Paige read it and said, "I'm mighty glad you stopped me."

Meet Robert Francis

Robert Francis had a love-hate relationship with poetry. "I do not like poetry. I dislike it. Much of it I detest," he wrote in his autobiography. Despite these sentiments, Francis devoted most of his life to writing poetry. He published more than a dozen books and taught at writing workshops across the country.

Robert Francis was born in Upland, Pennsylvania, in 1901 and died in 1987.

Meet Samuel Allen

Samuel Allen advises young writers to "find meaning in [your] surroundings and in the events that are part of [your] life." He adds, "No matter how humdrum one's life may be, there is meaning and poetry if one has the sight to see it." He still writes today, but laughingly confesses that "the muse doesn't visit as often as she used to."

Samuel Allen was born in Columbus, Ohio, in 1917.

The Base Stealer

Robert Francis

Poised between going on and back, pulled
Both ways taut like a tightrope-walker,
Fingertips pointing the opposites,
Now bouncing tiptoe like a dropped ball
Or a kid skipping rope, come on, come on,
Running a scattering of steps sidewise,
How he teeters, skitters, tingles, teases,
Taunts° them, hovers like an ecstatic bird,
He's only flirting, crowd him, crowd him,
Delicate, delicate, delicate, delicate—now!

---

8 To *taunt* is to challenge in a scornful, insulting way.

To Satch

Samuel Allen

Sometimes I feel like I will *never* stop
Just go on forever
Till one fine mornin
I'm gonna reach up and grab me a handfulla stars
Swing out my long lean leg
And whip three hot strikes burnin down the heavens
And look over at God and say
How about that!

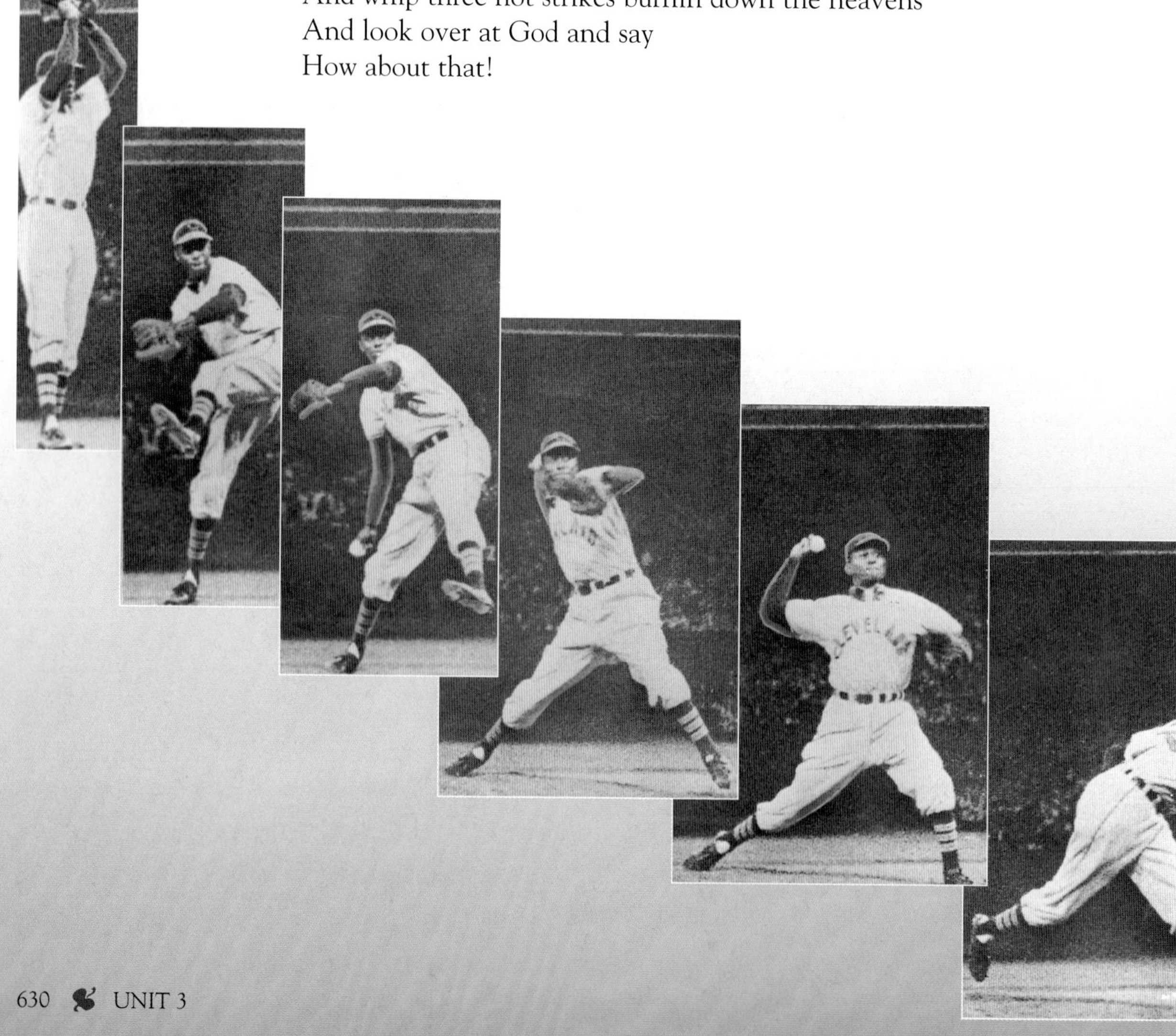

Responding to Literature

Personal Response

Which of the two players from the poems do you admire more? Why?

Analyzing Literature

The Base Stealer

Recall and Interpret

1. Identify several **similes** in the poem. (See Literary Terms Handbook, page R12.) What two things are being compared in each simile? What sense do these comparisons give you about the act of base stealing?
2. How would you explain the action described in lines 6–9 in your own words?
3. What do you think the speaker is describing in the last two lines of the poem? How do you know?

Evaluate and Connect

4. How does the use of **repetition** affect the **tone,** or atmosphere, of the poem? Give several examples.
5. Why do you think the poet chose not to reveal the outcome of the action?
6. Some people think base stealing is the most exciting part of a baseball game. What aspect of your favorite sport do you find most exciting? How does that compare with the description in this poem?

To Satch

Recall and Interpret

7. What do you think the speaker is referring to in lines 1–2? How would you describe the speaker based on these two lines?
8. What does the speaker plan to do "one fine mornin"? What might you infer about the speaker's outlook on life from this description?
9. What do you think the poet's attitude is toward the speaker? Explain.

Evaluate and Connect

10. How does the Background information on page 628 help you better understand this poem?
11. Evaluate how the use of **imagery** adds to your understanding and appreciation of the poem. (See Literary Terms Handbook, page R6.)
12. Many fans admired Satchel Paige. Think of an athlete whom you admire. What do you admire most about this person?

Literary ELEMENTS

Hyperbole

Hyperbole is a figure of speech in which an obvious overstatement or exaggeration is made for either serious or comic effect. When the speaker in "To Satch" says, "I'm gonna reach up and grab me a handfulla stars," the reader knows he cannot really grab stars–yet the exaggeration conveys the speaker's high level of skill and exuberant love of pitching a baseball.

1. Find another example of hyperbole in Allen's poem, and describe its effect.
2. Is there hyperbole in "The Base Stealer"? Explain.
3. Write your own example of hyperbole in a line or two, and share it with a classmate.

- See **Literary Terms Handbook,** p. R6.

Literature and Writing

Writing About Literature

Evaluate Poetic Form Both poems were written as a single stanza. Why do you think the poets chose this form instead of breaking their poems into more than one stanza? What effect does the use of a single, uninterrupted stanza create in these poems? List your ideas, and then develop them in a paragraph or two.

Creative Writing

To ??? Review your answer to question 12 on page 631. Write a letter to this person or to someone else you admire, saying what you admire about him or her. In your letter, you might want to focus on the aspect of the person's accomplishments that you admire the most. If you wish, share your letter with the class.

Extending Your Response

Literature Groups

Poetic Portrayal As a group, discuss the ways Francis and Allen portray the energy and confidence of the base stealer and Satch. Consider diction, punctuation, and such poetic devices as repetition, figurative language, and sound devices. Then look back at your responses to the Reading Focus on page 628, and choose one experience that most of the group can identify with. Discuss how you would create a poem similar to "The Base Stealer" or "To Satch" about that experience. Share either your ideas or your poem with the rest of the class.

Interdisciplinary Activity

Sports History: African American Athletes For many years, African American athletes such as Leroy "Satchel" Paige were excluded from participating at certain levels of professional sports. Use the library or the Internet to learn about the struggles and triumphs of such African American athletes as boxer Joe Louis, track stars Jesse Owens and Wilma Rudolph, and baseball player Jackie Robinson. Share your findings.

Learning for Life

Sportscasting Imagine that you are a radio or television sportscaster covering the events described in the two poems. Write a brief description of each one for your sportscast and deliver it to the class.

Reading Further

You might also enjoy the poem "Touchdown" from *Every Round and Other Poems,* Allen's most recent volume of poetry, which also includes "To Satch."

Save your work for your portfolio.

Listening, Speaking, and Viewing

Oral Interpretation of a Poem

Have you ever heard poets recite their work, either in person or on recordings? If you have, you probably gained a deeper understanding and appreciation of the poems you heard. But anyone can prepare and deliver an oral presentation of a favorite poem, based on his or her own interpretation of the work.

Preparing Your Oral Interpretation

Follow these steps as you prepare your oral interpretation of a poem.

- As you read the poem silently, think about who the speaker might be. Whose "voice" do you hear? Does it belong to the poet, to an unidentified person, or to a character the poet has created? (In some poems, the speaker may be an animal or even a thing.) What is the speaker's tone, or attitude toward the subject of the poem? Think about how you might use your voice to convey that tone.
- Read through the poem again, this time focusing on your own reaction to it. What emotions do you experience as you read? What ideas and questions come to mind? Jot down your responses to the poem, and look up any unfamiliar words. Has the poet used imagery or figurative language? Make notes about how the poet's choice of language helps convey the intended meaning. Think about what words, phrases, or sentences you will emphasize in your oral interpretation.
- Notice how the poet has used rhyme, rhythm, and alliteration. How do these devices affect you? How do they affect the mood of the poem? Consider how you will emphasize sound devices as you recite or read the poem aloud.
- Remember to pause at the end of a line only if there is a punctuation mark or a natural pause there. Otherwise, read through the ends of lines, even rhyming lines, until you reach a proper place to pause.
- Practice reciting or reading the poem aloud. Experiment with your voice, using volume, speed, and other vocal devices to convey your own interpretation of the poem. Remember that your goal is to help the listener "hear" the poem as you do.

ACTIVITY

Prepare an oral interpretation of a poem that has captured your imagination. You might choose "The Base Stealer," "To Satch," or another poem you have read in this unit. Follow the suggestions given above as you practice reciting or reading the poem aloud. Then share your oral interpretation with a group. After everyone in your group has made his or her oral interpretation, discuss your understanding of each one.

MEDIA connection

Magazine Article

Your current actions can affect your future life, but there will always be some things you can't control. In this article, an athlete contemplates the player strike that may end his long baseball career.

Making Hay

by Tom Verducci—*Sports Illustrated*, September 12, 1994

The bushes need trimming. The barn out back is in need of repair. The green '57 Chevy, the first car he ever called his own, stands like some beleaguered sentry over the backyard, awaiting a fresh coat of paint before it becomes his eldest son's car. The carpet must be cleaned (thanks to the puppy) and the hay over at the cattle ranch needs to be baled, and surely he cannot forget his promise to take the three boys fishing. There is much for Rich (Goose) Gossage to do, and goodness knows he has the time to get around to all of it.

There is no ball game tonight, and there might never be another one for Gossage, who, though seated on a chair in front of his Colorado Springs house, appears prepared should one, like a brushfire, break out.

"For me [playing baseball has] been like going to Disneyland and riding the best ride in the whole place and never getting off. That's what I wish people understood. We're players. There's nothing we'd rather be doing than playing baseball right now."

Gossage is housebound because of a player strike that is now in its fourth week, with no sign that it will end anytime soon.

Someday there will be baseball in major league cities again. There is no recovery, though, of a ballplayer's most precious commodity: time. It runs out especially quickly if you're a 43-year-old pitcher and four teams in the past five years have already decided you're finished.

Twenty-four years have passed since that day he ran home to the one-bedroom house on Beacon Street in Colorado Springs, flung open the door and announced, "Mom, I've got a job working as a counselor at the summer camp!" Mother Goose had replied, "Son, you've got another job. There's a man here from the Chicago White Sox, and he says they've drafted you in the ninth round." So overwhelmed was the boy that he ran off alone into the mountains and cried.

Gazing now upon the same range of mountains, he knows that it might all be over, this heart-racing ride of a major league career.

Analyzing Media

1. Based on this article, how do you think Gossage would describe himself? What appears to be the most important part of his life?
2. What interests are most important to you now? Do you think these interests will still be important to you in a few years? Why or why not?

Before You Read

Ex-Basketball Player and *Miss Rosie*

Reading Focus

Is it better to achieve greatness and then fall from glory, or never to be great at all?

Chart It! List the pros and cons of both sides of this issue in a comparison chart like the one shown. Consider examples of once-great people you've known or heard about, such as actors, musicians, or athletes.

To achieve greatness, but fall from glory		To never be great at all	
Pros	Cons	Pros	Cons

Setting a Purpose Read about two characters who have known glory.

Building Background

Did You Know?

- In 1926 a premium brand of gasoline called Esso was first marketed in the United States. Today, Esso is known in the United States as Exxon; around the world, however, there are still Esso subsidiaries and service stations. At the time that Esso gasoline was common in the United States, packaged candies such as Necco Wafers, Nibs, and jujubes (jo͞o′ jo͞obs′) (Juju Beads) were popular, and people drank *phosphates,* beverages made with carbonated water and fruit syrup, much like modern soft drinks.
- In addition to writing poetry, Lucille Clifton has written nearly twenty books for children: "Well, I had six kids in seven years, and when you have a lot of children, you tend to attract children, and you see so many kids, you get ideas from that. And I have such a good memory from my own childhood, my own time. I have great respect for young people; I like them enormously." Although Clifton often writes about the effects of poverty, unemployment, and lack of education in black communities, she says her books "celebrate life."

Meet John Updike

John Updike has been admired and criticized for writing about ordinary life and ordinary characters. He believes, however, ". . . either nobody is a hero or everyone is. I vote for everyone." Updike has written scores of novels, poems, short stories, and essays. Many of his novels have appeared on best-seller lists.

John Updike was born in Pennsylvania in 1932.

Meet Lucille Clifton

Lucille Clifton has said, "In the bigger scheme of things the universe is not asking us to *do* something, the universe is asking us to *be* something." True to her words, Clifton is many things: a writer, teacher, mother, and spokesperson for the African American family, especially young people and women.

Lucille Clifton was born in New York in 1936.

Ex-Basketball Player

John Updike

Pearl Avenue runs past the high-school lot,
Bends with the trolley tracks, and stops, cut off
Before it has a chance to go two blocks,
At Colonel McComsky Plaza. Berth's Garage
Is on the corner facing west, and there,
Most days, you'll find Flick Webb, who helps Berth out.

Flick stands tall among the idiot pumps—
Five on a side, the old bubble-head style,°
Their rubber elbows hanging loose and low.
One's nostrils are two S's, and his eyes
An E and O. And one is squat, without
A head at all—more of a football type.

Once Flick played for the high-school team, the Wizards.
He was good: in fact, the best. In '46
He bucketed° three hundred ninety points,
A county record still. The ball loved Flick.
I saw him rack up thirty-eight or forty
In one home game. His hands were like wild birds.

---

8 ***Bubble-head style*** **refers to early gas station pumps that were sometimes topped with lighted glass globes.**

15 Flick ***bucketed,*** **or scored, 390 points playing basketball.**

Gas, 1940. Edward Hopper. Oil on canvas, 20¼ x 40¼ in. The Museum of Modern Art, New York. Mrs. Simon Guggenheim Fund.

He never learned a trade, he just sells gas,
Checks oil, and changes flats. Once in a while,
As a gag, he dribbles an inner tube,
But most of us remember anyway.
His hands are fine and nervous on the lug wrench.
It makes no difference to the lug wrench, though.

Off work, he hangs around Mae's Luncheonette.
Grease-gray and kind of coiled, he plays pinball,
Smokes those thin cigars, nurses lemon phosphates.
Flick seldom says a word to Mae, just nods
Beyond her face toward bright applauding tiers°
Of Necco Wafers, Nibs, and Juju Beads.

---

29 A sports stadium has *tiers,* or rows, of seats arranged one above another. Many restaurants have tiers of candies stacked near the cash register.

Yellow Hat, 1936. Norman Lewis. Oil on burlap, 36½ x 26 in. Collection of Loide Lewis and the late Reginald Lewis.

Viewing the painting: How does the woman in the painting compare with your image of the speaker in the poem? with your image of the young Miss Rosie? Which characteristics are the same and which are different?

Miss Rosie

Lucille Clifton

When I watch you
wrapped up like garbage
sitting, surrounded by the smell
of too old potato peels
or
when I watch you
in your old man's shoes
with the little toe cut out
sitting, waiting for your mind
like next week's grocery
I say
when I watch you
you wet brown bag of a woman
who used to be the best looking
gal in Georgia
used to be called the Georgia Rose
I stand up
through your destruction
I stand up

Responding to Literature

Personal Response
If you could speak to the characters in the poems, what would you say to them?

Analyzing Literature

Ex-Basketball Player

Recall and Interpret

1. Who is Flick Webb? What does the speaker remember about him? How would you characterize the speaker's attitude toward Flick's high school accomplishments?
2. How has Flick's life changed since high school and why?
3. What qualities does the speaker notice in Flick that reveal his past glory? Provide details from the poem.
4. Explain what happens in the poem's last stanza. How do you think the speaker views Flick as an adult? Use details from the poem to support your response.

Evaluate and Connect

5. Look again at the description of the street in the first stanza. Evaluate the meaning and effect of this image.
6. Think about your response to the Reading Focus on page 635. Do you think Flick's talent changed his life for the better or worse? Explain.

Miss Rosie

Recall and Interpret

7. Who is the speaker describing in this poem? What is the subject's current state, and how is it different from what she once was?
8. What do lines 9–10 imply about Miss Rosie?
9. In your opinion, what does the speaker think about Miss Rosie? What effect does Miss Rosie's life have on the speaker's life?

Evaluate and Connect

10. Clifton uses details that appeal to the senses to describe Miss Rosie. Give an example of a **sensory detail** in the poem, explaining what sense it appeals to and its effect.
11. How might you react to seeing someone you know fall into a state similar to Miss Rosie's? Explain.
12. In your opinion, does this poem present a stronger picture of Miss Rosie or of the speaker? Support your response with details from the poem.

Literary Criticism

Ronald Baughman writes of "Miss Rosie" that "the poem . . . functions both as a lament for the woman destroyed and as a tribute to the new black woman who rises from the ashes of her predecessor's destruction." With your classmates, discuss how the poem serves as both a lament and a tribute. What do you learn about the woman who has been "destroyed"? How does the speaker "rise from the ashes"?

Literary ELEMENTS

Tone

Tone is the reflection of a writer's or speaker's attitude toward the subject. In a poem, tone may be expressed through particular words, details, structure, and other poetic devices that convey certain emotions and that evoke an emotional response in the reader. For example, in "Ex-Basketball Player," the poet's use of basketball jargon helps create a familiar, conversational tone. To identify the tone of a poem, read the poem aloud and listen to how your voice sounds. The tone in your voice may reflect the tone of the poem.

1. How would you describe the tone of "Miss Rosie"? List the emotions that the tone conveys.
2. Does the tone of "Ex-Basketball Player" change in the poem, or does it stay the same? Support your response with details from the poem.

- See **Literary Terms Handbook,** p. R13.

Literature and Writing

Writing About Literature

Analyzing Approaches In "Ex-Basketball Player," the speaker tells readers about Flick Webb, the subject of the poem. In "Miss Rosie," the speaker addresses Miss Rosie directly. Write two or three paragraphs analyzing how effective each approach is at conveying a sense of the subject. Then examine how effective each poem might be if the approaches were switched–that is, what would "Ex-Basketball Player" be like if the speaker addressed Flick directly? How would the impact of Clifton's poem change if the speaker told readers about Miss Rosie? Discuss which approach seems more powerful to you and why.

Creative Writing

Speaking for Themselves Write a journal entry from the point of view of either Flick Webb or Miss Rosie. What might they say about their past and present circumstances? You may make up details, as long as they are consistent with the poems' representations.

Extending Your Response

Literature Groups

Value Statements In your group, discuss what these poems suggest about the value of beauty and athletic ability in our society. As a group, develop a statement that you think reflects each poet's views on these social values. Use details from the poems and your own experiences in formulating your statements. Then be ready to support your group's statements as you compare them with those of other groups.

Interdisciplinary Activity

Sports: Stats Just how great a player was young Flick Webb? Do some research to check out high school basketball records for 1946. Would scoring 390 points in a season have been outstanding then, or merely good? Would Flick have broken any records? If possible, look at your school's yearbook from 1946 or newspapers to get the hometown story. Share your discoveries with the class.

Performing

Different Perspectives Prepare a monologue in which you tell about Flick from the point of view of the secondary characters Berth or Mae. You may invent details as long as they don't contradict those in the poem. Perform your piece for the class.

Save your work for your portfolio.

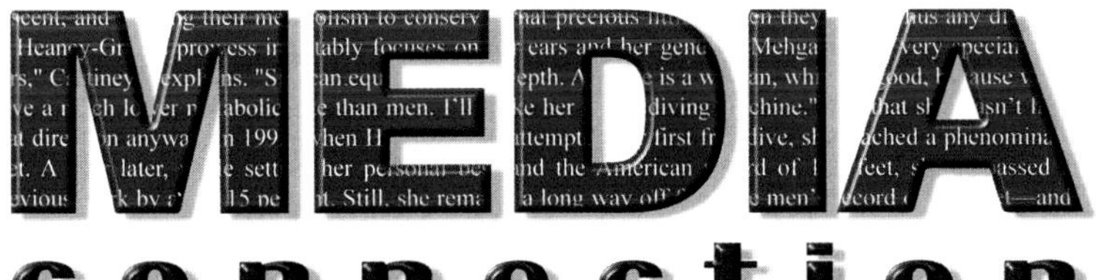

Interview

After hearing Lucille Clifton read her poetry, Bill Moyers interviewed her about her writing and her life. During the conversation, she discusses how she has managed to turn bad times into positive experiences.

Lucille Clifton

from *The Language of Life*

by Bill Moyers

MOYERS: The audience was really with you last night, riding every current of pleasure and surprise. I kept asking myself, should poetry *be* this much fun?

CLIFTON: I hope so. It *can* be fun, but that doesn't mean it's not serious. I'm very serious.

MOYERS: What happens to you when the audience comes back to you the way they did last night?

CLIFTON: Well, I sort of ride that energy. I often don't know what I'm going to read until I get in front of people, then I try to feel out where it seems to be going for them, and for me as well.

MOYERS: So, you're improvising—in a way.

CLIFTON: Well, I'm improvising what poems to read, yes. I often have a feeling for what I want to hear so I usually include a couple of those poems, but I also try to feel out what this particular group of people needs or wants or what poem should follow this one. It's like riding a wave, or what I like to think riding a wave must be like.

MOYERS: Listening to you recite your poems I imagined you having had a very hard life.

CLIFTON: I don't know if I think I've had a hard life, but I *have* had a challenging life. Everybody's life is more difficult than people think. . . . [P]oetry's probably saved my life. It has been *the* stable thing, something to love. . . . I think poetry has been the one faithful, good thing.

MOYERS: By doing *what* for you? Exactly what does it mean to sit and wrestle with those words until they line up on the page just the way you want them?

CLIFTON: I'm not sure that's how it happens exactly. I have a feeling that sometimes rather than wrestle and look for words, you have to be still and let them come. I was not trained as a poet, and I've never taken poetry lessons or had workshops. Nobody taught me anything much, really. So, I learned how to learn, and what I learned is that I could be still and allow the world and the impressions and the feelings—I'm very good with feelings—to come to me, and I could use our language to write them down.

MOYERS: You're good with feelings?

CLIFTON: I never learned to cut feelings off. I never learned that you were supposed to contain your feelings if you were an educated person, a sophisticated person. I did learn that I had to see things wholly and I learned to feel wholly as well, especially the complexities of what it means to be human and the complexities of what it means to be me.

Analyzing Media

1. Does Clifton think her life has been hard? Would she think your life is hard? What quality does she believe can help ease life's difficulties?
2. How do Clifton's strategies for coping with life compare with your own strategies?

Before You Read

The Road Not Taken and *We Are Many*

Reading Focus

How would you visualize your life's journey? Can you picture it as a road?

Illustrate Draw a picture of a road that depicts your life's journey. Show where you have been and where you think you are going. Mark and label five spots along the road where you have made or expect to make significant choices.

Setting a Purpose Read to see how the speakers in two poems reflect upon their life journeys.

Building Background

Did You Know?

- Robert Frost found delight and inspiration in the commonplace tasks and diversions associated with working on his New England farm: mending a wall, taking a walk through the woods, picking apples, or meeting a couple of tramps. Frost's poems, which contain rustic images and are deceptively simple, often present a moral problem or a question about life that the reader is left to ponder.
- Pablo Neruda was influenced in his decision to be a writer by the renowned Chilean poet, Gabriela Mistral. Mistral taught Neruda at the Temuco school, where she was headmistress, in southern Chile. With Mistral's encouragement and support, Neruda, a railroad worker's son, was able to pursue his passion for poetry.
- Both Frost and Neruda had reservations about their chosen profession. Robert Frost once confided, "Sometimes I have my doubts about words altogether. . . . They are worse than nothing unless they do something, unless they amount to deeds." Pablo Neruda at times expressed envy of the craftsperson who shapes tangible materials into objects of art. The poet's hand, he said, "grasps nothing but paper and pen, and gropes for the words to accommodate thoughts and feelings."

Meet Robert Frost

Robert Frost once said "A poem should begin in delight and end in wisdom." Frost, who in his youth worked at odd jobs, was invited to read his poem "The Gift Outright" at John F. Kennedy's presidential inauguration ceremony in 1961. Frost is the only American poet to be awarded four Pulitzer Prizes.

Robert Frost was born in 1874 in San Francisco. He died in 1963.

Meet Pablo Neruda

"Anyone who hasn't been in the Chilean forest doesn't know this planet. I have come out of that landscape, . . . to go singing through the world." Neruda, a spokesman for the poor and working class, found inspiration in simple objects, and even fashioned a piece of driftwood into a work table at which he wrote many of his poems. Neruda received the Nobel Prize for Literature in 1971.

Pablo Neruda was born Neftalí Ricardo Reyes Basoalto in 1904. He died in 1973.

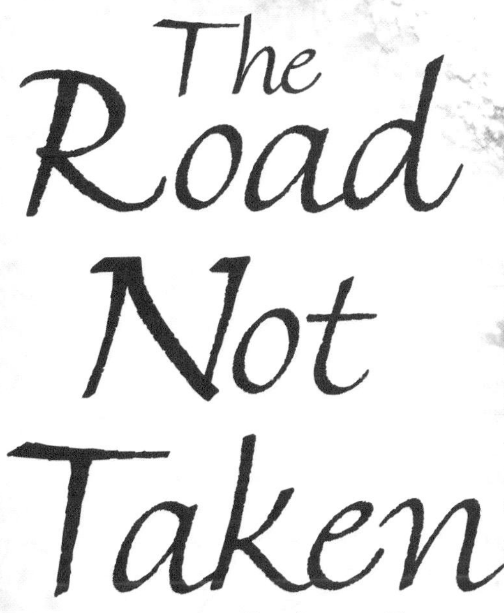

The Road Not Taken

Robert Frost

Two roads diverged° in a yellow wood,
And sorry I could not travel both
And be one traveler, long I stood
And looked down one as far as I could
To where it bent in the undergrowth;

Then took the other, as just as fair,
And having perhaps the better claim,
Because it was grassy and wanted wear;
Though as for that the passing there
Had worn them really about the same,

And both that morning equally lay
In leaves no step had trodden black.
Oh, I kept the first for another day!
Yet knowing how way leads on to way,
I doubted if I should ever come back

I shall be telling this with a sigh
Somewhere ages and ages hence:
Two roads diverged in a wood, and I—
I took the one less traveled by,
And that has made all the difference.

---

1 *Diverged* means that the roads go off in different directions.

We Are Many

Pablo Neruda

Translated by Alastair Reid

Of the many men whom I am, whom we are,
I cannot settle on a single one.
They are lost to me under the cover of clothing.
They have departed for another city.

When everything seems to be set
to show me off as a man of intelligence,
the fool I keep concealed on my person
takes over my talk and occupies my mouth.

On other occasions, I am dozing in the midst
of people of some distinction,
and when I summon my courageous self,
a coward completely unknown to me
swaddles° my poor skeleton
in a thousand tiny reservations.°

When a stately home bursts into flames,
instead of the fireman I summon,
an arsonist° bursts on the scene,
and he is I. There is nothing I can do.
What must I do to distinguish myself?
How can I put myself together?

All the books I read
lionize° dazzling hero figures,
always brimming with self-assurance.
I die with envy of them;
and, in films where bullets fly on the wind,
I am left in envy of the cowboys,
left admiring even the horses.

---

13 To *swaddle* is to wrap or bind with cloth.

14 Here, *reservations* means "doubts" or "hesitations."

17 An *arsonist* is someone who intentionally sets fire to a building.

22 To look upon or to treat people as celebrities is to *lionize* them.

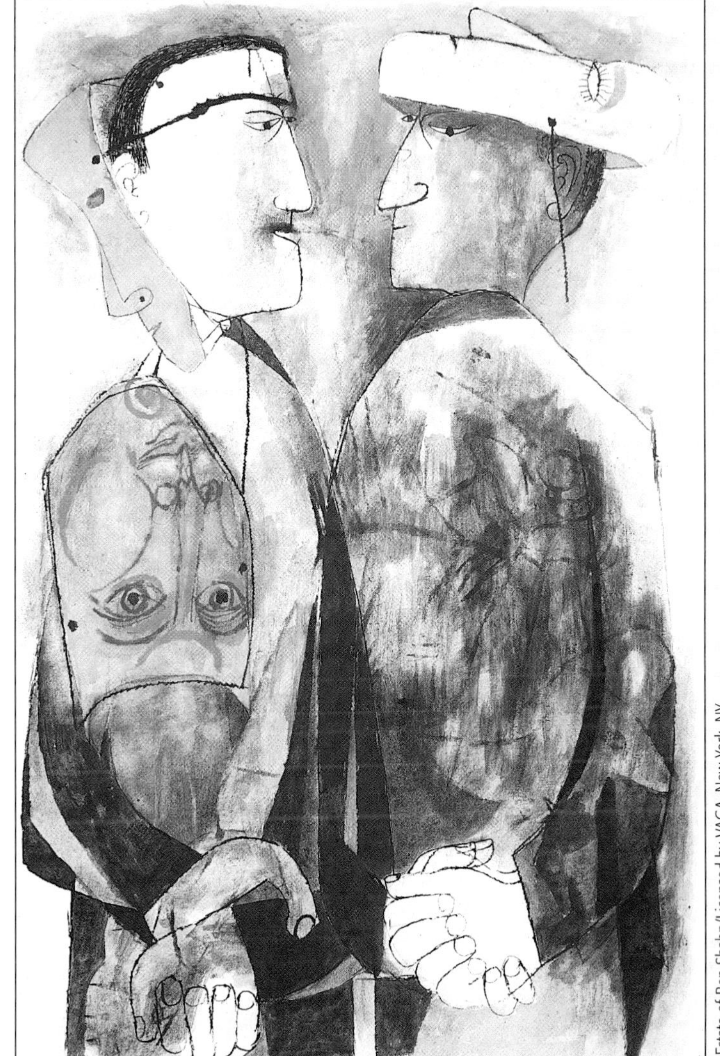

Conversations, 1958. Ben Shahn. Watercolor on paper, 39¼ x 27 in. Collection of Whitney Museum of American Art, New York. Purchase, with funds from the Friends of the Whitney Museum of American Art. 58.21.

Viewing the Painting: What ideas from "We Are Many" do you see represented in this painting? Explain.

But when I call upon
  my dashing being,
out comes the same
  old lazy self,
and so I never know just who I am,
nor how many I am, nor who we will be being.
I would like to be able to touch a bell
and call up my real self, the truly me,
because if I really need my proper self,
I must not allow myself to disappear.

While I am writing, I am far away;
and when I come back, I have already left.
I should like to see if the same thing happens
to other people as it does to me,
to see if as many people are as I am,
and if they seem the same way to themselves.
When this problem has been thoroughly explored,
I am going to school myself so well in things
that, when I try to explain my problems,
I shall speak, not of self, but of geography.

Responding to Literature

Personal Response

Which speaker do you identify with more closely? Why?

Analyzing Literature

The Road Not Taken

Recall and Interpret

1. What lines explain the decision the speaker makes? On what does the speaker base his decision?
2. What **sensory details** does Frost use to help you visualize the two roads? How are the roads alike? How are they different? (See Literary Terms Handbook, page R11.)
3. What name does the speaker give to the road he has decided to take? What do you think the two roads **symbolize** or represent? Explain.

Evaluate and Connect

4. **Theme Connections** Look at the illustration you created for the Reading Focus on page 642. Describe a time when you were faced with choices that affected your future. How does the poem reflect your own inner conflict over having to make two relatively equal choices?
5. Why do you think Frost entitled this poem "The Road Not Taken," rather than "The Road Taken"? Support your answer with details from the poem.

We Are Many

Recall and Interpret

6. What is the speaker's dilemma in "We Are Many"? How does the poet illustrate the speaker's problem?
7. What character traits does the speaker exhibit? Which traits would he like to exhibit?

Evaluate and Connect

8. **Hyperbole** is intentional exaggeration. This figure of speech may be used to achieve a humorous effect or to emphasize a serious situation. Identify one example of hyperbole in "We Are Many" and explain why the poet may have used it.
9. What is the predominant **mood,** or attitude, of the speaker in this poem? How does Neruda achieve this mood? How does the mood affect your own attitude toward the speaker's problem? (See Literary Terms Handbook, page R8.)
10. Do you think that the speaker's dilemma is realistic? Have you ever felt like the speaker does? Explain.

Literary Criticism

John T. Ogilvie writes that "The Road Not Taken" could be read as a "commentary on the price of the poet's dedication. The two roads that 'diverged in a yellow wood' represent a critical choice between two ways of life. The poet takes 'the one less traveled by,' the lonelier road, which, we can presume leads deeper into the wood." Write a letter to Ogilvie explaining in detail why you agree or disagree with his interpretation.

Literary ELEMENTS

Lyric Poem

A **lyric poem** is a short poem in which a speaker expresses intense personal thoughts and feelings. Lyric poetry got its name from the *lyre,* a stringed instrument that was used to accompany the singer of a lyric poem in ancient Greece. A lyric poem is melodic in its pattern of rhythm and may have rhymed or unrhymed verse. While a lyric poem might be about an object, a person, or an event, the focus of the lyric poem is on an emotional experience of the speaker, which may or may not be the poet. For example, the speaker in "The Road Not Taken" expresses his or her thoughts and feelings on the subject of making a decision about which path to follow.

1. Describe the emotions expressed by each poem's speaker toward the subject.
2. Which poem do you think is more melodic? Why?

- See Literary Terms Handbook, p. R7.

Literature and Writing

Writing About Literature

Understanding Connections Neruda and Frost wanted the general public to feel comfortable reading and listening to their poetry. Write one or two paragraphs explaining how you think the poets connect to ordinary people through the poems "The Road Not Taken" and "We Are Many." Use details from the poems to illustrate your ideas.

Personal Writing

Difficult Choices Write about a time when you were in a situation like that of one of the speakers in "The Road Not Taken" or "We Are Many." In a few paragraphs, or in a poem modeled on one of the poems above, describe your dilemma, how you faced it, and how you resolved it.

Extending Your Response

Literature Groups

Understanding Meaning Frost suggested that "The Road Not Taken" was simply about a friend with whom he took frequent walks. After their walks, the friend usually regretted that they had not taken a different path. Do you think this is all Frost wanted readers to learn from this poem? What does this poem teach you about life? Working with your group, discuss these questions and share your findings with the class.

Interdisciplinary Activity

Music: Songs of Life Find a piece of contemporary music related to the ideas explored in "The Road Not Taken" or "We Are Many." With your group, come to a consensus about how the song's message relates to one of the two poems. Then, play the song and present your ideas for the class.

Learning for Life

Career Choices What path might you choose in life? Where would you look for information on career possibilities? Use the Internet and the library to put together a source list on a career or on how to choose a career. Present your findings in a chart or poster and share it with the class.

Reading Further

You might also enjoy these works:

Listening: "Birches" and "The Road Not Taken" are read by Robert Frost in Volume One of *In Their Own Voices: A Century of Recorded Poetry.*

Poem: "Quartz opens its eyes in the snow," from *Las piedras del cielo / Stones of the Sky* by Pablo Neruda.

Save your work for your portfolio.

Before You Read

The Floral Apron and *My Mother Pieced Quilts*

Reading Focus

What things in your home have special value or significance to your family?

Journal Think of a cherished item in your home, such as a photograph, piece of furniture, or holiday decoration. Describe the item, and tell why it is important to your family.

Setting a Purpose Read about how two different household items take on great significance for the speakers.

Building Background

Did You Know?

- A plentiful, inexpensive seafood in China, squid is often called a "poor man's lobster." Cleaning squid is not difficult, but it is time-consuming because squid are so small. The cook first removes the head and tentacles, peels back the purple skin, and slits the body to remove the cartilage and the jellylike inner material. A popular way to prepare squid is to roll it in batter and fry it in hot oil. Squid has a firm, chewy texture and a mild flavor.
- Cleavers are large knives with wide, heavy blades. Cleavers are important and common tools in Chinese food preparation. Complicated chopping techniques are such a distinctive feature of Chinese cuisine that dishes are sometimes named according to the shapes and sizes into which the ingredients are cut.
- Most quilts have three layers: a top layer of pieced-together patchwork or design units, a middle layer of filler or batting, and a bottom layer of cotton or muslin. The top layer takes the longest to sew and often consists of a complex, colorful design. Traditionally, pieces of fabric for the top layer are cut from the family's old, discarded clothing.

Meet Marilyn Chin

Born to Chinese parents, Marilyn Chin was raised in Portland, Oregon, by her mother and grandmother. She believes that people like herself, Americans from all over the world, have important stories to tell: "We're breaking new ground, and *this* is the voice of America. My voice is one of the *many* voices of America."

Marilyn Chin was born in 1955.

Meet Teresa Palomo Acosta

"The poem 'My Mother Pieced Quilts' came to me at an early age—as I literally passed my hands along them . . . when I awoke on cold winter mornings," says Teresa Palomo Acosta. Later, as an adult, she was able to write the poem "fairly quickly," after "carrying its images inside" for so long. Acosta, who grew up in a small town in Texas, says she writes about everyday life from her own point of view as a Chicana woman.

Teresa Palomo Acosta was born in 1949.

The Floral Apron

Marilyn Chin

The woman wore a floral apron around her neck,
that woman from my mother's village
with a sharp cleaver in her hand.
She said, "What shall we cook tonight?
Perhaps these six tiny squids
lined up so perfectly on the block?"

She wiped her hand on her apron,
pierced the blade into the first.
There was no resistance,
no blood, only cartilage
soft as a child's nose. A last
iota of ink° made us wince.

Suddenly, the aroma of ginger and scallion°
fogged our senses,
and we absolved° her for that moment's
barbarism.
Then, she, an elder of the tribe,
without formal headdress, without elegance,
deigned° to teach the younger
about the Asian plight.

And although we have traveled far
we would never forget that primal lesson—
on patience, courage, forbearance,°
on how to love squid despite squid,
how to honor the village, the tribe,
that floral apron.

Girl in Blue Sweater, 1991. Huang Jinsheng. Oil on canvas, 21⅝ x 17¾ in. Private collection.

---

12 The *iota* (ī ō′ tə) *of ink* is a very small quantity of the squid's ink.

13 Young green onions are called *scallions.*

14 In *absolving* the woman, they freed her of guilt or blame.

17 *Deigned* means "willing to do something beneath one's normal level of dignity."

21 To have *forbearance* is to show self-control and restraint, especially when provoked.

My Mother Pieced Quilts

Teresa Palomo Acosta

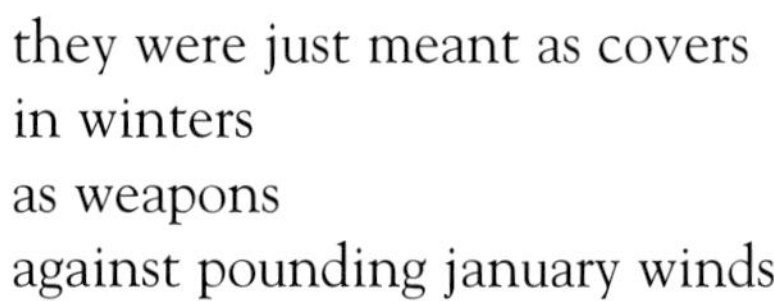

they were just meant as covers
in winters
as weapons
against pounding january winds

but it was just that every morning I awoke to these
october ripened canvases
passed my hand across their cloth faces
and began to wonder how you pieced
all these together
these strips of gentle communion cotton and flannel nightgowns
wedding organdies
dime store velvets

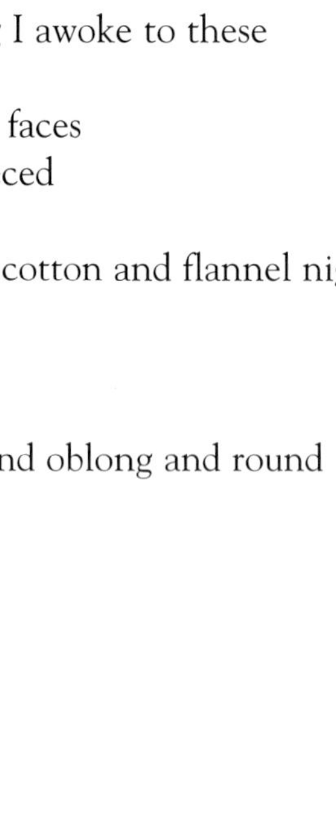

how you shaped patterns square and oblong and round
positioned
balanced
then cemented them
with your thread
a steel needle
a thimble

His Grandmother's Quilt. Phoebe Beasley. Collage, 30 x 40 in. Collection of John and Eunice Johnson.

how the thread darted in and out
galloping along the frayed edges, tucking them in
as you did us at night
oh how you stretched and turned and re-arranged
your michigan spring faded curtain pieces
my father's santa fe work shirt°
the summer denims, the tweeds of fall

in the evening you sat at your canvas
—our cracked linoleum floor the drawing board
me lounging on your arm
and you staking out the plan:
whether to put the lilac purple of easter against the red plaid of winter-going-
into-spring
whether to mix a yellow with blue and white and paint the
corpus christi° noon when my father held your hand
whether to shape a five-point star from the
somber black silk you wore to grandmother's funeral

you were the river current
carrying the roaring notes
forming them into pictures of a little boy reclining
a swallow flying
you were the caravan master at the reins
driving your threaded needle artillery across the mosaic° cloth bridges
delivering yourself in separate testimonies.

oh mother you plunged me sobbing and laughing
into our past
into the river crossing at five
into the spinach fields
into the plainview cotton rows
into tuberculosis wards
into braids and muslin dresses
sewn hard and taut to withstand the thrashings of twenty-five years

stretched out they lay
armed/ready/shouting/celebrating

knotted with love
the quilts sing on

---

25 A *Santa Fe work shirt* was named for the Santa Fe Railroad.
34 *Corpus Christi* (kôr′ pəs kris′ tē), Texas, is a port city on the Gulf of Mexico.
42 Here, *mosaic* refers to variously colored bits of materials.

Responding to Literature

Personal Response

What do you find most memorable, interesting, or powerful about these poems? Share your response with a classmate.

Analyzing Literature

The Floral Apron

Recall and Interpret

1. Who is wearing the floral apron? What is she doing in the first two stanzas? How does the speaker react to the woman's actions?
2. What happens in the third stanza? How does the attitude of the observers change? Why does it change?
3. What lesson does the speaker describe in stanza four? What do you think it means "to love squid despite squid"?
4. What does the floral apron seem to **symbolize,** or represent, to the speaker in the last line? Explain.

Evaluate and Connect

5. Theme Connections In your opinion, how did the speaker's experience affect his or her sense of identity?
6. What lessons about life have you learned in a kitchen? How do these lessons compare with the lesson the speaker learns?

My Mother Pieced Quilts

Recall and Interpret

7. Who made the quilts? What was the quilts' original purpose?
8. What childhood memories or associations do the quilts bring to the speaker's mind? What have the quilts come to **symbolize,** or represent, to the speaker? Give details from the poem to support your answer.
9. What two things does the speaker compare the mother to in lines 37–43? What is your interpretation of these comparisons? Explain.
10. In line 53, what do you think the speaker means by the statement that the quilts are "armed/ready/shouting/celebrating"? How do the quilts "sing on"?

Evaluate and Connect

11. What are the speaker's feelings toward his or her mother? What lines or details support your views?
12. What common household activities, such as gardening, carpentry, and cooking, are practiced in your household? Which of these, in your opinion, is most likely to leave a lasting impression in your life? Explain why.

Literary ELEMENTS

Imagery

Imagery is descriptive language that represents a feeling, triggers a memory or idea, or evokes a sensory experience. For example, an effective image might help a reader visualize a baseball game, hear an old woman laugh, feel the texture of a stone, smell rotting potatoes, or taste a sweet melon. In addition to creating vivid pictures, images also convey ideas and feelings. Teresa Palomo Acosta creates a compelling image of her mother sewing when she says her mother's thread "darted in and out / galloping along the frayed edges, tucking them in / as you did us at night." These lines show how skillful, confident, and loving the mother was, both in sewing and taking care of her children. In "The Floral Apron," Chin uses an image of a child's soft nose to convey the texture of the raw squid and to reveal the speaker's squeamishness.

1. Find two other examples of imagery in "My Mother Pieced Quilts." Explain their meaning and effect.
2. In your opinion, what is the most effective image in "The Floral Apron"? Why is it effective?

- See **Literary Terms Handbook,** p. R6.

Literature and Writing

Writing About Literature

Character Sketch Think about each speaker's personal observations about identity. What do they reveal about the speaker? Write a character sketch of one of the speakers based on what you know directly and what you can infer from the poem. Share and compare character sketches with a classmate.

Creative Writing

Prized Possession Reread the journal entry you wrote in response to the Reading Focus on page 648. Then write a letter to your family or to a specific family member telling your thoughts about the significant family item and what it means to you.

Extending Your Response

Literature Groups

Women Teachers The woman at the heart of each of these poems possesses important qualities, skills, and knowledge. What does each woman know? What does each woman teach and to whom? Work with your group to create a chart comparing and contrasting these women according to as many criteria as you can identify in both poems. Share your chart with the class.

Interdisciplinary Activity

Family and Consumer Sciences: Presentation Prepare a brief presentation in which you explain and, if possible, demonstrate a home art or craft, such as cooking, sewing, woodworking, canning, soap-making, or gardening.

Learning for Life

Design a Quilt Create a quilt block (section of several individual pieces) or a visual representation of a quilt block in any medium of your choice. Like the quilts in the poem, your design should represent an image or images that are meaningful to you.

Reading Further

You might enjoy this book and video:

An interview with Marilyn Chin in Bill Moyer's video series and companion book *The Language of Life: A Festival of Poets.*

Save your work for your portfolio.

Before You Read

A *Bus Along St. Clair: December* and *Freeway 280*

Reading Focus

What natural places have you seen or heard about that existed in the midst of an urban environment?

Discuss Think of such a place, and, with your group, discuss the following questions. How do people, animals, and nature adapt to urban environments? What do they lose? What do they gain?

Setting a Purpose Read two poems that explore what happens when people build over natural places.

Building Background

Did You Know?

- Margaret Atwood believes that "a voice is a gift; it should be cherished and used. . . . Powerlessness and silence go together." In her poetry, stories, and novels, Atwood speaks in her wry, intelligent voice and explores social concerns, such as isolation from nature and the destructiveness of gender roles.
- Although strongly influenced by her Spanish-speaking heritage, Lorna Dee Cervantes writes mainly in English because it is the language she spoke at home growing up: "I think to write poetry, you have to write in the language of your childhood, and the language you dream in." Spanish words, especially the names of trees and plants, often communicate meaning more precisely or poetically than English words. *Albaricoqueros* (äl bär′ ē kō kā′ rōs) are apricot trees; *cerezos* (ser ā′ zōs) are cherry trees; *nogales* (nō gä′ lās) are walnut trees. *Espinaca* (es′ pē nä′ kə) is spinach; *verdolagas* (ver′ dō lä′ gäs) is purslane; *yerbabuena* (yer′ bə bwā′ nə) is mint.
- The titles of both poems contain references to major cities. St. Clair is a densely urban, primarily commercial street in Toronto, Canada. Freeway 280 runs from San Jose, California, where Cervantes grew up, to San Francisco, California, where she was born.

Meet Margaret Atwood

As a child, Canadian poet and novelist Margaret Atwood spent summers in the woods, where her father, an entomologist, studied insects and her mother read to her. Often alone, Atwood spent much of her time reading: "I became a reading addict, and have remained so ever since." Today she is an internationally known and respected writer.

Margaret Atwood was born in 1939.

Meet Lorna Dee Cervantes

Mexican American Lorna Dee Cervantes clearly states who she is: "I'm a Chicana writer, I am a feminist writer, I am a political writer." Cervantes became a political activist in the feminist and Hispanic American cultural movements and she formed her own small press to publish the works of Hispanic American women writers. Today, Cervantes continues to run Mango Publications and to write poetry.

Lorna Dee Cervantes was born in 1954.

A Bus Along St. Clair: December

Margaret Atwood

It would take more than that to banish
me: this is my kingdom still.

Turn, look up
through the gritty window: an unexplored
wilderness of wires

Though they buried me in monuments
of concrete slabs, of cables
though they mounded a pyramid
of cold light over my head
though they said, We will build
silver paradise with a bulldozer

it shows how little they know
about vanishing: I have
my ways of getting through.

Right now, the snow
is no more familiar
to you than it was to me:
this is my doing.
The gray air, the roar
going on behind it
are no more familiar.

I am the old woman
sitting across from you on the bus,
her shoulders drawn up like a shawl;
out of her eyes come secret
hatpins, destroying
the walls, the ceiling

Turn, look down:
there is no city;
this is the center of a forest

your place is empty

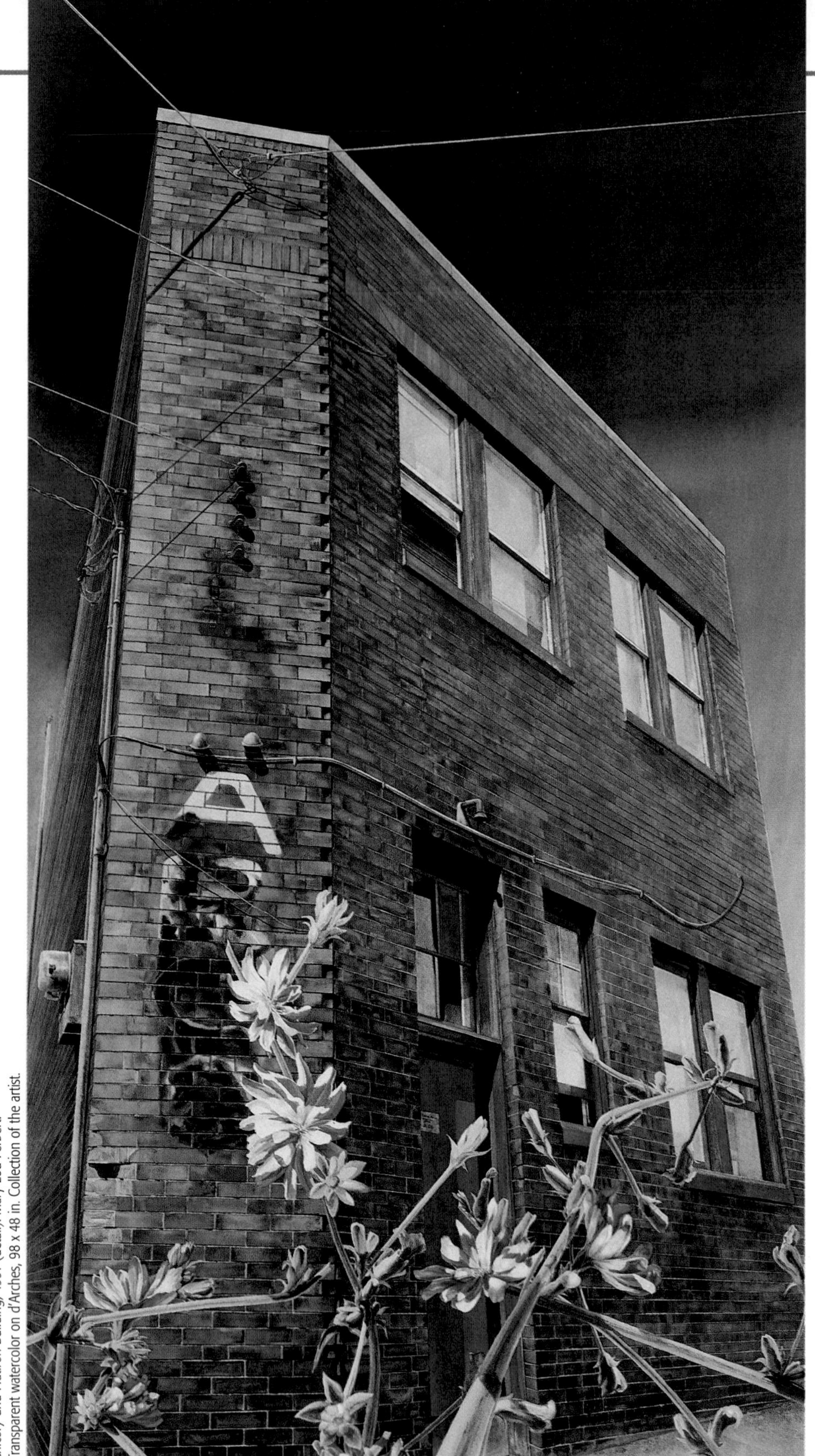

Chicory and Flatiron Building, 1991 (detail). Mary Lou Ferbert.
Transparent watercolor on d'Arches, 98 x 48 in. Collection of the artist.

Freeway 280

Lorna Dee Cervantes

Las casitas° near the gray cannery,
nestled amid wild abrazos° of climbing roses
and man-high red geraniums
are gone now. The freeway conceals it
all beneath a raised scar.

But under the fake windsounds of the open lanes,
in the abandoned lots below, new grasses sprout,
wild mustard remembers, old gardens
come back stronger than they were,
trees have been left standing in their yards.
Albaricoqueros, cerezos, nogales . . .
Viejitas° come here with paper bags to gather greens.
Espinaca, verdolagas, yerbabuena . . .

I scramble over the wire fence
that would have kept me out.
Once, I wanted out, wanted the rigid lanes
to take me to a place without sun,
without the smell of tomatoes burning
on swing shift° in the greasy summer air.

Maybe it's here
en los campos extraños de esta ciudad°
where I'll find it, that part of me
mown under
like a corpse
or a loose seed.

---

1 *Las casitas* (läs cə sē′ təs) is Spanish for "little houses."
2 *Abrazos* (ə brä′ zōs) is Spanish for "embraces" or "hugs."
12 *Viejitas* (vē′ e hē′ təs) means "old women" in Spanish.
19 In factories, hospitals, and some businesses the *swing shift* is the work period from midafternoon to midnight, between the day and night shifts.
21 *en los campos extraños de esta ciudad* (en lōs cäm′ pōs eks′ trä nyōs′ dā es′ tə sē′ oo däd′) In English, this is "in the strange fields of this city."

Responding to Literature

Personal Response

Describe an image that stays in your mind after reading the poems.

Analyzing Literature

A Bus Along St. Clair: December

Recall and Interpret

1. What is the **setting,** or place, at the beginning of this poem? What is the general atmosphere of this place? Support your answer with specific details from the poem.
2. According to the third stanza, what has happened to the speaker? Who might the speaker be in this poem? Explain and support your response.
3. In the last five stanzas, what does the speaker tell the person being addressed? What message do the speaker's words convey to you?

Evaluate and Connect

4. What does the title add to your understanding of the poem?
5. What do you think the speaker's last statement, "your place is empty" means? Do you agree with the speaker? Why or why not?
6. Which of the images in the poem best matches your own experiences of being in a dense urban area?

Freeway 280

Recall and Interpret

7. What does the speaker say that the freeway conceals? What might have gone on there in the past?
8. In stanza two, what remains despite the freeway? What does their presence tell you about them?
9. What did the speaker want from the freeway? How does she or he seem to feel about it now? Give details from the poem to support your answers.

Evaluate and Connect

10. Theme Connections Do you think the speaker will find "that part of me" that he or she is hoping to find in line 22? Why or why not?
11. In your opinion, how do the Spanish words enhance Cervantes's poem? How would the poem be different without them?
12. Think about your response to the Reading Focus on page 654. How does your group's view of urban environments compare with the views expressed in this poem?

Literary ELEMENTS

Speaker

Like the narrator in a work of prose, the **speaker** in a poem is the voice that communicates with the reader. The speaker may be a fictional person, an animal or thing, or even the voice of the poet. Often a poet invents a speaker with a particular identity in order to create a desired impact or impression. For example, the speaker in "Freeway 280" uses many Spanish words and expressions, indicating to the reader that the speaker could be Cervantes herself or someone with a similar background. The speaker's words also create a particular tone. The speaker in "A Bus Along St. Clair: December" addresses the reader angrily and powerfully, expressing a tone of indignation and perhaps vengeance.

1. How effectively does the speaker in "A Bus Along St. Clair: December" convey the poem's message? Use evidence from the poem to support your answer.
2. Describe the speaker's tone in "Freeway 280."

- See **Literary Terms Handbook,** p. R12.

Literature and Writing

Writing About Literature

Comparing Themes There are similarities between these poems, but how close are they in **theme,** or message? In a paragraph, state the main theme of each poem. Then write another paragraph or two discussing how the themes are alike and how they are different. Use specific details from the poems to elaborate on your thoughts.

Creative Writing

Along for the Ride Suppose the speaker in "A Bus Along St. Clair: December" shows up in your community on some form of public or private transportation. What might the speaker have to say? To whom might the speaker's words be addressed? Record the speaker's remarks as a poem, a monologue, or a dialogue.

Extending Your Response

Literature Groups

A Dim View of Progress Both speakers present views of the industrialized world. How do they make their case? Work with your group to find details in each poem that suggest how construction and building affect the world. Then decide how convincing, as well as how realistic, each speaker's case is. Share your opinions and your reasons with other groups.

Listening and Speaking

Understanding the Past Interview older relatives, friends, or neighbors who lived in your community a long time ago. Ask them to show you old photographs and describe what their neighborhood was like, what changes they've seen, and what they think about the changes. Share your findings.

Interdisciplinary Activity

Science: Close to Home As land is developed for human use, animal populations may move, decline, or become extinct. Working with a partner, contact your state or local park district, or local chapters of environmental organizations, to find out the status of animal species in your area. Present your findings in a chart or map.

Reading Further

You might enjoy these poems:

"The Ottawa River by Night" and "Bored" from *morning in the burned house,* new poems by Margaret Atwood.

Save your work for your portfolio.

Before You Read

Making a Fist and *What We Believe*

Reading Focus

How might a parent or other adult explain a difficult concept to a young child? What kinds of details should be told and what, if anything, should be left out?

Quickwrite Briefly write about which methods you think might work best in explaining things to young children. Give examples of when you think a factual approach is best and when you'd suggest a story or a fictional approach.

Setting a Purpose Read to find out how two speakers talk about things that are difficult to explain.

Building Background

Did You Know?

- To make a fist, the muscles in the hands have to contract. To contract, a muscle needs a signal from the brain, transmitted through the nervous system, as well as energy and oxygen, carried by the blood. When a person is dying, the heart stops pumping blood to the peripheral nervous system, which controls the hands and other extremities of the body. Therefore, making a fist becomes impossible.

- There are many Native American stories that explain the origin of horses. Apaches and Navajos were some of the first peoples to obtain horses. Their traditions suggest that horses were formed from colored clay. Similarly, a Skidi Pawnee story tells of a young boy who forms a pony out of mud and brings it to life.

Meet Naomi Shihab Nye

"I believe poetry is as basic to our lives . . . and to education as anything else there could possibly be," says Naomi Shihab Nye (shi′ häb nē). To promote her belief, Nye travels around the world, reading poetry and visiting schools. Growing up with a Palestinian father and an American mother, Nye lived in Missouri, the Middle East, and Texas. Nye sees poetry as a uniting force among people and cultures everywhere.

Naomi Shihab Nye was born in 1952.

Meet Anita Endrezze

Half Yaqui Indian and half European, Anita Endrezze (en′ drə zē) often writes about her Yaqui heritage, capturing the rhythms of the natural world and exploring relationships between humans and nature. Endrezze was raised in Hawaii and the western United States and attended college in Washington, where she later built a log cabin in a pine forest with her husband.

Anita Endrezze was born in 1952.

MAKING A FIST

Naomi Shihab Nye

For the first time, on the road north of
Tampico,°
I felt the life sliding out of me,
a drum in the desert, harder and harder
to hear.
I was seven, I lay in the car
watching palm trees swirl a sickening
pattern past the glass.
My stomach was a melon split wide inside
my skin.

"How do you know if you are going
to die?"
I begged my mother.
We had been traveling for days.
With strange confidence she answered,
"When you can no longer make a fist."

Years later I smile to think of that journey,
the borders we must cross separately,
stamped with our unanswerable woes.
I who did not die, who am still living,
still lying in the backseat behind all my
questions,
clenching and opening one small hand.

---

1 *Tampico* (tam pē′ kō) is a port city on Mexico's east coast.

Fritzmobile, 1984. Frank Romero. Acrylic on canvas, 66 x 108 in. Private collection.

Dakota Teaching, c. 1951. Oscar Howe. Watercolor, 13¾ x 21⅛. The Phillbrook Museum of Art. Museum Purchase 1951.8.

WHAT WE BELIEVE

Anita Endrezze

We believe in a land where sweating horses
kick up the dust, forming clay ponies
that sigh with red and yellow breaths.

We believe in a grass-weaver,
whose fingers make gentle blankets,
trusting in green, yellow, and brown.

We believe the horses will wear our blankets,
will drift forever past our campfires,
listening to us telling stories of long ago.

We believe that long ago we were horses
and grass, that our stories are our children's
dreams. We are waiting for the sound of hoof-beats

to rise from our throats and for the tall grasses
to stamp and snort in the wind. What we believe
will always be—and always be true.

Responding to Literature

Personal Response

With which poem do you more closely identify? Why?

Analyzing Literature

MAKING A FIST

Recall and Interpret

1. What does the speaker say he or she was feeling at the beginning of the poem? What do you think the third line is describing?
2. What does the speaker ask? Do you think the mother might have intended more than one meaning with her answer? Explain.
3. In your own words, state what the speaker is thinking and doing in the last stanza.

Evaluate and Connect

4. Why, do you think, is the speaker still carrying the memory of that road trip? Have you had a similarly memorable experience from your early childhood? Explain.
5. Do you agree with the speaker's comments and conclusion in the last stanza? Cite specific lines and give reasons.
6. **Theme Connections** In your opinion, does this poem present positive or negative observations about life? Support your answer with lines from the poem.

WHAT WE BELIEVE

Recall and Interpret

7. What do the speakers in this poem believe? What do their beliefs tell you about them?
8. In what does the grass-weaver trust? What do you think this trust means?
9. What are the speakers waiting for? Why do they have to wait?
10. What is the speakers' concluding comment? What is the meaning of that comment?

Evaluate and Connect

11. How do lines 12–14 affect the rest of the poem? Explain.
12. After reading the poem, what do you think the speakers value? Do you share any of these values? Why or why not?

Literary ELEMENTS

Symbol

A **symbol** is a sign that represents, or stands for, something else. In poetry and other forms of literature, a symbol is a word or phrase that conveys an idea or a range of ideas beyond its literal meaning. For example, in "Making a Fist," when the speaker refers to "that journey," she or he is talking about both a literal journey taken as a child and the larger journey of life. In "What We Believe," the blankets the grass-weaver makes for the horses might symbolize the care and respect the speakers feel toward the horses.

1. What does making a fist symbolize to the speaker in "Making a Fist"? Do you think this is an effective symbol? Why or why not?
2. What might the colors mentioned throughout "What We Believe" symbolize? How do these symbols affect the poem overall? Explain and support your answer.

- See **Literary Terms Handbook,** p. R13.

Literature and Writing

Writing About Literature

Comparing Observations In both poems, the speakers express strong observations about life. Briefly characterize the observations expressed in each poem. Then discuss similarities and differences between the two observations and how they affect the speakers' approach to life.

Personal Writing

Living Through It Using your response to the Reading Focus on page 660 as a starting point, write a few paragraphs about a time when an adult explained a difficult concept to you. Did the explanation help you to understand? Was it a good or memorable explanation? How could the explanation be improved? If you wish, share your writing with a classmate.

Extending Your Response

Literature Groups

Pass It Along Which of these two poems would you be more likely to recommend to another reader? Within your group, share what you think are the main ideas expressed in the two poems. Discuss which ideas seem most important to you and which ones you think could really benefit someone else. Share your group's conclusions with the class.

Internet Connection

Yaqui Culture Endrezze's poem reflects her Yaqui Indian heritage. Look on the Internet to find out more about Yaqui culture. Find out in what part of North America the Yaqui originally lived, what Yaqui art is like, and what life is like for Yaqui Indians today.

Performing

Performance Piece Work with a partner or several other students to prepare a dramatic reading or enactment of one of the poems. Use voices, movements, music, and props to help convey the poem's words, actions, mood, and meaning. Share your performance with the class.

Reading Further

You might enjoy these works:

"Thank You in Arabic" from *Never in a Hurry,* a collection of Nye's essays.

"The Girl Who Loved the Sky," a poem by Anita Endrezze from *Harper's Anthology of 20th Century Native American Poetry.*

Save your work for your portfolio.

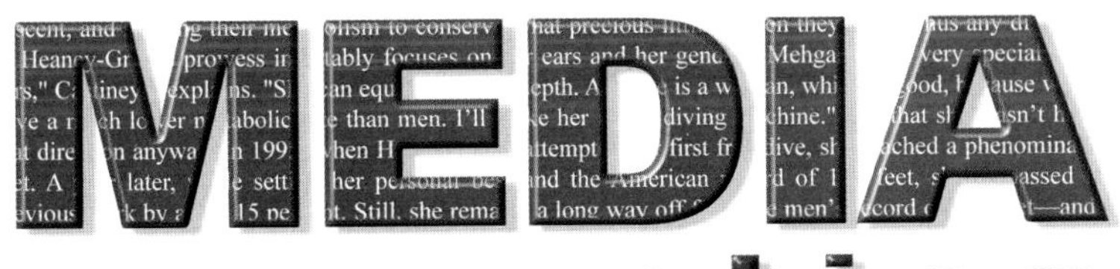

Travel Guide

When two cultures collide, misunderstandings sometimes occur. The more you know about the foreign cultures you come into contact with, the easier it is to blend in with them.

The Culturally Sensitive Traveler

from *Asia Through the Back Door*

by Rick Steves and Bob Effertz with John Gottberg

You can be a "Beautiful American." Your fate as a tourist lies in your own hands.

Cultural No No's

Before you land, you should at least know a few things that would shock the locals. Then you can decide whether you want to do just that or to fit in. The following are some cultural faux pas [social blunders] that apply to most places in Asia.

Saving Face

You'll be taking giant steps backward if you get angry, if you raise your voice and shout when you're not getting the service you expect or are otherwise frustrated. Not only will you be causing the person on whom you vent your anger a loss of face [embarrassment] but you yourself will lose respect in their eyes, which you can't expect to regain.

Body Language

The following gestures are regarded as universally offensive or obscene throughout Asia: pointing with your forefinger (use your open hand); beckoning someone (including a taxi) with a crooked forefinger (use your whole hand, palm down, waving toward you); making a fist and hitting it against your open palm.

Many Asians feel the head is the home of the soul. Resist patting even small children on the beanie; it's disrespectful.

If someone laughs or smiles at a seemingly inappropriate moment, don't be surprised. Smiles and laughter are used to cover up embarrassment and shock as well as to show happiness. In many Asian cultures (as well as in America), strong feelings are not shown in public.

In general, dress conservatively. In temples and mosques, anticipate modesty dress codes: keep your upper arms and back covered, and don't wear shorts. You may need to take your shoes off before entering a religious place. If in doubt, watch what the locals are doing.

When visiting a private home, be observant. In many countries, you'll remove your shoes before you enter.

Analyzing Media

1. Which cultural taboo do you think the average American would have the most trouble avoiding during a visit to Asia? Why would avoiding the taboo be difficult?
2. If you were planning a visit to another country, what else could you do to help ensure that you would be a "culturally sensitive traveler"?

Before You Read

Foreign Ways and *Song for My Name*

Reading Focus

If you visited another country and spent some time with the people there, what things about yourself, besides your language, might reveal that you are an American?

List Ideas Use your journal to list the clues that point to your national identity.

Setting a Purpose Read to find out how two speakers reveal their cultural identities.

Building Background

Did You Know?

- Chinese is different from most Western languages in that the words have only one syllable and do not in themselves contain varying stresses. Since many Chinese words sound alike, speakers convey different meanings by using tonal variations–words are said at high or low pitches, or at pitches that vary by rising or falling. Chinese consists of many different dialects, including Mandarin, which is China's official national language.

- Historically, the Chickasaw people are known for their tall, strong bodies and very dark eyes and hair, which the women typically wore in braids. The Chickasaw traditionally have lived in harmony with nature and used the cycles of the moon to measure time. During European colonization of North America, the Chickasaw and other Native American cultures had begun to decline. By the twentieth century, the Chickasaw people had been driven from their ancestral land, and centuries of Chickasaw tradition were lost. Major centers of the Chickasaw Nation exist today in Oklahoma.

Meet Diana Chang

The daughter of a Chinese father and a European-Asian mother, Diana Chang spent her childhood in China but moved to New York City when she was in high school. Although her works reveal her Chinese influences, she considers herself "an American writer whose background is Chinese."

Diana Chang was born in New York City in 1934.

Meet Linda Hogan

"If you believe that the earth, and all living things, and all the stones are sacred, your responsibility really is to protect those things," says Linda Hogan. Although Hogan belongs to the Chickasaw tribe, she grew up outside the Indian community. Today, Hogan expresses her commitment to Chickasaw values through her writings about relationships between humans and other species and as a volunteer for wildlife rehabilitation.

Linda Hogan was born in Denver, Colorado, in 1947.

Foreign Ways

Diana Chang

If I were in China this minute
and running after a friend
spied across from the hotel
I was staying at

waving to him, say
calling his name in Mandarin

Still they'd know me—
the body giving the person away
betrays a mind
of its own—

my voice from Duluth°
my lope with its prairie air

11 *Duluth* is a port city on Lake Superior in Minnesota; its citizens are mostly of northern European descent.

Night Lights of Kowloon. Dong Kingman. Watercolor, 22 x 22 in. Private collection.

Song for My Name

Linda Hogan

Before sunrise
think of brushing out an old woman's
dark braids.
Think of your hands,
fingertips on the soft hair.

If you have this name,
your grandfather's dark hands
lead horses toward the wagon
and a cloud of dust follows,
ghost of silence.

That name is full of women
with black hair
and men with eyes like night.
It means no money
tomorrow.

Such a name my mother loves
while she works gently
in the small house.
She is a white dove
and in her own land
the mornings are pale,
birds sing into the white curtains
and show off their soft breasts.

If you have a name like this,
there's never enough water.
There is too much heat.
When lightning strikes, rain
refuses to follow.
It's my name,
that of a woman living
between the white moon
and the red sun, waiting to leave.
It's the name that goes with me
back to earth
no one else can touch.

Seated Woman, 1990. Robert C. Gorman. Oil pastel drawing.

Viewing the painting: What specific images, words, or impressions from the poem do you think this painting reflects? Cite the line and explain the connection.

Responding to Literature

Personal Response

Which lines from each of the two poems made the most impression on you? Why?

Analyzing Literature

Foreign Ways

Recall and Interpret

1. What does the speaker imagine doing in the first two stanzas? What does this reveal about him or her?
2. In the third stanza, who would know the speaker? Why?
3. Where is the speaker's home? What else do the last two lines reveal?

Evaluate and Connect

4. Think about your response to the Reading Focus on page 666. Which of the clues that reveal the speaker's identity are similar to those that might reveal your own?

Song for My Name

Recall and Interpret

5. What details about family members does the speaker present in the first three stanzas? What do these facts suggest about the speaker's life?
6. What information about her mother does the speaker give in the fourth stanza? Why, do you think, does her mother love her name?
7. What conditions does the speaker's name evoke in the last stanza? What might her references to the moon, the sun, and the earth mean? Explain.

Evaluate and Connect

8. What effect does Hogan create by the **repetition** of the word "name" throughout the poem? (See Literary Terms Handbook, page R10.) In what ways is this poem a "song" for her name?

Literary ELEMENTS

Sensory Details

Sensory details are words, phrases, or images that convey sensory experiences–seeing, hearing, tasting, touching, and smelling. "Song for My Name," for example, appeals to the sense of touch as the speaker says, "Think of your hands, / fingertips on the soft hair."

1. Find three other sensory details in "Song for My Name." Tell what sense(s) each appeals to, and what effect each creates.
2. To what senses does "Foreign Ways" appeal? Explain and give examples.

- See **Literary Terms Handbook**, p. R11.

Writing Workshop

Creative Writing: Poem

Many of the poems you have read in Theme 8 paint striking portraits of distinctive characters–a base runner poised to steal a base, an old woman who's lost her youthful beauty, a mother who stitched her family's history into her quilts. **In this workshop, you will write a poem about a person–real or fictional–who has interested or inspired you.**

- As you write your poem, refer to the **Writing Handbook**, pp. R58–R71.

Evaluation Rubric

By the time you complete this Writing Workshop, you will have

- written a poem about a real or fictional person
- chosen the type of poem that best conveys your subject
- used sound devices and poetic elements to convey your ideas
- used precise, vivid language
- presented a poem that is free of unintentional errors in grammar, usage, and mechanics

The Writing Process

PREWRITING

Prewriting Tip

Scan your journal, a scrapbook, or a photo album to find people you might write about.

Explore ideas

The following suggestions might help you find a subject for your poem.

- Skim the poems in Theme 8. Do any of the characters in these poems remind you of someone you want to write about?
- Think of people in occupations or situations that intrigue you. Could you write about a soccer player, a drummer, or a coach?
- Jot down names of people who have made strong impressions on you. Have you admired a friend? Envied a character from a book?

Consider your purpose

The type of poem you write will depend on what aspects of the character you want to describe. Use the following chart as a guide.

Use this type of poem . . .	Which is defined as a . . .	If you want to . . .
lyric poem	poem in which the speaker expresses personal thoughts and feelings	describe the character or your feelings about him or her
dramatic poem	poem that consists entirely of a dialogue or monologue	show how the character thinks or feels about something
narrative poem	poem that tells a story	show what a character does or how he or she behaves

Choose your audience

Do your readers already know your character? If not, think about what background information you will need to convey for your poem to make sense.

Freewrite about your character

Most poems are concise—they are shorter than stories or essays. However, this doesn't mean that poets have little to say about their subject. To find the most precise, exciting words and phrases, poets usually draw from a large store of material. You can create a store of material by freewriting about your character. The springboards below can help get you started.

- What colors come to mind when you think of your character? What smells? What sounds?
- If your character were an animal, which one would he or she be? Why do you think so?
- Describe your character in action as if you were watching him or her. Describe that same action from his or her point of view.

STUDENT MODEL

> At first the music is soft, but then it soars, and he gracefully raises his arms, runs with pointed toes across the stage, and leaps into the air. His legs fly into perfect splits when he jumps. My heart is pounding. He doesn't even look like he's sweating as he completes endless pirouettes and tours jetés, jumping and spinning. When his solo is finished, he welcomes his partner, a beautiful female dancer portraying Giselle, into his arms.

Complete Student Model on p. R117.

Review poetry elements

Poetic elements can help you convey sights, sounds, and emotions. For descriptions of these elements, turn to Genre Focus: Poetry on pages 578–579.

Consider using sound devices:

Sound Device	STUDENT MODEL
alliteration	decision to defect
assonance	plan on the fact
repetition	straining, straining, straining
onomatopoeia	thumping feet

Complete Student Model on p. R117.

DRAFTING

DRAFTING TIP

Finding the right word can be one of the most difficult aspects of writing poetry. Keep a thesaurus, a dictionary, and a rhyming dictionary handy as you draft and revise.

Experiment

Take a playful approach in drafting your poem. Experiment with words, phrases, and sound effects, and don't pressure yourself to create a perfect poem immediately. Try different rhyme schemes and different line and stanza lengths. Read your writing aloud to see if it has a rhythmic flow. The rhythm you create should suit your subject. It might be fast or slow, smooth or choppy.

STUDENT MODEL

You are the greatest dancer of your
  generation
And, I believe, of all time
I still remember the first time I saw you
I was six years old.
Later, years later, I saw you again.
You were Albrecht, wooing Giselle
with arabesques and shining, whirling turns
that drove the crowd around me mad.
We were all frozen by you.
Your incredible passion and performances.
Your bravery.
You have inspired me for years now,
flying, leaping, spinning, planning, leaving,
sacrificing your own country
where your mother must have waited to hear
  the crowd,
straining, straining, straining to hear our
  applause
all the way across the wide, deep blue ocean.

Complete Student Model on p. R117.

Write your draft

Writing a poem is a little like solving a puzzle. If you fit the right words in the right places, the picture suddenly appears. However, you may spend a lot of time trying to fit the wrong words in the wrong places. Accept that possibility, and as you draft, feel free to make changes.

Use imagery to heighten the effect

Poetry relies on **imagery.** The images that a poet creates in words can trigger a memory or evoke a response similar to a physical sensation. Read each of the lines of your poem and put yourself into the moment. Add a word or phrase that you associate with how you feel.

REVISING

Revising Tips

Vague, general words can ruin a poem. Replace them with precise, specific words.

Your poem doesn't have to rhyme or follow a certain rhythm, but use rhyme and rhythm if they will strengthen the effect.

Take another look

As you revise, ask yourself where you can use poetic techniques such as figurative language and sound devices to enhance the reader's experience of the poem. Use the **Rubric for Revising** to guide your work.

Have a writing conference

Read your poem aloud to a writing partner. Ask your listener to be aware of any places where you can improve your use of imagery and sound devices to make the poem more engaging. Then go through the **Rubric for Revising** with your listener.

STUDENT MODEL

You taught me, as well, about ~~the~~ hard ~~times~~ [ships].
You taught me that no matter how high you
 can jump
No matter how many tour jetés you spin,
no matter how fast your legs fly into splits,
Or how great of a dancer you are,
Life can still [test you in cruel ways.] ~~be hard for people sometimes.~~
Your decision to defect~~, to leave your own~~
 ~~country for life:~~
At the airport, [a scramble] ~~all~~ of ~~the~~ secret service
 agents,
Shout~~ing~~[s] and the revving of airplane
 engines, chaos,
The plan you must have worked out in
 advance.
Did you plan on the fact
That you might never see your ~~very own~~
 mother again?
Thanks to you, I never look to my talents
To protect me from life.

Complete Student Model on p. R117.

Rubric for Revising

Your revised poem should have
- ☑ a real or fictional person as its subject
- ☑ a poetic form that effectively conveys your subject
- ☑ figurative language, sensory details, and other poetic elements that help create vivid images
- ☑ a strong use of rhythm and/or other sound devices to evoke specific impressions
- ☑ line and stanza lengths that effectively match your subject
- ☑ an ending that provides a sense of completeness for readers

Your revised poem should be free of
- ☑ unnecessary or confusing lines or expressions
- ☑ unintentional errors in grammar, usage, and mechanics

EDITING/PROOFREADING

PROOFREADING TIP

There are no ironclad rules for punctuation and capitalization in poetry. Follow the rules that make sense for your poem, keeping readability in mind.

Although poets sometimes depart from conventional rules of grammar for effect, unintentional mistakes are still distracting. The **Proofreading Checklist** on the inside back cover can help you catch errors in your poem.

Grammar Hint

Use punctuation to indicate the pauses that you want your readers to make in reading your poem. A period, an exclamation point, or a question mark calls for the longest pause. A comma calls for the shortest.

LONG PAUSES, SLOW PACE: *Leaping. Spinning. Whirling.*

SHORT PAUSES, QUICK PACE: *Leaping, spinning, whirling*

- For more about punctuation, see **Language Handbook,** pp. R26–R28.

Complete Student Model

For a complete version of the model developed in this workshop, refer to **Writing Workshop Models**, p. R117.

STUDENT MODEL

```
Your decision to defect:
at the airport, a scramble of secret
    service agents,
shouts, and the revving of airplane
    engines,
Chaos,
```

Complete Student Model on p. R117.

PUBLISHING/PRESENTING

PRESENTING TIP

When reading your poem aloud, be sure to speak loudly and clearly.

Consider holding a class poetry festival featuring readings of student poems. Each student might tell about the source of inspiration for his or her poem and describe how the poem developed.

Reflecting

What did you find most difficult about writing this poem? What was most gratifying? How has writing a poem changed your appreciation of the poems you have read? Answer these questions in your journal.

Save your work for your portfolio.

Theme 9 Observations and Expressions

How observant are you? Do you notice small details or do you tend to take in the "big picture"? Do you find ways to share what you see? Poets—among the world's best observers—use language to express what they feel as well as what they witness. In this theme you'll encounter poetry that examines everything from minute details to cosmic events.

THEME PROJECTS

Learning for Life

Get Out the News Turn the language of poetry into the language of everyday life.

1. Choose two poems from this theme. How might the events they describe be recounted in a newspaper article?
2. Write a newspaper article about each poem's events. Be objective; focus on facts rather than opinions.
3. Read the news stories aloud to the class. Ask your classmates to identify the poems.

Internet Connection

Poetic Resource Online poetic activity abounds.

1. Using a keyword such as "poetry" and a search engine such as Yahoo! or Excite, research Web sites that may be of interest to poets, such as journals that allow poets to submit their work online, chat rooms for writers, sites that give bibliographic information on famous poets, and more.
2. Present your most interesting findings in a database or poster. Make sure you describe each site and list its address.

"There sleeps Titania sometime of the night lull'd in flowers . . . ," 1994. Carmen Garcia. Etching, 57 x 76 cm. Private collection.

Before You Read

Night Clouds and *Tiger Year*

Reading Focus

Close your eyes and picture the night sky. What do you see?

Freewrite In your journal, freewrite about your impressions of the night sky; write for five minutes without stopping.

Setting a Purpose Read to see how the night sky affects the speakers of two poems.

Building Background

Did You Know?

- In the early 1900s, Amy Lowell was a leader of a poetic movement known as **Imagism.** Poets create an image when they describe or portray something, such as a feeling, an idea, or a sensory experience, in vivid language. Imagist poets believed that an image in a poem should be so precise, so concrete, that it immediately evokes in the reader all the emotion and meaning of the poem. The Imagists were inspired by the precision and simplicity of the Japanese haiku and believed that imagery was the essence of poetry. Lowell and other Imagist poets experimented with new verse forms, unusual rhythms, and surprising themes.
- The Chinese calendar is based on the cycles of the moon. A new year begins with the second new moon of the winter season. According to Chinese legend, a designated animal rules over each year within a twelve-year cycle. The twelve animals are, in order: rat, ox, tiger, hare, dragon, snake, horse, sheep, monkey, rooster, dog, and pig. Numerous cultures hold claim to the origins and sequence of the twelve-animal cycle. One legend says that Buddha invited all the animals to visit him before he departed Earth. Only these twelve animals showed up, arriving in this order. In Chinese tradition the animal ruling in the year a person is born influences that person's personality. The year in which Laura Iwasaki was born—1950—was the Year of the Tiger.

Meet Amy Lowell

"I do not suppose that anyone [who is] not a poet can realize the agony of creating a poem. Every nerve, even every muscle, seems strained to the breaking point." Despite her words about the writing process, Amy Lowell was known as a dedicated, versatile poet, who wrote more than 650 poems. Her first major collection, *A Dome of Many-Colored Glass*, was published in 1912. In 1926, a year after her death, Lowell was awarded the Pulitzer Prize.

Amy Lowell was born in Massachusetts in 1874 and died in 1925.

Meet Laura Iwasaki

Asian American poet Laura Iwasaki grew up in Los Angeles, California. She attended the University of Hawaii where she majored in pharmacology. After college, Iwasaki traveled throughout South America and then moved back to Los Angeles to live.

Laura Iwasaki was born in Hawaii in 1950.

Diamonds in the Sky. Eric Sloane (1905–1985). Oil on board, 50 x 52 in. Courtesy of the Estate of Eric Sloane and the Michael Wigley Galleries Ltd., Santa Fe.

Night Clouds

Amy Lowell

The white mares of the moon rush along the sky
Beating their golden hoofs upon the glass Heavens;
The white mares of the moon are all standing on their hind legs
Pawing at the green porcelain doors of the remote Heavens.
Fly, Mares!
Strain your utmost,
Scatter the milky dust of stars,
Or the tiger sun will leap upon you and destroy you
With one lick of his vermilion° tongue.

---

9 The color *vermilion* is vivid red to reddish orange.

Tiger Year

Laura Iwasaki

new moon,
you lie
in shadow—
traveling over the face
of silent water

as planets circle in the gathering dark
like pale insects
around the opened throats of flowers.

see how the stars are blossoming
one by one:
as if merely to breathe.

they blossom for you,
defining your way
through the clear night air
with hands as pure and bright as clouds.

will you hurry to my season?
it is time:
you bring the light.

Responding to Literature

Personal Response

What images from these poems remain with you after reading?

Analyzing Literature

Night Clouds

Recall and Interpret

1. In your own words, tell what the speaker is describing in lines 1–4. What is the emotional impact of the speaker's description? Explain.
2. Summarize the advice that the speaker gives in lines 5–7. What does the speaker imply will happen in lines 8–9 if this advice is not followed?
3. What, do you think, is the overall **theme,** or message, of this poem? What words or lines from the poem imply this message?

Evaluate and Connect

4. **Theme Connections** Recall how you pictured the night sky for the Reading Focus on page 676. How does Lowell's observation of the night sky compare with yours?
5. Which lines from the poem do you find the most creative or unusual? Why? Support your answer with specific details from the poem.

Tiger Year

Recall and Interpret

6. Whom or what does the speaker address? What is the speaker describing in the first two stanzas?
7. What image does the speaker present in lines 9–15? What does this suggest about the poet's view of the night sky?
8. What do you think the speaker means in the last stanza? Support your response with details from the poem.

Evaluate and Connect

9. How would you summarize the speaker's **tone** or attitude toward the subject of this poem? How does the tone affect your reading of the poem? Explain.
10. In what ways does this poem alter or add to your appreciation of the sky? Explain.

Literary Criticism

Reviewer William Lyon Phelps writes that Lowell's "chief forte is description, owing to her extraordinary sensitivity to sounds, colors, and smells." With a group of classmates, list examples of Lowell's vivid descriptions in "Night Clouds." Discuss why the descriptions make this poem a good example of Imagism.

Literary ELEMENTS

Figurative Language

Figurative language conveys meaning beyond the literal definition of a word. In these two poems, Lowell and Iwasaki use three types of figurative language: **similes,** which compare two unlike things using *like* or *as*; **metaphors,** which compare two or more things that have something in common; and **personification,** the giving of human qualities to nonhuman things. For example, Iwasaki uses the simile "planets circle in the gathering dark / like pale insects / around the opened throats of flowers" to compare planets to insects. The simile suggests that the planets seem to be alive and appear to have a reason for their movements.

1. What other figurative language does Iwasaki use in "Tiger Year"? List at least one example of each type and explain its effect.
2. How does metaphor make Lowell's poem "Night Clouds" lively and vivid?

- See **Literary Terms Handbook,** p. R5.

Literature and Writing

Writing About Literature

Compare and Contrast Poetic Elements In two or three paragraphs, compare and contrast "Night Clouds" and "Tiger Year," considering similarities and differences in language, subject matter, form and structure, imagery, and theme. Cite examples from the poems.

Creative Writing

Sky Poem Choose an object in the sky–day or night, near or far. Think of at least two images that the object suggests. Then, using those images, write a short poem about the object you chose. Try to describe the images in a way that conveys your ideas about this object.

Extending Your Response

Literature Groups

Strong Yet Fragile In your group, discuss how "Night Clouds" conveys both the strength and fragility of the night sky. Use specific details from the poem to support your ideas. Then list other elements or events in the sky that might support this contrast. Share your list with the class.

Interdisciplinary Activity

Science: Explaining Terms Choose a line from one of the poems that contains a reference to the sky, the stars, clouds, insects, or the planets. Use library resources or the Internet to find scientific information about the reference. Then write a few paragraphs in which you summarize the information and explain whether or not it helps your understanding or alters your appreciation of the poem.

Learning for Life

Comparison Report Search the Internet or library references to identify a work of art that illustrates the imagery in one of the poems or that conveys a similar meaning or message. Prepare a brief report to explain your choice to the class. Create a comparison chart with pictures of the art work and your comments to illustrate your points.

Reading Further

You might enjoy the following poems by Amy Lowell and Laura Iwasaki.

"Music," from *The Complete Poetical Works of Amy Lowell,* illustrates how reality can be transformed by the imagination.

"Geography," by Laura Iwasaki, is filled with images of space and time. It appears in *Counterpoint, Perspectives on Asian America* by Emma Gee.

Save your work for your portfolio.

INTERDISCIPLINARY CONNECTION

ASTRONOMY

Phases of the Moon

As you read "Tiger Year," did you wonder how long it takes for a new moon to "bring the light"? It takes just a day. The night after a darkened new moon, a sliver of light appears in the sky.

Moonlight is actually reflected sunlight. As the moon revolves around the earth, varying amounts of its sunlit surface are visible. A new moon occurs when the moon is between the sun and the earth; the sun lights only the side facing away from the earth. A full moon occurs when the earth is between the moon and the sun, allowing sunlight to flood the entire surface of the moon facing the earth. The moon travels around the earth in about 29½ days, completing the cycle from new moon to full moon and back to new moon again.

Since ancient times, people have studied the phases of the moon and planned important activities, such as planting and harvesting, around the lunar cycle. Even today, some people use the lunar cycle to time fishing trips, haircuts, medical treatments, and many other ventures.

As the moon is "growing," or changing from a new moon to a full moon, it is called a **waxing moon.** As it is "shrinking," or changing from a full moon back to a new moon, it is called a **waning moon.** A **crescent moon** is banana-shaped; a **gibbous moon** is roughly oval.

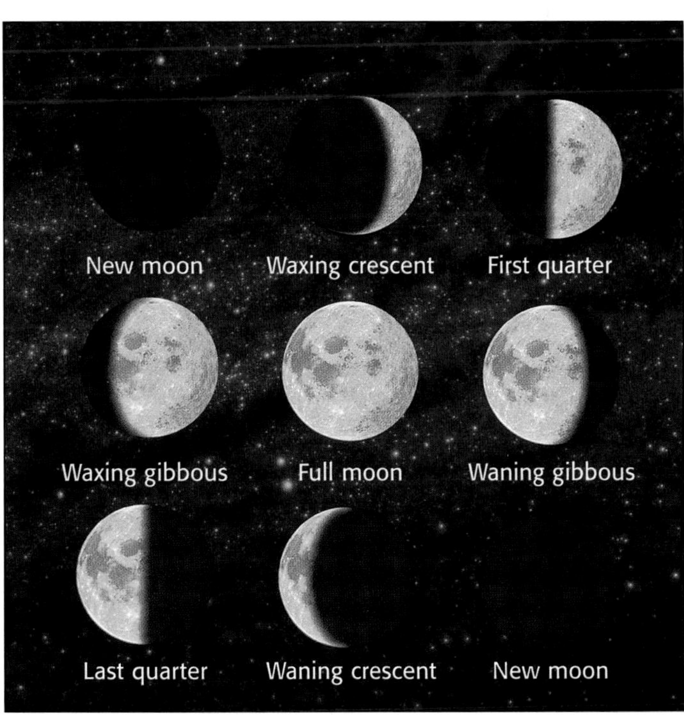

Phases of the moon

Activity

Some people believe that human emotions and energy levels are influenced by the lunar cycle. Why not find out for yourself? Follow one lunar cycle and keep a record of the phases of the moon and how you felt and acted. Compare your record with those of your classmates and see what conclusions you can draw.

Before You Read

For Poets and *Reapers*

Reading Focus

In your mind's eye, picture an area of open land that has no buildings on it.

Journal In your journal, describe the scene you are visualizing. Include everything you "see," such as plants, animals, rocks, and perhaps even people.

Setting a Purpose Read to share the speakers' observations and images of people interacting with the natural world.

Building Background

Did You Know?

- "The stuff of poetry is life itself," says African American poet Al Young. From childhood on, Young's life has included both urban and rural influences. Growing up in Detroit, he absorbed the city's working-class culture and Motown music. At his grandparents' home in rural Mississippi as a youth, Young came under the sway of "the mystery of natural things."

- A *scythe* is a tool with a long, curved blade attached to a long handle. It may be used for cutting tall grasses or for *reaping,* or harvesting, grain by hand. The movement of a reaper wielding a scythe is graceful and rhythmic. Holding the scythe in front of his or her body, the reaper moves it back and forth in wide, sweeping arcs. Like much other farm labor, the work of reaping by hand is exhausting: the same motion is repeated hundreds and thousands of times, and the work is performed in a stooped-over position.

Meet Al Young

Novelist, screenwriter, and poet, Al Young says that part of the American dream is the yearning to be somewhere else. Following that impulse, he moved to California and has made that state his home. Believing that poetry and music go together, Young sometimes bursts into song when giving poetry readings.

Al Young was born in 1939 in Ocean Springs, Mississippi.

Meet Jean Toomer

"Life is mystery in motion," said Jean Toomer, a poet, novelist, and philosopher who spent much of his own life seeking to understand the mysteries of human existence. This quest took Toomer to Georgia in 1921, where he found his ancestral roots in the richly textured culture of blacks living in the American South. Toomer celebrated this culture in *Cane,* a book of poetry and fiction.

Jean Toomer was born in 1894 in Washington, D.C., and died in 1967.

For Poets

Al Young

Stay beautiful
but don't stay down underground too long
Don't turn into a mole
or a worm
or a root
or a stone

Come on out into the sunlight
Breathe in trees
Knock out mountains
Commune° with snakes
& be the very hero of birds

Don't forget to poke your head up
& blink
think
Walk all around
Swim upstream

Don't forget to fly

---

10 To *commune* means to exchange feelings and ideas with someone else.

Reapers

Jean Toomer

Black reapers with the sound of steel on stones
Are sharpening scythes. I see them place the hones°
In their hip-pockets as a thing that's done,
And start their silent swinging, one by one.
Black horses drive a mower through the weeds,
And there, a field rat, startled, squealing bleeds.
His belly close to ground. I see the blade,
Blood-stained, continue cutting weeds and shade.

---

2 The fine-grained stones used to sharpen any kind of blade are called *hones.*

Responding to Literature

Personal Response

What was your reaction to each poem? Share your reaction with your classmates.

Analyzing Literature

For Poets

Recall and Interpret

1. What advice does the speaker give in the first stanza? What do you think the speaker means by this advice?
2. What does the speaker tell poets in the second stanza? What do these lines suggest to you about the speaker's views of people and nature?
3. Express in your own words what the speaker says in the last two stanzas. In your opinion, why might the advice be important for poets? for non-poets?

Evaluate and Connect

4. What is the **tone** of this poem? (See Literary Terms Handbook, page R13.) How does the tone help convey the poet's message?
5. If you took the advice offered in this poem, how might your life change?

Reapers

Recall and Interpret

6. Describe in your own words what the reapers do.
7. What attitude do the reapers seem to have toward their work? What words or phrases convey that attitude?
8. Summarize what happens in the last four lines of the poem. What connections do you see between the reapers and the horses? Explain.

Evaluate and Connect

9. How would you characterize the way in which the accident with the field rat is described? How does the **style** of the description affect your reaction to the event? (See Literary Terms Handbook, page R12.)
10. Theme Connections What observations does the poet make in this poem? What message do you think he is conveying? Explain.

Literary Criticism

Critic Motley Deakin remarks that "the general effect of [Toomer's] poetry is a loosening of poetic structures, a movement towards prose." Do you agree with this critic's analysis? Why or why not? Write a paragraph or two supplying examples to support your response to these questions.

Literary ELEMENTS

Sound Devices

Poets use sound devices to help develop the mood or tone of a poem and to draw attention to particular words or ideas. One type of sound device is **alliteration,** the repetition of sounds, usually consonant sounds, at the beginning of words. As you read "Reapers" aloud, you can hear alliteration in the repetition of the *st* sound in the first line: "*st*eel on *st*one." Another type of sound device is **assonance,** the repetition of vowel sounds in a line of poetry. You can hear assonance in the repetition of the long *e* sound in "a f*ie*ld rat, startled, squ*ea*ling bl*ee*ds."

1. Identify another example of alliteration and one of assonance in "Reapers." How do these examples affect your reading of the poem?
2. Find an example of assonance in "For Poets." What does it add to the poem?

- See **Literary Terms Handbook,** p. R12.

Literature and Writing

Writing About Literature

Comparing Tone The **tone** of a poem is the emotional attitude that the speaker takes toward the subject. In a paragraph, compare the tone of "Reapers" with that of "For Poets." Identify words and phrases that convey the tone in each poem.

Creative Writing

Poem Use the description that you wrote for the Reading Focus on page 682 as the starting point for a one- or two-stanza poem about the object you described. Choose the most vivid words from your description, and add **sound devices** such as **alliteration** and **assonance.** Share your poem with the class.

Extending Your Response

Literature Groups

Powerful Images The power of these poems lies largely in their vivid imagery. In your group, choose the lines from each poem that you find most powerful or memorable. Discuss what makes these lines so compelling, then with your group, design an illustration for each poem based on the lines you choose. Make the lines of poetry part of your design.

Interdisciplinary Activity

History: Reaping Research the history behind Jean Toomer's poem. What time period is he probably referring to? Who were the reapers? Where did they reap? What were their living and working conditions? Present your findings in a brief report to the class.

Internet Connection

Poet Profiles Search the Internet for more information about Al Young and Jean Toomer. Use what you find to create a poster profile of one of the two poets, conveying what you find most interesting about him or his life.

Reading Further

You might also enjoy these works by Al Young and Jean Toomer:

Poems: "Sweet Sixteen Lines" and "Son" in *Heaven: Collected Poems 1958–1990,* by Al Young, capture some of the varied feelings of youth.

"November Cotton Flower" and "Storm Ending" in *Cane,* by Jean Toomer, offer other brief portraits of southern culture and landscape.

Save your work for your portfolio.

Before You Read

Three Haiku and *Two Tanka*

Reading Focus

Do most beautiful things last for a long time? Or are most beautiful objects impermanent or temporary? Is something more beautiful if it lasts only a short while?

Quickwrite Briefly describe an object of beauty. It may be an item you possess or something in nature. As you describe the object, consider how its permanence or impermanence affects your appreciation of the object.

Setting a Purpose Read to see how two Japanese poets use ancient literary forms to describe the beauty in nature.

Building Background

Did You Know?

- **Haiku** is an unrhymed Japanese verse form consisting of seventeen syllables that are arranged in three lines. The first and third lines have five syllables each; the second line has seven syllables. Traditionally, the goal of haiku is to suggest large ideas, using the simplest and fewest words. Although they leave much to the reader's imagination, haiku poets use explicit and evocative words to lead readers in the right direction. Matsuo Bashō, perhaps the greatest haiku poet of all time, said that a good poem should "seem light as a shallow river flowing over its sandy bed."
- **Tanka** is an unrhymed Japanese verse form that consists of five lines. The first and third lines have five syllables each; the other lines have seven syllables each. Tanka is considered the basic form of Japanese poetry. Most tanka focus on a single thought or idea related to love or to an appreciation of nature, a common theme in Japanese poetry. Because the poems are so short and simple, tanka poets, like haiku poets, must rely on precise, direct language to suggest ideas. A tanka can have different meanings for different readers, depending on the life experiences of the reader.
- Some translations of haiku and tanka may lose the poet's original syllable count when the poems are translated into English.

Meet Matsuo Bashō

"Don't follow in the footsteps of the old poets, seek what they sought." Matsuo Bashō's words echo his approach to life. Using traditional Japanese verse forms of his time, Bashō began his writing career in his twenties. By his early thirties he was considered a *haiku* master. During the last ten years of his life, Bashō perfected the simple and direct haiku style.

Matsuo Bashō was born in 1644 in Iga-Uen, Japan. He died in 1694.

Meet Lady Ise

Considered one of the Thirty-six Poetic Geniuses of Japan, Lady Ise enjoyed the celebrity status and fame that accompanied literary accomplishment in ancient Japan. She served in Emperor Uda's court and was known there for her literary works. Much of her poetry is found in a collection of Japanese poetry known as the *Kokin Wakashū*, or *Kokinshū*, published around the year 905. It was the first in a series of imperially commissioned collections of Japanese poetry.

Lady Ise lived in Japan from approximately 875–938.

Flowers and grasses of the seasons: Autumn, c. 1840s.
Seisei Kiitsu. Ink and colors on silk, approx. 1032 x 346 mm.
The British Museum, London.

Three Haiku

Matsuo Bashō

Translated by Robert Hass

It would melt
in my hand—
the autumn frost.

First day of spring—
I keep thinking about
the end of autumn.

Spring!
a nameless hill
in the haze.

Two Tanka

Lady Ise

Translated by Willis Barnstone

Hanging from the branches of a green
willow tree,
the spring rain
is a
thread of pearls.

Translated by Etsuko Terasaki
with Irma Brandeis

Lightly forsaking°
the Spring mist as it rises,
the wild geese are setting off.
Have they learned to live
in a flowerless country?

1 *Forsaking* means turning away from or abandoning.

Responding to Literature

Personal Response

Which of the images in these poems seems most familiar to you? Describe the image in your journal and explain why you think it seems familiar.

Analyzing Literature

Three Haiku

Recall and Interpret

1. What does the first haiku describe? What does this image make you think about autumn?
2. What is the second haiku about? What sentiment might the poet be trying to evoke?
3. What things does the speaker name in the third haiku? What might this combination of things suggest about daily life?

Evaluate and Connect

4. Theme Connections Which haiku do you find most expressive? Support your choice with examples from the poems.
5. Refer to the description you wrote for the Reading Focus on page 686. How well do you think the speaker's descriptions and observations capture the beauty of nature? Do you think the impermanence of nature affects the message of the haiku?

Two Tanka

Recall and Interpret

6. What two things are compared in the first tanka? What insights about these things does the comparison bring to mind?
7. What natural events does the speaker present in the second tanka? How do these events contribute to the **mood,** or atmosphere, of the tanka?
8. What question does the speaker ask in the second tanka? What might be the meaning of this question?

Evaluate and Connect

9. In what ways do the images of spring in the two tanka reflect your own observations of spring? Explain.
10. In your opinion, which tanka offers more for you to think about? Why?

Extending Your Response

Writing About Literature

Haiku and Tanka Use the information provided in the Background section on page 686, as well as the form and content of the Bashō and Lady Ise poems you have read, to help you write three haiku or tanka of your own. Share your poems with other students.

Interdisciplinary Activity

Art: Visualizing Poetry Search the Internet or library references for a work of art or create your own to reflect the theme in one of the Bashō or Lady Ise poems.

Save your work for your portfolio.

Press Conference Transcript

Have you ever wanted to leave your mark by accomplishing something special that people would remember? Read the February 18, 1998, press conference with U.S. gold medalist Nikki Stone to hear her comments after winning the freestyle aerial in Nagano, Japan.

U.S. Aerialists Are Golden

I wore number four today, and February 4th was my birthday. Every time I've blown the candles out on my birthday cake my wish has come true. I wished I would make the team a few years ago, and I did. I wished I would win a World Championship, and I did. And I wished this year that I would win the Olympic gold, and now I did.

My first jump I felt really good. The weather was right, the wind was mellow, it felt good in the air and the landing was good. I tried to stay calm and tell myself "you have another jump to do." O[n] my second jump I did a wind check and I think I heard Wayne [Hilterbrand, U.S. ski aerialist head coach] yell louder than he ever had[:] "REACH for the landing."

Two years ago I was the most miserable person you've ever met. Things got turned around, though. But coming here to win a gold medal does make [life] that much sweeter. Every time I went out to the gym I just kept saying, "gold medal, gold medal, gold medal."

Last year at [the] Worlds [Championship] here I set my focus to show everyone that I wasn't 10th best.

I think the guys are just getting scared that the girls are catching up.

On my second jump my nerves were definitely stronger. My form wasn't as good and I just said, "hey, just land this thing."

We've got great coaches, great facilities and a great program in the United States. . . .

[return from back injury]

When I got back in the gym, I just kept telling myself "gold medal, gold medal, gold medal." I got myself to the Olympics and I got myself a gold medal.

[waiting for final scores]

I was nervous, I was definitely nervous. I was thinking gold or silver, but I wanted us to win as many gold medals as we can.

This was my goal in life. I don't know what I'm going to do now.

It feels good to prove a lot of people wrong.

Analyzing Media

1. What personal qualities helped Stone to succeed?
2. Have you or someone you know attempted to reach a difficult goal? Explain.

Before You Read

A Motto from Poets: Leave Stone and *Constantly risking absurdity*

Reading Focus

What ideas come to mind when you hear the word *poet?*

Map It! Create a cluster map. Surround the word *poet* with words and phrases that express your ideas about what poets are like and what they do.

Setting a Purpose Read to discover how two speakers view the work of a poet.

Building Background

Did You Know?

- While still a teenager, Roberto Fernández Retamar interviewed the renowned American author Ernest Hemingway, who was living near Havana, Cuba, at the time. This interview was Fernández Retamar's first published work, a piece that he later described as "unreadably adolescent." The young man declined Hemingway's offer to assist him in getting his poetry published; he says he felt too embarrassed to accept the famous author's help.
- Lawrence Ferlinghetti is perhaps best known for the role he played in promoting the Beat Movement of the 1950s. The Beats were a group of writers who wanted to take art away from academia and bring it to the people in the streets. Beatniks—as the followers of this movement were dubbed—wore shabby clothing and used the "hip" language of jazz musicians to show their unconventionality. The Beat poets, who included Ferlinghetti, Allen Ginsberg, and Gregory Corso, created poetry that was meaningful and powerful yet free of the rigidity of conventional poetry.

Meet Roberto Fernández Retamar

After Roberto Fernández Retamar graduated from high school at the top of his class, his parents rewarded him by sending him to New York City. "I had just turned seventeen," he said, "and although I had not yet published a single line, I felt certain . . . that I was a poet." Fernández Retamar has since become one of Cuba's most respected and influential writers.

Roberto Fernández Retamar was born in 1930 in Havana, Cuba.

Meet Lawrence Ferlinghetti

The early years of Lawrence Ferlinghetti's life were plagued by the loss of his parents and other family. However, a wealthy family let Ferlinghetti stay in their home and also financed his education. Ferlinghetti became associated with the Beat Movement and produced volumes of powerful poetry.

Lawrence Ferlinghetti was born in 1919 in Yonkers, New York.

A Motto from Poets: Leave Stone

Roberto Fernández Retamar
Translated by Tim Reynolds

A motto° from poets: leave stone
alone, it won't grow; try
trees, working their way up
and up into air.
And there they inscribe their names magnificent
in the sun as banners
But it is rock that keeps when trees
are ash, or furniture; you eat, or sleep, or lie
dead among the painted detritus° of trees.
And all the time there's some stone
somewhere, planted, not
bigger, not
smaller, carrying still
across its livid° frontage some savage
scrawl, some few letters
of someone long gone who,
one afternoon, graved° them there,
laughing, dreaming, remembering.

---

1 A *motto* is a saying that expresses a guiding principle.
9 *Detritus* (di trī′ təs) is the accumulated remains of something destroyed, eroded, or discarded.
14 Here, *livid* means "pale or grayish-blue."
17 The person who *graved* the letters carved them into the stone.

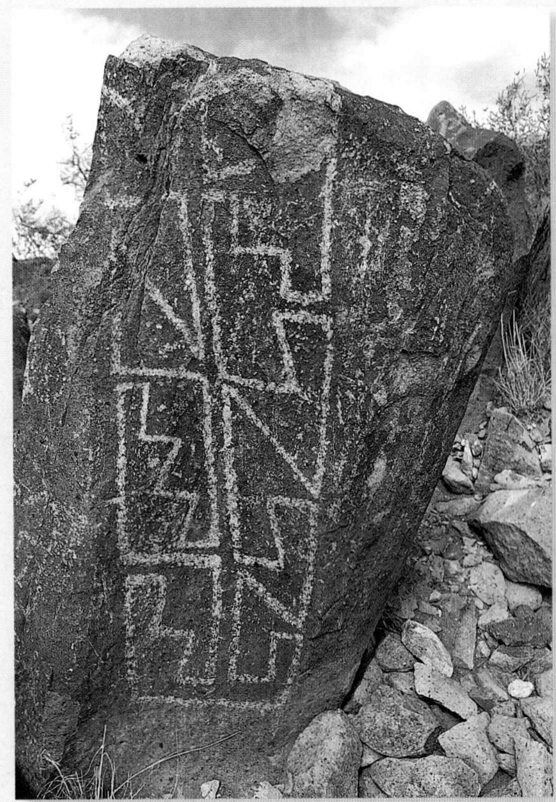

Petroglyphs on exposed stones,
Arches National Park, UT.
Gerry Ellis, photographer.

Constantly risking absurdity

Lawrence Ferlinghetti

Constantly risking absurdity°
and death
whenever he performs
above the heads
of his audience
the poet like an acrobat
climbs on rime°
to a high wire of his own making
and balancing on eyebeams°
above a sea of faces
paces his way
to the other side of day
performing entrechats°
and sleight-of-foot tricks
and other high theatrics
and all without mistaking
any thing
for what it may not be

For he's the super realist
who must perforce° perceive
taut truth
before the taking of each stance or step
in his supposed advance
toward that still higher perch
where Beauty stands and waits
with gravity
to start her death-defying leap

And he
a little charleychaplin° man
who may or may not catch
her fair eternal form
spreadeagled° in the empty air
of existence

1 absurdity: being ridiculously unreasonable or irrational.

7 rime: an old way of spelling **rhyme.**

9 eyebeams: a play on "I-beam," an iron or steel construction beam that looks like a capital *I*, and that construction workers sometimes walk across.

13 entrechat (ôn′ trə shä′): in ballet a jump during which the dancer crosses the legs a number of times, alternately back and forth.

20 perforce: by force of circumstances.

29 charleychaplin man: Charlie Chaplin, a star of silent movies, most famous for his tragic-comic character known as "The Little Tramp."

32 spreadeagled: arms and legs spread wide, suggesting the appearance of an eagle with stretched out wings and legs.

Responding to Literature

Personal Response

Sketch the image from the poem that made the strongest impression on you.

Analyzing Literature

A Motto from Poets: Leave Stone

Recall and Interpret

1. What is the "motto from poets" that the speaker expresses in lines 1–4? What do you think this motto means?
2. How does Fernández Retamar use **personification** (see Literary Terms Handbook, page R9) in line 5? To whom might the speaker be comparing the personified object? Explain.
3. What characteristics does the speaker attribute to stone and to trees in lines 7–9? What do these lines convey about the speaker's attitude toward stone and trees?
4. Restate lines 10–18 in your own words. What ideas do you think the speaker is trying to convey in these lines? Explain.

Evaluate and Connect

5. How does the extended comparison between stone and trees help you understand the **theme,** or main idea, of this poem?
6. Do you think poets should adopt the motto expressed in this poem? Why or why not?
7. If you wanted to leave a message for future generations, what material or technique would you use to record your message? Explain your choice.

Constantly risking absurdity

Recall and Interpret

8. In the extended comparison in this poem, to whom does the speaker compare the poet? How are the two alike, according to the speaker?
9. What occupations are suggested by the references to *eyebeams, entrechats,* and *sleight-of-foot tricks?* What might these occupations have in common with the job of poet?
10. Who is the "super realist" in line 19? What is his ultimate goal? What must he do to approach it, and how likely is he to attain it?

Evaluate and Connect

11. Evaluate the poet's choice of title. How does it help you better understand the poem's **theme,** or main idea? Explain.
12. Have you ever tried to do something that involved "risking absurdity"? Explain.
13. **Theme Connections** In your opinion, does the speaker accurately portray the poet's task? Give reasons for your answer.
14. Find examples of **sound devices** and evaluate how their use affects your understanding and appreciation of the poem. (See Literary Terms Handbook, page R12.)

Literary ELEMENTS

Epic Simile

An **epic simile** is an extended simile that typically uses the words *like* or *as* to compare two things in an elaborate or detailed way. Epic similes usually compare a complex action, rather than a simple thing, with another complex action, and the comparison continues for several lines. For example, in "Constantly risking absurdity," Lawrence Ferlinghetti uses a variety of detailed images and actions to compare a poet to an acrobat.

1. What details for comparison does Ferlinghetti present in lines 9–12? In your opinion, what idea does the speaker express in these lines?
2. How does Ferlinghetti's epic simile, comparing the work of a poet to the risk-taking act of an acrobat, contribute to your understanding of the work of a poet?

- See **Literary Terms Handbook,** p. R12.

Literature and Writing

Writing About Literature

Describe a Poet and the Poet's Task Use the ideas expressed in the two poems you have just read to expand and revise the cluster map you created in the Reading Focus on page 690. Then write a paragraph or two describing your concept of a poet and the poet's task.

Personal Writing

My Motto Write a personal motto—a saying that expresses a principle that guides your behavior and outlook on life. Explain how you arrived at your motto and why you think it is a good guiding principle. If you wish, explain your motto to your classmates.

Extending Your Response

Literature Groups

Secret Meanings Lawrence Ferlinghetti once suggested that the poet's duty is "to uncover the secret meaning of things." Assuming that statement is valid, do you think Fernández Retamar and Ferlinghetti have fulfilled their duty in the poems you have just read? Use specific details from the poems as you discuss this question in your group. Share and compare your ideas with the members of another group.

Internet Connection

Multimedia Presentation Work with a small group of classmates to create a multimedia presentation about the Beat poets. Do research to get information about the authors. Find poems, articles, critical reviews, recordings, and other materials to use in your presentation. Plan and deliver your presentation for the class.

Performing

Beatnik Poetry Reading Research the Beat poets of the 1950s. Then prepare and perform a Beatnik poetry reading. Choose an unconventional poem of the Beatnik era that is meaningful to you, and read it aloud with expression for the class. If you wish, dress the part of a Beatnik poet.

Reading Further

You might also enjoy these poems:

Poems: "London, Rainy Day," from *Open Eye, Open Heart,* by Lawrence Ferlinghetti, describes life on a rainy morning in London.

"400-Meter Freestyle," from *Maxine Kumin, Selected Poems, 1960–1990,* reveals a swimmer's race to the finish.

"Fireworks," from *John Updike, Collected Poems, 1953–1993,* gives different perspectives about a fireworks display.

Save your work for your portfolio.

Writing Skills

Using Simile and Metaphor

If you look up the word *love* in a dictionary, you may find that the definition doesn't do justice to that exalted emotion. Poets and other writers often express meaning beyond the literal definition by using **similes** and **metaphors,** figurative language that compares seemingly unlike things to reveal new truths about them. A **simile** uses *like* or *as* to compare the two things. A **metaphor** makes a comparison without using *like* or *as*. Notice how Lawrence Ferlinghetti uses simile and metaphor.

> the poet like an acrobat
> climbs on rime
> to a high wire of his own making
> and balancing on eyebeams
> above a sea of faces
> paces his way
> to the other side of day
> performing entrechats
> and sleight-of-foot tricks
> and other high theatrics
> and all without mistaking
> any thing
> for what it may not be

The first line of this excerpt contains a simile. Ferlinghetti uses the word *like* to compare a poet to an acrobat. He then extends this simile throughout the poem by describing the poet's activities in terms of those of the acrobats. Ferlinghetti also uses metaphor. In the second line of this excerpt, the poet/acrobat is said to "climb on rime." Here, Ferlinghetti uses an **implied metaphor,** or a metaphor in which one of the things being compared is suggested rather than directly stated. The rime (rhyme) is being implicitly compared to the ladder an acrobat would use to ascend to the high wire. In other words, the rime is just a tool to get somewhere else; it is not an end in itself.

To arrive at effective comparisons in your writing, let your mind free-associate. Use simile and metaphor to startle a reader into a deeper understanding of the meaning you want to convey.

EXERCISE

Using at least one simile, one metaphor, and one implied metaphor, write sentences that describe each of the following things.

1. an emotion 2. a sound 3. an activity 4. a type of physical pain

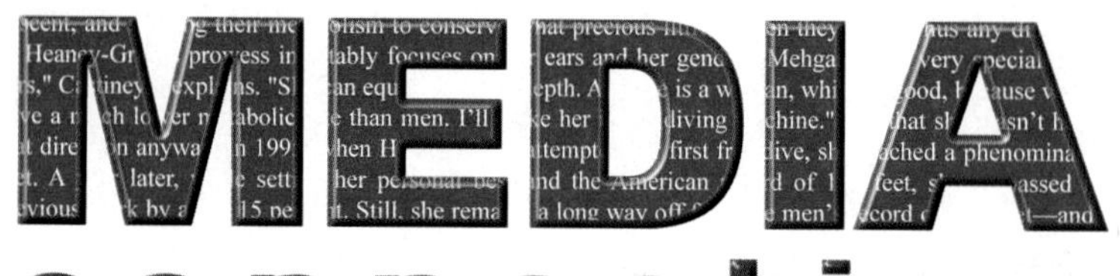

Newspaper Article

Jazz is an art form based on rhythm, teamwork, and improvisation. Because basketball relies on these three qualities as well, one jazz musician has been able to combine the music with the sport.

Hoops Picks Up a Jazz Beat

by Melita Marie Garza—*Chicago Tribune*, April 7, 1998

Douglas Ewart and Fred Hopkins swayed and paced under the basketball nets in the Washington Park gym while nine kids dribbled and shot to the duo's saxophone and acoustic bass.

"Get back in line; get back in line," admonished Ewart, as the kids started shooting randomly at the gym's six hoops. "Keep bouncing; keep bouncing. C'mon, man, let's keep to the same tempo."

Ewart, 51, is one of several prominent jazz artists who has taken up a challenge from the Chicago Park District and the Jazz Institute of Chicago to help bring jazz music to children.

"They told me they wanted to have concerts and get young people in the neighborhoods to attend," said Ewart, who quickly caught on that he would be competing for the kids' attention with the No. 1 pastime at the park—basketball.

Ewart has fashioned a musical score with the beat of children's basketballs and the tempo of jazz.

The piece is part of a Park District and Jazz Institute project called JazzCity.

Ewart, who stands 5 feet, 5 inches, doesn't even play basketball, and the kids, whose musical tastes run to rap and rhythm and blues, had rarely, if ever, heard improvisational jazz.

By the end of the second rehearsal, it was clear that the boys and girls in the gym would never hear a basketball bounce in the same way.

"It gave me a rhythm to dribble the ball," Eric Lewis, 12, a 5th grader at Carter School, said of his experience in going one-on-one with jazz and basketball. "The music gave me a happy feeling inside," Lewis said.

"There are many parallels between 'the game' and the music," said Ewart.

"Each form demonstrates individual and collective capacity, the combination of movement and sound. Players and musicians also have to combine discipline with spontaneity," he said.

Jazz artist Douglas Ewart plays one of his homemade instruments in the Washington Park gym.

The new experience was not lost on Max Costello, 12, 6th grader at Dulles School. "I thought it was really, really cool. It made basketball and music come together."

Analyzing Media

1. Do you think Ewart was playing music for the kids, or was he making music with them? Explain your answer.
2. Why did Ewart choose a basketball court as the place to introduce the kids to jazz? What skills of his make it possible for him to do this?

Before You Read

let my spirit fly in time and *Jazz Fantasia*

Reading Focus

If you could use only words to capture the mood or effects of a piece of music, how would you do it?

Discuss With a partner, identify a piece of instrumental music that you both enjoy. Discuss ways to express it in words.

Setting a Purpose Read to learn how two poets use words to convey the spirit and rhythms of jazz.

Building Background

Did You Know?

- *Jazz* is the name given to many styles of music that share certain characteristics, the most important of which is improvisation. In music, improvisation is the act of inventing a new version of a melody while playing it.
- Esteves's poem reflects the jazz of the 1950s and 1960s, when saxophonist John Coltrane and other musicians pioneered new sounds. Coltrane was known for his creative improvisations, which he played with great emotional power.
- When Sandburg published "Jazz Fantasia" in 1920, the jazz era was underway. Rooted in the musical traditions of African Americans, jazz evolved from ragtime and the blues into the New Orleans style: an upbeat, lively sound created by an ensemble of reed and brass instruments, plus drums. Experimental New Orleans musicians, such as jazz trumpeter and singer Louis Armstrong, moved to Chicago, where Sandburg lived, and influenced local jazz artists. One of Armstrong's most original types of improvisation was *scat singing:* using the voice, without words, to imitate the sounds of an instrument.

Louis Armstrong

Meet Sandra María Esteves

"I am two parts," says Sandra María Esteves (ā stā′ vās) in her poem "Here." Born in the Bronx in New York City, Esteves belongs to the "Nuyorican" group of poets, so called because they live in New York and have Puerto Rican heritage. Much of Esteves's early poetry explores her Afro-Caribbean roots; her later work includes the experiences of other ethnic groups.

Sandra María Esteves was born in 1948.

Meet Carl Sandburg

Nicknamed the "Poet of the People," Carl Sandburg was a distinguished poet, novelist, journalist, and historian. In exuberant free verse and song, he wrote about everyday life in America on subjects ranging from the prairie to steel factories. An accomplished guitarist, he also sang and studied regional music. Sandburg produced the most famous biography of Abraham Lincoln ever written.

Carl Sandburg was born in 1878 and died in 1967.

let my spirit fly in time

Sandra María Esteves

let my spirit fly in time
the outer world spaceless
no boundaries
deep, black rhythms and John Coltrane
fast movin' notes flying into space
the open eye
and peace descends across the earth
Sahara
black desert
rivers moving in line towards the sunrise
one
rivers moving over mountains and highways
going to the sunrise
rivers flowing
black flowers
ebony flowers
velvet
magic rivers flowing closer and closer
towards the sunrise

sun beating down
deep base laying down step down
base laying down life roots deep breaths
ancient stones glittering red ruby
jewels running deep running deep
running deep rivers towards the sunrise

lightening clouds
thundering wars
charcoal juju° heat soul
flow thru rivers moving towards the sunrise

poetry and sun music

---

28 *Juju* (jü′ jü) is a type of Nigerian pop music that features singing, guitars, and traditional drums.

Jazz Fantasia

Carl Sandburg

Drum on your drums, batter on your banjoes,
sob on the long cool winding saxophones.
Go to it, O jazzmen.

Sling your knuckles on the bottoms of the happy
tin pans, let your trombones ooze, and go husha-
husha-hush with the slippery sand-paper.

Moan like an autumn wind high in the lonesome tree-
tops, moan soft like you wanted somebody terrible,
cry like a racing car slipping away from a motorcycle
cop, bang-bang! you jazzmen, bang altogether drums,
traps, banjoes, horns, tin cans—make two people fight
on the top of a stairway and scratch each other's eyes
in a clinch tumbling down the stairs.

Can the rough stuff . . . now a Mississippi steamboat
pushes up the night river with a hoo-hoo-hoo-oo . . .
and the green lanterns calling to the high soft stars
. . . a red moon rides on the humps of the low river
hills . . . go to it, O jazzmen.

Rhapsody in Blue, c. 1925. Miguel Covarrubias. Oil on canvas, 25¼ x 31 in. Private collection.

Responding to Literature

Personal Response

Make a list of words that show your reaction to one or both of these poems.

Analyzing Literature

let my spirit fly in time

Recall and Interpret

1. What is the speaker in this poem thinking about in the first five lines? What clues tell you this?
2. What is the poem describing in lines 6–19? What do you think these images might stand for?
3. What comparisons does the speaker make in lines 20–29? Explain the impact of line 30.

Evaluate and Connect

4. Theme Connections Would you call this poem an observation, an expression, or both? Explain your answer.
5. In your opinion, does the poem as a whole appeal more to one of the five senses than to the others? What is the effect of the sensory appeal? Support your response with evidence from the poem.
6. In what ways is this poem like a piece of music? In what ways is it different from music?

Jazz Fantasia

Recall and Interpret

7. In the first two stanzas, what does the speaker want the jazzmen to do? What do these instructions tell you about the speaker?
8. How does the **tone** of the poem change from the beginning of the third stanza to the end of that stanza? How does this change reflect the sounds of jazz?
9. What differences do you see between the images in the last stanza and those in the rest of the poem? Based on all these images, how would you summarize Sandburg's message?

Evaluate and Connect

10. One definition of *fantasia* is "a fanciful musical composition not conforming to strict style or form." Why is "Jazz Fantasia" an appropriate title of this poem? Give evidence from the poem to support your answer.
11. In your opinion, which sensory images in this poem best convey a sense of lively, rhythmic music like jazz? Explain your choices.
12. Why might a jazz fan or any music fan like or dislike this poem? Explain.

Literary ELEMENTS

Onomatopoeia

Onomatopoeia is the use of a word or phrase that imitates or describes the sound it names. When Carl Sandburg writes, "go husha- / husha-hush with the slippery sand-paper," he is actually imitating the sound of sandpaper as it is rubbed against a surface. By using onomatopoeia, poets call attention to sounds and draw readers into the mood or message of the poem through their sense of hearing. Onomatopoeia can make the sounds of the poem seem almost musical, and it can stimulate images in readers' minds. The use of onomatopoeia may make a poem more lively and fun to read.

1. Identify two other examples of onomatopoeia in "Jazz Fantasia."
2. How does the use of onomatopoeia in this poem affect your reading of the poem?

- See **Literary Terms Handbook,** p. R9.

Literature and Writing

Writing About Literature

Analyzing Structure Both Esteves and Sandburg have used unusual structures in their poems. Look at how each poet has used punctuation, line breaks, stanzas, and placement of words on the page to express their thoughts and feelings about music. In two to four paragraphs, analyze the ways the structure of each poem helps convey the poet's message and contributes to your enjoyment of the poem.

Creative Writing

Musical "Composition" Think about your response to the Reading Focus on page 697. Then develop a word composition that somehow "plays" or "sings" or depends on sound for its power and effect. If you wish, you can model your work on Sandburg's or Esteves's example or create a jingle, slogan, riddle, or newspaper headline.

Extending Your Response

Literature Groups

Definitive Analysis Following are a few of the many definitions Carl Sandburg wrote for *poetry:*

"Poetry is an echo asking a shadow dancer to be a partner."

"Poetry is a type-font design for an alphabet of fun, hate, love, death."

"Poetry is the silence and speech between a wet struggling root of a flower and a sunlit blossom of that flower."

"Poetry is the capture of a picture, a song, or a flair, in a deliberate prism of words."

In your group, discuss each of these definitions and decide which one best applies to these poems. Share your opinion and reasons with another group.

Performing

All That Jazz Work with a partner or a small group to interpret and perform one of these poems. You may choose to bring the poem to life by setting it to music, dancing to it, creating a dramatic reading, or using sound, words, music, or movement together or separately, in another way.

Interdisciplinary Activity

Music History: Jazz Time Work with a small group to create a time line showing the history of jazz. You might borrow informative headings from a comprehensive encyclopedia article to highlight events and dates. You might also download images from the Internet or photocopy illustrations to add interest to your jazz history.

Save your work for your portfolio.

Writing Workshop

Descriptive Writing:
Extended Metaphor

Have you ever explained one thing by comparing it to something else? Writers typically use comparisons to help a reader see things in a new light and to show their own attitude toward a subject. One type of comparison, a metaphor, speaks of a subject as though it were something else. When a metaphor continues throughout a paragraph, a stanza, or an entire work, it is called an extended metaphor. **In this workshop, you will write an extended metaphor.**

- As you write your extended metaphor, refer to the **Writing Handbook,** pp. R58–R71.

EVALUATION RUBRIC

By the time you complete this Writing Workshop, you will have

- focused on a particular subject to create an extended metaphor
- conveyed clear connections and deeper meanings by comparing one thing to another
- included vivid images, precise language, and sensory details
- concluded with a clear, final impression of your subject
- presented an extended metaphor that is free of errors in grammar, usage, and mechanics

The Writing Process

PREWRITING

PREWRITING TIP

Metaphors will be easier to create for a subject that has a strong personal meaning for you than for a subject that does not interest you.

Explore ideas

A metaphor compares two things by identifying one with the other. A simile directly states that one thing is *like* another, but a metaphor implies the comparison; it suggests a shared quality between two things. An *extended* metaphor goes even further. It continues the comparison throughout a paragraph, a stanza, or an entire work.

You might choose to write about an abstract subject, such as *loyalty* or *greed.* Or you might decide to write about an event, a person, a scene—even a relationship. To get yourself thinking about your subject metaphorically, try thinking of the topic as if it were

- an animal, like the cloud-mares in "Night Clouds."
- a person, like the poet-acrobat in "Constantly risking absurdity."
- a place, like the spring-hill in the third of Bashō's three haiku.
- a kind of weather, like the music-wind in "Jazz Fantasia."

Consider your purpose

The purpose of your essay is to describe your subject. The purpose of the extended metaphor is to create connections and deeper meanings by comparing your subject to something else. Keep in mind, though, that your audience will probably not have made exactly the same observations about your subject that you have made. You will want to craft your metaphor to help your audience see from your perspective.

Make a plan

Once you've chosen a subject that you feel strongly about, think about the point you want to make. Consider the kind of emotional response you have for your subject and why. An idea web like the one shown can help you identify those feelings.

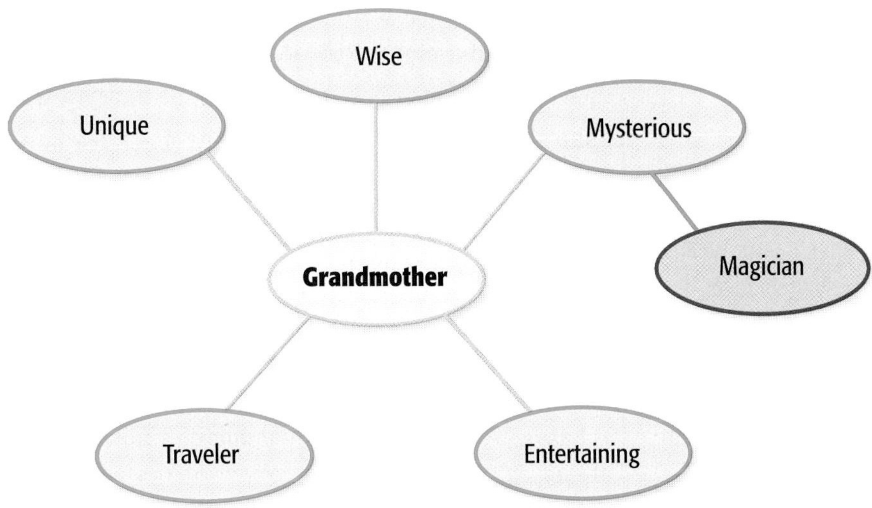

Reread your idea web, looking for any concrete things on which you can build your metaphor. Choose something that you have close, personal experience with, something that people can experience fully with their senses. Freewrite to develop ideas of how your subject is like that concrete thing. Then underline any words or phrases that are especially descriptive of your topic or your feelings about it. Perhaps one will lead you to your extended metaphor.

As you read the student model below, notice that the student chose "Magician" as the concrete thing on which to build the extended metaphor.

STUDENT MODEL

MAGICIAN: sometimes wears a black tuxedo or a cape, carries a wand, has a bag of tricks, pulls things out of the air, hides things up a sleeve, makes things disappear and reappear, has magical props or devices (mirrors, trapdoors, deck of cards, hat, scarves), entertains you, dazzles you, appeals to kids, very mysterious and wonderful

Complete Student Model on p. R119.

DRAFTING

Drafting Tips

Experiment. Try something new. Try something daring. You can always change or cut words or ideas in the revision.

Follow your plan, but don't feel that it has you on a leash. Shift from the plan if a good new idea comes along.

Write your draft
Jump right into your draft. Use a thesaurus for additional ideas for the extended metaphor.

Stay flexible
Let your writing and your thinking work together. If your writing suggests new ideas, let the new ideas change the direction of what you write. This will help you focus on the point you're trying to make.

STUDENT MODEL

FIRST DRAFT

My grandmother is like a magician. She doesn't wear special clothes to perform her magic, but she's still a magician. Since I was a kid, I've watched her with awe. She can make things appear. Plus, she's been known to come up missing all of a sudden. (Later, we find out she's just taken a trip.)

SECOND DRAFT

My grandmother is a magician. She doesn't wear a black tuxedo, or a cape, or carry a wand, but she does have an air of mystery about her. She can make things appear out of nowhere, pulling surprises out of her bag of tricks. She can even disappear on a moment's notice.

Complete Student Model on p. R119.

REVISING

Revising Tip

Make sure the images in your metaphor work together. For example, don't mix metaphors by calling something an airplane and then later describing a helicopter.

Evaluate your work
Set your draft aside for a while. Then read it slowly, marking places that you think should be improved. Using the **Rubric for Revising** to guide you, make revisions to your draft.

Have a writing conference
Read your extended metaphor aloud to a group of students or to your family. Then use the **Rubric for Revising** to prompt constructive comments about your work. Discuss parts of the extended metaphor that aren't clear and jot down notes for later changes.

STUDENT MODEL

A magician may ~~have things like his magic playing~~ pull a deck of cards and a hat, out of the bag but my grandmother has items stowed away inside in her huge black purse, too. When I look inside there I see a ~~huge mess~~ mysterious clutter of things: lipsticks, compacts with mirrors, travel brochures for different countries. Her purse ~~is like a treasure chest~~ contents become magical.

Complete Student Model on p. R119.

Rubric for Revising

Your revised extended metaphor should have

- ☑ a clear focus on a particular subject
- ☑ a comparison that helps your readers see your subject differently
- ☑ a concise topic sentence that expresses the comparison you are about to make
- ☑ vivid details and examples

Your revised extended metaphor should be free of

- ☑ confusing or awkward passages
- ☑ errors in grammar, usage, and mechanics

EDITING/PROOFREADING

Edit your essay carefully. Work your way through the entire essay several times, looking for one kind of error each time. Use the **Proofreading Checklist** on the inside back cover to help you find and correct errors in grammar, usage, mechanics, and spelling.

PROOFREADING TIP

Reading your essay backwards, one word at a time, will help you to look at each word and to spot spelling errors more easily.

Grammar Hint

Make sure that each pronoun's antecedent–the noun to which the pronoun refers–is clearly stated. Clarify an unclear pronoun reference either by rewording the sentence or by eliminating the pronoun altogether.

UNCLEAR REFERENCE: I ask for a shell, and my brother asks for a baseball card. Sooner or later it appears on my pillow.

CLEAR: I ask for a shell, and my brother asks for a baseball card. Sooner or later a new shell appears on my pillow.

- For more on pronouns, see **Language Handbook,** p. R20.

STUDENT MODEL

Once, when we were waiting at the doctor's office, she pulled out a pack of candy hearts and a needle and thread ~~out of her purse~~ and taught me how to make a candy heart necklace ~~out of it~~. Another time, she taught me how to build a castle out of poker chips.

Complete Student Model on p. R119.

Complete Student Model

For a complete version of the model developed in this workshop, refer to **Writing Workshop Models,** p. R119.

PUBLISHING/PRESENTING

You might read your metaphor aloud for a class discussion. Or, with your classmates, make a booklet that contains each student's extended metaphor. Display the booklet in your classroom.

PRESENTING TIP

To illustrate your essay, draw a picture or cartoon that depicts the subject metaphorically.

Reflecting

When people share their feelings, they often are trying to help others see things from another point of view. What did you learn as you wrote your extended metaphor?

Save your work for your portfolio.

Unit Assessment

Personal Response

1. Which of the poems in this unit did you find the most interesting?
2. Which poems did you find the most moving or inspiring?
3. As a result of the work you have done in this unit, what new ideas do you have about the following?
   - what the elements of poetry are
   - how a poet combines elements to communicate a theme or main idea
   - how to work with other students in pairs or in groups

Analyzing Literature

Comparing Elements of Poetry Choose two poems from this unit and compare at least two basic elements, such as *speaker, lines and stanzas, rhythm and meter, rhyme, sound devices, imagery,* and *figures of speech.* For help in understanding the elements of poetry, see Genre Focus: Poetry on page 578. At the end of your comparison, explain how those elements work in each poem to make the words sing.

Evaluate and Set Goals

Evaluate

1. What was your strongest contribution to group activities as you worked through this unit?
2. What was your most challenging task in this unit?
   - How did you approach this task?
   - What was the result?
3. How would you assess your work in this unit, using the following scale? Give at least two reasons for your assessment.
   4 = outstanding **3** = good **2** = fair **1** = weak

Set Goals

1. Choose a goal to work toward in Unit 4. It could involve reading, writing, speaking, researching, or working in a group.
2. Discuss your goal with your teacher.
3. Jot down three or four steps that you will take to achieve your goal.
4. Decide at which points in the next unit you will stop and assess your progress toward your goal.

 Build Your Portfolio

Select Choose two pieces of writing that you did in this unit and include them in your portfolio. Use these questions to help you make your selection.
- Which piece are you most satisfied with?
- Which one did you find most challenging to write?
- Which piece are you most likely to share?
- Which one led you to new discoveries as you wrote?

Reflect Write brief notes for the two pieces you selected. These questions can help you.
- What did this writing teach you?
- What changes would you make if you were just beginning the piece?

Reading on Your Own

You might also be interested in the following books.

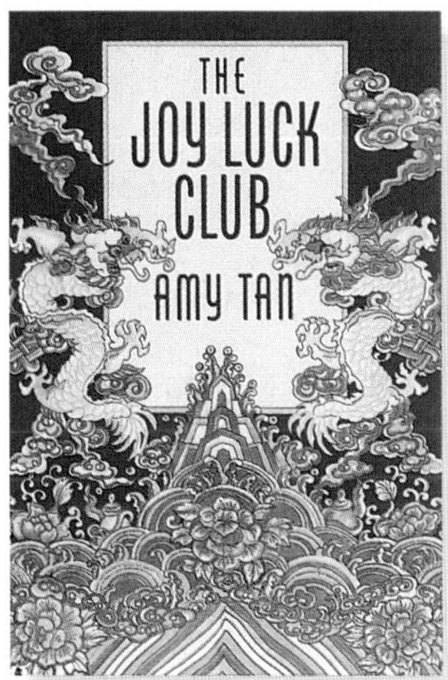

The Joy Luck Club
by Amy Tan For forty years, four Chinese mothers gather in San Francisco to socialize, talking about their lives and their Chinese American daughters. The daughters are establishing their own identities in a different culture from that of their mothers. A fierce love carries both generations to an understanding of each other's needs.

A Poetry Handbook
by Mary Oliver In this highly readable handbook, Oliver empowers the student of poetry and demonstrates that "out of writing, and the rewriting, beauty is born." Citing works from other poets, such as Elizabeth Bishop, T. S. Eliot, William Carlos Williams, and Lucille Clifton, Oliver demonstrates that writing good poetry is a craft.

The Space Between Our Footsteps: Poems and Paintings from the Middle East
selected by Naomi Shihab Nye This collection of the works of more than one hundred poets and artists from nineteen Middle Eastern countries explores themes that include exile, family, childhood, journeys, and joy. Award-winning poet and anthologist Naomi Shihab Nye pairs poems with full-color art from the countries represented.

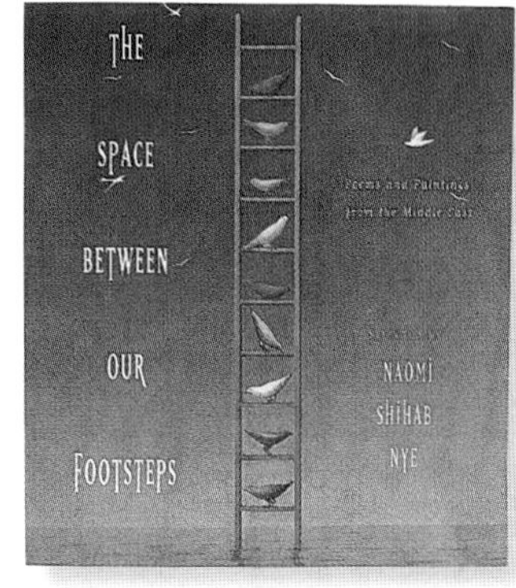

A Haiku Menagerie: Living Creatures in Poems and Prints
by Stephen Addiss with Fumiko and Akira Yamamoto Showing how fascinating the smallest animal or insect can be, this collection of Japanese haiku features master poets' insights into the natural world. More than forty-eight woodblock prints illustrate the creatures described in the poems. The poems are presented both in English translation and the original Japanese.

Reading and Analyzing Test Questions

Read the passage and choose the word or group of words that belongs in each space. Mark the letter for your answer on your paper.

> If you get a chance __(1)__ a trip to Egypt, you must make time to see the Great Pyramids!
>
> No one knows exactly how the pyramids were built. No ancient society __(2)__ the technology that would have been needed to produce them. Scientists are left to speculate as to how ancient architects could have designed such perfectly aligned structures. The stones in each pyramid are fitted so __(3)__ together that it's impossible to drive a knife blade between __(4)__, and the cement between the stones is stronger than the stones themselves. The inside chambers, which used to be filled with treasure, __(5)__ masterfully constructed. There are air passages to allow excellent circulation and hallways to provide easy access to burial chambers.
>
> The Great Pyramids of Egypt are truly a wonderful sight to behold. It is no wonder that __(6)__ are considered part of the Seven Wonders of the World. Don't miss them!

1 **A** take
B to take
C taking
D took

2 **F** should have had
G shouldn't have had
H should hardly have had
J shouldn't never have had

3 **A** tightest
B tighter
C tight
D tightly

4 **F** it
G their
H its
J them

5 **A** is
B are
C is being
D has been

6 **F** it
G you
H they
J he

Read the passage and decide which type of error, if any, appears in each underlined section. Mark the letter for your answer on your paper.

Ranada leaned into her swing <u>and felt the ball hit, the center of her racquet.</u> (7) <u>Her shot flew strait as an arrow toward the net, brushing</u> (8) the top edge as it flew over. On the other side of the court, Jessica looked startled as the ball rocketed toward her like a rifle shot.

<u>The tennis ball hit Jessicas racquet so hard</u> (9) she could feel the impact up to her shoulder. <u>The crowd on either side of the stadium let out a roar of suprise.</u> (10)

Ranada returned the volley, but Jessica's previous effort made her slow to react. Ranada smiled slowly, as she realized <u>she had finally won the Pinefield high school Tennis Championship.</u> (11) She raised her racquet <u>and ran off the court to celabrate.</u> (12)

7 A Spelling error
B Capitalization error
C Punctuation error
D No error

8 F Spelling error
G Capitalization error
H Punctuation error
J No error

9 A Spelling error
B Capitalization error
C Punctuation error
D No error

10 F Spelling error
G Capitalization error
H Punctuation error
J No error

11 A Spelling error
B Capitalization error
C Punctuation error
D No error

12 F Spelling error
G Capitalization error
H Punctuation error
J No error

STOP

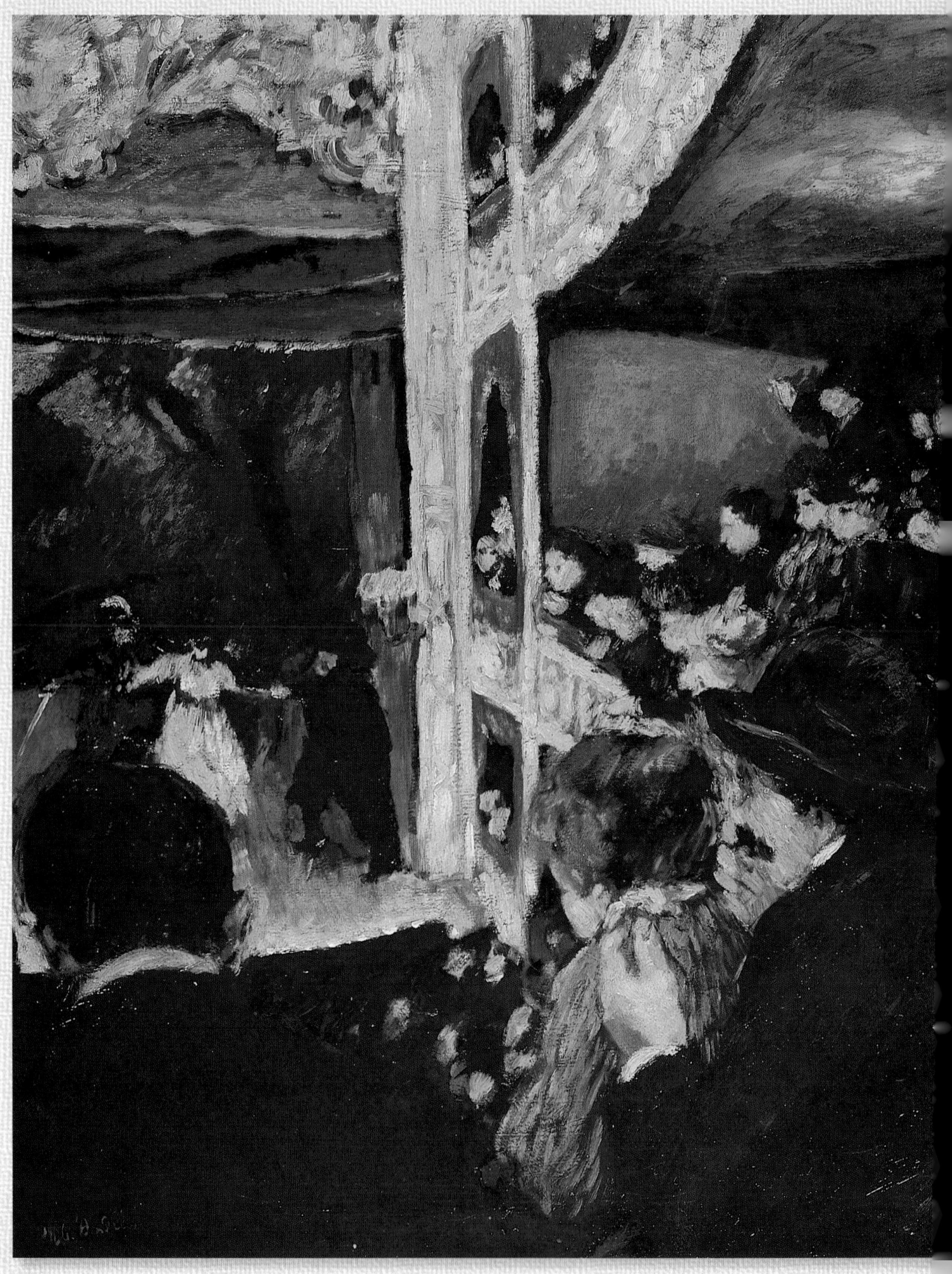

Au Theatre. Albert Andre (1869–1954).

UNIT FOUR

Drama

"Drama . . . makes the point, ceaselessly, that our lives are now; there is no history that is not now."

—Joyce Carol Oates

Theme 10

Loyalty and Betrayal

Genre Focus

Drama

A play, or **drama,** is a story told mainly through the words and actions of characters and is intended to be performed by actors. Feature films can be dramas, as well as many television programs. Although drama shares certain elements with other kinds of narrative, it also has elements that are specifically characteristic of drama alone. Knowing about these elements can help you appreciate and discuss plays that you see and read.

When playwrights develop a script for a play, they include **stage directions** to help actors, directors, and readers visualize what is to be happening on stage. These directions are interspersed between the lines of dialogue, and are usually printed in italics and enclosed in parentheses or brackets. The directions explain how characters should look, speak, act, and move on the stage; they also specify details of the stage set, such as lighting, props, and sound effects.

This chart describes the key elements of drama with models from the play *The Ring of General Macías*, which appears on pages 879–893.

ELEMENTS OF DRAMA

MODEL: *The Ring of General Macías*

Characters

The cast of characters is listed at the beginning of a play and might include a short description of each character. The playwright may further describe a character when he or she first appears in the play. Audiences learn about characters through their actions and through the dialogue.

CHARACTERS
MARICA: the sister of General Macías
RAQUEL: the wife of General Macías
ANDRÉS DE LA O: a captain in the Revolutionary Army
CLETO: a private in the Revolutionary Army
BASILIO FLORES: a captain in the Federal Army

Setting

Typically, the setting is described at the beginning of a play. Additional details might appear throughout the play, such as at the beginning of acts and scenes, when the setting changes.

PLACE: *Just outside Mexico City*
TIME: *A night in April, 1912*

Plot

The plot of a drama, like the plots of other narratives, is the series of related events that revolve around a central conflict. The conflict may be a struggle between people, ideas, or other forces.

The Ring of General Macías tells the story of a Mexican general's wife who is confronted with an opportunity to save her husband's life at the cost of betraying the government's side in the Mexican Revolution. She is torn between her love for her husband and her sense of honor and duty.

Dialogue

Most plays consist largely of dialogue, or conversation between the characters. The dialogue helps reveal the plot and characters of the play.

RAQUEL. Yes. Tell me, captain, do you think it possible to love a person too much?

ANDRÉS. Yes, señora. I do.

RAQUEL. So do I. Let us drink a toast, captain—to honor. To bright and shining honor.

Acts and Scenes

Many plays are divided into acts and scenes, which indicate a change in location or the passage of time. One-act plays take place in one location over a brief, continuous span of time.

The Ring of General Macías is a one-act play.

Active Reading Strategies

Drama

To actively read a script, you use the stage directions and the dialogue to visualize and hear the play in your mind. When you interact with the words, you create the performance in your mind. Use these strategies when you read a play to help you understand and appreciate what you are reading.

• For more about reading strategies, see **Reading Handbook,** pp. R78–R107.

VISUALIZE As you read, picture in your mind all the elements described in the script.

Ask yourself . . .

- What does this scene look like? Is this like a place I've seen or been in before?
- What does this character look like?
- What does this gesture or movement look like? How would I interpret the gesture or movement?
- What might the character's facial expressions convey?

LISTEN Imagine how each character says his or her lines. Sometimes stage directions will give hints about how a line should be delivered. Other times, readers must infer how the line sounds from the words and the context of the play.

Ask yourself . . .

- What tone of voice would the character use here?
- Which words would the character emphasize?
- How loudly or quickly would the person speak this line?

QUESTION Note the questions you have as you read, and see if those questions are answered as you read on.

Ask yourself . . .

- Why does this action take place in this setting?
- What is really happening here? Do I understand the plot so far?
- Why did the character say or do this?
- Why are other characters reacting as they do?
- Will these props be important?

CONNECT Find connections between the characters and events in the play and the people and events in your own life.

Think to yourself . . .

- Whom does this character remind me of?
- When have I felt or acted like this?
- How would my friends and I react in a similar situation?
- This stage set reminds me of . . .

PREDICT Use clues in the dialogue and stage directions to guess what will happen next.

Think to yourself . . .

- What is this character likely to do next?
- How might this conflict be resolved?
- What will the other characters do?

INTERPRET Think about the characters, what they do, and what happens to them. Assess why the characters act as they do.

Say to yourself . . .

- What does this character's actions or words indicate about his or her personality and values?
- What effects do the characters' decisions have on their lives?
- What philosophy about life or people is the playwright conveying?

EVALUATE Form opinions and make judgments about what you are reading.

Ask yourself . . .

- Are the characters, plot, and dialogue believable? clever? funny?
- Do the stage set and the actor's movements contribute to the play or distract from it?

Applying the Strategies

Read the next selection, an excerpt from the play *Big River,* using the Active Reading Model in the margins. Then choose another play and practice using all of these strategies.

Before You Read

from *Big River: The Adventures of Huckleberry Finn*

Reading Focus

How much would you risk to help a friend in need? Would you risk danger? punishment? your reputation?

Journal Reflect on your sense of loyalty and commitment to friends. Then, in your journal, tell what you'd be willing to risk for a friend.

Setting a Purpose Read to see how the classic literary character Huck Finn responds to a friend in need.

Building Background

The Time and Place

The events in this play take place around the 1840s, before the Civil War (1861–1865), on an island in the Mississippi River between Missouri and Illinois.

Did You Know?

- Based on Mark Twain's classic novel *The Adventures of Huckleberry Finn,* the musical play *Big River* recounts the adventures of Huck, a teenaged boy who fakes his own death to escape from his drunken, abusive father, and Jim, a runaway from enslavement. In this scene from the play, Huck acknowledges that he will probably be called a "dirty abolitionist" for his decision. Abolitionists campaigned to end the practice of slavery, and some were despised in areas where slavery was viewed as an economic necessity.
- In the late 1700s, laws known as "fugitive slave laws" made it illegal to assist runaway enslaved people or to prevent those who owned them from recovering them. Anyone caught helping enslaved people escape faced severe punishment.

Elderly Ex-Slave, May 1941. Jack Delano. Black-and-white photography. Greene County, Georgia, U.S.A.

Meet William Hauptman

"Writing is hard work," says one-time actor William Hauptman. Hauptman switched from acting to playwriting in graduate school. He traces his love of theater to his childhood days in the oil boomtown of Wichita Falls, Texas, where he saw plays, magic shows, and dramatic readings in the city auditorium. Although he has also written screenplays, television scripts, short stories, and a novel, Hauptman is best known as the author of the Tony Award-winning musical *Big River,* which first appeared on Broadway in 1985. His other writings include the short story collection *Good Rockin' Tonight* and the novel *The Storm Season.*

William Hauptman was born in 1942 in Wichita Falls, Texas.

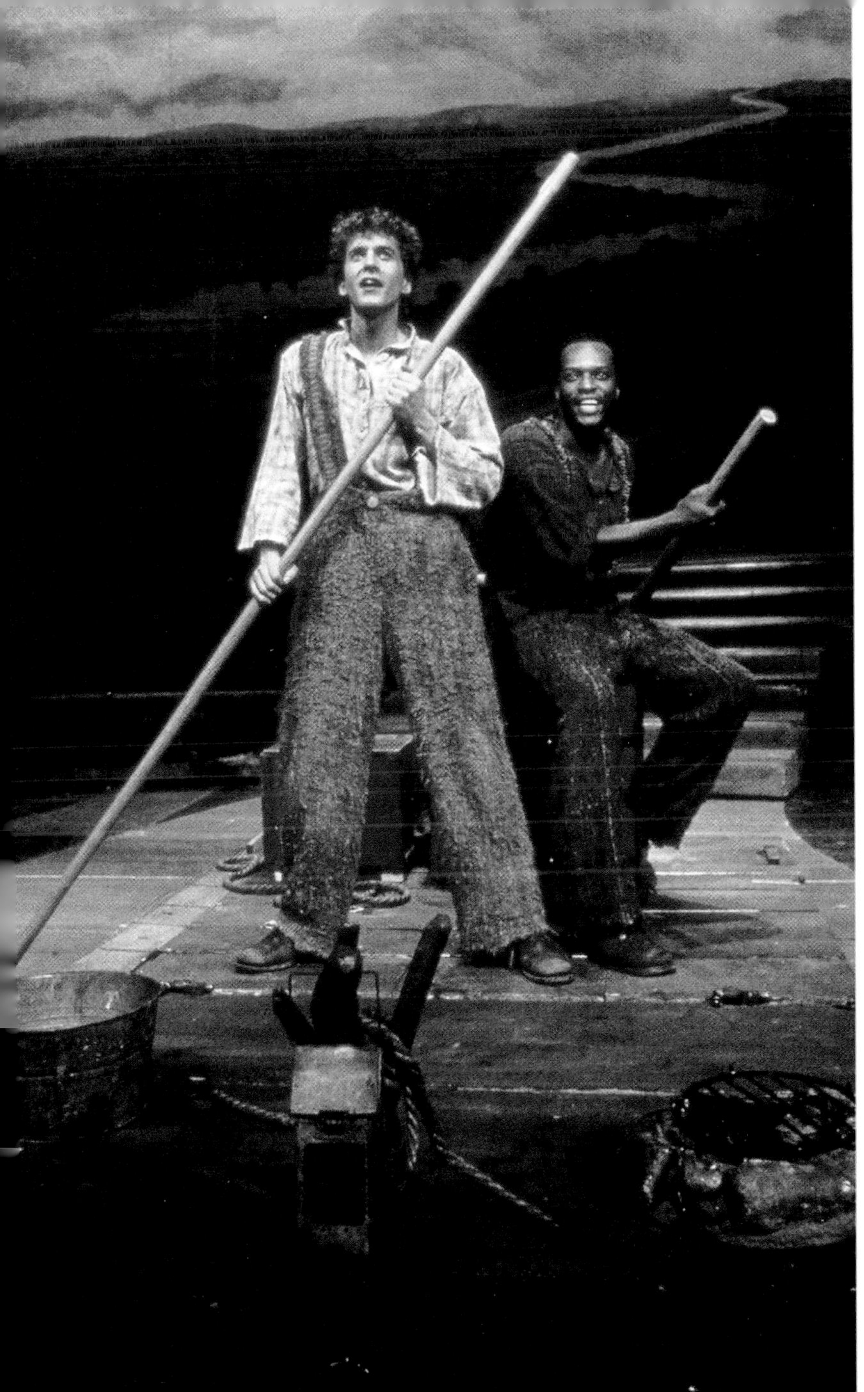

from BIG RIVER: The Adventures of Huckleberry Finn

William Hauptman

Active Reading Model

CHARACTERS

JIM (ADULT) HUCK (13–14)

HUCK has just set off on his own when he comes face to face with JIM.

HUCK. Hello, Jim!

JIM. Get back in the river where you belong, and don't do nothing to ole Jim, who was always your friend!

Active Reading Model

LISTEN

Notice the distinctive speech of Jim and Huck. What tone of voice do you imagine them using here?

VISUALIZE

Picture in your mind the makeshift camp that Jim has built on the river island.

QUESTION

Why has Jim run off?

HUCK. Jim, I'm not dead! I'm alive—and ever so glad to see you!

JIM. You ain't a ghost, is you?

HUCK. Touch me—I'm solid enough. I had to run away from Pap. He got the *delirium tremens*[1] and tried to stab me with his Barlow-Knife. So I faked the whole thing.

[*JIM just keeps staring. HUCK addresses the audience.*]

I talked along, but Jim just stood there. Finally he says—

JIM. See those birds flyin' low? That means rain. Let's go to my camp.

HUCK. I followed Jim to a lean-to he'd built on the Illinois side.

[*A flash of lightning and a roll of thunder. They cross to a lean-to. An enormous catfish hangs from a line. There is a trunk and a raft of logs nearby.*]

You got a great place here, Jim! That must be the biggest catfish ever pulled out of the Mississippi River!

JIM. [*Taking out knife and cutting down the fish.*] Found him on my trotline[2] this morning. I was just getting ready to clean him up.

HUCK. I never seen a bigger one . . . what's all this?

JIM. Trash come floating down on the high water.

HUCK. [*Opening the trunk.*] Here's a calico gown . . . and some seegars . . .[3] there must be a flood somewheres upriver . . . and look at this raft!

JIM. That came floating down, too.

HUCK. Jim? What *are* you doing here?

JIM. You wouldn't tell on me if I was to tell you?

HUCK. Blamed if I would, Jim.

JIM. Huck—I run off.

HUCK. Jim!

JIM. You said you wouldn't tell.

HUCK. And I'll stick to it, Jim, honest Injun. People can call me a dirty abolitionist and despise me for it—that don't make no difference. I ain't a-going to tell and I ain't a-going back there anyways—so let's hear about it.

JIM. Miss Watson always say she won't sell me. But I notice lately there's been a slave trader around the place considerable. The night you was killed, I creep to the door, and I hear the missus telling the

1. *Delirium tremens* is a temporary form of mental disturbance usually caused by excessive drinking of alcohol. The condition is often accompanied by restlessness, violent shaking, and terrifying hallucinations.
2. Jim's *trotline* is a fishing line suspended across a stream with many baited hooks hung at intervals along it.
3. This is Huck's way of pronouncing *cigars*.

Active Reading Model

Widow Douglas[4] she's going to sell me down to New Orleans. She don't want to, but she can get eight hundred dollars for me, and it's such a big stack of money, she can't refuse. I never hear the rest. I light out.

[*He cuts open the belly of the catfish—bloodlessly—and several objects spill out.*]

Big fish like this eat all sorts of trash in his years.

HUCK. I'll say. Here's a spool.

JIM. And a horseshoe.

HUCK. [*Picks up a hard little sphere.*] What's this?

JIM. Must a been in there a long time to coat it over so.

[*JIM cuts open the sphere and hands HUCK a coin.*]

HUCK. It's gold.

JIM. What sort of writing is that on it?

HUCK. Spanish . . . I think. This is a Spanish d'bloon,[5] Jim, it's pirate gold! Why I reckon this fish could be a hundred years old. Do you reckon so, Jim?

JIM. [*Nodding.*] He go along on the bottom. Eat the little ones. Get older and older and bigger and bigger. He here before people come maybe. Before this was a country. When there was nothing here but that big river . . .

[*He grabs HUCK's arm.*]

I'm going down that river, Huck. To Cairo,[6] where the Mississippi joins the Ohio. Then I'm following the Ohio north, to the Free States. I'm going down on that raft, and I'm getting my freedom!

HUCK. I'm going with you, Jim!

JIM. You get in a powerful lot of trouble, helping Jim. You might find yourself hangin' from a cottonwood tree.

HUCK. You can't do it alone. But if I came along, I can tell people you belong to me, and they won't bother you.

JIM. [*Greatly moved.*] You'd do that for Jim? Then you a friend, Huck.

EVALUATE
Is it realistic that a catfish could swallow a horseshoe? Why do you think the writer included this detail?

CONNECT
What would you do in Huck's situation?

INTERPRET
What is Jim's definition of *friend?* Do you agree that Huck really is a friend? Why or why not?

---

4. Jim had belonged to *Miss Watson,* an unpleasant woman whose sister is the good *Widow Douglas. The night you was killed* refers to the night Huck made it appear that he had been murdered so that he could run away without being pursued.
5. *D'bloon* refers to a doubloon, a gold coin used in Spain and by Spanish colonists in the Americas.
6. This *Cairo* is a river port at the southern tip of Illinois, where people pronounce it (kā′ rō).

Responding to Literature

Personal Response

What is your reaction to Jim and his quest for freedom?

Active Reading Response

Look back at the strategies described in the Active Reading Model on pages 717–719. Which Active Reading Strategy was most helpful to you in understanding this scene from the play?

Analyzing Literature

Recall and Interpret

1. How does Jim first react to seeing Huck? Why?
2. Why is Huck on the island? Why is Jim there?
3. What is Jim's plan? What is Huck's response to Jim's plan?
4. Based on his words and actions, how would you describe Jim? What does he value? What kind of person is Huck? Give evidence from the play to support your answers.

Evaluate and Connect

5. In what ways are Jim and Huck alike?
6. An **aside** is a comment made by a character who is heard by the audience but not by the other characters onstage. What is the purpose of Huck's aside in this scene? (See Literary Terms Handbook, page R1.)
7. Look back at the writing you did for the Reading Focus on page 716. Knowing the potential consequences of your actions, would you have made the same decision that Huck makes at the end of this scene? Why or why not?
8. Whom do you identify with most in this scene, Huck or Jim? Why?

Literary ELEMENTS

Dialect

Dialect is a variation of language spoken by a particular group, often within a particular region. Dialects differ in pronunciation, grammar, and vocabulary from the standard form of a language. Huck and Jim speak dialects of English common in the small river towns in northeastern Missouri in the mid-1800s. For example, Huck pronounces cigars, *seegars,* and says "there must be a flood *somewheres*" instead of *somewhere.*

1. Find three other examples of dialect in this scene. Rewrite the examples in standard English.
2. What does the use of dialect add to your reading of this scene?

- See **Literary Terms Handbook,** p. R3.

Extending Your Response

Interdisciplinary Activity

Art and Drama: Set Designers Wanted With a partner, consider the relevance of setting and time frame to this play's meaning. Then, design a set for this scene from *Big River.* Work to convey the essential elements of the setting in a clear and simple way. Then share your set design with your classmates.

Literature Groups

Analyzing Motivation Does Huck act purely out of friendship for Jim? What other reasons might he have for wanting to go with Jim? Discuss these questions in your group and share your responses with your classmates. Be prepared to justify your responses.

Save your work for your portfolio.

Theme 10 Loyalty and Betrayal

Has a friend ever betrayed you? Have you, yourself, ever been the betrayer? Loyalty is a highly valued trait, but perhaps, sometimes, there are justifiable reasons to turn against someone. The plays in this theme will take you into a world where the line between loyalty and betrayal sometimes becomes blurred.

THEME PROJECTS

Performing

Time Travel Show how the themes in *Julius Caesar* can be applied to a different time.

1. Choose a monologue from *Julius Caesar* and show how it could relate to another time or historical event, for example, the American Revolution, the American Civil War, the 1960s, or the present.
2. Rewrite the monologue so that it is relevant to the period you have chosen.
3. Perform your revised monologue for the class.

Interdisciplinary Project

Art: Comic Strip With a partner, choose any scene from this theme and depict it as a comic strip.

1. Together, discuss what kind of illustrations and how much dialogue are necessary to re-create the drama of the scene.
2. Consider having one person act as a writer and create the script that will be used in the comic. The other person could act as the artist and draw the panels, including captions and word bubbles to fill with dialogue.
3. Share your comic strip with your classmates.

Othello, Desdemona and Emilia, 1867. Daniel Maclise. Oil on canvas, 130 x 87 cm. Johannesburg Art Gallery, South Africa.

Viewing the art: Do you think the characters portrayed in this scene from Shakespeare's tragedy *Othello* are the betrayers or the betrayed? Why?

Literature FOCUS

Classical Greek Drama

The sun has not yet risen over Athens, but the city's narrow streets are already alive with people. Chatting excitedly, family parties carry with them provisions for the long day ahead: baskets of food, cushions, blankets to ward off the chill March air. This happy crowd streams toward the Acropolis, the rocky hill that towers over the city. Those who look up can make out the snowy columns of the Parthenon silhouetted against the morning sky. But it is not for this elegant temple on the summit that the travelers are bound. Their journey stops on the lower slopes of the Acropolis, at the gates of the Theater of Dionysos. The crowd slows to a crawl, for it seems that the entire city is trying to squeeze through the entryways. Inside, however, there is room for everyone. Banked up the slopes of the hill are curving tiers of stone benches. The spectators check their admission tokens to find their designated sections. They spread out their cushions and watch the eastern sky. The sun is rising. The first play is about to begin.

Theater was far more than entertainment for the people of ancient Greece. It was part of their religion, a way of displaying loyalty to their city-state, and a method of honoring local heroes. It was also a major social event, a thrilling competition, and a place where important philosophical issues could be aired.

Origins

Like most great traditions, Greek drama began very simply. For centuries the people of Greece had loved to sing and dance as a way of worshiping their gods and celebrating important occasions. When work was done, a circular threshing floor, used for separating the grains of wheat from their inedible husks, made an ideal space for people to rejoice in the harvest with circle dances and songs that Greek people still enjoy. Over the centuries, these circle dances developed into the **dithyramb,** a religious ritual performed by a chorus of men wearing masks. Special arenas were established for these rituals at the base of hills, allowing spectators to sit on the slopes and watch the performance unobstructed. A theater was taking shape, with a circular stage and seating, but as yet there were no plays.

Terra-cotta grinning mask. 6th century B.C., Motya.

An Athenian poet called Thespis is traditionally credited with inventing what we now call drama. In 534 B.C. he discovered that a dithyramb could be creatively expanded by adding a character separate from the chorus of male singers. Thus the first actor appeared on the circular stage, and with him there emerged a whole new world of possibilities for writers. Now there could be dialogue, an exchange of ideas, even a lively argument. Clearly the spectators approved, because drama continued to develop and grow in popularity.

In the early fifth century B.C., the great dramatist Aeschylus (525–456 B.C.) added a second actor to the stage; within a few years, his rival Sophocles (496–406 B.C.) answered with a third. The chorus remained, but the audience's attention had shifted from the chants and dances of a group to the lives and struggles of individuals. European theater was born.

The Theaters

The theaters that graced Greek cities of the late fifth century were not buildings at all. Instead, architects had merely adapted the hillside and circle of the ancient dances. An early innovation was to add a few wooden benches curving around the lower slopes for the comfort of important spectators. Then the circular dancing area, known as the **orchestra,** might be paved with stones so that the chorus members would have a more formal place to perform. Another early addition was the **skene,** a rectangular building made of wood, which faced the audience from the opposite side of the orchestra and had several doors opening out toward the audience. This building provided changing rooms for actors and a place to store props.

Theater design naturally evolved from these early innovations. Wooden seats gave way to stone, not just for the privileged front-row customers, but for the entire audience. Benches of stone curved around the hillside with gangways radiating up from the orchestra, creating wedge-shaped seating areas. It was not long before the wooden skene was replaced by a permanent building of stone. This provided a formal backdrop to the action and served as a built-in piece of stage scenery, such as a palace or a temple, from which actors could make their entries. As the centuries progressed, theaters became more decorative and complex, but for more than a thousand years, they maintained their basic elements: a circle for the actors, a slope for the spectators, and the open air for a roof.

Chorus, Actors, and Stage Sets

What would you have seen from the benches of an ancient Greek theater? Dominating the area below the spectators, and partly surrounded by the curved seating, was the great circle of the orchestra. More than sixty-five feet in diameter, this was the domain of the **chorus,** which would enter at the beginning of the drama and remain throughout the performance. Only men were allowed to perform. As they had for centuries, choruses chanted and danced, though now they moved in lines rather than the traditional circle. Their role was to comment on the action of the play, reacting to the plot with expressive, stylized dances. A single musician, playing a type of pipe called the **aulos,** accompanied the chorus. The **choragos,** or leader of the chorus, sometimes participated in the dialogue and generally represented the

Two statuettes of elderly comic actors. c. 375–350 B.C., Attica.

typical responses of an ordinary citizen to the events of the play.

The enormous size of Greek theaters influenced the style of acting. Up to fifteen thousand spectators could watch performances in the Theater of Dionysos in Athens. Perched in the upper rows of seats, a spectator was more than fifty-five yards from the action below. The actors' gestures had to be exaggerated and dramatic, for no one in the back row could have interpreted slight movements.

All the participants, except the musician, wore masks. Made of wool, linen, wood, plaster or other perishable materials, none of these masks have survived, but enough paintings remain to give us an idea of what they were like. In the mid-fifth century, the time of Sophocles, masks were fairly realistic representations of human faces. In later centuries, masks grew in size and became less realistic, featuring deep eye sockets and wide, gaping mouths, making actors appear larger against the background skene. Typically, tragic actors wore striking, richly decorated robes that set them apart from the audience. Chorus members wore more conventional costumes, which identified the roles they were playing: soldiers, priests, mourners, or even—in the case of comedies—frogs, birds, or wasps.

Performances were full of color and movement but were lacking the scenery and technical magic that modern audiences would expect from a major production. The skene, directly behind the actors, served as a palace, temple, cave, or whatever other structure the spectators were asked to imagine. It is likely that painted panels were sometimes installed in front of the skene, but they could do little more than provide a decorative backdrop in such a huge space. Actors made their entrances and exits through doors of the skene, and probably remained at the far end of the orchestra, where a low wooden platform may have raised them a foot or two above the ground. In later centuries, this platform was built up to stand several feet above ground level—the forerunner of the modern theater stage.

The lighting, of course, was natural, and there were very few props. A hunter might carry a bow; an old man, a stick; a soldier, a sword and shield; but these props served more as symbols to identify the character's role in the play than to provide an imitation of life. The violence—murder, suicide, and battles—almost always occurred offstage. Typically, a messenger would appear after the event and describe in gory detail what had just happened.

The Plays

During the fifth century B.C., known as the golden age of Greek drama, four playwrights emerged as the greatest Greek dramatists: Aeschylus, Sophocles, Euripides (480–406 B.C.), and Aristophanes (448–385 B.C.). These masters—all from Athens—wrote plays in verse, based on themes familiar to their audiences. They retold myths, rewrote history, and ridiculed politicians. Aristophanes, the sole comic writer among the four Athenian masters, boldly and uproariously satirized society, politics, and even the gods, landing himself in legal trouble for doing so. However, his three great contemporaries were all tragic poets, whose plays capture humankind's timeless struggle to find the purpose of life and to achieve self-understanding.

Central to the **tragedy** is the fall of a great man (or woman, though her part would have been acted by a man)—the **tragic hero,** whose fate is brought about by a flaw within his or her own character. The aim of the tragic hero was to inspire audiences to examine their own lives, to define their beliefs, and to cleanse their emotions of pity and terror through compassion for the character.

Relief in honor of Euripides. Late Hellenistic period. Height: 60 cm. Archaeological Museum, Istanbul, Turkey.

Theater as Festival

Plays in ancient Greece were never performed day after day for a "season" as they often are now. Instead, drama was the centerpiece of annual festivals that were partly religious and partly political. In one such festival, three tragic poets competed for first prize. Each author had to write and direct three tragedies and a farce; these four offerings would then be performed on a single day. Ten judges, chosen at random from among prominent citizens, were responsible for selecting a winner, but the crowd took an intense interest in the results, making their opinions loudly known and no doubt influencing the outcome with their emotional reactions. Sophocles came away with first prize at least eighteen times and never placed lower than second. There were also competitions for best comic poet, best tragic actor, and best comic actor.

Theater was far more than a popularity contest for the people of Athens, however. Audiences cared deeply for the content of the plays. People would memorize and quote their favorite passages, and there are many accounts of crowds being moved to tears by an emotional performance.

Nearly 2,500 years have passed since the golden age of Greek drama, but it is safe to say that any stage, television, or movie production we enjoy today owes its existence to that open theater, those pioneering actors, the dedicated poets, and the passionate audiences of ancient Greece.

Before You Read

Antigone

Reading Focus

Do you know of someone who had to act bravely in order to do what was right?

Discuss Think of an example of someone who, in your opinion, acted bravely. Share your story with the rest of the class.

Setting a Purpose Read to learn about a character who courageously stands up for what she believes is right.

Building Background

The Time and Place

This play takes place in ancient Greece, in the city of Thebes, which is about thirty miles northwest of Athens. At the time, Thebes was one of the greatest cities of Greece.

Did You Know?

The Greeks of Sophocles's day believed that if a corpse was not buried or cremated according to a strict ritual, his or her soul might not get to Hades, the underworld of the dead, but would wander the earth, bringing shame upon its survivors and angering the gods. To leave a body unburied was a terrible insult to the family of the deceased.

Vocabulary Preview

repulse (ri puls′) *n.* an act of beating back or driving away, as with force; p. 728

arrogance (ar′ ə gəns) *n.* overbearing pride; p. 745

perverse (pər vurs′) *adj.* determined to go against what is reasonable, expected, or desired; contrary; p. 752

absolve (ab zolv′) *v.* to free from guilt or blame; p. 752

prevail (pri vāl′) *v.* to be superior in power or influence; succeed; p. 754

defile (di fīl′) *v.* to spoil the purity of; to make dirty or unclean; p. 758

Meet Sophocles

Sophocles, a handsome, athletic youth skilled in music, was only sixteen when he was chosen to lead a chorus in honor of Greece's victory at the Battle of Salamis. He studied music under Lamprus, the most acclaimed musician of his time, and tragedy, musical composition, and choreography under Aeschylus, the great writer of tragedy. During his ninety years, Sophocles wrote 123 dramas, winning 24 of 30 competitions. Other credits include inventing "scene paintings" and adding a third actor to dramas. He was also elected one of the ten military commanders of Athens and served on embassies to foreign states.

Sophocles was born about 496 B.C. at Colonus, a village near Athens. He died in Athens in 406 B.C.

ANTIGONE

Sophocles

Translated by Dudley Fitts and Robert Fitzgerald

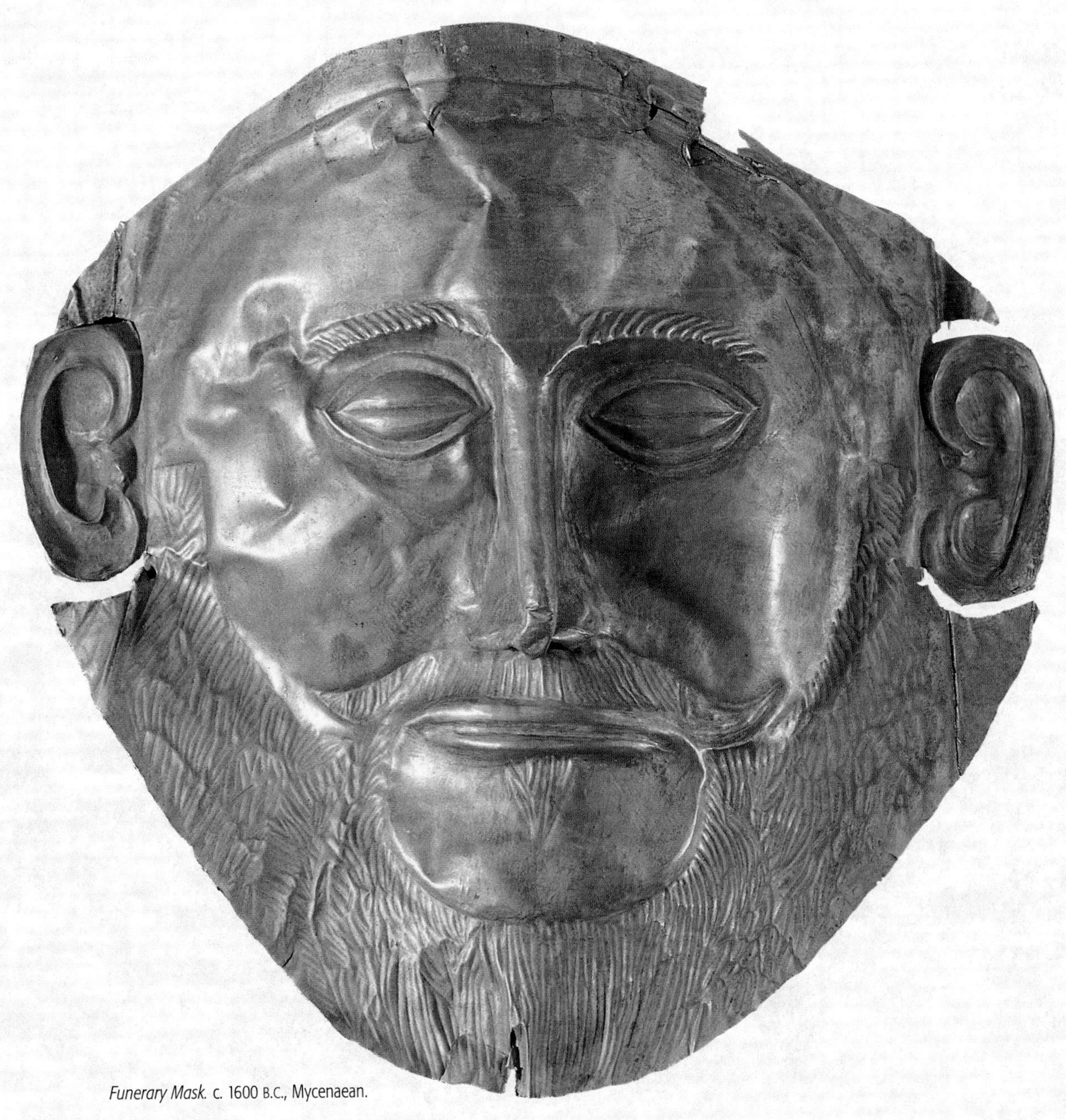

Funerary Mask. c. 1600 B.C., Mycenaean.

CHARACTERS

ANTIGONE: daughter of Oedipus

ISMENE: daughter of Oedipus

EURYDICE: wife of Creon

CREON: King of Thebes, uncle of Antigone and Ismene

HAIMON: son of Creon

TEIRESIAS: a blind prophet

A SENTRY

A MESSENGER

CHORUS: elders of Thebes

CHORAGOS: leader of the Chorus

SCENE: *Before the palace of* CREON, *King of Thebes. A central double door, and two lateral doors. A platform extends the length of the façade, and from this platform three steps lead down into the* "orchestra," *or chorus-ground.* **TIME:** *Dawn of the day after the repulse of the Argive army from the assault on Thebes.*

Vocabulary

repulse (ri puls′) *n.* an act of beating back or driving away, as with force

Theatre of Ancient Epidaurus. Mid-4th century B.C. to Hellenistic period. Palaia Epidaurus, Greece.

Prologue

[ANTIGONE and ISMENE enter from the central door of the Palace.]

ANTIGONE.° Ismene,° dear sister,
You would think that we had already suffered enough
For the curse on Oedipus:°
I cannot imagine any grief
That you and I have not gone through. And now—
Have they told you of the new decree of our King Creon?

ISMENE. I have heard nothing: I know
That two sisters lost two brothers, a double death
In a single hour; and I know that the Argive army°
Fled in the night; but beyond this, nothing.

ANTIGONE. I thought so. And that is why I wanted you
To come out here with me. There is something we must do.

ISMENE. Why do you speak so strangely?

ANTIGONE. Listen, Ismene:
Creon buried our brother Eteocles
With military honors, gave him a soldier's funeral,
And it was right that he should; but Polyneices,
Who fought as bravely and died as miserably,—
They say that Creon has sworn
No one shall bury him, no one mourn for him,
But his body must lie in the fields, a sweet treasure
For carrion birds to find as they search for food.
That is what they say, and our good Creon is coming here
To announce it publicly; and the penalty—
Stoning to death in the public square!
There it is,
And now you can prove what you are:
A true sister, or a traitor to your family.

ISMENE. Antigone, you are mad! What could I possibly do?

ANTIGONE. You must decide whether you will help me or not.

ISMENE. I do not understand you. Help you in what?

ANTIGONE. Ismene, I am going to bury him. Will you come?

ISMENE. Bury him! You have just said the new law forbids it.

ANTIGONE. He is my brother. And he is your brother, too.

ISMENE. But think of the danger! Think what Creon will do!

ANTIGONE Creon is not strong enough to stand in my way.

ISMENE. Ah sister!

1 **Antigone:** (an tig′ ə nē). **Ismene:** (is mē′ nē).

3 **Oedipus:** (ed′ ə pəs).

8–9 **two sisters . . . Argive army:** After the death of Oedipus, King of Thebes (thēbz), his sons, Eteocles (ē tē′ ə klēz′) and Polyneices (pä′ lə nī′ sēz), struggled to gain the throne. Argos, a rival city-state, sent its army in support of Polyneices. Before the Argive (ar′ jīv) army was driven back, both Eteocles and Polyneices were killed in battle. Creon (krē′ on), their uncle and Oedipus's brother-in-law, became king.

Oedipus died, everyone hating him
For what his own search brought to light, his eyes
Ripped out by his own hand; and Jocasta died,
His mother and wife at once: she twisted the cords
That strangled her life;° and our two brothers died,
Each killed by the other's sword. And we are left:
But oh, Antigone,
Think how much more terrible than these
Our own death would be if we should go against Creon
And do what he has forbidden! We are only women,
We cannot fight with men, Antigone!
The law is strong, we must give in to the law
In this thing, and in worse. I beg the Dead
To forgive me, but I am helpless: I must yield
To those in authority. And I think it is dangerous business
To be always meddling.

ANTIGONE. If that is what you think,
I should not want you, even if you asked to come.
You have made your choice, you can be what you want to be.
But I will bury him; and if I must die,
I say that this crime is holy: I shall lie down
With him in death, and I shall be as dear
To him as he to me.
It is the dead,
Not the living, who make the longest demands:
We die for ever . . .
You may do as you like,
Since apparently the laws of the gods mean nothing to you.

ISMENE. They mean a great deal to me; but I have no strength
To break laws that were made for the public good.

ANTIGONE. That must be your excuse, I suppose. But as for me,
I will bury the brother I love.

ISMENE. Antigone,
I am so afraid for you!

ANTIGONE. You need not be:
You have yourself to consider, after all.

ISMENE. But no one must hear of this, you must tell no one!
I will keep it a secret, I promise!

ANTIGONE. Oh tell it! Tell everyone!
Think how they'll hate you when it all comes out
If they learn that you knew about it all the time!

37–41 **Oedipus died . . . her life:** Oedipus had killed Laïos (lī′ əs), the king of Thebes at the time, and married the queen, Jocasta (jō kas′ tə). Together, they had four children—Antigone, Ismene, and two sons. When it was revealed that Oedipus had, without realizing it, killed his own father and married his own mother, he blinded himself, was banished from Thebes, and died, and Jocasta hanged herself.

ISMENE. So fiery! You should be cold with fear.

ANTIGONE. Perhaps. But I am only doing what I must.

ISMENE. But can you do it? I say that you cannot.

ANTIGONE Very well: when my strength gives out, I shall do no more.

ISMENE. Impossible things should not be tried at all.

ANTIGONE. Go away, Ismene:
I shall be hating you soon, and the dead will too,
For your words are hateful. Leave me my foolish plan:
I am not afraid of the danger; if it means death,
It will not be the worst of deaths—death without honor.

ISMENE. Go then, if you feel that you must.
You are unwise,
But a loyal friend indeed to those who love you.

[*Exit into the Palace.* ANTIGONE *goes off, L. Enter the* CHORUS.]

Antigone. Marie Spartali Stillman (1844–1927). Simon Carter Gallery, Woodbridge, Suffolk, U.K.

Viewing the art: What characters are portrayed here? How does this image differ from the storyline that you've read so far?

Parodos°

CHORUS. Now the long blade of the sun, lying
Level east to west, touches with glory
Thebes of the Seven Gates. Open, unlidded
Eye of golden day! O marching light
Across the eddy and rush of Dirce's stream,°
Striking the white shields of the enemy
Thrown headlong backward from the blaze of morning!

CHORAGOS. Polyneices their commander
Roused them with windy phrases,
He the wild eagle screaming
Insults above our land,
His wings their shields of snow,
His crest their marshalled helms.

CHORUS. Against our seven gates in a yawning ring
The famished spears came onward in the night;
But before his jaws were sated with our blood,
Or pinefire took the garland of our towers,
He was thrown back; and as he turned, great Thebes—
No tender victim for his noisy power—
Rose like a dragon behind him, shouting war.

CHORAGOS. For God° hates utterly
The bray of bragging tongues;
And when he beheld their smiling,
Their swagger of golden helms,
The frown of his thunder blasted
Their first man from our walls.

CHORUS. We heard his shout of triumph high in the air
Turn to a scream; far out in a flaming arc
He fell with his windy torch, and the earth struck him.
And others storming in fury no less than his
Found shock of death in the dusty joy of battle.

CHORAGOS. Seven captains at seven gates
Yielded their clanging arms to the god
That bends the battle-line and breaks it.°
These two only, brothers in blood,
Face to face in matchless rage,
Mirroring each the other's death,
Clashed in long combat.

CHORUS. But now in the beautiful morning of victory
Let Thebes of the many chariots sing for joy!

Parodos (**păr′ ə dos**): the first "song" of the Chorus.

5 Dirce's stream: This stream, which flows past Thebes, was named after a murdered queen.

21 God: Here, "God" refers to Zeus (**zo͞os**), the king of the gods, who used thunderbolts to strike down the invading Argives.

32–34 Seven captains . . . breaks it: The Thebans offered the captains' armor **(arms)** as a sacrifice to Ares (ā′ rēz), the god of war.

With hearts for dancing we'll take leave of war:
Our temples shall be sweet with hymns of praise,
And the long night shall echo with our chorus.

SCENE 1

CHORAGOS. But now at last our new King is coming:
Creon of Thebes, Menoikeus'° son.
In this auspicious° dawn of his reign
What are the new complexities
That shifting Fate° has woven for him?
What is his counsel? Why has he summoned
The old men to hear him?

[Enter CREON *from the Palace,* C. *He addresses the* CHORUS *from the top step.]*

CREON. Gentlemen: I have the honor to inform you that our Ship of State, which recent storms have threatened to destroy, has come safely to harbor at last,° guided by the merciful wisdom of Heaven. I have summoned you here this morning because I know that I can depend upon you: your devotion to King Laïos was absolute; you never hesitated in your duty to our late ruler Oedipus; and when Oedipus died, your loyalty was transferred to his children. Unfortunately, as you know, his two sons, the princes Eteocles and Polyneices, have killed each other in battle; and I, as the next in blood, have succeeded to the full power of the throne.

I am aware, of course, that no Ruler can expect complete loyalty from his subjects until he has been tested in office. Nevertheless, I say to you at the very outset that I have nothing but contempt for the kind of Governor who is afraid, for whatever reason, to follow the course that he knows is best for the State; and as for the man who sets private friendship above the public welfare,—I have no use for him, either. I call God to witness that if I saw my country headed for ruin, I should not be afraid to speak out plainly; and I need hardly remind you that I would never have any dealings with an enemy of the people. No one values friendship more highly than I; but we must remember that friends made at the risk of wrecking our Ship are not real friends at all.

These are my principles, at any rate, and that is why I have made the following decision concerning the sons of Oedipus:

2 **Menoikeus** (me noi′ kē əs)

3 **auspicious:** favorable, indicating good fortune.

5 **Fate:** The ancient Greeks believed that three sisters, called the Fates, controlled human destiny. The first sister was said to spin the thread of human life, the second decided its length, and the third cut it.

8–10 **Gentlemen . . . at last:** The expression "Ship of State" likens a nation to a ship under sail. In reassuring the citizens of Thebes that the "storms" are over, Creon is referring to the Argive invasion and the many troubles in the house of Oedipus.

Eteocles, who died as a man should die, fighting for his country, is to be buried with full military honors, with all the ceremony that is usual when the greatest heroes die; but his brother Polyneices, who broke his exile to come back with fire and sword against his native city and the shrines of his fathers' gods, whose one idea was to spill the blood of his blood and sell his own people into slavery—Polyneices, I say, is to have no burial: no man is to touch him or say the least prayer for him; he shall lie on the plain, unburied; and the birds and the scavenging dogs can do with him whatever they like.

This is my command, and you can see the wisdom behind it. As long as I am King, no traitor is going to be honored with the loyal man. But whoever shows by word and deed that he is on the side of the State,—he shall have my respect while he is living, and my reverence when he is dead.

CHORAGOS. If that is your will, Creon son of Menoikeus,
You have the right to enforce it: we are yours.

CREON. That is my will. Take care that you do your part.

CHORAGOS. We are old men: let the younger ones carry it out.

CREON. I do not mean that: the sentries have been appointed.

CHORAGOS. Then what is it that you would have us do?

CREON. You will give no support to whoever breaks this law.

CHORAGOS. Only a crazy man is in love with death!

CREON. And death it is; yet money talks, and the wisest
Have sometimes been known to count a few coins too many.

[*Enter* SENTRY *from L.*]

SENTRY. I'll not say that I'm out of breath from running, King, because every time I stopped to think about what I have to tell you, I felt like going back. And all the time a voice kept saying, "You fool, don't you know you're walking straight into trouble?"; and then another voice: "Yes, but if you let somebody else get the news to Creon first, it will be even worse than that for you!" But good sense won out, at least I hope it was good sense, and here I am with a story that makes no sense at all; but I'll tell it anyhow, because, as they say, what's going to happen's going to happen, and—

CREON. Come to the point. What have you to say?

SENTRY. I did not do it. I did not see who did it. You must not punish me for what someone else has done.

Marble gravestone of Sosinos from Gortyna, a bronze founder. Classical Greek, Attic period, last quarter of the 5th century B.C. Louvre Museum, Paris.

Viewing the art: What might Antigone and Ismene have wanted depicted on Polyneices's gravestone if they had been allowed to bury their brother properly?

CREON. A comprehensive defense! More effective, perhaps,
If I knew its purpose. Come: what is it?

SENTRY. A dreadful thing . . . I don't know how to put it—

CREON. Out with it!

SENTRY. Well, then;
The dead man—
Polyneices—

[*Pause. The* SENTRY *is overcome, fumbles for words.* CREON *waits impassively.*]

out there—
someone,—
New dust on the slimy flesh!

[*Pause. No sign from* CREON.]

Someone has given it burial that way, and
Gone . . .

[*Long pause.* CREON *finally speaks with deadly control.*]

CREON. And the man who dared do this?

SENTRY. I swear I
Do not know! You must believe me!
Listen:
The ground was dry, not a sign of digging, no,
Not a wheeltrack in the dust, no trace of anyone.
It was when they relieved us this morning: and one of them,
The corporal, pointed to it.
There it was,
The strangest—
Look:
The body, just mounded over with light dust: you see?
Not buried really, but as if they'd covered it
Just enough for the ghost's peace. And no sign
Of dogs or any wild animal that had been there.

And then what a scene there was! Every man of us
Accusing the other: we all proved the other man did it,
We all had proof that we could not have done it.
We were ready to take hot iron in our hands,
Walk through fire, swear by all the gods,
It was not I!
I do not know who it was, but it was not I!

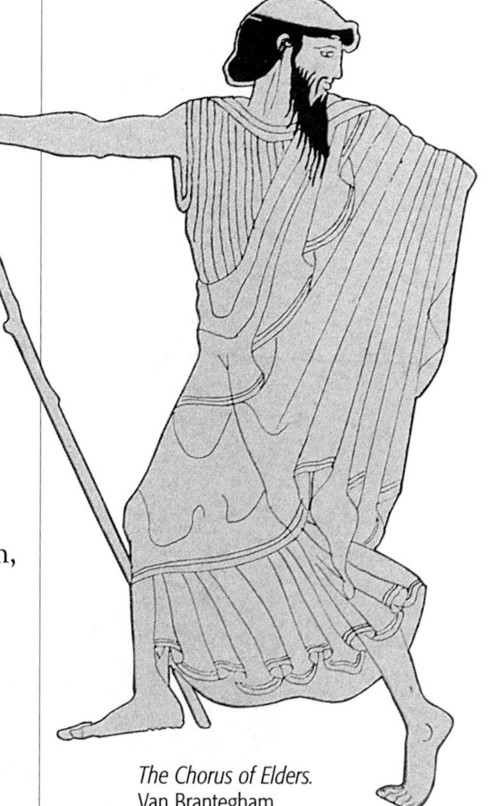

The Chorus of Elders. Van Brantegham Collection, Brussels.

[*CREON's rage has been mounting steadily, but the* SENTRY *is too intent upon his story to notice it.*]

And then, when this came to nothing, someone said
A thing that silenced us and made us stare
Down at the ground: you had to be told the news,
And one of us had to do it! We threw the dice,
And the bad luck fell to me.° So here I am,
No happier to be here than you are to have me:
Nobody likes the man who brings bad news.

CHORAGOS. I have been wondering, King: can it be that the gods have done this?

CREON. [*Furiously.*] Stop!
Must you doddering wrecks
Go out of your heads entirely? "The gods!"
Intolerable!
The gods favor this corpse? Why? How had he served them?
Tried to loot their temples, burn their images,
Yes, and the whole State, and its laws with it!
Is it your senile opinion that the gods love to honor bad men?
A pious thought!—
No, from the very beginning
There have been those who have whispered together,
Stiff-necked anarchists, putting their heads together,
Scheming against me in alleys.° These are the men,
And they have bribed my own guard to do this thing.
[*Sententiously.*] Money!
There's nothing in the world so demoralizing as money.
Down go your cities,
Homes gone, men gone, honest hearts corrupted,
Crookedness of all kinds, and all for money!
[*To* SENTRY.] But you—!
I swear by God and by the throne of God,
The man who has done this thing shall pay for it!
Find that man, bring him here to me, or your death
Will be the least of your problems: I'll string you up
Alive, and there will be certain ways to make you
Discover your employer before you die;
And the process may teach you a lesson you seem to have missed:
The dearest profit is sometimes all too dear:
That depends on the source. Do you understand me?
A fortune won is often misfortune.

103–104 We threw . . . to me: Like tossing a coin, throwing dice is a way to determine something randomly. In this case, it is who must do what no one wants to do.

117–120 A pious . . . in alleys: Anarchy is a state of disorder and confusion or lawlessness, often due to the absence of governmental authority. Anarchists believe that all forms of government are unjust and should be resisted. Here, Creon calls those who oppose him anarchists.

SENTRY. King, may I speak?

CREON. Your very voice distresses me.

SENTRY. Are you sure that it is my voice, and not your conscience?

CREON. By God, he wants to analyze me now!

SENTRY. It is not what I say, but what has been done, that hurts you.

CREON. You talk too much.

SENTRY. Maybe; but I've done nothing.

CREON. Sold your soul for some silver: that's all you've done.

SENTRY. How dreadful it is when the right judge judges wrong!

CREON. Your figures of speech
May entertain you now; but unless you bring me the man,
You will get little profit from them in the end.

[*Exit* CREON *into the Palace*.]

SENTRY. "Bring me the man"—!
I'd like nothing better than bringing him the man!
But bring him or not, you have seen the last of me here.
At any rate, I am safe!

[*Exit* SENTRY.]

ODE° 1

CHORUS. Numberless are the world's wonders, but none
More wonderful than man; the stormgray sea
Yields to his prows,° the huge crests bear him high;
Earth, holy and inexhaustible, is graven°
With shining furrows where his plows have gone
Year after year, the timeless labor of stallions.

The lightboned birds and beasts that cling to cover,
The lithe° fish lighting their reaches of dim water,
All are taken, tamed in the net of his mind;
The lion on the hill, the wild horse windy-maned,
Resign to him; and his blunt yoke has broken
The sultry shoulders of the mountain bull.

Words also, and thought as rapid as air,
He fashions to his good use; statecraft is his,
And his the skill that deflects the arrows of snow,

Ode: a song chanted by the Chorus.

3 **prows:** ships.

4 **graven:** formed or shaped with a chisel; sculpted.

8 **lithe:** easily bent; flexible.

The spears of winter rain: from every wind
He has made himself secure—from all but one:
In the late wind of death he cannot stand.

O clear intelligence, force beyond all measure!
O fate of man, working both good and evil!
When the laws are kept, how proudly his city stands!
When the laws are broken, what of his city then?
Never may the anarchic man find rest at my hearth,
Never be it said that my thoughts are his thoughts.

SCENE 2

[*Re-enter* SENTRY *leading* ANTIGONE.]

CHORAGOS. What does this mean? Surely this captive woman
Is the Princess, Antigone? Why should she be taken?

SENTRY. Here is the one who did it! We caught her
In the very act of burying him.—Where is Creon?

CHORAGOS. Just coming from the house.

[*Enter* CREON, C.]

CREON. What has happened?
Why have you come back so soon?

SENTRY. [*Expansively.*] O King,
A man should never be too sure of anything:
I would have sworn
That you'd not see me here again: your anger
Frightened me so, and the things you threatened me with;
But how could I tell then
That I'd be able to solve the case so soon?

No dice-throwing this time: I was only too glad to come!

Here is this woman. She is the guilty one:
We found her trying to bury him.
Take her, then; question her; judge her as you will.
I am through with the whole thing now, and glad of it.

CREON. But this is Antigone! Why have you brought her here?

SENTRY. She was burying him, I tell you!

CREON. [*Severely.*] Is this the truth?

SENTRY. I saw her with my own eyes. Can I say more?

CREON. The details: come, tell me quickly!

SENTRY. It was like this:
After those terrible threats of yours, King,
We went back and brushed the dust away from the body.
The flesh was soft by now, and stinking,
So we sat on a hill to windward and kept guard.
No napping this time! We kept each other awake.
But nothing happened until the white round sun
Whirled in the center of the round sky over us:
Then, suddenly,
A storm of dust roared up from the earth, and the sky
Went out, the plain vanished with all its trees
In the stinging dark. We closed our eyes and endured it.
The whirlwind lasted a long time, but it passed;
And then we looked, and there was Antigone!
I have seen
A mother bird come back to a stripped nest, heard
Her crying bitterly a broken note or two
For the young ones stolen. Just so, when this girl
Found the bare corpse, and all her love's work wasted,
She wept, and cried on heaven to damn the hands
That had done this thing.
And then she brought more dust
And sprinkled wine three times for her brother's ghost.

We ran and took her at once. She was not afraid,
Not even when we charged her with what she had done.
She denied nothing.
And this was a comfort to me,
And some uneasiness: for it is a good thing
To escape from death, but it is no great pleasure
To bring death to a friend.
Yet I always say
There is nothing so comfortable as your own safe skin!

CREON. [*Slowly, dangerously.*] And you, Antigone,
You with your head hanging,—do you confess this thing?

ANTIGONE. I do. I deny nothing.

CREON. [*To* SENTRY.] You may go.

[*Exit* SENTRY.]

[*To* ANTIGONE.] Tell me, tell me briefly:
Had you heard my proclamation touching this matter?

Peplos Kore from the Athenian Acropolis. c. 530 B.C., Greek. Three-quarters life-size. The Acropolis Museum, Athens.

Viewing the sculpture: How does the woman shown here compare with your image of Antigone? In what ways are they the same? In what ways are they different?

ANTIGONE. It was public. Could I help hearing it?

CREON. And yet you dared defy the law.

ANTIGONE. I dared.
It was not God's proclamation. That final Justice
That rules the world below makes no such laws.

Your edict,° King, was strong,
But all your strength is weakness itself against
The immortal unrecorded laws of God.
They are not merely now: they were, and shall be,
Operative for ever, beyond man utterly.

I knew I must die, even without your decree:
I am only mortal. And if I must die
Now, before it is my time to die,
Surely this is no hardship: can anyone
Living, as I live, with evil all about me,
Think Death less than a friend? This death of mine
Is of no importance; but if I had left my brother
Lying in death unburied, I should have suffered.
Now I do not.
You smile at me. Ah, Creon,
Think me a fool, if you like; but it may well be
That a fool convicts me of folly.

CHORAGOS. Like father, like daughter: both headstrong, deaf to reason!
She has never learned to yield.

CREON. She has much to learn.
The inflexible heart breaks first, the toughest iron
Cracks first, and the wildest horses bend their necks
At the pull of the smallest curb.
Pride? In a slave?
This girl is guilty of a double insolence,
Breaking the given laws and boasting of it.
Who is the man here,
She or I, if this crime goes unpunished?
Sister's child, or more than sister's child,
Or closer yet in blood—she and her sister
Win bitter death for this!
[*To* SERVANTS.] Go, some of you,
Arrest Ismene. I accuse her equally.
Bring her: you will find her sniffling in the house there.

59 edict: an official order or decree issued by a person in authority.

Her mind's a traitor: crimes kept in the dark
Cry for light, and the guardian brain shudders;
But how much worse than this
Is brazen boasting of barefaced anarchy!

ANTIGONE. Creon, what more do you want than my death?

CREON. Nothing.
That gives me everything.

ANTIGONE. Then I beg you: kill me.
This talking is a great weariness: your words
Are distasteful to me, and I am sure that mine
Seem so to you. And yet they should not seem so:
I should have praise and honor for what I have done.
All these men here would praise me
Were their lips not frozen shut with fear of you.
[*Bitterly.*] Ah the good fortune of kings,
Licensed to say and do whatever they please!

CREON. You are alone here in that opinion.

ANTIGONE. No, they are with me. But they keep their tongues in leash.

CREON. Maybe. But you are guilty, and they are not.

ANTIGONE. There is no guilt in reverence for the dead.

CREON. But Eteocles—was he not your brother too?

ANTIGONE. My brother too.

CREON. And you insult his memory?

ANTIGONE. [*Softly.*] The dead man would not say that I insult it.

CREON. He would: for you honor a traitor as much as him.

ANTIGONE. His own brother, traitor or not, and equal in blood.

CREON. He made war on his country. Eteocles defended it.

ANTIGONE. Nevertheless, there are honors due all the dead.

CREON. But not the same for the wicked as for the just.

ANTIGONE. Ah Creon, Creon,
Which of us can say what the gods hold wicked?°

116 Which . . . wicked: Note Antigone's belief that people cannot understand the thinking of the gods.

CREON. An enemy is an enemy, even dead.

ANTIGONE. It is my nature to join in love, not hate.

CREON. [*Finally, losing patience.*] Go join them, then; if you must have your love,
Find it in hell!

CHORAGOS. But see, Ismene comes:

[*Enter* ISMENE, *guarded.*]

Those tears are sisterly, the cloud
That shadows her eyes rains down gentle sorrow.

CREON. You too, Ismene,
Snake in my ordered house, sucking my blood
Stealthily—and all the time I never knew
That these two sisters were aiming at my throne!
Ismene,
Do you confess your share in this crime, or deny it?
Answer me.

ISMENE. Yes, if she will let me say so. I am guilty.

ANTIGONE. [*Coldly.*] No, Ismene. You have no right to say so.
You would not help me, and I will not have you help me.

ISMENE. But now I know what you meant; and I am here
To join you, to take my share of punishment.

ANTIGONE. The dead man and the gods who rule the dead
Know whose act this was. Words are not friends.

ISMENE. Do you refuse me, Antigone? I want to die with you:
I too have a duty that I must discharge to the dead.

ANTIGONE. You shall not lessen my death by sharing it.

ISMENE. What do I care for life when you are dead?

ANTIGONE. Ask Creon. You're always hanging on his opinions.

ISMENE. You are laughing at me. Why, Antigone?

ANTIGONE. It's a joyless laughter, Ismene.

ISMENE. But can I do nothing?

ANTIGONE. Yes. Save yourself. I shall not envy you.
There are those who will praise you; I shall have honor, too.

ISMENE. But we are equally guilty!

ANTIGONE. No more, Ismene.
You are alive, but I belong to Death.

CREON. [*To the* CHORUS.] Gentlemen, I beg you to observe these girls:
One has just now lost her mind; the other,
It seems, has never had a mind at all.

ISMENE. Grief teaches the steadiest minds to waver, King.

CREON. Yours certainly did, when you assumed guilt with the guilty!

ISMENE. But how could I go on living without her?

CREON. You are.
She is already dead.

ISMENE. But your own son's bride!

CREON. There are places enough for him to push his plow.
I want no wicked women for my sons!°

ISMENE. O dearest Haimon, how your father wrongs you!

CREON. I've had enough of your childish talk of marriage!

CHORAGOS. Do you really intend to steal this girl from your son?

CREON. No; Death will do that for me.

CHORAGOS. Then she must die?

CREON. [*Ironically.*] You dazzle me.
—But enough of this talk!

154–156 She is . . . sons: Here's a new complication: Antigone is engaged to marry Creon's son, Haimon. Thus, punishing her means punishing him, a fact that doesn't appear to bother Creon greatly.

Throne room, in the palace at Knossos.

[*To GUARDS.*] You, there, take them away and guard them well:
For they are but women, and even brave men run
When they see Death coming.

[*Exit ISMENE, ANTIGONE, and GUARDS.*]

ODE 2

CHORUS. Fortunate is the man who has never tasted God's vengeance!
Where once the anger of heaven has struck, that house is shaken
For ever: damnation rises behind each child
Like a wave cresting out of the black northeast,
When the long darkness under sea roars up
And bursts drumming death upon the windwhipped sand.
I have seen this gathering sorrow from time long past
Loom upon Oedipus' children: generation from generation
Takes the compulsive rage of the enemy god.
So lately this last flower of Oedipus' line
Drank the sunlight! but now a passionate word
And a handful of dust have closed up all its beauty.

What mortal arrogance
Transcends° the wrath of Zeus?
Sleep cannot lull him, nor the effortless long months
Of the timeless gods: but he is young for ever,
And his house is the shining day of high Olympos.°
All that is and shall be,
And all the past, is his.
No pride on earth is free of the curse of heaven.

The straying dreams of men
May bring them ghosts of joy:
But as they drowse, the waking embers burn them;
Or they walk with fixed eyes, as blind men walk.
But the ancient wisdom speaks for our own time:
Fate works most for woe
With Folly's fairest show.
Man's little pleasure is the spring of sorrow.

14 **Transcends:** is greater or better than.

17 **Olympos:** Zeus and the other gods and goddesses were believed to live on Mount Olympus.

Vocabulary
arrogance (ar′ə gəns) *n.* overbearing pride

Responding to Literature

Personal Response

How do you feel about Antigone's decision?

Analyzing Scenes 1 and 2

Recall

1. What new law has Creon just enacted? What does Antigone propose doing about it?
2. What does Creon announce from the palace steps?
3. What news does the sentry bring on his first visit to Creon? How does the king react?
4. Why does the sentry lead Antigone into Creon's presence on his second visit? How does she explain her actions?
5. What does Ismene try to share with Antigone? How does Antigone answer her?

Interpret

6. In explaining her plans to Ismene, Antigone says that "this crime is holy." What do you think she means?
7. What does Creon's speech suggest about his values? Explain.
8. What can you infer about Creon's personality from his reaction to the sentry's first report?
9. Compare and contrast what Antigone holds to be important with what Creon values.
10. How has Ismene changed since the beginning of the play? Why, do you think, has she done so?

Evaluate and Connect

11. How does Antigone's action compare with the one you described for the Reading Focus on page 726? Explain.
12. Do you think it would still be possible for Creon and Antigone to resolve their differences at the end of scene 1? Why or why not?
13. How do the choragos and chorus affect your understanding and enjoyment of the play?
14. What is your reaction to the sentry in scene 1? What purpose or purposes does he seem to serve in the play?
15. If you were in a similar situation, would you be more likely to respond as Antigone does or as Ismene does? Explain.

Conflict: Protagonist and Antagonist

The **conflict** in a work of literature is a struggle between opposing forces. One force, the **protagonist,** is the central character and is often the character with whom the audience sympathizes or identifies. Any character or force that opposes the protagonist is called an **antagonist.** Sometimes the protagonist and antagonist are two characters who oppose each other, such as Antigone and Creon. However, a conflict could exist between a character and nature; between a character and society; or between ideas, values, or emotions within a character's own mind.

1. Review the prologue of *Antigone,* up to the *Parodos* on page 732. Identify two conflicts, citing the protagonist and antagonist in each. Which conflict do you think is more important? Explain.
2. In scene 1, line 138, the sentry asks Creon, "Are you sure that it is my voice, and not your conscience?" Do you think that he has hit upon the truth in identifying this conflict? Explain.

- See **Literary Terms Handbook,** p. R3.

Literature and Writing

Writing About Literature

Comparing Viewpoints Skim scenes 1 and 2 for a sentence or phrase spoken by Antigone that you feel best expresses her viewpoint. Copy the sentence and underneath it write a paragraph summarizing her side of the argument with Creon. On another sheet of paper, do the same for Creon, making his case against Antigone. Compare your summaries with those of other students in the class.

Creative Writing

I've Got a Problem Imagine that you are Ismene, desperately in need of advice about your sister Antigone. Write a letter to the "Personal Problem" page of the *Thebes Gazette.* Tell your story without giving away who you are or revealing the names and positions of the other characters.

Extending Your Response

Literature Groups

Getting to Know Her Write at least two questions that you would like to ask Antigone. In your group, share your questions, and then discuss how you think Antigone might answer. Finally, select one person from your group to play the part of Antigone and to respond to questions from other groups. Be prepared to justify your responses based on scenes 1 and 2.

Interdisciplinary Activity

Art: Making Masks Greek drama was performed by actors wearing masks. Using cardboard, papier mâché, fabric, or other materials, make a mask that covers your entire face and expresses the dominant personality trait of one of the characters of *Antigone.* Use yarn for hair, and make sure to include eye holes and a substantial mouth opening.

Internet Connection

Surfing to Ancient Greece Generate several questions to research about ancient Greece. Then, search the Internet for answers. You might narrow your search by using keywords such as Thebes, Acropolis, Theatre of Dionysos. Prepare a report on any interesting findings and present it to the class.

Learning for Life

Incident Report Imagine that the sentry has to write a formal report for a superior officer about his discovery of Antigone's "crime." Describe the incident as accurately as possible in modern English. Make sure that you stick to the sentry's point of view. Invent details if necessary, but be careful not to contradict the text.

Save your work for your portfolio.

Reconstruction of Greek theater masks.

SCENE 3

CHORAGOS. But here is Haimon, King, the last of all your sons.
Is it grief for Antigone that brings him here,
And bitterness at being robbed of his bride?

[*Enter* HAIMON.]

CREON. We shall soon see, and no need of diviners.° —Son,
You have heard my final judgment on that girl:
Have you come here hating me, or have you come
With deference° and with love, whatever I do?

4 diviners: people who predict the future.

7 deference: respect and honor due to another.

HAIMON. I am your son, father. You are my guide.
You make things clear for me, and I obey you.
No marriage means more to me than your continuing wisdom.

CREON. Good. That is the way to behave: subordinate
Everything else, my son, to your father's will.
This is what a man prays for, that he may get
Sons attentive and dutiful in his house,
Each one hating his father's enemies,
Honoring his father's friends. But if his sons
Fail him, if they turn out unprofitably,
What has he fathered but trouble for himself
And amusement for the malicious?
So you are right
Not to lose your head over this woman.
Your pleasure with her would soon grow cold, Haimon,
And then you'd have a hellcat in bed and elsewhere.
Let her find her husband in Hell!
Of all the people in this city, only she
Has had contempt for my law and broken it.

Do you want me to show myself weak before the people?
Or to break my sworn word? No, and I will not.
The woman dies.
I suppose she'll plead "family ties." Well, let her.
If I permit my own family to rebel,
How shall I earn the world's obedience?
Show me the man who keeps his house in hand,
He's fit for public authority.
I'll have no dealings
With law-breakers, critics of the government:
Whoever is chosen to govern should be obeyed—

Must be obeyed, in all things, great and small,
Just and unjust! O Haimon,
The man who knows how to obey, and that man only,
Knows how to give commands when the time comes.
You can depend on him, no matter how fast
The spears come: he's a good soldier, he'll stick it out.

Anarchy, anarchy! Show me a greater evil!
This is why cities tumble and the great houses rain down,
This is what scatters armies!

No, no: good lives are made so by discipline.
We keep the laws then, and the lawmakers,
And no woman shall seduce us. If we must lose,
Let's lose to a man, at least! Is a woman stronger than we?

CHORAGOS. Unless time has rusted my wits,
What you say, King, is said with point and dignity.

HAIMON. [*Boyishly earnest.*] Father:
Reason is God's crowning gift to man, and you are right
To warn me against losing mine. I cannot say—
I hope that I shall never want to say!—that you
Have reasoned badly. Yet there are other men
Who can reason, too; and their opinions might be helpful.
You are not in a position to know everything
That people say or do, or what they feel:
Your temper terrifies them—everyone
Will tell you only what you like to hear.
But I, at any rate, can listen; and I have heard them
Muttering and whispering in the dark about this girl.
They say no woman has ever, so unreasonably,
Died so shameful a death for a generous act:
"She covered her brother's body. Is this indecent?
She kept him from dogs and vultures. Is this a crime?
Death?—She should have all the honor that we can give her!"

This is the way they talk out there in the city.

You must believe me:
Nothing is closer to me than your happiness.
What could be closer? Must not any son
Value his father's fortune as his father does his?
I beg you, do not be unchangeable:
Do not believe that you alone can be right.

The Armentum Rider. c. 550 B.C., Greek. Bronze, height: 23.6 cm. The British Museum, London.

The man who thinks that,
The man who maintains that only he has the power
To reason correctly, the gift to speak, the soul—
A man like that, when you know him, turns out empty.

It is not reason never to yield to reason!

In flood time you can see how some trees bend,
And because they bend, even their twigs are safe,
While stubborn trees are torn up, roots and all.
And the same thing happens in sailing:
Make your sheet fast, never slacken,—and over you go,
Head over heels and under: and there's your voyage.
Forget you are angry! Let yourself be moved!
I know I am young; but please let me say this:

The ideal condition
Would be, I admit, that men should be right by instinct;
But since we are all too likely to go astray,
The reasonable thing is to learn from those who can teach.

CHORAGOS. You will do well to listen to him, King,
If what he says is sensible. And you, Haimon,
Must listen to your father.—Both speak well.

CREON. You consider it right for a man of my years and experience
To go to school to a boy?

HAIMON. It is not right
If I am wrong. But if I am young, and right,
What does my age matter?

CREON. You think it right to stand up for an anarchist?

HAIMON. Not at all. I pay no respect to criminals.

CREON. Then she is not a criminal?

HAIMON. The City would deny it, to a man.

CREON. And the City proposes to teach me how to rule?

HAIMON. Ah. Who is it that's talking like a boy now?

CREON. My voice is the one voice giving orders in this City!

HAIMON. It is no City if it takes orders from one voice.

CREON. The State is the King!

HAIMON. Yes, if the State is a desert.

[*Pause.*]

CREON. This boy, it seems, has sold out to a woman.

HAIMON. If you are a woman: my concern is only for you.

CREON. So? Your "concern"! In a public brawl with your father!

HAIMON. How about you, in a public brawl with justice?

CREON. With justice, when all that I do is within my rights?

HAIMON. You have no right to trample on God's right.

CREON. [*Completely out of control.*] Fool, adolescent fool!
Taken in by a woman!

HAIMON. You'll never see me taken in by anything vile.

CREON. Every word you say is for her!

HAIMON. [*Quietly, darkly.*] And for you.
And for me. And for the gods under the earth.

CREON. You'll never marry her while she lives.

HAIMON. Then she must die.—But her death will cause another.

CREON. Another?
Have you lost your senses? Is this an open threat?

HAIMON. There is no threat in speaking to emptiness.

CREON. I swear you'll regret this superior tone of yours!
You are the empty one!

HAIMON. If you were not my father,
I'd say you were perverse.

CREON. You girlstruck fool, don't play at words with me!

HAIMON. I am sorry. You prefer silence.

CREON. Now, by God—!
I swear, by all the gods in heaven above us,
You'll watch it, I swear you shall!
[*To the* SERVANTS.] Bring her out!
Bring the woman out! Let her die before his eyes!
Here, this instant, with her bridegroom beside her!

HAIMON. Not here, no; she will not die here, King.
And you will never see my face again.
Go on raving as long as you've a friend to endure you.

[*Exit* HAIMON.]

CHORAGOS. Gone, gone.
Creon, a young man in a rage is dangerous!

CREON. Let him do, or dream to do, more than a man can.
He shall not save these girls from death.

CHORAGOS. These girls?
You have sentenced them both?

CREON. No, you are right.
I will not kill the one whose hands are clean.

CHORAGOS. But Antigone?

CREON. [*Somberly.*] I will carry her far away
Out there in the wilderness, and lock her
Living in a vault of stone. She shall have food,
As the custom is, to absolve the State of her death.

Vocabulary

perverse (pər vurs′) *adj.* determined to go against what is reasonable, expected, or desired; contrary

absolve (ab zolv′) *v.* to free from guilt or blame

And there let her pray to the gods of hell:
They are her only gods:
Perhaps they will show her an escape from death,
Or she may learn,
though late,
That piety shown the dead is pity in vain.

[*Exit* CREON.]

ODE 3

CHORUS. Love, unconquerable
Waster of rich men, keeper
Of warm lights and all-night vigil
In the soft face of a girl:
Sea-wanderer, forest-visitor!
Even the pure Immortals cannot escape you,
And mortal man, in his one day's dusk,
Trembles before your glory.

Surely you swerve upon ruin
The just man's consenting heart,
As here you have made bright anger
Strike between father and son—
And none has conquered but Love!
A girl's glance working the will of heaven:
Pleasure to her alone who mocks us,
Merciless Aphrodite.°

16 Aphrodite (af′ rə dī′ tē): the goddess of love and beauty.

SCENE 4

CHORAGOS. [*As* ANTIGONE *enters guarded.*] But I can no longer stand in awe of this,
Nor, seeing what I see, keep back my tears.
Here is Antigone, passing to that chamber
Where all find sleep at last.

ANTIGONE. Look upon me, friends, and pity me
Turning back at the night's edge to say
Good-by to the sun that shines for me no longer;
Now sleepy Death
Summons me down to Acheron,° that cold shore:
There is no bridesong there, nor any music.

CHORUS. Yet not unpraised, not without a kind of honor,
You walk at last into the underworld;

9 Acheron (ak′ ə ron): The Greeks believed that the souls of the dead inhabited an underworld bordered by the river Acheron.

Untouched by sickness, broken by no sword.
What woman has ever found your way to death?

ANTIGONE. How often I have heard the story of Niobe,
Tantalos' wretched daughter, how the stone
Clung fast about her, ivy-close: and they say
The rain falls endlessly
And sifting soft snow; her tears are never done.
I feel the loneliness of her death in mine.°

CHORUS. But she was born of heaven, and you
Are woman, woman-born. If her death is yours,
A mortal woman's, is this not for you
Glory in our world and in the world beyond?

ANTIGONE. You laugh at me. Ah, friends, friends,
Can you not wait until I am dead? O Thebes,
O men many-charioted, in love with Fortune,
Dear springs of Dirce, sacred Theban grove,
Be witnesses for me, denied all pity,
Unjustly judged! and think a word of love
For her whose path turns
Under dark earth, where there are no more tears.

CHORUS. You have passed beyond human daring and come at last
Into a place of stone where Justice sits.
I cannot tell
What shape of your father's guilt appears in this.

ANTIGONE. You have touched it at last: that bridal bed
Unspeakable, horror of son and mother mingling:
Their crime, infection of all our family!
O Oedipus, father and brother!
Your marriage strikes from the grave to murder mine.
I have been a stranger here in my own land:
All my life
The blasphemy of my birth has followed me.°

CHORUS. Reverence is a virtue, but strength
Lives in established law: that must prevail.
You have made your choice,
Your death is the doing of your conscious hand.

ANTIGONE. Then let me go, since all your words are bitter,
And the very light of the sun is cold to me.

15–20 How often . . . mine: Niobe (nī′ ō bē′), a former queen of Thebes, was punished by the gods for excessive pride. After all of her children were killed, she was turned to stone, but she continued to shed tears.

35–44 I cannot . . . followed me: Incest, or sexual relations between siblings or between parents and children, was a sin against the gods. Oedipus and Jocasta did not know, at the time, that they were committing incest, but their marriage was cursed nonetheless, and that curse now plagues their daughter, Antigone.

Vocabulary

prevail (pri vāl′) *v.* to be superior in power or influence; succeed

Lead me to my vigil, where I must have
Neither love nor lamentation;° no song, but silence.

[*CREON interrupts impatiently.*]

CREON. If dirges and planned lamentations could put off death,
Men would be singing for ever.
[*To the SERVANTS.*] Take her, go!
You know your orders: take her to the vault
And leave her alone there. And if she lives or dies,
That's her affair, not ours: our hands are clean.

ANTIGONE. O tomb, vaulted bride-bed in eternal rock,
Soon I shall be with my own again
Where Persephone° welcomes the thin ghosts underground:
And I shall see my father again, and you, mother,
And dearest Polyneices—
dearest indeed
To me, since it was my hand
That washed him clean and poured the ritual wine:
And my reward is death before my time!

And yet, as men's hearts know, I have done no wrong,
I have not sinned before God. Or if I have,
I shall know the truth in death. But if the guilt

52 **lamentation:** mournful outcry of sorrow or grief.

60 **Persephone** (pər sef′ ə nē): Persephone is the queen of the underworld of the dead.

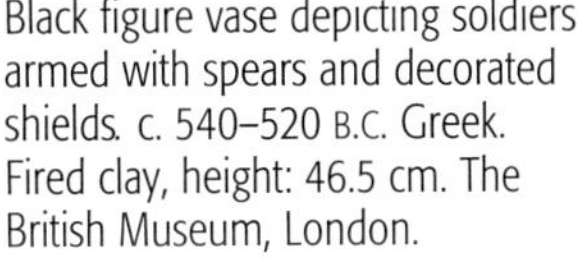

Black figure vase depicting soldiers armed with spears and decorated shields. c. 540–520 B.C. Greek. Fired clay, height: 46.5 cm. The British Museum, London.

Lies upon Creon who judged me, then, I pray,
May his punishment equal my own.

CHORAGOS. O passionate heart,
Unyielding, tormented still by the same winds!

CREON. Her guards shall have good cause to regret their delaying.

ANTIGONE. Ah! That voice is like the voice of death!

CREON. I can give you no reason to think you are mistaken.

ANTIGONE. Thebes, and you my fathers' gods,
And rulers of Thebes, you see me now, the last
Unhappy daughter of a line of kings,
Your kings, led away to death. You will remember
What things I suffer, and at what men's hands,
Because I would not transgress° the laws of heaven.
[*To the* GUARDS, *simply.*] Come: let us wait no longer.

[*Exit* ANTIGONE, *L., guarded.*]

80 **transgress:** break or violate.

ODE 4

CHORUS. All Danäe's beauty was locked away
In a brazen cell where the sunlight could not come:
A small room, still as any grave, enclosed her.
Yet she was a princess too,
And Zeus in a rain of gold poured love upon her.
O child, child,
No power in wealth or war
Or tough sea-blackened ships
Can prevail against untiring Destiny!°

And Dryas' son also, that furious king,
Bore the god's prisoning anger for his pride:
Sealed up by Dionysos in deaf stone,
His madness died among echoes.
So at the last he learned what dreadful power
His tongue had mocked:
For he had profaned the revels,
And fired the wrath of the nine
Implacable Sisters that love the sound of the flute.°

And old men tell a half-remembered tale
Of horror done where a dark ledge splits the sea
And a double surf beats on the gray shores:

1–9 **All Danäe's . . . Destiny:** The Chorus briefly relates three Greek legends. Danäe (dan′ ā ē′) was imprisoned by her father when it was foretold that she would bear a child who would kill him. After Zeus visited Danäe, she gave birth to Zeus's son, who did eventually kill his grandfather.

10–18 **And Dryas' . . . flute:** Dionysos (dī′ ə nī′ səs) is the god of wine and fertility, and the Implacable Sisters (also called the Muses) are the goddesses of the arts and sciences. After Dryas's son (King Lycurgus) objected to the worship of Dionysos, the Sisters imprisoned him and drove him mad.

How a king's new woman, sick
With hatred for the queen he had imprisoned,
Ripped out his two sons' eyes with her bloody hands
While grinning Ares watched the shuttle plunge
Four times: four blind wounds crying for revenge,

Crying, tears and blood mingled.—Piteously born,
Those sons whose mother was of heavenly birth!
Her father was the god of the North Wind
And she was cradled by gales,
She raced with young colts on the glittering hills
And walked untrammeled in the open light:
But in her marriage deathless Fate found means
To build a tomb like yours for all her joy.°

19–34 And old men . . . all her joy: It was King Phineus who imprisoned his first wife (the queen) and allowed his jealous new wife to blind the queen's sons. This horrible act was done under the gleeful gaze of Ares, the war god.

SCENE 5

[Enter blind TEIRESIAS, *led by a boy. The opening speeches of* TEIRESIAS *should be in singsong contrast to the realistic lines of* CREON.]

TEIRESIAS. This is the way the blind man comes, Princes,
Princes, Lock-step, two heads lit by the eyes of one.

CREON. What new thing have you to tell us, old Teiresias?

TEIRESIAS. I have much to tell you: listen to the prophet, Creon.

CREON. I am not aware that I have ever failed to listen.

TEIRESIAS. Then you have done wisely, King, and ruled well.

CREON. I admit my debt to you. But what have you to say?

TEIRESIAS. This, Creon: you stand once more on the edge of fate.°

CREON. What do you mean? Your words are a kind of dread.

1–8 This is . . . of fate: The blind prophet serves as the gods' agent, or go-between, in their dealings with people.

TEIRESIAS. Listen, Creon:
I was sitting in my chair of augury, at the place
Where birds gather about me. They were all a-chatter,
As is their habit, when suddenly I heard
A strange note in their jangling, a scream, a
Whirring fury; I knew that they were fighting,
Tearing each other, dying
In a whirlwind of wings clashing. And I was afraid.°
I began the rites of burnt-offering at the altar,
But Hephaistos failed me: instead of bright flame,
There was only the sputtering slime of the fat thighflesh
Melting: the entrails dissolved in gray smoke,
The bare bone burst from the welter. And no blaze!

11–17 I was sitting . . . afraid: Teiresias sits in his chair of augury to listen to the birds, whose sounds he interprets as messages from the gods, allowing him to foretell, or augur, the future. The birds' fighting is a very bad sign.

This was a sign from heaven. My boy described it,
Seeing for me as I see for others.

I tell you, Creon, you yourself have brought
This new calamity upon us. Our hearths and altars
Are stained with the corruption of dogs and carrion birds
That glut themselves on the corpse of Oedipus' son.
The gods are deaf when we pray to them, their fire
Recoils from our offering, their birds of omen
Have no cry of comfort, for they are gorged
With the thick blood of the dead.°
O my son,
These are no trifles! Think: all men make mistakes,
But a good man yields when he knows his course is wrong,
And repairs the evil. The only crime is pride.

18–32 I began . . . of the dead: Another bad sign: Hephaistos (hi fes′ təs), the god of fire, is withholding fire. Teiresias says that the gods are rejecting the Thebans' sacrificial offerings because the animals have fed on Polyneices's corpse.

Give in to the dead man, then: do not fight with a corpse—
What glory is it to kill a man who is dead?
Think, I beg you:
It is for your own good that I speak as I do.
You should be able to yield for your own good.

CREON. It seems that prophets have made me their especial province.
All my life long
I have been a kind of butt for the dull arrows
Of doddering fortune-tellers!
No, Teiresias:
If your birds—if the great eagles of God himself
Should carry him stinking bit by bit to heaven,
I would not yield. I am not afraid of pollution:
No man can defile the gods.
Do what you will,
Go into business, make money, speculate
In India gold or that synthetic gold from Sardis,°
Get rich otherwise than by my consent to bury him.
Teiresias, it is a sorry thing when a wise man
Sells his wisdom, lets out his words for hire!

50 synthetic gold from Sardis: The people of Sardis, the capital of ancient Lydia (in modern-day Turkey), invented metallic coinage, the "synthetic gold" that Creon speaks of.

TEIRESIAS. Ah Creon! Is there no man left in the world—

CREON. To do what?—Come, let's have the aphorism!°

55 aphorism: a concise statement of a general truth.

Vocabulary

defile (di fīl′) *v.* to spoil the purity of; make dirty or unclean

TEIRESIAS. No man who knows that wisdom outweighs any wealth?

CREON. As surely as bribes are baser than any baseness.

TEIRESIAS. You are sick, Creon! You are deathly sick!

CREON. As you say: it is not my place to challenge a prophet.

TEIRESIAS. Yet you have said my prophecy is for sale.

CREON. This generation of prophets has always loved gold.

TEIRESIAS. The generation of kings has always loved brass.

CREON. You forget yourself! You are speaking to your King.

TEIRESIAS. I know it. You are a king because of me.°

CREON. You have a certain skill; but you have sold out.

TEIRESIAS. King, you will drive me to words that—

CREON. Say them, say them!
Only remember: I will not pay you for them.

TEIRESIAS. No, you will find them too costly.

CREON. No doubt. Speak:
Whatever you say, you will not change my will.

TEIRESIAS. Then take this, and take it to heart!
The time is not far off when you shall pay back
Corpse for corpse, flesh of your own flesh.
You have thrust the child of this world into living night,
You have kept from the gods below the child that is theirs:
The one in a grave before her death, the other,
Dead, denied the grave. This is your crime:
And the Furies° and the dark gods of Hell
Are swift with terrible punishment for you.

Do you want to buy me now, Creon?

Not many days,
And your house will be full of men and women weeping,
And curses will be hurled at you from far
Cities grieving for sons unburied, left to rot
Before the walls of Thebes.

These are my arrows, Creon: they are all for you.

[*To* BOY.] But come, child: lead me home.
Let him waste his fine anger upon younger men.

64 I know . . . me: It was Teiresias who revealed the truth of Oedipus's relationship to Jocasta and thus set off the chain of events that led to Creon's becoming king.

77 Furies: three goddesses who avenge crimes.

Maybe he will learn at last
To control a wiser tongue in a better head.

[*Exit* TEIRESIAS.]

CHORAGOS. The old man has gone, King, but his words
Remain to plague us. I am old, too,
But I cannot remember that he was ever false.

CREON. That is true. . . . It troubles me.
Oh it is hard to give in! but it is worse
To risk everything for stubborn pride.

CHORAGOS. Creon: take my advice.

CREON. What shall I do?

CHORAGOS. Go quickly: free Antigone from her vault
And build a tomb for the body of Polyneices.

CREON. You would have me do this?

CHORAGOS. Creon, yes!
And it must be done at once: God moves
Swiftly to cancel the folly of stubborn men.

CREON. It is hard to deny the heart! But I
Will do it: I will not fight with destiny.

CHORAGOS. You must go yourself, you cannot leave
it to others.

CREON. I will go.
—Bring axes, servants:
Come with me to the tomb. I buried her, I
Will set her free.
Oh quickly!
My mind misgives—
The laws of the gods are mighty, and a man
must serve them
To the last day of his life!

[*Exit* CREON.]

Aphrodite. Greek, from eastern Turkey.

Paean°

CHORAGOS. God of many names

CHORUS. O Iacchos°
son
of Kadmeian Semele
O born of the Thunder!

Paean (pē′ ən): a song of praise, joy, or thanksgiving. Here, the Chorus praises Dionysos.

3 **Iacchos** (yä′ kəs): considered Thebes's special protector because his mother had been a Theban princess. The Chorus begs Dionysos to come to Thebes and drive out evil.

Guardian of the West
Regent
of Eleusis' plain
O Prince of maenad Thebes
and the Dragon Field by rippling Ismenos:°

CHORAGOS. God of many names

CHORUS. the flame of torches
flares on our hills
the nymphs of Iacchos
dance at the spring of Castalia:

from the vine-close mountain
come ah come in ivy:°
Evohé° *evohé!* sings through the streets of Thebes

CHORAGOS. God of many names

CHORUS. Iacchos of Thebes
heavenly Child
of Semele bride of the Thunderer!
The shadow of plague is upon us:
come
with clement° feet
oh come from Parnasos
down the long slopes
across the lamenting water

CHORAGOS. Io Fire! Chorister of the throbbing stars!
O purest among the voices of the night!
Thou son of God, blaze for us!

CHORUS. Come with choric rapture of circling Maenads
Who cry *Io Iacche!*
God of many names!

1–5 **God of . . . Ismenos:** The names of Dionysos refer to people and places associated with him. His mother, **Kadmeian Semele** (sem′ ə lē), was the daughter of Kadmos, a king of Thebes. His father was Zeus, who controlled thunder. This plain was the site of religious ceremonies performed in honor of Dionysos, and the river **Ismenos** ran near Thebes. The **maenads** (mē′ nadz) were Dionysos's devoted priestesses.

7–9 **the nymphs . . . come in ivy:** Dionysos was raised by **nymphs,** long-lived women who were associated with trees and other parts of nature. The **spring of Castalia** is on Parnasos, a holy mountain. The grape **vine** and **ivy** were symbols of Dionysos.

10 *Evohé:* "Hallelujah."

14 **clement:** forgiving; merciful.

Exodos°

[*Enter* MESSENGER, *L.*]

MESSENGER. Men of the line of Kadmos, you who live
Near Amphion's citadel:°
I cannot say
Of any condition of human life "This is fixed,
This is clearly good, or bad." Fate raises up,
And Fate casts down the happy and unhappy alike:
No man can foretell his Fate.

Exodos: the last part of the play.

2 **Amphion's citadel:** the wall around Thebes, which Amphion built by charming stones into place with music.

Take the case of Creon:
Creon was happy once, as I count happiness:
Victorious in battle, sole governor of the land,
Fortunate father of children nobly born.
And now it has all gone from him! Who can say
That a man is still alive when his life's joy fails?
He is a walking dead man. Grant him rich,
Let him live like a king in his great house:
If his pleasure is gone, I would not give
So much as the shadow of smoke for all he owns.

CHORAGOS. Your words hint at sorrow: what is your news for us?

MESSENGER. They are dead. The living are guilty of their death.

CHORAGOS. Who is guilty? Who is dead? Speak!

MESSENGER. Haimon.
Haimon is dead; and the hand that killed him
Is his own hand.

CHORAGOS. His father's? or his own?

MESSENGER. His own, driven mad by the murder his father had done.

CHORAGOS. Teiresias, Teiresias, how clearly you saw it all!

MESSENGER. This is my news: you must draw what conclusions you can from it.

CHORAGOS. But look: Eurydice, our Queen:
Has she overheard us?

[*Enter* EURYDICE *from the Palace,* C.]

EURYDICE. I have heard something, friends:
As I was unlocking the gate of Pallas'° shrine,
For I needed her help today, I heard a voice
Telling of some new sorrow. And I fainted
There at the temple with all my maidens about me.
But speak again: whatever it is, I can bear it:
Grief and I are no strangers.°

MESSENGER. Dearest Lady,
I will tell you plainly all that I have seen.
I shall not try to comfort you: what is the use,
Since comfort could lie only in what is not true?
The truth is always best.
I went with Creon
To the outer plain where Polyneices was lying,
No friend to pity him, his body shredded by dogs.

27 **Pallas:** the goddess of wisdom; also known as Athena.

32 **Grief and I . . . strangers:** Eurydice (yoo rid′ i sē) is referring to the death of Megareus (me gär′ ā o͞os), her older son, who died in the battle for Thebes.

We made our prayer in that place to Hecate°
And Pluto,° that they would be merciful. And we bathed
The corpse with holy water, and we brought
Fresh-broken branches to burn what was left of it,
And upon the urn we heaped up a towering barrow
Of the earth of his own land.
When we were done, we ran
To the vault where Antigone lay on her couch of stone.

39 Hecate (hek′ ə tē): another name for Persephone, the goddess of the underworld.

40 Pluto: another name for Hades, the god of the underworld.

Cult Statue of Aphrodite. 425–400 B.C., Greek. Limestone and marble, height: 7 ft. 6 in. The J. Paul Getty Museum, Los Angeles.

Viewing the sculpture: How does this sculpture reflect the mood of this scene? Explain.

One of the servants had gone ahead,
And while he was yet far off he heard a voice
Grieving within the chamber, and he came back
And told Creon. And as the King went closer,
The air was full of wailing, the words lost,
And he begged us to make all haste. "Am I a prophet?"
He said, weeping, "And must I walk this road,
The saddest of all that I have gone before?
My son's voice calls me on. Oh quickly, quickly!
Look through the crevice there, and tell me
If it is Haimon, or some deception of the gods!"

We obeyed; and in the cavern's farthest corner
We saw her lying:
She had made a noose of her fine linen veil
And hanged herself. Haimon lay beside her,
His arms about her waist, lamenting her,
His love lost under ground, crying out
That his father had stolen her away from him.

When Creon saw him the tears rushed to his eyes
And he called to him: "What have you done, child? Speak to me.
What are you thinking that makes your eyes so strange?
O my son, my son, I come to you on my knees!"
But Haimon spat in his face. He said not a word,
Staring—
And suddenly drew his sword
And lunged. Creon shrank back, the blade missed; and the boy,
Desperate against himself, drove it half its length
Into his own side, and fell. And as he died
He gathered Antigone close in his arms again,
Choking, his blood bright red on her white cheek.
And now he lies dead with the dead, and she is his
At last, his bride in the houses of the dead.

[*Exit* EURYDICE *into the Palace*.]

CHORAGOS. She has left us without a word. What can this mean?

MESSENGER. It troubles me, too; yet she knows what is best,
Her grief is too great for public lamentation,
And doubtless she has gone to her chamber to weep
For her dead son, leading her maidens in his dirge.

CHORAGOS. It may be so: but I fear this deep silence

[*Pause.*]

MESSENGER. I will see what she is doing. I will go in.

[*Exit* MESSENGER *into the Palace.*]

[*Enter* CREON *with attendants, bearing* HAIMON*'s body.*]

CHORAGOS. But here is the King himself: oh look at him,
Bearing his own damnation in his arms.

CREON. Nothing you say can touch me any more.
My own blind heart has brought me
From darkness to final darkness. Here you see
The father murdering, the murdered son—
And all my civic wisdom!

Haimon my son, so young, so young to die,
I was the fool, not you; and you died for me.

CHORAGOS. That is the truth; but you were late in learning it.

CREON. This truth is hard to bear. Surely a god
Has crushed me beneath the hugest weight of heaven,
And driven me headlong a barbaric way
To trample out the thing I held most dear.

The pains that men will take to come to pain!

[*Enter* MESSENGER *from the Palace.*]

MESSENGER. The burden you carry in your hands is heavy,
But it is not all: you will find more in your house.

CREON. What burden worse than this shall I find there?

MESSENGER. The Queen is dead.

CREON. O port of death, deaf world,
Is there no pity for me? And you, Angel of evil,
I was dead, and your words are death again.
Is it true, boy? Can it be true?
Is my wife dead? Has death bred death?

MESSENGER. You can see for yourself.

[*The doors are opened, and the body of* EURYDICE *is disclosed within.*]

CREON. Oh pity!
All true, all true, and more than I can bear!
O my wife, my son!

Statue of Chrysippus, the Greek philosopher. 3rd century B.C. Marble. Louvre Museum, Paris.

Viewing the sculpture: What emotions does this sculpture convey? How might these emotions compare with what Creon may be feeling at this point in the play?

MESSENGER. She stood before the altar, and her heart
Welcomed the knife her own hand guided,
And a great cry burst from her lips for Megareus dead,
And for Haimon dead, her sons; and her last breath
Was a curse for their father, the murderer of her sons.°
And she fell, and the dark flowed in through her closing eyes.

116 Was a curse . . . sons: Note that even though Haimon stabbed himself and Megareus died in battle, Eurydice blames Creon for their deaths.

CREON. O God, I am sick with fear.
Are there no swords here? Has no one a blow for me?

MESSENGER. Her curse is upon you for the deaths of both.

CREON. It is right that it should be. I alone am guilty.
I know it, and I say it. Lead me in,
Quickly, friends.
I have neither life nor substance. Lead me in.

CHORAGOS. You are right, if there can be right in so much wrong.
The briefest way is best in a world of sorrow.

CREON. Let it come,
Let death come quickly, and be kind to me.
I would not ever see the sun again.

CHORAGOS. All that will come when it will; but we, meanwhile,
Have much to do. Leave the future to itself.

CREON. All my heart was in that prayer!

CHORAGOS. Then do not pray any more: the sky is deaf.

CREON. Lead me away. I have been rash and foolish.
I have killed my son and my wife.
I look for comfort; my comfort lies here dead.
Whatever my hands have touched has come to nothing.
Fate has brought all my pride to a thought of dust.

[*As* CREON *is being led into the house, the* CHORAGOS *advances and speaks directly to the audience.*]

CHORAGOS. There is no happiness where there is no wisdom;
No wisdom but in submission to the gods.
Big words are always punished,
And proud men in old age learn to be wise.

Responding to Literature

Personal Response

In your opinion, what is the most tragic event of the play? Why?

Analyzing Scenes 3 to 5

Recall

1. Why has Haimon come to see his father? What does he try to persuade Creon to do? How does Creon respond?
2. To what punishment does Creon sentence Antigone? How does she respond? How does the chorus react to her?
3. What does Teiresias tell Creon? What does Creon accuse Teiresias of at first?
4. What does Creon set out to do after his conversation with Teiresias? What does he find?
5. What final events add to Creon's sorrow? How does he react?

Interpret

6. What does the discussion between Haimon and Creon reveal about their attitudes toward Antigone's actions? toward each other?
7. What reasons do the chorus and Antigone imply are responsible for her fate? What does this suggest about the inevitability of Antigone's fate?
8. In your opinion, what finally causes Creon to change his mind? Do you think he is motivated by compassion or by self-interest? Explain.
9. What do you think motivated Antigone and Haimon to act as they did?
10. What do you think is the main message, or lesson, of this play? Do you think Creon learned that message? Explain.

Evaluate and Connect

11. What examples of **foreshadowing** do you find in the play? Did they add to or detract from your enjoyment of the play? Why?
12. In scene 3, Creon says, "Whoever is chosen to govern should be obeyed– / Must be obeyed, in all things, great and small, / Just and unjust!" Do you agree with this statement? Explain your response.
13. How did you react to the dialogue between Creon and Haimon? Was it a realistic confrontation between a parent and child? Explain.
14. Audiences in ancient Greece would have understood the references to the house of Oedipus and to Greek mythology. How did these **allusions** affect your appreciation of the play?
15. What lesson do you take away from this play?

Literary **ELEMENTS**

Tragic Flaw

According to the Greek philosopher Aristotle (384–322 B.C.), the hero of a tragedy is a person of great ability who comes to grief because of a fault within his or her character: a **tragic flaw.** Pride, ambition, jealousy, self-doubt, and anger are among those human weaknesses that can defeat the tragic hero. Sometimes a tragic flaw can even be an excess of virtue, such as the love of honor or the pursuit of duty. *Antigone,* a play that Aristotle knew well, is one of the tragedies from which he derived his definition.

1. Reread Teiresias's warning to Creon (scene 5, lines 10–40). What flaw does he specifically identify in the king's character? Do you believe that this weakness is sufficient to cause the tragedy that results? Explain.
2. How would you describe Antigone's personality? Does she have a fault that might qualify as a tragic flaw? Is she, too, a tragic hero, or is she an innocent victim of Creon? Explain.

- See **Literary Terms Handbook,** p. R13.

Literature and Writing

Writing About Literature

Analyzing Bias Would Antigone's fate have been different if she had been a man? Review the play for statements that reveal Creon's and other characters' attitudes toward women and their role in Thebes society. Then write two or three paragraphs summarizing these attitudes and stating whether or not, in your opinion, bias against women affected Creon's judgment and Antigone's fate. Support your analysis with specific quotations and other details from the play.

Creative Writing

Here's What Happened Imagine that you have witnessed the day's terrible events in front of Creon's palace. That evening, your sixteen-year-old son or daughter asks you to explain why such a tragedy has occurred. How would you interpret to him or her what has happened? Write your account in modern English.

Extending Your Response

Literature Groups

Ranking Loyalty Much of the struggle in *Antigone* revolves around the question of which power or authority most deserves people's loyalty. In your group, review the speeches made by Creon, Antigone, the chorus, the choragos, and other characters, to determine where they think a person's loyalty should ultimately rest. Use specific citations from the play to support your ideas. Then rank each character's position on a line like the one shown. Feel free to add other kinds of loyalties to the line as they are needed. Finally, decide as a group where you think Sophocles himself should be placed on the continuum. Share your group's results with the rest of the class, and discuss any differences you find.

Religious law ———————————— **King's law**

Learning for Life

Genealogical Chart Skim scenes 3 and 4 for references to Antigone's ancestors. Then use resource materials on Greek drama, mythology, and legend to trace the genealogy, or family tree, of the House of Oedipus. Create a chart showing Antigone's ancestors, parents, and siblings and their relationships to one another. Indicate which relatives died untimely deaths–a possible result of the curse of Oedipus.

Interdisciplinary Activity

Drama: Stage Sets With a partner, design a stage set for *Antigone,* and create a diorama to show your design. You might choose to create the set for a presentation of the play as it would have been staged in ancient Greece, or you could choose to design a set for a more modern, contemporary staging. Display your diorama in your classroom.

Reading Further

If you enjoyed *Antigone,* you might also enjoy these works by Sophocles:

Plays: *Oedipus Rex,* the powerful tragedy of Oedipus, king of Thebes and father of Antigone. In this play, the curse of Oedipus, mentioned in *Antigone,* is explained.

Oedipus at Colonus, a sequel to *Oedipus Rex,* which recounts the final moments of the exiled king.

Literary Criticism

"Antigone," argues Roger D. Dawe, "represents the clash of two different philosophies shown through the medium of two conflicting personalities. Both sides, in their different ways, have right on their side, and therein lies the tragedy." Discuss the motivations behind Creon's and Antigone's actions. Do you find one or the other's philosophy to be more honorable? Explain and support your opinions.

Save your work for your portfolio.

Skill Minilessons

GRAMMAR AND LANGUAGE • Using the Dash

The dash is a form of punctuation that is often used where a comma is not quite strong enough. An author may use a dash to suggest hesitation in speech, to introduce an explanation, or to separate a phrase from the rest of a sentence, indicating a slight change of idea. For example, in scene 1 of *Antigone,* when the Sentry stammers, "The dead man–Polyneices–out there–someone,– / New dust on the slimy flesh!" the dashes show hesitation in his speech and also confusion in his thoughts.

PRACTICE Copy several passages from *Antigone* that include dashes, and read them to a partner. Discuss what purpose you think the dash serves in each case.

For more about dashes, see **Language Handbook,** p. R49.

READING AND THINKING • Identifying the Author's Purpose

Authors often write fiction or drama with a purpose: to entertain, to inform or teach a lesson, to tell a story, to try to persuade readers to accept an idea, or for a number of purposes. To identify an author's purpose, look carefully at the way a piece of literature is written, at your reactions to it, and at the message that seems to come across to you.

PRACTICE Review the passages of the play that seem most important to you. Then, on your paper, copy each of the following statements and write a sentence saying why you agree or disagree with the statement.

1. Sophocles wrote *Antigone* to entertain his audiences at the Greek festivals.
2. Sophocles probably intended his audience to learn from the lessons Creon and other characters learn in the play.
3. *Antigone* was intended solely as a way of teaching the history of a famous family from Thebes.

For more about inference, see **Reading Handbook,** p. R92.

VOCABULARY • Antonyms

Antonyms are words with opposite meanings. Identifying an antonym for a word helps you refine your understanding of that particular word. Also, because antonyms have opposite meanings, using them in your writing or speaking provides a good, clear way to present a contrast.

PRACTICE Write down a word that could go in each blank. It should be the best antonym you can think of for the underlined word. Use a dictionary as needed.

1. I expected a man of great arrogance, but he surprised me with his _______ .
2. Before the conquerors were driven out, they had defiled the temple, and it was now the job of the faithful to _______ it.
3. Sisters, even twin sisters, are not always alike. One may be completely _______ and the other, totally perverse.
4. Preparation, courage, and effort will help you prevail, but lacking any one of these will guarantee that you _______ .
5. You may _______ me now, but the facts, when they are known, will absolve me.

Reading & Thinking Skills

Monitoring Comprehension

Have you ever read a paragraph without registering the meaning of the words? Because not understanding one passage can hinder your understanding of later sections, it's important to monitor your comprehension. Check your understanding as you read by using these techniques:

- Slow your reading rate. Reread to clarify.
- Ask yourself *who, what, where, when, why,* and *how* questions.
- Paraphrase–restate in your own words–difficult passages.

Try these techniques on the following lines from Sophocles's *Antigone:*

> **Against our seven gates in a yawning ring**
> **The famished spears came onward in the night. . . .**

As you read the passage slowly, ask yourself questions. For example, after reading the first line, you might ask, "Whose seven gates are these?" To answer this question, you need to understand previous passages. If you are unable to answer the question, look back through the selection to find that Thebes is referred to as "Thebes of the Seven Gates." Then, think about "famished spears" as "hungry weapons of war," moving forward, or attacking. To paraphrase this passage, you might simply state, "The enemy launched an attack at night on the walled city of Thebes."

- For more about related comprehension skills, see **Reading Handbook,** pp. R82–R85.

EXERCISE

Read the following words spoken by Cassius to Brutus in Shakespeare's play *Julius Caesar.* Then write and answer three questions that you could use to monitor your comprehension of this passage.

> **Brutus and Caesar; what should be in that "Caesar"?**
> **Why should that name be sounded more than yours?**
> **Write them together, yours is as fair a name;**
> **Sound them, it doth become the mouth as well;**
> **Weigh them, it is as heavy; conjure with 'em,**
> **"Brutus" will start a spirit as soon as "Caesar."**
> **Now, in the names of all the gods at once,**
> **Upon what meat doth this our Caesar feed,**
> **That he is grown so great?**

Literature FOCUS

Understanding Shakespeare and Elizabethan Drama

On a typical summer afternoon, Londoners from all levels of Elizabethan society could be found heading to the suburb of Southwark. They would walk over the London Bridge or ferry across the River Thames, then trudge through a muddy field in the direction of an open-air building—the Globe Theater, where William Shakespeare's newest plays were performed. As trumpets sounded, those who had paid for seats found their way to them, while "groundlings" paid less and stood in the open yard around three sides of the stage. Vendors wandered through the crowd, selling beer, water, hazelnuts, oranges, and other snacks. No lights dimmed and no curtain was raised. Instead, actors simply walked onto the nearly bare stage. With Shakespeare's language, these players could capture the attention of the thousands of people who had come to see them.

The Globe Theatre, 1616. Cornelius de Visscher. Engraving. British Library, London.

The Age of Shakespeare

William Shakespeare lived and wrote during what is known as the English Renaissance, which lasted from about 1485 through the 1660s. This period is also known as the Elizabethan Age, named after Queen Elizabeth I, who ruled England from 1558 to 1603. During Elizabeth's reign, society celebrated poets, such as Edmund Spenser, and politicians and courtiers who surrounded the queen. Elizabethans would have been surprised to learn that their age would become best known for its theater, as most considered drama a less distinguished form of literature than poetry.

Elizabeth was a clever and powerful queen. She deftly eased religious conflicts that had plagued England for years, and her skill at international diplomacy helped safeguard England from its enemies abroad. The British economy grew rapidly, and London, the center of English business and government, was becoming the largest city in Europe.

Despite England's flourishing society, life was not easy for everyone. Catholics experienced religious persecution. English women were subject to many restrictions. In addition, most English people endured crowded living conditions and an unsatisfactory diet. Rich and poor alike were defenseless against frequent outbreaks of bubonic plague. In 1564, the year Shakespeare was born, nearly one-third of the residents in his hometown died from the plague.

After Elizabeth died in 1603, her cousin, King James of Scotland, took over the English throne. James, like Elizabeth, was a great supporter of literature and the arts, and he eventually became the direct patron of Shakespeare's theater company.

The Theater and the Stage

In the late 1500s, when Shakespeare began his career, English theater was going through major changes. For hundreds of years leading up to this time, professional actors, called "players," traveled the countryside, playing to audiences in towns and villages. They set up makeshift stages in public halls, marketplaces, and the courtyards of inns. Local officials, many of whom believed that "play-acting" violated biblical commandments, typically greeted acting companies with hostility.

Distrust of theater was so great that in 1574 the Common Council of London issued an order banishing players from London. To get around the order, actor James Burbage and his company of players built a playhouse in nearby Shorebridge. Completed in 1576, the building resembled the courtyard of an inn. Burbage's playhouse became the first public theater in England and was an immediate success, leading to the development of other public theaters over the next few years.

Shakespeare's company, the Lord Chamberlain's Men, performed at Burbage's theater until 1599, when they built their own playhouse, the Globe. Shakespeare referred to the Globe as "this wooden O," a term that led scholars to believe it was a circular building. The theater had three levels of galleries, covered by thatched roofs, overlooking an open courtyard. Projecting out into the yard was a platform stage about forty feet wide, with trapdoors for the entrance and exit of actors playing ghosts or other supernatural characters. At the back of the main stage was a small curtained inner stage used for indoor scenes. Above this stood a two-tiered gallery. The first tier was used to stage balcony and bedroom scenes; the second, to house musicians. Sound effects, such as the booming of thunder, were produced in a hut on top of the stage roof.

The Globe could hold about three thousand spectators. Members of the middle class and nobility typically sat in the galleries. Admission to the gallery benches was twopence. For sixpence (what a skilled laborer earned in a day), wealthier spectators could sit in a "lords' room" directly over the stage. Less well-to-do spectators, called "groundlings," could stand and watch from the courtyard for only a penny. Their close proximity to the stage created a noisy theatrical experience. Accounts of the time suggest that the groundlings did not hesitate to shout comments to the actors onstage. As theater became more profitable, its reputation improved. Eventually, Shakespeare's company received the support of Queen Elizabeth and, later, King James.

The Illusions of Theater

Because there was no artificial lighting, all performances at the Globe took place in the after-

The New Globe, London, interior.

noon. There were few props and no movable scenery. Shakespeare made up for the lack of scenery by inviting audiences to visualize the scenes based on descriptive passages spoken by the characters. For example, a character's description of a storm would help Elizabethan audiences visualize raging weather.

What the Elizabethan stage lacked in scenery, it made up for in costumes and other spectacles. Elizabethan audiences considered clothing an important indication of rank, so they demanded realistic costumes. Audiences also thought it immoral for women to appear on stage, so boys performed the female roles.

Shakespeare's Life

Nearly four centuries after the death of William Shakespeare, his plays are still performed around the world. In fact, Shakespeare's writings are more widely read and more often quoted than any other literature, aside from the Bible. Unfortunately, there are no biographies of Shakespeare from his own time. Most of the information we have comes from public records and comments by contemporaries such as Ben Jonson, a friend and rival playwright, who readily recognized Shakespeare's genius.

Shakespeare was born in 1564 in Stratford-upon-Avon, a small market town about one hundred miles from London. His father, a tradesman and landowner, was elected bailiff (the equivalent of a mayor) in 1567, and his mother came from a prosperous farming family. William was the third of at least eight children born to this couple. He was their first boy and their first child to survive past childhood. Most likely, he attended the local grammar school, where he would have studied Latin and classical literature. At age eighteen, Shakespeare married twenty-six-year-old Anne Hathaway. The couple had three children: Susanna, born in 1583, and twins Judith and Hamnet, born two years later. Hamnet, their only son, died when he was eleven.

Shakespeare moved to London sometime between 1585 and the early 1590s and worked as an actor and playwright. He was soon known for his comedies and historical plays. By 1594 he had joined a company of players called the Lord Chamberlain's Men, with whom he spent the remainder of his career. Although Shakespeare maintained his family home in Stratford, he himself spent much of each year in London.

Shakespeare eventually retired in Stratford and died in 1616. Seven years later, a group of friends brought out a collected edition of his works known as the *First Folio*. The volume played a crucial role in preserving his plays for future generations.

Reading Shakespeare

Shakespeare was a prolific writer. In addition to thirty-seven plays, he wrote two narrative

Painted frieze from the Great Chamber, c. 1585. Gilling Castle, Yorkshire, England.

poems, a series of sonnets, and other poetry. He excelled in all forms of drama. His tragic masterpieces include *Hamlet*, *Romeo and Juliet*, *Othello*, *Macbeth*, and *King Lear*. The beauty and richness of his language, as well as the universal issues his characters encounter, make his plays rewarding to read. However, some readers are intimidated by Shakespeare's use of language, which reflects English as it was spoken in Elizabethan times. The following suggestions may help you understand and enjoy his work:

- Some of the words in Shakespeare's plays are no longer used. Others have changed in meaning. Try to understand difficult words by looking at their context within a sentence or by consulting the side notes.
- Much of the dialogue in Shakespeare's plays is written as verse. These lines have a regular pattern of stressed and unstressed syllables. In order to follow such a pattern, Shakespeare often placed words in an unusual order within a sentence (for example, "Cassius from bondage will deliver Cassius"). If a sentence is confusing, try rearranging the words ("Cassius will deliver Cassius from bondage").
- Shakespeare's writing is full of imagery, figurative language, and wordplay. You might find a single metaphor or simile extended throughout an entire speech. Other speeches contain different metaphors and similes crowded together.

Shakespeare's *Julius Caesar*

Julius Caesar may be Shakespeare's most readable work. He probably wrote the play in 1599, the same year that the Globe Theater opened.

The Background *Julius Caesar* portrays a crucial period in history: Rome's transition from a republic to an empire. According to tradition, Rome became a republic about 509 B.C. and remained one for the next four and a half centuries. The Roman republic was governed by citizen assemblies: two elected consuls who could serve for just one year, and a powerful Senate, which proposed laws and oversaw officials.

The republic greatly expanded its territory and wealth through a series of foreign wars. However, as generals became more powerful from these wars, they began to ignore the Senate's authority. During its last fifty years, the republic was wracked by internal conflict.

In 60 B.C., Rome came under the control of a wealthy nobleman named Crassus and two generals, Pompey the Great and Julius Caesar. Crassus's death set off a power struggle between the generals. Caesar defeated Pompey in 48 B.C. To maintain order in Rome, Caesar seemed prepared to reestablish the monarchy.

Shakespeare's Retelling: Art and History Meet While Shakespeare based his play on historical sources, he also imaginatively reshaped history. He left out many incidents, changed the timing of events, and fleshed out details to make the story more exciting and powerful.

Today, with its clear style and exciting plot, *Julius Caesar* still appeals to a wide audience. In the play, Shakespeare confronts some of the most difficult issues of his or any other time: What form of government is best? When does power become tyranny? How can one balance personal concerns with the public interest? These and other important themes are at the heart of Shakespeare's play.

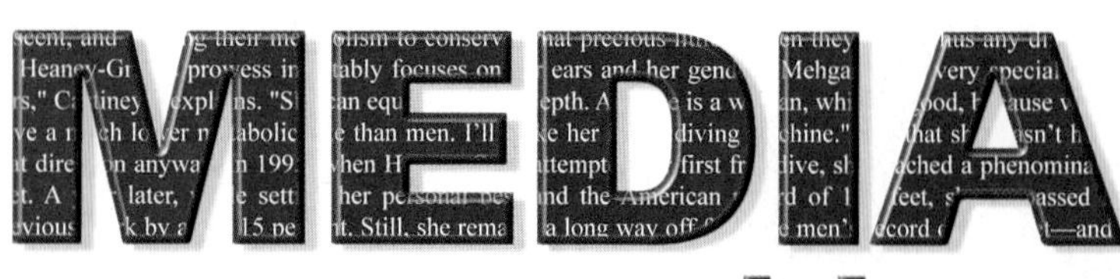

Rap

Shakespeare's "rhythm"—and Mark Antony's speech—takes on a whole new context in this student-written piece.

The Mark Antony Rap

by Beth—quoted in "The Shakespeare Frolic Project"
by Lawrence Baines, *The Clearing House*, March–April 1997

Hey everybody, listen up!
Caesar is gone, he's one dead pup.
His goodness is buried, but his evil lives on.
'Cause Brutus has you thinking that he done us
wrong.
Brutus called him greedy, he called him bad,
But that way of thinking has got me mad.
Brutus is okay. He's a real cool dude,
But all this stuff he's saying is pretty rude.
Caesar was my friend, he was my bud,
But Brutus says he's greedy, so you think he's a dud.
What about the stuff that Caesar did?
He filled the treasure chest right up to its lid.
He brought lots of prisoners back to Rome
And we got lots of money 'fore we sent 'era home.
So was that greedy? Was it bad?
Brutus says it was and we know he's tad.
You all know that I told Caesar that he should
Make himself the only king of this hood.
Three times I told him, three times he refused.
If Brutus says that's greedy, I'd say he's confused.

Analyzing Media

1. What mood do you think is conveyed in this rap? What elements help create this mood?
2. How would you costume Mark Antony for this piece?

Before You Read

The Tragedy of Julius Caesar

Reading Focus

Think of leaders of the country, of your state, of your community or school. What qualities do these leaders share?

Map It! Create a word web of qualities that you think are important for a leader. Share your ideas with the class.

Setting a Purpose Read to find out what leadership qualities several characters reveal.

Building Background

The Time and Place

Shakespeare's *Julius Caesar* is set in ancient Rome between 44 and 42 B.C.

Did You Know?

- Julius Caesar was an immensely gifted military leader and politician. Born in 100 B.C., he belonged to a noble family, but he often looked for political support among Rome's lower classes. His daring military adventures made him famous and wealthy. After conquering Gaul in western Europe, he defeated his rival Pompey and became dictator of Rome in 48 B.C. Between military campaigns, he undertook popular reforms of Roman government and society.

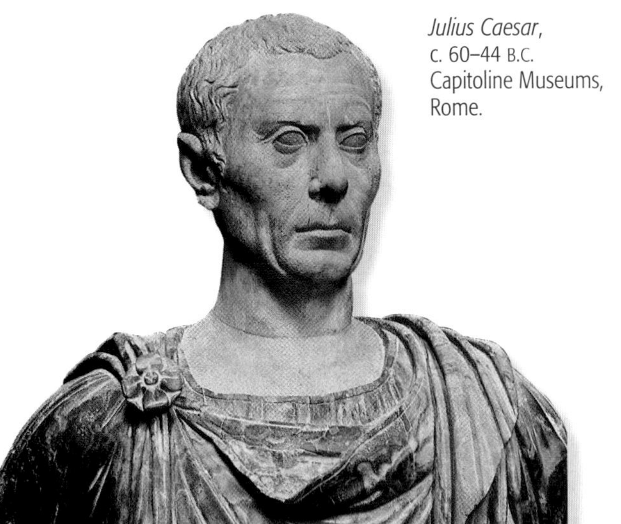

Julius Caesar, c. 60–44 B.C. Capitoline Museums, Rome.

- Caesar was a talented public speaker and writer whose war commentaries are considered literary classics. He introduced a new calendar, which is still used today in a slightly altered version. Although he could be charming, Caesar's arrogance and ambition created enemies in the Senate. A group of conspirators assassinated him in 44 B.C.
- Roman society was divided into several classes. Roman citizens, who had the right to vote, were either patricians (nobles) or plebeians (commoners). At first, only the noble landowners–the patricians–could hold office. But gradually the lower-class "commoners"–the plebeians–gained some political power and became represented in government by officials called tribunes.
- The Roman Senate watched over public officials and proposed new laws. Senators came from Rome's noble families. Popular assemblies enacted laws and elected public officials, including two powerful consuls responsible for the military. In times of emergency a dictator was appointed to replace the consuls for a brief period. Caesar acquired the title of dictator when he took control of Rome's government, although his powers exceeded those of a traditional dictator.

THE TRAGEDY OF JULIUS CAESAR

William Shakespeare

Tribute to Caesar. Andrea del Sarto (c. 1487–1530). Villa Medicea, Poggio a Caiano, Italy.

CHARACTERS

JULIUS CAESAR: ambitious military leader and politician; the most powerful man in Rome

CALPHURNIA: wife of Caesar

MARCUS BRUTUS: friend of Caesar, appointed by him to high office in the Roman government; a believer in the republic and member of the conspiracy against Caesar

PORTIA: wife of Brutus and daughter of a Roman patriot

CAIUS CASSIUS: brother-in-law of Brutus and member of the conspiracy against Caesar

MARK ANTONY: friend of Caesar, senator, and eloquent orator; member of the triumvirate, the three-man governing body that ruled Rome after Caesar's death

OCTAVIUS CAESAR: Caesar's great-nephew and official heir; member of the triumvirate

M. AEMILIUS LEPIDUS: military leader and member of the triumvirate

Conspirators Against Caesar

CASCA **METELLUS CIMBER** **TREBONIUS**
CINNA **DECIUS BRUTUS** **CAIUS LIGARIUS**

Senators

CICERO **PUBLIUS** **POPILIUS LENA**

Tribunes *(Public Officials)*

FLAVIUS **MURELLUS**

Officers in the Armies of Brutus and Cassius

LUCILIUS **MESSALA** **VOLUMNIUS**
TITINIUS **YOUNG CATO** **FLAVIUS**

Servants of Brutus

LUCIUS **CLITUS** **STRATO**
VARRUS **CLAUDIO** **DARDANIUS**

Others

A SOOTHSAYER (one who predicts the future)

ARTEMIDORUS OF CNIDOS: teacher of rhetoric

CINNA: a poet

PINDARUS: servant of Cassius

ANOTHER POET

SERVANTS TO CAESAR, ANTONY, AND OCTAVIUS; CITIZENS, GUARDS, SOLDIERS

ACT 1

SCENE 1. Rome. A street.

[*Enter* FLAVIUS, MURELLUS, *and certain* COMMONERS *over the stage*.]

FLAVIUS. Hence! Home, you idle creatures, get you home!
Is this a holiday? What, know you not,
Being mechanical,° you ought not walk
Upon a laboring day without the sign
Of your profession? Speak, what trade art thou?°

CARPENTER. Why, sir, a carpenter.

MURELLUS. Where is thy leather apron and thy rule?
What dost thou with thy best apparel on?
You, sir, what trade are you?

COBBLER. Truly, sir, in respect of° a fine workman, I am but, as you would say, a cobbler.°

MURELLUS. But what trade art thou? Answer me directly.

COBBLER. A trade, sir, that, I hope, I may use° with a safe conscience, which is indeed, sir, a mender of bad soles.

FLAVIUS. What trade, thou knave? Thou naughty knave, what trade?

COBBLER. Nay, I beseech you, sir, be not out° with me; yet, if you be out,° sir, I can mend you.

MURELLUS. What mean'st thou by that? Mend me, thou saucy fellow?

COBBLER. Why, sir, cobble you.

FLAVIUS. Thou art a cobbler, art thou?

COBBLER. Truly, sir, all that I live by is with the awl;° I meddle with no tradesman's matters, nor women's matters; but withal, I am indeed, sir, a surgeon to old shoes; when they are in great danger, I recover them. As proper men as ever trod upon neat's leather° have gone upon my handiwork.

FLAVIUS. But wherefore art not in thy shop today?
Why dost thou lead these men about the streets?

COBBLER. Truly, sir, to wear out their shoes, to get myself into more work. But indeed, sir, we make holiday to see Caesar and to rejoice in his triumph.°

2–5 Is this a . . . art thou: Flavius and Murellus, public officials, remind the laborers that they should be dressed in their work outfits rather than their best clothes.

3 mechanical: manual laborers.

10 in respect of: in comparison with.

11 cobbler: "clumsy worker" or "shoemaker." The Cobbler plays on the word's double meaning. Murellus and Flavius fail to understand his pun at first and keep pressing him to reveal a trade he has already identified.

13 use: practice.

16 out: angry.

16–17 if you be out: if your shoes are worn out.

22 awl: a tool for making holes in leather. The Cobbler puns on the words *all, awl,* and *withal,* which means "nevertheless."

26 neat's leather: cowhide. The Cobbler claims that his shoes have been worn by as fine men as ever walked in shoes.

31 triumph: triumphal celebration. (The triumph was held to celebrate Julius Caesar's defeat of two sons of Pompey the Great, his former rival. Caesar gained control over Rome when he defeated Pompey in 48 B.C.)

A shoemaker with hammer. 1st–3rd century A.D., Gallo-Roman. Tombstone relief. Musée Rolin, Autun, France.

Viewing the art: Based on what you've read about the cobbler in this scene, what representative elements might you add to a tombstone relief for him? Why?

MURELLUS. Wherefore rejoice? What conquest brings he home?
What tributaries° follow him to Rome,
To grace in captive bonds° his chariot wheels?
You blocks, you stones, you worse than senseless things!
O you hard hearts, you cruel men of Rome,
Knew you not Pompey? Many a time and oft
Have you climb'd up to walls and battlements,
To tow'rs and windows, yea, to chimney tops,
Your infants in your arms, and there have sate
The livelong day, with patient expectation,
To see great Pompey pass the streets of Rome;
And when you saw his chariot but° appear,
Have you not made an universal shout,
That Tiber° trembled underneath her banks
To hear the replication° of your sounds
Made in her concave shores?
And do you now put on your best attire?
And do you now cull out a holiday?°
And do you now strew flowers in his way,
That comes in triumph over Pompey's blood?°
Be gone!
Run to your houses, fall upon your knees,
Pray to the gods to intermit° the plague
That needs must light on this ingratitude.

FLAVIUS. Go, go, good countrymen, and, for this fault,
Assemble all the poor men of your sort;
Draw them to Tiber banks and weep your tears
Into the channel, till the lowest stream
Do kiss the most exalted shores of all.°

[*Exit all the* COMMONERS.]

See, whe'er their basest mettle be not mov'd;°
They vanish tongue-tied in their guiltiness.
Go you down that way towards the Capitol,
This way will I. Disrobe the images,
If you do find them deck'd with ceremonies.°

MURELLUS. May we do so?
You know it is the feast of Lupercal.°

FLAVIUS. It is no matter, let no images
Be hung with Caesar's trophies.° I'll about,
And drive away the vulgar° from the streets;
So do you too, where you perceive them thick.
These growing feathers pluck'd from Caesar's wing

33 **tributaries:** captured enemies who pay tribute, or ransom money, for their release.

34 **captive bonds:** the chains of prisoners.

43 **but:** only.

45 **Tiber:** a river running through Rome.

46 **replication:** echo.

49 **cull out a holiday:** pick out this day as a holiday.

51 **Pompey's blood:** Pompey's sons.

54 **intermit:** hold back.

58–60 **Draw them to . . . of all:** Flavius wants the commoners to weep into the Tiber until the river's lowest water reaches its highest banks.

61 **whe'er . . . mov'd:** whether their humble spirits have not been touched.

64–65 **Disrobe the images . . . ceremonies:** Flavius directs Murellus to remove any decorations from the statues.

67 **feast of Lupercal:** religious festival for a god worshiped by shepherds as a protector of flocks.

69 **trophies:** decorations honoring Caesar.

70 **vulgar:** common people.

Will make him fly an ordinary pitch,°
Who else would soar above the view of men
And keep us all in servile fearfulness.

[*They exit.*]

72–73 These growing . . . pitch: Plucking feathers from a bird's wings prevents it from flying. Flavius uses this metaphor for his plan to keep Caesar's power at an ordinary **pitch,** or height.

SCENE 2. Rome. A public place.

[*Enter* CAESAR, ANTONY *for the course*, CALPHURNIA, PORTIA, DECIUS, CICERO, BRUTUS, CASSIUS, CASCA, CITIZENS, *and a* SOOTHSAYER; *after them* MURELLUS *and* FLAVIUS.]

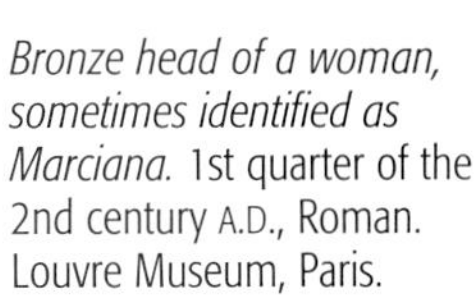

Bronze head of a woman, sometimes identified as Marciana. 1st quarter of the 2nd century A.D., Roman. Louvre Museum, Paris.

Viewing the sculpture: Describe the woman portrayed here. How might she reflect Calphurnia's feelings at this point in the drama?

CAESAR. Calphurnia!

CASCA. Peace, ho, Caesar speaks.

[*All fall silent as* CAESAR *calls for his wife.*]

CAESAR. Calphurnia!

CALPHURNIA. Here, my lord.

CAESAR. Stand you directly in Antonio's way
When he doth run his course. Antonio!

ANTONY. Caesar, my lord?

CAESAR. Forget not in your speed, Antonio,
To touch Calphurnia; for our elders say,
The barren, touched in this holy chase,
Shake off their sterile curse.°

6–9 Forget not . . . curse: Caesar, who has no children, refers to a traditional belief that barren women could become fertile if they were struck by leather thongs carried by runners who passed through Rome on the feast of Lupercal.

ANTONY. I shall remember;
When Caesar says, "Do this," it is perform'd.

CAESAR. Set on, and leave no ceremony out. [*Flourish.*]

SOOTHSAYER. Caesar!

CAESAR. Ha! Who calls?

CASCA. Bid every noise be still; peace yet again!

CAESAR. Who is it in the press° that calls on me?
I hear a tongue shriller than all the music,
Cry "Caesar!" Speak, Caesar is turn'd to hear.°

15 press: crowd.

17 turn'd to hear: Caesar turns his good ear to the Soothsayer (he was deaf in one ear).

SOOTHSAYER. Beware the ides of March.°

18 ides of March: March 15. In the Roman calendar, a day in the middle of every month was called the ides.

CAESAR. What man is that?

BRUTUS. A soothsayer bids you beware the ides of March.

CAESAR. Set him before me, let me see his face.

CASSIUS. Fellow, come from the throng, look upon Caesar.

CAESAR. What say'st thou to me now? Speak once again.

SOOTHSAYER. Beware the ides of March.

CAESAR. He is a dreamer, let us leave him. Pass.

[*They exit.* BRUTUS *and* CASSIUS *remain.*]

CASSIUS. Will you go see the order of the course?°

BRUTUS. Not I.

CASSIUS. I pray you do.

BRUTUS. I am not gamesome;° I do lack some part
Of that quick spirit that is in Antony.
Let me not hinder, Cassius, your desires;
I'll leave you.

CASSIUS. Brutus, I do observe you now of late;°
I have not from your eyes that gentleness
And show of love as I was wont to° have.
You bear too stubborn and too strange a hand
Over your friend that loves you.°

BRUTUS. Cassius,
Be not deceiv'd: if I have veil'd my look,
I turn the trouble of my countenance
Merely upon myself.° Vexed I am
Of late with passions of some difference,°
Conceptions only proper to myself,
Which give some soil, perhaps, to my behaviors;°
But let not therefore my good friends be griev'd
(Among which number, Cassius, be you one),
Nor construe any further° my neglect,
Than that poor Brutus, with himself at war,
Forgets the shows of love to other men.

CASSIUS. Then, Brutus, I have much mistook your passion,°
By means whereof this breast of mine hath buried
Thoughts of great value, worthy cogitations.°
Tell me, good Brutus, can you see your face?

BRUTUS. No, Cassius; for the eye sees not itself
But by reflection, by some other things.

CASSIUS. 'Tis just,
And it is very much lamented, Brutus,
That you have no such mirrors as will turn
Your hidden worthiness into your eye,
That you might see your shadow.° I have heard
Where many of the best respect in Rome
(Except immortal Caesar), speaking of Brutus
And groaning underneath this age's yoke,
Have wish'd that noble Brutus had his eyes.°

25 **order . . . course:** progress of the race.

28 **gamesome:** fond of games and sports.

32 **of late:** lately.

34 **was wont to:** used to.

35–36 **You bear . . . loves you:** Cassius uses the metaphor of a rider holding a tight rein on an unfamiliar horse to suggest Brutus's unfriendly behavior toward him.

37–39 **Be not . . . upon myself:** If I have seemed withdrawn, my displeased looks have been turned only on myself.

40 **passions of some difference:** conflicting emotions.

42 **Which give . . . behaviors:** Which might blemish my conduct.

45 **Nor . . . further:** Nor should you think any more of.

48 **mistook your passion:** misunderstood your feelings.

49–50 **By means . . . cogitations:** Because of this I have kept important thoughts to myself.

58 **shadow:** reflection.

58–62 **I have heard . . . eyes:** Cassius claims that many highly respected Roman citizens, groaning under the oppression of Caesar's rule, wished that Brutus would recognize his own worth.

BRUTUS. Into what dangers would you lead me, Cassius,
That you would have me seek into myself
For that which is not in me?

CASSIUS. Therefore, good Brutus, be prepar'd to hear;
And since you know you cannot see yourself
So well as by reflection, I, your glass
Will modestly discover to yourself
That of yourself which you yet know not of.°
And be not jealous on° me, gentle Brutus;
Were I a common laughter, or did use
To stale with ordinary oaths my love
To every new protester; if you know
That I do fawn on men and hug them hard,
And after scandal them; or if you know
That I profess myself in banqueting
To all the rout, then hold me dangerous.°

[*Flourish and shout.*]

BRUTUS. What means this shouting? I do fear the people
Choose Caesar for their king.

CASSIUS. Ay, do you fear it?
Then must I think you would not have it so.

BRUTUS. I would not, Cassius, yet I love him well.
But wherefore° do you hold me here so long?
What is it that you would impart to me?
If it be aught toward the general good,
Set honor in one eye and death i' th' other,
And I will look on both indifferently;°
For let the gods so speed° me, as I love
The name of honor more than I fear death.

CASSIUS. I know that virtue to be in you, Brutus,
As well as I do know your outward favor.°
Well, honor is the subject of my story:
I cannot tell what you and other men
Think of this life; but for my single self,
I had as lief not be as live to be
In awe of such a thing as I myself.°
I was born free as Caesar; so were you;
We both have fed as well, and we can both
Endure the winter's cold as well as he;
For once, upon a raw and gusty day,
The troubled Tiber chafing with her shores,°

68–70 **I, your . . . not of:** I, your mirror, will reveal without exaggeration what you do not yet know about yourself.

71 **jealous on:** suspicious of.

72–78 **Were I . . . dangerous:** If I were a laughingstock or used to cheaply offering my affection to anyone, or if you know me to slander men after fawning on them, or if you know me to proclaim friendship to the common crowd while drinking, then consider me dangerous.

83 **wherefore:** why.

85–87 **If it be aught . . . indifferently:** If it is anything that concerns the public welfare, I will face honor and death impartially.

88 **speed:** favor.

91 **favor:** appearance.

94–96 **for my single . . . myself:** Personally, I would rather not live than live in awe of another human being.

101 **chafing with her shores:** dashing into the shores (as if angry with them for their restraint).

Caesar said to me, "Dar'st thou,° Cassius, now
Leap in with me into this angry flood,
And swim to yonder point?" Upon the word,
Accoutred° as I was, I plunged in,
And bade him follow; so indeed he did.
The torrent roar'd, and we did buffet it
With lusty sinews,° throwing it aside
And stemming it with hearts of controversy;°
But ere we could arrive the point propos'd,
Caesar cried, "Help me, Cassius, or I sink!"
I, as Aeneas,° our great ancestor,
Did from the flames of Troy upon his shoulder
The old Anchises bear, so from the waves of Tiber
Did I the tired Caesar. And this man
Is now become a god, and Cassius is
A wretched creature, and must bend his body°
If Caesar carelessly but nod on him.
He had a fever when he was in Spain,
And when the fit was on him, I did mark
How he did shake—'tis true, this god did shake;
His coward lips did from their color fly,
And that same eye whose bend° doth awe the world
Did lose his° luster; I did hear him groan;
Ay, and that tongue of his that bade the Romans
Mark him, and write his speeches in their books,
Alas, it cried, "Give me some drink, Titinius,"
As a sick girl. Ye gods, it doth amaze me
A man of such a feeble temper should
So get the start of the majestic world,
And bear the palm alone.°

[*Shout. Flourish.*]

BRUTUS. Another general shout?
I do believe that these applauses are
For some new honors that are heap'd on Caesar.

CASSIUS. Why, man, he doth bestride the narrow world
Like a Colossus,° and we petty men
Walk under his huge legs, and peep about
To find ourselves dishonorable graves.
Men at some time are masters of their fates;
The fault, dear Brutus, is not in our stars,°
But in ourselves, that we are underlings.
Brutus and Caesar; what should be in that "Caesar"?

102 **Dar'st thou:** Do you dare?

105 **Accoutred:** dressed in armor.

108 **sinews:** muscles.

109 **stemming . . . controversy:** making headway against the river's flow in a spirit of rivalry.

112 **Aeneas** (i nē′ əs)**:** The legendary founder of Rome, who carried his father Anchises on his back as he fled the burning city of Troy after it was conquered by the Greeks.

117 **bend his body:** bow.

123 **bend:** glance, look.

124 **his:** its.

130–131 **So get the . . . alone:** get ahead of all others and carry the victor's prize himself.

136 **Colossus:** The Colossus of Rhodes, a gigantic statue of the Greek god Apollo in the harbor of Rhodes, was said to be so tall that ships could sail through its legs.

140 **stars:** fate (believed to be determined by the position of the stars and planets at someone's birth).

Why should that name be sounded more than yours?
Write them together, yours is as fair a name;
Sound them,° it doth become the mouth as well;
Weigh them, it is as heavy; conjure° with 'em,
"Brutus" will start a spirit as soon as "Caesar."
Now, in the names of all the gods at once,
Upon what meat doth this our Caesar feed,
That he is grown so great? Age,° thou art sham'd!
Rome, thou hast lost the breed of noble bloods!
When went there by an age, since the great flood°
But it was fam'd with more than with one man?°
When could they say, till now, that talk'd of Rome,
That her wide walks encompass'd but one man?
Now is it Rome indeed and room enough,°
When there is in it but one only man.
O! you and I have heard our fathers say
There was a Brutus once that would have brook'd
Th' eternal devil to keep his state in Rome
As easily as a king.°

BRUTUS. That you do love me, I am nothing jealous;°
What you would work me to, I have some aim.°
How I have thought of this, and of these times,
I shall recount hereafter. For this present,
I would not (so with love I might entreat you)
Be any further mov'd.° What you have said
I will consider; what you have to say
I will with patience hear, and find a time
Both meet° to hear and answer such high things.
Till then, my noble friend, chew° upon this;
Brutus had rather be a villager
Than to repute himself a son of Rome
Under these hard conditions as this time
Is like to lay upon us.

CASSIUS. I am glad that my weak words
Have struck but thus much show of fire from Brutus.

[*Enter* CAESAR *and his* TRAIN.]

BRUTUS. The games are done, and Caesar is returning.

CASSIUS. As they pass by, pluck Casca by the sleeve,
And he will (after his sour fashion) tell you
What hath proceeded worthy note today.°

BRUTUS. I will do so. But look you, Cassius,
The angry spot doth glow on Caesar's brow,

145 **Sound them:** say them.

146 **conjure:** call up spirits.

150 **Age:** the present era.

152 **great flood:** a time, according to Roman mythology, when a god let loose a flood that drowned all but two people.

153 **But it was . . . man:** That was not celebrated for more than one great man.

156 **Now is it . . . enough:** Cassius makes a pun on the words *Rome* and *room,* which were sometimes pronounced alike in Shakespeare's time.

159–161 **There was . . . king:** There once was a Brutus who would have accepted the devil ruling in Rome as easily as a king. (Cassius refers to Lucius Junius Brutus, who expelled the king and made Rome a republic in 509 B.C. Brutus claimed this hero as his ancestor.)

162 **am nothing jealous:** have no doubt.

163 **have some aim:** can guess.

167 **mov'd:** urged.

170 **meet:** suitable.

171 **chew:** ponder.

181 **What hath . . . today:** What noteworthy things have occurred today.

Julius Caesar is offered the crown by Marcus Antonius, but he prudently refuses it.

Viewing the art: What qualities of Caesar's does this painting depict? Do you think they are accurate? Why or why not?

And all the rest look like a chidden train;°
Calphurnia's cheek is pale, and Cicero°
Looks with such ferret° and such fiery eyes
As we have seen him in the Capitol,
Being cross'd in conference by some senators.

CASSIUS. Casca will tell us what the matter is.

CAESAR. Antonio!

ANTONY. Caesar?

CAESAR. Let me have men about me that are fat,
Sleek-headed men, and such as sleep a-nights.
Yond Cassius has a lean and hungry look,
He thinks too much; such men are dangerous.

ANTONY. Fear him not, Caesar, he's not dangerous,
He is a noble Roman, and well given.°

184 **chidden train:** scolded band of followers.

185 **Cicero:** a Roman senator famous for his oratory.

186 **ferret:** a weasel-like animal with red eyes.

197 **well given:** favorably disposed (toward Caesar).

CAESAR. Would he were fatter! But I fear him not.
Yet if my name were liable to fear,°
I do not know the man I should avoid
So soon as that spare Cassius. He reads much,
He is a great observer, and he looks
Quite through the deeds of men.° He loves no plays,
As thou dost, Antony; he hears no music;
Seldom he smiles, and smiles in such a sort
As if he mock'd himself, and scorn'd his spirit
That could be mov'd to smile at any thing.°
Such men as he be never at heart's ease
Whiles they behold a greater than themselves,
And therefore are they very dangerous.
I rather tell thee what is to be fear'd
Than what I fear; for always I am Caesar.
Come on my right hand, for this ear is deaf,
And tell me truly what thou think'st of him.

[*CAESAR and his TRAIN exit. CASCA stays.*]

CASCA. You pull'd me by the cloak, would you speak with me?

BRUTUS. Ay, Casca; tell us what hath chanc'd° today,
That Caesar looks so sad.°

CASCA. Why, you were with him, were you not?

BRUTUS. I should not then ask Casca what had chanc'd.

CASCA. Why, there was a crown offer'd him; and being offer'd him, he put it by° with the back of his hand, thus, and then the people fell a-shouting.

BRUTUS. What was the second noise for?

CASCA. Why, for that too.

CASSIUS. They shouted thrice; what was the last cry for?

CASCA. Why, for that too.

BRUTUS. Was the crown offer'd him thrice?

CASCA. Ay, marry, was't,° and he put it by thrice, every time gentler than other; and at every putting-by mine honest neighbors° shouted.

CASSIUS. Who offer'd him the crown?

CASCA. Why, Antony.

BRUTUS. Tell us the manner of it, gentle Casca.

CASCA. I can as well be hang'd as tell the manner of it; it was mere foolery, I did not mark° it. I saw Mark Antony offer

199 **if my name . . . fear:** if it were possible for me to fear anyone.

202–203 **looks . . . of men:** sees people's true motives in their actions.

206–207 **scorn'd . . . any thing:** scorned anyone who ever smiles.

216 **chanc'd:** happened.

217 **sad:** serious.

221 **put it by:** pushed it aside.

228 **marry, was't:** indeed it was.

229–230 **mine honest neighbors:** Casca refers ironically to his "honest neighbors," for whom he has contempt.

235 **mark:** pay attention to.

him a crown—yet 'twas not a crown neither, 'twas one of these coronets°—and as I told you, he put it by once; but for all that, to my thinking, he would fain° have had it. Then he offer'd it to him again; then he put it by again; but to my thinking, he was very loath to lay his fingers off it. And then he offer'd it the third time; he put it the third time by; and still as he refus'd it, the rabblement hooted, and clapp'd their chopp'd° hands, and threw up their sweaty nightcaps, and utter'd such a deal of stinking breath because Caesar refus'd the crown, that it had, almost, chok'd Caesar; for he swounded,° and fell down at it; and for mine own part, I durst not laugh, for fear of opening my lips and receiving the bad air.

CASSIUS. But, soft,° I pray you; what, did Caesar swound?

CASCA. He fell down in the market place, and foam'd at mouth, and was speechless.

BRUTUS. 'Tis very like, he hath the falling sickness.°

CASSIUS. No, Caesar hath it not; but you, and I,
And honest Casca, we have the falling sickness.

CASCA. I know not what you mean by that, but I am sure Caesar fell down. If the tag-rag people° did not clap him and hiss him, according as he pleas'd and displeas'd them, as they use to do the players in the theater, I am no true man.

BRUTUS. What said he when he came unto himself?

CASCA. Marry, before he fell down, when he perceiv'd the common herd was glad he refus'd the crown, he pluck'd me ope his doublet,° and offer'd them his throat to cut. And I had been a man of any occupation,° if I would not have taken him at a word,° I would I might go to hell among the rogues. And so he fell. When he came to himself again, he said, if he had done or said anything amiss, he desir'd their worships to think it was his infirmity. Three or four wenches, where I stood, cried, "Alas, good soul!" and forgave him will all their hearts. But there's no heed to be taken of them; if Caesar had stabb'd their mothers, they would have done no less.

BRUTUS. And after that, he came thus sad away?

CASCA. Ay.

CASSIUS. Did Cicero say anything?

CASCA. Ay, he spoke Greek.

237 **coronets:** small crowns.

238 **fain:** rather.

243 **chopp'd:** chapped.

246 **swounded:** fainted.

249 **soft:** wait a minute.

252 **'Tis very . . . falling sickness:** It's very likely that he has epilepsy.

256 **tag-rag people:** ragged mob.

261–262 **pluck'd . . . doublet:** ripped open his short jacket.

262–263 **And I . . . occupation:** If I had been "a man of action" (or "a laborer").

264 **a word:** his word.

CASSIUS. To what effect?

CASCA. Nay, and I tell you that, I'll ne'er look you i' th' face again. But those that understood him smil'd at one another, and shook their heads; but for mine own part, it was Greek to me.° I could tell you more news too; Murellus and Flavius, for pulling scarfs off Caesar's images, are put to silence.° Fare you well. There was more foolery yet, if I could remember it.

CASSIUS. Will you sup with me tonight, Casca?

CASCA. No, I am promis'd forth.

CASSIUS. Will you dine with me tomorrow?

CASCA. Ay, if I be alive, and your mind hold,° and your dinner worth the eating.

CASSIUS. Good, I will expect you.

CASCA. Do so. Farewell, both. [*Exit.*]

BRUTUS. What a blunt fellow is this grown to be!
He was quick mettle° when he went to school.

CASSIUS. So is he now in execution
Of any bold or noble enterprise,
However he puts on this tardy form.°
This rudeness is a sauce to his good wit,
Which gives men stomach to disgest° his words
With better appetite.

BRUTUS. And so it is. For this time I will leave you.
Tomorrow, if you please to speak with me,
I will come home to you, or, if you will,
Come home to me, and I will wait for you.

CASSIUS. I will do so. Till then, think of the world.°

[*Exit* BRUTUS.]

Well, Brutus, thou art noble; yet I see
Thy honorable mettle may be wrought
From that it is dispos'd;° therefore it is meet°
That noble minds keep ever with their likes;
For who so firm that cannot be seduc'd?
Caesar doth bear me hard,° but he loves Brutus.
If I were Brutus now and he were Cassius,
He should not humor° me. I will this night,
In several hands, in at his windows throw,
As if they came from several citizens,
Writings, all tending to the great opinion

279–280 **it was Greek to me:** I couldn't understand a word of it.

281 **put to silence:** barred from speaking in public (or perhaps exiled or executed).

286 **your mind hold:** you don't change your mind.

291 **quick mettle:** lively, clever.

294 **However . . . form:** Although he puts on this dull manner.

296 **disgest:** digest.

302 **the world:** the present state of affairs.

304–305 **Thy honorable . . . dispos'd:** Your honorable nature can be manipulated to go against its normal inclinations.

305 **meet:** appropriate.

308 **doth bear me hard:** dislikes me.

310 **humor:** influence.

The Barber Shop of Licinius, 1881. Gustave Clarence Rodolphe Boulanger. Oil on canvas, 71.1 x 102.2 cm.

Viewing the painting: How does this portrayal of a Roman street scene enhance your understanding of the play's setting?

That Rome holds of his name; wherein obscurely
Caesar's ambition shall be glanced at.°
And after this, let Caesar seat him sure,°
For we will shake him, or worse days endure. [*Exit.*]

310–315 I will . . . glanced at: Tonight I will throw letters in different handwriting, as if they came from several citizens, into Brutus's windows. The letters will relate that Brutus is highly regarded in Rome and will subtly hint at Caesar's ambition.

316 seat him sure: seat himself securely.

SCENE 3. A Roman street. One month later.

[*Thunder and lightning. Enter (from opposite sides)* CASCA *(with his sword drawn) and* CICERO.]

CICERO. Good even,° Casca; brought you Caesar home?
Why are you breathless? And why stare you so?

CASCA. Are not you mov'd, when all the sway° of earth
Shakes like a thing unfirm? O Cicero,
I have seen tempests, when the scolding winds
Have riv'd° the knotty oaks, and I have seen
Th' ambitious ocean swell and rage and foam,
To be exalted with° the threat'ning clouds;
But never till tonight, never till now,
Did I go through a tempest dropping fire.
Either there is a civil strife in heaven,
Or else the world, too saucy° with the gods,
Incenses them to send destruction.

1 even: evening.

3 sway: realm.

6 riv'd: split.

8 exalted with: raised as high as.

12 saucy: insolent.

CICERO. Why, saw you any thing more wonderful?

CASCA. A common slave—you know him well by sight—
Held up his left hand, which did flame and burn
Like twenty torches join'd; and yet his hand,
Not sensible of° fire, remain'd unscorch'd.
Besides—I ha' not since put up my sword—
Against the Capitol I met a lion,
Who glaz'd° upon me and went surly by,
Without annoying me. And there were drawn
Upon a heap° a hundred ghastly women,
Transformed with their fear, who swore they saw
Men, all in fire, walk up and down the streets.
And yesterday the bird of night° did sit
Even at noonday upon the marketplace,
Hooting and shrieking. When these prodigies°
Do so conjointly meet,° let not men say,
"These are their reasons, they are natural";
For I believe they are portentous things
Unto the climate that they point upon.°

CICERO. Indeed, it is a strange-disposed time;
But men may construe things after their fashion,
Clean from the purpose of the things themselves.°
Comes Caesar to the Capitol tomorrow?

CASCA. He doth; for he did bid Antonio
Send word to you he would be there tomorrow.

CICERO. Good night then, Casca; this disturbed sky
Is not to walk in.

CASCA. Farewell, Cicero. [*Exit* CICERO.]

[*Enter* CASSIUS.]

CASSIUS. Who's there?

CASCA. A Roman.

CASSIUS. Casca, by your voice.

CASCA. Your ear is good. Cassius, what night is this!°

CASSIUS. A very pleasing night to honest men.

CASCA. Who ever knew the heavens menace so?

CASSIUS. Those that have known the earth so full of faults.
For my part, I have walk'd about the streets,
Submitting me° unto the perilous night;
And thus unbraced,° Casca, as you see,
Have bar'd my bosom to the thunder-stone;°

18 **sensible of:** sensitive to.

21 **glaz'd:** stared.

22–23 **drawn . . . heap:** huddled together.

26 **bird of night:** screech owl.

28 **prodigies:** bizarre events.

29 **conjointly meet:** coincide.

31–32 **portentous . . . point upon:** bad omens for the place where they occur.

34–35 **But men may . . . themselves:** But people may interpret things in their own way, regardless of the real meaning of the things.

42 **what night is this:** what a night this is!

47 **Submitting me:** exposing myself.

48 **unbraced:** with jacket open.

49 **thunder-stone:** thunderbolt.

And when the cross blue lightning seem'd to open
The breast of heaven, I did present myself
Even in the aim° and very flash of it.

CASCA. But wherefore did you so much tempt the heavens?
It is the part of men to fear and tremble
When the most mighty gods by tokens° send
Such dreadful heralds to astonish° us.

CASSIUS. You are dull,° Casca; and those sparks of life
That should be in a Roman you do want,°
Or else you use not. You look pale, and gaze,
And put on fear, and cast yourself in wonder,
To see the strange impatience of the heavens;
But if you would consider the true cause
Why all these fires, why all these gliding ghosts,
Why birds and beasts from quality and kind,°
Why old men, fools, and children calculate,°
Why all these things change from their ordinance,
Their natures and preformed faculties,
To monstrous quality—why, you shall find
That heaven hath infus'd them with these spirits,
To make them instruments of fear and warning
Unto some monstrous state.°
Now could I, Casca, name to thee a man
Most like this dreadful night,
That thunders, lightens, opens graves, and roars
As doth the lion in the Capitol—
A man no mightier than thyself, or me,
In personal action, yet prodigious grown
And fearful,° as these strange eruptions are.

CASCA. 'Tis Caesar that you mean; is it not, Cassius?

CASSIUS. Let it be who it is; for Romans now
Have thews° and limbs like to their ancestors;
But, woe the while,° our fathers' minds are dead,
And we are govern'd with our mothers' spirits;
Our yoke and sufferance° show us womanish.

CASCA. Indeed, they say, the senators tomorrow
Mean to establish Caesar as a king;
And he shall wear his crown by sea and land,
In every place, save here in Italy.

CASSIUS. I know where I will wear this dagger then;
Cassius from bondage will deliver Cassius.°
Therein,° ye gods, you make the weak most strong;

52 **in the aim:** at the point where it was directed.

55 **tokens:** ominous signs.

56 **astonish:** stun with fear.

57 **dull:** stupid.

58 **want:** lack.

64 **from quality and kind:** act contrary to nature.

65 **calculate:** make prophecies.

66–71 **Why all these . . . state:** Cassius argues that things have changed from their normal behavior as a heavenly warning of some unnatural state of affairs.

77–78 **yet prodigious . . . fearful:** yet has become ominous and threatening.

81 **thews:** muscles.

82 **woe the while:** alas for these times.

84 **yoke and sufferance:** servitude and patient submission.

89–90 **I know . . . deliver Cassius:** Cassius says that he would rather kill himself than submit to Caesar.

91 **Therein:** in that way (referring to suicide).

Therein, ye gods, you tyrants do defeat;
Nor stony tower, nor walls of beaten brass,
Nor airless dungeon, nor strong links of iron,
Can be retentive to the strength of spirit;
But life, being weary of these worldly bars,
Never lacks power to dismiss itself.
If I know this, know all the world besides,
That part of tyranny that I do bear
I can shake off at pleasure.

[*Thunder still.*]

CASCA. So can I;
So every bondman in his own hand bears
The power to cancel his captivity.

CASSIUS. And why should Caesar be a tyrant then?
Poor man, I know he would not be a wolf,
But that he sees the Romans are but sheep;

Augustus and lictors, detail from the south frieze of the Ara Pacis Augustae. 13–9 B.C., Roman. Museum of the Ara Pacis, Rome.

Viewing the art: One of the duties of Roman officers called *lictors* was to accompany officials like Caesar in public appearances. What does this image suggest to you about the government of Rome in Caesar's time?

He were no lion, were not Romans hinds.°
Those that with haste will make a mighty fire
Begin it with weak straws. What trash° is Rome?
What rubbish and what offal?° when it serves
For the base matter° to illuminate
So vile a thing as Caesar! But, O grief,
Where hast thou led me? I, perhaps, speak this
Before a willing bondman; then I know
My answer must be made.° But I am arm'd,
And dangers are to me indifferent.

CASCA. You speak to Casca, and to such a man
That is no fleering° tell-tale. Hold, my hand.
Be factious for redress of all these griefs,°
And I will set this foot of mine as far
As who goes farthest.

CASSIUS. There's a bargain made.
Now know you, Casca, I have mov'd° already
Some certain of the noblest-minded Romans
To undergo with me an enterprise
Of honorable-dangerous consequence;
And I do know, by this they stay for me
In Pompey's Porch;° for now, this fearful night,
There is no stir or walking in the streets;
And the complexion of the element
[In] favor's like the work we have in hand,°
Most bloody, fiery, and most terrible.

[*Enter* CINNA.]

CASCA. Stand close awhile, for here comes one in haste.

CASSIUS. 'Tis Cinna, I do know him by his gait,
He is a friend. Cinna, where haste you so?

CINNA. To find out you. Who's that? Metellus Cimber?

CASSIUS. No, it is Casca, one incorporate°
To our attempts. Am I not stay'd for, Cinna?

CINNA. I am glad on't. What a fearful night is this!
There's two or three of us have seen strange sights.

CASSIUS. Am I not stay'd for? tell me.

CINNA. Yes, you are.
O Cassius, if you could
But win the noble Brutus to our party—

106 **hinds:** deer.

108 **trash:** "twigs" or "garbage."

109 **offal:** "chips of wood" or "garbage."

110 **base matter:** kindling.

112–114 **I, perhaps . . . be made:** Perhaps I am speaking to one who accepts his slavery; if so, I shall have to answer for my words (suggesting that Casca might inform on him).

117 **fleering:** sneering.

118 **Be factious . . . griefs:** Form a group to straighten out all these problems.

121 **mov'd:** persuaded.

125–126 **by this . . . Porch:** By this time they wait for me in the entrance to the theater built by Pompey.

128–129 **the complexion . . . in hand:** The condition of the sky appears similar to the work we have to do.

135 **incorporate:** joined.

CASSIUS. Be you content. Good Cinna, take this paper,
And look you lay it in the praetor's chair,
Where Brutus may but find it; and throw this
In at his window; set this up with wax
Upon old Brutus' statue.° All this done,
Repair° to Pompey's Porch, where you shall find us.
Is Decius Brutus and Trebonius there?

CINNA. All but Metellus Cimber, and he's gone
To seek you at your house. Well, I will hie,°
And so bestow these papers as you bade me.

CASSIUS. That done, repair to Pompey's theater.

[*Exit* CINNA.]

Come, Casca, you and I will yet ere day
See Brutus at his house. Three parts of him
Is ours already, and the man entire
Upon the next encounter yields him ours.°

CASCA. O, he sits high in all the people's hearts;
And that which would appear offense in us,
His countenance, like richest alchemy,
Will change to virtue and to worthiness.°

CASSIUS. Him, and his worth, and our great need of him,
You have right well conceited.° Let us go,
For it is after midnight, and ere day
We will awake him and be sure of him.

[*They exit.*]

142–146 **Good Cinna . . . statue:** Marcus Brutus held the office of praetor, a high-ranking judge who settled disputes brought before him. Cassius directs Cinna to leave one letter on Brutus's chair, throw a second into his window, and fasten a third onto the statue of the hero Lucius Junius Brutus.

147 **Repair:** go.

150 **hie:** hurry.

155–156 **the man . . . ours:** When we next meet him, he will be entirely in our hands.

159–160 **His countenance . . . worthiness:** Alchemy was the "science" of trying to turn base metals into gold. Casca says that Brutus's noble reputation will change the public's attitude toward their plot from condemnation to admiration.

162 **conceited:** understood.

Responding to Literature

Personal Response

Which characters in act 1 made the strongest impression on you? Why?

Analyzing Act 1

Recall and Interpret

1. After seeing the public celebrating Caesar's triumph, what do Flavius and Murellus do? Why do they respond this way?
2. Summarize the conversation between Cassius and Brutus in scene 2. What does Cassius seem to be most concerned about?
3. What incident does Casca describe to Cassius and Brutus? What is Casca's attitude toward the incident?
4. Describe Cassius's and Casca's reactions to the storm. What do their reactions reveal about them?
5. Whom do Cassius and Casca want to win over to their plan? Why might they feel it is important for this person to join them?

Evaluate and Connect

6. Do you think Shakespeare's portrayal of the commoners in act 1 is realistic? How does their wordplay in scene 1 affect you?
7. Do you think that the conspirators have good reasons for their reactions to Caesar? Explain your answer.
8. How would you describe the overall **mood** of act 1? Use specific details from the act to support your description.
9. **Internal conflict** is a struggle that takes place within a character. Describe an internal conflict that occurs in act 1. What effect does this conflict have on your appreciation of that character?
10. What similarities in leadership qualities do you see between any of the characters in act 1? How do those qualities compare with the ones you listed for the Reading Focus on page 777?

Literary ELEMENTS

Blank Verse

Blank verse is lines of verse written in unrhymed iambic pentameter. Each line of iambic pentameter has five metrical feet, and each foot, or iamb, consists of an unstressed syllable followed by a stressed syllable. Because blank verse is intended to sound like spoken language, its meter is often not perfectly regular. These lines from *Julius Caesar* are examples of blank verse with perfect iambic pentameter:

Lĕt mé / hăve mén / ăbóut / mĕ thát / ăre fát,
Slĕek-héad / ĕd mén, / ănd súch / ăs sléep / ă-níghts.

1. Find two other lines from act 1 written in blank verse with perfect iambic pentameter. Indicate the stressed and unstressed syllables.
2. Find two lines of blank verse with imperfect iambic pentameter. Show the stressed and unstressed syllables.

- See **Literary Terms Handbook,** p. R2.

Extending Your Response

Literature Groups

Impressive Expressions With your group, identify three segments of dialogue or monologue from act 1 that seem particularly effective or descriptive. Discuss the elements that make each segment memorable. Compare your passages and analyses with those of other groups.

Creative Writing

In My Opinion Write a newspaper editorial about an event in act 1. Include details from the play and present your opinions in a clear and well-argued analysis.

Save your work for your portfolio.

Writing Skills

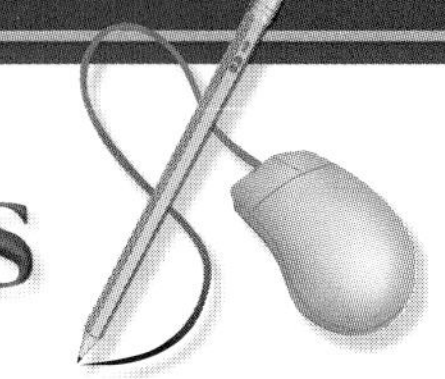

Effective Conclusions

Even if you make many great points in the body of an essay, your reader may be left with an unsatisfactory feeling if you don't sum up your argument in a **conclusion**–the final paragraph that pulls the piece together and lets the reader know you are finishing your argument. Here are a few possible ways to conclude an essay.

Possible Conclusion	When to Use
sum up the main points and restate your thesis	if you've presented a great deal of information
make a recommendation	if you've described a problem
make a prediction	if you've described a current situation
ask a question	if you want your reader to continue thinking about the material presented
express your own thoughts and impressions	if you've discussed a personal experience

Read the paragraph below to see how one student concludes an essay that compares and contrasts *Antigone* and *Julius Caesar.* Note how she sums up her main points and, in the last two sentences, restates her thesis or main idea.

Both *Antigone* and *Julius Caesar* deal with themes of loyalty and betrayal. However, in *Julius Caesar,* Cassius feels the need to convince Brutus to join him in betrayal, but Antigone does not feel the need to convince her sister Ismene. Cassius is looking for political power, while Antigone is trying to respect her brother and her gods. To me, these differences between main characters make *Antigone* a much more inspiring play. I learn more from reading about a selfless, brave person like Antigone than a selfish, power-hungry one like Cassius.

EXERCISE

On your paper, write the strategy that you might use to conclude essays on the following topics:

1. The first time you were separated from a parent
2. Destruction of the rain forest
3. Population growth in your community
4. Comparing and contrasting two films

ACT 2

SCENE 1. BRUTUS's garden. The ides of March.

[*Enter* BRUTUS *in his orchard.*]

BRUTUS. What, Lucius, ho!
I cannot, by the progress° of the stars,
Give guess how near to day. Lucius, I say!
I would it were my fault° to sleep so soundly.
When, Lucius, when? Awake, I say! What, Lucius!

[*Enter* LUCIUS.]

LUCIUS. Call'd you, my lord?

BRUTUS. Get me a taper° in my study, Lucius.
When it is lighted, come and call me here.

LUCIUS. I will, my lord.

[*Exit* LUCIUS.]

BRUTUS. It must be by his death;° and for my part,
I know no personal cause to spurn° at him,
But for the general.° He would be crown'd:
How that might change his nature, there's the question.
It is the bright day that brings forth the adder,°
And that craves° wary walking. Crown him that,°
And then I grant we put a sting in him
That at his will he may do danger with.
Th' abuse of greatness is when it disjoins
Remorse from power;° and, to speak truth of Caesar,
I have not known when his affections° sway'd
More than his reason. But 'tis a common proof°
That lowliness° is young ambition's ladder,
Whereto the climber-upward turns his face;
But when he once attains the upmost round,°
He then unto the ladder turns his back,
Looks in the clouds, scorning the base degrees
By which he did ascend. So Caesar may;
Then lest he may, prevent.° And since the quarrel
Will bear no color for the thing he is,
Fashion it thus: that what he is, augmented,

2 **progress:** position.

4 **I would . . . fault:** I wish it were my weakness.

7 **taper:** candle.

10 **his death:** Caesar's death.

11 **spurn:** strike out.

12 **the general:** the public good.

14 **adder:** poisonous snake.

15 **craves:** demands. **Crown him that:** If we crown him.

18–19 **Th' abuse . . . power:** Greatness is misused when it separates mercy from power.

20 **affections:** feelings, desires.

21 **a common proof:** a common occurrence.

22 **lowliness:** humility.

24 **upmost round:** top rung.

28 **Then lest . . . prevent:** Let us act in advance to prevent it.

Would run to these and these extremities;°
And therefore think him as a serpent's egg,
Which hatch'd, would as his kind grow mischievous,
And kill him in the shell.

[*Enter* LUCIUS.]

LUCIUS. The taper burneth in your closet,° sir.
Searching the window for a flint, I found
This paper thus seal'd up, and I am sure
It did not lie there when I went to bed.

[*Gives him the letter.*]

BRUTUS. Get you to bed again, it is not day.
Is not tomorrow, boy, the [ides] of March?

LUCIUS. I know not, sir.

BRUTUS. Look in the calendar, and bring me word.

LUCIUS. I will, sir. [*Exit.*]

BRUTUS. The exhalations° whizzing in the air
Give so much light that I may read by them.

[*Opens the letter and reads.*]

"Brutus, thou sleep'st; awake, and see thyself!
Shall Rome, etc. Speak, strike, redress!"°
"Brutus, thou sleep'st; awake."
Such instigations° have been often dropp'd
Where I have took them up.
"Shall Rome, etc." Thus must I piece it out:°
Shall Rome stand under one man's awe? What, Rome?
My ancestors did from the streets of Rome
The Tarquin° drive when he was call'd a king.
"Speak, strike, redress!" Am I entreated
To speak and strike? O Rome, I make thee promise,
If the redress will follow, thou receivest
Thy full petition at the hand of Brutus!°

[*Enter* LUCIUS.]

LUCIUS. Sir, March is wasted fifteen days.

[*Knock within.*]

BRUTUS. 'Tis good. Go to the gate, somebody knocks.

[*Exit* LUCIUS.]

Since Cassius first did whet° me against Caesar,
I have not slept.

28–31 **since the quarrel . . . extremities:** Since our complaints are not supported by Caesar's present behavior, we will have to put our case the following way: if given more power, Caesar's nature would lead him to such and such extremes.

35 **closet:** small private room.

44 **exhalations:** meteors.

47 **redress:** correct a wrong.

49 **instigations:** letters urging action.

51 **piece it out:** fill in the gaps in meaning.

54 **Tarquin** (tär′ kwin): the last king of Rome, driven out by Lucius Junius Brutus.

55–58 **Speak, strike . . . Brutus:** Brutus vows that Rome's petition for redress will be granted if it can be done through his words and actions.

61 **whet:** incite.

Grave-relief of the corn-merchant Lucius Ampudius Philomusu, with his wife and daughter, c. 15 B.C.–A.D. 5
Marble, 0.63 x 1.63 m. The British Museum, London.

Viewing the art: Which characters at this point in the play might have facial expressions similar to those portrayed in the relief? Why?

Between the acting of a dreadful thing
And the first motion,° all the interim is
Like a phantasma,° or a hideous dream.
The Genius and the mortal instruments°
Are then in council, and the state of a man,
Like to a little kingdom, suffers then
The nature of an insurrection.°

[*Enter* LUCIUS.]

LUCIUS. Sir, 'tis your brother° Cassius at the door,
Who doth desire to see you.

BRUTUS. Is he alone?

LUCIUS. No, sir, there are moe° with him.

BRUTUS. Do you know them?

LUCIUS. No, sir; their hats are pluck'd about their ears,
And half their faces buried in their cloaks,
That by no means I may discover° them
By any mark of favor.°

BRUTUS. Let 'em enter.

[*Exit* LUCIUS.]

They are the faction. O Conspiracy,
Sham'st thou° to show thy dang'rous brow by night,

64 **motion:** prompting.

65 **phantasma:** nightmare.

66 **Genius . . . instruments:** the mental and physical powers that allow someone to take action.

67–69 **the state . . . insurrection:** Brutus compares his conflicted state of mind to a kingdom paralyzed by civil unrest.

70 **brother:** brother-in-law. (Cassius is married to Brutus's sister, Junia.)

72 **moe:** more.

75 **discover:** identify.

76 **favor:** appearance.

78 **Sham'st thou:** Are you ashamed?

When evils are most free? O then, by day
Where wilt thou find a cavern dark enough
To mask thy monstrous visage? Seek none, Conspiracy;
Hide it in smiles and affability;
For if thou path, thy native semblance° on,
Not Erebus° itself were dim enough
To hide thee from prevention.°

[*Enter the* CONSPIRATORS, CASSIUS, CASCA, DECIUS, CINNA, METELLUS, *and* TREBONIUS.]

CASSIUS. I think we are too bold upon° your rest.
Good morrow,° Brutus, do we trouble you?

BRUTUS. I have been up this hour, awake all night.
Know I these men that come along with you?

CASSIUS. Yes, every man of them; and no man here
But honors you; and every one doth wish
You had but that opinion of yourself
Which every noble Roman bears of you.
This is Trebonius.

BRUTUS. He is welcome hither.

CASSIUS. This, Decius Brutus.

BRUTUS. He is welcome too.

CASSIUS. This, Casca; this, Cinna; and this, Metellus Cimber.

BRUTUS. They are all welcome.
What watchful cares do interpose themselves
Betwixt your eyes and night?°

CASSIUS. Shall I entreat a word?

[*They whisper.*]

DECIUS. Here lies the east; doth not the day break here?

CASCA. No.

CINNA. O, pardon, sir, it doth; and yon gray lines
That fret° the clouds are messengers of day.

CASCA. You shall confess that you are both deceiv'd.
Here, as I point my sword, the sun arises,
Which is a great way growing on the south,
Weighing the youthful season of the year.
Some two months hence, up higher toward the north
He first presents his fire, and the high east
Stands, as the Capitol, directly here.°

BRUTUS. Give me your hands all over,° one by one.

83 **path . . . semblance:** go about undisguised.

84 **Erebus** (er′ ə bəs)**:** in classical mythology, the dark place through which the dead pass on their way to Hades, the underworld.

85 **prevention:** discovery.

86 **too bold upon:** intruding upon.

87 **morrow:** morning.

98–99 **What watchful . . . night:** What cares keep you awake?

104 **fret:** interlace.

106–111 **Here, as I . . . directly here:** Casca insists that in the early spring the sun rises south of the spot pointed out by Decius and Cinna; it will rise farther north in about two months.

112 **all over:** all of you.

CASSIUS. And let us swear our resolution.

BRUTUS. No, not an oath. If not the face of men,
The sufferance of our souls, the time's abuse—
If these be motives weak, break off betimes,°
And every man hence to his idle bed.
So let high-sighted° tyranny range on
Till each man drop by lottery.° But if these
(As I am sure they do) bear fire° enough
To kindle cowards and to steel with valor
The melting spirits of women, then, countrymen,
What need we any spur but our own cause
To prick° us to redress? What other bond
Than secret Romans that have spoke the word
And will not palter?° and what other oath
Than honesty to honesty engag'd
That this shall be, or we will fall for it?°
Swear priests and cowards and men cautelous,°
Old feeble carrions,° and such suffering souls
That welcome wrongs; unto bad causes swear
Such creatures as men doubt; but do not stain
The even virtue of our enterprise,
Nor th' insuppressive mettle of our spirits,
To think that or our cause or our performance
Did need an oath;° when every drop of blood
That every Roman bears, and nobly bears,
Is guilty of a several bastardy,°
If he do break the smallest particle
Of any promise that hath pass'd from him.°

CASSIUS. But what of Cicero? Shall we sound him?°
I think he will stand very strong with us.

CASCA. Let us not leave him out.

CINNA. No, by no means.

METELLUS. O, let us have him, for his silver hairs
Will purchase us a good opinion,
And buy men's voices to commend our deeds.
It shall be said his judgment rul'd our hands;
Our youths and wildness shall no whit° appear,
But all be buried in his gravity.°

BRUTUS. O, name him not! Let us not break with him,°
For he will never follow anything
That other men begin.

114–116 If not . . . betimes: The sadness in people's faces, the suffering of our souls, the corruption of our age—if these are weak motives, let's give up at once.

118 high-sighted: arrogant.

119 drop by lottery: die by chance (at Caesar's whim).

120 bear fire: are spirited.

124 prick: spur.

126 palter: waver; deceive.

126–128 what other oath . . . for it: What other oath is needed than that of honest men who have pledged to each other that they will prevail or die trying?

129 cautelous: wary; crafty.

130 carrions: men no better than corpses.

132–136 do not stain . . . oath: Do not insult the steadfast virtue of our undertaking or the indomitable courage of our spirits to think that either our cause or our actions require an oath.

136–140 every drop . . . from him: Brutus claims that no one of true Roman blood would break a promise.

138 Is guilty . . . bastardy: is illegitimate.

141 sound him: find out his feelings.

148 no whit: not in the least.

149 gravity: dignity.

150 break with him: reveal our plot to him.

CASSIUS. Then leave him out.

CASCA. Indeed, he is not fit.

DECIUS. Shall no man else be touch'd but only Caesar?

CASSIUS. Decius, well urg'd. I think it is not meet
Mark Antony, so well belov'd of Caesar,
Should outlive Caesar; we shall find of him
A shrewd contriver; and you know, his means,°
If he improve them,° may well stretch so far
As to annoy us all; which to prevent,
Let Antony and Caesar fall together.

BRUTUS. Our course will seem too bloody, Caius Cassius,
To cut the head off and then hack the limbs—
Like wrath in death and envy afterwards;°
For Antony is but a limb of Caesar.
Let's be sacrificers, but not butchers, Caius.
We all stand up against the spirit of Caesar,°
And in the spirit of men there is no blood.
O that we then could come by° Caesar's spirit,
And not dismember Caesar! But, alas,
Caesar must bleed for it. And, gentle friends,
Let's kill him boldly, but not wrathfully;
Let's carve him as a dish fit for the gods,
Not hew him as a carcass fit for hounds;
And let our hearts, as subtle masters do,
Stir up their servants° to an act of rage,
And after seem to chide 'em. This shall make
Our purpose necessary, and not envious;
Which so appearing to the common eyes,
We shall be call'd purgers, not murderers.
And for Mark Antony, think not of him;
For he can do no more than Caesar's arm
When Caesar's head is off.

CASSIUS. Yet I fear him,
For in the ingrafted° love he bears to Caesar—

BRUTUS. Alas, good Cassius, do not think of him.
If he love Caesar, all that he can do
Is to himself—take thought and die° for Caesar.
And that were much he should,° for he is given
To sports, to wildness, and much company.

TREBONIUS. There is no fear in him;° let him not die,
For he will live and laugh at this hereafter.

158 **means:** abilities.

159 **improve them:** uses them fully.

164 **Like wrath . . . afterwards:** as if the killings were motivated by anger and malice.

167 **the spirit of Caesar:** what Caesar represents.

169 **come by:** get possession of.

176 **servants:** hands.

184 **ingrafted:** deep-rooted.

187 **take thought and die:** die from grief.

188 **that were much he should:** It is unlikely that he would do such a thing.

190 **no fear in him:** nothing to fear from him.

[*Clock strikes.*]

BRUTUS. Peace, count the clock.

CASSIUS. The clock hath stricken three.

TREBONIUS. 'Tis time to part.

CASSIUS. But it is doubtful yet
Whether Caesar will come forth today or no;
For he is superstitious grown of late,
Quite from the main opinion° he held once
Of fantasy, of dreams, and ceremonies.°
It may be these apparent prodigies,
The unaccustom'd terror of this night,
And the persuasion of his augurers°
May hold him from the Capitol today.

196 Quite from the main opinion: contrary to the strong opinion.

197 ceremonies: omens.

200 augurers: religious officials who interpreted omens to predict future events.

DECIUS. Never fear that. If he be so resolv'd,
I can o'ersway him; for he loves to hear
That unicorns may be betray'd with trees,
And bears with glasses, elephants with holes,
Lions with toils, and men with flatterers;°
But when I tell him he hates flatterers
He says he does, being then most flattered.
Let me work;
For I can give his humor the true bent,°
And I will bring him to the Capitol.

203–206 for he loves . . . flatterers: Decius refers to legends that the mythical unicorn could be tricked into charging a tree and getting its horn stuck, and that bears can be lured by mirrors. He also refers to trapping elephants in pits and using nets to catch lions, and tricking men with flattery.

210 give his . . . bent: put him in the right mood.

CASSIUS. Nay, we will all of us be there to fetch him.

BRUTUS. By the eight hour; is that the uttermost?°

213 uttermost: latest.

CINNA. Be that the uttermost, and fail not then.

METELLUS. Caius Ligarius doth bear Caesar hard,°
Who rated° him for speaking well of Pompey.
I wonder none of you have thought of him.

215 bear Caesar hard: strongly resents Caesar.

216 rated: rebuked.

BRUTUS. Now, good Metellus, go along by him.
He loves me well, and I have given him reasons;
Send him but hither, and I'll fashion° him.

220 fashion: persuade.

CASSIUS. The morning comes upon 's; we'll leave you, Brutus.
And, friends, disperse yourselves; but all remember
What you have said, and show yourselves true Romans.

BRUTUS. Good gentlemen, look fresh and merrily;
Let not our looks put on our purposes,
But bear it as our Roman actors do,
With untir'd spirits and formal constancy.°
And so good morrow to you every one.

224–227 look fresh . . . constancy: Brutus warns the others not to let their serious expressions show their intentions; they should carry out their plot appearing at ease and dignified.

[*They exit.* BRUTUS *remains.*]

Boy! Lucius! Fast asleep? It is no matter,
Enjoy the honey-heavy dew of slumber.
Thou hast no figures nor no fantasies,
Which busy care draws in the brains of men;
Therefore thou sleep'st so sound.

[*Enter* PORTIA.]

PORTIA. Brutus, my lord!

BRUTUS. Portia! what mean you? wherefore rise you now?
It is not for your health thus to commit
Your weak condition to the raw cold morning.

PORTIA. Nor for yours neither. Y'have ungently,° Brutus,
Stole from my bed; and yesternight at supper
You suddenly arose and walk'd about,
Musing and sighing, with your arms across;°

237 **ungently:** discourteously.

240 **across:** folded.

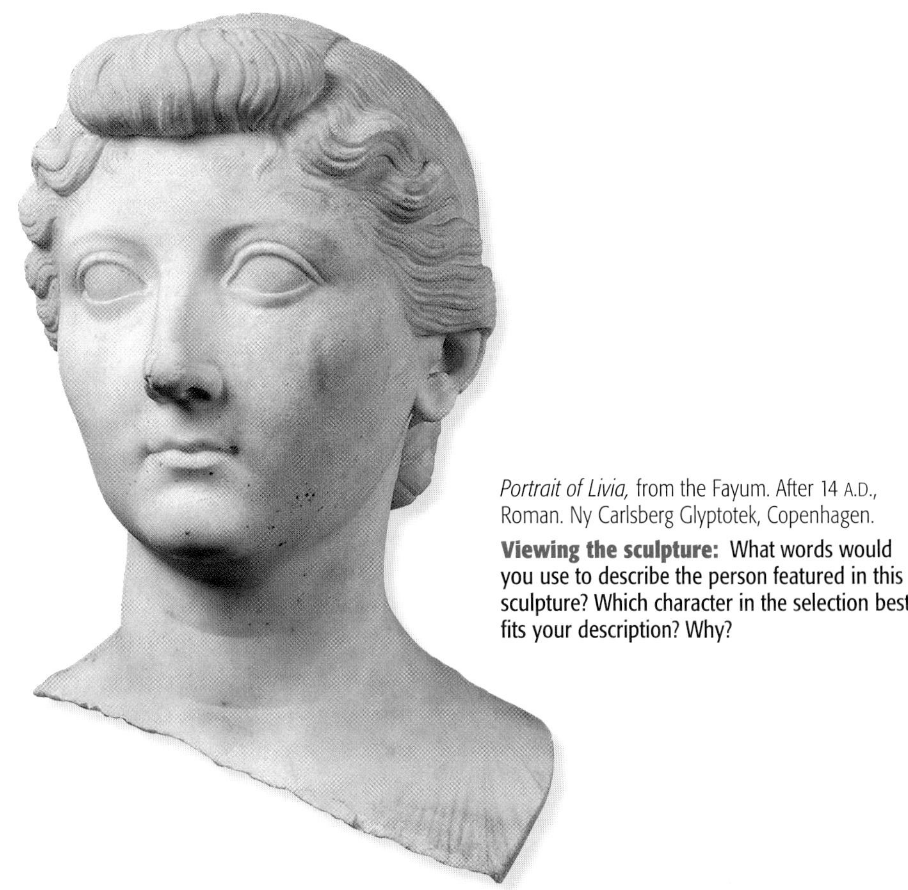

Portrait of Livia, from the Fayum. After 14 A.D., Roman. Ny Carlsberg Glyptotek, Copenhagen.

Viewing the sculpture: What words would you use to describe the person featured in this sculpture? Which character in the selection best fits your description? Why?

And when I ask'd you what the matter was,
You star'd upon me with ungentle looks.
I urg'd you further; then you scratch'd your head,
And too impatiently stamp'd with your foot.
Yet I insisted, yet you answer'd not,
But with an angry wafter° of your hand
Gave sign for me to leave you. So I did,
Fearing to strengthen that impatience
Which seem'd too much enkindled, and withal°
Hoping it was but an effect of humor,°
Which sometimes hath his° hour with every man.
It will not let you eat, nor talk, nor sleep,
And could it work so much upon your shape
As it hath much prevail'd on your condition,
I should not know you Brutus.° Dear my lord,
Make me acquainted with your cause of grief.

BRUTUS. I am not well in health, and that is all.

PORTIA. Brutus is wise and, were he not in health,
He would embrace the means to come by it.

BRUTUS. Why, so I do. Good Portia, go to bed.

PORTIA. Is Brutus sick, and is it physical°
To walk unbraced and suck up the humors
Of the dank morning?° What, is Brutus sick,
And will he steal out of his wholesome bed,
To dare the vile contagion of the night,
And tempt the rheumy and unpurged air°
To add unto his sickness? No, my Brutus;
You have some sick offense° within your mind,
Which by the right and virtue of my place,°
I ought to know of; and upon my knees
I charm you, by my once commended beauty,
By all your vows of love, and that great vow
Which did incorporate and make us one,
That you unfold to me, yourself, your half,
Why you are heavy, and what men tonight
Have had resort to you; for here have been
Some six or seven, who did hide their faces
Even from darkness.

BRUTUS. Kneel not, gentle Portia.

PORTIA. I should not need, if you were gentle Brutus.
Within the bond of marriage, tell me, Brutus,
Is it excepted I should know no secrets

246 **wafter:** waving.

249 **withal:** also.

250 **but an . . . humor:** only a passing mood.

251 **his:** its.

253–255 **And could . . . Brutus:** And if it could change your appearance as much as it has changed your state of mind, I would not recognize you as Brutus.

261 **physical:** healthy.

262–263 **humors . . . morning:** damp morning mist.

266 **tempt the . . . air:** risk the damp and impure air. (It was believed that the night air was dangerous to breathe because it wasn't purified by the sun's rays.)

268 **sick offense:** harmful disorder.

269 **by the right . . . place:** as your wife.

That appertain to you? Am I your self
But, as it were, in sort or limitation,°
To keep with you at meals, comfort your bed,
And talk to you sometimes? Dwell I but in the suburbs°
Of your good pleasure? If it be no more,
Portia is Brutus' harlot, not his wife.

BRUTUS. You are my true and honorable wife,
As dear to me as are the ruddy drops
That visit my sad heart.

PORTIA. If this were true, then should I know this secret.
I grant I am a woman; but withal
A woman that Lord Brutus took to wife.
I grant I am a woman; but withal
A woman well reputed, Cato's daughter.°
Think you I am no stronger than my sex,
Being so father'd and so husbanded?
Tell me your counsels, I will not disclose 'em.
I have made strong proof of my constancy,
Giving myself a voluntary wound
Here, in the thigh;° can I bear that with patience,
And not my husband's secrets?

BRUTUS. O ye gods!
Render me worthy of this noble wife! [*Knock.*]
Hark, hark, one knocks. Portia, go in a while,
And by and by thy bosom shall partake
The secrets of my heart.
All my engagements I will construe° to thee,
All the charactery of my sad brows.°
Leave me with haste.

[*Exit* PORTIA.]

Lucius, who's that knocks?

[*Enter* LUCIUS *and* CAIUS LIGARIUS.]

LUCIUS. Here is a sick man that would speak with you.

BRUTUS. Caius Ligarius, that Metellus spake of.
Boy, stand aside. [*Exit* LUCIUS.] Caius Ligarius, how?°

CAIUS. Vouchsafe° good morrow from a feeble tongue.

BRUTUS. O, what a time have you chose out, brave Caius,
To wear a kerchief!° Would you were not sick!

CAIUS. I am not sick, if Brutus have in hand
Any exploit worthy the name of honor.

283 **in sort or limitation:** after a fashion or within limits.

285 **suburbs:** outskirts.

295 **Cato's daughter:** Portia's father, Marcus Porcius Cato, killed himself rather than submit to Caesar's rule after Pompey was defeated.

299–301 **I have made . . . thigh:** Portia reveals that she intentionally cut her thigh before approaching Brutus to show her strong determination.

307 **construe:** explain.

308 **charactery of . . . brows:** what is written in my sad brows (the reasons I am sad).

312 **how:** how are you?

313 **Vouchsafe:** Please accept.

315 **kerchief:** a scarf (wrapped around an ill person's head to protect against drafts).

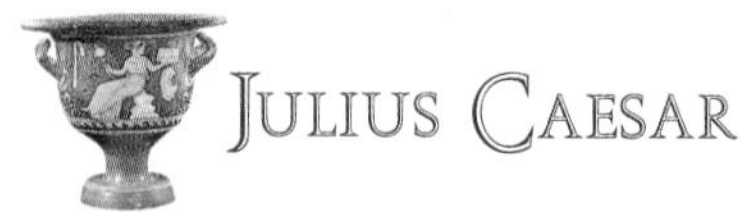

BRUTUS. Such an exploit have I in hand, Ligarius,
Had you a healthful ear to hear of it.

CAIUS. By all the gods that Romans bow before,
I here discard my sickness!
Soul of Rome!
Brave son, deriv'd from honorable loins!
Thou, like an exorcist,° hast conjur'd up
My mortified° spirit. Now bid me run,
And I will strive with things impossible,
Yea, get the better of them. What's to do?

BRUTUS. A piece of work that will make sick men whole.

CAIUS. But are not some whole that we must make sick?

BRUTUS. That must we also. What it is, my Caius,
I shall unfold to thee, as we are going
To whom it must be done.°

CAIUS. Set on your foot.°
And with a heart new-fir'd I follow you,
To do I know not what; but it sufficeth
That Brutus leads me on.

[*Thunder.*]

BRUTUS. Follow me, then. [*They exit.*]

323 **exorcist:** one who summons up spirits.

324 **mortified:** deadened.

330–331 **I shall . . . done:** They are going to Caesar's house to escort him to the Capitol.

331 **Set on your foot:** Go ahead.

SCENE 2. CAESAR's house. A few hours later.

[*Thunder and lightning. Enter* JULIUS CAESAR *in his nightgown.*]

CAESAR. Nor heaven nor° earth have been at peace tonight.
Thrice hath Calphurnia in her sleep cried out,
"Help, ho! they murther° Caesar!" Who's within?

[*Enter a* SERVANT.]

SERVANT. My lord?

CAESAR. Go bid the priests do present sacrifice,
And bring me their opinions of success.°

SERVANT. I will, my lord. [*Exit.*]

[*Enter* CALPHURNIA.]

CALPHURNIA. What mean you, Caesar? Think you to walk forth?
You shall not stir out of your house today.

CAESAR. Caesar shall forth; the things that threaten'd me
Ne'er look'd but on my back; when they shall see
The face of Caesar, they are vanished.

1 **Nor . . . nor:** neither . . . nor.

3 **murther:** murder.

5–6 **Go bid . . . success:** Tell the priests to make a sacrifice immediately, and bring me their interpretations of the results.

Portrait of a woman in encaustic on limewood with added gold leaf. c. A.D. 160–170, Roman period, Egypt. 44.3 x 20.4 cm. The British Museum, London.

Viewing the art: What qualities do you think this woman possesses? Which of these qualities do you think Portia or Calphurnia shares? Explain.

CALPHURNIA. Caesar, I never stood on ceremonies,°
Yet now they fright me. There is one within,
Besides the things that we have heard and seen,
Recounts most horrid sights seen by the watch.°
A lioness hath whelped° in the streets,
And graves have yawn'd,° and yielded up their dead;
Fierce fiery warriors fight upon the clouds
In ranks and squadrons and right form of war,°
Which drizzled blood upon the Capitol;
The noise of battle hurtled in the air;

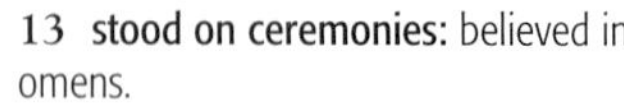

13 **stood on ceremonies:** believed in omens.

16 **watch:** night watchmen.

17 **whelped:** given birth.

18 **yawn'd:** opened.

20 **right form of war:** proper military formation.

The Ides of March. Sir Edward John Poynter (1836–1919). Manchester City Art Galleries, England.

Viewing the art: What is the mood of this piece? Does it support or contradict the mood created with each reference to the ides of March in the drama? Explain.

Horses did neigh, and dying men did groan,
And ghosts did shriek and squeal about the streets.
O Caesar, these things are beyond all use,°
And I do fear them.

CAESAR. What can be avoided
Whose end is purpos'd by the mighty gods?
Yet Caesar shall go forth; for these predictions
Are to the world in general as to Caesar.°

CALPHURNIA. When beggars die, there are no comets seen;
The heavens themselves blaze forth the death of princes.

CAESAR. Cowards die many times before their deaths,
The valiant never taste of death but once.
Of all the wonders that I yet have heard,
It seems to me most strange that men should fear,
Seeing that death, a necessary end,
Will come when it will come.

[*Enter a* SERVANT.]

What say the augurers?

SERVANT. They would not have you to stir forth today.
Plucking the entrails of an offering forth,
They could not find a heart within the beast.°

CAESAR. The gods do this in shame of° cowardice;
Caesar should be a beast without a heart
If he should stay at home today for fear.
No, Caesar shall not; Danger knows full well
That Caesar is more dangerous than he.
We [are] two lions litter'd in one day,°
And I the elder and more terrible;
And Caesar shall go forth.

CALPHURNIA. Alas, my lord,
Your wisdom is consum'd in confidence.
Do not go forth today; call it my fear
That keeps you in the house and not your own.
We'll send Mark Antony to the Senate House,
And he shall say you are not well today.
Let me, upon my knee, prevail in this.

CAESAR. Mark Antony shall say I am not well,
And for thy humor,° I will stay at home.

[*Enter* DECIUS.]

Here's Decius Brutus, he shall tell them so.

25 **use:** normal experience.

29 **Are to the . . . Caesar:** apply to everyone as well as to me.

39–40 **Plucking the . . . beast:** Augurers would examine the inner organs of a sacrificed animal to predict the future. The absence of a heart would be a strange and unfavorable omen.

41 **in shame of:** to shame.

44–46 **Danger knows . . . day:** Caesar uses two figures of speech, first personifying danger and then using the metaphor that he and danger are lions born on the same day.

56 **humor:** whim.

DECIUS. Caesar, all hail! good morrow, worthy Caesar,
I come to fetch you to the Senate House.

CAESAR. And you are come in very happy time°
To bear my greeting to the senators,
And tell them that I will not come today.
Cannot, is false; and that I dare not, falser;
I will not come today. Tell them so, Decius.

CALPHURNIA. Say he is sick.

CAESAR. Shall Caesar send a lie?
Have I in conquest stretch'd mine arm so far
To be afeard to tell graybeards the truth?°
Decius, go tell them Caesar will not come.

DECIUS. Most mighty Caesar, let me know some cause,
Lest I be laugh'd at when I tell them so.

CAESAR. The cause is in my will, I will not come:
That is enough to satisfy the Senate.
But for your private satisfaction,
Because I love you, I will let you know.
Calphurnia here, my wife, stays° me at home:
She dreamt tonight° she saw my statue,
Which, like a fountain with an hundred spouts,
Did run pure blood, and many lusty Romans
Came smiling and did bathe their hands in it.
And these does she apply for° warnings and portents
And evils imminent, and on her knee
Hath begg'd that I will stay at home today.

DECIUS. This dream is all amiss interpreted,
It was a vision fair and fortunate.
Your statue spouting blood in many pipes,
In which so many smiling Romans bath'd,
Signifies that from you great Rome shall suck
Reviving blood, and that great men shall press
For tinctures, stains, relics, and cognizance.°
This by Calphurnia's dream is signified.

CAESAR. And this way have you well expounded it.

DECIUS. I have, when you have heard what I can say;
And know it now: the Senate have concluded
To give this day a crown to mighty Caesar.
If you shall send them word you will not come,
Their minds may change. Besides, it were a mock
Apt to be render'd,° for someone to say,

60 in very happy time: at the right moment.

66–67 Have I . . . truth: Have I made such conquests to be afraid to tell old men the truth?

75 stays: keeps.

76 tonight: last night.

80 apply for: interpret as.

85–89 Your statue . . . cognizance: **Tinctures** are features added to a coat of arms; **relics** are the remains of saints; **cognizance** is a mark identifying one as a lord's follower. Decius interprets Calphurnia's dream as a sign of Caesar's prestige, with great men coming to him to show their political loyalty and reverence.

96–97 it were a . . . render'd: it would be a joke likely to be made.

"Break up the Senate till another time,
When Caesar's wife shall meet with better dreams."
If Caesar hide himself, shall they not whisper,
"Lo, Caesar is afraid"?
Pardon me, Caesar, for my dear dear love
To your proceeding° bids me tell you this;
And reason to my love is liable.°

CAESAR. How foolish do your fears seem now, Calphurnia!
I am ashamed I did yield to them.
Give me my robe, for I will go.

[*Enter* BRUTUS, LIGARIUS, METELLUS CIMBER, CASCA, TREBONIUS, CINNA, *and* PUBLIUS.]

And look where Publius is come to fetch me.

PUBLIUS. Good morrow, Caesar.

CAESAR. Welcome, Publius.
What, Brutus, are you stirr'd so early too?
Good morrow, Casca. Caius Ligarius,
Caesar was ne'er so much your enemy°
As that same ague° which hath made you lean.
What is't o'clock?

BRUTUS. Caesar, 'tis strucken eight.

CAESAR. I thank you for your pains and courtesy.

[*Enter* ANTONY.]

See, Antony, that revels long a-nights,°
Is notwithstanding up. Good morrow, Antony.

ANTONY. So to most noble Caesar.

CAESAR. Bid them prepare within;
I am to blame to be thus waited for.
Now, Cinna; now, Metellus; what, Trebonius,
I have an hour's talk in store for you;
Remember that you call on me today;
Be near me, that I may remember you.

TREBONIUS. Caesar, I will [*Aside.*] and so near will I be,
That your best friends shall wish I had been further.

CAESAR. Good friends, go in, and taste some wine with me,
And we, like friends, will straightway go together.

BRUTUS. [*Aside.*] That every like is not the same, O Caesar,
The heart of Brutus earns to think upon.°

[*They exit.*]

102–103 **my dear . . . proceeding:** my very deep desire for your advancement.

104 **liable:** subservient. Decius says that his love for Caesar forces him to say this, even though he may be overstepping himself.

112 **your enemy:** Caesar had recently pardoned Ligarius for his support of Pompey during the civil war.

113 **ague:** sickness.

116 **that revels long a-nights:** who carouses late into the night.

128–129 **That every . . . upon:** Brutus grieves to think that not everyone who appears to be a friend is a real friend.

SCENE 3. A street near the Capitol. Shortly afterward.

[*Enter* ARTEMIDORUS *(reading a paper)*.]

ARTEMIDORUS. "Caesar, beware of Brutus; take heed of Cassius; come not near Casca; have an eye to Cinna; trust not Trebonius; mark well Metellus Cimber; Decius Brutus loves thee not; thou hast wrong'd Caius Ligarius. There is but one mind in all these men, and it is bent against Caesar. If thou beest not immortal, look about you; security gives way to conspiracy.° The mighty gods defend thee!
Thy lover,° Artemidorus."
Here will I stand till Caesar pass along,
And as a suitor° will I give him this.
My heart laments that virtue cannot live
Out of the teeth of emulation.°
If thou read this, O Caesar, thou mayest live;
If not, the Fates with traitors do contrive.° [*Exit.*]

6–7 **security gives . . . conspiracy:** overconfidence opens the way for enemy plots.

8 **lover:** devoted friend.

10 **suitor:** person presenting a special request to a ruler.

12 **Out of . . . emulation:** beyond the reach of envy.

14 **contrive:** conspire.

SCENE 4. Another Roman street. Immediately after.

[*Enter* PORTIA *and* LUCIUS.]

PORTIA. I prithee, boy, run to the Senate House;
Stay not to answer me, but get thee gone.
Why dost thou stay?

LUCIUS. To know my errand, madam.

PORTIA. I would have had thee there and here again
Ere I can tell thee what thou shouldst do there°—
O constancy,° be strong upon my side;
Set a huge mountain 'tween my heart and tongue!
I have a man's mind, but a woman's might.
How hard it is for women to keep counsel!°—
Art thou here yet?

LUCIUS. Madam, what should I do?
Run to the Capitol, and nothing else?
And so return to you, and nothing else?

PORTIA. Yes, bring me word, boy, if thy lord look well,
For he went sickly forth; and take good note
What Caesar doth, what suitors press to him.
Hark, boy, what noise is that?

LUCIUS. I hear none, madam.

PORTIA. Prithee, listen well.
I heard a bustling rumor, like a fray,°
And the wind brings it from the Capitol.

4–5 **I would . . . do there:** You could go there and return here before I could explain what you should do there.

6 **constancy:** firmness.

9 **counsel:** a secret.

18 **bustling . . . fray:** noise of some activity such as a fight.

LUCIUS. Sooth,° madam, I hear nothing.

[*Enter the* SOOTHSAYER.]

PORTIA. Come hither, fellow; which way hast thou been?

SOOTHSAYER. At mine own house, good lady.

PORTIA. What is't a'clock?

SOOTHSAYER. About the ninth hour, lady.

PORTIA. Is Caesar yet gone to the Capitol?

SOOTHSAYER. Madam, not yet; I go to take my stand,
To see him pass on to the Capitol.

PORTIA. Thou hast some suit to Caesar, hast thou not?

SOOTHSAYER. That I have, lady, if it will please Caesar
To be so good to Caesar as to hear me:
I shall beseech him to befriend himself.

PORTIA. Why, know'st thou any harm's intended towards him?

SOOTHSAYER. None that I know will be, much that I fear may chance.
Good morrow to you. Here the street is narrow;
The throng that follows Caesar at the heels,
Of senators, of praetors, common suitors,
Will crowd a feeble man almost to death.
I'll get me to a place more void,° and there
Speak to great Caesar as he comes along.

[*Exit.*]

PORTIA. I must go in. Ay me! How weak a thing
The heart of woman is! O Brutus,
The heavens speed thee in thine enterprise!
Sure, the boy heard me—Brutus hath a suit
That Caesar will not grant.°—O, I grow faint.—
Run, Lucius, and commend me to my lord,°
Say I am merry. Come to me again,
And bring me word what he doth say to thee.

[*They exit separately.*]

20 **Sooth:** truly.

37 **void:** empty.

42–43 **Brutus hath . . . grant:** Portia makes up this excuse about Brutus's petition to explain her nervousness to Lucius.

44 **commend me to my lord:** send my regards to my husband.

Responding to Literature

Personal Response

Which character are you most sympathetic toward? Why?

Analyzing Act 2

Recall and Interpret

1. According to Brutus, why must Caesar be killed?
2. According to Brutus, why don't the conspirators need to swear an oath? What can you infer about Cassius, Casca, and Brutus in scene 1 as these conspirators make their plans?
3. Why does Brutus want to spare Antony's life? What opinion does he seem to hold of Antony?
4. Why does Calphurnia want Caesar to remain at home? In your opinion, why does Caesar eventually decide to go to the Capitol?
5. Why does Portia send her servant to the Capitol? What impression do you have of Portia and her relationship with Brutus? Support your response with details from the selection.

Evaluate and Connect

6. **Theme Connections** How do Brutus's intentions relate to the theme of loyalty and betrayal? Do you accept Brutus's justification for killing Caesar? Why or why not?
7. If you were one of the conspirators, would you agree with Brutus's recommendations or with Cassius's? Explain.
8. Calphurnia urges Caesar to act on her fears and remain at home. Do you agree with her reasoning? Why or why not?
9. Compare and contrast Portia and Calphurnia. How do they compare with women you know or with contemporary female characters?
10. What events or scenes in act 2 contribute to the **suspense?** Why?

Literary ELEMENTS

Soliloquies and Asides

Soliloquies are speeches delivered while a character is alone on stage. **Asides** are comments that a character makes to the audience that other characters on stage do not hear. Both of these theatrical devices are used frequently in Elizabethan drama to provide information to the audience and to reveal the characters' thoughts. For example, Cassius's soliloquy after his first meeting with Brutus (act 1, scene 2) reveals his plan to win over Brutus. It also influences the audience's opinion of Cassius.

1. What does Brutus reveal in his soliloquy at the beginning of act 2?
2. What does Trebonius mean in act 2, scene 2, lines 124–125? Why might Shakespeare have written these lines as an aside?

- See **Literary Terms Handbook,** pp. R12 and R1.

Extending Your Response

Writing About Literature

Characterization Shakespeare developed Caesar's character through his words and actions and through other characters' comments about him. Skim act 2 for examples of these three methods of characterization. In a paragraph explain whether Caesar's words and actions are consistent with what other characters say about him.

Performing

Act It Out! In a small group, choose a scene or a portion of a scene to perform for the class. Discuss different ways of delivering the dialogue. For example, decide whether a line should be spoken softly or with great emphasis. Give reasons for your choices. Perform your scene for the class.

Save your work for your portfolio.

Vo•cab•u•lar•y Skills

Homophones

The word **homophone** comes from the Greek *homo,* meaning "same," and *phone,* meaning "sound." Homophones are words that sound the same even though they are spelled differently and have different meanings.

When you are writing, using a homophone for the desired word can sometimes result in confusion. For example, you convey a totally different meaning if you write "a doctor who needs more *patience*" than if you wrote *patients.* Also, using homophones such as *marshal* instead of *martial,* or *profit* instead of *prophet,* can give the reader the impression that you are unaware of the difference in meaning or that you are careless.

If you use the wrong homophones in your writing, don't expect your computer to help you fix them. Computer programs that check spelling–and grammar–can be valuable. However, a computer probably won't tell you that you have used *rung* when you should have used *wrung,* because both of those are correctly spelled words.

Careful proofreading will help you eliminate any mistakes with homophones. Be especially careful with frequently overlooked homophones, such as *it's* and *its* or *who's* and *whose.* Thinking about the meaning of each homophone will help you use it correctly.

EXERCISE

List each underlined word on your paper. If the word is the correct one to use in the sentence, write *Correct.* If it is a homophone for the correct word, write the word that should have been used. Check definitions in a dictionary as needed.

The incredible feat of creating *Julius Caesar* involved making a number of choices. That the right choices were made seems clear from the fact that the play has born the test of time.

To lesson what would otherwise have been an impossibly long play, Shakespeare had to altar some historical facts. Certain events in *Julius Caesar* very from history, but this is mainly a matter of simplification. He also chose to center the play more on Brutus and his dual loyalties to Caesar and to Rome than on Caesar himself.

Shakespeare chose his hero well, as Brutus is a holy fascinating character. Although Cassius hates Caesar the man, Brutus hates only the tyranny he fears will result from Caesar's reign. It is this fear that leads him to conclude that Caesar must parish.

ACT 3

SCENE 1. The Capitol in Rome. The ides of March.

[*Flourish. Enter* CAESAR, BRUTUS, CASSIUS, CASCA, DECIUS, METELLUS, TREBONIUS, CINNA, ANTONY, PUBLIUS, POPILIUS, LEPIDUS, ARTEMIDORUS, *and the* SOOTHSAYER.]

CAESAR. The ides of March are come.

SOOTHSAYER. Ay, Caesar, but not gone.

ARTEMIDORUS. Hail, Caesar! Read this schedule.°

DECIUS. Trebonius doth desire you to o'er-read,
(At your best leisure) this his humble suit.

ARTEMIDORUS. O Caesar, read mine first; for mine's a suit
That touches Caesar nearer. Read it, great Caesar.

CAESAR. What touches us ourself shall be last serv'd.

ARTEMIDORUS. Delay not, Caesar, read it instantly.

CAESAR. What, is the fellow mad?

PUBLIUS. Sirrah,° give place.

CASSIUS. What, urge you your petitions in the street?
Come to the Capitol.

[*CAESAR enters the Capitol, the rest following.*]

POPILIUS. I wish your enterprise today may thrive.

CASSIUS. What enterprise, Popilius?

POPILIUS. Fare you well. [*Leaves him and joins* CAESAR.]

BRUTUS. What said Popilius Lena?

CASSIUS. He wish'd today our enterprise might thrive.
I fear our purpose is discovered.

BRUTUS. Look how he makes° to Caesar; mark him.

CASSIUS. Casca, be sudden, for we fear prevention.°
Brutus, what shall be done? If this be known,
Cassius or Caesar never shall turn back,°
For I will slay myself.

3 **schedule:** document.

10 **Sirrah:** an insulting form of address to an inferior.

18 **makes:** makes his way.

19 **be sudden . . . prevention:** be quick, for we fear that we will be stopped.

21 **turn back:** return alive.

BRUTUS. Cassius, be constant;°
Popilius Lena speaks not of our purposes,
For look he smiles, and Caesar doth not change.

CASSIUS. Trebonius knows his time; for look you, Brutus,
He draws Mark Antony out of the way.

[*ANTONY and TREBONIUS exit.*]

DECIUS. Where is Metellus Cimber? Let him go
And presently prefer° his suit to Caesar.

BRUTUS. He is address'd;° press near and second him.

CINNA. Casca, you are the first that rears your hand.

CAESAR. Are we all ready? What is now amiss
That Caesar and his Senate must redress?

METELLUS. Most high, most mighty, and most puissant° Caesar,
Metellus Cimber throws before thy seat
An humble heart. [*Kneeling.*]

CAESAR. I must prevent thee, Cimber.
These couchings and these lowly courtesies
Might fire the blood of ordinary men,
And turn preordinance and first decree
Into the [law] of children. Be not fond
To think that Caesar bears such rebel blood
That will be thaw'd from the true quality
With that which melteth fools—I mean sweet words,
Low-crooked curtsies, and base spaniel fawning.°
Thy brother by decree is banished;
If thou dost bend, and pray, and fawn for him,
I spurn thee like a cur° out of my way.
Know, Caesar doth not wrong, nor without cause
Will he be satisfied.°

METELLUS. Is there no voice more worthy than my own,
To sound more sweetly in great Caesar's ear
For the repealing of my banish'd brother?

BRUTUS. I kiss thy hand, but not in flattery, Caesar;
Desiring thee that Publius Cimber may
Have an immediate freedom of repeal.°

CAESAR. What, Brutus?

CASSIUS. Pardon, Caesar! Caesar, pardon!
As low as to thy foot doth Cassius fall,
To beg enfranchisement° for Publius Cimber.

22 **constant:** calm.

28 **presently prefer:** immediately present.

29 **address'd:** ready.

33 **puissant:** powerful.

36–43 **These couchings . . . fawning:** This kneeling and humble behavior might influence ordinary men and turn laws and decisions that have been firmly established into the whims of children. But don't be foolish enough to think that Caesar's emotions are so out of control that he will be swayed from the proper course with compliments, bowing, and fawning like a dog.

46 **spurn thee . . . cur:** kick you like a dog.

47–48 **Know . . . satisfied:** Caesar is not unjust, nor will he grant a pardon without good reason.

54 **freedom of repeal:** permission to be recalled from exile.

57 **enfranchisement:** restoration of his rights as a citizen.

Death of Julius Caesar. Guillaume Lethière (1760–1832). Oil on paper, 47.5 x 71.5 cm. Private collection.

Viewing the painting: What emotions do you see expressed here? Do you think the same emotions are expressed in this scene? Explain.

CAESAR. I could be well mov'd, if I were as you;
If I could pray to move, prayers would move me;
But I am constant as the northern star,
Of whose true-fix'd and resting quality
There is no fellow in the firmament.°
The skies are painted with unnumb'red sparks,
They are all fire and every one doth shine;
But there's but one in all doth hold his place.
So in the world: 'tis furnish'd well with men,
And men are flesh and blood, and apprehensive;°
Yet in the number I do know but one
That unassailable holds on his rank,
Unshak'd of motion; and that I am he,
Let me a little show it, even in this—
That I was constant° Cimber should be banish'd,
And constant do remain to keep him so.

CINNA. O Caesar—

CAESAR. Hence! Wilt thou lift up Olympus?°

DECIUS. Great Caesar—

CAESAR. Doth not Brutus bootless° kneel?

62 **no fellow in the firmament:** no equal in the heavens. (Because the North Star appears directly above the North Pole, it seems to be stationary; the other stars seem to change position as the earth rotates.)

67 **apprehensive:** capable of reason.

72 **constant:** determined.

74 **lift up Olympus:** try to do the impossible. (Olympus is a mountain in Greece; in classical mythology, it was the home of the gods.)

75 **bootless:** in vain.

CASCA. Speak hands for me!

[*They stab* CAESAR.]

CAESAR. *Et tu, Brute?*°—Then fall Caesar. [*Dies.*]

CINNA. Liberty! Freedom! Tyranny is dead!
Run hence, proclaim, cry it about the streets.

CASSIUS. Some to the common pulpits,° and cry out
"Liberty, freedom, and enfranchisement!"

BRUTUS. People, and senators, be not affrighted.
Fly not; stand still; ambition's debt is paid.°

CASCA. Go to the pulpit, Brutus.

DECIUS. And Cassius too.

BRUTUS. Where's Publius?

CINNA. Here, quite confounded with this mutiny.°

METELLUS. Stand fast together, lest some friend of Caesar's
Should chance—

BRUTUS. Talk not of standing. Publius, good cheer,
There is no harm intended to your person,
Nor to no Roman else. So tell them, Publius.

CASSIUS. And leave us, Publius, lest that the people,
Rushing on us should do your age some mischief.

BRUTUS. Do so; and let no man abide° this deed,
But we the doers.

[*All but the* CONSPIRATORS *exit. Enter* TREBONIUS.]

CASSIUS. Where is Antony?

TREBONIUS. Fled to his house amaz'd.°
Men, wives, and children stare, cry out and run,
As° it were doomsday.

BRUTUS. Fates,° we will know your pleasures.
That we shall die, we know, 'tis but the time,
And drawing days out, that men stand upon.°

CASCA. Why, he that cuts off twenty years of life
Cuts off so many years of fearing death.

BRUTUS. Grant that, and then is death a benefit.
So are we Caesar's friends, that have abridg'd
His time of fearing death. Stoop, Romans, stoop,
And let us bathe our hands in Caesar's blood
Up to the elbows, and besmear our swords.
Then walk we forth, even to the marketplace,

77 ***Et tu, Brute?:*** Latin for, "And you, Brutus?" (He is shocked that even Brutus would betray him.)

80 **pulpits:** platforms for public speaking.

83 **ambition's debt is paid:** Ambition received what was due to it.

86 **confounded with this mutiny:** confused by this uproar.

94 **abide:** pay the penalty for.

96 **amaz'd:** stunned.

98 **As:** as if.

98 **Fates:** in classical mythology, three goddesses who determined human destiny.

99–100 **'tis but . . . upon:** It is only the time of death and prolonging of life that men care about.

And waving our red weapons o'er our heads,
Let's all cry "Peace, freedom, and liberty!"

CASSIUS. Stoop then, and wash. How many ages hence
Shall this our lofty scene be acted over
In states unborn and accents yet unknown!

BRUTUS. How many times shall Caesar bleed in sport,°
That now on Pompey's basis° [lies] along
No worthier than the dust!

114 in sport: for entertainment. (These prophecies—of reenacting Caesar's assassination in countries not yet founded and in languages not yet known—are fulfilled by the performance of Shakespeare's play.)

115 Pompey's basis: the base of Pompey's statue.

CASSIUS. So oft as that shall be,
So often shall the knot of us be call'd
The men that gave their country liberty.

DECIUS. What, shall we forth?

CASSIUS. Ay, every man away.
Brutus shall lead, and we will grace his heels
With the most boldest and best hearts of Rome.

[*Enter a* SERVANT.]

BRUTUS. Soft, who comes here? A friend of Antony's.

SERVANT. Thus, Brutus, did my master bid me kneel;
Thus did Mark Antony bid me fall down;
And, being prostrate, thus he bade me say;
Brutus is noble, wise, valiant, and honest;°
Caesar was mighty, bold, royal, and loving.
Say, I love Brutus, and I honor him;
Say, I fear'd Caesar, honor'd him, and lov'd him.
If Brutus will vouchsafe° that Antony
May safely come to him, and be resolv'd°
How Caesar hath deserv'd to lie in death,
Mark Antony shall not love Caesar dead
So well as Brutus living; but will follow
The fortunes and affairs of noble Brutus
Thorough the hazards of this untrod state°
With all true faith. So says my master Antony.

126 honest: honorable.

130 vouchsafe: allow.

131 be resolv'd: receive a satisfactory explanation.

136 Thorough . . . state: through all the dangers of this new and uncertain state of affairs.

BRUTUS. Thy master is a wise and valiant Roman;
I never thought him worse.
Tell him, so please him come unto this place,
He shall be satisfied and, by my honor,
Depart untouch'd.

SERVANT. I'll fetch him presently.° [*Exit* SERVANT.]

BRUTUS. I know that we shall have him well to friend.°

142 presently: immediately.

143 well to friend: as a good friend.

CASSIUS. I wish we may; but yet have I a mind
That fears him much; and my misgiving still
Falls shrewdly to the purpose.°

[*Enter* ANTONY.]

BRUTUS. But here comes Antony. Welcome, Mark Antony.

ANTONY. O mighty Caesar! dost thou lie so low?
Are all thy conquests, glories, triumphs, spoils,
Shrunk to this little measure? Fare thee well.
I know not, gentlemen, what you intend,
Who else must be let blood,° who else is rank.°
If I myself, there is no hour so fit
As Caesar's death's hour, nor no instrument
Of half that worth as those your swords, made rich
With the most noble blood of all this world.
I do beseech ye, if you bear me hard,°
Now, whilst your purpled° hands do reek and smoke,
Fulfill your pleasure. Live a thousand years,
I shall not find myself so apt° to die;
No place will please me so, no mean of death,°
As here by Caesar, and by you cut off,
The choice and master spirits of this age.

BRUTUS. O Antony! beg not your death of us.
Though now we must appear bloody and cruel,
As by our hands and this our present act
You see we do, yet see you but our hands
And this the bleeding business they have done.
Our hearts you see not, they are pitiful;°
And pity to the general wrong of Rome—
As fire drives out fire, so pity pity—
Hath done this deed on Caesar.° For your part,
To you our swords have leaden° points, Mark Antony;
Our arms in strength of malice,° and our hearts
Of brothers' temper, do receive you in
With all kind love, good thoughts, and reverence.

CASSIUS. Your voice shall be as strong as any man's
In the disposing of new dignities.°

BRUTUS. Only be patient till we have appeas'd
The multitude, beside themselves with fear,
And then we will deliver you the cause°
Why I, that did love Caesar when I struck him,
Have thus proceeded.

145–146 **my misgiving . . . purpose:** My suspicions always turn out to be close to the truth.

152 **let blood:** killed. **rank:** swollen with disease. In Antony's metaphor, political corruption is like a disease that must be treated by drawing blood from the patient.

157 **bear me hard:** have a grudge against me.

158 **purpled:** blood-stained.

160 **apt:** ready.

161 **mean of death:** way of dying.

169 **pitiful:** full of pity.

170–172 **And pity . . . Caesar:** Brutus says that just as one fire can extinguish another, their pity for Rome overcame their pity for Caesar.

173 **leaden:** blunt.

174 **Our arms . . . malice:** our arms seemingly full of malice (because still blood-stained).

177–178 **Your voice . . . dignities:** You will have equal say in deciding who will hold political office.

181 **deliver you the cause:** explain.

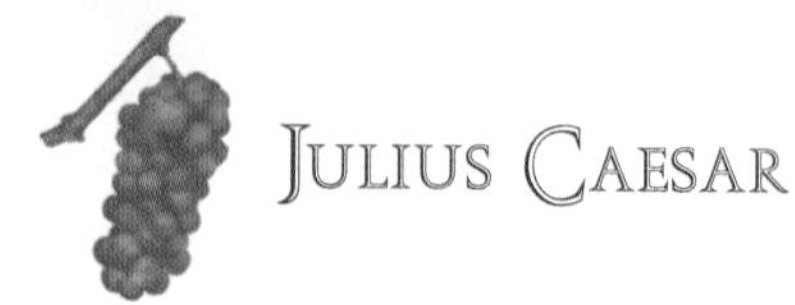

ANTONY. I doubt not of your wisdom.
Let each man render me his bloody hand.
First, Marcus Brutus, will I shake with you;
Next, Caius Cassius, do I take your hand;
Now, Decius Brutus, yours; now yours, Metellus;
Yours, Cinna; and, my valiant Casca, yours;
Though last, not least in love, yours, good Trebonius.
Gentlemen all—alas, what shall I say?
My credit° now stands on such slippery ground
That one of two bad ways you must conceit° me,
Either a coward or a flatterer.
That I did love thee, Caesar, O, 'tis true;
If then thy spirit look upon us now,
Shall it not grieve thee dearer than thy death,
To see thy Antony making his peace,
Shaking the bloody fingers of thy foes,
Most noble, in the presence of thy corse?°
Had I as many eyes as thou hast wounds,
Weeping as fast as they stream forth thy blood,
It would become me better than to close°
In terms of friendship with thine enemies.
Pardon me, Julius! Here wast thou bay'd,° brave hart,°
Here didst thou fall, and here thy hunters stand,
Sign'd in thy spoil,° and crimson'd in thy lethe.°
O world! thou wast the forest to this hart,
And this indeed, O world, the heart of thee.
How like a deer, strooken by many princes,
Dost thou here lie!

CASSIUS. Mark Antony—

ANTONY. Pardon me, Caius Cassius!
The enemies of Caesar shall say this:
Then, in a friend, it is cold modesty.°

CASSIUS. I blame you not for praising Caesar so,
But what compact mean you to have with us?
Will you be prick'd° in number of our friends,
Or shall we on,° and not depend on you?

ANTONY. Therefore I took your hands, but was indeed
Sway'd from the point by looking down on Caesar.
Friends am I with you all, and love you all,
Upon this hope, that you shall give me reasons
Why, and wherein,° Caesar was dangerous.

191 **credit:** reputation (because he was Caesar's friend).

192 **conceit:** judge, consider.

199 **corse:** corpse.

202 **close:** come to an agreement.

204 **bay'd:** cornered like a hunted animal. **hart:** male deer. Antony plays on the words *hart* and *heart* later in this speech.

206 **Sign'd in thy spoil:** marked with your slaughter. **lethe:** bloodstream. (In classical mythology, Lethe was a river in Hades, the underworld.)

213 **modesty:** restraint.

216 **prick'd:** marked down; counted.

217 **on:** proceed.

222 **wherein:** in what way.

Bedroom from the villa of P. Fannius Sinistor (detail of west wall). 1st century B.C., Roman. Fresco on lime plaster, height: (average) 8 ft. The Metropolitan Museum of Art, New York. Rogers Fund, 1903. 03.14.13.

Viewing the art: Do the details in this fresco reinforce or alter the images you have developed of Brutus's and Caesar's homes? Explain.

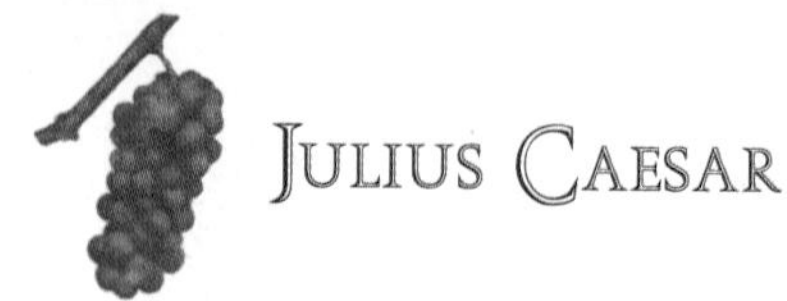

BRUTUS. Or else were this a savage spectacle.
Our reasons are so full of good regard°
That were you, Antony, the son of Caesar,
You should be satisfied.

ANTONY. That's all I seek;
And am moreover suitor° that I may
Produce° his body to the marketplace,
And in the pulpit, as becomes a friend,
Speak in the order° of his funeral.

BRUTUS. You shall, Mark Antony.

CASSIUS. Brutus, a word with you.
[*Aside to* BRUTUS.] You know not what you do. Do not consent
That Antony speak in his funeral.
Know you how much the people may be mov'd
By that which he will utter?

BRUTUS. By your pardon—
I will myself into the pulpit first,
And show the reason of our Caesar's death.
What Antony shall speak, I will protest°
He speaks by leave and by permission;
And that we are contented Caesar shall
Have all true rites and lawful ceremonies.
It shall advantage° more than do us wrong.

CASSIUS. I know not what may fall,° I like it not.

BRUTUS. Mark Antony, here, take you Caesar's body.
You shall not in your funeral speech blame us,
But speak all good you can devise of Caesar,
And say you do't by our permission;
Else shall you not have any hand at all
About his funeral. And you shall speak
In the same pulpit whereto I am going,
After my speech is ended.

ANTONY. Be it so;
I do desire no more.

BRUTUS. Prepare the body then, and follow us.

[*They exit.* ANTONY *remains.*]

ANTONY. O pardon me, thou bleeding piece of earth,
That I am meek and gentle with these butchers!
Thou art the ruins of the noblest man

224 **good regard:** sound considerations.

227 **am moreover suitor:** furthermore I ask.

228 **Produce:** bring forth.

230 **order:** ceremony.

238 **protest:** declare.

242 **advantage:** benefit.

243 **fall:** happen.

That ever lived in the tide of times.°
Woe to the hand that shed this costly blood!
Over thy wounds now do I prophesy
(Which like dumb mouths do ope their ruby lips
To beg the voice and utterance of my tongue)
A curse shall light° upon the limbs of men;
Domestic fury and fierce civil strife
Shall cumber° all the parts of Italy;
Blood and destruction shall be so in use,°
And dreadful objects so familiar,
That mothers shall but smile when they behold
Their infants quartered° with the hands of war;
All pity chok'd with custom of fell deeds;°
And Caesar's spirit, ranging° for revenge,
With Ate° by his side come hot from hell,
Shall in these confines with a monarch's voice
Cry "Havoc!"° and let slip the dogs of war,
That this foul deed shall smell above the earth
With carrion° men, groaning for burial.

[*Enter Octavius's* SERVANT.]

You serve Octavius Caesar, do you not?

SERVANT. I do, Mark Antony.

ANTONY. Caesar did write for him to come to Rome.

SERVANT. He did receive his letters and is coming,
And bid me say to you by word of mouth—
[*Seeing the body.*] O Caesar!—

ANTONY. Thy heart is big;° get thee apart and weep.
Passion, I see, is catching, [for] mine eyes,
Seeing those beads of sorrow stand in thine,
Began to water. Is thy master coming?

SERVANT. He lies tonight within seven leagues° of Rome.

ANTONY. Post° back with speed, and tell him what hath chanc'd.
Here is a mourning Rome, a dangerous Rome,
No Rome of safety for Octavius yet;
Hie hence,° and tell him so. Yet stay awhile,
Thou shalt not back till I have borne this corse
Into the marketplace. There shall I try,°
In my oration, how the people take
The cruel issue° of these bloody men,
According to the which thou shalt discourse

257 **the tide of times:** all of history.

262 **light:** fall.

264 **cumber:** burden; harass.

265 **in use:** common.

268 **quartered:** cut to pieces.

269 **custom of fell deeds:** familiarity with cruel deeds.

270 **ranging:** roving (like an animal in search of prey).

271 **Ate:** goddess of vengeance and strife.

273 **Havoc:** a battle cry to kill without mercy. (Only a king could give this order.)

275 **carrion:** dead and rotting.

282 **big:** swollen with grief.

286 **seven leagues:** twenty-one miles.

287 **Post:** Ride back quickly.

290 **Hie hence:** Go quickly from here.

292 **try:** test.

294 **cruel issue:** outcome of cruelty.

To young Octavius of the state of things.
Lend me your hand.

[*They exit (with* CAESAR*'s body).*]

SCENE 2. The Roman Forum, the city's great public square. A few days later.

[*Enter* BRUTUS *and* CASSIUS *with the* PLEBEIANS.]

PLEBEIANS. We will be satisfied!° Let us be satisfied!

BRUTUS. Then follow me, and give me audience, friends.
Cassius, go you into the other street,
And part the numbers.°
Those that will hear me speak, let 'em stay here;
Those that will follow Cassius, go with him;
And public reasons shall be rendered°
Of Caesar's death.

FIRST PLEBEIAN. I will hear Brutus speak.

SECOND PLEBEIAN. I will hear Cassius, and compare their reasons,
When severally° we hear them rendered.

[*Exit* CASSIUS *with some of the* PLEBEIANS. BRUTUS *goes into the pulpit.*]

THIRD PLEBEIAN. The noble Brutus is ascended; silence!

BRUTUS. Be patient till the last.°
Romans, countrymen, and lovers,° hear me for my cause, and be silent, that you may hear. Believe me for mine honor, and have respect to mine honor,° that you may believe. Censure° me in your wisdom, and awake your senses,° that you may the better judge. If there be any in this assembly, any dear friend of Caesar's, to him I say, that Brutus' love to Caesar was no less than his. If then that friend demand why Brutus rose against Caesar, this is my answer; Not that I lov'd Caesar less, but that I lov'd Rome more. Had you rather Caesar were living, and die all slaves, than that Caesar were dead, to live all free men? As Caesar lov'd me, I weep for him; as he was fortunate, I rejoice at it; as he was valiant, I honor him; but, as he was ambitious, I slew him. There is tears for his love; joy for his fortune; honor for his valor; and death for his ambition. Who is here so base that would be a bondman?° If any, speak, for him have I offended. Who is here so rude,° that would not be a Roman? If any, speak, for him have I offended. Who

1 **satisfied:** The common people **(plebeians)** demand a full explanation of the assassination.

4 **part the numbers:** divide the crowd.

7 **rendered:** presented.

10 **severally:** separately.

12 **last:** end of the speech.

13 **lovers:** dear friends.

15 **have respect . . . honor:** remember that I am honorable.

16 **Censure:** judge.

17 **senses:** reason.

28 **bondman:** slave.

29 **rude:** uncivilized.

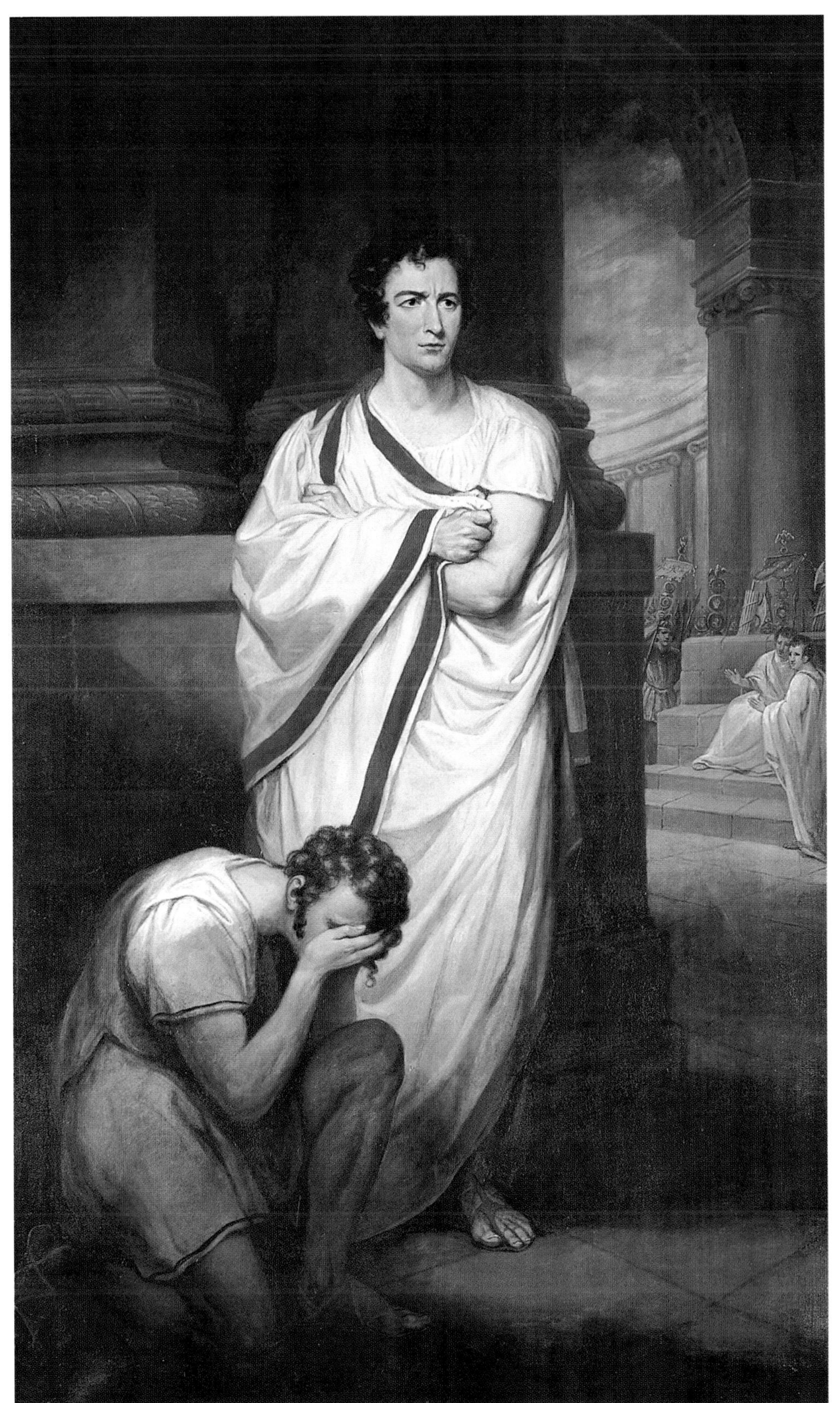

Edmund Kean as Brutus, 1819. James Northcote. Oil on canvas, 236.5 x 145 cm.

Viewing the painting: What, do you think, is Brutus thinking about? Why do you think so?

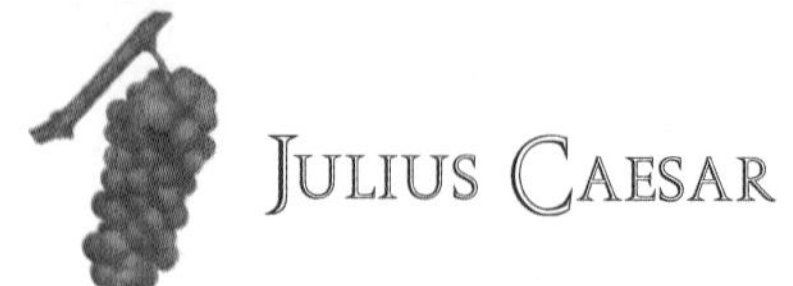

is here so vile that will not love his country? If any, speak, for him have I offended. I pause for a reply.

ALL. None, Brutus, none.

BRUTUS. Then none have I offended. I have done no more to Caesar than you shall do to Brutus. The question of his death is enroll'd in the Capitol;° his glory not extenuated,° wherein he was worthy; nor his offenses enforc'd,° for which he suffer'd death.

[*Enter* MARK ANTONY *(and others) with* CAESAR'S *body.*]

Here comes his body, mourn'd by Mark Antony, who, though he had no hand in his death, shall receive the benefit of his dying, a place in the commonwealth,° as which of you shall not? With this I depart, that, as I slew my best lover for the good of Rome, I have the same dagger for myself, when it shall please my country to need my death.

ALL. Live, Brutus, live, live!

FIRST PLEBEIAN. Bring him with triumph home unto his house.

SECOND PLEBEIAN. Give him a statue with his ancestors.

THIRD PLEBEIAN. Let him be Caesar.

FOURTH PLEBEIAN. Caesar's better parts°
Shall be crown'd in Brutus.

FIRST PLEBEIAN. We'll bring him to his house
With shouts and clamors.

BRUTUS. My countrymen—

SECOND PLEBEIAN. Peace, silence! Brutus speaks.

FIRST PLEBEIAN. Peace, ho!

BRUTUS. Good countrymen, let me depart alone,
And, for my sake, stay here with Antony.
Do grace to Caesar's corpse, and grace his speech
Tending to Caesar's glories,° which Mark Antony
(By our permission) is allow'd to make.
I do entreat you, not a man depart,
Save I alone, till Antony have spoke.

FIRST PLEBEIAN. Stay, ho, and let us hear Mark Antony.

THIRD PLEBEIAN. Let him go up into the public chair;°
We'll hear him. Noble Antony, go up.

ANTONY. For Brutus' sake, I am beholding° to you.

[*Goes into the pulpit.*]

35–36 The question . . . Capitol: The reasons for his death are recorded in the public archives of the Capitol.

37 extenuated: diminished.

38 enforc'd: exaggerated.

41 a place in the commonwealth: citizenship in a free republic.

48 parts: qualities.

55–56 Do grace . . . glories: Pay respect to Caesar's body and listen respectfully to Antony's speech dealing with Caesar's glories.

61 public chair: pulpit.

63 beholding: indebted.

FOURTH PLEBEIAN. What does he say of Brutus?

THIRD PLEBEIAN. He says, for Brutus' sake,
He finds himself beholding to us all.

FOURTH PLEBEIAN. 'Twere best he speak no harm of Brutus here!

FIRST PLEBEIAN. This Caesar was a tyrant.

THIRD PLEBEIAN. Nay, that's certain.
We are blest that Rome is rid of him.

SECOND PLEBEIAN. Peace, let us hear what Antony can say.

ANTONY. You gentle Romans—

[*The noise continues.*]

ALL. Peace, ho, let us hear him.

ANTONY. Friends, Romans, countrymen, lend me your ears!
I come to bury Caesar, not to praise him.
The evil that men do lives after them,
The good is oft interred° with their bones;
So let it be with Caesar. The noble Brutus
Hath told you Caesar was ambitious;
If it were so, it was a grievous fault,
And grievously hath Caesar answer'd° it.
Here, under leave° of Brutus and the rest
(For Brutus is an honorable man,
So are they all, all honorable men),
Come I to speak in Caesar's funeral.
He was my friend, faithful and just to me;
But Brutus says he was ambitious,
And Brutus is an honorable man.
He hath brought many captives home to Rome,
Whose ransoms did the general coffers° fill;
Did this in Caesar seem ambitious?
When that the poor have cried, Caesar hath wept;
Ambition should be made of sterner stuff:
Yet Brutus says he was ambitious;
And Brutus is an honorable man.
You all did see that on the Lupercal°
I thrice presented him a kingly crown,
Which he did thrice refuse.° Was this ambition?
Yet Brutus says he was ambitious;
And sure he is an honorable man.
I speak not to disprove what Brutus spoke,
But here I am to speak what I do know.

74 **interred:** buried.

78 **answer'd:** paid the penalty for.

79 **leave:** permission.

87 **general coffers:** public treasury.

93 **Lupercal:** See act 1, scene 1, line 67.

95 **Which he . . . refuse:** the incident described by Casca in act 1, scene 2, lines 234–242.

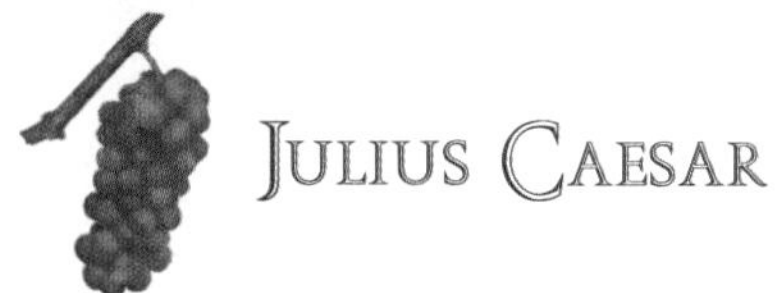

You all did love him once, not without cause;
What cause withholds you then to mourn for him?
O judgment, thou art fled to brutish beasts,
And men have lost their reason. Bear with me,
My heart is in the coffin there with Caesar,
And I must pause till it come back to me.

FIRST PLEBEIAN. Methinks there is much reason in his sayings.

SECOND PLEBEIAN. If thou consider rightly of the matter,
Caesar has had great wrong.

THIRD PLEBEIAN. Has he, masters?
I fear there will a worse come in his place.

FOURTH PLEBEIAN. Mark'd ye° his words? He would not take the crown,
Therefore, 'tis certain he was not ambitious.

110 **Mark'd ye:** Did you listen to?

FIRST PLEBEIAN. If it be found so, some will dear abide it.°

112 **dear abide it:** pay dearly for it.

SECOND PLEBEIAN. Poor soul, his eyes are red as fire with weeping.

THIRD PLEBEIAN. There's not a nobler man in Rome than Antony.

FOURTH PLEBEIAN. Now mark him, he begins again to speak.

ANTONY. But yesterday the word of Caesar might
Have stood against the world; now lies he there,
And none so poor to do him reverence.°
O masters! if I were dispos'd to stir
Your hearts and minds to mutiny and rage,
I should do Brutus wrong and Cassius wrong,
Who (you all know) are honorable men.
I will not do them wrong; I rather choose
To wrong the dead, to wrong myself and you,
Than I will wrong such honorable men.
But here's a parchment with the seal of Caesar;
I found it in his closet, 'tis his will.
Let but the commons° hear this testament—
Which, pardon me, I do not mean to read—
And they would go and kiss dead Caesar's wounds,
And dip their napkins° in his sacred blood;
Yea, beg a hair of him for memory,
And dying, mention it within their wills,
Bequeathing it as a rich legacy
Unto their issue.°

118 **none . . . reverence:** No one is humble enough to honor him.

128 **commons:** common people.

131 **napkins:** handkerchiefs. (Antony refers to the custom of dipping cloths in the blood of martyrs.)

135 **issue:** children.

FOURTH PLEBEIAN. We'll hear the will; read it, Mark Antony.

ALL. The will, the will! we will hear Caesar's will!

ANTONY. Have patience, gentle friends, I must not read it.
It is not meet° you know how Caesar lov'd you:
You are not wood, you are not stones, but men;
And being men, hearing the will of Caesar,
It will inflame you, it will make you mad.
'Tis good you know not that you are his heirs,
For if you should, O, what would come of it?

139 **meet:** proper.

FOURTH PLEBEIAN. Read the will, we'll hear it, Antony.
You shall read us the will, Caesar's will.

ANTONY. Will you be patient? Will you stay awhile?
I have o'ershot myself° to tell you of it.
I fear I wrong the honorable men
Whose daggers have stabb'd Caesar; I do fear it.

148 **o'ershot myself:** gone further than I intended.

FOURTH PLEBEIAN. They were traitors; honorable men!

ALL. The will! the testament!

SECOND PLEBEIAN. They were villains, murderers. The will, read the will!

ANTONY. You will compel me then to read the will?
Then make a ring about the corpse of Caesar,
And let me show you him that made the will.
Shall I descend? And will you give me leave?

ALL. Come down.

SECOND PLEBEIAN. Descend.

THIRD PLEBEIAN. You shall have leave.

[*ANTONY comes down from the pulpit.*]

The Artemision with Artemis Ephesia. A.D. 117, Roman. Silver, diameter: 2.7 cm. Kunsthistorisches Museum, Muenzkabinett, Vienna, Austria.

FOURTH PLEBEIAN. A ring, stand round.

FIRST PLEBEIAN. Stand from the hearse, stand from the body.

SECOND PLEBEIAN. Room for Antony, most noble Antony.

ANTONY. Nay, press not so upon me; stand far° off.

164 **far:** farther.

ALL. Stand back; room, bear back.

ANTONY. If you have tears, prepare to shed them now.
You all do know this mantle.° I remember
The first time ever Caesar put it on;
'Twas on a summer's evening, in his tent,
That day he overcame the Nervii.°
Look, in this place ran Cassius' dagger through;

167 **mantle:** cloak, toga.

170 **Nervii:** a fierce Gallic tribe defeated by Caesar in 57 B.C.

Mark Antony's funeral oration over the corpse of Caesar.

Viewing the art: How does the scene depicted here differ from events in the play? How is it the same?

See what a rent° the envious Casca made;
Through this the well-beloved Brutus stabb'd,
And as he pluck'd his cursed steel away,
Mark how the blood of Caesar followed it,
As rushing out of doors, to be resolv'd
If Brutus so unkindly knock'd or no;°
For Brutus, as you know, was Caesar's angel.°
Judge, O you gods, how dearly Caesar lov'd him!
This was the most unkindest cut of all;
For when the noble Caesar saw him stab,
Ingratitude, more strong than traitors' arms,
Quite vanquish'd him. Then burst his mighty heart,
And, in his mantle muffling up his face,
Even at the base of Pompey's statue
(Which all the while ran blood) great Caesar fell.
O, what a fall was there, my countrymen!
Then I, and you, and all of us fell down,
Whilst bloody treason flourish'd° over us.
O now you weep, and I perceive you feel
The dint° of pity. These are gracious drops.
Kind souls, what weep you when you but behold
Our Caesar's vesture wounded? Look you here, [*Lifting* CAESAR*'s mantle.*]
Here is himself, marr'd as you see with traitors.°

FIRST PLEBEIAN. O piteous spectacle!

SECOND PLEBEIAN. O noble Caesar!

THIRD PLEBEIAN. O woeful day!

FOURTH PLEBEIAN. O traitors, villains!

FIRST PLEBEIAN. O most bloody sight!

SECOND PLEBEIAN. We will be reveng'd.

ALL. Revenge! About! Seek! Burn! Fire! Kill! Slay!
Let not a traitor live!

ANTONY. Stay, countrymen.

FIRST PLEBEIAN. Peace there, hear the noble Antony.

SECOND PLEBEIAN. We'll hear him, we'll follow him, we'll die with him.

ANTONY. Good friends, sweet friends, let me not stir you up
To such a sudden flood of mutiny.
They that have done this deed are honorable.
What private griefs° they have, alas, I know not,

172 **rent:** rip.

176–177 **As rushing . . . no:** as if rushing outside to learn for certain whether or not Brutus so cruelly and unnaturally "knocked."

178 **angel:** favorite.

189 **flourish'd:** swaggered.

191 **dint:** force; blow.

192–194 **Kind souls . . . traitors:** In a dramatic gesture, Antony uncovers Caesar's mutilated body after remarking how much the commoners weep when they gaze merely upon Caesar's mutilated clothing.

209 **private griefs:** personal grievances. Antony suggests that the conspirators killed Caesar not for the public reasons Brutus has declared but rather for personal, and therefore less worthy, motives.

That made them do it. They are wise and honorable,
And will, no doubt, with reasons answer you.
I come not, friends, to steal away your hearts.
I am no orator, as Brutus is;
But (as you know me all) a plain blunt man
That love my friend, and that they know full well
That gave me public leave to speak of him.
For I have neither wit, nor words, nor worth,
Action, nor utterance, nor the power of speech
To stir men's blood;° I only speak right on.
I tell you that which you yourselves do know,
Show you sweet Caesar's wounds, poor, poor, dumb mouths,
And bid them speak for me. But were I Brutus,
And Brutus Antony, there were an Antony
Would ruffle up° your spirits, and put a tongue
In every wound of Caesar, that should move
The stones of Rome to rise and mutiny.

ALL. We'll mutiny.

FIRST PLEBEIAN. We'll burn the house of Brutus.

THIRD PLEBEIAN. Away then, come, seek the conspirators.

ANTONY. Yet hear me, countrymen, yet hear me speak.

ALL. Peace, ho, hear Antony, most noble Antony!

ANTONY. Why, friends, you go to do you know not what.
Wherein hath Caesar thus deserv'd your loves?
Alas, you know not! I must tell you then;
You have forgot the will I told you of.

ALL. Most true. The will! Let's stay and hear the will.

ANTONY. Here is the will, and under Caesar's seal:
To every Roman citizen he gives,
To every several° man, seventy-five drachmas.°

SECOND PLEBEIAN. Most noble Caesar! we'll revenge his death!

THIRD PLEBEIAN. O royal° Caesar!

ANTONY. Hear me with patience.

ALL. Peace, ho!

ANTONY. Moreover, he hath left you all his walks,
His private arbors and new-planted orchards,°
On this side Tiber; he hath left them you,
And to your heirs forever—common pleasures,°
To walk abroad and recreate yourselves.
Here was a Caesar! when comes such another?

217–219 **For I have . . . blood:** Antony claims that he doesn't have the cleverness **(wit)**, fluency **(words)**, high personal standing or reputation **(worth)**, gestures **(action)**, and manner of speaking **(utterance)** of a skilled orator.

224 **ruffle up:** enrage.

238 **several:** individual. **drachmas:** silver coins.

240 **royal:** most generous.

244 **orchards:** gardens.

246 **common pleasures:** public recreation areas.

FIRST PLEBEIAN. Never, never! Come, away, away!
We'll burn his body in the holy place,°
And with the brands° fire the traitors' houses.
Take up the body.

SECOND PLEBEIAN. Go fetch fire.

THIRD PLEBEIAN. Pluck down benches.

FOURTH PLEBEIAN. Pluck down forms,° windows,° anything.

[*Exit* PLEBEIANS *with the body.*]

ANTONY. Now let it work. Mischief, thou art afoot,
Take thou what course thou wilt!

[*Enter* SERVANT.]

How now, fellow?

SERVANT. Sir, Octavius is already come to Rome.

ANTONY. Where is he?

SERVANT. He and Lepidus° are at Caesar's house.

ANTONY. And thither will I straight to visit him;°
He comes upon a wish.° Fortune is merry,
And in this mood will give us anything.

SERVANT. I heard him say, Brutus and Cassius
Are rid° like madmen through the gates of Rome.

ANTONY. Belike° they had some notice of the people,
How I had mov'd them. Bring me to Octavius.

[*They exit.*]

SCENE 3. Shortly afterward. A street near the Forum.

[*Enter* CINNA *the poet, and after him the* PLEBEIANS.]

CINNA.° I dreamt tonight° that I did feast with Caesar,
And things unluckily charge my fantasy.°
I have no will to wander forth of doors,
Yet something leads me forth.

FIRST PLEBEIAN. What is your name?

SECOND PLEBEIAN. Whither are you going?

THIRD PLEBEIAN. Where do you dwell?

FOURTH PLEBEIAN. Are you a married man or a bachelor?

SECOND PLEBEIAN. Answer every man directly.

FIRST PLEBEIAN. Ay, and briefly.

FOURTH PLEBEIAN. Ay, and wisely.

250 **the holy place:** the site of the most sacred Roman temples.

251 **brands:** pieces of burning wood.

255 **forms:** benches. **windows:** shutters.

260 **Lepidus:** one of Caesar's generals.

261 **thither will . . . him:** I will go there immediately to visit him.

262 **upon a wish:** just as I had wished.

265 **Are rid:** have ridden.

266 **Belike:** probably.

1 **Cinna:** a well-known poet, not the same Cinna who helped kill Caesar. **tonight:** last night.

2 **things . . . fantasy:** my imagination is burdened with bad omens.

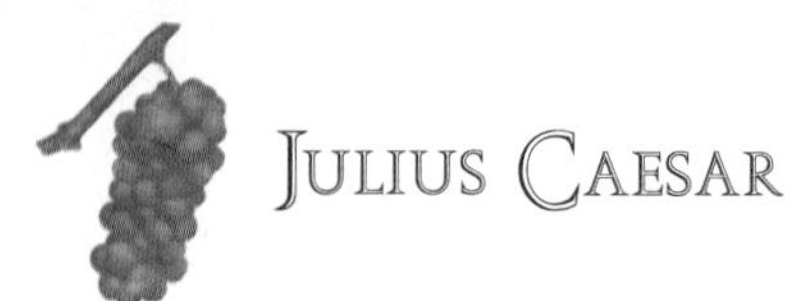

THIRD PLEBEIAN. Ay, and truly, you were best.°

CINNA. What is my name? Whither am I going? Where do I dwell? Am I a married man or a bachelor? Then, to answer every man directly and briefly, wisely and truly: wisely I say, I am a bachelor.

SECOND PLEBEIAN. That's as much as to say, they are fools that marry. You'll bear me a bang° for that, I fear. Proceed directly.

CINNA. Directly, I am going to Caesar's funeral.

FIRST PLEBEIAN. As a friend or an enemy?

CINNA. As a friend.

SECOND PLEBEIAN. That matter is answer'd directly.

FOURTH PLEBEIAN. For your dwelling—briefly.

CINNA. Briefly, I dwell by the Capitol.

THIRD PLEBEIAN. Your name, sir, truly.

CINNA. Truly, my name is Cinna.

FIRST PLEBEIAN. Tear him to pieces, he's a conspirator.

CINNA. I am Cinna the poet, I am Cinna the poet.

FOURTH PLEBEIAN. Tear him for his bad verses, tear him for his bad verses.

CINNA. I am not Cinna the conspirator.

FOURTH PLEBEIAN. It is no matter, his name's Cinna. Pluck but his name out of his heart, and turn him going.

THIRD PLEBEIAN. Tear him, tear him!
Come, brands, ho, firebrands! To Brutus', to Cassius'; burn all! Some to Decius' house, and some to Casca's; some to Ligarius'. Away, go!

[*All the* PLEBEIANS *exit (dragging off* CINNA*).*]

12 **you were best:** you had better.

18 **bear me a bang:** get a blow from me.

Responding to Literature

Personal Response

What was your reaction to Caesar's murder?

Analyzing Act 3

Recall and Intrepret

1. What action does Caesar refuse to take just before he is murdered? How would you describe his behavior in refusing?
2. What most surprises Caesar when he is attacked? What might Caesar have been thinking as he died?
3. How does Antony respond to the conspirators immediately after Caesar's murder? In your opinion, why does he behave this way?
4. Summarize the crowd's reactions to Brutus's and Antony's funeral speeches. What can you infer about the crowd from their reactions?
5. What was the content of Caesar's will? Why might Antony have made a point of reading the will to the people?

Evaluate and Connect

6. How did Caesar's behavior outside the Capitol just before he died affect your reaction to his death?
7. Did Antony's **soliloquy** (see page R12) after his discussion with the conspirators surprise you? Explain.
8. What is your opinion of Brutus? Has it changed since act 1? Explain.
9. Why might Shakespeare have chosen to include the scene of the attack on Cinna the poet? Do you know of a similar incident of mob violence? If so, how do the incidents compare?
10. If you had been an eyewitness to Caesar's murder and the following speeches, whose funeral speech would have moved you more, Brutus's or Antony's? Why?

Literary ELEMENTS

Prose

Prose is literature that is written in sentence and paragraph form. The dialogue in Shakespeare's plays is a mixture of verse and prose. Clowns, servants, and other lower-class characters usually speak in prose. Well-born characters often speak in verse, especially when making speeches.

However, Shakespeare's use of prose varies from play to play and even within plays. For example, Antony's address to the crowd at Caesar's funeral is in blank verse. Brutus's speech is in prose.

1. Why, do you think, did Shakespeare have his lower-class characters speak in prose rather than verse?
2. Why might Shakespeare have chosen to write Brutus's funeral oration in prose rather than verse?

- See **Literary Terms Handbook,** p. R10.

Extending Your Response

Literature Groups

The Art of Rhetoric With your group, analyze the techniques that Antony uses in his funeral speech. Does he portray Caesar's murder fairly, or does he distort the event? How does he use repetition, irony, and other rhetorical or persuasive techniques to make his point? What else does he do to win over his audience? Present to the class a list of techniques that Antony uses.

Creative Writing

In Cassius's Words Write a speech that Cassius might have delivered while Brutus gave his funeral speech. First consider Cassius's character and what he said earlier in the play about Caesar. Would Cassius make an emotional or a low-key speech? How might he justify his action?

Save your work for your portfolio.

ACT 4

SCENE 1. Antony's house in Rome. A year and a half after Caesar's death.

[*Enter* ANTONY, OCTAVIUS, *and* LEPIDUS.]

ANTONY. These many then shall die, their names are prick'd.°

OCTAVIUS. Your brother too must die, consent you, Lepidus?°

LEPIDUS. I do consent—

OCTAVIUS. Prick him down, Antony.

LEPIDUS. Upon condition Publius shall not live,
Who is your sister's son, Mark Antony.

1 **prick'd:** marked down on a list.

2 **Your brother . . . Lepidus:** Lepidus's brother was a prominent politician who sided with the conspirators after Caesar's assassination.

Interior of a Roman House/Home of Cornelius Rufus in Pompeii (Reconstruction). Artist unknown.

Viewing the art: What impressions of Roman life do you get from this scene? How do those impressions relate to the lives of the characters in the play?

ANTONY. He shall not live; look, with a spot I damn him.
But, Lepidus, go you to Caesar's house;
Fetch the will hither, and we shall determine
How to cut off some charge in legacies.°

LEPIDUS. What? shall I find you here?

OCTAVIUS. Or here or at the Capitol.

[*Exit* LEPIDUS.]

ANTONY. This is a slight unmeritable man,
Meet° to be sent on errands; is it fit,
The threefold world° divided, he should stand
One of the three to share it?

OCTAVIUS. So you thought him,
And took his voice who should be prick'd to die
In our black sentence and proscription.°

ANTONY. Octavius, I have seen more days than you,
And though we lay these honors on this man
To ease ourselves of divers sland'rous loads,°
He shall but bear them as the ass bears gold,
To groan and sweat under the business,
Either led or driven, as we point the way;
And having brought our treasure where we will,
Then take we down his load, and turn him off
(Like to the empty ass) to shake his ears
And graze in commons.°

OCTAVIUS. You may do your will;
But he's a tried and valiant soldier.

ANTONY. So is my horse, Octavius, and for that
I do appoint him store of provender.°
It is a creature that I teach to fight,
To wind,° to stop, to run directly on,
His corporal° motion govern'd by my spirit;
And in some taste° is Lepidus but so.
He must be taught, and train'd, and bid go forth;
A barren-spirited fellow; one that feeds
On objects, arts, and imitations,
Which, out of use and stal'd by other men,
Begin his fashion.° Do not talk of him
But as a property.° And now, Octavius,
Listen great things. Brutus and Cassius
Are levying powers; we must straight make head;
Therefore let our alliance be combin'd,

9 **cut off . . . legacies:** reduce the amount of money left to the people in Caesar's will.

13 **Meet:** fit.

14 **threefold world:** three parts of the Roman world. (In the autumn of 43 B.C., Antony, Octavius Caesar, and Lepidus formed a triumvirate—a committee of three—to rule Rome. They divided up among themselves territory that the Romans had conquered.)

15–17 **So you . . . proscription:** Octavius wonders why Antony asked Lepidus to name people who should be sentenced to death if he had so poor an opinion of him.

20 **divers sland'rous loads:** the burden of accusations for our various actions.

24–27 **And having . . . commons:** When Lepidus has brought our treasure where we want it, we will send him off to shake his ears and graze on public land like an unburdened donkey.

30 **appoint . . . provender:** allot him a supply of food.

32 **wind:** turn.

33 **corporal:** bodily.

34 **taste:** degree.

36–39 **A barren-spirited . . . fashion:** a man with no originality, one who indulges in curiosities, tricks, and fashions, which he takes up only after they have become outmoded.

40 **a property:** a mere tool.

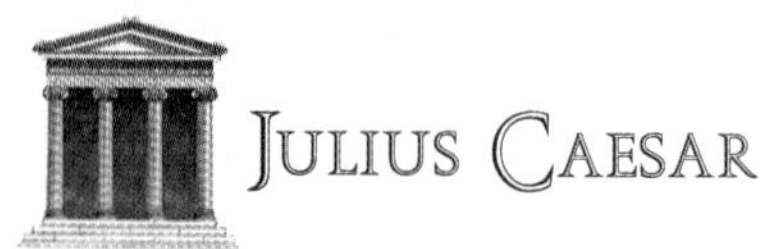

Our best friends made, our means stretch'd;
And let us presently go sit in council,
How covert matters may be best disclos'd,
And open perils surest answered.°

OCTAVIUS. Let us do so; for we are at the stake,
And bay'd about with many enemies,°
And some that smile have in their hearts, I fear,
Millions of mischiefs. [*They exit.*]

41–47 Listen great . . . answered: Listen to important matters. Brutus and Cassius are raising armies; we must press forward immediately. Therefore let us become united, choose our allies, and make the most of our resources. And let us decide at once how hidden threats may be uncovered and open dangers most safely confronted.

48–49 we are . . . enemies: Octavius's metaphor refers to bear-baiting, a popular entertainment in which bears were tied to stakes and surrounded by vicious dogs.

SCENE 2. A military camp near Sardis in Asia Minor. Several months later.

[*Drum. Enter* BRUTUS, LUCILIUS, LUCIUS, *and the army.* TITINIUS *and* PINDARUS *meet them.*]

BRUTUS. Stand ho!

LUCILIUS. Give the word ho! and stand.°

BRUTUS. What now, Lucilius, is Cassius near?

LUCILIUS. He is at hand, and Pindarus is come
To do you salutation from his master.

2 Give the . . . stand: Lucilius, one of Brutus's officers, tells his subordinates to pass on Brutus's command for the army to halt **(stand).** He has returned from Cassius's camp with Titinius, one of Cassius's officers, and Pindarus, Cassius's servant.

BRUTUS. He greets me well. Your master, Pindarus,
In his own change, or by ill officers,
Hath given me some worthy cause to wish
Things done undone,° but if he be at hand,
I shall be satisfied.°

PINDARUS. I do not doubt
But that my noble master will appear
Such as he is, full of regard and honor.

BRUTUS. He is not doubted. A word, Lucilius.
How he receiv'd you; let me be resolv'd.°

6–9 Your master . . . undone: Either a change in Cassius or the misconduct of his officers has given me good reason to wish I could undo what I have done. (Brutus is having some misgivings about having participated in the conspiracy because of incidents that have occurred in Cassius's army.)

10 be satisfied: receive an explanation.

14 resolv'd: informed.

LUCILIUS. With courtesy and with respect enough,
But not with such familiar instances,°
Nor with such free and friendly conference,°
As he hath us'd of old.

16 familiar instances: signs of friendship.

17 conference: conversation.

BRUTUS. Thou hast describ'd
A hot friend cooling. Ever note, Lucilius,
When love begins to sicken and decay
It useth an enforced ceremony.°
There are no tricks in plain and simple faith;
But hollow men, like horses hot at hand,
Make gallant show and promise of their mettle;

[*Low march within.*]

21 enforced ceremony: strained formality.

But when they should endure the bloody spur,
They fall their crests, and like deceitful jades
Sink in the trial.° Comes his army on?

LUCILIUS. They mean this night in Sardis to be quarter'd.
The greater part, the horse in general,°
Are come with Cassius.

[*Enter* CASSIUS *and his* POWERS.]

BRUTUS. Hark! He is arriv'd.
March gently on to meet him.

CASSIUS. Stand ho!

BRUTUS. Stand ho! Speak the word along.

FIRST SOLDIER. Stand!

SECOND SOLDIER. Stand!

THIRD SOLDIER. Stand!

CASSIUS. Most noble brother, you have done me wrong.

BRUTUS. Judge me, you gods! wrong I mine enemies?
And if not so, how should I wrong a brother.

CASSIUS. Brutus, this sober form° of yours hides wrongs,
And when you do them—

BRUTUS. Cassius, be content.
Speak your griefs softly; I do know you well.
Before the eyes of both our armies here
(Which should perceive nothing but love from us)
Let us not wrangle. Bid them move away;
Then in my tent, Cassius, enlarge your griefs,
And I will give you audience.°

CASSIUS. Pindarus,
Bid our commanders lead their charges off
A little from this ground.

BRUTUS. Lucius, do you the like, and let no man
Come to our tent till we have done our conference.
Let Lucilius and Titinius guard our door.

[*They exit.* BRUTUS *and* CASSIUS *remain and withdraw into* BRUTUS*'s tent, while* LUCILIUS *and* TITINIUS *mount guard without.*]

SCENE 3. BRUTUS's tent. A few minutes later.

CASSIUS. That you wrong'd me doth appear in this;
You have condemn'd and noted Lucius Pella
For taking bribes here of the Sardians;

23–27 **But hollow . . . trial:** Brutus compares insincere men to horses that are spirited at the start but drop their proud necks as soon as they feel the spur, failing like nags **(jades)** when put to the test.

29 **horse in general:** main part of the cavalry.

40 **sober form:** dignified manner.

47–48 **enlarge . . . audience:** Explain your grievances, and I will listen.

Wherein my letters, praying on his side,
Because I knew the man, was slighted off.°

BRUTUS. You wrong'd yourself to write in such a case.

CASSIUS. In such a time as this it is not meet
That every nice offense should bear his comment.°

BRUTUS. Let me tell you, Cassius, you yourself
Are much condemn'd to have an itching palm,°
To sell and mart° your offices for gold
To undeservers.

CASSIUS. I, an itching palm?
You know that you are Brutus that speaks this,
Or, by the gods, this speech were else your last.

BRUTUS. The name of Cassius honors this corruption,
And chastisement doth therefore hide his head.°

CASSIUS. Chastisement?

BRUTUS. Remember March, the ides of March remember:
Did not great Julius bleed for justice' sake?
What villain touch'd his body, that did stab
And not for justice? What? shall one of us,
That struck the foremost man of all this world
But for supporting robbers,° shall we now
Contaminate our fingers with base bribes?
And sell the mighty space of our large honors
For so much trash as may be grasped thus?
I had rather be a dog, and bay the moon,
Than such a Roman.

CASSIUS. Brutus, bait° not me,
I'll not endure it. You forget yourself
To hedge me in.° I am a soldier, I,
Older in practice, abler than yourself
To make conditions.°

BRUTUS. Go to; you are not, Cassius.

CASSIUS. I am.

BRUTUS. I say you are not.

CASSIUS. Urge me no more, I shall forget myself;
Have mind upon your health; tempt me no farther.

BRUTUS. Away, slight man!

CASSIUS. Is't possible?

1–5 **That you . . . off:** Cassius complains that Brutus publicly disgraced **(noted)** a man for taking bribes, ignoring Cassius's request for leniency.

7–8 **not meet . . . comment:** not fitting that each minor offense should be criticized.

10 **condemn'd to . . . palm:** blamed for being greedy.

11 **mart:** trade.

15–16 **The name . . . head:** Because you have become associated with this corruption, the bribe-takers go unpunished.

23 **supporting robbers:** Brutus now suggests that one of Caesar's offenses was to protect corrupt officials.

28 **bait:** provoke.

30 **hedge me in:** limit my freedom.

32 **conditions:** regulations.

BRUTUS. Hear me, for I will speak.
Must I give way and room to your rash choler?°
Shall I be frighted when a madman stares?

CASSIUS. O ye gods, ye gods, must I endure all this?

BRUTUS. All this? ay, more. Fret till your proud heart break.
Go show your slaves how choleric you are,
And make your bondmen tremble. Must I budge?°
Must I observe you?° Must I stand and crouch
Under your testy humor?° By the gods,
You shall digest the venom of your spleen
Though it do split you;° for, from his day forth,
I'll use you for my mirth, yea, for my laughter,
When you are waspish.

CASSIUS. Is it come to this?

BRUTUS. You say you are a better soldier;
Let it appear so; make your vaunting° true,
And it shall please me well. For mine own part,
I shall be glad to learn of noble men.°

CASSIUS. You wrong me every way; you wrong me, Brutus;
I said, an elder soldier, not a better.
Did I say "better"?

BRUTUS. If you did, I care not.

CASSIUS. When Caesar liv'd, he durst° not thus have mov'd° me.

BRUTUS. Peace, peace, you durst not so have tempted him.

CASSIUS. I durst not?

BRUTUS. No.

CASSIUS. What? durst not tempt him?

BRUTUS. For your life you
durst not.

CASSIUS. Do not presume too much upon my love,
I may do that° I shall be sorry for.

BRUTUS. You have done that you should be sorry for.
There is no terror, Cassius, in your threats;
For I am arm'd so strong in honesty
That they pass by me as the idle wind,
Which I respect not. I did send to you
For certain sums of gold, which you denied me;
For I can raise no money by vile means.
By heaven, I had rather coin my heart
And drop my blood for drachmas than to wring

39 **rash choler:** quick temper.

44 **budge:** flinch.

45 **observe you:** defer to you.

46 **testy humor:** irritable mood.

47–48 **digest . . . split you:** swallow the poison of your own anger, even if it makes you burst. (The spleen was thought to be the source of anger.)

52 **vaunting:** boasting.

54 **learn of noble men:** "learn from noble men" or "find out that you are noble."

58 **durst:** dared. **mov'd:** provoked.

64 **that:** something that.

From the hard hands of peasants their vile trash°
By any indirection.° I did send
To you for gold to pay my legions,
Which you denied me. Was that done like Cassius?
Should I have answer'd Caius Cassius so?
When Marcus Brutus grows so covetous
To lock such rascal counters° from his friends,
Be ready, gods, with all your thunderbolts,
Dash him to pieces!

CASSIUS. I denied you not.

BRUTUS. You did.

CASSIUS. I did not. He was but a fool that brought
My answer back. Brutus hath riv'd° my heart.
A friend should bear his friend's infirmities;°
But Brutus makes mine greater than they are.

BRUTUS. I do not, till you practice them on me.

CASSIUS. You love me not.

BRUTUS. I do not like your faults.

CASSIUS. A friendly eye could never see such faults.

BRUTUS. A flatterer's would not, though they do appear
As huge as high Olympus.

CASSIUS. Come, Antony, and young Octavius, come,
Revenge yourselves alone on Cassius,
For Cassius is aweary of the world;
Hated by one he loves, brav'd° by his brother,
Check'd like a bondman,° all his faults observ'd,
Set in a notebook, learn'd and conn'd by rote,°
To cast into my teeth. O, I could weep
My spirit from mine eyes! There is my dagger,
And here my naked breast; within, a heart
Dearer than Pluto's mine,° richer than gold:
If that thou be'st a Roman, take it forth.
I, that denied thee gold, will give my heart:
Strike as thou didst at Caesar; for I know,
When thou didst hate him worst, thou lovedst him better
Than ever thou lovedst Cassius.

BRUTUS. Sheathe your dagger.
Be angry when you will, it shall have scope;
Do what you will, dishonor shall be humor.°
O Cassius, you are yoked° with a lamb

74 **vile trash:** small sums of money.

75 **indirection:** dishonest means.

80 **rascal counters:** grubby coins.

85 **riv'd:** broken.

86 **bear . . . infirmities:** accept his friend's faults.

96 **brav'd:** challenged.

97 **Check'd like a bondman:** scolded like a slave.

98 **conn'd by rote:** memorized.

102 **Pluto's mine:** all the riches in the earth. (Pluto, the Roman god of the underworld, was often confused with Plutus, the god of wealth.)

108–109 **Be angry . . . humor:** Brutus says that he will give Cassius's anger free play **(scope)** and will consider his insults merely the result of a bad mood.

110 **yoked:** allied.

That carries anger as the flint bears fire,
Who, much enforced,° shows a hasty spark,
And straight° is cold again.

CASSIUS. Hath Cassius liv'd
To be but mirth and laughter to his Brutus
When grief and blood ill-temper'd° vexeth him?

BRUTUS. When I spoke that, I was ill-temper'd too.

CASSIUS. Do you confess so much? Give me your hand.

BRUTUS. And my heart too.

CASSIUS. O Brutus!

BRUTUS. What's the matter?

CASSIUS. Have you not love enough to bear with me,
When that rash humor which my mother gave me
Makes me forgetful?°

BRUTUS. Yes, Cassius, and from henceforth,
When you are over-earnest with your Brutus,
He'll think your mother chides, and leave you so.°

[*Enter a* POET *(to* LUCILIUS *and* TITINIUS *as they stand on guard)*.]

POET. Let me go in to see the generals;
There is some grudge between 'em; 'tis not meet
They be alone.

112 **enforced:** struck hard; irritated.

113 **straight:** immediately.

115 **blood ill-temper'd:** moodiness.

121 **forgetful:** forget myself.

122–123 **When you . . . so:** When you are too difficult with me, I will attribute it to the quick temper you inherited from your mother, and leave it at that.

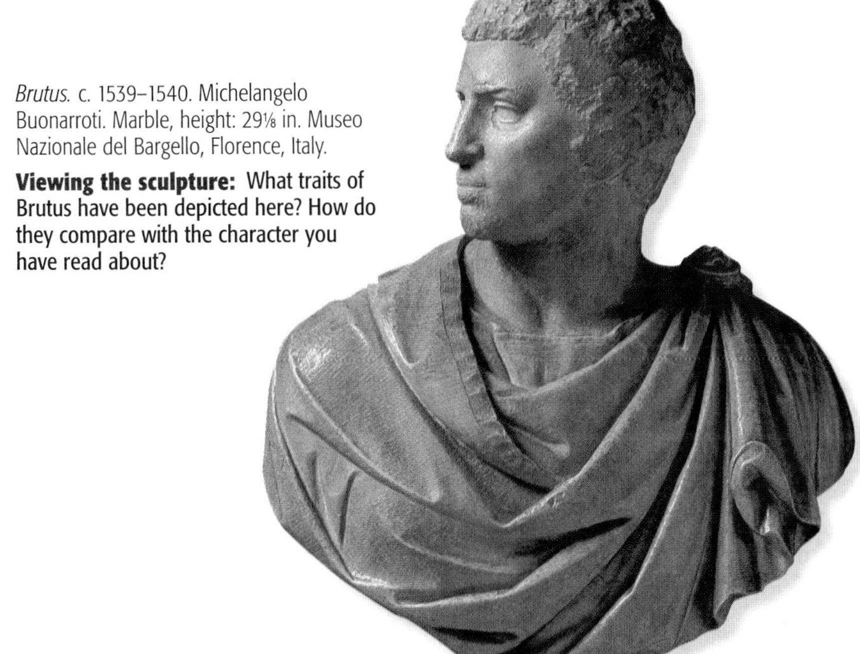

Brutus. c. 1539–1540. Michelangelo Buonarroti. Marble, height: 29⅛ in. Museo Nazionale del Bargello, Florence, Italy.

Viewing the sculpture: What traits of Brutus have been depicted here? How do they compare with the character you have read about?

LUCILIUS. You shall not come to them.

POET. Nothing but death shall stay me.

[*BRUTUS and CASSIUS step out of the tent.*]

CASSIUS. How now. What's the matter?

POET. For shame, you generals! what do you mean?
Love, and be friends, as two such men should be,
For I have seen more years, I'm sure, than ye.

CASSIUS. Ha, ha! how vilely doth this cynic° rhyme!

BRUTUS. Get you hence, sirrah! saucy fellow, hence!

CASSIUS. Bear with him, Brutus, 'tis his fashion.

BRUTUS. I'll know his humor when he knows his time.°
What should the wars do with these jigging° fools?
Companion,° hence!

CASSIUS. Away, away, be gone! [*Exit POET.*]

BRUTUS. Lucilius and Titinius, bid the commanders
Prepare to lodge their companies tonight.

CASSIUS. And come yourselves, and bring Messala with you
Immediately to us.

[*LUCILIUS and TITINIUS exit.*]

BRUTUS. [*To LUCIUS within.*] Lucius, a bowl of wine!

[*BRUTUS and CASSIUS return into the tent.*]

CASSIUS. I did not think you could have been so angry.

BRUTUS. O Cassius, I am sick of many griefs.

CASSIUS. Of your philosophy you make no use,
If you give place to accidental evils.°

BRUTUS. No man bears sorrow better. Portia is dead.

CASSIUS. Ha? Portia?

BRUTUS. She is dead.

CASSIUS. How scap'd I killing° when I cross'd you so?
O insupportable and touching° loss!
Upon what sickness?

BRUTUS. Impatient of° my absence,
And grief that young Octavius with Mark Antony
Have made themselves so strong—for with her death
That tidings came.° With this she fell distract,°
And (her attendants absent) swallow'd fire.°

133 **cynic:** rude fellow.

136 **I'll know . . . time:** I'll accept his quirks when he learns the proper time for them.

137 **jigging:** rhyming.

138 **Companion:** fellow (used here as a term of contempt).

145–146 **Of your . . . evils:** According to the philosophy Brutus studied, people should not accept chance misfortunes.

150 **How scap'd I killing:** How did I escape being killed?

151 **touching:** painful.

152 **Impatient of:** unable to endure.

154–155: **with her death . . . came:** I received news of her death and of their strength at the same time.

155 **distract:** insane.

156 **fire:** burning coals.

CASSIUS. And died so?

BRUTUS. Even so.

CASSIUS. O ye immortal gods!

[Enter Boy (LUCIUS) with wine and tapers.]

BRUTUS. Speak no more of her. Give me a bowl of wine.
In this I bury all unkindness, Cassius. *[Drinks.]*

CASSIUS. My heart is thirsty for that noble pledge.
Fill, Lucius, till the wine o'erswell the cup;
I cannot drink too much of Brutus' love.

[Drinks. Exit LUCIUS.]

BRUTUS. Come in, Titinius. *[Enter TITINIUS and MESSALA.]*
Welcome, good Messala.
Now sit we close about this taper here,
And call in question our necessities.°

CASSIUS. Portia, art thou gone?

BRUTUS. No more, I pray you.
Messala, I have here received letters
That young Octavius and Mark Antony
Come down upon us with a mighty power,°
Bending their expedition toward Philippi.°

MESSALA. Myself have letters of the selfsame tenure.°

BRUTUS. With what addition?

MESSALA. That by proscription° and bills of outlawry
Octavius, Antony, and Lepidus
Have put to death an hundred senators.

BRUTUS. Therein our letters do not well agree;
Mine speak of seventy senators that died
By their proscriptions, Cicero being one.

CASSIUS. Cicero one?

MESSALA. Cicero is dead,
And by that order of proscription.
Had you your letters from your wife, my lord?

BRUTUS. No, Messala.

MESSALA. Nor nothing in your letters writ of her?

BRUTUS. Nothing, Messala.

MESSALA. That methinks is strange.

BRUTUS. Why ask you? Hear you aught of her in yours?

165 **call . . . necessities:** discuss what we must do.

169 **power:** army.

170 **Bending . . . Philippi:** Directing their march toward Philippi (an ancient town in northern Greece).

171 **tenure:** basic meaning.

173 **proscription:** condemning to death.

MESSALA. No, my lord.

BRUTUS. Now as you are a Roman, tell me true.

MESSALA. Then like a Roman bear the truth I tell,
For certain she is dead, and by strange manner.

BRUTUS. Why, farewell, Portia. We must die, Messala.
With meditating that she must die once,°
I have the patience to endure it now.

MESSALA. Even so great men great losses should endure.

CASSIUS. I have as much of this in art as you,
But yet my nature could not bear it so.°

BRUTUS. Well, to our work alive.° What do you think
Of marching to Philippi presently?

CASSIUS. I do not think it good.

BRUTUS. Your reason?

CASSIUS. This it is;
'Tis better that the enemy seek us;
So shall he waste his means,° weary his soldiers,
Doing himself offense,° whilst we, lying still,
Are full of rest, defense, and nimbleness.

BRUTUS. Good reasons must of force give place to better:
The people 'twixt Philippi and this ground
Do stand but in a forc'd affection;°
For they have grudg'd us contribution.
The enemy, marching along by them,
By them shall make a fuller number up,
Come on refresh'd, new-added° and encourag'd;
From which advantage shall we cut him off
If at Philippi we do face him there,
These people at our back.

CASSIUS. Here me, good brother.

BRUTUS. Under your pardon.° You must note beside
That we have tried the utmost of our friends,°
Our legions are brimful,° our cause is ripe:
The enemy increaseth every day;
We, at the height, are ready to decline.
There is a tide in the affairs of men,
Which, taken at the flood, leads on to fortune;
Omitted, all the voyage of their life
Is bound in shallows and in miseries.°
On such a full sea are we now afloat,

181–195 Had you your . . . bear it so: This passage contradicts lines 147–158, where Brutus tells Cassius of Portia's death. Many scholars believe that the second passage was mistakenly printed in a revised version of the play. According to this theory, Shakespeare originally emphasized Brutus's philosophical composure, but in rewriting the play, he decided to offer a warmer view of Brutus grieving for his wife.

191 once: at some time.

194–195 I have as . . . so: Cassius says that although he shares Brutus's ideal of philosophical self-control, he could not practice it as Brutus does.

196 alive: "at hand" or "of the living."

200 waste his means: use up his supplies.

201 Doing himself offense: harming himself.

205 Do stand . . . affection: Are friendly toward us only because they have no choice.

209 new-added: reinforced.

213 Under your pardon: I beg your pardon (let me continue).

214 tried . . . friends: demanded from our allies all that they can give.

215 brimful: at full strength.

218–221 There is a . . . miseries: Brutus says that if men fail to act when the tide of fortune is flowing, they may never get another opportunity.

And we must take the current when it serves,
Or lose our ventures.

CASSIUS. Then with your will° go on;
We'll along ourselves, and meet them at Philippi.

BRUTUS. The deep of night is crept upon our talk,
And nature must obey necessity,
Which we will niggard with a little rest.°
There is no more to say?

CASSIUS. No more. Good night.
Early tomorrow will we rise, and hence.

BRUTUS. Lucius. [*Enter* LUCIUS.] My gown. [*Exit* LUCIUS.]
Farewell, good Messala.
Good night, Titinius. Noble, noble Cassius,
Good night, and good repose.

CASSIUS. O my dear brother!
This was an ill beginning of the night.
Never come such division 'tween our souls!
Let it not, Brutus.

[*Enter* LUCIUS *with the gown.*]

BRUTUS. Everything is well.

CASSIUS. Good night, my lord.

BRUTUS. Good night, good brother.

TITINIUS AND MESSALA. Good night, Lord Brutus.

BRUTUS. Farewell
every one.

[*Exit (all but* BRUTUS *and* LUCIUS*).*]

Give me the gown. Where is thy instrument?

LUCIUS. Here in the tent.

BRUTUS. What, thou speak'st drowsily?
Poor knave,° I blame thee not; thou art o'erwatch'd.°
Call Claudius and some other of my men,
I'll have them sleep on cushions in my tent.

LUCIUS. Varrus and Claudio!

[*Enter* VARRUS *and* CLAUDIO.]

VARRUS. Calls my lord?

BRUTUS. I pray you, sirs, lie in my tent and sleep;
It may be I shall raise° you by and by
On business to my brother Cassius.

224 **with your will:** as you wish.

227–228 **nature must . . . rest:** Human nature has its needs, which we will grudgingly satisfy **(niggard)** by resting briefly.

241 **knave:** lad. **o'erwatch'd:** tired from staying awake too long.

247 **raise:** awaken.

VARRUS. So please you, we will stand and watch your pleasure.°

BRUTUS. I will not have it so. Lie down, good sirs,
It may be I shall otherwise bethink me.°

[*VARRUS and CLAUDIO lie down.*]

Look, Lucius, here's the book I sought for so;
I put it in the pocket of my gown.

LUCIUS. I was sure your lordship did not give it me.

BRUTUS. Bear with me, good boy, I am much forgetful.
Canst thou hold up thy heavy eyes awhile,
And touch thy instrument a strain or two?°

LUCIUS. Ay, my lord, an't° please you.

BRUTUS. It does, my boy.
I trouble thee too much, but thou are willing.

LUCIUS. It is my duty, sir.

BRUTUS. I should not urge thy duty past thy might;
I know young bloods look for a time of rest.

LUCIUS. I have slept, my lord, already.

BRUTUS. It was well done, and thou shalt sleep again;
I will not hold thee long. If I do live,
I will be good to thee.

[*Music, and a song.*]

This is a sleepy tune. O murd'rous slumber!
Layest thou thy leaden mace° upon my boy,
That plays thee music? Gentle knave, good night;
I will not do thee so much wrong to wake thee.
If thou dost nod, thou break'st thy instrument;
I'll take it from thee; and, good boy, good night.
Let me see, let me see; is not the leaf turn'd down
Where I left reading? Here it is, I think.

[*Enter the GHOST OF CAESAR.*]

How ill this taper burns!° Ha! who comes here?
I think it is the weakness of mine eyes
That shapes this monstrous apparition.
It comes upon me. Art thou anything?
Art thou some god, some angel, or some devil,
That mak'st my blood cold, and my hair to stare?°
Speak to me what thou art.

GHOST. Thy evil spirit, Brutus.

---

249 stand . . . pleasure: stay awake and be ready to serve you.

251 It may be . . . me: I might change my mind.

257 touch thy . . . two: play a song or two. (Lucius probably plays the lute, a stringed instrument.)

258 an't: if it.

267–268 O murd'rous . . . mace: Officers used to touch a rod **(mace)** to a person's shoulder as a sign of arrest. Brutus calls the mace of deathlike **(murd'rous)** sleep "leaden" because of its heaviness.

275 How ill . . . burns: It was believed that candles burn dimly when a ghost appears.

280 stare: stand on end.

Shakespeare–Julius Caesar, Act IV Scene iii. Richard Westall (1765–1836). Line and stipple engraving with hand coloring, 646 x 459 mm. Fine Arts Museums of San Francisco.

Viewing the art: Who is pictured here? Based on what you've read, do you think the characters have been portrayed accurately? Why or why not?

BRUTUS. Why com'st thou?

GHOST. To tell thee thou shalt see me at Philippi.

BRUTUS. Well; then I shall see thee again?

GHOST. Ay, at Philippi.

BRUTUS. Why, I will see thee at Philippi then.

[*Exit* GHOST.]

Now I have taken heart thou vanishest.
Ill spirit, I would hold more talk with thee.
Boy! Lucius! Varrus! Claudio! Sirs, awake!
Claudio!

LUCIUS. The strings, my lord, are false.°

BRUTUS. He thinks he still is at his instrument.
Lucius, awake!

LUCIUS. My lord?

BRUTUS. Didst thou dream, Lucius, that thou so criedst out?

LUCIUS. My lord, I do not know that I did cry.

BRUTUS. Yes, that thou didst. Didst thou see anything?

LUCIUS. Nothing, my lord.

BRUTUS. Sleep again, Lucius. Sirrah Claudio!
[*To* CLAUDIO *and then* VARRUS.] Fellow thou, awake!

VARRUS. My lord?

CLAUDIO. My lord?

BRUTUS. Why did you so cry out, sirs, in your sleep?

BOTH. Did we, my lord?

BRUTUS. Ay. Saw you anything?

VARRUS. No, my lord, I saw nothing.

CLAUDIO. Nor I, my lord.

BRUTUS. Go and commend me° to my brother Cassius;
Bid him set on his pow'rs betimes before,°
And we will follow.

BOTH. It shall be done, my lord.

[*They exit.*]

291 **false:** out of tune.

306 **commend me:** send my regards.

307 **set on . . . before:** start his troops moving early, at the lead.

Responding to Literature

Personal Response

What do you think about the relationship between Brutus and Cassius?

Analyzing Act 4

Recall and Intrepret

1. How does the political situation in Rome following Caesar's murder compare with what it was under Caesar's rule?
2. Describe the main **conflict,** or struggle, between Brutus and Cassius in act 4. In your opinion, who is more to blame? Why?
3. What personal grief does Brutus relate to Cassius? How does this news affect Cassius?
4. What battle plan does Cassius propose? Why, do you think, does he agree to march to Philippi?
5. What unexpected visitor comes to Brutus's tent? How does Brutus react to this visitation? Explain.

Evaluate and Connect

6. What is your impression of Antony in act 4? Do his actions surprise you? Explain.
7. Why, do you think, did Shakespeare include the conflict between Cassius and Brutus?
8. Would you rather serve as a Roman soldier under Brutus or Cassius? Why? Which of them better displays the qualities you identified in your leadership web in the Reading Focus on page 777?
9. In your opinion, what is the purpose of the scene in Brutus's tent with Brutus and Lucius as Brutus prepares to sleep?
10. Based on your own experiences, what are some ways to prevent disagreements like the one between Cassius and Brutus?

Literary **ELEMENTS**

Foreshadowing

Playwrights and other authors use **foreshadowing** to prepare readers for events that will happen later. In act 2 of *Julius Caesar,* for example, Cassius suggests to Brutus that the conspirators should kill Mark Antony along with Caesar or else "we shall find of him / A shrewd contriver." In act 3, Cassius urges Brutus not to let Antony speak at Caesar's funeral. Cassius's fears later are shown to be well-founded, and Brutus's judgment is shown to be in error.

1. What may be foreshadowed by Cassius and Brutus disagreeing on a plan of military action?
2. What may be foreshadowed by Caesar's ghost appearing to Brutus and saying he will see Brutus at Philippi?

- See **Literary Terms Handbook,** p. R5.

Extending Your Response

Personal Writing

Still Friends? In your journal, describe an argument that you once had with a close friend. What caused the disagreement? How did you try to settle your differences? Were you able to remain friends with this person? Compare your personal experience with the dispute between Cassius and Brutus.

Interdisciplinary Activity

Social Studies: Army Life Use library resources and the Internet to research armies of ancient Rome. How were armies organized? Who was in charge? Where were the armies stationed? How were funds raised to support them? Present your findings to the class in an oral report.

Save your work for your portfolio.

ACT 5

SCENE 1. The Plains of Philippi in Greece. A few weeks later.

[*Enter* OCTAVIUS, ANTONY, *and their* ARMY.]

OCTAVIUS. Now, Antony, our hopes are answered.
You said the enemy would not come down,
But keep the hills and upper regions.
It proves not so: their battles° are at hand;
They mean to warn° us at Philippi here,
Answering before we do demand of them.°

ANTONY. Tut, I am in their bosoms,° and I know
Wherefore they do it. They could be content
To visit other places, and come down
With fearful° bravery, thinking by this face
To fasten in our thoughts that they have courage;°
But 'tis not so.

[*Enter a* MESSENGER.]

MESSENGER. Prepare you, generals,
The enemy comes on in gallant show;
Their bloody sign° of battle is hung out,
And something to be done immediately.

ANTONY. Octavius, lead your battle softly° on
Upon the left hand of the even° field.

OCTAVIUS. Upon the right hand I, keep thou the left.

ANTONY. Why do you cross me in this exigent?°

OCTAVIUS. I do not cross you; but I will do so.° [*March.*]

[*Drum. Enter* BRUTUS, CASSIUS, *and their* ARMY; LUCILIUS, TITINIUS, MESSALA, *and others.*]

BRUTUS. They stand, and would have parley.°

CASSIUS. Stand fast, Titinius; we must out and talk.

OCTAVIUS. Mark Antony, shall we give sign of battle?

ANTONY. No, Caesar, we will answer on their charge.°
Make forth, the generals would have some words.

OCTAVIUS. Stir not until the signal.

BRUTUS. Words before blows; is it so, countrymen?

4 **battles:** armies.

5 **warn:** defy.

6 **Answering before . . . them:** responding hostilely before we even challenge them to fight.

7 **am in their bosoms:** know what is in their hearts.

8–11 **They could . . . courage:** Antony dismisses his enemy's bravery as a false show **(face)**, saying that they would really prefer to be somewhere else.

10 **fearful:** "frightening" or "full of fear."

14 **bloody sign:** A red flag was flown from a Roman general's tent to signal the start of battle.

16 **softly:** slowly.

17 **even:** level.

19 **cross me in this exigent:** oppose me at this moment of crisis.

20 **I will do so:** I will do as I said. (Octavius insists on attacking from the right, which is usually the position of the most experienced general.)

21 **would have parley:** request a conference.

24 **answer on their charge:** respond when they attack.

OCTAVIUS. Not that we love words better, as you do.

BRUTUS. Good words are better than bad strokes, Octavius.

ANTONY. In your bad strokes, Brutus, you give good words;
Witness the hole you made in Caesar's heart,
Crying, "Long live! hail, Caesar!"

CASSIUS. Antony,
The posture of your blows are yet unknown;°
But for your words, they rob the Hybla° bees,
And leave them honeyless.

ANTONY. Not stingless too?

BRUTUS. O, yes, and soundless too;
For you have stol'n their buzzing, Antony,
And very wisely threat before you sting.

ANTONY. Villains! you did not so, when your vile daggers
Hack'd one another in the sides of Caesar.
You show'd your [teeth]° like apes, and fawn'd like hounds,
And bow'd like bondmen, kissing Caesar's feet;
Whilst damned Casca, like a cur, behind
Struck Caesar on the neck, O you flatterers!

CASSIUS. Flatterers? Now, Brutus, thank yourself;
This tongue had not offended so today,
If Cassius might have rul'd.°

OCTAVIUS. Come, come, the cause.° If arguing make us sweat,
The proof of it° will turn to redder drops.
Look,
I draw a sword against conspirators;
When think you that the sword goes up again?°
Never, till Caesar's three and thirty wounds
Be well aveng'd; or till another Caesar
Have added slaughter to the sword of traitors.°

BRUTUS. Caesar, thou canst not die by traitors' hands,
Unless thou bring'st them with thee.°

OCTAVIUS. So I hope;
I was not born to die on Brutus' sword.

BRUTUS. O, if thou wert the noblest of thy strain,°
Young man, thou couldst not die more honorable.

CASSIUS. A peevish schoolboy,° worthless of such honor,
Join'd with a masker and a reveler!°

ANTONY. Old Cassius still!

33 **The posture . . . unknown:** We don't know what kind of blows you will strike.

34 **Hybla:** an area in Sicily noted for its honey. (Cassius is reminding Antony of his "sweet" words to the conspirators after the assassination.)

41 **show'd your [teeth]:** grinned.

47 **If Cassius . . . rul'd:** if Cassius had had his way (when he argued that Antony should be killed).

48 **cause:** business at hand.

49 **The proof of it:** deciding the argument in battle.

52 **goes up again:** goes back into its sheath.

54–55 **till another . . . traitors:** until the conspirators have killed another Caesar (that is, Octavius himself).

56–57 **Caesar . . . thee:** Brutus suggests that all the traitors are on the side of Octavius and Antony.

59 **strain:** family.

61 **schoolboy:** Octavius was twenty-one at the time of the battle.

62 **a masker and a reveler:** one who indulges in lavish entertainment and drunken feasts.

OCTAVIUS. Come, Antony; away!
Defiance, traitors, hurl we in your teeth.
If you dare fight today, come to the field;
If not, when you have stomachs.°

[*Exit* OCTAVIUS, ANTONY, *and* ARMY.]

CASSIUS. Why, now blow wind, swell billow, and swim bark!
The storm is up, and all is on the hazard.°

BRUTUS. Ho, Lucilius, hark, a word with you.

[LUCILIUS *and (then)* MESSALA *stand forth.*]

LUCILIUS. My lord?

[BRUTUS *and* LUCILIUS *converse apart.*]

CASSIUS. Messala!

MESSALA. What says my general?

CASSIUS. Messala,
This is my birthday; as this very day
Was Cassius born. Give me thy hand, Messala;
Be thou my witness that against my will
(As Pompey was)° am I compell'd to set
Upon one battle all our liberties.
You know that I held Epicurus strong,°
And his opinion; now I change my mind,
And partly credit things that do presage.°
Coming from Sardis, on our former ensign°
Two mighty eagles fell, and there they perch'd,
Gorging and feeding from our soldiers' hands,
Who to Philippi here consorted° us.
This morning are they fled away and gone,
And in their steads do ravens, crows, and kites°
Fly o'er our heads, and downward look on us
As° we were sickly prey. Their shadows seem
A canopy most fatal, under which
Our army lies, ready to give up the ghost.

MESSALA. Believe not so.

CASSIUS. I but believe it partly,
For I am fresh of spirit, and resolv'd
To meet all perils very constantly.°

BRUTUS. Even so, Lucilius.°

CASSIUS. Now, most noble Brutus,
The gods today stand friendly, that we may,

66 **stomachs:** appetite for battle.

68 **all is . . . hazard:** Everything is at stake.

74 **As Pompey was:** Pompey was persuaded against his better judgment to fight at Pharsalus, where he was defeated by Caesar.

76 **held Epicurus strong:** have been a firm believer of Epicurus (a Greek philosopher whose followers did not believe in omens).

78 **presage:** foretell the future.

79 **former ensign:** foremost banner.

82 **consorted:** accompanied.

84 **kites:** hawks. (All three birds are omens of death.)

86 **As:** As if.

91 **constantly:** resolutely.

92 **Even so, Lucilius:** Brutus finishes his discussion with Lucilius.

Lovers in peace, lead on our days to age!°
But since the affairs of men rests still incertain,
Let's reason with the worst that may befall.°
If we do lose this battle, then is this
The very last time we shall speak together:
What are you then determined to do?

BRUTUS. Even by the rule of that philosophy
By which I did blame Cato for the death
Which he did give himself—I know not how,
But I do find it cowardly and vile,
For fear of what might fall, so to prevent
The time of life—arming myself with patience
To stay the providence of some high powers
That govern us below.°

CASSIUS. Then, if we lose this battle,
You are contented to be led in triumph
Thorough the streets of Rome?

BRUTUS. No, Cassius, no. Think not, thou noble Roman,
That ever Brutus will go bound to Rome;
He bears too great a mind.° But this same day
Must end that work the ides of March begun.
And whether we shall meet again I know not;
Therefore our everlasting farewell take:
Forever, and forever, farewell, Cassius!
If we do meet again, why, we shall smile;
If not, why then this parting was well made.

CASSIUS. Forever, and forever, farewell, Brutus!
If we do meet again, we'll smile indeed;
If not 'tis true this parting was well made.

BRUTUS. Why then, lead on. O, that a man might know
The end of this day's business ere it come!
But it sufficeth that the day will end,
And then the end is known. Come, ho, away!

[*BRUTUS, CASSIUS, and their ARMY withdraw to begin the battle.*]

93–94 The gods . . . age: May the gods remain friendly today, so that we, dear friends in peace with each other, may live to see old age.

96 Let's reason . . . befall: Let's consider the worst that can happen.

100–107 Even by the . . . below: Brutus says that according to his beliefs, suicide is cowardly (he refers to his father-in-law, Cato, who killed himself after Caesar's defeat of Pompey). He would endure his fate rather than cut short **(prevent)** his life because of what might happen.

110–112 Think not . . . mind: Brutus is suggesting that even though he rejects suicide, his pride would force him to commit such an act rather than allow himself to be paraded through the streets of Rome.

SCENE 2. The field of battle. Shortly afterward.

[*Alarm. Enter BRUTUS and MESSALA.*]

BRUTUS. Ride, ride, Messala, ride, and give these bills°
Unto the legions on the other side.°

[*Loud alarm.*]

1 bills: written orders.

2 legions on . . . side: other wing of troops (led by Cassius).

Let them set on at once; for I perceive
But cold demeanor° in Octavio's wing,
And sudden push gives them the overthrow.
Ride, ride, Messala, let them all come down.

[*They exit.*]

4 cold demeanor: lack of spirit.

SCENE 3. Another part of the battlefield. Several hours later.

[*Alarms. Enter* CASSIUS *and* TITINIUS.]

CASSIUS. O, look, Titinius, look, the villains° fly!
Myself have to mine own turn'd enemy.°
This ensign° here of mine was turning back;
I slew the coward, and did take it° from him.

1 villains: Cassius's own troops (who are retreating).

2 Myself have . . . enemy: I have turned to fighting my own men.

3 ensign: standard bearer.

4 it: the standard, or army flag.

TITINIUS. O Cassius, Brutus gave the word too early,
Who, having some advantage on Octavius,
Took it too eagerly. His soldiers fell to spoil,°
Whilst we by Antony are all enclos'd.

7 spoil: looting.

[*Enter* PINDARUS.]

PINDARUS. Fly further off, my lord, fly further off;
Mark Antony is in your tents,° my lord;
Fly, therefore, noble Cassius, fly far off.

10 tents: camp.

CASSIUS. This hill is far enough. Look, look, Titinius!
Are those my tents where I perceive the fire?

TITINIUS. They are, my lord.

CASSIUS. Titinius, if thou lovest me,
Mount thou my horse, and hide° thy spurs in him
Till he have brought thee up to yonder troops.
And here again, that I may rest assur'd
Whether yond troops are friend or enemy.

15 hide: dig.

TITINIUS. I will be here again, even with a thought.°

[*Exit.*]

19 even with a thought: as quick as a thought.

CASSIUS. Go, Pindarus, get higher on that hill;
My sight was ever thick;° regard Titinius,
And tell me what thou not'st about the field.

21 my sight . . . thick: I have always been nearsighted.

[PINDARUS *goes up.*]

This day I breathed first: time is come round,
And where I did begin, there shall I end;
My life is run his compass.° Sirrah, what news?

25 is run his compass: has come full circle.

PINDARUS. [*Above.*] O my lord!

CASSIUS. What news?

Trajan. After A.D. 108, Roman. Marble. Louvre Museum, Paris.

PINDARUS. Titinius is enclosed round about
With horsemen, that make to him on the spur,°
Yet he spurs on. Now they are almost on him.
Now, Titinius! Now some light.° O, he lights too!
He's ta'en! [*Shout.*] And, hark, they shout for joy.

CASSIUS. Come down; behold no more.
O, coward that I am, to live so long,
To see my best friend ta'en° before my face!

[*PINDARUS descends.*]

Come hither, sirrah.
In Parthia did I take thee prisoner,
And then I swore thee, saving of thy life,°
That whatsoever I did bid thee do,
Thou shouldst attempt it. Come now, keep thine oath;

29 make to . . . spur: ride quickly toward him.

31 some light: some of them dismount.

32 ta'en: taken prisoner.

38 swore thee . . . life: made you swear when I saved your life.

Now be a freeman, and with this good sword,
That ran through Caesar's bowels, search° this bosom.
Stand not° to answer; here, take thou the hilts,°
And when my face is cover'd, as 'tis now,
Guide thou the sword. [*PINDARUS stabs him.*] Caesar, thou art
reveng'd,
Even with the sword that kill'd thee. [*Dies.*]

PINDARUS. So, I am free; yet would not so have been,
Durst I have done my will. O Cassius,
Far from this country Pindarus shall run,
Where never Roman shall take note of him. [*Exit.*]

[*Enter TITINIUS and MESSALA.*]

MESSALA. It is but change,° Titinius; for Octavius
Is overthrown by noble Brutus' power,
As Cassius' legions are by Antony.

TITINIUS. These tidings will well comfort Cassius.

MESSALA. Where did you leave him?

TITINIUS. All disconsolate,
With Pindarus his bondman, on this hill.

MESSALA. Is not that he that lies upon the ground?

TITINIUS. He lies not like the living. O my heart!

MESSALA. Is not that he?

TITINIUS. No, this was he, Messala,
But Cassius is no more. O setting sun,
As in thy red rays thou dost sink tonight,
So in his red blood Cassius' day is set!
The sun of Rome is set. Our day is gone,
Clouds, dews,° and dangers come; our deeds are done!
Mistrust of my success° hath done this deed.

MESSALA. Mistrust of good success° hath done this deed.
O hateful error, melancholy's child,°
Why dost thou show to the apt° thoughts of men
The things that are not? O error, soon conceiv'd,
Thou never com'st unto a happy birth,
But kill'st the mother that engend'red thee!°

TITINIUS. What, Pindarus? Where art thou, Pindarus?

MESSALA. Seek him, Titinius, whilst I go to meet
The noble Brutus, thrusting this report
Into his ears; I may say "thrusting" it;
For piercing steel and darts° envenomed

42 **search:** penetrate.

43 **Stand not:** don't wait. **hilts:** sword handles.

51 **but change:** only an exchange of fortune. (Pindarus was mistaken when he reported Titinius's capture—he had in fact come upon Brutus's troops.)

64 **dews:** Dews were considered unhealthy.

65 **Mistrust of my success:** Fear of my mission's outcome.

66 **Mistrust of good success:** Fear of how the battle would turn out.

67 **O hateful . . . child:** Messala suggests that Cassius's melancholy temperament caused him to misperceive events.

68 **apt:** ready (to be deceived).

71 **the mother . . . thee:** the mind that conceived the error.

76 **darts:** arrows.

Shall be as welcome to the ears of Brutus
As tidings of this sight.

TITINIUS. Hie you, Messala,
And I will seek for Pindarus the while.

[*Exit* MESSALA.]

Why didst thou send me forth, brave Cassius?
Did I not meet thy friends? and did not they
Put on my brows this wreath of victory,
And bid me give it thee? Didst thou not hear their shouts?
Alas, thou hast misconstrued everything.
But hold thee, take this garland on thy brow;
Thy Brutus bid me give it thee, and I
Will do his bidding. Brutus, come apace,°
And see how I regarded° Caius Cassius.
By your leave, gods!—this is a Roman's part;°
Come, Cassius' sword, and find Titinius' heart. [*Dies.*]

[*Alarm. Enter* BRUTUS, MESSALA, LUCILIUS, VOLUMNIUS, YOUNG CATO, *and* STRATO.]

BRUTUS. Where, where, Messala, doth his body lie?

MESSALA. Lo, yonder, and Titinius mourning it.

BRUTUS. Titinius' face is upward.

CATO.° He is slain.

BRUTUS. O Julius Caesar, thou art mighty yet!
Thy spirit walks abroad, and turns our swords
In our own proper° entrails. [*Low alarms.*]

CATO. Brave Titinius!
Look, whe'er he have not crown'd° dead Cassius!

BRUTUS. Are yet two Romans living such as these?
The last of all the Romans, fare thee well!
It is impossible that ever Rome
Should breed thy fellow.° Friends, I owe moe° tears
To this dead man than you shall see me pay.
I shall find time, Cassius; I shall find time.
Come, therefore, and to Thasos° send his body;
His funerals shall not be in our camp,
Lest it discomfort° us. Lucilius, come,
And come, young Cato; let us to the field.
Labio and Flavio set our battles on.
'Tis three a'clock; and, Romans, yet ere night
We shall try fortune in a second fight.

[*They exit.*]

87 **apace:** quickly.

88 **regarded:** honored.

89 **By your . . . part:** Titinius asks the gods to pardon him because he is cutting his life short to fulfill a Roman's duty **(part).**

93 **Cato:** Brutus's brother-in-law, the son of Marcus Cato.

96 **our own proper:** our very own.

97 **Look . . . crown'd:** see how he has crowned.

101 **fellow:** equal. **moe:** more.

104 **Thasos:** an island near Philippi.

106 **discomfort:** dishearten.

Base of the Column of Antoninus Pius. A.D.138–161, Roman. Vatican State.

Viewing the art: In what ways does this scene add to your understanding of the battles in this play?

SCENE 4. Another part of the battlefield. Shortly later.

[*Alarm. Enter* BRUTUS, MESSALA, *(young)* CATO, LUCILIUS, *and* FLAVIUS.]

BRUTUS. Yet, countrymen, O, yet hold up your heads!°
[*They exit.*]

CATO. What bastard doth not?° Who will go with me?
I will proclaim my name about the field.
I am the son of Marcus Cato,° ho!
A foe to tyrants, and my country's friend.
I am the son of Marcus Cato, ho!

[*Enter* SOLDIERS *and fight.*]

LUCILIUS. And I am Brutus, Marcus Brutus, I;
Brutus, my country's friend; know me for Brutus!°

[YOUNG CATO *is slain.*]

1 **Yet . . . heads:** Brutus urges his troops to keep fighting.

2 **What bastard doth not:** Who among us was born so low that he doesn't?

4 **Marcus Cato:** Portia's father.

7–8 **And I am . . . Brutus:** Lucilius impersonates his leader to divert the enemy's attention from the real Brutus.

O young and noble Cato, art thou down?
Why, now thou diest as bravely as Titinius,
And mayst be honor'd, being Cato's son.

FIRST SOLDIER. Yield, or thou diest.

LUCILIUS. Only I yield to die;
There is so much that thou wilt kill me straight:°
Kill Brutus, and be honor'd in his death.

FIRST SOLDIER. We must not. A noble prisoner!

[*Enter* ANTONY.]

SECOND SOLDIER. Room, ho! Tell Antony, Brutus is ta'en.

FIRST SOLDIER. I'll tell the news. Here comes the general.
Brutus is ta'en. Brutus is ta'en, my lord.

ANTONY. Where is he?

LUCILIUS. Safe, Antony, Brutus is safe enough.
I dare assure thee that no enemy
Shall ever take alive the noble Brutus;
The gods defend him from so great a shame!
When you do find him, or alive or° dead,
He will be found like Brutus, like himself.°

ANTONY. This is not Brutus, friend, but, I assure you,
A prize no less in worth. Keep this man safe,
Give him all kindness; I had rather have
Such men my friends than enemies. Go on,
And see whe'er Brutus be alive or dead,
And bring us word unto Octavius' tent
How everything is chanc'd.

[*They exit.*]

13 There is . . . straight: You have good reason to kill me immediately.

24 or . . . or: either . . . or.

25 like himself: behaving like his noble self.

SCENE 5. Another part of the field. Late in the day.

[*Enter* BRUTUS, CLITUS, DARDANIUS, VOLUMNIUS, *and* STRATO.]

BRUTUS. Come, poor remains of friends, rest on this rock.

CLITUS. Statilius show'd the torchlight,° but, my lord,
He came not back. He is or ta'en or slain.

BRUTUS. Sit thee down, Clitus; slaying is the word,
It is a deed in fashion.° Hark thee, Clitus. [*Whispering.*]

CLITUS. What, I, my lord? No, not for all the world.

BRUTUS. Peace then, no words.

CLITUS. I'll rather kill myself.

2 show'd the torchlight: signaled with a torch. (Statilius was sent out to see whether their camp was occupied by the enemy.)

5 It is . . . fashion: So many are being killed.

BRUTUS. Hark thee, Dardanius. [*Whispering.*]

DARDANIUS. Shall I do such a deed?

CLITUS. O Dardanius!

DARDANIUS. O Clitus!

CLITUS. What ill request did Brutus make to thee?

DARDANIUS. To kill him, Clitus. Look, he meditates.

CLITUS. Now is that noble vessel full of grief,
That it runs over even at his eyes.

BRUTUS. Come hither, good Volumnius; list° a word.

VOLUMNIUS. What says my lord?

BRUTUS. Why, this, Volumnius;
The ghost of Caesar hath appear'd to me
Two several° times by night; at Sardis once,
And this last night, here in Philippi fields.
I know my hour is come.

VOLUMNIUS. Not so, my lord.

BRUTUS. Nay, I am sure it is, Volumnius.
Thou seest the world, Volumnius, how it goes;°
Our enemies have beat us to the pit.°

[*Low alarms.*]

It is more worthy to leap in ourselves
Than tarry till they push us. Good Volumnius,
Thou know'st that we two went to school together;
Even for that our love of old, I prithee
Hold thou my sword-hilts, whilst I run on it.

VOLUMNIUS. That's not an office° for a friend, my lord.

[*Alarm still.*]

CLITUS. Fly, fly, my lord, there is no tarrying here.

BRUTUS. Farewell to you, and you, and you, Volumnius.
Strato, thou hast been all this while asleep;
Farewell to thee too, Strato. Countrymen,
My heart doth joy° that yet in all my life
I found no man but he was true to me.°
I shall have glory by this losing day
More than Octavius and Mark Antony
By this vile conquest shall attain unto.°
So fare you well at once, for Brutus' tongue
Hath almost ended his life's history.

15 **list:** hear.

18 **several:** separate.

22 **Thou seest . . . goes:** You see how things are going.

23 **pit:** a hole into which hunted animals are driven (also, a grave).

29 **office:** job.

34 **joy:** rejoice.

35 **no man . . . me:** no man to be unfaithful to me.

36–38 **I shall . . . unto:** I shall have more glory from this defeat than Octavius and Antony will achieve from their ignoble victory.

Trajan's Column, A.D. 112–113 (detail). Roman. Marble, height: approximately 68 m. Rome, Italy.
Viewing the art: What scene from the play is depicted here? Why do you think so?

Night hangs upon mine eyes; my bones would rest,
That have but labor'd to attain this hour.

[*Alarm. Cry within, "Fly, fly, fly!"*]

CLITUS. Fly, my lord, fly!

BRUTUS. Hence! I will follow.

[*CLITUS, DARDANIUS, and VOLUMNIUS exit.*]

I prithee, Strato, stay thou by thy lord,
Thou art a fellow of a good respect;°
Thy life hath had some smatch° of honor in it.
Hold then my sword, and turn away thy face,
While I do run upon it. Wilt thou, Strato?

STRATO. Give me your hand first. Fare you well, my lord.

BRUTUS. Farewell, good Strato. [*Runs on his sword.*] Caesar, now be still,
I kill'd not thee with half so good a will.

[*Dies.*]

45 **respect:** reputation.

46 **smatch:** taste.

[*Alarm. Retreat. Enter* ANTONY, OCTAVIUS, MESSALA, LUCILIUS, *and the* ARMY.]

OCTAVIUS. What man is that?

MESSALA. My master's man. Strato, where is thy master?

STRATO. Free from the bondage you are in, Messala;
The conquerors can but make a fire of him;
For Brutus only overcame himself,°
And no man else hath honor by his death.

LUCILIUS. So Brutus should be found. I thank thee, Brutus,
That thou hast prov'd Lucilius' saying true.

OCTAVIUS. All that serv'd Brutus, I will entertain them.°
Fellow, wilt thou bestow thy time with me?

STRATO. Ay, if Messala will prefer° me to you.

OCTAVIUS. Do so, good Messala.

MESSALA. How died my master, Strato?

STRATO. I held the sword, and he did run on it.

MESSALA. Octavius, then take him to follow thee,
That did the latest° service to my master.

ANTONY. This was the noblest Roman of them all;
All the conspirators, save only he,
Did that they did in envy of great Caesar;
He, only in a general honest thought
And common good to all, made one of them.°
His life was gentle,° and the elements
So mix'd in him that Nature might stand up
And say to all the world, "This was a man!"°

OCTAVIUS. According to his virtue let us use° him,
With all respect and rites of burial.
Within my tent his bones tonight shall lie,
Most like a soldier, ordered honorably.°
So call the field to rest, and let's away,
To part° the glories of this happy day.

[*All exit.*]

56 **Brutus . . . himself:** only Brutus conquered himself.

60 **entertain them:** take them into my service.

62 **prefer:** recommend.

67 **latest:** last.

71–72 **He, only . . . them:** He joined them only with honorable intentions for the public good.

73–75 **His life . . . man:** The Elizabethans believed that four elements (earth, water, air, and fire) in the body determined a person's temperament. Antony says that in Brutus the elements were perfectly balanced.

73 **gentle:** noble.

76 **use:** treat.

79 **ordered honorably:** with all due honor.

81 **part:** divide.

Responding to Literature

Personal Response

What went through your mind as you finished reading this play? Record your reactions in your journal.

Analyzing Act 5

Recall

1. What does Cassius confide to Messala before the battle?
2. What event leads to Cassius's death?
3. What does Brutus say about Caesar's spirit at Philippi?
4. What happens to Brutus at the end of the play? What do Antony and Octavius then say about Brutus?
5. What actions does Octavius take at the end of the play?

Interpret

6. Why do you think Cassius does not tell Brutus about his fears?
7. What might have influenced Cassius to accept Pindarus's report?
8. In what way does Brutus believe that Caesar is affecting events on the battlefield? Support your answer with evidence from act 5.
9. Compare Antony's speech at the end of the play with his discussion of Brutus at Caesar's funeral. How have his views of Brutus changed? Why have they changed?
10. What message do Octavius's actions suggest about honor and leadership? Explain.

Evaluate and Connect

11. According to Cassius, the last events of the play take place on his birthday. In your opinion, what does this information contribute to the last act?
12. Do you think that Antony and Octavius are motivated more by the desire for power or the wish to avenge Caesar's death? Explain, using evidence from the text.
13. What do you consider the most significant mistake committed at Philippi?
14. Do you agree with Antony that all the conspirators except for Brutus were motivated by envy? Support your opinion with examples from the play.
15. **Theme Connections** What loyalties would you say are strongest in this play? What betrayals seem the most damaging?

Tragedy and the Tragic Hero

A **tragedy** is a drama that ends in the downfall of its main character. The main character, or **tragic hero,** who suffers this fate is usually a high-ranking or respected person whose personality is marred by a fatal weakness or flaw, a **tragic flaw.** Fate or bad luck may work against this tragic hero, but usually his or her downfall is brought about by an error or a character flaw. Even if flawed, most tragic heroes are admirable individuals, and the audience regrets their loss.

Julius Caesar is an unusual tragedy because more than one character might be considered the tragic hero. Caesar is the title character, and his death is the central event in the play. However, the play focuses more on Brutus and ends with his death rather than Caesar's.

1. What is Caesar's tragic flaw? What is Brutus's tragic flaw?
2. In your opinion, which character is the tragic hero of the play? Explain your choice.

- See **Literary Terms Handbook,** p. R13.

Literature and Writing

Writing About Literature

Review Write a review of *Julius Caesar,* describing the play's strengths and weaknesses and discussing its major themes. Include a brief plot summary. Answer questions such as the following: Are the characters interesting and believable? How effectively did Shakespeare organize the plot? Why might Shakespeare have chosen to tell this story? Use quotes from the play and references to specific scenes in your analysis.

Creative Writing

A Historic Visit Imagine that you have an opportunity to interview the ghost of Caesar. You can find out how he feels about Brutus after the assassination, ask him to reveal which character he thinks should inherit his power, or get his response to the defeat of the conspirators at Philippi. Come up with a list of interesting questions, and then create answers that are appropriate for Caesar's character.

Extending Your Response

Literature Groups

Reading the Author's Mind Do you think Shakespeare was more sympathetic toward the conspirators or toward Antony and Octavius's alliance? Discuss this question in your group. Remember that instead of debating your own opinion, you are trying to figure out Shakespeare's opinions of the characters. Use evidence from the play to develop and support your position. Share your results with the class.

Learning for Life

Special Report Imagine that you are a reporter at the Battle of Philippi. Create a radio news report about the defeat of the conspirators. Describe important events in the battle, and provide information that will help listeners understand the outcome. Make sure to include sensory details that convey what it was like to be present at the battlefield. Present your news report to the class.

Interdisciplinary Activity

History: Rome After Caesar Are you curious about what happened after the assassination of Caesar and the deaths of the conspirators? Use resources such as books, CD-ROMs, and the Internet to find out about these events. Create a time line of Roman history beginning with the death of Julius Caesar and ending with the division of the Roman Empire in A.D. 395. Draw a map showing the extent of the empire at its height. Locate Philippi in Greece on the map.

Roman ruins—Celsus Library, Ephesus, Turkey A.D. 110–135

Reading Further

If you are interested in Shakespeare or Julius Caesar, you might enjoy these works:

Play: *Antony and Cleopatra,* by William Shakespeare, is a tragedy that portrays the struggle for power between Antony and Octavius.

Biography: *William Shakespeare,* by Andrew Gurr, is an accessible study of Shakespeare's life and times.

History: *Julius Caesar,* by Michael Grant, is a concise account of Caesar's life and career.

Viewing: A 1978 BBC television production of *Julius Caesar,* directed by Herbert Wise.

Save your work for your portfolio.

GRAMMAR AND LANGUAGE • Active and Passive Voice

The **voice** of a verb shows the relationship between the verb's subject and the action expressed by the verb. A verb is in the **active voice** when the subject of the sentence performs the action. A verb is in the **passive voice** when the action is performed on the subject. A passive verb always consists of a form of the verb *to be* plus a past participle. The following are examples of active and passive voice from *Julius Caesar.*

Active: "he sits high in all the people's hearts"
Passive: "we are governed with our mothers' spirits"

Writers often prefer using the active voice because it makes their writing sound more vigorous.

PRACTICE On your paper, write the verb that appears in each sentence and identify whether it is used in the active or passive voice.

1. Cassius flattered Brutus about his reputation.
2. Caesar mistrusted the lean Cassius.
3. Caesar was stabbed by Brutus in the Capitol.
4. Cicero and many other senators were executed.
5. Antony and Octavius defeated Brutus and Cassius at Philippi.

For more on verbs, see **Language Handbook,** p. R44.

READING AND THINKING • Visualizing

Visualizing the scenes of a play as you read can help the lines, actions, and characters come alive for you and can help you understand difficult passages. Typically, you can use the stage directions to get a sense of how the sets and characters should look. In addition, in Shakespeare's plays, the lines are particularly rich in descriptive details that you can visualize. For example, in act 1, Casca vividly describes a crowd scene: "the rabblement hooted, and clapp'd their chopp'd hands, and threw up their sweaty nightcaps, and utter'd such a deal of stinking breath because Caesar refus'd the crown." Can you see, hear, and smell the scene, even though it happened offstage?

PRACTICE Find a descriptive passage in *Julius Caesar.* On your paper, identify the scene and the details that help you visualize the scene. Which of the senses does the description appeal to?

For more on visualizing, see **Reading Handbook,** p. R84.

VOCABULARY • Analogies

An analogy is a type of comparison that is based on the relationships between things or ideas. Some analogies are based on a relationship that could be called "antonym variant." In this type of analogy, the paired words would be antonyms if they were the same part of speech.

healthy : illness :: weak : strength

A *healthy* person is the opposite of one with *illness;* a *weak* person is the opposite of one with *strength.*

To finish an analogy, decide what relationship exists between the first two things or ideas. Then apply that relationship to another pair of words and see if it is the same.

PRACTICE Complete each analogy.

1. confident : misgiving :: humble :
   a. doubt b. arrogance c. sensitivity
2. miserable : elation :: doubtful :
   a. joy b. concern c. faith
3. unchanged : modification :: intact :
   a. growth b. destruction c. preservation

For more on analogies, see **Communications Skills Handbook,** p. R77.

Word Processing: Creating Academic Reports

Word processing software often includes special templates and interactive instructions for the creation of term papers. Even without templates, you can adhere to the guidelines of the Modern Language Association (MLA) without much difficulty simply by using standard word processing features. Just a click of the mouse, for example, allows you to adjust such formatting features as fonts, line spacing, and margins.

Using the Keyboard and the Toolbar

Before you begin, spend a few minutes reviewing the important word processing features found on the sample toolbars and ruler shown below. Because computers and software packages differ, some tools may have different names or toolbar appearances. If you have trouble finding any of the keys, icons, or features, click on the **Help** feature.

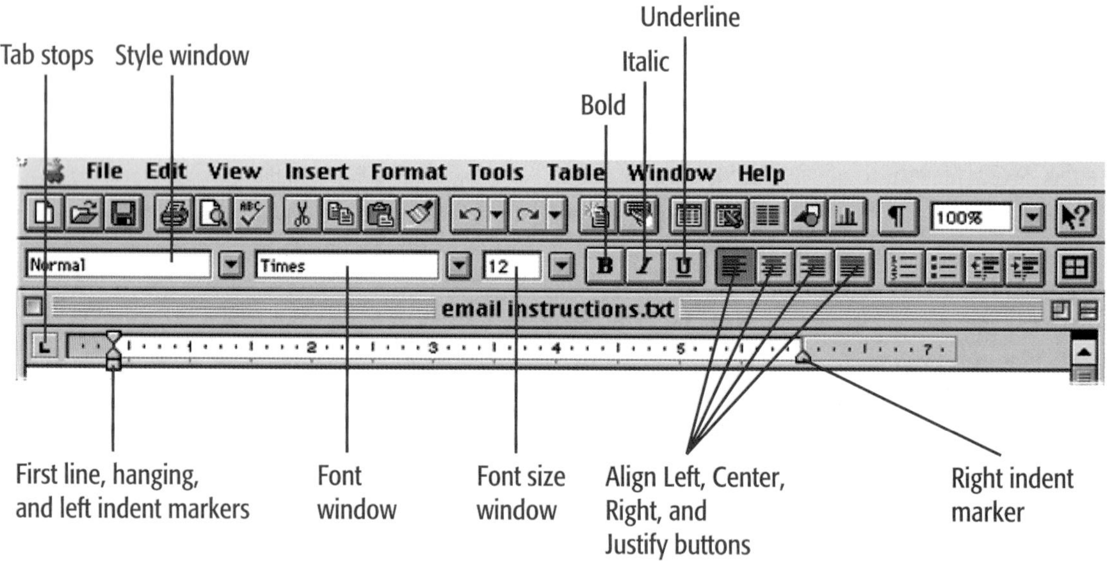

Creating an Academic Report According to MLA Guidelines

Select a report you wrote earlier in the year. Format the first page of your report according to the suggestions in the sample on the following page. Notice that a separate title page is not used in this format.

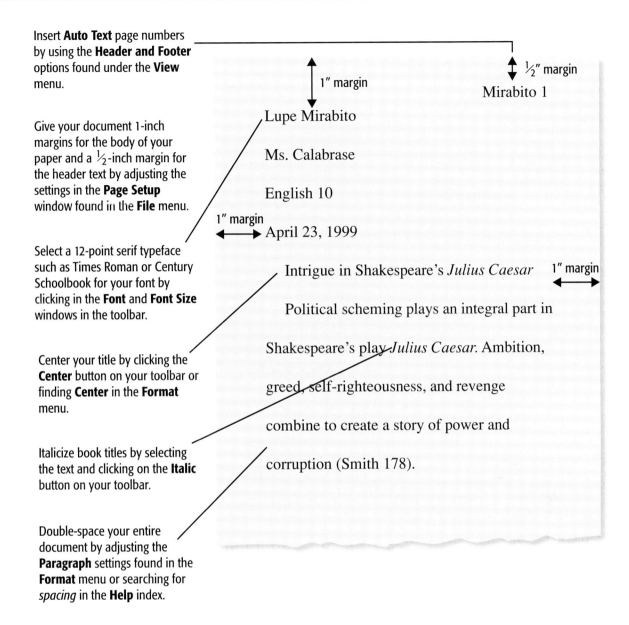

Insert **Auto Text** page numbers by using the **Header and Footer** options found under the **View** menu.

Give your document 1-inch margins for the body of your paper and a ½-inch margin for the header text by adjusting the settings in the **Page Setup** window found in the **File** menu.

Select a 12-point serif typeface such as Times Roman or Century Schoolbook for your font by clicking in the **Font** and **Font Size** windows in the toolbar.

Center your title by clicking the **Center** button on your toolbar or finding **Center** in the **Format** menu.

Italicize book titles by selecting the text and clicking on the **Italic** button on your toolbar.

Double-space your entire document by adjusting the **Paragraph** settings found in the **Format** menu or searching for *spacing* in the **Help** index.

1″ margin

½″ margin

Mirabito 1

Lupe Mirabito

Ms. Calabrase

English 10

1″ margin

April 23, 1999

Intrigue in Shakespeare's *Julius Caesar*

1″ margin

Political scheming plays an integral part in Shakespeare's play *Julius Caesar.* Ambition, greed, self-righteousness, and revenge combine to create a story of power and corruption (Smith 178).

ACTIVITY

1. Search the World Wide Web to find sample documents written in MLA style. You may also wish to browse the Modern Language Association's site at http://www.mla.org. For more help in setting up research papers, access http://www.researchpaper.com through your browser. See also Writing Handbook, pp. R64–R69.
2. Using one of the sites above or another Web site, find examples of the works-cited format for a poem found in an anthology, a newspaper article, a short story in a collection of stories, and an article from a CD-ROM encyclopedia.

INTERDISCIPLINARY LANGUAGE ARTS CONNECTION

The Romance Languages

When Shakespeare had Julius Caesar utter his famous last words, *"Et tu, Brute,"* it is hardly surprising that he used Latin. Latin was the official language not only of Rome but of most of the lands Caesar conquered. At the height of the Roman Empire, Latin was spoken throughout most of western Europe.

Like Caesar, however, Latin was not to dominate forever. In the conquered countries of the Roman Empire, people added words and pronunciations from their native languages to the Latin they spoke. Over several centuries, a distinct group of languages developed from the different dialects of everyday Latin spoken in the Roman provinces. A *dialect* is a regional variety of a language that has distinctive vocabulary, pronunciation, or grammar. Over time, a dialect may become so different from the standard language that it forms a distinct language. Starting in the ninth century, documents were produced in France—and later in Italy and Spain—in languages that looked similar to Latin but were different enough that they could be called separate languages. These new languages came to be called the *Romance languages* because of their Roman roots.

Today, five major languages are identified as Romance languages: French, Italian, Spanish, Portuguese, and Romanian. Because they all come from Latin, they have notable similarities. Many words in the Romance languages have the same or similar spellings. Notice the similarities in the examples in the box.

English	*to see*	*sweet*	*water*
Latin	videre	dulcis	aqua
French	voir	doux	eau
Italian	vedere	dolce	acqua
Spanish	ver	dulce	agua
Portuguese	ver	doce	água
Romanian	a vedea	dulce	apa

The Romance languages share other characteristics besides a Latin-based vocabulary. They also have a similar sentence structure. And in general, they have a pleasing, musical sound, partly because of the importance of vowel sounds, which are clear and precisely articulated. Spanish and Italian are especially phonetic, meaning that words are generally pronounced the way they are spelled. In French, by contrast, most final consonants are not pronounced. To foreigners' ears, the sound of most Romance languages is fast and fluid.

Throughout the world today, more than 900 million people speak one of the Romance languages as their mother tongue. In more ways than one, the culture of Julius Caesar lives on.

Activity

Languages often vary depending on where they are spoken. Choose a Romance language spoken in two widely separated places—such as French in France and in Quebec, Canada, or Spanish in Spain and in Mexico—and use reference materials to find out how pronunciation and vocabulary differ. What conclusions can you draw about how languages change and evolve?

MEDIA connection

Magazine Article

Engagement rings and heroes can come in very strange packages!

The Ring Finders of Philly

by Ralph Cipriano—*Good Housekeeping*, April 1996

The bride-to-be was heartbroken. There, at the bottom of the sewer grate, under five feet of stagnant water, sludge, and old soda cans, was the brand new ring she'd accidentally dropped. While standing at the corner of Thirteenth and Pine streets in Philadelphia, E. A. "Betsy" Alexander had yanked at the too-tight ring "and it flew up in the air" and, *plop*, fell into the sewer. *What kind of omen is this?* she thought to herself as she stared down at floating cigarette butts. Her wedding was less than two weeks away.

Retrieving the ring could have been a lost cause in many cities. But the Philadelphia Water Department has two heroes in Henry McGill, 53, and Charles Brooks, 46, who spend their days driving around the city in a mustard-colored Ford diesel truck, cleaning out sewers. Whenever anyone phones the switchboard at city hall to report he's dropped a valuable down a drain, the call immediately goes out for the rescue team of McGill and Brooks. Their specialty: grate-fishing.

In the last year alone, the two men have teased out at least two other rings. "You could call us the ring finders of Philadelphia," says Brooks. "And the marriage savers!"

Plucking out Betsy Alexander's ring was fairly routine. The partners, in blue uniforms and work boots, lifted the 70-pound cast-iron grate by hand and lowered a 250-pound hydraulic bucket into the sewer. Up came 50 pounds of slop, which they dumped on the roadside. Then they methodically combed through it with a rake and shovel until they found something bright and shiny.

Their "clients" are always grateful. Alexander, a composer who lives in Philadelphia's gentrified Society Hill section, brought each of the men a bouquet of roses and an invitation to her wedding.

But for McGill and Brooks it was all in a day's work.

Both men get a kick out of reuniting people with their valuables. "It makes you feel good," says McGill. Brooks concurs: "I leave with a sense of accomplishment."

Analyzing Media

1. Would you dig in a sewer full of sludge to retrieve your wedding ring or something of equal emotional value?
2. What's the most valuable or treasured item you've ever lost? What was your reaction to this loss?

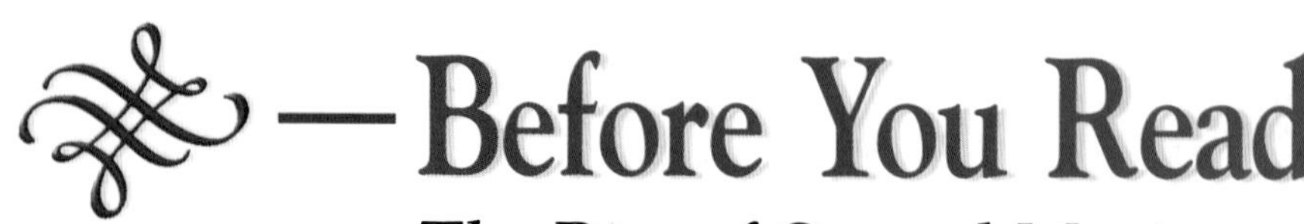

Before You Read

The Ring of General Macías

Reading Focus

In what situations do people exhibit bravery? What causes them to act bravely?

Map It! Create a cluster map about bravery. Include examples of actions that reveal bravery, people who can be considered brave, and possible reasons for acting bravely.

Setting a Purpose
Read to find out why several characters act bravely.

Building Background

The Time and Place
The events take place in a home just outside Mexico City on a night in April 1912, during the Mexican Revolution.

Did You Know?
The Mexican Revolution had its roots in the dictatorship of President Porfirio Díaz, who took power in 1876. Under Díaz, the majority of citizens–small farmers and laborers–suffered increasing hardship and repression. Meanwhile, land and wealth were accumulated by a small, elite class, many of whom were educated in Europe and who adopted European–especially French–fashions and manners. In 1910 armed resistance to Díaz's rule began, and by 1911 the dictator was forced to resign. The revolutionary struggle, which lasted for several more years, helped define Mexican identity.

Vocabulary Preview

regally (rē′ gəl lē) *adv.* in a grand, dignified manner befitting a king or queen; p. 883

ostentatiously (os′ tən tā′ shəs lē) *adv.* in a way intended to attract attention or impress others; p. 883

notorious (nō tôr′ ē əs) *adj.* widely and unfavorably known; p. 887

repressed (ri prest′) *adj.* held back or kept under control; restrained; p. 889

impertinent (im purt′ ən ənt) *adj.* inappropriately bold or forward; not showing proper respect or manners; p. 890

Meet Josephina Niggli

"Though we are all of the same clay, a jug is not a vase," says a Mexican proverb. Writer Josephina Niggli brought this understanding of people's differences to her writing of plays, poems, short stories, and novels. Although her parents were Scandinavian American, Niggli was born in Monterrey, Mexico, at the start of the Mexican Revolution. She grew up speaking both Spanish and English. Eventually, Niggli made the United States her home, but her early experiences in Mexico influenced much of her writing.

Josephina Niggli was born in 1910 and died in 1983.

The Ring of General Macías

A Drama of the Mexican Revolution

Josephina Niggli

La Tormenta, 1985. Gronk. Acrylic on canvas, 90 x 60 in. Kuwada/Grimm Collection.

CHARACTERS

MARICA (mär ē′ kə): the sister of General Macías

RAQUEL (rə kel′): the wife of General Macías

ANDRÉS DE LA O (än′ drās dā lə ō): a captain in the Revolutionary Army

CLETO (klā′ tō): a private in the Revolutionary Army

BASILIO FLORES (bə sēl′ yō flô′ rās): a captain in the Federal Army

PLACE: *Just outside Mexico City.*

TIME: *A night in April 1912.*

[The living room of General Macías's[1] *home is luxuriously furnished in the gold and ornate style of Louis XVI.*[2] *In the Right wall are French windows leading into the patio. Flanking these windows are low bookcases. In the Back wall is, Right, a closet door; and, Center, a table holding a wine decanter*[3] *and glasses. The Left wall has a door Upstage, and Downstage a writing desk with a straight chair in front of it. Near the desk is an armchair. Down Right is a small sofa with a table holding a lamp at the Upstage end of it. There are pictures on the walls. The room looks rather stuffy and unlived in.*

1. *Macías* (mä sē′ əs)
2. France's King *Louis XVI* lived a life of luxury and elegance until he was beheaded in 1793 during the French Revolution.
3. A *decanter* is a decorative bottle with a stopper.

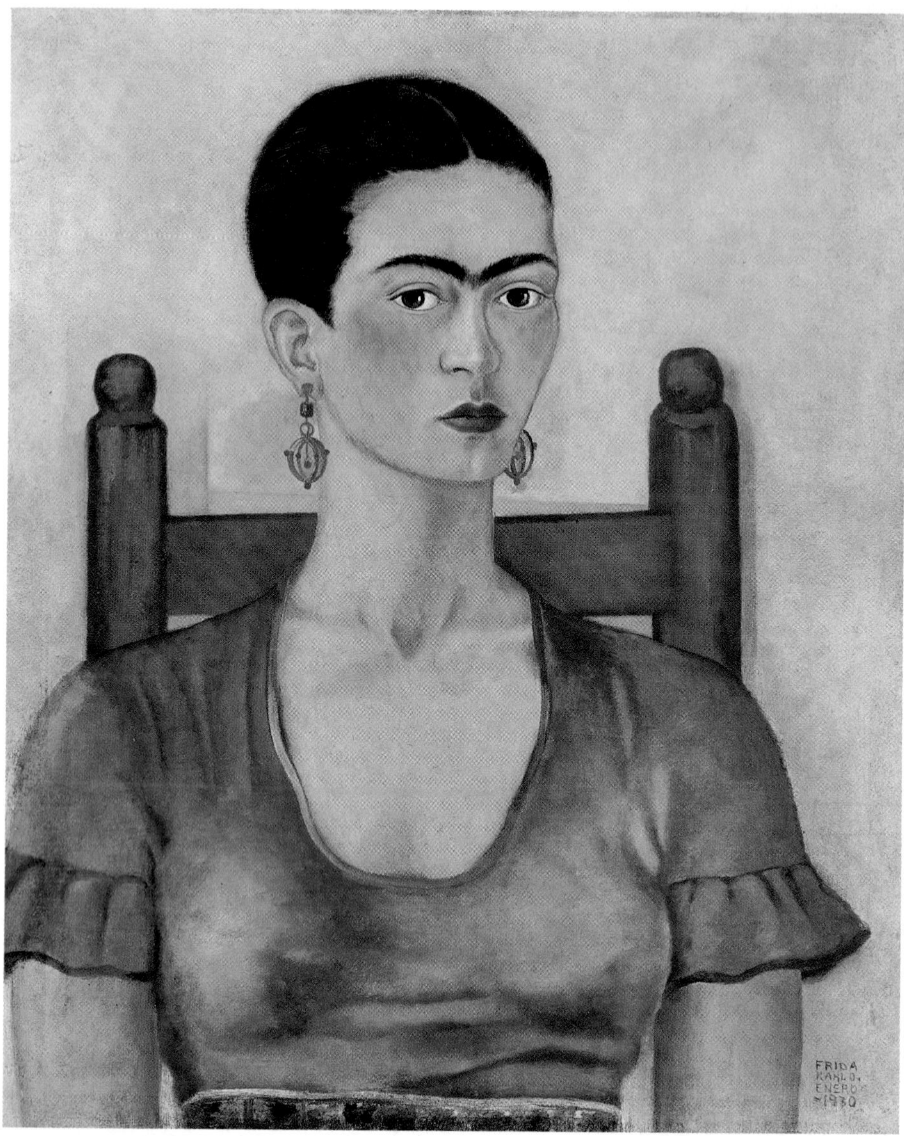

Self-Portrait, 1930. Frida Kahlo. Oil on canvas, 25½ x 21⅛ in. Museum of Fine Arts, Boston. Anonymous loan.

Viewing the painting: Is the woman portrayed here closer to the image you have developed of Marica or of Raquel? Explain.

When the curtains part, the stage is in darkness save for the moonlight that comes through the French windows. Then the house door opens and a young girl in negligee enters stealthily. She is carrying a lighted candle. She stands at the door a moment listening for possible pursuit, then moves quickly across to the bookcase Down Right. She puts the candle on top of the bookcase and begins searching behind the books. She finally finds what she wants: a small bottle. While she is searching, the house door opens silently and a woman, also in negligee, enters. (These negligees are in the latest Parisian style.) She moves silently across the room to the table by the sofa, and as the girl turns with the bottle, the woman switches on the light. The girl gives a half-scream and draws back, frightened. The light reveals her to be quite young—no more than twenty—a timid, dovelike creature. The woman has a queenly air, and whether she is actually beautiful or not, people think she is. She is about thirty-two.]

MARICA. [*Trying to hide the bottle behind her.*] Raquel! What are you doing here?

RAQUEL. What did you have hidden behind the books, Marica?

MARICA. [*Attempting a forced laugh.*] I? Nothing. Why do you think I have anything?

RAQUEL. [*Taking a step toward her.*] Give it to me.

MARICA. [*Backing away from her.*] No. No, I won't.

RAQUEL. [*Stretching out her hand.*] I demand that you give it to me.

MARICA. You have no right to order me about. I'm a married woman. I . . . I . . . [*She begins to sob and flings herself down on the sofa.*]

RAQUEL. [*Much gentler.*] You shouldn't be up. The doctor told you to stay in bed. [*She bends over* MARICA *and gently takes the bottle out of the girl's hand.*] It was poison. I thought so.

MARICA. [*Frightened.*] You won't tell the priest, will you?

RAQUEL. Suicide is a sin, Marica. A sin against God.

MARICA. I know. I . . . [*She catches* RAQUEL*'s hand.*] Oh, Raquel, why do we have to have wars? Why do men have to go to war and be killed?

RAQUEL. Men must fight for what they believe is right. It is an honorable thing to die for your country as a soldier.

MARICA. How can you say that with Domingo[4] out there fighting, too? And fighting what? Men who aren't even men. Peasants. Ranch slaves. Men who shouldn't be allowed to fight.

RAQUEL. Peasants are men, Marica. Not animals.

MARICA. Men. It's always men. But how about the women? What becomes of us?

RAQUEL. We can pray.

MARICA. [*Bitterly.*] Yes, we can pray. And then comes the terrible news, and it's no use praying any more. All the reason for our praying is dead. Why should I go on living with Tomás[5] dead?

RAQUEL. Living is a duty.

MARICA. How can you be so cold, so hard? You are a cold and hard woman, Raquel. My brother worships you. He has never even looked at another woman since the first day he saw you. Does he know how cold and hard you are?

RAQUEL. Domingo is my—honored husband.

MARICA. You've been married for ten years. And I've been married for three months. If Domingo is killed, it won't be the same for you. You've had ten years. [*She is crying wildly.*] I haven't anything . . . anything at all.

RAQUEL. You've had three months—three months of laughter. And now you have tears. How lucky you are. You have tears. Perhaps five months of tears. Not more. You're only twenty. And in five months Tomás will become just a lovely memory.

MARICA. I'll remember Tomás all my life.

RAQUEL. Of course. But he'll be distant and far away. But you're young . . . and the young need laughter. The young can't live on tears. And one day in Paris, or Rome, or even Mexico City, you'll meet another man. You'll marry again. There will be children in your house. How lucky you are.

MARICA. I'll never marry again.

RAQUEL. You're only twenty. You'll think differently when you're twenty-eight, or nine, or thirty.

MARICA. What will you do if Domingo is killed?

RAQUEL. I shall be very proud that he died in all his courage . . . in all the greatness of a hero.

4. *Domingo* (də ming′ gō)

5. *Tomás* (tō mäs′)

MARICA. But you'd not weep, would you? Not you! I don't think there are any tears in you.

RAQUEL. No, I'd not weep. I'd sit here in this empty house and wait.

MARICA. Wait for what?

RAQUEL. For the jingle of his spurs as he walks across the tiled hall. For the sound of his laughter in the patio. For the echo of his voice as he shouts to the groom to put away his horse. For the feel of his hand . . .

MARICA. [*Screams.*] Stop it!

RAQUEL. I'm sorry.

MARICA. You do love him, don't you?

RAQUEL. I don't think even he knows how much.

MARICA. I thought that after ten years people slid away from love. But you and Domingo—why, you're all he thinks about. When he's away from you he talks about you all the time. I heard him say once that when you were out of his sight he was like a man without eyes or ears or hands.

RAQUEL. I know. I, too, know that feeling.

MARICA. Then how could you let him go to war? Perhaps to be killed? How could you?

RAQUEL. [*Sharply.*] Marica, you are of the family Macías. Your family is a family of great warriors. A Macías man was with Ferdinand when the Moors were driven out of Spain. A Macías man was with Cortés when the Aztecans surrendered. Your grandfather fought in the War of Independence. Your own father was executed not twenty miles from this house by the French.[6] Shall his son be any less brave because he loves a woman?

MARICA. But Domingo loved you enough to forget that. If you had asked him, he wouldn't have gone to war. He would have stayed here with you.

RAQUEL. No, he would not have stayed. Your brother is a man of honor, not a whining, creeping coward.

MARICA. [*Beginning to cry again.*] I begged Tomás not to go. I begged him.

RAQUEL. Would you have loved him if he had stayed?

MARICA. I don't know. I don't know.

RAQUEL. There is your answer. You'd have despised him. Loved and despised him. Now come, Marica, it's time for you to go to bed.

MARICA. You won't tell the priest—about the poison, I mean?

RAQUEL. No. I won't tell him.

MARICA. Thank you, Raquel. How good you are. How kind and good.

RAQUEL. A moment ago I was hard and cruel. What a baby you are. Now, off to bed with you.

MARICA. Aren't you coming upstairs, too?

RAQUEL. No . . . I haven't been sleeping very well lately. I think I'll read for a little while.

MARICA. Good night, Raquel. And thank you.

RAQUEL. Good night, little one.

[*MARICA goes out through the house door Left, taking her candle with her. RAQUEL stares down at the bottle of poison in her hand, then puts it away in one of the small drawers of the desk. She next selects a book from the Downstage case and sits on the sofa to read it, but feeling chilly, she rises and goes to the closet, Back Right, and takes out an afghan.*[7] *Coming back to the sofa, she makes herself comfortable, with the afghan across her knees.*

6. In 1492 *Ferdinand* of Aragon defeated the *Moors,* a Muslim people from northwest Africa who had controlled most of Spain since the 700s. Through the *War of Independence,* Mexico won freedom from Spain in 1821. The *French* invaded and occupied Mexico City in 1863.

7. An *afghan* is a knitted or crocheted wool blanket.

Suddenly she hears a noise in the patio. She listens, then convinced it is nothing, returns to her reading. But she hears the noise again. She goes to the patio door and peers out.]

RAQUEL. [*Calling softly.*] Who's there? Who's out there? Oh! [*She gasps and backs into the room. Two men—or rather a man and a young boy—dressed in the white pajama suits of the Mexican peasants, with their sombreros tipped low over their faces, come into the room. Raquel draws herself up regally. Her voice is cold and commanding.*] Who are you, and what do you want here?

ANDRÉS. We are hunting for the wife of General Macías.

RAQUEL. I am Raquel Rivera de Macías.

ANDRÉS. Cleto, stand guard in the patio. If you hear any suspicious noise, warn me at once.

CLETO. Yes, my captain. [*The boy returns to the patio.*]

[*The man, hooking his thumbs in his belt, strolls around the room, looking it over. When he reaches the table at the back he sees the wine. With a small bow to* RAQUEL *he pours himself a glass of wine and drains it. He wipes his mouth with the back of his hand.*]

RAQUEL. How very interesting.

ANDRÉS. [*Startled.*] What?

RAQUEL. To be able to drink wine with that hat on.

ANDRÉS. The hat? Oh, forgive me, señora. [*He flicks the brim with his fingers so that it drops off his head and dangles down his back from the neck cord.*] In a military camp one forgets one's polite manners. Would you care to join me in another glass?

RAQUEL. [*Sitting on the sofa.*] Why not? It's my wine.

ANDRÉS. And very excellent wine. [*He pours two glasses and gives her one while he is talking.*] I would say Amontillado[8] of the vintage of '87.

RAQUEL. Did you learn that in a military camp?

ANDRÉS. I used to sell wines . . . among other things.

RAQUEL. [*Ostentatiously hiding a yawn.*] I am devastated.

ANDRÉS. [*Pulls over the armchair and makes himself comfortable in it.*] You don't mind, do you?

RAQUEL. Would it make any difference if I did?

ANDRÉS. No. The Federals are searching the streets for us, and we have to stay somewhere. But women of your class seem to expect that senseless sort of question.

RAQUEL. Of course I suppose I could scream.

ANDRÉS. Naturally.

RAQUEL. My sister-in-law is upstairs asleep. And there are several servants in the back of the house. Mostly men servants. Very big men.

ANDRÉS. Very interesting. [*He is drinking the wine in small sips with much enjoyment.*]

RAQUEL. What would you do if I screamed?

ANDRÉS. [*Considering the request as though it were another glass of wine.*] Nothing.

RAQUEL. I am afraid you are lying to me.

ANDRÉS. Women of your class seem to expect polite little lies.

8. *Amontillado* (ə môn′ til ä′ dō) is a kind of sherry, which is a strong wine.

Vocabulary

regally (rē′ gəl lē) *adv.* in a grand, dignified manner befitting a king or queen

ostentatiously (os′ tən tā′ shəs lē) *adv.* in a way intended to attract attention or impress others

RAQUEL. Stop calling me "woman of your class."

ANDRÉS. Forgive me.

RAQUEL. You are one of the fighting peasants, aren't you?

ANDRÉS. I am a captain in the Revolutionary Army.

RAQUEL. This house is completely loyal to the Federal government.

ANDRÉS. I know. That's why I'm here.

RAQUEL. And now that you are here, just what do you expect me to do?

ANDRÉS. I expect you to offer sanctuary to myself and to Cleto.

RAQUEL. Cleto? [*She looks toward the patio and adds sarcastically.*] Oh, your army.

CLETO. [*Appearing in the doorway.*] I'm sorry, my captain. I just heard a noise. [*RAQUEL stands. ANDRÉS moves quickly to her and puts his hands on her arms from the back. CLETO has turned and is peering into the patio. Then the boy relaxes.*] We are still safe, my captain. It was only a rabbit. [*He goes back into the patio. RAQUEL pulls away from ANDRÉS and goes to the desk.*]

RAQUEL. What a magnificent army you have. So clever. I'm sure you must win many victories.

ANDRÉS. We do. And we will win the greatest victory, remember that.

RAQUEL. This farce has gone on long enough. Will you please take your army and climb over the patio wall with it?

ANDRÉS. I told you that we came here so that you could give us sanctuary.

RAQUEL. My dear captain—captain without a name . . .

ANDRÉS. Andrés de la O, your servant. [*He makes a bow.*]

RAQUEL. [*Startled.*] Andrés de la O!

ANDRÉS. I am flattered. You have heard of me.

RAQUEL. Naturally. Everyone in the city has heard of you. You have a reputation for politeness—especially to women.

ANDRÉS. I see that the tales about me have lost nothing in the telling.

RAQUEL. I can't say. I'm not interested in gossip about your type of soldier.

ANDRÉS. Then let me give you something to heighten your interest. [*He suddenly takes her in his arms and kisses her. She stiffens for a moment, then remains perfectly still. He steps away from her.*]

RAQUEL. [*Rage forcing her to whisper.*] Get out of here—at once!

ANDRÉS. [*Staring at her in admiration.*] I can understand why Macías loves you. I couldn't before, but now I can understand it.

RAQUEL. Get out of my house.

ANDRÉS. [*Sits on the sofa and pulls a small leather pouch out of his shirt. He pours its contents into his hand.*] So cruel, señora, and I with a present for you? Here is a holy medal. My mother gave me this medal. She died when I was ten. She was a street beggar. She died of starvation. But I wasn't there. I was in jail. I had been sentenced to five years in prison for stealing five oranges. The judge thought it a great joke. One year for each orange. He laughed. He had a very loud laugh. [*Pause.*] I killed him two months ago. I hanged him to the telephone pole in front of his house. And I laughed. [*Pause.*] I also have a very loud laugh. [*RAQUEL abruptly turns her back on him.*] I told that story to a girl the other night and she thought it very funny. But of course she was a peasant girl—a girl who could neither read nor write.

She hadn't been born in a great house in Tabasco.[9] She didn't have an English governess.[10] She didn't go to school to the nuns in Paris. She didn't marry one of the richest young men in the Republic. But she thought my story very funny. Of course she could understand it. Her brother had been whipped to death because he had run away from the plantation that owned him. [*He pauses and looks at her. She does not move.*]

9. On the southern coast of the Gulf of Mexico, *Tabasco* is one of Mexico's thirty-five states.
10. A *governess* is a woman employed to teach children in a private household.

Are you still angry with me? Even though I have brought you a present? [*He holds out his hand.*] A very nice present—from your husband.

RAQUEL. [*Turns and stares at him in amazement.*] A present! From Domingo?

ANDRÉS. I don't know him that well. I call him the General Macías.

RAQUEL. [*Excitedly.*] Is he well? How does he look? [*With horrified comprehension.*] He's a prisoner . . . your prisoner!

ANDRÉS. Naturally. That's why I know so much about you. He talks about you constantly.

From Porfirismo to the Revolution, 1955–1966. David Alfaro Siqueiros. Mural (detail), Acrílico/triplay, 420 square meters. Museo National de Historia. Castillo de Chapultepec, Mexico City.

Viewing the art: How do the characteristics of these people help you understand the actions and attitudes of Andrés and Cleto?

RAQUEL. You know nothing about him. You're lying to me.

[*CLETO comes to the window.*]

ANDRÉS. I assure you, señora . . .

CLETO. [*Interrupting.*] My captain . . .

ANDRÉS. What is it, Cleto? Another rabbit?

CLETO. No, my captain. There are soldiers at the end of the street. They are searching all the houses. They will be here soon.

ANDRÉS. Don't worry. We are quite safe here. Stay in the patio until I call you.

CLETO. Yes, my captain. [*He returns to the patio.*]

RAQUEL. You are not safe here. When those soldiers come I shall turn you over to them.

ANDRÉS. I think not.

RAQUEL. You can't escape from them. And they are not kind to you peasant prisoners. They have good reason not to be.

ANDRÉS. Look at this ring. [*He holds his hand out, with the ring on his palm.*]

RAQUEL. Why, it's—a wedding ring.

ANDRÉS. Read the inscription inside of it. [*As she hesitates, he adds sharply.*] Read it!

RAQUEL. [*Slowly takes the ring. While she is reading her voice fades to a whisper.*] "D. M.—R. R.—June 2, 1902." Where did you get this?

ANDRÉS. General Macías gave it to me.

RAQUEL. [*Firmly and clearly.*] Not this ring. He'd never give you this ring. [*With dawning horror.*] He's dead. You stole it from his dead finger. He's dead.

ANDRÉS. Not yet. But he will be dead if I don't return to camp safely by sunset tomorrow.

RAQUEL. I don't believe you. I don't believe you. You're lying to me.

ANDRÉS. This house is famous for its loyalty to the Federal government. You will hide me until those soldiers get out of this district. When it is safe enough Cleto and I will leave. But if you betray me to them, your husband will be shot tomorrow evening at sunset. Do you understand? [*He shakes her arm. RAQUEL looks dazedly at him. CLETO comes to the window.*]

CLETO. The soldiers are coming closer, my captain. They are at the next house.

ANDRÉS. [*To RAQUEL.*] Where shall we hide? [*RAQUEL is still dazed. He gives her another little shake.*] Think, woman! If you love your husband at all—think!

RAQUEL. I don't know. Marica upstairs—the servants in the rest of the house—I don't know.

ANDRÉS. The General has bragged to us about you. He says you are braver than most men. He says you are very clever. This is a time to be both brave and clever.

CLETO. [*Pointing to the closet.*] What door is that?

RAQUEL. It's a closet . . . a storage closet.

ANDRÉS. We'll hide in there.

RAQUEL. It's very small. It's not big enough for both of you.

ANDRÉS. Cleto, hide yourself in there.

CLETO. But, my captain . . .

ANDRÉS. That's an order! Hide yourself.

CLETO. Yes, Sir. [*He steps inside the closet.*]

ANDRÉS. And now, señora, where are you going to hide me?

RAQUEL. How did you persuade my husband to give you his ring?

ANDRÉS. That's a very long story, señora, for which we have no time just now. [*He puts the ring and medal back in the pouch and thrusts it inside his shirt.*] Later I will be glad to give you all the details. But at present it is only necessary for you to remember that his life depends upon mine.

RAQUEL. Yes—yes, of course. [*She loses her dazed expression and seems to grow more queenly as she takes command of the situation.*] Give me your hat. [*ANDRÉS shrugs and passes it over to her. She takes it to the closet and hands it to CLETO.*] There is a smoking jacket hanging up in there. Hand it to me. [*CLETO hands her a man's velvet smoking jacket. She brings it to ANDRÉS.*] Put this on.

ANDRÉS. [*Puts it on and looks down at himself.*] Such a pity my shoes are not comfortable slippers.

RAQUEL. Sit in that chair. [*She points to the armchair.*]

ANDRÉS. My dear lady . . .

RAQUEL. If I must save your life, allow me to do it in my own way. Sit down. [*ANDRÉS sits. She picks up the afghan from the couch and throws it over his feet and legs, carefully tucking it in so that his body is covered to the waist.*] If anyone speaks to you, don't answer. Don't turn your head. As far as you are concerned, there is no one in this room—not even me. Just look straight ahead of you and . . .

ANDRÉS. [*As she pauses.*] And what?

RAQUEL. I started to say "and pray," but since you're a member of the Revolutionary Army I don't suppose you believe in God and prayer.

ANDRÉS. My mother left me a holy medal.

RAQUEL. Oh, yes, I remember. A very amusing story. [*There is the sound of men's voices in the patio.*] The Federal soldiers are here. If you can pray, ask God to keep Marica upstairs. She is very young and very stupid. She'll betray you before I can shut her mouth.

ANDRÉS. I'll . . .

RAQUEL. Silence! Stare straight ahead of you and pray. [*She goes to the French window and speaks loudly to the soldiers.*] Really! What is the meaning of this uproar?

FLORES. [*Off.*] Do not alarm yourself, señora. [*He comes into the room. He wears the uniform of a Federal officer.*] I am Captain Basilio Flores, at your service, señora.

RAQUEL. What do you mean, invading my house and making so much noise at this hour of the night?

FLORES. We are hunting for two spies. One of them is the notorious Andrés de la O. You may have heard of him, señora.

RAQUEL. [*Looking at ANDRÉS.*] Considering what he did to my cousin—yes, I've heard of him.

FLORES. Your cousin, señora?

RAQUEL. [*Comes to ANDRÉS and puts her hand on his shoulder. He stares woodenly in front of him.*] Felipe[11] was his prisoner before the poor boy managed to escape.

FLORES. Is it possible? [*He crosses to ANDRÉS.*] Captain Basilio Flores, at your service. [*He salutes.*]

RAQUEL. Felipe doesn't hear you. He doesn't even know you are in the room.

FLORES. Eh, it is a sad thing.

RAQUEL. Must your men make so much noise?

FLORES. The hunt must be thorough, señora. And now if some of my men can go through here to the rest of the house . . .

RAQUEL. Why?

FLORES. But I told you, señora. We are hunting for two spies . . .

RAQUEL. [*Speaking quickly from controlled nervousness.*] And do you think I have them

11. *Felipe* (fə lē′ pā)

Vocabulary
notorious (nō tôr′ ē əs) *adj.* widely and unfavorably known

hidden someplace, and I the wife of General Macías?

FLORES. General Macías! But I didn't know . . .

RAQUEL. Now that you do know, I suggest you remove your men and their noise at once.

FLORES. But, señora, I regret—I still have to search this house.

RAQUEL. I can assure you, captain, that I have been sitting here all evening, and no peasant spy has passed me and gone into the rest of the house.

FLORES. Several rooms open off the patio, señora. They needn't have come through here.

RAQUEL. So . . . you do think I conceal spies in this house. Then search it by all means. Look under the sofa . . . under the table. In the drawers of the desk. And don't miss that closet, captain. Inside that closet is hidden a very fierce and wicked spy.

FLORES. Please, señora . . .

RAQUEL. [*Goes to the closet door.*] Or do you prefer me to open it for you?

FLORES. I am only doing my duty, señora. You are making it very difficult.

RAQUEL. [*Relaxing against the door.*] I'm sorry. My sister-in-law is upstairs. She has just received word that her husband has been killed. They were married three months ago. She's only twenty. I didn't want . . .

MARICA. [*Calling off.*] Raquel, what is all that noise downstairs?

Wall with a Door and Tree (Muro con Puerta y Arbol). Pablo Burchard (1875–1964).

Viewing the painting: What is the mood of this painting? How does it compare with the mood in the play?

RAQUEL. [*Goes to the house door and calls.*] It is nothing. Go back to bed.

MARICA. But I can hear men's voices in the patio.

RAQUEL. It is only some Federal soldiers hunting for two peasant spies. [*She turns and speaks rapidly to* FLORES.] If she comes down here, she must not see my cousin. Felipe escaped, but her husband was killed. The doctor thinks the sight of my poor cousin might affect her mind. You understand?

FLORES. Certainly, señora. What a sad thing.

MARICA. [*Still off.*] Raquel, I'm afraid! [*She tries to push past* RAQUEL *into the room.* RAQUEL *and* FLORES *stand between her and* ANDRÉS.] Spies! In this house. Oh, Raquel!

RAQUEL. The doctor will be very angry if you don't return to bed at once.

MARICA. But those terrible men will kill us. What is the matter with you two? Why are you standing there like that? [*She tries to see past them, but they both move so that she can't see* ANDRÉS.]

FLORES. It is better that you go back to your room, señora.

MARICA. But why? Upstairs I am alone. Those terrible men will kill me. I know they will.

FLORES. Don't be afraid, señora. There are no spies in this house.

MARICA. Are you sure?

RAQUEL. Captain Flores means that no spy would dare to take refuge in the house of General Macías. Isn't that right, captain?

FLORES. [*Laughing.*] Of course. All the world knows of the brave General Macías.

RAQUEL. Now go back to bed, Marica. Please, for my sake.

MARICA. You are both acting very strangely. I think you have something hidden in this room you don't want me to see.

RAQUEL. [*Sharply.*] You are quite right. Captain Flores has captured one of the spies. He is sitting in the chair behind me. He is dead. Now will you please go upstairs!

MARICA. [*Gives a stifled sob.*] Oh! That such a terrible thing could happen in this house. [*She runs out of the room, still sobbing.*]

FLORES. [*Worried.*] Was it wise to tell her such a story, señora?

RAQUEL. [*Tense with repressed relief.*] Better that than the truth. Good night, captain, and thank you.

FLORES. Good night, señora. And don't worry. Those spies won't bother you. If they were anywhere in this district, my men would have found them.

RAQUEL. I'm sure of it.

[*The Captain salutes her, looks toward* ANDRÉS *and salutes him, then goes into the patio. He can be heard calling his men. Neither* ANDRÉS *nor* RAQUEL *moves until the voices outside die away. Then* RAQUEL *staggers and nearly falls, but* ANDRÉS *catches her in time.*]

ANDRÉS. [*Calling softly.*] They've gone, Cleto. [ANDRÉS *carries* RAQUEL *to the sofa as* CLETO *comes out of the closet.*] Bring a glass of wine. Quickly.

CLETO. [*As he gets the wine.*] What happened?

ANDRÉS. It's nothing. Just a faint. [*He holds the wine to her lips.*]

CLETO. She's a great lady, that one. When she wanted to open the closet door my knees were trembling, I can tell you.

Vocabulary

repressed (ri prest′) *adj.* held back or kept under control; restrained

ANDRÉS. My own bones were playing a pretty tune.

CLETO. Why do you think she married Macías?

ANDRÉS. Love is a peculiar thing, Cleto.

CLETO. I don't understand it.

RAQUEL. [*Moans and sits up.*] Are they—are they gone?

ANDRÉS. Yes, they're gone. [*He kisses her hand.*] I've never known a braver lady.

RAQUEL. [*Pulling her hand away.*] Will you go now, please?

ANDRÉS. We'll have to wait until the district is free of them—but if you'd like to write a letter to your husband while we're waiting . . .

RAQUEL. [*Surprised at his kindness.*] You'd take it to him? You'd really give it to him?

ANDRÉS. Of course.

RAQUEL. Thank you. [*She goes to the writing desk and sits down.*]

ANDRÉS. [*To* CLETO, *who has been staring steadily at* RAQUEL *all the while.*] You stay here with the señora. I'm going to find out how much of the district has been cleared.

CLETO. [*Still staring at* RAQUEL.] Yes, my captain.

[ANDRÉS *leaves by the French windows.* CLETO *keeps on staring at* RAQUEL *as she starts to write. After a moment she turns to him.*]

RAQUEL. [*Irritated.*] Why do you keep staring at me?

CLETO. Why did you marry a man like that one, señora?

RAQUEL. You're very impertinent.

CLETO. [*Shyly.*] I'm sorry, señora.

RAQUEL. [*After a brief pause.*] What do you mean: "a man like that one"?

CLETO. Well, you're very brave, señora.

RAQUEL. [*Lightly.*] And don't you think the general is very brave?

CLETO. No, señora. Not very.

RAQUEL. [*Staring at him with bewilderment.*] What are you trying to tell me?

CLETO. Nothing, señora. It is none of my affair.

RAQUEL. Come here. [*He comes slowly up to her.*] Tell me what is in your mind.

CLETO. I don't know, señora. I don't understand it. The captain says love is a peculiar thing, but I don't understand it.

RAQUEL. Cleto, did the general willingly give that ring to your captain?

CLETO. Yes, señora.

RAQUEL. Why?

CLETO. The general wanted to save his own life. He said he loved you and he wanted to save his life.

RAQUEL. How would giving that ring to your captain save the general's life?

CLETO. The general's supposed to be shot tomorrow afternoon. But he's talked about you a lot, and when my captain knew we had to come into the city, he thought perhaps we might take refuge here if the Federals got on our trail. So he went to the general and said that if he fixed it so we'd be safe here, my captain would save him from the firing squad.

RAQUEL. Was your trip to the city very important—to your cause, I mean?

CLETO. Indeed yes, señora. The captain got a lot of fine information. It means we'll win the

Vocabulary

impertinent (im purt′ ən ənt) *adj.* inappropriately bold or forward; not showing proper respect or manners

Two Women, 1929. Frida Kahlo. Oil on canvas, 27⅜ x 21 in. Private collection.

Viewing the painting: What different personalities do these two women convey? How do they reflect the differences between Raquel and Marica?

next big battle. My captain is a very clever man, señora.

RAQUEL. Did the general know about this information when he gave his ring to your captain?

CLETO. I don't see how he could help knowing it, señora. He heard us talking about it enough.

RAQUEL. Who knows about that bargain to save the general's life beside you and your captain?

CLETO. No one, señora. The captain isn't one to talk, and I didn't have time to.

RAQUEL. [*While the boy has been talking, the life seems to have drained completely out of her.*] How old are you, Cleto?

CLETO. I don't know, señora. I think I'm twenty, but I don't know.

RAQUEL. [*Speaking more to herself than to him.*] Tomás was twenty.

CLETO. Who is Tomás?

RAQUEL. He was married to my sister-in-law. Cleto, you think my husband is a coward, don't you?

CLETO. [*With embarrassment.*] Yes, señora.

RAQUEL. You don't think any woman is worth it, do you? Worth the price of a great battle, I mean?

CLETO. No, señora. But as the captain says, love is a very peculiar thing.

RAQUEL. If your captain loved a woman as much as the general loves me, would he have given an enemy his ring?

CLETO. Ah, but the captain is a great man, señora.

RAQUEL. And so is my husband a great man. He is of the family Macías. All of that family have been great men. All of them—brave and honorable men. They have always held their honor to be greater than their lives. That is a tradition of their family.

CLETO. Perhaps none of them loved a woman like you, señora.

RAQUEL. How strange you are. I saved you from the Federals because I want to save my husband's life. You call me brave, and yet you call him a coward. There is no difference in what we have done.

CLETO. But you are a woman, señora.

RAQUEL. Has a woman less honor than a man, then?

CLETO. No, señora. Please, I don't know how to say it. The general is a soldier. He has a duty to his own cause. You are a woman. You have a duty to your husband. It is right that you should try to save him. It is not right that he should try to save himself.

RAQUEL. [*Dully.*] Yes, of course. It is right that I should save him. [*Becoming practical again.*] Your captain has been gone some time, Cleto. You'd better find out if he is still safe.

CLETO. Yes, señora. [*As he reaches the French windows she stops him.*]

RAQUEL. Wait, Cleto. Have you a mother—or a wife, perhaps?

CLETO. Oh, no, señora. I haven't anyone but the captain.

RAQUEL. But the captain is a soldier. What would you do if he should be killed?

CLETO. It is very simple, señora. I should be killed, too.

RAQUEL. You speak about death so calmly. Aren't you afraid of it, Cleto?

CLETO. No, señora. It's like the captain says . . . dying for what you believe in—that's the finest death of all.

RAQUEL. And you believe in the Revolutionary cause?

CLETO. Yes, señora. I am a poor peasant, that's true. But still I have a right to live like a man, with my own ground, and my own family, and my own future. [*He stops speaking abruptly.*] I'm sorry, señora. You are a fine lady. You don't understand these things. I must go and find my captain. [*He goes out.*]

RAQUEL. [*Rests her face against her hand.*] He's so young. But Tomás was no older. And he's not afraid. He said so. Oh, Domingo—Domingo! [*She straightens abruptly, takes the bottle of poison from the desk drawer and stares at it. Then she crosses to the decanter and laces the wine with the poison. She hurries back to the desk and is busy writing when* ANDRÉS *and* CLETO *return.*]

ANDRÉS. You'll have to hurry that letter. The district is clear now.

RAQUEL. I'll be through in just a moment. You might as well finish the wine while you're waiting.

ANDRÉS. Thank you. A most excellent idea. [*He pours himself a glass of wine. As he lifts it to his lips she speaks.*]

RAQUEL. Why don't you give some to—Cleto?

ANDRÉS. This is too fine a wine to waste on that boy.

RAQUEL. He'll probably never have another chance to taste such wine.

ANDRÉS. Very well. Pour yourself a glass, Cleto.

CLETO. Thank you. [*He pours it.*] Your health, my captain.

RAQUEL. [*Quickly.*] Drink it outside, Cleto. I want to speak to your captain. [*The boy looks at* ANDRÉS, *who jerks his head toward the patio.* CLETO *nods and goes out.*] I want you to give my husband a message for me. I can't write it. You'll have to remember it. But first, give me a glass of wine, too.

ANDRÉS. [*Pouring the wine.*] It might be easier for him if you wrote it.

RAQUEL. I think not. [*She takes the glass.*] I want you to tell him that I never knew how much I loved him until tonight.

ANDRÉS. Is that all?

RAQUEL. Yes. Tell me, captain, do you think it possible to love a person too much?

ANDRÉS. Yes, señora. I do.

RAQUEL. So do I. Let us drink a toast, captain—to honor. To bright and shining honor.

ANDRÉS. [*Raises his glass.*] To honor. [*He drains his glass. She lifts hers almost to her lips and then puts it down. From the patio comes a faint cry.*]

CLETO. [*Calling faintly in a cry that fades into silence.*] Captain. Captain.

[ANDRÉS *sways, his hand trying to brush across his face as though trying to brush sense into his head. When he hears* CLETO *he tries to stagger toward the window but stumbles and can't quite make it. Hanging on to the table by the sofa he looks accusingly at her. She shrinks back against her chair.*]

ANDRÉS. [*His voice weak from the poison.*] Why?

RAQUEL. Because I love him. Can you understand that?

ANDRÉS. We'll win. The Revolution will win. You can't stop that.

RAQUEL. Yes, you'll win. I know that now.

ANDRÉS. That girl—she thought my story was funny—about the hanging. But you didn't . . .

RAQUEL. I'm glad you hanged him. I'm glad.

[ANDRÉS *looks at her and tries to smile. He manages to pull the pouch from his shirt and extend it to her. But it drops from his hand.*]

RAQUEL. [*Runs to French window and calls.*] Cleto. Cleto! [*She buries her face in her hands for a moment, then comes back to* ANDRÉS. *She kneels beside him and picks up the leather pouch. She opens it and, taking the ring, puts it on her finger. Then she sees the medal. She rises and, pulling out the chain from her own throat, she slides the medal on to the chain. Then she walks to the sofa and sinks down on it.*]

MARICA. [*Calling off.*] Raquel! Raquel! [RAQUEL *snaps off the lamp, leaving the room in darkness.* MARICA *opens the house door. She is carrying a candle which she shades with her hand. The light is too dim to reveal the dead* ANDRÉS.] What are you doing down here in the dark? Why don't you come to bed?

RAQUEL. [*Making an effort to speak.*] I'll come in just a moment.

MARICA. But what are you doing, Raquel?

RAQUEL. Nothing. Just listening . . . listening to an empty house.

QUICK CURTAIN

Responding to Literature

Personal Response

What did you find most surprising in this play? Share your reactions with a classmate.

Analyzing Literature

Recall

1. When the play opens, what two characters are on stage? What do they discuss?
2. Who enters the home of General Macías? Why do they come there?
3. How has Raquel felt about her husband? What does she learn about him from the intruders?
4. What does Raquel learn in her conversation with Cleto?
5. What does Raquel eventually do to the intruders?

Intrepret

6. Which of the two women in the play is wiser or more capable? How do you know?
7. In your own words, summarize the political differences between the intruders and General Macías and his wife.
8. How does the intruders' information about her husband affect Raquel? Use specific details from the selection to support your response.
9. What does Raquel's conversation with Cleto reveal about her values?
10. What conflicting thoughts and emotions does Raquel experience near the end of the play? Why do you think she does what she does? Support your ideas with details from the play.

Evaluate and Connect

11. **Theme Connections** Explain how this play concerns both loyalty and betrayal.
12. Think about your response to the Reading Focus on page 878. How do the characters in this play demonstrate bravery? Why do they act bravely? Add their actions to your cluster map.
13. In your opinion, is Raquel a heroine? Explain your answer.
14. In what ways does this play help an audience understand the early part of the Mexican Revolution?
15. What do the ring of General Macías and the medal of Andrés **symbolize** to their owners? What do they represent to Raquel?

Irony

Irony is a contrast between reality and what seems to be real. There are different kinds of irony, all of which can be found in this play. **Verbal irony** exists when a person says one thing but means another. For example, when Raquel says, "What a magnificent army you have," she actually means the opposite and is insulting Andrés de la O and Cleto. **Situational irony** occurs when a situation has an outcome that is the opposite of what someone has expected. **Dramatic irony** occurs when the audience has important information that the characters do not have. For example, the audience knows that Andrés de la O is sitting in the room where the Federal soldiers are searching for him, but the soldiers do not recognize him.

1. Find another example of verbal irony and dramatic irony in the play. Explain why each is ironic.
2. Which of the outcomes in this play is an example of situational irony? Explain your answer.

- See **Literary Terms Handbook,** p. R6.

Literature and Writing

Writing About Literature

Exploring Suspense When an audience is waiting anxiously to find out what happens next, the writer has created suspense. In this play, when does the audience experience suspense? What actions or developments cause the suspense? In two or three paragraphs, explore how Niggli's use of suspense helps to make the drama more exciting.

Creative Writing

Write a New Scene What happens next? Will General Macías be executed? Will Raquel continue the myth of her husband's bravery? How will she explain her earlier actions with the Federal soldiers? Write a new scene to extend the play, using the standard form for a play script. Use dialogue and stage directions that remain true to the personalities of the original characters.

Extending Your Response

Literature Groups

Codes of Honor Search the play for statements that reveal the characters' assumptions about what honor requires of men and women. Then, as a group, decide what you think the playwright's intention might have been. Do you think Niggli wants to make a point about male and female roles, or is her purpose to depict a historical situation in which male and female roles happened to overlap? Share your ideas with another group.

Performing

Making a Scene Choose one segment of this play, and work with a small group to bring it to life. First, assign parts. Then discuss staging: where you will perform, how you will enter and leave the stage set, and what simple furnishings and props you will need. Base your choices on the scene's setting and the message it conveys. Rehearse your segment. Then perform it for the class.

Learning for Life

Incident Report Imagine that you are an investigator sent to gather information and report on the death of Captain Andrés de la O. With a partner, create a report that clearly presents the facts of what happened.

Reading Further

For more about the Mexican Revolution, you might also be interested in the following work:

Revolution! Mexico 1910–1920, by Ronald Atkin, information about the causes, people, places, and effects of the Mexican Revolution.

Save your work for your portfolio.

VOCABULARY • Connotation

The definition of a word is called its **denotation.** The positive and negative associations of a word are called its **connotation.** Words with the same denotations can have different connotations. For example, *scrawny* and *slender* are both synonyms of *thin,* but the word *scrawny* suggests a malnourished skinniness, whereas the word *slender* suggests a pleasing slimness. The way a word is used reveals its connotation.

PRACTICE For each pair of synonyms, write a brief description of how the words' connotations differ.

1. *ambitious* and *pushy*
2. *frown* and *scowl*
3. *destiny* and *doom*
4. *fragile* and *flimsy*
5. *risk* and *menace*

Before You Read

Marked

Reading Focus

How can an individual stay true to what he or she believes?

List Ideas With a partner, make a list of personal values that could help someone remain true to himself or herself.

Setting a Purpose Read to discover how one mother suggests that her daughter remain true to herself.

Building Background

Did You Know?

Following Tradition In her poem "Marked," Carmen Tafolla uses the word *m'ija,* a contraction of the Spanish words *mi* ("my") and *hija* ("daughter"). By calling the reader *m'ija,* Tafolla follows the Mexican American tradition of addressing all readers as if they were her own children and makes the poem a message to the reader.

Idiom Meanings The phrase *make your mark,* or *make one's mark,* is an idiom, or common expression. Like many words and phrases, it has more than one meaning. For example, in a time when many people were illiterate, *to make one's mark* meant to sign something by drawing a symbol, such as a cross or X. *To make one's mark* also means "to achieve success or fame" or "to distinguish oneself." "When I speak about making your mark," says Carmen Tafolla, "I'm talking about . . . what you do with your life."

Adjective Meanings The adjective *marked* also has multiple meanings. When something is marked, it visibly reveals some special quality or characteristic. That characteristic may even be a flaw, or imperfection. In this poem, the poet mentions "turquoise / marked." Pure turquoise is a blue-green, sky blue, or green mineral. But most turquoise is not pure: it includes a pattern of brown or black veins of other minerals. These markings are technically flaws in the turquoise stone, yet many people think that the pattern is what makes a piece of turquoise unique and valuable.

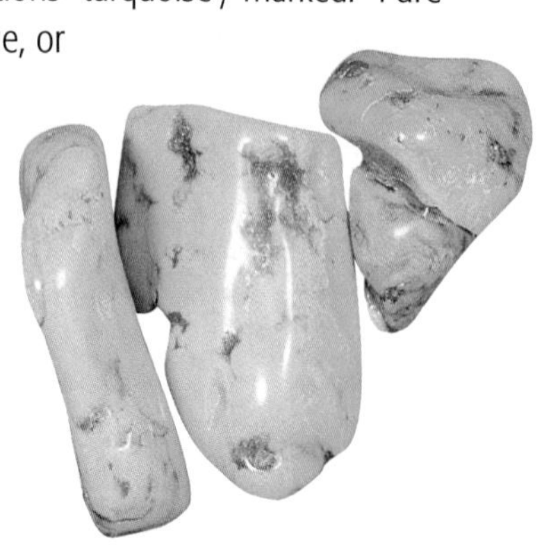

Meet Carmen Tafolla

"I have always told my children not to be ashamed to be who they are," says Carmen Tafolla (kär′ men tä fō′ yä). A native of San Antonio, Texas, Tafolla declares her identity in works ranging from poetry to screenplays. She explains that "as a Mexican American growing up in the 50s and 60s, I came from a group that was not often represented in textbooks. I saw no reflections of my own culture, and I longed to record the beauty and uniqueness of the culture that surrounded me." Tafolla is currently at work on her autobiography.

Carmen Tafolla was born in 1951.

Marked

Carmen Tafolla

Never write with pencil,
m'ija
It is for those
who would
erase.
Make your mark proud
and open,
Brave,
beauty folded into
its imperfection,
Like a piece of turquoise
marked.

Never write
with pencil,
m'ija.
Write with ink
or mud,
or berries grown in
gardens never owned,
or, sometimes,
if necessary,
blood.

Collage Series II, No. 3, 1993. Katherine S. Nemanich. Oil pastel on paper and board, 12 x 9 in. Private collection.

Responding to Literature

Personal Response

How do you react to the message in this poem? Record your response in your journal.

Analyzing Literature

Recall and Interpret

1. What instruction does the speaker give her daughter in the first line? What does she mean by "those who would erase"? In your opinion, why might the poet have chosen to repeat this instruction?
2. According to the speaker, what should the girl write with? What might these materials symbolize?
3. Where does a reference to the title word appear in the poem? In your opinion, why might the poet have chosen this word as the title?
4. The poet uses a **simile** in line eleven to describe the type of mark the girl is instructed to make. What things does the poet compare through this simile? What does the simile add to the idea of making one's mark? (See Literary Terms Handbook, page R12.)

Evaluate and Connect

5. **Theme Connections** Why might this poem appear in a group of selections about loyalty and betrayal?
6. Think about your response to the Reading Focus on page 896. How do the qualities you listed compare with the qualities the poem values?
7. In your opinion, what are examples of ways someone might follow the advice given in the poem?
8. Are there any situations for which you would not recommend someone to follow the advice in the poem? Explain your answer.

Literary **ELEMENTS**

Free Verse

Free verse is poetry that has no fixed pattern of meter, rhyme, line length, or stanza arrangement. For example, in "Marked," Tafolla has created two stanzas, but the stanzas are of unequal length: the first has twelve lines; the second has ten. Also, the words at the ends of lines–with two exceptions–do not rhyme, and the lines are composed of varying numbers of syllables.

1. Explain why you think Tafolla chose free verse to convey the message in this poem.
2. Why, do you think, did Tafolla use unusual spacing to set off words and phrases such as *and open, marked, or mud,* and *blood*?

- See **Literary Terms Handbook,** p. R5.

Extending Your Response

Literature Groups

Good or Bad Advice? With a group, share your opinions about the advice in this poem. Is the advice universally good, is it only good some of the time, or is it misleading or bad? Referring to the exact words of the poem, discuss the situations in which the advice might be most sound. Then compare your opinions with those of another group. Do any of their insights make you rethink your own?

Listening and Speaking

Mark My Words Working with a partner, think about how you would advise middle school students to make their mark in high school. Then state your advice in a short speech or two stanzas of free verse. Practice reading the work aloud, each of you reading specific passages. When you are ready, present your advice to another pair of students, and invite their reactions.

Save your work for your portfolio.

COMPARING selections

The Ring of General Macías
A Drama of the Mexican Revolution
and *Marked*

COMPARE **ROLES**

Both the play and the poem spotlight girls or women. Discuss these questions:

1. In what ways do both the play and the poem suggest or show that girls and women are capable of acting bravely or of fulfilling roles once reserved for men?
2. Do the concerns of these works relate to all women and girls, or to specific groups of them? Do the concerns relate similarly to men and boys? Give reasons for your answer.

Female firefighter, Colorado.

COMPARE **MESSAGES**

In *The Ring of General Macías,* Raquel takes two lives in wartime. In "Marked," part of the poem's advice is to make one's mark in, "if necessary, / blood." Tafolla says she is not advocating violence in this line, but she is suggesting that there are some things for which a person should be willing to give his or her life.

1. Consult media sources, including on-line information services, to find causes in the world today for which people are willing to risk their lives.
2. With a partner, discuss the causes you have researched. Then decide why a character in the play or the speaker in the poem might approve or disapprove of each one.

COMPARE **LOYALTIES**

Loyalty is important in both of these works, yet the object of that loyalty differs.

1. To whom or what do the main characters in the play believe they owe their loyalty? To whom does the speaker in the poem believe loyalty is owed?
2. What are some explanations for these differing ideas of loyalty?

Grammar Link

Misplaced or Dangling Modifiers

The position of a **modifier**–a word or phrase that describes something–determines what it modifies. For example, "Barking with joy, Fred was greeted by his long-lost dog" means that Fred has an unusual way of expressing himself. *Who* was barking with joy? If it was the dog, then the modifying phrase should be placed right next to "long-lost dog." The easiest way to do this is to restructure the sentence. "Barking with joy, the long-lost dog greeted Fred."

A *misplaced modifier* is one that is in the wrong place and, therefore, describes the wrong thing. A *dangling modifier* is one that is meant to modify a word or phrase, but that word or phrase is not present in the sentence. Such a modifier "dangles," attaching itself to nothing.

Correcting a misplaced or a dangling modifier is easy if you think about what you are saying.

Problem 1 A misplaced modifier
Raquel offers to open the closet door pretending to be unconcerned.

Solution The wrong noun is modified. The door is not pretending. Move the misplaced modifier as close as possible to the word it modifies.
Pretending to be unconcerned, Raquel offers to open the closet door.

Problem 2 A dangling modifier
Using poisoned wine, the honor of her husband was protected.

Solution The sentence contains no word for the modifier to logically modify. Rewrite the sentence to include a noun or pronoun for the modifier to modify.
Using poisoned wine, she protected the honor of her husband.

● For information about similar usage problems, see **Language Handbook,** p. R24.

EXERCISE

On your paper, rewrite the sentences to correct misplaced or dangling modifiers.

1. Raquel hears revolutionary soldiers reading on the couch in her living room.
2. Dressed in peasant clothing, Raquel knows who the men must be.
3. While opening a leather pouch, a story of starvation and brutality is told.
4. Andrés tells Raquel about hanging a judge laughing with amusement.
5. Searching all the houses, Cleto notices Federal soldiers.
6. Working quickly, a clever plan is put into action.
7. In the closet, Andrés tells Cleto to remain silent.
8. Captain Flores is hunting for two spies wearing his federal uniform.
9. Sitting as if in a trance, Flores does not realize that Andrés is the man he is seeking.
10. Cleverly responding to each new threat, the plan is successful.

LISTENING, SPEAKING, and VIEWING

Persuasive Speech

When Raquel in *The Ring of General Macías* convinces herself of the importance of "honor," she is speaking persuasively. Persuasive speaking skills are valuable tools, especially when your goal is to influence someone. For example, you might use these skills to convince a business owner to hire you or to present your views on an issue to a school newspaper reporter.

Preparing and Organizing the Speech

- Identify the issue and the stand you are taking. Jot down your thoughts and feelings about the issue.
- State your central claim. A claim statement will help you clarify your main purpose and focus your argument.
- Gather facts, examples, and observations you can use to help the audience see things your way. Rank this evidence by "order of importance."
- Explain how the evidence supports your claim. Then tell the audience why they should accept your evidence.
- Summarize your arguments, explaining why your central claim is the logical conclusion based on your evidence.

Presenting Your Speech

- On note cards, write the main ideas, important details, quotations, and statistics. Number the cards to keep them in order.
- Practice before an audience of relatives or close friends. Try out different tones of voice, gestures, and visual aids. Evaluate your audience's feedback.
- Speak clearly and at a normal pace. Emphasize your key points.
- Make eye contact with your listeners so they feel included.
- Maintain a natural, relaxed stance. Practice before a mirror so you can check your stance and gestures.

ACTIVITY

With a partner, identify two opposing positions on a controversial issue. Prepare a three- to five-minute persuasive speech in support of your side of the issue while your partner prepares a speech for the opposing side. For example, you might support the position that the minimum driving age should be raised, while your partner supports the current minimum driving age. With your partner, practice your speeches and present them to the class.

Writing Workshop

Expository Writing:
Compare-and-Contrast Essay

What makes one literary work stand above the rest? Perhaps the characters are more believable, or the theme is more striking. Maybe the style is better suited to the topic. You can write effective literary criticism by comparing and contrasting these and other elements of literature. Comparing means to discuss similarities between features. Contrasting means to discuss differences. **In this workshop, you will write an essay comparing and contrasting two literary works.**

- As you write your expository essay, refer to **Writing Handbook,** pp. R58–R71.

EVALUATION RUBRIC

By the time you complete this Writing Workshop, you will have

- included a thesis statement about the importance of the two works' similarities and differences
- provided evidence to support your thesis
- organized ideas in a logical, consistent order
- developed a conclusion that restates the thesis and demonstrates how it has been proved
- presented an essay that is free of errors in grammar, usage, and mechanics

The Writing Process

PREWRITING

PREWRITING TIP

It is often helpful to write down your initial impressions about a piece of literature as you read.

Explore ideas

Choose two literary works that develop the themes of loyalty and betrayal. You may wish to use a comparison frame to explore your ideas about the two works. Here is a frame created to compare and contrast *Antigone* and *The American.*

Literary Element	Questions	*Antigone*	*The American*
Theme	How is the theme of loyalty or betrayal addressed?	Antigone's loyalty to brother Polyneices; his betrayal of the state	Newman's loyalty to individual honor; Clair de Cintré's loyalty to family
Style	Formal or informal?	generally formal	somewhat formal
Tone	Serious? Sad? Humorous?	very serious; sad; sentry provides comic relief	light; sometimes sarcastic
Setting	What effect do time and place have?	right after battle; makes loyalty a key issue	France's aristocratic circles in 1868
Plot	What is the main conflict?	Antigone vs. Creon	Christopher Newman vs. the Bellegardes
Characters	How are they presented?	dialogue, actions, choral comments	dialogue, actions, narrator's comments

Consider your purpose

Your purpose is to compare and contrast the two literary works. However, there should be a purpose to your comparison. You should have a thesis about the importance of the similarities and differences. Consider the responses you wrote in the comparison frame; then decide how those similarities and differences affect the themes of loyalty and betrayal. Use your ideas to focus your thesis statement.

Choose an audience

The most important consideration here is whether or not the readers are familiar with both literary works. If they are, you can make indirect references to the works. If they are not, you will have to directly quote passages to support your points.

Make a plan

Organize your essay into a form that your readers can follow and understand. Be sure to provide the basic essay elements of introduction, body, and conclusion.

- In the introduction, state the thesis that you have formed about the importance of the similarities and differences between the two subjects.
- In the body, compare and contrast each element, with specific examples from the literary works. The chart shown below details two methods of organization: (1) by subject and (2) by feature.
- In the conclusion of your essay, restate your thesis and summarize your proof.

How to Organize a Compare-and-Contrast Essay	
By Subject	**By Feature**
Subject 1: *Antigone* Feature A: Theme Feature B: Setting Feature C: Plot **Subject 2: *The American*** Feature A: Theme Feature B: Setting Feature C: Plot	**Feature A: Theme** Subject 1: *Antigone* Subject 2: *The American* **Feature B: Setting** Subject 1: *Antigone* Subject 2: *The American* **Feature C: Plot** Subject 1: *Antigone* Subject 2: *The American*

The number of features being compared determines which method of organization to use. If many features are being compared, organize by feature. Otherwise, your reader may forget what you said about the first subject by the time you discuss the second subject.

Use your method of organization consistently. If you are organizing by subject, keep the features in the same order for each subject. If you are organizing by feature, discuss the features in the same sequence for both subjects.

DRAFTING

Drafting Tip

When comparing two items, use the comparative form of a modifier.

Refer to the Writing Skill "Effective Conclusions" on page 799 to help you draft your conclusion.

Write your draft

As you write, refer to your plan, but focus on getting your key points of comparison down. Don't worry about perfect organization at this stage.

Think of the reader

State each comparison or contrast. Use a term or phrase that clearly states the relationship, such as *like Antigone* or *unlike Newman.*

STUDENT MODEL

The American, a novel by Henry James, and *Antigone*, a play by Sophocles, have striking similarities in the way they explore the theme of loyalty and betrayal. However, *Antigone* gives more weight to the theme than *The American* does.

Complete Student Model on p. R120.

REVISING

Revising Tip

Check off points on your plan and in your draft to make sure no important points are missing.

Evaluate your work

Put your draft aside for a while. Later, read it as if your audience were reading it. Make note of any parts that you think need to be improved. Then use the **Rubric for Revising** to guide you as you revise your draft.

Have a writing conference

Work with a partner to improve your draft. As you read the draft aloud, pay special attention to organization and transitions. Go through the **Rubric for Revising** together. Then make the revisions that seem important to you.

STUDENT MODEL

The themes of both ~~also~~ ~~have something in common~~. They both ~~have characters who are forced to be pitted~~ against the system of the ~~particular~~ societies ~~that these people are~~ in, from those in Thebes to ~~France~~. In *The American*, Newman believes in the power of an individual to make his or her own ~~personal~~ decisions about what is ~~the~~ best ~~thing to do~~.

Complete Student Model on p. R120.

Rubric for Revising

Your revised persuasive essay should have

- ☑ a clear thesis statement giving your opinion of the way two literary works deal with the theme of loyalty and betrayal
- ☑ a consistent organization that compares and contrasts the theme, setting, and plot of each work
- ☑ adequate proof to support each comparison and contrast and to convince readers of the thesis
- ☑ a conclusion that restates the thesis and shows how it has been proved

Your revised essay should be free of

- ☑ passages that are confusing or that do not clearly support the thesis
- ☑ errors in grammar, usage, and mechanics

EDITING/PROOFREADING

Edit your essay to find and correct errors in grammar, usage, mechanics, and spelling. Use the **Proofreading Checklist** on the inside back cover to guide your work.

Grammar Hint

To avoid confusing your readers, place modifying words and phrases as close as possible to the words they modify. In the sentence below, the modifying phrase *like Neuman* should be placed near *Antigone,* the word it modifies.

MISPLACED: Antigone has values that are in conflict with those of the larger society like Newman.

CORRECT: Like Newman, Antigone has values that are in conflict with those of the larger society.

- For more about modifiers, see **Language Handbook,** p. R24.

Complete Student Model

For a complete version of the model developed in this workshop, refer to **Writing Workshop Models**, p. R120.

STUDENT MODEL

The narrator of *The American* often calls Newman "our friend" when ~~he is telling the reader about~~ describing something ~~he~~ Newman did or said, and this comes across as gossipy. Also, the narrator often seems amused by Newman ~~often~~ telling us about how silly or naive ~~his~~ Newman's thoughts are. In *Antigone*, however, the author doesn't seem to find anything amusing about Antigone at all.

Complete Student Model on p. R120.

PUBLISHING/PRESENTING

A week or so before your presentation to the class, you could distribute copies of your essay. This will make it possible for your classmates to prepare for a discussion of the points you have made.

PRESENTING TIP

Begin an oral presentation by reading a significant passage from each literary work.

Reflecting

What new insights have you gained by comparing and contrasting these works? How can such comparisons between works be useful? Jot down your responses.

Identify techniques from this workshop that you could use in other compare-and-contrast writing, such as in history essays. What you've learned here can help you there.

Save your work for your portfolio.

Unit Assessment

Personal Response

1. Which of the plays in this unit would you like to see turned into a film? What actors would you want to star in the leading roles? Explain your choices.
2. How did your work in this unit enhance your skills in the following areas?
   - understanding dialogue that is very different from your own speech
   - identifying elements of drama
   - discussing different interpretations of a line, scene, or play
   - working cooperatively with your classmates

Analyzing Literature

Comparing Two Elements Choose two plays from this unit, and compare them based on one of the elements of drama you studied in the Genre Focus on pages 712–713. For example, you might choose to compare and contrast the character traits of Creon in *Antigone* with those of Caesar in *Julius Caesar,* explaining how the traits of these two characters influence the final outcome of their stories.

Evaluate and Set Goals

Evaluate

1. What was your most valuable contribution to the class as you worked through this unit?
2. What assigned task in this unit did you find most challenging?
   - How did you approach this task?
   - What was the outcome?
3. How would you assess your work in this unit, using the following scale? Give at least two reasons for your assessment.
   4 = outstanding **3** = good **2** = fair **1** = weak

Set Goals

1. Choose a goal to work toward in Unit 5. Concentrate on any skill you wish to improve, such as reading, writing, speaking, or working in a group.
2. Discuss your goal with your teacher.
3. Write down three steps you will take to help you achieve your goal.
4. Plan checkpoints at specific intervals in the unit to assess your progress toward your goal.
5. Include a self-evaluation plan to determine whether you have reached your goal.

Build Your Portfolio

Select Choose two pieces of writing you did in this unit and include them in your portfolio. The following questions can help you make your selection:

- Which pieces do you think would be most interesting to an outside reader?
- Which pieces demonstrate the greatest amount of thought?
- Which pieces demonstrate the greatest amount of creativity?
- Which pieces contain your most polished writing?

Reflect Write some notes to accompany the pieces you selected. Use these questions to guide you.

- What is the strongest aspect of the piece?
- What was the most helpful comment you received regarding this piece? How did you incorporate that comment into the final version?
- How might the skills you used in writing this piece help you with your future writing?

Reading on Your Own

You might also be interested in the following books.

The Adventures of Huckleberry Finn
by Mark Twain The adults in Huck Finn's life fail to appreciate his mischievous and fun-loving attitude. Hungry for comradeship, he befriends the runaway slave, Jim, and together they escape the constrictions of the small town to raft down the Mississippi River. Jim helps Huck learn the nature of friendship and the meaning of freedom.

The Post Office
by Rabindranath Tagore An illustrated edition of Tagore's play about an adopted child named Amal. Confined to his home as the result of an illness, Amal's only entertainment is watching the neighborhood as he sits at his open window. As Amal engages in conversations with the townspeople who stroll by, he expresses amazing insight into life.

Seven Against Thebes
by Aeschylus Prehistoric Thebes is under siege by an Argive army led by Polyneices, son of Oedipus and brother of Eteocles. Eteocles pledges to save Thebes and fiercely defend its seven gates against the Argive army's seven armored chiefs and their warriors. Trying to avoid disaster, the Theban women warn Eteocles to stay away from the seventh gate.

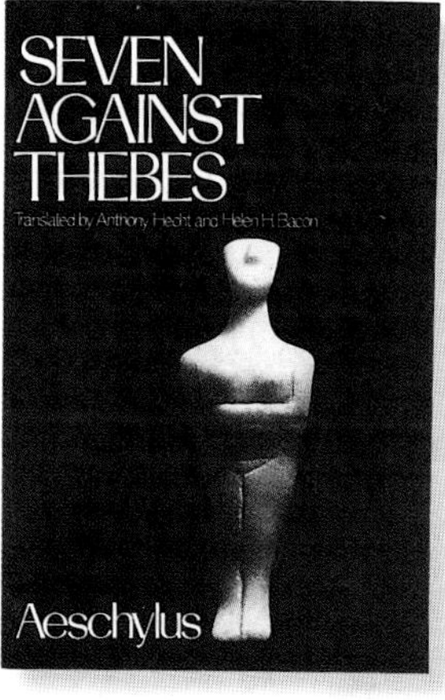

Shakespeare
by F. E. Halliday This illustrated biography of Shakespeare gives details about the playwright's life and plays and presents fascinating information about the history of the theater. Reproductions of documents, maps, and illustrations enliven the text. Included are contemporary photographs of Shakespeare's grave in Stratford and other historic sites.

Reading and Analyzing Test Questions

Read the following passage. Then read each question on page 909. Decide which is the best answer to each question. Mark the letter for that answer on your paper.

Benny Wins a Trip

Congratulations to Benny Thompson! Benny has won the Model United Nations Junior Citizen Essay contest. Everyone in his class was required to submit a 500-word personal interpretation of the phrase, "Everyone is a citizen of the world." A prolific writer, Benny drafted several essays and then chose one to polish for his official entry. The end result was a creative adaptation of the American Pledge of Allegiance to the Flag that asserted Benny's loyalty to the planet Earth as a federation of nations. "I pledge allegiance to the Earth as a citizen of its united nations . . ." Benny began. His essay focused on the responsibilities every person has to the causes of civic responsibility, education, racial harmony, and the advancement of the human race. Quite a piece of work!

As a reward, Benny will receive an all-expenses-paid trip to New York City to visit the United Nations and receive an award on the floor of the General Assembly. The itinerary for his trip is reprinted below.

TRAVEL ITINERARY

Thursday, August 8

3:10 P.M.	(CDT) Flight 605 leaves Bush Intercontinental Airport
7:40 P.M.	(EDT) Flight 605 lands at La Guardia Airport in New York City
8:00 P.M.	Shuttle to hotel arrives in the pick-up lane outside gate F
8:30 P.M.	Check-in at the Manhattan Towers Hotel
8:45 P.M.	Dinner at Ricardo's Italian Bistro

Friday, August 9

8:00 A.M.	Breakfast at the Towers Spotlight Cafe in the Manhattan Towers Hotel
9:00 A.M.	Tour leaves for the Statue of Liberty
12:00 NOON	Lunch at the Liberty Park Pavilion
2:00 P.M.	A "Meet and Greet" juice bar with other essay winners from around the country in the lobby of the Del Monico Theater on Broadway
3:00 P.M.	Broadway show (to be determined)
6:00 P.M.	Dinner in Chinatown
8:00 P.M.	Special taping of "The Eli Wetterman Show" at Network Studios

Saturday, August 10

8:00 A.M.	Breakfast at the Towers Spotlight Cafe in the Manhattan Towers Hotel
9:00 A.M.	Tour of the United Nations complex
12:00 NOON	Meet for lunch at the "Let Us Beat Swords into Plowshares" statue
1:00 P.M.	Special Awards Ceremony on the Floor of the General Assembly Hall
3:00 P.M.	Press Conference and Photo Session in the General Assembly Lobby
5:00 P.M.	Round-robin discussion among essay finalists on the topic: "Spaceship Earth: Are We Running Out of Fuel?" Scheduled for Conference Room 1A of the Manhattan Towers Hotel
8:00 P.M.	Dinner at the famous Waterfront Steak House

Sunday, August 11

8:30 A.M.	Continental breakfast in the central piazza of the Manhattan Towers Hotel (buffet will be set up on the terrace)
10:00 A.M.	Check out of hotel rooms
10:30 A.M.	Meet shuttle bus bound for La Guardia Airport
12:04 P.M.	(EDT) Flight 502 takes off from La Guardia Airport
2:50 P.M.	(CDT) Flight 502 lands at Bush Intercontinental Airport

1 The main idea of the passage is that —

A Benny plans a visit to New York

B all the students in Benny's class are required to enter a contest

C Benny has been invited to join the United Nations

D everyone learns that Benny has won a trip

2 While he is in New York, Benny will most likely —

F not see the United Nations complex

G decide to go to college in New York

H not see the Statue of Liberty

J not have much free time

3 How does the author of this piece feel about Benny's essay?

A Discouraged

B Enthusiastic

C Critical

D Neutral

4 The word prolific in this passage indicates that Benny —

F is a well-known writer

G hates to revise his writing

H produces a lot of writing

J is reluctant to write

5 Which is the best summary of the schedule for Friday, August 9th?

A Benny will visit the Statue of Liberty.

B Benny will receive his award.

C Benny will see a Broadway show.

D Benny will enjoy many New York activities.

6 The information in the passage suggests that the trip's organizers have arranged for —

F transit to and from each activity

G a visit with the mayor of New York

H Benny to have a trip every year

J free souvenirs to be distributed

STOP

St. George: The Rescue, 1903. Maximilian Liebenwein. Brush and ink, gouache and gold paint on board, 89 x 69.5 cm.

UNIT FIVE

Legends

***"I loved best
the evening meal,
for that was the time old
legends were told."
—Zitkala-Ša***

Theme 11

Heroism

pages 913–993

Literature FOCUS

Legends

Just who was King Arthur? Several well-known stories describe him as a king in shining armor who gathered around him the best and bravest knights of England. There is another Arthur story, too, that tells about an amazing warrior who led British forces against Roman armies. These tall tales and romances may have developed around a historical figure, but, as often happens, the legend is now better known than the man.

People frequently use the words "legend" and "myth" as if the two words mean the same thing, but there is an important difference between them. Whereas both myths and legends tell traditional stories about a very distant past, **myths** center on religious or supernatural material. They try to explain the great mysteries of human experience, such as the origins of life, the existence of evil, and the shape of the universe. Mythical heroes are the gods and creatures who inhabited the world in a time "before time." No one can historically date a myth.

Robin Hood by N. C. Wyeth.

Legends, on the other hand, are more historically based. Although these stories may contain exaggerated, magical, or supernatural elements, they are set in a particular time and place, and they focus on people who might have existed. Robin Hood was a real person; so was Sundiata, the African leader who ruled the Kingdom of Mali (see page 934). King Arthur may have been a real man too, although no one knows for sure.

Originally, legends, like myths, were passed on from generation to generation by word of mouth. For this reason, these stories are classified as **folklore**—they are part of a community's culture that is maintained without reliance on the written word. Folklore helps define a culture's unique identity. Local legends, however, can also become part of other regions' legends. **The Arthurian legends**—the body of stories about the king—were passed on orally both in England and in France. Another popular legend that became widely distributed and adapted—the folktale of a marksman who shot an apple from his son's head—is based on a Swiss hero, William Tell.

As different storytellers recounted these and other tales over and over again, each person added his or her own slight variation, and the content of the legends probably shifted. Legends may not get written down until hundreds of years after they originated. Perhaps this explains why stories based on actual people and events end up containing very little information that is historically verifiable.

ACTIVITY

As you read the stories of King Arthur and other heroes in this theme, identify the exaggerated, magical, or supernatural elements in each legend. What do these elements add to the story?

Theme 11 Heroism

The shining quality of true heroes can last through the ages. In this theme, you'll meet legendary characters who use their extraordinary strength and bravery in the service of causes larger than themselves. Who do you think are the heroes in today's world?

THEME PROJECTS

Learning for Life

Nominate a Hero Which character from this theme deserves to win an International Hero award?

1. Write a letter to the International Hero nominating committee, telling them what you think a hero is and which character should win the award.
2. In order to persuade the committee, provide detailed information about your nominee's heroic achievements. Explain why he or she deserves the award by comparing him or her with the other heroes in this theme.
3. Present your argument in business letter format.

Interdisciplinary Project

History What conclusions can you draw about how each time period influenced the legends in this theme?

1. Research to find out what life was like for African royalty in the 1200s, for British knights and nobility in the 1400s, and for Cheyenne warriors in the 1800s.
2. Look for information about everyday details. How did people occupy themselves during the day? What did people eat? What did they wear? To what music did they listen?
3. Summarize your findings and conclusions in a series of posters.

Human Achievement, 1983. Tsing-Fang Chen. Acrylic on canvas, 66 x 96 in. Lucia Gallery, New York.

Before You Read

from *Le Morte d'Arthur*

Reading Focus

Who is your hero? What makes that person a hero to you?

Idea Web Make an idea web for the word *hero.* In the branching ovals, write words and phrases describing the qualities of a hero. Compare your ideas with those of your classmates.

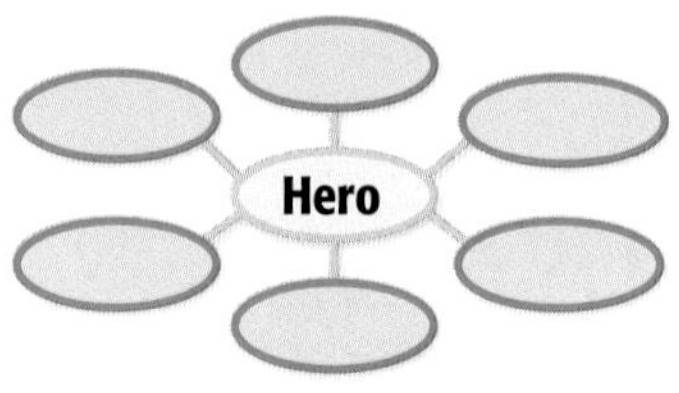

Setting a Purpose Read to discover the qualities of some legendary heroes.

Building Background

The Time and Place
King Arthur's England as described in *Le Morte d'Arthur* is likely a blend of fact and fiction. The time period and location of the legendary land have been difficult for historians to confirm. It is true, however, that jousting and sword fighting were popular sports among the nobility of Europe in 1470 when *Le Morte d'Arthur* was written. Of course, the monsters that Sir Thomas Malory wrote about are pure fantasy.

Thomas, Lord Berkeley. 14th century. Brass relief. St. Mary the Virgin, Wotton under Edse, England.

Did You Know?
Knights and noblemen in late medieval Europe (twelfth to fifteenth centuries) tried to behave according to a strict code of chivalry, a word derived from the French *chevalier,* meaning horseman. A chivalrous knight, however, was more than a skilled rider. He also strove to be generous to the weak and courteous to women.

Meet Sir Thomas Malory

Details of the author's life were few even in the fifteenth century. A knight named Thomas Malory is known to have lived at the time the book was written, but not enough evidence exists to be sure he was the author. Sir Thomas Malory, commonly accepted as the author, had lots of time to write his book. He spent several years in prison for crimes ranging from stealing animals to attempted murder. In one incident he was accused of stealing 7 cows, 2 calves, 335 sheep, and a farmer's cart. At the end of *Le Morte d'Arthur*, which he wrote in a London prison, he urged his readers to pray for his safe release.

Sir Thomas Malory was born about 1405 and died in London in 1471. His book was completed between 1469 and 1470 and first published in 1485.

Vocabulary Preview

accost (ə kôst′) *v.* to approach and speak to, especially in an aggressive manner; p. 916

abashed (ə basht′) *adj.* self-conscious; embarrassed or ashamed; p. 917

inscribe (in skrīb′) *v.* to write, carve, or mark on a surface; p. 919

ignoble (ig nō′ bel) *adj.* of low birth or position; without honor or worth; p. 920

tumultuous (too mul′ cho͞o əs) *adj.* wildly excited, confused, or agitated; p. 920

prowess (prou′ is) *n.* great ability or skill; p. 921

from

Le Morte d'Arthur

Sir Thomas Malory

retold by Keith Baines

Uther, Igraine and the Duke of Cornwall, 1498. Woodcut by the Arthur-cutter for Wynkyn de Worde's *Malory.*

The Tale of King Arthur

KING UTHER[1] PENDRAGON,[2] RULER OF ALL BRITAIN, had been at war for many years with the Duke of Tintagil in Cornwall when he was told of the beauty of Lady Igraine,[3] the duke's wife. Thereupon he called a truce and invited the duke and Igraine to his court, where he prepared a feast for them, and where, as soon as they arrived, he was formally reconciled to the duke through the good offices of his courtiers.

---

1. *Uther* (o͞o′ thər)
2. In ancient Britain, *Pendragon*, meaning "supreme leader," was a title attached after a ruler's name.
3. *Igraine* (ē grān′)

In the course of the feast, King Uther grew passionately desirous of Igraine and, when it was over, begged her to become his paramour.[4] Igraine, however, being as naturally loyal as she was beautiful, refused him.

"I suppose," said Igraine to her husband, the duke, when this had happened, "that the king arranged this truce only because he wanted to make me his mistress. I suggest that we leave at once, without warning, and ride overnight to our castle." The duke agreed with her, and they left the court secretly.

The king was enraged by Igraine's flight and summoned his privy council.[5] They advised him to command the fugitives' return under threat of renewing the war; but when this was done, the duke and Igraine defied his summons. He then warned them that they could expect to be dragged from their castle within six weeks.

Did You Know?
Sally ports were the gates or openings in the castle walls through which the duke's troops could make sudden attacks.

The duke manned and provisioned[6] his two strongest castles: Tintagil for Igraine, and Terrabyl, which was useful for its many sally ports, for himself. Soon King Uther arrived with a huge army and laid siege to Terrabyl; but despite the ferocity of the fighting, and the numerous casualties suffered by both sides, neither was able to gain a decisive victory.

Still enraged, and now despairing, King Uther fell sick. His friend Sir Ulfius came to him and asked what the trouble was. "Igraine has broken my heart," the king replied, "and unless I can win her, I shall never recover."

"Sire," said Sir Ulfius, "surely Merlin the Prophet could find some means to help you? I will go in search of him."

Sir Ulfius had not ridden far when he was accosted by a hideous beggar. "For whom are you searching?" asked the beggar; but Sir Ulfius ignored him.

"Very well," said the beggar, "I will tell you: You are searching for Merlin, and you need look no further, for I am he. Now go to King Uther and tell him that I will make Igraine his if he will reward me as I ask; and even that will be more to his benefit than to mine."

"I am sure," said Sir Ulfius, "that the king will refuse you nothing reasonable."

"Then go, and I shall follow you," said Merlin.

Well pleased, Sir Ulfius galloped back to the king and delivered Merlin's message, which he had hardly completed when Merlin himself appeared at the entrance to the pavilion. The king bade him welcome.

"Sire," said Merlin, "I know that you are in love with Igraine; will you swear, as an anointed[7] king, to give into my care the child that she bears you, if I make her yours?"

The king swore on the gospel that he would do so, and Merlin continued: "Tonight you shall appear before Igraine at Tintagil in the likeness of her husband, the duke. Sir Ulfius and I will appear as two of the duke's knights: Sir Brastius and Sir Jordanus. Do not question either Igraine or her men, but say that you are sick and retire to bed. I will fetch you early in the morning,

4. A man's lover or mistress is his *paramour*.
5. A *privy council* is the group of a ruler's closest advisors. (*Privy* comes from the same Latin root as *private.*)
6. The duke supplied *(provisioned)* the castles with food and goods.
7. An *anointed* king was believed to have been chosen by God to be king.

Vocabulary
accost (ə kôst′) *v.* to approach and speak to, especially in an aggressive manner

Merlin the Magician, c. 1352. Manuscript illustration. Ms. Add. Meladius, 12228, fol 202v. The British Library, London.

Viewing the art: How do you think Igraine might have reacted if she knew what Uther Pendragon and Merlin were planning? Explain.

and do not rise until I come; fortunately Tintagil is only ten miles from here."

The plan succeeded: Igraine was completely deceived by the king's impersonation of the duke, and gave herself to him, and conceived Arthur. The king left her at dawn as soon as Merlin appeared, after giving her a farewell kiss. But the duke had seen King Uther ride out from the siege on the previous night and, in the course of making a surprise attack on the king's army, had been killed. When Igraine realized that the duke had died three hours before he had appeared to her, she was greatly disturbed in mind; however, she confided in no one.

Once it was known that the duke was dead, the king's nobles urged him to be reconciled to Igraine, and this task the king gladly entrusted to Sir Ulfius, by whose eloquence[8] it was soon accomplished. "And now," said Sir Ulfius to his fellow nobles, "why should not the king marry the beautiful Igraine? Surely it would be as well for us all."

The marriage of King Uther and Igraine was celebrated joyously thirteen days later; and then, at the king's request, Igraine's sisters were also married: Margawse, who later bore Sir Gawain, to King Lot of Lowthean and Orkney; Elayne, to King Nentres of Garlot. Igraine's daughter, Morgan le Fay, was put to school in a nunnery; in after years she was to become a witch, and to be married to King Uryens of Gore, and give birth to Sir Uwayne of the Fair Hands.

A few months later it was seen that Igraine was with child, and one night, as she lay in bed with King Uther, he asked her who the father might be. Igraine was greatly abashed.

"Do not look so dismayed," said the king, "but tell me the truth and I swear I shall love you the better for it."

"The truth is," said Igraine, "that the night the duke died, about three hours after his death, a man appeared in my castle—the exact image of the duke. With him came two others who appeared to be Sir Brastius and

8. Here, *eloquence* is speech or writing that is expressive, stirring, and effective.

Vocabulary

abashed (ə basht′) *adj.* self-conscious; embarrassed or ashamed

Sir Jordanus. Naturally I gave myself to this man as I would have to the duke, and that night, I swear, this child was conceived."

"Well spoken," said the king; "it was I who impersonated the duke, so the child is mine." He then told Igraine the story of how Merlin had arranged it, and Igraine was overjoyed to discover that the father of her child was now her husband.

Sometime later, Merlin appeared before the king. "Sire," he said, "you know that you must provide for the upbringing of your child?"

"I will do as you advise," the king replied.

"That is good," said Merlin, "because it is my reward for having arranged your impersonation of the duke. Your child is destined for glory, and I want him brought to me for his baptism. I shall then give him into the care of foster parents who can be trusted not to reveal his identity before the proper time. Sir Ector would be suitable: he is extremely loyal, owns good estates, and his wife has just borne him a child. She could give her child into the care of another woman, and herself look after yours."

Sir Ector was summoned, and gladly agreed to the king's request, who then rewarded him handsomely. When the child was born he was at once wrapped in a gold cloth and taken by two knights and two ladies to Merlin, who stood waiting at the rear entrance to the castle in his beggar's disguise. Merlin took the child to a priest, who baptized him with the name of Arthur, and thence to Sir Ector, whose wife fed him at her breast.

Two years later King Uther fell sick, and his enemies once more overran his kingdom, inflicting heavy losses on him as they advanced. Merlin prophesied that they could be checked only by the presence of the king himself on the battlefield, and suggested that he should be conveyed there on a horse

Merlin & Arthur. W. Goscombe John. Bronze, height: 22⅞ in. National Museum of Wales, Cardiff.

Viewing the sculpture: Which of Merlin's characteristics do you think this sculpture portrays?

litter.[9] King Uther's army met the invader on the plain at St. Albans, and the king duly appeared on the horse litter. Inspired by his presence, and by the lively leadership of Sir Brastius and Sir Jordanus, his army quickly defeated the enemy and the battle finished in a rout.[10] The king returned to London to celebrate the victory.

But his sickness grew worse, and after he had lain speechless for three days and three nights Merlin summoned the nobles to attend the king in his chamber on the following morning. "By the grace of God," he said, "I hope to make him speak."

In the morning, when all the nobles were assembled, Merlin addressed the king: "Sire, is it your will that Arthur shall succeed to the throne, together with all its prerogatives?"[11]

The king stirred in his bed, and then spoke so that all could hear: "I bestow on Arthur God's blessing and my own, and Arthur shall succeed to the throne on pain of forfeiting my blessing."[12] Then King Uther gave up the ghost. He was buried and mourned the next day, as befitted his rank, by Igraine and the nobility of Britain.

During the years that followed the death of King Uther, while Arthur was still a child, the ambitious barons fought one another for the throne, and the whole of Britain stood in jeopardy. Finally the day came when the Archbishop of Canterbury, on the advice of Merlin, summoned the nobility to London for Christmas morning. In his message the Archbishop promised that the true succession to the British throne would be miraculously revealed. Many of the nobles purified themselves during their journey, in the hope that it would be to them that the succession would fall.

The Archbishop held his service in the city's greatest church (St. Paul's), and when matins[13] were done the congregation filed out to the yard. They were confronted by a marble block into which had been thrust a beautiful sword. The block was four feet square, and the sword passed through a steel anvil which had been struck in the stone, and which projected a foot from it. The anvil had been inscribed with letters of gold:

WHOSO PULLETH OUTE THIS SWERD
OF THIS STONE AND ANVLYD IS RIGHTWYS
KYNGE BORNE OF ALL BRYTAYGNE

The congregation was awed by this miraculous sight, but the Archbishop forbade anyone to touch the sword before mass had been heard. After mass, many of the nobles tried to pull the sword out of the stone, but none was able to, so a watch of ten knights was set over the sword, and a tournament proclaimed for New Year's Day, to provide men of noble blood with the opportunity of proving their right to the succession.

Sir Ector, who had been living on an estate near London, rode to the tournament with Arthur and his own son Sir Kay, who had been recently knighted. When they arrived at the tournament, Sir Kay found to his annoyance that his sword was missing from its sheath, so he begged Arthur to ride back and fetch it from their lodging.

9. The king was to be carried *(conveyed)* on a stretcher *(litter)* pulled by a horse.
10. A *rout* (rout) is an overwhelming defeat.
11. *Prerogatives* (pri rog′ ə tivz) are the rights and privileges belonging solely to a particular person (such as a king) or group.
12. *Forfeiting my blessing* means that Uther is withholding his blessing if Arthur does not eventually become king.
13. *Matins* (mat′ inz) are morning prayers.

Vocabulary

inscribe (in skrīb′) *v.* to write, carve, or mark on a surface

Arthur found the door of the lodging locked and bolted, the landlord and his wife having left for the tournament. In order not to disappoint his brother, he rode on to St. Paul's, determined to get for him the sword which was lodged in the stone. The yard was empty, the guard also having slipped off to see the tournament, so Arthur strode up to the sword, and, without troubling to read the inscription, tugged it free. He then rode straight back to Sir Kay and presented him with it.

Sir Kay recognized the sword, and taking it to Sir Ector, said, "Father, the succession falls to me, for I have here the sword that was lodged in the stone." But Sir Ector insisted that they should all ride to the churchyard, and once there bound Sir Kay by oath to tell how he had come by the sword. Sir Kay then admitted that Arthur had given it to him. Sir Ector turned to Arthur and said, "Was the sword not guarded?"

"It was not," Arthur replied.

"Would you please thrust it into the stone again?" said Sir Ector. Arthur did so, and first Sir Ector and then Sir Kay tried to remove it, but both were unable to. Then Arthur, for the second time, pulled it out. Sir Ector and Sir Kay both knelt before him.

"Why," said Arthur, "do you both kneel before me?"

"My lord," Sir Ector replied, "there is only one man living who can draw the sword from the stone, and he is the true-born King of Britain." Sir Ector then told Arthur the story of his birth and upbringing.

"My dear father," said Arthur, "for so I shall always think of you—if, as you say, I am to be king, please know that any request you have to make is already granted."

Sir Ector asked that Sir Kay should be made Royal Seneschal,[14] and Arthur declared that while they both lived it should be so. Then the three of them visited the Archbishop and told him what had taken place.

All those dukes and barons with ambitions to rule were present at the tournament on New Year's Day. But when all of them had failed, and Arthur alone had succeeded in drawing the sword from the stone, they protested against one so young, and of ignoble blood, succeeding to the throne.

The secret of Arthur's birth was known only to a few of the nobles surviving from the days of King Uther. The Archbishop urged them to make Arthur's cause their own; but their support proved ineffective. The tournament was repeated at Candlemas and at Easter,[15] and with the same outcome as before.

Finally at Pentecost,[16] when once more Arthur alone had been able to remove the sword, the commoners arose with a tumultuous cry and demanded that Arthur should at once be made king. The nobles, knowing in their hearts that the commoners were right, all knelt before Arthur and begged forgiveness for having delayed his succession for so long. Arthur forgave them, and then, offering his sword at the high altar, was dubbed first knight of the realm. The coronation took place a few days later, when Arthur swore to rule justly, and the nobles swore him their allegiance.

14. In medieval times, the *Royal Seneschal* (sen′ ə shəl) managed the king's estate, ran his household, and sometimes also had official state duties or a military command.
15. *Candlemas* and *Easter* are Christian festivals; *Candlemas* is celebrated on February 2 and *Easter* in early spring.
16. *Pentecost*, a religious observance, is the seventh Sunday after Easter.

Vocabulary

ignoble (ig nō′ bel) *adj.* of low birth or position; without honor or worth
tumultuous (too mul′ cho͞o əs) *adj.* wildly excited, confused, or agitated

Camelot, 1984. Alan Lee.

Viewing the painting: What does this painting tell you about Camelot? How does the depiction here compare with the Camelot described in the selection?

The Tale of Sir Launcelot du Lake

When King Arthur returned from Rome he settled his court at Camelot, and there gathered about him his knights of the Round Table, who diverted[17] themselves with jousting and tournaments. Of all his knights one was supreme, both in prowess at arms and in nobility of bearing, and this was Sir Launcelot, who was also the favorite of Queen Gwynevere, to whom he had sworn oaths of fidelity.[18]

One day Sir Launcelot, feeling weary of his life at the court, and of only playing at arms, decided to set forth in search of adventure. He asked his nephew Sir Lyonel to accompany him, and when both were suitably armed and mounted, they rode off together through the forest.

At noon they started across a plain, but the intensity of the sun made Sir Launcelot feel sleepy, so Sir Lyonel suggested that they should rest beneath the shade of an apple tree that grew by a hedge not far from the road. They dismounted, tethered their horses, and settled down.

"Not for seven years have I felt so sleepy," said Sir Launcelot, and with that fell fast asleep, while Sir Lyonel watched over him.

Soon three knights came galloping past, and Sir Lyonel noticed that they were being pursued by a fourth knight, who was one of the most powerful he had yet seen. The pursuing knight overtook each of the others in turn, and as he did so, knocked each off his horse with a thrust of his spear. When all three lay stunned he dismounted, bound them securely to their horses with the reins, and led them away.

Without waking Sir Launcelot, Sir Lyonel mounted his horse and rode after the knight, and as soon as he had drawn close enough, shouted his challenge. The knight turned about and they charged at each other, with the result that Sir Lyonel was likewise flung from his horse, bound, and led away a prisoner.

17. Here, *diverted* means "amused; entertained."
18. Launcelot swore his loyalty and devotion *(fidelity)* to Gwynevere.

Vocabulary
prowess (prou′ is) *n.* great ability or skill

The victorious knight, whose name was Sir Tarquine, led his prisoners to his castle, and there threw them on the ground, stripped them naked, and beat them with thorn twigs. After that he locked them in a dungeon where many other prisoners, who had received like treatment, were complaining dismally.

Meanwhile, Sir Ector de Marys, who liked to accompany Sir Launcelot on his adventures, and finding him gone, decided to ride after him. Before long he came upon a forester.

"My good fellow, if you know the forest hereabouts, could you tell me in which direction I am most likely to meet with adventure?"

"Sir, I can tell you: Less than a mile from here stands a well-moated castle. On the left of the entrance you will find a ford where you can water your horse, and across from the ford a large tree from which hang the shields of many famous knights. Below the shields hangs a caldron, of copper and brass: strike it three times with your spear, and then surely you will meet with adventure—such, indeed, that if you survive it, you will prove yourself the foremost knight in these parts for many years."

"May God reward you!" Sir Ector replied.

The castle was exactly as the forester had described it, and among the shields Sir Ector recognized several as belonging to knights of the Round Table. After watering his horse, he knocked on the caldron and Sir Tarquine, whose castle it was, appeared.

How Four Queens Found Sir Lancelot Sleeping, 1908. William Frank Calderon. Oil on canvas, 48 x 72 in. Private collection.

Viewing the painting: What can you tell about Launcelot based on the contrast in the painting between him and the queens and their retinue?

They jousted, and at the first encounter Sir Ector sent his opponent's horse spinning twice about before he could recover.

"That was a fine stroke; now let us try again," said Sir Tarquine.

This time Sir Tarquine caught Sir Ector just below the right arm and, having impaled him on his spear, lifted him clean out of the saddle, and rode with him into the castle, where he threw him on the ground.

"Sir," said Sir Tarquine, "you have fought better than any knight I have encountered in the last twelve years; therefore, if you wish, I will demand no more of you than your parole[19] as my prisoner."

"Sir, that I will never give."

"Then I am sorry for you," said Sir Tarquine, and with that he stripped and beat him and locked him in the dungeon with the other prisoners. There Sir Ector saw Sir Lyonel.

"Alas, Sir Lyonel, we are in a sorry plight. But tell me, what has happened to Sir Launcelot? for he surely is the one knight who could save us."

"I left him sleeping beneath an apple tree, and what has befallen him since I do not know," Sir Lyonel replied; and then all the unhappy prisoners once more bewailed their lot.

While Sir Launcelot still slept beneath the apple tree, four queens started across the plain. They were riding white mules and accompanied by four knights who held above them, at the tips of their spears, a green silk canopy, to protect them from the sun. The party was startled by the neighing of Sir Launcelot's horse and, changing direction, rode up to the apple tree, where they discovered the sleeping knight. And as each of the queens gazed at the handsome Sir Launcelot, so each wanted him for her own.

19. A knight's *parole* was his pledge to fulfill certain conditions in exchange for full or partial freedom.

"Let us not quarrel," said Morgan le Fay. "Instead, I will cast a spell over him so that he remains asleep while we take him to my castle and make him our prisoner. We can then oblige him to choose one of us for his paramour."

Sir Launcelot was laid on his shield and borne by two of the knights to the Castle Charyot, which was Morgan le Fay's stronghold. He awoke to find himself in a cold cell, where a young noblewoman was serving him supper.

"What cheer?"[20] she asked.

"My lady, I hardly know, except that I must have been brought here by means of an enchantment."

"Sir, if you are the knight you appear to be, you will learn your fate at dawn tomorrow." And with that the young noblewoman left him. Sir Launcelot spent an uncomfortable night but at dawn the four queens presented themselves and Morgan le Fay spoke to him:

"Sir Launcelot, I know that Queen Gwynevere loves you, and you her. But now you are my prisoner, and you will have to choose: either to take one of us for your paramour, or to die miserably in this cell—just as you please. Now I will tell you who we are: I am Morgan le Fay, Queen of Gore; my companions are the Queens of North Galys, of Estelonde, and of the Outer Isles. So make your choice."

"A hard choice! Understand that I choose none of you, lewd sorceresses[21] that you are; rather will I die in this cell. But were I free, I would take pleasure in proving it against any who would champion[22] you that Queen Gwynevere is the finest lady of this land."

"So, you refuse us?" asked Morgan le Fay.

20. *What cheer?* was the same as asking "How are you?"
21. Launcelot accuses the women of being unchaste *(lewd)* witches *(sorceresses)*.
22. As a verb, *champion* means "to defend a person or cause."

"On my life, I do," Sir Launcelot said finally, and so the queens departed.

Sometime later, the young noblewoman who had served Sir Launcelot's supper reappeared.

"What news?" she asked.

"It is the end," Sir Launcelot replied.

"Sir Launcelot, I know that you have refused the four queens, and that they wish to kill you out of spite. But if you will be ruled by me, I can save you. I ask that you will champion my father at a tournament next Tuesday, when he has to combat the King of North Galys, and three knights of the Round Table, who last Tuesday defeated him ignominiously."[23]

"My lady, pray tell me, what is your father's name?"

"King Bagdemagus."[24]

"Excellent, my lady, I know him for a good king and a true knight, so I shall be happy to serve him."

"May God reward you! And tomorrow at dawn I will release you, and direct you to an abbey which is ten miles from here, and where the good monks will care for you while I fetch my father."

"I am at your service, my lady."

As promised, the young noblewoman released Sir Launcelot at dawn. When she had led him through the twelve doors to the castle entrance, she gave him his horse and armor, and directions for finding the abbey.

"God bless you, my lady; and when the time comes I promise I shall not fail you."

Sir Launcelot rode through the forest in search of the abbey, but at dusk had still failed to find it, and coming upon a red silk pavilion, apparently unoccupied, decided to rest there overnight, and continue his search in the morning. . . .

As soon as it was daylight, Sir Launcelot armed, mounted, and rode away in search of the abbey, which he found in less than two hours. King Bagdemagus' daughter was waiting for him, and as soon as she heard his horse's footsteps in the yard, ran to the window, and, seeing that it was Sir Launcelot, herself ordered the servants to stable his horse. She then led him to her chamber, disarmed him, and gave him a long gown to wear, welcoming him warmly as she did so.

King Bagdemagus' castle was twelve miles away, and his daughter sent for him as soon as she had settled Sir Launcelot. The king arrived with his retinue[25] and embraced Sir Launcelot, who then described his recent enchantment, and the great obligation he was under to his daughter for releasing him.

"Sir, you will fight for me on Tuesday next?"

"Sire, I shall not fail you; but please tell me the names of the three Round Table knights whom I shall be fighting."

"Sir Modred, Sir Madore de la Porte, and Sir Gahalantyne. I must admit that last Tuesday they defeated me and my knights completely."

"Sire, I hear that the tournament is to be fought within three miles of the abbey. Could you send me three of your most trustworthy knights, clad in plain armor, and with no device,[26] and a fourth suit of armor which I myself shall wear? We will take up our position just outside the tournament field and watch while you and the King of North Galys enter into combat with your followers; and then, as soon as you are in difficulties, we will come to your rescue, and show your opponents what kind of knights you command."

This was arranged on Sunday, and on the following Tuesday Sir Launcelot and the three

23. The woman's father was defeated shamefully or dishonorably *(ignominiously).*

24. *Bagdemagus* (bag′ də mag′ əs)

25. The king's *retinue* is the group of people who accompany and serve him.

26. Armor with no *device* has no ornamental design.

knights of King Bagdemagus waited in a copse,[27] not far from the pavilion which had been erected for the lords and ladies who were to judge the tournament and award the prizes.

The King of North Galys was the first on the field, with a company of ninescore knights; he was followed by King Bagdemagus with fourscore knights, and then by the three knights of the Round Table, who remained apart from both companies.[28] At the first encounter King Bagdemagus lost twelve knights, all killed, and the King of North Galys six.

With that, Sir Launcelot galloped on to the field, and with his first spear unhorsed five of the King of North Galys' knights, breaking the backs of four of them. With his next spear he charged the king, and wounded him deeply in the thigh.

"That was a shrewd blow," commented Sir Madore, and galloped onto the field to challenge Sir Launcelot. But he too was tumbled from his horse, and with such violence that his shoulder was broken.

Sir Modred was the next to challenge Sir Launcelot, and he was sent spinning over his horse's tail. He landed head first, his helmet became buried in the soil, and he nearly broke his neck, and for a long time lay stunned.

Finally Sir Gahalantyne tried; at the first encounter both he and Sir Launcelot broke their spears, so both drew their swords and hacked vehemently at each other. But Sir Launcelot, with mounting wrath, soon struck his opponent a blow on the helmet which brought the blood streaming from eyes, ears, and mouth. Sir Gahalantyne slumped forward in the saddle, his horse panicked, and he was thrown to the ground, useless for further combat.

27. A *copse* is a thicket of trees.

28. One *score* is twenty, so more than 260 knights have gathered.

Sir Launcelot took another spear, and unhorsed sixteen more of the King of North Galys' knights, and with his next, unhorsed another twelve; and in each case with such violence that none of the knights ever fully recovered. The King of North Galys was forced to admit defeat, and the prize was awarded to King Bagdemagus.

That night Sir Launcelot was entertained as the guest of honor by King Bagdemagus and his daughter at their castle, and before leaving was loaded with gifts.

"My lady, please, if ever again you should need my services, remember that I shall not fail you."

The next day Sir Launcelot rode once more through the forest, and by chance came to the apple tree where he had previously slept. This time he met a young noblewoman riding a white palfrey.

Did You Know?
A *palfrey* is a gentle saddle horse, especially one trained for a woman rider.

"My lady, I am riding in search of adventure; pray tell me if you know of any I might find hereabouts."

"Sir, there are adventures hereabouts if you believe that you are equal to them; but please tell me, what is your name?"

"Sir Launcelot du Lake."

"Very well, Sir Launcelot, you appear to be a sturdy enough knight, so I will tell you. Not far away stands the castle of Sir Tarquine, a knight who in fair combat has overcome more than sixty opponents whom he now holds prisoner. Many are from the court of King Arthur, and if you can rescue them, I will then ask you to deliver me and my companions from a knight who distresses us daily, either by robbery or by other kinds of outrage."

"My lady, please first lead me to Sir Tarquine, then I will most happily challenge this miscreant[29] knight of yours."

When they arrived at the castle, Sir Launcelot watered his horse at the ford, and then beat the caldron until the bottom fell out. However, none came to answer the challenge, so they waited by the castle gate for half an hour or so. Then Sir Tarquine appeared, riding toward the castle with a wounded prisoner slung over his horse, whom Sir Launcelot recognized as Sir Gaheris, Sir Gawain's brother and a knight of the Round Table.

"Good knight," said Sir Launcelot, "it is known to me that you have put to shame many of the knights of the Round Table. Pray allow your prisoner, who I see is wounded, to recover, while I vindicate[30] the honor of the knights whom you have defeated."

"I defy you, and all your fellowship of the Round Table," Sir Tarquine replied.

"You boast!" said Sir Launcelot.

At the first charge the backs of the horses were broken and both knights stunned. But they soon recovered and set to with their swords, and both struck so lustily that neither shield nor armor could resist, and within two hours they were cutting each other's flesh, from which the blood flowed liberally. Finally they paused for a moment, resting on their shields.

"Worthy knight," said Sir Tarquine, "pray hold your hand for a while, and if you will, answer my question."

"Sir, speak on."

"You are the most powerful knight I have fought yet, but I fear you may be the one whom in the whole world I most hate. If you are not, for the love of you I will release all my prisoners and swear eternal friendship."

"What is the name of the knight you hate above all others?"

"Sir Launcelot du Lake; for it was he who slew my brother, Sir Carados of the Dolorous Tower, and it is because of him that I have killed a hundred knights, and maimed[31] as many more, apart from the sixty-four I still hold prisoner. And so, if you are Sir Launcelot, speak up, for we must then fight to the death."

"Sir, I see now that I might go in peace and good fellowship, or otherwise fight to the death; but being the knight I am, I must tell you: I am Sir Launcelot du Lake, son of King Ban of Benwick, of Arthur's court, and a knight of the Round Table. So defend yourself!"

"Ah! this is most welcome."

Now the two knights hurled themselves at each other like two wild bulls; swords and shields clashed together, and often their swords drove into the flesh. Then sometimes one, sometimes the other, would stagger and fall, only to recover immediately and resume the contest. At last, however, Sir Tarquine grew faint, and unwittingly lowered his shield. Sir Launcelot was swift to follow up his advantage, and dragging the other down to his knees, unlaced his helmet and beheaded him.

Sir Launcelot then strode over to the young noblewoman: "My lady, now I am at your service, but first I must find a horse."

Then the wounded Sir Gaheris spoke up: "Sir, please take my horse. Today you have overcome the most formidable knight, excepting only yourself, and by so doing have saved us all. But before leaving, please tell me your name."

"Sir Launcelot du Lake. Today I have fought to vindicate the honor of the knights of the Round Table, and I know that among Sir Tarquine's prisoners are two of my brethren, Sir Lyonel and Sir Ector, also your own brother, Sir Gawain. According to the shields there are also: Sir Brandiles, Sir

29. A *miscreant* knight is an evil, villainous one.

30. Launcelot wishes to defend against opposition, or *vindicate*, the honor of Tarquine's prisoners.

31. To *maim* is to injure seriously or horribly.

Galyhuddis, Sir Kay, Sir Alydukis, Sir Marhaus, and many others. Please release the prisoners and ask them to help themselves to the castle treasure. Give them all my greetings and say I will see them at the next Pentecost. And please request Sir Ector and Sir Lyonel to go straight to the court and await me there."

When Sir Launcelot had ridden away with the young noblewoman, Sir Gaheris entered the castle, and finding the porter in the hall, threw him on the ground and took the castle keys. He then released the prisoners, who, seeing his wounds, thanked him for their deliverance.

"Do not thank me for this work, but Sir Launcelot. He sends his greetings to you all, and asks you to help yourselves to the castle treasure. He has ridden away on another quest, but said that he will see you at the next Pentecost. Meanwhile, he requests Sir Lyonel and Sir Ector to return to the court and await him there."

"Certainly we shall not ride back to the court, but rather we shall follow Sir Launcelot wherever he goes," said Sir Ector.

"And I too shall follow him," said Sir Kay.

The prisoners searched the castle for their armor and horses and the castle treasure; and then a forester arrived with supplies of venison, so they feasted merrily and settled down for the night in the castle chambers—all but Sir Ector, Sir Lyonel, and Sir Kay, who set off immediately after supper in search of Sir Launcelot.

Launcelot Slays the Caitiff Knight Sir Tarquin and Rescues the Fair Lady and the Knights in Captivity, 1954–1955. Frank Cadogan Cowper. Oil, 40½ x 32 in. Private collection.

Viewing the painting: What knightly qualities does this painting express? Explain.

Sir Launcelot and the young noblewoman were riding down a broad highway when the young noblewoman said they were within sight of the spot where the knight generally attacked her.

"For shame that a knight should so degrade his high calling," Sir Launcelot replied. "Certainly we will teach him a much-needed lesson. Now, my lady, I suggest that you ride on ahead, and as soon as he molests you, I will come to the rescue."

Sir Launcelot halted and the young noblewoman rode gently forward. Soon the knight appeared with his page, and seized the young noblewoman from her horse; she cried out at once, and Sir Launcelot galloped up to them.

. . . you are the bravest and gentlest knight I have known.

"Scoundrel! what sort of knight do you think you are, to attack defenseless women?"

In answer the other knight drew his sword. Sir Launcelot did likewise, and they rushed together. With his first stroke Sir Launcelot split open the knight's head, down to the throat.

"Let that be your payment, though long overdue," said Sir Launcelot.

"Even so; he certainly deserved to die. His name was Sir Percy of the Forest Sauvage."

"My lady, do you require anything more of me?"

"No, good Sir Launcelot; and may the sweet Lord Jesu[32] protect you, for certainly you are the bravest and gentlest knight I have known. But pray tell me one thing: why is it you do not take to yourself a wife? Many good ladies, both high born and low born, grieve that so fine a knight as yourself should remain single. It is whispered, of course, that Queen Gwynevere has cast a spell over you so that you shall love no other."

"As for that, people must believe what they will about Queen Gwynevere and me. But married I will not be, for then I should have to attend my lady instead of entering for tournaments and wars, or riding in search of adventure. And I will not take a paramour, both for the fear of God and in the belief that those who do so are always unfortunate when they meet a knight who is purer of heart; for whether they are defeated or victorious in such an encounter, either result must be equally distressing and shameful. I believe that a true knight is neither adulterous nor lecherous."[33]

Sir Launcelot then took his leave of the young noblewoman, and for two days wandered alone through the forest, resting at night at the most meager of lodgings. On the third day, as he was crossing a bridge, he was accosted by a churlish porter,[34] who, after striking his horse on the nose so that it turned about, demanded to know by what right Sir Launcelot was riding that way.

"And what right do I need to cross this bridge? Surely, I cannot ride beside it," said Sir Launcelot.

"That is not for you to decide," said the porter, and with that he lashed at Sir Launcelot with his club. Sir Launcelot drew his sword, and after deflecting the blow, struck the porter on the head and split it open.

At the end of the bridge was a prosperous-looking village, overtopped by a fine castle.

32. *Jesu* (jā′ zo͞o) is a form of *Jesus.*

33. A true knight is pure. He doesn't commit adultery *(adulterous)*, nor is he preoccupied with indecent thoughts and desires *(lecherous)*.

34. Here, the gatekeeper *(porter)* is bad-tempered and very rude *(churlish)*, especially toward the poor horse!

As Sir Launcelot advanced he heard someone cry: "Good knight, beware! You have done yourself no good by killing the chief porter of the castle."

Sir Launcelot rode on regardless, through the village and into the castle court, which was richly grassed. Thinking to himself that this would be a good place for combat, Sir Launcelot tied his horse to a ring in the wall and started across the lawn. Meanwhile people were peering at him from every door and window, and again he heard the warning: "Good knight, you come here at your peril!"

Before long two giants appeared, fully armed except for their heads, and brandishing huge clubs. Together they rushed at Sir Launcelot, who raised his shield to defend himself, and then struck at one of the giants and beheaded him. Thereupon the second giant roared with dismay and fled into the forest, where Sir Launcelot pursued him. In a few minutes, Sir Launcelot drew abreast of the giant and struck him on the shoulder with a blow that carried through to the navel, and the giant dropped dead.

When Sir Launcelot returned to the castle, he was greeted by threescore ladies, who all knelt before him.

"Brave knight! we thank you for delivering us. Many of us have been prisoners for seven years now, and although we are all high born, we have had to work like servants for our keep, doing silk embroidery. Pray tell us your name, so that our friends can know who has saved us."

"My ladies, I am called Sir Launcelot du Lake."

"Welcome, Sir Launcelot! It was you alone whom the giants feared, and you alone who could have overcome them. How often have we prayed for your coming!"

"My ladies, please greet your friends for me; and when I pass through this country again, grant me what hospitality you may feel is my due. Please recompense[35] yourselves from the castle treasure, and then insure that the castle is restored to the rightful owner."

"Sir Launcelot, this is the castle of Tintagil, and belonged formerly to the duke of that name. But after his death, Igraine, who had been his wife, was made queen by King Uther Pendragon, to whom she bore Arthur, our present king."

"And so, after all, I know the owner of this castle. My ladies, I bless you, and farewell."

Always in quest of adventure, Sir Launcelot rode through many different countries, through wild valleys and forests, and across strange rivers; and at night he slept where he could, often in the roughest of lodgings. Then one day he came to a well-kept house where the lady offered him the best of hospitality. After supper he was taken to his chamber, which overlooked the front door, and there Sir Launcelot disarmed and fell comfortably asleep.

He was awakened a short time later by a tremendous knocking at the door below, and looking through the window recognized Sir Kay in the moonlight, and three knights galloping toward him with drawn swords. The moment they got to the house, they dismounted and set upon Sir Kay, who turned about and drew his sword to defend himself. Sir Launcelot hastily armed, saying to himself: "If they kill Sir Kay I shall be a party to his death, for three against one is unjust."

He let himself down from the window by means of his sheet, and then challenged the three attackers, whispering to Sir Kay to stand by while he dealt with them. Sir Kay did as he was advised, and then Sir Launcelot, with

35. **Launcelot invites the ladies to *recompense* themselves, or divide the treasure among themselves as a way to make up for their treatment by the giants.**

seven tremendous blows, brought all three knights to their knees and begging for mercy.

"Your lives will be spared if you yield to Sir Kay," said Sir Launcelot.

"Sir, it is surely you to whom we should yield, since we could easily have overcome Sir Kay."

"If you wish to be spared, you will go as prisoners of Sir Kay, and yield to Queen Gwynevere."

Each of the knights then swore on his sword to abide by the conditions of his surrender, and Sir Launcelot knocked once more at the door of the house.

"Why, I thought you were safely in bed," said the landlady, recognizing Sir Launcelot as she opened the door.

"Madam, I was, but then I had to jump out of the window and rescue this comrade of mine."

As they came into the light, Sir Kay recognized Sir Launcelot and thanked him humbly for twice saving his life.

"It was no more than I should have done, but come up to my chamber; you must be tired and hungry."

When Sir Kay had eaten, he lay on Sir Launcelot's bed, and they slept together until dawn. Sir Launcelot woke first, and rising quietly, clad himself in Sir Kay's armor, and then, mounting Sir Kay's horse, rode away from the house.

When Sir Kay awoke, he was astonished to find that Sir Launcelot had exchanged armor with him, but then he realized he had done it so that he should ride home unmolested, while Sir Launcelot encountered his opponents. And when Sir Kay had taken his leave of the landlady he rode back to the court without further incident.

For several days Sir Launcelot rode through the forest, and then he came to a countryside of low meadows and broad streams. At the foot of a bridge he saw three pavilions, and a knight standing at the entrance to each, with a white shield hanging above, and a spear thrust into the ground at one side. Sir Launcelot recognized the three knights, who were from Arthur's court, as Sir Gawtere, Sir Raynolde, and Sir Gylmere. However, he rode straight past them, looking neither to right nor to left, and without saluting them.

"Why, there rides Sir Kay, the most overbearing[36] knight of all, in spite of his many defeats. I think I will challenge him and see if I cannot shake his pride a little," said Sir Gawtere.

He then galloped up to Sir Launcelot and challenged him. They jousted, and Sir Gawtere was flung violently from the saddle.

"That is certainly not Sir Kay," said Sir Raynolde. "For one thing, he is very much bigger."

"Probably it is some knight who has killed Sir Kay and is riding in his armor," Sir Gylmere replied.

"Well, since he has overcome our brother we shall have to challenge him. But I think it must be either Sir Launcelot, Sir Tristram, or Sir Pelleas; and we may not come well out of this."

Sir Gylmere challenged Sir Launcelot next, and was also overthrown. Then Sir Raynolde rode up to him.

"Sir, I would prefer not to challenge a knight so powerful as you, but since you have probably killed my brothers, I am obliged to; so defend yourself!"

They jousted; both broke their spears and they continued the combat with swords. Sir Gawtere and Sir Gylmere recovered, and attempted to rescue their brother, but Sir

36. An *overbearing* person is excessively proud and superior in attitude and behavior.

Launcelot saw them in time, and using more strength than hitherto, struck each off his horse again. At this, Sir Raynolde, badly wounded as he was, and with blood streaming from his head, picked himself up and once more rushed at Sir Launcelot.

"Sir, I should let things be," said Sir Launcelot. "I was not far away when you were knighted, and I know you to be worthy: therefore do not oblige me to kill you."

"May God reward you!" Sir Raynolde replied. "But speaking both for myself and my brothers, I would prefer to know your name before yielding to you, because we know very well that you are not Sir Kay, whom any one of us could have overcome."

"That is as may be; but I still require that you yield to Queen Gwynevere at the next Pentecost, and say that Sir Kay sent you."

The three brothers took their oath, and Sir Launcelot left them. He had not ridden much further when, coming to a glade, he found four more knights of the Round Table: Sir Gawain, Sir Ector, Sir Uwayne, and Sir Sagramour le Desyrus.

"Look!" said Sir Sagramour, "there rides Sir Kay. I will challenge him."

Sir Sagramour first, then each of the other knights in turn, challenged Sir Launcelot, and was flung from his horse. Sir Launcelot left them gasping on the ground, and said to himself as he rode away: "Blessed be the maker of this spear; with it I have tumbled four knights off their horses." Meanwhile the four knights were picking themselves up and consoling each other.

"To the devil with him! He is indeed powerful," said one.

"I believe that it must be Sir Launcelot," said another.

"Anyhow, let him go now; we shall discover when we return to Camelot," said a third, and so on. . . .

Sir Launcelot returned to Camelot two days before the feast of Pentecost, and at the court was acclaimed[37] by many of the knights he had met on his adventures.

Sir Gawain, Sir Uwayne, Sir Ector, and Sir Sagramour all laughed when they saw him in Sir Kay's armor, but without the helmet, and readily forgave his joke at their expense.

Sir Gaheris described to the court the terrible battle Sir Launcelot had fought with Sir Tarquine, and how sixty-four prisoners had been freed as a result of his victory.

Sir Kay related how Sir Launcelot had twice saved his life, and then exchanged armor with him, so that he should ride unchallenged.

Sir Gawtere, Sir Gylmere, and Sir Raynolde described how he had defeated them at the bridge, and forced them to yield as prisoners of Sir Kay; and they were overjoyed to discover that it had been Sir Launcelot nevertheless.

Sir Modred, Sir Mador, and Sir Gahalantyne described his tremendous feats in the battle against the King of North Galys; and Sir Launcelot himself described his enchantment by the four queens, and his rescue at the hands of the daughter of King Bagdemagus. . . .

And thus it was, at this time, that Sir Launcelot became the most famous knight at King Arthur's court.

37. Launcelot was *acclaimed*, or greeted with loud, enthusiastic praise.

Responding to Literature

Personal Response

What was your reaction to the world of King Arthur and his knights? If you could be transported there for a day, would you go? Why or why not?

Analyzing Literature

Recall

1. What does Merlin ask in return for granting King Uther his wish?
2. What events lead Arthur to pull the sword from the stone? What happens after he retrieves the sword?
3. Why is Sir Tarquine so determined to kill Sir Launcelot?
4. What rumor does the "young noblewoman" say has been circulating about why Sir Launcelot has never married?
5. Why does Sir Launcelot exchange armor with Sir Kay? What is the result of this action for Sir Launcelot?

Interpret

6. Why, do you think, does Merlin insist upon the reward he requested for helping Uther?
7. What does Arthur's behavior immediately after pulling the sword tell you about him? How might Arthur's rule be different from Uther's?
8. Why, do you suppose, does Sir Launcelot reveal his identity to Sir Tarquine, knowing that the ensuing fight will be to the death?
9. What does Sir Launcelot's explanation for not marrying tell you about his values?
10. What do you learn about Sir Kay's character in "The Tale of King Arthur" that **foreshadows** (see page R5) what his fellow knights think of him in "The Tale of Sir Launcelot du Lake"?

Evaluate and Connect

11. Do the characters of King Uther Pendragon and Igraine seem realistic? Why or why not?
12. If you had been one of the nobles, would you have proclaimed the young Arthur king as described in "The Tale of King Arthur"? Explain.
13. How do the relationships between men and women in the selections compare with gender roles in society today?
14. Compare your reaction to the violence in the selection with your response to violence in television programs and video games. Explain.
15. Theme Connections Does Sir Launcelot fit your description of a hero that you noted in the Reading Focus on page 914? Explain.

Literary ELEMENTS

Dialogue

Much of *Le Morte d'Arthur* is related through **dialogue,** the written conversation between characters. Dialogue gives readers a sense of a character's personality and feelings, and helps readers focus on important scenes. In "The Tale of King Arthur," for example, the reader realizes the importance of King Uther's feelings when Uther says, "Igraine has broken my heart, and unless I can win her, I shall never recover."

1. Reread the scene on page 920 in which Sir Ector realizes that Arthur has removed the sword from the stone. Why, do you suppose, has the author chosen to use dialogue here?
2. Which passage of dialogue do you find particularly effective or striking? Why?

- See **Literary Terms Handbook,** p. R3.

Literary Criticism

"Arthur," observes critic Jeffrey Helterman, "institutes a code of behavior which stresses always succoring ladies . . . and never taking up battles for a wrongful cause." With a partner, find examples from the "Tale of Sir Launcelot du Lake" of knights following this code of behavior. What can you infer from the code about the values held by this society?

Literature and Writing

Writing About Literature

Character Sketch Briefly list the principal adventures of Sir Launcelot. Then make a note of Launcelot's character traits revealed by these incidents. Based on these notes, write a description of Sir Launcelot.

Creative Writing

Boy to Become King? Imagine that you are a reporter sent back in time to report on the events involving Arthur and the sword. Write a news story, using "quotations" from people who witnessed the events.

Extending Your Response

Literature Groups

Your Move Develop a board game based on the adventures of knights of the Round Table. Start by listing the conflicts met by Sir Launcelot and his resolutions of those situations. Then brainstorm additional difficulties and outcomes that could have occurred in Camelot. Write the goal and rules of the game and sketch a game board. Share your game with other groups.

Performing

A Manner of Speaking What might Arthur say to the nobles and knights at his coronation? Jot down a few notes and determine how your delivery will be in character. Then deliver Arthur's "inaugural address" to the class.

Interdisciplinary Activity

Music: Rock 'n' Rollin' Knights Choose a type of music—rock, blues, jazz, folk, rap—and write lyrics to retell the tale of Arthur or Sir Launcelot. Perform your song for the class. Then explain how your choice of music and performance techniques suits the content of the tale.

Reading Further

You might enjoy this legendary tale of heroes:

Sir Gawain and the Green Knight, written by an unknown poet, tells the extraordinary adventure of Sir Gawain.

Save your work for your portfolio.

VOCABULARY • Etymology

An etymology traces the development of a word since its earliest recorded usage. For example, *accost* comes from the Middle French *coster,* derived from the Latin *ad,* meaning "to," and *costa,* meaning "side" or "rib." Originally, to *accost* someone meant to be by that person's side. Eventually it came to mean "to approach," and then, over time, it came to mean "to approach and speak to, especially in an aggressive manner." The etymology of *accost* shows the change in the word's meaning and spelling over time.

Now study these etymologies of words from *Le Morte d'Arthur:*

oblige: from the Middle English *obligen,* from the Old French *obliger,* from the Latin *obligare,* meaning "to bind to," from *ob,* meaning "toward," and *ligare,* "to bind."

tumultuous: from the Middle English *tumulte,* from the Middle French, from the Latin *tumultus,* from the Latin *tumere,* "to swell," akin to the Sanskrit *tumula,* meaning "noisy."

PRACTICE Use the etymologies given above to answer the questions.

1. Which word is LEAST likely to have come from the same root as *oblige—ligament, league,* or *legend?*
2. Which word is MOST likely to have come from the same root as *accost—coast, cost,* or *costume?*
3. Which word is MOST likely to have come from the same root as *tumultuous—tumble, tumor,* or *tomb?*

Before You Read

from *Sundiata*

Reading Focus

What helps you gain the extra confidence and energy that you need to perform well in events such as a crucial game, an exam, or a driving test?

Quickwrite Recall a challenging situation. Write for five minutes, explaining the situation and telling how you prepared to face it.

Setting a Purpose Read to learn how a legendary hero prepares his troops for battle.

Building Background

The Time and Place

According to legend, the ancient Kingdom of Mali (mä′ lē) was established by a hero named Sundiata in approximately 1230. This territory included a large part of present-day West Africa. At a time when bandits roamed through other areas, Mali was known as a safe and orderly place. "Neither traveler nor inhabitant in it has anything to fear from robbers or men of violence," wrote an early Arab visitor.

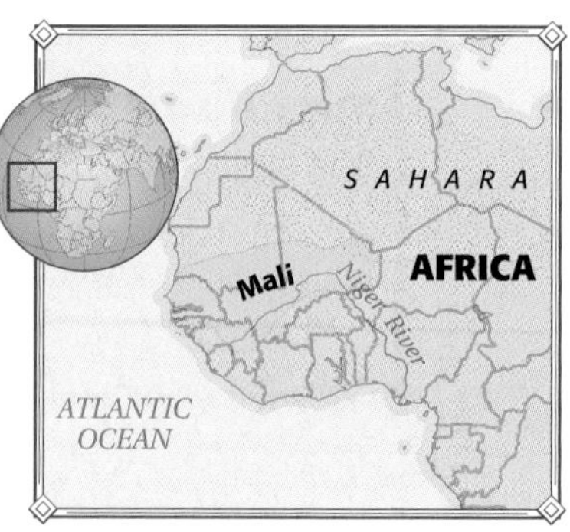

Did You Know?

An important member of an African king's household was the *griot* (grē′ ō). At a time when the people of Mali could not read or write, the *griot* was a sort of living history book who recalled for the court the great deeds of the past and recited the country's traditions and laws.

Vocabulary Preview

vanquish (vang′ kwish) *v.* to conquer or overcome; p. 937

scrupulous (skrōō′ pyə ləs) *adj.* thoroughly attentive to even the smallest details; precise; p. 937

elude (i lōōd′) *v.* to avoid or escape, especially through cleverness or quickness; p. 937

confidante (kon′ fə dant′) *n.* a person who is entrusted with secrets or private affairs; p. 938

perpetuate (pər pech′ ōō āt′) *v.* to cause to continue to be remembered; p. 938

Meet the Storyteller

"Listen to my word, you who want to know; by my mouth you will learn the history of Mali."

So said Mamadou Kouyaté (ma′ mä dōō kōō yä′ tā), the African storyteller, or *griot*, who, in the 1950s, narrated *Sundiata* (sōōn dyä′ tə) for D. T. Niane, a folklore scholar. *Sundiata* has no single author. It is a tale that has been passed down orally by skilled poets from generation to generation. As the storyteller Kouyaté put it, "Without us the names of kings would vanish into oblivion, we are the memory of mankind."

Most cultures have stories that originate in oral tradition. *Mahābhārata* and *Rāmāyaṇa* are two stories about the codes of conduct in war and romance in ancient India. *Egils saga* portrays adventurous tales of murder, family feuds, and warfare in medieval Iceland and Norway.

from Sundiata

Recorded by D. T. Niane

Translated by G. D. Pickett

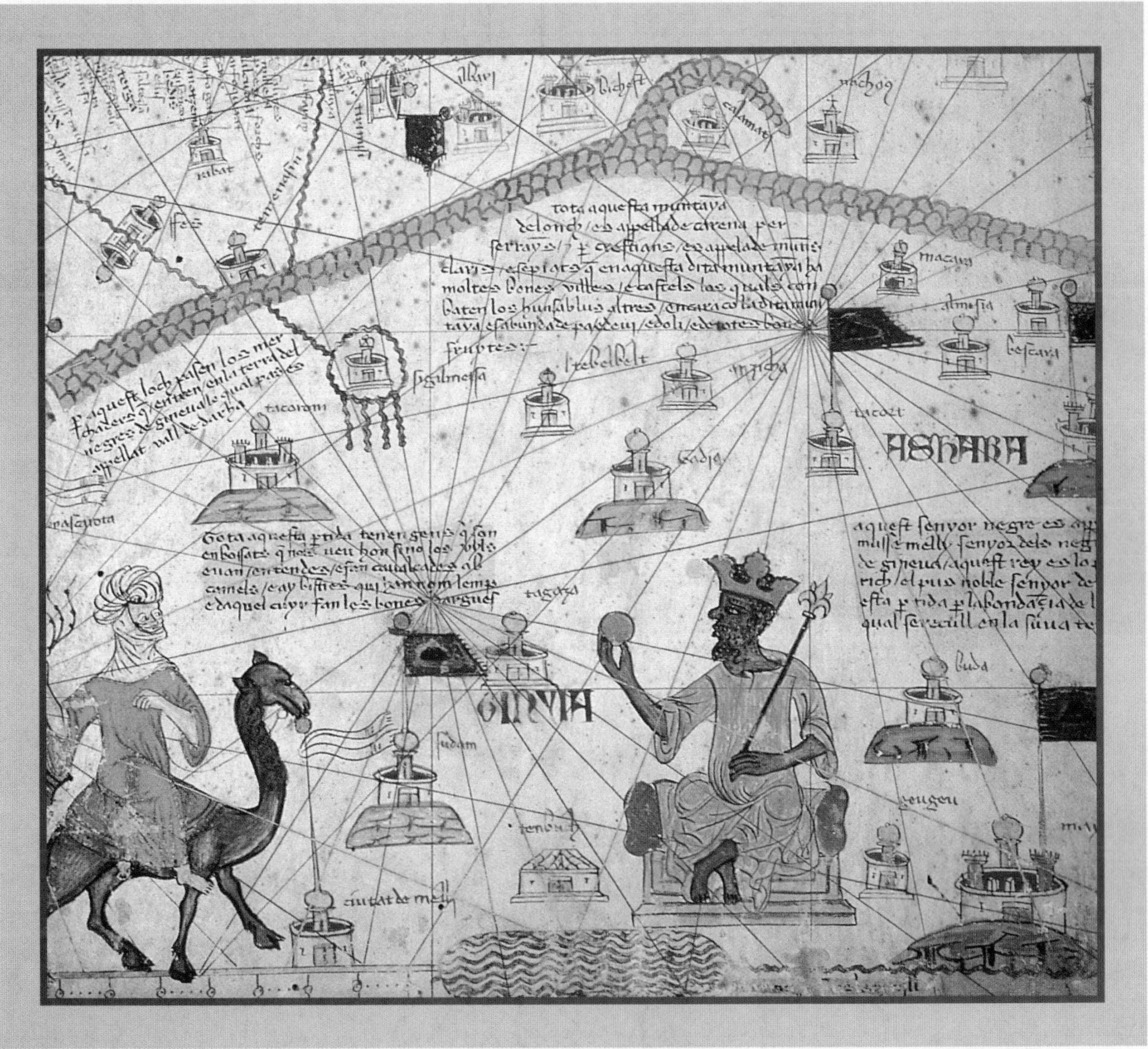

The Catalan Atlas, c. 1375 (detail). Attributed to Cresques Abraham. Vellum, 65 x 300 cm. Bibliotheque Nationale de France, Paris.

Even before he was born, Sundiata was destined for greatness. Acting on the instructions of a soothsayer,[1] his father, the king of Mali, had married a hideous, hunchbacked woman named Sogolon. As foretold, the couple had a son. It seemed, however, that the boy was unlikely to become a great leader as had been predicted. The young Sundiata could not even walk. He and his ugly mother became the object of cruel jokes and jealous abuse by the old king's first wife. At the age of seven, Sundiata suddenly reacted to an insult by standing up and tearing a tree from the ground. He instantly became the center of attention, a boy with great charm and the strength of ten men. Among his constant companions were the princes Fran Kamara and Kamandjan.[2] Even more important to him was his griot, Balla Fasséké,[3] who taught him the history of his people and of the world beyond.

Still fearing persecution from the jealous queen, Sogolon escaped with Sundiata to neighboring Ghana. There the amazing boy grew up. In his absence, Mali was taken over by the king of Sosso, a cruel sorcerer named Soumaoro,[4] whose secret chamber was tapestried with human skins and adorned with the skulls of his enemies. Soumaoro captured Balla Fasséké and Sundiata's half-sister, Nana Triban.[5] Enraged by Soumaoro's barbarism, Sundiata raised an army and prepared to restore his country to its rightful people. Although he succeeded in defeating Soumaoro in a great battle, he could not capture or kill the man himself, for the magician had the power to appear and disappear at will. While Sundiata rested in the town of Sibi,[6] Soumaoro once again raised a powerful army. The two prepared to meet in a final battle.

1. A *soothsayer* is someone who claims to be able to foretell the future.
2. *Kamara* (kä′ mä rä), *Kamandjan* (kä′ män jän)
3. *Balla Fasséké* (bä′ lä fä sä′ kā)
4. *Soumaoro* (so͞o′ mər ō)
5. *Nana Triban* (nä′ nä tri′ bän)
6. *Sibi* (si′ bē)

SUNDIATA and his mighty army stopped at Sibi for a few days. The road into Mali lay open, but Soumaoro was not yet vanquished. The king of Sosso had mustered a powerful army and his sofas were numbered by the thousand. He had raised contingents[7] in all the lands over which he held sway and got ready to pounce again on Mali.

With scrupulous care, Sundiata had made his preparations at Sibi. Now he had sufficient sofas to meet Soumaoro in the open field, but it was not a question of having a lot of troops. In order to defeat Soumaoro it was necessary first of all to destroy his magical power. At Sibi, Sundiata decided to consult the soothsayers, of whom the most famous in Mali were there.

On their advice Djata[8] had to sacrifice a hundred white bulls, a hundred white rams and a hundred white cocks. It was in the middle of this slaughter that it was announced to Sundiata that his sister Nana Triban and Balla Fasséké, having been able to escape from Sosso, had now arrived. Then Sundiata said to Tabon Wana, "If my sister and Balla have been able to escape from Sosso, Soumaoro has lost the battle."

Leaving the site of the sacrifices, Sundiata returned to Sibi and met his sister and his griot.

"Hail, my brother," said Nana Triban.

"Greetings, sister."

"Hail Sundiata," said Balla Fasséké.

"Greetings, my griot."

After numerous salutations, Sundiata asked the fugitives to relate how they had been able to elude the vigilance of a king such as Soumaoro. But Triban was weeping for joy. Since the time of their childhood she had shown much sympathy towards the crippled child that Sundiata had been. Never had she shared the hate of her mother, Sassouma Bérété.

"You know, Djata," she said, weeping, "for my part I did not want you to leave the country. It was my mother who did all that. Now Niani is destroyed, its inhabitants scattered, and there are many whom Soumaoro has carried off into captivity in Sosso."

She cried worse than ever. Djata was sympathetic to all this, but he was in a hurry to know something about Sosso. Balla Fasséké understood and said, "Triban, wipe away your tears and tell your story, speak to your brother. You know that he has never thought ill of you, and besides, all that was in his destiny."

Nana Triban wiped her tears away and spoke.

"When you left Mali, my brother sent me by force to Sosso to be the wife of Soumaoro, whom he greatly feared. I wept a great deal at the beginning but when I saw that perhaps all was not lost

Bearded Male Figure. 14th century, Djenne. Terra-cotta, height: 38.1 cm. The Detroit Institute of Arts.

Viewing the sculpture: What personal characteristics does this sculpture convey to you? Which character from the selection possesses similar traits? Explain.

7. The *sofas* are soldiers or warriors, and *contingents* are additional troops.
8. *Djata* (dyä′ tə) is a shortened form of *Sundiata*.

Vocabulary

vanquish (vang′ kwish) *v.* to conquer or overcome
scrupulous (skroo̅′ pyə ləs) *adj.* thoroughly attentive to even the smallest details; precise
elude (i lo̅o̅d′) *v.* to avoid or escape, especially through cleverness or quickness

Archer Figure. Inland Delta Region, Mali. Ceramic, height: 61.9 cm. National Museum of African Art. Museum Purchase, 86-12-1.

I resigned[9] myself for the time being. I was nice to Soumaoro and was the chosen one among his numerous wives. I had my chamber in the great tower where he himself lived. I knew how to flatter him and make him jealous. Soon I became his confidante and I pretended to hate you, to share the hate which my mother bore you. It was said that you would come back one day, but I swore to him that you would never have the presumption[10] to claim a kingdom you had never possessed, and that you had left never to see Mali again. However, I was in constant touch with Balla Fasséké, each of us wanting to pierce the mystery of Soumaoro's magic power. One night I took the bull by the horns and said to Soumaoro: 'Tell me, oh you whom kings mention with trembling, tell me Soumaoro, are you a man like others or are you the same as the jinn[11] who protects humans? No one can bear the glare of your eyes, your arm has the strength of ten arms. Tell me, king of kings, tell me what jinn protects you so that I can worship him also.' These words filled him with pride and he himself boasted to me of the might of his Tana. That very night he took me into his magic chamber and told me all.

"Then I redoubled my zeal to show myself faithful to his cause, I seemed more overwhelmed than him. It was even he who went to the extent of telling me to take courage, that nothing was yet lost. During all this time, in complicity[12] with Balla Fasséké, I was preparing for the inevitable flight. Nobody watched over me any more in the royal enclosure, of which I knew the smallest twists and turns. And one night when Soumaoro was away, I left that fearsome tower. Balla Fasséké was waiting for me at the gate to which I had the key. It was thus, brother, that we left Sosso."

Balla Fasséké took up the story.

"We hastened to you. The news of the victory of Tabon made me realize that the lion had burst his chains. Oh son of Sogolon, I am the word and you are the deed, now your destiny begins."

Sundiata was very happy to recover his sister and his griot. He now had the singer who would perpetuate his memory by his

9. When Nana *resigned* herself, she gave in without resistance or complaint.
10. Here, *presumption* means "excessive boldness in thought or conduct."
11. In Arab folklore, a *jinn*, or genie, was an angel-like spirit that had magical powers and could take on human or animal form.
12. People acting in *complicity* are involved together, as accomplices in a crime or, as here, in secret activities.

Vocabulary

confidante (kon′ fə dant′) *n.* a person who is entrusted with secrets or private affairs
perpetuate (pər pech′ o͞o āt′) *v.* to cause to continue to be remembered

words. There would not be any heroes if deeds were condemned to man's forgetfulness, for we ply our trade to excite the admiration of the living, and to evoke the veneration[13] of those who are to come.

Djata was informed that Soumaoro was advancing along the river and was trying to block his route to Mali. The preparations were complete, but before leaving Sibi, Sundiata arranged a great military review in the camp so that Balla Fasséké, by his words, should strengthen the hearts of his sofas. In the middle of a great circle formed by the sofas, Balla Fasséké extolled[14] the heroes of Mali. To the king of Tabon he said: "You whose iron arm can split ten skulls at a time, you, Tabon Wana, king of the Sinikimbon and the Djallonké,[15] can you show me what you are capable of before the great battle is joined?"

The griot's words made Fran Kamara leap up. Sword in hand and mounted on his swift steed he came and stood before Sundiata and said, "Maghan Sundiata, I renew my oath to you in the sight of all the Mandingoes gathered together. I pledge myself to conquer or to die by your side. Mali will be free or the smiths[16] of Tabon will be dead."

The tribes of Tabon shouted their approval, brandishing their weapons, and Fran Kamara, stirred by the shouts of the sofas, spurred his charger and charged forward. The warriors opened their ranks and he bore down on a great mahogany tree. With one stroke of his sword he split the giant tree just as one splits a paw-paw.[17] The flabbergasted army shouted, "Wassa Wassa . . . Ayé . . . "

Then, coming back to Sundiata, his sword held aloft, the king of Tabon said, "Thus on the Niger plain will the smiths of Tabon cleave those of Sosso in twain."[18] And the hero came and fell in beside Sundiata.

Turning towards Kamandjan, the king of Sibi and cousin of the king of Tabon, Balla Fasséké said, "Where are you, Kamandjan, where is Fama Djan? Where is the king of the Dalikimbon Kamaras? Kamandjan of Sibi, I salute you. But what will I have to relate of you to future generations?"

Before Balla had finished speaking, the king of Sibi, shouting his war cry, started his fiery charger off at full gallop. The sofas, stupefied, watched the extraordinary horseman head for the mountain that dominates[19] Sibi. . . . Suddenly a tremendous din filled the sky, the earth trembled under the feet of the sofas and a cloud of red dust covered the mountain. Was this the end of the world? . . . But slowly the dust cleared and the sofas saw Kamandjan coming back holding a fragment of a sword. The mountain of Sibi, pierced through and through, disclosed a wide tunnel!

Admiration was at its highest pitch. The army stood speechless and the king of Sibi, without saying a word, came and fell in beside Sundiata.

Balla Fasséké mentioned all the chiefs by name and they all performed great feats; then the army, confident in its leadership, left Sibi.

13. To *evoke veneration* is to call up feelings of deep respect.
14. Balla highly praised *(extolled)* the heroes.
15. *Sinikimbon* (si′ nē kim′ bōn), *Djallonké* (jä lôn′ kā)
16. The *Mandingoes* were various peoples who inhabited the upper and middle Niger River valley. *Smiths* make or repair metal objects, such as swords, but Fran Kamara is speaking figuratively, referring to his sword-bearing troops.

17. *Paw-paw* is a banana-like fruit.
18. To *cleave in twain* is to split in two.
19. The mountain *dominates* Sibi because it towers over the city.

Responding to Literature

Personal Response

What do you think might happen next in this story? Share your predictions with your classmates.

Analyzing Literature

Recall and Interpret

1. What does Sundiata first plan to do in order to defeat Soumaoro? Later, what does he do before leaving Sibi? What do his methods suggest about him as a leader?
2. How does Nana Triban get information from Soumaoro about his magic powers? What is her purpose in getting this information?
3. **Theme Connections** Who escapes with Nana Triban? What does the narrator mean by saying, "There would not be any heroes if deeds were condemned to man's forgetfulness . . ."?
4. What astonishing deeds do Fran Kamara and Kamandjan perform at the urging of Balla Fasséké? Why do Balla Fasséké's words cause the warriors to react as they do?

Evaluate and Connect

5. What do you think of the way Nana Triban handles Soumaoro? Can you imagine such a situation taking place today? Explain.
6. Why do you think Sundiata has such a strong desire to be remembered by future generations? For what would you like to be remembered?
7. What knowledge of human nature does Balla Fasséké reveal through his speeches? Does our society today have any methods comparable to Balla Fasséké's? Explain.
8. Compare and contrast your response to the Reading Focus on page 934 with the way Sundiata prepares his army for the battle.

Literary ELEMENTS

Tall Tale

Sundiata is a **tall tale,** a type of folklore in which the deeds of one or more characters are wildly exaggerated but told seriously–as if the deeds were true. As with Sundiata and the other kings gathered in Sibi, the heroes of tall tales are likeable characters whose extraordinary traits enable them to perform improbable feats. For example, when Balla Fasséké acclaims the heroes in camp, he convincingly describes the king of Tabon as one "whose iron arm can split ten skulls at a time."

1. In your opinion, which of the heroes in *Sundiata* possesses the most extraordinary trait? Give one example of how that trait is exaggerated in the tall tale.
2. Why, do you think, are the heroes in *Sundiata* likeable?

- See **Literary Terms Handbook,** p. R13.

Extending Your Response

Creative Writing

Tall Tales According to the final paragraph of this excerpt, Balla Fasséké inspires all the chiefs of Sundiata's army to perform "great feats." Only two of these feats are described, however. Invent three other characters, give them suitable names, and describe what fantastic feats they might perform to impress the troops and win fame.

Learning for Life

On the Eve of Battle Imagine that you are Sundiata trying to prepare his army for battle. Write a memo to Balla Fasséké, instructing him on how to address the troops. Include a convincing explanation for your request. Share your memo with the class.

Save your work for your portfolio.

COMPARING *selections*

from Le Morte d'Arthur and *from* Sundiata

COMPARE **HEROES**

Which character better fits your description of a hero, Sir Launcelot or Sundiata? Draw and complete a chart like the one shown.

Your description of a hero:	
Heroic quality of Sir Launcelot:	
Specific detail from story:	
Heroic quality of Sundiata:	
Specific detail from story:	
Conclusion: Which character better fits your definition of a hero? Why?	

COMPARE **THEMES**

Like many legendary tales, both *Le Morte d'Arthur* and *Sundiata* share themes of magic, romance, and heroism. Each work, however, treats these themes in a distinctive style. Discuss the following questions with your class.

1. In which work, would you say, does magic play a more important role? Support your answer with specific examples.
2. How do the exploits of Arthur's knights compare with the feats of Kamara and Kamandjan?
3. Are the relationships between men and women presented differently in the two legends? Explain.

How Four Queens Found Sir Lancelot Sleeping, 1908 (detail).

COMPARE **IMAGES**

Working with your group, decide which images from *Le Morte d'Arthur* and *Sundiata* you would show on videotape case covers for feature films of these stories. Then, write the text and draw a rough sketch for each case cover. Discuss the similarities and differences between the covers with other groups.

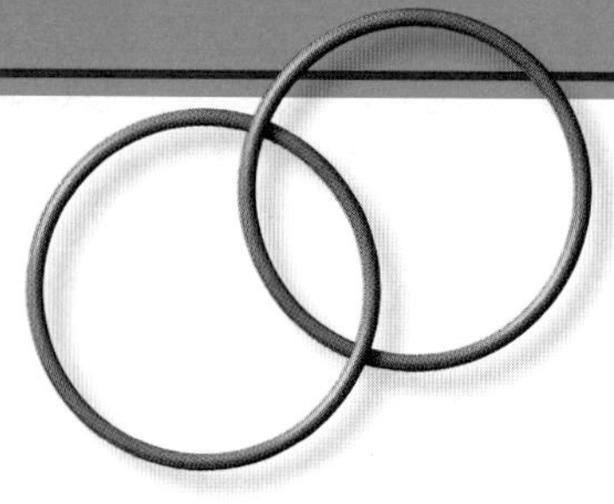

Grammar Link

Missing Commas with Nonessential Elements

There are many kinds of **grammatical elements**–words, phrases, and clauses–that can be part of a sentence. In some sentences, these elements are "essential," that is, they are necessary to the meaning of the sentence. Those elements that are *not* essential to the meaning of the sentence must be set off with commas.

Essential: The knight who defeated the most challengers was Launcelot.
Nonessential: Launcelot, who was famous and feared, went in search of adventure.

In the first example, the underlined section identifies which knight the sentence is about. It gives necessary information about a noun *(knight).* Therefore, it is essential to the meaning of the sentence. In the second example, the underlined section gives "extra" information about a noun *(Launcelot).* It could be left out without changing the meaning of the sentence. Therefore, it is nonessential and must be set off with commas.

Problem Missing commas with a nonessential element:
The greatest knight Launcelot slept under a tree.
His companions who were also knights rode off.
There was to be sure much adventure to be found.
Medieval England was well rather short on law and order.

Solution Set off a nonessential element with commas:
The greatest knight, Launcelot, slept under a tree.
His companions, who were also knights, rode off.
There was, to be sure, much adventure to be found.
Medieval England was, well, rather short on law and order.

● For more about commas with nonessential elements, see **Language Handbook,** p. R26.

EXERCISE

Rewrite incorrect sentences, adding necessary commas. If the sentence is correct, write *Correct.*

1. Soumaoro the king of Sosso was Sundiata's enemy.
2. The woman who was Soumaoro's favorite wife was Sundiata's half-sister.
3. Sundiata's griot Balla Fasséké escaped from Sosso with Nana Triban.
4. The royal enclosure filled with twists and turns was no challenge for Nana Triban.
5. Another benefit in fact was that she had a key to the gate.

Writing Skills

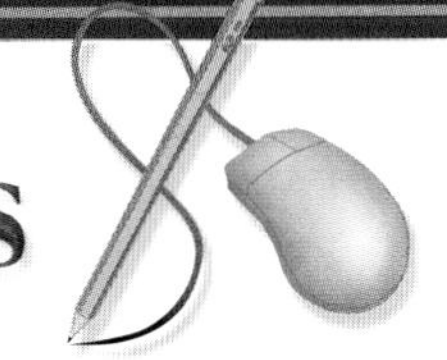

Main Idea and Supporting Details

Novelist George Orwell wrote, "Good prose is like a window-pane." To make your writing as clear as glass, make sure each paragraph expresses one main idea supported by details.

The **main idea,** or focus, of a paragraph should be presented in a direct statement–that is, in a **topic sentence.** All the other sentences in the paragraph are to give details that prove, clarify, or expand the main idea. These details will include examples, quotations, and facts. Read the following paragraph from a personal response to the story "Arthur Becomes King."

> **The author adds humor to the story by emphasizing the human characteristics of his characters. For example, the noblemen don't speak in the formal, stilted language that I've heard kings, princes, and lords use. King Pellinore sounds like a common gossip when he says "It's the very latest news." His fragmented dialogue is true of the way people speak when they're very excited and in a hurry to tell gossip. The way the characters interrupt and don't listen carefully to each other leads to misunderstandings and confusion—just as in real life. Finally, the characters mix up their words, substituting one word for another, which causes the reader to envision something very different from the intended meaning.**

In the paragraph above, the first sentence states the main idea and also hints at what the paragraph will say about it. Each of the other sentences supports the main idea.

Although a topic sentence often appears at the beginning of a paragraph, as in the example above, it can appear anywhere in a paragraph.

- Begin a paragraph with a topic sentence to let the reader know what's to come.
- End a paragraph with a topic sentence to summarize the main idea and reinforce the reader's understanding of the main idea.

EXERCISES

1. Write a paragraph with a topic sentence and supporting details that describe your ideal getaway place–a place you like to go to think things through.
2. Look in your portfolio for a paragraph you have written. Reread the paragraph, and underline the topic sentence. Then rewrite the paragraph, moving the topic sentence to a new position. How does moving the topic sentence affect the paragraph? What other adjustments, if any, did you have to make? Why?

Before You Read

The Passing of Arthur

Reading Focus

When have you found it difficult to part with something you wished you could keep?

Journal What special meaning did the object have? Did you find a substitute or consider it irreplaceable? In your journal, describe the object and tell how you reacted to giving it up.

Setting a Purpose Read to learn how two characters part with something important.

Building Background

The Time and Place

"The Passing of Arthur" is one of a series of twelve long poems called *Idylls of the King,* which tells about the legendary King Arthur and his knights of the Round Table. The *Idylls* takes place in early medieval times in England. This excerpt is set in Lyonnesse, a legendary land located off the southwestern coast of England. King Arthur has just been wounded–and most of his knights have been killed–in a battle against Arthur's evil nephew, Modred. The lone surviving knight, Sir Bedivere, takes the wounded king to the ruins of a chapel near the battlefield.

Battle between King Arthur and Modred. 15th century, from the St. Albans Chronicle. English, with Flemish illuminations.

Did You Know?

Different stories are told about the source of Excalibur, King Arthur's sword, which plays a major role in "The Passing of Arthur." In one account, Arthur miraculously draws the sword from a stone as a young boy to prove his royalty. In another version, the Lady of the Lake, a magical being who lives in a castle in a lake, gives the sword to Arthur. In *Idylls of the King,* Tennyson adopts the latter version of the story and relates that Arthur is instructed to take the sword and then to cast it away later in his life.

Meet Alfred, Lord Tennyson

"The vision of Arthur . . . came upon me when, little more than a boy, I first lighted upon Malory."

After his initial exposure to Sir Thomas Malory's *Le Morte d'Arthur* in boyhood, Tennyson longed to write a "whole great poem" on the Arthurian legend. One of twelve children, Tennyson and his brothers often played knights of the Round Table. Tennyson worked on *Idylls of the King,* a verse rendition of the Arthur legend, over several years. A popular poet, he became poet laureate of Great Britain in 1850.

Alfred, Lord Tennyson was born in Somersby in Lincolnshire, England, in 1809. He died in 1892. "The Passing of Arthur" was first published in 1842.

The Passing of Arthur

from Idylls of the King

Alfred, Lord Tennyson

Morte d'Arthur, 1862. James Mulcaster Carrick. Oil on canvas, 39¼ x 54 in. Private collection.

The Passing of Arthur

Then spake King Arthur to Sir Bedivere:
"The sequel° of to-day unsolders° all
The goodliest fellowship of famous knights
Whereof this world holds record. Such a sleep
They sleep—the men I loved. I think that we
Shall never more, at any future time,
Delight our souls with talk of knightly deeds,
Walking about the gardens and the halls
Of Camelot,° as in the days that were.
I perish by this people which I made,—
Tho' Merlin° sware that I should come again
To rule once more—but let what will be be,
I am so deeply smitten thro' the helm°
That without help I cannot last till morn.
Thou therefore take my brand° Excalibur,
Which was my pride; for thou rememberest how
In those old days, on summer noon, an arm
Rose up from out the bosom of the lake,
Clothed in white samite,° mystic,° wonderful,
Holding the sword—and how I row'd across
And took it, and have worn it, like a king;
And, wheresoever I am sung or told
In aftertime, this also shall be known.
But now delay not; take Excalibur,
And fling him far into the middle mere;°
Watch what thou seest, and lightly° bring me word."

To him replied the bold Sir Bedivere:
"It is not meet,° Sir King, to leave thee thus,
Aidless, alone, and smitten thro' the helm—
A little thing may harm a wounded man;
Yet I thy hest° will all perform at full,
Watch what I see, and lightly bring thee word."

So saying, from the ruin'd shrine he stept,
And in the moon athwart° the place of tombs,
Where lay the mighty bones of ancient men,
Old knights, and over them the sea-wind sang
Shrill, chill, with flakes of foam. He, stepping down
By zigzag paths and juts of pointed rock,
Came on the shining levels of the lake.

There drew he forth the brand Excalibur,
And o'er him, drawing it, the winter moon,

2 **sequel:** the result or consequence. **unsolders** (un sod′ ərz): separates.

9 **Camelot:** the site of King Arthur's court.

11 **Merlin:** a magician who counseled King Arthur.

13 **smitten thro' the helm:** struck through the helmet.

15 **brand:** sword.

19 **samite:** a heavy silk fabric. **mystic:** mysterious.

25 **middle mere** (mēr): the middle of the lake.

26 **lightly:** speedily.

28 **meet:** suitable or proper.

31 **hest:** command.

34 **athwart:** across.

Brightening the skirts of a long cloud, ran forth
And sparkled keen with frost against the hilt;°
For all the haft° twinkled with diamond sparks,
Myriads of topaz-lights,° and jacinth-work°
Of subtlest° jewellery. He gazed so long
That both his eyes were dazzled as he stood,
This way and that dividing the swift mind,
In act to throw; but at the last it seem'd
Better to leave Excalibur conceal'd
There in the many-knotted water-flags,°
That whistled stiff and dry about the marge.°
So strode he back slow to the wounded King.

Then spake King Arthur to Sir Bedivere:
"Hast thou perform'd my mission which I gave?
What is it thou hast seen? or what hast heard?"

And answer made the bold Sir Bedivere:
"I heard the ripple washing in the reeds,
And the wild water lapping on the crag."°

To whom replied King Arthur, faint and pale:
"Thou hast betray'd thy nature and thy name,
Not rendering true answer, as beseem'd°
Thy fealty,° nor like a noble knight;
For surer sign had follow'd, either hand,
Or voice, or else a motion of the mere.
This is a shameful thing for men to lie.
Yet now, I charge thee, quickly go again,
As thou art lief° and dear, and do the thing
I bade thee, watch, and lightly bring me word."

Then went Sir Bedivere the second time
Across the ridge, and paced beside the mere,
Counting the dewy pebbles, fixt in thought;
But when he saw the wonder of the hilt,
How curiously and strangely chased,° he smote
His palms together, and he cried aloud:

"And if indeed I cast the brand away,
Surely a precious thing, one worthy note,°
Should thus be lost for ever from the earth,
Which might have pleased the eyes of many men.

43–44 **hilt, haft:** names for a sword's handle.

45 **topaz** (tō′ paz), **jacinth** (jā′ sinth): precious gems.

46 **subtlest:** most finely crafted.

51 **water-flags:** marsh plants.

52 **marge:** edge.

59 **crag:** the rocky shore.

62–63 **beseem'd / Thy fealty:** was appropriate to your loyalty or duty.

68 **lief** (lēf): beloved.

74 **chased:** engraved.

77 **worthy note:** deserving admiration.

What good should follow this, if this were done?
What harm, undone? Deep harm to disobey,
Seeing obedience is the bond of rule.
Were it well to obey then, if a king demand
An act unprofitable, against himself?
The King is sick, and knows not what he does.
What record or what relic of my lord
Should be to aftertime, but empty breath
And rumors of a doubt? But were this kept,
Stored in some treasure-house of mighty kings,
Some one might show it at a joust of arms,
Saying: 'King Arthur's sword, Excalibur,
Wrought° by the lonely Maiden of the Lake.
Nine years she wrought it, sitting in the deeps
Upon the hidden bases of the hills.'
So might some old man speak in the aftertime
To all the people, winning reverence.
But now much honor and much fame were lost."

So spake he, clouded with his own conceit,°
And hid Excalibur the second time,
And so strode back slow to the wounded King.

Then spoke King Arthur, breathing heavily:
"What is it thou hast seen? or what hast heard?"

And answer made the bold Sir Bedivere:
"I heard the water lapping on the crag,
And the long ripple washing in the reeds."

To whom replied King Arthur, much in wrath:°
"Ah miserable, and unkind, untrue,
Unknightly, traitor-hearted! Woe is me!
Authority forgets a dying king,
Laid widow'd of the power in his eye
That bow'd the will. I see thee what thou art,
For thou, the latest-left of all my knights,
In whom should meet the offices° of all,
Thou wouldst betray me for the precious hilt;
Either from lust of gold, or like a girl
Valuing the giddy pleasure of the eyes.
Yet, for a man may fail in duty twice,
And the third time may prosper, get thee hence;

92 **Wrought:** shaped by hand.

98 **conceit:** thought, idea, or concept.

106 **wrath:** anger.

113 **offices:** duties and responsibilities.

But, if thou spare to fling Excalibur,
I will arise and slay thee with my hands."

Then quickly rose Sir Bedivere, and ran,
And, leaping down the ridges lightly, plunged
Among the bulrush beds, and clutch'd the sword,
And strongly wheel'd and threw it. The great brand
Made lightnings in the splendor of the moon,
And flashing round and round, and whirl'd in an arch,
Shot like a streamer of the northern morn,°
Seen where the moving isles of winter° shock
By night, with noises of the Northern sea.
So flash'd and fell the brand Excalibur;
But ere he dipt the surface, rose an arm
Clothed in white samite, mystic, wonderful,
And caught him by the hilt, and brandish'd him
Three times, and drew him under in the mere.
And lightly went the other to the King.

Then spoke King Arthur, drawing thicker breath:
"Now see I by thine eyes that this is done.
Speak out; what is it thou hast heard, or seen?"

And answer made the bold Sir Bedivere:
"Sir King, I closed mine eyelids, lest the gems
Should blind my purpose, for I never saw,
Nor shall see, here or elsewhere, till I die,
Not tho' I live three lives of mortal men,
So great a miracle as yonder hilt.
Then with both hands I flung him, wheeling him;
But when I look'd again, behold an arm,
Clothed in white samite, mystic, wonderful,
That caught him by the hilt, and brandish'd him
Three times, and drew him under in the mere."

And answer made King Arthur, breathing hard:
"My end draws nigh; 't is time that I were gone.
Make broad thy shoulders to receive my weight,
And bear me to the margin;° yet I fear
My wound hath taken cold, and I shall die."

So saying, from the pavement he half rose,
Slowly, with pain, reclining on his arm,

127 **streamer of the northern morn:** the northern lights.

128 **isles of winter:** floating ice or icebergs.

153 **margin:** the land bordering the lake.

How Sir Bedivere Cast the Sword Excalibur Into the Water, 1893–1894. Aubrey Beardsley. Illustration for *Le Morte d'Arthur*, London: Dent.

Viewing the art: What does this image convey about Sir Bedivere's feelings on returning Excalibur to the lake? Does the poem convey the same emotions? Explain.

And looking wistfully° with wide blue eyes
As in a picture. Him Sir Bedivere
Remorsefully regarded thro' his tears,
And would have spoken, but he found not words;
Then took with care, and kneeling on one knee,
O'er both his shoulders drew the languid° hands,
And rising bore him thro' the place of tombs.

But, as he walk'd, King Arthur panted hard,
Like one that feels a nightmare on his bed
When all the house is mute. So sigh'd the King,
Muttering and murmuring at his ear, "Quick, quick!
I fear it is too late, and I shall die."
But the other swiftly strode from ridge to ridge,
Clothed with his breath, and looking, as he walk'd,
Larger than human on the frozen hills.
He heard the deep behind him, and a cry
Before. His own thought drove him like a goad.°
Dry clash'd his harness° in the icy caves
And barren chasms,° and all to left and right
The bare black cliff clang'd round him, as he based
His feet on juts of slippery crag that rang
Sharp-smitten with the dint of armed heels°—
And on a sudden, lo, the level lake,
And the long glories of the winter moon!

Then saw they how there hove° a dusky barge,
Dark as a funeral scarf from stem to stern,
Beneath them; and descending they were ware°
That all the decks were dense with stately forms,
Black-stoled, black-hooded, like a dream—by these
Three queens with crowns of gold—and from them rose
A cry that shiver'd to the tingling stars,
And, as it were one voice, an agony
Of lamentation, like a wind that shrills
All night in a waste land, where no one comes,
Or hath come, since the making of the world.

Then murmur'd Arthur, "Place me in the barge."
So to the barge they came. There those three queens
Put forth their hands, and took the King, and wept.
But she that rose the tallest of them all
And fairest laid his head upon her lap,

157 **wistfully:** with sad longing; yearningly.

162 **languid:** weak; lacking vitality.

173 **goad:** a sharp stick used for driving cattle.

174 **Dry clash'd his harness:** His armor creaked or grated.

175 **barren chasms** (kaz′ əmz): lifeless cracks or gorges.

178 **dint of armed heels:** impact of armored feet.

181 **hove:** floated into sight.

183 **ware:** aware.

The Passing of Arthur, 1875. Julia Margaret Cameron. Sepia-toned photograph to illustrate *Idylls of the King and other poems.*

Viewing the art: How would you describe the tone of this photograph? Is the same tone reflected in the poem's description of Arthur's departure in the barge? Explain.

And loosed the shatter'd casque,° and chafed° his hands,
And call'd him by his name, complaining loud,
And dropping bitter tears against a brow
Striped with dark blood; for all his face was white
And colorless, and like the wither'd moon
Smote by the fresh beam of the springing east;°
And all his greaves and cuisses° dash'd with drops
Of onset;° and the light and lustrous curls—
That made his forehead like a rising sun
High from the dais-throne—were parch'd with dust,
Or, clotted into points and hanging loose,
Mixt with the knightly growth that fringed his lips.
So like a shatter'd column lay the King;
Not like that Arthur who, with lance in rest,
From spur to plume a star of tournament,
Shot thro' the lists° at Camelot, and charged
Before the eyes of ladies and of kings.

Then loudly cried the bold Sir Bedivere:
"Ah! my Lord Arthur, whither shall I go?

197 **casque** (kask): helmet. **chafed:** restored warmth by rubbing.

202 **Smote . . . east:** struck by the first light of dawn.

203 **greaves and cuisses** (kwis′ əs): pieces of armor covering the legs.

204 **onset:** the early stages of dying, signified by spattered blood from battle wounds.

212 **lists:** the field in which tournaments took place.

Where shall I hide my forehead and my eyes?
For now I see the true old times are dead,
When every morning brought a noble chance,
And every chance brought out a noble knight.
Such times have been not since the light that led
The holy Elders with the gift of myrrh.°
But now the whole Round Table° is dissolved
Which was an image of the mighty world;
And I, the last, go forth companionless,
And the days darken round me, and the years,
Among new men, strange faces, other minds."

And slowly answer'd Arthur from the barge:
"The old order changeth yielding place to new,
And God fulfils himself in many ways,
Lest one good custom should corrupt the world.
Comfort thyself; what comfort is in me?
I have lived my life, and that which I have done
May He within himself make pure! but thou,
If thou shouldst never see my face again,
Pray for my soul. More things are wrought by prayer
Than this world dreams of. Wherefore, let thy voice
Rise like a fountain for me night and day.
For what are men better than sheep or goats
That nourish a blind life within the brain,
If, knowing God, they lift not hands of prayer
Both for themselves and those who call them friend?
For so the whole round earth is every way
Bound by gold chains about the feet of God.
But now farewell. I am going a long way
With these thou seest—if indeed I go—
For all my mind is clouded with a doubt—
To the island-valley of Avilion;°
Where falls not hail, or rain, or any snow,
Nor ever wind blows loudly; but it lies
Deep-meadow'd, happy, fair with orchard lawns
And bowery hollows° crown'd with summer sea,
Where I will heal me of my grievous wound."

So said he, and the barge with oar and sail
Moved from the brink, like some full-breasted swan
That, fluting a wild carol ere her death,°
Ruffles her pure cold plume, and takes the flood°

220–221 **the light . . . myrrh:** the light from a star guided the **holy Elders,** the three kings who came to see the baby Jesus. They brought precious gifts, including *myrrh,* a fragrant substance used in incense and perfumes.

222 **Round Table:** the association of King Arthur and his knights; also the circular table at which they sat.

247 **Avilion:** an alternate spelling of *Avalon.* Medieval legends describe this island, and its castle, as being "not far on this side of paradise."

251 **bowery hollows:** shallow valleys shaded by overhanging trees and vines.

255 **fluting . . . death:** According to legend, a swan sings just before it dies.

256 **flood:** the deep water.

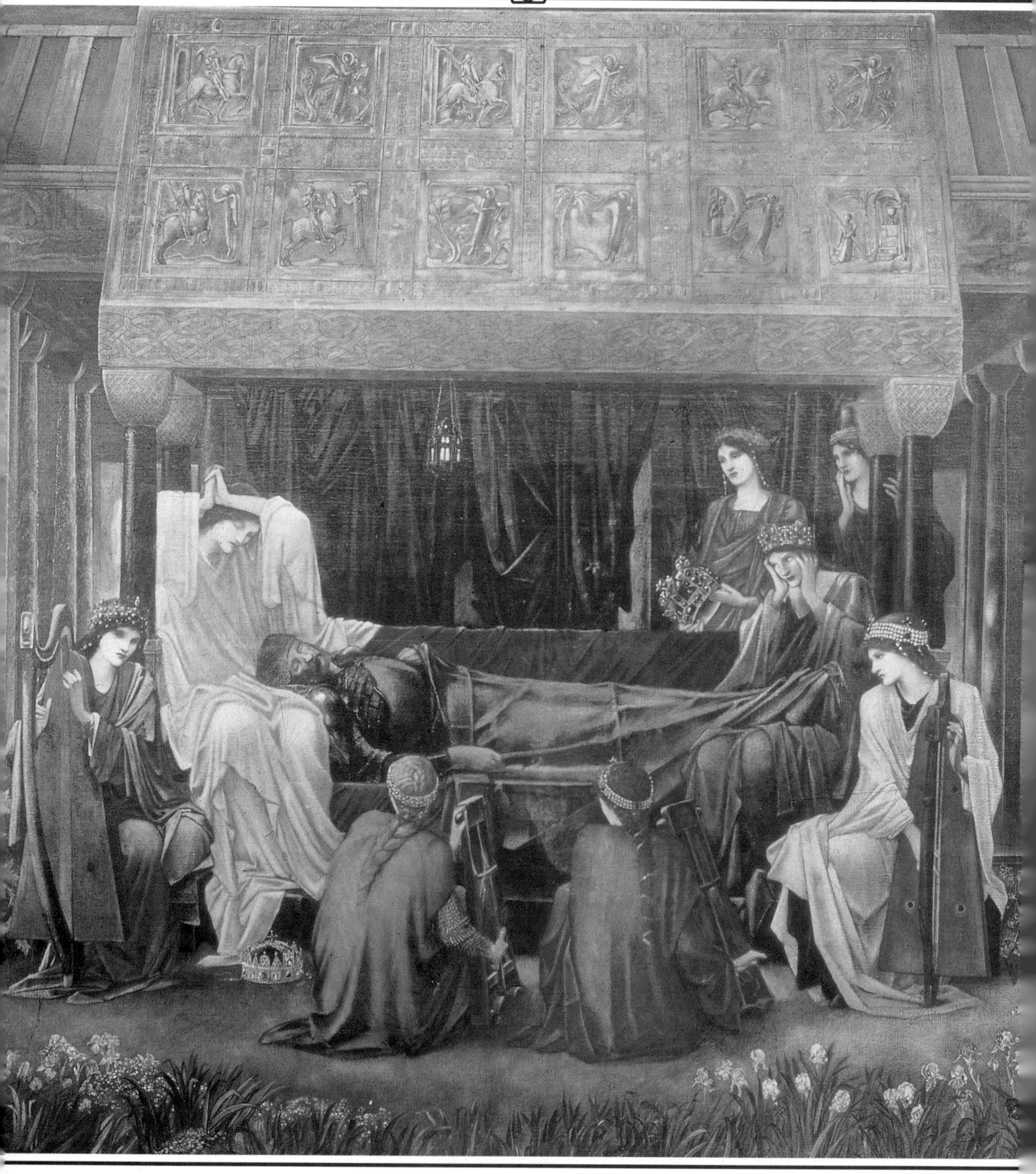

With swarthy webs. Long stood Sir Bedivere
Revolving many memories, till the hull
Look'd one black dot against the verge of dawn,
And on the mere the wailing died away.

But when that moan had past for evermore,
The stillness of the dead world's winter dawn
Amazed him, and he groan'd, "The King is gone."
And therewithal came on him the weird rhyme,
"From the great deep to the great deep he goes."°

265 "From the great deep . . . goes": the last line of a rhyme that Merlin recites in "The Coming of Arthur" from *Idylls of the King,* in answer to a question about Arthur's origin.

266 clomb: climbed.

Whereat he slowly turn'd and slowly clomb°
The last hard footstep of that iron crag,
Thence mark'd the black hull moving yet, and cried:
"He passes to be king among the dead,
And after healing of his grievous wound
He comes again; but—if he come no more—
O me, be yon dark queens in yon black boat,
Who shriek'd and wail'd, the three whereat we gazed
On that high day, when, clothed with living light,
They stood before his throne in silence, friends
Of Arthur, who should help him at his need?"°

272–276 yon dark queens . . . at his need: "The Coming of Arthur" describes three queens who appeared when Arthur was crowned king.

Then from the dawn it seem'd there came, but faint
As from beyond the limit of the world,
Like the last echo born of a great cry,
Sounds, as if some fair city were one voice
Around a king returning from his wars.

Thereat once more he moved about, and clomb
Even to the highest he could climb, and saw,
Straining his eyes beneath an arch of hand,
Or thought he saw, the speck that bare the King,
Down that long water opening on the deep
Somewhere far off, pass on and on, and go
From less to less and vanish into light.
And the new sun rose bringing the new year.

The Sleep of Arthur in Avalon, 1880–1898 (detail). Edward Burne-Jones. Oil on canvas, 9 ft 3 in x 21 ft 2 in. Museo de Arte de Ponce, Puerto Rico.

Viewing the painting: What do the expressions and activities of the people in this painting suggest to you about people's regard for Arthur?

Responding to Literature

Personal Response

How did you react to Sir Bedivere's comments about the passing away of the age of King Arthur and his knights?

Analyzing Literature

Recall

1. As this excerpt begins, what is King Arthur's condition and what thoughts does he express?
2. What does King Arthur direct Sir Bedivere to do with the sword?
3. Summarize how Sir Bedivere reacts to King Arthur's order and what he does with Excalibur.
4. Where does Sir Bedivere escort King Arthur? What happens there?
5. How does Sir Bedivere react to Arthur's leaving, and how does Arthur respond?

Interpret

6. Judging from what he says in the first stanza, how does King Arthur feel about the passing of Camelot? Use details from the poem to support your answer.
7. Why does King Arthur give the order regarding the sword?
8. How does Sir Bedivere justify his failure to follow Arthur's orders? Cite lines from the poem to support your response.
9. What might the barge and the three queens **symbolize,** or represent?
10. How would you characterize Arthur's feelings about his impending death? How do his feelings compare with Sir Bedivere's?

Evaluate and Connect

11. Do you think Sir Bedivere is justified in hesitating to follow King Arthur's orders regarding Excalibur? Why or why not?
12. Tennyson had once intended to name his poem sequence *The False and the True* instead of *Idylls of the King.* Based on the characters in this poem, how well do you think the original title applies?
13. How do the reactions you described in the Reading Focus on page 944 compare with Sir Bedivere's reactions to parting, both with the sword and with the era of the Round Table? Explain.
14. With whom do you identify more, King Arthur or Sir Bedivere? Why?
15. The **mood** of this poem has been described as pessimistic but hopeful. Citing specific details, explain how Tennyson creates this contradictory mood. (See Literary Terms Handbook, page R8.)

Literary ELEMENTS

Narrative Poetry

Narrative poetry tells a story. It evolved from the oral tradition of passing down stories from generation to generation. Narrative poetry contains many of the same elements as a short story, such as setting, characters, plot, conflict, and theme. The two main types of narrative poetry are the **ballad** and the **epic.** Typically, ballads tell in a simple, dramatic way a popular, usually tragic, story or legend. Epics, such as *Idylls of the King,* run longer and use elevated or stately language, such as, "It is not meet, Sir King, to leave thee thus, / Aidless, alone, and smitten thro' the helm." Epics celebrate the great deeds of legendary heroes such as King Arthur.

1. Summarize the plot of "The Passing of Arthur."
2. Identify an internal and an external conflict in the narrative.

- See **Literary Terms Handbook,** p. R8.

Anglo-Saxon and Celtic jewelry. 1st–7th century A.D. Bronze.

Literature and Writing

Writing About Literature

Evaluate Character Behavior Tennyson held true to the concept that faith and commitment must stand at the center of the human character or else character will falter and fail. Write an evaluation of the way Tennyson presents ideas of faith and commitment to oneself and one's fellow human beings in "The Passing of Arthur." Share your evaluation with the class.

Creative Writing

The Last Knight What do you think happens to Sir Bedivere, the last of King Arthur's knights, after the events described in this excerpt? Write a **narrative**—in verse or prose—telling what becomes of Sir Bedivere.

Extending Your Response

Literature Groups

A Hero for All Time? Critic William Vaughn Moody and poet Robert Morss Lovett said that *Idylls of the King* "spoke more eloquently to Victorian than to modern readers." Do you agree or disagree? What qualities does Tennyson bestow on Arthur that might put him out of touch with today's readers? What heroic qualities does he have that give him timeless appeal? What traits would you add to or take away from Arthur to make him more appealing as a hero today? Discuss these questions in your group. Share your group's ideas with the rest of your classmates.

Learning for Life

Long Live the King Use details in "The Passing of Arthur" and information you learned from previously read works or from research to write King Arthur's obituary for *The Arthurian Times.* In preparation, you might read obituaries of celebrated leaders of modern times and note the kinds of information typically included, such as a brief biographical account, the circumstances of the person's death, personal accomplishments, quotations attributed to the person, and tributes from people close to the person.

Interdisciplinary Activity

Art: Magazine Cover Imagine that *Idylls of the King* has been made into a twelve-week television miniseries. Design a television guide magazine cover that promotes the last episode, which is based on "The Passing of Arthur."

Reading Further

If you enjoyed "The Passing of Arthur," you might want to read these other poems by Tennyson:

The other eleven poems in *Idylls of the King.*

"Merlin and the Gleam" from *A Collection of Poems by Alfred Tennyson.*

Save your work for your portfolio.

Literary Criticism

Into *Idylls of the King*, observes one critic, "[Tennyson] poured his deepening feelings of the desecration of decency and of ancient English ideals by the gradual corruption of accepted morality." In a class discussion, explore how the events and sentiments in "The Passing of Arthur" might be symbolic of the "desecration of decency and of ancient English ideals." Point to specific passages from the selection to support your opinions.

St. Mawes Castle, Cornwall, 1821. John Chessell Buckler. Watercolor over pencil on paper, 25.4 x 35.6 cm. Mallett Gallery, London.

Skill Minilessons

GRAMMAR AND LANGUAGE • Subject-Verb Agreement

An **inverted sentence** is one in which the subject follows the verb. "The Passing of Arthur" contains many inverted sentences, such as: "So strode he back slow to the wounded King." Following standard word order, the line would read: "He strode back slowly to the wounded King." The verb in an inverted sentence must always agree with the subject in number and person.

PRACTICE On your paper, underline the simple subject in each of the following sentences. Then write the form of the verb in parentheses that agrees with the subject.

1. With his dying breaths (issue, issues) the noble King Arthur orders to cast away Excalibur.
2. Upon his shoulders (carry, carries) Sir Bedivere the weight of the wounded king.
3. There (was, were) three queens upon the barge.
4. (Does, Do) these stories still enchant readers?
5. Among King Arthur's knights (was, were) Sir Launcelot.

APPLY Underline the subject and the verb in three examples of inverted sentences in "The Passing of Arthur."

● For more about subject-verb agreement, see **Language Handbook,** p. R17.

READING AND THINKING • Paraphrasing

When you paraphrase a passage, you tell what happens in your own words. You can improve your comprehension of "The Passing of Arthur" by restating difficult passages in your own words. Study this example.

> "The sequel of today unsolders all / The goodliest fellowship of famous knights / Whereof this world holds record."
>
> *What follows from today is the breakup of the best association of knights the world has ever seen.*

PRACTICE On your paper, paraphrase the following passage from "The Passing of Arthur."

> "Authority forgets a dying king, / Laid widow'd of the power in his eye / That bow'd the will. I see thee what thou art, / For thou, the latest-left of all my knights, / In whom should meet the offices of all, / Thou wouldst betray me for the precious hilt; / Either from lust of gold, or like a girl / Valuing the giddy pleasure of the eyes."

● For more about paraphrasing, see **Reading Handbook,** p. R91.

VOCABULARY • Semantic Mapping

To learn a new or difficult word, try making a **semantic map**—a simple diagram that explains the meaning of the word. A semantic map consists of a definition, a few synonyms, and an example of the word used in context.

sequel
- **Definition:** what follows something
- **Synonyms:** result, consequence, outcome
- **Example:** He suffered nightmares as a sequel of the battle.

PRACTICE Using a dictionary, create a semantic map for each of the following words.

1. unsolder
2. mystic
3. fealty
4. wistfully
5. languid

APPLY Find five unfamiliar words in "The Passing of Arthur" and create semantic maps for them.

INTERDISCIPLINARY CONNECTION

GEOGRAPHY

Arthurian Sites of England

The magical stories of King Arthur and his knights live on not only in literature but also in the geography of England. From the former county of Cornwall on the southwestern coast to the far northern reaches of England stretch sites where King Arthur is believed to have fought, ruled, and died. These sites, whether actual haunts of a historical person or part of a myth, help keep King Arthur's story—and his mystique—alive.

According to legend, Arthur was conceived at **Tintagil,** where a ruined castle still stands. Only a few miles inland, the village of **Slaughter Bridge** lays claim to being the site where Arthur waged his final battle. Nearby is **Bodmin Moor**, where a pond called **Dozmary Pool** lies. Into this pond Sir Bedivere supposedly cast Arthur's sword, Excalibur.

1 **Tintagil:** King Uther and Lady Igraine conceive Arthur.
2 **Slaughter Bridge:** Modred wounds Arthur.
3 **Bodmin Moor:** Sir Bedivere casts Excalibur into Dozmary Pool.
4 **Glastonbury Tor:** Arthur dies on the Isle of Avilion.
5 **Cadbury Castle:** Arthur holds court in Camelot.

The **Isle of Avilion,** Arthur's supposed burial place, may actually be a hill called the Tor near the small town of **Glastonbury.** In Celtic folklore, Avilion was an enchanted island. Long ago, the Tor was surrounded by watery marshland. From most angles, it would have appeared as an island rising from the marshy mists.

Glastonbury also features the ruins of a medieval abbey, or monastery. In 1191 monks at the **Glastonbury Abbey** claimed that they had discovered King Arthur's grave. Digging in their cemetery, they supposedly unearthed a lead cross bearing the Latin words "Here lies buried the renowned King Arthur in the Isle of Avilion." Deeper down, they found a coffin containing the bones of a tall man with a damaged skull.

And what about **Camelot,** Arthur's supposed kingdom? The most famous of the reputed sites of Camelot is **Cadbury Castle,** a hill-fort near the village of South Cadbury. Excavations at the site showed that a large fortress stood on the hill during the supposed time of Arthur. A local legend has it that on Christmas Eve, hoofbeats can be heard as the ghosts of King Arthur and his knights gallop on horses through the ancient gateway of the castle.

The lure of King Arthur remains entrenched in English culture and geography.

Activity

Find out more about the Arthurian legends behind these and other sites. Look for information on the Internet and in encyclopedias, books, and journals. You may even write to a tourist bureau in England for information. Then compile your research in a travel brochure outlining a tour of Arthurian England.

MEDIA connection

Screenplay

Humor can be found even in serious material. Read the following excerpt from the screenplay *Monty Python and the Holy Grail* to see how the weighty themes in King Arthur's legends can be spoofed.

from Monty Python and the Holy Grail

by John Cleese, Graham Chapman, Terry Gilliam, Eric Idle, Terry Jones, and Michael Palin

SIR LAUNCELOT
Look, my liege!

[*Trumpets.*]

ARTHUR
Camelot!

SIR GALAHAD
Camelot!

LAUNCELOT
Camelot!

PATSY
It's only a model.

ARTHUR
Shh! Knights, I bid you welcome to your new home. Let us ride . . . to . . . Camelot!

[*In medieval hall.*]

KNIGHTS [*Singing.*]
We're knights of the Round Table.
We dance whene'er we're able.
We do routines and chorus scenes
With footwork impeccable.
We dine well here in Camelot.
We eat ham and jam and spam a lot.

[*Dancing.*]

We're knights of the Round Table.
Our shows are formidable,
But many times we're given rhymes
That are quite unsingable.
We're opera mad in Camelot.
We sing from the diaphragm
a lot.

[*In dungeon.*]

PRISONER
[*Clap clap clap clap.*]

[*In medieval hall.*]

KNIGHTS [*Tap-dancing.*]
In war we're tough and able,
Quite indefatigable.
Between our guests we sequin vests and
impersonate Clark Gable.
It's a busy life in Camelot.

MAN
I have to push the pram a lot.

[*Outdoors.*]

ARTHUR
Well, on second thought, let's not go to Camelot. It is a silly place.

KNIGHTS
Right. Right.

Analyzing Media

Do you think this scene is funny? Does familiarity with the legends of King Arthur make this scene more funny or less so? Explain your answer.

Before You Read

Arthur Becomes King

Reading Focus

How would you react if you were suddenly given great responsibility?

Sharing Ideas Jot down your thoughts about how you would react to a sudden change in your status. How might your friends react?

Setting a Purpose Read to see how one character reacts to a sudden change in status.

Building Background

The Time and Place

This story takes place *somewhere* in England at *some time* during the medieval period when men wore armor and fought with swords. The author refers to the setting simply as "an imaginary world."

Did You Know?

Jousting was one of the most popular sports in Europe during the fourteenth and fifteenth centuries. Jousting involved two armored horsemen charging at each other with lowered spears, or lances. Their goal was to knock their opponent off his horse. Sometimes the jousters merely broke their lances; occasionally they were injured or killed. King Henry II of France died after a jousting tournament in honor of his daughter's marriage.

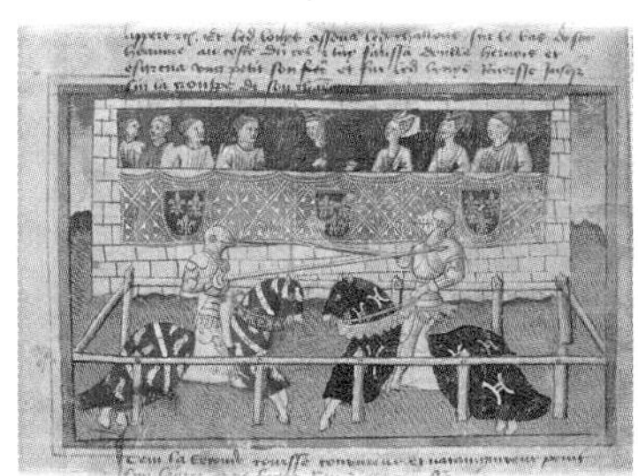

Vocabulary Preview

petulantly (pech′ ə lənt lē) *adv.* crankily; in an annoyed way; p. 964
indignantly (in dig′ nənt lē) *adv.* with quiet, dignified anger in response to something unjust, mean, or unworthy; p. 964
vulgar (vul′ gər) *adj.* characterized by a lack of good breeding or good taste; common; crude; p. 966
sumptuous (sump′ cho͞o əs) *adj.* costly and magnificent; p. 967
desolate (des′ ə lit) *adj.* deserted or uninhabited; p. 967
combatant (kəm bat′ ənt) *n.* one trained for, or engaged in, combat; p. 969
throng (thrông) *v.* to move or gather in large numbers; crowd together; p. 969
ruefully (ro͞o′ fəl ē) *adv.* regretfully; sorrowfully; p. 970

Meet T. H. White

Terence Hanbury White had an unhappy childhood mainly because his parents frequently fought and occasionally became violent. In a letter to a friend, White wrote that *The Once and Future King* "is more or less a kind of wish-fulfillment of the things I should like to have happened to me when I was a boy."

A scholar of medieval life, White worked as a schoolteacher for six years before quitting to write full time. He became reclusive, avoiding human company and doting on his many pets.

T. H. White was born in Bombay, India, in 1906, but lived most of his life in England. He died in 1964. The Sword in the Stone, *the first of four novels in the volume of* The Once and Future King, *was published in 1938.*

Arthur Becomes King

from The Once and Future King

T. H. White

KING PELLINORE ARRIVED for the important week-end in a high state of flurry.

"I say," he exclaimed, "do you know? Have you heard? Is it a secret, what?"

"Is what a secret, what?" they asked him.

"Why, the King," cried his majesty. "You know, about the King?"

"What's the matter with the King?" inquired Sir Ector. "You don't say he's comin' down to hunt with those demned hounds of his or anythin' like that?"

"He's dead," cried King Pellinore tragically. "He's dead, poor fellah, and can't hunt any more."

Sir Grummore stood up respectfully and took off his cap of maintenance.

"The King is dead," he said. "Long live the King."

Everybody else felt they ought to stand up too, and the boys' nurse burst into tears.

"There, there," she sobbed. "His loyal highness dead and gone, and him such a respectful gentleman. Many's the illuminated picture I've cut out of him, from the Illustrated Missals,[1] aye, and stuck up over the mantel. From the time when he was in swaddling bands, right through them world towers till he was a-visiting the dispersed areas as the world's Prince Charming, there wasn't a picture of 'im but I had it out, aye, and give 'im a last thought o' nights."

"Compose yourself, Nannie," said Sir Ector.

"It is solemn, isn't it?" said King Pellinore, "what? Uther the Conqueror, 1066 to 1216."

"A solemn moment," said Sir Grummore. "The King is dead. Long live the King."

"We ought to pull down the curtains," said Kay, who was always a stickler[2] for good form, "or half-mast the banners."

1. Here, *illuminated* refers to a style of decorating a book in gold, silver, and bright colors; *missals* are, in actuality, prayer books. The writer is pulling the reader's leg here (and will again later) by inserting bits of modern culture into his fictional medieval world. The *Illustrated Missals* seems to be a tabloid–style periodical featuring stories about knights and members of royalty.
2. A *stickler* is someone who insists on having things done in a certain way.

Knights and Ladies Ride Out to a Tourney in London. Late 15th century. Manuscript illustration from *Froissart's Chronicle.*

"That's right," said Sir Ector. "Somebody go and tell the sergeant-at-arms."[3]

It was obviously the Wart's duty to execute this command, for he was now the junior nobleman present, so he ran out cheerfully to find the sergeant. Soon those who were left in the solar could hear a voice crying out, "Nah then, one two, special mourning fer 'is lite[4] majesty, lower awai on the command Two!" and then the flapping of all the standards, banners, pennons, pennoncells, banderolls, guidons, streamers and cognizances which made gay the snowy turrets of the Forest Sauvage.[5]

"How did you hear?" asked Sir Ector.

"I was pricking through the purlieus of the forest after that Beast, you know, when I met with a solemn friar of orders gray,[6] and he told me. It's the very latest news."

3. A *sergeant-at-arms* preserves order and performs minor official duties, for example, at meetings of a court or a legislature.
4. As a small boy, Arthur was nicknamed *Wart.* The *solar,* or solarium, is a sunny room or porch. The speaker's accent turns *late,* meaning "recently deceased," into *lite.*
5. The *standards . . . cognizances* are variously shaped flags flying from the small towers, or *turrets,* of Sir Ector's castle, *Forest Sauvage* (sō vazh′). The French word *sauvage* means "savage; wild."
6. The forest's *purlieus* (pur′ lo͞oz) are its edges, and the *friar of orders gray* is a Roman Catholic monk.

"Poor old Pendragon," said Sir Ector.

"The King is dead," said Sir Grummore solemnly. "Long live the King."

"It is all very well for you to keep on mentioning that, my dear Grummore," exclaimed King Pellinore petulantly, "but who is this King, what, that is to live so long, what, accordin' to you?"

"Well, his heir," said Sir Grummore, rather taken aback.[7]

"Our blessed monarch," said the Nurse tearfully, "never had no hair. Anybody that studied the loyal family knowed that."

"Good gracious!" exclaimed Sir Ector. "But he must have had a next-of-kin?"

"That's just it," cried King Pellinore in high excitement. "That's the excitin' part of it, what? No hair and no next of skin, and who's to succeed to the throne? That's what my friar was so excited about, what, and why he was asking who could succeed to what, what? What?"

"Do you mean to tell me," exclaimed Sir Grummore indignantly, "that there ain't no King of Gramarye?"

"Not a scrap of one," cried King Pellinore, feeling important. "And there have been signs and wonders of no mean[8] might."

"I think it's a scandal," said Sir Grummore. "God knows what the dear old country is comin' to. Due to these lollards and communists,[9] no doubt."

"What sort of signs and wonders?" asked Sir Ector.

"Well, there has appeared a sort of sword in a stone, what, in a sort of a church. Not in the church, if you see what I mean, and not in the stone, but that sort of thing, what, like you might say."

"I don't know what the Church is coming to," said Sir Grummore.

"It's in an anvil," explained the King.

"The Church?"

"No, the sword."

"But I thought you said the sword was in the stone?"

"No," said King Pellinore. "The stone is outside the church."

"Look here, Pellinore," said Sir Ector. "You have a bit of a rest, old boy, and start again. Here, drink up this horn of mead[10] and take it easy."

"The sword," said King Pellinore, "is stuck through an anvil which stands on a stone. It goes right through the anvil and into the stone. The anvil is stuck to the stone. The stone stands outside a church. Give me some more mead."

"I don't think that's much of a wonder," remarked Sir Grummore. "What I wonder at is that they should allow such things to happen. But you can't tell nowadays, what with all these Saxon agitators."

"My dear fellah," cried Pellinore, getting excited again, "it's not where the stone is, what, that I'm trying to tell you, but what is written on it, what, where it is."

"What?"

7. To be *taken aback* is to be suddenly surprised or startled.
8. Here, *mean* means "humble or modest," so signs and wonders of *no mean might* actually have considerable symbolic importance.
9. *Lollards* are lazy good-for-nothings. The writer is also slyly mocking people of his own era by having Sir Grummore see or suspect *communists* nearly everywhere.
10. *Mead* is an alcoholic drink made from honey and, here, is served in a vessel made from the horn of an animal.

Vocabulary

petulantly (pech′ ə lənt lē) *adv.* crankily; in an annoyed way

indignantly (in dig′ nənt lē) *adv.* with quiet, dignified anger in response to something unjust, mean, or unworthy

Did You Know?
The *pommel* of a sword is a knob at the end of the hilt, or handle.

"Why, on its pommel."

"Come on, Pellinore," said Sir Ector. "You just sit quite still with your face to the wall for a minute, and then tell us what you are talkin' about. Take it easy, old boy. No need for hurryin'. You sit still and look at the wall, there's a good chap, and talk as slow as you can."

"There are words written on this sword in this stone outside this church," cried King Pellinore piteously, "and these words are as follows. Oh, do try to listen to me, you two, instead of interruptin' all the time about nothin', for it makes a man's head go ever so."

"What are these words?" asked Kay.

"These words say this," said King Pellinore, "so far as I can understand from that old friar of orders gray."

"Go on, do," said Kay, for the King had come to a halt.

"Go on," said Sir Ector, "what do these words on this sword in this anvil in this stone outside this church, say?"

"Some red propaganda, no doubt," remarked Sir Grummore.

King Pellinore closed his eyes tight, extended his arms in both directions, and announced in capital letters, "Whoso Pulleth Out This Sword of this Stone and Anvil, is Rightwise King Born of All England."

"Who said that?" asked Sir Grummore.

"But the sword said it, like I tell you."

"Talkative weapon," remarked Sir Grummore sceptically.

"It was written on it," cried the King angrily. "Written on it in letters of gold."

"Why didn't you pull it out then?" asked Sir Grummore.

"But I tell you that I wasn't there. All this that I am telling you was told to me by that friar I was telling you of, like I tell you."

"Has this sword with this inscription been pulled out?" inquired Sir Ector.

"No," whispered King Pellinore dramatically. "That's where the whole excitement comes in. They can't pull this sword out at all, although they have all been tryin' like fun, and so they have had to proclaim a tournament all over England, for New Year's Day, so that the man who comes to the tournament and pulls out the sword can be King of all England for ever, what, I say?"

"Oh, father," cried Kay. "The man who pulls that sword out of the stone will be the King of England. Can't we go to the tournament, father, and have a shot?"

"Couldn't think of it," said Sir Ector.

"Long way to London," said Sir Grummore, shaking his head.

"My father went there once," said King Pellinore.

Kay said, "Oh, surely we could go? When I am knighted I shall have to go to a tournament somewhere, and this one happens at just the right date. All the best people will be there, and we should see the famous knights and great kings. It does not matter about the sword, of course, but think of the tournament, probably the greatest there has ever been in Gramarye, and all the things we should see and do. Dear father, let me go to this tourney, if you love me, so that I may bear away the prize of all, in my maiden fight."

"But, Kay," said Sir Ector, "I have never been to London."

"All the more reason to go. I believe that anybody who does not go for a tournament like this will be proving that he has no noble blood in his veins. Think what people

King Arthur and the 30 Kingdoms, 1307. Illustration from Peter Langtoft's *Chronicle of England.* The British Library, London.

Viewing the art: How does this image help you picture the knights gathered with Sir Ector?

will say about us, if we do not go and have a shot at that sword. They will say that Sir Ector's family was too vulgar and knew it had no chance."

"We all know the family has no chance," said Sir Ector, "that is, for the sword."

"Lot of people in London," remarked Sir Grummore, with a wild surmise. "So they say."

He took a deep breath and goggled at his host with eyes like marbles.

"And shops," added King Pellinore suddenly, also beginning to breathe heavily.

"Dang it!" cried Sir Ector, bumping his horn mug on the table so that it spilled. "Let's all go to London, then, and see the new King!"

They rose up as one man.

"Why shouldn't I be as good a man as my father?" exclaimed King Pellinore.

"Dash it all," cried Sir Grummore. "After all, damn it all, it is the capital!"

"Hurray!" shouted Kay.

"Lord have mercy," said the nurse.

At this moment the Wart came in with Merlyn, and everybody was too excited to notice that, if he had not been grown up now, he would have been on the verge of tears.

"Oh, Wart," cried Kay, forgetting for the moment that he was only addressing his squire, and slipping back into the familiarity of their boyhood. "What do you think? We are all going to London for a great tournament on New Year's Day!"

"Are we?"

"Yes, and you will carry my shield and spears for the jousts, and I shall win the palm[11] of everybody and be a great knight!"

"Well, I am glad we are going," said the Wart, "for Merlyn is leaving us too."

"Oh, we shan't need Merlyn."

"He is leaving us," repeated the Wart.

"Leavin' us?" asked Sir Ector. "I thought it was we that were leavin'?"

11. Kay hopes to win praise. In ancient time, a *palm* leaf or branch was often used as a symbol of victory or rejoicing.

Vocabulary

vulgar (vul′ gər) *adj.* characterized by a lack of good breeding or good taste; common; crude

"He is going away from the Forest Sauvage."

Sir Ector said, "Come now, Merlyn, what's all this about? I don't understand all this a bit."

"I have come to say Good-bye, Sir Ector," said the old magician.

"Tomorrow my pupil Kay will be knighted, and the next week my other pupil will go away as his squire. I have outlived my usefulness here, and it is time to go."

"Now, now, don't say that," said Sir Ector. "I think you're a jolly useful chap whatever happens. You just stay and teach me, or be the librarian or something. Don't you leave an old man alone, after the children have flown."

"We shall all meet again," said Merlyn. "There is no cause to be sad."

"Don't go," said Kay.

"I must go," replied their tutor. "We have had a good time while we were young, but it is in the nature of Time to fly. There are many things in other parts of the kingdom which I ought to be attending to just now, and it is a specially busy time for me. Come, Archimedes,[12] say Good-bye to the company."

"Good-bye," said Archimedes tenderly to the Wart.

"Good-bye," said the Wart without looking up at all.

"But you can't go," cried Sir Ector, "not without a month's notice."

"Can't I?" replied Merlyn, taking up the position always used by philosophers[13] who propose to dematerialize. He stood on his toes, while Archimedes held tight to his shoulder—began to spin on them slowly like a top—spun faster and faster till he was only a blur of grayish light—and in a few seconds there was no one there at all.

"Good-bye, Wart," cried two faint voices outside the solar window.

"Good-bye," said the Wart for the last time—and the poor fellow went quickly out of the room.

The knighting took place in a whirl of preparations. Kay's sumptuous bath had to be set up in the box-room, between two towel-horses and an old box of selected games which contained a worn-out straw dart-board—it was called fléchette[14] in those days—because all the other rooms were full of packing. The nurse spent the whole time constructing new warm pants for everybody, on the principle that the climate of any place outside the Forest Sauvage must be treacherous to the extreme, and, as for the sergeant, he polished all the armor till it was quite brittle and sharpened the swords till they were almost worn away.

At last it was time to set out.

Perhaps, if you happen not to have lived in the Old England of the twelfth century, or whenever it was, and in a remote castle on the borders of the Marches[15] at that, you will find it difficult to imagine the wonders of their journey.

The road, or track, ran most of the time along the high ridges of the hills or downs, and they could look down on either side of them upon the desolate marshes where the snowy reeds sighed, and the ice crackled, and the duck in the red sunsets quacked loud on

12. *Archimedes* (är′ kə mē′ dēz) is Merlyn's pet owl.

13. Magicians and sorcerers were sometimes referred to as *philosophers,* those who pursue wisdom and logical reasoning.

14. In French, *fléchette* (flā shet′) means "a small arrow; dart."

15. *Marches* is a variation of *marshes.*

Vocabulary

sumptuous (sump′ cho͞o əs) *adj.* costly and magnificent

desolate (des′ ə lit) *adj.* deserted or uninhabited

View on the Coast of Cornwall, Frank Goodwin (1848–1873).
Viewing the painting: What similarities do you find between the country depicted here and the one described in the selection? Explain.

the winter air. The whole country was like that. Perhaps there would be a moory marsh on one side of the ridge, and a forest of a hundred thousand acres on the other, with all the great branches weighted in white. They could sometimes see a wisp of smoke among the trees, or a huddle of buildings far out among the impassable reeds, and twice they came to quite respectable towns which had several inns to boast of, but on the whole it was an England without civilization. The better roads were cleared of cover for a bow-shot[16] on either side of them, lest the traveller should be slain by hidden thieves.

They slept where they could, sometimes in the hut of some cottager who was prepared to welcome them, sometimes in the castle of a brother knight who invited them to refresh themselves, sometimes in the firelight and fleas of a dirty little hovel with a bush tied to a pole outside it—this was the sign-board used at that time by inns—and once or twice on the open ground, all huddled together for warmth between their grazing chargers. Wherever they went and wherever they slept, the east wind whistled in the reeds, and the geese went over high in the starlight, honking at the stars.

London was full to the brim. If Sir Ector had not been lucky enough to own a little land in Pie Street, on which there stood a respectable inn, they would have been hard put to it to find a lodging. But he did own it, and as a matter of fact drew most of his dividends from that source, so they were able to get three beds between the five of them. They thought themselves fortunate.

16. A *bow-shot* measured about 400 yards, roughly the distance an old English longbow could shoot an arrow. The roadsides were cleared of trees and shrubs, or *cover.*

On the first day of the tournament, Sir Kay managed to get them on the way to the lists at least an hour before the jousts[17] could possibly begin. He had lain awake all night, imagining how he was going to beat the best barons in England, and he had not been able to eat his breakfast. Now he rode at the front of the cavalcade,[18] with pale cheeks, and Wart wished there was something he could do to calm him down.

For country people, who only knew the dismantled tilting[19] ground of Sir Ector's castle, the scene which met their eyes was ravishing. It was a huge green pit in the earth, about as big as the arena at a football match. It lay ten feet lower than the surrounding country, with sloping banks, and the snow had been swept off it. It had been kept warm with straw, which had been cleared off that morning, and now the close-worn grass sparkled green in the white landscape. Round the arena there was a world of color so dazzling and moving and twinkling as to make one blink one's eyes. The wooden grandstands were painted in scarlet and white. The silk pavilions of famous people, pitched on every side, were azure and green and saffron and checkered. The pennons and pennoncells which floated everywhere in the sharp wind were flapping with every color of the rainbow, as they strained and slapped at their flagpoles, and the barrier down the middle of the arena itself was done in chessboard squares of black and white. Most of the combatants and their friends had not yet arrived, but one could see from those few who had come how the very people would turn the scene into a bank of flowers, and how the armor would flash, and the scalloped sleeves of the heralds[20] jig in the wind, as they raised their brazen trumpets to their lips to shake the fleecy clouds of winter with joyances and fanfares.

"Good heavens!" cried Sir Kay. "I have left my sword at home."

"Can't joust without a sword," said Sir Grummore. "Quite irregular."

"Better go and fetch it," said Sir Ector. "You have time."

"My squire will do," said Sir Kay. "What a damned mistake to make! Here, squire, ride hard back to the inn and fetch my sword. You shall have a shilling if you fetch it in time."

The Wart went as pale as Sir Kay was, and looked as if he were going to strike him. Then he said, "It shall be done, master," and turned his ambling palfrey against the stream of newcomers. He began to push his way toward their hostelry[21] as best he might.

"To offer me money!" cried the Wart to himself. "To look down at this beastly little donkey-affair off his great charger and to call me Squire! Oh, Merlyn, give me patience with the brute, and stop me from throwing his filthy shilling in his face."

When he got to the inn it was closed. Everybody had thronged to see the famous tournament, and the entire household had followed after the mob. Those were lawless days and it was not safe to leave your house—or even to go to sleep in it—unless you were certain that it was impregnable. The wooden shutters bolted

17. The *lists* was the field or area in which knights fought tournaments. The *jousts* were formal battles between mounted knights armed with long spears or other weapons.
18. A procession of people on horseback (or in vehicles) is a *cavalcade*.
19. Jousting is also called *tilting*.
20. At tournaments, *heralds* carried challenges between knights, made proclamations, and trumpeted the stages of competition.
21. Wart is riding a gentle saddle horse *(palfrey)* toward the inn *(hostelry)*.

Vocabulary

combatant (kəm bat′ ənt) *n.* one trained for, or engaged in, combat
throng (thrông) *v.* to move or gather in large numbers; to crowd together

over the downstairs windows were two inches thick, and the doors were double-barred.

"Now what do I do," asked the Wart, "to earn my shilling?"

He looked ruefully at the blind little inn, and began to laugh.

"Poor Kay," he said. "All that shilling stuff was only because he was scared and miserable, and now he has good cause to be. Well, he shall have a sword of some sort if I have to break into the Tower of London.

"How does one get hold of a sword?" he continued. "Where can I steal one? Could I waylay some knight, even if I am mounted on an ambling pad,[22] and take his weapons by force? There must be some swordsmith or armorer in a great town like this, whose shop would be still open."

He turned his mount and cantered off along the street. There was a quiet churchyard at the end of it, with a kind of square in front of the church door. In the middle of the square there was a heavy stone with an anvil on it, and a fine new sword was stuck through the anvil.

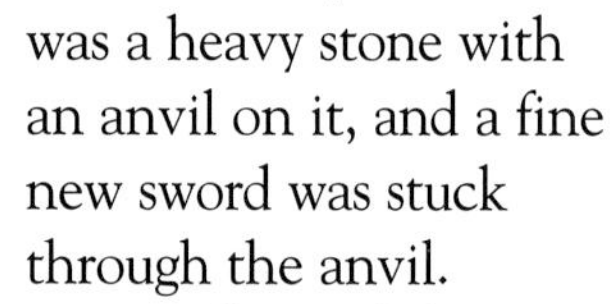

Did You Know?
A *lych-gate* (lich′ gāt) is a roofed gateway to a churchyard.

"Well," said the Wart, "I suppose it is some sort of war memorial, but it will have to do. I am sure nobody would grudge Kay a war memorial, if they knew his desperate straits."[23]

He tied his reins round a post of the lych-gate, strode up the gravel path, and took hold of the sword.

"Come, sword," he said. "I must cry your mercy and take you for a better cause.

"This is extraordinary," said the Wart. "I feel strange when I have hold of this sword, and I notice everything much more clearly. Look at the beautiful gargoyles of the church, and of the monastery which it belongs to. See how splendidly all the famous banners in the aisle are waving. How nobly that yew[24] holds up the red flakes of its timbers to worship God. How clean the snow is. I can smell something like fetherfew and sweet briar—and is it music that I hear?"

It was music, whether of pan-pipes or of recorders, and the light in the churchyard was so clear, without being dazzling, that one could have picked a pin out twenty yards away.

"There is something in this place," said the Wart. "There are people. Oh, people, what do you want?"

Nobody answered him, but the music was loud and the light beautiful.

"People," cried the Wart, "I must take this sword. It is not for me, but for Kay. I will bring it back."

There was still no answer, and Wart turned back to the anvil. He saw the golden letters, which he did not read, and the jewels on the pommel, flashing in the lovely light.

"Come, sword," said the Wart.

He took hold of the handles with both hands, and strained against the stone. There was a melodious consort[25] on the recorders, but nothing moved.

The Wart let go of the handles, when they were beginning to bite into the palms of his hands, and stepped back, seeing stars.

22. To *waylay* is to lie in wait for and attack. Wart's *pad,* or pad horse, is trained for slow, steady road travel and wouldn't do well in a quick getaway.
23. *Straits* is a troublesome or difficult situation.
24. The church's *gargoyles* are ornaments in the form of outlandish creatures, its *monastery* is a residence for monks, and the *yew* is a type of evergreen tree.
25. Here, *consort* means "a harmony of sounds."

Vocabulary
ruefully (ro͞o′ fəl ē) *adv.* regretfully; sorrowfully

The Faithful Knight in Equal Field Subdues his Faithless Foe. Frederick and Pickford Marriot (1860–1941).
Viewing the painting: How might the Merlin's advice about "not letting go" apply to these jousters?

"It is well fixed," he said.

He took hold of it again and pulled with all his might. The music played more strongly, and the light all about the churchyard glowed like amethysts;[26] but the sword still stuck.

"Oh, Merlyn," cried the Wart, "help me to get this weapon."

There was a kind of rushing noise, and a long chord played along with it. All round the churchyard there were hundreds of old friends. They rose over the church wall all together, like the Punch and Judy[27] ghosts of remembered days, and there were badgers and nightingales and vulgar crows and hares and wild geese and falcons and fishes and dogs and dainty unicorns and solitary wasps and corkindrills and hedgehogs and griffins and the thousand other animals he had met. They loomed round the church wall, the lovers and helpers of the Wart, and they all spoke solemnly in turn. Some of them had come from the banners in the church, where they were painted in heraldry,[28] some from the waters and the sky and the fields about—but all, down to the smallest shrew mouse, had come to help on account of love. Wart felt his power grow.

"Put your back into it," said a Luce (or pike) off one of the heraldic banners, "as you once did when I was going to snap you up.[29] Remember that power springs from the nape of the neck."

"What about those forearms," asked a Badger gravely, "that are held together by a chest? Come along, my dear embryo,[30] and find your tool."

A Merlin sitting at the top of the yew tree cried out, "Now then, Captain Wart, what is the first law of the foot? I thought I once heard something about never letting go?"

26. The light was the violet color of quartz crystals called *amethysts.*
27. The main characters in a puppet show, *Punch and Judy* have been popular with English audiences for centuries.
28. The animals in *heraldry* are painted on banners showing coats of arms, designs that represent noble families and their histories.
29. *Luce* is an old name for the pike, a fish that can grow to more than four feet long and that normally eats other fish.
30. The fertilized egg of an organism is an *embryo,* but the word can also refer to someone or something in the beginning stage of development.

"Don't work like a stalling woodpecker," urged a Tawny Owl affectionately. "Keep up a steady effort, my duck, and you will have it yet."

A white-front said, "Now, Wart, if you were once able to fly the great North Sea, surely you can co-ordinate a few little wing-muscles here and there? Fold your powers together, with the spirit of your mind, and it will come out like butter. Come along, Homo sapiens, for all we humble friends of yours are waiting here to cheer."

The Wart walked up to the great sword for the third time. He put out his right hand softly and drew it out as gently as from a scabbard.[31]

There was a lot of cheering, a noise like a hurdy-gurdy[32] which went on and on. In the middle of this noise, after a long time, he saw Kay and gave him the sword. The people at the tournament were making a frightful row.

"But this is not my sword," said Sir Kay.

"It was the only one I could get," said the Wart. "The inn was locked."

"It is a nice-looking sword. Where did you get it?"

"I found it stuck in a stone, outside a church."

Sir Kay had been watching the tilting nervously, waiting for his turn. He had not paid much attention to his squire.

"That is a funny place to find one," he said.

"Yes, it was stuck through an anvil."

"What?" cried Sir Kay, suddenly rounding upon him. "Did you just say this sword was stuck in a stone?"

"It was," said the Wart. "It was a sort of war memorial."

Sir Kay stared at him for several seconds in amazement, opened his mouth, shut it again, licked his lips, then turned his back and plunged through the crowd. He was looking for Sir Ector, and the Wart followed after him.

"Father," cried Sir Kay, "come here a moment."

"Yes, my boy," said Sir Ector. "Splendid falls these professional chaps do manage.

The Boyhood of Arthur, 1851. John Callcott Horsley. Oil on canvas. Walker Galleries, Harrogate, UK.

Viewing the painting: How does this portrayal of Arthur compare or contrast with the character of Arthur in the selection?

31. A *scabbard* is a case for the blade of a sword.
32. The *hurdy-gurdy* is a musical instrument shaped somewhat like a guitar but played by turning a hand crank that causes a revolving wheel to make the strings vibrate.

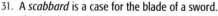

Why, what's the matter, Kay? You look as white as a sheet."

"Do you remember that sword which the King of England would pull out?"

"Yes."

"Well, here it is. I have it. It is in my hand. I pulled it out."

Sir Ector did not say anything silly. He looked at Kay and he looked at the Wart. Then he stared at Kay again, long and lovingly, and said, "We will go back to the church."

"Now then, Kay," he said, when they were at the church door. He looked at his first-born kindly, but straight between the eyes. "Here is the stone, and you have the sword. It will make you the King of England. You are my son that I am proud of, and always will be, whatever you do. Will you promise me that you took it out by your own might?"

Kay looked at his father. He also looked at the Wart and at the sword.

Then he handed the sword to the Wart quite quietly.

He said, "I am a liar. Wart pulled it out."

As far as the Wart was concerned, there was a time after this in which Sir Ector kept telling him to put the sword back into the stone—which he did—and in which Sir Ector and Kay then vainly tried to take it out. The Wart took it out for them, and stuck it back again once or twice. After this, there was another time which was more painful.

He saw that his dear guardian[33] was looking quite old and powerless, and that he was kneeling down with difficulty on a gouty knee.

"Sir," said Sir Ector, without looking up, although he was speaking to his own boy.

"Please do not do this, father," said the Wart, kneeling down also. "Let me help you up, Sir Ector, because you are making me unhappy."

"Nay, nay, my lord," said Sir Ector, with some very feeble old tears. "I was never your father nor of your blood, but I wote well ye are of an higher blood than I wend[34] ye were."

"Plenty of people have told me you are not my father," said the Wart, "but it does not matter a bit."

"Sir," said Sir Ector humbly, "will ye be my good and gracious lord when ye are King?"

"Don't!" said the Wart.

"Sir," said Sir Ector, "I will ask no more of you but that you will make my son, your foster-brother, Sir Kay, seneschal[35] of all your lands?"

Kay was kneeling down too, and it was more than the Wart could bear.

"Oh, do stop," he cried. "Of course he can be seneschal, if I have got to be this King, and, oh, father, don't kneel down like that, because it breaks my heart. Please get up, Sir Ector, and don't make everything so horrible. Oh, dear, oh, dear, I wish I had never seen that filthy sword at all."

And the Wart also burst into tears.

33. Merlyn had arranged for Sir Ector to be Arthur's *guardian* and to raise him as his son. Neither Ector nor Wart knew that the baby's biological father was Britain's King Uther.

34. *Wote* and *wend* are past-tense forms of two obsolete verbs—*wot,* meaning "to know," and *ween,* meaning "to suppose, believe, or expect."

35. In medieval times, the *seneschal* (sen′ ə shəl) managed the king's estate, ran his household, and sometimes also had official state duties or a military command.

Responding to Literature

Personal Response

How did you react to the Wart's behavior at the beginning of the excerpt? at the middle? at the end? How might you have behaved differently?

Analyzing Literature

Recall

1. Why has the death of King Uther thrown the country into a state of excitement?
2. What news does the Wart announce to Sir Ector and Kay?
3. Why is the Wart unable to bring Sir Kay's sword back to him?
4. How does the Wart know immediately that the sword in the stone is no ordinary sword?
5. Who does Sir Kay claim pulled the sword from the stone? What is the Wart's response?

Interpret

6. What effect does the death of the old king have upon Sir Ector and his companions? Explain.
7. What can you infer about the Wart's relationship with Merlyn? Support your answer with details from the text.
8. Why, do you suppose, does the Wart silently obey Sir Kay's order to fetch his sword?
9. How does the author build the plot to a **climax** (see page R2) during the scene in which the Wart pulls the sword from the stone?
10. What does the Wart's response to Sir Kay suggest to you about Arthur's character and future leadership?

Evaluate and Connect

11. Does it seem realistic to you that the characters fail to notice the Wart's sadness about Merlyn's departure? Explain.
12. How does the author's use of **repetition** in the first churchyard scene affect your appreciation of the story?
13. Why might the author have portrayed Sir Ector as a wise and loving father?
14. Think about your response to the Reading Focus on page 961. Do Sir Ector's and Sir Kay's reactions to the Wart's sudden "promotion" seem true to life? Explain.
15. **Theme Connections** In your opinion, what is the author saying about heroes?

Literary ELEMENTS

Tone

Tone suggests a writer's or speaker's attitude toward the subject. When you read a selection, think about the attitude it conveys. Is it solemn? silly? frightening? angry? To identify an author's tone, consider the imagery, syntax, sound devices, and connotations being used. For example, King Pellinore says, "Oh, do try to listen to me, you two, instead of interruptin' all the time about nothin', for it makes a man's head go ever so." Pellinore's casual language and frustration suggest a humorous, down-to-earth view of nobility that is contrary to its frequent portrayal as being haughty and intelligent.

1. What is the subject of the first page of the selection? What tone is taken toward the subject? Identify two examples from the page that convey this tone.
2. Choose a passage in which the tone is different from that of the opening scene. How has the author made the tone different? Why, do you suppose, has he changed his tone?

- See **Literary Terms Handbook,** p. R13.

Literature and Writing

Writing About Literature

Character Analysis No one is more surprised than the Wart to find that he is to be King of England. Does the Wart have what it takes to be a good king? Look through the selection for signs that young Arthur possesses superior qualities. Then brainstorm a list of "kingly" traits that you detect in the Wart. Write a brief analysis of his character based on your list, and share it with the class.

Creative Writing

Father and Son This passage ends with both Sir Ector and Sir Kay on their knees before the Wart, their future king. What is going through their minds? Imagine a scene later that evening when Sir Ector and Kay are alone. What will they say to each other about the sudden elevation of the Wart from squire to king? Write their brief dialogue, using language and content that reflects each character.

Extending Your Response

Literature Groups

Memorable Moments Which scenes do you continue to think about? A specific element, such as humor, emotion, description, realism, or fantasy, can make a scene vivid. Skim the selection for two scenes that are the most memorable for you, and identify why they made an impression. As you share your choices with the group, discuss other group members' thoughts and feelings about the scenes. Compare your group's impressions with those of other groups.

Learning for Life

Hear Ye! Hear Ye! "They . . . have had to proclaim a tournament all over England, for New Year's Day, so that the man who comes to the tournament and pulls out the sword can be King of all England for ever," whispers King Pellinore. Make a scroll, announcing specific details of the tournament. Read your announcement to the class, and then post it for all to read.

Performing

Reenactment With two classmates, act out the story from the scene when Sir Kay sends the Wart to fetch his sword. Improvise dialogue for each scene, staying true to the content and to each character's manner of speaking. Rehearse the reenactment and perform it for the class.

Reading Further

If you'd like to read other adventures, you might enjoy these epics:

The Hobbit, The Fellowship of the Ring, The Two Towers, and *The Return of the King,* by J. R. R. Tolkien, describe adventures of heroes who set out to save Middle Earth from evil.

Save your work for your portfolio.

GRAMMAR AND LANGUAGE • Sentence Fragments

A sentence fragment is a word group written as a sentence but lacking either a subject, a verb, or both. Because sentence fragments are grammatically incorrect and often hard to understand, writers tend to avoid using them. However, authors may use sentence fragments in dialogue, where they can create the sound of natural speech. For example, in "Arthur Becomes King," Sir Kay expresses a desire to go to London. "Long way to London," Sir Grummore replies. His statement lacks a subject and a verb, but it's the kind of clipped, fragmentary comment you might hear in real speech.

PRACTICE Copy a passage from "Arthur Becomes King" that includes several sentence fragments. With a partner, replace these fragments with complete sentences; then discuss how this changes the effect of the dialogue.

APPLY Find a passage of dialogue that you have written. Where did you use sentence fragments? Where might the addition of sentence fragments make your dialogue sound more natural?

- For more about sentence fragments, see **Language Handbook,** p. R14.

READING AND THINKING • Making Inferences

Experienced readers pay attention to a character's dialogue, appearance, and behavior in order to gain information about the character that is not directly stated in the text of a story. In "Arthur Becomes King," for example, Sir Kay is described as looking "white as a sheet." He tells a lie but later admits the truth. These clues help readers to infer that Sir Kay is jealous and ambitious but essentially honest.

PRACTICE Tell a classmate what you have inferred about the Wart. Then work with your partner to find clues in the story's dialogue and descriptions that verify your impression or cause you to change it.

- For more about making inferences, see **Reading Handbook,** p. R92.

VOCABULARY • Dictionary Skills: Definitions

Many words, such as *vulgar,* have several meanings. A dictionary will supply all (or most) of the meanings a word has, but the person using the dictionary must figure out which of those meanings is the appropriate one for a certain use of the word. For any multiple-meaning word, you must pay attention to the context that the word appears in to know which meaning is appropriate.

Here is a sample dictionary entry for the word *desolate* as an adjective.

desolate *adj.* **1.** solitary; lonely: *one desolate child on the playground.* **2.** uninhabited; deserted: *a desolate shack.* **3.** ruined or destroyed: *left desolate by the tornado.* **4.** unhappy; miserable; wretched: *an abandoned puppy's desolate howl.*

PRACTICE Decide which meaning of *desolate* is used in each sentence and write the number of that meaning.

1. The plains stretched before our wagon, *desolate* and forbidding.
2. On the bluff, the only sign of life was a *desolate* tree.
3. I finally found a *desolate* beach that fulfilled my need for privacy.
4. Learning that our grandparents were moving away left us feeling *desolate.*
5. Sherman's men marched through Georgia and the Carolinas, leaving towns, fields, and farms *desolate* in their wake.

Vo•cab•u•lar•y Skills

Idioms

Kay is desperately eager to go to London. "Think what people will say about us," he says, "if we do not go and have a shot at that sword." If you knew the meaning of every English word but had never heard the phrase *have a shot at,* what would you think Kay was proposing?

A word or phrase that has a special meaning different from its ordinary meaning is called an **idiom.** The phrase *have a shot at* is so familiar to most speakers of English that we know immediately that it means "have a try at" or "make an effort." Unfamiliar idioms, however, can sometimes be confusing.

Often you can understand unfamiliar idioms by thinking about the ordinary meanings of the words.

nipped in the bud	stopped at an early stage
a slap on the wrist	a very mild punishment
to wrap it up	to finish
to know the ropes	to be familiar with a method or procedure

Some idioms cannot be interpreted so easily. Why does *stuck up* mean "conceited"? Why does *take it with a grain of salt* mean "accept a statement, but with some doubt as to its complete truthfulness"? If you didn't already know what those idioms mean, how could you figure out their meanings?

When you come across an unfamiliar idiom, context clues can be helpful. Although context may not reveal the precise meaning of an idiom, it will almost always hint at the meaning.

EXERCISE

To figure out the meaning of each idiom, think about the ordinary meanings of the underlined words, use context clues, or do both. Then write a short definition or a phrase that could be substituted for the idiom. Use a dictionary as needed.

1. Kay is sure that things will go swimmingly for him in the tournament competitions.
2. Kay's snobbiness is a shock to Wart and temporarily puts him out of sorts.
3. Wart is willing to play second fiddle to Kay, but not to be looked down on.
4. Kay realizes what sword he has been given and, with an eye to the main chance, claims that he took it from the stone.
5. Kay's conceit might be understandable, but lying about how he got the sword is beyond the pale.

Technology Skills

Citing Electronic Sources

If you use the Internet when conducting research for a report on literature, art, or another subject in the humanities, use the following guidelines for citing your sources and preparing your bibliography or works-cited list. The guidelines are based on the style recommended by the Modern Language Association (MLA). The American Psychological Association (APA) and American Medical Association (AMA) guidelines, which differ somewhat, may be used when writing about scientific subjects, but check with your teacher first and use the guidelines he or she prefers.

The information in each works-cited entry should appear in the order listed below, but note that no source will include every item listed. The box on the next page provides sample entries you may use as models.

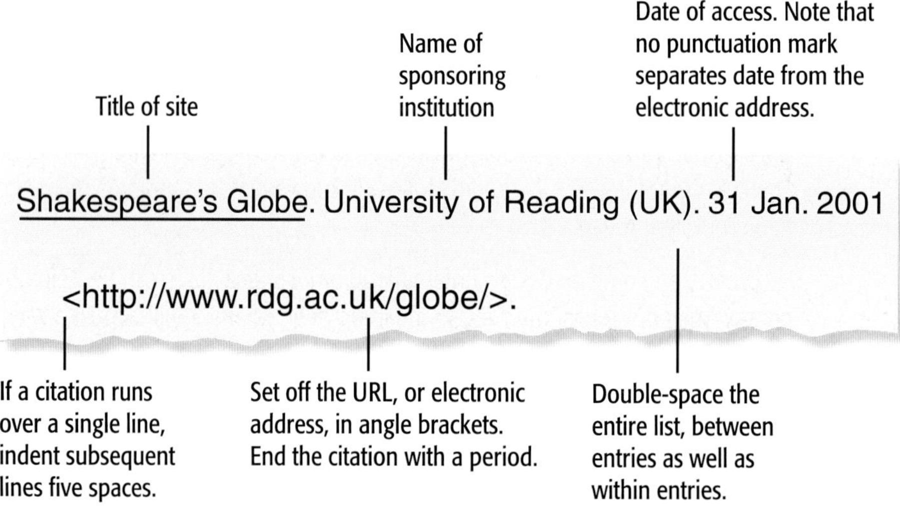
Title of site
Name of sponsoring institution
Date of access. Note that no punctuation mark separates date from the electronic address.
Shakespeare's Globe. University of Reading (UK). 31 Jan. 2001
<http://www.rdg.ac.uk/globe/>.
If a citation runs over a single line, indent subsequent lines five spaces.
Set off the URL, or electronic address, in angle brackets. End the citation with a period.
Double-space the entire list, between entries as well as within entries.

1. **Name** of author, editor, or translator of the source (last name first), followed by an abbreviation, such as *ed.* or *trans.,* if appropriate
2. **Title**
   - of a poem, short story, article, or other short work (in quotation marks)
   - of a book (underlined)
   - of a scholarly project, database, periodical, or site (underlined). If a personal or professional site has no title, use a description, such as *Home page* (with no underlining or quotation marks)
3. **Name** of the editor or translator of the text (if relevant and if not cited earlier), preceded by the appropriate abbreviation, such as *Ed.* or *Trans.*

TECHNOLOGY TIP

Since Web sites change frequently, be sure to print out any pages that you use for your research and that you will need to include in your list of works cited.

4. **Publication information**
- date of latest posting and institution or organization sponsoring the site
- place and date of original version
- version number, volume number, or other identifying number
- reference to pages, paragraphs, or sections used (such as *pp. 47-52* or *pars. 1-14*)

3. For a posting to a **discussion list,** the name of the list and the description *Online posting*

4. Date when the researcher accessed the source

5. Electronic address, or URL, of the source (in angle brackets)

Sample Entries for List of Works Cited

Professional Site

Shakespeare's Globe. 28 June 2000. University of Reading (UK). 31 Jan 2001 <http://www.rdg.ac.uk/globe>.

Personal Site

Brennan, Mark. *The Huckleberry Finn Web Site.* 3 Feb. 1997 <http://ourworld.compuserve.com/homepages/MBrennan/homepage.html>.

Book

Twain, Mark. *The Celebrated Frog of Calaveras County, and Other Sketches*. Ed. John Paul. New York: C. H. Webb, 1867. About.com. 31 Jan. 2001 <http://mark-twain.miningco.com/library/texts/bl_jf_contents.htm>.

Poem

Bevington, Louise Sarah. "Cloud-Climbing." *Poems, Lyrics, and Sonnets*. London: Eliot Stock, 1882. 30 Aug. 1996, Indiana U. 31 Jan. 2001 <http://www.indiana.edu/~letrs/vwwp/bevington/bevpoems.html>.

Article in a Reference Database

"Sonnet." *Concise Columbia Electronic Encyclopedia.* Infonautics 2000. 26 Jan. 2001 <http://www.encyclopedia. com>.

Article in a Journal

Fox, Robert Elliot. "Shaping an African American Literary Canon." *Postmodern Culture* 9.1 (Sept. 1996): 19 pars. 23 Feb. 1999 <http://www.iath.virginia.edu/pmc/998/9.1.r_fox.html>.

Article in a Magazine

Bennehum, David S. "Coming of Age in Cyberspace." 28 Oct. 1998. *Atlantic Online.* 31 Jan. 2001 <http://www.theatlantic.com/unbound/digicult/dc981028.htm>.

Posting to a Discussion List

Renshaw, Scott. "Review of *William Shakespeare's Romeo and Juliet.*" Online posting. 28 Oct. 1996. Usenet. 4 Nov. 1996 <http://www.usenet.com>.

For more on documenting sources, see Writing Handbook, pages R64–R69.

EXERCISES

1. Think of a topic for a research paper. Then do a Web search for information on your topic. Find a significant fact from each of at least six electronic sources and write the corresponding citations. You might work with a partner to choose a topic. Then compare information and citations after completing your research independently.

2. With a small group, do a Web search for organizations other than the MLA that offer style guides for citing electronic sources. For instance, you might search for the guidelines provided by the Alliance for Computers and Writing or for the American Psychological Association (APA). What differences in citation style do you see?

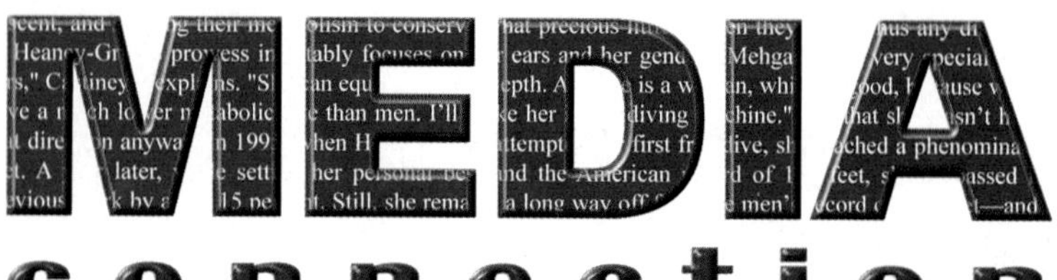

connection

Theme Song Lyrics

Wonder Woman has "lived" to be the legendary, superhero star of a comic book and a television series since her creation during World War II as a fighter against the enemies of the free world. Here's a little piece of that history.

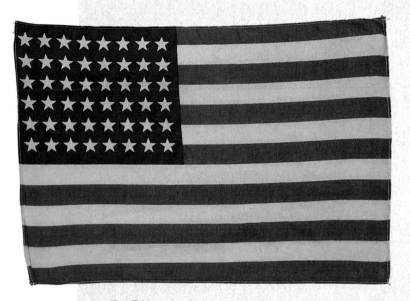

The official American flag from 1912–1959 had 48 stars.

Wonder Woman

Wonder Woman!
Wonder Woman!

Now the world is ready for you
and the wonders you can do
Make a hawk a dove
stop a war with love
Make a liar tell the truth

Wonder Woman!
Get us out from under, Wonder
Woman

All our hopes are pinned upon you
and the magic that you do
Stop a bullet cold
make the Axis fold
change their minds and change
the world

Wonder Woman!
Wonder Woman!

You're a wonder, Wonder Woman!

Analyzing Media

1. Does the image of Wonder Woman on the comic book cover match the idea of Wonder Woman in the television show's theme song? Explain.
2. What do you think is the most wondrous thing Wonder Woman can do? Why?

Wonder Woman
NOVEMBER No. 23
SENSATION COMICS
10¢
A SUPERMAN DC PUBLICATION
FRUIT AND VEGETABLES
SALE
IN THIS ISSUE
Wonder Woman's
LESSON TO BULLIES!
HARRY G. PETER

Before You Read

Where the Girl Rescued Her Brother

Reading Focus

Whom have you heard or read about who responded heroically in a time of crisis? What made their actions heroic?

Heroic Act Checklist What elements are common to acts of heroism? Create a checklist that could be used to identify heroic acts. Share your checklist with the class.

Setting a Purpose Read to see how a young woman responds heroically in a time of crisis.

Building Background

The Time and Place

The characters and events described in this story are based on fact. The battle that sparked these events took place on June 17, 1876, at Rosebud Creek in southern Montana.

Did You Know?

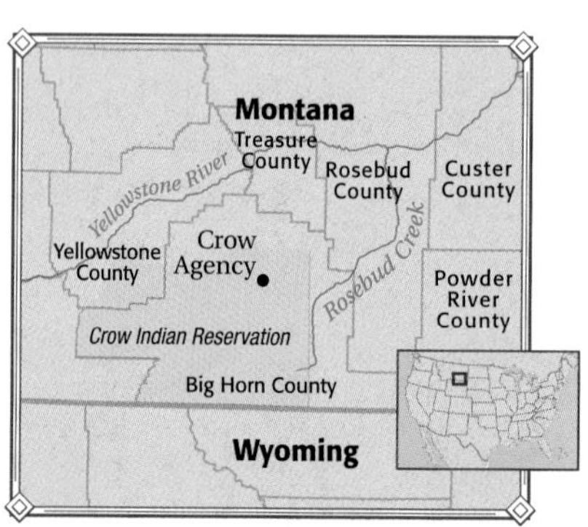

When gold was discovered in the Black Hills of South Dakota in the early 1870s, miners rushed into the area, heedless of the treaty that had previously guaranteed the Sioux people exclusive possession of the land. The miners' total disregard for the rights of Native Americans spurred skirmishes between the two groups. As a result, Brigadier General George Crook of the United States Army ordered the Sioux to leave the area, but Sioux chiefs Sitting Bull and Crazy Horse ignored the order. After a series of unprovoked attacks on his people, Sitting Bull summoned the Sioux, Cheyenne, and certain Arapaho to Montana. Soon after, this confederation surprised Crook's troops at Rosebud Creek. That battle is described, in part, in "Where the Girl Rescued Her Brother."

Vocabulary Preview

confront (kən frunt′) *v.* to come face-to-face with; to oppose; p. 984
vault (vôlt) *v.* to jump; spring; p. 985
strategic (strə tē′ jik) *adj.* highly important to an intended goal; p. 986

Meet Joseph Bruchac and Gayle Ross

Joseph Bruchac (bro͞o shak′), a Native American writer and storyteller, was raised by his grandparents. "My grandmother kept our house filled with books," he said, but it was from his grandfather that Bruchac learned the power of storytelling. "It is his voice that I often hear when I begin to tell a story."

Joseph Bruchac was born in 1942 in Saratoga Springs, New York.

Native American storyteller and writer Gayle Ross is a direct descendent of Chief John Ross, a Cherokee nation leader during the 1800s. Gayle Ross says that she and Bruchac "have been taught that stories are living spirits and that the role of the storyteller is to care for the tales in our keeping."

Gayle Ross was born in Denton, Texas, in 1951. "Where the Girl Rescued Her Brother" first appeared in The Girl Who Married the Moon *in 1994.*

Where the Girl Rescued Her Brother

Joseph Bruchac
& Gayle Ross

Cheyenne Woman. Greg Perillo.

IT WAS THE MOON when the chokecherries were ripe. A young woman rode out of a Cheyenne camp with her husband and her brother. The young woman's name was Buffalo Calf Road Woman. Her husband, Black Coyote, was one of the chiefs of the Cheyenne, the people of the plains who call themselves Tsis-tsis-tas, meaning simply "The People." Buffalo Calf Road Woman's brother, Comes-in-Sight, was also one of the Cheyenne chiefs, and it was well-known how close he was to his sister.

Like many of the other young women of the Cheyenne, Buffalo Calf Road Woman was respected for her honorable nature. Although it was the men who most often went to war to defend the people—as they were doing on this day—women would accompany their husbands when they went to battle. If a man held an important position among the Cheyenne, such as the keeper of the Sacred Arrows, then his wife, too, would have to be of the highest moral character, for she shared the weight of his responsibility.

Buffalo Calf Road Woman was well aware of this, and as she rode by her husband she did so with pride. She knew that today they were on their way to meet their old allies, the Lakota.[1] They were going out to try to drive back the *veho,* the spider people who were trying to claim all the lands of the Native peoples.

---

1. The *Lakota* were the largest group of the Sioux peoples. Their traditional hunting grounds were in the western Dakotas and Nebraska.

The Cheyenne had been worried about the *veho,* the white people, for a long time. They had given them that name because, like the black widow spider, they were very beautiful but it was dangerous to get close to them. And unlike the Cheyenne, they seemed to follow a practice of making promises and not keeping them. Although their soldier chief Custer had promised to be friendly with the Cheyenne, now he and the others had come into their lands to make war upon them.

Buffalo Calf Road Woman wore a robe embroidered with porcupine quills. The clothing of her brother and her husband, Black Coyote, was also beautifully decorated with those quills, which had been flattened, dyed in different colors, folded, and sewed on in patterns. Buffalo Calf Road Woman was proud that she belonged to the Society of Quilters. As with the men's societies, only a few women—those of the best character—could join. Like the men, the women had to be strong, honorable, and brave. Buffalo Calf Road Woman had grown up hearing stories of how Cheyenne women would defend their families when the men were away. The women of the Cheyenne were brave, and those in the Society of Quilters were the bravest of all.

Buffalo Calf Road Woman smiled as she remembered one day when the women of the Society of Quilters showed such bravery. It was during the Moon of Falling Leaves. A big hunt had been planned. The men who acted as scouts had gone out and located the great buffalo herd. They had seen, too, that there were no human enemies anywhere near their camp. So almost none of the men remained behind.

On that day, when all the men were away, a great grizzly bear came into the camp. Such things seldom happened, but this bear was one that had been wounded in the leg by a white fur-trapper's bullet. It could no longer hunt as it had before, and hunger brought it to the Cheyenne camp, where it smelled food cooking.

When the huge bear came walking into the camp, almost everyone scattered. Some women grabbed their little children. Old people shut the door flaps of their tepees, and the boys ran to find their bows and arrows. Only a group of seven women who had been working on the embroidery of an elk-skin robe did not run. They were members of the Society of Quilters, and Buffalo Calf Road Woman was among them. The seven women put down their work, picked up the weapons they had close to hand, and stood to face the grizzly bear.

Now of all of the animals of the plains, the only one fierce enough and powerful enough to attack a human was the grizzly. But confronted by that determined group of women, the grizzly bear stopped in its tracks. It had come to steal food, not fight. The head of the Society of Quilters stepped forward a pace and spoke to the bear.

"Grandfather," she said, her voice low and firm, "we do not wish to harm you, but we will protect our camp. Go back to your own home."

The grizzly shook its head and then turned and walked out of the camp. The women stood and watched it as it went down through the cottonwoods and was lost from sight along the bend of the stream.

Buffalo Calf Road Woman turned her mind away from her memories. They were close to Rosebud Creek. The scouts had told them that a great number of the *veho* soldiers would be there and that the Gray Fox,

Vocabulary

confront (kən frunt′) *v.* to come face-to-face with; to oppose

Dress. 19th century, Southern Cheyenne. Buckskin, elk teeth, glass beads, tin cones, and yellow and red pigments, length: 48 in., width: 35 in. Smithsonian Institution, Washington, D.C.

General George Crook, was in command. The Cheyenne had joined up now with the Oglala,[2] led by Crazy Horse. The Lakota people were always friends to the Cheyenne, but this man, Crazy Horse, was the best friend of all. Some even said that he was one of their chiefs, too, as well as being a war leader of his Oglala.

There were Crow and Shoshone[3] scouts with Crook, and the *veho* had many cannons. The Lakota and the Cheyenne were outnumbered by the two thousand men in Crook's command. But they were prepared to fight. They had put on their finest clothes, for no man should risk his life without being dressed well enough so that if he died, the enemy would know a great warrior had fallen. Some of the men raised their headdresses three times, calling out their names and the deeds they had done. Those headdresses of eagle feathers were thought to give magical protection to a warrior. Other men busied themselves painting designs on their war ponies.

Now they could hear Crook's army approaching. The rumble of the horses' hooves echoed down the valley, and there was the sound of trumpets. War ponies reared up and stomped their feet. Many of the Cheyenne men found it hard to put on the last of their paint as their hands shook from the excitement of the coming battle.

Crazy Horse vaulted onto his horse and held up one arm. "*Hoka Hey,*" he cried. "It is a good day to die."

Buffalo Calf Road Woman watched from a hill as the two lines of men—the blue soldiers to one side, and the Lakota and Cheyenne to the other—raced toward each other. The battle began. It was not a quick fight or an easy one. There were brave men on both sides. Two Moons, Little Hawk, Yellow Eagle, Sitting Bull, and Crazy Horse were only a few of the great warriors who fought for the Cheyenne and the Lakota. And Crook, the Gray Fox general of the whites, was known to be a tough fighter and a worthy enemy.

Buffalo Calf Road Woman's husband, Black Coyote, and her brother, Comes-in-Sight, were in the thick of the fight.

---

2. Also a Sioux people, the *Oglala* (ō glä′ lə) lived in what is now South Dakota.
3. The *Crow* and *Shoshone* (shə shō′ nē) peoples lived primarily in the Rocky Mountains.

Vocabulary
vault (vôlt) *v.* to jump; spring

The odds in the battle were almost even. Although the whites had more soldiers and guns, the Lakota and the Cheyenne were better shots and better horsemen. Had it not been for the Crow and Shoshone scouts helping Crook, the white soldiers might have broken quickly from the ferocity of the attack.

From one side to the other, groups of men attacked and retreated as the guns cracked, cannons boomed, and smoke filled the air. The war shouts of the Lakota and the Cheyenne were almost as loud as the rumble of the guns. The sun moved across the sky as the fight went on, hour after hour, while the confusion of battle swirled below.

Then Buffalo Calf Road Woman saw something that horrified her. Her brother had been drawn off to one side, surrounded by Crow scouts. He tried to ride free of them, but his pony went down, struck by a rifle bullet and killed. Now he was on foot, still fighting. The Crow warriors were trying to get close, to count coup[4] on him. It was more of an honor to touch a living enemy, so they were not firing their rifles at him. And he was able to keep them away with his bow and arrows. But it was clear that soon he would be out of ammunition and would fall to the enemy.

Buffalo Calf Road Woman waited no longer. She dug her heels into her pony's sides and galloped down the hill. Her head low, her braids streaming behind her, she rode into the heart of the fight. Some men moved aside as they saw her coming, for there was a determined look in her eyes. She made the long howling cry that Cheyenne women used to urge on the warriors. This time, however, she was the one going into the fight. Her voice was as strong as an eagle's. Her horse scattered the ponies of the Crow scouts who were closing in on her brother, Comes-in-Sight. She held out a hand; her brother grabbed it and vaulted onto the pony behind her. Then she wheeled, ducking the arrows of the Crow scouts, and heading back up the hill.

That was when it happened. For a moment, it seemed as if all the shooting stopped. The Cheyenne and the Lakota, and even the *veho* soldiers, lowered their guns to watch this act of great bravery. A shout went up, not from one side but from both, as Buffalo Calf Road Woman reached the safety of the hilltop again, her brother safe behind her on her horse. White men and Indians cheered her.

So it was that Buffalo Calf Road Woman performed the act for which the people would always remember her. Inspired by her courage, the Cheyenne and Lakota drove back the Gray Fox—Crook made a strategic withdrawal.

"Even the *veho* general was impressed," said the Cheyenne people. "He saw that if our women were that brave, he would stand no chance against us in battle."

So it is that to this day, the Cheyenne and the Lakota people do not refer to the fight as the Battle of the Rosebud. Instead, they honor Buffalo Calf Road Woman by calling the fight Where the Girl Rescued Her Brother.

4. Among some Native Americans, to *count coup* (kōō) was to touch a living enemy and get away safely—an act requiring both skill and courage.

Vocabulary

strategic (strə tē′ jik) *adj.* highly important to an intended goal

Responding to Literature

Personal Response

Were you surprised by the response of those who witnessed Buffalo Calf Road Woman's bravery at Rosebud Creek? Why or why not?

Analyzing Literature

Recall

1. Who are Black Coyote, Comes-in-Sight, and Buffalo Calf Road Woman going to meet?
2. What clothing is Buffalo Calf Road Woman wearing on her journey?
3. What happened during the encounter with the grizzly bear?
4. Describe the scene at Rosebud Creek when Buffalo Calf Road Woman and her husband and her brother arrive.
5. What do the Cheyenne believe is the reason for the outcome of the battle?

Interpret

6. Why are the Cheyenne people worried about the *veho?* How do the Cheyenne view the *veho's* actions?
7. What special meaning does Buffalo Calf Road Woman's clothing have? Why is she feeling proud?
8. Why is the story about the grizzly bear significant to Buffalo Calf Road Woman?
9. What do you infer from the battle preparations of Native Americans about their attitude toward fighting and battle?
10. What do Buffalo Calf Road Woman's actions suggest about her character and skills?

Evaluate and Connect

11. How do the Cheyenne people seem to view the role of women in their society? Do you think their views are typical for other Americans of that historical time period? Why or why not?
12. Why might the authors have included the bear story in their tale?
13. Were you surprised by the **climax** and the **resolution** of the story? Why or why not? (See Literary Terms Handbook, pages R2 and R10.)
14. Theme Connections Look at the checklist you made for the Reading Focus on page 982. Based on what you wrote, would you say that Buffalo Calf Road Woman's actions are heroic? Explain.
15. If you were a close friend of Buffalo Calf Road Woman and realized what she was about to do, would you have tried to stop her? Explain.

Literary ELEMENTS

Suspense

Suspense is the tension that builds in a story to make readers wonder what will happen next. Writers build suspense by providing **sensory details** of what the characters see, hear, touch, taste, or smell and by relying on readers' prior knowledge of details and events. Suspense in the bear story, for example, is developed with details such as "almost none of the men remained," "huge bear," and "hunger." When readers combine these details with their prior knowledge of the strength of a grizzly bear, the stress of hunger, and the feeling of fear, the suspense builds.

1. What sensory details in the battle scene describe the ferocity of the battle and the toughness of both sides?
2. What prior knowledge did you rely on to add to the suspense in the battle scene?
3. How do these sensory details and your prior knowledge build suspense in the battle scene of "Where the Girl Rescued Her Brother"?

- See **Literary Terms Handbook,** p. R13.

Literature and Writing

Writing About Literature

Analyze the Narrator's Perspective A narrator can influence readers' perceptions through **subjective details** that reveal personal opinions and feelings. In one or two paragraphs, show how subjective details influence your response to this story.

Creative Writing

In Bookstores Now! Imagine that you work in the marketing department of a book publishing company. How would you advertise this story on its book jacket? Write a brief summary of the story, including tantalizing details of the setting, characters, and events.

Extending Your Response

Literature Groups

Defining Roles Gayle Ross has written, "In this changing world, with the roles of men and women being constantly redefined, I believe it is important that our definitions be based on mutual respect and the acceptance of our common humanity." In your group, discuss how this story supports Ross's views. Share your group's ideas with the class.

Interdisciplinary Activity

Social Studies: Mapping Historic Sites Find out more about Native American societies who tried to protect their lands. Research the Plains Indians and then create a map showing the territories of each group and the sites of their historic battles. Share your map with the class.

Listening and Speaking

Storytelling Time Listen to recordings by storytellers to identify the techniques they use to make stories come alive. Then use the techniques to tell the story to an audience.

Reading Further

You might enjoy these works by Joseph Bruchac and Gayle Ross:

Folktale: "The Girl Who Almost Married an Owl," from *The Girl Who Married the Moon,* is a Native North American tale about two sisters who encounter a trickster.

Poetry: "Coming Back," by Joseph Bruchac from *Harper's Anthology of 20th Century Native American Poetry,* edited by Duane Niatum, captures the importance of Native North American history.

Save your work for your portfolio.

VOCABULARY • Synonyms—Shades of Meaning

Not all synonyms, or words that have similar meanings, are correct in every context. Some words, such as *doubt,* are general in their meaning. Sometimes you need to be more specific. *Suspicion* and *skepticism* are synonyms of *doubt,* but *suspicion* means "mistrust," and *skepticism* can mean "an attitude of not admitting that something is true."

When choosing a synonym for a word, check the dictionary for both its literal meaning and its suggested meaning.

PRACTICE Select the underlined synonym that is appropriate to each context.

1. To catch a mouse, does a cat pounce or vault?
2. Does a person hop or vault over a four-foot fence?
3. Is a baseball coach's batting lineup an example of tricky or strategic planning?
4. Is taking detailed notes in class a diplomatic or strategic move for students?
5. Do friends who meet accidentally encounter or confront each other?

Reading & Thinking Skills

Identifying Sequence

When you make a telephone call, you pick up the receiver, listen for a dial tone, and press the digits of a telephone number. These steps must be done in the right order, or **sequence,** so the call can go through.

Similarly, the events in narrative writing–writing that tells a story–happen in a sequence so readers can understand the passage of time in the story. Most narratives are related in **chronological,** or time, order. Transition words and phrases that show time, such as *then, next,* or *three days later,* help readers keep track of the chronology.

Sometimes authors interrupt the chronological order with a **flashback,** or a scene that took place prior to the current events. A sentence or phrase usually signals the beginning of a flashback. Another sentence or phrase signals a return to the chronological order of events.

In "Where the Girl Rescued Her Brother," Buffalo Calf Road Woman rides to the site of a battle, watches the battle, and then saves her brother. This chronological sequence of events is interrupted by a flashback to an earlier event. The sentence "Buffalo Calf Road Woman smiled as she remembered one day when the women . . . showed such bravery" signals the beginning of a flashback about an encounter with a grizzly bear. The sentence "Buffalo Calf Road Woman turned her mind away from her memories" signals the end of the flashback.

● For more about sequence, see **Reading Handbook,** p. R89.

EXERCISE

Read the following passage from *Sundiata.* Then complete the items that follow.

> **She cried worse than ever. Djata was sympathetic to all this, but he was in a hurry to know something about Sosso. Balla Fasséké understood and said, "Triban, wipe away your tears and tell your story, speak to your brother. You know that he has never thought ill of you, and besides, all that was in his destiny."**
>
> **Nana Triban wiped her tears away and spoke.**
>
> **"When you left Mali, my brother sent me by force to Sosso to be the wife of Soumaoro, whom he greatly feared. I wept a great deal at the beginning but when I saw that perhaps all was not lost I resigned myself for the time being. I was nice to Soumaoro and was the chosen one among his numerous wives."**

1. Which events in the passage occur in the present? List those events in chronological order.
2. Write the sentence that signals the beginning of a flashback. Then list the events of the flashback in chronological order.

Writing Workshop

Expository Writing: Biographical Research Paper

Have you ever wondered how a particular hero got to be so brave, selfless, or strong, or how someone's heroic action affected the life of others? One of the best ways to find out about a subject is to research it.

In this workshop, you will write a brief biographical research paper about some aspect of a hero's life. You will give credit to your sources by citing them in your paper and in a list of works cited.

- As you write your research paper, refer to the **Writing Handbook,** pp. R58–R69.

EVALUATION RUBRIC

By the time you complete this Writing Workshop, you will have

- developed a thesis statement that summarizes your findings about a specific hero
- supported your main points with well-documented facts and statistics
- Effectively organized your ideas in a logical order
- concluded by restating your thesis
- presented a research paper that is free of errors in grammar, usage, and mechanics

The Writing Process

PREWRITING

PREWRITING TIP

Brainstorm to make a list of your favorite heroes, then choose one of them to investigate.

Decide on a topic

The stories of King Arthur rely both on legend and on fact, but a research paper must rely only on fact. For this reason, it is important that you choose a topic about which a fair amount is known. However, a research paper must also be specific. If you provide *too* much information about your topic, you run the risk of writing a paper that is too general. Do some preliminary research at the library or on the Internet, then decide whether you need to expand or limit your topic. You might use a chart like the one below that a student began for a paper on Nelson Mandela.

Consider your purpose

Your main purpose will be to provide information about the hero you choose. You will state a thesis about some aspect of the person's life and then support the thesis by providing a factual account of the aspect you chose.

Choosing a Topic		
Too broad	**Limited**	**Too limited**
Nelson Mandela's life	Nelson Mandela's role in creating a new South African vision	Nelson Mandela's early childhood

Choose an audience
Your audience is anyone who might be interested in learning facts about your subject.

Formulate questions
Write four or five research questions to discover, organize, and support what you know and what you need to learn about your topic. As the student has done in the model at right, ask *what, why,* and *how.* Modify your questions as you gather information.

STUDENT MODEL

- Why did Nelson Mandela act heroically?
- What risks did he take?
- How did he manage to achieve what he did?
- Who was affected by his actions?

Complete Student Model on p. R121.

Gather information
Keep your research questions in mind as you compile information from primary and secondary sources from the library and the Internet. Look for books, periodicals, and Web sites that contain important facts, relevant statistics, or interesting quotes on your topic. Use your subject's name as a keyword in your searches, but also try using more general terms, such as the historical time period.

Take notes
Many researchers use index cards to create a working bibliography and to take notes. See the **Writing Handbook,** pages R65–R66, for help with these steps in the research process.

Make an outline
A working outline–one that you continue to write and revise as you conduct your research–can help you organize your information. The writer of the model shown below organized information in chronological order. You might also organize information to show the order of its importance or to show cause and effect.

STUDENT MODEL

From Prisoner to President

I. Background
   A. The apartheid system
   B. Nelson Mandela's personal background
II. Struggle for racial justice
   A. Involvement with the African National Congress
   B. 1962 arrest and imprisonment
   C. His principles regarding freedom
III. Acts of heroism when released from prison
   A. Negotiated the Record of Understanding
   B. Won the Nobel Peace Prize
   C. Became president of South Africa

Complete Student Model on p. R121.

DRAFTING

DRAFTING TIP

See the Writing Skills page, "Main Idea and Supporting Details," on page 943, for help with organizing individual paragraphs.

Develop a thesis statement

State your thesis in the introduction. Ask yourself the following questions to help you develop your thesis statement.

What significant ideas surfaced during my research?
How could I state my research findings in one sentence?

STUDENT MODEL

Nelson Mandela's refusal to compromise his vision for a democratic, non-racist South Africa has made him a worldwide hero.

Complete Student Model on p. R121.

Write your draft

Begin drafting, using your outline as a guide. For each heading in your outline, write at least one paragraph. Don't let details stall you, and don't worry about finding "perfect" phrasing.

REVISING

REVISING TIP

Tighten your paper by deleting anything that doesn't support your thesis.

Evaluate your work

Review your notes and reconsider your thesis. As you wrote your draft, your paper may have headed in a different direction from your original thesis. Revise your thesis if necessary. Next, use your thesis and the **Rubric for Revising** to guide your revision. Refer to **Writing Handbook** page R68 for help with formatting your list of works cited.

Have a writing conference

Work with a revision partner. Read your research papers to each other. Then use the **Rubric for Revising** to offer suggestions for improving each other's work.

RUBRIC FOR REVISING

Your revised research paper should have
- ☑ a clear thesis statement
- ☑ details, facts, and examples to elaborate on your thesis
- ☑ an effective, consistent organization
- ☑ a conclusion that restates the thesis and ends with a final observation
- ☑ a works-cited list and appropriate documentation for quotations and facts

Your revised paper should be free of
- ☑ irrelevant details
- ☑ errors in grammar, usage, and mechanics

STUDENT MODEL

Nelson Mandela was born [in 1918] in the Transkei[, a region on South Africa's southeastern coast]. His father was the village chief. Mandela was being groomed to take his father's place[when] he rebelled against an arranged marriage and fled to Johannesburg ~~by train. He was going~~ to pursue a [law] career.

Complete Student Model on p. R121.

EDITING/PROPROOFREADING

After revising your draft, type or print a new copy of it with your corrections included. Then you can give your paper one final proofreading, checking citations, grammar, spelling, punctuation, and word use.

Grammar Hint

Do not use an apostrophe with possessive personal pronouns.

INCORRECT: A true hero is someone who saves a life at the risk of his or her's.

CORRECT: A true hero is someone who saves a life at the risk of his or hers.

- For more on punctuating possessive forms, see **Language Handbook,** p. R25.

PROOFREADING TIP

Use the **Proofreading Checklist** on the inside back cover to help you mark errors that you find.

TECHNOLOGY TIP

People usually make more mistakes when they proofread on the computer monitor. Print out a copy of your paper to proofread it.

STUDENT MODEL

Nelson Mandela is a favorite hero of mine who are some of your's?

Complete Student Model on p. R121.

Complete Student Model

For a complete version of the model developed in this workshop, refer to **Writing Workshop Models,** p. R121.

PUBLISHING/PRESENTING

Most research papers have a cover sheet that shows the title of the paper, the writer's name, and other identifying information. If you decide to present your paper orally, adapt it to make the ideas easier for your listeners to absorb. Shorten sentences and add visual aids that will break up the delivery of the text. Be sure to include a list of works cited in your paper.

PRESENTING TIP

Photographs enrich a biographical research paper.

Reflecting

In your journal, reflect on the effect your subject's heroism might have on your future actions or attitudes.

Which was the more difficult part of this assignment, the research or the writing? What did you learn from this experience that might help you conduct research in the future?

Save your work for your portfolio.

Unit Assessment

Personal Response

1. If someone were looking for exciting reading matter, which of the legends in this unit would you recommend? Explain your answer.
2. How did your work in this unit enhance your skills in the following areas?
   - connecting events from the past to your life in the present
   - figuring out the meanings of unfamiliar words and phrases
   - explaining your ideas in writing
   - working on your own to complete assignments

Analyzing Literature

Comparing Versions of Arthur Although a real Arthur may have walked the earth, the King Arthurs that you have read about are partially products of their authors' imaginations. Compare representations of King Arthur from two or more selections. What aspects of his character remain constant? What aspects vary? How might the times in which the selections were written have affected the images of the Arthur they portray? Use examples from the selections to illustrate your comparison.

Evaluate and Set Goals

Evaluate

1. How well did you meet the goals you set for yourself regarding this unit?
   - What helped you meet these goals?
   - What were the setbacks in accomplishing these goals?
2. What was your most meaningful contribution to a group project?
3. How would you assess your work in this unit, using the following scale? Give at least two reasons for your assessment.
   4 = outstanding **3** = good **2** = fair **1** = weak

Set Goals

1. Choose a goal to work toward in Unit 6. Concentrate on any skill you wish to improve, such as reading, writing, speaking, or working in a group.
2. Discuss your goal with your teacher.
3. Write down three steps you will take to help you achieve your goal.
4. Plan checkpoints at specific intervals in the unit to assess your progress toward your goal.
5. Include a self-evaluation plan to determine whether you have reached your goal.

Build Your Portfolio

Select Choose two pieces of writing you did in this unit, and include them in your portfolio. The following questions can help you make your selection.

- Which piece did people respond to most favorably?
- Which piece most clearly expresses your ideas?
- Which piece did you spend the most time revising?
- Which piece shows the most improvement in your writing?

Reflect Write notes for each piece you include in your portfolio. Consider the following issues.

- At the beginning of the writing process, what were your major concerns? How did you address them?
- What were your sources of inspiration?
- What do you think are general strengths of your writing? What do you have problems with? How does this piece fit with those trends?

Reading on Your Own

You might also be interested in the following books.

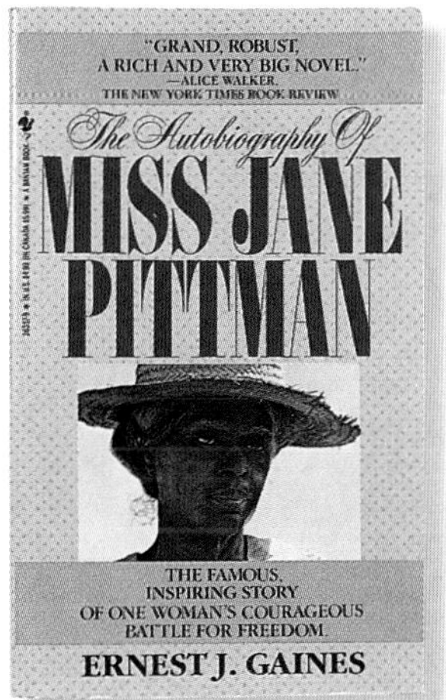

The Autobiography of Miss Jane Pittman

by Ernest J. Gaines Having lived 110 years, Jane Pittman is a woman with many stories to tell. Born into slavery, she lives through the Civil War, Reconstruction, life on a Southern plantation, and the Civil Rights movement of the 1960s. Her strength and courage serve as models to those around her.

The Light Beyond the Forest

by Rosemary Sutcliff The Knights of the Round Table set out in search of a holy relic known as the Holy Grail. This is a tale of heroism and adventure, in which Sir Lancelot, Sir Galahad, and the other knights struggle against great dangers to reach their goal. Only the most perfect knight succeeds.

Cut from the Same Cloth: American Women of Myth, Legend, and Tall Tale

by Robert D. San Souci Discover America's unheralded heroines who are as strong-willed and clever as their male counterparts. San Souci retells fifteen folktales, ballads, and stories about legendary women, representing such cultures as African American, Anglo American, Inuit, Hawaiian, Mexican American, and Native American.

The Talking Earth

by Jean Craighead George Do cultural traditions belong in our modern, technological world? Billie Wind finds the answer to this question when she ventures off alone into the Florida Everglades as punishment for doubting her Seminole tribe's legends. Her adventure teaches her that her tribe's legends are important—especially in today's world.

California English–Language Arts

Reading and Analyzing Test Questions

Read the passage and decide which type of error, if any, appears in each underlined section. Mark the letter for your answer on your paper.

> Dear Ben,
>
> Please forgive me for not having written sooner. This camping trip has been a busy one. It's very hard to find time to sit down (1) and compose a letter. The counselors here at camp sunshine have given me (2) many new responsibilities. I never complain, though? (3) Camp life agrees with me. It's a great place to go after a hard year at School. (4) I know that if you see this place, you'll agree.
>
> Your idea to come visit me during the last week of August sounds great! How can I help with the preparations. (5) Send me whatever details you think I'll need, and let's get you out here at your earliest convenence. (6) I'm excited to see you after all this time!
>
> Your friend,
>
> Veronica

1 A Spelling error
B Capitalization error
C Punctuation error
D No error

2 F Spelling error
G Capitalization error
H Punctuation error
J No error

3 A Spelling error
B Capitalization error
C Punctuation error
D No error

4 F Spelling error
G Capitalization error
H Punctuation error
J No error

5 A Spelling error
B Capitalization error
C Punctuation error
D No error

6 F Spelling error
G Capitalization error
H Punctuation error
J No error

Read the passage. Some sections are underlined. The underlined sections may be one of the following:

- Incomplete sentences
- Run-on sentences
- Correctly written sentences that should be combined
- Correctly written sentences that do not need to be rewritten

Choose the best way to write each underlined section. On your paper mark the letter for your answer. If the underlined section needs no change, mark the choice "Correct as is."

<u>The development of new types of blacksmith techniques in medieval times led to the widespread use of steel armor to protect soldiers during wartime.</u> (7) <u>The earliest version of armor was called mail. Mail was clunky and heavy.</u> (8) It deflected weapons but also slowed the wearer down. Blacksmiths soon found that the more motion and quickness armor allowed, the less protection it provided. <u>For instance, full plate mail sometimes weighed 75 pounds. Or more.</u> (9) A knight wearing a suit of plate mail might walk through a hailstorm of arrows and slingshots unharmed, but he was far too encumbered to fight against a single pikeman or lancer.

7 **A** The development of new types of blacksmith techniques in medieval times. Led to the widespread use of steel armor to protect soldiers during wartime.

B To develop certain types of blacksmith techniques in medieval times led blacksmiths to the widespread use of steel armor to protect soldiers during wartime.

C The development of certain types of blacksmith techniques in medieval times leading to the widespread use of steel armor to protect soldiers during wartime.

D Correct as is

8 **F** The earliest version of armor was called mail, and it was clunky and heavy.

G The earliest version of armor was called mail, but it was clunky and heavy.

H The earliest version of armor—called mail—was clunky and heavy.

J Correct as is

9 **A** For instance, full plate mail sometimes weighing 75 pounds, or more.

B For instance, full plate mail sometimes weighed 75 pounds, more or less.

C For instance, full plate mail sometimes weighed 75 pounds or more.

D Correct as is

STOP

La Valse hesitation. René Magritte. Oil on canvas, 13⅞ x 18 in. Private collection.

UNIT SIX

Humor

"Humor may not be laughter,
it may not even be a smile;
it is a point of view,
an attitude toward experience."

—Howard Thurman

Literature FOCUS

Humor

Are you quick to laugh? Do you enjoy the lighter side of life and poke fun at your own idiosyncrasies? If so, you probably have a good sense of humor.

Many writers of humor simply want to entertain their readers—to give them a smile or a laugh. However, writers can also use humor as an effective way to point out human weaknesses, social ills, or the absurd aspects of daily life.

Writers create humor by twisting what readers expect into the ridiculous or unexpected. The following techniques can help create a comic effect:

- **Hyperbole** is extravagant exaggeration for the sake of emphasis. For example: Her eyes were as big as saucers.
- **Understatement** is representing something as less than it actually is, for example, saying that something is "not bad" when it's really great. Understatement is the opposite of hyperbole.
- **Irony** is a contrast between reality and what seems to be real. There are several forms of irony. **Situational irony** exists when the actual outcome of a situation is the opposite of someone's expectations. **Verbal irony** exists when a person says one thing and means another. **Dramatic irony** occurs when the audience has important information that characters in a literary work do not have.
- **Satire** is a form of writing that exposes personal, social, or political failings to ridicule or scorn, often in an effort to correct them.
- **Pun** is a play on words, or a joke based on words with several meanings or on words that sound alike but have different meanings.

Dilbert reprinted by permission of United Feature Syndicate, Inc.

- **Parody** is a form of writing that closely imitates the style of an author or a literary work for the sake of ridicule or comic effect. Parodies are designed to mock the work or form they imitate.
- **Sarcasm** consists of cutting, often unkind or ironic, remarks made to show disapproval or to taunt. For example: I wouldn't expect *you* to understand.

ACTIVITY

As you read the selections in this unit, look for examples of comic techniques and think about the writer's purpose in using them.

Theme 12 Comic Perspectives

What things strike you as funny? What television programs make you laugh? What do you enjoy most about your favorite comedian? Although personal taste in humor can vary, there are some topics that most people find amusing. In this theme, you'll read humorous writing—fiction and nonfiction—that recounts both unusual and commonplace experiences that can make you laugh.

THEME PROJECTS

Performing

Comedy Show Which selections from this theme could become amusing skits?

1. Working with a group, choose the funniest scenes from three or four selections and rewrite them in the form of skits.
2. Use existing dialogue and add your own to capture and condense the essential humor of the pieces. Include minimal props and consider using pantomime.
3. Perform your skit sequence as a comedy show for other groups.

Interdisciplinary Project

Art: Comic Strips Choose four anecdotes or episodes from the selections in this theme. Adapt the episodes to a series of comic strips.

1. Rewrite and condense the episodes. Keep the essential details and humor.
2. Create comical visual representations of the characters and events. If you like, use computer software to produce images.
3. Compile your comic strips into a comic book, and create an enticing and descriptive cover.

Fishing, 20th century. Brad Holland. Private collection.

Before You Read

Let's Sweat!

Reading Focus

What is your attitude toward sports? Are you mildly interested or wildly enthusiastic as an observer? as a participant?

Discuss Consider how you react to sports and fitness programs. Who or what influences your attitudes? With your group, discuss how and why people become interested or uninterested in sports and fitness.

Setting a Purpose Read a personal essay to find out how Nikki Giovanni became interested in sports.

Building Background

The Time and Place

Nikki Giovanni wrote this essay in the 1980s, a period in which Americans became aware of the many benefits of participation in sports and fitness programs.

Did You Know?

Although attitudes toward women in sports have changed, especially in the last twenty-five years, emphasis at the school and amateur levels is still on male participation. However, research indicates that young women, as well as young men, who are athletic and participate in sports and fitness programs are more likely to have higher self-esteem to do better academically in high school and college, and to have greater aspirations toward leadership roles at work and in their communities than their nonathletic peers.

Vocabulary Preview

impending (im pen′ ding) *adj.* about to occur; p. 1003
intone (in tōn′) *v.* to speak in a singing tone or monotone; recite; p. 1003
ultimately (ul′ tə mit lē) *adv.* at last; finally; p. 1004
heyday (hā′ dā) *n.* period of greatest strength, popularity, or prosperity; p. 1005

Meet Nikki Giovanni

In the 1960s, award-winning poet, essayist, and teacher Nikki Giovanni joined the Black Arts movement to promote African American rights and racial equality. Her writings during this period have been described as "militant" and "combative." In 1995 and 1996, she underwent successful surgery and treatment for lung cancer. The experience compelled her to determine what kind of writing she wanted to leave behind. "I decided laughter was the most important thing," she concluded.

Nikki Giovanni was born in 1943 in Knoxville, Tennessee. "Let's Sweat!" appears in Sacred Cows . . . And Other Edibles, *a collection of stories published in 1988.*

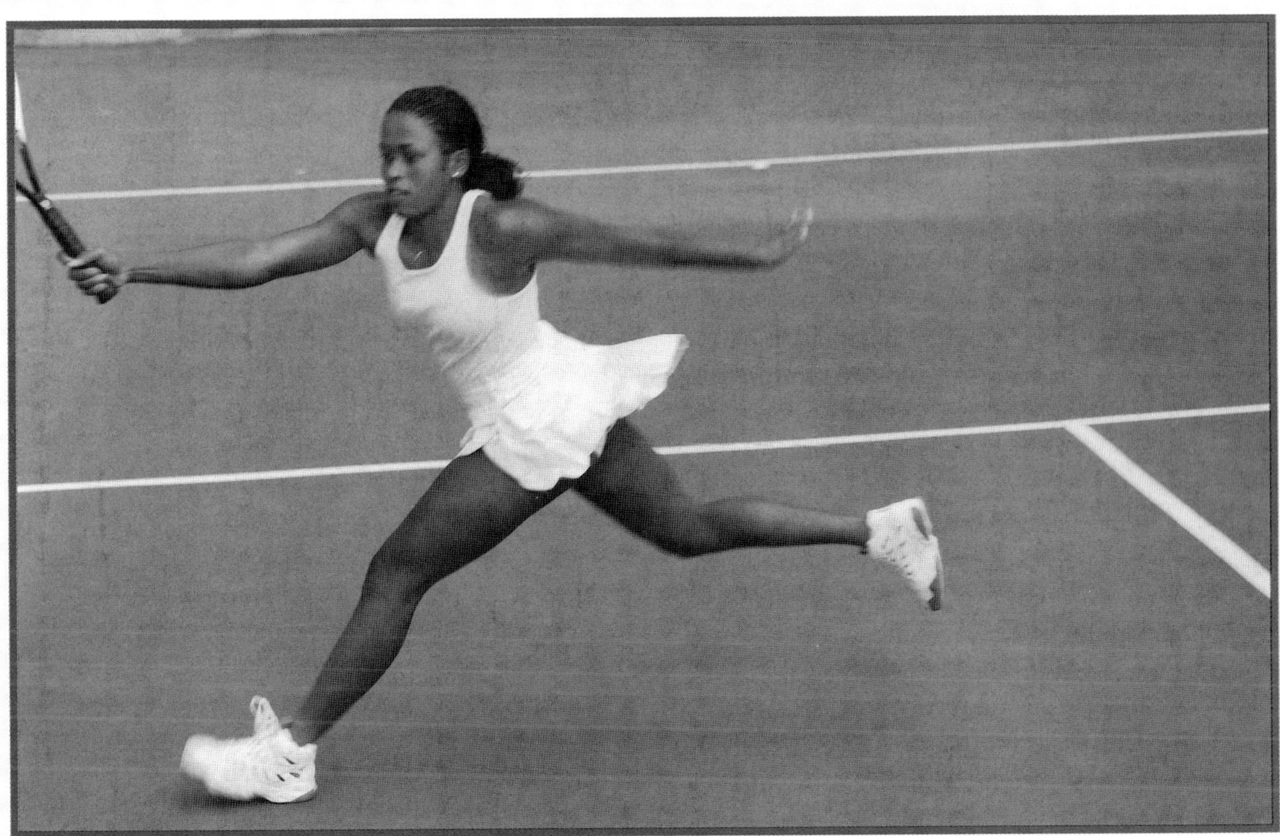

Chanda Rubin. Annie Leibovitz, photographer.

Let's Sweat!

Nikki Giovanni

Like most poets, I carry a two-hole folder with me almost compulsively.[1] It's not that I carry my ideas around so that should the occasion arise I can pull it out and say, in regard to some impending problem, "Oh well, a stitch in time saves nine." I do not have profound idioms at occasions of great distress so that I can intone: "It's always darkest before the dawn."

1. She acts *compulsively;* that is, the urge to carry the folder is compelling and irresistible.

Vocabulary

impending (im pen′ ding) *adj.* about to occur

intone (in tōn′) *v.* to speak in a singing tone or monotone; recite

No. It's just that like most writers I think I think best when I'm not actually thinking about it, so I carry a book that allows me to put either something I have thought up as being very clever or, most likely, something that someone else said that I would one day like to use. Steve Krieder, running back for the Cincinnati Bengals, once said in response to the question "Why do you think the fans came out in – twenty degree weather to watch a football game?" "I think it's a failure of our educational system." I think that is neat. I love sports, too; but any fool who would sit in Riverfront Stadium in twenty below-zero weather to watch a game that was being televised anyway indeed has been let down by our public school system. I haven't found a way to work that into a poem, but with any luck and lots of persistence I will ultimately be able to achieve it. You don't see too many good poems on football. Baseball has "Casey At The Bat," but when you think sports, that's about it. Tennis needs a national poem. So does soccer. Any reader out there who's a soccer fan should really think about it because soccer is an international game and you could get a real chance to show off your Latin, Greek, Spanish, English, ancient Gaelic.[2] It could be a real intellectual *tour de force*,[3] as it were. I mention my folder because, in fact, I want to talk about sports. My folder, which is bright orange, has a mock license plate saying POETIC LICENSE,[4] which is normal since I do poetry. But right below that is a white and orange circle that states: BODY BY SCANDINAVIAN. It's true. I've joined the Spa Revolution.

You may rightfully wonder why a forty-three-year-old woman would suddenly decide she can no longer get along without getting her body in shape. And that is exactly the point. If people know anything about the writing profession they know that all we do is sit and read or sit and write or sit and talk or sit on planes to go sit and do all of the above. I personally know writers whose legs give out if they have to go up one flight of stairs and now refuse to lecture at certain universities because the schools lack elevators. That's simply being in bad shape. . . . Dear young writer out there, you must sweat.

I guess you are wondering how I got into sports in the first place. I was visiting my father and mother one fall when a bunch of my dad's friends came over. Laughing loudly . . . they plopped themselves in front of the television and began to talk in numbers and letters. RBI's 35; ERA 3.56; HR 15; only 21 percent against left-handers and other things I didn't understand. It seemed so unlike my father to have gone into the stock market. I went into the living room and asked what was going on. It was friendly. I mean, I wasn't meddling or anything—just curious. You know the look you get when people think you are not quite bright? well, five men turned to my father: "And that's the famous one, huh?" And they all burst out laughing. My father was mortified. "We're watching the World Series, sweetie," he said sweetly. That should have been my clue to go on, as he never called me "sweetie" unless I had done something extremely stupid and he was exercising great patience to not scream, "Lughead, what do you think is going on?" I then, with

2. *Gaelic* (gā′ lik), an ancient language, is still spoken in some parts of Ireland and Scotland.
3. The French term *tour de force* means "a feat of extraordinary strength or skill."
4. The license plate plays on the actual meaning of *poetic license,* which refers to a writer's intentional variation from a rule or standard for the sake of effect.

Vocabulary

ultimately (ul′ tə mit lē) *adv.* at last; finally

the smile, I'm sure, of the terminally stupid, asked, "Oh, who's playing?" The room literally shook with laughter. I, naturally, beat a hasty retreat. The Giovannis are a close but competitive family. I determined from then on that the next time I came to visit I would know the sport, who was playing and what all those little numbers meant. From then on instead of reading the front page I turned to sports first. I cribbed a *Sports Illustrated* anywhere I could. I even purchased *Sporting News* and, during Hagler's[5] heyday (though the Marvelous One may think he is still in his heyday) read *Boxing News*.

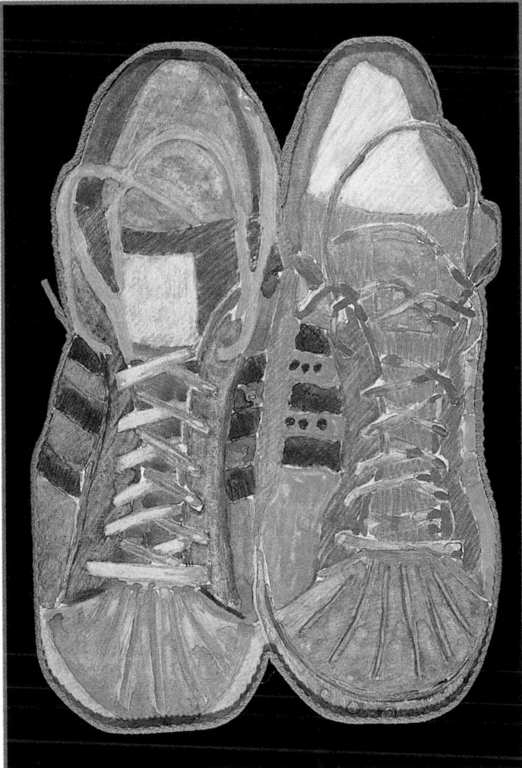

Shoe Series #2, 1982–1983. Marilee Whitehouse-Holm. Acrylic, 24 x 18 in. Private collection.

Viewing the painting: Do you think the wearer of these shoes is a sports observer or a participant, as described by Nikki Giovanni? Why?

Since I travel a lot I also made a great discovery. Alone in a hotel room on the road I would usually tune in *Tonight* or one of the talk shows. I can't stand violence and no lone woman in her right mind would look at *Hawaii Five-O* or any of those pictures where women are stalked and brutally killed. I learned, and I'm lucky cable came in when it did, that I could catch the West Coast games live. I'll bet I know more about the Phoenix Suns during that period than any poet from the East Coast. I do have to confess I never became a Lakers fan but I kind of appreciate Houston—unless they're playing the Celtics. I could come back to a cold, empty hotel room in the middle of February and tune in something to cheer about. I could catch boxing, West Coast tennis, gymnastics—hell, fencing, if it came to that. I never did get into hockey because my major sports requirement is that I have to be able to see the ball, but I'm working on golf. Ahhh, but bowling. I love to watch bowling. You get a big, usually black, ball going down a clearly defined lane. I could sit and munch Planter's peanuts and cheer my little head off. . . . Sports is fun. We expect the men to want to go shopping to pick out curtains but we don't feel the same obligation to understand why you punt on fourth down. We want the guys to marvel at the cleanliness of our homes but we don't want to know what a cleanup hitter is. Come on, girls. Let's be fair. It's time to quit being jealous of our jogging mates and join in.

5. Marvin *Hagler* was a middleweight boxing champion in 1980.

Vocabulary

heyday (hā′ dā) *n.* period of greatest strength, popularity, or prosperity

Responding to Literature

Personal Response

What did you especially like about this selection? Why?

Analyzing Literature

Recall

1. Why does Nikki Giovanni carry a two-hole folder all the time?
2. What "movement" has she joined in her forties? What advice does Giovanni give young writers?
3. Summarize the circumstances that sparked Giovanni's interest in sports.
4. What TV programs does Giovanni not like to watch? What is her favorite sport to watch? What is Giovanni's major sports requirement?
5. What does she encourage women to do at the end of the selection?

Intrepret

6. What do you think Giovanni means when she says, "Like most writers I think I think best when I'm not actually thinking about it"?
7. What is the purpose of the "movement" that Giovanni has joined? What reasoning might be behind her advice to young writers?
8. What does her reaction to the incident at her parents' home tell you about Giovanni's personality?
9. What can you infer about Giovanni from her television viewing and sports preference?
10. What contradiction in women's expectations of men does Giovanni point out at the end of the selection?

Evaluate and Connect

11. **Theme Connections** What is the overall **theme,** or message, of this selection? Evaluate Giovanni's use of humor to get this message across.
12. Do you agree with Giovanni's concluding comments? In what ways do these comments apply to you or your peers? Explain.
13. Consider the discussion you participated in for the Reading Focus on page 1002. How has this selection affected your interest in sports as an observer and as a participant?
14. What word or words would you use to describe Giovanni's **tone** in this selection? Cite specific lines from the essay to support your description. (See Literary Terms Handbook, page R13.)
15. What does this selection reveal about the roles of young women who grew up in the 1950s and 1960s? In your opinion, how do these roles compare with those of women who grew up in the 1980s and later?

Literary ELEMENTS

Personal Essay

The **personal essay** is an informal essay in which the writer reveals one or more personal experiences, uses a light, conversational tone, and presents personal views on an issue. Often, a personal essay will contain humor as well as specific details from the writer's life in order to help readers personalize the events, relating them to experiences in their own lives. In "Let's Sweat," for example, Nikki Giovanni describes in detail how the circumstances surrounding a visit to her parents' house encouraged her interest in sports and fitness. While reading Giovanni's essay, the reader may have made a connection by saying, "Yes. Something like that happened to me once. I know just how that feels."

1. Identify two or three specific details in Giovanni's personal narrative that make people, places, and events come to life.
2. Do you think a short story could convey Giovanni's message as effectively as the personal essay? Why or why not?
3. Do you think her humorous approach strengthens or weakens her points? Explain.

- See **Literary Terms Handbook,** p. R4.

Literature And Writing

Writing About Literature

Comparing Attitudes In what ways are your attitudes and experiences regarding sports like those of Nikki Giovanni? What is your reaction to the final sentence? Write one or two paragraphs comparing your attitudes with Giovanni's and explaining your reaction. Cite specific details from the selection. Share your writing with a small group of students.

Creative Writing

Write a Sports Poem Giovanni points out that just about every sport, except baseball, is lacking a national poem. Write a poem that tells an exciting story about an American sport of your choice. You may want to obtain a copy of "Casey at the Bat" and use that poem as a model for your writing. Share your poem in a group poetry reading.

Extending Your Response

Literature Groups

Evaluate the Writing In your group, discuss the following questions and evaluate Nikki Giovanni's personal essay, supporting your opinions with details from the essay. Is her essay coherently organized? How does she personalize the experiences described? How does she present events to achieve her purpose? Share your findings with other groups.

Performing

Create a Commercial Encourage people to get in shape and stay fit. In your group, create, write, and perform for the class a 20- to 30-second television commercial targeted at a male and female audience in the age-group of your choice.

Learning for Life

Sports Opportunity Report Most professional sports are male-dominated events. Which sports offer the most opportunities for women to compete professionally? Use the Internet and current periodicals to research this and your own questions about sports opportunities for women. Summarize your findings in a chart or brief report for the class.

Reading Further

If you enjoyed "Let's Sweat!" you might want to read these poems from *The Selected Poems of Nikki Giovanni.*

Poems: "Choices" and "a poem for langston hughes."

Save your work for your portfolio.

VOCABULARY • The Latin Root *pend*

The word *impending* comes from the Latin prefix *in-*, meaning "in" and the root *pend,* meaning "to hang." When something is about to happen, especially if it is threatening, we often say it is "hanging over" us. An *impending* event is hanging over you.

This root is found in several familiar words. One's pants can be kept hanging by means of *suspenders.* A *dependent* is someone who *depends* on you, in a sense, or "hangs" on you.

PRACTICE Use your knowledge of the root *pend* to answer the questions.

1. Which animal has *pendulous* ears–a rabbit, a basset hound, or a bird?
2. Which of the following is a *pendent* source of light–a chandelier, a flashlight, or the sun?
3. Which device keeps time by using a *pendulum* –a wristwatch, a sun dial, or a grandfather clock?

MEDIA connection

Comic Strip

Some people think cats are the most intelligent, friendly pets. Others feel the same about dogs. Are you a "cat person" or a "dog person"?

Garfield

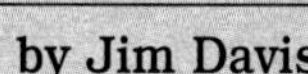

by Jim Davis

Analyzing Media

1. Describe what you think the cartoonist's relationships with his pets might be like. Explain how you came to your conclusions.
2. Do you agree with the depiction of cats and dogs shown in this comic strip? Explain.

Before You Read

From A Cat's Garden of Verses

Reading Focus

Have you ever put new words to a song or an advertising jingle? Was your version more humorous than the original?

Quickwrite Rewrite the words to a jingle you've heard on the radio or on television to make it humorous. Share your new jingle with a partner.

Setting A Purpose Read to enjoy the result of putting new words to old rhymes.

Building Background

Did You Know?

- Robert Louis Stevenson is the author of such classic works as *Treasure Island, Kidnapped,* and *The Strange Case of Dr. Jekyll and Mr. Hyde.* His poems in *A Child's Garden of Verses* were quite popular at the turn of the century (1900). Children grew up hearing his familiar poems, such as the following:

  Happy Thought

  The world is so full of a number of things,
  I'm sure we should all be as happy as kings.

- People often anthropomorphize their pets, pretending that the pet views life as a human would. In "From A Cat's Garden of Verses," Henry Beard pretends that the author of the poems is the cat belonging to Robert Louis Stevenson.
- Felines, or members of the cat family, include lions, tigers, jaguars, and wild and domestic cats. Wild felines are meat-eating animals who survive by hunting and eating smaller animals. Domesticated cats, like their cousins in the wild, still have the instinct to stalk and catch smaller animals, especially small rodents and birds.

Meet Henry Beard

Humor writer Henry Beard has written numerous hilarious books on topics from cats to golf. He also was cofounder of *National Lampoon*, a magazine that poked fun at national institutions and political figures of the 1970s. Beard admits that his most annoying habit is "avoiding answering the really tough questions." This is evident in his response to a question about the secret of comedy. "I'm glad I'm a humor writer instead of a comedian," he said, "because if someone hates me, they have to put the tomato in a box and send it to me. They can't throw it at me."

Henry Beard was born in 1945. Robert Louis Stevenson's cat is only one of the talented feline poets introduced in Beard's Poetry for Cats: The Definitive Anthology of Distinguished Feline Verse *published in 1994.*

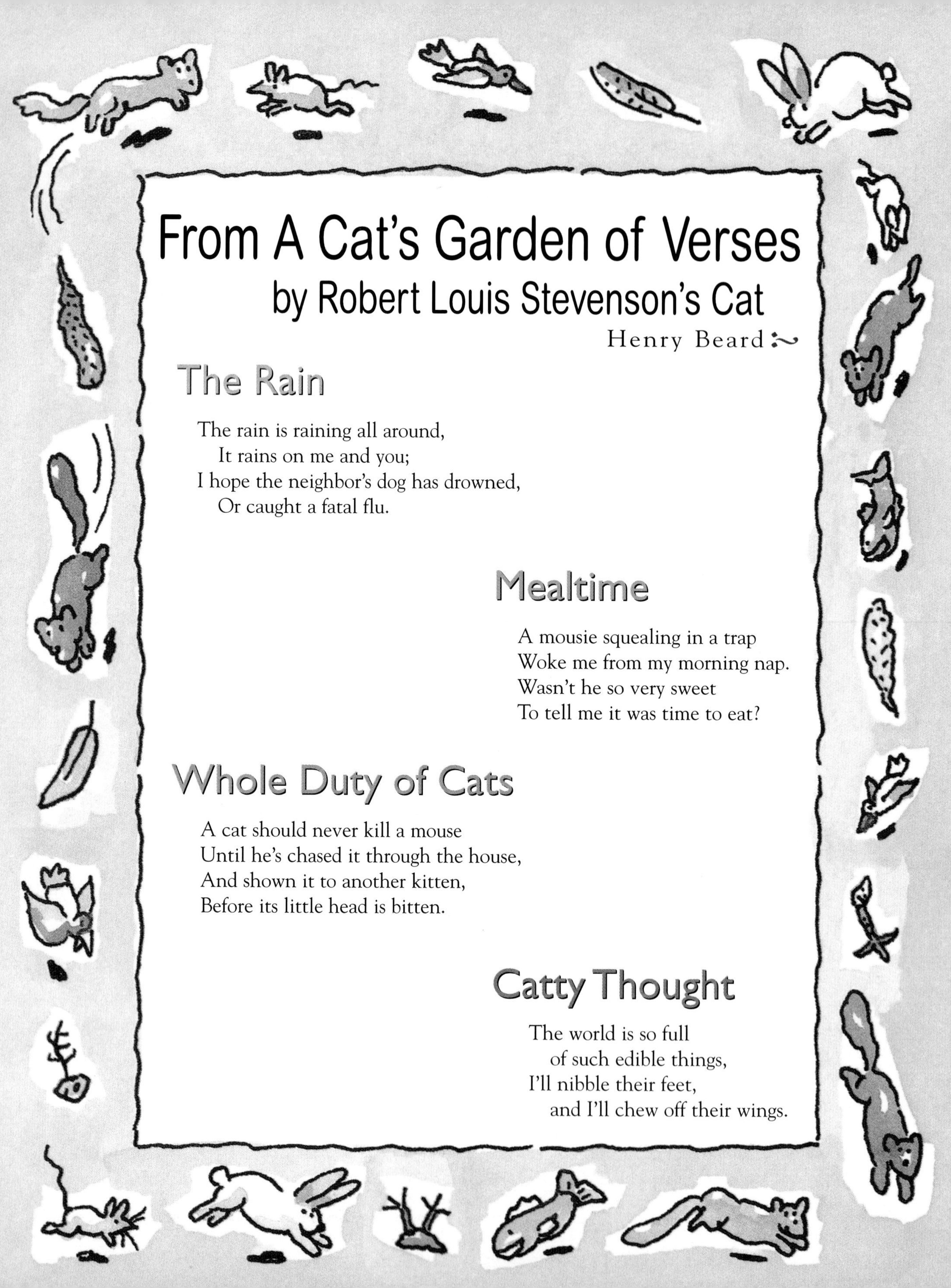

From A Cat's Garden of Verses
by Robert Louis Stevenson's Cat

Henry Beard

The Rain

The rain is raining all around,
  It rains on me and you;
I hope the neighbor's dog has drowned,
  Or caught a fatal flu.

Mealtime

A mousie squealing in a trap
Woke me from my morning nap.
Wasn't he so very sweet
To tell me it was time to eat?

Whole Duty of Cats

A cat should never kill a mouse
Until he's chased it through the house,
And shown it to another kitten,
Before its little head is bitten.

Catty Thought

The world is so full
  of such edible things,
I'll nibble their feet,
  and I'll chew off their wings.

Responding to Literature

Personal Response

Which of Beard's poems did you like the best? Explain why.

Analyzing Literature

Recall and Intrepret

1. What wish does the speaker of "The Rain" make? Why is the speaker's wish humorous?
2. What are the poems "Mealtime," "Whole Duty of Cats," and "Catty Thought" about? On the basis of these poems, what subjects seem to be of special interest to the speaker?
3. From the content of all four poems, describe the cat characteristics that might have inspired Beard to write each poem.
4. What conclusions can you draw about the personality and character of Stevenson's cat from these poems? Explain.

Evaluate and Connect

5. **Verbal irony** occurs when a speaker says one thing and means another. Explain how the use of verbal irony in "Mealtime" adds to the humor of the poem.
6. **Theme Connections** On a humor scale of one to ten, evaluate the level of humor in each of these poems. Explain your evaluation.
7. Beard uses **alliteration** and **assonance** throughout these poems. What effects do the alliteration and assonance have? Give examples. (See Literary Terms Handbook, page R1.)
8. Look back at the humorous song or jingle you wrote in the Reading Focus on page 1009. Do you think the subject matter of Beard's poems would be good material for a cat food company's advertising jingle? Why or why not?

Literary ELEMENTS

Parody

A **parody** is a humorous piece of writing that imitates the style and ideas of an author. For example, compare Beard's "The Rain" with Stevenson's "Rain" shown here.

Rain

The rain is raining all around,
It falls on field and tree,
It rains on the umbrellas here,
And on the ships at sea.

Both poems have similar titles, the same first line, and the same rhythm and meter. However, Stevenson's speaker is a child while Beard's speaker is a cat.

1. Evaluate how effectively Beard imitates Stevenson's poem.
2. Is Beard's poem a good parody of Stevenson's poem? Explain.

- See **Literary Terms Handbook,** p. R9.

Extending Your Response

Listening and Speaking

Parody Review With a partner, present a critic's review of these parodies for your class. Discuss the tone, rhyme, rhythm, point of view, and humor in Beard's poems and whether you find them effective or not. Use details from the poems to support your points. Conclude with a recommendation to read or not to read Beard's work.

Creative Writing

Write a Parody Parody a poem by a favorite writer. Think of a different theme and subject for the parody. Approach the new subject in a silly manner while maintaining the style and characteristics of the original work. Read both poems aloud to the class.

Save your work for your portfolio.

Database: Critical Viewing Skills

Are television characters believable–or are they stereotypes, characters who are not developed as individuals but, rather, presented as types (such as the cranky old man, the helpless woman, or the confused teenager)? By analyzing how the visual media portray various groups of people, you can become a more critical viewer.

Start with a Few Favorites

Think about some of your favorite television characters. Record the names of at least six characters from TV shows. After each name, write a brief description of the character. Include his or her most prominent physical or emotional characteristics.

Reviewing Database Tools

A database is a collection of data that is organized so that information can be referenced in various ways. Review the major functions of databases. Remember that database software differs from product to product. The directions given here may need to be adapted.

TERM	FUNCTION
Database	A collection of information arranged in predetermined ways
Table	The form in which data appears
Field Names	Column headings
Fields	Columns that hold data
Records	Rows of data
Table Helpers or Wizards	Features that walk you through the creation of a table by using preset formats

Building a Critical-Viewing Database

1. Work with a partner. To begin, open your database program.
2. Go to the **File** menu, and select **New.** (If your software opens with a dialogue box asking you to choose between opening an existing database or starting a new one, opt for a new one with a blank database.) If you're asked what sort of database you would like to create, select **Table.** You will also be asked if you wish to see your table in Design or Datasheet view. Select **Design** view so that you can name your fields.
3. Once in Design view, you will be asked to create and describe field names. Under field name, type in each heading listed below. Select **Text** as your data type.

   TV Show   Character   Gender   Description   Ethnicity   Stereotype?

4. Next, switch to Datasheet view by using the pull-down **View** menu. If you are asked if you want the database program to set a primary key for you, select **no.** If asked if you want to save the table, choose **yes;** save to disk or to the shared directory of your network. You will then be taken to the table you created.

5. You and your partner can now enter the names of characters and their descriptions. Decide whether each character is a multifaceted realistic character or a stereotype. You may use the following as a guide for entries in the Ethnicity column.

Native American	Asian American	Australian	African American
Middle Eastern	Pacific Islander	European	Hispanic American

6. After examining your data, decide whether each character is developed as an individual or as a collection of stereotypic traits. Ask yourself questions such as the following.
   - Are the characters presented as unique individuals or as types?
   - How are various ethnic groups portrayed on TV? Are any underportrayed?
   - Are females and males equally likely to be stereotyped? Are the types of stereotypes for males and females similar or different?
   - Is the age or physical condition of a character made an issue? How?

7. Discuss with your partner the number and kinds of stereotypes you've discovered in TV shows. What conclusions can you come to on the basis of your data?

TECHNOLOGY TIP

Use the Help function of your database program to learn how to manipulate your data. For example, you could select to see only the female characters from your datasheet, or only the African American characters, or only those you marked as stereotypes.

	Show	Character	Gender	Ethnic Heritage	Description	Stereotype?
▶	Brady Bunch	Marsha Brady	female	European American	Pretty, self-centered blond	yes
	Star Trek	Dr. McCoy	male	European American	Grumpy but loyal crew member	yes
	Cosby	Dr. Huxtable	male	African American	Paternal, funny, often befuddled	no
	I Love Lucy	Lucy Ricardo	female	European American	Pretty, funny, often-blundering wife	yes
	The Simpsons	Apu	male	Asian American	Friendly, funny accent	yes
	Seinfeld	Kramer	male	European American	Totally bizarre, clumsy, funny	no
	ER	Carol Hathaway	female	European American	Dedicated, friendly, caring	no
*						

ACTIVITIES

1. Combine your data with the data of the other partners in your class. Print out the results and distribute copies to class members to use in a discussion of the kinds of stereotypes found on television. Consider whether current TV shows are more likely or less likely than older shows to include stereotypes.

2. With a group, create a database to acquire information about stereotyping in a particular TV genre, such as dramas, sitcoms, music and variety shows, documentaries, or commercials. Present your findings to the class.

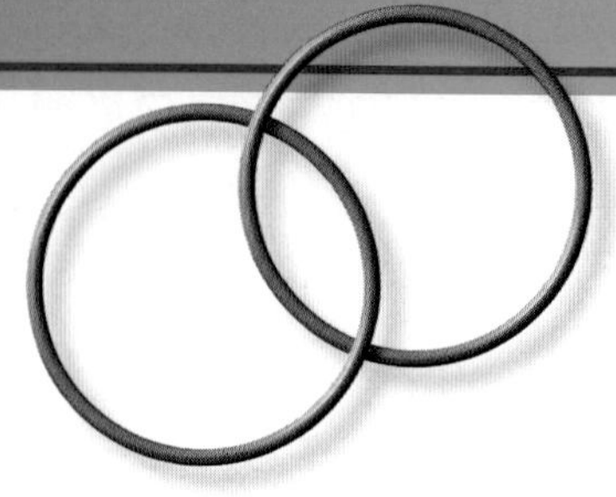

Grammar Link

Missing or Misplaced Possessive Apostrophes

An important use of the apostrophe is to form the possessive of nouns and some pronouns. To form the possessive, add either an apostrophe or an apostrophe and *-s.*

Problem 1 Singular nouns that end in *s*
This witness story of fishing in Alaska is a personal account.

Solution To make the possessive form of a singular noun ending in *s,* add an apostrophe and *-s.*
This witness's story of fishing in Alaska is a personal account.

Problem 2 Plural nouns ending in *-s*
He claims that both bears heads were bigger than a steering wheel.

Solution If a plural noun ends in *-s,* make it possessive by adding only an apostrophe.
He claims that both bears' heads were bigger than a steering wheel.

Problem 3 Plural nouns not ending in *-s*
His teeths chattering was caused by cold and fear.

Solution If a plural noun does not end in *-s,* add an apostrophe and *-s.*
His teeth's chattering was caused by cold and fear.

Problem 4 Pronouns
The next story about someones brush with death is his.

Solution Form the possessive of an indefinite pronoun (for example, *someone* or *everybody*) by adding an apostrophe and *-s.* Apostrophes are not used with possessive pronouns, such as *hers* and *theirs.*
The next story about someone's brush with death is his.

● For more information on apostrophes, see **Language Handbook,** pp. R25–R26.

EXERCISES

1. Write the possessive form of each word.
   a. children b. Massachusetts c. crisis d. hunters e. no one
2. If the sentence is correct, write *C.* If the sentence is incorrect, rewrite it correctly.
   a. Some fishermens stories are called fish tales.
   b. Not everyones tale is as believable as ours.
   c. Perhaps it's fishermens and hunters ways to exaggerate.

Before You Read

Appetizer

Reading Focus

Think about a surprising or frightening encounter you've had with an animal.

Freewrite Briefly write about a time when you were surprised or frightened by an animal. What were the circumstances? How did you react? What did the animal do?

Setting A Purpose Read this short story to find out what happens when the narrator encounters a bear.

Building Background

The Time and Place

"Appetizer" takes place in the Alaskan wilderness, sometime in the unspecified present.

Did You Know?

Brown bears have long, shaggy coats that range in color from blond to black, as well as stout bodies, massive heads, and long claws. Thought by some biologists to be as intelligent as such primates as monkeys or baboons, brown bears have a sense of smell as good as a bloodhound's, jaws capable of snapping small tree trunks, and the ability to sprint up to thirty-five miles an hour. Brown bears eat fish, mammals, nuts, berries, herbs, and grasses, but will feed exclusively on salmon when it is available, sometimes eating more than a dozen in a few hours.

Vocabulary Preview

consternation (kon′ stər nā′ shən) *n.* amazement or dismay that throws one into confusion; p. 1017
raptly (rapt′ lē) *adv.* in a deeply interested way; attentively; p. 1019
bereft (bi reft′) *adj.* robbed or deprived; p. 1019
impropriety (im′ prə pri′ ə tē) *n.* an improper act or behavior; p. 1019
profound (prə found′) *adj.* intense and complete; p. 1021
expedient (iks pē′ dē ənt) *n.* a useful method for bringing about a desired result; p. 1022

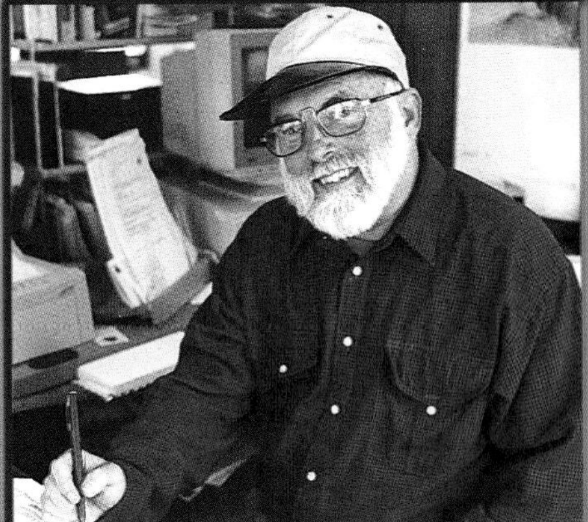

Meet Robert Abel

"I feel the planet is threatened, that writing should attempt to define and respond to this emergency, not with hysteria, but with some vision of a workable, maybe even beautiful future."

Writing about things "that matter" is a responsibility that fiction writer Robert Abel feels strongly about. In addition to writing fiction of various genres, Abel has worked as a reporter, a teacher, a fiction editor for a small press, and a volunteer firefighter. He is also a fisherman.

Robert Abel was born in Painesville, Ohio, in 1941.

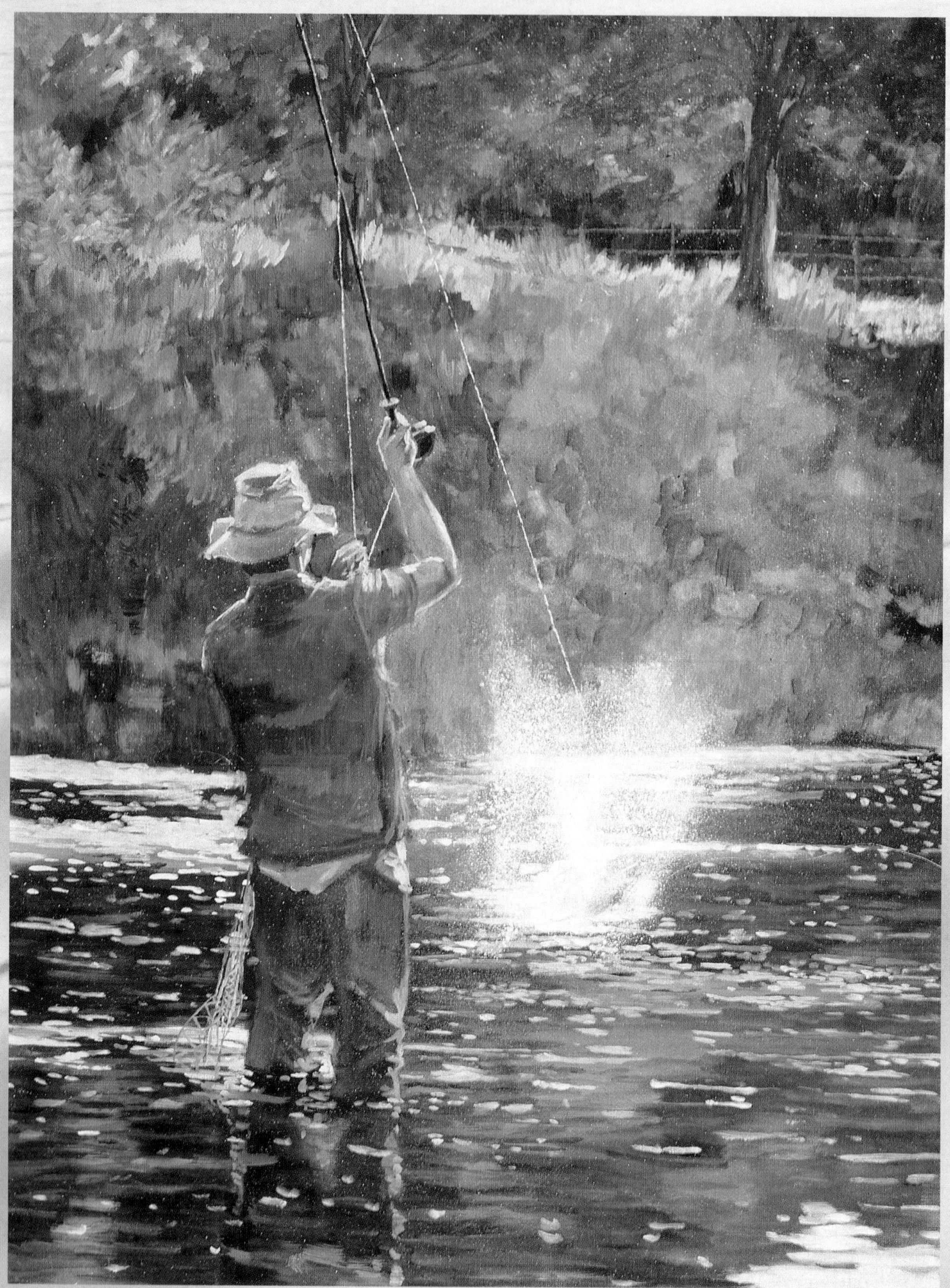

Fly Fishing. Rosemary Lowndes. Oil on canvas. Private collection.

Appetizer

Robert H. Abel

I'M FISHING THIS BEAUTIFUL stream in Alaska, catching salmon, char and steelhead, when this bear lumbers out of the woods and down to the stream bank. He fixes me with this half-amused, half-curious look which says: You are meat.

The bear's eyes are brown and his shiny golden fur is standing up in spikes, which shows me he has been fishing, too, perhaps where the stream curves behind the peninsula of woods he has just trudged through. He's not making any sound I can hear over the rumble of the water in the softball-sized rocks, but his presence is very loud.

I say "his" presence because temporarily I am not interested in or able to assess the creature's sex. I am looking at a head that is bigger around than my steering wheel, a pair of paws awash in river bubbles that could cover half my windshield. I am glad that I am wearing polarized fishing glasses so the bear cannot see the little teardrops of fear that have crept into the corner of my eyes. To assure him/her I am not the least bit intimidated, I make another cast.

Immediately I tie into a fat Chinook.[1] The splashing of the fish in the stream engages the bear's attention, but he/she registers this for the moment only by shifting his/her glance. I play the fish[2] smartly and when it comes gliding in, tired, pink-sided, glittering and astonished, I pluck it out of the water by inserting a finger in its gill—something I normally wouldn't do in order not to injure the fish before I set it free, and I do exactly what you would do in the same situation—throw it to the bear.

The bear's eyes widen and she—for I can see now past her huge shoulder and powerful haunches that she is a she—turns and pounces on the fish with such speed and nimbleness[3] that I am numbed. There is no chance in hell that I, in my insulated waders,[4] am going to outrun her, dodge her blows, escape her jaws. While she is occupied devouring the fish—I can hear her teeth clacking together—I do what you or anyone else would do and cast again.

God answers my muttered prayer and I am blessed with the strike of another fat salmon, like the others on its way to spawning grounds upstream. I would like this fish to survive and release its eggs or sperm to perpetuate the salmon kingdom, but Ms. Bear has just licked her whiskers clean and has now moved knee-deep into the water and, to my consternation, leans against me rather like a large and friendly dog, although her ears are at the level of my shoulder and her back is broader than that of any horse I have ever seen. Ms. Bear is intensely interested in the progress of the salmon toward us, and her head twists and twitches as the fish circles, darts, takes line away, shakes head, rolls over, leaps.

1. Native to the northern Pacific, the *Chinook* (shi nook′) is also called the king salmon.
2. To *play the fish* is to keep it on the line until it exhausts itself.
3. The bear's *nimbleness* is its ability to move lightly, quickly, and easily.
4. The writer's *waders* are waterproof trousers that have boots for legs.

Vocabulary

consternation (kon′ stər nā′ shən) *n.* amazement or dismay that throws one into confusion

Appetizer

With a bear at your side, it is not the simplest thing to play a fish properly, but the presence of this huge animal, and especially her long snout, thick as my thigh, wonderfully concentrates the mind. She smells like the forest floor, like crushed moss and damp leaves, and she is as warm as a radiator back in my Massachusetts home, the thought of which floods me with a terrible nostalgia. Now I debate whether I should just drift the salmon in under the bear's nose and let her take it that way, but I'm afraid she will break off my fly and leader[5] and right now that fly—a Doctor Wilson number eight—is saving my life. So, with much anxiety, I pretend to take charge and bring the fish in on the side away from the bear, gill and quickly unhook it, turn away from the bear and toss the fish behind me to the bank.

The bear wheels and clambers upon it at once, leaving a vortex[6] of water pouring into the vacuum of the space she has left, which almost topples me. As her teeth snack away, I quickly and furtively regard my poor Doctor Wilson, which is fish-mauled now, bedraggled, almost unrecognizable. But the present emergency compels me to zing it out once again. I walk a few paces downstream, hoping the bear will remember an appointment or become distracted and I can sneak away.

5. The *fly,* or *lure,* is artificial bait consisting of a hook with materials tied on to resemble insects. It is connected to the fishline by the *leader,* a length of nylon.

6. Here, *vortex* means "a small whirlpool."

Autumn Morning–Grizzly, 1985. Ron Parker. Acrylic on Masonite, 24 x 40 in.

Viewing the painting: What atmosphere does this painting convey? In what ways does it suit the opening scene of the story? Explain.

But a few seconds later she is leaning against me again, raptly watching the stream for any sign of a salmon splash. My luck holds; another fish smacks the withered Wilson, flings sunlight and water in silver jets as it dances its last dance. I implore the salmon's forgiveness: something I had once read revealed that this is the way of all primitive hunters, to take the life reluctantly and to pray for the victim's return. I think my prayer is as urgent as that of any Mashpee or Yoruban, or Tlingit or early Celt,[7] for I not only want the salmon to thrive forever, I want a superabundance of them now, right now, to save my neck. I have an idea this hungry bear, bereft of fish, would waste little time in conducting any prayer ceremonies before she turned me into the main course my salmon were just the appetizer for. When I take up this fish, the bear practically rips it from my hand, and the sight of those teeth so close, and the truly persuasive power of those muscled, pink-rimmed jaws, cause a wave of fear in me so great that I nearly faint.

My vertigo subsides[8] as Ms. Bear munches and destroys the salmon with hearty shakes of her head and I sneak a few more paces downstream, rapidly also with trembling fingers tie on a new Doctor Wilson, observing the utmost care (as you would, too) in making my knots. I cast and stride downstream, wishing I could just plunge into the crystalline water and bowl away like a log. My hope and plan is to wade my way back to the narrow trail a few hundred yards ahead and, when Ms. Bear loses interest or is somehow distracted, make a heroic dash for my camper. I think of the thermos of hot coffee on the front seat, the six-pack of beer in the cooler, the thin rubber mattress with the blue sleeping bag adorning it, warm wool socks in a bag hanging from a window crank, and almost burst into tears, these simple things, given the presence of Ms. Hungry Bear, seem so miraculous, so emblematic of the life I love to live. I promise the gods—American, Indian, African, Oriental—that if I survive I will never complain again, not even if my teenage children leave the caps off the toothpaste tubes or their bicycles in the driveway at home.

"Oh, home," I think, and cast again.

Ms. Bear rejoins me. You may or may not believe me, and perhaps after all it was only my imagination worked up by terror, but two things happened which gave me a particle of hope. The first was that Ms. Bear actually belched—quite noisily and unapologetically, too, like a rude uncle at a Christmas dinner. She showed no signs of having committed any impropriety, and yet it was clear to me that a belching bear is probably also a bear with a pretty-full belly. A few more salmon and perhaps Ms. Bear would wander off in search of a berry dessert.

Now the second thing she did, or that I imagined she did, was to begin—well, not *speaking* to me exactly, but *communicating* somehow. I know it sounds foolish, but if you were in my shoes—my waders, to be more precise—you might have learned bear talk pretty quickly, too. It's not as if the bear were speaking to me in complete sentences and English

7. These names refer to early peoples of North America *(Mashpee)*, Africa *(Yoruban)*, and Europe *(Celt)*.
8. *Vertigo subsides* means that the dizziness decreases.

Vocabulary

raptly (rapt′ lē) *adv.* in a deeply interested way; attentively
bereft (bi reft′) *adj.* robbed or deprived
impropriety (im′ prə prī′ ə tē) *n.* an improper act or behavior

words such as "Get me another fish, pal, or you're on the menu," but in a much more indirect and subtle way, almost in the way a stream talks through its bubbling and burbling and rattling of rocks and gurgling along.

Believe me, I listened intently, more with my mind than with my ears, as if the bear were telepathizing,[9] and—I know you're not going to believe this, but it's true, I am normally not what you would call an egomaniac[10] with an inflated self-esteem such that I imagine that every bear which walks out of the woods falls in love with me—but I really did truly believe now that this Ms. Bear was expressing feelings of, well, *affection*. Really, I think she kinda liked me. True or not, the feeling made me less afraid. In fact, and I don't mean this in any erotic or perverse kind of way, but I had to admit, once my fear had passed, my feelings were kinda mutual. Like you might feel for an old pal of a dog. Or a favorite horse. I only wish she weren't such a big eater. I only wish she were not a carnivore, and I, carne.[11]

Now she nudges me with her nose.

"All right, all right," I say. "I'm doing the best I can."

Cast in the glide behind that big boulder, the bear telepathizes me. *There's a couple of whoppers in there.*

I do as I'm told and wham! the bear is right! Instantly I'm tied into a granddaddy Chinook, a really burly fellow who has no intention of lying down on anybody's platter beneath a blanket of lemon slices and scallion shoots, let alone make his last wiggle down a bear's gullet. Even the bear is excited and begins shifting weight from paw to paw, a little motion for her that nevertheless has big consequences for me as her body slams against my hip, then slams again.

Partly because I don't want to lose the fish, but partly also because I want to use the fish as an excuse to move closer to my getaway trail, I stumble downstream. This fish has my rod bent into an upside-down *U* and I'm hoping my quick-tied knots are also strong enough to take this salmon's lurching and his intelligent, broadside swinging into the river current—a very smart fish! Ordinarily I might take a long time with a fish like this, baby it in, but now I'm putting on as much pressure as I dare. When the salmon flips into a little side pool, the bear takes matters into her own hands, clambers over the rocks, pounces, nabs the salmon smartly behind the head and lumbers immediately to the bank. My leader snaps at once and while Ms. Bear attends to the destruction of the fish, I tie on another fly and make some shambling headway downstream. Yes, I worry about the hook still in the fish, but only because I do not want this bear to be irritated by anything. I want her to be replete[12] and smug and doze off in the sun. I try to telepathize as much. Please, Bear, sleep.

Inevitably, the fishing slows down, but Ms. Bear does not seem to mind. Again she belches. Myself, I am getting quite a headache and know that I am fighting exhaustion. On a normal morning of humping along in waders over these slippery softball-sized rocks, I would be tired in any case. The added emergency is foreclosing on my energy reserves. I even find myself getting a little angry, frustrated at least, and I marvel at the bear's persistence, her inexhaustible doggedness. And appetite. I catch fish, I toss them to her. At supermarket prices, I calculate she has eaten about six hundred dollars worth of fish. The calculating gives me something to think about besides my fear.

9. The bear seems to be communicating mentally, or *telepathizing*.
10. An *egomaniac* believes that his or her activities and interests are of extreme importance to everyone else.
11. A *carnivore* (kär′ nə vôr′) eats meat, which, in Spanish, is *carne* (kär′ nā).
12. If she's *replete*, she's eaten plenty of food.

At last I am immediately across from the opening to the trail which twines back through the woods to where my camper rests in the dapple shade of mighty pines. Still, five hundred yards separate me from this imagined haven. I entertain the notion perhaps someone else will come along and frighten the bear away, maybe someone with a dog or a gun, but I have already spent many days here without seeing another soul, and in fact have chosen to return here for that very reason. I have told myself for many years that I really do love nature, love being among the animals, am restored by wilderness adventure. Considering that right now I would like nothing better than to be nestled beside my wife in front of a blazing fire, this seems to be a sentiment in need of some revision.

Now, as if in answer to my speculations, the bear turns beside me, her rump pushing me into water deeper than I want to be in, where my footing is shaky, and she stares into the woods, ears forward. She has heard something I cannot hear, or smelled something I cannot smell, and while I labor back to shallower water and surer footing, I hope some backpackers or some bear-poaching Indians are about to appear and send Ms. Bear a-galloping away. Automatically, I continue casting, but I also cannot help glancing over my shoulder in hopes of seeing what Ms. Bear sees. And in a moment I do.

It is another bear.

Unconsciously, I release a low moan, but my voice is lost in the guttural[13] warning of Ms. Bear to the trespasser. The new arrival answers with a defiant cough. He—I believe it is a he—can afford to be defiant because he is half again as large as my companion. His fur seems longer and coarser, and though its substance is as golden as that of the bear beside me, the tips are black and this dark surface ripples and undulates over his massive frame. His nostrils are flared and he is staring with profound concentration at me.

Now I am truly confused and afraid. Would it be better to catch another salmon or not? I surely cannot provide for two of these beasts and in any case Mister Bear does not seem the type to be distracted by or made friendly by any measly salmon tribute. His whole bearing—pardon the expression—tells me my intrusion into this bear world is a personal affront[14] to his bear honor. Only Ms. Bear stands between us and, after all, whose side is she really on? By bear standards, I am sure a rather regal and handsome fellow has made his appearance. Why should the fur-covered heart of furry Ms. Bear go out to me? How much love can a few hundred dollars worth of salmon buy? Most likely, this couple even have a history, know and have known each other from other seasons even though for the moment they prefer to pretend to regard each other as total strangers.

How disturbed I am is well illustrated by my next course of action. It is completely irrational, and I cannot account for it, or why it saved me—if indeed it did. I cranked in my line and lay my rod across some rocks, then began the arduous process of pulling myself out of my waders while trying to balance myself on those awkward rocks in that fast water. I tipped and swayed as I tugged at my boots, pushed my waders down, my arms in the foaming, frigid water, then the waders also filling, making it even more difficult to pull my feet free.

13. The bear's warning has a low, harsh, raspy or *guttural* quality.

14. An *affront* is a challenge or deliberate insult.

Vocabulary

profound (prə found′) *adj.* intense and complete

Appetizer

I emerged like a nymph from a cocoon, wet and trembling. The bears regarded me with clear stupefaction,[15] as if one of them had casually stepped out of his or her fur. I drained what water I could from the waders, then dropped my fly rod into them, and held them before me. The damned rocks were brutal on my feet, but I marched toward the trail opening, lifting and dropping first one, then the other leg of my waders as if I were operating a giant puppet. The water still in the waders gave each footfall an impressive authority, and I was half thinking that, well, if the big one attacks, maybe he'll be fooled into chomping the waders first and I'll at least now be able to run. I did not relish the idea of pounding down the trail in my nearly bare feet, but it was a damn sight better way to argue with the bear than being sucked from my waders like a snail from its shell. Would you have done differently?

Who knows what the bears thought, but I tried to make myself look as much as possible like a camel or some other extreme and inedible form of four-footedness as I plodded along the trail. The bears looked at each other, then at me as I clomped by, the water in the waders making an odd gurgling sound, and me making an odd sound, too, on remembering just then how the Indians would, staring death in the eye, sing their death song. Having no such melody prepared, and never having been anything but a bathtub singer, I chanted forth the only song I ever committed to memory: "Jingle Bells."

Yes, "Jingle Bells," I sang, "jingle all the way," and I lifted first one, then the other wader leg and dropped it stomping down. "Oh what fun it is to ride in a one-horse open sleigh-ay!"

The exercise was to prove to me just how complicated and various is the nature of the bear. The male reared up, blotting out the sun, bellowed, then twisted on his haunches and crashed off into the woods. The female, head cocked in curiosity, followed at a slight distance, within what still might be called striking distance whether I was out of my waders or not. Truly, I did not appreciate her persistence. Hauling the waders half full of water before me was trying work and the superfluous thought struck me: suppose someone sees me now, plumping along like this, singing "Jingle Bells," a bear in attendance? Vanity, obviously, never sleeps. But as long as the bear kept her distance I saw no reason to change my *modus operandi*.[16]

When I came within about one hundred feet of my camper, its white cap gleaming like a remnant of spring snow and beckoning me, I risked everything, dropped the waders and sped for the cab. The bear broke into a trot, too, I was sure, because although I couldn't see her, had my sights locked on the gleaming handle to the pickup door, I sure enough could hear those big feet slapping the ground behind me in a heavy rhythm, a terrible and elemental beat that sang to me of my own frailty, fragile bones and tender flesh. I plunged on like a madman, grabbed the camper door and hurled myself in.

I lay on the seat panting, curled like a child, shuddered when the bear slammed against the pickup's side. The bear pressed her nose to the window, then curiously, unceremoniously licked the glass with her tongue. I know (and you know) she could have shattered the glass with a single blow, and I tried to imagine what I should do if indeed she resorted to this simple expedient.

15. The bears' *stupefaction* (stōō′ pə fak′ shən) is a state of overwhelming astonishment.

16. The Latin phrase *modus operandi* means "method of operation."

Vocabulary

expedient (iks pē′ dē ənt) *n.* a useful method for bringing about a desired result

Two Fish, 1992. John S. Bunker. Mixed media, 20 x 15 in.
Viewing the painting: What sense of the river and the salmon do you get from this painting?

Fisherman that I am, I had nothing in the cab of the truck to defend myself with except a tire iron, and that not readily accessible behind the seat I was cowering on. My best defense, obviously, was to start the pickup and drive away.

Just as I sat up to the steering wheel and inserted the key, however, Ms. Bear slammed her big paws onto the hood and hoisted herself aboard. The pickup shuddered with the weight of her, and suddenly the windshield was full of her golden fur. I beeped the horn loud and long numerous times, but this had about the same effect as my singing, only caused her to shake her huge head, which vibrated the truck terribly. She stomped around on the hood and then lay down, back against the windshield, which now appeared to have been covered by a huge shag rug.

Could I believe my eyes?

No, I could not believe my eyes. My truck was being smothered in bear. In a moment I also could not believe my ears—Ms. Bear had decided the camper hood was the perfect place for a nap, and she was *snoring,* snoring profoundly, her body twitching like a cat's. Finally, she had responded to my advice and desires, but at the most inappropriate time. I was trapped. Blinded by bear body!

My exhaustion had been doubled by my sprint for the camper, and now that I was not in such a desperate panic, I felt the cold of the water that had soaked my clothes and I began to tremble. It also crossed my mind that perhaps Mister Bear was still in the vicinity, and if Ms. Bear was not smart enough, or cruel enough, to smash my window to get at me, he just might be.

Appetizer

Therefore, I started the engine—which disturbed Ms. Bear not a whit[17]—and rolled down the window enough to stick my head out and see down the rocky, limb-strewn trail. I figured a few jolts in those ruts and Ms. Bear would be off like a shot.

This proved a smug assumption. Ms. Bear did indeed awaken and bestir herself to a sitting position, a bit like an overgrown hood ornament, but quickly grew quite adept at balancing herself against the lurching and jolting of my truck, which, in fact, she seemed to enjoy. Just my luck, I growled, to find the first bear in Alaska who wanted a ride into town. I tried some quick braking and sharp turn maneuvers I thought might send her tumbling off, but her bulk was so massive, her paws so artfully spread, that she was just too stable an entity. She wanted a ride and there was nothing I could do about it.

When I came out of the woods to the gravel road known locally as the Dawson Artery, I had an inspiration. I didn't drive so fast that if Ms. Bear decided to clamber down she would be hurt, but I did head for the main road which led to Buckville and the Buckville Cannery. Ms. Bear swayed happily along the whole ten miles to that intersection and seemed not to bat an eye when first one big logging truck, then

17. A *whit* is a tiny amount.

Hauling in the Nets, 1930. Martha Walter. Watercolor, 15 x 22 in. David David Gallery, Philadelphia.

Viewing the painting: How do the activities shown in this painting compare with the activities at the Buckville Cannery described in the story?

another plummeted[18] by. I pulled out onto the highway, and for the safety of both of us—those logging trucks have dubious brakes and their drivers get paid by the trip[19]—I had to accelerate considerably.

I couldn't see much of Ms. Bear except her back and rump as I had to concentrate on the road, some of which is pretty curvy in that coastal area, shadowed also by the giant pines. But from the attitude expressed by her posture, I'd say she was having a whale, or should I say a salmon of a time. I saw a few cars and pickups veering out of the oncoming lane onto the shoulder as we swept by, but I didn't have time, really, to appreciate the astonishment of their drivers. In this way, my head out the window, Ms. Bear perched on the hood, I drove to the Buckville Cannery and turned into the long driveway.

Ms. Bear knew right away something good was ahead for she rose on all fours now and stuck her nose straight out like a bird dog on a pheasant. Her legs quivered with nervous anticipation as we approached, and as soon as I came out of the trees into the parking area, she went over the front of the camper like someone plunging into a pool.

Don't tell me you would have done any differently. I stopped right there and watched Ms. Bear march down between the rows of cars and right up the truck ramp into the cannery itself. She was not the least bit intimidated by all the noise of the machines and the grinders and stampers in there, or the shouting of the workers.

18. Here, *plummeted* means "plunged; dropped quickly and steeply."

19. The trucks' *dubious* brakes are of questionable quality, and the drivers speed so that they can make as many trips as possible.

Now the Buckville Cannery isn't that big—I imagine about two dozen people work there on any given day—and since it is so remote, has no hurricane fence around it, and no security guard. After all, what's anybody going to steal out of there besides a few cases of canned salmon or some bags of frozen fish parts that will soon become some company's cat food? The main building is up on a little hill and conveyors run down from there to the docks where the salmon boats pull in—the sea is another half mile away—and unload their catch.

I would say that in about three minutes after Ms. Bear walked into the cannery, twenty of the twenty-four workers were climbing out down the conveyors, dropping from open windows, or charging out the doors. The other four just hadn't got wind of the event yet, but in a little while they came bounding out, too, one fellow pulling up his trousers as he ran. They all assembled on the semicircular drive before the main office and had a union meeting of some vigor.

Myself, I was too tired to participate, and in any case did not want to be held liable for the disturbance at the Buckville Cannery, and so I made a U-turn and drove on into Buckville itself where I took a room above the Buckville Tavern and had a hot shower and a really nice nap. That night in the Tap and Lounge I got to hear many an excited story about the she-bear who freeloaded at the cannery for a couple of hours before she was driven off by blowing, ironically enough, the lunch whistle loud and long. I didn't think it was the right time or place to testify to my part in that historical event, and for once kept my mouth shut. You don't like trouble any more than I do, and I'm sure you would have done about the same.

Responding to Literature

Personal Response

What did you like best about this story? Discuss your thoughts with a classmate.

Analyzing Literature

Recall

1. How does the author describe the bear in the beginning of the story? What adjectives does he use? What verbs?
2. What does the narrator do after first noticing the bear? Why?
3. What does the narrator hope the bear will do after eating the fish? What will this allow him to do?
4. How does the narrator get to his truck?
5. How does the narrator finally rid himself of the bear?

Intrepret

6. What can you infer about the **narrator** from his description of the bear? (See Literary Terms Handbook, page R8.) How does the narrator really feel about the bear? about the situation?
7. What does the narrator mean when he says that his actions are "exactly what you would do"? Explain.
8. Based on what the narrator wants to happen to the bear, what kind of person do you think he is?
9. Why, do you think, does the narrator succeed in reaching his truck? What character traits does he exhibit through his actions? Explain.
10. In your opinion, are the narrator's actions at the end of the story consistent with those at the beginning? Why or why not?

Evaluate and Connect

11. Which passages in the story are the funniest? What makes them funny? In what different ways does the author create humor? Give examples to support your responses.
12. The narrator frequently suggests that he did exactly what any of his readers would have done. Do you agree with him? Why or why not?
13. Think about your response to the Reading Focus on page 1015. How does your experience compare with the narrator's? Explain.
14. The choice the narrator made at the end of the story saved him, but it was risky. Do you think he did the right thing? Explain.
15. Could this story actually have happened? Evaluate the author's choice of details and events, telling how realistic or believable they seem.

Literary ELEMENTS

Rising Action

Rising action is the part of a plot where complications to the conflict develop and tension and suspense build. Rising action draws the reader along to the climax of the plot. In "Appetizer," the plot begins when the narrator sees the bear. The action begins to rise when the narrator tosses the bear the first salmon. As action rises, the plot becomes more suspenseful as events combine to complicate the narrator's situation.

1. Together with a partner, chart the rising action of the story using a time line format. How do events and situations build on each other?
2. What point is most suspenseful? Where in the story does that point occur? Do you like the arrangement? Why or why not?

- See **Literary Terms Handbook,** p. R11.

Literature and Writing

Writing About Literature

Narrative Style In "Appetizer," the narrator's style is conversational and informal. He directly addresses the audience as though he were talking to a close friend. Write a short analysis of the effect of the narrator's style. How does this style contribute to the overall tone of the story? Support your analysis with examples from the story.

Creative Writing

The Other Side of the Story How would the bear tell this story? Rewrite Abel's story from the point of view of the female bear, telling how she remembers events, what she thought of the narrator, and so on. Try to create a distinctive character and voice for the bear. Read your story aloud to a classmate.

Extending Your Response

Literature Groups

The Man, the Bear, the Salmon It has been said that humor is "the juxtaposition of the incongruous"; that is, the positioning together of things that really don't belong together. In "Appetizer," the author presents a very funny recounting of what could have been a terrifying event. In your group, discuss the incongruous events that combine to make the story so humorous. Evaluate the ways in which other literary techniques contribute to make the story funny, such as personification or slapstick visual comedy. As a group, decide what you feel works best in this story, and share your reasons with the class.

Internet Connection

Bear Facts In many parts of the United States, bears such as grizzlies are endangered animals. Do some online research to find out more about these highly intelligent and fascinating animals and what is being done to protect them. Share your findings with the class.

Learning for Life

Bear Etiquette As their natural food sources diminish, bears have become increasingly drawn to campgrounds to find food. Contact the National Park Service for suggestions on how to deal with bears in the wilderness. Make a chart of your findings to share with the class.

Save your work for your portfolio.

VOCABULARY • Old Words

Someone who is *bereft* has been robbed or deprived of something important to him or her. The prefix *be-*, means "away," and *reft* is the past tense or past participle of *reave,* which means "to seize or rob." *Reave* and *reft* used to be common words in English; now they are almost never used. Sometimes, as with *bereft,* a word that was formed from another word remains active in the language while the original word fades from use. Another example of this is found in *ruthless,* which was formed from the now-archaic word *ruth,* meaning "mercy."

PRACTICE Examine the following old words and their meanings. Then write three sentences, each one containing at least two old words from the list below. Add appropriate endings to reflect plurals, verb tense, and modifiers.

flerk: to twitch
blutter: to blurt out
teenful: irritating
snawk: to smell
purfle: to decorate
fonkin: a little fool
whifling: an unimportant creature
pingle: to eat with little appetite
spuddle: to act important with little cause
boonfellow: a close companion

MEDIA connection

Magazine Article

Have you ever looked up a word in a thesaurus and been surprised at the number of synonyms listed? Wen Smith finds a humorous use for one such list.

Too Much Spice

by Wen Smith—*The Saturday Evening Post,* July/August 1997

Letters from readers pour into the wordshop, often with helpful suggestions. On Friday a particularly suggestive one poured in.

"You write a lot of dialogue," the reader wrote, "and you mostly use the word *said,* as in 'I *said,*' 'my wife *said,*' 'Charlie *said.*' Aren't there other words you could use for *said?*"

I showed the letter to my wife.

"I agree," she agreed. "You do use *said* a lot."

"OK, I'm guilty," I pleaded. "But I like to keep the writing simple."

"There are plenty of other words for *said,*" she indicated.

"Look," I whined, "if I use a lot of synonyms for *said,* the words will get more attention than the ideas."

"Just for variety's sake," she urged, "you might use one now and then."

"Nonsense," I reasoned. "Elegant variation is a mark of bad writing."

"Why?" she insisted.

"*Said* is a straightforward, generic word," I pontificated. "It fits almost any line of dialogue."

"But it's such a rich language," she marveled. "You may as well spend some of the riches."

"I remember," I reminisced, "how Ring Lardner once made fun of pretentious variations for *said.* He wrote a story with the infamous line '"Shut up!" he *explained.*'"

"He was just being funny," she opined.

"He showed how variations on *said* can be stretched too far, like a rubber band," I snapped.

"I suppose you're right," she conjectured.

"Of course I'm right," I snickered.

I imagined writing things like "'Somebody's been sleeping in my bed,' she broke in," or "'You're a nut,' he cracked."

"Anyway, good usage keeps things simple," I elucidated. "Why use *proclaimed* when it's just a remark, not a proclamation?"

"But your reader does have a point about repeating *said,*" my wife persisted.

"Variety may be the spice of life," I confessed, "but too much spice spoils the broth."

"You mean too many cooks," she simmered.

"It's better to repeat *said,*" I repeated, "than to reach too far for a synonym."

"Why not do one article using some of those synonyms," she suggested, "just to see how it comes out."

Analyzing Media

1. Do you agree with the author of this article or with his wife? Why?
2. What dialogue tags do you use most often in your writing? After reading this article, how might you change your use of dialogue tags in your future writing?

Before You Read

from *An American Childhood*

Reading Focus

Think of someone you know who views life with a comic perspective or has a great sense of humor. What makes them so funny?

Chart It! Make a chart like the one shown. In the first column, list names of people who you think are truly funny. You might include family members and friends, celebrities, and characters from stories you've read. In the second column, jot down what makes these people funny.

Funny people	What makes them funny?

Setting a Purpose Read an autobiographical account to learn about a person with a sense of humor.

Building Background

The Time and Place

This selection is set in Pittsburgh, Pennsylvania, in the 1950s.

Did You Know?

Most middle-class married women in the 1950s did not work outside the home or pursue their own careers. Women who were fortunate or wealthy enough to attend college were generally assumed to be looking for a husband. Even a well-educated married woman of the 1950s was expected to be content to take care of her husband and children.

Vocabulary Preview

tremulously (trem′ yə les lē) *adv.* in a trembling or vibrating way; p. 1030

connoisseur (kon′ ə sur′) *n.* one who has expert knowledge in a particular area, such as wine, food, or the arts; p. 1031

eschew (es cho͞o′) *v.* to keep apart from (something disliked or harmful); avoid; p. 1032

advocate (ad′ və kāt′) *v.* to publicly support; p. 1032

stolid (stol′ id) *adj.* showing little or no emotion; p. 1034

ostracism (os′ trə siz′ əm) *n.* exclusion from a group or society; p. 1035

Meet Annie Dillard

"I didn't want to write about me . . . just a book about noticing that you're living," said author and naturalist Annie Dillard about her motivation for writing *An American Childhood*. Much of Dillard's work, including *Pilgrim at Tinker Creek* for which she won the 1975 Pulitzer Prize for Nonfiction, is reflective and autobiographical. Dillard's parents encouraged her to be curious and to observe the world around her. The result is that whether Dillard is describing a grasshopper on her window or discussing her family's quirky idiosyncrasies, she displays a keen attention to detail and a fascination with life.

Annie Dillard was born in 1945 in Pittsburgh, Pennsylvania. An American Childhood *was published in 1987.*

from An American Childhood

Annie Dillard

ONE SUNDAY AFTERNOON Mother wandered through our kitchen, where Father was making a sandwich and listening to the ball game. The Pirates were playing the New York Giants at Forbes Field. In those days, the Giants had a utility infielder[1] named Wayne Terwilliger. Just as Mother passed through, the radio announcer cried—with undue drama—"Terwilliger bunts one!"

"Terwilliger bunts one?" Mother cried back, stopped short. She turned. "Is that English?"

"The player's name is Terwilliger," Father said. "He bunted."

"That's marvelous," Mother said. "'Terwilliger bunts one.' No wonder you listen to baseball. 'Terwilliger bunts one.'"

For the next seven or eight years, Mother made this surprising string of syllables her own. Testing a microphone, she repeated, "Terwilliger bunts one"; testing a pen or a typewriter, she wrote it. If, as happened surprisingly often in the course of various improvised gags, she pretended to whisper something else in my ear, she actually whispered, "Terwilliger bunts one." Whenever someone used a French phrase, or a Latin one, she answered solemnly, "Terwilliger bunts one." If Mother had had, like Andrew Carnegie,[2] the opportunity to cook up a motto for a coat of arms,[3] hers would have read simply and tellingly, "Terwilliger bunts one." (Carnegie's was "Death to Privilege.")

She served us with other words and phrases. On a Florida trip, she repeated tremulously, "That . . . is a royal poinciana." I don't remember the tree; I remember the thrill in her voice. She pronounced it carefully, and spelled it. She also liked to say "portulaca."[4]

The drama of the words "Tamiami Trail" stirred her, we learned on the same Florida trip. People built Tampa on one coast, and they built Miami on another. Then—the height of visionary[5] ambition and folly—they piled a slow, tremendous road through the terrible Everglades to connect them. To build the road, men stood sunk in muck to their armpits. They fought off cottonmouth moccasins and six-foot

1. In this context, *utility* means "useful generally rather than in a specialized function." So, a *utility infielder* is capable of playing shortstop or first, second, or third base.

2. Based in Pittsburgh, *Andrew Carnegie* (1835–1919) made a fortune in the steel industry and donated $350 million to social and educational institutions.

3. A *coat of arms* is an arrangement of symbols on a shield that, along with a motto, represents one's ancestry.

4. Both the *royal poinciana* and the *portulaca* (pôr′ chə la′ kə) are native to the tropics and bear bright flowers.

5. Here, *visionary* refers to imagining something in perfect but unrealistic form. People had foreseen the benefits of connecting the two cities but overlooked practical considerations involved in constructing the road.

Vocabulary

tremulously (trem′ yə ləs lē) *adv.* in a trembling or vibrating way

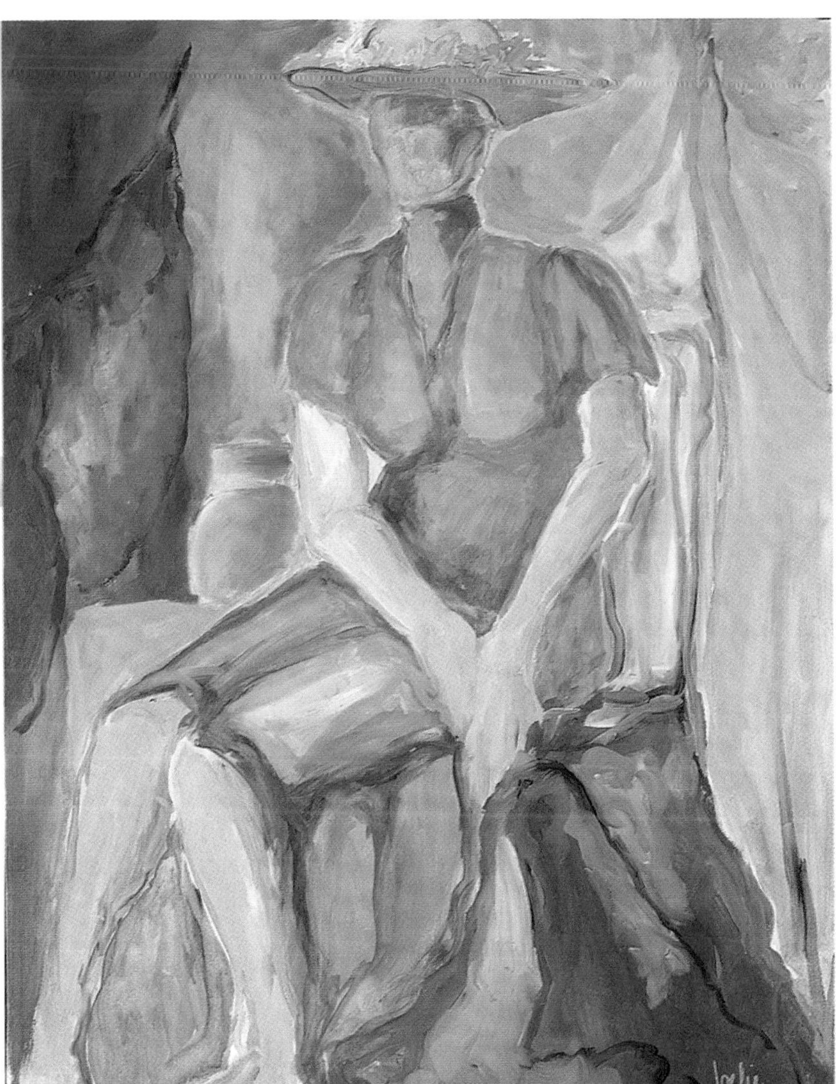

Woman in Blue, 1995. Leslie Braddock. Acrylic on canvas, 60 x 48 in. Private collection.

Viewing the painting: What techniques does the artist use to capture the character of the woman in this painting? What techniques does Annie Dillard use to portray the character of Mother in the opening of the selection?

alligators. They slept in boats, wet. They blasted muck with dynamite, cut jungle with machetes; they laid logs, dragged drilling machines, hauled dredges, heaped limestone. The road took fourteen years to build up by the shovelful, a Panama Canal in reverse, and cost hundreds of lives from tropical, mosquito-carried diseases. Then, capping it all, some genius thought of the word Tamiami: they called the road from Tampa to Miami, this very road under our spinning wheels, the Tamiami Trail. Some called it Alligator Alley. Anyone could drive over this road without a thought.

Hearing this, moved, I thought all the suffering of road building was worth it (it wasn't my suffering), now that we had this new thing to hang these new words on—Alligator Alley for those who like things cute, and, for connoisseurs like Mother, for lovers of the human drama in all its boldness and terror, the Tamiami Trail.

Back home, Mother cut clips from reels of talk, as it were, and played them back at leisure. She noticed that many Pittsburghers confuse "leave" and "let." One kind relative brightened our morning by mentioning why she'd brought

Vocabulary

connoisseur (kon′ ə sur′) *n.* one who has expert knowledge in a particular area, such as wine, food, or the arts her son to visit: "He wanted to come with me, so I left him." Mother filled in Amy and me on locutions we missed. "I can't do it on Friday," her pretty sister told a crowded dinner party, "because Friday's the day I lay in the stores."[6]

(All unconsciously, though, we ourselves used some pure Pittsburghisms. We said "tele pole," pronounced "telly pole," for that splintery sidewalk post I loved to climb. We said "slippy"—the sidewalks are "slippy." We said, "That's all the farther I could go." And we said, as Pittsburghers do say, "This glass needs washed," or "The dog needs walked"—a usage our father eschewed; he knew it was not standard English, nor even comprehensible English, but he never let on.)

"Spell 'poinsettia,'" Mother would throw out at me, smiling with pleasure. "Spell 'sherbet.'" The idea was not to make us whizzes, but, quite the contrary, to remind us—and I, especially, needed reminding—that we didn't know it all just yet.

"There's a deer standing in the front hall," she told me one quiet evening in the country.

"Really?"

"No. I just wanted to tell you something once without your saying, 'I know.'"

Supermarkets in the middle 1950s began luring, or bothering, customers by giving out Top Value Stamps or Green Stamps.[7] When, shopping with Mother, we got to the head of the checkout line, the checker, always a young man, asked, "Save stamps?"

"No," Mother replied genially, week after week, "I build model airplanes." I believe she originated this line. It took me years to determine where the joke lay.

Anyone who met her verbal challenges she adored. She had surgery on one of her eyes. On the operating table, just before she conked out, she appealed feelingly to the surgeon, saying, as she had been planning to say for weeks, "Will I be able to play the piano?" "Not on me," the surgeon said. "You won't pull that old one on me."

It was, indeed, an old one. The surgeon was supposed to answer, "Yes, my dear, brave woman, you will be able to play the piano after this operation," to which Mother intended to reply, "Oh, good, I've always wanted to play the piano." This pat scenario bored her; she loved having it interrupted. It must have galled[8] her that usually her acquaintances were so predictably unalert; it must have galled her that, for the length of her life, she could surprise everyone so continually, so easily, when she had been the same all along. At any rate, she loved anyone who, as she put it, saw it coming, and called her on it.

She regarded the instructions on bureaucratic forms as straight lines.[9] "Do you advocate the overthrow of the United States government by force or violence?" After some thought she wrote, "Force." She regarded children, even babies, as straight men.[10] When Molly learned to crawl, Mother delighted in buying her gowns with drawstrings at the bottom, like

6. *Locutions* are forms or styles of verbal expression. Where this woman said she had to *lay in the stores*, Mother might have said she had to go grocery shopping.
7. *[Top Value . . . Stamps]* Stores gave customers a certain number of stamps per dollar spent. These stamps were saved up and later exchanged for merchandise.
8. Here, *galled* means "irritated."
9. *Bureaucratic* refers to the rigidly formal paperwork and procedures involved in dealing with government officials and agencies. For Mother, these things were setups for jokes—the *straight lines* that led to punch lines.
10. *Straight men* are people who assist comedians by feeding them straight lines or serving as objects of fun.

Vocabulary

eschew (es chōō′) *v.* to keep apart from (something disliked or harmful); avoid
advocate (ad′ və kāt′) *v.* to publicly support

Did You Know?
Swee'pea is the baby in "Popeye" cartoons.

Swee'pea's, because, as she explained energetically, you could easily step on the drawstring without the baby's noticing, so that she crawled and crawled and crawled and never got anywhere except into a small ball at the gown's top.

When we children were young, she mothered us tenderly and dependably; as we got older, she resumed her career of anarchism.[11] She collared us into her gags. If she answered the phone on a wrong number, she told the caller, "Just a minute," and dragged the receiver to Amy or me, saying, "Here, take this, your name is Cecile," or, worse, just, "It's for you." You had to think on your feet. But did you want to perform well as Cecile, or did you want to take pity on the wretched caller?

During a family trip to the Highland Park Zoo, Mother and I were alone for a minute. She approached a young couple holding hands on a bench by the seals, and addressed the young man in dripping[12] tones: "Where have you been? Still got those baby-blue eyes; always did slay me. And this"—a swift nod at the dumbstruck young woman, who had removed her hand from the man's—"must be the one you were telling me about. She's not so bad, really, as you used to make out. But listen, you know how I miss you, you know where to reach me, same old place. And there's Ann over there—see how she's grown? See the blue eyes?"

And off she sashayed,[13] taking me firmly by the hand, and leading us around briskly past the monkey house and away. She cocked an ear back, and both of us heard the desperate man begin, in a high-pitched wail, "I swear, I never saw her before in my life. . . ."

On a long, sloping beach by the ocean, she lay stretched out sunning with Father and friends, until the conversation gradually grew tedious, when without forethought she gave a little push with her heel and rolled away. People were stunned. She rolled deadpan and apparently effortlessly, arms and legs extended and tidy, down the beach to the distant water's edge, where she lay at ease just as she had been, but half in the surf, and well out of earshot.

She dearly loved to fluster people by throwing out a game's rules at whim[14]—when she was getting bored, losing in a dull sort of way, and when everybody else was taking it too seriously. If you turned your back, she moved the checkers around on the board. When you got them all straightened out, she denied she'd touched them; the next time you turned your back, she lined them up on the rug or hid them under your chair. In a betting rummy game called *Michigan*, she routinely played out of turn, or called out a card she didn't hold, or counted backward, simply to amuse herself by causing an uproar and watching the rest of us do double takes and have fits. (Much later, when serious suitors came to call, Mother subjected them to this fast card game as a trial by ordeal; she used it as an intelligence test and a measure of spirit. If the poor man could stay a round without breaking down or running out, he got to marry one of us, if he still wanted to.)

She excelled at bridge, playing fast and boldly, but when the stakes were low and the hands dull, she bid slams[15] for the devilment

11. Here, *anarchism* refers to active resistance against what's oppressive and undesirable.
12. *Dripping* here refers to using excessive charm or appeal.
13. She *sashayed* or walked in a way that showed a seeming lack of interest.
14. The phrase *at whim* means "suddenly and unexpectedly."
15. When she *bid slams*, Mother "went for broke," betting that she would win every or all but one of the tricks in a round of play.

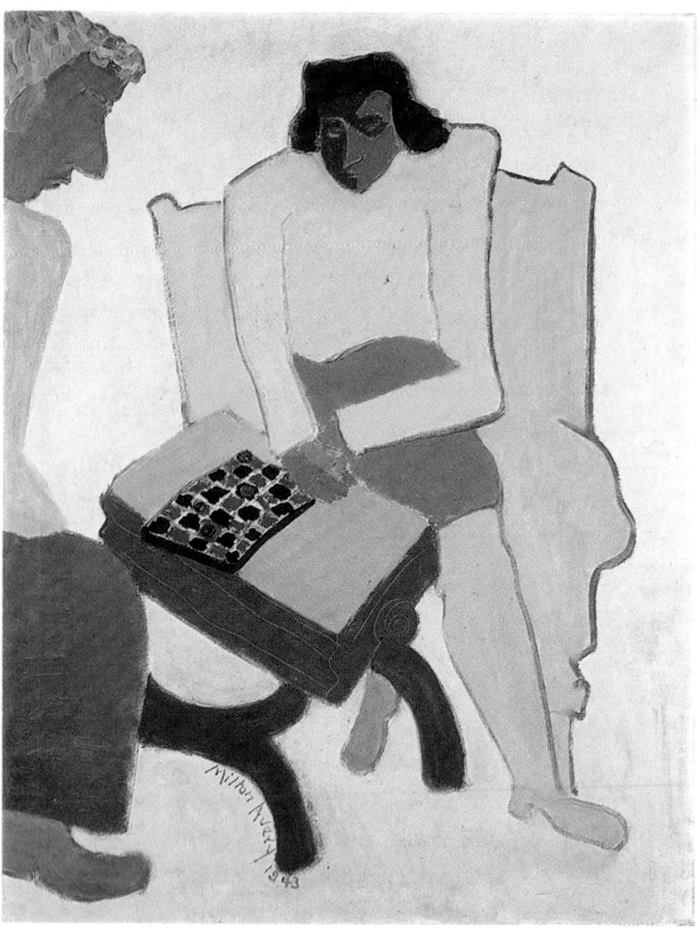

Checker Players, 1943. Milton Avery. Oil on canvas, 36 x 28 in. Private collection.

Viewing the painting: Look at the expressions and attitudes of these checker players. How do you think their game compares with one between Mother and an opponent? Explain.

of it, or raised her opponents' suit to bug them, or showed her hand, or tossed her cards in a handful behind her back in a characteristic swift motion accompanied by a vibrantly innocent look. It drove our stolid father crazy. The hand was over before it began, and the guests were appalled. How do you score it, who deals now, what do you do with a crazy person who is having so much fun? Or they were down seven, and the guests were appalled. "Pam!" "Dammit, Pam!" He groaned. What ails such people? What on earth possesses them? He rubbed his face.

She was an unstoppable force; she never let go. When we moved across town, she persuaded the U.S. Post Office to let her keep her old address—forever—because she'd had stationery printed. I don't know how she did it. Every new post office worker, over decades, needed to learn that although the Doaks' mail is addressed to here, it is delivered to there.

Mother's energy and intelligence suited her for a greater role in a larger arena—mayor of New York, say—than the one she had. She followed American politics closely; she had been known to vote for Democrats. She saw how things should be run, but she had nothing to run but our household. Even there, small minds bugged her; she was smarter than the people who designed the things she had to use all day for the length of her life.

"Look," she said. "Whoever designed this corkscrew never used one. Why would anyone sell it without trying it out?" So she invented a better one. She showed me a drawing of it.

The spirit of American enterprise never faded in Mother. If capitalizing and tooling up[16] had been as interesting as theorizing and thinking up, she would have fired up a new factory every week, and chaired several hundred corporations.

"It grieves me," she would say, "it grieves my heart," that the company that made one superior product packaged it poorly, or took the wrong tack[17] in its advertising. She knew,

16. *Capitalizing and tooling up* has to do with providing the finances and equipment necessary to start up a new business or factory.
17. The company took the wrong course of action or *tack*.

Vocabulary

stolid (stol′ id) *adj.* showing little or no emotion

as she held the thing mournfully in her two hands, that she'd never find another. She was right. We children wholly sympathized, and so did Father; what could she do, what could anyone do, about it? She was Samson[18] in chains. She paced.

She didn't like the taste of stamps so she didn't lick stamps; she licked the corner of the envelope instead. She glued sandpaper to the sides of kitchen drawers, and under kitchen cabinets, so she always had a handy place to strike a match. She designed, and hounded workmen to build against all norms,[19] doubly wide kitchen counters and elevated bathroom sinks. . . . She drew plans for an over-the-finger toothbrush for babies, an oven rack that slid up and down, and—the family favorite—Lendalarm. Lendalarm was a beeper you attached to books (or tools) you loaned friends. After ten days, the beeper sounded. Only the rightful owner could silence it.

She repeatedly reminded us of P. T. Barnum's dictum:[20] You could sell anything to anybody if you marketed it right. The adman who thought of making Americans believe they needed underarm deodorant was a visionary. So, too, was the hero who made a success of a new product, Ivory soap. The executives were horrified, Mother told me, that a cake of this stuff floated. Soap wasn't supposed to float. Anyone would be able to tell it was mostly whipped-up air. Then some inspired adman made a leap: Advertise that it floats. Flaunt it. The rest is history.

She respected the rare few who broke through to new ways. "Look," she'd say, "here's an intelligent apron." She called upon us to admire intelligent control knobs and intelligent pan handles, intelligent andirons and picture frames and knife sharpeners. She questioned everything, every pair of scissors, every knitting needle, gardening glove, tape dispenser. Hers was a restless mental vigor that just about ignited the dumb household objects with its force.

Torpid[21] conformity was a kind of sin; it was stupidity itself, the mighty stream against which Mother would never cease to struggle. If you held no minority opinions, or if you failed to risk total ostracism for them daily, the world would be a better place without you. . . .

She simply tried to keep us all awake. And in fact it was always clear to Amy and me, and to Molly when she grew old enough to listen, that if our classmates came to cruelty, just as much as if the neighborhood or the nation came to madness, we were expected to take, and would be each separately capable of taking, a stand.

18. In the Bible, *Samson* told Delilah the secret of his extraordinary strength, that his hair had never been cut. He fell asleep, she got out her clippers, and his enemies soon had Samson chained up in prison.

19. Here, the *norms* are rules, standards, and accepted practices.

20. In the 1800s, *Barnum* presented many popular entertainments, founded what is now the Ringling Brothers and Barnum & Bailey Circus, and staged sensational publicity stunts. The actual words of his famous saying *(dictum)* were, "There's a sucker born every minute."

21. Something that's *torpid* is dull and lifeless.

Vocabulary

ostracism (os′ trə siz′ əm) *n.* exclusion from a group or society

Responding to Literature

Personal Response

What questions would you like to ask the author about her mother?

Analyzing Literature

Recall

1. Why are the terms "Terwilliger bunts one" and "Tamiami Trail" important to Mother?
2. Mother found humor in situations that ordinarily would not be funny. Give an example and explain why the situation was comical.
3. Describe two incidents that illustrate how Mother's unexpected behavior flustered people.
4. What bothered Mother about certain products and tools? Which products did she admire?
5. According to Dillard, what did Mother expect of her daughters?

Interpret

6. What do Mother's reactions to and use of the phrase "Terwilliger bunts one" suggest about her personality?
7. What can you infer about Mother's philosophy of life from the way she responds to serious questions and situations?
8. Do you think Mother cared about the consequences of her actions? Explain.
9. Explain what Dillard means when she says that the "spirit of American enterprise never faded in Mother."
10. Based on everything Dillard has said about Mother, what words would you use to describe Mother's character and values? Explain.

Evaluate And Connect

11. An **anecdote** is a brief account of an event. Give examples of anecdotes from the selection and evaluate their use.
12. Identify places in the selection that illustrate Annie Dillard's attention to detail. How do these details enhance your appreciation of the selection?
13. **Theme Connections** Recall the chart you created in the Reading Focus on page 1029. Would you add Mother to your chart? Would you add Dillard herself? Why or why not?
14. What was your immediate response to Mother's treatment of the young couple at the zoo? How would you have felt in Dillard's place?
15. How does Mother compare with your mental picture of an ideal mother? Explain.

Literary **ELEMENTS**

Hyperbole

Writers use **hyperbole,** or extreme exaggeration, to emphasize a point or to create a certain effect, such as humor. Hyperbole is a figure of speech. It is not meant to be read literally. Sometimes you have to analyze a reference to understand the exaggeration and to get the effect. For example, when Annie Dillard says that "Mother's energy and intelligence suited her for a greater role in a larger arena–mayor of New York, say," she does not actually mean that her mother should have been mayor of New York City. She is using hyperbole. Because New York City is one of the largest, most complex cities of the world to govern, Dillard wants her readers to imagine what it would be like to live with someone who has the energy to run a city like New York.

Find these examples of hyperbole on page 1035 in the selection. Then explain their meaning and humorous effect.

1. "She was Samson in chains."
2. "Hers was a restless mental vigor . . ."
3. "Torpid conformity was a kind of sin . . . the mighty stream . . ."

- See **Literary Terms Handbook,** p. R6.

Literature and Writing

Writing About Literature

Define a Character Trait "My mother was always completely irrepressible," Dillard was quoted as saying in a magazine article. Look up and write the dictionary definition of the word *irrepressible.* Then write a brief assessment of how well Dillard illustrates her mother's "irrepressible" quality. Support your evaluation with details from the story. Share your evaluation with classmates.

Creative Writing

Boyfriend Beware! Dillard says that her mother challenged her daughters' dates to ridiculous card games to test their intelligence and measure their spirit. How might those young men have felt? How might her daughters have reacted? Write the dialogue that might have taken place between Mother, Annie as a young teenager, and one of Annie's hopeful boyfriends.

Extending Your Response

Literature Groups

Life with Mother Working with your group, divide a piece of paper into two columns. In the first column, write the traits that you like about Mother and the reasons it would be fun to live with her. In the second column, write the traits that could make life with Mother difficult. Then discuss the following questions with your group. What impressions about her mother is Dillard conveying? How might Dillard have reacted to her mother as a child? As an adult? What conclusions can you draw about the family's life with Mother? Share your ideas with your classmates.

Learning for Life

Customer Response Choose a commercial product that Mother mentions in the selection. Pretend you are Mother and write a letter to the manufacturer. Explain what you liked or did not like about the product and why you would or would not use it again. Share your letter with the class.

Interdisciplinary Activity

Art: The Mother of Invention Picture one of Mother's inventions, such as the "Lendalarm." Create an illustrated advertisement for one of her products.

Save your work for your portfolio.

VOCABULARY • The Latin Root *voc*

The word *advocate* comes from the Latin prefix *ad-*, meaning "to," and the root *voc,* meaning either "to call" or "voice." An *advocate* is a defender, someone "to call to" for aid.

The root *voc,* which is also spelled *vok,* is found in many English words. A *vocal* response is spoken; a *vocation* (or career) is often referred to as "a calling." A *vociferous* group of students are noisy due to a great deal of talking or shouting.

The following are some of the prefixes that have been attached to *voc* or *vok* to create words:

re-:	back	*pro-:*	forth
e-:	out	*con-:*	together

PRACTICE Use the meanings of *voc/vok* and the prefixes shown above to answer the questions.

1. Does a *provocative* statement ignore, arouse, or soothe the listener's feelings?
2. Would a driver's license be *revoked* because the driver passed a test or broke a law?
3. Is a *convocation* a secret plan, a method of travel, or an assembly?
4. Would a teacher *evoke* a correct answer by giving hints or by grading a paper?

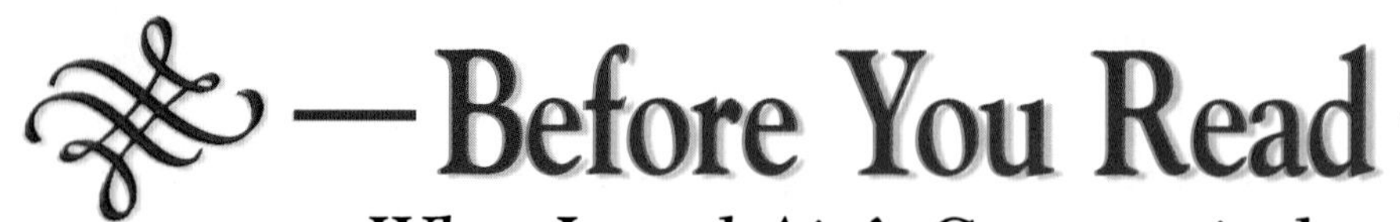

Before You Read

What Is and Ain't Grammatical

Reading Focus

What are your thoughts about the use of good grammar? Which grammar rules don't make sense to you? How do you react when you hear the word *ain't?*

Freewrite At the top of a sheet of paper, write "My Thoughts About English Grammar." For two minutes jot down whatever comes to mind about English grammar. Do not edit your thoughts.

Setting A Purpose Read an essay to learn about the comic perspective one writer takes toward grammar.

Building Background

Did You Know?

- Grammar is the study of the way that words come together to form phrases and sentences. American English grammar consists of rules aimed at helping you speak and write the standard dialect of American English so that your ideas are clear and understandable.
- According to Dave Barry, "Just about anything's a topic for a humor column: any event that occurs in the news, anything that happens in daily life—driving, shopping, reading, eating. You can look at just about anything and see humor in it somewhere."
- Most people find Dave Barry's columns and books extremely funny, but occasionally he receives complaints from people he calls "the humor-impaired, who are infuriated that I have written something that's not literally true."

Vocabulary Preview

prospective (prə spek′ tiv) *adj.* probable or expected; future; p. 1039
drone (drōn) *v.* to talk in a dull, monotonous tone; p. 1040
enlightening (en līt′ ən ing) *adj.* giving or revealing knowledge or wisdom; p. 1041

Meet Dave Barry

"I always wanted to write when I was a kid; it just never occurred to me that you could have a job that didn't involve any actual work."

Dave Barry's first job as a writer was for a small suburban newspaper where he wrote about the local "hot issues"—sewage and zoning. He eventually decided that writing humor might be a fun way to pay the bills. Barry's talent for finding humor in almost any topic led to his enormous success. In 1988 he was awarded the Pulitzer Prize for Distinguished Commentary. His weekly column is syndicated in hundreds of newspapers.

Dave Barry was born in Armonk, New York, in 1947.

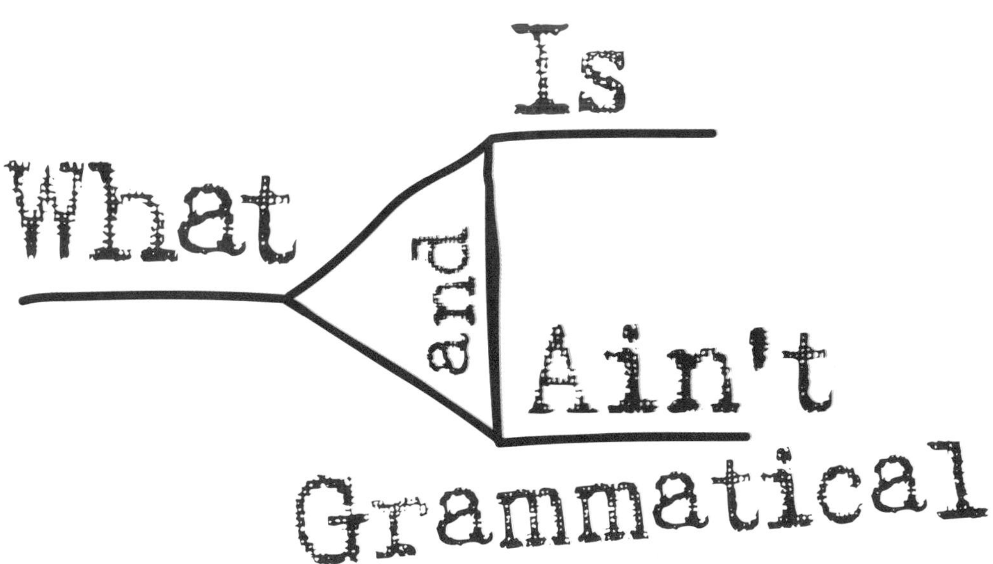
What
Is
and
Ain't
Grammatical

Dave Barry

I CANNOT OVEREMPHASIZE the importance of good grammar.

What a crock. I could easily overemphasize the importance of good grammar. For example, I could say: "Bad grammar is the leading cause of slow, painful death in North America," or "Without good grammar, the United States would have lost World War II."

The truth is that grammar is not the most important thing in the world. The Super Bowl is the most important thing in the world. But grammar is still important. For example, suppose you are being interviewed for a job as an airplane pilot, and your prospective employer asks you if you have any experience, and you answer: "Well, I ain't never actually flied no actual airplanes or nothing, but I got several pilot-style hats and several friends who I like to talk about airplanes with."

If you answer this way, the prospective employer will immediately realize that you have ended your sentence with a preposition. (What you should have said, of course, is "several friends with whom I like to talk about airplanes.") So you will not get the job, because airline pilots have to use good grammar when they get on the intercom and explain to the passengers that, because of high winds, the plane is going to take off several hours late and land in Pierre, South Dakota, instead of Los Angeles.

Vocabulary

prospective (prə spek′ tiv) *adj.* probable or expected; future

SOMETIMES I LIE AWAKE AT NIGHT, AND I ASK, "IS IT ALL WORTH IT?"

THEN A VOICE SAYS, "WHO ARE YOU TALKING TO?"

THEN ANOTHER VOICE SAYS, "YOU MEAN, 'TO WHOM ARE YOU TALKING?'"

NO WONDER I LIE AWAKE AT NIGHT!
2-6
SCHULZ

We did not always have grammar. In medieval England, people said whatever they wanted, without regard to rules, and as a result they sounded like morons. Take the poet Geoffrey Chaucer, who couldn't even spell his first name right. He wrote a large poem called *Canterbury Tales,* in which people from various professions—knight, monk, miller, reever, riveter, eeler, diver, stevedore, spinnaker, etc.—drone on and on like this:

In a somer sesun whon softe was the sunne
I kylled a younge birde ande I ate it on a
bunne.

When Chaucer's poem was published, everybody read it and said: "My God, we need some grammar around here." So they formed a Grammar Commission, which developed the parts of speech, the main ones being nouns, verbs, predicants, conjectures, particles, proverbs, adjoiners, coordinates, and rebuttals. Then the commission made up hundreds and hundreds of grammar rules, all of which were strictly enforced.

When the colonists came to America, they rebelled against British grammar. They openly used words like "ain't" and "finalize," and when they wrote the Declaration of Independence they deliberately misspelled many words. Thanks to their courage, today we Americans have only two rules of grammar:

Rule 1. The word "me" is always incorrect.

Most of us learn this rule as children, from our mothers. We say things like: "Mom, can

Vocabulary
drone (drōn) *v.* to talk in a dull, monotonous tone

Bobby and me roll the camping trailer over Mrs. Johnson's cat?" And our mothers say: "Remember your grammar, dear. You mean: 'Can Bobby and *I* roll the camping trailer over Mrs. Johnson's cat?' Of course you can, but be home by dinnertime."

The only exception to this rule is in formal business writing, where instead of "I" you must use "the undersigned." For example, this business letter is incorrect:

"Dear Hunky-Dory Canned Fruit Company: A couple days ago my wife bought a can of your cling peaches and served them to my mother who has a weak heart and she damn near died when she bit into a live grub. If I ever find out where you live, I am gonna whomp you on the head with a ax handle."

This should be corrected as follows:

". . . If the undersigned ever finds out where you live, the undersigned is gonna whomp you on the head with a ax handle."

Rule 2. You're not allowed to split infinitives.

An infinitive is the word "to" and whatever comes right behind it, such as "to a tee," "to the best of my ability," "tomato," etc. Splitting an infinitive is putting something between the "to" and the other words. For example, this is incorrect:

"Hey man, you got any, you know, spare change you could give to, like, me?"

The correct version is:

". . . spare change you could, like, give to me?"

The advantage of American English is that, because there are so few rules, practically anybody can learn to speak it in just a few minutes. The disadvantage is that Americans generally sound like jerks, whereas the British sound really smart, especially to Americans. That's why Americans are so fond of those British dramas they're always showing on public television, the ones introduced by Alistair Cooke.[1] Americans *love* people who talk like Alistair Cooke. He could introduce old episodes of "Hawaii Five-O" and Americans would think they were extremely enlightening.

So the trick is to use American grammar, which is simple, but talk with a British accent, which is impressive. This technique is taught at all your really snotty private schools, where the kids learn to sound like Elliot Richardson.[2] Remember Elliot? He sounded extremely British, and as a result he got to be Attorney General, Secretary of State, Chief Justice of the Supreme Court and Vice President *at the same time*.

You can do it, too. Practice in your home, then approach someone on the street and say: "Tally-ho, old chap. I would consider it a great honour if you would favour me with some spare change." You're bound to get quick results.

1. *Alistair Cooke* was the British-born host of public television's *Masterpiece Theater*.
2. *Elliot Richardson* was born in Boston. During the 1970s, he held four Cabinet offices (more than any other person) and served as ambassador to Great Britain. However, he did NOT hold these positions all at the same time, he was NEVER the vice president, and he did NOT serve on the Supreme Court.

Vocabulary
enlightening (en līt′ ən ing) *adj.* giving or revealing knowledge or wisdom

Responding to Literature

Personal Response

What is your opinion of Barry's comic perspective? Respond in your journal.

Analyzing Literature

Recall and Interpret

1. According to Dave Barry, why is good grammar important to know and use? Who do you think he is poking fun at with his explanation?
2. What does Barry say was the purpose of the Grammar Commission? Why did it come into existence? What did it leave behind? According to Barry, what is ironic about the formation of the Commission?
3. How did the colonists, according to Barry, show their defiance of British dominance? Why does Barry think that we Americans owe the original colonists our gratitude?
4. Explain Grammar Rules 1 and 2. What does Barry make fun of in Rule 1? What is **ironic** about Barry's explanation of Rule 2? (See page R6.)
5. Explain Barry's trick for speaking American English impressively. What point do you think he is trying to make here?

Evaluate and Connect

6. **Theme Connections** The purpose of **satire** usually is to amuse readers by exposing the follies of people or societies. Evaluate the use of **satire** in this selection. (See Literary Terms Handbook, page R11.)
7. How do your thoughts about grammar in the Reading Focus on page 1038 compare with Barry's? Cite examples from the selection.
8. What can you infer about Barry's knowledge of grammar? In your opinion, would he be a good grammar teacher? Explain.

Literary ELEMENTS

Allusion

An **allusion** is a reference in a work to a person or event outside the work. When readers recognize the reference, they make a connection between it and a point the writer is making. For example, when Barry says, "Without good grammar, the United States would have lost World War II," he is making an allusion to a historic event. Readers should recognize the absurdity in suggesting that grammar affected the outcome of World War II.

1. What allusion does Barry make about the spelling of Chaucer's name? What effect does this allusion have?
2. Find three other allusions in the selection. Explain them.

- See **Literary Terms Handbook,** p. R1.

Extending Your Response

Literature Groups

Grammar Teacher In several of Barry's "corrected" versions of grammar mistakes, he includes other grammar errors. Working with your group, correct as many errors as you can find. Then discuss the following questions: Why, do you suppose, does Barry include these errors? What do they add to the essay? Do you think he intends for his readers to detect these errors? Share the results of your discussion with your classmates.

Learning for Life

What Do You Think of This? In a 1995 interview, Dave Barry said that many of his ideas come from readers. "They are my reporters and they are quite good at it," he said. "They have an eye for the weird." In a letter to Dave Barry, suggest a topic for a future column. Explain why you think the topic suits his style and sense of humor.

Save your work for your portfolio.

COMPARING selections

from *An American Childhood* | What Is and Ain't Grammatical

COMPARE THEMES

In both *An American Childhood* and "What Is and Ain't Grammatical," the authors focus on the same subject: how we use language. Discuss these questions:

1. How are Mother's and Barry's attitudes toward language similar? How are they different?
2. How are Dillard's and Barry's messages about the use of language similar? Support your response with evidence from the selections.

COMPARE APPROACHES

Suppose that you are the talk show host for a television program featuring Mother and Barry as guests.

- Working in a group of three, prepare interview questions and responses that will allow Barry and Mother to express their views on the delights and absurdities of language. Be sure that Mother's and Barry's attitudes and ideas come across in the interview.
- Practice your interview and then present it to the class.

COMPARE TECHNIQUES

Dillard and Barry use a variety of techniques to achieve humor, including irony, satire, hyperbole (exaggeration), and allusion.

- Find examples in the two selections of each humor technique used by the authors. Record the examples in a chart like the one shown, and decide whether one author's use of a technique is more effective than the other author's.
- Share your chart and ideas with a small group of classmates.

Technique	Dillard example	Barry example
irony		
satire		
hyperbole		
allusion		

Before You Read

The Car We Had to Push

Reading Focus

What misadventures or silly situations have occurred in your family or a friend's family?

Journal In your journal, briefly write about a humorous episode or event that you have heard about or experienced.

Setting a Purpose Read to enjoy the humorous misadventures of one family.

Building Background

Thurber House

The Time and Place

James Thurber wrote *My Life and Hard Times,* the collection containing "The Car We Had to Push," in the middle of the Great Depression, although he never mentions economic conditions. The story takes place in his hometown, Columbus, Ohio.

Did You Know?

The critic Charles Holmes says Thurber's *My Life and Hard Times* "is obviously a special kind of autobiography, existing somewhere between the world of fact and the world of fantasy." Many of the characters and events in the book are based on the actual world of Thurber's boyhood. But, says Holmes, by weaving "a cross-pattern of absurd and fanciful details" into that world, Thurber subtly transformed it into a strange new world, "where confusion and eccentricity are the primary ways of life."

Vocabulary Preview

repercussion (rē′ pər kush′ ən) *n.* an effect or result of some action or event; p. 1045

unkempt (un kempt′) *adj.* in a neglected state; not combed or groomed; untidy; p. 1045

exhortation (eg′ zôr tā′ shən) *n.* a strong appeal or warning; p. 1045

contend (kən tənd′) *v.* to declare or maintain as a fact; argue; p. 1047

resonant (rez′ ə nənt) *adj.* having a full, rich sound; p. 1049

lucid (lo͞o′ sid) *adj.* clear-headed; mentally alert; p. 1049

Meet James Thurber

"I write humor the way a surgeon operates," explained James Thurber, "because it is a livelihood . . . and because I have the hope it may do some good." Thurber began his writing career in the 1920s, working as a newspaper columnist and reporter. Joining the staff of the *New Yorker* magazine in 1927, he soon began producing the humorous stories and essays that made his reputation. Despite blindness in one of his eyes, Thurber often filled notepads with cartoons. When E. B. White submitted them to the *New Yorker,* they were promptly accepted. Besides stories and essays, Thurber wrote a history of the *New Yorker.*

James Thurber was born in 1894 and died in 1961.

The Car We Had to Push

James Thurber

It took sometimes as many as five or six. James Thurber. Illustration from *My Life and Hard Times,* 1933.

MANY AUTOBIOGRAPHERS, among them Lincoln Steffens and Gertrude Atherton,[1] describe earthquakes their families have been in. I am unable to do this because my family was never in an earthquake, but we went through a number of things in Columbus that were a great deal like earthquakes. I remember in particular some of the repercussions of an old Reo we had that wouldn't go unless you pushed it for quite a way and suddenly let your clutch out. Once, we had been able to start the engine easily by cranking it, but we had had the car for so many years that finally it wouldn't go unless you pushed it and let your clutch out. Of course, it took more than one person to do this; it took sometimes as many as five or six, depending on the grade of the roadway and conditions underfoot. The car was unusual in that the clutch and brake were on the same pedal, making it quite easy to stall the engine after it got started, so that the car would have to be pushed again.

My father used to get sick at his stomach pushing the car, and very often was unable to go to work. He had never liked the machine, even when it was good, sharing my ignorance and suspicion of all automobiles of twenty years ago and longer. The boys I went to school with used to be able to identify every car as it passed by: Thomas Flyer, Firestone-Columbus, Stevens Duryea, Rambler, Winton, White Steamer, etc. I never could. The only car I was really interested in was one that the Get-Ready Man, as we called him, rode around town in: a big Red Devil with a door in the back. The Get-Ready Man was a lank unkempt elderly gentleman with wild eyes and a deep voice who used to go about shouting at people through a megaphone to prepare for the end of the world. "GET READY! GET READ-Y!" he would bellow. "THE WORLLLD IS COMING TO AN END!" His startling exhortations would come up, like summer

1. Besides their autobiographies, *Steffens* wrote nonfiction books and articles; *Atherton* wrote novels. Their major works were published between 1898 and 1936.

Vocabulary

repercussion (rē′ pər kush′ ən) *n.* an effect or result of some action or event

unkempt (un kempt′) *adj.* in a neglected state; not combed or groomed; untidy

exhortation (eg′ zôr tā′ shən) *n.* a strong appeal or warning thunder, at the most unexpected times and in the most surprising places. I remember once during Mantell's production of "King Lear" at the Colonial Theatre, that the Get-Ready Man added his bawlings to the squealing of Edgar and the ranting of the King and the mouthing of the Fool, rising from somewhere in the balcony to join in. The theatre was in absolute darkness and there were rumblings of thunder and flashes of lightning offstage. Neither father nor I, who were there, ever completely got over the scene, which went something like this:

EDGAR: Tom's a-cold.—O, do de, do de, do de!—Bless thee from whirlwinds, star-blasting, and taking . . . the foul fiend vexes!

[*Thunder off.*]

LEAR: What! Have his daughters brought him to this pass?—

GET-READY MAN: Get ready! Get ready!

EDGAR: Pillicock sat on Pillicock-hill:—
Halloo, halloo, loo, loo!

[*Lightning flashes.*]

GET-READY MAN: The Worllld is com-ing to an End!

FOOL: This cold night will turn us all to fools and madmen!

EDGAR: Take heed o' the foul fiend: obey thy paren—

GET-READY MAN: Get *Rea*-dy!

EDGAR: Tom's a-*cold!*

GET-READY MAN: The *Worr*-uld is coming to an end! . . .

They found him finally, and ejected him, still shouting. The Theatre, in our time, has known few such moments.

But to get back to the automobile. One of my happiest memories of it was when, in its eighth year, my brother Roy got together a great many articles from the kitchen, placed them in a square of canvas, and swung this under the car with a string attached to it so that, at a twitch, the canvas would give way and the steel and tin things would clatter to the street. This was a little scheme of Roy's to frighten father, who had always expected the car might explode. It worked perfectly. That was twenty-five years ago, but it is one of the few things in my life I would like to

The Get-Ready Man. James Thurber. Illustration from *My Life and Hard Times,* 1933.

live over again if I could. I don't suppose that I can, now. Roy twitched the string in the middle of a lovely afternoon, on Bryden Road, near Eighteenth Street. Father had closed his eyes and, with his hat off, was enjoying a cool breeze. The clatter on the asphalt was tremendously effective: knives, forks, can-openers, pie pans, pot lids, biscuit-cutters, ladles, eggbeaters fell, beautifully together, in a lingering, clamant[2] crash. "Stop the *car!*" shouted father. "I can't," Roy said. "The engine fell out." "God Almighty!" said father, who knew what *that* meant, or knew what it sounded as if it might mean.

It ended unhappily, of course, because we finally had to drive back and pick up the stuff and even father knew the difference between the works of an automobile and the equipment of a pantry. My mother wouldn't have known, however, nor *her* mother. My mother, for instance, thought—or, rather, knew—that it was dangerous to drive an automobile without gasoline: it fried the valves, or something. "Now don't you dare drive all over town without gasoline!" she would say to us when we started off. Gasoline, oil, and water were much the same to her, a fact that made her life both confusing and perilous. Her greatest dread, however, was the Victrola—we had a very early one, back in the "Come Josephine in My Flying Machine" days. She had an idea that the Victrola might blow up. It alarmed her, rather than reassured her, to explain that the phonograph was run neither by gasoline nor by electricity. She could only suppose that it was propelled by some newfangled and untested apparatus which was likely to let go at any minute, making us all the victims and martyrs of the wild-eyed Edison's dangerous experiments.[3] The telephone she was comparatively at peace with, except, of course, during storms, when for some reason or other she always took the receiver off the hook and let it hang. She came naturally by her confused and groundless fears, for her own mother lived the latter years of her life in the horrible suspicion that electricity was dripping invisibly all over the house. It leaked, she contended, out of empty sockets if the wall switch had been left on. She would go around screwing in bulbs, and if they lighted up she would hastily and fearfully turn off the wall switch and go back to her *Pearson's* or *Everybody's*,[4] happy in the satisfaction that she had stopped not only a costly but a dangerous leakage. Nothing could ever clear this up for her.

Did You Know?
Victrola is the trademark name of a record player; early models were hand-cranked, just as wind-up toys are. Electric phonographs were first produced in the 1920s.

Our poor old Reo came to a horrible end, finally. We had parked it too far from the curb on a street with a car line. It was late at night and the street was dark. The first streetcar[5] that came along couldn't get by. It picked up the tired old automobile as a terrier might seize a rabbit and drubbed it

2. Anything *clamant* (klā′ mənt) is noisy and demanding attention.

3. *Martyrs* are those who suffer or die for a cause. The *dangerous experiments* of Thomas A. *Edison* produced inventions that changed the world, including the light bulb, the first practical phonograph (1877), and important improvements to the telephone.
4. These were popular magazines of the early 1900s.
5. Since a *streetcar* runs on rails, it can't avoid things in its path.

Vocabulary
contend (kən tend′) *v.* to declare or maintain as a fact; argue

Electricity was leaking all over the house. James Thurber. Illustration from *My Life and Hard Times,* 1933.

unmercifully, losing its hold now and then but catching a new grip a second later. Tires booped and whooshed, the fenders queeled and graked, the steering wheel rose up like a spectre and disappeared in the direction of Franklin Avenue with a melancholy whistling sound, bolts and gadgets flew like sparks from a Catherine wheel.[6] It was a splendid spectacle but, of course, saddening to everybody (except the motorman of the streetcar, who was sore). I think some of us broke down and wept. It must have been the weeping that caused grandfather to take on so terribly. Time was all mixed up in his mind; automobiles and the like he never remembered having seen. He apparently gathered, from the talk and excitement and weeping, that somebody had died. Nor did he let go of this delusion. He insisted, in fact, after almost a week in which we strove mightily to divert him, that it was a sin and a shame and a disgrace on the family to put

6. A *spectre* is a ghost or ghostly vision. The *Catherine wheel* is a firework that, when lighted, spins like a pinwheel and spouts colorful sparks and flames.

the funeral off any longer. "Nobody is dead! The automobile is smashed!" shouted my father, trying for the thirtieth time to explain the situation to the old man. "Was he drunk?" demanded grandfather, sternly. "Was who drunk?" asked father. "Zenas," said grandfather. He had a name for the corpse now: it was his brother Zenas, who, as it happened, *was* dead, but not from driving an automobile while intoxicated. Zenas had died in 1866. A sensitive, rather poetical boy of twenty-one when the Civil War broke out, Zenas had gone to South America—"just," as he wrote back, "until it blows over." Returning after the war had blown over, he caught the same disease that was killing off the chestnut trees in those years, and passed away. It was the only case in history where a tree doctor had to be called in to spray a person, and our family had felt it very keenly; nobody else in the United States caught the blight. Some of us have looked upon Zenas' fate as a kind of poetic justice.

Now that grandfather knew, so to speak, who was dead, it became increasingly awkward to go on living in the same house with him as if nothing had happened. He would go into towering rages in which he threatened to write to the Board of Health unless the funeral were held at once. We realized that something had to be done. Eventually, we persuaded a friend of father's, named George Martin, to dress up in the manner and costume of the eighteen-sixties and pretend to be Uncle Zenas, in order to set grandfather's mind at rest. The impostor looked fine and impressive in side-burns and a high beaver hat, and not unlike the daguerreotypes of Zenas in our album. I shall never forget the night, just after dinner, when this Zenas walked into the living room. Grandfather was stomping up and down, tall, hawk-nosed, round-oathed. The newcomer held out both his hands. "Clem!" he cried to grandfather. Grandfather turned slowly, looked at the intruder, and snorted. "Who air *you*?" he demanded in his deep, resonant voice. "I'm Zenas!" cried Martin. "Your brother Zenas, fit as a fiddle and sound as a dollar!" "Zenas, my foot!" said grandfather. "Zenas died of the chestnut blight in '66!"

Did You Know?
Daguerreotypes (də ger′ ə tīps′) are photographs made by exposing light to silver-coated copper plates; Louis Daguerre invented the process in France in the mid-1800s.

Grandfather was given to these sudden, unexpected, and extremely lucid moments; they were generally more embarrassing than his other moments. He comprehended before he went to bed that night that the old automobile had been destroyed and that its destruction had caused all the turmoil in the house. "It flew all to pieces, Pa," my mother told him, in graphically describing the accident. "I knew 'twould," growled grandfather. "I allus told ye to git a Pope-Toledo."

Vocabulary
resonant (rez′ ə nənt) *adj.* having a full, rich sound
lucid (lo͞o′ sid) *adj.* clear-headed; mentally alert

Responding to Literature

Personal Response

Which event or character in the story did you find funniest? Share your reactions with a classmate.

Analyzing Literature

Recall

1. Who is the narrator, and what is his relationship to the story?
2. Who owned the car? Why did it have to be pushed?
3. What did the narrator's mother fear about the car? What other inventions did she fear? Why?
4. What eventually happened to the car?
5. Who was Zenas? How is Grandfather confused about him? How is Grandfather's confusion finally settled?

Intrepret

6. Describe the narrator's **tone,** or attitude, toward the people and events he describes. Support your answer with details from the selection.
7. What is the narrator's "happiest" memory of the car? What does considering this happy memory reveal about his personality?
8. What can you infer about the mother, based on her fears?
9. How does the car's end relate to the overall **mood,** or atmosphere, of the story? Explain. (See Literary Terms Handbook, page R8.)
10. Why might Grandfather's lucid moments be "more embarrassing than his other moments"? Explain.

Evaluate and Connect

11. Why, do you think, does Thurber include the Get-Ready Man in the story? What effect does this part of the story create?
12. Do you think the title accurately tells what the story is about? Why or why not? If you were to give the story another title, what would you choose? Support your choice with evidence from the story.
13. Think about your response to the Reading Focus on page 1044. In what ways are the events in this story similar to the ones you described?
14. Why were people during the narrator's childhood suspicious of "new-fangled" machines like cars, telephones, and electric appliances? Were any of their fears justified? Do similar attitudes exist today? Explain.
15. What qualities in this story do you think helped lead to Thurber's enormous popular success during his lifetime? Cite examples from the story to support your opinion.

Literary ELEMENTS

Characterization

A writer reveals the personality of a character through **direct** and **indirect** methods of **characterization.** In direct characterization, the writer makes statements directly describing a character's traits, words, or actions. Thurber uses direct characterization when he writes, "The Get-Ready Man was a lank unkempt elderly gentleman with wild eyes and a deep voice." In indirect characterization, the writer reveals aspects of a character through his or her words and actions, as well as through what other characters say and think about the character. Indirect characterization requires readers to interpret details or events. Thurber uses indirect characterization when he has Grandfather suddenly confirm, "Zenas, my foot! Zenas died of the chestnut blight in '66!"

1. Find another example of indirect characterization in the story. What does it show about the character?
2. Give an example of direct characterization that describes the narrator. What does it reveal about him?
3. Why, do you think, does Thurber use both methods of characterization? What effects does he create by doing so?

- See **Literary Terms Handbook,** p. R2.

Literature and Writing

Writing About Literature

Analyzing Humor How does Thurber use the car as the "vehicle" for holding the story together? In two or three paragraphs, explain how Thurber uses anecdotes about the car to present details about characters and events and, most of all, to make his readers laugh.

Personal Writing

Funny Characters Which **character** in Thurber's story do you find most believable? Which is the most humorous? Which contributes the most to the story? In your journal, describe the qualities of your favorite characters and tell why you think those characters are important to the story.

Extending Your Response

Literature Groups

Defining Humor What, in your opinion, makes writing funny? Is it what the characters say or how they view things? Is it the events that occur or how they affect the characters? Discuss these questions with your group. Then refer to the story, and analyze specific elements that contribute to the story's humor. List your findings, and share them with other groups.

Listening and Speaking

Newscast Choose a passage or anecdote from the story, and prepare it as a news story that might be broadcast on radio or television. Rehearse your news presentation and present it, in an appropriate reporting style, for the class.

Learning for Life

Accident Report Prepare a written report describing the details of the accident between the parked car and the passing streetcar. Include a diagram showing the locations of the vehicles involved and the likely resting place of the car parts. Also record facts that the streetcar driver might have conveyed to you when describing the incident.

Reading Further

You might enjoy these works by James Thurber:

Short Stories: In "The Letters of James Thurber" and "Here Lies Miss Groby" from *My World—and Welcome to It,* Thurber takes a humorous look at his writing and his way of thinking.

"An Outline of the Byrd Report," from *People Have More Fun Than Anybody,* humorously points out that the "value" of ice and land in Antarctica takes on different meanings in the scientific community and in the U.S. Senate.

Save your work for your portfolio.

VOCABULARY • The Latin Root *ject*

The word *eject* comes from the Latin prefix *e-*, meaning "out", and the root *ject,* meaning "to throw." Many English words contain the *ject* root. When pilots *eject* from an airplane, they are thrown out of it.

If you *reject* an offer, you throw it back. When people are *subjected* to cruel treatment, they are thrown under it.

The following prefixes can be attached to *ject*:
inter-: between *tra-*: across *pro-*: forward

PRACTICE Use the meanings of *ject* and the prefixes given to answer the questions.

1. What kind of device uses a *projectile*—a slingshot, a pulley, or a jackhammer?
2. Which object has a *trajectory*—a fence, a tower, or a fly ball?
3. When would a joke be *interjected* into a speech—at the beginning, in the middle, or at the end of it?

Reading & Thinking Skills

Synthesizing

If you rearrange the furniture in your bedroom so that you can look at each piece from a different angle and in a different position, you have not only created something new, but you may have improved the way in which the room works for you. You may see it as a more beautiful or interesting place.

When you combine the things you know to create something new, you are **synthesizing.** Synthesizing is an important thinking skill, because when you synthesize, you rearrange the understandings you have, making them richer and more complete.

Any time you look for patterns or connections within a story and put them together in a new way, you are synthesizing. Once you've done the work of reading a story and understanding it, you can enrich your understanding through a variety of thinking skills that broaden and deepen your enjoyment of an author's work.

In "The Car We Had to Push," for example, the narrator begins by stating that his family never encountered an earthquake, but "went through a number of things in Columbus that were a great deal like earthquakes." He goes on to tell many anecdotes about his family and how technological changes shook the family in much the same way an earthquake shakes people's lives. Once you understand the pattern of how these events are related, you can envision how the family's fear and confusion about new technology might bring about other humorous escapades. Your understanding of the story allows you to envision ways to extend and enrich what you know.

- For more about related comprehension strategies, see **Reading Handbook,** pp. R82–R89.

ACTIVITIES

1. Think about your understanding of the narrator's mother and the way she responds to different machines, ranging from the Reo to the Victrola and the telephone. Now pretend that she is your mother and that you have to explain to her how to leave a message on someone's telephone answering machine. With a partner, create a humorous dialogue between you and "Mom." Decide how the conversation will play out before you begin and think back to how Thurber creates humor in the interactions of his characters. When your dialogue is finished, perform it for the rest of the class.
2. The narrator's grandfather is a particularly humorous character in Thurber's story because, while he is generally confused, he also has moments when his understanding of events is clear and precise. And because the family never knows when those moments will come, they can never be sure of his responses in any given situation. With this in mind, and from the point of view of the narrator or another character in the story, write a humorous anecdote about taking grandfather to run an errand.

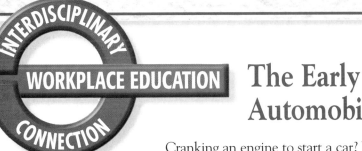

The Early Automobile

Cranking an engine to start a car? Pushing a car to get it moving? Exploding cars? After reading "The Car We Had to Push," you may wonder if the early cars were as crotchety as James Thurber makes them sound. The answer is both yes and no. At the time of Thurber's story, the automobile was still young and experiencing growing pains.

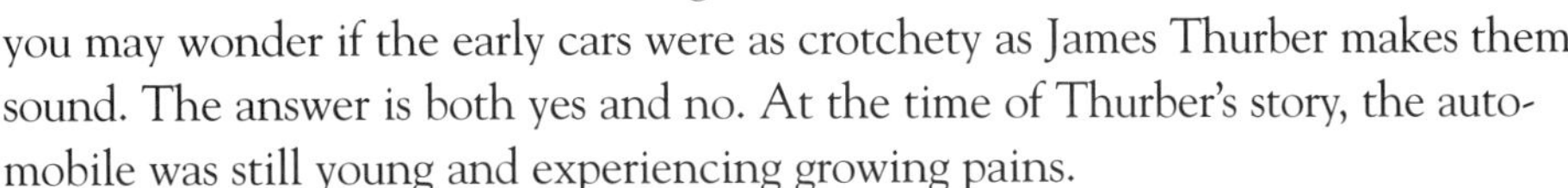

In his fear of an exploding car, Thurber's father may have been remembering the early steam cars of the 1800s, which did sometimes blow up. By the early 1900s, however, most cars had internal combustion engines fueled by gasoline. Although these cars did not typically explode, they did have their problems. Most had to be started manually with a crank that the motorist inserted into the front of the engine and turned until the engine started. Hand-cranking took time and muscle—and it was potentially dangerous. The hand-crank was replaced when the Cadillac engineering team developed an electric self-starter with a storage battery and generator. Batteries and generators led to additions such as electric headlights.

Keeping cars going was another problem. Places to buy gasoline were scarce. The wise motorist brought along an extra can of gasoline—and a ruler to measure the amount of gasoline in the tank.

Motorists also faced the probability of tire blowouts. Rubber patches and a hand pump helped, but early automobiles frequently had to be towed by a team of horses. Because of these problems, early motorists became the object of jokes, like this one from a 1904 issue of *Life* magazine:

"Yes, I enjoy my automobile immensely."

"But I never see you out."

"Oh, I haven't got that far yet. I am just learning to make my own repairs."

Within a Century: The 1906 Reo and a 1996 Automobile

Thurber's car, the Reo, got its name from the initials of Ransom Eli Olds, who designed the first Oldsmobile and later founded the Reo Motor Car Company. The Reo was one of the most popular cars of its time. This chart compares the Reo with a typical car of the 1990s.

Automobile	1906 Reo Model M	Typical 1996 Automobile
Cylinders	2	6
Horsepower	16	160
Top speed	25 miles per hour	over 100 miles per hour
Price	$2,000	about $19,000

Activity

Find a magazine advertisement for your favorite model of a modern car. Then investigate an early model car, such as the Oldsmobile Runabout, the Winton, the Locomobile, or the Model T. Create a magazine advertisement for the early model car, highlighting its features and price. Display both advertisements on a poster. Point out the similarities and the differences in features and price of the two models.

Before You Read

How I Changed the War and Won the Game

Reading Focus

Have you ever been in a situation where you could tell someone anything and he or she would believe it?

Journal In your journal, tell about a person you've had influence over. Explain why you had such influence, how you used it, and how it made you feel.

Setting a Purpose Read this autobiographical sketch to learn how someone uses her influence over others.

Building Background

The Time and Place

This story recalls events that occurred in a suburban neighborhood in California during World War II.

Did You Know?

World War II officially began in 1939, when Germany, Italy, and Japan joined together to form the Axis powers in an aggressive campaign to conquer large areas of the world. While Japan took over Southeast Asia, the Philippines, and other Pacific Islands, Germany swept through Europe, occupying Poland, Norway, Denmark, and France and moving on to North Africa. After Japan bombed the U.S. naval base at Pearl Harbor in 1941, the United States entered the war, joining Britain and Russia to form the Allied powers. As the war waged abroad, Americans at home feared a Japanese invasion on the West Coast.

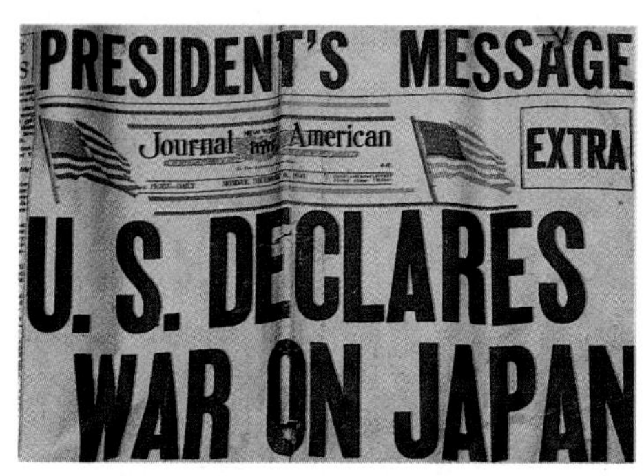
PRESIDENT'S MESSAGE

Journal American

EXTRA

U. S. DECLARES WAR ON JAPAN

Vocabulary Preview

coerce (kō urs′) *v.* to pressure or push into doing something, as by force or authority; p. 1055

pilgrimage (pil′ grə mij) *n.* a long journey, especially to a holy place or for a religious purpose; p. 1055

whim (hwim) *n.* a sudden notion or fanciful idea; p. 1056

Meet Mary Helen Ponce

Chicana writer Mary Helen Ponce grew up in the 1940s in Pacoima, a working-class Mexican American community outside of Los Angeles, California. Ponce remembers having a happy childhood, playing kickball with friends and writing and reading a lot: "I first began writing in grammar school. . . . I have read from 3–5 books every week for most of my life. . . . I think I wanted to be a writer at an early age but had no one to emulate." Ponce wrote *Hoyt Street: Memories of a Chicana Childhood* "to show the beauty, richness, and diversity of Mexican American/Chicano culture."

Mary Helen Ponce was born in 1938.

How I Changed the War and Won the Game

Mary Helen Ponce

DURING WORLD WAR II I used to translate the English newspaper's war news for our adopted grandmother Doña[1] Luisa and her friends. All were elderly ladies, señoras de edad,[2] who could not read English, only their native Spanish. Every afternoon they would gather on Doña Luisa's front porch to await Doña Trinidad's son who delivered the paper to her promptly at five o'clock. There, among the geraniums and pots of yerbabuena[3] I would bring to them the news of the war.

At first I enjoyed this as the señoras welcomed me as a grown-up. They would push their chairs in a semi-circle; the better to hear me. I sat in the middle on a banquito[4] that was once a milk crate. I don't remember how I began to be their translator but because I was an obedient child, and at eight a good reader, I was somehow coerced or selected.

I would sit down, adjust my dress, then slowly unwrap the paper, reading the headlines to myself in English, trying to decide which news stories were the most important, which to tell first. Then I would translate these into my best Spanish for Doña Luisa and her friends. The news of a battle would bring sighs of "Jesús, María, y José" from the ladies. They would roll their eyes towards heaven as they implored the Lord to protect their loved ones from danger. In return they vowed to light candles or make a *manda,*[5] a pilgrimage, to la Virgen de San Juan in the nearby town of Sunland.[6] Once I had read the highlights of the war I was allowed to go play with my friends.

1. In Spanish cultures, *Doña* (dōn′ yə) is a form of respectful address for a married woman, like the English "Madam."
2. *señoras de edad* (sen yôr′ əs dā ā′ däd)
3. Literally "good herb," *yerbabuena* (yer′ bə bwā′ nə) is in the mint family.
4. A *banquito* (bän kē′ tō) is a little bench.
5. *manda* (män′ də)
6. *La Virgen de* (lä ver′ hen dā) *San Juan* is a name for Mary, the mother of Jesus. In many locations throughout the centuries, Mary has reportedly appeared in visions to groups and individuals. Apparently, a shrine honoring one of these visions had been built in *Sunland* (which is now part of Los Angeles).

Vocabulary

coerce (kō urs′) *v.* to pressure or push into doing something, as by force or authority

pilgrimage (pil′ grə mij) *n.* a long journey, especially to a holy place or for a religious purpose

Sandia/Watermelon. Carmen Lomas Garza. Gouache on Arches paper, 20 x 28 in. Collection of Dudley D. Brooks and Tomas Ybarra-Frausto, New York.

Viewing the art: In what ways might this family reflect the narrator's family?

One day we had an important ballgame going. Our team was losing, it was my turn at bat. Just then Doña Luisa called me. It was time for las noticias![7] Furious at this interruption, yet not daring to disobey, I dropped the bat, ran to the porch, ripped open the paper, pointed to the headlines, and in a loud voice proclaimed: "Ya están los japoneses en San Francisco, . . . los esperan en Los Angeles muy pronto." The Japanese have landed in San Francisco, and should soon be in Los Angeles.

"Jesús María y José, la Sangre de Cristo, Ave María Purísima," chanted the ladies as I dashed off to resume my game. "Dios mío, ya vámonos, vamos a la iglesia a rezarle al Señor,"[8] they cried as chairs were pushed aside.

After this I was able to translate according to whim, . . . and depending on whether or not I was up to bat when the paper came.

7. *Las noticias* (läs nō′ ti sē′ əs) is the news.

8. The ladies' chant is "Jesus, Mary, and Joseph, Blood of Christ, Hail Mary, the Holy Virgin," followed by "My God, let's go, let's go to the church to pray to the Lord."

Vocabulary

whim (hwim) *n.* a sudden notion or fanciful idea

Responding to Literature

Personal Response

Do you approve of what the narrator did? Why or why not? Discuss your reaction with a classmate.

Analyzing Literature

Recall

1. What daily job did the narrator perform for her adopted grandmother and the other old women in her neighborhood?
2. At first, how did the narrator feel about her job?
3. How did the women usually react to the things they heard?
4. What was the wrong information that the narrator gave the women? Why did she give that information?
5. What happened after the narrator misled the women? How did the misinformation affect the narrator?

Interpret

6. Explain why, considering the **setting** of this piece, the narrator's job was so important to the women. (See Literary Terms Handbook, page R11.)
7. How did the narrator's attitude about her job change? Why did it change?
8. What do the women's daily reactions reveal about their lives and concerns?
9. Why, do you suppose, don't the women immediately know that they have been tricked?
10. How did the narrator react after misleading the women? What was her attitude? Cite evidence to support your answer.

Evaluate and Connect

11. Think about your response to the Reading Focus on page 1054. How does the situation described by the narrator compare with your situation?
12. What does the story reveal about the narrator's personality? What traits do you think she possesses?
13. If you had been in the narrator's situation, do you think you would have done the same thing? Why or why not?
14. Were you surprised that the narrator got away with doing her job "according to whim"? Why or why not?
15. Does what happened in this story seem true to life? Why or why not?

Diction

Diction is the choice of words in a piece of writing. Writers use different types of diction to establish setting, convey meaning, and create different tones, moods, and images. In "How I Changed the War and Won the Game," Ponce uses a mixture of English and Spanish words and expressions to convey the Mexican American culture of her childhood. Through her diction, Ponce brings authenticity and humor to her setting and characters.

1. Give an example from the story in which diction helps convey character and explain its effect.
2. Find three or four examples of direct or everyday language in the story.
3. What does the direct and mostly everyday language add to the story?

- See **Literary Terms Handbook,** p. R3.

Literature and Writing

Writing About Literature

Character Sketch What information about the author's childhood can you infer from this autobiographical sketch? On the basis of what you've learned from the story, write a brief character sketch of the author as a child. Consider what is directly revealed about her and what is implied. Compare your character sketch with those of other students.

Personal Writing

No Laughing Matter Sometimes the jokes we play on others don't have innocent or humorous results. Have you ever played a joke or misled someone in a way that wasn't funny? Do you know someone who has? Briefly write about an instance of a prank's negative consequences. If you wish, share your piece with the class.

Extending Your Response

Literature Groups

Autobiography How does this short piece of writing reveal so much information about the narrator and her world? Working with your group, analyze what makes this an example of good autobiographical writing. List the techniques that Ponce uses to convey information in so few words. Share your analysis with other groups.

Learning for Life

Remembering WWII Interview older relatives and/or friends who remember World War II. Find out how the war affected their lives. Ask them what it was like when the Japanese bombed Pearl Harbor and when the United States dropped atomic bombs on Japan.

Internet Connection

More About the War Do some on-line research about World War II, particularly what it was like for Americans at home. For example, how did people on the West Coast prepare for a possible Japanese invasion?

Reading Further

You might enjoy these works by Mary Helen Ponce:

Autobiography: "Doña Luisa," from *Hoyt Street: Memories of a Chicana Childhood,* relates Ponce's memories of her "adopted grandmother."

Short Story: "The Permanent," from *Taking Control,* shows how a woman changes her ways after recognizing her own prejudices.

Save your work for your portfolio.

VOCABULARY • Analogies

An analogy is a type of comparison that is based on the relationships between things or ideas. A relationship is reflected in the first pair of words. Figure out what that relationship is and then find another pair of words that reflects the same relationship. Express the relationship in reasonably clear terms.

For more about analogies, see **Communications Skills Handbook,** p. R77.

PRACTICE Choose the word pair that best completes each analogy.

1. urge : coerce ::
   a. coax : resist
   b. promise : intend
   c. attempt : succeed
   d. nudge : shove
   e. flatter : compliment

2. pilgrimage : journey ::
   a. voyage : tour
   b. sermon : speech
   c. glance : inspection
   d. inning : game
   e. discovery : invention

Vo•cab•u•lar•y Skills

Analyzing Words

There are many kinds of clues that can be used to determine the meaning of an unfamiliar word. Some, called "context clues," occur outside the word itself, in the sentence or paragraph the word appears in. There may also be internal clues to a word's meaning–a familiar prefix, base word, root, or suffix. Neither context clues nor internal clues, when they exist, will always be enough to provide the precise meaning of a word, but they can help.

The sentence "She falsified the news report she gave her aunts" provides no context clues for the meaning of *falsified.* The word itself, however, provides all the clues you need. Most important, the base word *false* is familiar. In addition, the suffix *-fy,* meaning "to make," is familiar from such words as *purify.* Clearly, the girl "made the news report false."

Even if a word does not have a base word that you know, it may contain one or more word parts that are familiar from other words. For example, look at *perturbed* in the sentence "Her aunts were perturbed by the news." If you think about *disturb* and *turbulence,* you should realize that being *perturbed* has something to do with being upset.

Although analyzing an unfamiliar word is not a substitute for looking it up in a dictionary, there are two reasons to try to do it. First, you may get a good idea of what the word means. Second, when you break a word into pieces and put it back together, you notice its parts, and that can help you remember its meaning.

● For more about using context clues, see **Reading Handbook,** p. R78.

EXERCISE

Analyze the underlined words on the left, using whatever clues they contain that help you. Try to match each one to its meaning on the right.

1. a <u>biped</u> animal
2. an <u>inimitable</u> style
3. the <u>malodorous</u> room
4. his rapid <u>ascendancy</u>
5. a <u>contradictious</u> person
6. a <u>contributory</u> factor
7. a <u>thermal</u> spring
8. the parts' <u>adhesion</u>
9. her <u>demented</u> state
10. his <u>exhibitionism</u>

a. hot
b. rise
c. insane
d. helpful
e. bad-smelling
f. argumentative
g. two-footed
h. tendency to show off
i. cannot be copied
j. ability to stick together

Writing Skills

Using Effective Language

Whether you want your readers to laugh, cry, or think, the best way to capture and hold their attention is to use effective language. For many writers, using effective language means using words that are definite, specific, and concrete instead of words that are general, vague, and abstract. The following table shows some examples of noneffective and effective language.

Noneffective		Effective	
General:	*period of time*	Specific:	*one week*
Vague:	*monetary reward*	Definite:	*hundred dollar bonus*
Abstract:	*discomfort*	Concrete:	*sharp pain*

Notice how Mary Helen Ponce uses effective language to create a vivid, interesting scene in this excerpt from "How I Changed the War and Won the Game."

> **"All were elderly ladies, *señoras de edad,* who could not read English, only their native Spanish. Every afternoon they would gather on Doña Luisa's front porch to await Doña Trinidad's son who delivered the paper to her promptly at five o'clock. There, among the geraniums and pots of yerbabuena I would bring to them the news of the war."**

Ponce's words draw readers in by creating a compelling impression of her childhood experience. She discusses specific people—*elderly ladies, Doña Luisa, Doña Trinidad*—rather than a general group, and she describes precisely what languages these ladies can and can't read. She uses definite words, such as *everyday* and *promptly at five o'clock* instead of vague words, such as *regularly.* In addition, Ponce uses concrete details, such as *the geraniums and pots of yerbabuena,* to help make the setting seem real.

Make your own writing more effective by replacing vague and abstract words and phrases with more specific and vivid ones. Keep your writing clear and direct.

EXERCISE

Rewrite the following passage, using your imagination to replace general, vague, and abstract language with more specific, concrete, and definite words.

> Some people from the club would go together to the regular home game. They had a strong feeling for their team and used their particular skills to encourage their team's members to play well. People who wanted the opposing team to do well didn't care for the presence of this enthusiastic group.

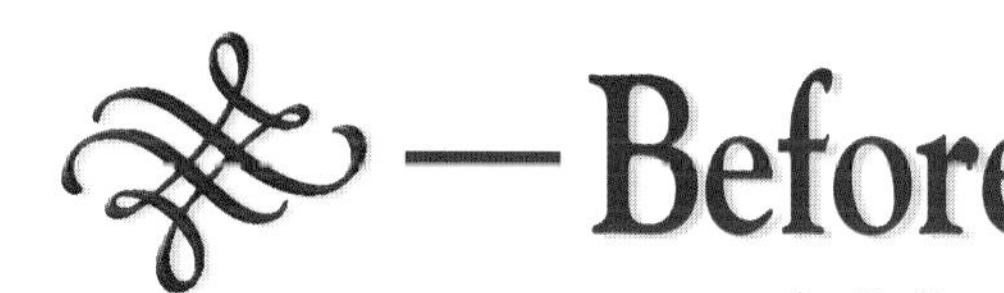

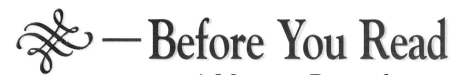

Before You Read

A Marriage Proposal

Focus Activity

Think of a time when you or someone you know had carefully prepared for a special event only to have the plans fall apart.

Journal Describe the plans and how and why they were altered. At the time, did you laugh when the plans fell apart?

Setting A Purpose Read the play *A Marriage Proposal* to see what happens when one man's plans fall apart.

Background

The Time and Place

Chekhov set this one-act play in the late 1800s in the Russian provinces, or countryside. At this time in Russia, the serfs had been freed, the Bolshevik revolution was less than twenty years away, and yet aristocratic farmers still depended on servants to do the work on their large estates.

Did You Know?

While studying medicine at the University of Moscow, Chekhov sold hundreds of articles to comic magazines to provide income for his family. He was not proud of these writings. Critics, however, see in Chekhov's early writings the revolutionary techniques that flourished in his later works. Chekhov focused on his characters' inner thoughts—how they felt about their lives and their relationships with other characters.

Vocabulary Preview

pompous (pom′ pəs) *adj.* showing an exaggerated sense of self-importance; p. 1063

affable (af′ ə bəl) *adj.* friendly, gracious, and pleasant; p. 1063

hypochondriac (hī′ pə kon′ drē ak′) *n.* one whose worry over health is so great that it brings on the imagined symptoms of an illness; p. 1063

impudence (im′ pyə dəns) *n.* speech or behavior that is aggressively forward or rude; p. 1067

oblivious (ə bliv′ ē əs) *adj.* unmindful or unaware; not noticing; p. 1072

Meet Anton Chekhov

At age sixteen, Anton Chekhov (chek′ ôf) lived alone and supported himself. His grocer father had gone bankrupt and rushed the rest of the family to Moscow to avoid debtor's prison. Three years later Chekhov joined his family to study medicine on scholarship at the University of Moscow. Although he received his medical degree, his writing was more important to him. Chekhov once said, "I try to catch every sentence, every word you and I say, and quickly lock all these sentences and words away in my literary storehouse because they might come in handy."

Anton Chekhov was born in 1860 and died in 1904. A Marriage Proposal *was first published between 1888 and 1890.*

Golden Autumn in the Village, 1889. Isaak Ilyich Levitan. Oil on canvas, 43 x 67.2 cm. State Russian Museum, St. Petersburg.

A Marriage Proposal

Anton Chekhov

Translated by Theodore Hoffman

CHARACTERS

STEPAN STEPANOVITCH CHUBUKOV (ste pän′ ste pä′ nô vich choo boo′ kôf): a landowner; elderly, pompous but affable

IVAN VASSILEVITCH LOMOV (i vän′ vä sil′ ē yich lô′ môf): a landowner and Chubukov's neighbor; healthy, but a hypochondriac; nervous, suspicious

NATALIA STEPANOVNA (nä täl′ yə ste pä nôv′ nə): Chubukov's daughter; twenty-five but still unmarried

SCENE: Chubukov's mansion—the living room

[LOMOV *enters, formally dressed in evening jacket, white gloves, top hat. He is nervous from the start.*]

Vocabulary

pompous (pom′ pəs) *adj.* showing an exaggerated sense of self-importance

affable (af′ ə bəl) *adj.* friendly, gracious, and pleasant

hypochondriac (hī′ pə kon′ drē ak′) *n.* one whose worry over his or her health is so great that it brings on the imagined symptoms of an illness

CHUBUKOV. [*Rising.*] Well, look who's here! Ivan Vassilevitch! [*Shakes his hand warmly.*] What a surprise, old man! How are you?

LOMOV. Oh, not too bad. And you?

CHUBUKOV. Oh, we manage, we manage. Do sit down, please. You know, you've been neglecting your neighbors, my dear fellow. It's been ages. Say, why the formal dress? Tails, gloves, and so forth. Where's the funeral, my boy? Where are you headed?

LOMOV. Oh, nowhere. I mean, here; just to see you, my dear Stepan Stepanovitch.

CHUBUKOV. Then why the full dress, old boy? It's not New Year's, and so forth.

LOMOV. Well, you see, it's like this. I have come here, my dear Stepan Stepanovitch, to bother you with a request. More than once, or twice, or more than that, it has been my privilege to apply to you for assistance in things, and you've always, well, responded. I mean, well, you have. Yes. Excuse me, I'm getting all mixed up. May I have a glass of water, my dear Stepan Stepanovitch? [*Drinks.*]

CHUBUKOV. [*Aside.*] Wants to borrow some money. Not a chance! [*Aloud.*] What can I do for you my dear friend?

LOMOV. Well, you see, my dear Stepanitch. . . . Excuse me, I mean Stepan my

Return from the Fair, 1883. Illarion Mikhailovich Pryanishnikov. Oil on canvas, 48.5 x 71.5 cm. State Russian Museum, St. Petersburg.

Viewing the painting: What does this painting suggest to you about rural life in Russia in the 1800s? How does this view affect your understanding of the play?

Dearovitch. . . . No, I mean, I get all confused, as you can see. To make a long story short, you're the only one who can help me. Of course, I don't deserve it, and there's no reason why I should expect you to, and all that.

CHUBUKOV. Stop beating around the bush! Out with it!

LOMOV. In just a minute. I mean, now, right now. The truth is, I have come to ask the hand. . . . I mean, your daughter, Natalia Stepanovna, I, I want to marry her!

CHUBUKOV. [*Overjoyed.*] Great heavens! Ivan Vassilevitch! Say it again!

LOMOV. I have come humbly to ask for the hand. . . .

CHUBUKOV. [*Interrupting.*] You're a prince! I'm overwhelmed, delighted, and so forth. Yes, indeed, and all that! [*Hugs and kisses* LOMOV.] This is just what I've been hoping for. It's my fondest dream come true. [*Sheds a tear.*] And, you know, I've always looked upon you, my boy, as if you were my own son. May God grant to both of you His Mercy and His Love, and so forth. Oh, I have been wishing for this. . . . But why am I being so idiotic? It's just that I'm off my rocker with joy, my boy! Completely off my rocker! Oh, with all my soul I'm. . . . I'll go get Natalia, and so forth.

LOMOV. [*Deeply moved.*] Dear Stepan Stepanovitch, do you think she'll agree?

CHUBUKOV. Why, of course, old friend. Great heavens! As if she wouldn't! Why she's crazy for you! Good God! Like a love-sick cat, and so forth. Be right back. [*Leaves.*]

LUMOV. It's cold. I'm gooseflesh all over, as if I had to take a test. But the main thing is, to make up my mind, and keep it that way. I mean, if I take time out to think, or if I hesitate, or talk about it, or have ideals, or wait for real love, well, I'll just never get married! Brrrr, it's cold! Natalia Stepanovna is an excellent housekeeper. She's not too bad looking. She's had a good education. What more could I ask? Nothing. I'm so nervous, my ears are buzzing. [*Drinks.*] Besides, I've just got to get married. I'm thirty-five already. It's sort of a critical age. I've got to settle down and lead a regular life. I mean, I'm always getting palpitations,[1] and I'm nervous, and I get upset so easy. Look, my lips are quivering, and my eyebrow's twitching. The worst thing is the night. Sleeping. I get into bed, doze off, and, suddenly, something inside me jumps. First my head snaps, and then my shoulder blade, and I roll out of bed like a lunatic and try to walk it off. Then I try to go back to sleep, but, as soon as I do, something jumps again! Twenty times a night, sometimes. . . .

[*NATALIA STEPANOVNA enters.*]

NATALIA. Oh, it's only you. All Papa said was: "Go inside, there's a merchant come to collect his goods." How do you do, Ivan Vassilevitch?

LOMOV. How do you do, dear Natalia Stepanovna?

NATALIA. Excuse my apron, and not being dressed. We're shelling peas. You haven't been around lately. Oh, do sit down. [*They do.*] Would you like some lunch?

LOMOV. No thanks, I had some.

NATALIA. Well, then smoke if you want. [*He doesn't.*] The weather's nice today . . . but yesterday, it was so wet the workmen couldn't get a thing done. Have you got much hay in? I felt so greedy I had a whole field done, but now I'm not sure I was right. With the rain it could rot, couldn't it? I should have waited. But why are you so dressed up? Is there a

1. If Lomov does, in fact, get *palpitations,* he experiences rapid, irregular heartbeats, which are often caused by stress or nervousness.

dance or something? Of course, I must say you look splendid, but. . . . Well, tell me, why are you so dressed up?

LOMOV. [*Excited.*] Well, you see, my dear Natalia Stepanovna, the truth is, I made up my mind to ask you to . . . well, to, listen to me. Of course, it'll probably surprise you and even maybe make you angry, but. . . . [*Aside.*] It's so cold in here!

NATALIA. Why, what do you mean? [*A pause.*] Well?

LOMOV. I'll try to get it over with. I mean, you know, my dear Natalia Stepanovna that I've known, since childhood, even, known, and had the privilege of knowing, your family. My late aunt, and her husband, who, as you know, left me my estate, they always had the greatest respect for your father, and your late mother. The Lomovs and the Chubukovs have always been very friendly, you might even say affectionate. And, of course, you know, our land borders on each other's. My Oxen Meadows touch your birch grove. . . .

NATALIA. I hate to interrupt you, my dear Ivan Vassilevitch, but you said: "my Oxen Meadows." Do you really think they're yours?

LOMOV. Why of course they're mine.

NATALIA. What do you mean? The Oxen Meadows are ours, not yours!

LOMOV. Oh, no, my dear Natalia Stepanovna, they're mine.

NATALIA. Well, this is the first I've heard about it! Where did you get that idea?

LOMOV. Where? Why, I mean the Oxen Meadows that are wedged between your birches and the marsh.

NATALIA. Yes, of course, they're ours.

LOMOV. Oh, no, you're wrong, my dear Natalia Stepanovna, they're mine.

NATALIA. Now, come, Ivan Vassilevitch! How long have they been yours?

LOMOV. How long! Why, as long as I can remember!

NATALIA. Well, really, you can't expect me to believe that!

LOMOV. But, you can see for yourself in the deed, my dear Natalia Stepanovna. Of course, there was once a dispute about them, but everyone knows they're mine now. There's nothing to argue about. There was a time when my aunt's grandmother let your father's grandfather's peasants use the land, but they were supposed to bake bricks for her in return. Naturally, after a few years they began to act as if they owned it, but the real truth is. . . .

NATALIA. That has nothing to do with the case! Both my grandfather and my great-grandfather said that their land went as far as the marsh, which means that the Meadows are ours! There's nothing whatever to argue about. It's foolish.

LOMOV. But I can show you the deed, Natalia Stepanovna.

NATALIA. You're just making fun of me. . . . Great Heavens! Here we have the land for hundreds of years, and suddenly you try to tell us it isn't ours. What's wrong with you, Ivan Vassilevitch? Those meadows aren't even fifteen acres, and they're not worth three hundred rubles, but I just can't stand unfairness! I just can't stand unfairness!

LOMOV. But, you must listen to me. Your father's grandfather's peasants, as I've already tried to tell you, they were supposed to bake bricks for my aunt's grandmother. And my aunt's grandmother, why, she wanted to be nice to them. . . .

NATALIA. It's just nonsense, this whole business about aunts and grandfathers and grandmothers. The Meadows are ours! That's all there is to it!

LOMOV. They're mine!

NATALIA. Ours! You can go on talking for two days, and you can put on fifteen evening coats and twenty pairs of gloves, but I tell you they're ours, ours, ours!

LOMOV. Natalia Stepanovna, I don't want the Meadows! I'm just acting on principle. If you want, I'll give them to you.

NATALIA. I'll give them to *you!* Because they're ours! And that's all there is to it! And if I may say so, your behavior, my dear Ivan Vassilevitch, is very strange. Until now, we've always considered you a good neighbor, even a friend. After all, last year we lent you our threshing machine, even though it meant putting off our own threshing until November. And here you are treating us like a pack of gypsies. Giving me my own land, indeed! Really! Why that's not being a good neighbor. It's sheer impudence, that's what it is. . . .

LOMOV. Oh, so you think I'm just a land-grabber? My dear lady, I've never grabbed anybody's land in my whole life, and no one's going to accuse me of doing it now! [*Quickly walks over to the pitcher and drinks some more water.*] The Oxen Meadows are mine!

NATALIA. That's a lie. They're ours!

LOMOV. Mine!

NATALIA. A lie! I'll prove it. I'll send my mowers out there today!

LOMOV. What?

NATALIA. My mowers will mow it today!

LOMOV. I'll kick them out!

NATALIA. You just dare!

LOMOV. [*Clutching his heart.*] The Oxen Meadows are mine! Do you understand? Mine!

NATALIA. Please don't shout! You can shout all you want in your own house, but here I must ask you to control yourself.

LOMOV. If my heart wasn't palpitating the way it is, if my insides weren't jumping like mad, I wouldn't talk to you so calmly. [*Yelling.*] The Oxen Meadows are mine!

NATALIA. Ours!

LOMOV. Mine!

NATALIA. Ours!

LOMOV. Mine!

[*Enter* CHUBUKOV.]

CHUBUKOV. What's going on? Why all the shouting?

NATALIA. Papa, will you please inform this gentleman who owns the Oxen Meadows, he or we?

CHUBUKOV. [*To* LOMOV.] Why, they're ours, old fellow.

LOMOV. But how can they be yours, my dear Stepan Stepanovitch? Be fair. Perhaps my aunt's grandmother did let your grandfather's peasants work the land, and maybe they did get so used to it that they acted as if it was their own, but. . . .

CHUBUKOV. Oh, no, no . . . my dear boy. You forget something. The reason the peasants didn't pay your aunt's grandmother, and so forth, was that the land was disputed, even then. Since then it's been settled. Why, everyone knows it's ours.

LOMOV. I can prove it's mine.

CHUBUKOV. You can't prove a thing, old boy.

LOMOV. Yes, I can!

CHUBUKOV. My dear lad, why yell like that? Yelling doesn't prove a thing. Look, I'm not

Vocabulary
impudence (im′ pyə dəns) *n.* speech or behavior that is aggressively forward or rude

after anything of yours, just as I don't intend to give up anything of mine. Why should I? Besides, if you're going to keep arguing about it, I'd just as soon give the land to the peasants, so there!

LOMOV. There nothing! Where do you get the right to give away someone else's property?

CHUBUKOV. I certainly ought to know if I have the right or not. And you had better realize it, because, my dear young man, I am not used to being spoken to in that tone of voice, and so forth. Besides which, my dear young man, I am twice as old as you are, and I ask you to speak to me without getting yourself into such a tizzy, and so forth!

LOMOV. Do you think I'm a fool? First you call my property yours, and then you expect me to keep calm and polite! Good neighbors don't act like that, my dear Stepan Stepanovitch. You're no neighbor, you're a land grabber!

CHUBUKOV. What was that? What did you say?

NATALIA. Papa, send the mowers out to the meadows at once!

CHUBUKOV. What did you say, sir?

NATALIA. The Oxen Meadows are ours, and we'll never give them up, never, never, never, never!

LOMOV. We'll see about that. I'll go to court. I'll show you!

CHUBUKOV. Go to court? Well, go to court, and so forth! I know you, just waiting for a chance to go to court, and so forth. You pettifogging[2] cheater, you! All of your family is like that. The whole bunch of them!

LOMOV. You leave my family out of this! The Lomovs have always been honorable, upstanding people, and not a one of them was ever tried for embezzlement,[3] like your grandfather was.

CHUBUKOV. The Lomovs are a pack of lunatics, the whole bunch of them!

NATALIA. The whole bunch!

CHUBUKOV. Your grandfather was a drunkard, and what about your other aunt, the one who ran away with the architect? And so forth.

NATALIA. And so forth!

LOMOV. Your mother limped! [*Clutches at his heart.*] Oh, I've got a stitch in my side. . . . My head's whirling. . . . Help! Water!

CHUBUKOV. Your father was a gambler.

NATALIA. And your aunt was queen of the scandalmongers![4]

LOMOV. My left foot's paralyzed. You're a plotter. . . . Oh, my heart. It's an open secret that in the last elections you brib. . . . I'm seeing stars! Where's my hat?

NATALIA. It's a low-mean, spiteful. . . .

CHUBUKOV. And you're a two-faced, malicious schemer!

LOMOV. Here's my hat. . . . Oh, my heart. . . . Where's the door? How do I get out of here? . . . Oh, I think I'm going to die. . . . My foot's numb. [*Goes.*]

CHUBUKOV. [*Following him.*] And don't you ever set foot in my house again!

NATALIA. Go to court, indeed! We'll see about that!

[*LOMOV staggers out.*]

CHUBUKOV. The devil with him! [*Gets a drink, walks back and forth excited.*]

NATALIA. What a rascal! How can you trust your neighbors after an incident like that?

2. A *pettifogging* person squabbles over unimportant matters or uses mean, tricky methods. Originally, the word described inferior lawyers who did these things.

3. *Embezzlement* is the act of stealing money entrusted to one's care; a bank official, for example, might embezzle funds from customers' accounts.

4. People who spread vicious gossip are *scandalmongers.*

Self-portrait in an Interior, Sokolniki, 1916–1917. Nina Simonovich-Efimova. Oil on canvas, 26 x 19⅝ in. Efimov Museum, Moscow.

Viewing the painting: How does this setting compare with your vision of the play's setting so far? Explain.

CHUBUKOV. The villain! The scarecrow!

NATALIA. He's a monster! First he tries to steal our land, and then he has the nerve to yell at you.

CHUBUKOV. Yes, and that turnip, that stupid rooster, has the gall[5] to make a proposal. Some proposal!

NATALIA. What proposal?

CHUBUKOV. Why, he came to propose to you.

NATALIA. To propose? To me? Why didn't you tell me before?

CHUBUKOV. So he gets all dressed up in his formal clothes. That stuffed sausage, that dried up cabbage!

NATALIA. To propose to me? Ohhhh! [*Falls into a chair and starts wailing.*] Bring him back! Back! Go get him! Bring him back! Ohhhh!

CHUBUKOV. Bring who back?

NATALIA. Hurry up, hurry up! I'm sick. Get him! [*Complete hysterics.*]

CHUBUKOV. What for? [*To her.*] What's the matter with you? [*Clutches his head.*] Oh, what a fool I am! I'll shoot myself! I'll hang myself! I ruined her chances!

NATALIA. I'm dying. Get him!

CHUBUKOV. All right, all right, right away! Only don't yell!

[*He runs out.*]

NATALIA. What are they doing to me? Get him! Bring him back! Bring him back!

[*A pause.* CHUBUKOV *runs in.*]

CHUBUKOV. He's coming, and so forth, the snake. Oof! You talk to him. I'm not in the mood.

NATALIA. [*Wailing.*] Bring him back! Bring him back!

CHUBUKOV. [*Yelling.*] I told you, he's coming! What agony to be the father of a grown-up daughter. I'll cut my throat some day, I swear I will. [*To her.*] We cursed him, we insulted him, abused him, kicked him out, and now . . . because you, you. . . .

NATALIA. Me? It was all your fault!

CHUBUKOV. My fault? What do you mean my fau . . . ? [LOMOV *appears in the doorway.*] Talk to him yourself! [*Goes out.* LOMOV *enters, exhausted.*]

LOMOV. What palpitations! My heart! And my foot's absolutely asleep. Something keeps giving me a stitch in the side. . . .

NATALIA. You must forgive us, Ivan Vassilevitch. We all got too excited. I remember now. The Oxen Meadows are yours.

LOMOV. My heart's beating something awful. My Meadows. My eyebrows, they're both twitching!

NATALIA. Yes, the Meadows are all yours, yes, yours. Do sit down. [*They sit.*] We were wrong, of course.

LOMOV. I argued on principle. My land isn't worth so much to me, but the principle. . . .

NATALIA. Oh, yes, of course, the principle, that's what counts. But let's change the subject.

LOMOV. Besides, I have evidence. You see, my aunt's grandmother let your father's grandfather's peasants use the land. . . .

NATALIA. Yes, yes, yes, but forget all that. [*Aside.*] I wish I knew how to get him going. [*Aloud.*] Are you going to start hunting soon?

LOMOV. After the harvest I'll try for grouse.[6] But oh, my dear Natalia Stepanovna, have you heard about the bad luck I've had? You know my dog, Guess? He's gone lame.

---

5. *Gall,* a synonym for *impudence,* means "shocking boldness; scornful disrespect."

6. A fowl-like bird, the *grouse* is often hunted for game or food.

NATALIA. What a pity. Why?

LOMOV. I don't know. He must have twisted his leg, or got in a fight, or something. [*Sighs.*] My best dog, to say nothing of the cost. I paid Mironov 125 rubles for him.

NATALIA. That was too high, Ivan Vassilevitch.

LOMOV. I think it was quite cheap. He's a first class dog.

NATALIA. Why Papa only paid 85 rubles for Squeezer, and he's much better than Guess.

LOMOV. Squeezer better than Guess! What an idea! [*Laughs.*] Squeezer better than Guess!

NATALIA. Of course he's better. He may still be too young but on points[7] and pedigree,[8] he's a better dog even than any Volchanetsky owns.

LOMOV. Excuse me, Natalia Stepanovna, but you're forgetting he's overshot, and overshot dogs are bad hunters.

NATALIA. Oh, so he's overshot, is he? Well, this is the first time I've heard about it.

LOMOV. Believe me, his lower jaw is shorter than his upper.

NATALIA. You've measured them?

LOMOV. Yes. He's all right for pointing, but if you want him to retrieve. . . .

NATALIA. In the first place, our Squeezer is a thoroughbred, the son of Harness and Chisel, while your mutt doesn't even have a pedigree. He's as old and worn out as a peddler's horse.

LOMOV. He may be old, but I wouldn't take five Squeezers for him. How can you argue? Guess is a dog, Squeezer's a laugh. Anyone you can name has a dog like Squeezer hanging around somewhere. They're under every bush. If he only cost twenty-five rubles you got cheated.

NATALIA. The devil is in you today, Ivan Vassilevitch! You want to contradict everything. First you pretend the Oxen Meadows are yours, and now you say Guess is better than Squeezer. People should say what they really mean, and you know Squeezer is a hundred times better than Guess. Why say he isn't?

LOMOV. So, you think I'm a fool or a blind man, Natalia Stepanovna! Once and for all, Squeezer is overshot!

NATALIA. He is not!

LOMOV. He is so!

NATALIA. He is not!

LOMOV. Why shout, my dear lady?

NATALIA. Why talk such nonsense? It's terrible. Your Guess is old enough to be buried, and you compare him with Squeezer!

LOMOV. I'm sorry, I can't go on. My heart . . . it's palpitating!

NATALIA. I've always noticed that the hunters who argue most don't know a thing.

LOMOV. Please! Be quiet a moment. My heart's falling apart. . . . [*Shouts.*] Shut up!

NATALIA. I'm not going to shut up until you admit that Squeezer's a hundred times better than Guess.

LOMOV. A hundred times worse! His head. . . . My eyes . . . shoulder . . .

NATALIA. Guess is half-dead already!

LOMOV. [*Weeping.*] Shut up! My heart's exploding!

NATALIA. I won't shut up!

[*CHUBUKOV comes in.*]

7. Natalia is referring to her dog's physical characteristics and ancestry. In dog shows today, a dog is judged on specific characteristics, or *points.* Each breed has point standards that cover everything from skull shape and tail length to eye color and hair texture.

8. A dog's ancestry, or *pedigree,* is proof that a dog is a purebred.

CHUBUKOV. What's the trouble now?

NATALIA. Papa, will you please tell us which is the better dog, his Guess or our Squeezer?

LOMOV. Stepan Stepanovitch, I implore you to tell me just one thing: Is your Squeezer overshot or not? Yes or no?

CHUBUKOV. Well what if he is? He's still the best dog in the neighborhood, and so forth.

LOMOV. Oh, but isn't my dog, Guess, better? Really?

CHUBUKOV. Don't get yourself so fraught up,[9] old man. Of course, your dog has his good points—thoroughbred, firm on his feet, well sprung ribs, and so forth. But, my dear fellow, you've got to admit he has two defects; he's old and he's short in the muzzle.

LOMOV. Short in the muzzle? Oh, my heart! Let's look at the facts! On the Marusinsky hunt my dog ran neck and neck with the Count's, while Squeezer was a mile behind them. . . .

CHUBUKOV. That's because the Count's groom hit him with a whip.

LOMOV. And he was right, too! We were fox hunting; what was your dog chasing sheep for?

CHUBUKOV. That's a lie! Look, I'm going to lose my temper . . . [*Controlling himself.*] my dear friend, so let's stop arguing, for that reason alone. You're only arguing because we're all jealous of somebody else's dog. Who can help it? As soon as you realize some dog is better than yours, in this case our dog, you start in with this and that, and the next thing you know—pure jealousy! I remember the whole business.

LOMOV. I remember too!

9. The expression *fraught up* means "excited; charged up."

CHUBUKOV. [*Mimicking.*] "I remember too!" What do you remember?

LOMOV. My heart . . . my foot's asleep . . . I can't . . .

NATALIA. [*Mimicking.*] "My heart . . . my foot's asleep." What kind of a hunter are you? You should be hunting cockroaches in the kitchen, not foxes. "My heart!"

CHUBUKOV. Yes, what kind of a hunter are you anyway? You should be sitting at home with your palpitations, not tracking down animals. You don't hunt anyhow. You just go out to argue with people and interfere with their dogs, and so forth. For God's sake, let's change the subject before I lose my temper. Anyway, you're just not a hunter.

LOMOV. But you, you're a hunter? Ha! You only go hunting to get in good with the count, and to plot, and intrigue, and scheme. . . . Oh, my heart! You're a schemer, that's what!

CHUBUKOV. What's that? Me a schemer? [*Shouting.*] Shut up!

LOMOV. A schemer!

CHUBUKOV. You infant! You puppy!

LOMOV. You old rat!

CHUBUKOV. You shut up, or I'll shoot you down like a partridge! You fool!

LOMOV. Everyone knows that—oh, my heart—that your wife used to beat you. . . . Oh, my feet . . . my head . . . I'm seeing stars . . . I'm going to faint! [*He drops into an armchair.*] Quick, a doctor! [*Faints.*]

CHUBUKOV. [*Going on, oblivious.*] Baby! Weakling! Fool! I'm getting sick. [*Drinks water.*] Me! I'm sick!

NATALIA. What kind of a hunter are you? You can't even sit on a horse! [*To her father.*] Papa,

Vocabulary
oblivious (ə bliv′ ē əs) *adj.* unmindful or unaware; not noticing

what's the matter with him? Look, papa! [*Screaming.*] Ivan Vassilevitch! He's dead.

CHUBUKOV. I'm choking, I can't breathe. . . . Give me air.

NATALIA. He's dead! [*Pulling* LOMOV's *sleeve.*] Ivan Vassilevitch! Ivan Vassilevitch! What have you done to me? He's dead! [*She falls into an armchair. Screaming hysterically.*] A doctor! A doctor! A doctor!

CHUBUKOV. Ohhhh. . . . What's the matter? What happened?

NATALIA. [*Wailing.*] He's dead! He's dead!

CHUBUKOV. Who's dead? [*Looks at* LOMOV.] My God, he is! Quick! Water! A doctor! [*Puts glass to* LOMOV's *lips.*] Here, drink this! Can't drink it—he must be dead, and so forth. . . . Oh what a miserable life! Why don't I shoot myself! I should have cut my throat long ago! What am I waiting for? Give me a knife! Give me a pistol! [LOMOV *stirs.*] Look, he's coming to. Here, drink some water. That's it.

LOMOV. I'm seeing stars . . . misty . . . Where am I?

CHUBUKOV. Just you hurry up and get married, and then the devil with you! She accepts. [*Puts* LOMOV's *hand in* NATALIA's.] She accepts and so forth! I give you my blessing, and so forth! Only leave me in peace!

LOMOV. [*Getting up.*] Huh? What? Who?

CHUBUKOV. She accepts! Well? Kiss her!

NATALIA. He's alive! Yes, yes, I accept.

CHUBUKOV. Kiss each other!

LOMOV. Huh? Kiss? Kiss who? [*They kiss.*] That's nice. I mean, excuse me, what happened? Oh, now I get it . . . my heart . . . those stars . . . I'm very happy, Natalia Stepanovna. [*Kisses her hand.*] My foot's asleep.

NATALIA. I . . . I'm happy too.

CHUBUKOV. What a load off my shoulders! Whew!

NATALIA. Well, now maybe you'll admit that Squeezer is better than Guess?

LOMOV. Worse!

NATALIA. Better!

CHUBUKOV. What a way to enter matrimonial bliss! Let's have some champagne!

LOMOV. He's worse!

NATALIA. Better! Better, better, better, better!

CHUBUKOV. [*Trying to shout her down.*] Champagne! Bring some champagne! Champagne! Champagne!

CURTAIN

Responding to Literature

Personal Response

How did you like the ending of the play? Discuss your reaction with a classmate.

Analyzing Literature

Recall

1. Why has Lomov come to Chubukov's house?
2. What is the cause of the first argument?
3. What is the second argument about?
4. How do the first and second arguments end?
5. Summarize the ending of the play.

Interpret

6. Why, do you think, is Lomov so nervous? What does his behavior tell you about his personality?
7. Why, in your opinion, does the first argument start so easily?
8. What do the arguments reveal about the participants? Explain, using details from the play to support your ideas.
9. What attitudes toward marriage does the play reveal?
10. What, do you think, does the ending suggest about the characters' future lives?

Evaluate and Connect

11. **Theme Connections** In your opinion, which is the worse-case scenario: Lomov's planned marriage proposal that fell apart or the special event you described in the Reading Focus on page 1061? Why? Do you see humor in the altered plans of either event? Explain.
12. Compare and contrast the bickering between characters in the play with similar interactions you have witnessed between people. How is it the same? How is it different?
13. In your opinion, are Lomov and Natalia a good match for each other? Do you think they should marry? Why or why not?
14. Does the **dialogue,** or speech, in Chekhov's play seem realistic to you? Why or why not? Find specific examples from the play to support your response. (See Literary Terms Handbook, page R3.)
15. Chekhov's aristocratic characters seem to be in their own little world; they have no interaction with people outside the Russian provinces. Do you think people today are more aware of problems in society outside their communities? Explain.

Literary ELEMENTS

Farce

A type of comedy in which characters are put into ridiculous situations is called **farce.** In farce an author uses physical action, exaggeration, improbable events, and surprises to make the audience laugh. Farce is one way to make fun of human traits and social customs. In *A Marriage Proposal,* for example, Chekhov has Lomov continually complain about physical ailments in order to poke fun at people with imaginary illnesses.

1. List three examples of statements made by the characters that made you laugh. Tell what you think Chekhov is making fun of in each example.
2. Identify three points in this play that you found particularly funny. Why are they humorous? What techniques of farce does Chekhov use to create each situation?

- See **Literary Terms Handbook,** p. R5.

Literary Criticism

One theme that predominates in Chekhov's fiction, argues a critic, is "the ironical misunderstandings, disillusionments, and cross-purposes that make up the human comedy in general." Write an analysis of "A Marriage Proposal," exploring how this theme is developed in the play.

Literature and Writing

Writing About Literature

Analyzing Dialogue Chekhov masterfully develops his characters' personalities through **dialogue.** Analyze the dialogue for each of the characters in the play. In a paragraph for each character, explain how Chekhov portrays the character through his or her speech. Support your ideas with dialogue from the play.

Creative Writing

Diary Entry Pretend that you are one of the characters writing an entry in your diary later that day. Jot down the character's thoughts about the day's events and his or her expectations for the future. Try to match your writing style to the character's personality and way of speaking.

Extending Your Response

Literature Groups

How Ironic This play contains situational irony (what appears likely to happen is not what happens) and dramatic irony (what appears true to a character is not what the audience knows to be true). Find one good example of each type of irony in the play. Discuss your examples with your group. Then discuss how different audiences–teenagers, single adults, married couples, socialites, homeowners–may react differently to the ironic situations. Share your findings.

Interdisciplinary Activity

Drama: Design the Set Using graph paper or computer software, draw a floor plan of the stage as you envision it. On the plan, place the various furnishings, stage props, and exits. Then select a scene and mark the characters' positions and movements across the stage.

Learning for Life

Cooperation Consultant Pretend that you are in training to become a consultant. Your class has just viewed a videotape of *A Marriage Proposal.* With a partner, make a list of the character traits–positive and negative–that you see in Lomov and Natalia, citing evidence from the play. Then, suggest how each character might compromise or change to bring positive attributes to their marriage.

Reading Further

You might enjoy reading the following short story by Anton Chekhov:

"The Darling," translated by David Magarshack from *Lady with Lapdog and Other Stories,* is a tale about love and marriage and the life of an innocent young woman.

Save your work for your portfolio.

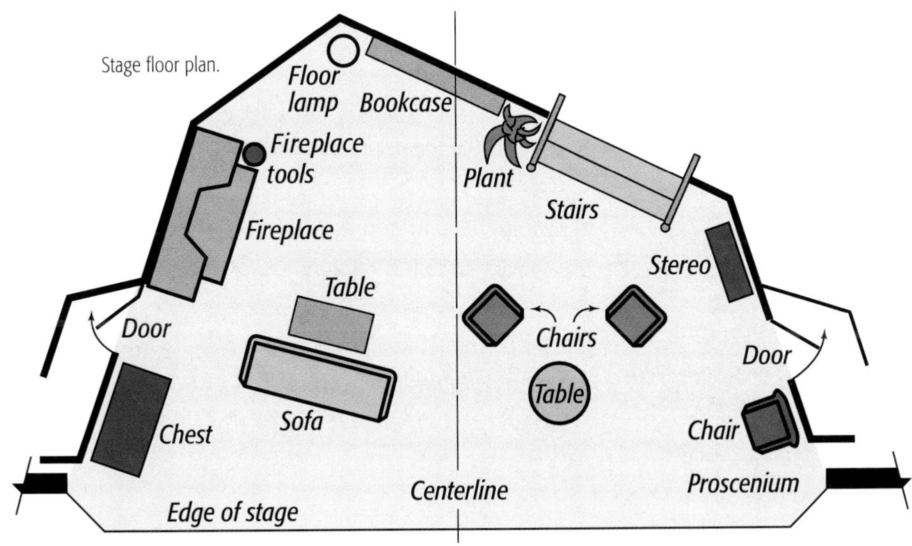

Stage floor plan.

Skill Minilessons

GRAMMAR AND LANGUAGE • Sentence Varieties

A **complex sentence** has one main clause and one or more subordinate clauses.

Main clause	Subordinate clause
Chubukov greets Lomov warmly	when he enters the room.

A **compound-complex sentence** has more than one main clause and at least one subordinate clause.

Main clause

Lomov wants to propose, |

Main clause	Subordinate clause
but he is not sure	that Natalia will accept.

● For more about sentence types, see **Language Handbook,** pp. R14–R16.

PRACTICE On your paper, write *complex* or *compound-complex* to identify each sentence.

1. Chubukov reassures his neighbor that Natalia is crazy for him.
2. Lomov does not love Natalia, but he thinks that marriage will regulate his life.
3. Before Lomov has a chance to propose, he and Natalia argue, and he grabs his hat and rushes out the door.
4. Natalia is beside herself when she discovers the reason for Lomov's visit.
5. Although they eventually kiss and declare their happiness, the argument about the better dog is unresolved.

READING AND THINKING • Responding

Responding while you are reading helps you step right inside a work. By responding with your immediate reactions such as "Oh! That was . . . " or "I'd like to ask the writer why . . . ," you give yourself a chance to spontaneously react to what you're reading and to enjoy it more. Responding is just one more way of reacting as you read.

PRACTICE Choose two segments of dialogue from *A Marriage Proposal* and write comments responding to each one.

● For related comprehension skills, see **Reading Handbook,** pp. R83–R85.

VOCABULARY • Etymology

The histories of some words are like very short stories. *Hypochondriac* comes from the Greek *hypo-,* meaning "under," and *chondros,* which is part of the sternum, or breastbone. The Greeks believed that the abdomen (which is below the breastbone) was where feelings of depression originated, so people who felt bad but were not really sick had something wrong in that part of the body.

Here are the etymologies of some other words from *A Marriage Proposal.*

affable: from the Latin *ad-,* "to," and *fari,* "to speak"
impudent: from the Latin *in-,* "not," and *pudere,* "shame"
pompous: from the Greek *pompé,* "solemn procession"

PRACTICE Use the given etymologies to answer the questions.

1. Which event would be most likely to involve pomp—a circus parade, a president's inauguration, or a school field trip?
2. Would the kind of rudeness called *impudence* be most likely to result from ignorance, excessive curiosity, or deliberate discourtesy?
3. Which word is most likely to have come from the same root as *affable—fable, fabric,* or *fare?*

Listening, Speaking, and Viewing

Readers Theater

A fun way to share your understanding of a literary work is through **Readers Theater,** in which a reader or a group of readers presents a performance by reading a script prepared from a poem, novel, short story, or play. Through voice, facial expressions, and controlled but meaningful gestures and stances, the readers create an imaginary stage peopled with interesting characters. A reader of Lomov's role in the opening scene of *A Marriage Proposal,* for example, might speak in a trembling voice and use facial expressions and gestures to show how nervous he is.

Preparing Your Reading

- Choose passages for reading that are interesting and that have strong emotional appeal.
- Reduce all descriptive and informative material to a minimum, leaving only compelling situations that lead up to a dramatic climax.
- Prepare a narrator's part that will include introductory or descriptive material and a summary of important parts of the work that you are omitting.

Rehearsing Your Reading

Practice reading your script with the other readers in your play.

- Discuss lines that need a change in emphasis. Mark changes on the script.
- Have each reader experiment with a suitable vocal style and movements that suggest the posture and location of each character when he or she speaks.
- Check that the narrator is effective and reads in a clear, strong voice with a sense of timing and climax.

Performing Your Reading

- Speak in a strong voice and put expression into each word. To project your voice so all the audience can hear, imagine that you are speaking to a person at the back of the room.
- Lengthen your pauses and exaggerate your gestures and facial expressions to be sure viewers get your message.

ACTIVITY

With a group of students, present part or all of one of the selections in this theme as Readers Theater. Prepare your script and rehearse. Then present your reading to the class.

Writing Workshop

Expository Writing: Feature Article

Feature articles are informative pieces in newspapers and magazines that take a more informal approach to their topics than news stories do. A feature writer draws the reader into a topic to inform, explain, *and* entertain and takes a more personal point of view than a newswriter does. **In this workshop, you will write a feature article on the humourous aspects of an event.**

- As you write your expository article, refer to the **Writing Handbook,** pp. R58–R63.

EVALUATION RUBRIC

By the time you complete this Writing Workshop, you will have

- written a feature article focusing on the humourous aspects of an event
- developed a strong "hook" in the introduction to grab readers' attention
- organized the article either by order of importance/interest or in chronological order
- used anecdotes, quotes, examples, and descriptions to entertain and inform readers
- concluded the article with a final insight or summary statement
- presented a feature article that is free of errors in grammar, usage, and mechanics

The Writing Process

PREWRITING

PREWRITING TIP

Narrow down a general topic to the single aspect that will intrigue readers most.

Explore ideas

Feature articles can cover many topics: sports heroes, science breakthroughs, tips on buying cars—even encounters with bears. Be alert and open to ideas in newspaper and magazine articles and on TV talk shows and newsmagazine programs. In your journal, make a list of the ideas you come across. Then explore the humourous side of each topic, adding notes to your list. To start, you may want to consider the topics presented in selections in this unit, such as the following:

- Information and misinformation, as in "What Is and Ain't Grammatical"
- Interpersonal relationships, as in "A Marriage Proposal"
- A child's view of adults, as in "How I Changed the War and Won the Game" and the selection from *An American Childhood*
- Attitudes toward machines and technology, as in "The Car We Had to Push"
- An unforgettable personal experience, as in "Appetizer"

Consider your purpose

Your purpose is to convey information about a topic of your choice and to give the information a personal touch. In addition, you want to entertain your readers and make them laugh. Consider the topics and humourous aspects you listed in your journal; then decide which of those ideas will both inform and entertain your readers.

Choose an Audience
Your feature article should be geared toward a broad audience–readers of magazines and newspapers. Because you can't assume that every reader is interested in or knows about your topic, you'll have to capture readers' attention and then provide some background.

Plan your opening
Consider making the lead paragraph an intriguing "hook." Think of a way to grab your readers' attention immediately. You might try one of these ideas:

- Relate a humorous anecdote.
- State a surprising statistic.
- Provide a vivid description.
- Use a provocative quote.

Collect the facts
With your story idea in mind, begin gathering facts by listing a few questions to direct your research.

Organize
Organize the article in a way that will grab and hold your readers' interest. The chart below shows two methods of organization for a feature article: (1) order of importance or interest and (2) chronological order.

Methods of Organization

		STUDENT MODEL
Order of importance or interest	Present details in order of increasing (or decreasing) importance or interest.	Is it bad luck to break a mirror in France? Is Friday the 13th considered unlucky in Russia? I found out—the hard way—about the superstitions of other countries on a trip to Europe last summer.
Chronological order	Describe an event or a process in sequence as it occurs over time.	When Teresa knocked on our door, my father opened it and put out his hand to shake Teresa's, but she just started laughing. Still laughing, she walked inside the room to sit down. Finally, she stopped laughing and apologized. "Russians are so superstitious!" she said. "It is bad luck to shake hands in a doorway!"

Complete Student Model on p. R123.

DRAFTING

DRAFTING TIPS

To engage your readers, put yourself in their shoes and anticipate questions they might ask.

Keep the reader reading

To keep the article lively, use a mixture of anecdotes, quotes from people you interviewed, descriptions, and explanations. Tease readers with bits of information in each paragraph so they continue reading.

Write your draft

As you write, follow your plan, choosing the most interesting details. Feel free to depart from your plan if you think of something that will make the article more interesting. A feature article doesn't have to be as tightly focused as a report or news story.

STUDENT MODEL

That afternoon, we visited a famous museum. We looked at sculptures, crowns, and other artifacts until I could barely stand it. At one point, I started whistling out of habit, and suddenly one of the guards, an old lady in a brown uniform, started yelling at me. "She's just trying to save you trouble later, " Teresa said. "Some Russians believe that whistling indoors will cause your family to be poor."

Complete Student Model on p. R123.

REVISING

REVISING TIP

If you've drafted on a computer, revising on a hard copy may help you spot problems.

Evaluate your work

Read your article and watch for confusing or boring parts. Look for opportunities to add humorous twists to your article. Using the **Rubric for Revising**, make revisions to your draft.

Have a writing conference

Read the draft aloud to someone who isn't familiar with the topic. Then work through the **Rubric for Revising** again to improve your feature article.

RUBRIC FOR REVISING

Your revised feature article should have

- a strong hook and a humorous introduction to grab readers' interest
- accurate facts, lively anecdotes, vivid details, and engaging quotes to entertain and inform readers
- a clear organizing strategy that makes the sequence of events clear to readers
- varied sentence lengths and rhythms to add interest to the writing
- a conclusion that includes a final insight or summary statement

Your revised feature article should be free of

- irrelevant details
- errors in grammar, usage, and mechanics

STUDENT MODEL

~~Plus~~ Next, we travelled to Italy. We stayed in Florence with a large Italian family. Over a huge dinner of pasta, meat, and vegetables, I asked them if they were familiar with American superstitions, such as broken mirrors or walking under a ladder. They shook their heads and laughed at me—the same way I had laughed at the Russian ~~ones~~ superstitions!

Complete Student Model on p. R123.

EDITING/PROOFREADING

Revise your feature article until it is lively, interesting, and informative. Using the **Proofreading Checklist** on the inside back cover of this book as a guide, make as many "passes" through the manuscript as needed to look for each type of error.

Grammar Hint

Adjective clauses are an efficient means of giving your readers background information. Be sure to set off nonrestrictive, or nonessential, adjective clauses with commas.

INCORRECT: We met Marie who was our new translator at an outdoor café.

CORRECT: We met Marie, who was our new translator, at an outdoor café.

- For more on using commas, see **Language Handbook,** pp. R26-28.

Complete Student Model

For a complete version of the student model developed in this workshop, refer to **Writing Workshop Models,** p. R123.

STUDENT MODEL

In Paris we stayed with a very nice translator named Marie. Marie smiled when I asked her about local superstitions. She said, "Yes, we have many superstitions in France. For example, if a black cat crosses in front of you, it is bad luck." Marie, who didn't seem to believe in this superstition herself, was surprised to hear that some Americans, like some French people, are wary of black cats.

Complete Student Model on p. R123.

PUBLISHING/PRESENTING

For presentation to the class, you could put your feature article together with those of other students in a class magazine. To reach a larger audience, you might submit the article to a school newspaper, a local magazine or newspaper, or a national publication.

PRESENTING TIP

Enliven and clarify your feature article with illustrations, photographs, maps, and diagrams.

Reflecting

In your journal, reflect on what you like and dislike about your finished article. What would you change in the article? How would you adapt the article for a different audience (much younger, for example) or for a different medium (a TV newsmagazine program, for example)? Jot down your ideas about ways to change the focus of your article.

Save your work for your portfolio.

Unit Assessment

Personal Response

1. Which selection in this unit do you think is the funniest? Why? Is there a selection that you think doesn't belong in a unit devoted to humor? Explain.
2. What new ideas did your work in this unit help you to develop about the following?
   - recognizing and creating different kinds of humor
   - working with others to generate ideas
   - discussing your reactions and opinions
   - using your writing to grab readers' attention

Analyzing Literature

Evaluating Types of Humor Humor is very subjective–what one person finds hilarious may not amuse another person at all. The authors in this unit create humor through a variety of methods, such as irony, farce, and hyperbole. Which method of humor do you think was used most effectively in this unit? Support your answer with an example of that method from a selection.

Evaluate and Set Goals

Evaluate

1. In which of the following areas did this unit help you to improve the most? Explain.
   - reading
   - writing
   - speaking
2. Which two tasks were the most challenging for you in this unit? What strategies did you use to meet each challenge? How will you approach similar tasks in the future?
3. How would you assess your work in this unit, using the following scale? Give at least two reasons for your assessment.
   4 = outstanding 3 = good 2 = fair 1 = weak

Set Goals

1. With your teacher, identify a habit or skill that you would like to improve upon in the future.
2. In your notebook, write down at least three things you can do to improve that habit or skill.
3. Create a checklist you can use to assess your progress in achieving your goal.

Build Your Portfolio

Select Choose two pieces of writing you did in this unit and include them in your portfolio. The following questions can help you make your selection.

- Which piece do you think shows your most clever thinking?
- Which piece is the liveliest or most humorous?
- Which piece is most focused and best organized?
- Which piece represented the biggest challenge?

Reflect Include a note with each piece that you place in your portfolio. Consider addressing any of the following issues.

- How did your writing process for the piece differ from your usual process?
- What aspects of the piece did you change in revision? What would you change if you were to revise again?
- How does this piece compare with writing you have done in previous units?

Reading on Your Own

You might enjoy these books.

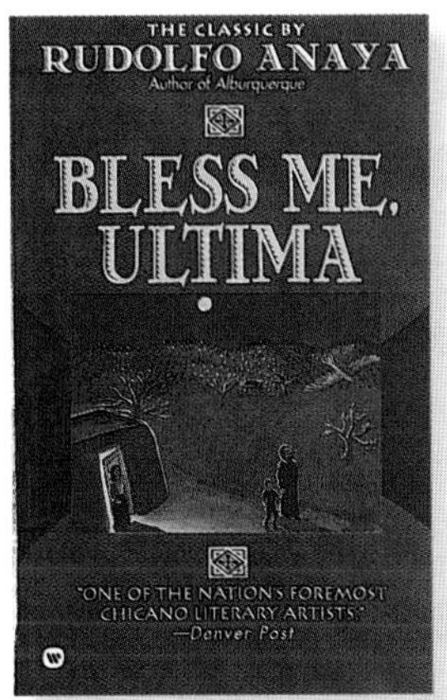

Bless Me, Ultima
by Rudolfo Anaya Antonio Marez struggles for meaning in his young life. Should he fulfill his mother's dreams or pursue a more adventurous life as his father did? Can he survive the cultural conflicts both within and beyond his small town? With the help of Ultima, a *curandera* who cures with herbs and magic, Antonio finds the meaning of life.

Novio Boy: A Play
by Gary Soto Rudy, a ninth grader, finally has a date with Patricia, an eleventh grader, and takes her to a restaurant in their Mexican American community. When Rudy's best friend, his "crazy" guitar-playing uncle, and his mother show up, Rudy worries that they might embarrass him, and he pretends not to know them.

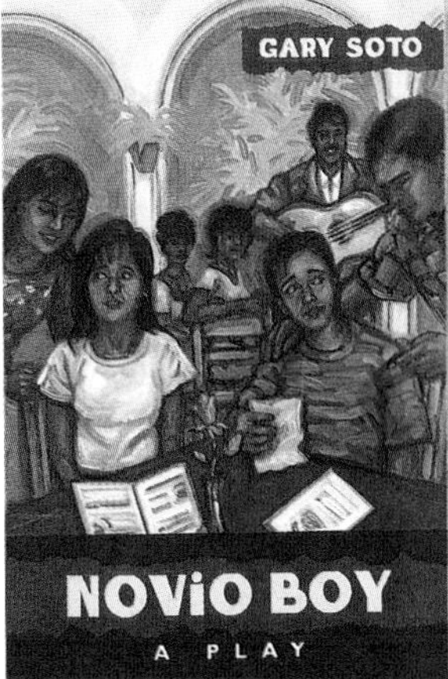

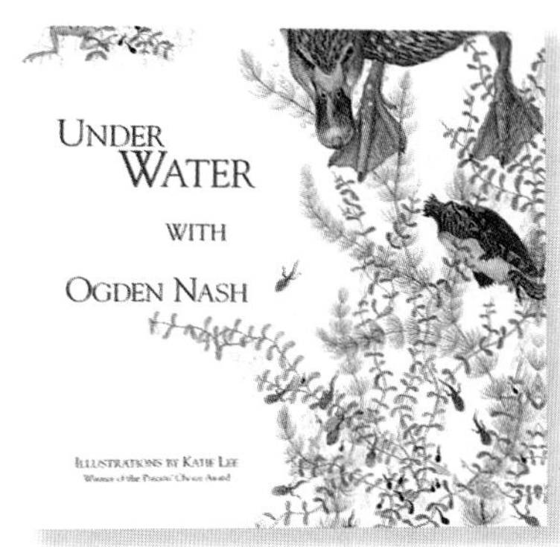

Under Water with Ogden Nash
by Ogden Nash In this collection of twenty-six delightful humorous poems, Ogden Nash writes about sea creatures such as the turtle, the jellyfish, the squid, and the shark. Detailed color drawings by award-winning zoological illustrator Katie Lee are paired with the poems.

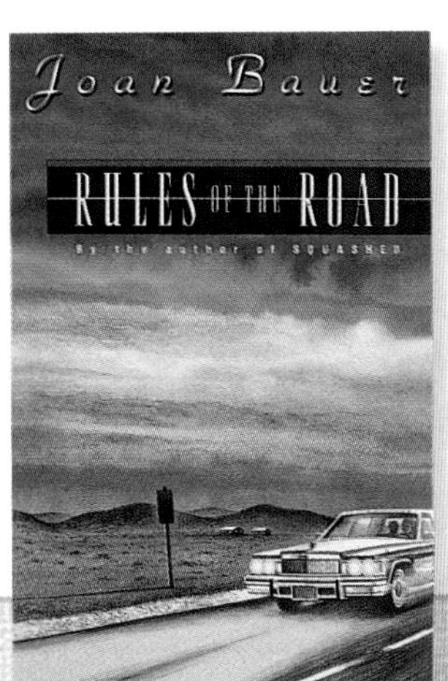

Rules of the Road
by Joan Bauer In this poignant yet funny novel, Jenna Boller, a sophomore with an after-school job selling shoes, agrees to take on the additional task of driving the store president, Mrs. Gladstone, on a business trip. As they journey all summer long from Chicago to Dallas, Jenna offers her own amusing rules for the "highway of life."

California English–Language Arts

Reading and Analyzing Test Questions

Read the following passage. Then read each question on page 1085. Decide which is the best answer to each question. Mark the letter for that answer on your paper.

LETTER 1

To the Editor of the Weeville *Post-Intelligencer*:

Shame on the Weeville Commissioner of Parks and Recreation! Ms. Phibbs has once again proven to the community at large that she is completely out of touch with the needs and desires of our citizenry. This year's proposed program for the Summer Fun Music Series in Memorial Park is the most ridiculous line-up I've ever seen. And I thought last year's was bad!

Does Ms. Phibbs *really* think that the majority of Weeville citizens enjoy rock music? This is apparently the case: five of the eight music presentations scheduled for the summer feature loud, boisterous, rowdy rock and roll bands–which isn't music at all! My dear wife Mercedes and I like to keep our minds open. We went to last year's concert series even when we didn't know the groups playing. How shocked we were when we had to put plugs in our ears to keep from going deaf! Even worse than the band, though, were the screaming hordes of youngsters who threw things at the stage and caused every manner of mayhem.

And now Ms. Phibbs wants to force-feed Weeville another round of this stuff the kids of today are calling music? What ever happened to Perry Como? What about the Boston Pops? What's wrong with a little Beethoven now and then? These are the *real* tastes of Weeville's citizens. And if Ms. Phibbs doesn't like it, she can just hand in her resignation and move somewhere else.

Yours sincerely,

Ezra T. Fitzgerald

LETTER 2

Dear Editor,

This year's Summer Fun Music Series looks to be the best one ever! Kudos to the Parks and Recreation Department, and especially to its Commissioner, Ms. Phibbs, for creating an excellent roster of musicians!

What my friends and I most appreciate is the deliberate realignment of Weeville's focus when it comes to planning community events. It's about time somebody woke up and treated Weeville's younger citizens with more courtesy and respect. When I noticed that my favorite band was slated to appear in Memorial Park August 5th this year, I nearly leapt out of my shoes! *This* is the kind of commitment Weeville citizens deserve from their elected officials and their planning committees. Last year's series, I have to say, disappointed me with its schedule of musicians who performed primarily music for older generations. Sure, some people still listen to Mozart, Bach, and Chopin, but there is a growing population whose tastes are somewhat different.

Once again, thank you, Ms. Phibbs. You've truly shown the young people of Weeville that they are important in the eyes of the town officials!

Yours very truly,

Raymond Q. Sunvil

1 The Summer Fun Music Series is under the direction of —

A the Commissioner of Parks and Recreation

B the Director of Memorial Park

C the Mayor of Weeville

D a committee made up of Bach, Mozart, and Chopin

2 The word kudos in Letter 2 most nearly means —

F shame

G good luck

H praise

J good-bye

3 The writer of Letter 1 most likely views the writer of Letter 2 as —

A a fellow music-lover

B a member of the Parks and Recreation Commission

C a respected musician

D a poorly behaved youngster

4 The author of Letter 2 cites Mozart, Bach, and Chopin as composers whose music —

F does not reflect the tastes of many younger people

G should be performed at the Summer Fun Music Series

H is not appreciated by anyone

J causes the audience to behave poorly and throw things

5 The author of Letter 1 uses which of the following as evidence that the performers at this year's Summer Fun Concert Series have been poorly selected?

A The fact that works by Mozart, Bach, and Chopin are not on the program

B The amount of money the performers are being paid by the Parks and Recreation Department

C The behavior of some people who attended last year's concert series

D The number of concerts planned as part of the series

6 The authors of both letters would likely describe themselves as —

F members of the Parks and Recreation Commission

G music lovers

H friends of Ms. Phibbs

J fans of Bach, Mozart, and Chopin

STOP

Reference Section

Literary Terms Handbook

A

Act A major division of a play. Many modern plays have two or three acts; some shorter plays have only one. Although Shakespeare did not separate his plays into acts, each play was later divided into five acts. Acts can contain one or more scenes.

See page 713.
See also SCENE.

Alliteration The repetition of sounds, most often consonant sounds, at the beginnings of words. Alliteration gives emphasis to words. For example, Robert Francis uses alliteration in the following lines from "The Base Stealer":

Running a scattering of steps sidewise,

How he teeters, skitters, tingles, teases . . .

See pages 579, 606, and 685.
See also SOUND DEVICES.

Allusion A reference in a work of literature to a character, place, or situation from history or from another work of literature, music, or art. For example, in "Constantly risking absurdity," Lawrence Ferlinghetti refers to a poet as "a little charleychaplin man." This allusion is to Charlie Chaplin, a famous film comedian.

See pages 526 and 1042.

Analogy A comparison based on a similarity between things that are otherwise dissimilar. A writer may use an analogy to explain something abstract or unfamiliar. For example, in the following lines from *King Lear,* William Shakespeare makes an analogy between the fate of insects and of humans:

As flies to wanton boys, are we to the gods,—
They kill us for their sport.

See also METAPHOR, SIMILE.

Antagonist A character or force that opposes the protagonist, or central character, in a story or drama. The reader is generally meant not to sympathize with the antagonist. For example, in "Chee's Daughter" by Juanita Platero and Siyowin Miller, Old Man Fat is the antagonist, opposing Chee.

See pages 2 and 746.
See also CHARACTER, CONFLICT, PROTAGONIST.

Aside In a play, a comment made by a character to the audience or another character but not heard by the other characters on stage. The speaker turns to one side, or "aside," away from the action on stage. Asides reveal what a character is thinking or feeling. For example, act 1, scene 2, of Shakespeare's *Julius Caesar* includes the following exchange:

CAESAR. Be near me, that I may remember you.

TREBONIUS. Caesar, I will [*Aside.*] and so near will I be,
That your best friends shall wish I had been further.

See page 818.
See also SOLILOQUY.

Assonance The repetition of same or similar vowel sounds in stressed syllables that end with different consonant sounds. For example, the short *i* sound is repeated in this line from Shakespeare's "Shall I Compare Thee to a Summer's Day?":

So long lives this, and this gives life to thee.

See pages 579 and 685.
See also SOUND DEVICES.

Atmosphere The emotional quality, or mood, of a piece of writing, especially a mood established in part by the setting.

See page 486.
See also MOOD.

Author's purpose An author's intent in writing a literary work. For example, the author may want to inform, entertain, persuade, tell a story, or express an opinion.

See pages 423, 538, and 770.
See also DICTION, STYLE, THEME.

Autobiography The story of a person's life written by that person. For example, *Farewell to Manzanar* is Jeanne Wakatsuki Houston's autobiography.

See pages 422 and 472.
See also BIOGRAPHY, MEMOIR, NONFICTION.

B

Ballad A narrative song or poem. Folk ballads, which usually recount an exciting or dramatic episode, were passed on by word of mouth for generations before being written down. Literary ballads are written in imitation of folk ballads.

See page 956
See also NARRATIVE POETRY.

Biography The account of a person's life written by another person. Biographies can be short or book-length.

See page 422
See also AUTOBIOGRAPHY, MEMOIR, NONFICTION.

Blank verse Poetry or lines of dramatic verse written in unrhymed **iambic pentameter,** which is a meter made up of five iambic feet to a line of verse. Each foot consists of one unstressed (˘) syllable followed by one stressed (´) syllable. Shakespeare wrote most of his plays largely in blank verse. The following line, spoken by Mark Antony in act 3, scene 1, of Shakespeare's *Julius Caesar,* is an example of blank verse.

Ŏ pár/dŏn mé, / thŏu bléed/ĭng piéce / ŏf eárth.

See page 798.
See also FOOT, METER, RHYTHM.

C

Character An individual in a literary work. **Main characters** are the most important to a work and **minor characters** are less important. A character who shows varied and sometimes contradictory traits, such as the daughter in Amy Tan's "Two Kinds," is called a **round character.** A character who reveals only one personality trait is called a **flat character.** A **stereotype** is a flat character of a familiar and often-repeated type, such as Old Man Fat in Juanita Platero and Siyowin Miller's "Chee's Daughter." A **dynamic character** changes during the story, as does Luis in Judith Ortiz Cofer's "Catch the Moon." A **static character,** such as Luis's father, remains primarily the same.

See pages 2, 124, 231, 492, and 712.
See also CHARACTERIZATION.

Characterization The methods a writer uses to reveal the personality of a character. In **direct characterization** the writer makes direct statements about a character's personality. In **indirect characterization** the writer reveals a character's personality through the character's words and actions and through what other characters think and say about the character.

See pages 231 and 1050.
See also CHARACTER.

Chorus In classical Greek drama, an actor or group of actors who comment on the main events in the play. Choruses in ancient Greece also sang and danced. The leader of the chorus was called the **choragos**. In *Antigone* by Sophocles, the chorus is identified as the elders of Thebes.

See page 723.

Climax The point of greatest emotional intensity, interest, or suspense in a narrative. Also called the **turning point,** the climax usually comes near the end of a story and often presents a resolution to the conflict. In "Through the Tunnel," by Doris Lessing, the climax occurs when Jerry finally goes through the tunnel.

See pages 3 and 86.
See also CONFLICT, PLOT.

Colloquial language A type of language used in everyday speech but not used in formal speech or formal writing. The expressions "That's cool" and "I'm out of here" are colloquial expressions.

See page 170.
See also DICTION, STYLE.

Comedy A type of drama that is humorous and typically has a happy ending. Comedy often pokes fun at peoples' faults and limitations in order to teach something about human nature.

See page 1074.
See also DRAMA, FARCE, HUMOR, SATIRE.

Comic relief A humorous scene or incident in an otherwise serious or tragic work. Comic relief breaks the tension yet emphasizes the unfolding tragedy. In scene 1 of *Antigone,* for example, the sentry's lines typically provide comic relief.

Conflict The struggle between opposing forces in a story or play. An **external conflict** exists when a character struggles against some outside force, such as another person, nature, society, or fate. In Doris Lessing's "Through the Tunnel," for example, when Jerry tries to swim through the tunnel, he is involved in an external conflict with nature. An **internal conflict** exists within the mind of a character who is torn between opposing feelings or goals. Jerry wrestles with an internal conflict when he tries to overcome his own fear in order to swim through the tunnel.

See pages 3, 59, 86, 275, and 429.
See also ANTAGONIST, PLOT, PROTAGONIST.

Connotation The suggested or implied meanings associated with a word beyond its dictionary definition, or **denotation.**

See page 72.
See also DENOTATION.

Consonance The repetition of consonant sounds before and after different vowels, as in the following lines from "My Mother Pieced Quilts" by Teresa Paloma Acosta:

as weapons

against pounding january winds

See page 579.
See also SOUND DEVICES.

Couplet Two consecutive rhyming lines of poetry, sometimes forming a stanza. For example, the following lines from "Shall I Compare Thee to a Summer's Day?" by William Shakespeare make up a couplet:

So long as men can breathe, or eyes can see,
So long lives this, and this gives life to thee.

See also STANZA.

Creative nonfiction Nonfiction that applies some of the devices of fiction to convey ideas about real issues. "The Angry Winter" by Loren Eiseley, is an example of creative nonfiction.

See page 560.
See also FICTION, NONFICTION.

D

Denotation The literal or dictionary meaning of a word. Literal language seeks to convey denotation, or exact meaning.

See page 72.
See also CONNOTATION.

Dénouement. See FALLING ACTION.

Description Writing that uses carefully selected details to help the reader picture settings, events, and characters. Almost all writing, fiction and nonfiction, contains elements of description.

See pages 112, 264, and 359.
See also IMAGERY.

Dialect A variety of a language or manner of speaking belonging to a specific group, often within a particular region. Dialects may differ in vocabulary, pronunciation, and grammatical form. Authors use dialect to help establish setting and to develop characters. In *Big River: The Adventures of Huckleberry Finn,* for example, William Hauptman uses dialect to help create characters who lived in a small river town in Missouri in the mid-1800s.

See page 720.

Dialogue Written conversation between characters in a literary work. These lines from Susan Beth Pfeffer's "As It Is with Strangers" are an example of dialogue:

"Yeah, sure," Jack said. "Have you lived here long?"
"Since the divorce," I said. "Eight years ago."

See pages 44, 302, 713, and 932.
See also MONOLOGUE.

Diction The writer's choice of words; an important element in the writer's voice or style. Good writers choose their words carefully to convey a particular meaning or feeling. These lines from "A Child's Christmas in Wales" give an example of Dylan Thomas's diction:

All the Christmases roll down toward the two-tongued sea, like a cold and headlong moon bundling down the sky that was our street. . . .

See page 1057.
See also STYLE, TONE, VOICE.

Drama Literature intended to be performed before an audience by actors on a stage. Most drama before the modern period can be divided into two basic types: tragedy, such as Shakespeare's *Julius Caesar,* and comedy, such as Chekhov's *A Marriage Proposal*. The two basic parts of a drama are its dialogue and its stage directions.

See pages 712–713.
See also COMEDY, DIALOGUE, PROPS, STAGE DIRECTIONS, TRAGEDY.

Dramatic irony. See IRONY.

Dramatic monologue A form of dramatic poetry in which one speaker addresses a silent listener in an intense or emotional situation. "First Lesson" by Philip Booth, is a dramatic monologue in which a father speaks to a silent daughter.

See also DRAMATIC POETRY, MONOLOGUE.

Dramatic poetry Poetry which uses elements of drama. One or more characters speak to other characters, themselves, or the reader. Dramatic poetry usually includes a tense situation or emotional conflict.

See also DRAMATIC MONOLOGUE, SPEAKER.

Dynamic character. See CHARACTER.

E

Elegy An extended, usually formal poem in which the speaker mourns a death or other great loss.

Epic A long narrative poem that traces the adventures of a larger-than-life hero. Epics intertwine myths, legends, and history, reflecting the values of the societies in which they originate. In epics, gods and goddesses often intervene in the affairs of humans.

See page 956.
See also FOLKLORE, HERO, LEGEND, MYTH, NARRATIVE POETRY.

Epic simile. See SIMILE.

Essay A short work of nonfiction on a single topic. The purpose of an essay is to communicate an idea or opinion. A **formal essay** is serious and impersonal. An **informal essay** entertains while it informs, usually in a light, conversational style. Many informal essays, or **personal essays,** reflect upon an experience in the writer's life, as in "Living Well, Living Good" by Maya Angelou and "The Tucson Zoo" by Lewis Thomas.

See pages 422, 423, and 1006.
See also EXPOSITION, NONFICTION.

Exaggeration. See HYPERBOLE.

Exposition An author's introduction of the characters, setting, and situation at the beginning of a story, novel, or play. For example, Edgar Allan Poe's "The Masque of the Red Death" opens with very straightforward exposition.

See pages 3 and 551.
See also ESSAY, PLOT.

Extended metaphor. See METAPHOR.

F

Fable A short, usually simple tale that teaches a moral and sometimes uses animal characters. Themes are usually stated explicitly, as in Aesop's fables.

See also LEGEND, MORAL, PARABLE, THEME.

Falling action In a play or story, the action that follows the climax. The falling action may show the results of the climax. It may also include the **dénouement** (dā′ nōō män′), a French word meaning "unknotting." The dénouement, or **resolution,** explains the plot or unravels the mystery.

See page 3.
See also PLOT, RISING ACTION.

Farce A type of comedy that provokes laughter by placing one-dimensional, or flat, characters in ridiculous situations. An example is Anton Chekhov's *A Marriage Proposal.*

See page 1074.
See also COMEDY, HUMOR, STEREOTYPE.

Fiction Literature in which situations and characters are invented by the writer. Aspects of a fictional work might be based on fact or experience, such as Amy Tan's "Two Kinds." Fiction includes both short stories, such as Stephen Vincent Benét's "By the Waters of Babylon," and novels, such as T. H. White's *The Once and Future King.*

See pages 2–3.
See also CREATIVE NONFICTION, NONFICTION, NOVEL, SCIENCE FICTION, SHORT STORY.

Figurative language Language or expressions that are not literally true but express some truth beyond the literal level. Figurative language appears in all kinds of writing, but is especially prominent in poetry. Types of figurative language called **figures of speech** include hyperbole, metaphor, personification, simile, and understatement.

See pages 579 and 680.
See also HYPERBOLE, IMAGERY, METAPHOR, OXYMORON, PERSONIFICATION, SIMILE, SYMBOL, UNDERSTATEMENT.

Flashback An account of an event that happened before a story began. A flashback interrupts the chronological sequence of story events, but gives readers information that may help explain the main events of the story. For example, in Leslie Marmon Silko's "Lullaby," the narrator includes a flashback to the day Ayah and Chato found out that Jimmie had died.

See pages 339 and 422.

Foil A character whose traits contrast with those of another character. By using a foil, a writer calls attention to the strengths or weaknesses of a main character. For example, the self-controlled Octavius is a foil for the excitable Mark Antony in Shakespeare's *Julius Caesar.*

See also CHARACTER.

Folklore The traditional beliefs, customs, stories, songs, and dances of a culture. Folklore is passed down through oral tradition and is based in the concerns of ordinary people.

See page 912.
See also EPIC, FOLKTALE, LEGEND, MYTH.

Folktale A traditional story passed down orally long before being written down. Commonly the author of a folktale is anonymous. Folktales include animal stories, trickster stories, fairy tales, myths, legends, and tall tales.

See also LEGEND, MYTH, ORAL TRADITION.

Foot The basic unit in the measurement of rhythm in poetry. A foot usually contains one stressed syllable (ʹ) and one or more unstressed syllables (˘).

See pages 578 and 589.
See also METER, RHYTHM, SCANSION.

Foreshadowing The use of clues by the author to prepare readers for events that will happen later in a story.

See pages 326 and 857.
See also PLOT, RISING ACTION, SUSPENSE.

Frame story A plot structure that includes the telling of a story within a story. The frame is the **outer** story, which usually precedes and follows the **inner** and more important story.

Free verse Poetry that has no fixed pattern of meter and rhyme. Free verse often uses sound devices and a rhythm similar to that of human speech. "A Blessing" by James Wright is an example of free verse.

See pages 627 and 898.
See also RHYTHM.

G

Genre A category of literary work characterized by a particular form or style. Some examples of literary genre are novel, short story, poetry, drama, nonfiction, essay, and epic. The term also refers to subcategories of literary work. For example, fantasy, magical realism, mystery, romance, and science fiction are genres of fiction. "A Sound of Thunder" by Ray Bradbury belongs to both the short story and science-fiction genres.

See pages 2–3, 422–423, 578–579, and 712–713.

H

Haiku A Japanese poetry form that has three lines and seventeen syllables. The first and third line have five syllables each; the middle line has seven syllables. Bashō's haiku are famous examples of the haiku form.

See page 686.
See also TANKA.

Hero The main character in a literary work, typically one whose admirable character or noble deeds arouse the admiration of the reader. Although the word *hero* is applied only to males in traditional usage (the female term is *heroine*), contemporary usage applies the term to both sexes. For example, Buffalo Calf Road Woman is the hero of "Where the Girl Rescued Her Brother" by Joseph Bruchac and Gayle Ross.

See pages 768 and 956.
See also EPIC, PROTAGONIST, ROMANCE, TRAGEDY.

Humor The quality of a literary work that makes the characters and their situations seem funny, amusing, or ludicrous. Humorous writing can be equally effective in fiction and nonfiction.

See page 1000.
See also COMEDY, FARCE, PARODY, PUN, SATIRE.

Hyperbole A figure of speech that uses exaggeration to express strong emotion, make a point, or evoke humor. For example, in the following lines from Isak Dinesen's "The Ring," Lise uses hyperbole when she thinks about the difference between her husband and herself:

"What a baby he is! I am a hundred years older than he."

See pages 632, 1000, and 1036.
See also FIGURATIVE LANGUAGE.

I

Iambic pentameter. See BLANK VERSE, METER.

Imagery The "word pictures" that writers create to help evoke an emotional response. To create effective images, writers use **sensory details,** or descriptions that appeal to one or more of the five senses: sight, hearing, touch, taste, and smell. For example, the following lines from "Through the Tunnel" by Doris Lessing use imagery to make an underwater scene vivid:

A few inches above them the water sparkled as if sequins were dropping through it. . . . It was like swimming in flaked silver.

See pages 70, 579, 653, and 676.
See also FIGURATIVE LANGUAGE.

Inversion Reversal of the usual word order in a prose sentence or line of poetry, for emphasis or variety. An example of this occurs in the final line of Shakespeare's sonnet "Shall I Compare Thee to a Summer's Day?"

So long lives this, and this gives life to thee.

Irony A contrast or discrepancy between appearance and reality, or between what is expected and what actually happens.

In **situational irony** the actual outcome of a situation is the opposite of someone's expectations–for example, the ending of "The Happy Man's Shirt" by Italo Calvino.

In **verbal irony** a person says one thing and means another. For example, in Shakespeare's *Julius Caesar,* Mark Antony uses verbal irony when he praises Brutus and the conspirators to the crowd at Julius Caesar's funeral; he is actually trying to turn the people against them.

In **dramatic irony** the audience has important information that characters in a literary work do not have. Dramatic irony also occurs in *Julius Caesar* when Caesar's wife warns him not to go to the Senate. The audience knows of the murder plot, although Caesar and his wife do not.

See page 372, 894, and 1000.
See also PARADOX.

L

Legend A traditional story handed down from the past and believed to be based on historical events and an actual hero. Most legends are exaggerated and gain elements of fantasy over the years. For example, "Where the Girl Rescued Her Brother" by Joseph Bruchac and Gayle Ross is a legend.

See pages 92 and 912.
See also EPIC, FABLE, FOLKLORE, FOLKTALE, MYTH.

Local color The use of specific details to evoke a particular region. In "The Californian's Tale," for example, Mark Twain recreates the mining country of California by describing the speech, dress, and habits of his characters.

See page 409.

Lyric poem Verse that expresses the thoughts and feelings of a single speaker. A lyric poem is usually short and creates a single, unified impression. Lyric poems in this book include Robert Hayden's "Those Winter Sundays" and Marilyn Chin's "The Floral Apron."

See page 647.

M

Magical realism Fiction that combines fantasy and realism; usually associated with contemporary Latin American writers. Magical realism inserts fantastic, sometimes humorous, events into a very believable, ordinary reality. "The Waltz of the Fat Man" by Alberto Alvaro Rios is an example of this genre.

See page 385.

Memoir An autobiographical narrative; an account of an event or period emphasizing the author's personal experience of it.

See page 422 and 440.
See also AUTOBIOGRAPHY.

Metaphor A figure of speech that compares two or more things that have something in common. In contrast to a simile, a metaphor implies the comparison instead of stating it directly, hence there is no use of connectives such as *like* or *as*. An **extended metaphor** continues the comparison throughout a paragraph, a stanza, or an entire work. The following example of a metaphor is from Naomi Shihab Nye's poem "Making a Fist":

My stomach was a melon split wide inside my skin.

See pages 579, 599, 680, 695, and 702–705.
See also ANALOGY, FIGURATIVE LANGUAGE, SIMILE.

Meter A regular pattern of stressed and unstressed syllables that gives a line of poetry a predictable rhythm. The unit of meter within a line is called a **foot.** Each type of foot has a unique pattern of stressed (´) and unstressed (˘) syllables:

iamb (˘´) as in *complete*
trochee (´˘) as in *trouble*
anapest (˘˘´) as in *intervene*
dactyl (´˘˘) as in *majesty*
spondee (´´) as in *baseball*

A particular meter is named for the type of foot and the number of feet per line. For example, **trimeter** has three feet per line, **tetrameter** has four feet, **pentameter** has five feet, and **hexameter** has six feet. The most common meter in English poetry is **iambic pentameter** as in this line from Shakespeare's *Julius Caesar:*

O par/don me, / thou bleed/ing piece / of earth.

See pages 578 and 589.
See also FOOT, RHYTHM, SCANSION.

Monologue A long speech or written expression of thoughts by one character in a literary work. The burial speeches of Brutus and Antony in act 3, scene 2, of *Julius Caesar* by Shakespeare are monologues.

See page 456.
See also DIALOGUE, DRAMATIC MONOLOGUE, SOLILOQUY.

Mood The emotional quality or atmosphere of a story. For example, Edgar Allan Poe uses graphic details of disease and death to establish a mood of horror in the beginning of "The Masque of the Red Death."

See pages 352 and 395.
See also ATMOSPHERE, SETTING, TONE.

Moral A practical lesson about right and wrong conduct.

See page 105.
See also FABLE, PARABLE.

Motif A significant word, description, idea, or image that is repeated throughout a literary work and is related to its theme. For example, in "A Swimming Lesson" Jewelle Gomez repeats the word *rhythm* to convey a message about life.

See page 498.

Myth A traditional story of anonymous origin that deals with goddesses, gods, heroes, and supernatural events. Elements of Sophocles' *Antigone* draw on the traditional mythology of ancient Greece.

See page 912.
See also EPIC, FOLKLORE, FOLKTALE, LEGEND.

N

Narration The kind of writing or speech that tells a story. Narration is used not only in novels, short stories, and narrative poetry, but also can be an important element in biographies, autobiographies, and essays.

See also NARRATIVE POETRY, NARRATOR.

Narrative poetry Verse that tells a story. Narrative poetry includes ballads, epics, and shorter poems that are usually more selective and concentrated than a prose story. For example, "Eldorado" by Edgar Allan Poe is a narrative poem.

See pages 584 and 956.
See also BALLAD, EPIC, NARRATION.

Narrator The person who tells a story. In some cases the narrator is a character in the story–for example, John in "By the Waters of Babylon" by Stephen Vincent Benét. At other times the narrator stands outside the story, as in "Catch the Moon" by Judith Ortiz Cofer.

See pages 2 and 134.
See also NARRATION, POINT OF VIEW, SPEAKER.

Nonfiction Literature about real people and events. Among the categories of nonfiction are biographies, autobiographies, and essays. For example, "An American Childhood" by Annie Dillard is nonfiction.

See pages 422–423.
See also AUTOBIOGRAPHY, BIOGRAPHY, CREATIVE NONFICTION, ESSAY, FICTION.

Novel A book-length fictional prose narrative. Because of its length, the novel has greater potential to develop plot, character, setting, and theme than does a short story.

See also FICTION, SHORT STORY.

O

Octave An eight-line stanza. The term is used mainly to describe the first eight lines of a **Petrarchan,** or **Italian, sonnet.** The octave usually presents a situation, idea, or question and rhymes *abbaabba*.

See also SESTET, SONNET, STANZA.

Ode An elaborate **lyric poem** expressed in a dignified and sincere way. Odes are imaginative as well as intellectual. Examples of the ode can be found in Sophocles' *Antigone*.

See also LYRIC POEM.

Onomatopoeia The use of a word or phrase that imitates or suggests the sound of what it describes. Some examples are *buzz, murmur, crack, swish.*

See pages 579 and 701.
See also SOUND DEVICES.

Oral tradition Literature that passes by word of mouth from one generation to the next.

See also FOLKLORE, FOLKTALE.

Oxymoron A figure of speech consisting of two seemingly contradictory terms. Some examples are "bright darkness," "wise fool," and "hateful love."

See also FIGURATIVE LANGUAGE, PARADOX.

P

Parable A simple story pointing to a moral or religious lesson. A parable differs from a fable in that its characters are usually people rather than animals.

See also FABLE, MORAL.

Paradox A situation or statement that seems to be impossible or contradictory but is nevertheless true, either literally or figuratively. An example is George Bernard Shaw's observation that "youth is wasted on the young."

See also IRONY, OXYMORON.

Parallelism The use of a series of words, phrases, or sentences that have similar grammatical form. Parallelism emphasizes the items that are arranged in the similar structures.

See also REPETITION.

Parody A humorous imitation of another, usually serious work. Behavior, customs, literature, or music can all be parodied. Henry Beard's *A Cat's Garden of Verses* is a parody of Robert Louis Stevenson's poetry.

See pages 1000 and 1011.
See also HUMOR.

Personal essay. See ESSAY.

Personification A figure of speech in which an animal, object, force of nature, or idea is given human qualities or characteristics. William Shakespeare personifies death in this line from "Shall I Compare Thee to a Summer's Day?":

Nor shall Death brag thou wand'rest in his shade

See pages 579, 614, and 680.
See also FIGURATIVE LANGUAGE.

Plot The sequence of events in a narrative work. The plot begins with **exposition,** which introduces the story's characters, setting, and conflicts. The **rising action** adds complications to the story's conflicts, or problems, leading to the **climax,** or **turning point,** which is the moment of highest emotional pitch. The **falling action** is the logical result of the climax; the **resolution,** sometimes called the **dénouement,** presents the final outcome.

See pages 3, 86, and 713.
See also CLIMAX, CONFLICT, EXPOSITION, FALLING ACTION, FORESHADOWING, RESOLUTION, RISING ACTION.

Poetry A form of literary expression distinguished from prose chiefly in its emphasis on the line as the unit of composition. Many other traditional characteristics of poetry apply to some poems but not to others: emotionally charged, imaginative language; use of figurative language; division into stanzas; rhyme; and regular metrical pattern.

See pages 578–579.

Point of view The relationship of the narrator, or storyteller, to the story. In a story with **first-person point of view,** the story is told by one of the characters, referred to as "I." The reader generally sees everything through that character's eyes. In a story with a **limited third-person point of view,** the narrator is outside the story and reveals the thoughts of only one character, but refers to that character as "he" or "she." In a story with a **third-person omniscient point of view,** the narrator is outside the story and knows everything about the characters and events.

See pages 2, 18, 164, 212, and 295.
See also NARRATOR, SPEAKER.

Props Theater slang (a shortened form of *properties*) for objects and elements of the scenery of a stage play or movie set.

See also DRAMA, STAGE DIRECTIONS.

Prose Literature that is written in sentence and paragraph form. Essays, short stories, most plays, novels, and magazine articles are examples of prose. The dialogue in Shakespeare's play *Julius Caesar* is a mixture of verse and prose.

See page 841.
See also ESSAY, SHORT STORY.

Protagonist The central character in a story, drama, or dramatic poem. Usually the action revolves around the protagonist, who undergoes the main conflict. Tiffany is the protagonist in Susan Beth Pfeffer's "As It Is with Strangers."

See pages 2 and 746.
See ANTAGONIST, CHARACTER, CONFLICT, HERO.

Pun A humorous play on two or more meanings of the same word or on two different words with the same sound. In act 1 of *Julius Caesar,* Shakespeare includes several puns. For example, the Cobbler says, "All that I live by is with the awl," punning on the words *awl* and *all*.

See page 1000.
See also HUMOR.

Q

Quatrain A four-line stanza. The quatrain is the most common stanza form in English poetry; it may be unrhymed or have a variety of rhyme schemes. The most common rhyme scheme is *abab* as in this quatrain from "The Glory of the Day Was in Her Face" by James Weldon Johnson:

The glory of the day was in her face, *a*
The beauty of the night was in her eyes. *b*
And over all her loveliness, the grace *a*
Of Morning blushing the early skies. *b*

See page 589.
See also RHYME SCHEME, STANZA.

R

Realism A literary manner that seeks to portray life as it really is lived. More specifically, realism was a nineteenth-century literary movement that usually focused on everyday middle-class or working-class conditions and characters.

Refrain A line or lines repeated at intervals in a poem or song, usually at the end of a stanza.

See also REPETITION, STANZA.

Repetition A literary device in which sounds, words, phrases, lines, or stanzas are repeated for emphasis in a poem, a speech, or another piece of writing. Repetition increases the unity in a work. When a line or stanza is repeated in a poem, it is called a **refrain.**

See also PARALLELISM, REFRAIN, RHYME.

Resolution The part of a plot that concludes the falling action by revealing or suggesting the outcome of the conflict. It is sometimes called **dénouement.**

See page 3.
See also CONFLICT, FALLING ACTION, PLOT.

Rhyme The repetition of the same stressed vowel sounds and any succeeding sounds in two or more words. **End rhymes** occur at the ends of lines of poetry. Rhyme that occurs within a single line is called **internal rhyme. Slant rhymes** occur when words include sounds that are similar but do not rhyme exactly. Slant rhyme usually involves some variation of **consonance** (the repetition of consonant sounds) or **assonance** (the repetition of vowel sounds).

See page 579.
See also ASSONANCE, CONSONANCE, REPETITION, RHYME SCHEME, SOUND DEVICES.

Rhyme scheme The pattern that end rhymes form in a stanza or in a poem. The rhyme scheme is designated by the assignment of a different letter of the alphabet to each new rhyme. For example, in these lines from "Eldorado" by Edgar Allan Poe, the rhyme scheme is *aabccb:*

Gaily bedight, *a*
A gallant knight *a*
In sunshine and in shadow, *b*
Had journeyed long, *c*
Singing a song, *c*
In search of Eldorado. *b*

See also QUATRAIN, RHYME, SONNET.

Rhythm The pattern of beats created by the arrangement of stressed and unstressed syllables, especially in poetry. Rhythm can be regular, with a predictable pattern of meter, or irregular. Rhythm can give a poem a musical quality. It can also emphasize certain words or ideas to help convey meaning.

See page 578.
See also BLANK VERSE, FOOT, FREE VERSE, METER, RHYME, SCANSION.

Rising action The part of a plot where complications to the conflict develop and increase reader interest.

See pages 3 and 1026.
See also CLIMAX, FALLING ACTION, FORESHADOWING, PLOT.

Romance A story concerning a knightly hero, his exciting adventures, and pursuit of love. The King Arthur legend is featured in many romances composed by medieval poets.

See also HERO.

S

Satire Writing that exposes and ridicules the vices or follies of people or societies. Satire may take the form of poetry, drama, or prose fiction or nonfiction. Luisa Valenzuela uses satire in "The Censors."

See pages 221 and 1000.
See also COMEDY, HUMOR.

Scansion The analysis of the meter of verse; also called scanning a poem. To scan a line of poetry means to note stressed and unstressed syllables and to divide the line into its feet, or rhythmical units.

See also FOOT, METER, RHYTHM.

Scene A subdivision of an act in a play. Each scene usually takes place in a specific setting and time.

See page 713.
See also ACT.

Science fiction Fiction dealing with the impact of real or imagined scientific or technological advances on human or alien societies of the past, present, or future. "A Sound of Thunder" by Ray Bradbury is an example of science fiction.

See also FICTION, GENRE.

Sensory details Evocative words that convey sensory experiences–seeing, hearing, tasting, touching, and smelling. Sensory details make writing come alive by helping readers experience what is being described.

See pages 70, 669, and 987.
See also IMAGERY.

Sestet A six-line poem or stanza; also the final six lines of a **Petrarchan,** or **Italian, sonnet.** In a sonnet, the sestet provides a resolution, comment, or answer to the question or situation posed earlier in the poem.

See also OCTAVE, SONNET, STANZA.

Setting The time and place in which the events of a story, novel, or play occur. Setting includes the ideas, customs, beliefs, and values of the time and place. The setting often helps create an atmosphere, or mood. For example, the setting of "The False Gems" by Guy de Maupassant is Paris in the late 1870s or early 1880s.

See pages 2, 153, 395, and 712.
See also ATMOSPHERE, MOOD.

Short story A brief fictional narrative in prose. Elements of the short story include **plot, character, setting, point of view,** and **theme**.

See pages 2–3 and 308–312.
See also FICTION.

Simile A figure of speech using *like* or *as* to compare seemingly unlike things. For example, this simile appears in Amy Tan's story "Two Kinds":

And she also did a fancy sweep of a curtsy, so that the fluffy skirt of her white dress cascaded to the floor like the petals of a large carnation.

An **epic simile** is a long, elaborate comparison that continues for several lines. It is a feature of epic poems, but is found in other poems as well. Lawrence Ferlinghetti's poem "Constantly risking absurdity" is an example of an epic, or extended, simile.

See pages 579, 594, 680, and 694.
See also ANALOGY, FIGURATIVE LANGUAGE, METAPHOR.

Situational irony. See IRONY.

Soliloquy A long speech spoken by a character in a dramatic work, who is typically alone on stage. This speech reveals the private thoughts and emotions of the character. For example, Antony vows his revenge of Caesar's murder in a soliloquy in Shakespeare's *Julius Caesar,* act 3, scene 1.

See page 818.
See also MONOLOGUE.

Sonnet A lyric poem of fourteen lines, almost always written in iambic pentameter and typically following strict patterns of stanza divisions and rhymes.

The **Shakespearean,** or **English, sonnet** consists of three **quatrains,** or four-line stanzas, followed by a **couplet,** or pair of rhyming lines. The rhyme scheme is usually *abab, cdcd, efef, gg.* The rhyming couplet often presents a conclusion to the issues or questions presented in the three quatrains. "Shall I Compare Thee to a Summer's Day?" is a Shakespearean sonnet.

In the **Petrarchan,** or **Italian, sonnet,** fourteen lines are divided into two stanzas, the eight-lined **octave** and the six-lined **sestet.** The sestet usually responds to a question or situation posed by the octave. The rhyme scheme for the octave is usually *abbaabba;* for the sestet the rhyme scheme is usually *cdecde.*

See pages 586 and 589.
See also OCTAVE, RHYME SCHEME, SESTET.

Sound devices Techniques used to emphasize particular sounds in writing or to create a sense of rhythm.

See pages 579 and 685.
See also ALLITERATION, ASSONANCE, CONSONANCE, ONOMATOPOEIA, RHYME.

Speaker The voice that communicates with the reader of a poem, similar to the narrator in a work of prose. Often a poet invents a speaker with a particular identity in order to create a desired impact. For example, the speaker in "The Rain," by Henry Beard, is a cat.

See pages 578 and 659.
See also DRAMATIC POETRY, NARRATOR, TONE.

Stage directions Instructions written by the dramatist to describe the appearance and actions of characters, as well as the sets, props, costumes, sound effects, and lighting for a play.

See page 712.
See also DRAMA, PROPS.

Stanza A group of lines forming a unit in a poem.

See page 578.
See also COUPLET, OCTAVE, QUATRAIN, SESTET.

Stereotype A character who is not developed as an individual but as a collection of traits and mannerisms supposedly shared by all members of a group.

See also CHARACTER, FARCE.

Stream of consciousness A writing technique which allows a character's or narrator's thoughts and feelings to flow in an uninterrupted manner.

Style The author's choice and arrangement of words and sentences in a literary work. Style can reveal an author's purpose in writing and attitude toward his or her subject and audience.

See page 255.
See also AUTHOR'S PURPOSE, DICTION, TONE, VOICE.

Suspense A feeling of curiosity, uncertainty, or even dread about what is going to happen next. Writers increase the level of suspense in a story by giving readers clues to what might happen. In "The Monkey's Paw" by W. W. Jacobs, suspense builds as the reader realizes how the monkey's paw makes wishes come true.

See pages 182 and 987.
See also FORESHADOWING, MOOD.

Symbol Any object, person, place, or experience that means more than what it is. Symbolism is the use of images to represent internal realities. Swimming through the tunnel, for example, is a symbolic act for Jerry in Doris Lessing's "Through the Tunnel." The act means that he is growing up.

See pages 243 and 664.
See also FIGURATIVE LANGUAGE.

T

Tall tale A type of folklore in which the deeds of one or more characters are wildly exaggerated but told seriously, as if the deeds were true. "Sundiata" is an example of a tall tale.

See page 940.
See also FOLKLORE, FOLKTALE.

Tanka Unrhymed Japanese verse form that consists of five lines. The first and third lines have five syllables each; the other lines have seven syllables each.

See page 686.
See also HAIKU.

Theme The central message of a story, poem, novel, or play that readers can apply to life. Some works have a **stated theme,** which is expressed directly. More commonly, works have an **implied theme,** which is revealed gradually. To discover an implied theme in a short story, the reader might look at the experiences of the main character and the lessons he or she learns.

See pages 3, 35, and 492.
See also AUTHOR'S PURPOSE, FABLE.

Thesis The main idea of a work of nonfiction. The thesis may be stated directly or implied.

See pages 423 and 513.

Tone A reflection of a writer's or speaker's attitude toward the subject. A writer's tone may convey a variety of attitudes, including sympathy, objectivity, seriousness, irony, sadness, bitterness, or humor. For example, Alice Childress's light, humorous tone in "Mrs. James" contrasts with Isabel Allende's solemn tone in "And of Clay Are We Created."

See pages 195, 306, 640, and 974.
See also ATMOSPHERE, DICTION, MOOD, SPEAKER.

Turning point. See CLIMAX.

Tragedy A play in which a main character, or **tragic hero,** suffers a downfall. That character typically is a person of dignified or heroic stature. The downfall may result from outside forces or from a weakness within the character, which is known as a **tragic flaw.** For example, *Antigone* by Sophocles is a tragedy which describes the downfall of a king, Creon.

See pages 768 and 871.
See also DRAMA, HERO.

Tragic flaw. See TRAGEDY.

U-V

Understatement Language that makes something seem less than it really is. Understatement may be used to insert humor or to focus the reader's attention on something the author wants to emphasize.

See pages 285 and 1000.
See also FIGURATIVE LANGUAGE.

Verbal irony. See IRONY.

Voice An author's distinctive use of language to convey the author's or narrator's personality to the reader. Voice depends on elements of style, such as **diction** and **tone.**

See page 566.
See also DICTION, STYLE, TONE.

Language Handbook

Troubleshooter

The Troubleshooter will help you recognize and correct errors that you might make in your writing.

Sentence Fragment

Problem: A fragment that lacks a subject

The snow is very deep. Is hard to shovel. *frag*

Solution: Add a subject to the fragment to make it a complete sentence.

The snow is very deep. It is hard to shovel.

Problem: A fragment that lacks a complete verb

The marathon winner received her awards. A trophy and a check. *frag*

The speaker addressed the unruly audience. Nobody listening to him. *frag*

Solution A: Add a complete verb or a helping verb and other words as needed to make the sentence complete.

The marathon winner received her awards. A trophy and a check were presented to her.

The speaker addressed the unruly audience. Nobody was listening to him.

Solution B: Combine the fragment with another sentence. Add a comma to set off a nonessential appositive or a comma and a conjunction to separate two main clauses in a compound sentence.

The marathon winner received her awards, a trophy and a check.

The speaker addressed the unruly audience, but nobody was listening to him.

Problem: A fragment that is a subordinate clause

Our teacher was late for school. Because she had a flat tire on the way. *frag*

I am eating spaghetti. Which is one of my favorite foods. *frag*

Solution A: Combine the fragment with another sentence. Add a comma to set off a nonessential clause.

Our teacher was late for school because she had a flat tire on the way.

I am eating spaghetti, which is one of my favorite foods.

Solution B: Rewrite the fragment as a complete sentence, eliminating the subordinating conjunction or the relative pronoun and adding a subject or other words necessary to make a complete thought.

Our teacher was late for school. She had a flat tire on the way.

I am eating spaghetti. It is one of my favorite foods.

Problem: A fragment that lacks both a subject and a verb

Kendra traveled all day and arrived in town. At nine o'clock. *frag*

Solution: Combine the fragment with another sentence.

Kendra traveled all day and arrived in town at nine o'clock.

Rule of Thumb: Sentence fragments can make your writing hard to understand. Be sure to check that every sentence has a subject and a verb.

Run-on Sentence

Problem: Comma splice—two main clauses separated by only a comma

We had dinner at a Chinese restaurant, I liked the cashew chicken. *run-on*

Solution A: Replace the comma with an end mark of punctuation, such as a period or a question mark, and begin the new sentence with a capital letter.

We had dinner at a Chinese restaurant. I liked the cashew chicken.

Solution B: Place a semicolon between the two main clauses.

We had dinner at a Chinese restaurant; I liked the cashew chicken.

Solution C: Add a coordinating conjunction after the comma.

We had dinner at a Chinese restaurant, and I liked the cashew chicken.

Problem: Two main clauses with no punctuation between them

The hurricane headed out to sea then it turned back toward land. *run-on*

Solution A: Separate the main clauses with an end mark of punctuation, such as a period or a question mark, and begin the second sentence with a capital letter.

The hurricane headed out to sea. Then it turned back toward land.

Solution B: Separate the main clauses with a semicolon.

The hurricane headed out to sea; then it turned back toward land.

Solution C: Add a comma and a coordinating conjunction between the main clauses.

The hurricane headed out to sea, but then it turned back toward land.

Problem: Two main clauses with no comma before the coordinating conjunction

I went to the mall on Saturday and my sister went with me. *run-on*

Solution: Add a comma before the coordinating conjunction to separate the two main clauses.

I went to the mall on Saturday, and my sister went with me.

Rule of Thumb: It often helps to have someone else read your writing to see if it is clear. Since you know what the sentences are supposed to mean, you might miss the need for punctuation.

Lack of Subject-Verb Agreement

Problem: A subject that is separated from the verb by an intervening prepositional phrase

The herd of wild horses (sweep) across the plains. *agr*

Even the youngest horses in the herd (keeps) up with the rest. *agr*

Solution: Make the verb agree with the subject, not with the object of a preposition. The subject of a sentence is never the object of a preposition.

The herd of wild horses sweeps across the plains.

Even the youngest horses in the herd keep up with the rest.

Problem: A predicate nominative that differs in number from the subject

Those three actors (is) the entire cast of the play. *agr*

The entire cast of the play (are) those three actors. *agr*

Solution: Ignore the predicate nominative, and make the verb agree with the subject of the sentence.

Those three actors are the entire cast of the play.

The entire cast of the play is those three actors.

Problem: A subject that follows the verb

In this cage (lives) six gerbils. *agr*

There (goes) two of them now. *agr*

Solution: In an inverted sentence, look for the subject *after* the verb. Then make sure the verb agrees with the subject.

In this cage live six gerbils.

There go two of them now.

Rule of Thumb: Reversing the order of an inverted sentence might help you decide on the correct verb form: "Six gerbils live in this cage."

Problem: A collective noun as the subject

The school band (practice) two days a week. *agr*

The group (has) different opinions on the subject. *agr*

Solution A: If the collective noun refers to a group as a whole, use a singular verb.

The school band practices two days a week.

Solution B: If the collective noun refers to each member of a group individually, use a plural verb.

The group have different opinions on the subject.

Problem: A noun of amount as the subject

Twenty dollars (are) the price they advertised. *agr*

Five one-dollar bills (is) in my wallet. *agr*

Solution: Determine whether the noun of amount refers to one unit and is therefore singular, or whether it refers to a number of individual units and is therefore plural.

Twenty dollars is the price they advertised.

Five one-dollar bills are in my wallet.

Problem: A compound subject that is joined by *and*

Macaroni and cheese (are) his favorite meal. *agr*

Vegetables and meat loaf (is) in the refrigerator. *agr*

Solution A: If the parts of the compound subject belong to one unit or if both parts refer to the same person or thing, use a singular verb.

Macaroni and cheese is his favorite meal.

Solution B: If the parts of the compound subject do not belong to one unit or if they refer to different people or things, use a plural verb.

Vegetables and meat loaf are in the refrigerator.

Problem: A compound subject that is joined by *or* or *nor*

Neither those cats nor that dog (belong) to me. *agr*

Solution: Make the verb agree with the subject that is closer to it.

Neither those cats nor that dog belongs to me.

Problem: A compound subject that is preceded by *many a, every,* or *each*

Every boy and girl here live in the neighborhood. *agr*

Solution: When *many a, every,* or *each* precedes a compound subject, the subject is considered singular. Use a singular verb.

Every boy and girl here lives in the neighborhood.

Problem: A subject that is separated from the verb by an intervening expression

Jermaine's dog, as well as Andrea's parrot, do a lot of tricks. *agr*

Solution: Certain intervening expressions, such as those beginning with *as well as, in addition to,* and *together with,* do not change the number of the subject. Ignore such expressions between a subject and its verb, and make the verb agree with the subject.

Jermaine's dog, as well as Andrea's parrot, does a lot of tricks.

Problem: An indefinite pronoun as the subject

Each of the activities are open to the public. *agr*

Solution: Determine whether the indefinite pronoun is singular or plural, and make the verb agree with it. Some indefinite pronouns are singular–*another, anyone, everyone, one, each, either, neither, anything, everything, something,* and *somebody.* Some are plural–*both, many, few, several,* and *others.* Some can be singular or plural–*some, all, any, more, most,* and *none*–depending on the noun to which they refer.

Each of the activities is open to the public.

Lack of Pronoun-Antecedent Agreement

Problem: A singular antecedent that can be either male or female

A family doctor sometimes refers his patient to a specialist. *ant*

Solution A: Traditionally, a masculine pronoun was used to refer to an antecedent that might be either male or female. This usage ignores or excludes females. Reword the sentence to use *he or she, him or her,* and so on.

A family doctor sometimes refers his or her patient to a specialist.

Solution B: Reword the sentence so that both the antecedent and the pronoun are plural.

Family doctors sometimes refer their patients to specialists.

Solution C: Reword the sentence to eliminate the pronoun.

A family doctor sometimes refers a patient to a specialist.

Problem: A second-person pronoun that refers to a third-person antecedent

Sarah is going to a school that trains (you) to repair computers. *ant*

Solution A: Use the appropriate third-person pronoun.

Sarah is going to a school that trains her to repair computers.

Solution B: Use an appropriate noun instead of a pronoun.

Sarah is going to a school that trains people to repair computers.

Problem: A singular indefinite pronoun as an antecedent

Neither of the boys brought (their) sleeping bag. *ant*

Solution: *Another, any, every, one, each, either, neither, anything, everything, something,* and *somebody* are singular; they therefore require singular personal pronouns even when followed by a prepositional phrase that contains a plural noun.

Neither of the boys brought his sleeping bag.

Rule of Thumb: To help yourself remember that pronouns such as *each, either, every,* and *neither* are singular, think *each one, either one, every one,* and *neither one.*

Lack of Clear Pronoun Reference [Unclear Antecedent]

Problem: A pronoun reference that is weak or vague

The sculptor was carving, (which) we admired. *ref*

A flock of birds roosted in that tree last year, and (it) was very noisy. *ref*

Solution A: Rewrite the sentence, adding a clear antecedent for the pronoun.

The sculptor was carving a statue of a bear, which we admired.

Solution B: Rewrite the sentence, substituting a noun for the pronoun.

A flock of birds roosted in that tree last year, and their chattering was very noisy.

Problem: A pronoun that could refer to more than one antecedent

Roberto and his grandfather caught six fish, and he cleaned them all. *ref*

The toxic waste the factory dumped in the river made the people avoid it. *ref*

Solution A: Rewrite the sentence, substituting a noun for the pronoun.

Roberto and his grandfather caught six fish, and Roberto cleaned them all.

Solution B: Rewrite the sentence, making the antecedent of the pronoun clear.

The people avoided the river because of the toxic waste the factory dumped in it.

Problem: The indefinite use of *you* or *they*

The movie's characters seem so real that you get caught up in the story. *ref*

In New Orleans they have a Mardi Gras celebration every year. *ref*

Solution A: Rewrite the sentence, substituting a noun for the pronoun.

The movie's characters seem so real that the audience gets caught up in the story.

Solution B: Rewrite the sentence, eliminating the pronoun entirely.

The city of New Orleans has a Mardi Gras celebration every year.

Shift in Pronoun

Problem: An incorrect shift in person between two pronouns

I like to sit next to the window, where you can enjoy the scenery. *pro*

Eduardo and Lily are learning to search the World Wide Web, where you can find information on many topics. *pro*

When you surf the Web, one might come up with inaccurate data. *pro*

Solution A: Replace the incorrect pronoun with a pronoun that agrees with its antecedent.

I like to sit next to the window, where I can enjoy the scenery.

Eduardo and Lily are learning to search the World Wide Web, where they can find information on many topics.

When you surf the Web, you might come up with inaccurate data.

Solution B: Replace the pronoun with an appropriate noun.

Eduardo and Lily are learning to search the World Wide Web, where students can find information on many topics.

Shift in Verb Tense

Problem: An unnecessary shift in tense

Laurent goes across town by bus and worked at his job all afternoon.

When the clock struck twelve, Cinderella's coach turns back into a pumpkin.

Solution: When two or more events occur at the same time, be sure to use the same verb tense to describe each event.

Laurent goes across town by bus and works at his job all afternoon.

When the clock struck twelve, Cinderella's coach turned back into a pumpkin.

Problem: A lack of correct shift in tenses to show that one event precedes or follows another

By the time my aunt finally got here, we waited for an hour.

Solution: When two events have occurred at different times in the past, shift from the past tense to the past perfect tense to indicate that one action began and ended before another past action began.

By the time my aunt finally got here, we had waited for an hour.

Rule of Thumb: When you need to use more than one verb tense in a sentence, it may help to first jot down the sequence of events you're writing about. Be clear in your mind which action happened first.

Incorrect Verb Tense or Form

Problem: An incorrect or missing verb ending

Have you ever milk a cow? *tense*

I did two months ago, when I visit my uncle's farm. *tense*

Solution: Add *-ed* to a regular verb to form the past participle and the past tense.

Have you ever milked a cow?

I did two months ago, when I visited my uncle's farm.

Problem: An improperly formed irregular verb

Jon seeked advice from all his friends. *tense*

Sheila nearly freezed before we built a warm fire. *tense*

Solution: Irregular verbs form their past and past participles in some way other than by adding *-ed.* Memorize these forms, or look them up in a dictionary.

Jon sought advice from all his friends.

Sheila nearly froze before we built a warm fire.

Problem: Confusion between the past form and the past participle

We've went to that beach many times. *tense*

Haskell has chose the bike he wants. *tense*

Solution: Use the past participle of an irregular verb, not the past form, when you use the auxiliary verb *have.*

We've gone to that beach many times.

Haskell has chosen the bike he wants.

Problem: Improper use of the past participle

He begun his assignment. *tense*

The tardy bell rung before I got through the door. *tense*

Solution A: The past participle of an irregular verb cannot stand alone as a verb. Add a form of the auxiliary verb *have* to the past participle to form a complete verb.

He has begun his assignment.

The tardy bell had rung before I got through the door.

Solution B: Replace the past participle with the past form of the verb.

He began his assignment.

The tardy bell rang before I got through the door.

Misplaced or Dangling Modifier

Problem: A misplaced modifier

Jungle cats frighten many people with big teeth and claws. *mod*

Floating over the park, Megan saw a red balloon. *mod*

The boy on the skateboard jumped the curb racing down the street. *mod*

Solution: Modifiers that modify the wrong word or that seem to modify more than one idea in a sentence are called misplaced modifiers. Move the misplaced phrase as close as possible to the word or words it modifies.

With big teeth and claws, jungle cats frighten many people.

Megan saw a red balloon floating over the park.

Racing down the street, the boy on the skateboard jumped the curb.

Problem: Incorrect placement of the adverb *only*

Juana only goes to movies on the weekend. *mod*

Solution: Place the adverb *only* immediately before the word or group of words it modifies.

Only Juana goes to movies on the weekend.

Juana goes only to movies on the weekend.

Juana goes to movies only on the weekend.

Rule of Thumb: Note that each time *only* is moved, the meaning of the sentence changes. Check to be sure that your sentence conveys your intended meaning.

Problem: A dangling modifier

Walking through the museum, the paintings were from many different countries. *mod*

By studying every night, the examination was easily passed. *mod*

Solution: Rewrite the sentence, adding a noun to which the dangling phrase clearly refers. Often you will have to add other words or change the form of the verb to complete the meaning of the sentence.

Walking through the museum, Arthur noticed paintings from many different countries.

By studying every night, the student passed the examination easily.

Missing or Misplaced Possessive Apostrophe

Problem: Singular nouns

That womans daughter is Doris best friend. *poss*

Solution: Use an apostrophe and *-s* to form the possessive of a singular noun or a proper name, even if the noun ends in *s.*

That woman's daughter is Doris's best friend.

Problem: Plural nouns ending in *-s*

Her twin daughters jackets are just alike. *poss*

Solution: Use an apostrophe alone to form the possessive of a plural noun that ends in *-s.*

Her twin daughters' jackets are just alike.

Problem: Plural nouns not ending in *-s*

This store carries a good selection of mens suits. *poss*

Solution: Use an apostrophe and *-s* to form the possessive of a plural noun that does not end in *-s.*

This store carries a good selection of men's suits.

Problem: Pronouns

In this organization everyones opinion counts. *poss*

Are these skates your's or her's? *poss*

Solution A: Use an apostrophe and -*s* to form the possessive of a singular indefinite pronoun.

In this organization everyone's opinion counts.

Solution B: Do not use an apostrophe with any of the possessive personal pronouns.

Are these skates yours or hers?

Problem: Confusion between *its* and *it's*

Its a long way from your house to mine. *cont*

The airplane had ice on it's wings. *poss*

Solution A: Use an apostrophe to form the contraction of *it is.*

It's a long way from your house to mine.

Solution B: Do not use an apostrophe to form the possessive of *it.*

The airplane had ice on its wings.

Missing Commas with Nonessential Elements

Problem: Missing commas with nonessential participles or participial phrases

Sonya exhausted from her long trip went to bed early. *com*

Solution: Determine whether the participle or participial phrase is essential to the meaning of the sentence or not. If it is not essential, set off the phrase with commas.

Sonya, exhausted from her long trip, went to bed early.

Problem: Missing commas with nonessential adjective clauses

My oldest cousin who visits us every summer is one grade ahead of me in school. *com*

Solution: Determine whether the clause is essential to the meaning of the sentence or not. If it is not essential, set off the clause with commas.

My oldest cousin, who visits us every summer, is one grade ahead of me in school.

Problem: Missing commas with nonessential appositives

In Chaco Canyon a site in New Mexico we saw the ruins of huge structures built by the Anasazi. *com*

Solution: Determine whether the appositive is essential to the meaning of the sentence or not. If it is not essential, set off the appositive with commas.

In Chaco Canyon, a site in New Mexico, we saw the ruins of huge structures built by the Anasazi.

Rule of Thumb: To determine whether a word, phrase, or clause is essential, try reading the sentence without it.

Problem: Missing commas with interjections and parenthetical expressions

Judith as you know will be sixteen tomorrow. *com*

Hey don't forget to bring the ice cream. *com*

Solution: Set off the interjection or parenthetical expression with commas.

Judith, as you know, will be sixteen tomorrow.

Hey, don't forget to bring the ice cream.

Missing Commas in a Series

Problem: Missing commas in a series of words, phrases, or clauses

Last summer Hideki visited relatives in Tokyo Kyoto and Kobe. ∆ com

We followed the trail along the river across a wooden bridge and up a steep hill. ∆ com

Alex dribbled the ball then he passed it to Dominic and Dominic scored the goal. ∆ com

The library is open for people who want a book to read people who are looking for specific information and people who need a quiet place to study. ∆ com

The little boy complained whined and cried until his mother picked him up. ∆ com

Solution: When there are three or more elements in a series, use a comma after each element, including the element that precedes a conjunction.

Last summer Hideki visited relatives in Tokyo, Kyoto, and Kobe.

We followed the trail along the river, across a wooden bridge, and up a steep hill.

Alex dribbled the ball, then he passed it to Dominic, and Dominic scored the goal.

The library is open for people who want a book to read, people who are looking for specific information, and people who need a quiet place to study.

The little boy complained, whined, and cried until his mother picked him up.

Rule of Thumb: When you're having difficulty with a rule of usage, try rewriting the rule in your own words. Then check with your teacher to be sure you have grasped the concept.

Troublesome Words

This section will help you choose between words that are often confusing. It will also alert you to avoid certain words and expressions in school or business writing.

a, an

Use the article *an* when the word that follows begins with a vowel sound. Use *a* when the word that follows begins with a consonant sound.

An exercise mat lay in **a** corner of the room.

Use the article *a* when the word that follows begins with a sounded *h* or a *u* with the long sound ("yew"). Use *an* when the word that follows begins with an unsounded *h* or a *u* with the short sound.

A hungry family will not wait **an** hour for dinner.

An umpire wears **a** uniform.

a lot, alot

The expression *a lot* means "a large amount" or "a great deal" (as in "I like him a lot") and should always be written as two words. Some authorities discourage its use in formal English.

A lot of people arrived early for the big game.

Many people arrived early for the big game.

accept, except

Accept is a verb meaning "to receive" or "to agree to." *Except* is occasionally used as a verb, but more often it is used as a preposition meaning "but."

Sally will **accept** the award.

Everybody was invited **except** Bob.

affect, effect

Affect is a verb meaning "to cause a change in" or "to influence." *Effect* as a verb means "to bring about or accomplish." As a noun, *effect* means "result" or "that which has been brought about."

Incorrect answers will **affect** your test score.

Diligent study will **effect** a rise in your test score.

Diligent study will have a good **effect** on your test score.

ain't

Ain't is never used in formal speaking or writing unless you are quoting the exact words of a character or real person. Instead of using *ain't,* say or write *am not, is not,* or use contractions: *I'm not, she's not, she isn't, they aren't.*

Cassandra **is not** going to the dance.

all ready, already

All ready, written as two words, is an adjective phrase that means "completely ready." *Already,* written as one word, is an adverb that means "before" or "by this time."

By the time supper was **all ready,** the guests had **already** arrived.

all right, alright

The expression *all right* should be written as two words.

Let's see if the man who fell down is **all right.**

Rule of Thumb: Dictionaries are good guides to the usage of a word. Even though some dictionaries do list the single word *alright,* they indicate that it is not a preferred spelling.

all together, altogether

All together means "in a group." *Altogether* is an adverb meaning "completely" or "on the whole."

They worked on the project **all together.**

Their work was **altogether** excellent.

amount, number

Use *amount* to refer to a quantity that cannot be counted. Use *number* to refer to things that can be counted.

A great **amount** of water went over the falls.

A great **number** of logs went over the falls.

Rule of Thumb: Use *amount* to refer to fluids, materials, and gases.

anxious, eager

Anxious means "uneasy or worried about some event or situation." *Eager* means "having a keen interest" or "feeling impatient for something expected."

Gus is **anxious** about the outcome of the difficult test.

Berta is **eager** to see her grades because she knows she did well.

a while, awhile

An article and a noun form the expression *a while.* Often the preposition *in* or *for* precedes *a while,* forming a prepositional phrase. The single word *awhile* is an adverb.

He'll arrive in **a while.** He'll work for **a while.**

He'll work **awhile** after he arrives.

being as, being that

Although the expressions *being as* and *being that* sometimes replace *because* or *since* in informal conversation, you should always avoid them in formal speaking and writing.

Because she made excellent grades, Sylvia skipped a year in school.

Since Carlos is already at home, let's visit him there.

beside, besides

Beside means "next to." *Besides* means "moreover" or "in addition to."

Clark sat **beside** me at dinner.

Besides having a fine dinner, we also ate dessert.

between, among

Use *between* when comparing one person or thing with another person or thing or with an entire group. Use *among* to show a relationship in which more than two persons or things are considered as a group.

He had to choose **between** the movie and the play.

What are the differences **between** a woodpecker and other birds?

There are differences **among** various kinds of birds.

bring, take

Bring means "to carry from a distant place to a closer one." *Take* means "to carry from a nearby place to a more distant one."

Bring me a copy of the newspaper when you come here tomorrow.

The cab will **take** you to the airport from here.

can, may

Can implies the ability to do something. *May* implies permission to do something or the possibility of doing it.

You **may** go to the movie if you **can** pay the price of a ticket.

Rule of Thumb: Although *can* is sometimes used in place of *may* in informal speech, you should distinguish between them when speaking and writing formally.

can't hardly, can't scarcely

Can't hardly and *can't scarcely* are considered double negatives, since *hardly* and *scarcely* by themselves have a negative meaning. Do not use *hardly* and *scarcely* with *not* or *-n't*.

Tamera **can hardly** reach the shelf.

Gabriel **can scarcely** believe he won the contest.

capital, capitol

Use *capital* to refer to the city that is the center of government of a state or country, to money or other assets, or to a capital letter. Use *capitol* to refer to the building in which a state or national legislature meets.

Our class took a trip to Washington, D.C., the nation's **capital.**

We toured the **capitol,** where the legislature was in session.

complement, compliment

A *complement* is something that makes a thing complete. A *compliment* is an expression of praise or admiration.

The CD-ROM is the **complement** of the textbook.

The teacher's **compliment** pleased Jade.

compose, comprise

Compose means "to form by putting together." *Comprise* means "to contain, embrace."

Water is **composed** of hydrogen and oxygen.

The United States **comprises** fifty states.

continual, continuous

Continual describes repetitive action with pauses. *Continuous* describes an action that continues with no interruption in space or time.

Whenever we get together, Jorge and I have **continual** discussions about science.

My interest in the subject has been **continuous** for as long as I can remember.

could of, might of, must of, should of, would of

The helping verb *have,* not the preposition *of,* should follow *could, might, must, should,* or *would.*

Midori **could have** climbed the rope if she had tried.

Isabel **must have** heard that song before.

different from, different than

The expression *different from* is generally preferred to *different than.*

Chess is **different from** checkers.

emigrate, immigrate

Emigrate means "to leave one country to settle in another." Use *from* with *emigrate. Immigrate* means "to enter a country in order to live there permanently." Use *to* or *into* with *immigrate.*

Nikolai plans to **emigrate** from the Ukraine.

Nikolai plans to **immigrate** to the United States.

Rule of Thumb: Remember that the *e-* in *emigrate* comes from *ex-* ("out of"); the *im-* in *immigrate* comes from *in-* ("into").

ensure, assure, insure

Ensure means to make sure of something, to guarantee it. *Assure* means to reassure someone, to remove doubt. *Insure* means to cover something with insurance or to secure it.

Please take action to **ensure** the prompt arrival of the package.

Can you **assure** me that everything has been taken care of?

You must **insure** the car before you can drive it.

farther, further

Farther refers to physical distance. *Further* refers to time or degree.

Now the comet is moving **farther** and **farther** away from Earth.

Think **further** back in time and see what you can remember.

There is nothing **further** to say.

fewer, less

Fewer is generally used to refer to things or qualities that can be counted. *Less* is generally used to refer to things or qualities that cannot be counted. In addition, *less* is sometimes used with figures that are regarded as single amounts or single quantities.

Fewer people attended the movie this week than last week.

There is **less** water in this swimming pool than in the one at school.

You can eat lunch at this restaurant for **less** than ten dollars. [The money is treated as a single sum, not as individual dollars.]

good, well

Good is often used as an adjective meaning "pleasing" or "able." *Well* may be used as an adverb of manner telling how ably something is done or as an adjective meaning "in good health."

This meal tastes **good.** [adjective after a linking verb]

Claudia swims **well.** [adverb of manner]

Because José has the flu, he is not **well** enough to come to school. [adjective meaning "in good health"]

had of

The word *of* should not be used between *had* and a past participle.

I wish I **had seen** that television show.

hanged, hung

When your meaning is "put to death by hanging," use *hanged* in the past tense. In all other cases, use *hung.*

Many countries **hanged** convicted murderers in the nineteenth century.

Rachel **hung** her hat on the peg.

in, into

Use *in* when you mean "inside" or "within." Use *into* to indicate movement or direction from outside to a point within.

Melissa is already **in** the theater.

I hurried **into** the theater because it was nearly time for the play to begin.

irregardless, regardless

Both the prefix *ir-* and suffix *-less* have negative meanings. When they are used together, they produce a double negative, which is incorrect. Therefore, you should use *regardless* rather than *irregardless.*

Riad listens to whatever people say, **regardless** of their opinions.

learn, teach

Learn means "to gain knowledge." *Teach* means "to instruct" or "to give knowledge to."

Emil **learns** well from his professor.

Mr. Musser **teaches** us our spelling lessons.

leave, let

Leave means "to go away; depart." *Let* means "to allow" or "to permit." With the word *alone* you may use either *let* or *leave.*

Francesca wanted to **leave** the party.

Ryugen **lets** me use his CDs.

Leave me alone. **Let** me alone.

lend, loan

Lend is a verb. *Loan* is a noun. Although *loan* is sometimes used informally as a verb, *lend* is preferable.

I will **lend** you my calculator if you return it tomorrow.

Thank you for the **loan.**

like, as

Use *like,* a preposition, to introduce a prepositional phrase. Use *as,* a subordinating conjunction, to introduce a subordinate clause. Many authorities believe that *like* should not be used before a clause in formal English.

Werner looks **like** his brother.

Mildred baby-sits tonight, **as** she always does on Fridays.

Rule of Thumb: *As* can be a preposition in some cases, as in *He posed as a secret agent.*

loose, lose

Use the adjective *loose* (lo͞os) when you mean "free," "not firmly attached," or "not fitting tightly." Use the verb *lose* (lo͞oz) when you mean "to have no longer," "to misplace," or "to fail to win."

In spite of the city's leash laws, Miguel lets his dog run **loose.**

Marlene doesn't want to **lose** another set of keys.

passed, past

Passed is the past and the past participle form of *pass. Past* is used as a noun, an adjective, a preposition, or an adverb.

The blue car **passed** the bicycle. [verb]

History is a study of events in the **past.** [noun]

Ian took a long vacation this **past** summer. [adjective]

The grocery store is just **past** the gas station. [preposition]

The puppies woke up when their mother walked **past.** [adverb]

precede, proceed

Use *precede* when you mean "to go or come before." Use *proceed* when you mean "to continue" or "to move along."

July **precedes** August.

The line of customers will **proceed** slowly.

principal, principle

Principal, as an adjective, means "the most important or first in rank." As a noun, it is the title of the head of a school. *Principle* is a noun that means "a fundamental truth or general law."

My **principal** objection to the TV set is its price.

The school **principal** fully supports our club's activities.

My research project was set up according to strict scientific **principles.**

raise, rise

The verb *raise* means "to cause to move upward" or "to lift up." It always takes an object. The verb *rise* means "to get up" or "to go up." It is an intransitive verb and never takes an object.

The soldiers **raise** the flag at dawn every morning.

Your temperature will **rise** if you do vigorous exercise.

reason . . . is that, because

Because means "for the reason that." Therefore, do not use *because* after *reason . . . is.* Use either *reason . . . is that* or *because* alone.

The **reason** there is no baseball game today **is that** it is raining.

There is no baseball game today **because** it is raining.

respectfully, respectively

Use *respectfully* to mean "with respect." Use *respectively* to mean "in the order named."

Saul spoke **respectfully** to his boss.

Gareth and Alice are third and fourth in line, **respectively.**

says, said	
Says is the present-tense, third-person singular form of the verb *say. Said* is the past tense of *say.* Do not use *says* when you are referring to the past.	Sebastian **says** he is going downtown. Yesterday Sebastian **said** he was going downtown.
sit, set	
Sit means "to be seated." It rarely takes an object. *Set* means "to put" or "to place," and it generally takes an object. When *set* is used to mean "the sun is going down," it does not take an object.	Sara is going to **sit** on the park bench. **Set** the groceries down on the kitchen table. The sun **set** at seven o'clock this evening.
than, then	
Than is a conjunction. Use it in comparisons. *Then* is an adverb used to mean "soon afterward," "the time mentioned," "at another time," "for that reason," "in that case," and "besides."	The task is more complex **than** you think it is. Alicia is better at math **than** Claudio is. Rashad will go to the party, and **then** I will join him. By **then** you will be very hungry. Andres was only five years old **then.** If you can't answer the question, **then** Sheila will.
their, they're, there	
Their is the possessive form of *they. They're* is the contraction of *they are. There* means "in that place." *There* is also sometimes used as an interjection, expressing a sense of completion.	It's **their** business, not ours. Ask them whether **they're** going to join us. You will find your book **there** on your desk. **There!**
to, too, two	
Use *to* when you mean "in the direction of." Also, use *to* before a verb to form an infinitive. Use *too* when you mean "also" or "excessively." *Two* is the number that comes after one.	We will drive **to** the mall. I need **to** buy new shoes. My brother will come along, **too.** I bought only **two** ice cream cones.
toward, towards	
These words are interchangeable; as prepositions, they both mean "in the direction of."	She drove **toward** her house. She drove **towards** her house.
where . . . at	
Do not use *at* after a question with *where.*	**Where** are my keys?

whereas, while

Both *whereas* and *while* can be used as conjunctions meaning "although." *Whereas* also means "it being the fact that." *While* can be used as a conjunction indicating a period of time.

I spent the afternoon at work, **whereas** you went swimming.

Miryam's brother and sister like vanilla, **while** she prefers chocolate.

Whereas everyone is in agreement, we can adjourn this meeting.

Roberto reviewed the lesson **while** Marisela finished her research paper.

Rule of Thumb: The conjunction *whereas* is usually reserved for very formal usage.

who, whom

Use the nominative case pronoun *who* for the subject.

Who knocked on the door?

Tell me **who** can solve this problem. [subject of the noun clause]

Who do you think can solve the problem?

Rule of Thumb: When a question contains an interrupting expression such as *do you think,* it helps to omit the interrupting phrase to determine whether to use *who* or *whom.*

Use the objective pronoun *whom* for the direct or indirect object of a verb or the object of a verbal.

Whom are you describing? [direct object]

They gave **whom** the award? [indirect object]

Giovanni told me **whom** he saw. [direct object of the verb *saw*]

Whom does the teacher want to nominate for student council? [object of the verbal *to nominate*]

Rule of Thumb: When speaking informally, people often use *who* instead of *whom* in sentences like *Who are you describing?* In writing and formal speech, distinguish between *who* and *whom.*

Use the objective pronoun *whom* for the object of a preposition.

Giovanni is a person with **whom** I have much in common. [object of the preposition *with*]

Grammar Glossary

This glossary will help you quickly locate information on parts of speech and sentence structure.

A

Abstract noun. *See* Noun chart.

Action verb. *See* Verb.

Active voice. *See* Voice.

Adjective A word that modifies a noun or pronoun by limiting its meaning. An adjective may answer one of these questions: *What kind? Which one? How many? How much?* Adjectives appear in various positions in a sentence. (The *exciting* story held my attention. That story is *exciting.*)

Many adjectives have different forms to indicate **degree of comparison.** *(happy, happier, happiest)*

The **positive degree** is the simple form of the adjective. *(strong, much)*

The **comparative degree** compares two persons, places, things, or ideas. *(stronger, more)*

The **superlative degree** compares more than two persons, places, things, or ideas. *(strongest, most)*

A **predicate adjective** follows a linking verb and further identifies the subject. (The animals are *hungry.*)

A **noun used as an adjective** answers one of these questions: *What kind? Which one?* (*government* building, *physics* lesson) In some cases possessive nouns are used as adjectives. (*Asa's* car)

A **proper adjective** is formed from a proper noun and begins with a capital letter. Proper adjectives are often created by using the following suffixes: *-an, -ian, -n, -ese,* and *-ish.* *(Indonesian)*

Adjective clause. *See* Clause chart.

Adverb A word that modifies a verb, an adjective, or another adverb by making its meaning more specific. Adverbs answer the questions *How? When? Where?* and *To what degree?* When modifying a verb, an adverb may appear in various positions in a sentence. (The cattle disappeared *rapidly* over the hill. *Suddenly,* not a single one was in sight.) When modifying an adjective or another adverb, an adverb appears directly before the modified word. (The cowboy was *quite* annoyed that he had to find them.) The negatives *no, not,* and the contraction *-n't* are adverbs. (Nakia's score was *no* better than mine.) Other negative words, such as *nowhere, hardly,* and *never,* can function as adverbs of time, place, and degree. (I *never* imagined that they would win the game.)

Some adverbs have different forms to indicate degree of comparison. *(slowly, more slowly, most slowly)*

The **comparative** form of an adverb compares two actions. *(more quickly, better)*

The **superlative** form compares three or more actions. *(most quickly, best)*

Adverb clause. *See* Clause chart.

Antecedent. *See* Pronoun.

Appositive A noun or a pronoun placed next to another noun or pronoun to identify or give additional information about it. (My cousin *Lonnie* is going to Guatemala this summer.)

Appositive phrase. *See* Phrase.

Article The adjective *a, an,* or *the.*

Indefinite articles (*a* and *an*) refer to one of a general group of persons, places, or things. (We saw *a* fish.)

The **definite article** *(the)* indicates that the noun is a specific person, place, or thing. (It swam under *the* log.)

Auxiliary verb. *See* Verb.

B

Base form. *See* Verb tense.

Clause A group of words that has a subject and a predicate and is used as part of a sentence. Clauses fall into two categories: *main clauses*, which are also called *independent clauses*, and *subordinate clauses*, which are also called *dependent clauses*.

A **main clause** has a subject and a predicate and can stand alone as a sentence. There must be at least one main clause in every sentence. *(I can't wait to see your new dog. I will arrive in a few minutes.)*

A **subordinate clause** has a subject and a predicate, but it cannot stand alone as a sentence. A subordinate clause makes sense only when attached to a main clause. Many subordinate clauses begin with subordinating conjunctions or relative pronouns. (Ethan got a high grade *because he was well prepared*.) The chart on this page shows the main types of subordinate clauses.

Collective noun. *See* Noun chart.

Common noun. *See* Noun chart.

Comparative. *See* Adjective, Adverb.

Complement A word or phrase that completes the meaning of a verb. The four basic kinds of complements are *direct objects*, *indirect objects*, *object complements*, and *subject complements*.

A **direct object** answers the question *What?* or *Whom?* after an action verb. (Hiro likes his *job* and his *car.* Hiro brings *me* to school every day.)

An **indirect object** answers the question *To whom? For whom? To what?* or *For what?* after an action verb. (Adebesi gave the *museum* an authentic Nigerian drum.)

An **object complement** answers the question *What?* after a direct object. An object complement is a noun, a pronoun, or an adjective that completes the meaning of a direct object by identifying or describing it. (We elected her *chairperson* of the committee. Our group considers the award *ours*. Angela finds science *fascinating*.)

A **subject complement** follows a subject and a linking verb. It identifies or describes a subject. The two kinds of subject complements are *predicate nominatives* and *predicate adjectives*.

A **predicate nominative** is a noun or pronoun that follows a linking verb and gives more information about the subject. (Those three students are *athletes*. The guard is *he*.)

A **predicate adjective** is an adjective that follows a linking verb and gives more information about the subject. (Laura is *athletic*. Your painting looks *finished* to me.)

Complex sentence. *See* Sentence.

Compound-complex sentence. *See* Sentence.

Compound sentence. *See* Sentence.

Conjunction A word that joins single words or groups of words.

A **coordinating conjunction** *(and, but, or, nor, for, yet)* joins words or groups of words that are equal in grammatical

TYPES OF SUBORDINATE CLAUSES			
Clause	**Function**	**Example**	**Begins with . . .**
Adjective clause	Modifies a noun or pronoun in the main clause	The story *that I just read* is by Amy Tan.	A relative pronoun such as *that, which, who, whom,* or *whose*
Adverb clause	Modifies a verb, an adjective, or an adverb in the main clause	Beryl went to the movie *after she finished studying.*	A subordinating conjunction such as *after, although, because, if, since, when,* or *where*
Noun clause	Serves as a subject, an object, or a predicate nominative in the main clause	*Whoever writes a great deal* often draws on personal experience.	Words such as *how, that, what, whatever, when, where, which, who, whom, whoever, whose,* or *why*

importance. (Toshio *and* Linda entered their projects in the science fair.)

Correlative conjunctions *(both . . . and, just as . . . so, not only . . . but also, either . . . or, neither . . . nor)* work in pairs to join words and groups of words of equal importance. (Rosa *not only* won the race *but also* set a new school record.)

A **subordinating conjunction** *(after, although, as soon as, because, before, if, in order that, since, than, though, until, when, while)* joins a dependent idea or clause to a main clause. (We should leave *as soon as* we can get ready.)

Conjunctive adverb An adverb used to clarify the relationship between clauses of a compound sentence. (The team lost the game last night; *consequently*, they will not play in the tournament.)

Coordinating conjunction. *See* Conjunction.

Correlative conjunction. *See* Conjunction.

D

Definite article. *See* Article.

Demonstrative pronoun. *See* Pronoun.

Direct object. *See* Complement.

E F

Emphatic form. *See* Verb tense.

Future tense. *See* Verb tense.

G

Gerund A verb form that ends in *-ing* and is used as a noun. A gerund may function as a subject, an object of a verb, or the object of a preposition. (*Studying* is not my favorite way to spend an evening. However, I have improved my grades by *studying*.)

Gerund phrase. *See* Phrase.

I

Indirect object. *See* Complement.

Infinitive A verb form that begins with the word *to* and functions as a noun, an adjective, or an adverb. (We were happy *to leave. To compose* was her ambition.) When *to* precedes a verb, it is not a preposition but instead signals an infinitive.

Infinitive phrase. *See* Phrase.

Intensive pronoun. *See* Pronoun.

Interjection A word or phrase that expresses emotion or exclamation. An interjection has no grammatical connection to other words in the sentence. Commas follow mild interjections; exclamation points follow stronger ones. (*Oh*, I forgot. *Wow!*)

Interrogative pronoun. *See* Pronoun.

Intransitive verb. *See* Verb.

Inverted order In a sentence written in *inverted order,* the predicate comes before the subject. Some sentences are written in inverted order for variety or special emphasis. (In the very center of the clearing *stood* a *deer*.) The subject also generally follows the predicate in a sentence that begins with *there* or *here.* (There *were* several *deer* beside the stream. Here *comes* the *bus* now.) Questions, or interrogative sentences, are generally written in inverted order. In many questions, an auxiliary verb precedes the subject and the main verb follows it. (*Has Edwin announced* the contest results?) Questions that begin with *who* or *what* follow normal word order.

Irregular verb. *See* Verb tense.

L M

Linking verb. *See* Verb.

Main clause. *See* Clause.

N O

Nominative pronoun. *See* Pronoun chart.

Noun A word that names a person, a place, a thing, or an idea. The chart on the next page shows the main types of nouns.

Noun clause. *See* Clause chart.

Noun of direct address. *See* Noun chart.

Number A noun, pronoun, or verb is *singular* in number if it refers to one, *plural* if it refers to more than one.

Objective pronoun. *See* Pronoun.

Participle A verb form that can function as an adjective. Present participles always end in *-ing*. (The audience applauded the *dancing* couple.) Although most past participles end in *-ed*, some take other forms. (We looked over the colorfully *wrapped* packages. We admired the tastefully *hung* ornaments.)

Passive voice. *See* Voice.

Past tense. *See* Verb tense.

Perfect tenses. *See* Verb tense.

Personal pronoun. *See* Pronoun.

Phrase A group of words that acts as a single part of speech in a sentence.

An **appositive phrase** is an appositive along with any modifiers. If not essential to the meaning of the sentence, an appositive phrase is set off by commas. (The Mayan weavers displayed their works, *a variety of handbags and clothing*.)

A **gerund phrase** includes a gerund and any complements and modifiers needed to complete its meaning. (*Studying every evening* has helped me improve my grades.)

An **infinitive phrase** includes the infinitive and any complements and modifiers. (Armand found it hard *to pitch strikes consistently*.)

A **participial phrase** contains a participle and any complements and modifiers necessary to complete its meaning. (*Freshly shorn of his luxuriant locks*, the new army recruit scowled at his reflection in the mirror.)

A **prepositional phrase** consists of a preposition, its object, and any modifiers of the object. A prepositional phrase can function as an adjective, modifying a noun or a pronoun. (We went to the movie *at the new theater*.) A prepositional phrase can also function as an adverb when it modifies a verb, an adverb, or an adjective. (Soccer has become very popular *in our town*.)

A **verb phrase** consists of one or more auxiliary verbs followed by a main verb. (The campers *should have noticed* the approaching storm.)

Positive degree. *See* Adjective.

Possessive noun. *See* Noun chart.

Predicate The verb and any objects, complements, or modifiers that say something about the subject of a sentence.

A **simple predicate** is a verb or verb phrase that tells something about the subject. (Some fish *swim* rapidly.)

A **complete predicate** includes the simple predicate and any words that modify it. (The López family *moved here in January*.) In some sentences the simple predicate and the complete predicate are the same. (Fish *swim*.)

A **compound predicate** has two or more verbs or verb phrases that are joined by a conjunction

TYPES OF NOUNS

Noun	Function	Examples
Abstract noun	Names an idea, a quality, or a characteristic	beauty, liberty, thoughtfulness
Collective noun	Names a group of things or people	class, orchestra
Common noun	Names a general type of person, place, thing, or idea	cousin, river, era, theory
Noun of direct address	Identifies the person or persons being spoken to	*Students,* please line up in single file.
Possessive noun	Shows possession, ownership, or the relationship between two nouns	the *child's* toy
Predicate noun	Follows a linking verb and gives information about the subject	Akira is the *winner.*
Proper noun	Names a particular person, place, thing, or idea	Aunt Rebecca, Japan, Renaissance

and share the same subject. (The puppies *ran and played*.) In a compound predicate that contains verb phrases, do not repeat the auxiliary verb (or verbs) before the second verb. (Neither the puppy nor the kitten *has been adopted* or *given* a name.)

Predicate adjective. *See* Adjective, Complement.

Predicate nominative. *See* Complement.

Preposition A word that shows the relationship of a noun or pronoun to some other word in the sentence. Prepositions include *about, above, across, among, as, behind, below, beyond, but, by, down, during, except, for, from, into, like, near, of, on, outside, over, since, through, to, under, until, with.*

A **compound preposition** is made up of more than one word. *(according to, ahead of, because of, by means of, in addition to, in spite of, on account of)* (*According to* scientific studies, the temperature of the earth is rising.)

Prepositional phrase. *See* Phrase.

Present tense. *See* Verb tense.

Progressive form. *See* Verb tense.

Pronoun A word that takes the place of a noun, a group of words acting as a noun, or another pronoun.

The word or group of words that a pronoun refers to is called its **antecedent**. (In the following sentence, *Carlos* is the antecedent of the pronoun *he. When Carlos lived in Colorado, he learned to ride horseback*.)

A **demonstrative pronoun** points out specific persons, places, things, or ideas. *(this, that, these, those)*

An **indefinite pronoun** refers to persons, places, or things in a more general way than a noun does. *(all, another, any, both, each, either, enough, everything, few, many, most, much, neither, nobody, none, one, other, others, plenty, several, some)*

An **intensive pronoun** adds emphasis to another noun or pronoun. If an intensive pronoun is omitted, the meaning of the sentence will be the same. (I *myself* took responsibility for the decision.)

An **interrogative pronoun** is used to form questions. *(who? whom? whose? what? which?)*

A **personal pronoun** refers to a specific person or thing. Personal pronouns have three cases: nominative, objective, and possessive. The case depends upon the function of the pronoun in a sentence. The chart on this page shows the case forms of the various personal pronouns.

A **reflexive pronoun** reflects back to a noun or pronoun used earlier in the sentence, indicating that the same person or thing is involved. (I taught *myself* to speak a little Spanish by listening to some of my friends.)

A **relative pronoun** is used to begin a subordinate clause. *(who, whose, whomever, that, what, whom, whoever, whomever, whichever, whatever)*

Proper adjective. *See* Adjective.

Proper noun. *See* Noun chart.

R

Reflexive pronoun. *See* Pronoun.

Relative pronoun. *See* Pronoun.

PERSONAL PRONOUNS			
Case	**Singular**	**Plural**	**Function in Sentence**
Nominative	I, you, she, he, it	we, you, they	subject or predicate nominative
Objective	me, you, her, him, it	us, you, them	direct object, indirect object, or object of a preposition
Possessive	my, mine, your, yours, her, hers, his, its	our, ours, your, yours, their, theirs	replacement for the possessive form of a noun

S

Sentence A group of words expressing a complete thought. Every sentence has a subject and a predicate. Sentences can be classified by function or by structure. The chart on this page shows the categories by function; the following subentries describe the categories by structure. *See also* Clause, Predicate, Subject.

A **simple sentence** has only one main clause and no subordinate clauses. *(Alana writes.)* A simple sentence may contain a compound subject or a compound predicate or both. *(Alana and Tony write. Alana writes and reads. Alana and Tony write and read.)* The subject and the predicate can be expanded with adjectives, adverbs, prepositional phrases, appositives, or verbal phrases. *(Alana, an excellent writer, vividly conveys her experiences through the use of concrete nouns and adjectives.)* As long as the sentence has only one main clause, however, it remains a simple sentence.

A **compound sentence** has two or more main clauses. Each main clause has its own subject and predicate, and these main clauses are usually joined by a comma and a coordinating conjunction. *(Alana likes to write, and Tony enjoys reading.)* Semicolons may also be used to join the main clauses in a compound sentence. *(Some of Alana's writing is difficult to read; Tony prefers her simpler writing.)*

A **complex sentence** has one main clause and one or more subordinate clauses. *(Tony likes Alana's poems because they sparkle with exciting images.)*

A **compound-complex sentence** has two or more main clauses and at least one subordinate clause. *(Tony read the essay, which was written by Alana, and he spoke favorably about it.)*

Simple predicate. *See* Predicate.

Simple subject. *See* Subject.

Subject The part of the sentence that tells what the sentence is about.

A **simple subject** is the main noun or pronoun in the subject. (The large *fish* swims slowly.)

A **complete subject** includes the simple subject and any words that modify it. *(The family that lives in the brick house moved here recently.)* In some sentences, the simple subject and the complete subject are the same. (*Fish* swim.)

A **compound subject** consists of two or more simple subjects joined by a conjunction. The subjects share the same verb. (*Dogs, cats, hamsters, and gerbils* are popular pets.)

Subordinate clause. *See* Clause.

Subordinating conjunction. *See* Conjunction.

Superlative degree. *See* Adjective, Adverb.

T

Tense. *See* Verb tense.

Transitive verb. *See* Verb.

TYPES OF SENTENCES

Sentence Type	Function	Ends with . . .	Examples
Declarative sentence	Makes a statement	A period	The rain is falling steadily.
Exclamatory sentence	Expresses strong emotion	An exclamation point	How exciting the play was! What an excellent cast!
Imperative sentence	Gives a command or makes a request	A period or an exclamation point	Please close the windows. Hurry!
Interrogative sentence	Asks a question	A question mark	Is that book a mystery? Will you write your report on that book? Why do you like that book so much?

Verb A word that expresses action or a state of being. *(move, feels, said)*

An **action verb** tells what someone or something does. Action verbs can express either physical or mental action. (She *runs* five miles per week. She *plans* in advance.)

An **auxiliary verb,** or helping verb, is a verb that accompanies the main verb to form a verb phrase. (I *have* studied.) The forms of *be* and *have* are the most common auxiliary verbs *(am, is, are, was, were, being, been; has, have, had, having).* Other auxiliaries include *can, could, do, does, did, may, might, must, shall, should, will, would.*

An **intransitive verb** is an action verb that is *not* followed by a word that answers the question *What?* or *Whom?* (Josie *travels* frequently.)

A **linking verb** expresses a state of being by linking the subject of a sentence with a word or expression that identifies or describes the subject. (Mary Cassatt *is* a well-known American painter.) The most commonly used linking verb is *be* in all its forms *(am, is, are, was, were, will be, been, being).* Other linking verbs include *appear, become, feel, grow, look, remain, seem, sound, smell, stay, taste.*

A **transitive verb** is an action verb that is followed by a word or words that answer the question *What?* or *Whom?* (Dwight *watched* the action with great interest.)

Verb phrase. *See* Phrase.

Verb tense The tense of a verb indicates when the action or state of being occurs–in the present, past, or future. All verb tenses are formed from the four principal parts of a verb: a base form *(swim),* a present participle *(swimming),* a simple past form *(swam),* and a past participle *(swum).*

A **regular verb** forms its simple past and past participle by adding *-ed* to the base form. *(jump, jumped, jumped)*

An **irregular verb** forms its past and past participle in some other way. *(drive, drove, driven; begin, began, begun)*

In addition to present, past, and future tense, there are three perfect tenses.

The **present perfect tense** expresses an action or condition that occurred at some indefinite time in the past. This tense also shows an action or condition that began in the past and continues into the present. (My grandfather *has worked* here for two years.)

The **past perfect tense** indicates that one past action or condition began and ended before another past action started. (Roger *had seen* that movie three times before I saw it once.)

The **future perfect tense** indicates that one future action or condition will begin and end before another future event starts. Use *will have* or *shall have* with the past participle of a verb. (By Thursday he *will have seen* the sequel, too.)

The **progressive form** of a verb expresses a continuing action with any of the six tenses. To make the progressive forms, use the appropriate tense of the verb *be* with the present participle of the main verb. (They *are walking.* They *will have been walking.*)

The **emphatic form** adds special force, or emphasis, to the present or past tense of a verb. For the emphatic form, use *do, does,* or *did* with the base form. (I *do walk* to school every day.)

Verbal A verb form that functions in a sentence as a noun, an adjective, or an adverb. The three kinds of verbals are gerunds, infinitives, and participles. *See* Gerund, Infinitive, Participle.

Voice The voice of a verb depends on whether the subject performs the action or receives the action of the verb.

A verb is in the **active voice** if the subject of the sentence performs the action. (Kara *trained* the black horse.)

A verb is in the **passive voice** if the subject of the sentence receives the action of the verb. (The black horse *was trained* by Kara.)

Mechanics

Capitalization

This section will help you recognize and use correct capitalization in sentences.

Rule	Example
Capitalize the first word in any sentence, including a direct quotation that is a sentence. Capitalize a sentence in parentheses unless it is included in another sentence.	He said, "We should leave now." We were looking for Laurel Avenue, where we thought Juanita lived. (There was no Laurel Avenue.)
Rule of Thumb: Since people do not always speak in complete sentences, written dialogue may contain sentence fragments. In dialogue, capitalize the first word of each fragment and each complete sentence. For example: "Late for class," Ferris mumbled.	
Always capitalize the pronoun *I* no matter where it appears in the sentence.	No matter where I live, I'll always remember my home at the edge of the desert.
Capitalize proper nouns, including these:	
a. names of individuals, personal titles used in direct address, and personal titles preceding a name or describing a relationship	Robert Penn Warren; Class President Iris Mura; Uncle Bill
b. names of ethnic groups, national groups, political parties and their members, and languages	African Americans; Hopi; the Democratic Party; a Republican; Vietnamese
c. names of organizations, institutions, companies, monuments, bridges, buildings, and other structures	Red Cross; North Carolina State University; the Museum of Science and Industry; Microsoft; Vietnam Memorial; Golden Gate Bridge
d. trade names and names of documents, awards, and laws	Macintosh; the Constitution of the United States; Nobel Prize; the Fifth Amendment
e. geographical terms and regions or localities	Lake Superior; Main Street; Palisades Park; North Dakota; the Northwest
f. names of planets and other heavenly bodies	Earth; Mars
g. names of ships, planes, trains, and spacecraft	USS *Enterprise;* the *Orient Express; Apollo 13*
h. names of most historical events, eras, calendar items, and religious items	World War One; Middle Ages; Saturday; Judaism; Methodists; Bible; Yom Kippur; God

Rule	Example
i. titles of literary works, publications, works of art, and musical compositions	"Sound of Thunder"; *New Yorker*; *Little Dancer*; *Concerto for Orchestra*
j. specific names of school courses	Algebra I
Rule of Thumb: Do not capitalize the names of subjects (He studied *algebra.*) or seasons of the year (Ian enjoys *winter.*)	
Capitalize proper adjectives (adjectives formed from proper nouns).	Spanish rice; Vidalia onions; Freudian theory; Buddhist meditation

Punctuation

This section will help you use these elements of punctuation correctly.

Rule	Example
Use a **period** at the end of a declarative sentence or an imperative sentence (a polite command).	His lecture was fascinating. Please take your seats.
Use an **exclamation point** to show strong feeling or after a forceful command.	Oh, no! What a disaster! Listen to me!
Use a **question mark** to indicate a direct question.	Is it time for class?
Use a **colon:** a. to introduce a list (especially after words such as *these,* or *as follows*) and to introduce material that explains, illustrates, or restates previous material	Toni Morrison's works include the following novels: *The Bluest Eye*, *Song of Solomon*, and *Beloved.* We must say it again: the customer is always right.
Rule of Thumb: Do not use a colon between the verb and its complement. A colon must follow a complete sentence.	
b. to introduce a long or formal quotation	In *Richard III*, the title character says: "Now is the winter of our discontent / Made glorious summer by this sun of York. . . ."
c. in precise time measurements, biblical chapter and verse references, and business letter salutations	12:45 P.M. 9:24 A.M. 2 Sam. 14:13–14 Eccles. 2:16 Dear Mrs. Clay: Dear Sir:

Rule	Example
Use a **semicolon:**	
a. to separate main clauses that are not joined by a coordinating conjunction	Tipping is considered proper at a restaurant; the rate is between fifteen and twenty percent.
b. to separate main clauses joined by a conjunctive adverb or by *for example* or *that is*	Herman Melville's earlier novels were fairly simple adventure stories; however, in his later works, he dealt with more complex themes.
c. to separate the items in a series when these items contain commas	Three signers of the Declaration of Independence were Thomas Jefferson, who wrote the document; Benjamin Franklin, who discovered that lightning consisted of electricity; and George Washington, who became our first president.
d. to separate two main clauses joined by a coordinating conjunction when such clauses already contain several commas	Manny, who traveled all the way from Fairbanks, Alaska, attended the reunion; but Teri, a local resident, did not.
Use a **comma:**	
a. between the main clauses of a compound sentence	The snow is already three feet deep, and it is still coming down.
b. to separate three or more words, phrases, or clauses in a series	Jefferson, Franklin, and Washington were three signers of the Declaration of Independence.
c. between coordinate modifiers	Sally is a shrewd, witty person.
d. to set off parenthetical expressions, interjections, and conjunctive adverbs	We might, in fact, go to the beach tomorrow. Oh, what a good idea! We spent all our money yesterday; consequently, we will stay home today.
e. to set off direct quotations	"My vacation," said Jana, "was great."
f. to set off long introductory prepositional phrases	From their hammocks in the trees, the hunters watched the boars.

Rule of Thumb: Use a comma after a short introductory prepositional phrase only if the sentence would be misleading without it.

Rule	Example
g. to set off nonessential words, clauses, and phrases, such as	
–adverbial clauses	Because I'm going to Mexico this summer, I need to work on my Spanish.
–adjective clauses	Alejo Carpentier, who wrote *The Lost Steps*, was born in Havana in 1904.
–participles and participial phrases	Joe, laughing, showed me the comic strip.
	Dashing along the sidewalk, I caught the bus.
–infinitive phrases	I didn't like that film very much, to tell the truth.
–prepositional phrases	The novel, from beginning to end, bored and depressed me.
–appositives and appositive phrases	Maxine Hong Kingston, an author and university lecturer, won the National Book Award for *China Men*.

Rule of Thumb: Nonessential elements can be removed without changing the meaning of the sentence.

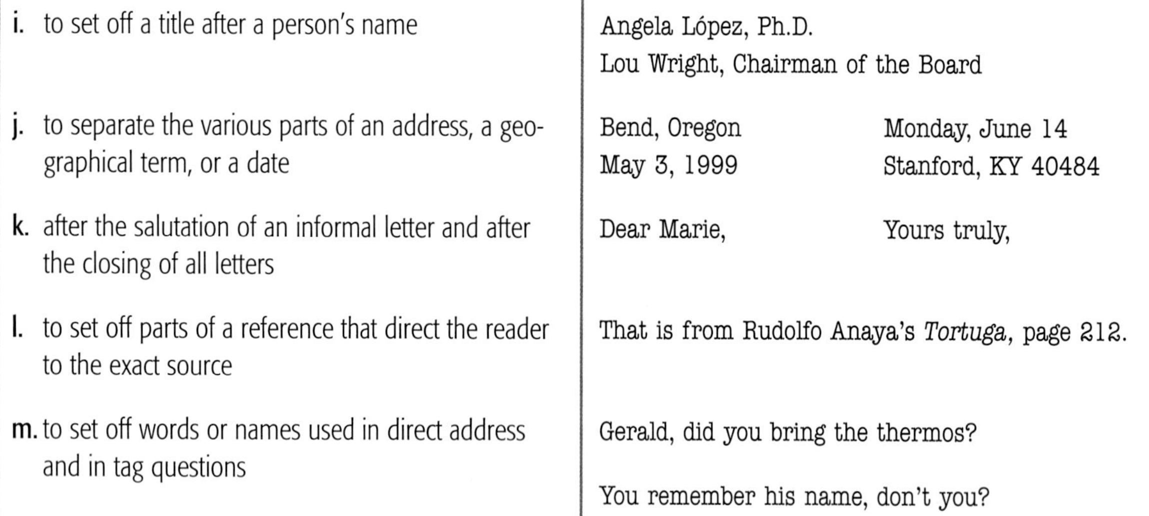

Rule	Example
h. to set off an antithetical phrase	Daffodils, not crocuses, are my favorite flowers.
i. to set off a title after a person's name	Angela López, Ph.D. Lou Wright, Chairman of the Board
j. to separate the various parts of an address, a geographical term, or a date	Bend, Oregon Monday, June 14 May 3, 1999 Stanford, KY 40484
k. after the salutation of an informal letter and after the closing of all letters	Dear Marie, Yours truly,
l. to set off parts of a reference that direct the reader to the exact source	That is from Rudolfo Anaya's *Tortuga*, page 212.
m. to set off words or names used in direct address and in tag questions	Gerald, did you bring the thermos? You remember his name, don't you?

Rule	Example
Use a **dash** to signal a change in thought or to emphasize a parenthetical comment.	Julie was unhappy—actually she was devastated—when she lost her new bracelet. Izanami's voice was cheerful—more like it had been in happier days.
Rule of Thumb: A good test of the correct use of dashes is to delete the information that the dashes set off. If the remaining sentence retains its basic meaning, then the dashes were properly used. If the remaining sentence has lost crucial information, then the dashes were improperly used.	
Use **parentheses** to set off supplemental material. Punctuate within the parentheses only if the punctuation is part of the parenthetical expression.	The Maya (who lived in Mexico and Central America) built remarkable stone structures. The Maya built remarkable stone structures. (They lived in Mexico and Central America.) We crept along the hallway (why were we so afraid?) until we reached the door at the end.
Use **quotation marks:** **a.** to enclose a direct quotation, as follows:	Secretary of State Madeleine Albright called her job "a great privilege."
When a quotation is interrupted, use two sets of quotation marks.	"One difference was apparent from the outset," a World War II news analyst said of radio. "It was the first time the peoples of the world could hear a war actually breaking out."
Use single quotation marks for a quotation within a quotation.	Ursula Le Guin wrote, "'Happens all the time,' says Coyote. 'That's what myths do. They happen all the time.'"
In writing dialogue, begin a new paragraph and use a new set of quotation marks every time the speaker changes.	"How about luncheon tomorrow?" "I'm afraid that's impossible." "How about dinner tomorrow evening?"
b. to enclose titles of short works, such as stories, poems, essays, articles, chapters, and songs	"Why I Live at the P.O." is a story by Eudora Welty.

Rule	Example
c. to enclose unfamiliar slang terms and unusual expressions	"Fuzzy logic" is a term applied to certain mathematical processes.

Rule of Thumb: A good way to tell whether question marks and exclamation points go inside or outside quotation marks is to take the direct quotation out of the sentence and see how it would be punctuated if it stood alone. If it would end with a question mark or exclamation point, then that mark of punctuation should go within the quotation marks. If the new sentence would end with a period, then the question mark or exclamation point should go outside the quotation marks.

Rule	Example
Use **italics**: a. for titles of books, lengthy poems, plays, films, television series, paintings and sculptures, long musical compositions, court cases, names of newspapers and magazines, ships, trains, airplanes, and spacecraft (Italicize and capitalize *a, an,* and *the* at the beginning of a title only when they are part of the title.)	*Star Wars* [film]; *Under Milk Wood* [play] *Man at the Crossroads* [painting] *Discover* [magazine] *Apollo 13* [spacecraft] *Air Force One* [airplane] *The Lost Steps* [book] the *Los Angeles Times* [newspaper]
b. for foreign words and expressions that are not used frequently in English	He came up with the perfect word, the *mot juste.*
c. for words, letters, and numerals used to represent themselves	In that sentence, use *adapt*, not *adopt.* There is no *6* in this list.
Use an **apostrophe**: a. for a possessive form, as follows: Add an apostrophe and *-s* to all singular indefinite pronouns, singular nouns, plural nouns not ending in *-s,* and compound nouns. Add only an apostrophe to a plural noun that ends in *-s.*	someone's jacket; California's coastline; the women's books; the boss's desk my brother-in-law's computer; the Chief of Police's office; the race car driver's accident the waves' continuous motion
If two or more persons possess something jointly, use the possessive form for the last person named. If they possess it individually, use the possessive form for each one's name.	Penn and Teller's magic act Romeo and Juliet's problem Picasso's and Braque's cubist paintings Ford's and Chrysler's minivans

Rule	Example
b. to express amounts of money or time that modify a noun	twenty dollars' worth; one day's vacation (You can use a hyphenated adjective instead: a one-day vacation.)
c. in place of omitted letters or numerals	it's [it is, it has] the floods of '97
d. to form the plural of letters, numerals, symbols, and words used to represent themselves (use an apostrophe and -*s*)	*9*'s *x*'s and *y*'s #'s
Use a **hyphen**: **a.** after any prefix joined to a proper noun or proper adjective	mid-Atlantic post-Impressionist
b. after the prefixes *all-, ex-,* and *self-* joined to any noun or adjective; after the prefix *anti-* when it joins a word beginning with *i;* after the prefix *vice-* (except in *vice president*); and to avoid confusion between words that begin with *re-* and look like another word	ex-teammate self-taught anti-imperialist vice-principal re-view the picture review the book re-lay the flooring relay the message
Rule of Thumb: Remember that the prefix *anti-* requires a hyphen when followed by a word that begins with *i* in order to prevent spelling words with two successive *i*'s. Otherwise, *anti* does not require a hyphen except before a capitalized word.	
c. in a compound adjective that precedes a noun	a five-year-old car her mud-encrusted boat
d. in any spelled-out cardinal or ordinal numbers up to *ninety-nine* or *ninety-ninth* and with a fraction used as an adjective	fifty-six seventy-first three-quarters majority
e. to divide a word at the end of a line between syllables	com-plete hang-man big-gest search-ing

LANGUAGE HANDBOOK

Abbreviations

This section will help you learn how to use abbreviations, which are shortened forms of words.

Rule	Example
Use only one period if an abbreviation occurs at the end of a sentence. If the sentence ends with a question mark or exclamation point, use the period and the second mark of punctuation.	I called Terika Harvey, M.D. Have you ever been outside the U.S.A.? This temple was built around 1000 B.C.!
Capitalize abbreviations of proper nouns and abbreviations related to historical dates.	Edward R. Murrow; First Ave. 1000 B.C.; A.D. 502; C.E. 502
Use all capital letters and no periods for abbreviations that are pronounced letter by letter or as words.	NAFTA; FBI; NATO YWCA; NAACP; NBA UN; CIA; AFL-CIO
When addressing mail, use the U.S. Post Office abbreviations (two capital letters, no periods).	AK (Alaska); CT (Connecticut) HI (Hawaii); ME (Maine) MA (Massachusetts); TX (Texas)
Use abbreviations for some personal titles.	Ms. Goodwin; Gen. Anderson; Dr. Julia Marshall
Abbreviate units of measure used with numerals in technical or scientific writing, but not in ordinary prose. Use a period after an abbreviation of an English unit of measure, but not after a metric unit.	ft. (foot); g (gram) gal. (gallon); m (meter) in. (inch); mm (millimeter)

Rule of Thumb: In a letter it is appropriate to use a state abbreviation in the address. In other forms of writing, such as expository writing, spell out the name of a state.

Numbers and Numerals

This section will help you understand when to use numerals and when to spell out numbers.

Rule	Example
In general, spell out cardinal and ordinal numbers that can be written in one or two words.	More than three thousand people came to the lecture by physicist Stephen Hawking.
Spell out any number that occurs at the beginning of a sentence.	Two hundred eighty-one books have been added to the library.
In general, use numerals (numbers expressed in figures) to express numbers that would be written in more than two words. Extremely large numbers are often expressed as a numeral followed by the word *million* or *billion.*	The library has recently added 281 new books to its collection. The department store chain had a first-quarter income of $32.3 million.
If related numbers appear in the same sentence, use all numerals.	Of the 124 hotels and motels in the resort area, more than 100 have their own restaurant.
Use numerals to express amounts of money, decimals, and percentages.	$2.53 21.5 students per class 0.6% 12 percent
Use numerals to express the year and day in a date and to express the precise time with the abbreviations *A.M.* and *P.M.*	Robert was born January 17, 1979. Yemane has a job interview on March 4 at 9:00 A.M.
Spell out a number to express a century when the word *century* is used, or a decade when the century is clear from the context. When a century and a decade are expressed as a single unit, use numerals followed by *-s.*	In the twentieth century many things changed, especially during the sixties. Some people look back upon the 1950s with nostalgia.
Use numerals for streets and avenues numbered above ten and for all house, apartment, and room numbers.	411 Eighth Avenue 310 West 72nd Street Room 205 Apartment 2H
Use numerals to express page, paragraph, stanza, and line numbers.	See page 325, paragraph 2, for that information. In stanza 4, lines 19, 21, and 23 rhyme.

Spelling

The following basic rules, examples, and exceptions will help you master the spelling of many words.

ie and ei

Many writers find the rules for certain combinations of letters, like *ie* and *ei,* difficult to remember. One helpful learning strategy is to develop a rhyme to remember a rule. Look at the following rhyme for the *ie* and *ei* rule.

Rule	Example
Put *i* before *e,* except after *c,* or when sounded like *a,* as in *neighbor* and *weigh.*	relief, thief, piece, brief receipt, deceit, perceive sleigh, deign, heir, rein, beige, vein

EXCEPTIONS: seize, leisure, weird, height, either, forfeit, protein, counterfeit, sleight.

-cede, -ceed, and -sede

Because various combinations of letters in English are sometimes pronounced the same way, it is often easy to make slight spelling errors. Except for the exceptions below, spell the *sēd* sound at the end of words as *cede:*

precede accede intercede

EXCEPTION: One word uses *-sede* to spell the final *sēd* sound: supersede.

EXCEPTION: Three words use *-ceed* to spell the final *sēd* sound: proceed, exceed, succeed.

Unstressed vowels

Notice the vowel sound in the second syllable of the word *or-i-gin.* This is the unstressed vowel sound; dictionary pronunciation spellings use the *schwa* symbol (ə) to indicate it. Because any of several vowels can be used to spell this sound, you might find yourself uncertain about which vowel to use. Try thinking of a related word in which the syllable containing the vowel sound is stressed.

Unknown Spelling	Related Word	Correct Spelling
dram_tize	dramatic	dramatize
rev_rence	revere	reverence
simil_r	similarity	similar
distr_bution	distribute	distribution

Adding prefixes

When adding a prefix to a word, keep the original spelling of the word. If the prefix forms a double letter, keep both letters.

dis + count = discount
ir + responsible = irresponsible
mis + spell = misspell

Suffixes and the silent *e*

Many English words end in a silent letter *e.* Sometimes the *e* is dropped when a suffix is added. When adding a suffix that begins with a consonant to a word that ends in silent *e,* keep the *e.*

hope + ful = hopeful
arrange + ment = arrangement

COMMON EXCEPTIONS: awe + ful = awful; judge + ment = judgment

When adding the suffix *-y* or a suffix that begins with a vowel to a word that ends in silent *e,* usually drop the *e.*

shade + y = shady
force + ible = forcible

COMMON EXCEPTION: mile + age = mileage

When adding a suffix that begins with *a* or *o* to a word that ends in *ce* or *ge,* keep the *e* so the word will retain the soft *c* or *g* sound.

peace + able = peaceable
manage + able = manageable
courage + ous = courageous

When adding a suffix that begins with a vowel to a word that ends in *ee* or *oe,* keep the *e.*

foresee + able = foreseeable
flee + ing = fleeing
tiptoe + ing = tiptoeing

Suffixes and the final *y*

When adding a suffix to a word that ends in a consonant + *y,* change the *y* to *i* unless the suffix begins with *i.* Keep the *y* in a word that ends in a vowel + *y.*

try + ed = tried
stay + ing = staying
copy + ing = copying
fry + ed = fried
display + ed = displayed
joy + ous = joyous

LANGUAGE HANDBOOK

Doubling the final consonant

When adding a suffix to a word that ends in a consonant, double the final consonant if it is preceded by a single vowel and the word is one syllable, if the accent is on the last syllable and remains there even after the suffix is added, or if the word is made up of a prefix and a one-syllable word.

shop + ing = shopping
compel + ing = compelling
misstep + ed = misstepped
stop + age = stoppage
concur + ent = concurrent
reset + ing = resetting

Do not double the final consonant if the accent is not on the last syllable or if the accent shifts when the suffix is added. Also do not double the final consonant if it is preceded by two vowels or by another consonant. If the word ends in a consonant and the suffix begins with a consonant, do not double the final consonant.

develop + ing = developing
swoop + ing = swooping
remind + ed = reminded
travel + ing = traveling
rain + ing = raining
faith + ful = faithful

Adding *-ly* and *-ness*

When adding *-ly* to a word that ends in a single *l,* keep the *l,* but when the word ends in a double *l,* drop one *l.* When adding *-ness* to a word that ends in *n,* keep the *n.*

ideal + ly = ideally
full + ly = fully
mean + ness = meanness
real + ly = really
dull + ly = dully
keen + ness = keenness

Forming compound words

When joining a word that ends in a consonant to a word that begins with a consonant, keep both consonants.

rain + fall = rainfall
key + board = keyboard
year + book = yearbook
stair + case = staircase

Forming plurals

English words form plurals in many ways. Most nouns simply add *-s.* The following chart shows other ways of forming plural nouns and some common exceptions to the pattern.

GENERAL RULES FOR FORMING PLURALS		
If a noun ends in	**Rule**	**Example**
ch, s, sh, x, z	add *-es*	church, churches
a consonant + *y*	change *y* to *i* and add *-es*	baby, babies
o or a vowel + *y*	add only *-s*	radio, radios day, days
a consonant + *o* common exceptions	generally add *-es* but sometimes add only *-s*	tomato, tomatoes halo, halos
f or *ff* common exceptions	add *-s* change *f* to *v* and add *-es*	reef, reefs; riff, riffs leaf, leaves
lf	change *f* to *v* and add *-es*	shelf, shelves
fe	change *f* to *v* and add *-s*	life, lives

A few plurals are exceptions to the rules in the previous chart, but they are easy to remember. The following chart lists these plurals and some examples.

SPECIAL RULES FOR FORMING PLURALS	
Rule	**Example**
To form the plural of proper names and one-word compound nouns, follow the general rules for plurals.	López, Lópezes Farraday, Farradays newspaper, newspapers
To form the plural of hyphenated compound nouns or compound nouns of more than one word, make the most important word plural.	father-in-law, fathers-in-law oil well, oil wells attorney general, attorneys general
Some nouns have unusual plural forms.	woman, women mouse, mice ox, oxen
Some nouns have the same singular and plural forms.	sheep deer series

Writing Handbook

The Writing Process

The writing process consists of five stages that take you from choosing a topic to presenting a finished piece of writing. These stages are *prewriting*, *drafting*, *revising*, *editing/proofreading*, and *publishing/presenting*. You do not need to follow them in a strict order but can move back and forth among them as your ideas develop. For example, before revising your first draft, you might present it to a friend in order to get feedback; or you might go back to prewriting in order to rethink your topic or gather more information.

The Writing Process

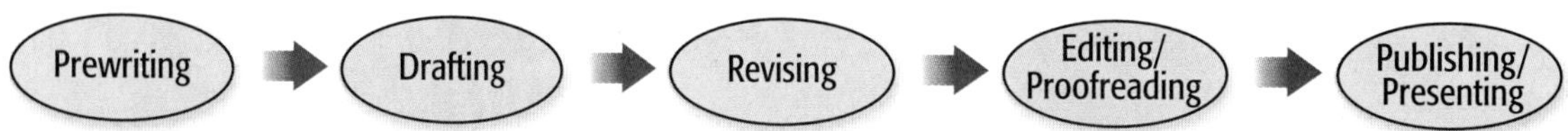

Prewriting

In the prewriting stage, you explore topic ideas, choose a topic, gather information, and begin to organize your material.

Exploring ideas

Ask yourself the following questions before you begin exploring topic ideas.

- What is my general purpose? Am I writing to fulfill an assignment? Am I writing for a personal reason?
- What audience do I have in mind? My teacher? My classmates? Younger children? The general public?
- What do my purpose and audience determine about the length of my paper? the kinds of topics that are appropriate? the tone and language of my writing (formal or informal; serious or light; objective or personal)?

Once you have given some thought to these questions, the following techniques can help you find a topic to write about.

- Scan your memory for interesting, funny, or moving personal experiences.
- Flip through a variety of magazines and newspapers.
- Browse through a library catalog.
- Brainstorm for topics with a group of classmates.

Choosing a topic

When you have several possible topics in mind, ask yourself these questions about each one.

- Is this a topic that I am interested in?
- Does it fulfill my assignment or my own purpose for writing?
- Is it appropriate for the length of paper I plan to write? Would I need to narrow or broaden this topic?
- Do I know enough about this topic, or can I find enough information?

Gathering information

How you gather your information will depend upon the kind of paper you are writing.

If you are writing a personal essay, all of the information may come from your own experiences and feelings. Try one or both of the following techniques.

- Freewriting Set a time limit of ten minutes, and write down everything that comes to mind on your topic. You might want to list your thoughts and images under general headings or make a cluster diagram.
- Discussion Talk about your topic with one or more people. Take notes on your ideas as they come to you. Encourage your listeners to ask you questions.

If you are writing a report or a persuasive essay, you will probably need to locate pertinent factual information and take notes on it. You may consult library resources, such as books, magazines, and newspapers, as well as the Internet and other on-line resources. You may also choose to interview people with experience or specialized knowledge related to your topic. (See Research Paper Writing, pp. R64–R69.)

Organizing your material

Determine the main points, subtopics, or events you will be writing about, and choose a general order in which to present them.

Sometimes the best order will be self-evident. For example, a biography usually calls for chronological order, and a description of a place may lend itself to spatial order, such as from near to far or from low to high. For other kinds of writing, such as science reports, you may need to experiment to find the best order.

After deciding on the general order, make a rough outline. It can be as simple as a list, or include headings and subheadings.

Drafting

In the drafting stage, use your notes and outline to write a rough version of your paper. Drafting is an opportunity to explore and develop your ideas.

Tips for drafting

- You might want to write your draft very quickly, capturing the rapid flow of your ideas; or you might wish to work more slowly, rethinking and revising as you write. Choose the approach that works better for you.
- Whether you work quickly or slowly, don't focus on details. Concentrate on developing the main ideas. At this stage, just circle or annotate minor points that need more work.
- Keep your purpose in mind, and use your outline as a general guideline. At the same time, try to stay flexible. If part of your outline doesn't work, omit it. If better ideas occur to you as you write, feel free to change your direction.

Revising

After you have finished your first draft, set it aside for a while. Then reread it, and look for ways to improve and refine it. This is the point at which peer review can be most helpful.

Using peer review

Ask one or more of your classmates to read your draft. Here are some specific ways in which you can direct their responses.

- Have readers tell you in their own words what they have read. If you do not hear your ideas restated, you will want to revise for clarity.
- Ask readers to tell you what parts of your writing they liked best and why. You may want to expand those elements when you revise.
- Discuss the ideas in your writing with your readers. Have them share their own ideas about the topic. Include in your revision any new insights you gain.
- Ask readers for their suggestions in specific areas, such as organization, word choice, or examples.

You may want to take notes on your readers' suggestions so you will have a handy reference as you revise. Finally, weigh your peer responses carefully. Compare them with your own insights. Use what is most helpful to write the revised draft.

Editing/Proofreading

In the editing stage, you polish your revised draft and proofread it for errors in grammar and spelling. Use this proofreading checklist to help you check for errors, and use the proofreading symbols in the chart below to mark places that need corrections.

- ☑ Have I avoided run-on sentences and sentence fragments and punctuated sentences correctly?
- ☑ Have I used every word correctly, including plurals, possessives, and frequently confused words?
- ☑ Do verbs and subjects agree? Are verb tenses correct?
- ☑ Do pronouns refer clearly to their antecedents and agree with them in person, number, and gender?
- ☑ Have I used adverb and adjective forms and modifying phrases correctly?
- ☑ Have I spelled every word correctly, and checked the unfamiliar ones in a dictionary?

Proofreading Symbols		
⊙	Lieut Brown	Insert a period.
∧	No one came the party.	Insert a letter or a word.
≡	I enjoyed paris.	Capitalize a letter.
/	The Class ran a bake sale.	Make a capital letter lowercase.
⁀ ‿	The campers are home sick.	Close up a space.
(sp)	They visited N.Y. (sp)	Spell out.
∧ ∧	Sue please come I need your help.	Insert a comma or a semicolon.
∩∪	He enjoyed feild day.	Transpose the position of letters or words.
#	alltogether	Insert a space.
ℓ	We went to to Boston.	Delete letters or words.
∨ ∨ ∨	She asked, Who's coming?	Insert quotation marks or an apostrophe.
/=/	mid January	Insert a hyphen.
¶	"Where?" asked Karl. "Over there," said Ray.	Begin a new paragraph.

Publishing/Presenting

There are a number of ways you can share your work. You could publish it in a magazine, a class anthology, or another publication, or read your writing aloud to a group. You could also join a writer's group and read one another's works.

Writing Modes

Writing may be classified as expository, descriptive, narrative, or persuasive. Each of these classifications, or modes, has its own purpose.

Expository Writing

Expository writing explains and compares. There are six types of expository writing. The kind of essay you write depends on your goal.

As you write an expository piece, use the checklist shown here as a guide.

- ☑ **Does my opening contain attention-grabbing details or intriguing questions to hook the reader?**
- ☑ **Are my explanations complete, clear, and accurate?**
- ☑ **Have I presented information in a logical order?**
- ☑ **Have I included specific, relevant details?**
- ☑ **Have I defined any unfamiliar terms and concepts?**
- ☑ **Have I made comparisons clear and logical?**
- ☑ **Have I used language and details appropriate for my intended audience?**

Type	Definition	Example
Process explanation	Explains how something happens, works, or is done, using step-by-step organization	How the human brain stores memories
Cause and effect	Identifies the causes and/or effects of something and examines the relationship between causes and effects	Causes of skin cancer
Comparison and contrast	Examines similarities and differences to find relationships and draw conclusions	The safety features of U.S. cars compared with those of imported models
Definition	Explains a term or concept by listing and examining its qualities and characteristics	The "Trail of Tears"
Classification	Organizes subjects into categories and examines the qualities or characteristics of those categories	Kinds of snakes native to this area
Problem and solution	Examines aspects of a complex problem and explores or proposes possible solutions	Providing community-wide access to parks and playgrounds

Descriptive Writing

Good descriptive writing creates word pictures of people, places, things, and experiences. It includes carefully chosen details that appeal to the reader's senses. Descriptive passages are a part of many kinds of writing, including novels, short stories, informative essays, biographies, poems, and persuasive speeches.

Use this checklist when you write a descriptive passage.

- ☑ Did I use an introduction that grabbed the reader?
- ☑ Were the images I used clear and striking?
- ☑ Did I organize details carefully and consistently?
- ☑ Did I use exact, energetic verbs to enliven my description?
- ☑ Did I write from a vantage point that makes sense?
- ☑ Have I used precise, vivid word choices?
- ☑ Have I created a strong, unified impression?

Narrative Writing

A narrative, whether fictional or nonfictional, tells a story. Narratives include novels and short stories as well as biographies, memoirs, narrative poems, and histories. Narratives typically include a setting, characters, and a plot, which revolves around a conflict of some sort.

As you write your narrative, use this checklist as a guide.

- ☑ Did I introduce characters, setting, plot, and conflict?
- ☑ Did I include descriptions and dialogue appropriate for the characters–whether fictional or nonfictional?
- ☑ Did I present a clear and consistent point of view?
- ☑ Is the conflict or complication interesting to my audience?
- ☑ Did I use mood, foreshadowing, or dialogue to move the story along?
- ☑ Is the writing vivid and expressive?
- ☑ Did I end in a way that satisfies my audience?

Persuasive Writing

Persuasive writing expresses a writer's opinion and tries to make readers agree with it, change their own opinion, and perhaps even take action. Effective persuasive writing uses strong, reliable evidence to support the claims. Persuasive writing is used in newspaper editorials, letters of complaint, advertisements, product evaluations, and many other applications.

This checklist offers a guide for writing a persuasive piece.

- ☑ Is my position stated in a clear thesis statement?
- ☑ Is the supporting evidence convincing?
- ☑ Have I anticipated and responded to opposing viewpoints?
- ☑ Are my facts and opinions relevant and credible?
- ☑ Does the conclusion relate to the evidence?
- ☑ Is the tone appropriate?
- ☑ Have I used strong, specific words to support my argument?
- ☑ Did I end with a strong call to action?

Research Paper Writing

A research paper presents the findings and conclusions of an inquiry into primary and secondary sources. Unlike personal essays in which you present your own thoughts and feelings, a research paper requires that you go beyond personal experience to search for facts, gather data, and evaluate evidence in order to draw a conclusion.

Types of Research Papers

Research papers can take many forms. Some of the most common approaches to writing a research paper are listed below. In some cases you might combine approaches, perhaps by evaluating the research of others and then conducting original research.

- A **summary** explores a topic by summing up the opinions of other writers. The author of the paper does not express an opinion about the subject.
- An **evaluative paper** states an opinion and backs it up with evidence found in primary and secondary sources.
- An **original paper** involves research that leads to new insights or information about the topic.

Making a plan

- Schedule ample time for your research. A good research paper can't be written in a weekend. Sketch out a schedule that allows several weeks for the completion of your paper.
- Select a general topic that interests and motivates you.
- Do some preliminary research to build background and identify available resources.
- To set a clear path for research, generate three to seven research questions to answer first. In trying to answer these questions, you will discover other questions. Let your central idea guide you in selecting questions–the answers will emerge later in the course of your research.
- Refine and/or focus the topic as appropriate.
- Examine the topic. Look at the material from various points of view. Don't worry if some angles lead to dead ends. At this point just try to think critically about the topic from several perspectives.

Choosing and evaluating sources

Kinds of sources There are two kinds of sources–primary and secondary.

A **primary source** is a firsthand account of an event–an account by someone who has actually experienced or observed the event–for example, the slave narrative written by Olaudah Equiano.

A **secondary source** is one written by a person who has done extensive research on the topic and who has interpreted primary sources. Although most sources on a topic will be secondary, make use of primary sources when they are available.

Criteria for evaluation Examine sources critically. As you search for sources, select those that are authoritative and timely.

- Choose those authors who have written widely on a subject and whose work in their field is recognized.
- Use articles from well-respected newspapers or scholarly journals; do not use material from popular magazines unless it can be verified in another source.
- Try to find the most recently published information on your topic.
- Be especially careful in evaluating on-line sources. Anyone can create a Web site; therefore, the information found in such a source is not always reliable. Before using information from on-line sources, apply the criteria identified for print materials.

Because every source you use is written by a person with particular interests, knowledge, and values, be alert to the author's perspective. Try to get sources that approach your topic from various points of view.

Preparing a working bibliography

A working bibliography is a record of the books, articles, and other sources you will consult for your paper. For each source you find, follow these steps:

1. Skim it to see if it has any useful information. Also look at tables of contents, indexes, chapter titles, and graphic aids to efficiently locate information.
2. If it does, record on an index card all the information needed for compiling the list of works. Be sure to include the author's name and the title.
3. Number your cards in the upper right-hand corner so you can keep them in order. You can also write yourself notes on the cards.

See the sample cards below for a book, a magazine, and an on-line article.

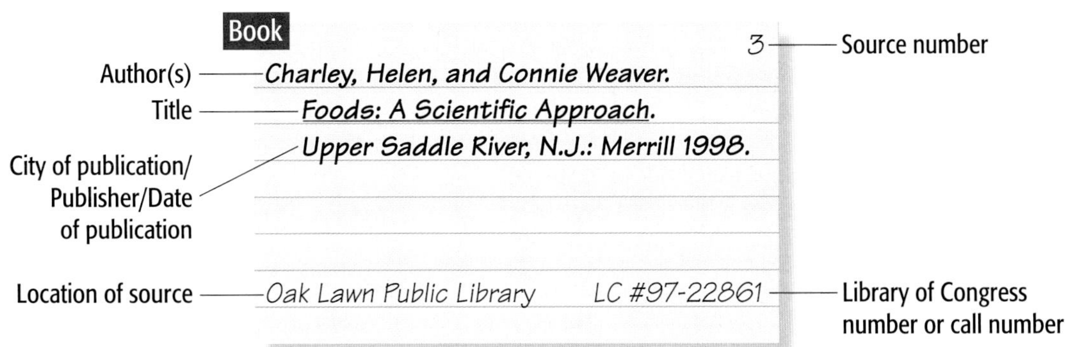

WRITING HANDBOOK

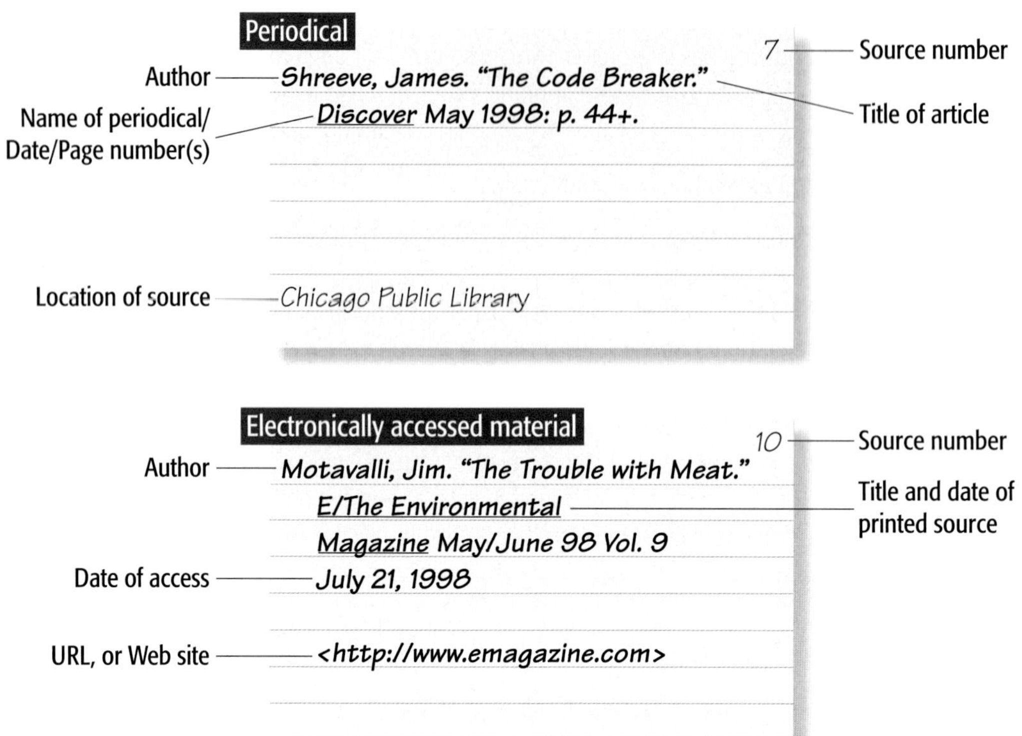

Taking careful notes

Use index cards when you take notes, and follow these guidelines:

- As you find information that you can use, note it on a card.
- In the upper right-hand corner of the note card, write the number of the source from the working bibliography.
- Place any exact words from the source in quotation marks.
- If you jot your own thoughts down on note cards, initial them so you can distinguish your own opinions from those that come from other sources.

> **Important** Avoid plagiarism. Plagiarism is using someone else's ideas or statements and presenting them as your own. Even when unintentional, plagiarism is a serious offense. Keep clearly documented notes so you know where you found each piece of information.

The card at the right shows what a completed note card will look like. Include the source number and the number of the page on which you found your information.

10

E. coli bacteria have become more widespread in the past thirty years. Eating infected food can result in hemolytic uremic syndrome (HUS), a condition that is life threatening.
"Meat-borne pathogens like Salmonella entenditis can be traced to 'factory farms.'"
p. 29

Developing an outline

Organize your note cards to develop a working outline.

- As you take notes, look for ways to classify the facts and ideas you find. For example, look for similar features, such as two facts about the role of an individual in a historical event, or two causes of the same effect.
- Begin to group the note cards as you classify them. As you make decisions on how to organize your cards, you are developing the headings you need to write a working outline.
- If some cards do not fit with any others, set them aside. Later you can decide whether to keep or discard them.

The following partial outline is based on chronological development. Note that in an outline, you cannot have a single subheading. If you have a *I,* you must have a *II;* if you have an *A,* you must have a *B,* and so on.

Sample Outline

Women in the Workplace

I. Prior to World War II

A. Factors limiting women's employment outside the home

B. Types of jobs assigned to women

C. Percentage of women in the work force

II. From 1945 to 1975

A. Factors promoting women's employment outside the home

B. Continuing limitations

1. Gender-specific job titles (secretary vs. executive assistant)

2. Salary discrepancies for identical work by men and women

Writing a thesis statement

- To develop a thesis statement, rewrite your central idea into a concise, tightly focused sentence that describes your topic and your approach to it. Even though this thesis statement may change slightly in later stages of your writing process, it will provide a clear direction for your writing.
- The kind of thesis statement you use will depend upon the type of paper you write: summary, evaluative, original, or a combination of two or more types.

After you have made an outline and written a thesis statement, you are ready to proceed with drafting. As you draft your paper, be sure to document the information you include.

Documenting sources

The information in your research paper must be properly documented. By citing your sources accurately, you acknowledge those people whose ideas you are using. You do not have to cite the source of common knowledge, such as that the Andes are in South America or that the Magna Carta was signed in 1215. Widely known proverbs, famous quotations, and simple definitions are also considered common knowledge.

In-text citations The Modern Language Association (MLA) recommends using citations in the text of your writing that refer readers to a list of works cited at the end of the paper. The citation should appear at the end of the quotation or other material. The chart below shows the MLA style of documenting various sources.

Type of Source	Citation Style
Author named in text "According to M. Harte, . . ."	Page number in parentheses (52)
Author not named in text	Author's last name and page number in parentheses (Coogan 322)
More than one author is cited	Name all in text or authors' names and page number in parentheses (Lee, Sanford, Berlig 234)
No author listed	Title and page number in parentheses ("Lively Bacteria" 64)
More than one work in list by same author	Include words from title in reference (Sutford "Planetary Threat")
Quotation from another work	Use "qtd. in" (qtd. in Coogan 320)
Work from anthology	Cite author, not anthology editor
Novels; plays; poems	Page and chapter (43, ch. 8); part and line number (2:12–14); act and scene plus line number, if applicable (3.2:11–18)
Multivolume work	Include volume number (Durand 2:167)

Note: For material accessed on CD-ROM or on-line databases, follow the style of in-text references for print materials. See below for the style of their inclusion in works cited.

Compiling a list of works cited

At the end of your text, provide an alphabetized list of works cited.

- Include complete publishing information for each source.
- Cite only those sources from which you actually used information.
- Arrange entries in alphabetical order according to the author's (or editor's) last name. Write the last name first.
- If an entry runs more than one line, indent five spaces every line after the first.

Works Cited

One author — Barber, Elizabeth Wayland. *Women's Work: The First 20,000 Years.* New York: Norton, 1995. — Book

Bolz, Diane M. "Women and Flight." *Smithsonian* July 1997: 90+. — Magazine

Two or more authors — Brown, Clair, and Joseph A. Pechman. *Gender in the Workplace.* Washington, D.C.: Brookings, 1987. — Reverse only the first author's name.

No author given — "The Convention on the Elimination of All Forms of Discrimination Against Women." United Nations Division for Advancement of Women. 9 Mar. 2001 <http://www.un.org/womenwatch/daw/cedaw/conven.htm>. — Alphabetize by title, disregarding the word *a, an,* or *the* at the beginning of a title.

Online source — *Rosie the Riveter: Women Join the Industrial Workforce.* 4 Dec. 1999. American Airpower Heritage Museum. 1 Feb. 2001 <http://www.airpowermuseum.org/frrosier.html>. — Include sponsor of the site, date of access, and URL.

More than one work by an author — Ware, Susan. *Letter to the World: Seven Women Who Shaped the American Century.* New York: Norton, 1998.

---. *Modern American Women: A Documentary History.* Belmont, California: Wadsworth, 1988. — Use three hyphens followed by a period in place of the author's last name.

Note: Titles of books and magazines are in italic type or underlined; titles of articles are placed in quotation marks.

Preparing a manuscript

Follow the guidelines of the Modern Language Association when you prepare the final copy of your research paper.

- Heading On separate lines in the upper left-hand corner of the first page, include your name, your teacher's name, the course name, and the date.
- Title Center the title on the line below the heading.
- Numbering Number the pages one-half inch from the top of the page in the right-hand corner. Write your last name before each page number after the first page.
- Spacing Use double-spacing throughout.
- Margins Leave one-inch margins on all sides of every page.

Business and Technical Writing

Business and technical writing are kinds of expository writing that explain information and processes to people within various professions.

Business writing includes documents such as letters, memorandums, reports, briefs, proposals, and articles for business publications. Business writing must be clear, concise, accurate, and correct in usage.

Technical writing is expository writing that informs readers about specialized areas of science and technology, such as anthropology, biology, chemistry, computer science, engineering, electronics, and psychology. Technical writing is practical and objective, focusing on the technical content rather than on the author's perspective on the subject. Technical writing encompasses user guides and manuals, data sheets describing software or equipment, operator's manuals, business reports, and writing for newsletters in fields such as business, health, and science.

Writing a business letter

- Use proper business letter form.
- Whenever possible, address your letter to a specific person.
- Explain exactly what you are requesting in a businesslike tone.

The letter below illustrates the block form, a popular style for a business letter.

Alan Shephard High School
123 Washington Way
Oak Center, IL 60308
August 27, 20_

Carol Bosley
TV Channel 2
1 Merchandise Mart
Chicago, IL 60602

Dear Ms. Bosley:

On March 15, Alan Shephard High School will have its semiannual career day. We cordially invite you to address the students on the career of broadcast journalism.

The program is scheduled for 2 P.M. We anticipate that you will speak for twenty to thirty minutes with an additional time for questions. We are inviting two other speakers in the areas of business and science. If the time conflicts with other commitments you may have, we will be happy to adjust our schedule.

We would appreciate your prompt response to Dr. Harry Belding, Principal. The school phone number is 708-536-9887, or you may respond by E-mail to shephard@ilsch.edu.

Yours truly,

Peter Bianco

Sending a memo

A memo (memorandum) is a concise means of communicating information. A memo begins with a header that provides basic information, followed by the text of the message. It does not have a formal closing.

TO: Cycle Club members

FROM: Josie Brown

SUBJECT: Parks and Recreation Department Activities

DATE: June 4, 20__

The Parks and Recreation Department is happy to announce the opening of a brand new trail for bicyclists. (See map at the bottom of this page.)

Writing a proposal

A proposal describes a project the writer wishes to undertake. It is presented to the person or persons responsible for making a decision in that area. For example, a proposal might be written to a school administrator suggesting a fundraising project or to a business manager about a change in procedures. A proposal includes an overview of the idea and the reasoning behind the plan.

Purpose: To replace the old and unreliable sound system in the Roosevelt High School auditorium at an estimated cost of $2,000.

Proposal: The Drama Club proposes a fundraising event: a readers theater production entitled *Shakespeare's Lovers*, to be presented on the small stage in the study hall.

Proposed Budget

Expenditures	
Publicity: posters, mailings, etc.	$25
Programs (computer class)	NC
Tickets	$20
Refreshments (parent donations)	NC
Income	
Ticket sales (200 at $5)	$1000
Program ads	$300
Net proceeds	$1255
Schedule	
Approval of proposal	March 16
Preparation of program	March 17–April 12
Publicity campaign kickoff, ticket order	March 20
Performance dates	April 13, 14, 15

Using Electronic Resources

Computers and computer networks are changing the ways in which people gather information. If you have access to a personal computer at home or in school, you can find information in two ways—through CD-ROMs or through the Internet.

CD-ROM

CD-ROMs (compact disc-read-only memory), which store a variety of information, can be purchased in stores or through mail-order catalogs. CD-ROMs may include sound, photographs, and video, as well as text. Types of information available in this form include the following:

- general reference books–encyclopedias, almanacs, histories
- literature collections and biographies
- news reports from various sources
- back issues of magazines

The Internet

The Internet is, as its name implies, an extensive network that links computers. To access the Internet, you must purchase the services of an Internet service provider. Many Internet service providers are available.

The Internet gives you access to a wealth of information from universities, news organizations, researchers, government organizations, institutions, and individual experts in various fields. It also enables you to visit Web sites created by people who may or may not offer legitimate information and/or useful opinions.

Browsing the Web When you browse the Web, you search electronically for World Wide Web sites related to a particular subject.

Using a search engine Although you can browse the Web at large, you can narrow your search for selected information by using a search engine. When you select a specific search engine, it will identify a list of subject areas from which to choose.

Evaluating a Web site Consider the source of the material you locate when deciding whether the information on a Web site is reliable. Although many sites are maintained by educational institutions and other authorities, anyone can create a Web site and post information—or misinformation—on it. To evaluate a Web site, ask yourself these questions:

- Do I recognize the name of the author?
- Is the site associated with a well-known university or other reputable organization?
- Can the information be substantiated in another source?
- Is the writer citing a fact or offering an opinion?

Terms to know

On-line information services are commercial services that provide many resources: chat forums; bulletin boards; databases; publications; reference materials; news, weather, and sports; and E-mail and Internet access.

The World Wide Web (WWW) is a global system that uses the Internet. It allows a user to create and link fields of information, to retrieve related documents, and to access the data in any order.

Downloading is using a computer modem to transfer a copy of a file from a distant computer to your computer.

A **Web site** is a group of one or more related Web pages that are accessible on the Internet. A **Web page** is a file that contains the information you view when you access a Web site. When you search the World Wide Web, you use a **Web browser** to access Web sites that carry the information you are searching for.

Computerized Library Resources

Electronic research is often faster than traditional methods and allows access to a wide spectrum of material. It has become an essential research tool. Public libraries, as well as school and university libraries, offer a variety of ways to do research electronically.

Catalogs Most libraries have computerized catalogs. By typing in a title or an author's name, you can find out if the library has the book, how many copies are in the library's collection, if the book is currently available, and if not, when it will be returned. In large library systems, the computer also provides the name of other libraries from which the desired book is available.

Electronic databases Your library may provide access to electronic databases through on-line information services. These databases are being continually updated. One helpful database available in many libraries is InfoTrac®, which provides an index and abstracts—short summaries—of articles from many periodicals. Other magazine indexes, some of which contain the full text of selected articles, may also be available.

Some libraries have an extensive collection of CD-ROMs. Ask the librarian what is available at your library and how to access the information.

Study and Test-Taking Skills

Study Skills

Taking notes and budgeting study time are essential skills for success as a student.

Taking notes in class

Keeping notes on classroom lectures and teachers' directions gives you a written record of important information. Here are some tips for note taking.

- Use loose-leaf paper if possible, so you can easily add and remove pages from your notebook. Use a different notebook for each subject to help organize your notes, and use a fresh page for every class. Write the name of the class and the date at the top of the page.
- Listen carefully for the main ideas, and record them in your own words. Do not try to write down every word. Also, be alert for signal words and phrases such as *most importantly, remember this,* and *to summarize.*
- Spend at least twice as much time listening as writing. Don't risk missing an important point while writing.
- Leave space around your notes to add more information later. Try leaving a wide left-hand margin to write in key points or an informal outline.
- As soon as possible after class, reread your notes and fill in any missing information while it is fresh in your mind. Exchange notes with a peer and jot down any key points he or she has that you may have missed.
- Take notes on your reading assignments. Your textbook can provide a framework for understanding the material presented by your teacher. Try using the text's headings and subheadings to create a basic outline.
- A good way to review your notes is to use them in an active way. Recopy or type your notes to help you commit the key points to memory.

Using study time wisely

- Study in the same place each day. Choose a place that is quiet and free from distractions.
- If discussion helps you to learn, try to find a study partner.
- Divide large assignments into smaller tasks.
- Make a monthly assignment calendar. Write down due dates, test dates, and notes about upcoming assignments so you can see at a glance what work you need to do and when, and so you can plan ahead for busy times.
- At the beginning of your study period, when your attention and energy are at their highest levels, work on the assignments you find hardest.
- Take a short break after completing each task. Stay alert by stretching, walking, or having a light snack.
- Review material before stopping. Even a short review will greatly increase the amount of material you are able to remember.

Preparing for Classroom Tests

This section will help you learn how to prepare for classroom tests.

Thinking ahead

Write down information about an upcoming test–when it will be given, what it will cover, and so on–so you can plan your study time effectively.

- Review your quizzes, homework assignments, class notes, and handouts. Look at end-of-chapter review questions in your textbook.
- Develop your own questions about main ideas and important details, and practice answering them.
- Make studying an active process. Rather than simply rereading your notes or a chapter, try summarizing the material or creating an outline, a list of characters, or a time line. Include details from your lecture notes and your reading so you will be able to see connections between them.
- Form study groups. Explaining information to a peer is one of the best ways to learn the material.
- Remember that students who are well rested and who eat a regular meal the morning of a test usually score higher than others.

Taking objective tests

Objective tests ask questions with specific, correct answers. Test time is usually limited, so use your time efficiently. First, read the directions carefully and ask questions if any are unclear. Then try to respond to each item on the test, starting with the easier ones. You can always come back to the more difficult ones later. Finally, try to save some time to review your test before turning it in.

Below are tips on answering specific kinds of objective test items.

- **Multiple-choice** Read all the answer choices provided before choosing one; even if the first one seems nearly correct, a later choice may be a better answer. Be cautious when choosing responses that contain absolute words such as *always, never, all,* or *none.* Since most generalizations have exceptions, absolute statements are often incorrect.
- **True/False** If *any* part of the item is false, the correct answer is "false."
- **Short-answer** Use complete sentences to help you write a clear response.
- **Fill-in** Restate fill-ins as regular questions to clarify what is being asked.
- **Matching** Note in the directions whether some responses can be used more than once or not used at all.

Taking subjective (essay) tests

Subjective tests typically require you to write an essay. Your grade is based more on how well you make your point than on whether you choose a correct answer.

When you receive the test, first read it through. Determine how much time to spend on each question. Then jot down ideas on scratch paper. Reread the question to make sure you are answering it. Develop a rough outline for your essay.

In the first paragraph, include a **thesis statement** that tells the main idea of your essay. Follow with paragraphs that provide **evidence** for your thesis. Give as much information as possible, including examples and illustrations where appropriate. Then finish with a **conclusion** that highlights the evidence you have provided and restates your thesis. If you have time left, **proofread** and neatly make corrections.

Preparing for Standardized Tests

Standardized tests are designed to be administered to very large groups of students, not just those in a particular class. Three of the most widely known standardized tests, all part of the college application process, are the ACT (American College Testing), the PSAT (Preliminary Scholastic Assessment Test), and the SAT (Scholastic Assessment Test). The strategies in this handbook refer specifically to the PSAT and SAT tests, but they also can apply to preparing for the ACT and other standardized tests.

The PSAT is generally administered to students in the 11th grade, though some schools offer it to students in the 10th grade as well. This test is designed to predict how well you will do on the SAT. For most students, the PSAT is simply a practice test. Those who perform exceptionally well on the 11th grade PSAT, however, will qualify for National Merit Scholarship competition.

The Scholastic Assessment Tests consist of the SAT-I: Reasoning Test and a variety of SAT-II: Subject Tests. The SAT-I is a three-hour test that evaluates your general verbal and mathematics skills. The SAT-II: Subject Tests are hour-long tests given in specific subjects and are designed to show specifically how much you have learned in a particular subject area.

Tips for taking standardized tests

- Skip difficult questions at first. Standardized tests are usually timed, so first answer items you know. You can return later to those you skipped.
- Mark only your answers on the answer sheet. Most standardized tests are scored by a computer, so stray marks can be read as incorrect answers.
- Frequently compare the question numbers on your test with those on your answer sheet to avoid putting answers in the wrong spaces.
- If time permits, check your answers. If you are not penalized for guessing, fill in answers for any items you might have skipped.

Preparing for the PSAT and the SAT-I

The verbal sections of the PSAT and SAT-I contain sentence completion items, reading comprehension questions, and analogies.

Sentence completion

Sentence completion items provide a sentence with one or two blanks and ask you to select the word or pair of words that best fits in the blank(s).

Start by reading the sentence and filling in your own word to replace the blank. Look for words that show how the word in the blank is related to the rest of the sentence–*and, but, since, therefore, although.* Then pick the word from the answer choices that is closest in meaning to your word. If you have trouble coming up with a specific word to fill in the blank, try to determine whether the word should be positive or negative. If you can eliminate even one answer choice, take a guess at the answer.

Reading comprehension

In Reading Comprehension, a series of questions follows each passage.

Read the passages quickly and spend your time working on the questions. You get points for answering questions correctly, not for reading passages thoroughly. Briefly summarize the passage. This will help you answer questions based on the passage as a whole. For specific questions based on details, return to the passage. Reading Comprehension is like an open-book test; you are expected to look at the passage while answering the questions. Finally, if you can eliminate even one answer choice, take a guess at the answer.

Analogies

Nearly half of the items on the verbal sections of the PSAT and SAT-I are designed to test your vocabulary. Therefore, the more words you know, the higher your score will be. Refer to pages R86–R87 of the **Reading Handbook** for information on how to build your vocabulary.

One type of vocabulary-based question is the analogy, which tests your ability to grasp the relationships between concepts. The best way to pinpoint the relationship is to connect the words in a simple sentence that defines one of the words. Some of the most common relationships seen on the PSAT and the SAT-I are shown below.

Relationship	Example
Cause and effect	heat : perspiration :: sadness : tears
A person to the normal action of that person	comedian : amuse :: journalist : write
An object to its normal function	telescope : magnify :: aircraft : fly
User to tool	teacher : book :: carpenter : hammer
Degree	terrified : frightened :: destitute : poor
Object to characteristic	water : wet :: brick : hard
Class to subclass (or subclass to class)	grain : rye :: music : rap

Reading Handbook

The Reading Process

Being an active reader is a very important part of being a lifelong learner. It is also an ongoing task. Good reading skills build on each other, overlap, and spiral around in much the same way that a winding staircase goes round and round while leading you to a higher place.

This handbook is designed to help you find and use the tools you'll need before, during, and after reading.

Vocabulary Development

Word identification and vocabulary skills are key building blocks in reading and in the comprehension process. By learning to use a variety of strategies to build your word skills and vocabulary, you will become a stronger reader.

Using context to determine meaning

The very best way to expand and extend your vocabulary is to read widely, listen carefully, and participate in a rich variety of discussions. When reading on your own, though, you can often figure out the meanings of new words by looking at their **context,** the other words and sentences that surround them. For example:

> *Contiguous* countries, such as the United States and Canada, usually have border patrols.

Although you may not know the meaning of *contiguous,* you can figure out from the phrase *such as the United States and Canada* that the word means "adjoining."

Tips for Using Context

- **Look for clues such as**
  - –a synonym or an explanation of the unknown word in the sentence.
    Elise's shop specialized in ***millinery,*** *or* ***hats for women.***
  - –a reference to what the word is or is not like.
    An ***archaeologist,*** *like a* ***historian,*** *deals with the past.*
  - –a general topic associated with the word.
    The ***cooking*** *teacher discussed the best way to* ***braise*** *meat.*
  - –a description or action associated with the word.
    He used the ***hoe*** *to* ***dig*** *up the garden.*
- **Predict a possible meaning.**

- **Determine whether the meaning makes sense in terms of the whole passage.**
- **Be aware the writer may be using**

  –a word with **multiple meanings.**

  Some of the group will play games; others will attend a play.

  –**figurative language,** such as **similes,** which use *like* or *as* to compare two unlike things, and **metaphors,** which compare two unlike things without using *like* or *as.*

  The leaves rustled like silk as they drifted to the ground. (simile)
  The bullets of rain pelted the sidewalk. (metaphor)

  –**idioms,** expressions that have a meaning apart from the literal one.

  I'm just pulling your leg is an idiom used about joking with someone.

  Hint: If you come across an idiom with an unfamiliar meaning, look in the dictionary under the main word in the phrase. Many dictionaries list idioms after the definitions.

  –**technical vocabulary,** words that require an understanding of the specific terms of a specialized field.

  Be sure to clean your ***mouse*** *from time to time to make the* ***cursor*** *move smoothly.*

● For more on figurative language, see **Literary Terms Handbook,** p. R5.

Using word parts and word origins

Another way to determine the meaning of a word is to take the word itself apart. If you understand the meaning of the **base,** or **root,** part of a word and also know the meanings of key syllables added either to the beginning or end of the base word, you can usually figure out what the word means.

Word Part	Definition	Example
Base or root	the most basic part of a word	*voc* means "call" *Convoke* means "call together."
Prefix	a syllable placed before a base word to change or add to its meaning	*inter-* means "between" *Intervene* means "come between."
Suffix	a syllable placed after a base word to create a new meaning	*-less* means "without" *Hopeless* means without hope

Word origins Since Latin, Greek, and Anglo-Saxon roots are the basis for much of our English vocabulary, having some background in one of these languages can be a useful vocabulary tool. For example, *astronomy* comes from the Greek root *astro,* which means "relating to the stars." *Stellar* also has a meaning referring to stars, but its origin is Latin. Knowing root words in other languages can help you determine meanings, derivations, and spellings in English.

Using vocabulary references

Dictionaries A dictionary provides the meaning or meanings of a word. Look at the sample dictionary entry below to see what other information it provides.

help (help) **helped** or *(archaic)* **holp, helped** or *(archaic)* **hol-pen, help-ing.** *v.t.* **1.** to provide with support, as in the performance of a task; be of service to: *He helped his brother paint the room.* ▲ also used elliptically with a preposition or adverb: *He helped the old woman up the stairs.* **2.** to enable (someone or something) to accomplish a goal or achieve a desired effect: *The coach's advice helped the team to win.* **3.** to provide with sustenance or relief, as in time of need or distress; succor: *The Red Cross helped the flood victims.* **4.** to promote or contribute to; further. *The medication helped his recovery.* **5.** to be useful or profitable to; be of advantage to: *It might help you if you read the book.* **6.** to improve or remedy: *Nothing really helped his sinus condition.* **7.** to prevent; stop: *I can't help his rudeness.* **8.** to refrain from; avoid: *I couldn't help smiling when I heard the story.* **9.** to wait on or serve (often with *to*): *The clerk helped us. The hostess helped him to the dessert.* **10. cannot help but.** *Informal* cannot but. **11. so help me (God).** oath of affirmation. **12. to help oneself to.** to take or appropriate: *The thief helped himself to all the jewels.* *–v.i.* to provide support, as in the performance of a task; be of service. *–n.* **1.** act of providing support, service, or sustenance. **2.** source of support, service, or sustenance. **3.** person or group of persons hired to work for another or others. **4.** means of improving, remedying, or preventing. [Old English *helpan* to aid, succor, benefit.] **Syn.** *v.t.* **1. Help, aid, assist** mean to support in a useful way. **Help** is the most common word and means to give support in response to a known or expressed need or for a definite purpose: *Everyone helped to make the school fair a success.* **Aid** means to give relief in times of distress or difficulty: *It is the duty of rich nations to aid the poor.* **Assist** means to serve another person in the performance of his task in a secondary capacity: *The secretary assists the officer by taking care of his correspondence.*

Thesauruses These references provide synonyms and often antonyms. Some dictionaries and thesauruses are available on CD-ROM and on the Internet.

Glossaries Many textbooks and technical works contain condensed dictionaries that provide an alphabetical listing of words used in the text and their specific definitions. The example on page R81 is from a social studies textbook.

Glossary

A

abolitionist 1800s reformer who worked to end slavery (p. 342)
acid rain acid precipitation in the form of rain (p. 1016)
agribusiness large farming operation that includes the cultivation, processing, storage, and distribution of farm products (p. 869)
amendment alteration to the Constitution (p. 160)
amnesty act of a government by which pardon is granted to an individual or groups of persons (p. 445)
anarchism a belief in no direct government authority over society (p. 531)
anarchist one who opposes all forms of government (p. 616)

Identifying word relationships

Determining the relationships of words to each other also aids comprehension. Some special word relationships include analogies, synonyms, antonyms, denotation, and connotation.

- **Denotation** A denotation expresses the exact meaning of a word. A word may have more than one denotation, but all of its denotations will be listed in the dictionary. Notice, for example, all the denotations for the word *help* listed in the dictionary entry on page R80.
- **Connotation** Connotation refers to an emotion or an underlying value that accompanies a word's dictionary meaning. When the word *leper* is used, you know that the word refers to someone suffering from a specific disease, but its connotation includes feelings of disgust or pity and suggests separation from familiar surroundings.

TRY THE STRATEGIES

Play a game of Word Clues. Each player chooses a word that has been used in class in the past two weeks and coins a nonsense word to represent it. Player One writes a sentence on the board using his or her nonsense word in an appropriate context. Players who can identify the word from the context raise their hands. Each scores five points for a correct identification. If no one is able to identify the word, Player One supplies a synonym or antonym for it. Players who identify the word correctly after the second clue score three points. If no one identifies the word, Player One gets a one-point penalty and the next player repeats the procedure. When time is up, the player with the most points wins.

Comprehension Strategies

Reading comprehension means understanding–deriving meaning from–what you have read. Using a variety of strategies can help you improve your comprehension and make reading more interesting and more fun.

Previewing

Before beginning a selection, it's helpful to **preview** what you are about to read.

- **Read** the title, headings, and subheadings of the selection.
- **Look** at the illustrations and notice how the text is organized.
- **Skim** the selection; that is, take a quick glance at the whole thing.
- **Decide** what the author's purpose might be.
- **Predict** what the selection will be about.
- **Set a purpose** for your reading.

Establishing a purpose for reading

To get the greatest benefit from what you read, you should **establish a purpose for reading.** Some purposes for reading are

- to enjoy
- to find information, to discover
- to interpret
- to follow directions or take action
- to be persuaded about an issue
- to appreciate a writer's craft
- to find models for your own writing

Vary your reading strategies to fit the different purposes you have when you read. If you are reading for entertainment, you might read quickly, but if you read to gather information or follow directions, you might read more slowly, take notes, construct a graphic organizer, or reread sections of text.

TRY THE STRATEGIES

Look through a newspaper or a magazine at home or at the library. Preview three or four articles using the strategies listed under Previewing. Then decide what your purpose for reading would be for each of the articles selected. Which of the articles should you read slowly? Which might you read quickly? In a small group, discuss your purposes for reading and why your reading speed would differ from article to article.

Drawing on personal background

Good reading is an interactive process between the writer and each different person reading a selection. Even the youngest child has a body of information and personal experiences which are important and uniquely his or her own. When you draw on your personal background, combining it with the words on a page, you create meaning in a selection. Drawing on this personal background is also called **activating prior knowledge.** To expand and extend your prior knowledge, share it in active classroom discussions.

Ask yourself questions like these:

- What do I know about this topic?
- What familiar places have similar settings?
- What experiences have I had that compare or contrast with what I am reading?
- What characters from life or literature remind me of the characters or narrator in the selection?

Making and verifying predictions

As you read, take educated guesses about story events and outcomes; that is, **make predictions** before and during reading. Using your prior knowledge and the information you have gathered in your preview, you can predict what you will learn or what might happen in a selection. Then use information you gather as you read to adjust or **verify your predictions.** Have you ever read a mystery, decided who committed the crime, and then changed your mind as more clues emerged? You were adjusting your predictions. Or did you shriek with delight or smile smugly when you found out you guessed the murderer? You were verifying your predictions. Careful predictions and verifications increase your comprehension of a selection.

TRY THE STRATEGIES

Find a selection from your social studies or science textbook. First, preview the title, illustrations, and available headings and subheadings to determine what the piece might be about or what might happen. On your own paper, write your predictions about what you will read. Then, as you read, revise your predictions based on new information and your own background or prior knowledge.

Monitoring and modifying reading strategies

No matter what your purpose for reading, your most important task is to understand what you have read. Try having a conversation with yourself as you work through a selection. **Check,** or **monitor, your understanding,** using the following strategies:

- Summarize
- Clarify
- Ask questions
- Predict what will come next

This might be done once or twice in an easy, entertaining selection, or after every paragraph in a nonfiction selection, dense with new concepts.

One way of questioning yourself is to pretend that you are the teacher trying to determine if your students have understood the main ideas of a selection. What questions would you ask? Be sure that you can answer those questions before you read on.

Tips for Monitoring Understanding

- Reread.
- Make a graphic organizer, such as a chart or a diagram, to help sort out your thoughts.
- Consult other sources, including text resources, teachers and other students.
- Write comments or questions on another piece of paper for later review or discussion.

Use or modify whatever strategy fits your learning style, but don't settle for not understanding. Be an active reader.

Visualizing

Try to form a mental picture of scenes, characters, and events as you read. Use the details and descriptions the author gives you. According to your imagination and the text, what do the characters look like? What does the setting look like? Can you picture the steps in a process when you read nonfiction? If you can **visualize** what you read, selections will be more interesting. When someone reads aloud to you, try sketching what you're hearing–you'll be more likely to recall it later.

Constructing graphic organizers

Graphic organizers help you reconstruct ideas in a visual way, so you can remember them later on. You might make a **chart** or **diagram,** showing the information the author provides.

Venn diagrams When mapping out a comparison-and-contrast text structure, you can use a Venn diagram. The outer portions of the circles will show how two characters, ideas, or items contrast, or are different, and the overlapping part will show how they are similar, or compare them.

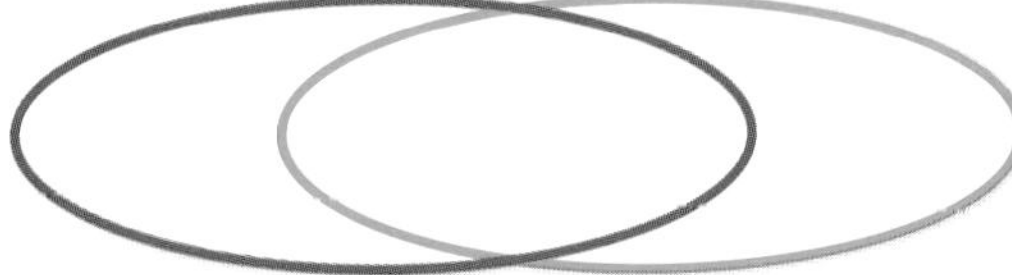

Flow charts To help you keep track of the sequence of events, use a flow chart. Arrange ideas or events in their logical, sequential order. Then draw arrows between your ideas to indicate how one idea or event flows into another. Look at the following flow chart to see how you can map out story events in chronological order or show cause and effect relationships.

Web To help you determine a main idea and supporting details, use a web. Surround the main idea with examples or supporting details. Then create additional circles, branching off from the supporting details, to add related thoughts.

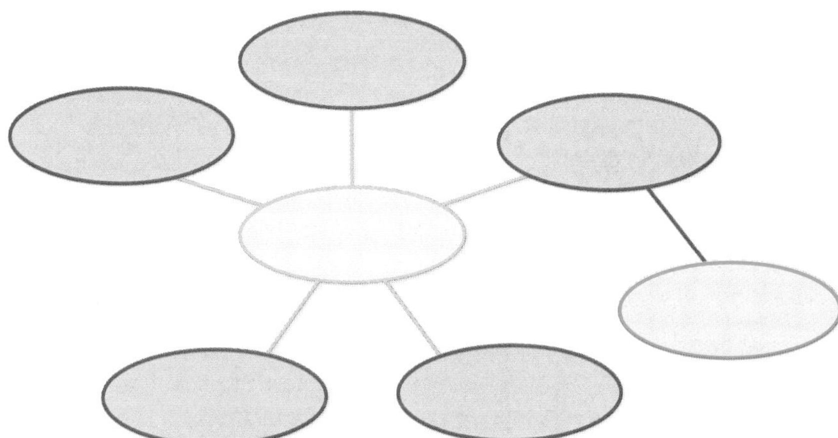

Analyzing text structures

Writers organize their written work in various ways, depending on their topic and purpose. Finding and analyzing that pattern of organization or **text structure** helps you to understand what an author is trying to say. Here are three important ways that writers structure or organize text:

Kind of Organization	Purpose	Clues
Comparison and contrast	To determine similarities and differences	Words and phrases like *similarly, on the other hand, in contrast to, but, however*
Cause and effect	To explore the reasons for something and to examine the results of events or actions	Words and phrases like *because* and *as a result*
Chronological order	To present events in time order	Words and phrases like *first, next, then, later,* and *finally*

Writers may embed one kind of structure within another, but it is usually possible to identify one main pattern of organization that will help you discover an author's purpose and will focus your attention on the important ideas in the selection.

Read the following example. Analyze the text structure used.

Two high school athletes who have attracted the attention of state high school tennis fans are Cleo Whittington and Tessa Levine. Two great players could hardly be more different. Cleo is a left-hander who depends on her lightning serve and ground strokes to overpower her opponents. Tessa is right-handed, hits her backhand with two hands, and outlasts other players with an endless stream of smooth shots as if she were a human backboard. Cleo displays her emotions, while Tessa is known for her blank expression on the court.

Cleo was born in Jamaica, but she and her family moved here when she was in eighth grade. Although she had not played tennis in Jamaica, she seemed to have been born with a tennis racquet in her hand. In her freshman year, she tried out for the tennis team. After one month, she was moved to the varsity team because no other freshman girls offered her competition.

Tessa, on the other hand, grew up playing tennis with her family. She began playing in tournaments at age nine. Her goal has always been to make a name for herself as a tennis pro.

Throughout their years in high school, Cleo and Tessa have been friendly rivals. Both were delighted when they were chosen to represent their school in the Regional Junior Championship Tournament at Forest Park on Long Island.

What is the basic text structure of the previous paragraphs? How do you know? What words help you to see the structure? How could you show this information on a graphic organizer?

TRY THE STRATEGIES

Find a selection in your literature, social studies, or science textbook and determine its text structure. Look for important clues. Use the chart on page R86 to help you in your determination.

Interpreting graphic aids

Graphic aids provide an opportunity to see and analyze information at a glance. Some effective graphic aids include maps, charts, tables, and diagrams. To interpret any of these graphic aids, you need to understand how the information presented is organized.

Reading a map Maps are flat representations of land, with other features included. A **compass rose** helps a reader to determine direction. A **legend** explains the map's symbols, while a **scale** shows the relationship of the map size to the land represented. A map may show physical features, political divisions, or historical data.

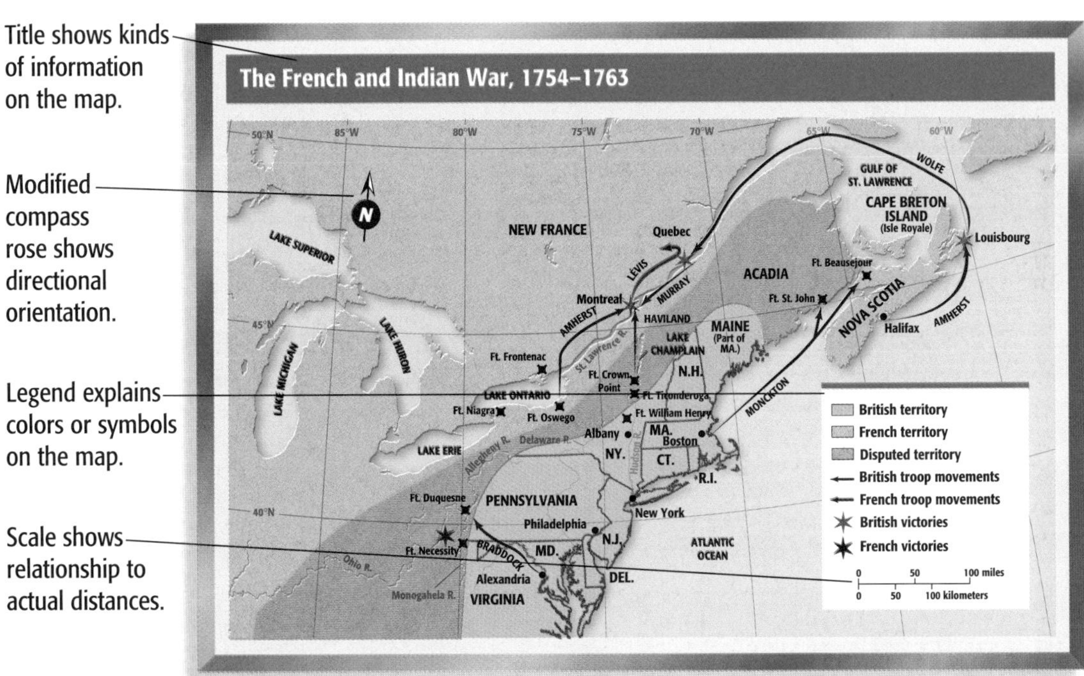

Refer to the map to answer these questions. What route did British General Wolfe take to reach Quebec? Where did the French secure victories?

Reading a chart Charts help you compare and analyze information. In charts or tables, information is presented in rows and columns.

Video Rentals and Sales (in millions)		
Year	Video Rental	Video Sales
1986	$3,308	$810
1987	$4,168	$1,004
1988	$5,210	$1,483
1989	$6,096	$2,240
1990	$6,645	$2,800

Title of chart — Column heads — Data

Between which two years did video rentals make the biggest jump? What conclusions can you draw about video sales over the five years from 1986 to 1990? Based on the trend shown on this chart, how might you expect the number of video rentals to have changed over the next five years, to 1995?

Reading a graph The relationship between two or more elements can be shown in a graph, using dots, bars, or lines. Look at the title of the graph and the labels. Be sure you understand what they mean. The labels on the bottom of line graphs tell you what each vertical line represents. In this case, the lines represent different years, and the vertical labels refer to thousands of automobiles. The source, shown below the graph, tells you where the data comes from. The title of this graph tells you that you will be comparing auto sales in the years from 1920 to 1929.

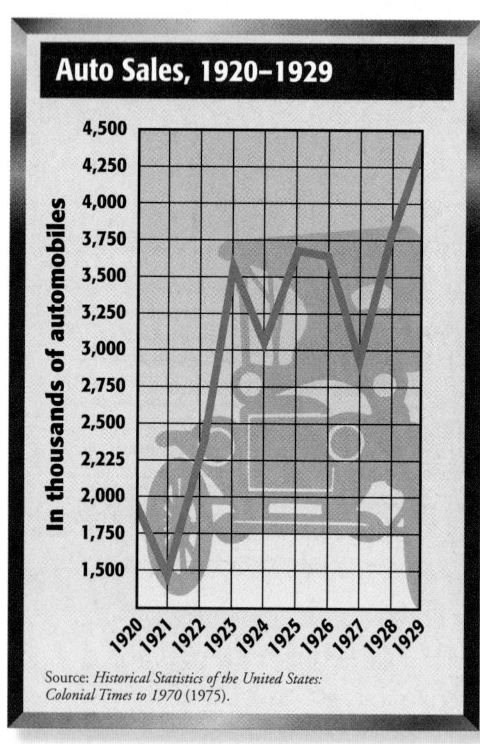

Source: *Historical Statistics of the United States: Colonial Times to 1970* (1975).

In what year were auto sales the lowest? How many cars were sold in 1925?

Reading a diagram A diagram illustrates the parts of an item. You might see a diagram of a bicycle, for instance, with arrows identifying the name of each part. Diagrams can also illustrate how a process functions. The diagram below illustrates how heat energy is turned into electricity.

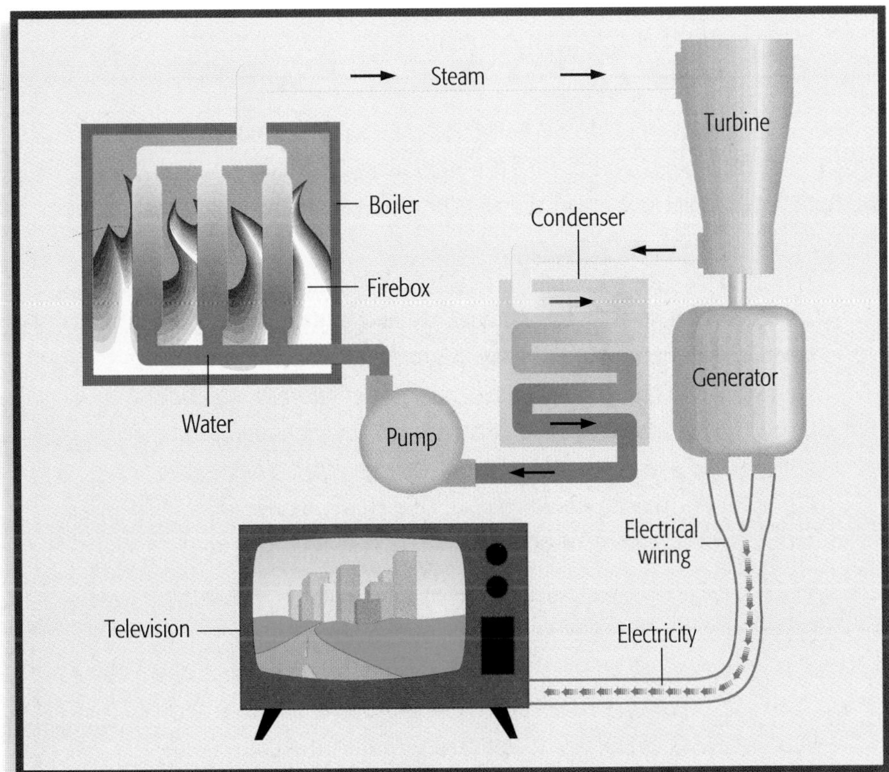

TRY THE STRATEGIES

In your social studies or science text, locate a section that uses a graphic aid. What kind of information is presented graphically? Read and interpret the information using the graphic aid, and then, on your paper, explain why the visual representation successfully presents the material.

Sequencing

The order in which thoughts are arranged is called **sequence.** A good sequence is logical, given the ideas presented. Three common forms of sequencing are

- Chronological order
- Spatial order
- Order of importance

Recognizing the sequence of something is particularly important when **following complex written directions.** If a written sequence is illogical or incomplete, or if you fail to precisely follow steps in a given order, you may be unable to complete an important task such as taking a test or locating a destination when driving a car.

Identifying main ideas and supporting details

As you read, it is important to identify the **main idea** of a paragraph or passage. Works of fiction and nonfiction can express one or more main ideas. In a single paragraph, the main idea will be the thought that organizes that paragraph and around which all other sentences are built. Some writers directly state the main idea in a topic sentence, while others imply the main idea with examples and other clues.

Read a paragraph carefully. Then decide if one sentence states the main, organizing thought, or if that thought is implied. Once you identify the main idea, you can use the **supporting details** to learn additional information about the main idea.

The next big breakthrough in fighting lung cancer may be as simple as a beam of light. **Doctors are now experimenting with lasers to kill tumors in patients.** *The new treatment is called photodynamic therapy. Most patients prefer the new treatment to the old style of operation. It's faster, less frightening for the patient, and even costs less. The method is still being studied, but the early results hold promise. One study showed a success rate of almost eighty percent.*

The treatment works like photosynthesis in plants, using light to set off a chemical reaction. *First the patient is injected with a drug that is sensitive to light. The drug travels through the bloodstream to cancerous cells. Then a scope is slid into the lung, where it emits a red-light laser. The light causes the drug to change into a form of oxygen that inflames the tumor. As the cancer cells die, they fall away from the lung like dead skin.*

Main idea

Supporting details

Main idea

Chronological order

Supporting details

Paraphrasing

When you **paraphrase,** you put something you've read into your own words. You might paraphrase just the main ideas, or you might retell an entire story in your own words. You need to understand something thoroughly in order to put it into your own words, so paraphrasing is a useful strategy for reviewing and for judging if you've understood what you've read.

- **Original** Doctors are now experimenting with lasers to kill tumors in patients. The new treatment is called photodynamic therapy. Most patients prefer the new treatment to the old style of operation. It's faster, less frightening for the patient, and even costs less. The method is still being studied, but the early results hold promise.
- **Paraphrase** Patients are enjoying a new experimental laser therapy used to treat tumors. It's not scary, it's quicker and cheaper, and it seems to work.

Summarizing

When you **summarize** you relate the main ideas of a selection in a logical sequence and in your own words. You are combining three skills in one. To create a good summary, include all the main ideas. Answer who, what, where, why, how, and when if that information is included in the passage. Do not include anything that is not important. A good summary can be easily understood by someone who has not read the whole text or selection. If you're not sure if an idea is a main idea or a detail, try taking it out of your summary. Does your summary still sound complete?

Look at the following summary of the passage on photodynamic therapy.

> There's a new photodynamic laser treatment that kills tumors and is quicker and cheaper than surgery. Patients like the therapy, and studies indicate that it works. Like photosynthesis in plants, the treatment uses light to set off a chemical reaction. The laser triggers a drug that kills the cancer cells and makes the tumor fall away.

TRY THE STRATEGIES

Read "The Angry Winter" on page 558 of your text. On separate paper, list the main ideas of the selection. Under each main idea, list the major supporting details that explain it. Use this information to write a summary of what you have read. Be sure that you do not use the writer's words. Paraphrase the writer's ideas in your own words.

Drawing and supporting inferences

Authors don't always directly state what they want you to understand in a selection. By providing clues and interesting details, they imply certain information. Whenever readers combine those clues with their own background and knowledge, they are drawing an inference. An **inference** involves using your reason and experience to come up with an idea, based on what an author implies or suggests. The following active reading behaviors help you infer:

- **Predicting** When you predict what a story will be about, or guess what will happen next, you are drawing an inference.
- **Drawing conclusions** A conclusion is a general statement you can make and explain with reasoning, or with supporting details from a text. If you read a story describing a sport where five players bounce a ball and throw it through a hoop, you may conclude that the sport is basketball.
- **Making generalizations** When readers make generalizations, they draw an inference that can apply to more than one item or group. This inference has a more general scope than a prediction or a conclusion. If you read articles

about how the Sioux people revere the crane and how the Cherokee believe strongly in protecting our natural resources, you might generalize that Native Americans respect nature.

What is most important when drawing inferences is to be sure that you have accurately based your guesses on supporting details from the text, as well as on your own knowledge. If you cannot point to a place in the selection to help back up your inference, you may need to rethink your guess.

Having walked home from school in a cool rain, Patricia trudged inside and tossed her wet coat on the throw rug. Her umbrella stood dripping in the entryway. "Patty, did you shut the front door?" her father called from his study down the hall. "Yes, Dad," she replied, and slowly moved back to pull the door closed. Her father was always checking up on her. Then she turned on the TV in the living room and went to the kitchen to make a snack. Patricia removed the mustard, lettuce, and bologna from the refrigerator and began looking for the bread. The theme song of her favorite afternoon TV show enticed her back into the living room.

At the first commercial break, Patricia decided to take a nice hot bath. In the bathroom off the back hallway, she turned on the tub faucet and tested the water several times with two fingers to make sure it was the correct temperature. Over the rush of the faucet she could hear the laugh track on TV, and she returned to the living room sofa.

It wasn't long before the phone rang. Patricia's best friend, Trudy, had a lengthy story to tell about that new boy from Idaho. Patricia sat watching TV and yawning and nodding at Trudy's story, feeling glad that she hadn't a worry in the world.

It wasn't until she noticed her dog's wet paws that a growing awareness came over her. Just then she heard her father's booming voice.

What inferences might you draw from the paragraphs above? What supporting details would support your inferences? Can you make a prediction or draw a conclusion from the information given? Is there enough information to support a generalization? Why or why not?

TRY THE STRATEGIES

Together with several other students, silently read several pages from a selection none of you has previously read. On your own paper, write down any inferences you can draw from the material you read. Compare your inferences within your group.

Using study strategies

All students face important studying tasks. Finding the right strategy will depend on the task you face. You may need to study for a quiz or a test, or make a class presentation with a group or by yourself. In each case you will want to pick the strategy which is most efficient and which helps you to organize and remember the material you need. Some useful study strategies include:

- **Skimming and scanning** If you want to refresh your memory about a passage you've read or get a general overview of new material, **skim** the pages by glancing quickly over the entire selection. It will focus your attention on the main ideas and the author's purpose. If you need to go back and find a particular piece of information, **scan** the selection, looking for key words or phrases that will point you to the specific information you need. You don't need to look at the whole selection. As you scan, look for section headings or terms in **boldface** type.
- **Using and creating study guides** It is often helpful to use end of chapter questions to guide you while you read. You can also create your own guide by turning headings and subheadings into questions to answer as you read. Don't forget to consider captions underneath illustrations when thinking up questions to help focus your attention. Use the guide to help you review aloud or silently.
- **Reviewing** Active readers go back over selections again and again. They combine their notes, outlines, and study guides to provide themselves with different ways of approaching the same information. The more you review information from different angles, the better you'll recall it when you need to.
- **Using KWL** A KWL is a good device for charting expository information. Make three columns on a page. Label the first column *What I Know,* the second column *What I Want to Know,* and the third column *What I Learned.* You can also add more columns to record places where you found information and places where you can look for more information.

TRY THE STRATEGIES

Skim a few chapters in a history textbook to find examples of comparison and contrast, chronological order, and cause and effect. Make graphic organizers to create a visual presentation of the ideas you have just read. Use these organizers to study the material.

For more about study strategies, see **Communications Skills Handbook,** pp. R74–R77.

Reading silently for sustained periods

What things keep you on track when you read? Do you need total silence to concentrate well, or does some soft background music help you stay focused? Whatever your preference, it is important to avoid distractions or interruptions when you have to read silently for any length of time.

Tips for Reading Silently

- Be sure you're comfortable, but not too comfortable.
- Once your external surroundings are set, it's important to maintain your concentration and check your comprehension regularly.
- Using a study guide or a concept web can help you get through difficult nonfiction passages. Your teacher may provide a guide, or you can use questions from the end of the material to guide you.
- When you read fiction, a story map or other graphic organizer will help you stay focused on the important elements of the selection.
- Take regular breaks when you need them, and vary your reading rate with the demands of the text.

TRY THE STRATEGIES

Choose one or more longer selections in this book. Block out a period of time during which you won't be interrupted. Make sure you are in a comfortable spot where you can concentrate. Read silently until you finish the selection. Then use the **Responding to Literature** questions that follow the selection to monitor your comprehension.

Reading Across Texts and Cultures

One of the most important student tasks is to read widely and to integrate information from different sources to create new knowledge. Throughout this text you have read both classic and contemporary works, looking at themes from different perspectives, from different cultures, and for different purposes. As a citizen of the world, and not just your own country, you have examined world literature through the eyes of history and with a view toward the future. Every time you discussed a selection, interpreted a theme, or analyzed a writer's purpose, you created new knowledge for yourself and your classmates.

Reading in varied sources

Depending on the type of source material they are creating, writers may use a variety of styles and settings to tell the same story or cover the same subject. Each source gives specific information in a particular way. For instance, if you were researching the American artist Georgia O'Keeffe, you might first locate some basic facts about her in a book on art history. A biography might give you additional details about her life. Then, if you searched her personal writings, such as letters and diaries, you would collect information from the artist's own perspective. Whatever sources you use, it's important to be able to organize and evaluate information, combining or synthesizing what you learn from varied sources to create something for your own purposes.

For instance, to learn about the history of your hometown or region, you might read and refer to a variety of texts:

- Consult a **map** to discover the boundaries and relative positions of the geographical features of your town.
- Look up **diaries** and **journals** of long-time and former residents to gain valuable insights into different times and places.
- Find **speeches** made in the town on special occasions. These recorded public comments can showcase the style of the orator, as well as provide information about a topic, an area, or a group of people.
- Refer to the Internet and other **electronic media** that can lead you to a variety of sources and allow you to find a broader base of information about a subject.
- Try to find old **letters, memoranda, newspapers, magazines,** and **textbooks** that may provide valuable information not generally available in other sources.
- Ask a librarian or the curator of a local museum about **special collections** of posters or other resources that might offer information on your subject.

Read the following paragraphs from two kinds of primary sources. Then answer the questions that follow.

> Lincoln used to go to bed ordinarily [between] ten and eleven o'clock, unless he happened to be kept up by important news, in which case he would frequently remain at the War Department till one or two. He rose early. When he lived in the country at the Soldiers' Home, he would be up and dressed, eat his breakfast (which was extremely frugal, an egg, a piece of toast, coffee, etc.), and ride into Washington, all before eight o'clock. In the winter at the White House he was not quite so early.
>
> *—John Hay, one of Lincoln's private secretaries*

Four score and seven years ago our fathers brought forth on this continent, a new nation, conceived in Liberty, and dedicated to the proposition that all men are created equal.

Now we are engaged in a great civil war, testing whether that nation, or any nation so conceived and so dedicated, can long endure. We are met on a battlefield of that war. We have come to dedicate a portion of that field, as a final resting place for those who gave their lives that that nation might live. . . .

But in a larger sense, we can not dedicate—we can not consecrate—we can not hallow—this ground. The brave men, living and dead, who struggled here, have consecrated it, far above our poor power to add or detract. . . . It is rather for us to be here dedicated to the great task remaining before us—that from these honored dead we take increased devotion to that cause for which they gave the last full measure of devotion—that we here highly resolve that these dead shall not have died in vain—that this nation, under God, shall have a new birth of freedom—and that government of the people, by the people, for the people, shall not perish from the earth.

—Abraham Lincoln, from his address delivered at the dedication of the cemetery at Gettysburg, November 19, 1863

Which source would be better to use in a report on Lincoln as president of the United States? Which source would be better to use in a report on Abraham Lincoln's private life? How does reading across these texts provide a more complete picture of Abraham Lincoln?

TRY THE STRATEGIES

With a partner, select a topic that interests you, and research it in several kinds of sources. Compare the information from each source. Then organize and combine your information to present it to the class in some new form.

Recognizing distinctive and shared characteristics of cultures

When reading literature from different world cultures, you will find common themes about human nature. You will also see the ways in which distinctive characteristics of cultures increase your appreciation of those themes while enriching the understanding, knowledge, and enjoyment you have for your own roots. Fairytales, for example, often have counterparts in different cultures, so reading an Egyptian, a Native American, and an Asian version of "Cinderella" enhances your understanding of the story and also shows you the beauty and subtleties of different cultural traditions. Notice the similarities and differences in the elements of the Cinderella story in the four cultures charted at the top of page R97.

Culture	Heroine	Supernatural elements	Special clothing	Outcome
American/ European	Cinderella, mistreated stepchild	Fairy godmother	Glass slippers	Marries the prince
Zuni (Native American)	Turkey girl, turkey herder	Sacred turkeys	White doeskin robes	Returns to rags because she breaks her promise
Egyptian	Rhodopis, Greek slave girl	Falcon	Rose-red slippers	Marries the Pharaoh
Hmong (Asian)	Jouanah, despised stepchild	Dead mother's spirit	Special sandals	Finds love and happiness

Literary Response

Whenever you share your thoughts and feelings about something you've read, you are responding to text. Since we are all different people, though, we respond in different ways. Everyone has a learning style. Some learn best when speaking and writing, while others enjoy moving around or creating something artistic. What you do when you read can take different forms. Some responses to reading can include discussions, journals, oral interpretations, and dramatizations.

Responding to informational and aesthetic elements

You respond to what you read with both your mind and your emotions. To respond intellectually, think about whether ideas are logical and well supported. To respond emotionally, ask yourself how you feel about a selection.

Tips for Interpreting and Responding to Literature

- **Discuss** what you have read and share your views of the selections with your teacher and other students in the class.
- **Keep a journal** about what you read. Record your thoughts, feelings, or what you have learned in a journal. Write down what impresses you as well as what questions you have.
- **Read aloud** to yourself or with others. Poetry and drama make particularly good read-aloud materials, but even nonfiction passages can become clearer if troublesome passages are read orally.
- **Take part in dramatizations** and **oral interpretations.** Present characters through actions and dialogue. Use your voice, facial expressions, and body language to convey meaning. A **readers theater** is one kind of dramatic presentation in which students take different parts and read through a play or other fictional work.

Using text elements to defend personal interpretations

Whatever your response to a selection or your interpretation of a theme, you must be sure to use elements of the text to support those responses and interpretations. You need to provide details given by the writer to back up your interpretation. If you can't provide those text proofs, you may need to rethink your response.

Often you are asked to write about the selections you read. It is not enough to say, "I really liked the main character." You must know why you liked him or her. Look for specific descriptions. What did you find interesting about a story's setting? What details created certain feelings in you?

Comparing personal responses with authoritative views

Critics' reviews may encourage you to read a book, see a film, or attend a performance. They may also warn you that whatever is reviewed is not acceptable entertainment or is not valued by the reviewer.

Ask yourself the following questions:

- Would I go to a movie if it got a bad review from critics?
- Would I read a book if a reviewer said that it was a waste of time?
- Do I ever disagree with reviewers?

Deciding whether or not to value a review depends on the credibility of the reviewer, and also on your own personal viewpoints and feelings. Be sure that as you read authoritative reviews, you determine if the writer's opinions are supported with adequate and accurate details. Read the following model.

Review of *Titanic*

Directed by James Cameron

The Abyss

It's $200 million-plus worth of old-fashioned melodrama in a state-of-the-art package. It's both the shortest 3 ½ hours you'll ever spend at the movies and spectacle of such magnitude that it's hard to imagine feeling you didn't get your time and money's worth. It begins with eerie underwater images of the *Titanic* remains, resting beneath the Atlantic since its close encounter with an iceberg in 1912. The footage comes courtesy of a salvage expedition led by Brock Lovett (Bill Paxton), whose hidden purpose is to recover a fabulous blue diamond. The gem was bought by caddish roue Cal Hockley (Billy Zane) for his fiancée Rose (Kate Winslet), and apparently lost—with the girl—in the wreck. Imagine Lovett's surprise when he's contacted by a 101-year-old woman (Gloria Stuart) who claims to be the missing Rose and offers to tell all about what happened that cold, dreadful night. Everybody knows the plot in broad outlines:

The *Titanic*—marvel of modern engineering and floating monument to hubris—will sink, and more than half its passengers will die ("Not the better half," says the hissably shallow Cal) because there aren't enough lifeboats for them. The drama is in the details, and Cameron pays lip service to the human tragedy: women and children saved while their men stay behind to die; first-class passengers ushered into lifeboats while steerage passengers are held below; the band playing "Nearer My God to Thee" as the icy water rises; individual acts of valor and cowardice that have been told and retold in books, movies and even songs. Cameron concocts a fictional romance between poor little rich girl Rose and penniless free-spirit Jack Dawson (Leonardo DiCaprio), the better to highlight the brutal class struggle and give tragedy a dewy young face. But his heart is in the spectacle: The drama is clichéd, if competently effective, but Cameron's dissolves from the *Titanic's* rusted hulk to her brand spanking new decks is breathtaking, even poetic. And the sight of the great ship foundering on the black, black sea, its massive stern rising up from the water like a whale's tail, is simply unforgettable. You can cavil that it doesn't look real—who in this digital age believes seeing is believing?—but think about it: It probably didn't look real that night 85 years ago either.

—Maitland McDonagh, *TV Guide*

If you have seen the film, answer these questions:

- Is the review balanced? Does it refer to both the positive and negative aspects of the film?
- What does the reviewer like best about the film?
- How does the reviewer evaluate weaker parts of the film?
- If you disagree with the reviewer, what do you think the reviewer failed to recognize in the film that might have influenced what he or she wrote?

If you have not seen the film, answer these questions:

- Based on this review, would you go to see this film? Why or why not?
- What evidence can you find that the reviewer is reliable?
- Does he or she back up his or her opinions with facts?
- What bias, if any, does the reviewer reveal?

TRY THE STRATEGIES

In the weekend newspaper or on the Internet, find a review of a recent film. Use the ideas above to evaluate the review. If you have not seen the film, would the review influence you to see it? Why or why not? If you have seen the film, in what ways do you agree with the review? In what ways do you disagree?

Analysis and Evaluation

Active readers want to go beyond a simple understanding of the words on a page. They want to do more than recall information or interpret thoughts and ideas. When you read, you will want to read critically, forming opinions about characters and ideas and making judgments using your own prior knowledge and information from the text.

Analyzing characteristics of texts

To be a critical reader and thinker, start by analyzing the characteristics of the text. Some text characteristics can include:

- **Structure** Writers use patterns of organization to clearly present main ideas or themes. By figuring out what text structure a writer has used—for instance, chronological order, comparison-contrast, or cause and effect—you can better understand a writer's message. Look at the structure to unlock the meaning.
- **Word choices** Writers select words according to their connotations, which carry emotional or implied meanings, as well as their denotations, or dictionary meanings. A writer who uses the words *blabbed, tattled,* or *gossiped* to describe what someone said has a different attitude from a writer who uses the words *reported, narrated,* or *documented.* Looking at word choices helps you determine the writer's attitude about a topic and establishes a general mood within a piece of writing.
- **Intended audience** Most selections are written with a specific audience in mind. A speech at a pep rally would have a different style from one given by a diplomat at the United Nations. Similarly, writers must know their audiences in order to write material that is appropriate and interesting to the people who will read it.

As you read, look for the structure and word choices a writer uses to characterize his or her writing. Determine the intended audience for each selection you read.

Evaluating the credibility of sources

Would you take an article on nuclear fission seriously if you knew it was written by a comedic actor? If you need to rely on accurate information, it helps to know who wrote the selection and if that writer is qualified to speak with authority. How did the writer become informed?

Tips for Determining Credibility of a Source

- Look at the possible motivation of the writer. (If a reporter, for instance, writes an article about the rise in crime rate, you might find the story believable. If you found out, though, that the reporter has a close relative who is a police officer, and who wants a raise in pay, you might begin to question the truth, or credibility, of the article.)

- Check on the background of the writer. Do some research on the Internet, for example, to discover whether the writer is an authority in his or her field. Writers sometimes slant the facts in their work to convince readers to agree with them.
- Look at the statements the writer makes. Is the information fact or opinion? Can the writer's statements be proved by other sources?
- Consider the publication in which an article appears. Is it a well-known journal or respected newspaper?
- Ask the opinion of a librarian or teacher—someone who is likely to be familiar with a particular writer.

Look at the model below and think about the writer's motive or purpose.

> Do you need a flu shot but you're not crazy about being stuck with a needle? Imagine getting vaccinated with a simple nasal spray. Sound too good to be true? Scientists at a California company have created a spray mist that works as a vaccine for influenza. The spray contains a mild strain of a live virus. The virus, which can survive in the cool temperature of the nose and throat but not in the warmer areas of the body, causes the immune system to respond with infection-fighting activity in the nose and throat, where flu germs often attack. Several studies have proved that the spray works. So why get jabbed when you can get the same effect from a light mist? Your arm will thank you for it!

Has the writer included mostly factual statements or opinions? How can you tell?

How would it affect your opinion about this story if the author were

- president of the company that is marketing the new nasal spray vaccine?
- a medical expert on viruses?
- a student who saw the new product on a television news magazine program?

TRY THE STRATEGIES

Read the selection from *Farewell to Manzanar,* on page 460 of your text. Is this author credible? How do you know? Can you determine the author's motive for writing the selection? Is the information in the selection fact or opinion?

Analyzing logical arguments and modes of reasoning

When you analyze works you've read, ask yourself whether the reasoning behind the writer's views are logical. Two kinds of logical reasoning are

Inductive Reasoning By observing a limited number of particular cases, a reader arrives at a general or universal statement. This logic moves from the specific to the general.

Deductive Reasoning This logic moves from that which is general to that which is specific. The reader takes a general statement and, through reasoning, applies it to specific situations.

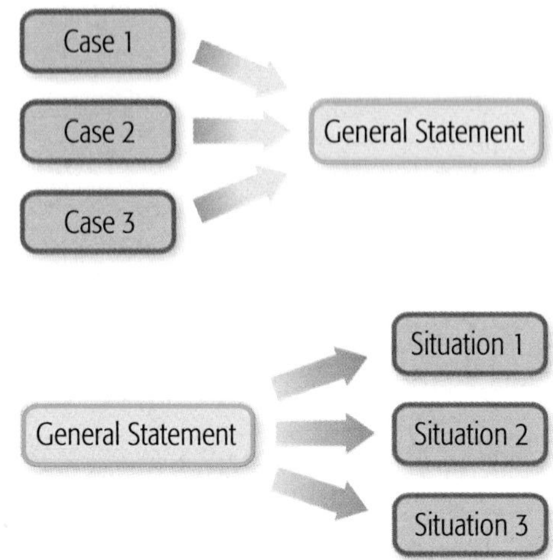

Identifying errors in logic

Whether reading an editorial, listening to a speech, or evaluating a commercial, watch out for these errors in logic:

- **Bare assertion** A claim is made and is not backed up with reasons.
  Go-Car-Go is the best gas on the market.
- **Oversimplifying** One cause or solution is given for a situation without the consideration of other factors.
  Annice wouldn't be so tired if she got to bed on time.
- **Begging the question** The writer assumes in a statement or definition the very point to be proved. Another name for this fallacy is circular reasoning.
  Teenagers cannot be trusted because they are irresponsible.
- **Either/or reasoning** This fallacy consists in reducing all options to two extremes.
  If you don't approve of capitalism, you must be a Communist.
- **Red herring** A side issue is introduced that distracts from the issue under discussion.
  You won't like that play. The lead actor owns that terrible restaurant on Third Street.

Sometimes writers neglect to support their arguments with facts, relying instead on opinions or generalizations. If ideas are not supported with facts, reasoning can become cloudy. When you interpret speeches and other persuasive writing, be sure to question the logic of the writer to determine whether the reasoning is faulty.

Analyzing bias and persuasive techniques

A writer shows a **bias** when he or she demonstrates a strong, personal, and sometimes unreasonable opinion. A writer who shows bias is inclined to a particular way of thinking. Editorials, documentaries, and advertisements commonly show bias. Writers use **persuasive techniques** when they try, through their writing, to get readers to believe a certain thing or to act in a particular way. A writer may have a strong personal bias and yet compose a persuasive essay that is logical and well supported. On the other hand, writers can be less than accurate in order to be persuasive. As a good reader, you'll need to judge whether a writer's bias influences his or her writing in negative or positive ways.

Look at some ways writers can misuse evidence in order to persuade:

- **Impressing with large numbers** Sometimes called the bandwagon appeal, this kind of argument relies on large numbers or references to *everybody* to be convincing.
  Over 5,000,000 satisfied customers have bought our product.
  Everybody raves about the new sports utility vehicle.
- **Irrelevant appeals to authority** An authority can only provide evidence in his or her own field. Dr. Joyce Brothers, for example, is not a competent authority in the field of breakfast cereals.
  Dr. Joyce Brothers says you won't be disappointed in the taste of Munchy Crunchies.
- **Appeal to popular sentiment** Some speakers or writers associate the point they are making with an item that enjoys popular appeal.
  Brushing with Toothful Polish is as important as drinking bottled water.

How well does the following paragraph persuade?

> There really is no need to build a new high school in our town. Another new school would only mean higher taxes for everyone. With all the new families moving into our community, it would be better to build more shopping malls. That would provide more jobs. Teachers have always been able to handle thirty or thirty-five students in a classroom. Besides, residents who no longer have children in school should not have to pay for all this fancy education. Vote "No" on the school referendum.

What bias does the writer show? With a partner, analyze the logic of the author's persuasive technique. How well are the writer's ideas supported?

TRY THE STRATEGIES

Find and read an editorial in the local newspaper. On your own paper, write a brief analysis of the writer's persuasive techniques. What kind of reasoning did the writer use? Was the writer biased?

Inquiry and Research

Asking and answering questions is at the very heart of being a good reader. You will need to read actively in order to research a topic assigned by a teacher. More often, you will need to generate an interesting, relevant, and researchable question on your own and locate appropriate print and nonprint information from a wide variety of sources. Then categorize that information, evaluate it, and organize it in a new way in order to produce some kind of research project for a specific audience. Finally, draw conclusions about your original research question. These conclusions may lead you to other areas for further inquiry.

It sounds like a lot, but when you generate a question of strong interest to you, the process is fun and very worthwhile.

Generating relevant and interesting questions for research

Finding a good research question or topic is a very important first step and deserves your careful attention. Whether you are researching an assigned topic or a topic you have selected, start by generating questions.

Tips for Generating Research Questions

- Think of a question or topic of interest to you.
- Choose a question that helps you focus your study on one main idea.
- Be sure your question is not too broad or too narrow.
  Too broad: How can we be ecologically more responsible?
  Better: What have Americans done in the last five years to preserve the Amazon rain forest?

Locating appropriate print and nonprint information

In your research, try to use a variety of sources. Because different sources present information in different ways, your research project will be more interesting and balanced when you read in a variety of sources. The following are some helpful print sources for research:

- **Textbooks** Texts include any book used as a basis for instruction or a source of information.
- **Book indices** A book index contains an alphabetical listing of books. Some book indices list books on specific subjects; others are more general. For example, H. W. Wilson's *Cumulative Book Index* lists hardcover and paperback books of fiction and nonfiction. Other indices list a variety of resources.
- **Periodicals** Magazines and journals are periodicals, publications issued at regular intervals, but less frequently than daily. One way of locating information in magazines is to use the *Readers' Guide to Periodical Literature.* This guide is available in print form in most libraries. Here is a subject entry from the *Readers' Guide*:

Subject — DIGITAL TELEVISION

Title of article — At war for 'eyeballs' [approved FCC standards for digital television] R. Coorsh. il *Consumers' Research Magazine* v80 p6 F '97

Author — Battle lines [computer-televisions] J. Brinkley. il *Video* v21 p20 Jl/Ag '97

Magazine title — Bill Gates, the cable guy [wants to design set-top boxes and modems for digital TV] E. Lesly and A. Cortese. il *Business Week* p22-4 Jl 14 '97

Volume number · Page number(s) · Date of publication

- **Technical manuals** A manual is a guide or handbook intended to give instruction on how to perform a task or operate something. A vehicle owner's manual might give information on how to operate and service a car.
- **Reference books** These books include encyclopedias and almanacs, and are books used to locate specific pieces of information.
- **Electronic encyclopedias, databases, and the Internet** There are many ways to locate extensive information using your computer. Infotrac®, for instance, acts as an on-line readers guide. CD-ROM encyclopedias can provide easy access to all subjects.
- **Nonprint information** This includes anything that is not written down. Some good nonprint sources of information are films, videos, and recorded interviews.

Organizing and converting information

As you gather information from different sources, taking careful notes, you'll need to think about how to **synthesize** the information, that is, convert it into a unified whole, as well as how to change it into a form your audience will easily understand and that will meet your assignment guidelines.

First, ask yourself what you want your audience to know. Then, think about a pattern of organization, a structure that will best show your main ideas. You might ask yourself questions like the following:

- When comparing items or ideas, what graphic aids can I use?
- When showing the reasons something happened and the effects of certain actions, what text structure would be best?
- How can I briefly and clearly show important information to my audience?
- Would an illustration or even a cartoon help to make a certain point?

TRY THE STRATEGIES

Read a nonfiction selection from Unit 2 of your text. Based on a topic in the selection, create a question you would use as a focus for a research paper. Determine what kinds of sources you would use to gather information. Then plan how you would organize the material, including the graphic aids. Share your research plan with the class.

Adapting researched material for presentation

How should you present the material you've gathered? Before you decide, think about your audience and purpose. Who will receive this information? What is your purpose? When you change the information you've located in order to tell or show someone else, you are adapting your research material for presentation. There are many options you might consider:

- Written or oral report
- Interview
- Debate
- Dramatic presentation

● For more on publishing/presenting, see **Writing Handbook,** p. R61.

Drawing conclusions from gathered information

After you've spent considerable time looking at a research question, you will certainly form opinions about your topic. A conclusion is a general statement that you'll make about the information you have found. It is important to explain your conclusions with good reasons and with supporting details from your sources.

Read the following excerpts and the conclusion that follows:

> Many scientists believe that acid deposition contributes to deforestation and soil degradation. It is known to dramatically accelerate the deterioration of buildings, including landmarks such as the Acropolis in Athens, the Taj Mahal in India, and the Statue of Liberty in New York City.
>
> —*National Geographic Information Central*

> It is not only plants and animals that suffer when the air is polluted. Buildings, sculptures, paintings, metal, glass, paper, leather, textiles, and rubber all deteriorate rapidly if exposed to sulphur dioxide, nitrogen oxides, or ozone.
>
> —*Norwegian Pollution Control Authority*

> The chemical content of acid rain is in itself dangerous to fish and other freshwater organisms. Another, equally important reason why fish populations are depleted, impoverished, or, as is often the case, wiped out altogether, is that acid water leaches toxic aluminum from the soils and bedrock. . . .
>
> —*Green Issues*

Conclusion: If acid rain is not controlled, both natural resources and art treasures may be lost to future generations.

Tips for Drawing Conclusions

- Don't try to twist the facts to match your original idea.
- Don't make sweeping generalizations that go beyond the facts you've gathered.
- Be prepared to adjust your original question to reflect the information you've located. Recognize that your conclusions might be different from what you originally thought they might be.
- Be sure to accurately record where you've gotten your information.
- Never present as your own ideas that aren't yours.
- Cite sources completely. If you're using a quote from someone, or if you want to present an idea taken from another source, be sure to use the proper notations.

TRY THE STRATEGIES

Read three or four articles about the same topic or current event. Compare the information and take careful notes. Then decide how you could organize and convert your information to support a reasonable conclusion, drawn from your reading.

● For more on citing sources and conducting research, see **Writing Handbook,** pp. R64–R69.

Writing Workshop Models

The following Writing Workshop Models are complete versions of the student models developed in the Writing Workshops at the end of each theme in this book. Use these models as examples of how one student might have responded to the assignments in the Writing Workshops.

Theme 1, pages 136–140

Personal Writing: Reflective Essay

A Battle for Dignity

"With All Flags Flying" by Anne Tyler is a story about an eighty-two-year-old man who is struggling to preserve his dignity in the face of old age and death. At first I thought he was a selfish, uncaring old man who did not love his family; however, after reading the story again and reflecting on it, I realized that the man does love his family but doesn't show his love because he believes that love leads to dependence and loss of dignity.

When the story begins, the main character (who is known only as "the old man") realizes that he can no longer live by himself. He has grown too weak; his body is failing him. He packs a few things in a paper bag and hitches a ride to his daughter's house in Baltimore. He tells Clara, his daughter, that he wants to go live in an old folks' home. She refuses to hear of it and insists that he stay with her and her family. But she can't change his mind, and finally she has to drive him there.

At first, my feelings toward the old man were only anger and frustration. I couldn't understand his position. My sympathies went to Clara and her family. Clara obviously cares about the old man, since she cries in the car all the way to the nursing home. Her husband reminds the old man that they bought the big house so there would be room for him to come live with them. The old man never tells Clara or her family that he loves them, and he never acts as though he appreciates their kindness.

There was one thing that puzzled me: Mr. Pond and the old man's discussion. Mr. Pond is the old man's roommate at the old-age home. After Clara leaves, the old man tells Mr. Pond that he doesn't think people should "'hang around making burdens of themselves, hoping to be loved.'" Mr. Pond answers, "'If you don't care about being loved, how come it would bother you to be a burden?'" Mr. Pond's question really made me think. Could not becoming "a burden" to his family be the old man's way of showing his love?

Mr. Pond's comment convinced me that the old man really does love his family and, for his own reasons, is trying not to show it. When I read the story again, I found evidence to support my new opinion. The old man believes that people choose the type of old age they will have. He thinks that "most . . . were weak, and chose to be loved at any cost. He had seen women turn soft and sad, anxious to please, and had watched with pity and impatience their losing battles." This passage is revealing: We see the connection the man makes between the choice to be "loved at any cost" and the weakness and defeat (the "losing battles") that this choice leads to. We are told that this old man has chosen "independence" for his old age. In his logic, independence means he has to prevent himself from needing love. This explains a lot about how he acts toward his family. When Clara and her daughter leave the old folks' home, he watches them because there is "no reason not to." This means, I think, that he can show his love now that they are gone. There is no one to see his weakness, so he won't be a burden to anyone.

I think the old man is fighting a battle to retain his dignity in old age. We learn from the last lines of the story that he prays to "not give in" and to "continue gracefully till the moment of my defeat," which shows his struggle with old age and death in terms of a "battle." The problem is that the old man sees the need for love as a weakness that could cause him to lose this battle. This is a sad situation both for the old man and for his family because they lose the most precious thing they have—time.

When I first read "With All Flags Flying," I thought it was the story of an uncaring, selfish old man who didn't know how to love. After thinking more about his situation, I began to understand that the old man does love his family but he can't show it. I believe this is because he wants to be strong and independent in his old age and because he believes letting himself need love will make him weak. Even though I still feel frustrated with the old man's way of thinking, I believe that the story is a realistic—and tragic—portrayal of the choices that old people face.

Theme 2, pages 234–238

Persuasive Writing: Letter to the Editor

Say No! to School Uniforms

Dear Editor:

The article on school uniforms that appeared in Tuesday's issue of your newspaper made me angry. The article said that our school board is considering adopting school uniforms in the high schools as a way to decrease violence in the schools and to improve test scores. As a tenth grader in one of our schools, I believe that this policy would be wrong. The way a person dresses is a matter of individual expression, which—like freedom of speech—is protected by the U.S. Constitution.

We are taught in school that the United States is great because it was founded on the belief that every individual has rights, including freedom of speech. Choice of dress is a type of individual expression—and therefore of "speech." How can the school endorse a policy that would deprive its students of their constitutional rights?

One of the goals of a school is to prepare us for being citizens of a democracy. A democracy can exist only in an environment in which everyone tolerates a diversity of opinions, ideas, and ways of life. I think school uniforms would create an atmosphere of intolerance of diversity. Adopting school uniforms, therefore would jeopardize our future success as good citizens of this country. The ACLU agrees with my position. On its Web site, the director of the New York Civil Liberties Union says, "A student's choice of dress is an expressive activity. It should be no concern to the school."

Some people argue that school uniforms would stop violence in the schools and improve test scores. These people believe that if students spent less time thinking about clothes, they would spend more time on their school work. Your article reports that the Long Beach school district saw a 36 percent decrease in crime the year after the school uniforms were passed. But the article also says that the Long Beach school district made other changes as well, such as assigning more hall monitors. Perhaps these changes were responsible for the drop in the crime rate. According to Nadine Strossen, president of the ACLU, "There's no evidence that school uniforms have any effect."

Freedom of individual expression is at the heart of our country's political system and way of life. To give it up is too great a price to pay for something that we are not even sure works.

I urge readers of this newspaper to write to members of the school board, asking them to decrease violence in the schools and improve test scores in ways that do not interfere with students' freedom of individual expression.

Theme 3, pages 308–312

Narrative Writing: Short Story

Ballet Blues

Tina stood in front of the broad one-story building and looked at the glass doors with the black-lettered sign: Ruzinsky's Dance School. She gazed at the photos of colorfully dressed dancers gliding across a brightly lit stage. She had looked at that sign and those pictures so many times as the bus went by, wishing she could go inside. Now she was about to.

Tina was going to lie and say that she was her best friend, Maria. Maria's mother had signed her up for a ballet class, and Maria had begged Tina to go in her place. Maria hated ballet.

"No one will know," said Maria. "Just say you are me. You always wanted to study ballet anyway."

It was true. Ever since Tina could remember, she had had pictures of ballerinas hanging on the walls of her room. But her mother had never been able to afford lessons. Although Tina had qualms about lying, Maria had convinced her to go through with the plan.

A little bell rang as she pushed the door open and stepped inside. She was in a hot, empty office. Just then a tall, pale lady with black hair and a lot of makeup came through the office door. Tina tried hard to look as if she belonged there.

"Who are you?" asked the woman, smiling.

"Maria," said Tina. "Maria Arsuaga. I'm here for the 4:30 class."

The woman sat down at her desk and flipped open a big book. "Now I remember. Your mother called and said we needed to work on your posture." She looked Tina over. "Hmm, that's strange. Your posture looks quite good."

Tina blushed. She tried to slouch a bit. She was scared she would be discovered before she even got to take one ballet class! But Ms. Ruzinsky just laughed and shook her long hair. "Well, one can always have better posture!" Tina watched her make a mark next to Maria's name in the book.

The class began at 4:30 exactly. The studio was big and air-conditioned. Tina wore the pink tights, black leotard, and ballet slippers Maria's mother had bought for Maria. Everything was a little big. Tina recognized one other girl in the class—Giselle Turner, a spoiled girl with brown curly hair who lived on Maria's block. Giselle never talked to Tina at school, and now she pretended not to notice Tina.

Ms. Ruzinsky started the class by lining the students up at the barre, a wooden railing attached to the walls at about waist level. Ms. Ruzinsky told them to rest their hands lightly on the barre, never to grab it. She told them to imagine an invisible thread running from the top of their heads to the ceiling. Tina closed her eyes and imagined as hard as she could.

Next Ms. Ruzinsky taught them how to stand in first position, with their feet turned out. She showed them how to point their feet and extend a leg straight in front of them and then draw it in quickly, all in time to a beat she clapped out. Tina was learning so much. She couldn't wait to tell Maria everything.

Suddenly Ms. Ruzinsky called out: "Maria! You are the only one who understands the exercise. Come to the center of the floor and demonstrate."

Tina felt proud and scared at once. She went to the middle of the floor and stood in front of Ms. Ruzinsky. She turned her feet out into first position.

Just then, Giselle ran forward and shouted, "She's not Maria! Her name is Tina. She doesn't belong here!"

Ms. Ruzinsky looked confused. She looked at Tina like she was going to ask her a question. Suddenly Tina knew she couldn't lie, no matter how much she wanted to take ballet. She turned and ran out of the studio into the dressing room. Feeling humiliated, she pulled on her clothes as quickly as she could and headed for the door.

But Ms. Ruzinsky stood in her way. "I'm really in trouble now," thought Tina.

"Is your name really Tina?" Ms. Ruzinsky asked her kindly.

Tina nodded and began to cry.

"Why did you lie?"

Tina told Ms. Ruzinsky everything. She told her

about Maria not wanting to take ballet and how she had always wanted to but her mother had no money for classes.

Ms. Ruzinsky looked thoughtful. Then she said, "I have an idea, Tina. What if I give you a scholarship?"

"A scholarship?" cried Tina in delight. She had never been more excited. She almost jumped into Ms. Ruzinsky's arms. The teacher laughed.

"Okay, go get changed again and come back to class. And I want both you and Maria at class next week!"

"You bet!" said Tina, trying to point her feet as she skipped down the hallway.

Theme 4, pages 412–415

Expository Writing: Critical Response

"Lullaby"

The short story "Lullaby," by Leslie Marmon Silko, is about Ayah, an aging Navajo woman who waits for, looks for, and finally takes care of her husband, Chato. While she waits for and then searches for Chato, Ayah reflects on her memories, both happy and painful. She remembers her childhood and her children. She remembers how one child died and two were taken from her because they had tuberculosis. She recalls the difficulties and indignities that her husband, Chato, endured while working for the white men. In "Lullaby," Silko conveys aspects of Navajo culture—a deep connection with nature, a strong tie to family, a reliance on tradition—and demonstrates how these cultural elements affect Ayah. Silko reflects Navajo culture in her story through unusual similes and through beautifully crafted descriptions.

For example, in the story's first sentence, Silko uses a simile to show how Ayah sees the world symbolically through the tradition of weaving: "The snow in the wind gave off its own light. It came in thick tufts like new wool—washed before the weaver spins it."

Silko then uses description to show how the tradition of weaving is handed down from one generation to the next. Ayah thinks "about the weaving and the way her mother had done it. . . . She could see it clearly. She had been only a little girl . . . And while she combed the wool, her grandma sat beside her, spinning . . . Her mother worked at the loom . . ." These lines also show that strong family ties are important to Ayah. She comforts herself with pleasant family memories such as these when she does not want to think about the more painful memories of her dead son, Jimmie.

Details about the natural world give insights into Ayah's life. For example, the yarn for weaving is dyed in "boiling black pots full of beeweed petals, juniper berries, and sage." This detail is followed by a beautiful, haunting simile: "The blankets . . . were soft and woven so tight that rain rolled off them like birds' feathers."

The vivid details Silko uses to describe Ayah's memories reflect Ayah's connection to nature and tradition. Ayah remembers the "high buckskin leggings that they wrapped over their elkhide moccasins" when she was young. She recalls how she walked "a step behind her mother" when they "walked to the old stone hogan together" when Ayah was ready to give birth. In her house, strips of venison are hung up to dry.

Later, Silko uses a graphic simile to illustrate Ayah's past fears of what the English-speaking doctors would do to her children: "She was frightened by the way they looked at the children, like the lizard watches the fly." Ayah then fled with her children into the comfort of nature, into the "the foothills of juniper trees and black lava rock" where "the sun warmth relaxed her and took the fear and anger away."

Through description, the author also shows the reader how Ayah and her family face the challenges and consequences of generations of poverty. Their cows are "skinny." Their house is a "boxcar shack." Ayah grew up in an "old hogan with a dirt roof and rock walls." They live in an area of "dry sandy arroyos where sparse grass grew."

At the end of the story, Ayah sings Chato a traditional lullaby that likens earth, sky, rainbow, and wind to mother, father, sister, and brother. Thus, Silko's ending reinforces her use of beautiful descriptive and figurative language to reflect the deep connection with nature, family, and tradition that characterizes Navajo culture. Despite the many deep troubles that Ayah has endured, she—like many Navajo—is able to take comfort in her cultural heritage and to derive strength from it.

Theme 5, pages 500–504

Narrative Writing: Autobiographical Incident

Daffy, the Duck

It was a warm spring evening, and I was eight years old. I was helping my mom set the table for dinner when I heard my dad pull our van into the driveway. He had gone to buy some mulch for our flower garden.

As I heard his familiar steps on the stairs, I also heard some unfamiliar sounds—"peep! peep! peep!" There my dad stood in the doorway with a little box. Inside was a fluffy, yellow, terrified duckling that was trying to disappear by huddling into a little ball.

My mom looked at my dad with that "Oh, no, honey!" look she gets in her eyes at times. But my dad just laughed and shrugged his shoulders.

"I went to Arcadian Gardens for the mulch, and they were selling these little guys for Easter. I just couldn't resist!" he said, gently petting the duckling.

I went crazy. Wow, a pet! I had been pleading for a pet for ages. I'm embarrassed to admit that I gave the duckling a very corny name, but I guess you do things like that when you're eight. She looked as yellow as daffodils, so I called her "Daffy."

Well, maybe her name was not original, but having a pet duck in the suburbs sure was! I had seen dogs being walked and the occasional cat trying to catch bugs in the grass. But a duck? Now that was different.

Looking back on it now, I think owning something so unusual and fragile really affected me. Feeling different is hard when you're eight, but with Daffy it was all right. I was proud to be responsible for something so helpless and young. Besides, she followed me everywhere, as faithful as any dog.

My dad built a big cage for her out of wood and wire mesh, and we kept her cage in the basement. Daffy's favorite haunt was down there too: our deep utility sink in the laundry room. Every day I'd fill the sink and give Daffy a boost, and she would paddle around and around, splashing water all over the place. When she was finished, I would set her back down. She would waddle with her slick webbed feet across the linoleum floor until she caught sight of her cage. Then she would settle in, curl up in a ball, and take a little snooze.

Daffy and I also had fun outside. One neighbor had a little pond where Daffy often took a dip. Or we would take walks around the block; she wore a tiny kitten collar and leash. At times she would free herself and go quacking madly in the opposite direction while I frantically tried to catch her.

My favorite memory of Daffy was when my great-grandmother visited us during the summer. Gramma loved to fall asleep in a lounge chair in our backyard. Daffy would waddle across the grass to sit underneath the lounge chair, quacking softly as she enjoyed the cool shade.

I had Daffy for only four months, but it felt like forever. We had to give her away when she became too big and difficult to keep in the house. We gave her to a woman who lived on a farm with a big pond and lots of other ducks for Daffy to paddle and splash around with.

The best part about Daffy, though, was what happened after Daffy. Once my mom and dad saw that I could take care of a pet responsibly, we always had a houseful. Normal pets—goldfish, a cat, two gerbils. And just last week, Dad, who always did have an eye for the unique and exotic, brought home an iguana. The adventures continue.

Descriptive Writing: Observational Report

Today's Charles Bridge

My father was born in Prague, Czechoslovakia. In 1969 he escaped the Communist regime and came to the United States. Until 1989 when the Communist government fell, he couldn't return to his homeland, but now we can visit our relatives every year. Prague has become more popular as a tourist destination, and new hotels, restaurants, and stores are opening each year. Capitalism is now in full swing in Prague. Last summer I spent an afternoon watching all the activity on the Charles Bridge, a busy tourist spot that links one side of the city to the other.

The bridge was packed when I arrived. A steady stream of people flowed over it. The atmosphere was like a carnival, with musicians performing and artists selling their wares. The day was hot, and the air smelled sticky and sweet, like spilled soda. I found an empty place to sit next to a statue on the stone bridge wall. I heard many languages but could only recognize three: English, Czech, and German. From where I sat, I could see the gothic-looking bridge gates, the majestic castle and Kampa Island, an island in the Vltava River that is big enough for houses and streets. A big German tour group of about fifty people stood in front of me listening to their tour guide. An American family with two kids passed by. Another group of people passed speaking to each other in a language I didn't recognize until I realized it was English with a strange accent.

Musicians performed all along the bridge. A little way down on my left, a teenager sang some Beatles songs I recognized. A few people tossed money in his hat, but not many people stopped to listen to him. On my right, a five-man band with an accordion and a trumpet played. It sounded like a professional wedding band. A crowd would gather around the band for a couple of songs and then, all at once, mysteriously disperse.

The sun got too hot after a while. I got up and started walking toward our hotel in Old Town Square. I hadn't heard much Czech while I was sitting on the bridge, except from the people selling things. So, on my way back, I listened for my father's language. An old lady looking up at one of the statues of the saints was praying in Czech, and I saw a group of Czech kids my own age hanging out. They were speaking Czech, but they were dressed like the kids in my hometown, with baggy shirts and pants.

I felt hot and dizzy. My father had once told me that the Charles Bridge was known as a romantic place when he was growing up. From my observations, I can say that the Charles Bridge is no longer a place for lovers, but only a place for tourists to pass one another and enjoy the friendly spirit of Prague.

Theme 7, pages 616–620

Business Writing: Interview

Lucille's Loves

It's not only movie stars who get married multiple times. My great aunt Lucille gives Elizabeth Taylor a run for her money: At ninety-two years old, she has been married three times. But Lucille has never been divorced; all three of her husbands have died. I talked to Lucille about love and loss since she obviously has experienced a lot of each.

I visited Lucille in her comfortable room in a nursing home in Riverdale, New York, where she has lived since her last husband died seven years ago. I asked her if she had always wanted to be married. In reply, Lucille told me she grew up in a family of five girls. "It was wonderful growing up with so many sisters," she said. "But we were competitive. We made bets about which one of us would get married first." Lucille's younger sister won, but Lucille soon followed her. She married Fred Millikan in 1926, when she was nineteen. Fred drowned two years later in a boating accident. Lucille was in mourning for several years, until she moved to New York City to become a singer. "I never would have become a singer if Fred hadn't died," she said. In New York, she met another musician, named Harold Wilson, and they got married. They were married for thirty years and had three children. Harold died of a heart attack in 1961, when Lucille was only fifty-four. In 1974, she married Bernie, the only one of her husbands I ever knew. He died several years ago.

I asked Lucille what she had learned about love from being married so many times. Lucille said she's learned that you can love people in such different ways. I asked her to elaborate. "I didn't know Fred very well when I married him," she said. "It was more of an infatuation than a deep love. But love grows deeper only when it is tested. I like to think that our love would have grown." Harold Wilson was the longest love of Lucille's life. "We spent thirty wonderful years together, and I'm grateful for every one of them." Her last marriage, said Lucille, was more sedate. "We were trusted companions and best friends. It was what we needed at that time in our lives—after all, I was 67 and he was 74 when we met!" I asked Lucille if she thought there was only one true love out there for each person. She shook her head and told me that love has as much to do with timing as with Mr. Right.

Lucille has always been open about talking about her feelings, so I felt that I could ask her about her losses too. I asked her what it was like in the years between being married. She said she never felt quite herself. "It was too quiet. I am one of those people who works better in a team. A marriage is like a team." I asked her if she could describe the feeling of grief at losing a husband. "It's like losing half of you," she said. She also said that there is a positive aspect to grief: "It puts everything in perspective. Before I lost Harry, I always worried about the little things, but afterward, I realized that nothing matters except having your loved ones around you."

Talking to Lucille, I learned a lot about the power of love and coping with loss. I asked her if she had any advice for those of us with less experience in love. She just smiled and said, "Keep your eyes open. You never know who you'll meet!"

Theme 8, pages 670–674

Creative Writing: Poem

Still Suspended in Air

I have followed your career since before
I was born.
The greatest dancer of your generation.
My parents were your fans.
They took me to see you when I was six years old
and I still remember your tours jetés—
jumping and spinning—
in an endless circle,
driving forward the hand of time.

Years later I saw you again.
As Albrecht, you wooed Giselle
with arabesques and shining, whirling turns
that drove the crowd mad.
You danced as if you were caught in a tornado wind
until we were all transfixed—
the audience, the other dancers, me.

When you held Giselle as she was dying
as if you were trying to grasp a setting sun,
you were telling me what
no one else would have told me:
that love inspires madness.

You taught me, as well, about hardship.
You taught me that no matter how high you can jump
no matter how many tours jetés you can spin,
no matter how fast your legs fly into splits,
life can test you in cruel ways.
Your decision to defect:
at the airport—scrambling secret service agents,
shouting, revving airplane engines, chaos,
the plan you must have worked out in advance.
Did you think about the fact
that you might never see your mother again?
Thanks to you, I never look to my talents
to protect me from pain.

Your mother must have been able
to hear the echoes of the encores all the way
across the ocean,
from the American audiences, trying
to love you more than she could.

I was jealous of the others
who loved you as passionately as I did,
all those showering claps and bravo!'s and thumping feet,
rocking the stage from which you gracefully bowed.
But now, ten years after I first saw you,
long after the others have replaced you with a new idol,
you are still suspended in my mind
above the stage, in mid-air,
your legs cutting the air into shreds
with the precision of a surgical knife.

Theme 9, pages 702–705

Descriptive Writing: Extended Metaphor

My Grandmother, the Magician

My grandmother is a magician. She doesn't wear a black cape or carry a wand, but she does mystify by making things appear out of thin air, pulling surprises out of her bag of tricks, and disappearing on a moment's notice.

It's my grandmother's sly generosity that makes it seem as if she conjures up things out of thin air. Every time she visits us, she asks me what I want. She smiles and tells me to whisper in her ear. I always ask for a shell for my shell collection; my brother asks for a baseball card for his card collection. Soon afterwards my shell appears magically on my pillow or bookshelf, and my brother finds a rare rookie card tucked away on his desk. I have never seen her sneaking into our rooms—she is very stealthy. When I ask her how she manages to sneak around without being seen, she says she turns invisible! She's joking, of course, but sometimes I still wonder how she gets into our rooms without anyone's noticing. Is it a trick of mirrors? Is there a secret trapdoor underneath my bedroom rug? And where do all the shells and the cards come from? Does she hide them up her sleeve? One thing's for sure: No matter how hard we look, we can't find them in her bag of tricks.

Yes, my grandmother has a bag of tricks. A magician may pull a deck of cards and a hat out of the bag, but my grandmother has things stowed away in her huge black purse. When I look inside, I see a mysterious clutter of things: lipsticks, compacts with mirrors, travel brochures for a bunch of countries. In her hands, her purse items become magical. She can always find something in her purse to entertain us. Once when we were waiting at the doctor's office, she pulled out a pack of candy hearts and a needle and thread and taught me how to make a candy-heart necklace. Another time she taught me how to build a castle out of poker chips. One of her tricks is blowing giant soap bubbles. When I was a kid, she used to dazzle me with this trick while I was taking a bath. She would unwrap her special soap that smelled like lavender. Then she would lather up the soap, make a circle with her thumb and forefinger, and blow through the circle. Out would come a bubble as big as a small house!

My grandmother has a mysterious side as well. She will disappear without a trace for several months. Every year she goes on a long trip to a faraway place. Last year she went to China. When she came back, she looked as if she had traded identities with an old lady. Her hair, which is usually bright red, was gray because she thought no hairdressers in China would know how to dye her hair. She always comes back with lots of exotic presents for me and my brother—puppets and teapots and other strange, wonderful things.

My grandmother leaves us spellbound. She keeps enthralling me, even though I am not a kid anymore. She is a unique person because laws don't seem to apply to her as they do to other people. She can travel whenever she wants, wherever she wants. With all the tricks she knows, she is able to turn any situation into an exciting one. She never tells the secret of her best trick—how she manages to enjoy life so much.

Theme 10, pages 902–905

Expository Writing: Compare-and-Contrast Essay

The American and *Antigone*

Despite having been written more than two thousand years apart, *The American* (a novel by Henry James) and *Antigone* (a play by Sophocles) have striking similarities in their treatment of the issues of loyalty and betrayal. However, *Antigone* imparts a greater moral weight to the theme than does *The American*.

The plots of the two works both involve a family torn apart by questions of loyalty. Antigone must decide whether she will violate the law Creon lays down forbidding anyone to bury her brother's body. She decides that she must be true to her own values, even at the risk of death, so she betrays Creon by trying to bury her brother. As a result, she is put to death.

While Antigone is in conflict with her uncle, Christopher Newman (the hero of *The American*) is in conflict with the family of the woman he wants to marry. Newman, a rich American businessman, falls in love with an aristocratic French woman, Madame de Cintre. The same way that Creon, King of Thebes, makes rules that govern his City, Madame de Cintre's mother makes rules to govern her family. For example, no one in the family can marry a "commercial person"—that is, a businessman. When Madame de Cintre is forbidden by her mother to marry Newman, she decides she cannot betray her mother. Newman tries—but fails—to convince Madame de Cintre that her happiness is more important than her family's honor.

However, the main theme of *The American* turns out to be the right to revenge versus the obligation to behave honorably. After Madame de Cintre rejects Newman, he learns a terrible secret about her family and must decide whether he will use it to get his revenge. At the end, he decides that he can't betray his own belief in fair play and consideration for others, and he burns up the incriminating evidence.

On the other hand, the main theme of *Antigone* involves pitting the value system of the main character against the value system of her society. Antigone believes in the laws of the gods that say a body must be buried. However, Creon has decreed that the body of Antigone's brother can't be buried because he was a traitor to Thebes. Antigone says, "The immortal unrecorded laws of God. / They are not merely now: they were, and shall be, / Operative for ever, beyond man utterly." (2. 61–63) Thus, Antigone decides she must go against her family's wishes and be loyal to the higher laws of the gods. She pays with her life for her loyalty to her values, but Newman never faces this choice between life and death.

Furthermore, *Antigone* has a tone of great moral seriousness, while *The American* has a light, sometimes sarcastic tone. The narrator of *The American* often calls Newman "our friend" when describing something Newman did or said, and this comes across as gossipy. The narrator also often seems amused by Newman, telling us about how silly or naive his thoughts are. In *Antigone,* however, the author doesn't seem to find anything amusing about Antigone: She is facing a serious, tragic choice. The second ode begins with the words "Fortunate is the man who has never tasted God's vengeance!" The tone of this line is filled with gravity and seems to support Antigone in her belief that the laws of the gods are greater than those of the mortals.

Despite the similarities between *The American* and *Antigone,* the latter work carries a much greater moral weight. Antigone must pay for her principles with her life, but Newman never has to make such a grave decision. *Antigone* resonates long after the play is finished. The variations in tone deepen the difference between the two works: *The American* is entertaining, but *Antigone* is a lasting and important work of literature.

Expository Writing: Biographical Research Paper

From Prisoner to President: Nelson Mandela's Vision and the Creation of a New South Africa

Not many years ago South Africa was a racist, undemocratic country, and Nelson Mandela was in prison serving a life sentence for treason. Today South Africa is a democratic nation; Mandela was elected its first president after the change. It has been Mandela's refusal to compromise his vision for a democratic South Africa that has made this new South Africa possible—and has made Mandela a hero all around the world.

Nelson Mandela was born in 1918 in Transkei, a region on South Africa's southeastern coast. His father was a village leader (Brief). The young Mandela was being groomed to become the village chief, but he fled to Johannesburg to avoid an arranged marriage and to pursue a law career (Graham 392). In Johannesburg, Mandela became involved with the African National Congress (ANC), a political group that opposed apartheid. Apartheid was the National Party's system of rule. Although black South Africans made up about three-fourths of the country's population, under apartheid laws they were not allowed to vote, to marry white people, or to live in the same neighborhoods as white people. The ANC used forms of nonviolent resistance, such as boycotts, strikes, and civil disobedience, to challenge apartheid policies.

As the ANC became more powerful, the National Party government began cracking down on the organization. The government especially targeted Mandela, who had become an important ANC leader. "During the whole of the fifties, Mandela was the victim of various forms of repression" (*Mandela,* 4). In 1962 officials arrested Mandela for organizing a strike and for leaving the country without valid travel documents. During his trial, Mandela acted like a hero: He never denied the charges but instead used the opportunity to express his principles and his views on the government. He argued that he was neither legally nor morally bound to obey laws created by a parliament in which, as a black, he had no representation (Graham 394). Since treason against the government was punishable by death, Mandela risked his life to express this belief in the individual's right to political representation and moral freedom. Mandela's passionate defense of democratic ideals made him a symbol all around the world of the struggle for freedom against oppression. Despite his eloquent defense, he was sentenced to five years in prison without parole. While serving his prison term, more serious charges were made against him. He was then convicted of treason and sentenced to life in prison with no chance of parole.

Mandela survived in prison for twenty-seven years. Even in prison he did not compromise his principles. For example, at one point the government offered to release him if he would agree to settle in his "tribal homeland" of Transkei. Mandela rejected their terms, stating that he would accept only unconditional freedom (*Mandela,* 5).

In 1989 F. W. de Klerk became president. Mandela described de Klerk as "a man who saw change as necessary and inevitable" (Graham, 394). He was right. In a speech before parliament on February 2, 1990, de Klerk lifted the ban on the ANC and overturned many apartheid laws. A week later, on February 11, de Klerk released Mandela from prison. This was "one of the most dramatic news events of the year" (Graham 395). Mandela was declared an international hero.

Now Mandela could put his principles into action. At the Convention for a Democratic South Africa, a multiparty effort, he and de Klerk signed the Record of Understanding. The record formalized their agreement that a single freely elected assembly would draft a new constitution and serve as the transitional legislature.

Their negotiations also bore another fruit: A date was set for the first free, open elections in the history of South Africa! For these accomplishments, Mandela and de Klerk jointly received the 1993 Nobel Peace Prize. No one was surprised when the ANC won the election by capturing 62.6 percent of the popular vote (Graham 395); Mandela was elected the first president of the new South Africa.

As president, Mandela did not give in to the same exclusionary tendencies as his predecessors. He stayed true to his belief in a representative democracy that respects all its citizens. In his cabinet, he included members of opposition political parties—even the National Party. Mandela also preached forgiveness and reconciliation between whites and blacks. He made non-racialism the country's guiding principle. In 1996 South Africa adopted a new constitution that legally encodes the principles that Mandela spent three decades in prison for. The constitution includes a wide-ranging bill of rights. Among the rights it guarantees are freedom of religion, belief, and opinion; freedom of the press; and freedom of political activity.

From prison to the presidency, Mandela held to his vision of a South Africa that offered freedom and protection to all its people, black and white. It was his commitment to this vision—in speaking for his principles during a hostile government trial, in negotiating with de Klerk, and presiding as a fair-minded president—that guided the new South Africa into existence. As he said in his inaugural address, "Out of the experience of an extraordinary human disaster that lasted too long must be born a society of which all humanity will be proud" (*Inaugural* 1).

Works Cited

"A Brief Biography of Nelson Mandela." *South Africa Explored.* 4 Nov. 2000 <http://www.sa-venues.com/nelson_mandela.htm>.

Graham, Judith, ed. Current Biography Yearbook 1995. New York: Wilson, 1995.

Inaugural Speech, Pretoria [Mandela]–5/10/94. 30 Jan. 2001 <http://www.sas.upenn.edu/African_Studies/Articles_Gen/Inaugural_Speech_17984.html>.

Mandela, Nelson Rolihlahla. African National Congress. 3 Nov. 2000 <http://www.anc.org.za/people/mandela.html>.

Expository Writing: Feature Article

A Superstitious Traveler

Is it bad luck to break a mirror in France? Is Friday the 13th considered unlucky in Russia? I found out—the hard way—about the superstitions of other countries on a trip to Europe last summer. My father and I visited Russia, Italy, and France. We stayed at friends' houses everywhere except Russia. Being hosted by friends allowed me to see local customs close-up.

When we arrived in Russia, we went to our hotel to freshen up. My father's friend Teresa rapped on our door, and my father opened it. He put out his hand to shake, but Teresa just looked up and burst into loud nervous laughter. She hurried into the room and plopped down in a large overstuffed chair. She couldn't stop laughing. Finally she apologized. "We Russians are so superstitious!" she said. "It is bad luck to shake hands in a doorway!" My father laughed, and so did I. Then he and Teresa shook hands in the middle of the room. Later we all went to a giant museum, where we walked around looking at paintings for hours. At one point, I started to whistle. Suddenly one of the guards, a sharp-looking old lady in a brown uniform, yelled something at me in Russian. Teresa explained, "She is only trying to protect you. Some Russians believe that whistling indoors will cause your family to be poor."

Next we traveled to Italy. We stayed in Florence with a large Italian family. Over a huge dinner of pasta, meat, and vegetables, I asked our hosts if they were familiar with American superstitions, such as broken mirrors or walking under a ladder. They shook their heads and laughed at me—the same way I had laughed at the Russian superstitions! I asked them to tell me some Italian superstitions. They told me about the "malocchio," which means "evil eye." They said that in southern Italy you can still put a curse on someone by giving *malocchio.* To give an evil eye, you put your hand in a fist and point your index finger and pinky in someone's direction. They said that although they didn't consider themselves superstitious, they would still be nervous if someone made the evil eye at them. I said I felt the same way about walking under a ladder.

The last country we visited was France. By now I was asking everyone we met about local superstitions. I was fascinated. We stayed in Nice for a few days, but all the French people I met there said they couldn't think of any French superstitions. Then we left Nice and went to Paris. In Paris we stayed with a translator named Marie. Marie smiled when I asked her about local superstitions. She said, "Yes, we have many superstitions in France. For example, if a black cat crosses in front of you, it is bad luck. It is also bad luck—for seven years—if you break a mirror." It took me a moment to recognize the superstitions I am familiar with. Then my father and I looked at each other and laughed. I said, "I guess we are getting close to home now!"

Hearing Marie tell me the superstitions that I grew up with should have struck a chord—but at that moment, all I could think was how strange it all sounded. After taking a tour of so many foreign superstitions, I can tell you that one set of superstitions sounds as crazy as any other.

Glossary

This glossary lists the vocabulary words found in the selections in this book. The definition given is for the word as it is used in the selection; you may wish to consult a dictionary for other meanings of these words. The key below is a guide to the pronunciation symbols used in each entry.

a	at	**ō**	hope	**ng**	sing
ā	ape	**ô**	fork, all	**th**	thin
ä	father	**oo**	wood, put	**th** (underlined)	this
e	end	**o͞o**	fool	**zh**	treasure
ē	me	**oi**	oil	**ə**	ago, taken, pencil, lemon, circus
i	it	**ou**	out	**′**	indicates primary stress
ī	ice	**u**	up	**′**	indicates secondary stress
o	hot	**ū**	use		

A

abashed (ə basht′) *adj.* self-conscious; embarrassed or ashamed; p. 917

abeyance (ə bā′ əns) *n.* a state of temporary inactivity; p. 363

absolve (ab zolv′) *v.* to free from guilt or blame; p. 752

abstract (ab′ strakt) *adj.* thought of apart from any specific example or case; theoretical; p. 510

abyss (ə bis′) *n.* an immeasurably deep hole; vast emptiness; nothingness; p. 547

accost (ə kôst′) *v.* to approach and speak to, especially in an aggressive manner; p. 916

acquiesce (ak′ wē es′) *v.* to consent or agree to without protest; p. 270

acrid (ak′ rid) *adj.* irritating or upsetting; p. 30

admonish (ad mon′ ish) *v.* to warn, as against a specific action; p. 448

advocate (ad′ və kāt′) *v.* to publicly support; p. 1032

affable (af′ ə bəl) *adj.* friendly, gracious, and pleasant; p. 1063

affluent (af′ lo͞o ənt) *adj.* wealthy; prosperous; p. 509

agenda (ə jen′ də) *n.* a program or schedule of things to be done; p. 522

albeit (ôl bē′ it) *conj.* although; even if; p. 219

alleviate (ə lē′ vē āt′) *v.* to make easier to bear; relieve; lessen; p. 467

amenable (ə mē′ nə bəl) *adj.* responsive; able to be controlled; p. 40

amiably (ā′ mē ə blē) *adv.* in a friendly, good-natured way; p. 173

anteroom (an′ tē ro͞om′) *n.* a small room serving as a waiting area or entrance to a larger, main room; p. 101

appal (ə pôl′) *v.* to fill with horror or dismay; shock; p. 393

apparition (ap′ ə rish′ ən) *n.* something strange or unexpected that comes suddenly into view, as a ghost; p. 229

apprehension (ap′ ri hen′ shən) *n.* fear of what may happen; anxiety; p. 253

appurtenance (ə purt′ ən əns) *n.* an optional article or piece of equipment that adds to one's convenience or comfort; accessory; p. 117

arrogance (ar′ ə gəns) *n.* overbearing pride; p. 745

arrogant (ar′ ə gənt) *adj.* full of self-importance; haughty; p. 403

arroyo (ə roi′ ō) *n.* a dry gully or stream bed; p. 331

articulate (ar tik′ yə lāt) *v.* to put into words; express clearly and effectively; p. 521

assuage (ə swāj′) *v.* to lessen in intensity; diminish; p. 291

atonement (ə tōn′ mənt) *n.* something done to make up for a sin, injury, or loss; p. 163

attribute (at′ rə būt) *n.* a quality or characteristic of a person or thing; p. 565

augment (ôg ment′) *v.* to make greater; increase; p. 559

avaricious (av′ ə rish′ əs) *adj.* greedy; p. 177

B

bade (bād) *v.* past tense of *bid,* to command, order, or ask; p. 96

banality (bə nal′ ə tē) *n.* something that is trite; p. 511

banter (ban′ tər) *n.* good-natured, witty joking or teasing; p. 30

benevolence (bə nev′ ə ləns) *n.* kindness; generosity; p. 496

bereaved (bi rēvd′) *adj.* sad and forlorn due to a loss, such as the death of a loved one; p. 379

bereft (bi reft′) *adj.* robbed or deprived; p. 1019

beseeching (bi sēch′ ing) *adj.* begging; asking earnestly; p. 81

blasphemous (blas′ fə məs) *adj.* showing disrespect or scorn for God or anything sacred; p. 394

boding (bōd′ ing) *n.* a warning or indication, especially of evil; p. 253

brash (brash) *adj.* boldly disrespectful; p. 90

C

cataclysm (kat′ ə kliz′ əm) *n.* a disaster, usually one that causes sudden and violent change; p. 344

cavernous (kav′ ər nəs) *adj.* large and spacious, like a cavern; p. 122

chic (shēk) *adj.* attractive, tasteful, and fashionable in style; p. 301

chronic (kron′ ik) *adj.* lasting a long time or returning repeatedly; p. 121

clientele (klī′ ən tel′) *n.* clients or customers considered as a group; p. 301

coerce (kō urs′) *v.* to pressure or push into doing something, as by force or authority; p. 1055

combatant (kəm bat′ ənt) *n.* one trained for, or engaged in, combat; p. 969

commandeer (kom′ ən dēr′) *v.* to seize for use by the military or government; p. 39

commodious (kə mō′ dē əs) *adj.* having or containing ample room; spacious; p. 490

compassionate (kəm pash′ ə nit) *adj.* having or showing sympathy for another's suffering or misfortune, combined with a desire to help; p. 522

conceive (kən sēv′) *v.* to form a mental image or idea of; imagine; p. 230

confidante (kon′ fə dant′) *n.* a person who is entrusted with secrets or private affairs; p. 938

confront (kən frunt′) *v.* to come face-to-face with; to oppose; p. 984

connoisseur (kon′ ə sur′) *n.* one who has expert knowledge and a sense of what is best in a particular area, such as wine, food, or the arts; p. 1031

conscientiously (kon′ shē en′ shəs lē) *adv.* thoughtfully and carefully; p. 76

consequent (kon′ sə kwent′) *adj.* following as a result or effect; p. 378

constancy (kon′ stən sē) *n.* the quality of being unchanging; faithfulness; loyalty; p. 427

consternation (kon′ stər nā′ shən) *n.* amazement or dismay that throws one into confusion; p. 1017

contemplate (kon′ təm plāt′) *v.* to give intense attention to; consider carefully; p. 132

contend (kən tənd′) *v.* to declare or maintain as a fact; argue; p. 1047

contrition (kən trish′ ən) *n.* sorrow for one's sin or wrongdoing; repentance; p. 76

convivial (kən viv′ ē əl) *adj.* fond of merriment and parties with good company; sociable; p. 491

convoluted (kon′ və lo͞o′ təd) *adj.* turned in or wound up upon itself; coiled; twisted; p. 201

convulsive (kən vul′ siv) *adj.* sudden and violent; p. 84

correlate (kôr′ ə lāt′) *v.* to bring (one thing) into relation (with another thing); calculate; p. 320

coterie (kō′ tər ē) *n.* a small group of people who share a particular interest and often meet socially; p. 448

countenance (koun′ tə nəns) *n.* the face; p. 391

credence (krēd′ əns) *n.* belief, especially in the reports or statements of others; p. 451

credulity (kri do͞o′ li tē) *n.* a tendency to believe or accept something too readily; p. 176

crevice (krev′ is) *n.* a narrow crack into or through something; p. 335

D

daft (daft) *adj.* without sense or reason; crazy; silly; p. 435

dally (dal′ ē) *v.* to linger; delay; waste time; p. 260

dauntless (dônt′ lis) *adj.* fearless; courageous; daring; p. 390

debasement (di bās′ mənt) *n.* the state of being lowered in quality, value, or character; degradation; p. 565

decapitate (di kap′ ə tāt′) *v.* to cut off the head of; p. 66

decree (di krē′) *n.* an order or decision made by a judge, monarch, or other official; p. 241

decrepit (di krep′ it) *adj.* broken down by long use or old age; p. 401

deference (def′ ər əns) *n.* courteous respect or regard for the judgment, opinions, or desires of another; p. 33

defile (di fīl′) *v.* to spoil the purity of; to make dirty or unclean; p. 758

definitive (di fin′ ə tiv) *adj.* conclusive; final; decisive; p. 230

deftness (deft′ nəs) *n.* the quality of being skillful and nimble; p. 205

derision (di rizh′ ən) *n.* mockery; ridicule; p. 364

designation (dez′ ig nā′ shən) *n.* a distinguishing name or mark; p. 464

desolate (des′ ə lit) *adj.* deserted or uninhabited; p. 967

detached (di tacht′) *adj.* not involved emotionally; neutral; p. 481

devastate (dev′ əs tāt) *v.* to destroy; overwhelm; p. 56

devoid (di void′) *adj.* not possessing; lacking (with *of*); p. 536

disconcerting (dis′ kən surt′ ing) *adj.* disturbing, confusing, or frustrating; p. 536

discordant (dis kôrd′ ənt) *adj.* not in agreement or harmony; p. 53

discreetly (dis krēt′ lē) *adv.* in a manner showing good judgment; cautiously; p. 145

disdain (dis dān′) *n.* a feeling of contempt for something or someone; scorn; p. 294

disperse (dis purs′) *v.* to go off in different directions; scatter; p. 129

distortion (dis tôr′ shən) *n.* an appearance of being twisted or bent out of shape; p. 338

divert (di vurt′) *v.* to draw attention away; distract; p. 558

doctrine (dok′ trin) *n.* a particular principle or position that is taught or supported, as of a religion; p. 13

doddering (dod′ ər ing) *adj.* trembling or shaking, as from age; p. 121

doggedly (dô′ gid lē) *adv.* stubbornly; firmly; p. 175

droll (drōl) *adj.* amusingly odd or fanciful; p. 291

drone (drōn) *v.* to talk in a dull, monotonous tone; p. 1040

E

ecosystem (e′ kō sis′ təm) *n.* a community of organisms together with their environment, functioning as a unit; p. 534

edifice (ed′ ə fis) *n.* a building, especially a large, important-looking one; p. 40

elation (i lā′ shən) *n.* a feeling of great joy; ecstasy; p. 564

elude (i lo͞od′) *v.* to avoid or escape, especially through cleverness or quickness; p. 937

endeavor (en dev′ ər) *n.* a strenuous attempt to accomplish something; p. 272

enhance (en hans′) *v.* to make greater, as in beauty or value; p. 260

enlightening (en līt′ ən ing) *adj.* giving or revealing knowledge or wisdom; p. 1041

enthralled (en thrôld′) *adj.* fascinated; charmed; p. 176

ephemeral (i fem′ ər əl) *adj.* short-lived; temporary; p. 534

equanimity (ek′ wə nim′ ə tē) *n.* the ability to remain calm and assured; p. 345

equilibrium (ēk′ wə lib′ rē əm) *n.* mental, emotional, or physical balance; p. 550

eschew (es cho͞o′) *v.* to keep apart from (something disliked or harmful); avoid; p. 1032

exclusively (iks klo͞o′ siv lē) *adv.* only; excluding any other; p. 462

exhortation (eg′ zôr tā′ shən) *n.* a strong appeal or warning; p. 1045

expedient (iks pē′ dē ənt) *n.* a useful method for bringing about a desired result; p. 1022

expend (iks pend′) *v.* to use up; consume; spend; p. 546

expendable (iks pen′ də bəl) *adj.* not strictly necessary; capable of being sacrificed without negative effect; p. 319

exultation (eg′ zul tā′ shən) *n.* joy; jubilation; p. 564

F

ferocity (fə ros′ ə tē) *n.* great fierceness; extreme intensity; p. 357

fiasco (fē as′ kō) *n.* a complete or humiliating failure; p. 56

flaunt (flônt) *v.* to display in a showy manner; p. 32

formidable (fôr′ mi də bəl) *adj.* causing fear, dread, or awe by reason of size, strength, or power; p. 400

fortitude (fôr′ tə to͞od′) *n.* firm courage or strength of mind in the face of pain or danger; p. 345

fortnight (fôrt′ nīt′) *n.* two weeks; p. 40

fortuitous (fôr to͞o′ ə təs) *adj.* fortunate; lucky; p. 549

furtive (fur′ tiv) *adj.* secret; shifty; sly; p. 11

G

gaudy (gô′ dē) *adj.* bright and showy to the point of being in bad taste; p. 26

gaunt (gônt) *adj.* extremely thin and hollow-eyed, as from hunger or illness; "looking like skin and bones"; p. 91

giddy (gid′ ē) *adj.* causing dizziness or lightheadedness; p. 151

gingerly (jin′ jər lē) *adv.* with extreme caution; carefully; p. 383

grapple (grap′ əl) *v.* to attempt to deal with; struggle; p. 519

grimace (grim′ is) *n.* a twisting of the face; p. 175

H

hale (hāl) *adj.* in good physical condition; healthy; p. 437

harass (hə ras′, har′ əs) *v.* to bother or annoy repeatedly; p. 63

heyday (hā′ dā) *n.* period of greatest strength, popularity, or prosperity; p. 1005

horde (hôrd) *n.* a large group; multitude; p. 160

hue (hū) *n.* a color; shade or tint; p. 241

humility (hū mil′ ə tē) *n.* the quality of being humble or modest; p. 91

hurtle (hurt′ əl) *v.* to move rapidly, especially with much force or noise; p. 403

hypochondriac (hī′ pə kon′ drē ak′) *n.* one whose worry over health is so great that it brings on the imagined symptoms of an illness; p. 1063

I

ideology (ī′ dē ol′ə jē) *n.* the ideas on which a political, economic, or social system is based; p. 511

ignoble (ig nō′ bel) *adj.* of low birth or position; without honor or worth; p. 920

impart (im pärt′) *v.* to give or share; p. 290

impeccable (im pek′ ə bəl) *adj.* free from error; flawless; p. 507

impending (im pen′ ding) *adj.* about to occur; p. 1003

impertinent (im purt′ ən ənt) *adj.* inappropriately bold or forward; not showing proper respect or manners; p. 890

impetuous (im pech′ o͞o əs) *adj.* rushing headlong into things; rash; p. 262

implicit (im plis′ it) *adj.* suggested but not directly stated; p. 163

imploring (im plôr′ ing) *adj.* asking earnestly; begging; p. 253

impotent (im′ pət ənt) *adj.* ineffective, powerless, or helpless; p. 160

impropriety (im′ prə pri′ ə tē) *n.* an improper act or behavior; p. 1019

improvised (im′ prə vīzd′) *adj.* invented, composed, or done without preparing beforehand; p. 201

impudence (im′ pyə dəns) *n.* speech or behavior that is aggressively forward or rude; p. 1067

incantation (in′ kan tā′ shən) *n.* words spoken in casting a spell; p. 262

incoherently (in′ kō hēr′ ənt lē) *adv.* in a confused, disconnected manner; unintelligibly; p. 547

incomprehensible (in′ kom pri hen′ sə bəl) *adj.* not understandable; p. 482

incredulous (in krej′ ə ləs) *adj.* unwilling or unable to believe; pp. 83

incur (in kur′) *v.* to acquire (something undesirable); bring upon oneself; p. 291

indifferently (in dif′ ər ənt lē) *adv.* in a way that shows a lack of feeling, concern, or care; p. 558

indignantly (in dig′ nənt lē) *adv.* with quiet, dignified anger in response to something unjust, mean, or unworthy; p. 964

indolence (ind′ əl əns) *n.* laziness; idleness; p. 27

indulge (in dulj′) *v.* to yield to a desire (by doing something); take pleasure (in); p. 299

inert (i nurt′) *adj.* without power to move or act; lifeless; p. 546

infamy (in′ fə mē) *n.* extreme wickedness or shameful evil; p. 163

inhibit (in hib′ it) *v.* to hold back one's natural impulses; restrain; p. 491

inscribe (in skrīb′) *v.* to write, carve, or mark on a surface; p. 919

inscrutable (in skro͞o′ tə bəl) *adj.* mysterious; p. 193

insular (in′ sə lər) *adj.* showing a limited point of view; p. 481

intact (in takt′) *adj.* entire; untouched, uninjured, and having all parts; p. 564

interlaced (in′ tər lāst′) *adj.* connected by or as if by being woven together; interwoven; p. 111

interminable (in tur′ mi nə bəl) *adj.* lasting, or seeming to last, forever; endless; p. 189

internment (in turn′ mənt) *n.* the act of restricting or being restricted to a particular place, especially during a war; p. 463

intimidate (in tim′ə dāt′) *v.* to make timid or fearful; bully; p. 480

intone (in tōn′) *v.* to speak in a singing tone or monotone; recite; p. 1003

intricacy (in′ tri kə sē) *n.* something that is complicated, involved, or confusing; p. 383

intrigue (in trēg′) *v.* to excite the curiosity or interest of; fascinate; p. 130

invaluable (in val′ ū ə bəl) *adj.* very great in value; p. 497

irrational (i rash′ ən əl) *adj.* contrary to reason; illogical; p. 464

irreproachable (ir′ i prō′ chə bəl) *adj.* free from blame or criticism; faultless; p. 218

J

judiciously (jo͞o dish′ əs lē) *adv.* in a way that shows good judgment; sensibly; p. 437

L

lament (lə ment′) *v.* to express sorrow or regret; p. 50

languor (lang′ gər) *n.* weakness; fatigue; p. 273

lethargy (leth′ ər jē) *n.* sluggish inactivity or drowsiness; p. 159

loll (lol) *v.* to hang down loosely; droop; p. 427

loom (lo͞om) *v.* to appear to the mind as large; to stand out prominently; p. 438

lucid (lo͞o′ sid) *adj.* clear-headed; mentally alert; p. 1049

lurk (lurk) *v.* to stay hidden, ready to attack; p. 438

M

mainstream (mān′ strēm′) *adj.* representing the most widespread attitudes and values of a society or group; p. 496

makeshift (māk′ shift′) *adj.* suitable as a temporary substitute for the proper or desired thing; p. 64

malicious (mə lish′ əs) *adj.* having or showing a desire to harm another; p. 407

manifest (man′ ə fest′) *v.* to make obvious or clear; show plainly; p. 378

materialistic (mə tēr′ ē ə lis′ tik) *adj.* overly concerned with material matters and worldly possessions; p. 250

mesmerizing (mez′ mə rīz ing) *adj.* fascinating; p. 51

meticulous (mi tik′ yə ləs) *adj.* characterized by great or excessive concern about details; p. 490

monologue (mon′ ə lôg′) *n.* a long speech made by one person; p. 131

monosyllabic (mon′ ə si lab′ ik) *adj.* having only one syllable; p. 121

mortify (môr′ tə fī′) *v.* to shame, humiliate, or embarrass; p. 301

muse (mūz) *v.* to think or reflect, especially in an idle manner; p. 546

myriad (mir′ ē əd) *n.* great or countless numbers; p. 81

N

notorious (nō tôr′ ē əs) *adj.* widely and unfavorably known; p. 887

O

obliterate (ə blit′ ə rāt′) *v.* to destroy completely; p. 91

oblivious (ə bliv′ ē əs) *adj.* unmindful or unaware; not noticing; p. 1072

obscurity (əb skyo͞or′ ə tē) *n.* darkness; dimness; p. 364

oppress (ə pres′) *v.* to control or govern by the cruel and unjust use of force or authority; p. 12

oppressive (ə pres′ iv) *adj.* hard to bear; distressing; p. 181

ostentatiously (os′ tən tā′ shəs lē) *adv.* in a way intended to attract attention or impress others; p. 883

ostracism (os′ trə siz′ əm) *n.* exclusion from a group or society; p. 1035

P

pall (pôl) *n.* a covering that darkens or conceals; atmosphere of gloom; p. 355

palpable (pal′ pə bəl) *adj.* capable of being touched or felt; p. 510

palpitating (pal′ pə tāt′ ing) *adj.* quivering; trembling; vibrating; p. 482

pandemonium (pan′ də mō′ nē əm) *n.* wild disorder and uproar; p. 347

pantry (pan′ trē) *n.* room or closet in which food and articles for preparing and serving food are kept; p. 305

paradox (par′ ə doks′) *n.* something that seems illogical, contradictory, or absurd, but that in fact may be true; p. 320

paraphernalia (par′ ə fər nāl′ yə) *n.* things used in a particular activity; equipment; p. 262

patriarch (pā′ trē ärk′) *n.* the male head of a family or group; p. 463

patronize (pā′ trə nīz) *v.* to be a customer of (a business), especially on a regular basis; p. 378

pent-up (pent′ up) *adj.* not expressed or released; held in; p. 206

perceive (pər sēv′) *v.* to be or become aware through the senses; p. 293

perilous (per′ ə ləs) *adj.* dangerous; risky; p. 151

permeated (pur′ mē ā′ təd) *adj.* filled with; p. 191

perpetuate (pər pech′ o͞o āt′) *v.* to cause to continue to be remembered; p. 938

perplexed (pər plekst′) *adj.* troubled with doubt or uncertainty; puzzled; p. 103

peruse (pə ro͞oz′) *v.* to read through or examine carefully; p. 450

perverse (pər vurs′) *adj.* determined to go against what is reasonable, expected, or desired; contrary; p. 752

pestilential (pes′ tə len′ shəl) *adj.* harmful; destructive; p. 274

petulantly (pech′ ə lənt lē) *adv.* crankily; in an annoyed way; p. 964

phenomena (fə nom′ ə nə′) *n.* facts, events, or conditions that can be known through the senses; p. 355

pilgrimage (pil′ grə mij) *n.* a long journey, especially to a holy place or for a religious purpose; p. 1055

pious (pī′ əs) *adj.* having either genuine or pretended religious devotion; p. 272

piqued (pēkt) *adj.* aroused to anger or resentment; offended; p. 262

plaintive (plān′ tiv) *adj.* expressing sorrow; mournful; sad; p. 133

pompous (pom′ pəs) *adj.* showing an exaggerated sense of self-importance; p. 1063

predecessor (pred′ ə ses′ ər) *n.* one who comes, or has come, before another in time; p. 249

presentiment (pri zen′ tə mənt) *n.* a feeling that something is about to happen; p. 344

presumably (pri zōō′ mə blē) *adv.* supposedly; probably; p. 279

presumptuous (pri zump′ chōō əs) *adj.* too forward; bold; p. 175

prevail (pri vāl′) *v.* to be superior in power or influence; succeed; p. 754

priceless (prīs′ lis) *adj.* of greater value than can be measured; p. 16

primeval (prī mē′ vəl) *adj.* of or having to do with the first or earliest age; primitive; p. 324

prodigal (prod′ i gəl) *adj.* recklessly wasteful; p. 280

prodigy (prod′ ə jē) *n.* an extraordinarily gifted or talented person, especially a child; p. 49

profound (prə found′) *adj.* intense and complete; p. 1021

profuse (prə fūs′) *adj.* great in amount; plentiful; p. 389

proliferation (prō lif′ ə rā′ shən) *n.* growth by rapidly producing new cells or offspring; p. 534

propriety (prə prī′ ə tē) *n.* the quality of being proper or appropriate; suitability; p. 379

prosaic (prō zā′ ik) *adj.* ordinary; commonplace; p. 177

prospective (prə spek′ tiv) *adj.* probable or expected; future; p. 1039

prowess (prou′ is) *n.* great ability or skill; p. 921

psalm (sälm) *n.* a sacred poem, song, or hymn; p. 111

R

rancor (rang′ kər) *n.* ill will; resentment; p. 291

raptly (rapt′ lē) *adv.* in a deeply interested way; attentively; p. 1019

rebuke (ri būk′) *v.* to scold sharply; p. 152

reciprocal (ri sip′ rə kəl) *adj.* given, felt, or shown in return; p. 133

reconciliation (rek′ ən sil′ ē ā′ shən) *n.* a settlement of a controversy or disagreement; p. 274

refrain (ri frān′) *n.* in a song or poem, a phrase or verse that is repeated regularly, especially at the end of each stanza; p. 242

regally (rē′ gəl lē) *adv.* in a grand, dignified manner befitting a king or queen; p. 883

rejuvenate (ri jōō′ və nāt′) *v.* to make fresh or young again; p. 158

relevant (rel′ ə vənt) *adj.* connected with the matter at hand; pertinent; meaningful; p. 521

relic (rel′ ik) *n.* an object that has survived decay, destruction, or the passage of time and is valued for its historic interest; p. 67

remonstrate (ri mon′ strāt) *v.* to say or plead in protest; argue; p. 290

repercussion (rē′ pər kush′ ən) *n.* an effect or result of some action or event; p. 1045

repressed (ri prest′) *adj.* held back or kept under control; restrained; p. 889

reprieve (ri prēv′) *v.* to give temporary relief, as from something unpleasant or difficult; p. 363

reproach (ri prōch′) *n.* blame; disgrace; discredit; p. 50

repulse (ri puls′) *n.* an act of beating back or driving away, as with force; p. 728

residue (rez′ ə dōō′) *n.* what remains after part is removed; p. 131

resilient (ri zil′ yənt) *adj.* capable of springing back into shape or position after being bent, stretched, or compressed; p. 321

resonant (rez′ ə nənt) *adj.* having a full, rich sound; p. 1049

retail (rē′ tāl) *v.* to sell directly to the consumer; p. 40

retinue (ret′ ən ōō′) *n.* the group of attendants or servants accompanying a person of rank or authority; p. 242

reveling (rev′əl ing) *adj.* taking great pleasure; p. 207

reverie (rev′ ər ē) *n.* fanciful thinking; daydream; p. 53

ruefully (ro͞o′ fəl ē) *adv.* regretfully; sorrowfully; p. 970

rustic (rus′ tik) *adj.* of, or relating to, the country; p. 226

S

sagacious (sə gā′ shəs) *adj.* having or showing wisdom and good judgment; p. 390

sanctity (sangk′ tə tē) *n.* the quality of deserving solemn respect as something not to be violated; p. 281

sashay (sa shā′) *v.* to walk or move in a way that shows indifference or a lack of interest; p. 305

scenario (si nār′ ē ō′) *n.* an outline or model of an expected or imagined series of events; p. 491

scrupulous (skro͞o′ pyə ləs) *adj.* thoroughly attentive to even the smallest details; precise; p. 937

scrutinize (skro͞ot′ ən īz) *v.* to look at closely; inspect carefully; p. 192

sedate (si dāt′) *adj.* quiet and restrained in style or manner; calm; p. 252

serenity (sə ren′ ə tē) *n.* calmness; peacefulness; p. 190

sever (sev′ ər) *v.* to break off; p. 249

sidle (sīd′ əl) *v.* to move sideways, especially in a way that does not attract attention or cause disturbance; p. 8

singular (sing′ gyə lər) *adj.* unusual or remarkable; p. 366

sinister (sin′ is tər) *adj.* threatening or suggesting evil; p. 178

skeptical (skep′ ti kəl) *adj.* having or showing doubt or suspicion; questioning; disbelieving; p. 193

slew (slo͞o) *n.* a large number or group; p. 242

solace (sol′ is) *n.* relief from sorrow or disappointment; comfort; p. 250

sparse (spärs) *adj.* thinly spread or distributed; p. 337

spasmodic (spaz mod′ ik) *adj.* sudden, violent, and temporary; p. 204

spawn (spôn) *v.* to bring forth; give birth; p. 358

spectral (spek′ trəl) *adj.* ghostlike; p. 393

speculate (spek′ yə lāt′) *v.* to guess; p. 523

sporadic (spə rad′ ik) *adj.* irregular; occasional; p. 160

squalor (skwol′ ər) *n.* wretchedness; misery and filth; p. 146

staidness (stād′ nəs) *n.* the state or quality of being serious, steady, or conservative in character; p. 219

stifling (stī′ fling) *adj.* smothering; suffocating; p. 189

stolid (stol′ id) *adj.* showing little or no emotion; not easily stirred or moved; p. 1034

strategic (strə tē′ jik) *adj.* highly important to an intended goal; p. 986

stridently (strīd′ ənt lē) *adv.* in a loud, harsh manner; shrilly; p. 437

subordinate (sə bôr′ də nāt′) *v.* to cause to be, or treat as, secondary, inferior, or less important; p. 471

subtle (sut′ əl) *adj.* not open or direct; not obvious; p. 121

subversive (sub vur′ siv) *adj.* seeking to weaken, destroy, or overthrow; p. 220

succor (suk′ ər) *n.* help; assistance; relief; p. 274

sumptuous (sump′ cho͞o əs) *adj.* costly and magnificent; p. 967

superfluous (soo pur′ flo͞o əs) *adj.* not needed; unnecessary; p. 496

supplication (səp′ lə kā′ shən) *n.* an earnest and humble request; p. 78

surmise (sər mīz′) *v.* to guess or conclude from little or no evidence; p. 33

T

taut (tôt) *adj.* tense; tight; p. 204

tedious (tē′ dē əs) *adj.* boring; tiresome; p. 534

temper (tem′ pər) *v.* to moderate by mingling with another thing; p. 427

tenaciously (ti nā′ shəs lē) *adv.* stubbornly; persistently; p. 160

tentative (ten′ tə tiv) *adj.* not fully worked out; uncertain; p. 357

tepid (tep′ id) *adj.* moderately or slightly warm; lukewarm; p. 483

theorize (thē′ ə rīz′) *v.* to form an idea that explains a group of facts; p. 380

throng (thrông) *v.* to move or gather in large numbers; crowd together; p. 969

tirade (tī rād′) *n.* a long, angry or scolding speech; p. 453

token (tō′ kən) *adj.* symbolic; p. 428

torturous (tôr′ chər əs) *adj.* causing pain or suffering; p. 496

totalitarian (tō tal′ ə tār′ ē ən) *adj.* characteristic of a government in which one political party has total control; p. 510

transient (tran′ shənt) *adj.* of temporary or brief duration; not lasting; p. 537

tremulously (trem′ yə les lē) *adv.* in a trembling or vibrating way; p. 1030

tribulation (trib′ yə lā′ shən) *n.* great misery or distress; suffering; p. 350

tumultuous (too mul′cho͞o əs) *adj.* wildly excited, confused, or agitated; p. 920

U

ulterior (ul tēr′ ē ər) *adj.* intentionally withheld or concealed; p. 219

ultimately (ul′ tə mit lē) *adv.* at last; finally; p. 1004

unconditional (un′ kən dish′ ən əl) *adj.* absolute; complete; p. 230

unimpeded (un′ im pē′ dəd) *adj.* not obstructed; unblocked; p. 211

unkempt (un kempt′) *adj.* in a neglected state; not combed or groomed; untidy; p. 1045

V

valid (val′ id) *adj.* acceptable; legitimate; p. 481

vanquish (vang′ kwish) *v.* to conquer or overcome; p. 937

vault (vôlt) *v.* to jump; spring; p. 985

vehemently (vē′ ə mənt lē) *adv.* strongly; intensely; passionately; p. 454

verandah (və ran′də) *n.* a long porch, usually with a roof, that extends along one or more sides of a house; p. 110

vermin (vur′ min) *n.* any animals that are harmful, destructive, or troublesome; p. 428

vexed (vekst) *adj.* impatient or angry; annoyed; p. 151

vintage (vin′ tij) *adj.* characterized by enduring appeal; classic; p. 64

void (void) *n.* an empty space; vacuum; p. 228

vulgar (vul′ gər) *adj.* characterized by a lack of good breeding or good taste; common; crude; p. 966

vulnerable (vul′ nər ə bəl) *adj.* easily damaged or hurt; p. 496

W

wane (wān) *v.* to decrease gradually; p. 148

wanton (wont′ ən) *adj.* shamelessly unrestrained; immoral; p. 392

wary (wār′ ē) *adj.* cautious; on the alert; p. 144

whim (hwim) *n.* a sudden notion or fanciful idea; p. 1056

whimsical (hwim′ zi kəl) *adj.* fanciful; curiously humorous; p. 467

wince (wins) *v.* to draw back slightly, as in pain; flinch; p. 119

wont (wōnt) *adj.* accustomed; used; p. 270

Z

zealously (zel′ əs lē) *adv.* eagerly; enthusiastically; p. 31

Spanish Glossary

A

abashed/avergonzado *adj.* abochornado; desconcertado; p. 917

abeyance/suspensión *s.* estado de inactividad temporal; p. 363

absolve/absolver *v.* liberar de culpa o responsabilidad; p. 752

abstract/abstracto *adj.* separado de un caso o ejemplo específico; teórico; p. 510

abyss/abismo *s.* sima; gran profundidad; vacío inmenso; p. 547

accost/abordar *v.* acercarse o dirigirse a alguien de manera brusca; p. 916

acquiesce/acceder *v.* aceptar o consentir sin protestar; p. 270

acrid/acre *adj.* irritante o desagradable; p. 30

admonish/regañar *v.* advertir en contra de una acción específica; amonestar; p. 448

advocate/abogar *v.* respaldar públicamente; p. 1032

affable/afable *adj.* amistoso, cordial y amable; p. 1063

affluent/afluente *adj.* acaudalado; próspero; p. 509

agenda/agenda *s.* programa o itinerario de cosas por hacer; p. 522

albeit/no obstante *conj.* aunque; si bien; sin embargo; p. 219

alleviate/aliviar *v.* hacer menos difícil; calmar; socorrer; p. 467

amenable/dispuesto *adj.* receptivo; dócil; p. 40

amiably/afablemente *adv.* de manera amistosa y cordial; p. 173

anteroom/antesala *s.* vestíbulo; pequeña sala de espera que conduce a la sala principal; p. 101

appal/pasmar *v.* llenar de horror o espanto; asombrar; p. 393

apparition/aparición *s.* algo extraño o inesperado que se aparece de repente, como un fantasma; p. 229

apprehension/aprensión *s.* temor de lo que pueda pasar; ansiedad; p. 253

appurtenance/accesorio *s.* artículo o pieza de equipo opcional que se adjunta por conveniencia o comodidad; adminículo; p. 117

arrogance/arrogancia *s.* orgullo desmedido; p. 745

arrogant/arrogante *adj.* lleno de vanidad; engreído; p. 403

arroyo/cauce *s.* en inglés quiere decir cauce seco de un río; en español, riachuelo; p. 331

articulate/expresar *v.* poner en palabras; decir algo clara y efectivamente; p. 521

assuage/mitigar *v.* reducir en intensidad; aliviar; p. 291

atonement/expiación *s.* acción para compensar un pecado, lesión o pérdida; p. 163

attribute/atributo *s.* cualidad o característica de una persona o cosa; p. 565

augment/aumentar *v.* agrandar; acrecentar p. 559

avaricious/avaro *adj.* codicioso o tacaño; p. 177

B

bade/ordenó *v.* pasado de *ordenar;* mandar; solicitar; p. 96

banality/banalidad *s.* trivialidad; insignificante o sin importancia; p. 511

banter/broma *s.* chanza ingeniosa y bien intencionada; p. 30

benevolence/benevolencia *s.* amabilidad; generosidad; p. 496

bereaved/afligido *adj.* triste y acongojado debido a una pérdida, tal como la muerte de un ser querido; p. 379

bereft/despojado *adj.* privado de algo; p. 1019

beseeching/suplicante *adj.* implorante; que ruega o pide con ansiedad; p. 81

blasphemous/blasfemo *adj.* que menosprecia o maldice a Dios o a cualquier figura sagrada; p. 394

boding/presagio *s.* advertencia o señal, particularmente de algo malo; p. 253

brash/insolente *adj.* atrevido; irrespetuoso; p. 90

C

cataclysm/cataclismo *s.* desastre que por lo general origina un cambio violento y repentino; p. 344

cavernous/cavernoso *adj.* grande y amplio como una caverna; p. 122

chic/chic *adj.* atractivo, distinguido y elegante; p. 301

chronic/crónico *adj.* que dura largo tiempo o que se repite constantemente; p. 121

clientele/clientela *s.* clientes o compradores fijos de un establecimiento comercial; p. 301

coerce/obligar *v.* presionar por medio de la fuerza o la autoridad; p. 1055

combatant/combatiente *s.* que participa en un combate o lucha; p. 969

commandeer/confiscar *v.* adueñarse de algo para uso militar o del gobierno; p. 39

commodious/espacioso *adj.* que tiene un amplio espacio; holgado; p. 490

compassionate/compasivo *adj.* que demuestra interés y preocupación por el sufrimiento o la desgracia de otros, así como deseo de ayudar; p. 522

conceive/concebir *v.* formarse una imagen o idea mental; imaginar; p. 230

confidante/confidente *s.* persona a la que se le confía un secreto o asunto privado; p. 938

confront/confrontar *v.* encontrarse cara a cara frente a alguien o algo; oponerse; p. 984

connoisseur/conocedor *s.* que sabe distinguir lo mejor de un sector específico, como vinos, comida o arte; experto en el tema; p. 1031

conscientiously/concienzudamente *adv.* de manera reflexiva y cuidadosa; p. 76

consequent/consecuente *adj.* como resultado o efecto de algo; p. 378

constancy/constancia *s.* cualidad de no cambiar; perseverancia; lealtad; p. 427

consternation/consternación *s.* asombro o aflicción que causa confusión; p. 1017

contemplate/contemplar *v.* pensar algo con mucha atención; considerar algo cuidadosamente; p. 132

contend/sostener *v.* declarar algo como hecho; p. 1047

contrition/contrición *s.* arrepentimiento por un pecado o mala acción que se ha cometido; remordimiento; p. 76

convivial/jovial *adj.* de buen ánimo; amigo de diversiones y fiestas; sociable; p. 491

convoluted/retorcido *adj.* enredado; complicado; abrupto; p. 201

convulsive/convulsivo *adj.* repentino y violento; p. 84

correlate/correlacionar *v.* relacionar una cosa con otra; p. 320

coterie/grupo *s.* camarilla; grupo pequeño de personas que comparten un interés particular y que se reúnen con frecuencia; p. 448

countenance/semblante *s.* rostro; cara; p. 391

credence/certeza *s.* convicción, particularmente en lo que dice o informa otra persona; p. 451

credulity/credulidad *s.* tendencia a creer o aceptar algo fácilmente; p. 176

crevice/grieta *s.* hendedura; ranura; p. 335

D

daft/tonto *adj.* necio; bobo; p. 435

dally/demorarse *v.* flojear; holgazanear; perder el tiempo; p. 260

dauntless/intrépido *adj.* sin miedo; valiente; atrevido; p. 390

debasement/degradación *s.* acción y efecto de degradar; bajar de categoría, calidad o valor; p. 565

decapitate/decapitar *v.* cortar la cabeza; p. 66

decree/decreto *s.* orden o decisión impartida por un juez, monarca u otro funcionario; p. 241

decrepit/decrépito *adj.* agotado por el uso o la ancianidad; achacoso; p. 401

deference/deferencia *s.* consideración o respeto hacia las opiniones o deseos de otra persona; p. 33

defile/mancillar *v.* manchar la pureza de algo; ensuciar; p. 758

definitive/definitivo *adj.* concluyente; final; decisivo; p. 230

deftness/destreza *s.* cualidad de ser hábil y ágil en algún oficio o actividad; p. 205

derision/escarnio *s.* mofa; burla; p. 364

designation/designación *s.* nombre o título de distinción; p. 464

desolate/desolado *adj.* desértico o inhabitado; p. 967

detached/indiferente *adj.* alejado emocionalmente; neutral; p. 481

devastate/devastar *v.* destruir; asolar; p. 56

devoid/desprovisto *adj.* carente; vacío; p. 536

disconcerting/desconcertante *adj.* inquietante, confuso o frustrante; p. 536

discordant/discordante *adj.* en desacuerdo; opuesto a; discorde; p. 53

discreetly/discretamente *adv.* de modo sensato y cuidadoso; p. 145

disdain/desdén *s.* desprecio hacia algo o alguien; menosprecio; p. 294

disperse/dispersar *v.* apartar lo que estaba unido; diseminar; p. 129

distortion/distorsión *s.* deformación; torcimiento; alteración; p. 338

divert/distraer *v.* alejar de la atención; desviar; p. 558

doctrine/doctrina *s.* principio o posición que se enseña o promueve, por ejemplo, de la religión; p. 13

doddering/tambaleante *adj.* tembloroso o vacilante, como una persona anciana al caminar; p. 121

doggedly/obstinadamente *adv.* de manera terca; firmemente; p. 175

droll/risible *adj.* que causa risa por raro o cómico; p. 291

drone/murmurar *v.* hablar monótonamente; ronronear; p. 1040

E

ecosystem/ecosistema *s.* comunidad de organismos con su medio ambiente que funcionan como una unidad; p. 534

edifice/edificio *s.* construcción alta o de aspecto imponente; p. 40

elation/regocijo *s.* gran alegría; júbilo; éxtasis; p. 564

elude/eludir *v.* evadir o escapar, particularmente mediante astucia o agilidad; p. 937

endeavor/empeño *s.* gran esfuerzo por conseguir algo; p. 272

enhance/realzar *v.* mejorar, ya sea en belleza, calidad o valor; p. 260

enlightening/ilustrativo *adj.* que da o revela conocimientos o sabiduría; p. 1041

enthralled/cautivado *adj.* fascinado; encantado; p. 176

ephemeral/efímero *adj.* de corta vida; temporal; p. 534

equanimity/calma *s.* ecuanimidad, igualdad y constancia de ánimo; p. 345

equilibrium/equilibrio *s.* estabilidad mental, emocional o física; p. 550

eschew/evitar *v.* evadir algo desagradable o peligroso; soslayar; p. 1032

exclusively/exclusivamente *adv.* únicamente; limitado; p. 462

exhortation/exhortación *s.* advertencia o llamado severo; p. 1045

expedient/expediente *s.* recurso; método útil para obtener un resultado deseado; p. 1022

expend/gastar *v.* consumir; p. 546

expendable/prescindible *adj.* que no es estrictamente necesario; que se puede sacrificar sin efectos negativos; p. 319

exultation/exultación *s.* regocijo; júbilo; p. 564

F

ferocity/ferocidad *s.* fiereza; de gran intensidad; p. 357

fiasco/fiasco *s.* fracaso total y humillante; p. 56

flaunt/ostentar *v.* hacer alarde; p. 32

formidable/formidable *adj.* que causa miedo o asombro por razón de su tamaño, fuerza o poder; p. 400

fortitude/fortaleza *s.* valor o entereza en medio del dolor o del peligro; p. 345

fortnight/quincena *s.* período de dos semanas; p. 40

fortuitous/fortuito *adj.* afortunado; imprevisto; p. 549

furtive/furtivo *adj.* secreto; cauteloso; sigiloso; p. 11

G

gaudy/chillón *adj.* brillante y llamativo al punto de ser de mal gusto; p. 26

gaunt/demacrado *adj.* muy delgado y ojeroso; con aspecto enfermizo; p. 91

giddy/vertiginoso *adj.* que causa mareo o vértigo; p. 151

gingerly/con cautela *adv.* con gran cuidado; sigilosamente; p. 383

grapple/abordar *v.* examinar un asunto para resolverlo; bregar por resolver algo; p. 519

grimace/mueca *s.* gesto de la cara; p. 175

H

hale/vigoroso *adj.* en buen estado físico; saludable; p. 437

harass/acosar *v.* molestar o perturbar repetidamente; p. 63

heyday/apogeo *s.* período de mayor fuerza, popularidad o prosperidad; p. 1005

horde/horda *s.* grupo grande; multitud; p. 160

hue/color *s.* matiz; sombra o tinte; p. 241

humility/humildad *s.* cualidad de ser humilde o modesto; p. 91

hurtle/abalanzarse *v.* precipitarse; moverse rápidamente, especialmente con fuerza y ruido; p. 403

hypochondriac/hipocondríaco *s.* persona que se preocupa tanto por su salud que se imagina síntomas de una enfermedad; p. 1063

I

ideology/ideología *s.* ideas en las que se basa un sistema político, económico o social; p. 511

ignoble/innoble *adj.* de bajo origen o posición; sin honor ni valor; p. 920

impart/impartir *v.* dar o compartir; p. 290

impeccable/impecable *adj.* libre de errores; sin falla; p. 507

impending/inminente *adj.* a punto de ocurrir; p. 1003

impertinent/impertinente *adj.* indebidamente atrevido o directo; que no muestra respeto ni buenos modales; p. 890

impetuous/impetuoso *adj.* que se apresura a hacer algo; fogoso; p. 262

implicit/implícito *adj.* que se sugiere pero no se establece directamente; p. 163

imploring/implorante *adj.* que pide con intensidad; que suplica; p. 253

impotent/impotente *adj.* inefectivo, incapaz o indefenso; p. 160

impropriety/impropiedad *s.* incorrección; indecencia; p. 1019

improvised/improvisado *adj.* inventado; hecho sin preparación; p. 201

impudence/impudencia *s.* palabra o conducta descarada o ruda; p. 1067

incantation/conjuro *s.* palabras dichas en un encantamiento o sortilegio; p. 262

incoherently/incoherentemente *adv.* de modo confuso o disparatado; p. 547

incomprehensible/incomprensible *adj.* que no se puede entender; p. 482

incredulous/incrédulo *adj.* que no puede o no quiere creer; p. 83

incur/incurrir *v.* hacerse merecedor de una pena o un castigo; contraer; p. 291

indifferently/indiferentemente *adv.* de modo que muestra falta de interés, afecto o preocupación; p. 558

indignantly/con indignación *adv.* con rabia y desprecio dignos ante algo injusto o malo; p. 964

indolence/indolencia *s.* pereza; apatía; p. 27

indulge/consentir *v.* ceder a un deseo; complacer; p. 299

inert/inerte *adj.* inactivo; sin poder moverse o actuar; sin vida; p. 546

infamy/infamia *s.* maldad o perversidad extrema; p. 163

inhibit/inhibir *v.* reprimir los impulsos naturales; refrenarse; p. 491

inscribe/inscribir *v.* escribir, tallar o marcar en una superficie; p. 919

inscrutable/inescrutable *adj.* misterioso; p. 193

insular/insular *adj.* que tiene un punto de vista limitado; habitante de una isla; p. 481

intact/intacto *adj.* entero; ileso; con todas sus partes completas; p. 564

interlaced/entrelazado *adj.* conectado; entretejido; p. 111

interminable/interminable *adj.* que no termina; que dura mucho tiempo; eterno; p. 189

internment/internamiento *s.* acción de restringir a un lugar, especialmente durante una guerra; p. 463

intimidate/intimidar *v.* atemorizar o asustar; desafiar; p. 480

intone/entonar *v.* dar determinado tono a la voz; recitar; p. 1003

intricacy/complejidad *s.* cualidad de complejo, complicado o confuso; p. 383

intrigue/intrigar *v.* despertar la curiosidad o el interés por algo; fascinar; p. 130

invaluable/invaluable *adj.* de gran valor; que no se puede calcular; p. 497

irrational/irracional *adj.* contrario a la razón; ilógico; p. 464

irreproachable/irreprochable *adj.* sin culpa o crítica; sin falta alguna; p. 218

J

judiciously/sensatamente *adv.* de modo prudente; con buen juicio; p. 437

L

lament/lamentar *v.* expresar pena o arrepentimiento; p. 50

languor/languidez *s.* debilidad; fatiga; p. 273

lethargy/letargo *s.* período en que unos animales permanecen en inactividad y reposo; sopor, modorra; p. 159

loll/recostar *v.* reclinar; inclinar el cuerpo o alguna cosa sobre otro objeto; colgar; p. 427

loom/vislumbrarse *v.* surgir amenazadoramente; cobrar mucha importancia; p. 438

lucid/lúcido *adj.* claro en el razonamiento; alerta; p. 1049

lurk/acechar *v.* ocultarse y prepararse para atacar; p. 438

M

mainstream/de la cultura dominante *adj.* actitudes y valores más representativos de una sociedad o grupo; p. 496

makeshift/provisional *adj.* sustituto temporal del objeto apropiado o deseado; p. 64

malicious/malicioso *adj.* tener o manifestar el deseo de perjudicar a otro; p. 407

manifest/manifestar *v.* presentar; dar a conocer; decir; p. 378

materialistic/materialista *adj.* más preocupado de asuntos y bienes materiales que de asuntos intelectuales o espirituales; p. 250

mesmerizing/hipnotizante *adj.* fascinante; p. 51

meticulous/meticuloso *adj.* que se caracteriza por gran o excesiva preocupación hacia los detalles; p. 490

monologue/monólogo *s.* discurso largo que pronuncia un individuo; conversación dominada por una sola persona; p. 131

monosyllabic/monosilábico *adj.* de una sola sílaba; p. 121

mortify/mortificar *v.* afligir o preocupar; humillar o avergonzar; p. 301

muse/meditar *v.* pensar o reflexionar, especialmente en forma abstraída; p. 546

myriad/miríada *s.* multitud o infinidad de personas, cosas o asuntos; p. 81

N

notorious/notorio *adj.* de mala fama; público y sabido por todos; p. 887

O

obliterate/arrasar *v.* borrar; destruir por completo; p. 91

oblivious/abstraído *adj.* distraído; ensimismado; que no presta atención a lo que ocurre a su alrededor; p. 1072

obscurity/obscuridad *s.* falta de luz y claridad; p. 364

oppress/oprimir *v.* controlar o gobernar mediante fuerza o autoridad cruel o injusta; p. 12

oppressive/agobiante *adj.* agobiante; opresor; sofocante; p. 181

ostentatiously/ostentosamente *adv.* de un modo que busca llamar la atención o impresionar a otros; p. 883

ostracism/ostracismo *s.* exclusión de un grupo o sociedad; p. 1035

P

pall/manto *s.* palio; objeto que obscurece o cubre y da una atmósfera sombría; p. 355

palpable/palpable *adj.* que se puede tocar o sentir; p. 510

palpitating/palpitante *adj.* que vibra o se estremece; tembloroso; p. 482

pandemonium/pandemonio *s.* zafarrancho; algarabía; desorden; p. 347

pantry/alacena *s.* cuarto o armario en el que se guardan víveres o comestibles; p. 305

paradox/paradoja *s.* frase o situación que parece ilógica, contradictoria o absurda, pero que puede ser cierta; contrasentido; p. 320

paraphernalia/parafernalia *s.* conjunto de cosas que se usan en una determinada actividad; equipo; p. 262

patriarch/patriarca *s.* líder o jefe masculino de una familia o grupo; p. 463

patronize/ir a un negocio *v.* comprar o utilizar los servicios de una tienda o compañía de manera habitual; p. 378

pent-up/reprimido *adj.* que no se expresa o divulga; contenido; p. 206

perceive/percibir *v.* notar o comprender a través de los sentidos; p. 293

perilous/peligroso *adj.* azaroso; con riesgos; p. 151

permeated/impregnado *adj.* saturado; lleno; p. 191

perpetuate/perpetuar *v.* hacer que se siga recordando; p. 938

perplexed/perplejo *adj.* dudoso o incierto; confuso; p. 103

peruse/leer con atención *v.* escudriñar; examinar algo cuidadosamente; p. 450

perverse/perverso *adj.* que contraría a propósito lo que es razonable, esperado o deseable; p. 752

pestilential/perjudicial *adj.* peligroso; nocivo; destructivo; p. 274

petulantly/malhumoradamente *adv.* de mal modo; de mal genio; p. 964

phenomena/fenómenos *s.* hechos, sucesos o condiciones que se pueden conocer a través de los sentidos; p. 355

pilgrimage/peregrinación *s.* viaje largo, especialmente a un lugar sagrado y con fines religiosos; p. 1055

pious/piadoso *adj.* devoto; beato; p. 272

piqued/resentido *adj.* disgustado; ofendido; p. 262

plaintive/quejumbroso *adj.* que expresa dolor; que se queja; triste; p. 133

pompous/pomposo *adj.* ostentoso; vanidoso; magnífico o espléndido; p. 1063

predecessor/predecesor *s.* que precede o viene antes; precursor; p. 249

presentiment/presentimiento *s.* sensación de que algo está por pasar; p. 344

presumably/probablemente *adv.* supuestamente; con probabilidad; p. 279

presumptuous/presuntuoso *adj.* demasiado directo; atrevido; p. 175

prevail/prevalecer *v.* ser superior en poder o influencia; triunfar; p. 754

priceless/inapreciable *adj.* de un valor tal que no se puede calcular; p. 16

primeval/primitivo *adj.* relativo a lo inicial o primero; rudimentario; p. 324

prodigal/pródigo *adj.* derrochador; p. 280

prodigy/prodigio *s.* persona extraordinariamente talentosa, especialmente un niño; p. 49

profound/profundo *adj.* intenso y completo; p. 1021

profuse/profuso *adj.* abundante; cuantioso; p. 389

proliferation/proliferación *s.* reproducción o rápido crecimiento; p. 534

propriety/corrección *s.* cualidad de ser correcto o apropiado; conveniencia; p. 379

prosaic/prosaico *adj.* ordinario; vulgar; p. 177

prospective/presunto *adj.* probable o posible; futuro; p. 1039

prowess/habilidad *s.* gran pericia o destreza; p. 921

psalm/salmo *s.* poema, canción o himno sagrado; p. 111

R

rancor/rencor *s.* resentimiento; odio; p. 291

raptly/apasionadamente *adv.* con profundo interés o atención; p. 1019

rebuke/regañar *v.* reprender severamente; p. 152

reciprocal/recíproco *adj.* que se da, se siente o se muestra a cambio de una actitud similar; p. 133

reconciliation/reconciliación *s.* arreglo de una controversia o desacuerdo; p. 274

refrain/estribillo *s.* en una canción o poema, una frase o verso que se repite regularmente, especialmente al final de cada estrofa; p. 242

regally/fastuosamente *adv.* de modo grandioso o suntuoso, propio de reyes; p. 883

rejuvenate/rejuvenecer *v.* renovar; dar nuevos ánimos, juventud o frescura; p. 158

relevant/relevante *adj.* relacionado con el asunto en cuestión; pertinente; significativo; p. 521

relic/reliquia *s.* objeto que ha sobrevivido al paso del tiempo y que se conserva y valora por su interés histórico; p. 67

remonstrate/objetar *v.* decir o replicar en protesta; argüir; p. 290

repercussion/repercusión *s.* efecto o resultado de una acción o un suceso; p. 1045

repressed/reprimido *adj.* que se contiene o mantiene bajo control; frenado; p. 889

reprieve/aliviar *v.* dar un respiro; posponer algo desagradable o difícil; p. 363

reproach/reprochar *s.* culpar; censurar; criticar; p. 50

repulse/repulsión *s.* acción de repeler o rechazar; p. 728

residue/residuo *s.* lo que queda después de que se consume o retira la mayor parte de algo; p. 131

resilient/flexible *adj.* capaz de volver a su forma o posición original después de que se tuerce, estira o comprime; p. 321

resonant/resonante *adj.* que tiene un sonido que retumba o suena muy fuerte; p. 1049

retail/vender al menudeo *v.* vender directamente al consumidor; p. 40

retinue/séquito *s.* grupo de asistentes o sirvientes que acompaña a una persona de rango o autoridad; p. 242

reveling/deleitable *adj.* que da deleite; p. 207

reverie/ensoñación *s.* sueño despierto; visión que encanta; p. 53

ruefully/desconsoladamente *adv.* tristemente; penosamente; p. 970

rustic/rústico *adj.* relativo al campo; rural; p. 226

S

sagacious/sagaz *adj.* sabio o sensato; p. 390

sanctity/santidad *s.* cualidad de santo o de algo que merece inmenso respeto; p. 281

sashay/andar con desgano *v.* moverse o caminar de un modo que muestra indiferencia o falta de interés; p. 305

scenario/guión *s.* esbozo o modelo de una serie de sucesos previstos o imaginarios; p. 491

scrupulous/escrupuloso *adj.* muy atento a los más pequeños detalles; preciso; p. 937

scrutinize/escrutar *v.* mirar muy de cerca; inspeccionar cuidadosamente; p. 192

sedate/sosegado *adj.* que se mantiene tranquilo y sereno por naturaleza; calmado; p. 252

serenity/serenidad *s.* calma; tranquilidad; p. 190

sever/cortar *v.* separar; p. 249

sidle/moverse furtivamente *v.* caminar o deslizarse de forma que no llame la atención o que no moleste; p. 8

singular/singular *adj.* único, peculiar o especial; p. 366

sinister/siniestro *adj.* amenazante o que sugiere maldad; p. 178

skeptical/escéptico *adj.* que manifiesta duda o sospecha; suspicaz; incrédulo; p. 193

slew/montón *s.* grupo grande o numeroso; p. 242

solace/solaz *s.* alivio de una pena o desilusión; consuelo; p. 250

sparse/esparcido *adj.* extendido o distribuido en una capa delgada; p. 337

spasmodic/espasmódico *adj.* repentino, violento y temporal; p. 204

spawn/generar *v.* engendrar; crear; p. 358

spectral/espectral *adj.* fantasmal; estremecedor; p. 393

speculate/especular *v.* adivinar; p. 523

sporadic/periódico *adj.* esporádico; ocasional; p. 160

squalor/miseria *s.* pobreza y suciedad; sordidez; p. 146

staidness/sobriedad *s.* estado o cualidad de ser serio, estable o conservador por naturaleza; p. 219

stifling/sofocante *adj.* asfixiante; que ahoga; p. 189

stolid/impasible *adj.* que muestra poca o ninguna emoción; que no se conmueve fácilmente; p. 1034

strategic/estratégico *adj.* muy importante para una meta determinada; p. 986

stridently/estridentemente *adv.* de manera aguda y ruidosa; chillonamente; p. 437

subordinate/subordinar *v.* someter; tratar como secundario, inferior o de menor importancia; p. 471

subtle/sutil *adj.* que no es abierto ni directo; que no es obvio; p. 121

subversive/subversivo *adj.* que busca debilitar, destruir o derrocar; p. 220

succor/socorrer *s.* ayudar; auxiliar; p. 274

sumptuous/suntuoso *adj.* costoso y magnífico; p. 967

superfluous/superfluo *adj.* que no es necesario; inútil; p. 496

supplication/súplica *s.* ruego o solicitud intensa y humilde; p. 78

surmise/suponer *v.* conjeturar o concluir con poca o ninguna evidencia; p. 33

T

taut/tirante *adj.* tenso; tieso; p. 204

tedious/tedioso *adj.* aburridor; fastidioso; p. 534

temper/templar *v.* moderar o atenuar mezclando con otra cosa; p. 427

tenaciously/tenazmente *adv.* tercamente; persistentemente; p. 160

tentative/tentativo *adj.* que aún no se define o se termina; incierto; p. 357

tepid/templado *adj.* ligeramente tibio; p. 483

theorize/teorizar *v.* formarse una idea que explica un conjunto de hechos; p. 380

throng/apiñar *v.* reunir en grandes cantidades; amontonar; p. 969

tirade/perorata *s.* discurso largo y furibundo; p. 453

token/simbólico *adj.* que representa algo; p. 428

torturous/atormentador *adj.* que causa mucho dolor o sufrimiento; p. 496

totalitarian/totalitario *adj.* característico de un gobierno en el que un partido político tiene control total; p. 510

transient/temporal *adj.* transitorio o de corta duración; p. 537

tremulously/trémulamente *adv.* de modo tembloroso o vibrante; p. 1030

tribulation/penuria *s.* tribulación, gran pena o problema; sufrimiento; p. 350

tumultuous/tumultoso *adj.* muy alterado, confuso o agitado; p. 920

U

ulterior/ulterior *adj.* oculto; p. 219

ultimately/últimamente *adv.* por último, finalmente; p. 1004

unconditional/incondicional *adj.* absoluto; completo; p. 230

unimpeded/ininterrumpido *adj.* sin obstrucción ni obstáculo; p. 211

unkempt/desaliñado *adj.* descuidado; sin peinar ni arreglar; desarreglado; p. 1045

V

valid/válido *adj.* aceptable; legítimo; p. 481

vanquish/subyugar *v.* conquistar o vencer; p. 937

vault/saltar *v.* dar una voltereta; rebotar; p. 985

vehemently/vehementemente *adv.* intensamente; apasionadamente; p. 454

verandah/barandal *s.* balcón largo, usualmente con techo, que se extiende a lo largo de uno o más costados de una casa; p. 110

vermin/sabandija *s.* cualquier animal que es dañino, destructivo o molesto; p. 428

vexed/molesto *adj.* fastidiado; impaciente o furioso; disgustado; p. 151

vintage/añejo *adj.* que se caracteriza por tener un atractivo duradero; clásico; p. 64

void/vacío *s.* espacio desocupado; p. 228

vulgar/vulgar *adj.* sin buena educación o buen gusto; tosco; ordinario; p. 966

vulnerable/vulnerable *adj.* que se daña o lastima fácilmente; p. 496

W

wane/declinar *v.* menguar; reducir poco a poco; p. 148

wanton/licencioso *adj.* que no se puede contener; indecente; inmoral; p. 392

wary/cauteloso *adj.* cuidadoso; prudente; p. 144

whim/capricho *s.* idea o deseo repentino e innecesario; antojo; p. 1056

whimsical/curioso *adj.* con un sentido del humor muy particular; p. 467

wince/recular *v.* retroceder ligeramente, como cuando se siente dolor; hacer una mueca de dolor; p. 119

wont/habituado *adj.* acostumbrado; p. 270

Z

zealously/ardorosamente *adv.* fervientemente; con mucho entusiasmo; p. 31

Index of Skills

References beginning with R refer to handbook pages.

Literary Concepts & Techniques

Reading & Thinking

Grammar and Language

Vocabulary

Writing

Listening, Speaking, and Viewing

Research and Study Skills

Media and Technology

Life Skills

Interdisciplinary Studies

Index of Authors and Titles

Index of Art and Artists

Acknowledgments

(Continued from page ii)

Literature

Unit 1

"Everyday Use" from *In Love & Trouble: Stories of Black Women,* copyright © 1973 by Alice Walker, reprinted by permission of Harcourt Brace & Company.

"Civil Peace" from *Girls at War and Other Stories* by Chinua Achebe. Copyright © 1972, 1973 by Chinua Achebe. Used by permission of Doubleday, a division of Random House, Inc.

"We, Too, Are One" by Michael Henningsen, from the *Weekly Alibi* Web site, reprinted by permission of the author.

"Two Kinds" Copyright © 1989 by Amy Tan. Reprinted by permission of Amy Tan and the Sandra Dijkstra Literary Agency.

"Catch the Moon" from *An Island Like You: Stories of the Barrio* by Judith Ortiz Cofer. Copyright © 1995 by Judith Ortiz Cofer. Reprinted by permission of the publisher, Orchard Books, New York.

Excerpt from "Where No One Has Gone Before?" by Paul Kvinta. *Outside* July 1997. Reprinted by permission of the author.

"Through the Tunnel" from *The Habit of Loving.* Copyright © 1954 by Doris Lessing. Reprinted by kind permission of Jonathan Clowes Ltd., London, on behalf of Doris Lessing. "Through the Tunnel" from *The Habit of Loving* by Doris Lessing. Copyright © 1955 by Doris Lessing. Originally appeared in the *New Yorker.* Copyright renewed. Reprinted by permission of HarperCollins Publishers, Inc.

"The Vision Quest," from *American Indian Myths and Legends* by Richard Erdoes and Alfonso Ortiz, editors. Copyright © 1984 by Richard Erdoes and Alfonso Ortiz. Reprinted by permission of Pantheon Books, a division of Random House, Inc.

"By the Waters of Babylon" by Stephen Vincent Benét, from *The Selected Works of Stephen Vincent Benét,* Holt Rinehart & Winston, Inc. Copyright © 1936 by Stephen Vincent Benét. Copyright renewed by Thomas C. Benét, Stephanie B. Mahin and Rachel Benét Lewis. Reprinted by permission of Brandt & Brandt Literary Agents.

"What I Have Been Doing Lately" from *At the Bottom of the River* by Jamaica Kincaid. Copyright © 1983 by Jamaica Kincaid. Reprinted by permission of Farrar, Straus & Giroux, Inc.

"With All Flags Flying" by Anne Tyler. Copyright © 1971 by Anne Tyler. Reprinted by the permission of Russell & Volkening as agents for the author.

"A Child, a Dog, the Night" by Amalia Rendic, from *Landscapes of a New Land.* Copyright © 1989 by White Pine Press.

"The Boar Hunt" by Jose Vasconceles, translated by Paul Waldorf, from *The Muse in Mexico: A Mid-Century Miscellany,* edited by Thomas Mabry Cranfill. Copyright © 1959. By permission of the University of Texas Press.

"Delicious Death" from *Desire,* copyright © 1998 by Alma Luz Villanueva (Bilingual Press, Arizona State University, Tempe, Arizona). Reprinted by permission of the author.

"Tuesday Siesta" from *No One Writes to the Colonel* by Gabriel Garcia Marquez. Copyright © 1968 in the English translation by Harper & Row Publishers, Inc. Reprinted by permission of HarperCollins Publishers, Inc.

"Holiday Traffic Brings Out Fear on Suspension Bridge," approved by Mark Silverman, Publisher and Editor. Reprinted with permission from The Detroit News.

"Contents of a Dead Man's Pocket" by Jack Finney. Reprinted by permission of Don Congdon Associates, Inc. Copyright © 1956 by the Crowell Collier Publishing Co., renewed 1984 by Jack Finney.

"The Censors" by Luisa Valenzuela. Copyright © Luisa Valenzuela. Luisa Valenzuela is a well-known Argentine novelist who has been extensively translated into English.

"The Ring" from *Anecdotes of Destiny* by Isak Dinesen. Copyright © 1958 by Isak Dinesen. Reprinted by permission of Random House, Inc. and The Rungstedlund Foundation.

"The Happy Man's Shirt" from *Italian Folktales, Selected and Retold by Italo Calvino,* copyright © 1956 by Giulio Einaudi editore, s.p.a., English translation by George Martin copyright © 1980 by Harcourt Brace & Company, reprinted by permission of Harcourt Brace & Company.

Excerpt from "What is the meaning of this: We ponder happiness" by Amanda Vogt. CHICAGO TRIBUNE, August 4, 1998 (a)/copyrighted Chicago Tribune Company. All rights reserved. Used by permission.

"An Astrologer's Day" from *The Grandmother's Tale and Selected Stories* by R. K. Narayan. Copyright © 1994 by R. K. Narayan. Reprinted by permission of the Wallace Literary Agency, Inc.

"As It Is With Strangers" by Susan Beth Pfeffer, copyright © 1989 by Susan Beth Pfeffer, from *Connections: Short Stories,* by Donald R. Gallo, Editor. Used by permission of Delacorte Press, a division of Random House, Inc.

"The Saleswoman" from *The Collected Stories of Colette,* edited by Robert Phelps, and translated by Matthew Ward. Translation copyright © 1983 by Farrar, Straus & Giroux, Inc. Reprinted by permission of Farrar, Straus & Giroux, Inc.

"Mrs. James" by Alice Childress. Reprinted by permission of the Flora Roberts Agency.

"Sound of Thunder" by Ray Bradbury. Reprinted by permission of Don Congdon Associates, Inc. Copyright © 1952 by the Crowell Collier Publishing Co., renewed 1980 by Ray Bradbury.

Excerpt from "Three Generations of Navajo Weavers," by Paul Zolbrod. INDIAN ARTIST, Fall 1997. Reprinted by permission of the author and Indian Artist.

"Lullaby" Copyright © 1981 by Leslie Marmon Silko. Reprinted from *Storyteller* by Leslie Marmon Silko, published by Seaver Books, New York, New York.

"And of Clay Are We Created" reprinted with the permission of Scribner, a Division of Simon & Schuster, from *The Stories of Eva Luna* by Isabel Allende, translated by Margaret Sayers Peden. Copyright © 1989 by Isabel Allende. English translation copyright © 1991 by Macmillan Publishing Company.

From "Colombia's Mortal Agony," by George Russell. Copyright © 1985, Time, Inc. Reprinted by permission.

"Winter Night" by Kay Boyle, reprinted by permission of the Estate of Kay Boyle and the Watkins/Loomis Agency.

"Waltz of the Fat Man" by Alberto Alvaro Rios. First published in *The Kenyon Review* – New Series, Summer 1991, Vol. XIII, No. 3. Reprinted by permission of the author.

"To Da-duh, in Memoriam" reprinted by permission of The Feminist Press at The City University of New York, from *Reena and Other Stories* by Paule Marshall. Copyright © 1983 by Paule Marshall.

Unit 2

Excerpt from *Travels with Charley* by John Steinbeck. Copyright © 1961, 1962 by The Curtis Publishing Co., © 1962 by John Steinbeck, renewed © 1990 by Elaine Steinbeck, Thom Steinbeck, and John Steinbeck IV. Used by permission of Viking Penguin, a division of Penguin Putnam, Inc.

A Child's Christmas in Wales by Dylan Thomas. Copyright © 1954 by New Directions Publishing Corp. Reprinted by permission of New Directions Publishing Corp.

Excerpts from "Destination Wales" reprinted by permission of Lonely Planet.

Reprinted with the permission of Simon & Schuster from *Kaffir Boy* by Mark Mathabane. Copyright © 1986 by Mark Mathabane.

Chapters 2–4 from *Farewell to Manzanar* by James D. and Jeanne Wakatsuki Houston. Copyright © 1973 by James D. Houston. Reprinted by permission of Houghton Mifflin Co. All rights reserved.

"By Any Other Name" from *Gifts of Passage* by Santha Rama Rau. Copyright 1951 by Vasanthi Rama Rau Bowers. Copyright renewed. Reprinted by permission of HarperCollins Publishers, Inc. "By Any Other Name" originally appeared in the *New Yorker.*

"Living Well. Living Good." from *Wouldn't Take Nothing For My Journey Now* by Maya Angelou. Copyright © 1993 by Maya Angelou. Reprinted by permission of Random House, Inc.

"A Swimming Lesson" from *Forty-Three Septembers* by Jewelle Gomez. Copyright © 1993 by Jewelle Gomez. Reprinted by permission of Firebrand Books, Ithaca, New York.

"Pizza in Warsaw, Torte in Prague" from *How We Survived Communism and Even Laughed* by Slavenka Drakulic. Copyright © 1991 by Slavenka Drakulic. Reprinted by permission of W. W. Norton & Company, Inc.

"I See the Promised Land" from *A Testament of Hope: The Essential Writings of Martin Luther King, Jr.,* reprinted by arrangement with The Heirs to the Estate of Martin Luther King Jr., c/o Writers House, Inc., as agent for the proprietor. Copyright © 1968 by the Estate of Martin Luther King.

Excerpt from "Exploring Antarctic Ice" by Jane Ellen Stevens, from *National Geographic,* May 1996. Reprinted by permission of the author.

Excerpt from *A Match to the Heart* by Gretel Ehrlich. Copyright © 1994 by Gretel Ehrlich. Reprinted by permission of Pantheon Books, a division of Random House, Inc.

Excerpt from "The Angry Winter" in *The Unexpected Universe,* Copyright © 1968 by Loren Eiseley, reprinted by permission of Harcourt Brace & Company.

"The Tucson Zoo" copyright © 1977 by Lewis Thomas, from *The Medusa and the Snail* by Lewis Thomas. Used by permission of Viking Penguin, a division of Penguin Putnam, Inc.

Unit 3

"One Perfect Rose" by Dorothy Parker, copyright 1929, renewed © 1957 by Dorothy Parker, from *The Portable Dorothy Parker* by Dorothy Parker, Introduction by Brendan Gill. Used by permission of Viking Penguin, a division of Penguin Putnam, Inc.

"Simile" from *Angle Geese and Other Poems* by N. Scott Momaday. Copyright © 1974 by N. Scott Momaday. Reprinted by permission of the author.

"The Glory of the Day Was in Her Face" from *Saint Peter Relates an Incident* by James Weldon Johnson. Copyright © 1917, 1921, 1935 by James Weldon Johnson, copyright renewed © 1963 by Grace Nail Johnson. Used by permission of Viking Penguin, a division of Penguin Putnam, Inc.

"Missing You" by Shu Ting, translated by Carolyn Kizer with Y. H. Zhao, from *A Splintered Mirror: Chinese Poetry from the Democracy Movement,* translated by Donald Finkel. Translation copyright © 1991 by Donald Finkel. Reprinted by permission of North Point Press, a division of Farrar, Straus & Giroux, Inc.

"First Lesson" from *Letter From A Distant Land* by Philip Booth. Copyright © 1957 by Philip Booth. Used by permission of Viking Penguin, a division of Penguin Putnam, Inc.

"Those Winter Sundays," copyright © 1966 by Robert Hayden, from *Collected Poems of Robert Hayden* by Frederick Glaysher, editor. Reprinted by permission of Liveright Publishing Corporation.

"Halfway House for Horses" by Melanie L. Stephens. Copyright © 1990 Time, Inc. Reprinted by permission.

"Horses Graze" from *Blacks* by Gwendolyn Brooks. Copyright © 1991 Gwendolyn Brooks Blakely. Reprinted by permission.

"A Blessing" by James Wright, from *The Branch Will Not Break* © 1963 by James Wright, Wesleyan University Press. By permission of University Press of New England.

"Afro-American Fragment" from *Collected Poems* by Langston Hughes. Copyright © 1994 by the Estate of Langston Hughes. Reprinted by permission of Alfred A. Knopf, Inc., a division of Random House, Inc.

"Heaven" from *Frameless Windows, Squares of Light: Poems by Cathy Song.* Copyright © 1988 by Cathy Song. Reprinted by permission of W. W. Norton & Company, Inc.

"The Base Stealer" by Robert Francis, from *The Orb Weaver.* Copyright © 1945, 1946, 1947, 1948, 1949, 1950, 1953, 1954, 1955, 1956, 1959, 1960 by Robert Francis. Published by University Press of New England.

"To Satch" from *Every Round and Other Poems.* Copyright © 1987 by Samuel Allen. Reprinted by permission of the author.

Reprinted courtesy of *Sports Illustrated,* September 12, 1994. Copyright © 1994, Time, Inc. "Making Hay" by Tom Verducci. All rights reserved.

"Ex-Basketball Player" from *The Carpentered Hen and Other Tame Creatures* by John Updike. Copyright © 1957, 1982 by John Updike. Reprinted by permission of Alfred A. Knopf Inc., a division of Random House, Inc.

"Miss Rosie," copyright © 1987 by Lucille Clifton. Reprinted from *Good Woman: Poems and a Memoir: 1969–1980* with the permission of BOA Editions, Ltd., 260 East Ave., Rochester, NY 14604.

From *The Language of Life: A Festival of Poets* by Bill Moyers. Copyright © 1995 by Public Affairs Television, Inc. and David Grubin Productions, Inc. Used by permission of Doubleday, a division of Random House, Inc.

"We Are Many" by Pablo Neruda, translated by Alastair Reid, from *Selected Poems.* Reprinted by permission of Jonathan Cape Ltd.

"The Floral Apron" was published in *The Phoenix Gone, The Terrace Empty* by Marilyn Chin. Copyright © 1994 by Marilyn Chin. Reprinted by permission of Milkweed Editions.

"My Mother Pieced Quilts" by Teresa Palomo Acosta. Reprinted by permission of the author.

"A Bus Along St. Clair: December" from *Selected Poems 1966–1984* by Margaret Atwood. Copyright © Margaret Atwood 1990. Reprinted by permission of Oxford University Press Canada.

"Freeway 280" by Lorna Dee Cervantes. Reprinted by permission of the publisher, Latin American Literary Review, Volume 5, 1977, Pittsburgh, Pennsylvania.

"Making a Fist" from *Hugging the Jukebox*. Copyright © 1982 by Naomi Shihab Nye. Reprinted by permission of the author.

"What We Believe" by Anita Endrezze, from *at the helm of twilight* (Broken Moon Press, 1992). Reprinted by permission of the author.

"Foreign Ways" by Diana Chang, copyright © 1994 by Diana Chang, reprinted by permission of the author.

"Song for My Name" from *Calling Myself Home.* Copyright © 1980 by Linda Hogan. Reprinted by permission of Sanford J. Greenburger & Associates.

"Tiger Year" by Laura Tokunaga Iwasaki. Reprinted by permission of the author.

"For Poets" copyright © 1968 and 1992 by Al Young; reprinted with permission of the author.

Bashō's Haiku: "First day of spring—," "It would melt," and "Spring!" from *The Essential Haiku,* edited and translated by Robert Hass. Copyright © 1994 by Robert Hass. First published by The Ecco Press in 1994. Reprinted by permission of The Ecco Press.

"Hanging from the branches of a green" by Lady Ise, from *A Book of Women Poets from Antiquity to Now* by Aliki and Willis Barnstone, editors. Copyright © 1980 by Schocken Books Inc. Reprinted by permission of Schocken Books, distributed by Pantheon Books, a division of Random House, Inc.

"U.S. Aerialists Are Golden" reprinted by permission of the United States Olympic Committee.

"A Motto from Poets: Leave Stone," by Roberto Fernandez Retamar, translated by Tim Reynolds. Reprinted by permission of the author and Agencia Literaria Latinoamericana.

"Constantly risking absurdity" by Lawrence Ferlinghetti from *A Coney Island of the Mind.* Copyright © 1958 by Lawrence Ferlinghetti. Reprinted by permission of New Directions Publishing Corp.

"Hoops Picks Up a Jazz Beat" by Melita Marie Garza. Copyright © Chicago Tribune Company. All rights reserved. Used with permission.

"let my spirit fly in time" by Sandra Maria Esteves. Copyright © 1974 Sandra Maria Esteves, reprinted with permission from the author.

Unit 4

Excerpt from *Big River,* with book by William Hauptman and music and lyrics by Roger Miller. Copyright © 1986 by William Hauptman. Used by permission of Grove/Atlantic, Inc.

"Antigone" from *Sophocles, the Oedipus Cycle: An English Version* by Dudley Fitts and Robert Fitzgerald, copyright © 1939 by Harcourt Brace & Company and renewed 1967 by Dudley Fitts and Robert Fitzgerald, reprinted by permission of the publisher. CAUTION: All rights, including professional, amateur, motion picture, recitation, lecturing, performance, public reading, radio broadcasts, and television are strictly reserved. Inquiries on all rights should be addressed to Harcourt Brace & Company, Permissions Department, Orlando, FL 32887-6777.

"The Ring Finders of Philly" by Ralph Cipriano. GOOD HOUSEKEEPING, April 1996. Reprinted by permission.

"Marked" from *Sonnets to Human Beings and Other Selected Works* by Carmen Tafolla. Copyright © 1992 by Carmen Tafolla.

Unit 5

Excerpt from *Le Morte d'Arthur* by Sir Thomas Malory, translated by Keith Baines. Copyright © 1967 by Keith Baines. Reprinted by permission of Clarkson M. Potter, a division of Crown Publishers, Inc.

Excerpt from *Sundiata* by D. T. Niane, translated by G. D. Pickett. Copyright © 1965 by Longmans, Green and Co. Reprinted by permission of Addison Wesley Longman Ltd.

"Arthur Becomes King" reprinted by permission of The Putnam Publishing Group and David Higham Associates, Ltd., from *The Once and Future King* by T. H. White. Copyright © 1939, 1940 by T. H. White; renewed © 1958 by T. H. White Proprietor.

"Where the Girl Rescued Her Brother" from *The Girl Who Married the Moon,* by Joseph Bruchac and Gayle Ross. Copyright © 1994 by Joseph Bruchac and Gayle Ross. Reprinted by permission of Bridgewater Books, an imprint of Troll Communications, L.L.C.

Unit 6

"Let's Sweat" from *Sacred Cows . . . and Other Edibles* by Nikki Giovanni. Copyright © 1988 by Nikki Giovanni. By permission of HarperCollins Publishers.

"The Rain," "Mealtime," "Whole Duty of Cats," and "Catty Thought" from *Poetry for Cats* by Henry Beard. Copyright © 1994 by Henry

Beard and John Boswell Associates. Reprinted by permission of Villard Books, a division of Random House, Inc.

"Appetizer" from *Ghost Traps.* Copyright © 1991 by Robert H. Abel. Reprinted by permission of The University of Georgia Press.

From "Too Much Spice" by Wen Smith. *Saturday Evening Post,* July–August 1997. Reprinted by permission of the author.

Excerpt from *An American Childhood* by Annie Dillard. Copyright © 1987 by Annie Dillard. Reprinted by permission of HarperCollins Publishers, Inc.

"What Is and Ain't Grammatical" from *Bad Habits: A 100% Fat-Free Book* by Dave Barry. Copyright © 1982, 1983 by Feature Associates. Reprinted by permission of the author.

"The Car We Had to Push" from *My Life and Hard Times* by James Thurber. Copyright © 1933 by James Thurber. Copyright © renewed 1961 by Helen Thurber and Rosemary A. Thurber. Reprinted by arrangement with Rosemary A. Thurber and the Barbara Hogenson Agency.

"How I Changed the War and Won the Game" by Mary Helen Ponce, first published in *Woman of Her Word,* edited by Evegelina Vigil (Houston: Arte Publico Press:University of Houston, 1985) Reprinted by permission of the author.

"A Marriage Proposal" by Anton Chekhov. Copyright © 1958 by Eric Bentley. Reprinted by permission of Applause Theatre Books.

Maps

Ortelius Design, Inc.

Photography

Abbreviation key: **AH**=Aaron Haupt Photography; **AP**=Archive Photos; **AR**=Art Resource, New York; **BAL**=Bridgeman Art Library, London/New York; **CB**=Corbis/Bettmann; **CI**=Christie's Images; **LPBC/AH**=book courtesy Little Professor Book Centers, photo by Aaron Haupt; **LOC**=Library of Congress; **SIS**=Stock Illustration Source; **SS**=SuperStock; **TSI**=Tony Stone Images.

Cover, front, back and i (bust)Scala/AR, (painting)Sotheby's Picture Library; **vii** (t–b)John Warden/TSI, Patricia Mollica/SS, David David Gallery, Philadelphia/SS, reproduced with permission of Curtis Brown Ltd, London, on behalf of the Estate of Dame Laura Knight. ©The Estate of Dame Laura Knight. Photograph by Michael Holford, courtesy Sotheby's Picture Library; **viii** CI/SS; **ix** John Cancalosi/Peter Arnold, Inc.; **x** (l)AKG London, (r)BAL; **xi** (t)Martin Dohrn/Photo Researchers, (b)CI; **xii** Photograph ©1986 The Metropolitan Museum of Art, New York; **xiii** (t)Columbus Museum of Art, Columbus OH, (b)Scala/AR; **xiv** CI/©Artists Rights Society (ARS), New York/ADAGP, Paris; **xv** CB; **xvii** (t)Sotheby's Picture Library/©Artists Rights Society (ARS) New York/ADAGP, Paris, (b)Erich Lessing/AR; **xviii** Sotheby's Picture Library; **xix** (t)Mallett Library, London/BAL, (b)Sotheby's Picture Library; **xx** CI/©1999 C. Herscovici, Brussels/Artists Rights Society (ARS) New York; **xxi** Dave Bartruff/Stock Boston; **xxvi** CI/SS; **4** AH; **6** (l)The Shelburne Museum, Shelburne VT (10-658). Photograph by Ken Burris. (r)Anthony Barboza/Black Images; **7** AH; **8** Gamma Liaison; **9** AR; **12** SS; **13** Mark E. Gibson; **14** AR; **15** Hulton-Getty; **17** SS; **19** Doug Martin; **21** Private collection/Diana Ong/SS; **22** Lee Kuhn/FPG; **23** Tom Till/TSI; **24** R.J. Erwin/Photo Researchers; **25** Jerry Jacka; **26** George Diebold/The Stock Market; **27** Glenn Short/TSI; **28** David David Gallery, Philadelphia/SS; **29** Mark Tomalty/Masterfile; **30** Adam Jones/Photo Researchers; **31** Randy Trine/Glencoe; **32** Steven Needham/Envision; **33** Jerry Jacka; **36** Lawrence Migdale/Photo Researchers; **38** World Wide Photos; **39** Masterfile; **40** The Image Bank; **41** Loiuse Grubb/The Image Works; **42** The Butler Institute of American Art; **43** Steven Needham/Envision; **45** Marvin T. Jones; **47** AP/Metronome Collection; **48** (l)Philip Schermeister/National Geographic Image Collection, (r)CB; **49** Doug Martin; **52** (l)FPG, (r)Stock Montage/SS; **54** SS; **55** Mark Burnett; **56** Clive Barda/Camrax Inc; **57** Wing Luke Asian Museum; **60** AKG Photo; **62** (l)Mike Dobel/Masterfile, (r)Miriam Berkley; **64** Cindy Lewis Photography; **65** SS; **67** Mark Steinmetz; **69** The Minneapolis Institute of Arts/©1999 C. Herscovici, Brussels/Artists Rights Society (ARS), New York; **71** Charles Mason/TSI; **74** Jims Edds; **75** (l)Mark M. Lawrence/The Stock Market, (r)Hulton-Getty; **77** (t)Richard J. Green/Photo Researchers, (b)David David Gallery, Philadelphia/SS; **79** Douglass Faulkner; **80** Kennan Ward/The Stock Market; **82** ©1997 Whitney Museum of American Art; **84** Greg Bliss/Masterfile; **85** SS; **88** (l)Michele Burgess/The Stock Market, (tr)courtesy Richard Erdoes, (br)courtesy Richard Erdoes; **89** Collection of Prof. Herbert T. Hoover, University of SD; **90** Hulton-Getty; **93** (t)SS, (b)Collection of Prof. Herbert T. Hoover, University of SD; **94** (l)NOAA/Science Photo Library/Photo Researchers, (r)AP/World Wide Photos; **96** David M. Schleser/Photo Researchers; **97, 101** CI; **103** Marlborough Gallery, New York; **108** (l)Ron Boudreau/TSI, (r)Anthony Barboza/Black Images; **109** Van Hoorick/SS; **114** (l)Hans Halberstadt/Photo Researchers, (r)Diana Walker/Gamma Liaison; **115** Frances M. Cox/Stock Boston; **116** WA State University Museum of Art; **121** National Portrait Gallery, Smithsonian Institution/AR; **122** The Stock Market; **125** Doug Martin; **127** Larry Moore/SIS; **128** Wilhelm Scholz/Photonica; **130, 132** CI; **133** Animals Animals/Susan Jones; **134** Mark Burnett; **141** James Wardell/Masterfile; **142** (l)Louise Freshman Brown/SS, (r)courtesy Special Collections, University of NH Library; **143** David David Gallery, Philadelphia/SS; **144–145** DeYoung/Stock Imagery; **149** Whitford & Hughes, London/BAL; **151** SS; **154** Manfred Danegger/TSI; **156** (l)Art Wolfe/TSI, (r)World Wide Photos; **158** Tony Morrison/South American Pictures; **159** CI; **161** St. Meyers/Okapia/Photo Researchers; **162** CI/©1999 Artists Rights Society (ARS), New York/ADAGP, Paris; **164** SS; **166** (l)David Weintraub/Photo Researchers, (r)courtesy the author; **167** John Cancalosi/Peter Arnold, Inc; **169** Gerald Peters Gallery, Sante Fe; **171** Tony Morrison/South American Pictures; **172** (l)Boden/Ledingham/Masterfile, (r)CB; **173** Doug Martin; **174** Fine Arts Museums of San Francisco; **176** Mark Steinmetz; **179** Fine Arts Museums of San Francisco; **188** Ledru/Sygma; **190** Roger Wood/Corbis; **191** CI/©1999 Artists Rights Society (ARS), New York/ADAGP, Paris; **194** Kactus Foto, Santiago, Chile/SS/©1999 Artists Rights Society (ARS), New York/ADAGP; **196** Robert Francis/South American Pictures; **197** SS; **198** (l)AKG Photo, (r)Wide World Photos; **199** Sheldon Memorial Art Gallery, University of NE-Lincoln; **203** VAGA; **206** Yvonne Jacquette/Brooke Alexander, Inc; **208, 209, 211** Mark Burnett; **215** Jerry Howard/Stock Boston; **216** Universal Press Syndicate; **217** (l)LOC/Corbis, (r)Miriam Berkley; **219** Adam McCauley/SIS; **220** Mark Burnett; **222** Bob Daemmrich/The Image Works; **224** (l)Fletcher Baylis/Photo Researchers, (r)Rie Nissen, courtesy Karen Blixen Museum, Denmark; **225** CI; **227** Kelmscott Farms; **228** Municipal Museum, Dole/Lauros-Giraudon, Paris/SS; **230, 232** SS; **239** Elsa Peterson/Stock Boston; **240** (l)SS, (r)Sovfoto/Eastfoto; **245** Telegraph Color Library/FPG; **247** (l)LOC/Corbis, (r)Motion Picture & TV Photo Archive;

248 Cedar Rapids Museum of Art; **250** Doug Martin; **251** Mark Burnett; **252** Museum of Fine Arts, Boston; **255** Gerry Whitmont/Australian Picture Library/Corbis Los Angeles; **256** The Huntington Library Art Collections and Botanical Gardens, San Marino CA/SS; **258** ©1998 Walter Chandoha; **259** (l)BAL, (r)Tara Heinemann/Globe Photos; **261** *Indian Star Chart,* c. 1840, The British Library, O.I.O.C. Or. 5259 ff,56v; **265** BAL; **267** Larry Moore/SIS; **268** Mansell/Time Inc; **269** National Museum 1992/E. Cornelius; **270** St. Meteys/Okapia/Photo Researchers; **271** SS; **276** James Wardell/Masterfile; **278** (l)AH, (r)courtesy Scholastic Press; **279** Portland Art Museum; **281** Art Students League of New York; **283** Portland Art Museum; **284** ©1995 The Metropolitan Museum of Art; **286** Jeff Greenburg/Photo Researchers; **288** (l)Bridgeman Art Library/SS/©1999 Artists Rights Society (ARS), New York/ADAGP, Paris, (r)CB; **289** Philadelphia Museum of Art; **290** Bill Frymire/Masterfile; **293** Kunsthalle Bremen; **294** SS; **296** David Sacks/FPG; **298** (l)Hulton-Getty, (r)AP/Popperfoto; **300** SS; **304** (l)AP, (r)courtesy Flora Roberts, Inc.; **305** Mark Burnett; **313** Didier Givois/Agence Vandystady/Photo Researchers; **314** Universal Press Syndicate; **315** (l)Damir Frkovic/Masterfile, (r)AP/SAGA/Frank Capri; **316–317** Jerry Bauer; **318** Gerry Ellis/ENP Images; **318–319** (border)Jerry Bauer/Glencoe file; **319, 320** Gerry Ellis/ENP Images; **320–321** (border)Jerry Bauer/Glencoe file; **321** (l)Martin Dohrn/Photo Researchers, Inc., (tc)Gerry Ellis/ENP Images, (r)image reproduced from *Eyewitness Books: Knight* with permission from DK Publishing, Inc. ©Dorling Kindersley Ltd, London; **322** (t)Gerry Ellis/ENP Images, (b)Jim Zuckerman/Corbis Los Angeles; **322–323** (border)Jerry Bauer/Glencoe file; **323, 324** Gerry Ellis/ENP Images; **324–325** (border)Jerry Bauer/Glencoe file; **325** Gerry Ellis/ENP Images; **328** Sandra Lee Tatum/Indian Artist Magazine; **329** (l)Science Photo Library/Photo Researchers, (r)Nancy Crampton; **330** The Lowe Art Museum, The University of Miami/SS; **331** (border)The Lowe Art Museum, The University of Miami/SS, (r)Paul Conklin/Uniphoto; **332–333** (border) The Lowe Art Museum, The University of Miami/SS; **333** Herb Levart/SS; **334** Jerry Jacka; **334–335** (border)The Lowe Art Museum, The University of Miami/SS; **336** Thomas Ives/The Stock Market; **336–337** (border)The Lowe Art Museum, The University of Miami/SS; **337** Jerry Jacka; **338** John Sanford/Science Photo Library/Photo Researchers, (border)The Lowe Art Museum, The University of Miami/SS; **341** National Archives; **342** (l)Rank Siteman/TSI, (r)AP/Horst Tappe; **345** CI/©1999 Artists Rights Society (ARS), New York/VEGAP, Madrid; **349** Peter Harholdt/SS; **354** (l)Everett Johnson/TSI, (r)Time Inc. Picture Collection; **355** Kevin Schafer/TSI; **356** Guido A. Rossi/Mt. Vesuvius; **356–357** Carol Guzy; **358, 360** Kevin Schafer/TSI; **362** (l)UPI/CB, (r)Fred Stein/Black Star; **363** Barry Seidman/The Stock Market; **364** Charles Philip/Corbis Los Angeles; **365** Marlborough Gallery, New York; **366** SS; **369** CI; **373** National Archives via Jeffrey L. Ethell Collection; **376** (l)David Hiser/TSI, (r)courtesy Chronicle Books; **377, 381** Marlborough Gallery, New York; **382** Walter H. Hodge/Peter Arnold, Inc; **384** Marlborough Gallery, New York; **386** Ron Chapple/FPG; **388** (l)The Image Works, (r)CB; **390** Manuel Bellver/Corbis; **391** Erich Lessing/AR; **393** Damir Frkovic/Masterfile; **398** Wide World Photo; **399** Private collection/Erol Samuel/SS; **401** Cindy Lewis Photography; **402** Erol Samuel/SS; **406** The Phillips Collection; **410** Richard Berenholtz/The Stock Market; **417** LPBC/AH; **420** Photograph ©1986 The Metropolitan Museum of Art; **424** AH; **426** (l)Animals Animals/Mickey Gibson, (r)CB; **431** Telegraph Colour Library/FPG; **432** AP; **433** Sotheby's Picture Library; **434** Reproduced with permission of Curtis Brown Ltd., London, on behalf of The Estate of Dame Laura Knight. ©The Estate of Dame Laura Knight. Photograph courtesy Sotheby's London; **436** (t)Animals Animals/Jim Tuten, (b)AH; **437** Salamander Picture Library; **438** (t)Agence Top/Envision, (b)Salamander Picture Library; **439** Tate Gallery, London/AR/©1999 Artists Rights Society (ARS), New York/DACS; **441** Chester Higgins Jr./Photo Researchers; **443** (l)Keith Wood/TSI, (r)John Lawrence/TSI; **444** William Campbell for Time, Inc.; **445** Louise Gubb/The Image Works; **447** Earth Scenes/S. Morris; **448** ©1995 Jason Laure; **451** Reuters/Juda Ngwenya/AP; **452** Louise Gubb/The Image Works; **453** Lauren Goodsmith/The Image Works; **459** Robert Scheer; **460–461** The National Archives/Corbis; **462** (l)CB, (r)Susan McCartney/Photo Researchers; **465** AH; **466** LOC/Corbis; **468** UPI/CB; **469** AH; **470** Hulton-Deutsch Collection/Corbis; **473** Phil Schermeister/Corbis; **475** Gerald R. Ford Library; **478** World Wide Photos; **479, 480** Michael Darter/Photonica; **481** SS; **483** (l)Roderick Johnson/Images of India, (r)Geoff Bryant/Photo Researchers; **484** Anil A. Dave/Dinodia/Images of India; **485** Dinodia Picture Agency/Images of India; **488** Jim Stratford/Black Star; **489** ©1992 The Metropolitan Museum of Art; **494** (l)courtesy RevereBeach.com, (r)Diane Sabin; **495, 496** Columbus Museum of Art, Columbus OH; **505** BAL; **506** (l)SS, (r)Filip Horvat/SABA; **508** Christian Vioujard/Gamma Liaison; **509** Spencer Jones/FPG; **510** Dimitar Altankov/Gamma Liaison; **511** Geoff Johnson/TSI; **515** CB; **516, 517** Flip Schulke/Corbis; **518** (l)Joachim Messerschmidt/FPG, (r)AKG Photo; **520** Charles Moore/Black Star; **523, 524** UPI/CB; **527** AP Photo/Richard Sheinwald; **529, 530** Scott Polar Research Centre, University of Cambridge; **531** Courtesy the author; **532–533** Maria Stenzel/National Geographic Image Collection; **533** Earth Scenes/G.L. Kooyman; **534** Animals Animals/P. Parks; **535** Maria Stenzel/National Geographic Image Collection; **536** (t)CB, (b)Scott Polar Research Centre, University of Cambridge; **539** Peter L. Chapman/Stock Boston; **541** Larry Moore/SIS; **543** (l)Cotton Coulson/Woodfin Camp, (r)Bill Webb; **544** Kent Wood/Photo Researchers; **546** ©Roy Ooms/Masterfile; **548** Jon Feingersh/The Stock Market; **549** ©Roy Ooms/Masterfile; **550** ©S.I. Greim/Stock Imagery; **552** A. Pasieka/Photo Researchers; **556** (l)Scala/AR, (r)CB; **557** ©1994 The Metropolitan Museum of Art; **559** ©1995 The Metropolitan Museum of Art; **562** Nancy Crampton; **563** Wayne Lankinen/DRK Photo; **565** Scott Camazine/Photo Researchers; **567** Wayne Lankinen/DRK; **573** LPBC/AH; **576** CI/©1999 Artists Rights Society (ARS), New York/ADAGP, Paris; **580–581** AH; **582** CB; **583** Collections/Robert Pilgrim; **585** Private collection/Daniel Nevins/SS; **586** CB; **587** David Bassett/TSI; **590** Photofest; **591** (l)David A. Harvey/©National Geographic Society, (tr)Nancy Crampton, (br)Corbis; **592** David David Gallery, Philadelphia/SS; **596** (l)UPI/CB, (tr)LOC/Corbis, (br)courtesy of Renditions, Research Centre for Translation, Chinese University of Hong Kong; **597** ©Malcolm S. Kirk/Peter Arnold, Inc; **602** (l)James Randklev/TSI, (tr)Peter Ralston, (br)Pach/CB; **603** Patricia Mollica/SS; **604** BAL; **608** John Eastcott/Yva Momatiuk/Stock Boston; **609** John Eastcott & Yva Momatiuk/Masterfile; **610** (l)Boltin Picture Library, (tr)CB, (br)Nancy Crampton; **611** ©The British Museum; **612** David Heald/©Solomon R. Guggenheim Foundation, New York (FN 38.529); **621** Diana Ong/SS; **622** (l)A.J. Russell/FPG, (tr)Corbis, (br)John Eddy; **623** Gerry Ellis/ENP Images; **624–625** Chris Shinn/TSI; **628** (l)John Garrett/TSI, (tr)Roger Viollet/Gamma Liaison, (br)Susan Rankaitis; **629** Al Tielemans/Duomo; **630** CB; **633** Larry Moore/SIS; **634** Ronald C. Modra/S.I. Picture Collection; **635** (t)Frank Capri/SAGA/AP, (b)Gerardo Somoza/Outline; **637** Photograph ©The Museum of Modern Art, New York; **638** Courtesy Bill Hodges Gallery; **641** William Abranowicz; **642** (l)Jeffrey Coolidge/The Image Bank, (tr)Ken Heyman/Woodfin Camp & Assoc., (br)MTI/Eastfoto; **643** ©Patrick Kennedy/Natural Selection; **645** Photograph copyright ©1998 Whitney Museum of American Art; **648** (l)©1993 Turner & DeVries/

The Image Bank, (tr)Niki Berg/Milkweed Editions, (br)courtesy the author; **649** CI; **650–651** Courtesy Phoebe Beasley Art Studio; **654** (l)SS, (tr)Patrick Harbron/Outline, (br)Georgia McInnis ©1990, Arte Publico Press; **655, 656** Courtesy the artist; **660** (l)Lionel Delevingne/Stock Boston, (tr)Gerardo Somoza/Outline, (br)courtesy the author; **661** Courtesy the artist; **662** The Philbrook Museum of Art, Tulsa OK; **663** file photo; **665** The Purcell Team/Corbis; **666** (l)Andrew Holbrooke/The Stock Market, (tr)Gordon Robotham, (br)Douglas Kent Hall; **667** Courtesy the artist; **668** Courtesy the Navajo Gallery, Taos NM; **675** BAL; **676** (l)David Nunuk/Natural Selections, (tr)AP/World Wide Photos, (br)©Chiyoko Iwasaki; **677** Michael Wigley Galleries; **678** SS; **681** Telegraph Color Library/FPG; **682** (l)Hulton-Getty/TSI, (tr)Everett Collection, (br)CB; **686** (l)The Cleveland Museum of Art/AP, (r)Tenri University, Japan; **687** ©The British Museum; **689** Mike Powell/Allsport; **690** (l)Fred W. McDarrah, (tr)Miriam Berkley, (br)Maya Alleruzzo/Sygma; **691** Gerry Ellis/ENP Images; **696** Charles Cherney/Chicago Tribune; **697** (l)L. Fried/The Image Bank, (tr)Arte Publico Press, (br)CB; **698** Doug Martin/Photo Researchers; **699** CI; **707** LPBC/AH; **710–711** Sotheby's Picture Library/©1999 Artists Rights Society (ARS), New York/ADAGP, Paris; **713** Barros & Barros/The Image Bank; **716** (l)LOC/CB, (r)courtesy the author; **717** ©1990 Martha Swope/Time Life Syndication; **721** BAL; **722** Museo Whitaker, Moyta/BAL; **723** Ashmolean Museum, Oxford/BAL; **725** Erich Lessing/AR; **726** (l)AP, (r)BAL; **727** Photo by Studio Kontos; **728** Scala; **731, 735** BAL; **736** Mary Evans Picture Library; **740** The Acropolis Museum, Athens; **744** Erich Lessing/AR; **747** ©Ronald Sheridan/Ancient Art and Architecture Collection; **750, 755** ©The British Museum; **760** Michael Holford; **763** The J. Paul Getty Museum, Los Angeles; **766** Giraudon/AR; **772** AR; **773** Collections/Nigel Hawkins; **774** BAL; **775** Berkeley Castle, Gloucestershire, UK/BAL; **776** AH; **777** Archiv/Photo Researchers; **778** Scala/AR; **780** Chase Manhattan Bank Archive; **781** AR/Erich Lessing; **782** Chase Manhattan Bank Archive; **783** BAL; **784, 786** Chase Manhattan Bank Archive; **788** Mary Evans Picture Library; **790** Chase Manhattan Bank Archive; **792** Sotheby's Picture Library; **794** Chase Manhattan Bank Archive; **795** Scala/Art Resource; **796, 797** Chase Manhattan Bank Archive; **800** Smithsonian Institution; **802** ©The British Museum; **804, 806** Smithsonian Institution; **807** Ny Carlsberg Glyptotek, Copenhagen; **808, 810** Smithsonian Institution; **811** ©The British Museum; **812** (t)Smithsonian Institution, (b)BAL; **814, 816, 817** Smithsonian Institution; **822** BAL; **827** ©1986 The Metropolitan Museum of Art; **831** Sotheby's Picture Library; **835** Erich Lessing/AR; **836** Mary Evans Picture Library; **842** A.K.G. Berlin/SS; **849** BAL; **855** Fine Arts Museums of San Francisco; **863** BAL; **866** Scala/Art Resource; **869** C.M. Dixon, Canterbury, Kent; **872** Tim Gibson/Envision; **877** SS; **878** Courtesy Western Carolina University; **879** Courtesy Daniel Saxon Gallery, Los Angeles; **880** Courtesy Museum of Fine Arts, Boston; **885** Courtesy CENIDIAP-INBA; **888** SS; **891** Private collection, courtesy of Mary-Anne Martin/Fine Art, New York; **896** (l)Biophoto Associates/Photo Researchers, (r)courtesy the author; **897** file photo; **899** Kenneth Redding/The Image Bank; **901** Larry Moore/SIS; **907** LPBC/AH; **910** Sotheby's Picture Library; **912** Brandywine River Museum, Chadds Ford, PA/SS; **913** Lucia Gallery, New York/TF Chen/SS; **914** Collections/George Wright; **915** Reproduced by courtesy of the Director and University Librarian, the John Rylands University Library of Manchester; **916** Collections/Roy Stedall-Humphryes; **917** AR; **918** Courtesy National Museums and Galleries of Wales; **921** ©Alan Lee. Photograph ©Derek Bayes; **922** CI; **925** Collections/Brian Shuel; **927** CI; **935** Bibliotheque Nationale de France, Paris; **937** Founders Society Purchase, Eleanor Clay Ford Fund for African Art. Photograph ©1998 The Detroit Institute of Arts; **938** Franko Khoury/National Museum of African Art; **941** CI; **944** (l)Lambeth Palace Library/BAL, (r)AP; **945** Sotheby's Picture Library; **950** By permission of The Houghton Library, Harvard University; **952** Hulton-Deutsch Collection/Corbis; **954–955** Museo de Arte de Ponce, Puerto Rico/BAL; **956** Bonham's London/BAL; **957** Mallett Gallery London/BAL; **960** AP; **961** (l)private collection/BAL, (r)Loomis Dean/Life Magazine; **963** British Library/BAL; **965** Lukasz Schuster/Wavel State Art Collection, Cracow/BAL; **966** British Library/BAL; **968** BAL; **970** Collections/Brian Shuel; **971** Sotheby's Picture Library; **972** BAL; **975** Richard T. Nowitz/Corbis; **980** Jeffrey S. Hall; **981** Wonder Woman is a trademark of DC Comics, copyright ©1998. All rights reserved. Used with permission; **982** (l)Martin Benjamin, (r)courtesy the author; **983** SS; **985** Catalogue No. 153048, Department of Anthropology, Smithsonian Institution; **995** LPBC/AH; **998–999** CI/©1999 C. Herscovici, Brussels/Artists Rights Society (ARS), New York; **1001** BAL; **1002** (l)Jim Cummins/FPG, (r)Michael Evans/New York Times Co./AP; **1003** Annie Leibovitz; **1005** SS; **1008** GARFIELD ©1997 Paws, Inc. Reprinted with permission of UNIVERSAL PRESS SYNDICATE. All rights reserved; **1009** (l)AH, (r)©Marion Ettlinger/Villard; **1010** From *Poetry for Cats* by Henry Beard. ©1994 by Henry Beard. Reprinted by permission of Villard Books, a division of Random House, Inc; **1015** (l)John Warden/TSI, (r)courtesy the author; **1016** BAL; **1018** Courtesy Mill Pond Licensing; **1023, 1024** SS; **1028** AH; **1029** Rollie McKenna; **1031** SS; **1033** Reprinted with permission of King Features Syndicate; **1034** CI/©1999 Milton Avery Trust/Artists Rights Society (ARS), New York; **1038** (l)AH, (r)Brian Smith/Outline; **1044** (l)Geoff Butler, (r)Wide World Photos; **1045, 1046** "The Car We Had to Push" from *My Life and Hard Times* ©1933, 1961 by James Thurber. Reprinted by arrangement with Rosemary A. Thurber and the Barbara Hogenson Agency; **1047** Dave Bartruff/Stock Boston; **1048** "The Car We Had to Push" from *My Life and Hard Times* ©1933, 1961 by James Thurber. Reprinted by arrangement with Rosemary A. Thurber and the Barbara Hogenson Agency; **1049** Mark Burnett; **1053** FPG; **1054** (l)Phyllis Picardi/Stock Boston, (r)courtesy the author; **1056** ©1986 Carmen Lomas Garza. Photo by Wolfgang Dietze; **1061** CB; **1062–1063, 1064** State Russian Museum/BAL; **1069** Courtesy Thames and Hudson, London; **1077** Larry Moore/SIS; **1083** LPBC/AH.